Metabolic Care
of the
Surgical Patient

By

FRANCIS D. MOORE, M.D.

Moseley Professor of Surgery, Harvard Medical School;
Surgeon-in-Chief, Peter Bent Brigham Hospital

Illustrated by

MILDRED CODDING, A.B., M.A.

Surgical Artist, Department of Surgery,
Harvard Medical School, Peter Bent Brigham Hospital

W. B. SAUNDERS COMPANY

Philadelphia and London

Metabolic Care of the Surgical Patient

This book is dedicated to

Dr. Robert Elman

Dr. Everett I. Evans

Dr. John S. Lockwood

. . . three friends who devoted their professional lives to the improvement of surgical care at the sacrifice of other more easily attained objectives; three surgeons whose work was prematurely cut short by death in their prime; three scientists who have enriched human knowledge.

Contents

An account is given of the chronic nutritional disorders seen in surgery and traceable to inadequate intake or absorption of nourishment. This includes the defect in body composition produced by malignancy and cachexia, the nature and dynamics of catabolism and anabolism in chronic disease. The effects of operation in the presence of chronic cachexia are described. The study of body composition is outlined.

Being an account of the metabolic effects of visceral disease in surgical patients and their management. The diseases of the gastrointestinal tract and its peritoneal coverings are described in greatest detail, since they are so commonly at fault in the metabolic disorders treated by surgery. Parenchymatous diseases of liver, kidneys, lungs, heart, and endocrine glands are also described as they relate to surgical care.

This section contains an account of the special metabolic problems encountered in the diagnosis and treatment of wounds of war, of similar injuries in civilian life, and of fractures which so often accompany such problems. Included as well is a detailed account of the treatment of burns.

A detailed table of contents will be found at the beginning of each Part of the book.

INTRODUCTION

"The present age is prolific of works on physiology; therefore in offering to the public another book relative to an important branch of this science, it will perhaps be necessary to assign my motives."

WILLIAM BEAUMONT, *Experiments and Observations on the Gastric Juice and the Physiology of Digestion,* Plattsburgh, N. Y. (Allen), 1833.

A. SURGERY IS RESPONSIBILITY

Our motives in presenting this book are, first, to bring together in one volume a distinct area of knowledge that has grown from many sources in the past fifteen years and, second, to provide from this knowledge the data that are of direct daily bedside assistance in the care of the sick.

The fundamental act of medical care is assumption of responsibility. Surgery has assumed responsibility for the care of a large section of human illness: a segment of disease which is largely acute, focal, or traumatic. This is responsibility for the care of the entire range of injuries and wounds, local infections, benign and malignant tumors, as well as a large fraction of those various pathologic processes and anomalies which are localized in the organs of the body. The study of surgery is a study of these diseases, the conditions and details of their care. The practice of surgery is the assumption of complete responsibility for the welfare of the patient suffering from these diseases.

The surgeon employs any effective means available to serve the patient best. In most instances, these means include an open dissection under anesthesia, as a surgical operation, together with supportive measures based on an understanding of the patient's bodily processes in recovery. These latter steps assist normal metabolic processes and correct abnormalities, so that the natural sequences of convalescence ensue. These aspects of surgery are included in the term "metabolic care."

The purpose of this book is to provide a general text and guidebook for metabolic care in surgery. The focus is entirely on the care of the patient. Although scientific and theoretical background of great interest underlies all aspects of surgical metabolism, such matters are discussed here only as a brief review (in each Part) or as they bear directly on that understanding required by the surgeon to discharge his responsibility to the patient.

B. SURGICAL JUDGMENT AND SURGICAL METABOLISM

Sick surgical patients do not oblige their doctors by separating "metabolic" from "tissue pathology" states. Their care is always a surgical problem in the truest sense; the whole problem must be solved together, not in sections. The loss of a patient by necrosis of a gangrenous loop of bowel is in nowise excused by the cleverness of his intravenous feedings or the normalcy of his extracellular chemistry.

It has become a commonplace to state that surgeons who have been taught the skillful use of instruments but who understand nothing else are limited in their usefulness to society. Now, with the swing of the pendulum, the other extreme is equally dangerous. A consultant who has an exclusive concern with the biochemical aspects of a surgical patient may fail to rescue that patient for lack of a wary and experienced eye towards the tissue disease and its operative treatment. No amount of potassium chloride will rescue the hypokalemic alkalotic patient whose pylorus remains indefinitely obstructed. No quantity of caloric nourishment or complicated protein supplements will save the life of the wasting patient whose subphrenic abscess presses for drainage. Here is the hazard when the metabolic care of a surgical patient is divorced from responsibility for the treatment of the tissue pathology from which the patient suffers. The surgeon, not his consultants, joins the two in his own right: clinical judgment and a nice balance between operative skill and metabolic wisdom are needed; metabolic care is a part of surgery, not a separate consideration. Therefore, the first rule of metabolic care is to understand the disease itself.

The relation between pathology and metabolism has another corollary: the techniques of conventional histologic pathology will not show us errors when they lie in the field of surgical metabolism. Surgical tissue disease produces a metabolic defect; the two together take the patient down the pathway of illness. The burned patient who dies anuric in the second week will show to the pathologist his burns, his nephrotic kidneys, and his basal pneumonitis. But he will not demonstrate under the microscope a plasma potassium of 8 mE. per l. or ventricular fibrillation. Deaths from anoxia, cardiac arrhythmias, and acute respiratory acidosis show the pathologist little. The conventional methods of morbid anatomy reveal defects only in the area of tissue change, defects often surprisingly innocent of the fatality, and their contemplation disappointing for the improvement of surgical practice. The "pathology of death" in surgical patients is remarkably repetitive and frequently includes degenerative vascular disease, interstitial pneumonitis, a nephrotic lesion, and

ileus. The actual causes of demise are often metabolic and will pass unseen unless we look for them in life. The surgical conscience must seek out its errors before the pathologist enters the scene.

The clinical and metabolic problems discussed in this book arise with disease caused by focal processes or massive trauma and remediable with the scalpel. This book as a whole deals with the metabolic aspects of care and it must assume in the reader a background knowledge of surgical disease and operative care; this is not a textbook of surgery.

C. BACKGROUND AND SCOPE OF THIS BOOK

The range of disorders included here covers most of the metabolic situations encountered on a general surgical service plus some of those seen in urology, orthopedics, and neurosurgery. We have allocated the topic of "fluid balance" to its place as one of several important categories of metabolic management in surgery. Problems of the blood volume, visceral disease, nutrition, and severe injury have equal importance in this book, as they do on a surgical ward. Discussions of the metabolic and endocrine care of specific malignant tumors and of most endocrine diseases are omitted. Both of these represent important areas of metabolic care in surgery but they are special pathologic entities whose inclusion would greatly lengthen this book.

Our work in this field began in 1941. In 1952 we brought together a group of metabolic studies, in a monograph entitled *The Metabolic Response to Surgery*. This was the report of an investigation of metabolism in surgery. It was not intended as a clinical guidebook, although the final chapter was devoted to bedside application of the observations made. In 1953 a theory of metabolism and its meaning in surgical convalescence was outlined in the Churchill Lecture, entitled "Bodily Changes in Surgical Convalescence." In the St. Mary's Lectures at the University of London (1955), these basic patterns of convalescence, endocrinology, and metabolism were related directly to the daily problems of clinical care in surgery. At the lectures given at the University of Pennsylvania (1956), the daCosta Oration (1955), the Sommer Lectures in Portland (1955), the Harvey Lecture (1956), the Lister Lecture (1956), the Cushing Lecture at McGill University (1957), and the McGuire Lectures at the Medical College of Virginia (1957), the attempted orderly arrangement of this material was further put to the test of public presentation. I wish to express my gratitude to these universities and surgical groups for such opportunities.

The present book is an extension of the above concepts to a wide range of clinical problems in surgery; it is based on the study and care of surgical patients. The intent is to avoid dogmatism and to base treatment on metabolic realities, not inductive theory. Whether he is concerned with "shock," "anemia," "starvation," "dehydration," "potassium deficiency," "pathologic bleeding," "protein depletion," "adrenal failure," or any one of a host of overworked and under-defined terms, the surgeon asks: "What is the evidence? What does this word really mean? Is it really so? What is the patient's response to the challenge of his disease?" This volume —hopefully—tries to answer some of those questions.

D. ORGANIZATION

Ideally, a book on metabolic care in surgery should be entirely a case book. Management of today's sick patient rests on the successful accomplishment of specific missions in the past. Because of the very complexity of this subject, an attempt to base such a report wholly on individual case studies would lead to confusion. For this reason, this work is divided into six parts, each housing its own table of contents, systematic discussion, notes from the literature, illustrations, clinical procedure, summaries, and case records. The case records document individual surgical stories that illustrate a variety of points. There is no attempt to include a case or cases for every category or problem under consideration.

This book deals only with those areas of surgical care in which we have had personal experience. If a discussion were to have been based wholly on a review of the literature, we have omitted it completely. Others who have given more study to such matters are better qualified to write of them. Although this book makes no pretense of covering the extensive literature of its subject, there is a representative bibliography.

E. ACKNOWLEDGMENTS

I am indebted to the Surgical Residents and Research Fellows who have worked with me during the past fifteen years. They have made many contributions to the conceptual development and detailed procedures of our surgical services and the surgical laboratory. Each one has a share of whatever of worth is in this book.

I am particularly indebted to the members of the Brigham staff who have provided direct assistance in checking over parts of the manuscript. For this help I would like to acknowledge my indebtedness to Dr. Frank Gardner for reviewing sections on blood volume and blood replacement, to Dr. Leroy D. Vandam for reviewing sections on anesthesia and pulmonary problems, to Dr. Dwight E. Harken, Dr. Robert E. Gross, and Dr. Harrison Black for reviewing the sections on cardiac surgery, to Dr. John M. Kinney for reviewing sections on energy exchange, the lung, and the liver, to Dr. Richard Warren for reviewing sections on gastrointestinal disease, to Dr. T. Bartlett Quigley for reviewing the section on trauma, to Dr. J. Hartwell Harrison for reviewing the section on the kidney, to Dr. Carl W. Walter for reviewing the section on blood banking and blood transfusion, to Dr. Chilton Crane for reviewing the cases of hepatic disease, to Dr. J. Shelton Horsley for reviewing the section on the pancreas, to Dr. Harold D. Levine for reviewing the section on the heart, myocardial irritability, electrolytes, and the electrocardiograph, and to Dr. Henry Banks for reviewing the section on fractures.

Dr. J. Hartwell Harrison, Dr. Lewis Dexter, Dr. Warren Guild, Dr. Eugene C. Eppinger, and Dr. William H. Schwartz, Jr., have reviewed large sections of the data on electrolyte patterns.

I am indebted to the several members of our clinical and research groups who have written up the data for the case studies which we have used. These include Dr. Louis

L. Smith, Dr. Richard E. Wilson, Dr. John M. Kinney, Dr. William G. Hammond, Dr. Mayo Johnson, Dr. Martin S. Litwin, Dr. J. Shelton Horsley, and Dr. A.W.R. Williamson.

The production of the book itself has been a task involving many people. I am particularly indebted to Miss Doris Lewis for her help in organizing the group who have worked on the book. Miss Codding's charts have made a contribution to our teaching. Mrs. Colin Davey has typed and retyped the manuscript many times. I am indebted also to Mrs. Donald Height, who has typed the final versions, Mrs. David Humez, who has checked the book for editorial form and construction, and to Dr. Stephen Reynolds and Mrs. Donald Goodrich, who have checked the bibliography. Most of the chemical determinations mentioned in the case studies have been carried out in my laboratory under the technical direction of Miss Margaret R. Ball with the assistance of Miss Caryl Magnus and Mrs. Trond Kaalstad. The surgical life leaves but a few hours in the working day for reading or writing; my gratitude to my family, for their patience, is boundless. Mrs. Moore has provided essential help, advice and encouragement throughout the long undertaking.

The support of the Atomic Energy Commission in the work of our own laboratories is acknowledged with gratitude. The Army, the United States Public Health Service, and The Commonwealth Fund have been of great assistance. The help of the Upjohn Company and Winthrop Laboratories, Inc., is again gratefully acknowledged.

This book is wholly based on experience in the study and care of the sick. We therefore again acknowledge our gratitude to those many patients who have, wittingly or unwittingly, contributed to human knowledge so that the care of others could be improved.

FRANCIS D. MOORE

Brookline, Mass.

CREDITS

The author expresses his acknowledgment to the following publications and publishers for the reproduction of certain of the illustrations: The Harvey Lectures, The Josiah Macy, Jr. Foundation, The Laurentian Hormone Conference (Academic Press), New England Journal of Medicine, the Journal of the American Medical Association, and the Annals of Surgery (J. B. Lippincott Co.). The Appendix is modified slightly from "The Metabolic Response to Surgery" (Moore and Ball, 1952, Charles C Thomas, Publishers).

The Normal Patient. Convalescence, and the Metabolism of Recovery

Contents of Part I

CHAPTER 1. THE RESTING NORMAL PATIENT

CHAPTER 2. CONVALESCENCE IN THE HEALTHY: CLOSED SOFT-TISSUE TRAUMA OF MODERATE SEVERITY

CHAPTER 3. COMMON VARIATIONS AND ABNORMALITIES OF CONVALESCENT METABOLISM; THE VERY YOUNG AND THE VERY OLD; "SURGICAL RISK"

CHAPTER 4. SURGICAL ENDOCRINOLOGY AND METABOLISM: NOTES FROM THE LITERATURE

CHAPTER 5. METABOLIC ACTIVATION AFTER INJURY; MEDIATORS THAT STIMULATE DIFFUSE BODILY CHANGES AFTER FOCAL INJURY

CHAPTER 6. THE THERAPEUTIC MEANING OF NORMAL CONVALESCENCE; THE QUESTION OF EARLY FEEDING; NITROGEN BALANCE; THE WOUND

CHAPTER 1

The Resting Normal Patient

On a surgical service serving a civilian population, one-half to two-thirds of the patients cared for are metabolically normal individuals prior to their operation or injury. This includes all of the patients who are injured while at work or going about their usual business, and a very large fraction of those patients having elective surgery for such conditions as benign tumors and ulcers, stone, peripheral venous disease, early cancer, orthopedic conditions, or congenital abnormalities. In wartime military surgery all of the patients are normal and active up to the time of their injury. This is one of the characteristic features of surgical metabolism as contrasted with the metabolic problems seen in internal medicine, where chronic visceral disease predominates. Knowledge of certain metabolic features of the normal human being is therefore basic to metabolic care in surgery; normal metabolism is characteristic of a large fraction of patients prior to their trauma and abnormal metabolism can best be understood with the normal clearly in mind.

For such a purpose we define a metabolically normal patient as one who was at his normal weight and work, asymptomatic, socially effective, and subjectively well up to the start of the acute surgical episode under consideration, be it elective operation, an acute surgical emergency, or unanesthetized trauma.

It is the purpose of this first chapter to present a brief introductory account of normal body composition, metabolism, and endocrinology. Certain areas of this normal biochemistry are taken up in much greater detail in subsequent sections of the book.

Section I. Body Composition

A. BODY WEIGHT

1. Determinants

The body weight and body build of the adult are primarily determined by genetic factors; the offspring resembles the parent. Sex, dietary habits, and exercise determine relative composition in terms of fat and lean tissue. The female body contains a higher percentage of body fat, the male, more lean muscular tissue, but in either, eating more than necessary is associated with an increase in fat, and active exercise throws the balance in the other direction with an increase in muscle.

2. Subdivisions

For the understanding of surgical metabolism, the body weight may be considered as composed of the following broad divisions.

Body fat: largely neutral storage fat, an anhydrous tissue, rich in caloric potential.

Lean body solids: consisting chiefly of skeletal solids (crystal lattice of bone) and the soft-tissue solids, the heaviest of which are the structure proteins in body protoplasm. Electrolyte weight, while of crucial importance in determining water distribution, is itself negligible—a few grams.

Body water and its subdivisions: intracellular water and *extracellular water*, the latter being divided into *interstitial fluid* and *plasma*.

The normal body weight fluctuates through the day as a function of ingestion and excretion of food and water. Weight is at its peak in the late afternoon or early evening. Through the night, from 1 to 2 kg. disappears by the insensible loss of water through the lungs and, as food is oxidized, by the exhalation of the resultant carbon dioxide and the urinary excretion of the water of oxidation.

Over the short term (anything less than forty-eight hours) appreciable gains in weight are due largely to increase in body water. The synthesis of new protoplasm proceeds so slowly that it is a cause of weight change discernible only over a period of several days or a week. Specifically, the synthesis of lean tissue rarely proceeds at a rate faster than 150 gm. per day (corresponding to 5 gm. of nitrogen). The accumulation of neutral fat can occur quite rapidly when there is forced feeding of fat and carbohydrate in underweight individuals.

Weight loss due to dissolution of tissue occurs much more rapidly than its gain, particularly after trauma or operation, when fat oxidation rates are markedly accelerated and tissue loss as rapid as 500 gm. a day is not uncommon. Rapid loss of water, as from the gastrointestinal tract, may produce weight loss approximately ten times as fast (5000 gm. a day). Short-term rapid weight loss should therefore signify desalting water loss or true dehydration, whichever fits the circumstances. A recent and continuing severe tissue trauma (particularly with infection) may account for about 500 gm. a day; the rest is water.

The frequent weighing of surgical patients is quite unnecessary if convalescence is proceeding satisfactorily. In many complicated situations such as acute illness, congestive heart failure, burns, renal failure, or extrarenal losses, frequent check of the patient's weight provides the closest measurement of changes in total body water and, by calcu-

lation, changes in tissue content. From these observations previous treatment can be evaluated and future plans based on a firm foundation.

B. TOTAL BODY WATER AND FAT

1. Interrelationships

The controlling components of body composition are the lean-tissue mass and the total body water. In normal individuals, the amount of water in the body varies according to the amount of lean tissue present. The lean tissues contain the oxidizing and energy-exchanging protoplasm and are composed largely of striated muscle and the parenchymatous viscera. The soft lean tissues are constant in their water content, containing approximately 73 per cent water. The rest of the body (other than the skeleton) consists of fat. This nonaqueous neutral fat therefore varies inversely to the proportion occupied by water. "The more fat the less water" is a rule which holds for any age. A short, round, obese female who may contain as much as 45 per cent fat has a very small total body water. Small losses of water will induce changes much more marked than equal losses in a strapping big man whose total water is much greater, yet the large cushion of fat is there as a reservoir both of calories and of water which arises when the fat is burned.

2. Measurement, Normal Values, and Ranges

The total body water is most easily measured by the dilution of heavy water or deuterium oxide. Extensive studies of the total body water in health and disease have been carried out since the first description of the method in 1946. An account of the theoretical interrelationships of water and fat and of the various types of tissue gain and loss seen in surgical disease will be found in Part IV.

In the normal adult male, total body water is 55 per cent of body weight, with an overall range of from 50 to 60 per cent, depending upon body build. The more obese man has a smaller body water whereas the lean, well-trained athlete has a somewhat higher value. The female, having the higher body fat, has a lower body water, the normal total body water in the female being in the range of 50 per cent of body weight with an over-all range of 45 to 55 per cent. There is thus a sex-linked differential with respect to total body water. In a study of the total body water for all ages, it was discerned that this sex differential appears at puberty, when the female grows more subcutaneous fat as a part of her normal body composition and the male puts on more skeletal muscle as a secondary sex characteristic ("steroidal growth").

Understanding these normal relationships is basic to an understanding of changes in acute and chronic illness, in which water may either be lost externally, gained by ingestion, or added as a result of fat oxidation and lean-tissue catabolism during the antidiuretic state produced by trauma or visceral disease. As we shall see later, a relative excess of body water is much commoner in surgical patients than any variety of dehydration.

C. THE LEAN TISSUES: PROTEIN, NITROGEN, POTASSIUM

1. The Lean-Tissue Mass

Strictly speaking, the lean body mass includes both the soft tissues and the nonfatty portion of cortical bone. We will deal with the latter separately, however, and for this reason consider the term "lean-tissue mass" to signify the soft lean tissues—the cellular tissues.

The largest masses of soft lean tissues are those of skeletal muscle. Heart, lungs, liver, spleen, gastrointestinal tract, and other parenchymatous and hollow viscera together comprise a mass that, in the male, is smaller than the total taken up by muscle. In an obese female the viscera predominate in lean-tissue mass. The total cellular protein of the body, not counting connective tissue or bone matrix, is about 8 kg., of which the great majority (7 kg., or 87 per cent) occurs in the form of skeletal muscle. Assuming that 1/30 of the wet weight of lean tissue is nitrogen, we may suppose that the soft-tissue cellular protein of 7 kg. contains 1120 gm. of nitrogen, or a total net weight of about 30 kg. of lean tissue. This coefficient is not constant for all lean tissues but is a close enough approxima-

tion for clinical calculation. All the energy exchange of the living body occurs by oxidation of carbon substrates in the lean body mass, and the size of this mass is therefore directly related to resting oxygen consumption, carbon dioxide production, basal metabolic rate, caloric requirements, creatinine excretion, and many other indices of total energy metabolism, including the total red cell volume.

Most of the weight of lean tissue is water; the rest is protein. The weight of salts is negligible. In addition to this large amount of protein (which is enclosed in cells) there are three other large masses of protein in the body: the solute protein (mostly plasma protein), the extracellular connective-tissue protein, and skeletal protein.

It is a common fallacy to assume that the total plasma protein or its concentration is somehow related to the over-all nitrogen balance or "protein reserves" of the body. There is very little evidence to support such a view. Indeed, the lean-tissue mass may gain or lose large amounts of protein without reflection in the concentration of plasma proteins or plasma albumin, and in the sense of an inactive storehouse there is no such thing as "protein reserve" in the body.

2. Potassium

In the adult male, the total body potassium is about 47 mE. per kg., or approximately 3200 mE. Somewhat over 98 per cent of this resides in the lean-tissue mass, in body cells, and, since body cells are largely those of striated muscle, this is the site of most of the potassium in the body. Only a small fraction, some 60 mE., exists in the extracellular fluid. In the female, with a somewhat smaller lean-tissue mass, the total body potassium ranges from 37 to 44 mE. per kg., averaging 40 mE. per kg.

The total exchangeable potassium is measured by isotope dilution. The findings in surgical disease, of great importance in the management of hyperkalemia and hypokalemia, will be found in Part III and Part IV.

The concentration of potassium within the body cells is not accurately known. It is probably in the general range of 130 to 160 mE. per l. of cell water. Taking a figure for the body as a whole, and realizing that there are certain areas of cell water which may contain a good deal less potassium, the average figure is about 150 mE. per l. Potassium is the predominant base of cell water and the total osmolality* of intracellular water is therefore roughly proportional to its potassium concentration. Since body cells do not tolerate osmotic gradients across their membranes, we may predict that when the osmolality of the extracellular phase is low (as in the hypotonic and low sodium states) the osmolality of intracellular water will also be low. Under such circumstances the intracellular concentration of potassium should also be low. By the same token a lowering of intracellular potassium concentration by potassium loss or water loading should be expected to produce hyponatremia and extracellular hypotonicity merely as a result of the operation of osmotic equilibrium.

The concentration of potassium outside of the cell, in the extracellular part of the body, lies between 3.9 and 4.4 mE. per l. Many influences bear upon the regulation of the extracellular potassium concentration, including the potassium intake and output, and the pH of the extracellular phase. In many situations seen in clinical practice the plasma potassium concentration does not reflect the total body potassium, and may even change in an inverse direction. In induced acidosis the plasma potassium rises, and in induced alkalosis it falls abruptly, both of these changes occurring quite aside from any alterations in body content, absorption, or excretion. Rapid removal of the potassium from the body will slowly lower the plasma potassium concentration. Alkalosis hastens this lowering. Failure of the kidneys to excrete potassium will result in a rise in plasma potassium concentration, particularly if aci-

dosis coexists or new potassium is added to the system.

Potassium is one of many intracellular electrolytes. Others are phosphate, sulfate, calcium, magnesium, and an important series of trace minerals and electrolytes. Potassium so predominates in the cation constitution of intracellular water, however, that it may be thought of as the primary intracellular electrolyte.

Potassium can leave the cell in three different relationships, all three of which may occur in the surgical patient in the course of convalescence.

(1) *Cell Death.* The entire cell may break down, with release of all its nitrogen and its potassium. In this case the relationship of the potassium to nitrogen in the released fluid should be approximately that of the cell itself: 3 mE. of potassium per gm. of nitrogen. This is the change that predominates in crush, gangrene, necrosis, and cell death.

(2) *Cell Atrophy.* "Atrophy" may take place, with the cells remaining the same in number but of smaller size and normal composition. This is the change that occurs in striated muscle early in starvation and cachexia. The muscle still functions, but it is smaller and ultimately weaker. The cell remains isotonic.

(3) *Base Exchange.* A more subtle alteration in the cell may come about, with discharge of part of its potassium and water but only a small portion of its protein matrix. This yields a negative balance with a high potassium:nitrogen ratio. It is seen early after severe injury. It is associated with hypotonicity, and there may be a concomitant shift of cations across the cell membrane. Exchange of potassium for hydrogen and sodium occurs under a variety of circumstances. The amount of protein leaving the cell depends on the setting. It is assumed that when intracellular potassium is lost, cellular osmolality has to be maintained by the migration of hydrogen and sodium into the cell. Cellular pH falls, extracellular pH may rise. This sequence occurs in severe cachexia and in potassium loss and after severe injury, in which case cellular matrix is also lost. After

---

* "Osmolarity" is defined as osmolar concentration per unit total volume. "Osmolality" is osmolar concentration per unit total water; it is this which body cells "feel" and respond to, and which the clinical osmometer measures. Numerical differences between the two are minor; the term "osmolality" is used throughout.

severe injury more potassium than matrix is lost initially, resulting in a negative balance characterized by a high potassium:nitrogen ratio (up to 15 mE. per gm.). Aciduria and extracellular alkalosis are favored by this combination.

D. THE EXTRACELLULAR PHASE: SODIUM, CHLORIDE, AND CONNECTIVE TISSUE

1. Definition

It is apparent that there is an area of body water not contained within cells, a significant fraction of which is found in the blood plasma. Its measurement has been approximated by the dilution of a large variety of ions and crystalloids. Discussion of this experimental work is found in Parts III and IV. The smallest volumes revealed for this phase of body water are those based on the dilution of crystalloids of high molecular weight, such as inulin, which yield a volume in the neighborhood of 15 per cent of the body weight (this figure includes the plasma). Somewhat larger volumes are recorded for the dilution of ions, the highest values of which are in the general neighborhood of 24 or 25 per cent of body weight. For clinical calculation in surgical care, an extracellular volume of 20 per cent of body weight is a valid first approximation. Unlike most of the other dimensions of body composition, which can be measured directly by carcass analysis in animals, the extracellular phase defies direct measurement. It also defies accurate definition; we will probably never achieve a universally acceptable "true" value.

The extracellular phase consists of the following subdivisions:

(1) the *plasma volume;*

(2) the *interstitial fluid,* such as lymph and other extracellular, extravascular liquids; and

(3) the *extracellular solids,* including extracellular structure material such as fascia, tendon, connective tissue, dermis (and other tissues which contain very few cells in relation to their mass), and much of cortical bone solids. These solids are of special interest because of their content of sodium and chloride, often in unusual relationships and not infrequently "bound" or not freely available.

The extracellular fluid is that area of body water engaged in transporting substances back and forth between the outside world and the body cells. It is the area in which body tonicity is determined largely by sodium content. It is the area in which acid-base and electrolyte changes have been most extensively studied and are described in the classic monograph by Gamble. The proteins circulating in this fluid are the solute proteins.

2. The Solute Proteins—Plasma Protein

The solute proteins are those proteins which normally exist in solution in the extracellular phase. Chief among these proteins is albumin. In addition, there is a variety of other proteins which have been isolated and identified but whose total mass is not great and whose oncotic significance is negligible. They are special-purpose proteins involved in immune responses, coagulation, hormone transport, and many other functions. These are the globulins, fibrinogen, and lipoproteins.

The solute proteins are usually referred to as the "plasma proteins," and this term will not be readily changed. Yet the fact of the matter is that only slightly more than half of the solute protein in the body is actually within the plasma at any one moment. The distribution of albumin in the body indicates that high concentrations of it occur in the lymph of liver, lungs, and gastrointestinal tract. There are large areas of the extracellular phase which contain proteins in lesser concentration. The term "solute proteins" indicates the fact that these substances are not confined to the plasma; the term "plasma proteins" gives the erroneous impression that they are. This distinction is particularly important with respect to colloid osmotic pressure.

The function of albumin in plasma is to exert colloid osmotic ("oncotic") pressure, yet a colloid in solution can only exert effective colloid osmotic pressure when that solution is facing a membrane impermeable to that colloid. Therefore, in those large areas of the body (liver, lungs, heart, gastrointestinal tract) where the lymph contains albumin in high concentration, the albumin exerts very little colloid osmotic pressure and there is virtually no colloid osmotic pressure gradient across the capillary; the capillary is very permeable to albumin.

The normal concentration of solute protein in the plasma is 6 to 7 gm. per 100 ml., the albumin fraction 4 to 5 gm. per 100 ml.

3. The Nonprotein Nitrogen and Its Fractions

Many nitrogen compounds of low molecular weight are involved in transit from various sites of ingestion or excretion, to and from the lean tissues, where protein synthesis and degradation is carried on. These nitrogen compounds are measured as "nonprotein nitrogen" in the blood. Nonprotein nitrogen consists of approximately 60 per cent urea nitrogen, along with a variety of compounds such as creatine, creatinine, other xanthines, amino acids, and polypeptides.

The normal value of blood nonprotein nitrogen is 15 to 30 mg. per 100 ml. The normal value for blood urea nitrogen is 7 to 15 mg. per 100 ml.

4. Sodium Content, Distribution, and Concentration

In both men and women, the total "active" sodium of the body is about 40 mE. per kg., or close to 2800 mE., in the adult. This is the amount of sodium measured by dilution of radioactive sodium, the radioactive isotope exchanging with body sodium through a mass of that weight; this is therefore referred to as the "total exchangeable" sodium. Of this total active sodium, approximately one-quarter occurs in the skeleton in a form which is evidently available in certain types of metabolic emergencies. Approximately 1500 mE. of sodium, in a normal man, is present in the extracellular phase at a concentration of about 138 to 145 mE. per l. of plasma, or approximately 150 mE. per kg. of extracellular water.

There is, in addition, a fraction of "nonexchangeable" sodium in the skeleton which is evidently deposited there with skeletal growth and which is inactive in later life.

It totals about 750 mE. in the adult. Some sodium is found normally, in low concentrations, in certain body cells such as muscle.

5. Chloride Content, Distribution, and Concentration

There is proportionally less chloride than sodium in the body. The ratio (by equivalence) in the extracellular fluid is approximately 3:2 (150 mE. per l. of sodium to 105 of chloride). There is much less chloride than sodium in the skeleton.

There is a very high concentration of chloride in one small area of body cells—the parietal cells of the stomach. The secretory cells of the rest of the gastrointestinal tract contain both sodium and chloride in high concentrations, as indicated by the fact that the fluids that issue forth from those cells contain these ions in concentrations close to that observed in plasma. In addition, disproportionally large amounts of chloride are found in association with certain connective tissue solids such as collagen.

6. Bicarbonate

Upon the hydration of carbon dioxide—a reaction proceeding readily in the presence of carbonic anhydrase—the carbonic acid so formed is immediately ionized into hydrogen ion and bicarbonate ion. The bicarbonate ion is then maintained in the extracellular phase at a concentration determined by external acid-base loads and governed by pulmonary and renal mechanisms. Carbon dioxide is freely diffusible; bicarbonate is not, but exists both inside and outside of cells.

This carbonic anhydrase mechanism provides hydrogen ion to exchange for sodium ion and potassium ion in the renal tubular cell; it provides carbon dioxide for pulmonary excretion (from dissolved carbonic acid and bicarbonate) and it provides the basis for the marked pH gradients observed in gastrointestinal secretions.

7. The Nature of Connective Tissue

The extracellular structural tissues of the body are remarkable in that they contain large amounts of protein—much of it collagen and elastin—with large amounts of chloride and sodium, yet with only small amounts of potassium. Examples of such tissues are tendon, fascia, ligamentous structures, periarticular structures, and the dermis. In wasting diseases, these structures tend to maintain a size close to normal while the fatty and lean cellular tissues are consumed. As will be described subsequently in the section on cachectic diseases, the starved patient is largely "skin, bones, and water." He is also "fascia and tendon," and a very large fraction of his body water is therefore extracellular.

8. Sodium:Potassium Relationships; Content and Concentration; Total Body Osmolality

In the normal adult male there is significantly less active sodium in the body than there is potassium, this ratio being approximately 0.8. In the female, because there is less body potassium, the ratio is very close to unity. In most chronic diseases, potassium leaves the body as the cell mass shrinks and, as mentioned briefly above, the extracellular phase remains the same size or actually increases, leading to inverted and high sodium: potassium ratios, a characteristic finding in the chronically ill patient. Ratios of 1.3 to 1 5 are commonly found in starvation from a variety of causes. In congestive heart failure and other fluid-accumulating diseases, the sodium:potassium ratio in the body may be as high as 1.9.

The relationships between concentrations of sodium and potassium are governed primarily by the fact that the body does not tolerate osmotic gradients across any surfaces or membranes. Certain cells are capable of building up very high pH gradients (an example can be found in the parietal cells of the stomach, which elaborate a secretion with a pH as low as 1.0). Other cells (such as muscle cells) build up very high concentration gradients of specific ions or other substances. The normal muscle cell maintains potassium in a very high concentration inside the cell and low concentration outside the cell, the reverse being the case for sodium. The maintenance of this gradient requires the expenditure of energy. This phenomenon applies also to phosphate, sulfate, chloride,

trace minerals, certain types of structure proteins, enzymes, and many other substances.

But, unlike these special gradients, the total osmolality of body fluids is the same throughout the body, according to the best of our present knowledge. The osmolality of a solution is a property determined by the concentration of all the molecules in solution and by their molecular weight and behavior; it is their osmolality which determines the "thirst" for water on the part of solutes in a biologic system. The normal osmolality of plasma water is approximately 295 mO. per kg. of water. Intracellular water presumably has the same osmolality.

Extracellular osmolality is almost wholly determined by the concentration of salts, since the sum of the known salt concentrations of plasma extracellular fluid accounts for all but a few (1 to 5) mO. of osmolality, the remainder being accounted for by the small concentration of crystalloids and proteins. In so far as losses or gains of sodium cannot be compensated for by other mechanisms, the sodium concentration of the extracellular fluid may be considered as a prime determinant of its osmolality and therefore of body osmolality. Similarly, certain types of potassium loss must lead to a low sodium concentration and extracellular hypotonicity. Under most conditions—there are important exceptions—the osmolality of the extracellular fluid (in mO. per l.), and therefore of total body water, is close to a numerical value of twice the plasma sodium concentration (in mE. per l.).

Protein contributes the entire colloid osmotic pressure of plasma and other body fluids; because the molecules are large and heavy, it contributes only a negligible quantity (1 to 3 mO. per l.) of total osmolality.

E. WATER CONTENT OF PHASES

Plasma is normally about 93 per cent water; the nonaqueous weight is protein. Sudden large changes in content of fat, protein, or crystalloids alter water content but not electrolyte concentration in that water. Ideally, sodium and chloride concentration should be expressed relative to plasma water in clinical work; means for so doing are not readily available.

Interstitial fluid varies in water content from about 94 per cent to 99.9 per cent depending on protein content.

Muscle tissue is about 73 per cent water.

Neutral fat is considered as having no water. In point of fact it does contain a small amount of water in its extracellular phase and in cell nuclei and protoplasm other than fat.

F. THE SKELETON

1. Size and Phases

The total weight of the skeleton (wet cortical, and trabecular bone) in the adult is approximately 7 to 10 kg. or 10 to 15 per cent of body weight. The skeleton contains much electrolyte and mineral with a low proportion (15 to 25 per cent) of water. From a biochemical point of view, the skeleton may be considered as falling into the following divisions.

a. The Extracellular Fluid Phase. This is a fraction of skeletal weight occupied by chloride at plasma concentrations, and an accompanying appropriate amount of sodium. This is no different from the extracellular phase of any other tissue. There is a very small intracellular phase in the bone-cell nuclei.

b. The "Exchangeable, Nonextracellular" Sodium Phase. This is a fraction of bone where sodium resides at high concentrations and in amounts over and above the total chloride of the skeleton. It is that fraction of skeletal sodium which exchanges with the isotope and which may be considered as "available" for certain types of metabolic emergencies, of which sodium-losing acidosis (as in low intestinal obstruction) appears to be the most prominent.

c. The "Nonexchangeable, Nonextracellular" Sodium Phase. This other fraction of sodium in the skeleton is characterized by being in an insoluble structural form. This sodium is not exchangeable with the isotope and is presumably deposited in these areas as skeletal growth proceeds and is, thereafter, turned over either not at all or at an exceedingly slow rate. As far as we know, it has no importance in surgical metabolism.

G. THE BLOOD VOLUME

1. The Plasma Volume

In normal healthy man the plasma volume, as measured by dye or colloid dilution, occupies from 3 to 5 per cent of body weight. Just as the total volume of body water varies inversely with the fat content and is smaller in women, so also the plasma volume is smaller in the obese and in the female. The plasma volume is often expressed as "ml. per kg.," a figure which is numerically the same as "per cent of body weight" with one more decimal place (i.e., 45 ml. per kg. is 4.5 per cent of body weight). This designation "per cent of body weight" treats the red cell volume (and other phase volumes) as an equal volume of water, without considering specific gravity.

2. The Red Cell Volume

The red cell volume is from 2 to 4 per cent of body weight.

3. The Blood Volume

The blood volume, being the sum of the plasma and red cell volumes, varies from 5 to 8 per cent of body weight. The blood volume figure at 10 per cent of body weight, formerly considered a normal value, is higher than is usually seen except in the extremely well-trained athlete, in people at high altitudes, or in various conditions (congestive heart failure, congenital cardiac disease, chronic pulmonary disease, polycythemia vera) in which the blood volume is pathologically enlarged. In the male, a blood volume figure of 7.0 per cent of body weight, and in the woman 6.5 per cent of body weight, come close to the norm for the normally-built individual.

As with the several other compartments of body water, the total blood volume varies inversely with obesity. An extremely obese man has a blood volume closer to the range of 5 or 6 per cent of body weight. An athlete in top condition with little fat may have a blood volume approaching 8 per cent of body weight.

4. Hematocrit Factors

The peripheral concentration of red blood cells can be measured in several different ways: the red blood cell count, the hemoglobin concentration, and the hematocrit. Where conditions of hyperchromic or hypochromic anemia do not occur acutely, these three measurements may be considered to vary as a linear function of each other, and all three of them measure, in effect, the peripheral concentration of red blood cells.

Sudden changes in plasma osmolality produce shrinkage or swelling of the red blood cell, which distorts the linear relationship among these three indices. Hypertonicity, for example, will lower the hematocrit slightly without altering either the hemoglobin concentration or red blood cell count. There will be the same number of cells in the blood and each will contain the same amount of hemoglobin but they will occupy a smaller volume. In certain circumstances, sudden changes in osmolality may introduce in these three indices of peripheral red cell concentrations nonlinear effects which make the effects of transfusion or other surgical therapy appear confusing. But such situations are rare and, generally speaking, the three measurements are parallel under the conditions seen in surgical care.

When blood is removed in a tube and spun down to a constant meniscus, there is always some trapped plasma in the cell fraction, increasing slightly the hematocrit reading. This "trapped plasma" is constant under ordinary laboratory conditions but tends to produce a slightly higher hematocrit than would be the "true" value for that tube of blood.

The relationship between the blood volume and the red cell volume is such as to indicate that the proportion of red cells in the total blood volume of the body as a whole is lower than it is in a peripheral large vessel, as, for instance, the antecubital vein. This relationship of the total red cell volume to the total blood volume is termed the whole body hematocrit (WBH), and it is consistently lower than the large vessel hematocrit (LVH). This is not an important factor in everyday surgical therapy but is of interest in relation to blood volume methods. These details are discussed more fully in Part II.

Section II.   Metabolism

A. PROTEIN, CARBOHYDRATE, FAT, CALORIES

1. Nitrogen Balance: Its Nature and Meaning

The normal adult male ingests approximately 12 gm. of nitrogen a day in the form of protein. This nitrogen represents approximately 75 gm. of dietary protein. Men doing heavy work eat more than this and females ordinarily eat somewhat less. This dietary protein is hydrolyzed in the gastrointestinal tract and absorbed into the portal circuit as a hydrolysate of protein, consisting of polypeptides and amino acids.

The normal individual, neither gaining nor losing weight (and at the lean-tissue mass determined by his genes and his exercise), excretes an amount of nitrogen equal to his intake. He is therefore referred to as in zero nitrogen balance. If he has an intake of 12 gm. a day, he may be expected to excrete 11 gm. in the urine and the remaining 1 gm. in the feces. The fecal nitrogen is fairly constant over a considerable range of dietary intakes, in the normal individual.

Urine nitrogen disposal is 60 per cent as urea at low nitrogen excretion levels, 90 per cent urea at high levels. Assuming a urine nitrogen at 10 gm., the partition is:

	Nitrogen (grams)
Urea	7.0
Ammonia	0.5
Uric acid	0.2
Creatinine	0.8
Amino acids	0.2
Enzymes	0.3
Miscellaneous	1.0

Urea with a molecular weight of 60 is, by weight, about one-half nitrogen. Therefore a blood urea nitrogen increment of 100 mg. per 100 ml. means 200 mg. per 100 ml. of urea, or 2000 mg. per l., or 16.6 mM. per l., or 16.6 mO. per l.

This balance of nitrogen is prone to fluctuate widely, depending on intake, output, and a number of other influences, of which surgical operation or traumatic injury is outstanding. Nitrogen balance changes can be interpreted as indicative of over-all net synthesis or degradation of protein, because there is normally in the body no storage site for inactive nitrogen compounds. The tiny fraction of body nitrogen represented by the blood urea nitrogen or nonprotein nitrogen represents merely a transitory form of nitrogen in the dynamic equilibrium between protein and its end-products. For this reason, an individual in grossly positive or negative nitrogen balance may be assumed quite justifiably to be making or breaking down large amounts of protein. Several important aspects of this contention must be examined more closely.

Protein can be synthesized in one site and broken down in another, simultaneously. An individual whose heart is enlarging and becoming hypertrophied as a phase of cardiac disease, while the rest of the lean tissues are wasting away in the cachexia of congestive heart failure, is an obvious case in point. There may be much more subtle gradations of this type of interplay. After trauma or hemorrhage there is extensive protein synthesis in the wound (and in hemoglobin and albumin) whereas body muscular tissues as a whole are breaking down. Nitrogen balance measurements consider the organism as a whole and record the net process without any indication as to the various shades and intermediates between synthesis and degradation.

When renal function is impaired, the significance of nitrogen balance is clearly altered. An individual making no urine whatsoever is incapable of being in very much of a negative nitrogen balance, regardless of the degree of tissue wasting. If he is taking no nitrogen in, the small loss in the feces, sweat, and vomitus represents his only egress of nitrogen. Such

an individual may be breaking down muscular tissues rapidly, particularly if he has just been severely wounded. In this case nitrogen compounds of low molecular weight, which would ordinarily appear in one form or another in the urine, build up in body water to produce the characteristic azotemia. Under this circumstance, over-all nitrogen balance is meaningless but one may contemplate—if not calculate—the "nitrogen balance" between the cells and the extracellular fluid: there is clearly a negative nitrogen balance of the cells themselves and the end-products are accumulating in the extracellular fluid.

When the patient is infused directly, usually by the intravenous route, with whole protein in the form of plasma protein, hydrolysates, or albumin, nitrogen balance temporarily loses its significance. This protein may be infused much more rapidly than the organism can metabolize and excrete it. This occurs in the plasma treatment of early burns. It takes time for metabolic processes to degrade the injected protein or albumin into smaller forms in which excretion can occur, and, for this reason, the patient can readily build up a "false positive" nitrogen balance which is devoid of the significance of tissue synthesis. Similarly, over the course of a few hours, it is possible to inject much more protein hydrolysate than the body can excrete; during this period a transient nitrogen positivity is built up which is associated with the accumulation of nitrogen compounds of low molecular weight in body fluid but which lacks an appropriate increase in the rate of protein synthesis. Amino acids and small polypeptides can be excreted in the urine as such, but the total rate of urine flow and the urine concentration are controlling factors in the rapidity with which this excretion can occur.

2. The Body Carbohydrate, Glycogen Formation, and Glycolysis

In sharp contrast to the large amounts of protein, fat, water, and salts in the body, the total body carbohydrate is very small. It has been estimated at approximately 400 gm. in the normal individual. This carbohydrate is largely present as glycogen in the liver and in muscle. Although carbohydrate represents the primary, preferred fuel of the body, the daily carbohydrate intake will be virtually as large as the total body carbohydrate. The life of carbohydrates in the body is short indeed. Their ingestion is shortly followed by hydrolysis to monosaccharides and then absorption. The majority of absorbed carbohydrate (around 55 per cent) enters rapidly into the energy cycle and is converted into thermal or kinetic energy by its combustion to carbon dioxide and water. This carbon dioxide leaves the body almost wholly via the lungs (approximately 90 per cent), only a tiny fraction of the total burned carbon being represented by urinary bicarbonate at ordinary urine pH.

When carbohydrate is ingested in excess of need, glycogen stores may be increased to some extent, particularly in the liver. Muscle glycogen is necessary for aerobic and anaerobic muscular contraction, whereas liver glycogen is more labile and may rightly be referred to as "storage carbohydrate." The glycogen deposited in liver can be rapidly broken down and indeed, after a short fast, particularly with stress after surgical operation or injury, the liver glycogen is reduced from normal concentrations to extremely low values in a matter of hours. Muscle glycogen is for muscle alone; liver glycogen is available for work anywhere.

The remaining excess carbohydrate is converted into fat, the predominant form of energy storage in the body.

3. The Deposition and Mobilization of Fat; Carbon Balance

In the normal person, deposition of fat signifies that the individual's caloric intake is in excess of daily work requirements; fat mobilization signifies the reverse, namely that the caloric needs of the organism are not wholly met by exogenous intake.

Under certain pathologic circumstances these generalizations are not valid, but through most of surgical metabolism they are. The late convalescent rate of deposition of fat is not very rapid in an individual eating a normal diet and not being force-fed or overeating for other purposes. It is in the general neighborhood of 50 to 150 gm. a day, corresponding to a weight gain of about a kg. a week (2.2 pounds per week). Such weight gain, of course, must be interpreted in the light of other body compositional changes. An individual in the convalescent phase of acute poliomyelitis, for instance, may still be undergoing atrophy of the lean muscular tissues while fat is increasing. The net daily weight gain is then less than the net fat deposition.

The mobilization of fat proceeds in starvation at rates of 75 to 100 gm. a day. As we shall see later, after surgical operation or injury the mobilization of fat occurs at much more rapid rates, up to 500 gm. per day. This "shift over" from exogenous carbohydrate intake to endogenous fat oxidation as the chief source of bodily energy is one of the basic metabolic phenomena of surgery. The greatly increased rate of fat oxidation which may be observed in certain patients under certain circumstances is an even more remarkable aspect of this energy shift. The energy balance sheet may be expressed on the basis of the total carbon intake and output; the total carbon oxidized is the basic indicator of energy production. In a normal day's intake there is about 185 gm. of carbon, this being returned largely as expired carbon dioxide (160 gm.) and the remainder in feces and urine, the amount in the latter depending to some extent on acid-base balance. After trauma the body's total production of energy, and therefore of carbon dioxide, goes up, at the expense of lean tissue and body fat, the carbon (i.e., energy) intake being very small in most instances.

A regular adult diet contains about 350 gm. of (dry) organic material. Protein is about 14 per cent nitrogen. Amino acids average about 52 per cent carbon, while carbohydrate is 44 per cent carbon and fat 77 per cent.

4. Caloric Needs and Their Satisfaction

The caloric needs of the subject may be judged by measuring his change in body weight and body composition under varying circumstances, by measuring his oxygen consumption (his "BMR," but hardly "basal," as explained on page 91) and nitrogen output, or, most accurately, by measuring simultaneously his oxygen consumption and carbon dioxide output. The adult in sedentary work eats about 2400 calories and maintains body weight at normal. With heavy muscular exercise or outdoor activity, caloric needs rise to the range of 3600 to 4000 calories per day. On the basis of oxygen consumption, it has been estimated that patients with severe sepsis and high fever and in the acute phase of burns may be burning substrates rapidly enough to produce as much as 3500 to 4500 calories per day. Normal resting adult heat production is about 80 calories per hour. This corresponds to a dietary intake of 1920 calories per day in a normal man. Other levels are:

	Cal. per hour
Sitting reading	105
Typing	140
Swimming	500
Running	570

There is thus approximately a factor of 5 in human caloric potential contrasting rest (awake) with maximum effort. Severe surgical illness appears to raise caloric needs considerably, along the full-scale potential, even though the patient is lying apparently quietly in bed.

Under certain circumstances this large caloric need can be met by mouth, but in acute illness this is rare. Most of the caloric requirements of the acutely ill patient are met by oxidation of the patient's own body fat. Nutriment given from other sources may, if trauma is not too recent or severe, "spare" some of his own fat or lean tissue. The lysis of cellular tissue such as muscle does produce some caloric supplement as the protein is burned, but this contribution is relatively small as compared with fat, not only because fat yields more calories per gram but because the protein content of wet tissue is comparatively small (about 27 per cent of the wet weight of the tissue).

An individual who is not eating and who is receiving small amounts of carbohydrate by vein (as for example an individual on a daily intravenous ration of 2000 ml. of 5 per cent dextrose in water) will receive some caloric supply from this source (in the given instance 400 calories). Although such calories are few in relation to total demand, there is some evidence that even they are important in "sparing" the further oxidation of nitrogen compounds. This is especially true in the resting individual; protein "sparing" may require larger amounts of carbohydrate in the postoperative patient, as described in Part IV. As far as known, the maximum protein-sparing and antiketogenic effect of carbohydrate, in the nondiabetic, is reached at intakes of 100 gm.

Individuals receiving large amounts of carbohydrate by vein inevitably lose some of this in the urine unless the carbohydrate is "covered" accurately by large amounts of insulin. This urinary sugar excretion is important chiefly in its osmotic effect since it removes water from the body, particularly if the urine osmolality is fixed at low or constant values by renal tubular disease or by antidiuresis. Its significance from the point of view of caloric loss is small since even a gross glycosuria in the face of glucose infusion represents only a small percentage of the total glucose infused.

The lysis of lean tissue and the oxidation of fat provide not only energy, but also sodium-free water, released from the cells. If normally excreted it merely acts as a water source—like the camel's hump. But if released during an antidiuretic phase of negative free water clearance, as occurs after operations and injuries, this new water dilutes the plasma solids and contributes to the dilutional hypotonicity so characteristically seen after surgery. After severe injury, tissue destruction may approach 500 gm. of fat and 500 gm. of lean tissue a day as the extreme upper limit. This provides a total of about 1 liter of new sodium-free water in the total body water. Water of oxidation can also be approximated as 10 ml. per 100 calories, if water is entirely endogenous. These aspects are discussed in full in Part III.

B. WATER AND SALT

1. Renal Function

With good hydration, the normal urea clearance is 60 to 100 ml. per minute. Using as reference the normal adult, with 1.73

square meters of surface, the normal glomerular filtration by either inulin or endogenous creatinine is for men 127 ml. per minute, for women 117 ml. per minute. The glomerular filtration rate is about 100 liters per square meter per day.

Based on measurements using Diodrast at low concentrations, the renal plasma flow is about 740 ml. per minute, equivalent to renal blood flow of about 1200 ml. per minute.

The normal kidneys contain about one million glomeruli each. In destructive disease, below a count of about 750,000 (total) the phenomena are those of continuous solute diuresis in the normal tubules that remain, yielding a poorly-processed urine of fixed concentration. Renal adjustments are inflexible, and the kidneys are unable to excrete acid normally.

About 125 ml. of glomerular filtrate is formed per minute, or 180 liters per day. In a typical urine:

	Filtered (mm./day)	Excreted (mm./day)	Reabsorbed	
			mm./day	percentage
Na	25,560	111	25,449	99.6
Cl	18,540	119	18,421	99.4
K	900	60	840	93.4

About one-fifth of the plasma reaching a glomerulus passes through into the tubular lumen as filtrate. The remainder passes on to the vessels supplying the tubular cells and thence into the renal vein.

Normal solute excretion is 750 mO. per square meter per day; in a diabetic, up to 3000 mO. per day.

It requires about 25 per cent of the normal glomeruli to excrete a normal nitrogen load as urea.

When the glomerular filtration rate falls below 20 ml. per hour, renal function is entirely the prey of filtration; "filtration failure" may be said to exist. Under other circumstances with high filtration and high volume, there may be azotemia and acidosis (but rarely true uremia). These latter may result from altered tubular function, on the one hand, or increased load of solute, on the other; in sepsis and after traumatic shock both are present and certain of the chemical indices of renal failure may coexist with high renal outputs. Many further details of renal function in surgery are discussed in Parts III and V.

2. Water Balance and Turnover

The "available new water" of a normal individual arises chiefly from water taken in as such. It totals approximately 1500 ml. a day. Water contained in foodstuffs accounts for another 250 ml. of water. The water of oxidation of the food (chiefly from the oxidation of the fat) accounts for a small increment of about 100 ml., depending on the nature of the food.

This water is then lost from the body chiefly through the urine (approximately 1200 ml. per day) and additionally through the lungs and skin. The ambient temperature and humidity, as well as bodily exercise, are predominant factors in cutaneous skin loss. In the resting surgical patient under hospital conditions at normal room temperature, the skin loss of water is not great (100 ml. per day). Pulmonary water loss is similarly not very large in such circumstances, in the male averaging 500 to 700 ml. per day and in the female about 300 to 500 ml. per day. This latter factor is subject to tremendous variation. In the patient with high fever and dyspnea, the pulmonary water loss may rise rapidly to figures over 3000 ml. per day. Such large water losses impose large caloric demands on the organism through provision for the heat of vaporization, as well as large water demands.

The dynamics of water excretion through the kidney represents an area in physiology and biochemistry of which recent advance has given us a much clearer understanding. The kidney cannot excrete water without some solute (solids in solution) and similarly cannot excrete solute without water (except in the form of renal stones!). The normal kidney can adjust its total flow and solute concentration over a wide range, but one of the characteristics of renal function in the sick surgical patient is the distortion of these homeostatic boundaries within which the kidney operates. The range of concentration tends to be fixed, rendering the excretion of water obligatory if solute excretion is high.

This makes the surgical patient vulnerable to the dehydrating effect of solute diuresis.

3. Sodium and Potassium Balance; Potassium: Nitrogen Ratio

The normal individual eats between 100 and 250 mE. of sodium per day. This rather great variation depends on the degree of saltiness he enjoys in his food. This sodium is excreted almost entirely in the urine; sodium turnover takes place via the extracellular phase. The amount of sodium taken in per day is, however, only about 10 per cent of the active sodium in the body, and if small tracer amounts of sodium are added to the diet it is found that the sodium "turnover" is very small, as one would expect with a small daily intake in relation to a large body pool, exactly the reverse of the carbohydrate situation. Another characteristic of sodium metabolism is the wide fluctuation in balance from day to day. If a normal individual is allowed to drink water and have food ad lib., it will be found that his sodium balance swings up and down from day to day, going through a range from about +75 mE. to −75 mE. This episodic nature of sodium balance probably has no very profound significance and is related merely to "happen-chance" variations in the rate of water and salt intake with overlappings of the twenty-four-hour period, but it does cause random weight fluctuations which may be confusing if this factor is not appreciated. If the balance is noted over "metabolic periods" of three to seven days, this variability disappears.

If the extracellular sodium concentration remains constant, the loss of 75 mE. of sodium indicates the loss of approximately 500 ml. of extracellular fluid (and 500 gm. of weight). It is therefore clear that sudden changes in sodium balance will, other things being equal, produce variations in weight which are due to alterations in total body water. These sodium-induced weight changes must be taken into consideration in viewing the short-term relationship of body weight to metabolic balance. Even if the sodium concentration undergoes gross changes during sodium loss as, for example, falling from 140 to 120 mE.

per l., the loss of large amounts of sodium still indicates the loss of very large amounts of water, in this case somewhat less than if the concentration remained constant.

Potassium balance is rather less prone to random fluctuations than is sodium balance. One might predict this from the site of potassium in the body and the fact that the entire body cell mass cannot fluctuate as rapidly in either direction as can the extracellular volume or concentration. A normal man eats about 100 mE. of potassium a day and excretes about 95 mE. in the urine, 5 mE. in the feces. The potassium balance from day to day is quite constant—approximating zero in the normal individual. Potassium turnover is also very slow, because the daily intake constitutes such a small fraction of the total pool in which it is diluted.

The relationship of potassium to nitrogen in the balance is of interest. As previously mentioned, the two coexist in certain muscular cells at a ratio of about 3 mE. of potassium per gm. of nitrogen. In tendon, connective tissue, and dermis, there is much more protein per unit of potassium. If an individual is losing tissue largely composed of skeletal muscle cells, one might then expect the over-all balance ratio to have a potassium : nitrogen relationship similar to that of muscle. This is observed quite frequently in certain types of starvation and in chronic weight change in surgery. In most acute convalescent situations the potassium : nitrogen ratio departs rather markedly in one direction or another from the so-called lean-tissue ratio. Early after injury the K : N ratio is high; later (especially in burns) it is very low.

C. ACID-BASE REGULATION

All earth-dwelling vertebrates live under constant threat of two enemies: dehydration and acidosis. The kidney protects us against the former; both kidney and lung join to combat acidosis. This has two results:

(1) disease of kidney or lung leads to acidosis;

(2) we have few physiologic compensations for alkalosis.

The principal acid-base regulatory mechanisms are three in number: the blood and body buffers, respiratory ventilation, and renal excretion.

1. The Blood and Body Buffers

The buffering capacity of a solution is defined as the ability of that solution to take up or discharge hydrogen ion per unit change in pH. A large-capacity buffer accepts much hydrogen ion with little change in pH. The chief buffer systems in blood are those of hemoglobin and of the bicarbonate system. When the ratio of bicarbonate to carbonic acid in the blood changes, the pH changes; and the relation between the two may be used as an expression of the pH. This is because the normal pH of blood is close to the pk of the bicarbonate buffer pair. Under conditions of ordinary surgical disease, the buffering capacity of the blood does not undergo any change except as the buffers are taken up by acidosis itself, or base loss. Anemia reduces the content of a most important buffer: hemoglobin.

In considering the blood buffers as contributing to the capacity of the whole body to take up and discharge hydrogen ion, we are apt to neglect the fact that the extracellular fluid as a whole contains all the blood buffers (except the hemoglobin group). The total capacity of the extracellular phase is therefore greater than that of the blood alone. Intracellular buffer systems are not well understood (except for the red cell) but they are very large in buffer capacity and account for the fact that the total buffering capacity of the body as a whole is far greater than that of the extracellular fluid and blood combined. In uremia, the acid load is 75 mE. per day; there is 1000 mE. of buffer base to deal with this load in the body as a whole.

2. Pulmonary Ventilation

The primary pulmonary mechanism of acid-base regulation depends upon the ventilatory capacity of the lungs to remove carbon dioxide from the blood. The actual loss of hydrogen ion is via the water molecule. As this is done, more carbon dioxide and water are formed from carbonic acid. For this reason, large amounts of carbonic acid are removed from the body through the lungs every day, without change in the total carbon dioxide or bicarbonate concentration. This normal process requires carbonic anhydrase and normal pulmonary blood flow and ventilation. It may be greatly accelerated in response to the formation of large amounts of carbonic acid, as is found after the oxidation of a large amount of carbohydrate or fat, or in acidosis due to accumulation of hydrogen ion with some other anion. In either case the lung then blows off carbon dioxide and water as a compensatory mechanism, lowering the total carbon dioxide and bicarbonate in the blood and producing the picture of metabolic acidosis, in which there is accumulation of hydrogen ion with fixed anions such as chloride or keto-acid and a low blood bicarbonate, total carbon dioxide, carbon dioxide combining power, and carbon dioxide tension.

While the kidney excretes 45 mM. of fixed acid per day, the lung removes 12,000 to 20,000 mM. of CO_2 per day.

Under conditions of hyperventilation, the excess carbon dioxide (and water which carries the hydrogen ion) may be exhaled more rapidly than it is formed, to produce a respiratory alkalosis. Under conditions of diminished ventilation the accumulation of hydrogen ion and carbon dioxide produces, by the same token, a respiratory acidosis. This is a common and hazardous occurrence in surgery.

3. Renal Excretion

The renal excretion of hydrogen ion occurs in several forms, of which the most important are ammonia, dihydrogen phosphate, and carbonic acid. All hydrogen excretion save that of ammonia depends upon the hydration of carbon dioxide so as to provide available hydrogen ion; this process requires carbonic anhydrase. In the case of ammonia, the rate of synthesis and excretion of ammonia (in preference to the electrically neutral urea) is governed in part by blood pH and mediated through the glutamine-arginine system of liver and kidney. The renal regulation of acid-base balance is thus a complex one requiring normal renal tubular function and blood supply as well as glomerular filtration. Both are missing in severe injury.

The monohydrogen–dihydrogen phosphate system of buffers accounts for the urinary excretion of hydrogen ions and is governed by phosphatase and by carbonic anhydrase, which makes the hydrogen ion available, from carbon dioxide and water, to hydrogenate monohydrogen phosphate. The bicarbonate–carbonic acid system is under the control of carbonic anhydrase in the renal tubule just as it is in the lung. At a urinary pH below 6.5, it is an unimportant buffer pair. The sum total of these mechanisms is the production of an acid urine and the excretion of a urine of low pH and high titratable acidity in the face of an acid load.

This complex renal regulation of acid-base balance is impaired when there is acute or chronic tubular disease, as is the case in shock or nephrosclerosis, or when the kidney is under strong influence of steroid or antidiuretic hormone as after trauma or operation. When the body is under the influence of adrenal steroids, particularly aldosterone, sodium is being reabsorbed more completely than normal and to a greater extent than chloride, and the renal compensation to alkalosis is markedly impaired. This is a mechanism of great importance in the occurrence of hypokalemic alkalosis in the postoperative patient, when sodium (bicarbonate) excretion is markedly reduced despite the "need" of the body to excrete it in large amounts.

The renal regulation of acid-base balance requires a normal urine volume. Under conditions of maximal distal renal tubular water resorption (dehydration) or diminished glomerular filtration (shock), acid-base regulation is impaired since there is not enough urine formed to excrete the accumulating hydrogen ion. Acidosis occurs readily.

Section III.   Endocrinology

A. PITUITARY HORMONE ACTION

1. Anterior Pituitary

Most of the anterior pituitary hormones, with the possible exception of growth hormone, appear to act directly on a target endocrine gland. The hormone product of this target gland in turn inhibits the pituitary output of its tropic hormone. Thus, a feedback relationship is set up which is self-regulating.

The substance considered to be homogenous, and identified as growth hormone or "somatotropin," has a profound effect on the intermediary metabolism of carbohydrate, fat, and protein, and under certain circumstances it seems to favor skeletal growth and the synthesis of protein. For this reason, its importance in the processes of convalescence may be considerable. It is rather species-specific. At the present time, we are unable to identify the importance of this substance in terms of surgical care; patients recover from total hypophysectomy quite satisfactorily without the administration of any growth-hormone–like substances. But they absolutely require corticosteroids to survive the procedure and live normally thereafter.

In the light of current knowledge of the metabolic care of surgical patients, the ACTH-hydrocortisone system is the most important anterior pituitary relationship. ACTH is a protein hormone or hormones characterized as having a low molecular weight. The substance is sufficiently species-nonspecific so that ACTH of beef or hog origin has a potent effect in man. The assay of ACTH in peripheral blood has recently become available, and from this evidence, as well as the study of adrenal responses, it is suggested that ACTH output is not constant throughout the day but fluctuates from hour to hour and is more prominent in the morning hours. After any type of physical injury, there is an increase in the output of ACTH from the pituitary. This results in a sudden and large increase in the production, by the adrenal, of its various steroid hormones. The electrolyte-active principles (such as aldosterone) appear to be less under pituitary influence than the others, but are also increased in secretion after injury.

There is reason to believe that severe trauma interferes with the pituitary production of gonadotropic hormones after an initial surge, though this has not been conclusively proven by assay.

2. Posterior Pituitary

The posterior pituitary appears to be a storage site for antidiuretic hormone. The significance of the posterior pituitary in its production is not as great. When the posterior pituitary is removed, the subject does not inevitably develop diabetes insipidus so long as certain hypothalamic centers (which can be demonstrated to contain a lipid-like material) are intact. The importance of antidiuretic hormone in the metabolism of convalescence is pointed up by the almost universal occurrence of antidiuresis after injury. This antidiuretic tendency is related to the occurrence of a urinary flow-solute relationship such as one finds under the maximal influence of antidiuretic hormone. It is, in turn, partly responsible for post-traumatic hypotonicity, as described in Part III.

B. ADRENALS

1. Adrenal Cortex

The adrenal cortex secretes a variety of steroid hormones, which can be divided into the following broad classes.

a. The 17-hydroxycorticoids of the hydrocortisone group. In man, hydrocortisone is the predominant steroid of this group. These compounds are active in the intermediary metabolism of carbohydrate, fat, and protein: they are "anti-inflammatory" and in large doses have a number of other tissue effects.

b. Aldosterone or electrocortin. This is a steroid which is particularly active in the metabolism of salt, recalling sodium bicarbonate from the renal tubule.

c. Steroids having estrogenic activity;

d. Steroids having androgenic activity;

e. Miscellaneous steroids. Some of these are relatively inactive biologically and some of them have progestational activity.

These steroids are released by the adrenal cortex into the adrenal vein and thence into the general circulation. Their fate thereafter is a complicated exercise in organic chemistry. The hormones suffer many changes, both by interconversion, whereby they acquire new biologic activity or lose their old activity, and by chemical destruction, reduction, and conjugation. The final excretory product in the urine may bear little or no chemical resemblance to the active hormone in the blood.

Surgical trauma is followed by a gross increase in the blood concentration of ACTH and of the hydrocortisone-like compounds The blood levels of adrenal hormones of the 17-hydroxycorticoid group (the cortisone steroids) can be measured accurately and show very large and sudden changes after injury. The urinary products are also measurable by a variety of chemical and biologic assays. The blood curve is probably more indicative of the actual level of the free hormone affecting the metabolism of body cells, whereas the urinary excretion curve may be a more accurate index of the total secretory activity of the adrenal cortex over a period of several days.

The mode of action of adrenal steroids is unknown. Many tissues do not function normally without them. Their action has been referred to as normalizing, since they produce changes toward normal, the exact direction of change being determined by the set of the cells or tissues before hormone action begins. They have also been thought of as permissive, in that their presence is essential to permit a tissue to exhibit changes initiated by another agency or stimulus. And finally they require the presence of other hormones (insulin, catechol amines) in order to demonstrate their maximum effect.

2. Adrenal Medulla

The adrenal medulla is probably the only site in the body for the production of epinephrine and is one of the many sites for the production of a closely related compound known as norepinephrine. Norepinephrine is also produced by many extra-adrenal sites, chiefly peripheral synapses and nerve-endings. Both of these catechol amines play an important role in emergencies through the maintenance of normal vasoconstrictive responses, cardiac output, and blood pressure. Heart rate and coronary flow are responsive to those substances, as are certain intermediary metabolic factors, such as the production of glucose from liver glycogen.

Under many circumstances, the production of these hormones is increased by surgical trauma. There appears to be an especially large increase when there is hemorrhage, shock, anoxia, or excessive emotional tension. The increase in peripheral blood level of these hormones is much more difficult to demonstrate than is their increased secretion into the adrenal vein blood or into the urine.

It appeared for some years that the catechol amines (epinephrine and norepinephrine) were capable of stimulating the production of adrenal cortical hormones via ACTH. Current evidence does not favor this hypothesis; but the catechol amines can lower the eosinophil count (formerly thought to be an evidence of adrenocortical discharge) without the intermediary action of anterior pituitary or adrenal cortex.

C. PITUITARY:ADRENAL RELATIONSHIPS

Substances and/or impulses arising in the periphery and communicated to the midbrain stimulate the pituitary to produce ACTH. This pathway of stimulus is activated after injury. In tissue culture this part of the brain can be shown to stimulate the pituitary-adrenal axis directly.

In the absence of the pituitary, the adrenal gradually undergoes atrophy and its secretory activity drops down to a low level. A similar change occurs upon the administration of an active steroid such as cortisone. The secretion of hydrocortisone first shows inhibition, and the inhibition of aldosterone follows slowly. After prolonged cortisone administration, this inhibition can easily be seen on gross or microscopic examination, and surgical convalescence may be threatened by the absence either of hydrocortisone or of aldosterone.

Prolonged severe illness or administration of large amounts of ACTH results in a prominent hypertrophy of the adrenal glands and a greatly increased production of 17-hydroxycorticoids. There is good evidence that there is increased production of adrenal androgens upon administration of ACTH. The evidence for increased production of estrogens is not as clear.

The secretion of aldosterone seems to be somewhat independent of ACTH effects, although not entirely so, since the administration of ACTH to a normal individual results in an immediate alteration in salt metabolism that is somewhat more prominent than one would predict on the basis of hydrocortisone alone.

The reciprocal regulatory activity of the pituitary-adrenal axis is therefore well documented, at least for pharmacologically administered hormones in the normal person. The evidence that the increase in free hydrocortisone in the blood produced, for instance, by surgical operation is followed by decreased ACTH output is not as conclusive.

A severe surgical injury such as a burn or extensive wound produces changes in almost all the bodily systems and metabolic processes. There are few endocrine relations in the body which do not appear to be altered after severe injury.

This introductory comment is necessarily brief; an account of details and the scientific evidence on which these accounts are based is to be found in the later chapters of this Part.

D. CONSERVATION OF WATER, SALT, AND FUNCTIONAL EXTRACELLULAR VOLUME

Two of the most prominent metabolic activities of normal man, already alluded to briefly, and considered to be due in part to endocrine activity, are the conservation of water and the conservation of salt. These act in concert to maintain the integrity of the volume of extracellular fluid and hence of the plasma and blood.

1. Normal Salt Conservation

As mentioned before, the normal individual excretes an intravenously administered load of sodium chloride rather slowly. An intravenously administered tracer dose of radioactive sodium, so small in total quantity that it does not affect the total body sodium but dilutes throughout its mass, is excreted in the urine only to the extent of 1 or 2 per cent in the first twenty-four hours; sodium turnover is slow. The body's economy of extracellular salt is geared to conservation of these substances and of the water which is retained with them, at isotonic osmolality and in normal volume.

The extent to which water and salt are reabsorbed in the proximal tubule is in part a function of flow rate. For this reason, where decreased glomerular filtration rate occurs, tubular resorption can be of maximum efficiency if blood flow is good. When very large amounts of filtrate are held in the tubule by nonresorbed solute (as in solute diuresis), tubular processing is very incomplete; water is carried out by solute, ion exchange is incomplete, so that hypertonicity and acidosis are common sequelae.

Reduction of the effective volume of extracellular fluid (and, of necessity, plasma) is a most important stimulus to increased aldosterone production, yet under conditions of even the most transient sodium loss, such as is produced by sweating on a hot day, aldosterone, a strong salt-conserving force, comes into the circulation in increased amounts, giving added impetus to normal salt conservation. This steroidal hormone is secreted by the adrenal cortex in amounts which may be of the order of magnitude of only one-thousandth of that found for the compound F group of hormones. But its activity in salt conservation is immense. In the resting state, renal tubular sodium resorption is only partially under the influence of aldosterone; in the stimulated state and at low flow rates the tubular sodium resorption is essentially 100 per cent complete, as stimulated by aldosterone.

An important and, in a sense, peculiar result accrues from the small size of the daily sodium excretion in relation to the large filtration. If tubular sodium resorption is fixed or maximal for any one of many reasons, a very small increase in sodium filtration (e.g., 2 per cent) will double or treble the total sodium excretion. Similarly, a small decrease in glomerular filtration rate will virtually eliminate sodium from the urine. Such changes may at times be of critical importance; in hypotonic expansion of the extracellular fluid such increases may be associated with operation of a volume-sensitive mechanism.

The renal dynamics of potassium metabolism are rather different. The 100 mE. per day of potassium excretion represents a high percentage of the total filtered potassium (about 93 per cent), partly because potassium is also secreted by the tubule. Under conditions of potassium loss or deprivation, renal potassium excretion continues for several days at levels as high as 40 mE. per day. It has been shown that with very prolonged potassium deprivation, the renal potassium loss may be as low as 1 to 5 mE. per day. It is also of interest that during a period of sharp potassium loading in cells, as is characteristically found in the early days of spontaneous postoperative anabolism, the urinary potassium loss is reduced to a very low figure. The same steroid forces which produce sodium conservation tend to increase potassium loss. This is true both of hydrocortisone and of aldosterone and relates to hydrogen ion exchange not only in the renal tubule but also throughout the body. The tendency to sodium conservation and potassium wastage which occurs after trauma suggests an aldosterone effect.

2. Water Conservation and Free Water Clearance

Losses of pure water from the body increase osmolality; tiny increases in osmolality stimulate an area (the osmoreceptor) in the midbrain which in turn stimulates the elaboration of antidiuretic hormone (ADH); urine osmolality is increased and volume reduced by dint of water resorption in the distal tubule. Among other earmarks of this antidiuretic state is the fact that urine volume becomes directly proportional to total solute excretion.

An excess of water, by an inverse mechanism, "releases" the tubule from the effect of ADH and a diuresis of dilute urine results. When this ADH effect is inappropriately maintained in the face of water loading, severe hypotonicity results. This occurs readily after injury or operation.

If the plasma osmolality is 285 mO. per l. (a normal value) and the urine is also 285 mO. per l., the subject is said to be in "zero free water clearance," meaning that he is, in net effect, neither adding nor subtracting water in processing the glomerular filtrate. If the urine is more concentrated (as is usually the case), one may calculate (from the osmotic U:P ratio and urine flow) the removal of water from the distal tubule in ml. per minute. This is called "negative free water clearance." It is the normal renal situation, an expression of resting antidiuretic "tone," and the normal negative free water clearance is 1 to 2 ml. per minute. The maintenance of negative free water clearance in the face of water loading and hypotonicity is the diagnostic trademark of inappropriate antidiuresis, an antidiuresis maintained when water excretion would seem called for. This is observed after injury and in chronic visceral disease.

When the urine osmolality falls below that of plasma there is a net excretion of more water than solute. This is "positive free water clearance." The maximum value is near 15 ml. per minute. This is diagnostic of "no anti-diuretic effect"; it is seen in water loading in normal persons, and in diabetes insipidus. It is virtually never seen in the early post-traumatic period.

Recent evidence has suggested a distal tubular site where water resorption is independent of antidiuretic hormone, but of low total capacity. Thus, when glomerular filtration is low (as in shock, for example), water resorption at this distal site may process the urine to an osmolality of, say, 500 mO. per l. (approximately a specific gravity of 1.018), even in the absence of antidiuretic hormone. This accounts for the long-known but poorly understood fact that severely dehydrated patients with diabetes insipidus elaborate a somewhat concentrated urine. It is also very important in considering and interpreting the osmolality of the urine in burns, shock, and early renal failure.

3. Maintenance of Volume

Only recently suspected, poorly delineated, yet of most remarkable surgical interest are those bodily mechanisms which maintain effective volume in the face of bodily changes which do not alter salt or solute concentration.

These mechanisms appear to act on the renal tubule by the resorption of water (activated by antidiuretic hormone) and sodium (by aldosterone) and also, when volume is severely threatened, by renal vasoconstriction (caused by catechol amines). There are seemingly additional effector mechanisms independent of these hormones. The location or nature of the "sensing" centers is unknown; they may be sensitive to arterial pressure, venous pressure, arteriovenous pressure difference, oxygenation, intracellular hydration, or some other stimuli as yet unknown.[*] They may be located in the periphery, in the right heart, or in the neck, or head, or in several places. Hemorrhage is the classic and commonest example of a "volume receptor" stimulus. Although there is no change in concentrations, osmolality, or glomerular filtration rate, a small hemorrhage excites near-maximal tubular resorption of water and salt, thus tending to preserve the volume of extracellular fluid, which in turn regulates volume of plasma and the blood pressure. Hemorrhage, continuing or unreplaced, may be responsible for continued post-traumatic retention of water and salt far beyond the apparent balance requirement for these substances. Adequate blood replacement may therefore do much to restore to normal the excretion of water and salt after surgical operations. Volume regulation is dealt with in greater detail in Part II and Part III.

The foregoing pages have been a brief account of the metabolic setting in which trauma occurs. The next three chapters will describe some of the alterations that ensue in this orderly arrangement when the patient suffers bodily injury or undergoes a surgical operation.

---

[*] The point must be emphasized that the regulation of effective extracellular and circulating blood volume probably resides in mechanisms sensitive to some stimulus other than volume itself. Such terms as "volume-sensitive" and "volume receptor" are merely convenient shorthand or slang for a variety of interlocking and poorly understood mechanisms.

CHAPTER 2

Convalescence in the Healthy:
Closed Soft-Tissue Trauma
of Moderate Severity

Introduction.   The Extent of Injury

However one wishes to consider trauma, and by whatever criteria one wishes to grade its severity, a range is apparent. Whether one looks at the patient right after the operation, asks him how he feels, takes his pulse, examines the anesthesia chart, counts the empties in the blood bank, analyzes the urine for hormones, talks to the nurse, or does serial plasma sodium determinations, by whatever criteria one might choose, one reconfirms the obvious fact that some injury is severe, some operations extensive, while others are slight. Surgical care in the post-traumatic state is governed in large part by the severity of the injury sustained, its nature as a wound, and the previous health of the individual.

Moderate operative trauma of the closed soft-tissue type, without fracture, in which primary healing occurs without infection, represents in a sense the civilian surgical "norm." The pattern of convalescence in this type of injury demonstrates the dynamic changes which we think of as the phases of convalescence, their endocrinology, metabolism, and clinical management. This norm provides a convenient backdrop for the contrasting patterns of other surgical trauma and it involves important changes in the normal system of body composition, metabolism, and endocrinology just described.

To grade or indicate the extent of trauma, a simple "scale of ten" was proposed (Moore and Ball, 1952) in which the lesser traumata, such as the repair of a small hernia, were regarded as scale 1 or 2 where the most extensive injuries, such as burns and multiple open wounds of soft parts and bone, occupied scale 9 or 10. At this high end of the scale were also included multivisceral cancer operations if difficult and sanguinous. In the midscale ranges were ordinary elective surgical traumata of the type induced by such operations as subtotal gastrectomy, prostatectomy, pneumonectomy, or colectomy. This simple scale of trauma has been a useful one in bringing into focus the various factors which influence the magnitude of the systemic response to trauma. Grant has graded surgical trauma according to the amount of tissue involved, using the volume of tissue indicated by the closed fist as a single unit; this represents a sort of rough grading of trauma as he has applied it to the study of shock.

Churchill expressed this concept in stating that the severity of a wound was the sum total or net vector of all factors acting in the direction of deterioration.

Howard (BCK, I)* and his group evolved a much more complex and thorough point system for the evaluation of a wound. A total of forty points was a maximum for a very severe wound carrying a very high mortality. The points were based on the anatomic nature of the wound, its duration, and the requirements for resuscitation as follows:

		Points
1. Nature of injury		
Simple penetration		1
Femoral or pelvic fractures		2
Other fractures		1
For each "fist" of tissue damaged		1
Ankle or wrist amputation		1
Calf or upper arm amputation		2
Middle or upper thigh amputation		3
Penetration of:		1 each
Stomach		
Duodenum		
Spleen		
Intestine		
Bladder		
Lungs		
Penetration of kidney		1.5
Nephrectomy		2
Liver laceration		1 to 3
Multiple intestinal perforations		2 to 3

2. Duration
   1 point per 2 hour interval before admission to site equipped for definitive surgery.
3. Resuscitation
   1 point for each 5 units of intravenous therapy needed in resuscitation.

By such a system, for example, a severe multiple-penetration injury involving the liver and intestine, with one supracondylar amputation and requiring seventeen units of blood for resuscitation, with four hours' duration before admission, would total sixteen points. Many patients with survival totaled twenty to thirty points; wounds of less than five points rarely presented any serious problem.

Such grading has been a useful device but

---

* The abbreviation "BCK" refers to the volumes entitled *Battle Casualties in Korea* (Howard, ed., 1955). The numeral refers to the volume. The abbreviation "BSSW" refers to the reports from the study of casualties in World War II published under the direction of the Board for the Study of the Severely Wounded. (Beecher, ed., 1952).

should not be taken too seriously. There is no accurate way to quantify the multiplicity of stimuli which enter the surgical experience. The stimuli to endocrine and metabolic change in the surgical patient are numerous if not innumerable. Pain and apprehension enter as neuropsychologic stimuli; sedative drugs, opiates, and anesthetics all influence the response of the body; starvation, immobilization, and hemorrhage are a part of the injury. And finally, the tissue trauma itself, be it primarily closed injury (as in elective surgery), open injury, fracture, or burn, is a most important stimulus to metabolic change. Any subsequent infection adds to the injury. When there is the passage of time between the injury (as in unanesthetized war wounds) and definitive surgery (the repair of soft parts, immobilization of fracture, control of bleeding, and removal of devitalized tissue), this passage of time profoundly influences the severity of the injury. Ensuing sepsis is a unique feature of trauma in its ability to stimulate metabolic change. If there is shock, the physiologic and metabolic response is influenced drastically by the hemodynamic changes which occur and by the tissue anoxia, which, if prolonged, leads to death.

A. GRADATION BY ACCRETION OF BIOLOGIC COMPONENTS

Thus a gradation of trauma might be elucidated which depends not only on cross-sectional tissue extent but also on those particular features which challenge survival most bitterly and stimulate bodily change most extensively. Acting on all these is the factor of duration between onset of trauma and the subsidence of maximal homeostatic tension. This latter subsidence occurs with the successful completion of definitive surgery.

When we thus grade the extent of trauma by this "weighted accretion of biologic components" we come up with a system which looks cumbersome, but can be broken down into three groups in ascending scale of significance to the patient.

Group I. Threshold Stimuli. These stimuli initiate endocrine and metabolic changes that are usually minor in extent, transient in duration, or both:

(1) non–tissue-traumatizing stress such as fear, pain, cold, fatigue;
(2) minor tissue injury;
(3) anesthesia and drugs;
(4) immobilization; and
(5) starvation.

Alterations in endocrine activity and the metabolism of carbohydrate, fat, protein, and minerals are discernible. Spontaneous recovery is the rule.

Group II. Threatening Challenges. These stimuli threaten the maintenance of homeostasis and summon a near-maximal response:

(1) extensive injury to tissue;
(2) bleeding, plasma loss (replaced or transient);
(3) fluid accumulation, traumatic edema, desalting water loss; and
(4) anoxia, hypercarbia.

These are strong stimuli to retention of water and salt, peripheral vasoconstriction, and tachycardia. Spontaneous recovery often occurs, but treatment is needed. Any one of them if prolonged or unrepaired can lead to a shocklike state or, in the case of anoxia and hypercarbia, sudden cardiac death.

Group III. Tissue-Killing Injury. These stimuli add the products of tissue degeneration and, in their turn, accelerate the rate of metabolic change associated with tissue lysis and catabolism:

(1) very extensive tissue injury;
(2) invasive sepsis;
(3) necrosis of tissue, either primary (crush, burn) or secondary (sepsis, gangrene); and
(4) shock with prolonged deficiency of blood flow.

These are stimuli which greatly speed the rate of bodily wasting. The toxic products of bacteria and dead tissue are added to the body fluids; tissues remote from the injury (liver, brain, kidney) suffer severe changes in shock. Maximum homeostatic tension builds up; spontaneous recovery is rare and treatment difficult.

B. PHASES OF CONVALESCENCE

The division of surgical convalescence into four phases has proved to be a useful device.

This division into several phases was outlined by the author in 1952. Some of the details of this description were revised three years later and the presentation here represents a further revision as further facts have become available. Every patient shows some departure in one way or another from this typical pattern; individual variation is great. The metabolic trends in the four phases represent the results of very strong inner forces in the convalescent organism. The identification and separation of the phases remain useful even though the duration of phases varies and the divisions may merge clinically with only a few clear landmarks. The duration of the various phases is highly variable according to the health of the individual and the nature of the trauma.

The ensuing account is based on an average male patient; in the female, metabolic and endocrine changes are less pronounced. The smaller lean-tissue mass may account in part for this, or there may be sex-linked factors in in the extent of endocrine or metabolic change.

The concept that there is an integrated endocrine-metabolic sequence in convalescence, and one of survival value to the organism, places convalescence among those adaptive endocrine-metabolic sequences (of which pregnancy is another example) in which certain normal functions are compromised to achieve a specific survival objective. In pregnancy such a sequence, of nine months' duration, results in the delivery of a normal infant and survival of the species. Systemic alterations appear to be devoted to a local tissue change (uterus, placenta) and growth (fetus), directed at the ultimate objective. In convalescence after injury the sequence may take three to twelve months and results in the functional rehabilitation of the patient, his return to normal activity, and survival of the individual. Systemic changes (loss of muscle, fat) are devoted to caloric needs and local growth (healing of the wound), all directed at the ultimate objective of survival. In the Darwinian sense, surgical metabolism is primarily concerned with the basic survival mechanisms of the individual.

Section I.   Injury—the First Phase

A. CLINICAL APPEARANCES

After an operation of the magnitude of pneumonectomy, total gastrectomy, combined abdominoperineal resection, total perineal prostatectomy, or esophagectomy, the patient is seen to lie quietly in bed after he arouses from anesthesia. He has a somewhat rapid pulse, a desire to be undisturbed, a lack of interest in his surroundings or visitors, a lack of interest in food. If left to his own devices, the patient will sleep a good deal more than usual. If pain from the incision is bothersome, he will try to find a comfortable position and will resist efforts to be moved. Within a few hours the tendency to tachycardia will become less apparent if blood loss has been quantitatively replaced, and by the next morning the pulse will be slower, although the temperature may be elevated a degree or so. Peristalsis audible for the first twelve to twenty-four hours may become diminished or absent for a day or two, depending on whether or not the trauma has involved the peritoneal cavity. If the trauma is extraperitoneal but rather severe, peristalsis will also be absent, but for a shorter time.

This initial phase after extensive surgery persists for from two to four days and corresponds approximately to a period when the endocrine and metabolic picture resembles that produced by adrenergic and adrenocortical hormones. Hence the term "adrenergic-corticoid" phase. A better term is the "phase of injury." It is this phase toward the elucidation of which so much study has been devoted; it is the phase of convalescence about which the most accurate information is currently available.

This duration of the first, or "injury," phase depends largely on the extent of the trauma, that extent measured in terms of its gradation by weighted biologic components. Any unreplaced blood loss, extensive fluid dislocation, or acid-base change (Group II stimuli) will deepen and prolong the response; any Group III changes (sepsis, necrosis, shock) immediately take it out of the range we have set up as our norm for descriptive purposes. Both here and in the succeeding account one is dealing with major surgery, with blood loss replaced and fluid accumulation minimal. This would be a mid-scale injury with Group II stimuli transient; an extensive gastrectomy for cancer would be an example.

A variation on the emotional appearance of the sick apathetic patient is the occasional individual exhibiting postoperative euphoria. In civilian surgery this results from psychologic factors, such as a feeling of relief that the long-apprehended operation is over, or a sense that it "was not as bad as I had thought," or a sense of relief from the fear of malignancy. Postoperative euphoria may be related to that noted in the study of the wounded, in which was observed a state of euphoria far outweighing the apparently painful or crippling aspects of the wound. This euphoria was due to a sense of relief on the part of the patient because he had not been killed and was relieved from the further travails of combat.

When in civilian surgery this is manifest, the patient seems euphoric for twenty-four to thirty-six hours. In such cases the traumatic episode later "catches up" with the patient. It may be helpful to warn the patient that while he feels so good the first day he still should not overload his stomach with food or become overinvolved in other endeavors. He will find on the third or fourth day that an emotional downswing will ensue, accompanied by malaise, loss of appetite, and occasionally abdominal distention, following which he will once again resume normal convalescence.

B. THE WOUND

The first few days after the operation occupy the first phase of wound healing, a phase when tensile strength is low. If the wound must be reopened, it falls apart as the sutures are removed. If unusual stress is placed on the wound, if the sutures are poorly selected, poorly placed, or poorly tied, a tensile disruption may occur.

This early period of wound healing, though tensile strength be low, is of importance to the wound. Accumulation of leucocytes and of plasma containing immune proteins deals with the minor bacterial contamination almost inevitable in the wound despite aseptic technique, which serves only to lower the dose and virulence of bacteria. There also accumulates in the wound during this period a coagulum of substances from which collagen fibrils are later formed. These substances— extracellular fluid with proteins, mucopolysaccharides, ascorbic acid, and amino acids later devoted to tissue synthesis—accumulate in the wound despite the fact that the patient is starving and that other tissues, particularly skeletal muscle, are wasting. Herein lies the concept of the high biologic priority of the early wound, a concept which acquires further meaning in relation to the excellent wound healing often seen in advanced cachexia.

In primary soft-tissue trauma of moderate magnitude, this period (when the wound is held together by sutures and looks very much as it did at the end of the operation) draws to a close as nitrogen loss decreases and eosinophils rise. Such anatomic-metabolic correlation is not always seen in other settings. In the presence of good preoperative nourishment the correlation of early healing with high urine nitrogen excretion rates remains true to form. The correlation with steroid activity is variable. The fact that large pharmacologic doses of cortisone inhibit fibroplasia in the experimental animal has led to the speculation that the early steroid peak may delay fibroplasia to allow removal of detritus, as well as to mobilize substrates for tissue rebuilding. The amount of steroid involved in the clinical setting is far lower than that employed in the animal experiments where healing is inhibited, yet such a mechanism may be a factor in this early amorphous phase of wound healing.

Motion or stress on the wound is painful during this period. Immobilization of the wound is sought by the patient, and often by the doctor.

C. EVIDENCES OF ENDOCRINE CHANGE

1. Adrenal Medulla

The most potent stimuli to sympathoadrenal secretion of epinephrine and norepineph-rine are psychologic stimuli (excitement, fear, or pain), anoxia, hemorrhage, and oligemic shock. Ether anesthesia is a strong stimulus to the secretion of the adrenal medulla.

The clinical evidences of adrenal medullary stimulation have been considered to be tachycardia, vasoconstriction, and sweating. Tachycardia and vasoconstriction are adrenergic in their end-organ mediation, while sweating is cholinergic although the nervous pathways involved are the sympathetic side of the autonomic nervous system. Injections of epinephrine or norepinephrine produce these changes in variable degrees without the sweating. The pale, blanched, pulsy, and sweating individual is the classic figure of the man facing an ordeal with fear for survival. Add hypotension and one has the picture of shock. Happily, this picture is only rarely seen in civilian surgery where the manners of the surgeon, his attendants, and the anesthetist are wise and merciful, and where the patient has confidence in the outcome of his surgical care. Occasionally the frightened child may show these evidences, though more often than not tachycardia alone is outstanding.

Where surgical shock occurs, this clinical adrenomedullary activity is intense and this observation may be the first clue that shock is imminent even if hypotension has not yet occurred. Since the diastolic blood pressure is a measure of peripheral resistance, a rise in diastolic blood pressure is commonly seen with the onset of peripheral vasoconstriction and is an evidence of sympathoadrenal stimulation, usually the result of decreased blood volume.

By chemical quantitation the urinary excretion of epinephrine and norepinephrine is found to be elevated for a day or two; the blood level is less constantly observed to be elevated.

2. Adrenal Cortex

Historically, the first suggestions of adrenal cortical activity discerned after trauma were the increased rate of nitrogen excretion, decreased rate of sodium excretion, and changes in urinary hormone activity by bioassay. Then came the description of the eosinophil changes, and more recently have come many assays of urinary and blood steroids. Since these latter are in a sense the primary chemical evidences, they will be discussed first. They may or may not correlate in point of time with the metabolic changes described a decade earlier.

After injury, afferent pathways both of the nervous and humoral type stimulate areas of the brain in the floor of the third ventricle. Via these nuclei the anterior pituitary is stimulated to release ACTH into the blood stream in increased amounts. Quantitative assay of this increased blood ACTH after trauma has recently become available. The neuroendocrine mediation of the stress response appears to be a primary homeostatic interaction between nervous tissue and the endocrine system.

a. Hydrocortisone. As a result of stimulation by ACTH after injury, the adrenal cortex secretes increased amounts of hydrocortisone into the peripheral blood. The normal blood level of 17-hydroxycorticoids (largely represented by hydrocortisone in the human subject) is between 5 and 15 mcg. per 100 ml. Within a few minutes after the start of ether anesthesia or a surgical procedure or both, this level rises abruptly to values between 30 and 80 mcg. per 100 ml., depending upon the extent of the trauma, the previous health of the individual, and the nature of the anesthetic agent used. Studies of adrenal vein blood in the dog have made it clear that this increased blood level is due to an increased secretory rate of the adrenal cortex.

When hydrocortisone is secreted into the circulating blood, it is removed from the circulation by several mechanisms, of which the most important are: (1) conjugation as the glucuronide, (2) reduction to dihydro- and tetrahydro-derivatives, (3) degradation, (4) excretion in the urine in the free or conjugated form, and (5) alteration, probably in the liver, to other steroidal configuration, including 17-ketosteroids.

The absolute peak of blood steroid concentration attained during the injury phase of surgical convalescence and the duration of this elevation are functions both of the absolute secretory rate of the adrenal cortex and the rate at which these many mechanisms clear the blood of the hormone. In the case we are considering as an example (elective primary severe soft-tissue surgery in the healthy), there is no operative shock to decrease circulation and inactivation of steroids, there is no overt liver disease, and there is no impairment of renal function other than those changes later to be described as characteristic of normal early post-traumatic physiology. Under these circumstances the peak in blood concentration of hydrocortisone is reached approximately six hours after the induction of anesthetic and from two to four hours after the completion of the operation. If the operation is done in the morning, this peak is attained in about the middle of the afternoon and by the next morning the free plasma corticoid has returned to normal. Measurement of the total plasma corticoid (the term "total" indicating that both the active free steroid and the inactive conjugates are measured) indicates that there is a later peak reached when inactive conjugates are considered. This would be expected from the fact that the drop in free plasma level is due in part to the gradual increase in concentration of conjugated steroids.

The excretion of steroid conjugates in the urine is increased by surgical trauma. The normal value for 17-hydroxycorticoids (free and conjugated) in the urine is 10 to 20 mg. in twenty-four hours. This is increased to ranges from 40 to 60 mg. per twenty-four hours over a period of two to four days in instances of moderately severe trauma such as we are considering here. The total amount of (conjugated) steroid excreted in the urine is probably a more accurate index of the total magnitude of the adrenal discharge than is the blood peak of free steroids. The latter is of more interest with respect to the mechanism by which this discharge occurs and its precise timing.

The urinary excretion of steroids then returns to normal and remains so for the rest of convalescence. There are occasions when rather low urinary steroid values have been observed some days after the peak.

There are a host of other documented evidences of increased steroid excretion after surgical injury, including urinary measurements by a variety of chemical and biologic techniques. These are mentioned in the section on the literature.

b. Eosinophils. Changes in the concentration of eosinophils in the peripheral blood are brought about by sudden changes in the concentration of adrenal hormones in the blood. The totally adrenalectomized subject on constant cortisone dosage will respond to trauma by a drop in eosinophils and his eosinophils will also fall in response to injections of epinephrine. Increases in steroid hormone concentration produce drops in the eosinophil count, but a maintained high steroid concentration will not necessarily keep the eosinophil count down. A fall in steroid level is often associated with a rise in eosinophils, but a prolonged low steroid level is not necessarily associated with a prolonged high eosinophil count. Apparently the rate of change of steroid concentration is a factor of importance in determining the eosinophil count.

In the normal resting individual the eosinophil count ranges from 100 to 300 per cu. mm., with extremes well beyond this range. In general a resting count above 1000 or below 50 cu. mm. is evidence of abnormality. As a surgical patient approaches the operating room, the eosinophil count will often fall 25 to 30 per cent below its starting values; the significance of this change must be viewed with some reservation since the technique for counting eosinophils is inaccurate at best. Shortly after the induction of anesthesia a transient eosinophilia will often be seen, with the count rising to 400 to 500 per cu. mm. before it then drops precipitously to values at or near zero. During surgical operations of moderate severity, the eosinophil count is substantially zero by the time the incision is being closed. The count then remains at this level for from two to four days before it starts its return upward. In many instances the drop in urinary excretion of 17-hydroxycorticoids will be seen to correlate nicely with the rise in blood eosinophils. In other instances this correlation is but poorly demonstrated.

The normal steroid fall and eosinophil rise three to seven days after major surgery is an event of importance in surgical convalescence, since it indicates the progression of convalescence out of the injury phase and on to the periods of anabolism.

The common and important abnormality of the eosinophil count in surgical patients does not relate to the postoperative high count of adrenal failure—a rather rare finding. Instead, it is the prolonged eosinopenia of the complicated surgical convalescence. The advent of sepsis, thrombophlebitis, wound dehiscence, renal failure, atelectasis, or other complications will maintain a low count. After operation of major magnitude a low eosinophil count after the sixth day should be regarded with suspicion as indicating the presence of a tissue complication which demands accurate diagnosis and effective treatment.

c. Aldosterone. The metabolic events occurring in this early phase of surgery would suggest that there is an increased secretion of aldosterone after trauma. There is evidence for this by bioassay but the correlation is not always perfect. It is of interest that aldosterone is an adrenal steroid whose production does not seem to be under the influence of ACTH to as great an extent as some of the other adrenal hormones. This might lead one to suspect that after trauma it need not necessarily be increased in amount unless there were extrarenal salt loss, decreased effective blood volume, or the production of a low plasma sodium concentration by extra-adrenal factors. The latter apparently occurs after surgery (primarily as a result of osmolar dilution) and when it does occur it often coexists with most marked reduction in urinary sodium excretion. It is difficult to know which limb of this paradox—sodium retention with a falling plasma sodium concentration— is primary and which is secondary. It is of interest that volume change rather than concentration change is the more potent stimulus to aldosterone production. Concentration change is a weak stimulant to aldosterone change. Realizing that trauma alters the inactivation of adrenal steroids, even though the liver is not seriously diseased, we can postulate that with small quantities of aldosterone circulating, only minor changes in the rate of aldosterone inactivation could produce a considerable alteration in the renal metabolism of sodium.

3. Other Endocrine Changes

a. Gonads. Gonadal function appears to be decreased after major trauma. Amenorrhea in the female, accompanied by masculine hair growth, and loss of libido in the male are characteristic. If a female is traumatized after the midpoint in the menstrual cycle, when a proliferative endometrium has been established under the influence of estrogens, some uterine bleeding, apparently the result of sudden estrogen withdrawal, will often follow closely after the trauma. Detailed documentation of changes either in pituitary gonadotropic hormones or in gonadal steroids is as yet lacking for surgical patients; there may be an initial upsurge of activity before the quiescent phase.

b. Thyroid. There is an increased oxygen consumption and energy conversion after severe trauma when there is fever. This is due to the operation of several components, of which tissue necrosis and infection are prominent. As will be mentioned below, many body components partake of this increased oxidation, but it seems to be mostly at the expense of body fat. Change could be produced by increased thyroid function, but there is little evidence that there is a systematic increase in thyroid function after trauma. Net energy interconversions result from the relation between caloric intake, glucocorticoid production, thyroid activity, gluconeogenesis, insulin production, and muscular or heat output, the latter seemingly increased in sepsis or after severe trauma. It would therefore be surprising if there were not some alteration in the balance of thyroid activity after injury; measurements of protein-bound iodine and of radioiodine uptake have demonstrated but few alterations, and consistent or predictable patterns of increase or decrease have not been described. Increases in oxygen consumption and carbon dioxide production at the expense of body tissues are readily produced by a variety of extrathyroidal factors, including infection, malignancy, and pregnancy. The magnitude of energy exchange after simple injury is itself unknown.

c. Pancreas. An increase in blood sugar is a sequel of sympathoadrenal stimulation. Excesses of glucocorticoids such as hydrocortisone also raise the blood sugar, owing in part to gluconeogenesis from protein and fat, and in part to their peripheral antagonism to the activity of insulin. As is the case with the thyroid, there is unquestionably a change in the endocrine relationships of the pancreas; there is no evidence as yet of a systematic alteration in its secretion.

d. Parathyroids. Systematic changes in calcium and phosphorus metabolism have only rarely been observed after trauma. If the trauma involves the skeleton and requires immobilization, losses of calcium occur, but they are not large. Hypocalcemia is not a regular accompaniment. Such changes do not suggest altered parathyroid function. Here again one must conclude that the biochemical situation is altered in a way that would be expected to produce a compensatory parathyroid functional change, but there is no evidence that such occurs.

D. METABOLISM AND BIOCHEMISTRY

1. Nitrogen

If renal function is maintained without the severe oliguria of shock or dehydration, with total urine flows in the range of 0.5 to 1.5 ml. per minute or greater, the absolute urine nitrogen excretion rate is increased after an operation such as we are considering here. Starvation alone does not result in an increased absolute urinary nitrogen excretion rate on zero intake. Instead it is associated with the maintenance of urinary nitrogen excretion at a normal or reduced rate (5 to 7 gm. a day after an initial output at rates up to 10 gm. a day) and a gradual further reduction to low values. After major trauma, and with zero intake, one may expect the urinary nitrogen to rise to values from 7 to 15 mg. per day for the first two to five days. If injury is more extensive, this may be increased as high as 20 gm. per day, and with fractures, burns, or major injury complicated by infection, the lysis of lean tissue produces extraordinary urinary nitrogen excretion rates as high as 30 gm. per day. This latter nitrogen excretion corresponds to 180 gm. of protein per day or approximately 1 kg. of wet lean tissue. This nitrogen comes largely from skeletal muscle.

This urinary nitrogen is excreted almost wholly as urea. Other nitrogenous fractions in the urine are of qualitative interest, and minor changes in amino acid pattern may be of significance in considering the etiology and teleology of increased muscle catabolism after trauma. But most of this excretory product follows the familiar nitrogen pathway, producing for excretion an electrically neutral crystalloid—urea—which freely permeates body cells and is not an effective osmolar solute in terms of antidiuretic activity.

In the example considered here, where there is soft-tissue trauma passing on to normal convalescence and healing, this period of increased urinary nitrogen excretion rate persists for from two to five days and correlates very loosely with the period of increased urinary excretion of corticosteroids and the period of lowering of the eosinophil count.

If large amounts of readily utilized calories and nitrogen are provided during this period, the amount of net nitrogen loss may be decreased. This phenomenon suggests that in moderate trauma, starvation plays an important role, a fact further borne out by the observation that in minor injury the rate of catabolism of lean tissue does not exceed that of starvation. That starvation is not the only factor is established by the fact that after severe injury this large urinary nitrogen excretion rate cannot be stopped even by the infusion of large supplements, while in starvation it is readily overcome by even subnormal intakes. When amino acids or polypeptides are supplied intravenously along with calories, the infusion may be conducted so rapidly that urinary loss cannot keep pace, in which case a zero or even slightly positive nitrogen balance may be produced. The change does not signify tissue synthesis; it is achieved only at the expense of very large total urinary nitrogen excretion rates. When infusion is stopped, the outpouring continues. The metabolic picture of anabolism characterized by prolonged positive nitrogen balance on low intakes and with low nitrogen excretion rates has not been produced in the immediate post-stress period, either by the administration of calories, nitrogen, or hormones, although all three will reduce the extent of loss. This interesting problem is discussed in greater detail in Chapter 4.

An increased rate of nitrogen excretion can be produced by the injection of ACTH, cortisone, or compound F and is initiated during a phase of convalescence that includes adrenal stimulation. This has led to the possibility that post-traumatic catabolism is due to this endocrine change. There are a host of evidences indicating that the nature of the wound, also, may profoundly alter the pattern of nitrogen excretion, particularly its duration as an open wound and its relation to changes in caloric intake. In addition, later changes in nitrogen occur independent of demonstrable alteration in corticosteroid production or excretion. The alterations in post-traumatic nitrogen pattern accompanying age and infirmity are also independent of steroid correlation. These interpretive aspects are reviewed in the section on the literature.

In the first five days after trauma of this magnitude, without sepsis and with blood loss fully replaced, the patient may be expected to lose about 50 gm. of nitrogen, representing about 312 gm. of protein, or 1500 gm. of wet lean tissue. This is approximately 4 per cent of body protein exclusive of connective tissue and bone. This wet lean tissue contains 1 liter of water; the protein breakdown yields 100 gm. of urea, which is excreted in the urine, 375 ml. of water, and 1250 calories.

If there is blood retained in serous cavities or tissue planes there will be a considerable increase in total nitrogen loss as the blood is broken down and the products excreted. Blood is a high-nitrogen tissue in relation to phosphorus and a low-calcium tissue in relation to bone. The excretion of its catabolic products therefore distorts balance in the direction of excess nitrogen loss.

As the injury phase draws to a close, the absolute rate of urinary nitrogen excretion and the degree of negative nitrogen balance diminish, often rather suddenly. This signalizes the start of the turning-point phase described in the next section.

2. Potassium

When cellular protoplasm breaks down, nitrogen and potassium are released as evidence of the lysis of the structure protein and loss of cellular water. The amount of potassium excreted in the first day after moderately severe trauma is approximately 70 to 90 mE. The following day there is somewhat less potassium in the urine, and with succeeding days the urinary potassium loss is sharply restricted until often, by the third to sixth day, positive potassium balance is reached. Characteristically, potassium balance returns to zero or positive long before nitrogen regains positivity.

The potassium:nitrogen ratio in normal muscle is 2.5 to 3.0 mE. potassium per gm. of nitrogen. Shortly after trauma, potassium is lost at a much greater rate than nitrogen (from 5 to 15 mE. per gm.). This disproportionate ratio suggests exchange of cell base (the potassium being in part replaced with hydrogen or sodium), or loss of more cell water than cell matrix. It is probable that the three processes go on at once: atrophy of muscle cells with balanced loss of the total cell material, some differential loss of cell electrolyte and water, and some exchange of potassium for sodium and hydrogen ion, the last process being quantitatively the least important in ordinary trauma. It is therefore not surprising to find that the potassium loss reverses itself sooner than nitrogen loss: cell water and electrolyte mend before cell reconstruction has commenced. Our interpretation of these events is that the sodium-potassium exchange (involving at the most 40 to 50 mE. of sodium) reverts rather rapidly and that any tendency to loss of cell water (loss of 500 to 750 ml.) also ceases rapidly, whereas the gradual change-over from catabolism to cell reconstruction or anabolism is somewhat slower and is reflected in the nitrogen changes and partly conditioned by wound closure and caloric intake.

For example, the potassium loss may total about 240 mE., more during the first days than later. This is a potassium:nitrogen ratio of 4.75 mE. per gm. as based on our example. This slight "excess" potassium loss accounts in part for the intracellular hypotonicity which must perforce accompany the hyponatremia. The plasma potassium concentration would rise slightly during this time, to 4.9 mE. per l.—a mild sodium-potassium shift in the plasma.

The tissue losing most of the nitrogen and potassium is skeletal muscle; there is no other tissue in the body that can support such a large loss. There is no evidence that viscera such as the heart, kidney, liver, lungs, or intestinal tract become smaller after trauma; under certain circumstances they enlarge. There is good clinical and laboratory evidence that the skeletal muscle mass becomes smaller after trauma. Indeed, after very severe trauma with a prolonged period of sepsis and illness, the skeletal muscle mass may decrease by a factor of 30 per cent or more, as measured either by body weight, nitrogen balance, exchangeable potassium, muscular strength, or the size of specific muscle groups. Striated muscle comprises the great mass of lean oxidizing protoplasm in the body. It is extensively sacrificed after severe injury and becomes the nitrogen donor for the body.

3. Sodium

In previously healthy individuals, the characteristic pattern of sodium metabolism after surgery is a decreased urinary excretion. To see this in perspective, one must again recall that the vast majority of filtered sodium is normally reabsorbed in the renal tubule and that the final concentration of sodium in the urine (regardless of the total amount) depends not alone on the renal handling of base but also on the rate of tubular reabsorption of water.

After extensive trauma, one commonly sees the urinary sodium excretion reduced from approximately 100 mE. per day to 1 mE. per day. This reduction may persist for several days and under certain circumstances may persist for several weeks. There are other instances in which the onset of sodium conservation is slow and does not begin until the second or third day after trauma. In such instances the loss of sodium by urine and skin on zero intake may be enough to initiate sodium conservation on the basis of deficit alone, independent of other post-traumatic changes. The reduction in sodium excretion occurs early in most cases. It may be most evident when expressed in relation to potassium excretion (decreased sodium:potassium ratio) or in relation to total solute (decreased sodium fraction of total solute). Here again, as in other post-traumatic changes, certain components of the surgical experience are specifically potent stimuli. In the case of sodium conservation these are traumatic edema, desalting, hemorrhage, and ether anesthesia. Any reduction in functional extracellular volume or in effective blood volume reduces urine sodium excretion by a variety of mechanisms discussed in Part III.

The metabolism of chloride generally parallels that of sodium except that sodium conservation is more intense than chloride. Where positive balance of both ions is seen, the positive balance of sodium is usually greater than that of chloride; where alkalosis is threatened by extrarenal chloride loss, post-traumatic conservation of sodium bicarbonate thus accentuates the defect.

4. Calories, Fat, and Energy

A period of caloric starvation follows severe injury or extensive operation. The patient's oral intake is restricted for several days. If the surgery involves the peritoneal cavity, the oral intake is restricted for a longer time than if the trauma is peripheral or extraperitoneal. If there is intravenous administration of 5 per cent dextrose, 100 to 400 calories are readily provided by this route. Despite this meager intake, the patient continues to exhibit oxygen consumption and production of carbon dioxide as well as normal or elevated body temperature. If loading of water and salt is not marked, he loses weight. It is therefore clear that substances from within the body are being oxidized, and at an increased rate of oxidative energy conversion, after severe injury.

The body carbohydrate (300 to 500 gm.), mostly present as liver glycogen, muscle glycogen, and circulating glucose in the extracellular fluid, is quickly burned after injury. It is estimated that within eight to sixteen hours after an extensive surgical operation, the readily available stores of preformed carbohydrate in the body have been consumed.

As the protein lost from muscle is degraded, two- and three-carbon fragments are produced that yield oxidative energy through their combusion. Where a certain type of six-carbon compound is thus produced and then oxidized, it is referred to as gluconeogenesis from protein. The amounts of energy produced from such sources are quite significant when the lysis of muscle tissue is so great as to produce urine nitrogen excretion rates of 15 to 20 gm. per day. One can calculate that where enough muscle tissue is broken down to produce the urinary excretion of 20 gm. of nitrogen in a day, the amount of energy thus produced is equivalent to 125 gm. of glucose or 500 calories.

Despite the significance of protein destruction as a caloric source, the chief site of energy conversion after injury is body fat. The first conclusive demonstration of this came in the documentation of decreased body weight far in excess of that accountable on the basis of negative nitrogen balance or change in body water after trauma. This destruction of body substance must occur through degradation and oxidation of fat, which accounts nicely for the increased energy production despite lack of exogenous calories. When 1 gm. of exogenous fat is burned, about 9 calories of energy are produced. The same is assumed to be true for endogenous fat. After major trauma the fat oxidation may approximate 250 to 500 gm. per day, accounting for the production of 2000 to 4500 calories. Starvation fat oxidation rates range from 75 to 150 gm. per day. Severe trauma produces an increase in the rate of energy production from fat greater than that to be predicted from starvation alone.

For example, let us suppose that the patient's body weight drops about 3.0 kg. (about 4.5 per cent of body weight in a 70-kg. man) in the first five days. Since we can account for 1500 gm. of this as wet lean tissue, and net water change is small, there has been about 1.5 kg. of fat burned. This is an approximate figure subject to revision should body water be increased by excessive infusion or lost pathologically. This fat provides 13,500 calories, or an average of 2700 calories per day (somewhat more the first day or two, less later). This fat oxidation provides about 1650 ml. of water. The total endogenous water in five days is therefore about 3000 ml. This fat loss is about 10 per cent of the patient's total body fat. Because of slight water retention (see below) this weight-loss derivation yields minimum figures for tissue flux.

5. Water Metabolism and Urine Flow

The oxidation of a kilogram of fat in the body produces somewhat more than 1000 ml. of water of oxidation. The lysis of 1 kg. of lean tissue yields about 730 ml. of cell water, and about 250 ml. from the water of oxidation of protein. If the patient is given no water, these are the chief sources of water production or "intake" in the body after trauma. Where water is administered by mouth after severe injury, absorption may be poor. Gastrointestinal propulsive and absorptive function is markedly reduced after injury. If water is given by rectum, by clysis, or by vein, it is then admitted to the internal environment to produce additional intake. Water loss through the lungs is increased during and right after trauma when the respiratory rate or temperature is increased. Increased loss through the skin would occur only when sweating is of some significance.

In addition to these various influences on body water, antidiuretic activity is induced after trauma (especially with ether anesthesia, blood loss, or fluid dislocation) and a restricted amount of urine is produced at relatively high urine osmolality, the total urine flow being a function of solute excretion. If an infusion of water is given, the antidiuretic force tends to inhibit the rate at which an administered load is excreted. There is thus a tendency to water retention after trauma. If exogenous water administration is brisk, the tendency to water retention has a profound effect on plasma osmolality and body weight, producing a decrease in osmolality

and an increase in weight (or diminution in the rate of loss predicted from change in tissue solids). Postoperative hypotonicity results from the addition of sodium-free water arising from exogenous sources or from the oxidation of cell tissue, protein, and fat during an antidiuretic period.

The absolute volume of urine flow after trauma is influenced by a variety of factors, but where treatment is simple and administration of water or glucose not excessive, the formation of 450 to 1000 ml. of urine on the day of operation is quite normal. A day or two later the urine production may be somewhat larger than this and a mild diuresis is experienced. The antidiuresis after surgery involves a negative free water clearance of 1 to 2 ml. per minute, with total urine flow at 0.25 to 0.5 ml. per minute. Urine flow becomes a linear function of urine solute excretion, also indicating lack of free water excretion. The urine concentration is usually seen in the mid-range (specific gravity 1.020, solute 750 mO. per l.). Only where there is dehydration or marked reduction in glomerular filtration rate is the urine very concentrated. Solute loading (provided, for example, by intravenous concentrated glucose, mannitol, urea, or microdextran) produces a urine of mid-concentration not altered by antidiuresis save to reduce flexibility of water concentration.

In the hypotensive, oligemic, and oliguric patient urine volume is a reflection of renal blood flow and glomerular filtration rate rather than tubular function. It is this fact that gives urine volume such importance in evaluating resuscitation.

The induction phase of anesthesia is often associated with a reduction in the glomerular filtration rate quite aside from any evident change in blood volume; but as anesthesia deepens and the patient stabilizes, glomerular filtration rate returns to normal. In normal convalescence after major operation, where blood loss is quantitatively replaced, there is no further systematic reduction in renal plasma flow or glomerular filtration rate. In more complicated situations, prolonged reduction in renal hemodynamics may be observed, with efferent arteriolar vasoconstriction. Such changes are associated with a decreased water and sodium excretion and a lowered sodium:potassium ratio, adding further to conservation of water and sodium produced by the normal water-and-salt-retaining mechanisms.

The particular components of injury which strongly stimulate antidiuresis, in addition to drugs, anesthetics, and tissue trauma, are volume reduction, dehydration, desalting, shock, and pain.

The net effect of the protein-nitrogen-fat-water-salt changes in the injury phase is an increase in the volume of the extracellular phase at the expense of the intracellular phase and fat. If there is traumatic edema, or sequestration of body water (as in burn, crush, peritonitis, intestinal obstruction) the increased total extracellular fluid may be associated with a decreased functional extracellular volume, rising hematocrit, and oligemia. These aspects are discussed in full in Parts II and III.

6. Concentration of Blood Constituents

In the situation under discussion, where visceral function previously has been normal, convalescence uncomplicated, and the administration of water not excessive, the changes in concentration of blood constituents are not marked, but their subtle directions indicate tendencies which may become exaggerated in abnormalities of convalescence.

The blood urea nitrogen rises slightly, but not out of the range of normal. This is evidence of a transient phase when the endogenous production of urea slightly outstrips the rate of urinary excretion.

The carbon dioxide content and combining power, and the blood pH, do not usually change significantly after trauma in the normal setting. If there is any change, it is a slight change in the direction of metabolic alkalosis unless respiratory exchange has been embarrassed. Poor ventilation under anesthesia adds respiratory acidosis to the picture; if peripheral flow is poor the hypoxic acidosis of increased blood lactate may become evident also. The net acid-base change is the net result of the interaction among these forces.

The blood sugar rises transiently but by the following day is normal. There is a decreased glucose tolerance during this period.

The plasma sodium concentration falls while the plasma potassium concentration rises. This characteristic post-traumatic shift of sodium and potassium starts the day of operation and reaches its maximum distortion on the first postoperative day when, after moderately severe trauma, a plasma potassium concentration of 4.8 to 5.0 mE. per l. and a sodium concentration of 130 to 135 mE. per l. are observed. The tendency of the concentration of these two ions to move inversely to each other is consistent in a very wide variety of pathologic conditions. The fall in plasma sodium concentration may be ascribed almost wholly to water retention and dilution but this could not account for a rise in plasma potassium concentration. There is loss of potassium across the cell surface after trauma, but this would not account for an increase in the plasma concentration if renal excretion kept pace. There is good evidence that changes in pH and a continuing respiratory acidosis would raise the plasma potassium concentration. There is inadequate evidence to indicate that this is the explanation of the post-traumatic sodium-potassium shift.

In our example, the plasma sodium concentration may be expected to fall from 140 mE. per l. to about 132 mE. per l., and the osmolality accordingly from 286 to 270 mO. per l. Let us suppose that external sodium loss has been small—100 mE. through tube, skin, and urine. The patient has been given no sodium. This dilutional hypotonicity indicates the net addition of somewhat less than 2 l. of salt-free water to the body. This is a maximum figure. Any movement of sodium out of the extracellular fluid accentuates hypotonicity without requiring new water. Insensible (lung, skin) loss of water in five days would be about 4 l.; urine volume about 3.5 l.

We are supposing that the patient was given 9.0 l. of water by vein and mouth during the first five days. Together with the endogenous water, this would have been more than enough to account for the slight dilution during a period of decreased free water excretion.

The over-all net change in body composition is thus small, but with loss of cell water into the extracellular fluid (with enlargement of the latter) and retention of additional water, as shown by the hypotonicity, the fraction of body weight occupied by water goes up slightly, from 60 per cent to 63 per cent.

E. CLINICAL MANAGEMENT

A recurring theme of this book and the predominant fact of surgical metabolism is that operative management, surgical technique, and metabolic care are inseparable and often synonymous. This is clearly seen here in the management of the first phase of convalescence in elective closed surgery. Here, as in many other settings, the most important single metabolic step is a good operation done at the right time for the right disease, and by the finest surgical technique.

1. Surgical Technique

The purpose of good surgical technique is to lighten the load of immune and scavenger work to be done in the wound and to lessen the likelihood of infection. A well-performed procedure hastens the close of the injury phase so that the gastrointestinal tract may proceed to its normal digestive and absorptive function, the patient resume painless and effective mobility without infection, and metabolism pass quickly on to anabolic rehabilitation. Devitalized structures included in crudely-placed sutures or roughly-handled tissue require a more prolonged activity of macrophages and leucocytes in the first phase of wound healing than does living tissue gently coapted by well-placed sutures; devitalized tissue, blood, and debris invite infection; blood in the wound places a burden of removal or organization on the early healing process; unreplaced blood loss or ileus-obstruction delays the onset of diuresis; blood and detritus left in the peritoneal cavity are irritating and produce a more prolonged ileus; blood in the pleural cavity inhibits normal respiratory excursion; excessive bacterial contamination, or contamination with

unusually virulent organisms, diverts the resources of the patient to the conquest of sepsis and modifies the endocrine and metabolic sequence in a way which hastens tissue wasting and delays healing. These—not some mythical nutritive or endocrine combat—are the important aspects of metabolic treatment early in convalescence. Their importance illustrates better than any other single consideration the inseparable nature of operative and metabolic care in surgery.

It is thus a primary rule of clinical management in the first phase of convalescence to accomplish the initial surgery in such a fashion that physiologic needs are met and that the response of the organism is not diverted from its normal objective or delayed from its schedule. In terms of elective closed surgery this admonition covers the whole range of skills which make for technical excellence: asepsis, accuracy of concept, gentleness with tissues, speed without wasteful haste, meticulousness without idle pokiness, and a merciful concern for the patient rather than an eye to the operating list, the clock, or the admiring onlookers. Honest and excellent operative technique truly provides the best metabolic care of the surgical patient.

2. Duration before Definitive Surgery

In terms of unanesthetized trauma and military surgery, a matter of first importance in surgical care is the amount of time elapsing between injury and definitive surgery, and the specific timing of the accomplishment of the objectives of definitive surgery. In uncompensated blood loss, shock, anoxia, excessive trauma, or invasive sepsis the gross exaggeration of endocrine and metabolic changes is of primary value in promoting survival, but once this is accomplished the endocrine and metabolic changes can no longer be regarded as beneficial. As the wounded man is resuscitated by blood replacement, immobilization of fractures, exteriorization of holed hollow viscera, or debridement of muscle wounds, his period of maximal stimulation ceases. The sooner this is accomplished, the less likely he is to descend in a spiral of sepsis, persistent shock and vasoconstriction, tissue anoxia, liver damage, intense steroid-induced muscle-wasting, renal failure, hyperkalemia, and death as a result of some or all of these factors. In such a circumstance, the very biochemistry responsible for survival in a normal setting (mobilization of cell water, for instance) contributes to demise. Clinical problems of this type are treated in detail in the chapters on massive wounds and shock; they are mentioned here to point up the relation of operating-room management and surgical judgment to clinical metabolism during the first phase of convalescence. Good surgery lightens the load. Successful definitive operation after unanesthetized trauma puts an end to the injury. The shorter the interval between onset of trauma and completion of definitive surgery, the less the hazard and the stimulus to bodily change. The same consideration holds as to duration in civilian surgery, but in miniature. In abdominal and thoracic operations undue prolongation of the open anesthetized dissection unquestionably adds to the total trauma.

3. Volume Restoration

Decrease in the functional extracellular fluid volume or effective blood volume is produced by dehydration or desalting, but most importantly by blood loss. These drops in volume, occurring during operation, should be quantitatively replaced at the time of loss so that the stimulus of volume reduction is not added to the body's burden after the procedure. As discussed in Part II, the replacement of the loss of 300 to 500 ml. of blood (or less) should not be done as a single 500 ml. intraoperative transfusion, but should be replaced later if at all. Losses of more blood than this should be replaced *pari passu*.

4. Care after Operation

After the wound has been closed, management of the type of patient under consideration here poses few problems. In uneventful major surgery involving primary closure of soft tissue, nature does most of our job. This seems to be the post-traumatic situation for which the trauma response was "designed": elective clean soft-tissue surgery in the healthy.

A nasogastric tube left in overnight the first night may remove some swallowed air and ameliorate the nausea which often follows anesthesia and surgery. Unless there is some reason to expect an unusual degree of ileus, or unless the surgeon wishes to inhibit peristaltic activity across a bowel anastomosis by proximal decompression, the tube is removed the morning after operation.

Medication for pain and for sleep should be entered separately; the patient should move regularly and start leg exercises as soon as possible; he may stand up the next day. Catheterization, if needed, with careful asepsis, is ordered. A short-term chart is maintained until the patient is awake and stable. An unconscious patient is always in danger of acute respiratory obstruction and must have close observation.

a. Infusion. The patient will not take much fluid by mouth in the first twenty-four hours, and if the operation is peritoneal or anastomotic, oral intake is to be avoided for a longer time. Renal water loss will not be great, as the kidney is under a variety of influences all of which tend to conserve water and extracellular salt. If the patient will take 300 to 500 ml. by mouth and retain it, there is no need for parenteral therapy. If not, and if the nasogastric tube is on suction and oral intake not imminent, the patient will get along better with an intravenous infusion. A total of 750 to 1500 ml. will suffice for the normal adult in whom neither fever, dyspnea, nor extrarenal loss increases the water requirement.

b. Salt in the Infusion? Whether or not this first postoperative infusion should contain any salt has become a matter for controversy. If it contains no salt and is overabundant in amount, exceeding the losses of water from kidney, lungs, and skin which it is designed to replace, it will cause dilutional hypotonicity, lowering sodium, chloride, and protein concentration and hematocrit. If it contains salt and is excessive in amount, it will dilute protein and red cells, but a lesser fall in sodium concentration will result. In older individuals or those with overt renal or heart disease, the positive sodium balance so readily established is only slowly unloaded and may be deleterious. The moral is clearly this: plan what you are trying to accomplish with these early infusions and do it accurately.

In most straightforward surgical situations, 5 per cent dextrose in water suffices, with the addition of 75 mM. of sodium chloride as 500 ml. of 5 per cent dextrose in normal saline. The inclusion of vitamins is common practice but in the previously well-nourished patient is an unnecessary expense. The use of potassium, larger amounts of sodium chloride, special salt solutions designed to forestall acid-base imbalance, whole blood, albumin, or plasma is unnecessary where preoperative nourishment has been normal, acid-base balance normal, and blood volume replacement adequate at the time of operation. The use of rectal infusion or hypodermoclysis has gone out of general use in this country. Where the intravenous route is impractical, they may be used to good advantage.

The administration of sodium during this phase is not necessarily injurious. The degree of loading and the state of the patient's circulatory system must be used as guides to determine any potential hazard. But whether or not any harm results, and regardless of the degree of positive balance, the giving of sodium in this early phase in amounts greater than physiologic need has four effects:

(1) an increase in the urinary excretion of sodium over that seen on a "no-sodium" routine;

(2) a strong tendency to positive balance;

(3) a further increase in the "sodium space" or area of body water available for sodium solution; and

(4) an intensification of any tendency toward alkalosis and/or hypokalemia if there has been loss of acid gastric juice.

c. Feeding. The duration of the necessity for parenteral supplementation depends wholly on the resumption of oral intake. Oral intake of fluid should wait until absorption is evident; intake of semisolid or solid food should wait until effective peristalsis is evident on auscultation or by the anal passage of flatus. Both of these events are delayed by intraperitoneal surgery, particularly if dissection is extensive, or by the manipulation of the bowel necessary in anastomotic operations.

Early feeding after trauma is desirable because it permits anabolism to begin as soon as possible. Premature feeding of fluids or food in any quantity results only in vomiting and distention. Premature overloading of the gastrointestinal tract results at the least in crampy pain and at the worst in wound disruption, thrombophlebitis from increased intra-abdominal pressure, decreased pulmonary ventilation and atelectasis, and aspiration pneumonitis. For these very good reasons, the nutritional objective of the early postoperative period is not some predetermined caloric intake. The nutritional objective of the early postoperative period is a scaphoid abdomen.

d. Control of Bacteria. The control of bacteria in the first phase of convalescence, in clean elective soft-tissue surgery, is best managed by effective asepsis at the time of surgery. Most clean operative wounds contain bacteria at the time of closure, yet heal without sepsis. The prophylactic use of antibiotics has few virtues and many faults. It is hazardous because normal flora are converted to resistance and any infection—even though clinically minor—may become one harboring antibiotic-resistant organisms in significant quantity. In contaminated wounds and in septic anatomic areas, antibiotics should be used.

e. Mobilization. Early mobilization of the patient results in much benefit if it is not done as a compulsive necessity. One occasionally witnesses the bodily levitation from bed to chair of an immobile patient; the sitting position accomplishes little. The only beneficiary is the nurse, who is able to answer an enthusiastic "yes" the next morning when the surgeon queries her about the patient's getting up. The patient meanwhile drowses on in his uncomfortable chair.

Early mobilization preserves from wasting that fraction of muscular effectiveness lost to immobilization. The early postoperative period is not one of vigor, ambition, or enthusiasm. Exercise in bed will sometimes accomplish as much for the feeble or cautious, and cost much less in fatigue.

Once the pain and surprise of the first rising is over, early mobilization lessens wound pain, muscular spasm, and rigidity and the backache caused by a hard bed. It is not uncommon to see a patient lying rigid and immobile in bed, afraid to move, who after the first wrench of rising will move about freely and be relaxed. Adequate assistance, external wound support, and avoidance of fatigue are important in early rising. Atelectasis, wound disruption, and thrombophlebitis may occur in surgical patients who have been mobilized early, but their incidence is no higher and has hopefully been reported as lower than in those confined to bed for a week or two.

f. Chemical Study. In the uncomplicated setting, the performance of frequent chemical analyses of the blood is unnecessary, unwise, and uneconomical. Where blood replacement was required at surgery, fever was elevated, or extrarenal loss borderline, a useful minimum consists of determination of the hematocrit, blood urea nitrogen, and sodium (or chloride) on the first or second postoperative day. Other than showing a mild hyponatremia, these data should be normal, and if not, appropriate study and therapy should be undertaken as described in the chapters on blood volume, visceral disease, and electrolyte abnormality.

As peristalsis and appetite return, one may observe that the wound is stronger, the eosinophils rising, the patient more alert, and urine nitrogen excretion diminished. These are the harbingers of the second phase of convalescence.

5. Is This Therapeutic Nihilism?

This clinical approach to uncomplicated early convalescence lays major emphasis on the performance of good operative surgery, which is the most important single therapeutic step both as regards the wound locally and the organism as a whole. For the patient who enters operation with serious organ disease or metabolic disturbance, or in whom early convalescence is complicated by infection, extrarenal losses, or other less common occurrences, treatment must be active and accurate. Such treatment is based on a knowledge of the normal first phase, and an understanding of what should be expected. In

dealing with a normal first phase, meddlesome treatment should be held to a minimum.

Attempts to alter the normal physiology of the first phase in normal convalescence by massive infusion of sugar, alcohol, amino acids, or by injection of testosterone, cortisone, or other hormones (a pinch of this, a dash of that) have yet to be proven effective either in terms of significant metabolic change or, more important, in terms of promoting the patient's welfare.

Several workers have been interested in providing considerable amounts of sodium so as to maintain flexibility of urine pH regulation, or urea so as to maintain a continuous solute diuresis. Both concepts are interesting, and may have something to recommend them in special cases. The studies done in their elucidation have been fruitful of important data. But such steps are not important as treatment in normal convalescence.

Others have taken quite the other view: that nothing at all need be done, that intravenous "drips" are a useless extravagance and the patient should be left quite alone until he is well. Here again the data developed are of unusual interest. The production of endogenous water provides some continuing urine volume. Weight loss is massive but the patient is not too badly off despite a rise in hematocrit and very large losses in body water—that is, so long as no complications or additional trauma components appear. Should such occur, the patient is extremely vulnerable.

A third school of thought has recommended extensive intravenous calorie-nitrogen treatment in an effort to obliterate completely all loss of weight or nitrogen.

All these interesting contributions are discussed elsewhere in this book. In terms of the treatment of the patient after uncomplicated elective closed surgery our policy is midway between the water-solute enthusiasts, the nitrogen-calorie proponents, and the watchful-waiting school. We feel there is little to gain for the patient by any of these and that a simple procedure, meeting important needs but avoiding meddlesome treatment, is best.

Section II. The Turning Point—the Second Phase

This transient phase of surgical convalescence, when the patient rounds the corner, was originally named the "corticoid-withdrawal phase" because it bore certain biochemical resemblances to the effects of sudden withdrawal of administered ACTH or corticoids after a short period of high dosage. A clinically descriptive name—"the turning point"—is better.

We are here considering the normal sequence after primary, moderately extensive, elective closed soft-tissue surgery in a previously well person. Under such circumstances (colectomy, gastrectomy, pneumonectomy, radical hysterectomy) this "turning-point" phase is clearly seen both clinically and metabolically and occurs about the third to seventh day after the operation, lasting one or two days. In septic fractures, wounds, burns where there is continuing infection, and in a host of more complex settings, the "turning point" is long postponed and may not be so clearly seen in the patient or demonstrable in the laboratory. Continued operation of trauma components in Group II (threatening challenges) and Group III (tissue-killing injury) prevents the occurrence of the "turning point."

A. CLINICAL APPEARANCES

This clinical *volte-face* has been recognized by surgeons since the advent of asepsis—if not before—as characteristically coming on the third postoperative day with the unsolicited greeting: "I feel better today."

The patient now takes an interest in his surroundings. Whether it be visitors, the radio, the menu, or lipstick, the patient evinces an interest in life again. Mobilization becomes easier, appetite and bowel function return, the wound is less painful. Any elevation in fever or pulse now returns to normal.

It is a period of increased ambition, but weakness still throttles activity. The desire to walk in the hall is quickly tempered by a return to bed with a sigh of relief; the radio is clicked off soon and the TV sooner; the big order from the house-diet menu goes half-eaten. The hospital still looks like a satisfactory place to be. The telephone is best left disconnected.

B. THE WOUND

This period is of critical importance for the wound, as it is the time during which the ground substance which has been gathering in the wound begins to acquire tensile strength by chemical and morphologic change: a local histochemical sequence by which an amorphous coagulum achieves the appearance of fibrillary structure and becomes fibrous tissue abounding in collagen.

Wound healing bears a close relation to systemic factors, the most certain being the relation to methionine and vitamin C. Ascorbic acid is both required and consumed in wound healing. Many of the factors which relate surgical metabolism to wound healing are but poorly understood; the matter that concerns us for this moment in convalescence is that a spontaneous change to nitrogen anabolism occurs at or just after the time that a clean primary soft-tissue wound regains its tensile integrity. This combination occurs under a variety of circumstances; in fractures, as we shall see later, it also occurs, but closer to the sixteenth than the sixth day. By "tensile integrity" we mean that stage of healing where the mechanical functions of the tensile tissues, disrupted by the wound, can again take strain or do their job: in skin, the sutures are removed, in bowel, peristalsis crosses the suture line, in fractures, the splint is safely removed. This well-advanced and effective healing process has usually occurred by the time nitrogen excretion is reduced and balance easily becomes positive. In elective soft-tissue surgery, this rapid assumption of tensile strength in the wound occurs between the fourth and the eighth day. Sutures are removed from the skin. The fascia has healed to the point of accepting tensile pull. Were the wound to be reopened earlier it would have fallen apart under the examining finger. If the wound is to be reopened now, it must be done with sharp instruments.

Wound dehiscence may occur as a manifestation of the failure of this tensile-strength–gaining phenomenon to occur. Three remarkable facts about wound dehiscence deserve mention. First, it occurs in apparently well-nourished people with nearly as great frequency as it does in the cachectic. Second, bursting factors and the use of stay sutures alter the time of clinical diagnosis but not the basic fault in true dehiscence. And finally, in a way we do not understand, prompt resuture often results in prompt healing that differs little in appearance or result from primary solid healing. The explanation of these occurrences on a unitary basis such as protein depletion or scurvy is most difficult.

C. EVIDENCE OF ENDOCRINE CHANGE

Adrenomedullary signs such as tachycardia, pallor, and sweating have long since passed. If they have not, the turning point will not be reached until they do.

Adrenocortical indices now return to normal. In some cases there is at this time a simultaneous fall in urinary excretion of total 17-hydroxycorticoids and a rise in eosinophils correlated with decreased urine nitrogen excretion and increased sodium excretion. Whether or not such a perfect set of correlations occurs, certain features of this turning-point phase are constant.

First, if trauma has been severe and response great enough to cause increased urine nitrogen excretion rate (to 15 gm. a day, for example), the patient regularly goes through a phase of decreasing nitrogen excretion on his way to anabolism—whether or not this may precede or follow the clinical turning point. When all the evidences occur together (fall in urinary corticosteroids, rise in eosinophils, reduction in nitrogen excretion, return of clinical vigor), the clinical, endocrine, and metabolic correlation is dramatic, and mechanistically appealing. Such correlation is frequently lacking.

Second, the patient quite clearly cannot make his turn if complications (sepsis, oliguria, bleeding) occur; they maintain continued endocrine activity, with maintained high steroid levels, low eosinophils, elevated nitrogen excretion, and clinical illness. A maintained low eosinophil count is the commonest surgical abnormality of eosinophils and denotes the presence of complicating pathology, including such commonplace changes as atelectasis, infection, or thrombophlebitis.

Third, the inhibition of water diuresis in response to loading, so characteristic of the first day or two, has ceased to be manifest. A diuresis of water and salt frequently occurs.

D. METABOLISM AND BIOCHEMISTRY

Reduction in urine nitrogen excretion rate may now occur very suddenly, passing within twenty-four hours from rates of 15 to 20 gm. per day to rates of 5 to 7 gm. per day. This occurs even in the absence of caloric intake. It indicates a reversal in the dynamics of protein metabolism away from catabolism and toward anabolism. Net protein synthesis cannot occur unless intake is adequate in amount and composition, with sufficient exogenous calories to supply the energy required by the patient's total metabolism, which now includes the energy needed not only for muscular work and body heat but also for protein synthesis. As intake rises, the expected positive balance of nitrogen is readily produced, indicating a net increase in body protein. The rate of nitrogen gain quickly (in two to three days) attains a value in the range of 3 to 5 gm. of nitrogen per 70 kg. of body weight per day. This corresponds to a gain of about 90 gm. of lean tissue per day, in an organism containing about 30 kg. of lean tissue; the lean tissue (largely skeletal muscle) reproduces itself at about the rate of 0.3 per cent per day. Under special circumstances to be described later, a more rapid rate of protein synthesis may occur.

In the first phase of convalescence, the oxidation of fat supplies energy for the body to maintain life, but protein synthesis is markedly inhibited, and catabolism occurs. It is a general rule of convalescent metabolism that when energy is derived wholly from endogenous fat oxidation, protein anabolism does not occur. To state this otherwise: one does not see positive nitrogen balance in the absence of exogenous caloric intake. The extent of this caloric intake must be sufficient to support the needs of the body and supply the energy for protein synthesis if the latter is to occur at its ceiling rate. For these reasons the second phase of convalescence cannot lead to protein synthesis unless adequate calories are supplied. Just as careful, accurate, effective aseptic surgery is the most important therapeutic step in the first phase of convalescence, so also the provision and absorption of an increasing and adequate exogenous diet is the key to success in the later phases.

For protein synthesis to occur maximally during the anabolic phases of convalescence, a calorie:nitrogen ratio of 200 is necessary. This is based on the ratio of nonprotein calories to total nitrogen in the diet. A calorie:nitrogen ratio of 100 or 150 will permit anabolism to start, but not at maximal rates, with intakes near 0.1:15.* A calorie: nitrogen ratio of 200 with an intake of 0.1:20 is based on a diet containing, for example, nonprotein calories of 1400, with 7 gm. of nitrogen. Such a diet might consist of 120 gm. of fat, 75 gm. of carbohydrate, and 45 gm. of protein. This is a low intake for an active adult but it is an example of the level of intake attainable in practical reality during the turning-point phase and the early days of the subsequent spontaneous anabolic phase. In another five days, this level can often be doubled. Expressed on the basis of body weight, this would be a diet of 20 calories (nonprotein calories) per kilo, and about 0.1 gm. nitrogen per kilo or, in the shorthand we employ, an intake of 0.1:20.

Diuresis of water and salt—or at least a cessation of the retentive tendency—occurs during the turning-point phase. The antidiuretic effect on water metabolism shows no correlation with steroid activity at this time. The reduced sodium excretion bears little relation to other metabolic events of the nitrogen-calorie group, possibly to be explained on the basis of a separate steroidal mechanism. If sodium conservation has been slow starting, it will persist through this phase; if sudden and marked, it may be

* This intake is indicated thus: 0.1:15 indicates an intake of 0.1 gm. nitrogen and 15 calories per kg. per day.

suddenly and markedly released during this period. For these reasons, one does not always observe a close correlation between diuresis of water and salt (an inconstant aspect of the "turning point") and the readiness to commence anabolism as indicated by reduction in urine nitrogen excretion.

Potassium upswing regularly precedes nitrogen increase. A reduction in urinary potassium excretion rate and the achievement of positive balance on low intake occur a day or two before the analogous events for nitrogen. This tendency is especially marked if early potassium loss has been brisk and at a high potassium:nitrogen ratio. The reloading is then also brisk, and differential, occurring before nitrogen reloading and at high potassium:nitrogen ratios.

Summarizing the net compositional change in our example, further nitrogen loss is minor as the intake swings upward and positivity is achieved. Fat oxidation continues but much more slowly; at the rate of 100 gm. a day, 900 calories and 920 ml. of water are provided. A diuresis may now occur with loss of water in excess of salt—a "water diuresis" characteristic of release from antidiuretic influences. The loss of 1 to 2 l. of "excess water" in three days returns the extracellular fluid volume toward normal and raises tonicity; sodium concentration rises to normal and potassium concentration falls. Potassium is reloaded in excess of nitrogen, restoring intracellular tonicity to normal. Body water fraction remains a little high as the lost fat has not yet been regained.

E. CLINICAL MANAGEMENT

Nutritional restraint appropriate in the first few postoperative days can now be replaced by dietary enthusiasm. Resumption of positive nitrogen balance is an absolute essential to clinical recovery, because of the muscular strength it bestows. Where gastrointestinal function will not return normally (in malfunctioning stoma, for instance), one sees an example of the meaning of failure to gain nitrogen positivity during the turning-point phase. The wound heals satisfactorily and the patient may be up and about. But lack of weight, strength, and vigor are persistent; convalescence is stalled in its normal progression; the patient remains suspended at the turning point, never proceeding on upward to recovery.

As the patient's appetite returns, he will take care of his intake well enough, providing his gastrointestinal tract is behaving normally and is anatomically able to do so. If intake cannot now be resumed, an entirely different picture unfolds: that of late postoperative starvation. This important pathologic variant is described in greater detail in Part IV.

The wound can regain its tensile strength and proceed to apparent and effective healing in the absence of any significant intake during this phase, providing the patient is not suffering from scurvy. This fact again points up the meaning of the concept of wound priority. These phases of convalescence (up to the seventh or eighth day after major surgery) cover a period when endogenous foodstuffs from the lysis of muscle and fat provide the basis of energy for muscular work and the substrates for tissue synthesis in the wound. Endocrine and metabolic changes have placed the wound at a high priority where it heals and does so at the expense of other tissues.

Until the era of metabolic study, it might have been argued that wounds did not heal without positive nitrogen balance, because all surgeons have occasionally seen disruption or dehiscence, sepsis, and convalescent failure in the starving patient. We are apt to forget the many patients with intestinal obstruction, ulcerative colitis, esophageal anastomoses, or just "no appetite," who have had no significant intake prior to the eighth or tenth day, and whose wounds have healed perfectly. Metabolic study of such patients has merely served to demonstrate that the patient in negative nitrogen balance for two or three weeks, while not exhibiting ideal convalescence and persistently weak and cachectic, is quite capable of healing his wound without fault. Healing is the rule; failure is the exception.

When the starving patient fails to heal his wound, it is most likely to be on the basis of avitaminosis C, infection, or edema. Conservation of water and salt is marked in starvation, and accentuates hypoproteinemia. Simple caloric starvation is not a cause of healing failure in man.

Although the wound can heal without food, the metabolic meaning of diet for the patient now is that he needs food to repair the inroads on muscle and fat made during the first phase. The wound can heal without food but the patient cannot get well unless he eats.

Other features of clinical management at this phase need little elaboration here. Increasing mobilization of the patient goes along with increasing diet, and as his nitrogen balance becomes consistently positive, he passes into the next phase of convalescence.

Section III. Muscular Strength—the Third Phase

After one or two days of turning the corner the patient now passes into a prolonged period (two to five weeks) marked by spontaneous anabolism and continuously positive nitrogen balance, indicating resynthesis of muscular tissue, accompanied by resumption of muscular strength and vigor.

A. CLINICAL APPEARANCES

This is the phase when the patient not only wants to go home, but is able to. Ambulation is no longer painful. The "ambition with weakness" of the turning-point phase is now replaced by "ambition with increasing strength." Appetite is good. Bowel habits return to normal.

B. THE WOUND

Normally the wound now ceases to be painful, but a sensation that the wound is present persists for many weeks or months. The narrow sutured incision seen when the sutures were removed, which called forth expressions of admiration for the surgeon's skill, now begins its normal broadening process, which is to leave it a raised red scar 2 to

4 mm. across for the next six to twelve months. This appearance is due to the proliferation of the fibrous tissue in the wound, a proliferation which, were it to be unchecked by normal regulatory processes, goes on to keloid formation. Tensile integrity is established; the function of soft tissues (skin, fascia, gastrointestinal tract) is resumed.

C. EVIDENCES OF ENDOCRINE CHANGE

The steroidal factors so easily demonstrated to undergo changes early have now returned to normal. We are left with one of the most interesting and important phases of surgical convalescence without identification of its characteristic endocrine setting. The consistent addition of nitrogen (which appears as muscle protein) suggests normal growth. Skeletal size remains constant except in children, in whom skeletal growth returns. This would suggest that some growth principle determines the set of the tissues in this phase of convalescence. Hormones directly necessary for normal growth are insulin, adrenal steroids, thyroxin, pituitary growth hormone, and, at puberty, gonadal hormones. Hormones act on tissues in concert. Various phases of surgical convalescence appear to represent settings predominant in specific endocrine factors. Identification of the endocrine setting of anabolism is unknown. The actions of growth hormone are many and widespread, but the diversion of energy to protein synthesis is one of its most characteristic effects. Androgenic and anabolic factors might also be in the ascendancy at this time because of the formation of muscular tissue. Proof of such a theory is lacking.

D. METABOLISM AND BIOCHEMISTRY

The gathering of nitrogenous compounds into the body and their synthesis into protein occurs at a steady rate. In most instances this rate is represented by a positive balance of about 2 to 5 gm. of nitrogen per 70 kg. per day in a previously healthy male. The most rapid sustained rates of spontaneous anabolism we have seen in surgical convalescence occurred at 10 to 15 gm. of nitrogen per 70 kg. per day.

This average rate (3 to 4 gm. of nitrogen per 70 kg. per day) represents a synthesis of lean tissue corresponding to approximately 90 to 120 gm. or 0.2 to 0.5 per cent of the lean body mass per day. Gain of weight at this time is at about this rate, suggesting that lean tissue (muscle protoplasm) is the chief tissue being reconstructed and that fat synthesis is not prominent. There is often evidence that a small additional amount of fat is lost as building of lean tissue starts, an indication that exogenous intake is not meeting the total caloric need.

This gain of 90 to 120 gm. a day is scarcely discernible if measured by ordinary means on a day-to-day basis. If careful weight measurements are made under constant conditions, this steady gain may be observed. In three days a pound is gained, a kilogram in a week. The total amount of nitrogen ultimately to be gained is remarkably adjusted to the amount lost in the initial phase, but as the rate of gain is only about $\frac{1}{3}$ to $\frac{1}{6}$ the rate of loss, it takes three to six times as long to repair the lean-tissue defect as it did to create it.

Presumably potassium is gained at a rate proportional to nitrogen—or at about 10 mE. per day. Balance studies must have a greater order of accuracy than is usually attainable to show such a small positive balance (10 per cent or so of the intake) on a consistent daily basis. This amount of potassium is readily provided in a balanced diet containing 10 to 15 gm. of nitrogen and 80 to 100 mE. of potassium as meat protein with assorted vegetables.

E. CLINICAL MANAGEMENT

For this phase of convalescence to proceed to the conclusion of its anabolic objective, so that lean tissues are rebuilt and the patient's synthetic processes can return to the normal dynamic equilibrium of wear, tear, and replacement, the patient must have food intake in excess of gross needs for bodily functions and external work. Adequate diet plus enough exercise to rebuild morale and muscle is the key to this phase of convalescence.

Where special methods (tube feedings, gastrostomy, jejunostomy) must be employed to provide these foodstuffs, one is no longer dealing with normal convalescence. Their use is only rarely needed and is described elsewhere in this book (Part IV); their purpose is to provide the building blocks for convalescent anabolism so that it may occur despite crippling gastrointestinal disease.

It is an important requirement for the completion of convalescent anabolism that external work should not be in excess of the caloric supply. A portion of the ingested caloric intake covers the energetics of protein synthesis and the forging of peptide linkages. It is clear that if the patient undertakes 1000 calories of wood-chopping a day on a 2400-calorie diet, he is not going to have as much energy left to rebuild his muscles as he would if he did less work and ate more food. By the same token, a month later, when muscle has been resynthesized, he will be stronger and healthier (and doubtless happier) if he eats within the bounds of his caloric work requirement and does some physical work each day. This particular feature of convalescent anabolism (avoidance of premature overwork) is recognized in the time-honored admonition to "take it easy for a while." It acquires importance in several settings, two of which stand out. First, after very extensive injury or surgery or where infection has furthered muscle wasting, a long period of muscle anabolism will be needed and a long period of convalescence should be allowed before returning to work and before ambitious rehabilitational muscle re-education should begin. And second, where food intake is perforce low (or poorly absorbed), muscle mass should be regained before returning to work.

Because testosterone produces nitrogen anabolism in normal people and because nitrogen anabolism is a feature of this phase of convalescence, the presumption has been made that some such anabolic agent should be used. There is no evidence that these agents help the normally anabolic patient. If intake of nourishment is inadequate, the slightly increased tendency toward nitrogen anabolism resulting from testosterone might improve muscular strength but there is no evidence for it. Putting a patient who is on poor food intake into positive nitrogen balance is not a great therapeutic triumph: the point is to get him eating and to increase his intake. If the hormone increases his appetite and interest in food it has served its purpose well. If not, it is wasted.

Section IV. Fat Gain—the Fourth Phase

The final period of convalescence is one of gain in body weight due to the accumulation of fat. It is a period when weight gain occurs over a period of several months without any gain in total body water, indicating the accumulation of the nonaqueous fraction of body weight—fat.

A. CLINICAL APPEARANCES

Normal strength returns; the patient goes back to his usual occupation. There is much about his appearance to suggest a recent hospital illness; he moves more gingerly than usual, sparing the wound, he looks underweight, and his clothes fit loosely.

As in the third phase, he will carry on with his weight gain to completion as long as caloric intake exceeds output. Now his weight gain is principally in fat. He is in zero nitrogen balance but in positive carbon balance and positive energy balance. If this goes on past his normal weight, he becomes exactly like any person taking in more calories than total work output, and passes by easy stages to obesity.

B. THE WOUND

At some time during or after this phase of convalescence, the wound ceases to be a raised convex red line, and becomes white, flat, broad, and ultimately concave with small wrinkled cross-striations in the epithelium overlying the white fibrous cicatrix. This change would suggest that local tissue activity in the wound now ceases and an indolent cicatrix remains, making little metabolic demand on the organism. Discomfort and a sense of stiffness in the wound only gradually disappear.

That the wound is still a special area is suggested by two things: first, the tendency of microorganisms (apparently blood-borne) to localize in it months or years later. Second is the fact alleged so frequently in accounts of eighteenth-century voyages, that in scurvy, old wounds break down, suggesting continued need for vitamin C to maintain intercellular substance in the cicatrix. This latter fact is not of great clinical importance in the twentieth century but is an example of a prolonged metabolic specialization in the wound. The old unhealed wound seen particularly in uncovered skin defects and nonunited fractures long after the completion of anabolism represents a special clinical problem. The synthetic designs of the organism have shifted to muscle, and away from the formation of new tissue in an area of recent trauma; the wound has fallen from the grace of high priority while yet unhealed, and now has a low priority in the body's economy.

C. EVIDENCES OF ENDOCRINE CHANGE

Other than the return of normal sexual function, there is little evidence of altered endocrine balance during this phase of convalescence. The return of gonadal function is signaled by the return of menstruation, which in turn signifies the return of ovulation in response to renewed pituitary stimulation.

D. METABOLISM AND BIOCHEMISTRY

We have not kept patients in the hospital for study on careful observation long enough to document by balance techniques the details of this final phase of convalescence. Instead, the identification of a final fat-gaining phase of convalescence is based on observations of a constant total body water during gain in body weight. The rate of fat gain averages in the neighborhood of 75 to 150 gm. a day, depending on caloric intake, absorption, and work. A person who has lost 5 kg. of fat will therefore require somewhat over a month to store away the adipose tissue lost. After severe injury or long preoperative weight loss this phase of reconstitution may occupy many months.

E. CLINICAL MANAGEMENT

The clinical management of this phase of normal convalescence lies wholly in the simple facts that caloric intake must exceed caloric output until "ideal weight" is regained, and that the patient should then resume exercise and avoid overeating in order to avoid obesity. The balance between caloric intake and energy output (the caloric balance or carbon balance) must be positive for the patient to gain his fat and lean tissue back to normal.

CHAPTER 3

Common Variations and Abnormalities of Convalescent Metabolism; the Very Young and the Very Old; "Surgical Risk"

In this chapter will be summarized ten common variations of the convalescent norm just described in detail. These variants will be described briefly and only to point out the contrasts that can be presented to the metabolic appearances of normal convalescence. With a few exceptions, these variations are pathologic. In several cases the abnormality derives from infection or from abnormal visceral function, either that existing prior to the injury, or that produced by the injury itself. In many instances these abnormal patterns of convalescent metabolism threaten the patient's survival, and extensive treatment is essential to recovery. In this regard, such convalescent sequences form a very striking clinical contrast to the normal, wherein complex treatment is unnecessary. Further details on the background and treatment of many of these convalescent variants form the main body of the remaining parts of this book.

Section I.   Clean Trauma with Healthy Viscera

1. Minor Injury

Examples. Hernia repair, appendectomy, cholecystectomy, fractured rib or ankle, or other minor clean traumata or operations.

Components. The components of such trauma are transient and limited to those of Group I (threshold stimuli). Anesthesia may under some circumstances be the most potent endocrine-metabolic activator involved. There is no significant reduction of effective extracellular and circulating blood volume.

Metabolism. The injury phase is very transient. Increase in the blood level of corticosteroids is slight and short-lived. Changes in nitrogen metabolism cannot be identified as in any sense beyond those seen in simple starvation. Changes in sodium, potassium, and water metabolism are those produced by the anesthesia used. The turning-point phase is not clearly identifiable. The phases of muscular regrowth and fat gain are transient and ill-defined because the previous catabolic loss has been negligible.

2. Single Hemorrhage without Shock or Tissue Trauma (See also Part II)

Examples. Bleeding ulcer, uterine bleeding, bladder hemorrhage.

Components. The components of such trauma are limited to acute reduction in effective circulating blood volume. This overshadows all other aspects when the hemorrhage is unaccompanied by tissue trauma, surgical operation, or anesthesia; renal vascular and tubular function responds by reduced renal hemodynamics and increased resorption of water and salt.

Metabolism. In the injury phase, the most striking changes involve reduction in the excretion of water and sodium, with a concomitant increase in aldosterone production and excretion of the catechol amines. Nitrogen loss from the body is mostly through the blood loss itself. If diet is not interrupted, nitrogen loading soon begins and the patient will remain in anabolism at a slow rate until the mass of lost blood is resynthesized. During the turning-point phase, diuresis is to be expected but is not clear-cut if there is no transfusion given. If blood transfusion is given, diuresis occurs as a manifestation of restored effective volume.

3. Operative Trauma in Severe Nutritional Depletion (See also Part IV)

Examples. Gastrectomy or colectomy in late malignancy, resection of bowel in regional enteritis or chronic ulcerative colitis.

Components. The components of such a trauma are essentially the same as those of moderate elective soft-tissue trauma in the healthy. They consist principally of tissue trauma, transient reduction in effective volume, and anesthesia.

Metabolism. In the previously depleted individual, the metabolic changes of the injury phase are quite different from the normal. There is less nitrogen loss; the absolute urinary nitrogen excretion rate rarely exceeds that observed in starvation alone. Nitrogen loading comes earlier and on lower intakes than in a healthy person. The endocrine changes of blood and urine corticosteroids, and the eosinophil changes, are normal. The reduction in water and sodium excretion with increased potassium excretion is intensified and prolonged over that seen in the normal individual. This depleted response might therefore be characterized as normal endocrinologically, but with minimal nitrogen changes and maximal water-and-salt changes. In the turning-point phase, nitrogen anabolism and diuresis of water and salt do not occur together, anabolism beginning sooner. Nitrogen anabolism is very prolonged and involves a considerable gain of weight over that noted before the operation, particularly if the operation has been successful in removing the cause of the preoperative starvation. So far as we know, there is no characteristic metabolic or endocrine change which may be identified as occurring only in patients with cancer.

4. Injury with Traumatic Edema (See also Parts III and VI)

Examples. Crush or fracture of mid-femur, early burn, pooling of intestinal fluids (as in ileus or obstruction), peritonitis, portal thrombosis.

Components. The components of such a trauma involve all the parameters of severe injury and especially the obligatory accumulation of extracellular fluid in a pathologic area with a resulting reduction in the effective extracellular and circulating blood volumes, although the total extracellular volume may actually be increased.

Metabolism. During the injury phase, alterations in corticosteroids, catechol amines, and nitrogen metabolism are very pronounced and depend on the nature of the injury. In massive skeletal trauma and burns, such changes are large and prolonged. Retention of salt and water is very prominent, since we are dealing here with both an acute reduction of extracellular volume and a general stimulus to water-and-salt retention. If whole protein (for example, plasma) is given in early treatment, a positive nitrogen balance results which is devoid of the significance of tissue synthesis. If adequate therapy is given to support effectual circulating volume, gain of weight is inevitable in the presence of traumatic edema. During the turning-point phase, diuresis with weight loss is prominent as the traumatic edema is being reabsorbed.

5. Extrarenal Loss (See also Part III)

Examples. Prolonged intestinal obstruction, pyloric obstruction, pancreatic fistula.

Components. The components of such traumata are dominated by the loss of extracellular water and salt and the associated reduction in effective extracellular and circulating blood volume. If the loss is very rapid, blood volume reduction occurs and the hematocrit rises. If the loss is slower, blood volume reduction is not as prominent as hypotonicity.

Metabolism. Nitrogen loss in bowel contents may be significant when the bowel loss is greatly exaggerated. With this exception the early metabolism is predominantly that of renal tubular conservation of water and salt. If blood volume is reduced, the renal vasculature also partakes in the genesis of reduced excretion. Following restoration of extracellular volume and diminution of loss, with return of peristaltic and absorptive function, there is diuresis and a return to anabolism. The duration of the anabolic process depends entirely on the extent of previous tissue loss and the level of alimentation.

Section II. Trauma with Sepsis or Visceral Disease

6. Postoperative Infection

Examples. Severe antibiotic-resistant wound infection after elective clean soft-tissue surgery.

Components. The components of such trauma are those of the original operation, with a subsequent prolonged occurrence of invasive infection with the resulting metabolic changes.

Metabolism. The injury phase initially looks quite normal. But as the infection arises there is a rise in corticosteroids, fall in eosinophils, and loss of nitrogen and potassium, and a tendency to hold sodium and water. The downswing of nitrogen loss will often be a mirror-image of the rising intensity of the septic processes as indicated by the swinging fever. The tendency to retain salt and water in invasive infection is traceable both to the sequestration of edema in the area of the spreading infection and the effects of this volume reduction on renal tubular function. Corticosteroid elevation is noticeable until the sepsis is adequately dealt with by drainage or exteriorization. Following this the turning-point and anabolic phases ensue normally.

7. Severe Open Injury with Sepsis (See also Part VI)

Examples. Infection following crushing injury, war wounds, automobile accidents, or bullet wounds.

Components. The components of such trauma here involve the full range of all three groups: the threshold stimuli, the threatening challenges of volume reduction or ventilatory inadequacy, and tissue-killing injury with necrosis, sepsis, and shock.

Metabolism. As a result of these strong stimuli, the metabolic and endocrine changes are maximal. Loss of nitrogen may represent several kilograms of lean wet tissue during the first few days. Renal function is reduced in all parameters, both tubular and vascular. There is a tendency to retain all normally excreted products, especially water, nitrogen, sodium, potassium, and phosphorus. Acute reduction in blood volume produces renal vasoconstriction. This is followed by diuresis if treatment is adequate. The injury-phase metabolism lasts as long as the acute invasive septic process is continued. When sepsis is controlled and fever returns to normal, the turning-point phase is manifested both by the diuresis of water and salt and by the tendency to strong nitrogen anabolism. Once anabolism begins in such patients, it is very intense and very prolonged. If the individual is young and healthy to begin with, the reconstruction of his body composition will be complete in about a year.

8. Acute Post-traumatic Renal Insufficiency (See also Part V)

Examples. Anuria following severe injury with hemorrhage and myoglobinuria, transfusion reaction with shock and hemoglobinuria.

Components. The components of this injury are wholly those of the initial trauma itself.

The occurrence of renal failure per se does not seem to alter metabolism within the body (other than in the renal parameters) until very late in its course. The nature of the trauma, rather than the renal pathology, may be said to determine the chemical anatomy of the subsequent anuria.

Metabolism. The metabolic changes, in keeping with the above, are determined by the nature of the trauma. The essentially complete lack of urinary excretion dominates the picture. Nitrogen compounds which would normally be excreted, together with intracellular electrolyte, accumulate in the plasma and are noted as the familiar azotemia and hyperkalemia of post-traumatic renal insufficiency. Acidosis is an important part of this picture, lacking only if there is large loss of acid from the stomach. The acidosis of renal insufficiency is made much worse by extrarenal loss of base. The tendency to anabolism may antedate diuresis and be discernible by a decreased rate of rise of the blood urea nitrogen, but the turning-point phase may be considered to arise with diuresis. The effect of dialysis on metabolism is most pronounced with respect to plasma electrolyte and acid-base changes, and is transient. After diuresis, dietary intake can begin and anabolism will soon result. The reconstructive phases of convalescence are very prolonged if lean-tissue wasting has been severe.

9. Operation in Congestive Heart Failure (See also Part V)

Examples. Valvuloplasty in late mitral stenosis.

Components. The components of such trauma are those of the operation itself. The pre-existent heart disease and its effect on renal tubular function and liver function make the response markedly abnormal, and the retention of water and salt are pronounced.

Metabolism. Thus, a tendency to gain weight and withdraw salt and water from the glomerular filtrate is the most prominent aspect of the injury phase. As in any other form of depletion, endocrine activity is normal, nitrogen loss is minimal, but water-and-salt changes very pronounced. The turning-point phase is characterized by diuresis. If the cardiac surgery has been effective and retention of water and salt prominent in the preoperative and early postoperative phase, this diuresis may be among the most spectacular seen in surgical convalescence and run from 5000 to 10,000 ml. in the course of a few days. The anabolic phases of convalescence carry on as visceral function is gradually restored. Final restoration of body composition to normal may take a year or more.

10. Terminal Malignancy (See also Part IV)

Examples. Late carcinoma of the stomach, late carcinoma of the colon, liver, or lung.

Components. If there is no operation this sequence is not really a traumatic stimulus and the metabolic sequence should not be analyzed wholly in terms of the biologic components of trauma. One is dealing primarily with the effect of caloric starvation characterized by an intake of calories less than that required for bodily maintenance while the intake of water and salt is continued.

Metabolism. Metabolism is therefore the picture of prolonged caloric starvation with its resultant retention of water and salt and with maintenance of water and salt intake, leading finally to a high body water volume with loss of fat and lean tissue, an increased extracellular phase progressing finally to starvation edema with hyponatremia and hypoproteinemia. A recovery phase does not occur unless such a late situation can be dealt with surgically and the tumor removed. Just before death there is a rise in endocrine metabolic activity with increased blood and urine corticosteroids, a fall in eosinophils, and a rise in nitrogen excretion. As previously mentioned, we know of no metabolic earmark which is characteristic of malignancy and malignancy alone.

Section III.   Endocrinology, Metabolism, and Treatment of Trauma in the Very Young

In this section some aspects of surgical care in infants and young children will be reviewed. Although discussed prior to the similar therapeutic detail in adults, the therapy properly follows the compositional, metabolic, and endocrine information.

Techniques for the surgical care of infants have grown out of intensive experience in the children's hospitals. Many of these techniques relate to the special problems of anesthesia and oxygenation, intravenous infusion, body temperature, and nutritional requirements (Gross, 1953).

Endocrine changes after trauma in the infant and child have not been extensively studied. The seemingly minimal metabolic change resulting from surgical trauma in the newborn suggests that this infant may be under some special influence which dampens endocrine activity or overresponsiveness. Were the newborn still to be circulating the high level of estrogens and 17-hydroxycorticosterone seen in the mother at delivery, some such picture of adequate peripheral steroid, together with minimal pituitary-adrenal activation, might be seen. If the infant maintained the mother's tendency to retain water and salt, marked conservation would result, and in some cases the extreme state of sclerema could, at least theoretically, result.

Until recently there have been comparatively few data available on the metabolic changes observed in infants. The monograph of Rickham (1957) points a new direction in this field. The surgical complexity of measuring metabolism in tiny infants is forbidding, yet a number of studies were completed successfully by Rickham.

Some of the special aspects of neonatal surgery may be summarized under the general headings of: (a) body composition, chemistry, and metabolism; (b) endocrinology; (c) therapeutic detail.

A. BODY COMPOSITION, CHEMISTRY, AND METABOLISM IN NEONATES AND INFANTS

The total body water volume is high in neonates. Friis-Hansen (1951) of our laboratories found in neonates a total body water volume of 70 to 80 per cent of body weight; an average of 76.7 per cent of body weight has been used. This means that there is a considerable accumulation of extracellular fluid in the neonate; such a high volume of total body water (well above normal lean-tissue content) must have this connotation. The extracellular fluid is indeed high, as shown by radiosodium dilution, which yields a figure of 42.6 per cent of body weight, and by thiocyanate, 41.2 per cent (Flexner *et al.*, 1947). The blood volume is also higher than in adults, averaging 8.5 per cent of body weight (Mollison *et al.*, 1950): the hematocrit is also high in full-term newborns, in the vicinity of 55 to 65 per cent.

A further increase in the volume of extracellular fluid ensues if fluid and salt are given. In one of the infants studied by Rickham there was a 12 per cent gain in extracellular fluid over a ten-day period. Sweat in the adult contains 15 to 60 mM. of sodium chloride per liter; in the infant it is lower. Swanson and Iob (1933) estimated that in an infant weighing 2.5 kg. the loss of sodium in sweat is only about 0.2 mE. per day. In the first days of life there is very little urine elaborated—about 20 ml. in the first two days. Almost any fluid therapy in this period will produce accumulation of water and a gain in weight. When to this proclivity is added the tendency to retain salt and water produced by operation and evidently seen in some infants (Rickham, 1957), it is clear that fluid therapy must be strictly limited.

The potassium:nitrogen relationship in infants and children is enigmatic, as was previously emphasized (Moore and Ball, 1952). The potassium:nitrogen ratio of the negative

Text continues on page 69.

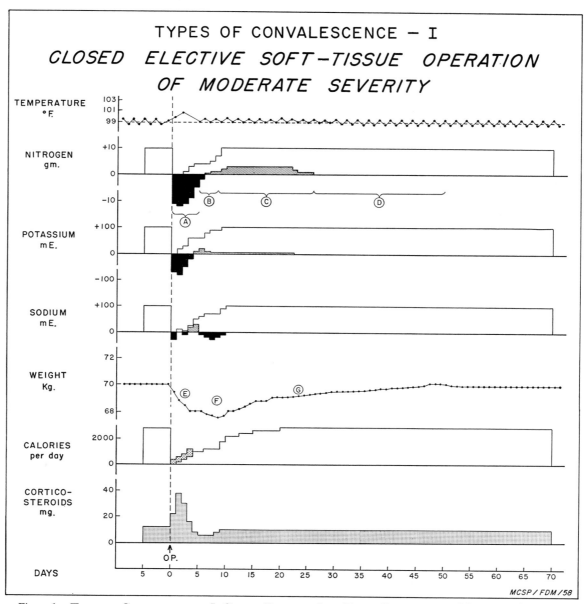

Figure 1.   Types of Convalescence. I. Closed Elective Soft-Tissue Operation of Moderate Severity

See facing page for detailed legend.

Figure 1. TYPES OF CONVALESCENCE. I. CLOSED ELECTIVE SOFT-TISSUE OPERATION OF MODERATE SEVERITY

In this and succeeding metabolic charts of this chapter the balances for nitrogen, potassium, and sodium are shown, together with changes in the patient's body weight, caloric intake, and corticosteroid excretion. These charts represent examples of what may be expected in several categories of convalescence. Individual variation is great. In all instances, the absolute balance is affected to some extent by the intake, this influence being most marked preoperatively and in the late postoperative period. Representative typical intakes are shown.

In all instances, the balances are "smoothed out" for ease of visual understanding. The daily fluctuations in intake and excretion are disregarded and straight lines are used, save where one may expect a daily stepwise change. Operative blood loss data and figures for blood transfusion are not included in most of these charts, in the interest of simplicity. Elsewhere in this book, these data are indicated after the method of Moore and Ball (1952). The charting convention is that of Moore and Ball (1952).*

Here is shown the typical mid-scale trauma of elective, closed, clean, civilian, soft-tissue operation.

This chart depicts the change one would expect to see in a man undergoing such an operation as combined abdominoperineal resection or uneventful gastrectomy. A woman would show a somewhat less florid response. On the nitrogen ordinate are shown letters indicating the characteristic four phases of convalescence. Preoperatively the patient is shown as being in zero balance.

* Intake is charted upward from zero, output downward from the top of the intake line. The resultant lower line is the balance. In these stylized introductory charts (Figures 1–8) the negative balance is marked in solid black and the positive balance is shaded, for ease of study.

A. The first or injury phase is characterized by loss of potassium and nitrogen and some tendency to conserve sodium. The timing of onset of sodium conservation is extremely variable and depends to a considerable extent on the anesthetic used.

B. The "turning point" phase is characterized chiefly by sharp reduction in nitrogen excretion rate despite increase in intake. Positive potassium balance is achieved before nitrogen balance. Sodium diuresis occurs at about this time and in this particular instance is not marked because sodium loading has not been marked.

C. Spontaneous nitrogen anabolism. In this instance, the duration of anabolism is only 17 days, this being sufficient to regain all the nitrogen lost.

D. The fat-gain phase is here depicted as of about 25 days' duration and sufficient to return the patient to his starting body weight, yielding an entire convalescent duration of approximately 50 days. This is achieved in patients with good preoperative status, whose gastrointestinal function quickly returns postoperatively, in whom there is no infection nor complication, and operative trauma of only moderate severity.

The weight curve shows at E the brisk weight loss associated with the early postoperative days. Loss of lean tissue accounts for about one-half of the weight loss and fat the other half. At F is seen the slight additional weight loss with sodium diuresis which may appear confusing at a time when the patient's intake is actually progressively rising.

The weight gained from this time forward is quite slow and represents first the laying down of lean tissue and later the restoration of fat.

The corticosteroid excretion pattern shows a single rise in the first phase, followed by a brief period of low normal excretion and then a normal pattern from that time forward.

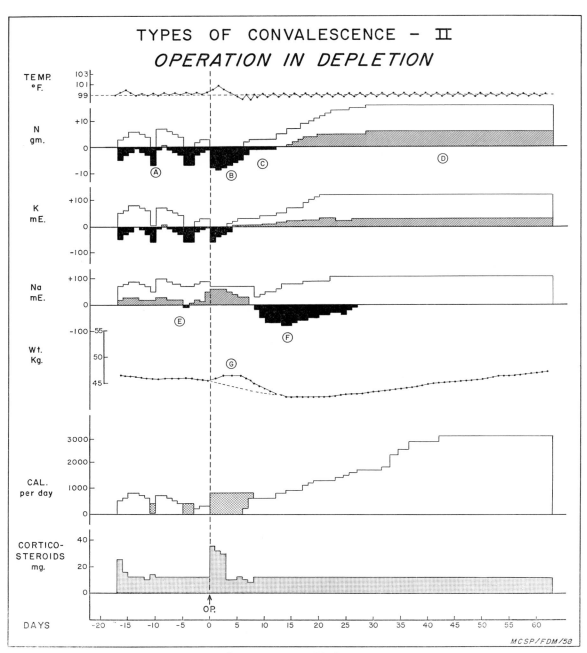

Figure 2.   TYPES OF CONVALESCENCE. II. OPERATION IN DEPLETION

See facing page for detailed legend.

Figure 2. Types of Convalescence. II. Operation in Depletion

This chart shows the sort of metabolic picture one may expect with uneventful, closed, soft-tissue surgery without infection in a patient who has previously been losing weight and is depleted prior to the operation. A typical example would be gastrectomy in partially obstructing carcinoma of the stomach with loss of 15 to 20 pounds of weight.

A. Preoperatively the patient is in negative nitrogen balance and shows a stepwise day-to-day change with the fluctuations in intake incident to work-up and X-rays. Note that balance is virtually a linear function of intake at this time. Were the patient to be more severely depleted, the same relationship would hold but the total nitrogen excretion each day would be considerably less.

B. The early postoperative nitrogen loss is not great and the absolute excretion rate is not increased, even by rather severe trauma.

C. The tendency to nitrogen conservation during the turning point phase is very striking and the patient goes to zero nitrogen balance and starts up into positive nitrogen balance on very low intakes, considerably lower than might be expected in a previously well patient.

D. As oral intake of nitrogen and calories progressively rises postoperatively, the gastrointestinal tract having been restored to normal continuity and function, the patient passes into very strongly positive nitrogen balance. One sees anabolism here rising to 6 gm. of nitrogen per day (8 gm./70 kg./day), a very high anabolic rate, characteristic of recovery in depletion.

E. The patient tends to be in positive sodium balance preoperatively and is not losing weight as rapidly as his nitrogen balance would indicate. This is confusing clinically and yields misleading information when the patient's preoperative status is judged wholly on the basis of weight change, uncorrected for sodium balance. Immediately after operation the patient goes into even more strongly positive sodium balance and it is in this type of patient that the plasma sodium:potassium concentration shift may be most marked, as described in Part III.

F. As the patient starts up into increasing caloric intake and better nutritional status than he has been in for many months, a prolonged sodium diuresis occurs. This may last as long as three or four weeks and may be associated with continued fall in weight or constant weight, despite rapidly increasing intake, a feature which again may be confusing clinically but of course indicates good metabolic recovery.

G. This patient shows some weight gain immediately after operation as a result of sodium loading. This sodium loading would be less marked were the patient given less sodium at this time. In the dotted line is shown the sort of weight curve which might be observed without sodium loading, a less rapid weight loss than one sees in normal convalescence in well nourished people.

Caloric intake is low preoperatively. It is maintained with ordinary rations of intravenous glucose postoperatively and then rises to a very high level for an individual of this weight, indicating very good restoration of gastrointestinal function and appetite, accounting for this patient's rapid anabolic recovery. Note that in such an individual anabolic recovery will ultimately go on for many kilograms greater than the immediate postoperative loss because the body is restoring normal weight as well as postoperative losses.

Corticosteroid excretion is unremarkable. Patients of this type show normal corticosteroid responses despite their rather dampened nitrogen change. Were 17-ketosteroid excretions to be recorded here, they would be found to be low throughout, and until convalescent anabolism has been accomplished. There would be an inconsequential rise with trauma.

See Part IV for a discussion of starvation and operation in depletion.

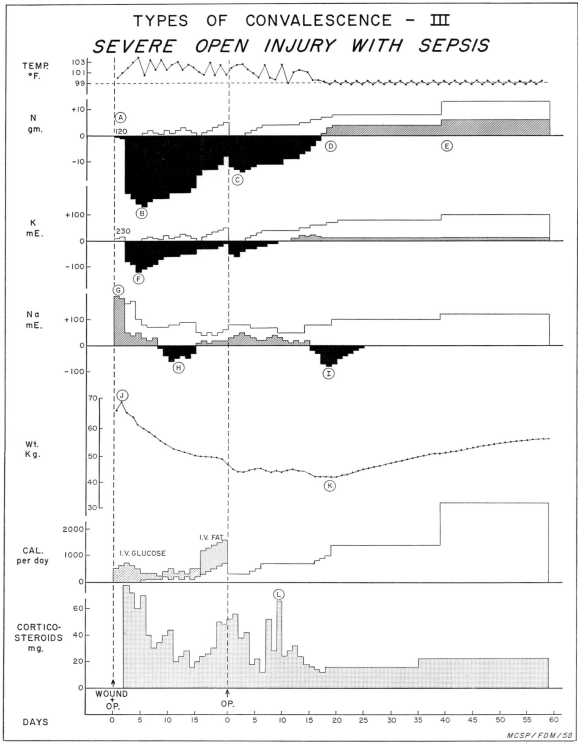

Figure 3.   Types of Convalescence. III. Severe Open Injury with Sepsis

See facing page for detailed legend.

Figure 3. TYPES OF CONVALESCENCE. III. SEVERE OPEN INJURY WITH SEPSIS

This chart depicts the sort of metabolic change that one may observe in a patient with severe, unanesthetized, open injury (automobile accident, war wound, industrial accident) followed by infection. An example would be a crushed pelvis with urinary extravasation, compound fracture of the tibia, and infection. Bullet wounds, traumatic amputations, and the like would demonstrate this sort of change with very large individual variation.

Temperature shows a spiking course for the first 35 days, coming back to normal after secondary operation and subsidence of infection. Secondary operation in such a case may take the form of drainage of an abscess, defunctioning colostomy, etc. In this instance the nitrogen and potassium content of the transfused red cells is indicated numerically above the columns.

A. The patient has an initial two-day period of oliguria during the lowered glomerular filtration rate of severe injury with shock and multiple transfusions. At the time of its occurrence, this oliguria is worrisome. But based on hourly urine outputs, an increasing response to replacement demonstrates the absence of severe parenchymatous damage. During oliguria renal metabolite excretion is cut off, and the products of catabolism build up in the extracellular fluid.

B. As renal function returns, a large nitrogen diuresis is demonstrated, resulting from the coexistence of three factors—the excretion of an unexcreted urea backlog, the excretion of blood in the tissues and the products of injured tissue, and the excretion of the continued catabolic product of severe injury and infection. During this extensive nitrogen loss, the patient's blood urea nitrogen may actually climb for a time as endogenous production of small molecular-weight nitrogen compounds outstrips the rate of their excretion. As this initial period progresses, nitrogen excretion rate becomes progressively less but is still above the starvation rate because of the presence of continuing fever and a strong catabolic process. Some of the nitrogen excreted arises from the destruction of blood in the tissues, the rest from muscle.

C. The secondary operation elicits a lesser increase in nitrogen excretion and about two weeks later, with subsidence of fever, a dramatic nitrogen conservation is seen (D). This is associated with or follows a marked clinical improvement, increasing intake, and a strong backswing of the eosinophil count. These events all taken together indicate the "turning point" in severe injury with sepsis.

E. This is then followed by prolonged anabolism, expected in such a case to last for many weeks and followed by a fat-gain phase lasting many months as the patient's extensive catabolism is restored by anabolic processes.

F. Similarly with potassium, there is an initial period of potassium retention during oliguria followed by marked diuresis as the kidneys open up. In such a case a rising plasma potassium concentration with falling sodium concentration is due in part to failure of excretion of potassium and water. The rate of potassium diuresis in such a case is greater than one would see had there been no period of oliguria, but the total excreted is no larger. Potassium balance becomes positive prior to nitrogen balance in this case, as in most other instances.

G. This patient shows a marked period of sodium conservation early on, due to the formation of traumatic edema in the area of the wound. The sodium administered at this time is the sodium found in both plasma and blood, as well as in mixed electrolyte solutions. After the initial accumulation of about 400 mE. of sodium in an area of traumatic edema, the patient's sodium accumulation is less rapid and the patient has two sodium diuresis periods. The first (H) is associated with the restoration of capillary permeability in the area of traumatic edema, and diuresis of the traumatic edema. The second period of sodium diuresis (I) is the definitive diuresis at the time of beginning intake, and represents the unloading of the entire sodium gain.

The weight curve shows the initial phase of weight gain due to traumatic edema (J), the same compositional change as that seen in an early burn but of less extent and much shorter duration. Following this there is prolonged weight-loss showing fluctuations according to additional losses of lean tissue and fat as balanced out by the rather marked changes in sodium balance. As in the previous figure there is a weight loss (K) even though the patient is beginning intake and anabolism, as the final post-traumatic sodium diuresis occurs.

Caloric intake is not adequate until about 20 days after the secondary operation. An attempt to increase caloric intake just before the second operation by administering intravenous fat is associated with an increase in total caloric intake and some reduction in nitrogen loss. Caloric intake finally reaches a satisfactory level long after the injury, as dietary rehabilitation is established.

Corticosteroid excretion shows little excretion during the early oliguric phase, followed by a prolonged period of high and fluctuating excretion, showing towards its end (L) spikes associated with daily spikes in fever.

Thereafter, with subsidence of fever and establishment of convalescent anabolism, the corticosteroid excretion is returned to a high normal range. Were 17-ketosteroid excretion to be measured in this patient, it would be found to be very low throughout the period until convalescent anabolism is an accomplished fact.

See Part VI for discussion of treatment of wounds.

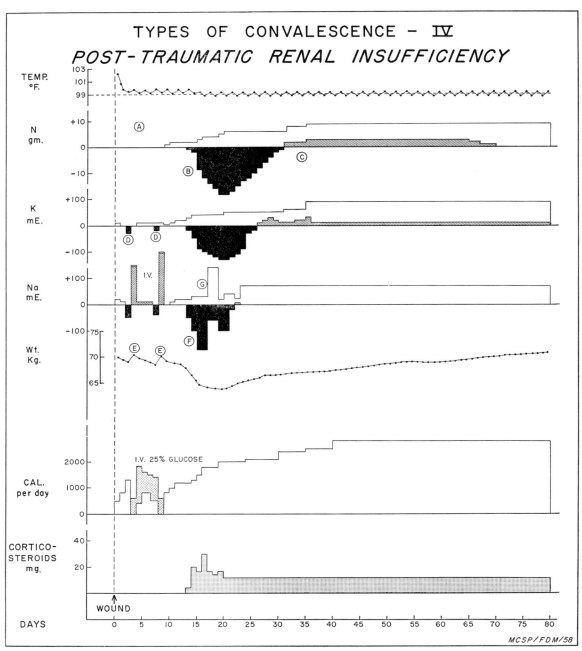

Figure 4.   TYPES OF CONVALESCENCE. IV. POST-TRAUMATIC RENAL INSUFFICIENCY

See facing page for detailed legend.

Figure 4. TYPES OF CONVALESCENCE. IV. POST-TRAUMATIC RENAL INSUFFICIENCY

In the previous chart was shown a patient with severe injury somewhat oliguric for two days. Here, by contrast, is shown a characteristic course for an individual with post-traumatic renal insufficiency such as one might se e after severe injury, with acute renal failure

In the instance depicted here, neither the trauma nor the renal insufficiency has been so severe as to be irreversible or fatal.

Temperature is not elevated after the first day or two, a most important favorable sign in post-traumatic renal insufficiency. Continued infection or surgical sepsis with a continuing high febrile course is a very unfavorable sign in post-traumatic renal insufficiency, chiefly because of the greatly accelerated accumulation of organic and inorganic acids and catabolic end-products when sepsis is superimposed.

A. Early nitrogen balance is shown as zero, with no intake and no output. There may, of course, be sligh t deviations from this if the patient has significant amounts of purulent discharge or extrarenal losses. Following this, diuresis commences on the 13th day and nitrogen diuresis gradually becomes established, finally excreting an amount of nitrogen commensurate with the expected negative balance for the previous thirteen days (plus small continuing losses) had rena₁ function been normal throughout. This, of course, am unts to a considerably greater daily nitrogen excretion than one would see in the same patient at this stage had there been no renal insufficiency.

This is followed (C) by a prolonged anabolic phase as the patient regains muscle mass in a typical anabolic period.

Potassium balance shows entirely analogous changes. Gastric intubation (D) has resulted in small potassium losses on two occasions. If the patient has large amounts of gastric acidity, such intubation may also be useful in removing hydrogen ion during an oliguric period.

Sodium balance shows comparatively little flux with the environment in the early period save for two episodes of extrarenal loss. In this chart is shown the metabolic effect of giving intravenous sodium to a patient with renal failure. There is essentially no loss with a resultant strongly positive balance and associated weight gain (E)

The diuresis period produces loss of sodium (F) which is significantly greater than the sodium previously gained. This suggests some obligatory tubular sodium loss during recovery from post-traumatic renal insufficiency, a loss which can in some instances be severely depleting, producing extracellular desalting water loss with a rising hematocrit. For this reason (G) sodium is given intravenously for two days during the diuresis phase.

Thereafter, the patient's sodium balance is depicted as being essentially zero.

The weight curve shows good maintenance of weight without significant gains save for the two intravenous periods (E). Then, with diuresis (G) there is a brisk weight loss as endogenously-produced water is excreted, followed by anabolic weight gain.

Caloric intake is maintained during the oliguric period by oral glucose, syrups, and the use of intravenous 25 per cent glucose. As diuresis is established, the oral caloric intake can become normal.

Corticosteroid excretion is zero during the oliguric phase and thereafter shows only a very small peak, the steroids retained in the body during the oliguric phase having been inactivated, conjugated, and destroyed by other mechanisms.

The changes of extrarenal dialysis are not shown on this chart. The metabolic change of dialysis is not striking quantitatively. During the six-hour period of dialysis there will be loss of considerable nitrogen and potassium, but the basic compositional situation is not altered until diuresis ensues.

See Part V for a discussion of renal insufficiency.

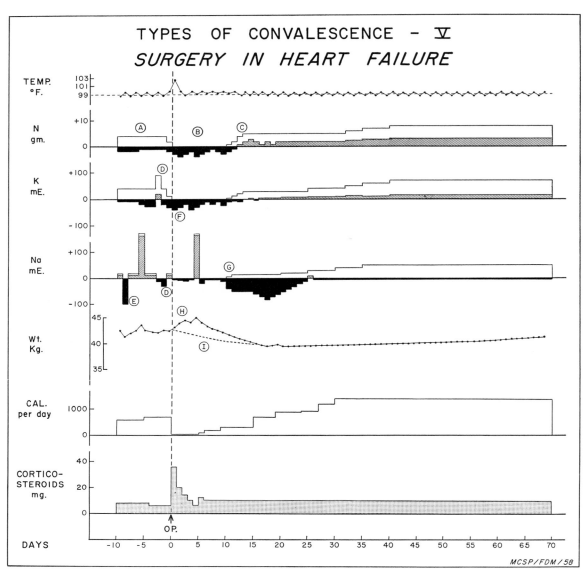

Figure 5. Types of Convalescence. V. Surgery in Heart Failure

See facing page for detailed legend.

Figure 5.   TYPES OF CONVALESCENCE. V. SURGERY IN HEART FAILURE

In this chart is depicted the sort of metabolic change one may expect in a woman with advanced mitral stenosis undergoing corrective operation. Temperature is essentially normal save for a slight elevation the day of operation and, thereafter, a rise usually due to inadequate clearing of bronchial secretion. Were the patient to have an extensively febrile or complicated course, a rather different metabolic picture would be seen.

Preoperatively, nitrogen balance (A) is consistently slightly negative. This has been going on for many months or years in such a patient, and is associated with the lean tissue wasting characteristic of late mitral stenosis. After operation (B) the total nitrogen excretion rate is very small in this depleted, cachectic person with imperfect circulatory dynamics. This is as small a negative nitrogen balance as one is apt to see after major thoracic surgery in the adult.

C. The turning point phase (nitrogen conservation and starting anabolism) going on to a prolonged anabolic phase of body compositional restoration is then characteristic. This does not occur without exogenous caloric intake and its occurrence is a very important metabolic sign of the success of the operative procedure. The anabolic restoration of body composition in such a patient as this may take as long as 12 to 18 months.

Potassium changes are entirely analogous to those seen in nitrogen. Shown at D is a single day's increase in potassium intake which may be associated with some significant sodium diuresis. Such a step must be entered into with some care in patients who carry a slightly elevated potassium concentration chronically, as is characteristic of mitral stenosis.

Sodium balance is generally positive preoperatively, a characteristic accompaniment of heart disease and of continuing nitrogen and potassium loss. The characteristic compositional change is that of consistent accumulation of extracellular fluid at the expense of intracellular fluid. This patient is on a low-sodium diet of 20 mE. per day but still shows some loading.

At (E) is shown the type of sodium diuresis which may be produced with mercurial diuretics, aminophylline, Diamox, or ammonium chloride.

Both before and after operation (days −6 and 6) are shown the typical effects of intravenous sodium, resulting in accumulation of water and salt and weight gain. If this is continued, it will result in pulmonary edema and is potentially fatal. Sodium changes early after operation are essentially those of no flux with the environment except when given intravenously.

At G, and concomitant with nitrogen and calorie loading (C), the patient starts in with a good brisk sodium diuresis. This is an extremely favorable sign, indicating success of operation and an excellent prognosis.

The weight curve shows some weight loss with mercurial diuresis, slowly regained, gain of weight with intravenous sodium, either pre- or postoperatively, and the period of weight gain immediately after operation due in this case to the inexorable tendency of these patients to gain weight if given water in any excessive amounts postoperatively. The dotted line at (H) demonstrates the sort of weight curve one would see with absolutely ideal balance of water and salt postoperatively.

Caloric intake preoperatively is at the very low level characteristic of patients in cardiac failure. Postoperatively as hemodynamic normalcy is restored, caloric intake increases towards a satisfactory level.

Corticosteroid excretion shows no particularly remarkable changes save for a normal postoperative response.

See Part V for a discussion of surgery in heart disease.

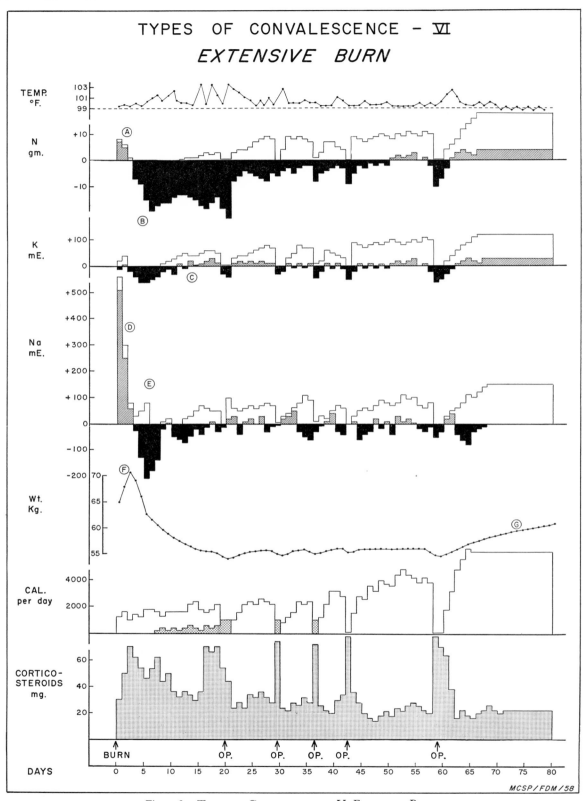

Figure 6.   Types of Convalescence. V. Extensive Burn

See facing page for detailed legend.

Figure 6. TYPES OF CONVALESCENCE. V. EXTENSIVE BURN

In this chart is depicted the sort of change one might observe in a burn of 35 to 40 per cent of body surface in a young adult male, with satisfactory convalescence and recovery, and without severe pulmonary, renal, or gastrointestinal complications.

The temperature chart shows a slowly rising temperature in the early days of the burn. This is a good sign indicating that invasive sepsis is not present early. The rise in fever is due to the presence of necrotic tissue. Thereafter there are a few days of spiking fever, associated initially with the presence of sloughing tissue and subsequently rising with excision and grafting procedures.

Nitrogen balance (A) shows the initial positive nitrogen balance of the plasma-treated burn. This merely represents the accumulation in the body of infused whole protein faster than it can be hydrolyzed metabolically and excreted. Following this (B) there is the severe nitrogen wasting of the burned patient. In this particular instance, negative nitrogen balance persists for about 50 days but the extreme losses are confined to the early 20 days.

The successive operations are shown, the first and the last both being extensive procedures. The first is a sharp debridement with extensive grafting, and the last an excision of some granulation tissue with extensive recoverage. The three other procedures represent dressing changes with grafting of open surfaces. Each operation is associated with a sharp drop in intake and some increased nitrogen wastage but there is rapid resumption of the over-all nitrogen curve as the patient resumes intake the day following the procedure. Any period of prolonged lack of intake after the twentieth day will be associated with nitrogen loss much greater than that shown here.

The potassium changes are characteristically similar to those of nitrogen. Potassium balance (C) becomes positive long before nitrogen and the potassium:nitrogen ratio for this prolonged initial period is therefore very low, a characteristic finding in burns.

The sodium balance shows at (D) the very marked, early positive sodium balance of the burned patient. This sodium is infused in the form of plasma, whole blood, and mixed electrolyte solutions. In this particular case the initial positive sodium balance at approximately 800 mE. is somewhat less than is often seen. This period of early positive sodium balance is followed (E) by sodium diuresis as the traumatic edema is mobilized and excreted. Thereafter the sodium balance shows wide stepwise swings with tendency to sodium accumulation after operative procedures and finally a diuresis as the wound is closed and the final anabolic phase established.

The weight curve shows the early weight gain (F) of the burned patient, here approximately 6 kg. in a 65 kg. individual, or 10 per cent of body weight. This is the weight gain which one expects in the burn patient treated by infusion of plasma or saline. In this particular instance, the sodium diuresis with associated weight drop starts at the third and fourth days and produces a fall in weight down to that level expected from tissue catabolism alone. There is a long "valley" in which weight is not gained until finally closure becomes established and the weight gain of anabolism ensues.

Caloric intake shows the stepwise changes and fluctuations with operation which are characteristic of the convalescent burn. In this patient caloric intake is finally established at about 6000 calories per day, a very optimal intake, permitting the earliest possible resumption of weight.

Corticosteroid excretion shows the prolonged elevated excretion of a burn during the phase of sepsis, catabolism, and beginning closure. Each operative procedure is associated with a sharp peak of steroid excretion, often a much higher peak than one would associate with a similar anesthesia and dressing in a normal individual. This suggests some adrenal hyperplasia, easily demonstrated by ACTH tests. As the later operations proceed, one sees no change in the eosinophil count or actually a rise, despite this very high rise in endogenous steroid production.

See Part VI for a discussion of the treatment of burns.

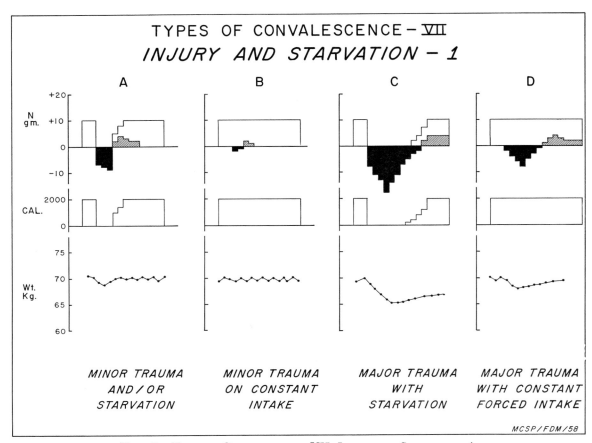

Figure 7.   TYPES OF CONVALESCENCE. VII. INJURY AND STARVATION. 1.

See facing page for detailed legend.

Figure 7. TYPES OF CONVALESCENCE. VII. INJURY AND STARVATION. 1.

In this and the succeeding chart are shown seven different types of situations which may be produced by various combinations of trauma, with and without intake of food by mouth. All of these, with the exception of the last (G), have been produced by clinical observation or investigation.

A. Minor operations and short-term starvation are metabolically indistinguishable when viewed within the narrow framework of nitrogen metabolism, caloric intake and weight change. In both instances (minor trauma and starvation) there is nitrogen loss in the starvation range followed by nitrogen gain. There is a short period of caloric interruption and there is a brisk weight loss followed by brisk resumption of weight.

B. Minor trauma is easily managed with constant dietary intake. In operations of lesser magnitude the maintenance of constant intake by mouth requires special nursing procedures, but can be accomplished. One then sees a slight tendency to nitrogen loss followed by gain, this being extremely variable. When the operative procedure is of little extent, the exact detail of this minor change of four to six days' duration depends on many other factors, including the sex of the patient (males tend to unload more nitrogen than females), the nature of the anesthesia (ether tends to produce more catabolism than other agents), the presence or absence of infection, and others. However, the principal conclusion, that constancy of diet essentially obliterates metabolic change in uneventful major surgery of lesser extent, is fully justified.

C. When a more severe injury or operation occurs without maintained intake, the characteristic sequence is observed: a loss of nitrogen greater than that seen in starvation alone. Here the loss of lean tissue and at combine to produce the observed weight loss.

D. Major trauma as in C but with constant intake. This experiment is much more difficult to carry out and has only rarely been recorded in the literature. In our experience, attempts to carry patients with very severe major injury or operation on constant oral intake have rarely been crowned with success. The alteration in function of the gastrointestinal tract shortly after trauma makes this difficult. When the materials are given intravenously, a somewhat similar picture might be expected as long as the balance between calories and nitrogen, and the chemical source of both, are ideally suited for human nutrition. In any event, what evidence there is suggests that the maintenance of constant intake through an episode of severe injury will do much to lessen the net catabolic loss of both nitrogen and fat and, of course, net weight loss. Note that the absolute nitrogen excretion rate on the second, third, and fourth postoperative days is the same in both C and D. However, in D (with maintained oral intake) this absolute increase in nitrogen excretion rate is carried downward from an intake of 10 gm. resulting in a considerably diminished net catabolic loss. The exact amount of caloric and nitrogen intake required to maintain a person in balance after severe injury is uncertain. In general we have found that normal individuals maintain their weight on intakes in the region of 0.1/30 (0.1 gm. of nitrogen per kilogram and 30 calories per kilogram per day). After moderate injury, intakes of 0.2/50 are required to maintain constancy of weight. After more severe injury, even higher intakes are rquired to maintain constancy of body mass. Clinical benefit of maintained intake after injury is uncertain.

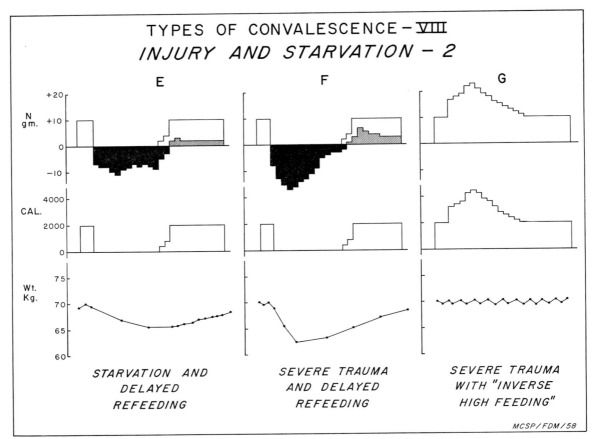

Figure 8. TYPES OF CONVALESCENCE. VIII. INJURY AND STARVATION. 2.

E. A more prolonged period of starvation produces a picture like that shown in A but more prolonged. With this longer period of starvation, the patient is starved long enough to show the nitrogen conservation of later starvation and occasionally seen in depleted surgical patients (see Figure 2). When the patient has reached this phase of starvation, he then shows the property of gaining nitrogen on very small intakes. This nitrogen conservation on refeeding, which we have termed "avidity for nitrogen," is a property of starvation after the first week or two. As the starved patient is refed, he very quickly goes into positive nitrogen balance and maintains it throughout anabolism. There is never any lag observed between resumed intake and resumed positive balance.

F. By contrast, when there is severe injury, with prolonged interruption of intake and resumed feeding, there is a greater loss of nitrogen and weight than with starvation alone. In this example, nitrogen conservation then begins several days before diet, a finding

characteristic of a severely injured patient in whom the stress factors (infection, tissue necrosis) abate before diet begins. This metabolic picture thus forms a contrast with starvation.

G. This diagram is strictly theoretical since we know of no example in the literature where this experiment has been carried out in man. This depicts a severe injury of the type which might be shown in F but with oral intakes raised up to very high levels, forming a mirror image of the expected nitrogen deficit. One might theorize that by such steps a patient after severe injury could indeed by maintained with *constant* body tissue mass. Whether or not such steps would be of any benefit to the patient remains uncertain. The resumption of muscular strength late in convalescence might be expected to be more facile and the period of reha bili tation shorter. Favorable effects on early convalescent recovery, on sense of well-being, or on wound healing would not be so readily expected. The hazards of overloading a postoperative stomach are obvious.

balance after trauma in newborns under three weeks of age is at the lean-tissue range, suggesting minimal differential potassium loss or potassium-sodium exchange. Subsequent positive potassium:nitrogen ratios are consistently high (4 to 8 mE. per gm.) even during normal growth, posing a problem as to interpretation of the disposition of the potassium. Fecal nitrogen losses may be relatively high in infants.

There is a tendency of newborns to show a consistent metabolic acidosis (Young *et al.*, 1941; Darrow, 1948) with an elevated plasma chloride (110 mE. per l., for example) and phosphorus, and a low carbon dioxide combining power (16 to 18 mM. per l., for example). This suggests an abnormality of the renal tubular function. In the postoperative period, retention of chloride is greater than sodium; a worsening of this hyperchloremic acidosis results.

In infants during the first three weeks of life there is a loss of weight—up to 20 per cent of body weight (Smith, 1951)—which does not appear to be accentuated by operation or food deprivation. It is of course obliterated by the administration of fluids. It may be due to insensible water loss. Newborn infants tolerate pure dehydration very well when it is due to unreplaced pulmonary water loss; they tolerate desalting water loss very poorly and will succumb rapidly to salt loss. In severe acid-loss alkalosis (as in pyloric stenosis) there is a hypokalemia and, not infrequently, tetany. The newborn may pass through a phase of very high gastric acidity (Miller, 1941) which is in the background of this change.

In newborn infants a normal adequate intake is 0.5 to 0.7 gm. of nitrogen per kg. per day and 80 calories per kg. per day. This is (by our shorthand) 0.5:80, a distortion of the adult equivalent (normally 0.1:30) in the direction of more nitrogen in relation to calories. Newborn infants tolerate short-term caloric starvation remarkably well.

In fact newborn infants probably quite normally get few calories or little nitrogen from mother's milk in the first seventy-two hours. They tolerate starvation well for two or three days. In esophageal atresia, the first few days (even up to eight days in one of Rickham's cases) of no intake, while preventing normal growth, do not seem to exact a penalty in terms of surgical survival.

Body temperature regulation fails to maintain a gradient with a cool environment (Smith, 1951). During and after operation temperature often falls to 90° to 94° F. unless preventive measures are taken; it is probable that this degree of hypothermia is beneficial when severe disease or extensive operation coexists.

B. ENDOCRINOLOGY

Newborns show a less marked drop in eosinophils in response to adrenocorticotropic hormone than do adults, but the response is variable (Jailer, 1951). The fetal adrenal cortex is only gradually replaced by adult cortex, starting at five days of age. Stoner *et al.* (1953) have shown a low steroid content, and urinary corticoid excretion is low. The possibility exists that maternal estrogen or corticosteroids hold pituitary and adrenal activation in check while at the same time providing basic support for trauma.

C. THERAPEUTIC DETAIL IN NEONATES, INFANTS, AND YOUNG CHILDREN

Infants are easily overloaded with water, salt, or blood. Small absolute errors in fluid administration (10 ml., for example) that are meaningless in the adult may be fatal in a three-pound premature infant. The intravenous route is preferable for administration if oral intake is interdicted, scalp veins or indwelling saphenous cannulae being used.

In infants the insensible water loss is 50 ml. per pound per day: in the postoperative period this rises to 100 ml. per pound per day. But replacement must be cautious. Rates near 30 ml. per pound per day to cover insensible loss are used in the first few days of life. Extrarenal desalting water loss is replaced volumetrically, using hypotonic saline solution. The basic daily requirement is therefore met at a level of about 40 to 50 ml. per pound per day of one-fifth normal saline solution. This is a ceiling rate. When the patient is debilitated or postoperative this ration may have to be cut to 10 to 15 ml. per pound. When deficits are present or there are large extrarenal losses continuing, these figures are revised upwards. An infusion burette should never contain more than 10 ml. per pound, so as to avoid overloading should the controls become inactive.

Provision of intravenous intakes must be done in small amounts, special pains being taken to see that accidental overadministration cannot occur. In newborns one or two slow syringe injections per day are to be preferred to a long intravenous infusion.

The blood chemical values needed to provide close check are not numerous. As in the adult, good metabolic care can be provided without complex or repetitive analyses. Intake, output, body weight, blood urea, hematocrit, and carbon dioxide combining power, or some other index of acid-base change, are the most important. Unlike the adult, the newborn simply cannot tolerate repetitive blood sampling for chemical check. Replacement of losses of salt and water is essential, with good attention to their ionic composition and acid-base significance. In some instances in the newborn, where salt is not being lost, it is advisable to withhold fluid administration completely for the first day.

There is some evidence that newborns destroy their own blood rapidly (Rickham); it would seem doubtful that this would apply to blood transfused. The rate of infusion of blood should rarely exceed 10 ml. per pound (25 ml. per kg.) per day (Bowman, 1950). This corresponds to 2000 ml. in an adult.

Measurements of operative blood loss are essential. The sponge-weight method developed by Dr. Gross (1949) particularly for infants is most useful. The method must be used with care and discrimination to yield good results in small infants. The changes in body weight of the patient provide a basis for estimation of the status of blood volume before and after extensive operations; other fluid factors are of course to be considered. Traumatic edema or blood in serous cavities provides weight without providing hemodynamic support and must also be considered and compensated for.

While a fall in temperature of 5° to 7° F. is permissible, well tolerated, and possibly beneficial during operation, the maintenance of high humidity is of great importance both during and after operation. Water loss and heat loss by vaporization are both prevented thereby. In 100 per cent humidity the insensible fluid loss is about 14 ml. per kg. per day (Rickham, 1957).

Body surface area is useful also as a basis for calculating total fluid needs, using the round figures of 1000 to 1500 ml. per twenty-four hours per square meter. This estimate can also be used for drugs. As a basis for calculating requirements either in the adult or child, it suffers largely from the fault of oversimplification, leading to neglect of the many other conditioning factors, particularly anesthesia, operation, fever, dyspnea, previous state of hydration, and salt loss.

The graph shown in Figure 9 is that used by Crawford and Talbot in calculating surface area. In infants, the ratio of surface area to weight is much higher than it is in children; this ratio falls most rapidly in the first year of life. Therefore, very small children require somewhat more therapy per unit weight. Our burn budget (see Part VI) is based on weight and is therefore slightly easier to adapt to children than is a rule-of-thumb formula, based on absolute treatment of volumes. The young child's burn treatment should be approached, as in the adult, with a realistic view of requirements and the use of every available guidepost along the way, the most useful of which are the body weight, capillary hematocrit, hourly urine output, and evaluation of the blood pressure (if possible) and peripheral circulatory integrity. Wallace (1949) has provided a guide-calculator for burn treatment in children.

Microchemical determinations are used in infants. The potassium concentration is often discovered to be elevated, possibly on the basis of tissue contamination in the method of collection of the blood. McGovern (1955) has presented the data needed for the use of the microhematocrit as performed on puncture blood.

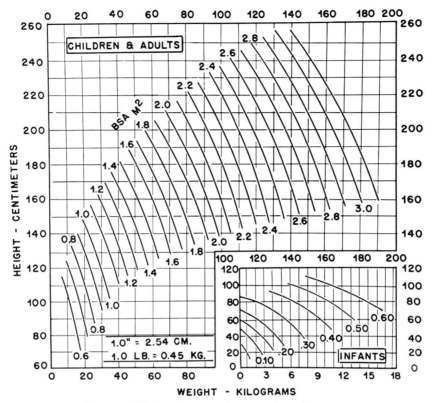

Figure 9. Height-Weight-Surface Area Diagram

In this diagram (taken from Talbot) are shown the surface areas for various heights and weights. The small insert at the lower right shows the more detailed figures for small infants.

Surface area does not make a practical standard for fluid therapy in adults. There are too many other variables, most particularly fever, dyspnea, sex, age, cardiac and renal function, all of which control the acceptable limitations of fluid therapy.

In the newborn or young infant, however, surface area provides a very helpful index of basic normal fluid requirements in the resting state, and these figures can then be modified for the pathologic situation at hand.

Section IV.   Metabolic Care in the Very Old: Brain, Lungs, Heart, and Kidneys

The surgical metabolism and ability of the elderly to accept and tolerate surgical trauma depend entirely on function of their visceral organs, brain, lungs, heart, and kidneys being the most important.

Physiologic aging differs from chronologic aging largely through the variation in extent of the ravages of degenerative vascular disease. This degeneration, in terms of surgical survival, is most keenly felt in brain, heart, and kidneys. These are the organs which are in areas of high-pressure blood flow. We might call them the "high-pressure, flow-sensitive" group. It is to these organs that one must look to evaluate the likelihood of survival in any individual case. By the same token, metabolic change after surgery in the elderly depends largely on the previous nutritive state and the function of these organs.

By contrast, the liver and lungs are in low-pressure circuits, and one rarely sees these organs suffer through the agency of degenerative vascular disease in aging per se. The liver is rarely at fault as a prime cause of poor surgical survival in the elderly, barring those cases in which it is diseased to begin with. The lungs suffer principally from a nonvascular syndrome of pulmonary insufficiency due to chronic bronchitis with decreased lung elasticity, asthma, emphysema, and senile bronchiectasis.

Post-traumatic endocrine activity in people over seventy-five seems to be quite normal. The same is true of their metabolic response. Where there is disease of heart and kidney both responses are modified: edema, hypoproteinemia, pulmonary insufficiency due to congestive heart failure, azotemia, and acidosis quickly predominate over the underlying metabolism.

Brain disease affects metabolism in a less spectacular way, but is often a most critical factor in recovery in the elderly. This points up the remarkable importance of normal mental and emotional responses in surgical recovery, especially in old people. The older patient whose eye is clear, understanding of his care adequate, and cooperation good will do much better than his brother suffering cerebrovascular disease (or oversedated), who lies in semicoma, restless, without normal reflexes of cough or swallowing. The latter patient represents the result of surgery superimposed on degenerative vascular disease of the brain, and recovery is very dubious with the most trivial insult.

The evaluation of the older patient prior to operation should thus be in terms of specific organ function, the design of his surgery based on the same, and the details of medication, anesthesia, and postoperative care based on the evolving response of brain, heart, kidneys, and lung.

In subsequent parts of this book many details of care in the elderly are further elaborated.

Section V. Surgical Risk: An Obsolete Concept

The term "surgical risk" took its origin from a period when major operation was rarely done except in dire emergency, elective operation was in its infancy, and any kind of operation was performed under conditions of inadequate oxygenation, poor relaxation, and with no blood replacement. The word "risk" is incomplete; it carries no connotation nor implication as to the alternative course offered should surgery be decided against. The word "risk" implies a "free choice," which rarely exists.

An example of poor risk might well be a patient in late congestive heart failure with enlarged liver, edema, pulmonary congestion only recently relieved, reduced vital capacity, marked wasting of tissue, and chronic invalidism. Yet, given the proper valvular lesion, the best possible treatment for this patient is a surgical operation. The alternative is a steadily downhill course even with excellent medical management, and death.

In a healthy young woman there is surely little "surgical risk" in cholecystectomy; yet, if the patient does not have gallstones the hazard of operation is excessive.

Clearly, then, the alternative course without operation is as important as the operative hazard in evaluating the advisability of operation. To focus attention on the ideal preoperative preparation of the patient and on the maximum dynamic physiologic improvement prior to operation is of much greater benefit to physician and patient alike than is the static evaluation of that obsolete and indefinable entity: surgical risk.

A better term for this concept is "the advisability of operation" and a better criterion arises from a comparison of the hazards of operative care with those of a continued course of nonoperative care.

CHAPTER 4

Surgical Endocrinology and Metabolism: Notes from the Literature

The surgeon, ever desirous of improving the care of his patient, and always on the lookout for new concepts that may be helpful to him in his responsibility to that patient, experiences the utmost difficulty in following the theories advanced by various scholars who concern themselves with endocrine matters. Although he may admire the consummate skill with which they demolish each other's hypotheses, he is confused by the data and readily admits that there seems to be no key to the truth, and very little of practical benefit resulting.

Despite this confusion as a new field of surgical biology opens up—namely, that of post-traumatic endocrinology and metabolism—let the surgical practitioner be warned not to be intimidated. He has a perfect right to insist that the work be carefully done, that the data be interpreted without bias, and that complicated laboratory methods be subjected constantly to chemical and theoretical check.

Much of the work in endocrinologic aspects of trauma has been done by surgeons whose training lay in other fields. Even the best authorities, when they move out of their fields of technical proficiency, are not free from subjective pressures, including many of which they are unconscious. One of these is a desire to find a simple explanation for a variety of facts. The concept of the "alarm reaction" advanced by Selye suffers from this fault; likewise the idea—nowhere very clearly formulated—that the adrenal cortex is re-sponsible for all post-traumatic metabolism. The concept of blood-sludging or of endo-toxin as explaining all the phenomena of shock likewise suffers from this premature search for a single explanation.*

There can be no question that a variety of endocrine activities are stimulated by trauma; alterations in intermediary metabolism and excretion of hormones also affect the result; certain types of tissue changes are especially noticeable after injury although their patho-genesis is quite varied, just as the biologic components of trauma are, themselves, varied. The chief problem at the bar for judgment now has to do with the relationship between the endocrine changes observed and the tissue or metabolic changes which occur with them. Does the endocrinology that we see and record after injury produce or favor the tissue changes which are concomitant?

In evaluating data on this point, the surgical reader has every right also to insist on certain general principles of interpretation as follows:

1. *Concomitance does not indicate causation.* The fact that nitrogen is lost while cortico-steroid excretion is increased does not signify that one causes the other. It makes it possible that the two are causally related, but it does not indicate such cause. As already mentioned in detail, there is much evidence to suggest that the nitrogen catabolic factors in trauma

---

* Cf. the paragraphs on religious controversy in Davies (1956).

are often not correlated with corticosteroid excretion at all. There is instead some sort of general association, possibly of the so-called permissive type. Since the first metabolic studies combining measurements of nitrogen change with those of endocrine change, the observation has been a commonplace that nitrogen anabolism occurs without any correlated corticosteroid alteration either downward or upward. There are many associations between the two; there are also many departures.

2. *Small differences between patients or experiments must not be overinterpreted.* One cannot interpret a blood steroid rise, for instance, of 32 micrograms per cent as being significantly greater than one of 30 micrograms per cent. Standard procedures for statistical evaluation of biologic data must be applied here as they are anywhere else. In many instances no person knows exactly the accuracy, reproducibility, and recovery rates of new hormone assays. In general, chemical methods for hormones are relatively inaccurate in the very low and very high ranges. Chemical methods are biologically nonspecific; biologic methods, by contrast, are chemically nonspecific.

3. *The abolition of a metabolic response by provision of special treatment does not indicate that such metabolism is free of endocrine origin.* Sodium reabsorption from the glomerular filtrate after injury is a good example here. It has been shown by virtually all who have worked in this field that if large amounts of sodium are given to the intraoperative or postoperative patient he will show a larger sodium excretion than if sodium is restricted. Such a finding casts relatively little light on the more basic question of whether or not aldosterone is concerned with post-traumatic renal sodium conservation. It is a very frequent occurrence in surgery that, with volume reduction or sodium loss, sodium reabsorption is greatly accentuated by the surgical procedure itself. Adrenal mechanisms in general are emergency mechanisms called into play when homeostasis is threatened; acute reduction in the volume of circulating extracellular fluid or blood is one of these emergencies. When such reduction is scrupulously avoided by special treatment, evidence of adrenal activation will naturally be much less prominent. The same is true for water reabsorption in relation to water administration.

A teleologic view of surgical endocrinology and metabolism points interesting directions for research and helps to focus in the surgeon's mind some of the relationships between the patient's own response and the surgical therapy he receives. Nonetheless, there is not space in this book for a teleologic interpretation of surgical endocrinology and metabolism, and this is not our purpose. Such views are available in the literature.

Instead, it is our intent in this chapter briefly to review the literature on this subject so that the reader may know where to seek out information on which knowledge of normal surgical endocrinology and metabolism is currently based and to discuss the relationship of endocrine changes to convalescent metabolism, a relationship that is currently unelucidated. Because it is difficult to find correlative reviews of this literature, the review here will be more detailed than in other sections of the book.

Finally, there will be a section devoted to a description of those aspects of surgical metabolism which seem to have special clinical meaning for the survival of the organism, wholly aside from a teleologic view of their origin. In this area, one of the most interesting problems is the relationship of nitrogen balance to food intake and to wound healing, and this will be discussed in Section VI of this chapter.

Section I.   Early Adrenocortical Changes after Trauma

A. URINE CORTICOIDS

Observations of an increase in excretion of cortical substance in the urine were the earliest ones which form a part of what we now recognize as normal postoperative endocrinology. The "classic period" in which these observations were being made by a variety of chemical and biologic techniques was during World War II. This began with the demonstration by Browne and his group (1944) of increased 17-ketosteroid excretion after trauma, and the work of Cope *et al.* (1943), showing increased 17-ketosteroid excretion in burns, and studies on a variety of patients in whom urinary studies were carried out by bioassay methods. This period included two events of special importance. One was the delivery by Albright of his Harvey Lecture (1942), comparing the postoperative changes to those seen in Cushing's disease, and the description and elaboration by Selye (1946) of the so-called "alarm reaction," a stress response held by him to be common and basic to a very wide variety of injuries or threats to survival, both acute and chronic. Both these concepts have required revision and many details have not gained wide acceptance; both were fertile sources of research.

Other workers whose publications occurred in this period included: Stevenson, Schenker, and Browne (1944), Talbot *et al.* (1947), Venning, Hoffmann, and Browne (1944), Shipley *et al.* (1946), Forbes *et al.* (1947).

The more recent period of urine corticoid study was the outgrowth of new analytic techniques and has been primarily devoted to a precise description of the changes in surgical injury. No reference is made here to studies on animals save as they have some special bearing on interpretation in man. Studies in man during this recent period (1947–1959) have been carried out by laboratories both in this country and abroad. The development of new methods has been of prime concern and the Porter-Silber reaction (1950) has been the basis for many quantitative studies of 17-hydroxycorticoids in the urine. The Porter-Silber reaction develops color with compounds E, F, and S. It is the basis for the method of Reddy, Jenkins, and Thorn (1952) (Reddy, 1954) for urinary corticoid study and for the Nelson-Samuels method of blood assay (1952). Like all colorimetry for assaying hormones, it is chemically specific but biologically nonspecific, since it is quite conceivable that other compounds having a certain chemical configuration may yield this color reaction without being of adrenal origin (Marks and Leftin, 1954).

Reports on the study of the urine of surgical patients by a variety of techniques in the past ten years are as follows: Bennett and Moore (1952), Conn *et al.* (1954), Nicholas *et al.* (1955), Hardy *et al.* (1953), Howard *et al.* (1955, a, b), Jabbour and Hardy (1954), Hayes (1952), Hayes and Coller (1952), Moore *et al.* (1955), Nicholas *et al.* (1953, 1954, 1955, 1956), Thorn *et al.* (1953, a, b), Thorn and Laidlaw (1954).

Little that is new in concept has come from these recent urinary studies, although they have defined the basic normal pattern of convalescent endocrinology. Studies of 17-hydroxycorticoids demonstrate increases with virtually all surgical trauma and in many instances show clear rises where the 17-ketosteroids show no change. The 17-hydroxycorticoid excretions correlate well with the eosinophil fall during the first four days after operation. Thereafter the correlation is less constant. The correlation with alterations in sodium and potassium excretion is not close. In an analysis of a small series of cases in our laboratory, a close correlation was found between the total 17-hydroxycorticoid excretion and the total urinary nitrogen excretion during the first four days after surgery (Moore *et al.*, 1955). Viewed in any other time relationship, this correlation was not as convincing. In many of our cases there is clear continuation of strong catabolic process after return of the urinary 17-hydroxycorticoids to normal.

B. BLOOD CORTICOIDS

With the development of the method of Nelson and Samuels, there have been reported a number of studies of the blood steroids after surgical injury and in disorders. These include Bliss *et al.* (1953), Eik-Nes *et al.* (1954, 1955), Elman *et al.* (1955), Franksson and Gemzell (1954), Franksson *et al.* (1954), Moncrief *et al.* (1954), Nelson *et al.* (1951), Sandberg *et al.* (1956), Steenburg (1954), Steenburg *et al.* (1956), Tyler *et al.* (1954), Moore (1955, 1957, 1958), Brown *et al*, (1954), Klein *et al.* (1955, a, b), Helmreich *et al.* (1957), Le Femine *et al.* (1957).

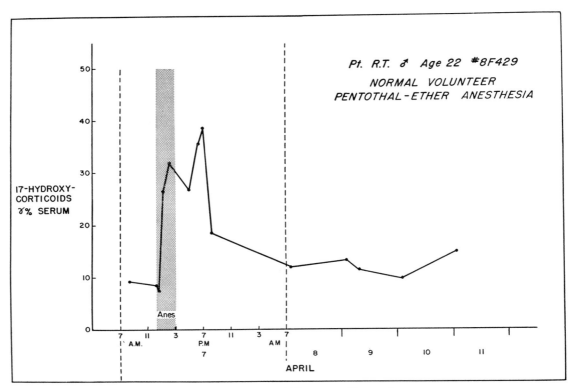

Figure 10. STEROID PHENOMENA. I. EFFECT OF ETHER ANESTHESIA

In this and in succeeding charts depicting the blood corticosteroid level, the measurements were carried out by the method of Nelson and Samuels. The concentrations are those of free 17-hydroxycorticosteroids in the serum.

In this chart is shown the effect of a short ether anesthesia on a normal volunteer. It will be observed that ether anesthesia is a strong but transient stimulus to increased secretion of corticosteroids from the adrenal.

The Nelson-Samuels method (1952) yields a measurement of the free blood 17-hydroxycorticoids which is quite accurate and reproducible and has been checked out by many laboratories (Harwood and Mason, 1956). It is our impression that in certain instances, particularly in extensive burns treated by antibiotics, one may, by this technique, see unreadable or excessive values which are probably artifactual.

A significant finding by the blood steroid method has been the sudden and very transient nature of the rise produced by surgical trauma. The sum of evidence at this time suggests that the rising limb of this curve, a very steep rise (often reaching a peak within a matter of minutes or hours after induction of anesthesia and the making of the incision), is due to the coincident activity of one major factor (increased adrenal secretion) and one minor factor (alterations in the intermediary metabolism of the hormone). The descending limb of the curve, however, is due to two major factors which are of almost equal importance. These are a decrease in the rate of adrenal secretion and an increased rate of conjugation and clearance from the blood by metabolism and disposal of the hormone. Studies of blood adrenocorticotropic hormone in man are still too sparse to permit of any correlation with these studies although there is a clear rise in blood ACTH after injury.

The work of Hume (1949, 1952, 1953) has shown that the anterior median eminence seems to be the important site for mediation of the pituitary and adrenal response to surgical trauma. The stalk, the bearer of the message to the pituitary and the hypophyseal portal system, is of primary importance in this transmission. The stalk is also the bearer of the neurones leading from the osmoreceptor, probably in the supraoptic nucleus, to the posterior pituitary, responsible for the release if not the secretion of antidiuretic hormone.

The peak of steroid concentration in the blood is usually passed and often back to a normal value at a time when the urinary excretion remains elevated. The urinary method recovers both free and conjugated hormone; in the urine the great majority of the material is reduced and conjugated as the glucuronide. It is altogether conceivable that increased adrenal function could occur and that the peripheral tissues could be exposed to an increased total amount of hormone, yet without an increase in blood concentration of the hormone, if urinary excretion were increased. Similarly the tissues could be exposed to an increase in blood concentration of steroid without change in rate of adrenal secretion if conjugation, clearance, and excretion were impaired. It is probable that the tissues are more responsive to change in concentration of hormones than to change in total secretion. The urinary studies give a better picture of total adrenal function as regards intensity and duration, whereas the blood curve yields precise information about the timing and mechanism of the change and the actual concentration affecting the metabolism in the tissues.

The development of improved methods for measuring 17-hydroxycorticosteroid conjugates in the blood has yielded data on the rate of appearance of blood conjugates after trauma and the probable site and mechanism of conjugation (Moncrief *et al.*, 1954; Weichselbaum and Margraf, 1955; Weichselbaum *et al.*, 1957; Klein *et al.*, 1955; Elman *et al.*, 1955; Reddy *et al.*, 1956).

The possibility that the patient suffering very prolonged chronic illness may have unusual steroid responses is suggested by the rise in eosinophils seen after operation late in burns, although there is no evidence of adrenal insufficiency. In one study from our laboratories (Moore, 1957), a patient late in the course of burn convalescence showed a remarkable rise in urinary steroid excretion on adrenocorticotropic hormone yet little rise in blood steroid or fall in eosinophils. This suggests facilitation of metabolism of

17-hydroxycorticosterone, and is reminiscent of the testosterone effect (Gemzell and Notter, 1956).

Alterations of steroid metabolism in liver disease and in other circumstances have been described by several workers (Tyler *et al.*, 1954; Brown *et al.*, 1954; Klein *et al.*, 1955, a, b; Sandberg *et al.*, 1956; Engel, 1955). Such alterations involve 17-hydroxycorticosterone, estrogens, and androgens. The altered disposal of 17-hydroxycorticosterone seen after trauma does not resemble that produced by liver disease, nor does it require overt liver disease for its occurrence. Studies of adrenal vein blood in the dog (Hume and Nelson, 1954; Walker *et al.*, 1959, a, b, c) and in man (Hardy and Turner, 1957) have added further evidence as to the timing and duration of adrenal activation after injury.

Various attempts to modify the blood steroid response have been recorded. The work of Gemzell and Notter (1956) is particularly interesting, since they have been able to damp out the response by pretreatment with testosterone. We have been unable to confirm all aspects of this work, whose clinical implications are not clear. As a general rule, failure to maintain an effective concentration of steroids in the blood after injury is associated with failure to maintain blood pressure.

C. ALDOSTERONE

The study of blood and urine corticoids has been largely descriptive, and is far ahead of quantitative information on aldosterone (Simpson *et al.*, 1952, 1953, 1954; Luetscher *et al.*, 1953, 1954, 1956; Bartter, 1956, a, b; Conn, 1955). The work of Llaurado (Llaurado, 1955; Cope and Llaurado, 1954; Llaurado and Woodruff, 1957; Llaurado, 1957, a, b), using a bioassay technique, has shown an increase in urinary excretion of aldosterone after surgical trauma. This has been confirmed by Zimmerman (1951; Zimmerman *et al.*, 1956, a, b). Correlation with sodium metabolism awaits further study. In Llaurado's work, a general correlation is suggested by the timing of both responses (sodium conservation and aldosterone secretion). Data on electrolyte metabolism after injury in relation to endocrine effects are found also in Johnson *et al.* (1950), Hardy (1950), Hayes and Coller (1952), Hayes (1952), Hayes *et al.* (1957), and Llaurado and Woodruff (1957). While dilutional hypotonicity might well cause sodium retention, hypotonic extracellular fluid expansion is not a strong stimulus to aldosterone secretion although acute volume reduction is a very strong stimulus. Llaurado has shown a close inverse correlation between urinary aldosterone content and urinary sodium:potassium ratio in postoperative patients. Zimmerman's demonstration of increased aldosterone excretion after operation (1956) was based on substantial increases found in the immediate postoperative period. Venning *et al.* (1955) failed to find this increase when the patients were studied at a later time.

In a subsequent paper, Zimmerman (1957) showed that large aldosterone excretions did not always correlate with "positive sodium balance" (urinary sodium:potassium ratios are not plotted so as to compare with Llaurado's data on this parameter). There was little correlation with plasma sodium concentration.*

---

* Further notes on aldosterone excretion in relation *to* surgical metabolism will be found in Part II.

D. OTHER STUDIES ON THE ADRENAL CORTEX

Other studies in man on the adrenal changes following trauma in man have consisted in paper chromatographic separation and identification of various adrenal compounds (Gold *et al.*, 1956, 1958) and several other biochemical approaches, including studies of carbon-14-labeled hormone and its disappearance curve. Eosinophil and leucocyte changes have been studied by Almy and Laragh (1949), Laragh and Almy (1948), Coppinger and Goldner (1950), Dalton and Selye (1939), Dingwall *et al.* (1954), Gabrilove (1950), Hills *et al.* (1948), Robbins *et al.* (1952), Roche *et al.* (1949, 1950), and Schoen (1953).

Elucidation of the role of the central nervous system and of activation of the pituitary-adrenal axis may be found in Hume (1949,

1952, 1953), Harris (1952), Hume and Wittenstein (1953).

In a recent review at the Laurentian Hormone Conference (Moore, 1957) current evidence is taken up as it bears on the endocrine phenomena observed after trauma and surgery. These data and conclusions will not be restated here; the reader is referred to that account for details.

The concept that an unusually prolonged adrenocortical response after a single trauma is the result of undesirable complications seems easily supported on both theoretical and practical grounds. Dingwall *et al.* (1954) studied eosinophil counts in fifty patients. They showed that in the cases of more severe injury there was a backswing rise to a somewhat higher level than in the lesser traumata. They also showed that a prolonged low count was usually due to the presence of surgical complications, often of an ominous nature. As measured by a prolonged lowering of the eosinophil count, such a response has been shown to be correlated with a poor prognosis in burns by Wight *et al.* (1953), and in head injury by Smolik *et al.* (1955).

Halme *et al.* (1957), in a very extensive study, show a clear sex difference between males and females as regards adrenocortical secretion after injury. Male patients consistently showed a larger and more prolonged urinary excretion of 17-hydroxycorticosterone and catechol amines. This is of especial interest relative to the greater excretion of nitrogen in the urine after injury in male patients.

Gold (1957) reviews the measurement and significance of blood corticoids and also concludes that the rise after surgery is due to increased secretion and impaired hepatic removal of 17-hydroxycorticosterone. His review makes no attempt to cover the various components of the surgical experience as stimuli or to differentiate them, nor to discuss their relation to metabolic change. Brown *et al.* (1957) have shown that reduction of steroids precedes conjugation; in liver disease it is the reduction, not the conjugation, which is adversely affected. In renal failure the conjugates accumulate in the body fluids. Peterson and Wyngaarden (1955) measured the hydrocortisone pool by the dilution principle using C[14]-labeled material. In normal subjects they found the pool to be 1.3 to 2.4 mg., with daily production around 20 mg. Under the administration of adrenocorticotropic hormone the pool goes up to 9 mg. and production to 181 mg. per day. Changes of this magnitude may be expected to occur in trauma, as judged by the alteration in blood and urine steroids.

Eik-Nes *et al.* (1955) studied a small group of surgical patients and showed the postanesthetic rise in free steroids, the further rise with trauma, the still further rise with adrenocorticotropic hormone, and an impaired ability to clear infused free hydrocortisone. The cases were a very mixed group; one, that of a patient with gallbladder disease having a simple cholecystectomy, showed a rise to 148 mcg. per 100 ml. and died thirty-six hours later. More information about this patient would be interesting: did she have hepatic artery ligature or pancreatitis? These initial studies have been amply confirmed in other laboratories.

There is growing evidence that in adrenal-ectomized man, trauma elicits a metabolic response that is close to normal as regards the familiar nitrogen-potassium-sodium changes, despite constancy of dosage of exogenous hormone replacement. Wilson (1955) and Mason (1955) bring this out in their discussion of Moore's paper (1955) at the Royal Society of Medicine. Mason (1955) discusses this at greater length. The basic problem here lies in the inconstancy of the blood levels: although exogenous dose may be constant, blood level is not.

The interpretation of these findings as

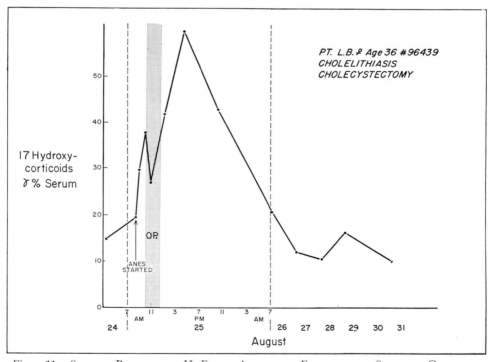

Figure 11. Steroid Phenomena. II. Ether Anesthesia Followed by Surgical Operation

Here the anesthesia was started and "held" for approximately an hour before the incision was made. It will be noted that ether itself produced a considerable rise in corticosteroid concentration in the serum. The operation of cholecystectomy produced a further rise.

By the next morning the corticosteroid concentrations were back down to an essentially normal range. Had the patient developed a complicated course, suffered sepsis or other complications, the steroid level would have remained high or would have risen again to a high value.

regards the metabolic significance of post-operative adrenocortical function is discussed in detail later on, but must be cautious for two reasons:

(1) When ACTH or cortisone is started up only a few days before surgery it may facilitate metabolic changes which reverse themselves later, regardless of trauma; if the dose has to be increased at the time of injury the meaning is of course clouded. This has been found to be especially true in the work of Jepson *et al.* (1956, 1957) wherein constancy of dose has little meaning in terms of constant blood level.

(2) More important than this is the fact that blood levels may change, conjugation be altered, or excretory pathways impaired, so that despite the constant dose, body cells are exposed to a changing concentration of active principles.

Robson *et al.* (1955, 1956) have also described studies after adrenalectomy and hypophysectomy, in which the "usual" metabolic changes occurred despite constancy of hormone dose and excretion of total Porter-Silber chromogens. Their tentative conclusion, like that of others who have studied these phenomena, is that the steroids are somehow permissive. They realize the possible pitfalls when the plasma-free and conjugated steroids are not also measured. After hypophysectomy there was a slight rise in urine corticosteroids.

The extreme variability of endocrine-metabolic responses after mixed trauma, and the fact that the first two hours of the adrenalectomy are no different from any other operation, make this field of clinical study a hazardous one for solid cause-and-effect conclusions. Correlations can be seen; mechanisms can be the subject of speculation and, occasionally, of inference. As pointed out elsewhere, evidence is good that the corticosteroids must be present to permit widespread changes after trauma; the basic question is what, then, causes the changes to occur? This is discussed in Chapter 5.

The normal level of conjugated steroid in the blood (as determined by acid hydrolysis) is 8.5 mcg. per 100 ml. over and above the average normal free hormone of around 13 mcg. per 100 ml. as described by several

laboratories. Klein *et al.* (1956) showed that liver disease of several types, either acute or chronic, was associated with a marked defect in the ability to convert orally administered cortisone into the reduced conjugate. They also studied some patients with liver disease undergoing surgery and found levels as high as 58 mcg. per 100 ml. of free hormone with no detectable conjugates, whereas their average normal values for surgical trauma were in the range of 52 mcg. per 100 ml. free and 21 mcg. per 100 ml. conjugates, four hours after operation.

At high levels of concentration the concentration of corticosteroids in red blood cells, as relative to plasma, is increased. Many cells of the body are not in equilibrium with plasma corticosteroid concentration; liver cells do appear to be in equilibrium with plasma.

Samuels suggests that the adrenal gland in elderly people produces less hydrocortisone, whether resting or stimulated. The studies from our laboratories, done by less refined techniques, appear to show a normal endocrine response to trauma in the elderly, at least in the sense of gross elevation of free blood corticosteroids. Monsaingeon (1957) has studied certain aspects of adrenal function in aged patients undergoing surgery. His data on eosinophil counts corroborate the findings of many groups that a later fall is ominous and a paradoxical post-traumatic rise is to be expected in chronic disease. The adrenal indices studied by Monsaingeon in the aged showed only a few deviations from the phenomena regarded as normal in the adult. The curves shown in his publication are among the most complete available. He studied the ACTH response during the height of eosinophil rebound and found the fall to be normal and certainly not that of any sort of adrenal insufficiency.

In dying patients, Monsaingeon described a late increase in the urinary secretion of corticosteroids reminiscent of the altered metabolism described by Gold *et al.* (1958). He describes also a very interesting phenomenon, that of extremely high eosinophils during cicatrization, as, for instance, in the healing of a varicose ulcer. This finding

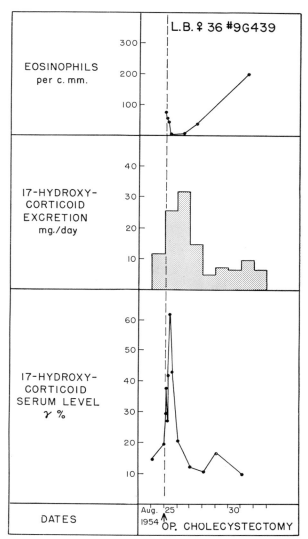

Figure 12. STEROID PHENOMENA. III. BLOOD AND URINE STEROIDS. 1.

Same patient as previous chart. It will be noted that the course of the blood corticosteroids over several days showed little change after the operation. The eosinophil count remained low for a day or two.

The urinary excretion of 17-hydroxycorticosteroids is measured by the method of Reddy, Jenkins, and Thorn. This is a measurement of the total 17-hydroxycorticosteroids in the urine. Most of this urinary steroid is in the conjugated form and a large majority of it is reduced to the tetrahydro derivative before conjugation.

It will be noticed that the peak of the urinary secretion comes the day after operation, indicating that the down-slope of the free blood steroid after operation is in part due to conjugation, hydrogenation, inactivation, and excretion of the steroid, as well as to its decreased output from the adrenal. This relationship is characteristic of clean, elective, civilian, soft-tissue operation without complications.

raises many interesting speculations concerning the endocrine setting of the scar-formation, fibrosis phase of wound healing. This phase is reminiscent of the "prophlogistic" phase of Selye's so-called "local adaptation," a phase characterized by low glucocorticoid-like and high STH-DOCA-like activity. His data certainly do not support the concept of adrenopause as a feature of normal aging.

Nicholas and Wilson (1953) observed some of the endocrine changes in 125 patients after skeletal injury, orthopedic operations, and related trauma. They found a rapid eosinophil rebound when the clinical management was effective in effecting reduction and fixation of skeletal trauma, without infection. Plaster immobilization, in itself, did not produce eosinopenia.

Symington *et al.* (1955) have described details of the lipid depletion seen in the adrenal cortex after surgical injury. They describe ribonucleic acid and alkaline phosphatase as occurring in adrenal glands that are actively producing steroids. In fatal severe burns there is an extreme lipid depletion. They equated this with the "exhausted gland" of Stoner *et al.* (1953) but feel (as we do on the basis of functional study) that such a gland is usually a very active producer of corticosteroids and resembles in many ways the gland under ACTH therapy. Most of Symington's cases were severe fatal burns or other acute fatal illnesses of short duration. His team studied 283 cases.

In addition, they describe the "normal lipid-laden adrenal" and the "focal lipid depletion" as two alternative patterns not infrequently seen. They found the normal lipid-laden glands in patients who died rapidly (as in coronary thrombosis) or in adrenals removed surgically (as from hypertensives). In nearly all cases, death had occurred less than eighteen hours after onset of trauma or disease in patients who showed this pattern at post mortem. In addition, all these patients were unconscious for many hours before death. The patients with focal lipid depletion had lived longer, and this seemed to be the picture of a gland in the presence of continuing severe disease.

In a later publication from the same group (Currie *et al.*, 1955) a study was undertaken of pituitary as well as adrenal histology. Marshall (1951) had brought forward evidence to show that ACTH is of basophilic origin, and Currie studied the histology of ACTH release. The patients in Currie's study had also died of a variety of diseases, both acute and chronic. In the pituitary, Currie used criteria of degranulation of the mucoid cells as an index of significant change in secretion. Extensive degranulation was associated with the acute traumata, while the more chronic "stresses" did not lead to degranulation. In a very general sort of way there was a correlation between pituitary degranulation and adrenal lipid depletion, but all combinations of association were found. The severe pituitary degranulation was most closely associated with very severe acute and rapidly fatal disease (severe injury, hemorrhage, burns, coronary thromboses). Degranulation of the mucoid cells was correlated with low eosinophil counts and an increase in urinary corticosteroid excretion. Currie postulates that a regular time sequence occurs in which the degranulation of the mucoid cells of the pituitary regularly precedes the lipid depletion of the adrenal.

Section II.   The Adrenal Medulla

The normal values for blood concentration of the catechol amines are: for epinephrine 0 to 1.5 mcg. per l. and for norepinephrine 1.5 to 5.0 mcg. per l. In pathologic states (stimulation, pheochromocytoma) these may rise to the general range of 5 and 25 mcg. per l. respectively.

The commonplace observation of vasoconstrictor activity together with tachycardia has led to the conviction that most forms of injury result in an increased secretion from the adrenal medulla of epinephrine and from the autonomic synapses of norepinephrine. In our experience, the traumatic stimuli which are most effective in calling forth reactions of this type are oligemic shock, acute anoxia, the excitement phase of a stormy ether induction, acute infection, and the combined neuropsychic stimuli of pain, fear, and apprehension. Oligemic shock may be caused by many changes in addition to external loss of whole blood, and many of these, such as desalting water loss, are effective in eliciting a cardiovascular response which resembles adrenal medullary activity.

In the last ten years there has been increasing interest in an attempt to document this adrenal medullary change by bioassay and biochemical methods, studying the blood and urine of man (Franksson *et al.*, 1954; von Euler, 1954, 1956; Aronow *et al.*, 1956; Manger *et al.*, 1954; Hammond *et al.*, 1956; Nickel *et al.*, 1954; Valk and Price, 1956; Aronow and Howard, 1955; Weil-Malherbe and Bone, 1953; Halme *et al.*, 1957). The short life of epinephrine and norepinephrine in the circulation—the substances being very rapidly destroyed by oxidation—and the fact that they are active in eliciting a tissue response in extremely low concentrations suggest that chemical methods may well have difficulty in demonstrating their true status in body fluids.

Epinephrine and norepinephrine disappear very rapidly from the circulation, 50 to 90 per cent having disappeared in three minutes after injection of tagged material.

Peripheral nerve tissue is the chief synthetic site for norepinephrine, the adrenal medulla for epinephrine. Only the levorotatory form is active.

The work of Goodall *et al.* (1957) has added much data to our understanding of the catechol amines. Although epinephrine and norepinephrine were synthesized in 1904, and although Elliott, Dale, Barger, Cannon and Rosenbleuth all worked intensively in the field it was not until 1946 that von Euler showed that norepinephrine was indeed the mediator in nerves and ganglia and the vasoconstrictor in the periphery. Wyngaarden, using C^{14}, showed that sympathetic nerves can make norepinephrine through a synthesis based on tyrosine as a starting material.

In burns Goodall *et al.* (1957) have shown

that the urinary excretion of both catechol amines remains elevated for a very long time after injury. Some patients died with very high outputs and others with remarkably low levels. As an example, the normal excretion of epinephrine is 15 mcg. per day; of norepinephrine 25 to 50 mcg. per day. In the first day after a burn, these levels rise to 600 to 700 mcg. of epinephrine, and 150 to 200 of norepinephrine. The normal adrenal glands contain but 200 to 800 mcg. of epinephrine and 50 to 150 mcg. of norepineph-

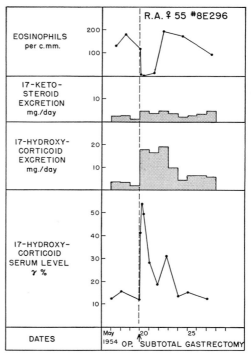

Figure 13. STEROID PHENOMENA. IV. BLOOD AND URINE STEROIDS. 2.

In this chart is shown the typical relationship between the blood free corticosteroid, the urinary 17-hydroxycorticosteroids, and the urinary 17-ketosteroids.

In trauma of only moderate severity, such as this straightforward subtotal gastrectomy, the changes in blood and urine steroids are characteristically transient as observed here.

The 17-ketosteroid is an end-product of hydrocortisone metabolism as well as of androgens, but does not show urinary elevations unless there is a very large amount of hydrocortisone being presented for metabolism, or unless there is some alteration in the intermediary pathway. Characteristically, trauma of moderate severity does not show much change in excretion of 17-ketosteroids.

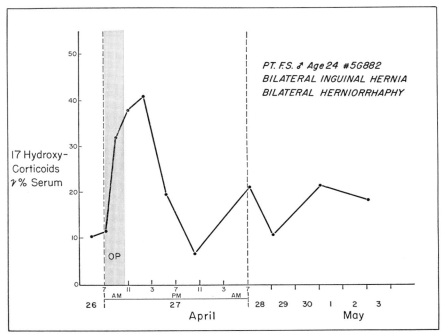

Figure 14. Steroid Phenomena. V. Effect of Lesser Operation

Here bilateral inguinal herniorrhaphy produces a rise in blood steroid somewhat less than that of cholecystectomy. One cannot predict the rise produced from the nature of the procedure itself. Blood loss, anesthesia, and duration of operation are important factors in the magnitude of the rise.

rine, the latter also produced in the periphery. At death, a few of the patients had values for urinary excretion as low as 7.8 mcg. of epinephrine and 18.0 mcg. of norepinephrine, suggesting some kind of block in synthesis or alteration in intermediary metabolism. In some of the fatal cases with low urinary values, the adrenals themselves were found essentially exhausted of catechols.

Hume has shown that ether alone produces a large rise in epinephrine in adrenal vein blood, while barbiturates lower it. Walker (1959), working in our laboratories, has shown a very considerable increase in adrenal vein catechol amines with hemorrhage alone. This is a very important parameter of the volume-regulating mechanism. This response is reversed by restoration of blood volume and dampened by barbiturate anesthesia. Trauma, shock, and severe agitation produce adrenal vein rises in catechol amine concentration which are not dampened immediately by blood replacement. Although barbiturate damps out the catechol amine rise following

hemorrhage, there is virtually no effect on the simultaneous rise in corticosteroids.

Studies on the urine (Franksson *et al.*, 1954) have shown that in uncomplicated surgical convalescence there is little evidence of increased adrenal medullary secretion, whereas blood loss and shock do produce increases in these substances. Chemical assay on the blood, carried out in our laboratories by Aronow's modification of the method of Weil-Malherbe and Bone, also failed to show changes in cases of uncomplicated surgery with ether and other anesthetics given alone and without other traumata (Hammond *et al.*, 1956, 1958). Our studies did, however, show remarkable rises in these substances in various traumatic conditions, including acute anoxia after a respiratory tract burn, and in severe ulcerative colitis prior to removal of the colon. This method may not be as sensitive as the method of Valk and Price (1956). Further studies are needed before we can measure quantitatively the alterations in man that have been assumed to be present. The method of Valk and Price shows some changes with ether anesthesia alone, changes that we did not detect with the modified method of Weil-Malherbe and Bone.

The work of Halme *et al.* (1957) has added rich data to the available literature on adrenomedullary changes after operation. The determinations were by bioassay on urine, using the response of the blood pressure of the cat and the rectal cecum of the hen as the testing systems for the two amines. They showed a very marked increase in urinary catechol amines after uneventful major surgery, raising the daily excretion of norepinephrine from normal values near 20 mcg. per twenty-four hours up to values near 50 mcg. per twenty-four hours. For epinephrine the increases were from normal values of 4 mcg. per twenty-four hours up to 16 mcg. per twenty-four hours. There was a marked sex difference, for the excretion of both catechol amines and the corticosteroids. The peak excretions in the male were from 50 to 100

per cent higher than the peaks for the female. The changes in 17-ketosteroid were much less pronounced, not infrequently showing little or no change. The authors find that the two categories of hormone (adrenomedullary and cortical) tend to correlate as regards postoperative increases in urinary excretion. They report, as an incidental observation, that in cesarean section there is no increase in corticosteroid excretion, and relate this to the lesser endocrine changes in women after trauma, their greater longevity, and better "tolerance" for disease.

For some years it was assumed that epinephrine or norepinephrine injected intravenously stimulated the hypothalamic-pituitary-adrenal-medullary system. There is now abundant evidence to show that while epinephrine may stimulate this system, it is not the only cause of ACTH secretion and eosinopenia after trauma (Pickford and Vogt, 1951). In addition, epinephrine will cause eosinopenia in the adrenalectomized subject

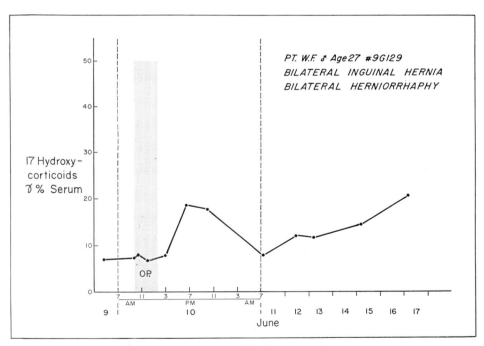

Figure 15. Steroid Phenomena. VI. Effect of Spinal Anesthesia

Here, a bilateral inguinal herniorrhaphy, similar to that carried out on the previous patient under ether anesthesia, is carried out under spinal anesthesia.

It will be noted that during the spinal anesthesia there is no rise in steroid in the blood whereas, when the anesthesia stops and wears off, there is some residual tendency to rise.

and, according to the work of Hume, epinephrine injection does not cause an increase in the amount of adrenocorticotropic hormone in the blood. An important area of interaction between the catechol amines and the glucocorticoids lies in the sensitization of tissues to glucocorticoid action by the presence of the catechol amines, and vice versa. The full significance of this fact in terms of surgical endocrinology is not clear as yet but, if both these substances are found to be increased after surgical injury, this synergistic action may ultimately turn out to be the basis of the normal ability of the subject to withstand hemorrhage. The role of aldosterone after hemorrhage seems to be concerned with movement of water and sodium, but this type of altered sensitivity may be important in vascular tone. Certainly both cortex and medulla are intimately concerned with homeostasis after isotonic volume reduction as in hemorrhage. Both hormones are needed to produce the ideal vascular response to hemorrhagic challenge; their interaction at the tissue level may also be affected by acid-base balance and electrolyte distribution.

Section III.   Antidiuresis and the Antidiuretic Hormone

Antidiuresis is a normal response to many trauma components: desalting, traumatic edema, dehydration, shock, and volume reduction from many causes. When these are overcome, normal water diuresis ensues. By contrast, the continuing antidiuresis of injury and operation (seen also in visceral disease and starvation) persists despite water loading not only in excess of needs but in sufficient quantity to produce severe hypotonicity. It is a continuous, seemingly inappropriate refusal to excrete water normally.

Verney (1946, 1948, 1954, 1958) has described the fundamental endocrinology of antidiuretic hormone. Perfused into the kidney, it produces a decrease in water excretion and an increase in electrolyte concentration. The infusion of hypertonic saline solution into the carotid produces the same effect. After hypophysectomy this response is reduced. A 2 per cent increase in effective osmotic pressure results in antidiuresis; sodium salts are effective, glucose less so, and urea ineffective. A 1 per cent decline in effective osmotic pressure of the carotid blood re-establishes diuresis. Verney has calculated that each osmoreceptor neurone (of which there are about 10^5) releases 12,000 molecules of antidiuretic hormone per second. He calculates that there are 2×10^{10} renal tubular cells, or 60 molecules of antidiuretic hormone per cell; the hormone probably acts on only a few of the tubular cells.

Verney has shown that neither the posterior pituitary, the carotid sinus, nor the carotid body is the site of the osmoreceptor; it is probably in the anterior hypothalamus. Verney's data show that the carotid-ligated dog, when salt-loaded, shows an increased excretion of water. In our opinion this reveals an underlying volume-sensitive mechanism, unmasked when osmoreception is blanked out by carotid ligature. Similarly, in a hypotonic dog, antidiuretic hormone causes an increased sodium excretion, normalized to low-flow antidiuresis by small sodium infusions.

The antidiuretic hormone consists of eight amino acids; the human will respond to one milliunit. "Vasopressin" is the pure hormone, and about 10 per cent of an administered dose appears in the urine. Evidently about 20 milliunits are in circulation normally and must be cleared before free water diuresis can occur. The resting rate of production is around 10 milliunits per hour. Ordinary dehydration of eighteen hours' duration increases this only at the rate of 1 to 2 milliunits per hour. Venous tourniquets and venesection do not increase antidiuretic hormone output (as measured by these techniques) if the subject is well hydrated. But if he is even slightly dehydrated, then small volume changes do induce an increase in output of antidiuretic hormone (Lewis, personal communication). Pain and emotion produce anti-

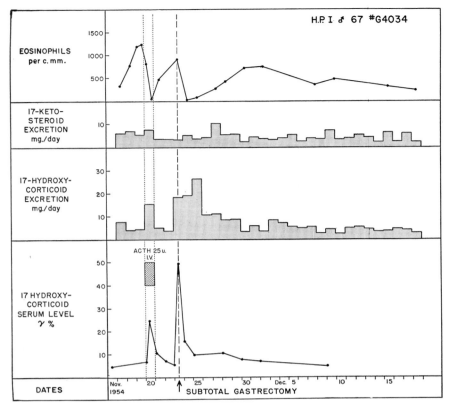

Figure 16. STEROID PHENOMENA. VII. CONTRAST OF OPERATION WITH ACTH STIMULATION

In this patient, adrenocorticotropin was given intravenously before operation. The effect on free blood steroid is a little less than is usually observed. The effect of operation, however, is to produce a higher peak in the blood free corticosteroid as well as a more prolonged increase in urinary excretion. This demonstrates that the blood steroid curve is an accurate index of the timing and mechanism of adrenal steroid changes, but the urinary excretion is a better measure of the total adrenal stimulation. It also indicates that operative trauma, in this instance, has been a greater stimulus to the adrenals than was a standard dose of adrenocorticotropin.

diuresis, but the hormone is difficult to demonstrate as elevated. Ether may act centrally or peripherally to block water excretion; morphine acts on the center itself. Postural hypotension as produced, for example, by vasodilators, produces antidiuresis through the stimulus to antidiuretic hormone release (Brun, Knudsen and Raskob, 1946).

That surgical injury alters the metabolism of water has been suggested from clinical evidence for some years (Cooper *et al.*, 1949; Moyer, 1950; Ariel, 1951). Close study of this phenomenon in many laboratories (Dudley *et al.*, 1954; deNiord and Hayes, 1954; Schlegel *et al.*, 1953, 1957) has shown that the change in water metabolism produced by injury is almost identical with that resulting

from the administration of Pitressin. Further, the administration of Pitressin together with a water load produces a uniform decrease in the plasma sodium concentration, a decrease often seen after surgery, particularly if water is provided in abundance, and occasionally when water is not provided externally (LeQuesne and Lewis, 1953; LeQuesne, 1954). In the latter circumstance, the new sodium-free water required to lower the plasma sodium concentration has come from within the body through the oxidation of fat and protein.

Eisen and Lewis (1954) used rats for the assay by which they found increased antidiuretic effect in human urine after surgical operations. The urine was filtered and diluted and injected intravenously. They found responses (after operations) in the general order of magnitude of 0.5 to 6.0 milliunits (of Pitressin-equivalence per ml.). In addition they carried out experiments on dogs in which the supraopticohypophyseal tracts had been sectioned and diabetes insipidus produced. Again, the human urine was injected intravenously. Control data lent significance to the findings. In general, the dog data showed less antidiuretic activity than did the rat method. Nicotine could be shown to produce circulating antidiuretic material by these techniques, as could the injection of Pitressin. Moderate dehydration gave a negative result.

Holden and his group (Cline et al., 1953) have found, in the urine of postoperative patients, antidiuretic substances, as shown by intraperitoneal bioassay in the rat. None of these substances has been shown absolutely to be identical with the antidiuretic hormone of the posterior pituitary, but the evidence is certainly strong that some such substance is at work. The almost identical actions of Pitressin and surgical trauma would suggest that this may well be the case, and if so it merely constitutes evidence, derived initially from metabolic change, that surgical injury stimulates the hypothalamus and the posterior lobe of the pituitary gland as well as the anterior lobe.

Dudley and Boling (unpublished observation) sought to quantify the appearance and significance of an antidiuretic substance in the blood of surgical patients. They established a delicate bioassay which will detect 10 milliunits per ml. of commercial Pitressin

(0.010 unit per ml.) on material injected intravenously. This is a more elegant technique than those dependent upon intraperitoneal injection, in which nonspecific noxious substances may cause antidiuresis unless the animal has diabetes insipidus. By this technique, no antidiuretic activity was identified. The significance of this is doubtful because of the extremely small concentrations in which antidiuretic hormone is active.

Kerrigan et al. (1955) provide a useful review of some of the aspects of the neurohypophyseal antidiuretic hormone-renal system as seen in daily fluid and electrolyte therapy.

It is of importance that the operation of hypophysectomy does not induce antidiuresis when Pitressin deficiency is the result of the procedure itself (as in diabetes insipidus after hypophysectomy). This further localizes the site of production of postoperative antidiuresis as being in the pituitary and brain.

The normal regulation of water output depends on a balance between the antidiuretic action of posterior pituitary hormones and the diuretic action of the hormones of the adrenal cortex. In adrenal cortical insufficiency there is marked antidiuresis relieved by cortisone. As shown so clearly by Ikkos et al. (1955), in hypophysectomized man there is a tendency to polyuria (diabetes insipidus), made much worse by the administration of cortisone. In both settings cortisone promotes diuresis. It would therefore appear that the postoperative antidiuretic stimulus must be very intense since it is evident in a setting where the concentration of blood corticoids is increased.

Section IV.   Thyroid and Energy Exchange

Severe surgical injury results in an increase in oxygen consumption. Such increases are not seen to a significant degree after ordinary surgical trauma of a mid-scale magnitude, but after burns (Cope et al., 1953) and perforated ulcers such changes are readily demonstrable. The role of infection and fever is of first importance but they are not the only factors involved. The studies of Cope and

his group have documented the extent of this increased turnover of oxidative energy and were accompanied by careful studies of radioiodine uptake in the gland and protein-bound iodine, none of which showed any systematic alteration suggesting a primary activation of the thyroid.

Animal studies (Bogoroch and Timiras, 1951; Paschkis et al., 1950; Williams et al.,

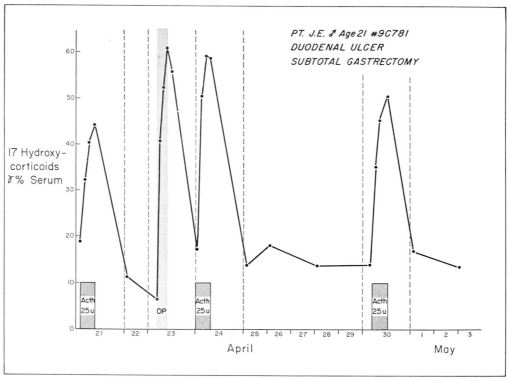

Figure 17. Steroid Phenomena. VIII. Effect of Operation on the Response to ACTH. 1.

Here, as in the previous chart, the effect of operation is contrasted with that of adrenocorticotropin, given both before and after operation.

Study of this chart will show that the effect of adrenocorticotropin on the blood steroid is considerably potentiated by the operation itself. The day after operation, the rise in free blood steroid produced by the same doses of adrenocorticotropin is considerably higher than it was before the operation. This suggests that the trauma itself has somehow altered the intermediary metabolism or disposal of the hydrocortisone hormones.

If we think of the disposal of the corticosteroids as involving a series of rate-limiting enzymatic conversions, one might rationalize this type of change by stating that these conversions were "crowded" or "taken up" by the steroid put out as a result of the trauma. An alternative explanation would be that the trauma changed the actual pathway of intermediary metabolism of the material.

By the seventh postoperative day the curve has returned to normal.

1949) have suggested that certain types of acute stress are associated with alterations in thyroid function. Considering the complex interrelationships among gonads and pituitary, adrenal, and thyroid glands it would be surprising if there were not some alteration in thyroid function after major surgery. The studies of Engstrom and Markardt (1955) are therefore of special interest. They studied twenty-four patients undergoing surgery ranging from minor to extensive. There were no detectable alterations, either acutely or chronically, in the serum precipitable iodine in these patients as a group. In three of the

patients who later died, the levels were normal after operation but fell to very low values just before death. A series of patients suffering severe chronic nonsurgical illness showed the same; there was a good correlation between the serum precipitable iodine and the serum albumin. A fall in the latter may have produced the changes seen in terminal illness.

Hayes and Goldenberg (Goldenberg *et al.*, 1955, a, b, and 1956) have been interested in the change in relation between thyroid and adrenal function induced by surgery. They have measured the serum butanol-

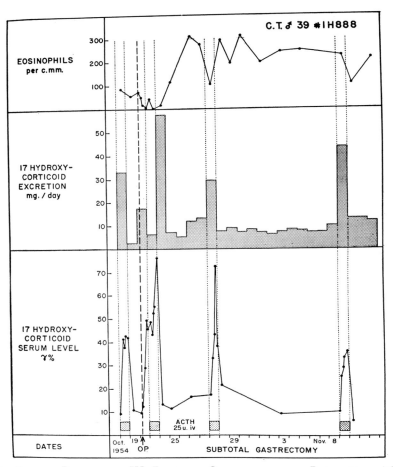

Figure 18. STEROID PHENOMENA. IX. EFFECT OF OPERATION ON THE RESPONSE TO ACTH. 2.

This study is similar to the previous one. Again a subtotal gastrectomy has been used as the model. It will be noticed that a standard dose of adrenocorticotropin produces a very considerably greater response after the operation than it does either before or on the 16th postoperative day.

extractable iodine as a measure of hormone level and the metabolism (including uptake) of radioiodine. They found no consistent pattern. One group (four out of thirteen patients in one study) showed an increased radioiodine uptake postoperatively as judged by the initial (one- and two-hour) readings. There was no change in the hormone level in the blood and no consistent pattern of urine excretion. Though this relation is unquestionably important, the data thus far certainly do not permit of any consistent interpretation even among the subgroups studied.

The studies of Shipley and MacIntyre (1954) have further documented the lack of systematic alteration in thyroid function after surgical trauma, at least as measured by these indices of circulating adrenal hormone and of thyroid avidity for radioiodine. Because the peripheral utilization of thyroid hormone may be changed after trauma and because systematic alterations may occur in thyroid function without alteration in level of thyroid hormone or change in radioiodine uptake, the reservation must be expressed that systematic alteration in thyroid function could ensue after trauma without being identified by any of these commonly-used methods for studying thyroid function. With this qualification, most of the studies to date do not show any alteration of thyroid function adequate to account for the observed increase in oxidative energy production. Perry and Gemmell (1949) and Blount and Hardy (1952) have further studied the thyroidal changes after injury.

In increased oxidative energy production after trauma, the oxygen is used to oxidize protein and fat, since the amount of stored carbohydrate in the body is quantitatively negligible and is burned within a few hours after severe injury. If the patient is given a diet which he can assimilate or if he is given intravenous injections of various oxidative substrates, then the pattern of oxygen utilization is altered. But in post-traumatic starvation—the most common situation during the first two to four days after severe injury, burns, war wounds, automobile accidents— the tissue burned consists of fat and protein, and, according to the data of Cope, a metabolic rate* as high as plus 80 per cent may be observed in burns. In a 70 kg. man of normal build, this indicates the production of about 5000 calories. If we assume a nitrogen excretion of about 20 gm. of nitrogen in the first day, we can then calculate the

---

* Because the post-traumatic situation is not "basal" in the sense that this word is used in metabolic rate measurements, the oxygen utilization here should properly be referred to as "metabolic rate" (MR) rather than "basal metabolic rate" (BMR).

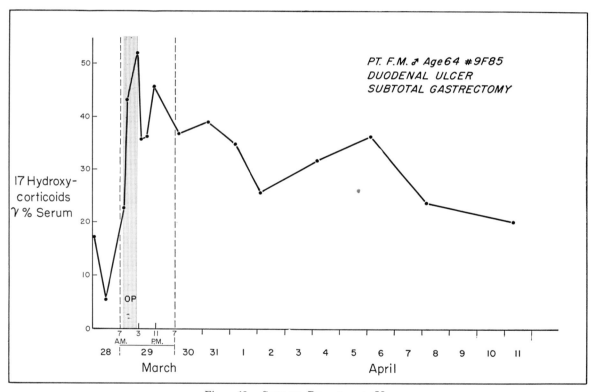

Figure 19. STEROID PHENOMENA. X.

Curve of blood corticosteroid concentrations in a patient undergoing subtotal gastrectomy for duodenal ulcer, in whom the postoperative course was complicated.

The patient had severe pain in the right upper quadrant with spasm and tenderness for four days after operation. Although afebrile during this period, he later ran a low-grade fever until approximately the eighth postoperative day. Neither the symptoms nor signs were severe enough to demand reexploration. It was presumed that he had a small area of peritonitis in the subhepatic region, which was handled without drainage. The blood steroid curve remained elevated for a period of about a week, and even at the end of this study has not returned to normal. The eosinophil count remained depressed throughout this time, as evidence of an abnormal postoperative course.

His later convalescence was uneventful.

amount of protein oxidized and the amount of calories produced from this protein oxidation. If we assume that the rest of the calories are produced from fat oxidation (an entirely justified assumption), we find that the rates of fat oxidation correlate nicely with weight loss. These crude approximations of oxidative energy production after injury also check out well with observations that have been made on change in body water and exchangeable potassium (Kinney and Moore, 1956).

An approximate balance sheet for the energy expenditure of a person with a metabolic rate of plus 80 per cent is shown below.

Oxygen Utilization:

Oxygen Consumption (MR +80) = 72 cal./sq.m./hr.
Oxygen Consumption   = 2990 cal./day

Tissues Burned:

20 gm. N = 120 gm. protein   = 500 cal./day
(120 gm. protein = 500 gm.
                  lean tissue)
              + 260 gm. fat   = 2490 cal./day
(Total weight loss = 760 gm.)
              Total Tissue Calories = 2990 cal./day

This is in the range of fat and lean tissue loss that we have often documented after severe injury and indicates the sort of tissue catabolism that provides the energy for this phase of convalescence.

The evidence is therefore solid as regards increased oxygen consumption and the substances that this oxygen oxidizes after severe injury. The unknowns are primarily in two areas. First, we do not know the actual number of calories produced by the oxidation of fat and endogenous protein. Endogenous protein oxidation does not produce the same amount of caloric value as would the combustion in vitro of this material because in vivo some of the carbon is excreted as urea with only one atom of oxygen rather than

two. The oxidative release of energy is therefore incomplete. The energy produced by oxidation of fat is usually considered to be 9 calories per gm. We have no evidence to show that endogenous fat oxidation is less rich in caloric energy, although precise evidence on this point is lacking.

In regard to energy exchange after trauma, the second broad aspect that is not understood at this time lies in the mechanism of its activation. There is nothing to suggest that adrenocortical secretory increases will produce such remarkable changes. Marked increase in thyroid function will produce such changes, and patients with severe thyrotoxicosis burn up their body stores of protein and fat at rapid rates that look like the postinjury state. Yet, thyroid function is not changed enough after injury to account for this increased oxidative energy production. Whatever its cause, whatever its mechanism, and whatever the precise caloric value of the body tissues which are burned, the changeover in energy production from basal levels of exogenous diet to very high caloric production from oxidation of body stores is one of the most drastic and most fundamental adjustments of the organism to injury.

Fever and infection (or both together) also speed up the rate of energy production and, by the same token, the rate of tissue catabolism in the face of low intake. A high fever with invasive sepsis is the most potent stimulus to tissue wasting. Both fever and infection play a role as biologic components in severe trauma. Yet here, as well as in injury alone, the mediator, activator, or "chemical messenger" that carries the message of catabolism from the infection to remote and uninvolved tissues remains unknown and is just as much of a challenge as is the chemical messenger arising from tissue trauma itself.

Section V.   The Gonads

The animal in winter, or the starved human being, has a marked reduction in reproductive vigor, a reduction that is restored to normal only with the return of adequate food

intake. The concept that starvation reduces reproductive activity finds support in the findings of lowered excretion of 17-ketosteroids in starving individuals. In patients

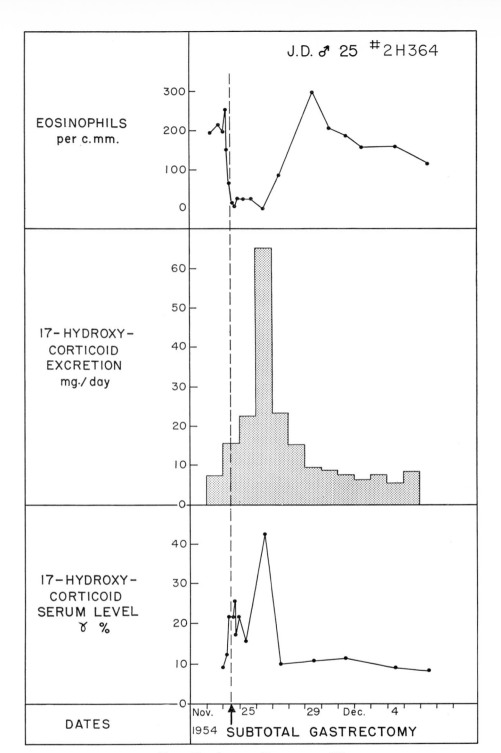

Figure 20. Steroid Phenomena. XI.

Findings in a patient having severe incisional pain following operation.

Like the patient shown in Figure 19, this patient's course following subtotal gastrectomy was complicated, but for a shorter time. On the second postoperative day the patient had severe pain in and around his incision. He was repeatedly examined because of apprehension over the possibility of intra-abdominal complications. There was no further elevation of fever or leucocyte count. With this bout of difficulty, the urinary steroid excretion rose to extremely high value as did the blood steroids. The eosinophil count remained low. The next day the patient was almost entirely asymptomatic and the steroid values show a return to normal convalescence. The nature of the episode was not explained. At its onset it suggested a severe septic complication or possibly acute pancreatitis; associated findings were lacking. Later convalescence was normal.

Page 93

after surgical injury who have been on sub-optimal intakes, it is therefore entirely conceivable that sexual function and/or the excretion of 17-ketosteroids may be lowered, and that such an effect may be due to starvation and bodily depletion rather than any primary effect of the injury itself. The studies of Sohval et al. (1951, 1952) indicate that immediately after surgical operation there is often a sudden increase in the production of follicle-stimulating hormone, as measured by bioassay of the urine. This then falls off to a low level and remains there for a long time. This change was found in eight of eighteen individuals studied by these workers. Their method of bioassay did not differentiate between pure follicle-stimulating hormone effects and effects contaminated by urinary estrogens. In the literature there are available very few such measurements of gonadal changes following surgical operation. Studies in our laboratory suggest the same train of events in terms of biologically determined androgens: an initial rise in secretion, very transient, followed by prolonged low levels.

The replenishing phase of surgical convalescence, in which body tissues are restored, body lean tissues resynthesized, and fat regained, is a phase of surgical convalescence the endocrine setting for which suggests the activity not only of growth hormone but also of the gonadal steroids, such as testosterone and estrogen. The female at puberty accumulates body fat to a much greater extent than the male, a fact that suggests that estrogenic substances have a secondary metabolic effect favoring the deposition of fat. The male at puberty greatly accelerates muscle regrowth, this growth of skeletal muscle being a secondary sex characteristic. There is therefore the possibility that the late phase of surgical convalescence represents the restoration of normal gonadal function with its associated alterations in body composition. There is no chemical evidence available at this time to confirm such an hypothesis. The return of menses during the later stages of convalescence from severe injury corroborates, as mentioned, the concept of gonadal renaissance at this time.

Section VI.   Metabolism Early in Convalescence

A. NITROGEN BALANCE

Works describing nitrogen and protein changes in man following injury include the following: Cuthbertson (1930, 1942, 1954), Mulholland et al. (1943), Browne et al. (1944, 1950), Howard (1945), Howard et al. (1944, 1945, 1946), Spence et al. (1946), Keeton et al. (1948), Moore (1948, 1953, 1955), Moore and Ball (1952), Baar and Topley (1956).

We have made no effort here to include mention of studies of nitrogen metabolism in animals, although many of these have formed an important aspect of the interpretive structure.

These alterations in nitrogen balance are accompanied by weight changes due to alterations in total body fat and total body water. Krieger et al. (1954) studied certain metabolic phenomena in patients with peritonitis of a variety of causes. Their results again showed the tremendous losses of nitrogen to which

these patients are prone. The research did not record body weights on many of these very sick patients but one may assume that wasting was severe. Emphasizing the factor of ileus, as well as the local accumulation of a protein-rich exudate in the peritoneal cavity, as interfering with intake and as a source of electrolyte loss, the investigators point out the tremendous importance of ample diet in avoiding extreme body wasting, a measure especially feasible as the acute septic phase passes by.

There have been several inquiries into the significance of this change in nitrogen balance, many of them being devoted to some artificial attempt to alter the nitrogen balance expected after injury. Comparatively few studies have been made of protein nutrition in relation to operative survival. Other than the obvious historical impression that starvation is undesirable, based on the fact that

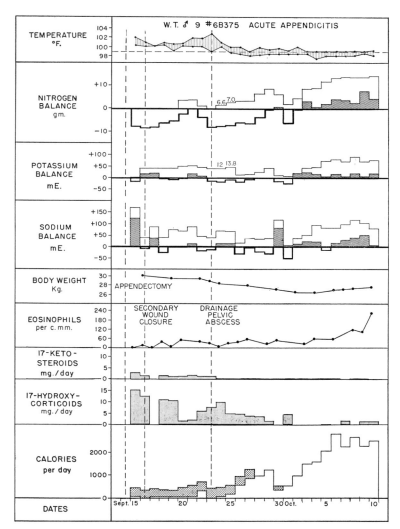

FIGURE 21. STEROID PHENOMENA. XII.

This chart of metabolism and endocrinology as observed in a young boy with appendicitis illustrates the effect on the urinary excretion of corticosteroids, and on the eosinophil count, of sepsis after the rupture of an acutely inflamed appendix.

On the ninth postoperative day, a pelvic abscess formed. Its formation can be seen in the gradually increasing urinary 17-hydroxycorticosteroid excretion and in the renewed intensity of nitrogen catabolism. It was then drained and some days later the patient started up into positive nitrogen balance, the eosinophils rose to normal, the urinary corticosteroid excretion fell to normal, and, with the subsidence of sepsis, the anabolism of convalescence ensued as indicated by the positive balance of nitrogen and the synthesis of protein that it signifies.

These three studies (Figures 19, 20, and 21) merely demonstrate that surgical complications summon corticosteroid repercussions which in turn subside as the surgical disease itself subsides, or is controlled by operation.

it is possible to starve to death, quantitative data relative to the effects of mild starvation in surgical recovery are rare.

The tendency to equate "nitrogen balance" with "plasma proteins" and these in turn with "body protein stores," and to assign to abnormalities of these three an almost mystical variety of surgical disorders ranging from poor wound healing to death itself, is demonstrated in many teaching reviews on the subject.*

As pointed out before, nitrogen loss must proceed for very long periods to produce hypoproteinemia. Variations in protein concentration are much more commonly a result of liver disease or altered body content of salt and water. Neither negative nitrogen balance nor hypoproteinemia can be demonstrated to have much influence per se on wound healing or recovery unless one wishes to note the remarkable surgical resilience of many malnourished patients. One must look beyond the nutritional platitudes of the textbooks to find the significance of nutrition in relation to surgery, whether or not it bears on plasma protein concentrations!

In one of the reviews mentioned above, loss of 4 pounds in eight days after a gastrectomy is regarded as evidence of the preoperative presence of subclinical edema despite the fact that (a) the patient had no edema, (b) his protein concentrations were normal, and (c) this is actually well within the range of postoperative weight loss reported for procedures of this magnitude by a number of students of the subject.

The repetition on many occasions of the statement that the plasma protein concentration reflects the state of body protein has misled many physicians and surgeons. Body protein resides in the lean body mass, largely striated muscle. There is really no "store" in the sense of inactive reserve. The lean body mass can undergo very wide changes in size with no change whatsoever in plasma protein concentration. Indeed, after major trauma there is catabolism of muscle proteins under

---

* A detailed review of further evidence bearing on the effects of starvation in surgical injury will be found in Chapter 6 of this Part, and in Part IV.

circumstances where plasma albumin may be undergoing an increased rate of synthesis.

There are a variety of evidences to indicate that while catabolism goes on in the major muscle masses after severe injury, there are many sites of protein anabolism whose activity is unquestionably increased after trauma. One might postulate that the total flux is increased by some sort of enzymatic activation, and that this results in increased release of nitrogen intermediates but also increased synthesis in many sites. The wound is one such site of synthesis. Plasma albumin is another. The data of Blocker (1955) showed that methionine is incorporated into plasma albumin at an increased rate after burns. Blocker's data also show the effect of high-nutrient feedings in reducing the total nitrogen losses after burns.

Hypoproteinemia due to hypoalbuminemia produces a lowered colloid osmotic pressure of the plasma, and it is harmful because of the increased tendency to transcapillary movement of water and salt into the interstitial spaces, with the production of edema. It may be due to a variety of causes, of which liver disease and the loading on of water and salt are among the commoner and starvation among the rarer causes.

B. NITROGEN INTERMEDIATES

Farr *et al.* (1942) showed that after operation there was a lowering of amino-acid nitrogen in the blood. Man *et al.* (1946) studied the changes in alpha-amino nitrogen and lipids in the plasma of surgical patients. A random group of thirty patients was investigated. All had sustained primary clean operations of only moderate magnitude except for one patient who had a stab wound of the chest, with shock. In many instances the nitrogen metabolism of these patients had previously been studied by Grossman *et al.* (1945). There was no correlation with nitrogen balance, the amino nitrogen being generally low even with large negative balances. They did find that a low resting value (below 4.0 mg. per 100 ml.) seemed to be associated with a poor or debilitated condition. In all but four, the alpha-amino nitrogen fell during the early postoperative period. There was a

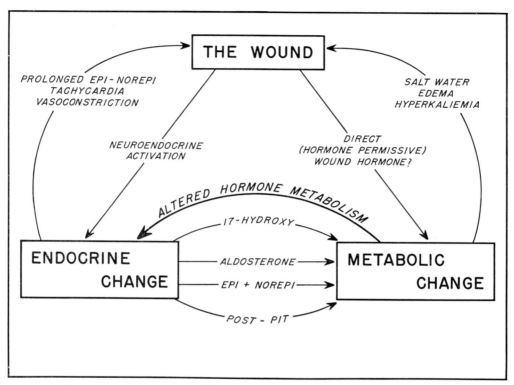

Figure 22. STEROID PHENOMENA. XIII. INTERRELATIONSHIPS IN SURGICAL ENDOCRINOLOGY

This is a summarizing chart of our current view of the interrelationship between the wound, the endocrine glands, and tissue metabolism after trauma. For a complete account the reader is referred to the Harvey Lecture (Moore, 1957).

It will be noted that the system involved is triphasic. The *wound*, as tissue injury, may affect the *endocrine glands*. Either of them may affect the peripheral *metabolism of tissue*, these latter being the effects we see clinically in the recovering patient, such as nitrogen loss, fat oxidation, and renal and hepatic changes.

As shown to the left in the chart, the wound directly affects the endocrines by neuro-endocrine mechanisms (via the peripheral nerves, the brain, and the pituitary), and the endocrine glands directly affect tissues through the intermediacy of at least four general types of hormones (corticosteroids, aldosterone, catechol amines, and posterior pituitary). In addition to this pathway, there appears to be a pathway by which the wound affects metabolic change directly, as shown to the right. This may occur through the nonendocrine mediators of trauma (such as anoxia, acidosis, low blood flow) or there may be other more subtle effects by which the wound affects metabolism. Under these circumstances, the hormones of the endocrine glands must be present

to permit these metabolic and tissue changes to occur. This activation involves the permissive action of the hormones.

In addition, both the endocrine changes and the metabolic changes occurring in the patient may, under unusual circumstances, make the injury of the wound potentially worse, through prolonged action of the catechol amines in reducing tissue perfusion, and through the tendency to hyperkalemia or to retain water and salt (which are damaging only if there is renal failure or if the surgeon overshoots the mark in therapy).

Finally, as suggested by the heavy arrow in the middle of the chart, there is evidence (some of which has been shown in the previous three charts) that the post-traumatic metabolism in itself alters the activation, inactivation, reduction, conjugation, and excretion of the adrenal hormones.

This complicated interaction exists as long as the wound is active as a challenge to homeostasis. The net effect is to support the circulation at the expense of the tissues. When definitive surgery repairs the wound so that it is no longer a challenge to the organism, this homeostatic tension returns to normal and the anabolism of convalescence ensues.

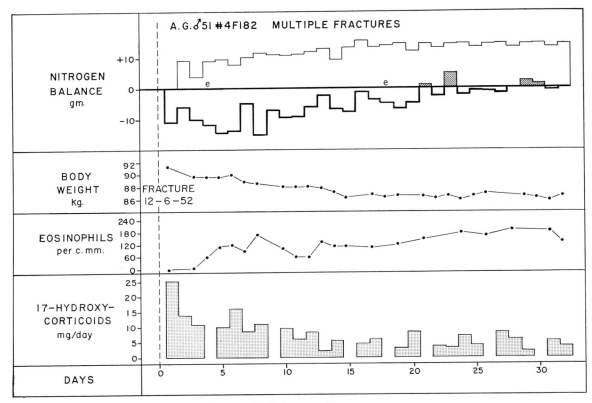

Figure 23. Multiple Fractures

This chart shows metabolic findings in a fifty-year-old man having multiple fractures, none of them involving major long bones. The patient had a fractured ankle, a fractured wrist, and a fractured tibial table. The period of nitrogen negativity is quite prolonged. By the fifteenth day the patient was taking an excellent dietary intake. The drop in weight, eosinophil course, and urinary steroid findings are quite normal. Had the patient had a midshaft femur fracture, his urinary nitrogen loss would have amounted to approximately 50 per cent more than this, due in part to the degradation and excretion of blood proteins in the tissues around the fracture.

correlation trend between severity of operation and fall in alpha-amino nitrogen. During recovery the level again rose. In all instances the plasma lipids fell postoperatively. This was not a large drop but it was consistent. This finding is of interest relative to the fact that plasma lipids increase slightly in starvation and water deprivation (Kartin *et al.*, 1944).

Everson and Fritschel (1951, 1952) took up this matter where Man *et al.* (1946) left off, and refined the study so as to differentiate the individual essential amino acids, using microbiologic assay. The results showed a transient drop in the essential (free) amino acids, most marked immediately after operation (137.7 mcg. per ml. of plasma as against

171.6 in the preoperative period), and then returning slowly towards normal, with threonine and arginine remaining low until the seventh day. Plasma dilution did not seem to be a factor. In dogs, ether anesthesia alone produced a drop fully as great as that seen in the operative patients.

Everson and Fritschel further reported on the surgical changes and the effects of nourishment, as suggested by the work of Man *et al.* (1946). They confirmed the lower values for the individual (free) essential amino acids in the malnourished patients. They found that a fall in free essential amino acids preceded any change in albumin concentration. The selective lowering of methionine and isoleucine suggested a specific amino-acid deficiency phenomenon and the possibility of therapeutic use of such materials. The urinary excretion values were normal. Youmans (1943) also emphasized that hypoalbuminemia is only a very late manifestation of protein starvation. Deficient diet reduces the amino-acid level in about six days. The fall due to surgery is more rapid but of the same order of magnitude. Conversely, high protein feedings for just a few days do not appreciably raise the lowered amino-acid levels seen in malnourishment. Sterling *et al.* (1955) showed that labeled protein in the circulation disappeared more rapidly in postoperative patients than in normal persons, despite lack of concentration change. They did not study nonoperated controls with starvation, anesthesia, or hemorrhage.

Other nitrogen studies include Margulis *et*

al. (1953) on electrophoretic patterns after surgery, and Walshe (1953) with particular reference to liver injury and its implications in nitrogen and amino-acid metabolism.

Shock (Hoar and Haist, 1944) and hemorrhage (Sayers *et al.*, 1945) raise the alpha-amino nitrogen level, as do injections of ACTH or adrenal hormones (Friedberg and Greenberg, 1947; Li *et al.*, 1949). It is of interest that insulin hypoglycemia lowers the blood level of alpha-amino nitrogen. Data on urinary studies by these same authors (unpublished) failed to show increases in excretion of amino acids adequate to account for the change. Epinephrine lowers the alpha-amino nitrogen level (Crismon *et al.*, 1940), and might be responsible for some lowering after trauma.

Nardi (1954) found an increased excretion of essential amino acids in the urine of

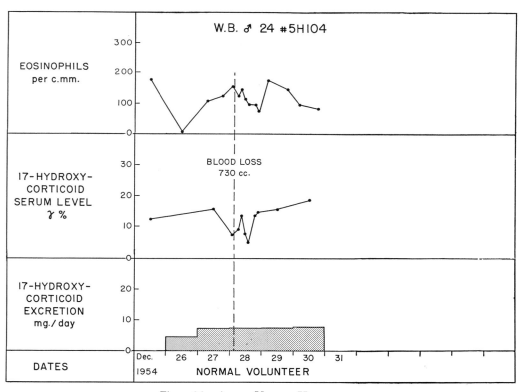

Figure 24. Acute Venous Hemorrhage

In this chart are shown the eosinophil count and steroid values in a patient having a venesection with loss of 730 ml. It will be noted that there is no discernible alteration by these indices. The patient's hematocrit dropped slowly during the first day, reaching an equilibrated lower value at the end of about twenty-two hours, proportional to the fraction of the erythrocyte volume lost. From Hammond *et al.* (unpub.).

severely burned patients, as well as an increase in nonessential amino acids. This was not always in linear relationship with total nitrogen excretion. An entirely analogous phenomenon was found after other surgical episodes and operations. More severe trauma or burn was followed by a more massive excretion of amino acids, particularly of the essential amino acids of higher molecular weights.

Levenson *et al.* (1955) have studied the plasma amino acids and their conjugates after severe battle wounds in five severely wounded patients. There were four deaths; shock and renal failure played a role. Despite severe azotemia in several, the total of free amino acids was normal. The investigators describe three groups: (1) glycine, histidine, threonine, proline, and glutamic acid, which stayed normal; (2) leucine, isoleucine, lysine, valine, tyrosine, and alanine, which rose early and then fell; and (3) phenylalanine, aspartic acid, and methionine, which rose in the first week to an even greater extent. In malnourishment the totals were low. In renal failure the amino-acid conjugates were high before dialysis and fell afterward, but the total amino-acid nitrogen was unchanged before and after dialysis.

Therapeutically, little has emerged from this field. Croft and Peters (1945) found a reduction in postburn nitrogen loss in rats fed methionine. Meyer *et al.* (1947) failed to confirm this, as did also Chanutin and Ludwig (1947). The "demand" theory of post-traumatic catabolism (i.e., the wound needs and receives some specific nitrogen compound from muscle) would favor some such application, but as yet nothing of practical usefulness has emerged.

These studies demonstrate that after extensive trauma there is an alteration in the pattern of amino-acid metabolism. The total urinary amino acid rises and certain essential amino acids may appear in the urine in greater concentration than previously. But the major amounts of urinary nitrogen appearing after trauma remain in the form of urea. These studies of nitrogen intermediates support the concept that, should such amino acids and nitrogen compounds of small molecular weight be required for synthesis of mucopolysaccharides or other collagen precursors in the wound, they are indeed available in increased amounts after injury.

No evidence that these nitrogen intermediates are of toxic significance has been forthcoming. Where large areas of muscle are physically destroyed, necrosed, or crushed, or after burns where the products of tissue destruction are directly released into the circulation, it is altogether conceivable that certain intracellular enzymes may be released, which are toxic in the extracellular phase. This is true, in a sense, of hemoglobin, myoglobin, and methemalbumin. Certainly the intracellular electrolytes (potassium, phosphate) are toxic (i.e., unfriendly to survival) when present in the extracellular fluid in abnormal amounts.

Creatinine excretion is a constant related to the size of the muscle mass and possibly the size of the lean body mass. Exercise, short-term fast, and large variations in urine volume do not affect this constant rate; yet alterations in renal function affect it profoundly, as creatinine (as a tubular solute) is unresorbed and is thus an index of glomerular filtration. In our experience the excretion of creatinine is a constant that is not altered acutely by ordinary civilian surgical operation. It is elevated for a few days after severe complex injury. In prolonged post-traumatic starvation it is lowered as muscle wastes away.

Howard's studies (BCK, I) show brisk increases in creatinine excretion, particularly in those casualties with severe muscle damage; wounds not involving masses of muscle were also capable of displaying this change. In many of these patients the plasma creatinine was elevated and the creatinine clearance above normal.

Although creatine is never a constituent of urine from normal individuals, it was universally present in patients suffering severe muscle injury, reaching levels as high as 3.9 gm. per day in some instances. When muscle damage was slight, creatine excretion was minimal.

This group of patients did not show regular or persistent lowering of glomerular filtration as measured by endogenous creatinine clear-

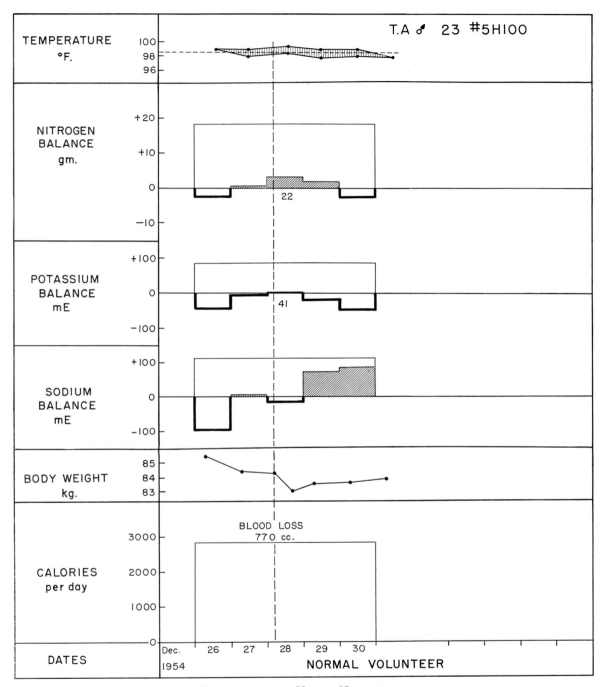

Figure 25. ACUTE VENOUS HEMORRHAGE

In this patient, as in that shown in the previous chart, a venesection was produced as an experimental procedure. It will be noticed that the alterations in nitrogen and potassium balance are not remarkable. The patient had a period of marked sodium conservation on the first and second day following the hemorrhage. Blood and urine steroid values in this patient were similar to those shown on the previous chart. From Hammond *et al.* (unpub.).

ance, but there was often a decrease on the first day.

Cuthbertson and Tompsett (1935) described a lowering of albumin concentration and increase of globulin after trauma. Hock-Legeti et al. (1953) demonstrated by more elegant methods a fall in albumin concentration and an increase in alpha-1 and alpha-2 globulins in 80 per cent of forty-five patients in the first four days. These were small changes. In our experience the early change in plasma protein concentration after operation has borne virtually no relation to the nitrogen balance; we have found that retention of salt and water has been the most potent cause of post-traumatic hypoprotein-emia Without control or measurement of these variables one cannot draw conclusions concerning the nature of hypoalbuminemia. Such a dilutional component cannot be invoked to explain an increase in the globulin fraction.

Frawley et al. (1955, a, b) investigated these changes in thirty-three Korean casualties. There was a progressive decline in the albumin:globulin ratio in nearly all patients, this progressing with time and reaching its low point of about 1.0 at the ninetieth hour, at which point the study was discontinued. This change was due to a decline in albumin and an increase in the alpha-1 and alpha-2 globulins. Beta and gamma globulins were unchanged. The tendency of traumatic edema fluid to be relatively rich in albumin as contrasted to the concentration of the large protein molecules may account for this difference.

Munro and Chalmers (1945) showed that when protein intake was reduced, there was a lesser protein loss after fracture (in rats). As mentioned above, this seems to find a clinical parallel. In the controversy as to whether steroid hormones are catabolic or antiana-bolic, there can be no question that the over-all effect of trauma is catabolic. For an antianabolic effect to be manifest, food must be taken. But in the traumatized patient on no diet whatsoever, amounts of nitrogen are mobilized within the body which may on occasion be two or three times as great as that seen in resting starvation.

The data of White and Roberts (1950) and of Roberts (1951, 1952, 1953) suggest that the adrenocortical hormones do in point of fact mobilize or "labilize" the tissue proteins. Roberts' data also suggest that when protein is labilized or translocated in the body as a result of adrenocortical activation, the over-all net result may be either anabolism or catabolism, depending upon the tissue requirement of the moment. He found that the labilization of tissue protein was directly under the control of the adrenal cortex. It was not clear whether or not this effect was primary or followed some other intermediate cause. These data and concepts from Roberts' work strike a familiar note in contemplating surgical metabolism. The concept that the effect of trauma was to "loosen" nitrogen refers to the same phenomenon. That an altered metabolism may labilize protein and facilitate either anabolism or catabolism is a particularly attractive theory to explain the phenomena seen after injury, because there is very brisk catabolism in certain areas, particularly skeletal muscle, while in other areas—the wound, albumin, hemoglobin—there is a definitely increased rate of anabolism. It therefore appears that the over-all nitrogen effect of trauma is not so much the destruction of body protein as it is an alteration in some enzymatic reaction which facilitates its moving in either direction, according to the demands of local sites or the over-all designs of the organism engaged in the struggle for survival. Roberts (like Browne and later ourselves) interprets his data as indicating that undamaged tissues make protein available for the repair of damaged structures. He also showed (in rats) that the release of protein to a plasma medium by liver and spleen, studied in vitro, was enhanced by preliminary treatment with adrenal cortical extract or ACTH.

There is no question but what a well-nourished animal or patient shows these effects more drastically than a poorly-nourished one. It is appealing to explain this again in the labilization or translocation theory; the well-nourished animal has more body protein available for labilization or translocation.

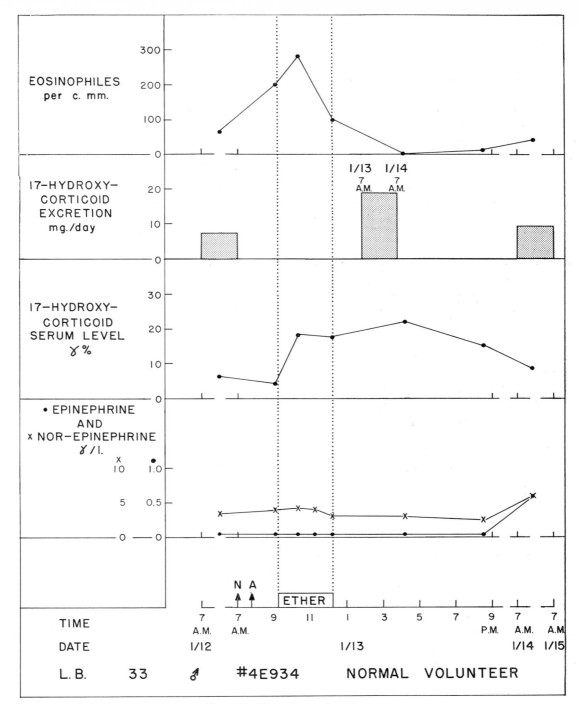

Figure 26. EFFECTS OF ANESTHESIA

In this chart are shown the effects of ether anesthesia, given to a normal volunteer, on the eosinophil count, the urinary corticosteroid excretion, the blood corticosteroid level and the plasma levels of epinephrine and norepinephrine as measured by the method of Weil, Malherbe, and Bone.

It will be noted that the ether anesthesia produces a small rise of blood corticosteroids in this patient (as in Figure 10) and a distinct rise in urinary steroid excretion, with a fall in the eosinophil count that is most marked about five hours after the administration of the anesthesia. There is no systematic alteration in the blood levels of epinephrine or norepinephrine, these values remaining normal throughout the period of observation.

C. ELECTROLYTES

Metabolic observations of changes in electrolyte excretion after surgery are surprisingly sparse, in view of the widespread acceptance of the existence of such changes and the widely-held assumptions in this regard. Other than the few studies published in our monograph some years ago, and a number of studies from these laboratories since, there is only a scattering of articles in which the electrolyte excretion pattern after surgery is observed in an untreated state. The studies of Hayes et al. (1957) are outstanding and unique in this regard. Many writers on this subject have introduced therapeutic steps and modifications and interpretations of these responses without, at least in their published works, ever having observed the untreated state. To a stranger approaching this field of work for the first time, it would appear surprising how much thought has been given to interpretation of post-traumatic electrolyte metabolism or attempts to modify it, in view of the very sparse reports of the actual facts observed in the natural state.

Sodium excretion after trauma can be expressed in absolute terms, in relation to potassium, or as the fraction of total solute. These variations of expression may have some interest with respect to endocrine mechanisms in body composition but they do not have any special clinical significance.

Alterations in the sodium:potassium ratio in the urine may result from alterations in aldosterone activity (though this is unproven), but the uncorrected sodium:potassium ratio in the patient's urine cannot be considered as a proper assay for aldosterone secretion.

The increased potassium excretion after injury is often very transient. In one publication of ours these changes were documented after a mixed series of bone and soft-tissue traumata (Moore, 1955) in civilian experience; it was found that the elevated potassium: nitrogen ratio usually persisted for only two or three days. One of the surprising aspects of metabolism after burns (Moore et al., 1950) is the extremely transient nature of the increased potassium excretion. This finding was corroborated extensively and described again by Reiss and his group in their careful and extensive studies of burn metabolism reported from Fort Sam Houston (Reiss et al., 1956).

The alterations in plasma concentration of sodium and potassium have been referred to several times in the literature. There are few systematic reports of these changes. The studies of Howard on plasma electrolyte changes in the wounded (1956) are of interest in this connection but involve a rather different phase of the problem, since many of the patients in his report had been in shock or were anuric or oliguric. Data on postoperative electrolyte changes may be found in Drucker et al. (1954), Winfield et al. (1951), and Moore (1958).

Several groups have noted a dilutional tendency as a cause of hyponatremia after trauma. Examination of the data shows that in many cases the potassium concentration rose slightly or (equally significant in hyponatremia) did not change at all.

The study of Hayes et al. (1957) is an extensive investigation of the postoperative renal handling of water and salt. Their studies on antidiuresis after injury corroborate a clear ADH-like effect, as shown by many others, changing positive free water clearance to negative regardless of solute load, and resulting in plasma dilution if water is overadministered. They showed, by sequential study, that the patients had regained their normal excretory ability by the fourth or fifth postoperative day, in most instances.

These studies provided a basis for calculating the dose of 5 per cent dextrose in water to be given intravenously each day, so as to provide adequate water for solute excretion but without plasma dilution.

Day of operation	—250 ml. per sq. meter
First postoperative day	—450 ml. per sq. meter
Second postoperative day	—480 ml. per sq. meter

They did not discern a sex difference in this requirement. They found it impossible to inhibit this ADH-like effect by the administration of alcohol at the time of anesthesia.

Hayes and his group also investigated insensible water loss and arrived at a basal estimate of 940 ml., of which 339 ml. would

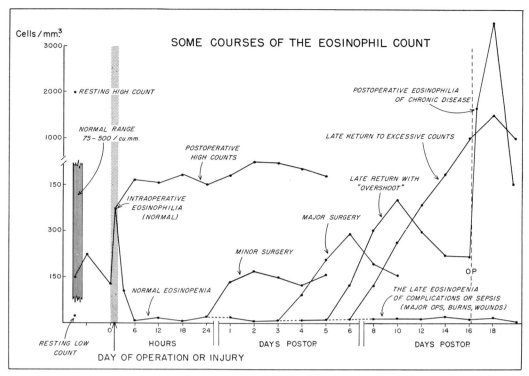

Figure 27. Some Courses of the Eosinophil Count

In this chart are shown a variety of time courses that may be taken by the eosinophil count in surgical patients. In only rare instances is the eosinophil count of clinical importance, but in those instances an understanding of the possible courses holds the key to proper evaluation.

Of particular importance are a resting high count (which may indicate subnormal adrenal function) and the late maintained low count which is so characteristic of continued complications in the surgical patient. The continued steroidal discharge of a complicated surgical course probably does not do the patient any harm in itself; it is merely another manifestation of the presence, in the patient, of continued, unresolved challenges to homeostasis.

The postoperative high count is important evidence of adrenal insufficiency if it coexists with high fever or hypotension or both.

be endogenous, leaving about 600 ml. to be given to cover this need. Measurements of weight were made with a very sensitive balance and showed that insensible loss was little changed by trauma, temperature (in a narrow range), or humidity. They arrived at a figure of 40.0 ± 5.1 gm. of water per square meter per hour, or 984 ml. per square meter per twenty-four hours; allowing for endogenous water this calculates out to 784 ml. per square meter per twenty-four hours, as needed from exogenous sources. As the rectal temperature goes over 99.6° F., a correction of +7 per cent per degree is to be included. If the ambient temperature is over 30° C., water loss is markedly reduced by skin covering. From these data the figure is set at 1000 ml. per square meter per day for the day of operation, plus 250 ml. added for each of the two succeeding days.

Hayes and his group showed that sodium restriction promotes aldosterone excretion (and presumably secretion) and sodium retention. As Zimmerman and others had shown in relation to sodium changes, and as Bartter showed relative to volume reduction, this change is not associated with pituitary-glucocorticoid changes—i.e., there is no eosinophil fall or 17-hydroxycorticosterone rise with the aldosterone discharge. Unfortunately, one cannot conclude from this that the pituitary is unconcerned with aldosteronal salt retention; one can only conclude that the aldosterone change may proceed maximally without 17-hydroxycorticosterone changes. There is other evidence, however, to suggest that both aldosterone stimulus and release may occur in the absence of the pituitary.

Acting on these data, the authors noted that patients given sodium throughout operation and convalescence had no tendency to retain sodium, whereas those given only water did. The ideal sodium load for this objective is about 50 mE. per square meter per day, according to their data. This calculates out to about 75 mE. per day (500 ml. of 0.85 per cent saline) in a normal adult. This corroborates Zimmerman's work (1951).

The authors did not happen to carry out the next step to demonstrate, as others have, that if the postoperative patient is given two or three times this much sodium he will retain it and develop hypoproteinemia, as at higher levels will the normal person; sodium loads are never excreted rapidly. After operation, whether for reasons of previous sodium restriction, acute volume reduction, anesthesia, or primary aldosteronal activity, the load is excreted even less well.

These data support the general policy that the operative patient's water and sodium needs should be met in realistic terms—"thinking in terms of balance"—neither depriving him nor overcrowding him with water or sodium salts. This is the common-sense view, and there is much evidence to support it.

D. CARBOHYDRATE, FAT, ENERGY; GUT AND LIVER FUNCTION

The extent of the change in carbohydrate metabolism engendered by uneventful major surgery is not accurately known at present. Glycogenolysis, hyperglycemia, gluconeogenesis, glycosuria, decreased glucose tolerance, and a worsening of diabetes mellitus are all known to occur particularly after very severe injury; in isolated instances they occur after less severe trauma. Ether is a stimulus to many such changes.

Rice et al. (1950) found a significant eleva-

tion of blood sugar (over 180 mg. per 100 ml.) early in the postoperative period in only six out of 200 "simple surgical cases," and in forty-three out of ninety-two "serious major" cases. No analysis of the pathologic conditions or surgical procedures is presented, but the general conclusion is reached that electrolyte imbalance of a wide variety of types is more common where the blood sugar is high. Both result from the same combinations of major surgery and metabolic disease. The tendency to compensatory hyponatremia which might be expected with a high crystalloid solute concentration is not illuminated by this report, and no mention is made of correlation with such a finding.

Studies of alterations in glucose and fructose metabolism after trauma are reported by Abbott et al. (1955), Ariel (1952), Beal (1954), Burns et al. (1953), Drucker et al. (1953), Elman and Weichselbaum (1951), Hayes and Brandt (1952), Howard (1955), Munro (1949, 1951), Weinstein and Roe (1953), and Wynn (1954). Documentation of the fat loss after trauma and its significance as determined by measurements of nitrogen balance or body water are to be found in Moore et al. (1952) and Paquin (1955).

One of the measurements which might appear to be the simplest to make in terms of post-traumatic metabolism—that of the patient's body weight and its interpretation in the light of nitrogen balance—has only rarely been made and recorded in the literature. Many studies (although seemingly unoriginal and repetitive) should be encouraged in this field to provide more basic facts from which therapy may grow. All of these studies join to show a picture of decreased glucose tolerance, glycogenolysis, transient tendency to glycosuria, transient accumulation of unburned carbohydrate intermediates, and increased fat oxidation.

Accumulation of unburned carbohydrate intermediates (lactate, pyruvate) produces metabolic acidosis and is in turn the product of anaerobiosis in tissue. High altitude anoxia, hemorrhage, shock, ischemia of muscle, and inadequate tissue perfusion of all types produce a hypoxic acidosis of this same genesis. Therefore, when one finds lacticacidemia in the surgical patient one should look for the site and cause of hypoxia. This is true whether one is dealing with anesthesia, or unusual situations such as extracorporeal circulation. In addition, respiratory alkalosis produces lacticacidemia.

In wounded patients, Howard (BCK, I) found the oral glucose tolerance curve to be diabetic and the insulin tolerance flattened (i.e., made resistant to insulin). Intestinal glucose absorption appeared to be unimpaired in these patients despite their other gastrointestinal abnormalities. Four of the patients studied developed an elevation of the blood amylase; three of these suffered trauma to the pancreas.

Gastrointestinal function was studied by Howard (BCK, II) through the absorption of deuterium oxide, which was severely impaired in abdominal wounds and less so in peripheral wounds. Peripheral vascular collapse impairs this function which, in view of the permeability of the gastrointestinal tract to water, is surely more a measure of gastrointestinal circulation than of cellular transference activity. This is not true of glucose absorption, which remained quite effective save for those patients with acute abdominal injuries.

Intravenously administered deuterium oxide (Schloerb *et al.*, 1950) equilibrates throughout body water; its rapidity is a measure of over-all circulation, but not a discriminating one because of the extreme permeability of tissues to deuterium. Only in severe hypotensive shock was the intravenous equilibrium prolonged. Absorption and redistribution of deuterium from subcutaneous or intramuscular sites is primarily a measure of local circulation to the part. With severe injury there was prolongation of absorption equilibria.

Baird *et al.* (1957) report a fall in plasma iron after a variety of surgical procedures, even of minor extent. This was most marked at forty-eight hours. This was not an absorptive defect nor a disorder of iron binding; there was no increased urinary excretion. This change appeared to be due to an alteration in iron distribution. One cannot help but wonder if it has to do with the localization of iron in inflammatory barriers as described by Wintrobe (Cartwright *et al.*, 1946, a, b, 1951).

The liver studies done in Korea (Howard, BCK, II) covered a wide variety of study methods. Nearly all showed changes in liver function, usually not severe and usually not of a sort that might be interpreted as compromising survival. Plasma bilirubin concentration was elevated in various patterns. The plasma hemoglobin of the stored blood was about 30 mg. per 100 ml. of plasma. Some small passive transfer of this moiety was observed. Retention of Bromsulphalein was increased transiently, particularly in association with shock.

There was depression in plasma prothrombin activity which was often biphasic, unresponsive to vitamin K, but evidently not of hemorrhagic proportions. This may have been due to the alterations in whole blood incident to storage, and was definitely related to the administration of stored blood. Cephalin flocculation was elevated for several days in the wounded man; fibrinogen synthesis was usually normal; albumin levels were not abnormal unless water and salt were over-administered.

In general, the liver was not the site of changes threatening to survival.

Nonfilling of the gallbladder was regularly seen in the seriously wounded in whom this function was tested. The dye was given intravenously. Both liver excretion and gallbladder absorption could be at fault here. Decreased gastrointestinal function and diminished absorption of deuterium oxide were also observed.

Cole and Leuchtenberger (1956) studied morphologic changes in the liver of dogs following operative trauma in the upper abdomen. They noted changes due to the trauma (not the anesthesia)—changes usually seen in livers actively engaged in protein synthesis; there was an increased tyrosine concentration in the cytoplasm. These changes were evident at three hours and support the concept of increased synthesis of hepatic protein (albumin ?) during a period of general cytoplasmic catabolism in skeletal muscle.

E. CHANGE IN BODY COMPOSITION

With the relatively small balance changes and tissue fluxes seen after moderate and uncomplicated trauma one would hardly expect large changes in body composition. Nonetheless trauma tends, to a greater or lesser extent depending on the magnitude and accretion of biologic components, to produce a compositional defect characterized by (1) an increase in the fraction of body weight occupied by the extracellular fluid (and plasma volume), at the expense of (2) intracellular fluid, which is mobilized, and (3) fat, which is burned. A relative expansion of total body water therefore occurs; that is, the water comes to occupy a larger fraction of body weight.

Lyon *et al.* (1949) reported a series of studies of the normal pattern of blood volume and extracellular fluid in postoperative patients. These patients exhibited the general tendency for a small (10 to 25 per cent) increase in volume of extracellular fluid unless desalting was clearly present. They showed this to be correlated with the falling chloride concentration and to be correlated loosely with changes in plasma volume— there being a plasma volume increase in uncomplicated surgical recovery. Where blood loss was brisk and hydration maintained the plasma volume increase was large, as one might predict. The changes in plasma volume did not correlate with, and were often the reciprocal of, the blood volume changes, the greatest plasma increase coming after the maximal blood loss. Although the authors did not inquire into mechanisms, these very nice studies epitomize a large mass of compositional data bearing on:

(1) the post-traumatic tendency to water retention with extracellular fluid expansion and solute dilution;

(2) the plasma volume rise in compensated blood volume loss;

(3) the need for adequate hydration to accomplish rise in plasma volume.

The authors also clearly re-emphasized that in normal hydration the stabilized hematocrit is a sensitive index of previous blood loss, and that a low postoperative plasma protein concentration does not mean "poor nutrition" or "depletion"; it means dilution. Very few data more recently elucidated or elaborately studied have added anything to these important conclusions.

That the acute surgical experience (of moderate magnitude) in healthy subjects does not grossly distort relationships between intracellular and extracellular fluids is suggested by the rapid recovery, small magnitude of the balance changes, and insignificant plasma chemical alterations. Stated otherwise, the bodily changes of normal convalescence after mid-scale trauma are small in terms of total body composition, involving but a small fraction of the total mass, though their understanding lies at the basis of surgical care. Burrows *et al.* (1955) have studied the matter by means of sodium and potassium dilution and the sulfate space and find no gross alterations in the acute surgical situation in the well nourished.

Greenberg and Laszlo (1955) showed that total body irradiation (for lymphoma) tended to increase the size of the extracellular fluid at the expense of the intracellular fluid, much as surgical trauma does. They did not carry out metabolic or endocrine studies. Certainly every evidence points to this as a basic bodily change seen in trauma of many types: irradiation, starvation, and cachexia.

DeCosse *et al.* (1956) have shown a sharp increase in the inulin space after operation, this seeming to occur at the expense of the intracellular phase. The authors conclude that the intracellular phase becomes hypertonic, the intracellular fluid diluting down the salt in the extracellular phase. Such a theory neglects the well-established fact that the cell does not tolerate nor exhibit any osmotic gradients across its surface. In addition, one need not postulate intracellular hypertonicity in assigning to intracellular water an important role as the diluent in post-traumatic hypotonicity. The lysis and catabolism of cells provides, to the extracellular fluid, water unassociated with sodium, as explained in detail in Part III. This water is partitioned throughout body water; its intracellular electrolyte (potassium, phosphate, sulfate) is excreted; the result is body hypotonicity. The data of DeCosse fit such a hypothesis, the expansion of extracellular fluid being in part "real" and in part an increased penetration of inulin into new areas such as traumatic edema and transcellular water.

Section VII.   Endocrinology and Metabolism Later in Convalescence

The literature on metabolism in late convalescence is scanty. There are only a few studies which show the late nitrogen anabolic phase of convalescence; several such from our laboratory are as yet unpublished. There are only a few studies of 17-hydroxycorticoid and 17-ketosteroid excretion in late convalescence and a few on hormone administration (see Part IV). The interpretation of late convalescence is based on this scanty evidence as filled out by the changes in total body water and weight which are characteristic of the "fat-gain phase" (Moore *et al.*, 1952).

The observation of late endocrinologic and metabolic changes after convalescence is very time-consuming, and it is difficult to convince patients of the necessity of remaining in the hospital for long metabolic studies. The dilutional study of body composition is particularly useful in such prolonged studies as shown in the data of Wilson *et al.* (1954). Such observations should be encouraged in order to achieve a better understanding of that most important phase of convalescence during which the patient regains his muscular strength and restores his social and economic usefulness.

Section VIII.   Endocrinology and Metabolism of the Biologic Components of the Surgical Experience

The components of the surgical experience are those biologic factors which can be separated and identified, and whose sum constitutes the totality of the injury. These are listed in our schema for grading the magnitude of trauma according to the weighted accretion of biologic components on page 110. The factor of duration operates on all these components, magnifying their effects as stimuli to widespread bodily change.

These components are, to recapitulate:

Group I. Threshold Stimuli

  (1) non–tissue-traumatizing stress such as fear, pain, cold, fatigue;
  (2) minor tissue injury;
  (3) anesthesia and drugs;
  (4) immobilization; and
  (5) starvation.

Group II. Threatening Challenges

  (1) extensive injury to tissue;
  (2) bleeding, plasma loss (replaced or transient);

  (3) fluid accumulation, traumatic edema, desalting water loss; and
  (4) anoxia, hypercarbia.

Group III. Tissue-Killing Injury

  (1) very extensive tissue injury;
  (2) tissue necrosis: crush, burn, gangrene;
  (3) sepsis; and
  (4) shock with prolonged deficiency of blood flow.

We are concerned here with the question of endocrine and metabolic changes related to these components as separate entities.

Such studies have been the basis for several investigations in our laboratory of the separate effects of starvation (Moore and Ball, 1952), gastric intubation (Moore *et al.*, 1955), ACTH (Moore and Ball), cortisone (Moore *et al.*, 1958), morphine (unpublished), anesthesia (Hammond *et al.*, 1958) and hemorrhage (unpublished).

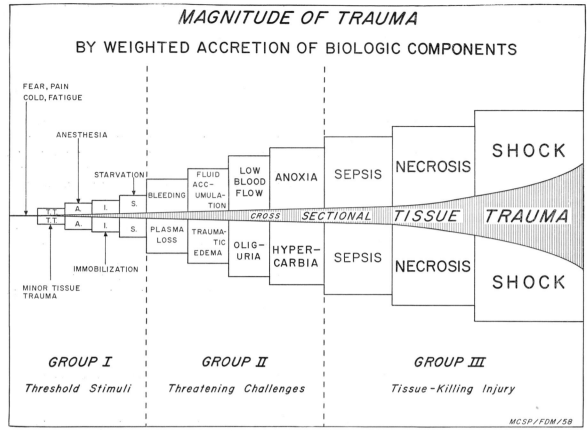

Figure 28. Magnitude of Trauma by Weighted Accretion of Biologic Components

The severity of an injury, its clinical, physiologic, and metabolic consequences, and its morbidity and mortality, are due to the summation of a number of factors that vary widely in the severity of their biologic implication for the organism.

The first group (to the left) are those "Threshold Stimuli" that produce minor changes of a traumatic variety. These include fear, pain, cold, fatigue, minor tissue trauma, anesthesia, starvation, and immobilization. Were any one of these stimuli to be of long duration or extreme severity, it might in itself be fatal. But, given its usual duration and magnitude, it constitutes but a small traumatic stimulus to the organism.

The second group (center), more severe in nature, are those "Threatening Challenges" which evoke a strong homeostatic response in the organism. These include bleeding, plasma loss, fluid accumulation, traumatic edema, low blood flow, oliguria, anoxia, and hypercarbia. These challenges produce physiologic and metabolic changes in the organism that are generally indistinguishable from those of moderately severe injury. The longer these challenges operate unopposed or uncorrected (examples would be bleeding or anoxia) the more severe is the injury and, like the "Threshold Stimuli," any of these acting long enough may in itself be fatal. All of these are correctable by the homeostatic wisdom of the body as long as the surgeon takes the necessary steps (examples would be blood replacement or tracheotomy) to permit homeostatic forces to act.

The third group of biologic components (to the right) determining the severity of an injury are those which result in necrosis and death of tissue. These "Tissue-killing Injuries" are sepsis, necrosis (as by occlusion of blood supply, crush, burn, or gangrene), and oligemic or traumatic shock. These produce dead tissues that release into the circulation the products of tissue necrosis as well as depriving the organism of the function of the organ undergoing ischemic necrosis. When any one of these three is present, the biologic response to trauma is much more profound than if not present. When any one of the three is present to an extensive degree, recovery is exceptional without early and accurate treatment. If all three are present to large degree, recovery is exceptional even with ideal treatment.

In the chart above, the weighted importance of these components is shown in a crude visual manner. Running through them all is cross-sectional tissue trauma. The biologic components of injury tend to increase as cross-sectional tissue trauma increases until, with very severe trauma, shock and necrosis are virtually inevitable.

A. ANESTHESIA

The metabolic effects of anesthesia alone are of interest in two broad connotations: first, the clinical selection of anesthetic agents in relation to possible metabolic consequences affecting the patient's primary disease, and second, the role of the anesthetic agent as a stimulus to the sum of metabolic changes which occur after the total surgical experience.

The studies of anesthesia, which must be carried out under anesthesia, but without trauma, demonstrate that ether anesthesia is a very potent stimulus to increase in steroid level in the blood. Other anesthetics partake of this property but to a lesser extent (Hammond *et al.*, 1958; Virtue *et al.*, 1957). Thiopental–nitrous oxide and curare anesthesia, as well as local and spinal anesthetic agents, are almost free of any effect upon the adrenal cortex. Morphine may stimulate the retention of water (de Bodo, 1944). Spinal anesthetic appears to delay the onset of the post-traumatic adrenal rise. Siker *et al.* (1956) and Moore *et al.* (unpublished) have carried out similar studies on anesthetic premedication. Data on adrenal medullary function after anesthesia include the work of Elmes and Jefferson (1942), Emmelin and Stromblad (1951), Watts (1955), Hammond *et al.* (1958), and Valk and Price (1956).

Metabolic data suggest that ether anesthesia alone is a strong stimulus to hyperglycemia (Bass *et al.*, 1953) and to the production of aldosterone and antidiuretic hormone (Hammond *et al.*, 1958). Other agents are less active. Pentobarbital may dampen adrenal response; spinal anesthesia and hypothermia (Egdahl *et al.*, 1955; Swan *et al.*, 1957; Bernhard *et al.*, 1956) definitely delay it. Hypothermia evidently reduces adrenal function by local effect; spinal anesthesia acts by both afferent and efferent denervation. Further data on renal vascular effects of anesthesia will be found in Shachman *et al.* (1952); Pringle *et al.* (1905), and Miles *et al.* (1952).

Drucker *et al.* (1952, a, b, 1953, 1955, 1957) studied the effects of ether anesthesia on carbohydrate metabolism. Their evidence suggests that ether interfered with the conversion of pyruvate, the pyruvate tolerance being decreased by ether anesthesia, and the production of lactate increased.

Miles and de Wardener (1952) found that under light anesthesia (cyclopropane and ether) there was a fall in cardiac output and visceral (including renal) blood flow but a rise in limb muscle flow. Then, after prolonged anesthesia, cardiac output fell even more, limb blood flow fell to normal, and visceral flow rose. But if the anesthesia were deepened markedly, all indices (cardiac output, renal blood flow, and muscle blood flow) fell. He showed that ether increases renal vasoconstriction and total renal resistance, a response abolished by denervation.

He also carried out carefully controlled experimental hemorrhage in man. The bleeding (800 to 1500 ml.) was carried out under anesthesia. In two patients, a profound hypotension occurred. As a general rule there was little change in renal blood flow. He found that the intrathoracic blood volume fell 400 ml. with a hemorrhage of about 1000 ml.; again there was no change in renal blood flow, although peripheral circulation was reduced. These results contrast with much other data but demonstrate that in as complex a system as an anesthetized, traumatized, and bled human being, the chance interplay of variables may produce exactly opposite end-results under seemingly similar conditions.

Surgical "depth" is a factor long considered to be a critical one in exacting a renal functional paid for its attainment. That this is not the case is suggested by several studies. Coller *et al.* (1943) studied inulin and Diodrast clearances during and after operation in twelve cases. The anesthetics used were ether and cyclopropane. Although no effort was made to separate the effects of the anesthetic from the surgical trauma, the authors concluded that the effect of the ether on glomerular filtration rate and renal blood flow is small or negligible so long as blood pressure is maintained. In one case there was surgical shock and in another (hernia) a hypotensive episode. In both these the glomerular filtration rate was markedly reduced. Although the data are small in number and the changes variable, the authors concluded that cyclopropane reduces glomerular filtration rate.

There seems to be an impression, possibly based on Craig *et al.* (1945), that in dogs deeper planes of anesthesia produce more marked changes in renal function. But the studies of both Burnett *et al.* (1949) and Habif *et al.* (1951) show maximal change in man at induction, with a progressive restoration toward normal as the operation proceeds and anesthesia deepens. Papper (1953, 1956) in his reviews recognizes this progressive improvement in renal hemodynamics as operation progresses but also restates the widespread concept, not always supported by the data, that "the deeper the plane the greater the change." Barring hemorrhage, shock, dehydration, or some other surgical or metabolic event, the most marked renal hemodynamic changes appear to be at the induction itself. This calls to mind neuroendocrine mechanisms (fright, stress, excitement phase) as being of greater importance than direct pharmacologic effect of the agent on the kidney.

Burnett *et al.* (1949) showed clear-cut diminution in glomerular filtration rate and effective renal plasma flow during anesthesia with ether and cyclopropane. They also showed the rather sudden effect at induction with a wearing off and even an increase to normal (or near normal) levels under maintained—and deeper—anesthesia. Their studies were nicely controlled to exclude premedication and operation as causes of the observed changes. The effects of cyclopropane were more marked except as regards total blood flow and water resorption, in which cases ether produced the more marked reductions. The filtration fraction rose. This and other studies (on lymph flow and omental vascular pattern) show that cyclopropane has more effect in diminishing capillary flow in several areas than has ether.

Habif *et al.* (1951), in a carefully controlled study of thirty-four patients, showed:

(1) a clear antidiuresis with Demerol, the urine flow falling with a rise in electrolyte concentration;

(2) a slight fall in glomerular filtration rate with Demerol;

(3) a marked fall in glomerular filtration rate with increased filtration fraction and increased tubular resorption of sodium, chlorine, and water, when cyclopropane and ether were added; and

(4) a very transient change in glomerular filtration rate, which disappeared when the patient regained consciousness.

Uneventful operation added little to this change. Any postoperative change must be tubular as glomerular filtration rate was normal.

The authors point out that this is a familiar response produced by a large variety of stimuli, mostly stressful, and that it may be a "diversionary vasoconstriction." Anesthesia was "held" on several patients in this study so that the phenomenon could be observed alone.

Etsten and Li (1955) studied thiopental anesthesia in man and found no change in cardiac output during hypnosis, but a 25 per cent decrease in deep surgical anesthesia. They used a dye-dilution method, and postulated that venous pooling plays a role in this change, as well as in the decrease in the stroke output and intrathoracic blood volume. It is noted that light thiopental anesthesia of the type used for induction produced few significant changes. Li and Etsten reported further studies on cardiac output in 1957.

Eckenhoff and his group (1955) have shown conclusively that any drug of a wide variety of opiate-narcotic-analgesics decreases effective ventilation (as measured by blood gas metabolism) wholly aside from changes in respiratory rate. These effects, plus the decrease in effective cough, are a severe hazard in the elderly.

Brewster *et al.* (1953) demonstrated that the administration of ether to the autonomic-blocked animal was fraught with cardiac hazards. These were abated by giving epinephrine. The authors concluded that "a major factor in the safety of ether anesthesia . . . is the quantitative reflex release . . . of epinephrine and norepinephrine." They did not present evidence to indicate that there actually is such a release.

Ether anesthesia tends to produce a mild metabolic acidosis with lacticacidemia (Beecher and Murphy, 1950); respiratory alkalosis or hyperventilation, or both, produce lacticacidemia; hypoventilation produces respiratory acidosis and anoxia, the latter also producing lacticacidemia as a feature of hypoxic (i.e., anaerobic) acidosis. Thus, anesthesia and ventilation produce variables of controlling importance in the acid-base balance of the anesthetized patient, as described further in Part III (Acid-Base Balance) and Part V (Lungs). Furthermore, the blood lactate is elevated in many circumstances where ventilation is abnormal or hypoxia severe.

B. HEMORRHAGE

Hemorrhage alone without shock is surprisingly free of any effect on adrenocortical 17-hydroxycorticosteroid function, as measured by urine and blood 17-hydroxycorticoid assay. The rather prolonged period of conservation of sodium and water that follows hemorrhage of about 750 ml. in a normal young male suggests that there may be other endocrine alterations in the secretion of aldosterone or antidiuretic hormone after this hemorrhage. As the blood is returned, endocrine activity subsides and diuresis ensues. Certainly as a stress, in the classic sense of that term, a brisk venous hemorrhage is surprisingly innocent of 17-hydroxycorticosteroid repercussions. Farrell (1958) and Bartter et al. (1956) showed that hemorrhage alone excites the production of aldosterone (see Part II).

Retention of sodium and water and the excretion of potassium are noteworthy. The metabolic effects of massive hemorrhage and shock include marked reduction of renal function, hypoxic acidosis, and the accumulation of metabolic intermediates and cell electrolyte.

In dogs a very brisk 17-hydroxycorticosteroid and epinephrine-norepinephrine response is seen (Hume and Nelson, 1955), in response to massive hemorrhage. Minor hemorrhage without shock is also a potent stimulus to output of epinephrine and norepinephrine in the adrenal vein of the dog (Walker et al., unpublished). In shock there are very few unaffected organs, tissues, endocrine glands, or metabolic processes. These are discussed in Part II (Shock) and Part VI (Treatment of Severe Injury).

C. OTHER COMPONENTS OF COMPLEX INJURY

Various non–tissue-traumatizing stresses have been studied for endocrine change (Thorn et al., 1953, a; Thorn and Laidlaw, 1954). In general the endocrine responses to cold, anoxia, fatigue, and athletic competition are minor and of duration not outlasting the stimulus.

Renold et al. (1951) studied the 1950 Harvard crew and found reduction in eosinophils; studies in 1953 and 1954 (Hill et al., 1956) showed only a very slight increase in urinary secretion of corticosteroids after the four-mile race. They noted that the coxswain and coach seemed to show as much adrenal stimulus as the crew, and concluded that what small degree of endocrine stimulus occurred was due to psychologic factors rather than muscular exertion. In some instances the urinary corticosteroid increase was as great or greater during pregame tension than it was during the race. The urinary uropepsin excretion was markedly elevated in several of the oarsmen. No adrenomedullary studies were undertaken in this group.

When contrasted with tissue trauma, it is remarkable how great a stress is associated with normal, subnormal, or only slightly elevated corticosteroid excretion.

Study of trauma without anesthesia (fracture, multiple injuries) demonstrates a full range of 17-hydroxycorticosteroids, catechol amines, and antidiuretic and salt-retaining responses (Moore et al., 1955; Hammond et al., 1958). Such observation necessarily includes other components such as blood loss, fluid accumulation, and pain.

The metabolic effects of immobilization (Dietrick et al., 1948) are particularly noteworthy with respect to calcium and phosphorus loss; nitrogen and electrolyte changes are fractional. The metabolic effects of infection are prominent, especially in the nitrogen-fat-energy area; body wasting is severe.

There has been increased interest in the psychiatric aspects of surgical patients in general and postoperative recovery in particular. Bliss *et al.* (1955, 1956) have studied the psychiatric aspects of mitral surgery, as have Fox *et al.* (1954).

Adrenocortical and psychiatric correlations are attractive for study; Bliss *et al.* (1956) have studied these relationships. Sturgis *et al.* (1956) have viewed anesthesia recovery patterns with reference to normal endocrine and metabolic phenomena, and as a guide to psychiatric prognosis. Deutsch (1942) was one of the early workers in this field, with her observations on psychologic phenomena in surgical patients. Jessner *et al.* (1952) studied the emotional implications of tonsillectomy and adenoidectomy in children.

CHAPTER 5

Metabolic Activation after Injury: Mediators That Stimulate Diffuse Bodily Changes after Focal Injury

Section I.   The Need to Postulate Mediators; Types of Mediators

When we look at a compound fracture it is apparent enough that mechanical forces disrupted and changed the tissue. When we look at the changing body composition remote from the injury, the changing nature of blood chemistry or urine secretion, the proximate cause of the alteration is not so clear. What forces, reflexes, mediators, or emissaries transmit the message of tissue injury to the uninjured tissues of the body?

In general there are two types of mediators. First, there are those which do not depend on the endocrine glands to initiate a diffuse change in bodily economy. Second, there are those which appear to depend on neuroendocrine activation.

Hormones are not the only chemical messengers which alter the metabolism of the body after injury. In recent years interest in endocrine changes after trauma has overshadowed study of those tissue factors that arise from the injury and affect the organism as a whole. These are the product of the anatomic injury itself and occur quite independently of any endocrine changes.

We can further characterize these two types of mediators. The nonendocrine mediators are largely harmful. They demand treatment, which is the basis of wound surgery. By contrast, the endocrine mediators are often helpful, and in most instances (with a few important exceptions) they do not require treatment. Indeed the significance of the endocrine mediators is best appreciated by the collapse that occurs in their absence.

The endocrine mediators are essential to survival, while the nonendocrine mediators underlie the basic rationale for treatment.

Section II.   The Nonendocrine Mediators That Arise from the Wound and Stimulate Diffuse Bodily Change; Their Relation to Wound Surgery

The nonendocrine phenomena that alter body metabolism diffusely after severe injury may be grouped under six headings.

(1) *Direct injury to the central nervous system*, with failure to ventilate (anoxia, acidosis), failure to cerebrate, and failure of vasoconstrictor mechanisms.

(2) *Injury to the airway*, with failure to ventilate, resulting also in anoxia and acidosis.

(3) *Loss of effective blood volume*, due either

to hemorrhage (internal or external) or sequestration of fluid or blood, leading to hypovolemic and hypotensive shock. This produces anoxia and acidosis, and the prolonged deficiency of flow leads to deficient organ function (liver, brain, kidney), accumulation of abnormal metabolites, and anaerobiosis in tissues.

(4) *Cross-sectional destruction of tissue*, with accumulation of extracellular fluid and plasma in the traumatized area, and release into the circulation of intracellular solutes, such as potassium, enzymes, and pigments.

(5) *Loss of the normal barriers to infection.* The skin and the mucous membranes line the body's exterior and interior, and protect it from the swarming bacteria of the outside world and the gastrointestinal tract. When these barriers are disrupted, contamination occurs, and in due course this contamination becomes infection.

(6) *Starvation.* All wounds of any magnitude are accompanied by starvation of at least transient nature. Starvation makes a contribution to the losses of body tissues. Starvation of the injured patient (or the postoperative surgical patient) after the first four to seven days becomes most significant in terms of retarded convalescence.

In Part VI are discussed the many surgical maneuvers by which these six sources of abnormal biochemistry are treated surgically to prevent the deterioration that results from their unimpeded progress. The successive steps of surgical care, starting with the simplest first-aid measures and following through major surgery to the last weeks of final convalescence, have as their objective the prevention or treatment of these six sources of disordered body metabolism, which arise directly from the wound itself. Effective wound surgery may be defined as an orderly approach to these six results of the wound. These are six mechanisms which, by a variety of biochemical modalities (acidosis, anoxia, toxicity, and energy-lack), transmit the message of injury to the tissues.

If the endocrine alterations now run their course without further stimulus, as they do in primary elective clean civilian surgery,

they quickly subside and convalescence proceeds.

In unanesthetized severe tissue injury they cannot subside because of the continued action of the specific systemic changes just described, the disordered biochemistry of the wound itself, the wound cycle. These maintain endocrine activity at a high rate and continue to threaten the patient by deficient neurologic function, blood flow, and oxygenation or by the development of acidosis or sepsis. As long as these systemic changes are active, the wound remains a continuing injury.

The major tactical steps of definitive surgery can be summarized as comprising six simple groups, corresponding to the six systemic effects of the wound itself; the wound cycle determines surgical tactics.

(1) *The Central Nervous System.* This tissue, which has virtually no power of regeneration, is treated by the removal of pressure, the removal of clots and detritus, the removal of foreign bodies, and the control of hemorrhage. Restoration of anatomic continuity is meaningful only in peripheral, fully myelinated nerves. Loss of protective reflexes and development of aspiration pneumonia must be considered as possible sequelae of injury to the brain and spinal cord.

(2) *Ventilatory Inadequacy.* With severe embarrassment, treatment must be started early or the patient will not survive to definitive surgery. In penetrating wounds of the jaw, the nasal bones, the face, the nose, or the throat, the development of edema may be slow, and the treatment of such injuries may inevitably require tracheotomy, best performed early. In crushing wounds of the chest, the flail chest, and in pressure pneumothorax, tracheotomy is also important. Water-seal chest drainage, the use of a high humidity atmosphere, expectorants, aminophylline, oxygen, bronchoscopy, artificial respiration—all have their meaning solely in terms of this chief threat to life: inadequate ventilation. Excessive infusions, particularly of salt, are avoided.

(3) *Hemorrhage, Prolonged Deficiency of Flow, and Shock.* This is treated by restoration of

effective blood volume to a level adequate for the maintenance of forward flow. This volume transfusion may be very large. If there is a major opening in the large-artery tree, it must be closed surgically as volume restoration is being started in order for the transfusion to be effective.

In the volume-flow-resistance relationship, there is a special distortion produced by anesthesia. Most anesthetic agents lower peripheral resistance, probably by direct effect on the myoneural mechanism responsible for arteriolar vasoconstriction. If a patient has just been restored to something resembling normal circulation by blood transfusion but is maintaining flow by a continued widespread vasoconstriction, then the induction of a general anesthetic agent may be followed by a secondary fall of pressure and flow to levels of deficiency that may be lethal. It is for this reason that the severely injured patient should be slightly overtransfused and should equilibrate his blood volume before going to the operating room.

(4) Tissue Disruption and Necrosis. Metabolic acidosis and release of intracellular substance result from tissue ischemia. Definitive surgery must leave behind only tissues with normal blood supply and a normal blood flow. If any tissues that do not answer this requirement are left in the patient, they alone may defeat survival by the development of sepsis. Their removal also prevents the further absorption of toxic intracellular substances such as electrolytes and enzymes. This is accomplished by the removal, cutting away, trimming, and amputation, when necessary, of devitalized tissues. This is debridement. The immobilization of fractures is important in the treatment of both volume reduction and tissue disruption because it puts a stop to laceration of nearby soft tissues and attendant local blood loss.

(5) Contamination Leading to Infection. After massive injury, effective definitive surgery alters the relationship of the patient to his bacteriologic environment so that severe invasive sepsis rarely occurs.

Invasive sepsis thrives: (1) where tissue is dead; (2) where mucosa-lined viscera leak into the tissues; and (3) where pressure can develop in the presence of bacterial invasion.

The tactics which prevent sepsis may therefore be listed under these three corresponding objectives: (1) debridement; (2) the closure, drainage, or exteriorization of holed hollow viscera; and (3) the establishment of adequate external drainage for those sources of infection or contamination which cannot be removed.

(6) Starvation. The closure, repair, or exteriorization of holed or obstructed hollow viscera is essential to the resumption of diet. It is the release from homeostatic tension and the return to normal of the endocrine and biochemical changes that permits appetite and food-taking to recommence after repair.

Section III.   The Endocrine Mediators; The Relationship of Postoperative Endocrinology to Metabolism

In the convalescent surgical patient there is a sequence of endocrine changes, and in that same patient there is a characteristic series of metabolic alterations. Has the metabolism resulted from the endocrine changes? Are the two a common result of some third force? Are they totally unrelated? Or does the metabolic change cause a compensatory endocrine alteration?

The relationship of the endocrine changes seen after injury to the metabolic alterations that we think of as the metabolism of convalescence is one that seems considerably more complicated now than it did at the time of World War II, when the possibility of a relationship was first considered.

In introducing any such discussion we should point out again that reduction in effective extracellular or circulating blood volume is a strong stimulant to the activity of vasopressin, catechol amines, corticosteroids, and aldosterone, and that the primary effect of trauma in the adrenal-deficient state is hypotension, shock, and unregulated loss of water and salt from the kidney. The maintenance of the circulation (pressure and flow) in the face of real or threatened volume reduction (typified by hemorrhage, shock, extrarenal loss, traumatic edema) is a primary endocrine-metabolic adjustment in surgical trauma.

A detailed discussion of this problem of endocrine-metabolic relations in surgical metabolism is beyond the scope of this book and at the time of this writing would surely be inconclusive. The reader is again referred to the Harvey Lecture (Moore, 1957) and the Laurentian Hormone Conference (Moore, 1957). It is our purpose in this section to review briefly certain important facts which bear on this controversial relationship.

A. WHAT RELATIONS MIGHT EXIST?

First of all, let us consider precisely what relationships we wish to describe. At the present time the following four relationships would seem worthy of consideration:

(1) the relationship of postoperative water retention (antidiuresis) to the secretion of antidiuretic hormone;

(2) the relationship of postoperative glycogenolysis, gluconeogenesis, and vasoconstriction to alterations in the catechol amines, epinephrine, and norepinephrine;

(3) the relationship of postoperative salt retention to aldosterone secretion; and

(4) the relationship of the nitrogen-potassium-carbohydrate-fat changes to alterations in the secretion or intermediary metabolism of hydrocortisone.

Most of the controversy that has waxed and waned over this question has concerned itself entirely with the fourth point above, overlooking the other three. The four points of reference are listed to indicate that any consideration of endocrine-metabolic alterations in surgery should take note of all the primary changes that are now known in sufficient detail to postulate any relationship at all.

1. Vasopressin and Catechol Amines

The first two of these (water–antidiuretic and catechol amine alterations) we may dispose of quickly. Although a circulating antidiuretic substance has been identified in the urine, there is no chemical evidence as yet that it is vasopressin. The circumstantial evidence is overpowering that post-traumatic antidiuresis is due to vasopressin secretion, and the renal effects are typical. Large changes in secretion of the catechol amines have been recorded in everyday surgical convalescence. Certain of the changes in vascular function and the metabolism of carbohydrates are characteristic of adrenal medullary activity. One may question whether the metabolic changes observed are due in fact to the alterations in secretion, to an alteration in the receptivity of the tissues, to alterations in the intermediary metabolism of the hormones involved, or to some outside or third agency, the hormone necessarily being present for the change to occur. There is little direct evidence on these questions.

2. Aldosterone

Turning now to aldosterone, we find evidences, both from the work of Ingle (1952) and from Mason (1955), that the adrenalectomized animal or man on constant doses of steroid replacement shows characteristic alterations in sodium balance. Interpretative problems are therefore the same as those surrounding the hydrocortisone changes. There is an increase in aldosterone secretion after trauma; there are widespread changes in sodium metabolism. Whether cause or effect is not clear; probably both are important. If reduction in effective extracellular or circulating blood volume is a prominent component of the injury, the increase in aldosterone secretion is predominantly a result of this component and the sodium transport a result of the aldosterone secretion. Decreased renal hemodynamics also decreases net sodium excretion, but not net tubular transport.

3. Hydrocortisone

It is with respect to the 17-hydroxycorticoid problem that most of the data have been developed and discussions recorded in the literature. The facts are about as follows.

a. Surgical Metabolism Occasionally Resembles That Which Follows Adrenal Stimulation. Injection of adrenocorticotropic hormone or compound F into normal human subjects produces changes that resemble the surgical experience in some respects; there are also many striking differences that have been recorded (Moore and Ball, 1952).

b. Surgical Trauma Excites Adrenal Secretion. Marked changes in adrenal secretion have been recorded after injury. These are changes not only in the urine but also in the blood and, on the basis of animal work (and fragmentary evidence in man), in the adrenal vein itself. There is no question but what there is an actual increase in adrenal function after trauma, whatever alteration in hormone disposal may later ensue.

c. Adrenalectomy, Plus Hormone, Yields a Normal Trauma Response. The adrenalectomized animal on constant replacement dosage and the adrenalectomized man under rather similar but less well controlled circumstances show a sequence of nitrogen, sodium, and potassium changes which are strongly reminiscent of the intact individual (see Section B below). This suggests that the adrenal hormones are permissive in their action and that some as yet unidentified agency initiates the metabolic change, the adrenal hormones merely permitting them to occur.

d. But Adrenalectomy Plus Hormone Does Not Yield a Constant Blood Level. Over and against this evidence, however, is the data from Steenburg and Ganong (1955) and Christenson, Shoemaker, and Moore (unpublished) that following trauma the adrenalectomized dog on constant doses of hydrocortisone shows a significant rise in hydrocortisone in the blood This suggests that some alteration in the intermediary pathway of the hormone is produced by the trauma so as greatly to potentiate its action in the tissues. Steenburg *et al.* (1956) also showed that the normal patient after trauma has a potentiated response to a standard dose of adrenocorticotropic hormone. There are other data (Gold *et al.*, 1956, 1958) demonstrating an alteration in intermediary pathway of the hormone after trauma. Taking all these things together, they indicate that after trauma the adrenalectomized animal on constant dose of hormone may not, in point of fact, be exposing the tissues to a constant level of the hormone. It is the concentration of hormone in the body fluids, not the total amount present, to which the tissues respond.

e. Adrenal Hormone Is Necessary for Life after Injury. In the total absence of adrenal hormones, survival is jeopardized and metabolism grossly abnormal. Survival is threatened because of failure of vascular homeostasis, metabolism is most remarkable in unregulated renal salt loss, and the clinical picture is that of shock.

Taking these five facts together, it is clear that the relationship of endocrine change to metabolic alteration is very intimate but that details are still *sub judice*. The assertion that something else causes changes in tissue metabolism after injury and that the adrenal hormones are permissive is very attractive because it fits in with much endocrine theory, but it leaves us uncertain as to the nature of this mysterious other agency, and it is that question which interests the surgeon the most.

It is not enough to assert that hormones are "permissive"; this still leaves unanswered the important question: what, then, initiates the metabolic change? In severe, open, unanesthetized trauma, the nonendocrine mediators could be such an initiating agency. In elective, clean, soft-tissue operations they are not very active and we must look elsewhere. The effect of anesthetic agents themselves and minor degrees of reduction in effective circulating extracellular or blood volume may be metabolic activators of importance in otherwise uneventful civilian, clean, soft-tissue trauma of moderate extent.

B. THE PROBLEM OF "CONSTANT REPLACEMENT VERSUS CONSTANT BLOOD LEVEL"

Cuthbertson (Campbell *et al.*, 1954) showed that adrenalectomized rats maintained on salt only did not show a normal response to fracture. When given cortisone pellets their response was "normalized," virtually regardless of the amount of steroid given. He made the very interesting observation—seemingly parallel to clinical experience—that the magnitude of the nitrogen response after injury appears to be a function of the basal urinary nitrogen excretion *before* the trauma.

These experiments of Cuthbertson summarize, confirm, and corroborate in one group most of the aspects of the so-called "primary versus permissive" concepts of adrenal relationships after trauma. One might interpret the trauma as releasing an active steroid hormone which then affects the tissues. But on closer examination it is apparent that the presence of adrenal cortex itself is unnecessary, so long as sufficient circulating hormone is present. This confirms the work of Ingle, Ward, and Kuizenga (1947) and the data of Ingle, Meeks, and Thomas (1951), Ingle and Nezamis (1950), Ingle (1952, a, b, 1954), Burns *et al.* (1953), and Engel (1952, 1955, 1957). Such data are in keeping with the permissive concept of adrenal action. Selye and Horava (1953) prefer the word "conditioning." This term is a gerund which connotes active participation rather than a passive role as suggested by the word "permissive."

A classic example of this conditioning is to be found in the experiments of Selye (1954), in which he showed that certain types of traumatic shock produced an increased blood sugar in the normal rat. But in the adrenalectomized rat, the same trauma produced hypoglycemia. If the adrenalectomized rat was then maintained on small amounts of adrenocortical extracts which in themselves did not cause any increase in blood sugar, the trauma in question produced a marked rise in blood sugar. Dr. Selye's conclusion, therefore, was that the metabolism resulting from trauma produced conditions which were favorable for the hyperglycemic effect of certain adrenocortical steroids. As we have pointed out elsewhere in this book, such a fact and such an explanation requires one further activation limb—namely, that activation mechanism by which a local trauma produces generalized alterations in metabolism whether through the intermediacy of the adrenal hormones themselves, or as a conditioning factor.

Cuthbertson reviews the evidence on accessory adrenal tissue in small laboratory animals and points out that one must be hesitant in the interpretation of certain experiments after adrenalectomy, because of the presence of accessory tissue.

The data of Mason (1955) and Jepson *et al.* (1957) are of interest in this regard. Mason found a normal sequence of postoperative metabolic changes (in nitrogen, sodium, potassium, calcium, and phosphorus) on constant cortisone dosage after adrenalectomy and constant adrenocorticotropic hormone after hypophysectomy. Jepson's paper suggests that normal nitrogen excretion was seen under similar circumstances. In neither instance were the blood levels measured, and in several of Jepson's cases considerable changes in urinary 17-hydroxycorticosterone were seen; the inhibitory effect of a few days of cortisone administered preoperatively was assumed to damp out endogenous stimulation completely, a conclusion which is not justified.

One of the basic observations involved in the concept that adrenal hormones are permissive in their action is this suggestion that tissue change occurs with adrenal constancy. The evidence for this in adrenalectomized animals or man is still not conclusive, since on constant doses of hydrocortisone the blood level is not constant after injury, as mentioned above. But if we look farther out in the convalescent pattern of normal man, we find many situations where metabolic sequences run out their course with constant hydrocortisone levels, constant at least by all the methods now available. Following a moderate trauma of the closed soft-tissue type, one can detect very few, if any, changes in indices of adrenal steroid function after the third postoperative day; some further backswing of eosinophils may occur for another day or two. After this time, the adrenal seems to have returned to its preoperative condition and from here on out to the final completion of convalescence (which may be as much as six months later) the entire sequence continues without adrenal change, including reversion to positive nitrogen balance, the maintenance of positive nitrogen balance until lean tissues are synthesized, and then the restoration of body fat. In the child, this characteristic pattern includes skeletal growth, returning the patient to the pre-injury normal growth curve. We need not, therefore, look only to the complicated laboratory situation of trauma in the adrenalectomized animal or man on constant replacement dosage in order to witness metabolic change after injury with adrenal constancy. It is a surgical commonplace. For this reason, whatever further evidence becomes available concerning the relationship of postoperative metabolism to endocrinology, it appears that the later phases of normal human convalescence occur quite normally without any alteration in adrenal steroids, as long as some steroid is present.

We may summarize these points:

(*1*) *In mild injury endocrine activation takes place largely along neural pathways.* Mild injury requires activation of the neuroendocrine mechanism in order to effect metabolic changes. The wound effect alone appears to be too inconsequential to initiate a diffuse change in metabolism.

(*2*) *Severe trauma affects remote tissues.* Very severe tissue injury can initiate widespread post-traumatic metabolic change by non-endocrine mediators and with little steroidal change as long as hormones of the pituitary and adrenal are present. In this sense, the adrenal hormones are permissive and the neuroendocrine pathway bypassed.

(*3*) *Adrenal hormone levels rise.* In severe injury, survival is threatened if the 17-hydroxycorticosterone hormone levels do not rise; they do rise because of an intense secretion of adrenal substances (produced by neuroendocrine activation) and because of reduced clearance of these substances from the blood.

(*4*) *Metabolism of hormone is changed by trauma.* In the adrenalectomized animal on constant dose of hormone, the hormone level in the blood also rises because of reduced clearance, reduced inactivation, reduced conjugation, or altered metabolic pathways.

(*5*) *The "run-off" of convalescence occurs without further 17-hydroxycorticosteroid stimulation.* In either case, with injury mild or severe, with or without adrenal activation, the metabolic sequence subsequently "runs out" its course to the completion of convalescence without

further detectable adrenal steroid change, and long after its return to normal. The point at which anabolism occurs and the extent to which fat is gained are determined by the stage to which wound healing has progressed, the presence or absence of infection, the diet, and the nature of the wound itself, whether burn, fracture, open or closed soft-tissue injury.

This interpretation invokes the neuroendocrine activation of adrenal function, the direct effect of hormones on tissues, and activation mechanisms from the wound itself. This third activation might act by one of three mechanisms.

(*1*) *Direct Effect.* The wound might initiate tissue metabolism by direct effect on the remote tissues.

(*2*) *Synergistic Effect.* The nonendocrine mediators might initiate diffuse metabolic change in the presence of raised levels of adrenal hormones but not in the presence of normal concentrations; there may be a synergistic effect possibly related to the catechol amines, which require normal corticosteroids for their peripheral vascular action.

(*3*) *Sensitizing Effect.* Some substance might act which did not affect the tissue directly save to sensitize it to the action of normal concentrations of adrenal hormones. Again, substances from the adrenal medulla, from the wound itself, systemic factors such as acidosis or anoxia, or hormones from the autonomic nervous tissue might so affect the tissues throughout the body that normal or slightly elevated levels of adrenal hormone could initiate very diffuse metabolic alterations.

C. THE PRIMACY OF VOLUME MAINTENANCE

Finally, it should be re-emphasized that the most important immediate homeostatic effect of the secretion of pituitary and adrenal hormones after injury is the maintenance of the circulation (blood pressure and tissue perfusion) despite the threat of volume reduction; when the hormones are lacking, hypotensive oligemic shock results.

This endocrine maintenance of the circulation occurs in part through metabolic agencies. Altered permeability of cells to cations (e.g., sodium, potassium) and crystalloids (nitrogen intermediates) accompanies response of the vascular muscle to the catechol amines. The more widespread metabolic result we see and measure (sodium conservation, nitrogen-potassium loss) may then be a by-product of circulatory homeostasis and might rightfully be expected to be most intense in those instances (sepsis, crush, necrosis, burns, shock) where volume reduction is most intense and circulatory homeostasis most severely challenged. Those same trauma components are the most active stimulants of post-traumatic 17-hydroxycorticosterone secretion and metabolic change. This suggests that the homeostatic response to threatened volume reduction is a primary endocrine-metabolic change after surgical trauma.

CHAPTER 6

The Therapeutic Meaning of Normal Convalescence; The Question of Early Feeding; Nitrogen Balance; The Wound

Section I.   Alterations in the Normal Sequence

Most of the metabolic changes which occur after surgery appear, in moderate trauma, to be of little adverse significance to the organism. The tendency to save sodium, the tendency to lose weight, and the tendency to lose nitrogen, for instance, do not, in themselves, have any adverse significance for the organism. There is no justification for stating that homeostasis is better if sodium is lost, weight is maintained, and nitrogen retained, although many efforts have been made to produce such modifications of post-traumatic metabolism. Such studies have been of interest and importance in understanding the metabolic mechanisms themselves and their interpretation, yet mere modification of the post-traumatic metabolism cannot be stated to improve homeostasis unless data are brought forth to support that contention in terms of the patient's well-being.

One could make out a good case for quite the opposite view: that normal metabolic change represents the optimal homeostasis and any departure from it is a deterioration. Again, data to support such a view would be necessary. With this in mind, one may then examine situations in which post-traumatic endocrine and metabolic changes are exaggerated or prolonged. This exaggeration or prolongation usually occurs as a result of persistent surgical disease. It is the complication, the shock, the infection, which exaggerate and prolong the "injury phase" of surgical metabolism. When this aspect is prolonged, it is certainly harmful to the organism. Such intensification or prolongation of postoperative metabolism as a result of continued injury, such as infection, justifies extensive efforts at treatment. Such treatment should be directed at the tissue disease (undrained pus, unreplaced blood loss, extrarenal loss) and not solely at its metabolic result.

The modification of post-traumatic metabolism by the administration of hormones remains largely unexplored territory. As is discussed in the following section on nitrogen balance and the wound, one cannot assume that transient negative nitrogen balance is in itself harmful or, if nitrogen excretion has been reduced, that thereby the patient is made better. Literature endorsing new anabolic hormones is based on the assumption—nowhere clearly stated—that if the patient is in zero or positive nitrogen balance, he is better off. Whether or not this statement is true depends entirely on the clinical setting and the rest of the details of the case.

Section II.   Changing the Balance by Early Feeding

The possibility that large dietary intakes could forestall, abort, or reverse the nitrogen changes seen after injury has been repeatedly studied over the past fifteen years. The question has four points of interest:

(1) Is post-traumatic nitrogen loss largely due to starvation?

(2) Is it harmful?

(3) Can it be prevented by feeding?

(4) If so, does this help the patient?

As to ease of feeding, following such an injury as a fracture there is transient difficulty in feeding, which arises only from the lack of appetite for food for a day or two and is indicated by diminished peristaltic activity. But in major surgery of face, neck, chest, and belly there is a real difficulty in feeding and a hazard in overstuffing a hesitant or rebellious stomach. In such cases therapeutic endeavors to overcome tissue loss require large intravenous intakes of nourishment in various forms, including glucose, fructose, invert sugar, fat, polypeptides, amino acids, and whole protein. The question is: is this effective, necessary, or helpful?

Peters (1944) in an early review said, "Administration of large excesses of protein (more than 100 to 125 gm. daily) immediately after injury is not indicated until some means is found to circumvent its immediate destruction; but throughout disease to provide generous supplies of food with adequate protein will insure against malnutrition." Grossman *et al.* (1945) described negative nitrogen balances despite high caloric nitrogen intakes in patients after operations and with infections. They found that in most cases further increasing the intake only increased the wastage with but poor effect on balance. Shaffer and Coleman in 1909 had shown, in typhoid fever, that nitrogen losses could be prevented by high caloric intakes; Coleman and duBois (1915) had shown the increased caloric need by calorimetry, but they found that even

when these needs were met, nitrogen loss persisted. Howard *et al.* (1944, b) could not overcome nitrogen loss with high caloric intakes, whereas Co Tui (1944), using high nitrogen and calorie intakes, could.

J. E. Howard's studies at Baltimore during World War II were among the early attempts to quantitate and then to modify the post-traumatic metabolism. In a group of six fracture patients (Howard *et al.*, 1944, a), an average loss of 200 gm. of nitrogen was found, over a thirty-five-day period. Fever, anesthesia, and drugs had little to do with these losses. The findings appeared to corroborate Cuthbertson's work of ten years before. The later anabolism was very slow in Howard's cases: 0.5 to 1.5 gm. of nitrogen per day. It was noted that during the phase of nitrogen loss the patients "did not feel inadequately fed," and that high-intake feeding was actively resisted and, if successfully forced, did no apparent good.

In an associated report (1944, b) Howard and his group studied the effects of diet on the post-traumatic nitrogen deficiency exhibited by fracture patients. They calculated that any nitrogen loss in excess of 10 gm. per day per 1.73 square meters was "due to factors other than starvation." In addition they assumed that normal anabolic relationships were involved when, on 10 gm. nitrogen and 1600 calories per day per 1.73 square meters (about 1.5/25, in terms of dietary shorthand), a person was in nitrogen equilibrium. They found that in the fractures "all negative nitrogen balances are greater than would be expected for dietary reasons alone and this is even more striking for the patients in whom diets higher in proteins were fed." In these patients it was not until the forty-first to the fifty-second day that their nitrogen dynamics returned to the normographic prediction. In the first nine days, feeding large intakes had no discernible effect on balance and, by the same token, greatly increased the urinary nitrogen excretion.

In the contrasting cases of soft-tissue surgery the losses were lesser and of shorter duration, but the unresponsiveness of nitrogen balance to elevated intake was equally clear. In one control pair the addition of 50 gm. of nitrogen and 8000 calories over a ten-day period in one had no effect on nitrogen balance as compared to the other.

The comments of Howard on high intravenous intakes and forced feeding in the early post-trauma period appear to us still to be valid and include the obvious and basic consideration that clinical utility depends not only on metabolic data ("achieving positive balance") but also on the question of whether achieving this balance is good for the patient. He points out the clear difference between early post-traumatic catabolic weight loss and starvation, and also the contrast with hyperthyroidism, in which calories have such a readily-demonstrated sparing action. Howard also confirmed the report of Cuthbertson on rats (1942, 1943) that protein depletion prior to surgery diminished rather than accentuated the post-traumatic loss.

In 1949 Werner and his group reported a careful study comparing short-term starvation with short-term postoperative loss. These studies were mostly in patients undergoing very moderate trauma (herniorrhaphy or cholecystectomy). In general, operation produced a slightly greater nitrogen loss than starvation alone, although this was not always the case. Prevention of nitrogen loss by isocaloric feeding was not readily accomplished. Both in these studies and in several subsequently (see below) the absolute magnitude of nitrogen loss after small major operations was not significantly greater than that seen in starvation, but it was less easily overcome.

Riegel *et al.* (1947) reported that plasma protein concentrations may rise despite negative nitrogen balance. They found that intakes near 0.3/30 (i.e., 0.3 gm. of nitrogen per kg. per day—about 21.0 gm. of nitrogen in an adult—and 30 calories per kg. per day) were needed to reverse nitrogen loss after injury. In starvation, restoration of nitrogen

balance is readily produced at intakes near 0.1/15. They concluded that the plasma protein concentration is no index of protein nutrition, that the real problem is, in forced feeding, not "balance," but vomiting, diarrhea, and distention, and that "forced feeding is not indicated."

As to intravenous intakes, Werner *et al.* (1949) showed that very large intravenous nitrogen intakes were required to achieve balance after operation. Wastage (in the sense of large urinary nitrogen losses) was extreme and clinical benefit dubious.

Beal *et al.* (1954) studied a small group of patients in relation to their ability to utilize administered nitrogen for protein synthesis. The method consisted in the maintenance of high intake levels after surgery in an experimental as compared with a control group of patients. There were only four patients from whom conclusions might be drawn. The effects were minor. In one, for instance, who was on the maintained postoperative intakes (about 12 gm. of nitrogen and 2400 calories), there was a prolonged negative nitrogen balance totaling about 80 gm.

Holden *et al.* (1957) again reopened this question with the most extensive and carefully-controlled studies yet reported. They showed a clear sex difference, males tending to lose more nitrogen than females.[*] In many of their patients after moderate operative injury (cholecystectomy, for example), by using a carefully-planned intravenous regimen near the 0.26/35 level, they were able to maintain a precarious balance, the patient lapsing back into large losses when infusions were stopped. As noted, the intakes given (0.3/30) were two to three times those required to prevent loss in simple starvation (0.1/15).

After severe trauma the loss of nitrogen is very large on zero intake, ranging from 15 to 25 gm. a day. There have been no reports of conscientious attempts to abate these losses in the first few days after trauma; later on, very large intakes are required for the main-

---

[*] This is of especial interest relative to the sex differences in postoperative adrenal function, long suspected but only recently proven (Halme *et al.*, 1957).

tenance of balance. As time passes, the post-operative requirements for attainment of balance fall day by day until, by the start of the anabolic phase (about the fourth to the seventh day), when urinary nitrogen loss is small, intakes in the vicinity of 0.1/15 will restore tissue synthesis and nitrogen balance.

Attempts to modify nitrogen balance by giving large amounts of calories and protein demonstrate that nitrogen balance on maintained intake after surgery resembles the result of forced feeding in the normal individual. By this is meant that as intakes go up, precariously positive balances are produced, but only at the expense of progressively larger urinary nitrogen excretions. In other words, there is an inefficient utilization of administered nitrogen compounds, urinary excretion being raised to high levels by high intakes and any net synthesis resulting being an extremely small portion of the whole. This inefficient utilization of high nitrogen intakes after trauma is to be contrasted sharply with the result of high nitrogen-calorie intakes after a period of starvation, or high nitrogen intakes after the spontaneous anabolic phase of surgery begins. In either of these latter two instances, increased nitrogen intake is not accompanied by increased loss of nitrogen in the urine but instead by a ready production of strongly positive and highly significant nitrogen balance. Indeed, the reaction of the freshly traumatized patient to high intakes of calories and nitrogen and its contrast with the same procedure in starvation constitutes one of the most clear-cut demonstrations that there is a fundamental metabolic difference between early post-traumatic catabolism and starvation.

A. IS THERE ANY BENEFIT TO BE DERIVED FROM EARLY FEEDING?

As to clinical benefit, there is no evidence available at present to show any clear gain to the patient, his wound, or his convalescence from these attempts to abort early postoperative nitrogen loss. Nor is there experimental evidence to indicate that such loss of body substance early after operation interferes with recovery.

Allende (1956) set up a study in dogs designed to mimic extreme total starvation (8 cal. per kg. per day, or about 560 cal. per day, as a relative human diet) with a reduction in all dietary features. This diet was maintained for twenty-eight to thirty-four days with a 25 per cent weight loss. A hemorrhagic and traumatizing operation was then standardized. In nineteen depleted dogs there were four deaths (one anesthesia death); none in the controls. The reduction in total plasma protein concentration was insignificant and recovery good in the depleted dogs. The curves are almost superimposable. But in the depleted dogs that died there was a greater reduction in albumin concentration and a rise in globulin, with a marked ratio reversal. After operation the controls returned to normal values a little less rapidly than the depleted animals. No liver histology is shown.

The painstaking study of Calloway et al. (1955) carried out in rats failed to demonstrate any effect whatsoever of upward variations in protein nutrition above a minimal level either on metabolism after injury, steroidal discharge (by adrenal weight), or wound healing. The only correlation was a lessened nitrogen excretion (i.e., loss) on the minimal nitrogen diets, and a more rapid accumulative balance (i.e., gain) on the larger diets in the late postoperative periods. The wounds showed no differences whatever at these levels. The authors state that "it is concluded that maintenance of a high plane of protein nutrition before injury is without obvious benefit to the animal in terms of wound healing as compared with minimal, adequate nutrition." Although such conclusions are anathema to many ardent surgical nutritionists, biologic facts must be evaluated realistically if surgical care is to be improved.

Further data are to be found in Levenson (1950) and Munro and Chalmers (1945). Andrews et al. (1956) tried to influence the healing of experimental burns in rats. Variation of twenty-fold in the protein content of diet had no effect on the rate of healing of full-thickness burns of about 10 per cent of body surface.

It is, again, difficult to avoid three general conclusions:

(1) The most damaging surgical effects of

semistarvation are to be found in such specific parameters as avitaminosis and water-loading.

(2) Semistarvation of a balanced sort and of moderate extent either pre- or postoperatively is surprisingly innocent of deleteriousness.

(3) Possibly more hazardous than either is obesity. It is of interest that while the trend in cardiovascular care is to suggest weight loss and the avoidance of obesity even in normal people, increasing evidence suggests that such a loss is not harmful in surgery, either.

B. FEEDING LATER IN CONVALESCENCE

The situation later on is quite different. All evidence points to the progressively greater importance of dietary intake as each week passes.

Not only is feeding of adequate diet a matter of clear importance later in convalescence, and a factor without which recovery does not proceed, but also it is accepted metabolically and new tissue synthesized with rapidity. Forsythe *et al.* (1955) studied the relation of nitrogen balance (retention) to nitrogen intake in individuals who had undergone prolonged malnutrition following severe battle wounds. They were studied very late in their convalescence. They showed a clear correlation of nitrogen gain with nitrogen intake, with calories reasonably well controlled. There was also a good correlation between nitrogen retention and the intake of nonprotein calories. There was no correlation between percentage of previous weight loss and tendency to retain nitrogen. The calorie: nitrogen ratios were in the range of 100 to 200. The positive nitrogen balances in some of the high-intake cases were truly remarkable, up to 15 gm. per day per 70 kg. The nitrogen intakes ranged around 0.2 to 0.8 gm. per kg. per day (which figured out to about 14 to 50 gm. total), with caloric intakes up to 3700 per day (i.e., intakes near 0.8/50). As the high intakes were begun, it took a few days for equilibrium to be reached; about 25 per cent of the dietary nitrogen was retained for anabolism in the most favorable circumstances. Indeed, the literature reviewed by these authors points to a rather constant fraction of nitrogen intake as being retained by malnourished individuals, around 20 to 25 per cent.* This is in sharp contrast, again, to the situation right after injury, when large intakes lead to progressively larger wastage. In some studies of high postoperative feeding in the early period nitrogen retention has been as little as 5 per cent of the intake, or has not been achieved at all.

As each week passes, this aspect of metabolism changes dynamically, as is so characteristic of many post-traumatic alterations. The achievement of balance requires progressively less intake and becomes progressively more important to the patient's welfare: his return of strength, morale, vigor, and even appetite itself. As each day passes the metabolic picture of early post-traumatic catabolism becomes less prominent and, if intake is not achieved, is replaced by the picture of post-traumatic starvation. This is described in greater detail in Part IV.

---

* This necessarily leads to a straight-line relationship for the data within these limits. This relationship is much more reliable than the relation of nitrogen retention to calories unless one concentrates on the low-calorie end of the scale, where caloric addition is reflected very strongly in nitrogen balance.

Section III. Wound Healing: Biochemical Changes and Nutritional Effects

A. LABORATORY DATA

The healing of wounds may be studied in terms of gross and microscopic morphology, by chemical sequences, or by the mechanical end-result: tensile strength. All three methods demonstrate a meaningful sequence involving three primary phenomena.

(1) There is an initial period when fluid and solutes (electrolyte, crystalloid, colloid) accumulate, and tensile strength is low.

(2) The change to strength is accompanied

by the microscopic appearance of fibrils and the chemical appearance of collagen.

(3) This sequence does not occur in the absence of vitamin C.

The picture one gets from such studies is that of the healing wound as a process obtaining a series of essential substrates from the metabolic pool. These substances include: (1) immune proteins (e.g., globulin), (2) oncotic proteins (e.g., albumin), (3) amino acids (e.g., methionine), (4) electrolytes (e.g., sodium, potassium, calcium), (5) mucopolysaccharides (e.g., hexosamine), (6) energy sources (e.g., glucose, 2-carbon fragments), and (7) ascorbic acid.

The wound then proceeds to a reorganization that involves two essential steps:

(1) the formation of collagen fibrils, and

(2) fibroblastic proliferation.

Collagen fibrils can be formed from the proper gel even without cells (and in vitro). But the invasion of blood vessels, the scavenging of detritus, and the formation of the proper pro-collagen gel require living tissue. The whole process requires vitamin C.

In the narrow sense that a parasitic process is one which looks to its own ends without regard to the needs of the host, the wound is parasitic; it acquires the needed substrates and vitamin C from the rest of the organism regardless of concomitant diet, and in a sense at the expense of the host tissues. Or, expressed another way, the host provides to the wound a large excess of these substances even though the body may be starving and its muscles wasting away.

If the organism has previously lacked vitamin C and is scorbutic at the time of wounding, then the wound also suffers along with the host, and the wound does not heal. If the host is in borderline scurvy, the wound will consume the available ascorbic acid and leave the host more scorbutic.

Any sort of relation to previous protein nourishment is much more difficult to demonstrate (in man), and it is a commonplace for the wound to heal to tensile integrity after trauma without dietary intake.

This is what is meant by the high biologic priority of the early wound. It is a very real phenomenon, and one whose endocrine and metabolic mediation remains to be identified.

By contrast, the late unhealed fracture or burn lies indolent in a body whose synthetic activities appear after several weeks to have been diverted to other objectives, particularly the regrowth of muscle and fat. Restoration of priority to the wound is not a matter of diet or vitamins, but of rewounding, with its significance locally, metabolically, and endocrinologically. This restores the wound to its favored place in the bodily economy.

The localization of substances in the wound is of prime interest in any consideration of the relationship of the wound to the rest of the body. In 1948 Localio *et al.* showed that there was an increased amount of sulfur in granulation tissue and this was, in part, methionine sulfur. Williamson's data (Williamson *et al.*, 1951, 1953, 1955, 1957) suggested that the presence of methionine was a feature of the resumption of tensile strength; methionine tagged with radiosulfur donates its sulfur to collagen from which it can later be recovered. In 1956 Dunphy *et al.* showed that in rats on a low-protein diet, methionine restored the hexosamine and later the collagen content as well as the tensile strength of wounds, as compared to the untreated controls.

In man, any such protein-deficient effect is very hard to demonstrate; yet any methionine reaching the early wound of the normal postoperative patient must come there from the patient's own tissues, since he is not eating at that time.

The sulfur-containing amino acids appear in the early wound before collagen; an injury increases urinary total sulfur and appears to release methionine into the extracellular fluid. On a protein-free diet, in the rat, methionine and cystine are the only amino acids that increase the rate of wound healing (Williamson and Fromm, 1953, 1955; Williamson, 1957; Localio *et al.*, 1949, 1956); evidently they do not become critical factors in the clinical situation, as the endogenous cystine-methionine donors provide more than the threshold amounts needed.

The studies of Dunphy and his coworkers have advanced and reopened the study of wound healing by new chemical techniques, and with particular reference to the formation of collagen and the development of tensile strength. Of central importance to this work was the demonstration by Udupa and Dunphy (1956) of an in vitro reaction by which ascorbic acid restored to normal the metachromatic activity of toluidine blue–chondroitin sulfate mixtures inhibited by albumin. This provided an in vitro basis for involving ascorbic acid in the histologic and histochemical sequences of wound healing. Metachromasia is related to the presence of sulfated acid polysaccharides in healing wounds. It is found between the third and ninth days, when hexosamines free of tensile property are yielding to collagen and tensile strength. It is absent in scurvy. This observation provided the stimulus for further chemical study of the wound (Dunphy *et al.*, 1956; Dunphy and Udupa, 1955; Dunphy, 1956; Udupa *et al.*, 1956; Edwards and Udupa, 1957; Edwards *et al.*, 1957) and to the development of the implanted plastic sponge as a device for sampling the regenerative chemistry of healing, an ingenious technique which holds much promise for the future. There is a possibility that these two "wound-specific substances" (ascorbic acid and methionine) are involved in related enzymatic conversions; under certain circumstances the feeding of methionine reduces the urinary wastage of ascorbic acid.

The involvement of hexosamines and mucopolysaccharides as prime movers in the early wound sequence gives additional interest to their changes in the blood after injury. Lanchantin *et al.* (1957) studied the plasma glycoproteins after burns, and found them elevated consistently and for a long time. Seromucoid accounts for a large fraction of this rise. The levels of plasma protein-bound hexose rose to twice those observed in normal individuals. Hexosamines also rose progressively. Dextran therapy may add interfering substances for these analyses, but if proper corrections are made the rises are found to remain significant. The postburn changes in glycoprotein outlast nitrogen catabolism; they are inverse to other protein alterations save for the alpha-1 and alpha-2 globulins, which also rise at this time.

These data confirm those of Keyser (1950 and 1952), Lanchantin and Deadrick (1957), Winzler (1955), Greenspan *et al.* (1951), Greenspan (1954), and Hamerman *et al.* (1956). Rosenthal *et al.* (1957) have shown that these substances may arise from the damaged tissue; Abercrombie *et al.* (1954) indicate a possible role in tissue repair. Such plasma polysaccharides and hexose-proteins have been found in a variety of visceral diseases (Seibert *et al.*, 1947, 1948), and specifically in hepatic disease (Greenspan *et al.*, 1951). Kushner *et al.* (1956) have shown a possible association with adrenocortical function; Chirico *et al.* (1956) have found elevations after operations. Weimer *et al.* (1955) have related them to the immune process.

Much of our knowledge of vitamin C metabolism in surgical patients arises from the long-continued study of Lund and his associates. They showed (Lund, 1939) that the blood ascorbate is lowered by surgical operations and then proceeded to produce scurvy in a volunteer subject (Crandon, Lund and Dill, 1940) by administration of vitamin-C-free diet for six months. It required 132 days of this diet to produce overt signs of scurvy. The white-cell ascorbate fell to zero long after the plasma ascorbate, and proved to be a much better index of the scorbutic state. At a time when the plasma ascorbate had been zero for forty-five days the wound healing was normal; when the white-cell ascorbate level was zero, wound healing failed completely but was restored to normal by parenteral vitamin C. Tissue and urine saturation curves were established and found to be good indices of the functional ascorbate content of tissues. They then showed (Lund, 1941) that wound disruption was more often associated with other factors than with avitaminosis C. In only three out of twelve disruptions was there significant scurvy. In the others, vitamin C data were within normal limits. Lund (1942) then showed the high frequency of subnormal levels of vitamin C in patients with gastric lesions. Only a few, however, could be regarded as being close to clinical scurvy. There was general agreement that high dosages of vitamin C were indicated in most surgical patients, at the time these data were developed, in the period 1939 to 1943 (Holman, 1940; Bartlett *et al.*, 1940). Toxicity and expense are low; the possibility of benefit high. Data developed since that time have corroborated this view.

Studies by this group several years later (Levenson *et al.*, 1946) showed that extensive trauma was associated also with low plasma levels of several water-soluble vitamins of the B group as well as | vitamin C, and that wounding a low-vitamin-C animal makes him actively scorbutic. The difficulty of correlating plasma levels with clinical manifestations remains. Present-day polyvitamin therapy is an outgrowth of the diagnostic difficulty pointed up by the studies of this period. While harmless, it is doubtless an unnecessary expense for many patients.

The morphology and chemistry of the early coagulum also have been studied by Brachfield and Kodicek (1951), Localio *et al.* (1948, 1949, 1956), Perez-Tamoyo and Ihnen (1953), Udupa *et al.* (1956), Van Den Brenk (1956), Williamson *et al.* (1951), and Williamson and Fromm (1953 and 1955). The tensile-strength collagen aspects have also been investigated by Taffel *et al.* (1951), Dunphy and Udupa (1955), and Howes *et al.* (1929).

One of the most important aspects of the early wound is its ability to abort infection despite the microorganisms that are almost inevitably present. Fresh surgical incisions made under sterile conditions usually show organisms on culture at the time of closure; only about 20 per cent are sterile. Fifty per cent will show staphylococci in current hospital practice (C. W. Howe, personal communication). The rate of sepsis, though a cause for great concern, is but a small proportion of these. Fresh traumatic wounds show both aerobic and anaerobic organisms on culture in the vast majority of instances. It is this latter fact, taken together with the widespread nature of the contamination and the induction of anaerobiosis by the development of shock, that makes prophylactic antibiotic therapy justified in trauma where it is not in the setting of uneventful elective civilian soft-tissue operation. Yet, even without antibiotics, clean healing is the rule if the surgeon is accurate and complete in his debridement. As pointed out repeatedly by many authors, antibacterial activity (leucocytes and immune proteins) is an important feature of the early wound.

B. CLINICAL ASPECTS

When one encounters a wound that fails to heal, either through the processes of early tensile disruption or later dehiscence, or because of chronic sepsis, one is prone to consider the etiology as being, at least in part, metabolic or nutritional. In some cases (e.g., avitaminosis C) this is clearly true. In most other instances, the wound does not seem to be adversely affected by the total postoperative adjustment or nutrition of the patient even though they are apparently adverse. In fact the wound seems to heal at the expense of the patient's tissues. It is our purpose here to try to define such facts as are now known relative to nitrogen, protein, and wound healing; the following ten propositions summarize certain clinical phenomena of wound healing.

Most wounds heal to completeness quite readily in the face of preoperative starvation.

It is such a commonplace for the patient who has lost from 12 to 25 per cent of his body weight to heal wounds quite satisfactorily that one can scarcely regard such a degree of inanition as unfriendly to or incompatible with normal wound healing. The specter of "protein depletion" is repeatedly raised. Any patient who has lost some weight is depleted of body protein, although his plasma protein concentration is quite normal. His wound heals well. There is good evidence that the plasma albumin concentration is but distantly related, if at all, to the total lean-tissue mass or nitrogen balance. It is further of interest that short-term provision of nitrogen nutriments, such as one might accomplish preoperatively, has only a very small fractional effect on total lean tissue and none on albumin concentration. The former is affected only by the slow pace of normal anabolism, the latter only by the diuresis of salt and water or by the repeated administration of concentrated human albumin.

By contrast, extreme preterminal cachexia is indeed associated with poor healing of wounds. Here there is also visceral disease (fatty liver), a severe compositional disorder (starvation edema), and specific deficiencies (vitamins A, B, C, D, K, essential amino acids, trace minerals). Yet, despite this galaxy of deficiencies it is a general rule that in the patient dying of cancer after operation the wound appears well healed in the face of severe inanition and widespread visceral involvement by malignancy.

The starving patient is neither healthy, strong, nor well. But failure of wound healing is not prominent in his catalogue of deficits, as described in Part IV. If wounds do not heal we should search elsewhere than his lack of macronutrients for the cause.

Wounds will heal to completeness in the face of a continuing negative nitrogen balance.

In patients who are having minor trauma, or in whom the stress is quite minimal and short-lived, a swing upward to positive nitrogen balance usually occurs before the wound is healed to tensile integrity. But in individuals having more extensive injuries, more extensive surgery, more extensive wounds, or some chronic stressing process such as injury followed by infection, the wound quite readily heals to completeness with the nitrogen balance still negative. On a civilian surgical service, the majority of wounds have regained their strength before net anabolism is achieved. The concept that nitrogen positivity is required for wound healing is thus untenable, as mentioned previously. It is more properly stated that convalescent nitrogen anabolism is necessary for the return to strength, vigor, and social usefulness of the patient, while the wound can heal without systemic anabolism.

The duration of nitrogen negativity after trauma seems to be related to the "normal expected time" for the return of the disrupted tissues to tensile integrity.

In soft-tissue wounds, return of "tensile integrity" (that point in time at which the normal tensile stress on the tissue can be borne by the healing wound) requires from four to ten days. The period of nitrogen negativity corresponds approximately to this. In skeletal trauma, a much longer period is required before tensile integrity is restored, particularly in fractures of the long bones,

and here also the period of nitrogen negativity is a good deal longer. The time required for the normal covering of a skin wound such as a burn is even longer and here, even in the absence of infection, the period of nitrogen negativity is considerably longer.

Wound disruption is produced by a disrupting force on the wound greater than the tensile strength of the sutures and the tissues in which they are placed, early after their placement; it may occur in any sort of nutritional setting. Wound dehiscence is a later phenomenon.

Mechanical "disruption" occurs in the first three or four days when disrupting force is greater than holding power. Wound "dehiscence" refers to a primary failure of wound healing characterized by the spontaneous opening of the wound at a later time, with less tensile stress than that found in wound disruption. The physical force required is a less prominent feature. It is our impression that the two are separate entities and of somewhat different etiology. One of the interesting things about wound dehiscence is the tendency of the wound to heal completely and spontaneously when resutured. Infection is not a prominent part of this process. No specific metabolic derangement has been identified either in disruption or dehiscence. They are somewhat commoner in people who seem poorly nourished, and they are particularly common in individuals who have unremoved cancer left behind in the abdomen. Possibly, in them, some distortion or abnormality of intra-abdominal pressure, as well as avitaminosis C, may be a factor.

Vitamin C deficiency is a specific factor inimical to wound healing.

This is the most important single nutritional factor known to be associated with the phenomena of wound healing. It evidently acts somewhere in the interval between the deposition of the ground substance and its conversion into tensile collagen fibrils. The fact that vitamin C does play a role in wound healing, that it is easily given, fairly inexpensive, and nontoxic, provides a major justification for its liberal use in surgical patients.

A low peripheral concentration of red blood cells is a specific factor inimical to wound healing.

This is particularly true in the resurfacing

of burns. Patients who have chronic open surface lesions do not heal them well in the presence of anemia. They will often be spurred to complete the healing process by adequate blood transfusion. Where the "take" of graft is involved, the mechanism of importance here may be the matter of oxygenation of the graft by the transport of more oxygen to the site; the same may be true of the growth of fibroblasts or epithelial cells. Whatever the mechanism, the patient with unhealed wounds should be watched for anemia and should be treated to produce a hematocrit over 40. Hypoferremia is also unfriendly to wound healing.

Hypoproteinemia is a specific factor in wound healing which cannot be equated with nitrogen balance.

The normal synthesis of plasma protein occurs most favorably when nitrogen and calorie provisions are adequate and nitrogen balance is positive. There is good evidence that plasma protein synthesis goes on in the face of negative nitrogen balance and that nitrogen balance and plasma albumin concentration show little if any interrelationship. Plasma protein, like the wound itself, has a high biologic priority; nitrogen-caloric starvation alone is not a frequent cause of hypoproteinemia. Indeed, severe degrees of body cachexia may be present with a normal plasma protein concentration. When the plasma protein concentration is low, the albumin fraction is usually low. The low colloid osmotic pressure then produces edema of fresh wounds. This edema may be acute or it may be that seen in the chronic unhealed wound, in which the granulations are watery and edematous. Despite the seeming rationale, the production of a normal colloid osmotic pressure by the use of concentrated albumin, by salt restriction, or by diuresis has not been shown to improve wound healing.

Invasive infection is a specific factor inimical to wound healing.

The relationship of infection to healing of the wound in cleanly incised abdominal wounds, thoracic wounds, or neck wounds is not an easy matter to state in general terms. Infection does not always prevent solid fascial healing. It is not at all uncommon to see wounds of the abdominal wall (including herniorrhaphy wounds) go on to solid healing despite the fact that sepsis has been present and has, for a time at least, constituted a clinical problem with fever and local redness, hot and chilly sensations, suggesting that an invasive organism is present. Following such a development, local wound drainage is followed by secure and normal wound healing of the inner layers. There is an obvious delay of healing of the subcutaneous layer—that layer most vulnerable to the development of sepsis—but this delay is produced by the mechanical presence of pus, by the passage of time required for leucocytic removal of the detritus, and for the production of normal granulation tissue (and healing by secondary intention), which occurs after drainage of the septic process.

In contrast to this favorable sequence, in which infection has produced an obvious delay in healing only of the superficial layers, are those instances where infection has involved all layers and has been followed by a gaping septic wound, through which bowel or lung may be seen and in which a sort of septic disruption of the wound has occurred. That this is a delaying factor in wound healing is perfectly evident. The wound has been destroyed. It also constitutes a continuing severe catabolic stimulus to the organism, as septic starvation. Anemia and hypoproteinemia are very readily produced in this type of infection with loss of red blood cells and protein in the exudate. Active measures of a nutritional sort, directed towards calorie, protein, and vitamin provision, are of more importance in relation to wound healing in this setting of invasive infection and septic starvation than in any other clinical situation. The effect of infection in delaying union of bone is obvious. The settings in tissues and metabolism which are favorable to healing may all be present but the infection produces a destructive effect which prevents normal union. When the infection is drained, the normal union then proceeds, leaving behind an increased amount of scarring and callus as evidence of the increased fibrotic reaction to the infection. When such infection occurs with prolonged drainage, hypoproteinemia, edema, and severe cachexia may result. Again in this situation, just as in that mentioned above, active measures of a nutritional type, focusing on calories, nitrogen, and vitamins, are of immediate importance to the healing of the wound. Infection consumes vitamin C, and a scorbutic state is quickly produced; large amounts are needed.

The significance of starvation in the rat cannot be equated with that in man.

The rat is, of Nature's beasts, one of the most sensitive to food deprivation. After seven days of starvation, a rat is in a critical state, eating its feces and cage-mates; after two weeks the fire of life burns low and survival is unlikely. Little wonder that after a week of starvation wounds heal poorly: it is analogous to a starved man near death, after months of total deprivation. A man after a week of starvation is still burning his fat and protein fairly comfortably; even if fed nothing he will have little severe hunger and will heal well. After months of severe deprivation and semistarvation with huge weight loss, man is still able to escape, compete, travel, fight, and heal, as centuries of literature will bear out. If rat is to be compared to man in nutritional and wounding experiments, some sort of time-correction is essential. His large storage depot of fat may have something to do with man's resistance to starvation.

Positive nitrogen balance and good general nutrition are absolutely essential to recovery, but not for the wound alone: for strength and rehabilitation.

This concept is dealt with in detail elsewhere, follows necessarily from the nature of convalescent anabolism.

In summary, then, we find that the relationship of nutrition to wound healing is not always clear-cut. Many wounds heal in semistarvation, in the presence of a negative nitrogen balance, and even in the presence of wound sepsis. Specific factors, such as vitamins or red blood cells, are often of more importance than more general nutritional factors such as calories or nitrogen balance. Vitamin C remains the only nutritional factor required from outside the body and identified as important in wound healing. One may truly contend that in wound healing the micronutrients (methionine, ascorbic acid) are more important than the macronutrients (calories, nitrogen, fat, carbohydrate, and protein).

Such a view as this may seem heterodox, iconoclastic, or even destructive of a due respect for nutrition. Quite the reverse. It is our conviction that such a view favors inquiry into the actual cause of wound failure in clinical surgery—a look beyond the platitudes about "protein depletion."

The Blood Volume: Hemorrhage, Plasma Loss, Transfusion, and Hypervolemia

Contents of Part II

CHAPTER 7.   THE BLOOD VOLUME IN HEALTH

CHAPTER 8.   ACUTE HEMORRHAGE WITHOUT SHOCK

CHAPTER 9. ACUTE HEMORRHAGE AND SHOCK

CHAPTER 10. THE BLOOD VOLUME, HEMORRHAGE, AND SHOCK; NOTES FROM THE LITERATURE

CHAPTER 11. ACUTE PLASMA LOSS AND ITS REPAIR

CHAPTER 12.   CHRONIC BLOOD LOSS AND THE BLOOD VOLUME IN CHRONIC DISEASE

CHAPTER 13.   STATES OF EXPANDED BLOOD VOLUME

CHAPTER 14.   BLOOD TRANSFUSIONS; RATES, ROUTES, AND HAZARDS; EFFECTS ON BLOOD VOLUME AND HEMATOCRIT

CHAPTER 15.   BLOOD TRANSFUSIONS; SPECIAL PROBLEMS IN MASSIVE, MULTIPLE TRANSFUSIONS: COAGULATION AND THE CITRATE LESION

CHAPTER 7

The Blood Volume in Health

Introduction.   Three Propositions

Acute loss of blood volume in the form of massive continuing hemorrhage is rapidly fatal. The mechanism of death is that of hypotension leading to deficiency of flow and acute tissue anoxia, lethal first to vital centers in the central nervous system and to the myocardium. Without oxygen here, the patient dies even though other individual organs or tissues remain viable, as can be shown by their subsequent survival on transplantation. Short of this exsanguination there are many other shades, degrees, rates, and types of blood loss, plasma loss, or blood excess, which will be dealt with in this part of the book.

The concept of a finite volume of blood circulating in the body, which can be measured at any instant, was a new and exciting one when it was first enunciated at the time of World War I. Study since that time has yielded quantitative information of importance in surgical care, and these data are the most important result of blood volume methods. The "bedside" use of these methods, in the sense of routine use, has never gained wide acceptance and has limitations that make such acceptance extremely unlikely.

As far as mass or volume of red blood cells is concerned, the concept of a finite volume is a sound one. The red-cell mass is a compartment of body composition with very finite "edges." Infusions that add to this volume remain there; the same cannot be said of the plasma volume. The constant exchange of water, electrolyte, crystalloids, and protein across the capillary makes the boundaries of the plasma volume much less definable and the volume effects of loss or of infusion less predictable. An understanding of this "liquid" property of the plasma volume, exchanging constantly across the capillary, is necessary for an understanding of its measurement and of the hematocrit.

This Part is arranged in sequence to consider first data on blood volume, followed by consideration of blood losses of increasing magnitude up to those producing oligemic shock. Acute plasma loss, chronic blood loss, and transfusion therapy are considered next. States of high blood volume are described briefly.

Three concepts that keep recurring in this Part are of basic importance in understanding blood volume support: (1) the space-occupying function of the red cell; (2) the tree of large arteries as a unicameral hydrostatic system; (3) output, pressure, and resistance.

A. THE SPACE-OCCUPYING FUNCTION OF THE RED BLOOD CELL

The size and shape of the erythrocyte is a consideration of such importance that it should be mentioned at the outset. The red blood cell occupies space in the blood volume in a way not shared by anything else that circulates in the blood vessels. Of itself it supports volume and presents resistance to flow, thus enhancing pressure. Most of the proteins and all of the electrolytes and crystalloids of the plasma can leave the plasma volume, crossing the capillary into the interstitial areas from which they originally came. This is not true of the red cell: the red cell is a thousand times as long and a billion times as heavy as the albumin molecule, and it is not in equilibrium with any other compartment of body fluid. Infused into the blood stream, it remains there, occupying volume, providing resistance to flow, and supporting pressure regardless of capillary permeability alterations short of frank hemorrhage.

The capacity of the red blood cell for carrying oxygen and for acting as a buffer is essential to life, but it is its size more than its hemoglobin-carrying or its carbon-dioxide buffering which makes it so important in the treatment of acute hemorrhage in surgical patients whose initial problem is volume reduction rather than hemodilution. Red blood cells placed in the blood volume "stay put"; they leak out only if frank hemorrhage continues, and it is the surgeon's job to put a stop to this. Thus, when one infuses blood one is infusing a heterogeneous system composed on the one hand of an aqueous phase, which shares a complex biochemical and hydrodynamic equilibrium with all the rest of body water, and on the other hand, a mass of rather large particles, which, once placed in the blood stream, continue to occupy volume, support pressure, and present resistance to flow so long as they are not lost externally or destroyed by immune mechanisms.

B. THE UNICAMERAL ARTERIAL TREE

A second concept of importance in surgical care is that of the arterial circulation—everything between the aortic valves and the peripheral resistance (arterioles)—as a unicameral hydrostatic system. By this is meant that in it no significant pressure gradients develop. If there is a hole in the aorta and pressure there falls to low levels or to zero, the pressure accordingly falls to about this same level in the whole arterial system. At two points in the system, the coronary ostia and the circle of Willis, arterial branches supply tissue that cannot tolerate anoxia, and it is at these points that death occurs.

While normal or nearly normal arterial pressure can be maintained with a wide range of venous pressures and, for a time at least, in the face of large venous hemorrhage, such is not the case with a large arterial hemorrhage. By the opening up of a large hole in the arterial tree between the heart and the arteriole, pressure is lost regardless of the continued operation of many homeostatic factors. This drastic loss of pressure affects coronary inflow; in massive arterial hemorrhage cerebral and myocardial anoxia therefore supervenes even before the changes we think of as "shock." If the body can stop the leak (in the aorta, mesenteries, or femoral artery) by its own ways (constriction, retraction, or clotting) or if the surgeon can apply hemostasis before irretrievable myocardial damage is done, the circulation may be soon restored. It is this unicameral nature of the large arterial tree that gives rise to the basic rule that in wounds of large arteries, homeostasis and hemostasis are inseparable; operation becomes itself a part of resuscitation.

C. OUTPUT, PRESSURE, AND RESISTANCE

Pressure is essential to force blood through organs; cardiac output initiates blood flow; but the blood flow of cardiac output cannot develop pressure unless it meets resistance. This resistance depends on an intact arterial-arteriolar anatomy with normal vasoconstrictor stimuli acting in a proper biochemical environment that permits the arteriole to constrict normally in response to catechol amines and steroids.

Cardiac output requires inflow of blood to the right heart, blood volume to work on, and coronary-myocardial blood supply carrying carbohydrate and oxygen to provide the energy for cardiac work.

Peripheral resistance requires an intact arterial tree of normal wall-elasticity. Peripheral resistance also requires normal or greater-than-normal tone of the peripheral arteriolar bed. Both of these require the operation of normal steroids and catechol amines or normal vascular muscle in a normal water-salt-acid milieu.

The above propositions are briefly stated. Each will appear recurrently in what follows, and is basic to circulatory homeostasis.

Section I.   Normal Values and Methods of Measurement

The central feature of blood volume therapy for surgical patients is a realistic estimate of the patient's normal volume, his volume in illness, and the changes in the latter volume produced by treatment. Some arithmetic can be applied to the data at hand and much good will come of it: an appreciation of what is to be expected from treatment and the meaning of alternative courses.

"Thinking in terms of volume" is here as important as "thinking in terms of balance" in such disorders as extrarenal loss or renal failure. The purpose of this part of the book is to provide a sound basis for "thinking in terms of volume."

An appreciation of the meaning of blood volume data in surgical patients depends to a large part on an understanding of the methods of measurement upon which those data are based. For this reason, although technical discussion of methods is usually avoided here, a brief account of blood volume technology follows.

A. THE BLOOD VOLUME AS A PHASE OF BODY COMPOSITION

It is only in recent years that we have begun to achieve a perspective in which the blood volume is appropriately considered, as it should be, as a phase of body composition and not as an isolated entity. Studies have shown several things.

(1) The erythrocyte volume is a special division of the mass of lean tissue; although the cells are not nucleated, they arise from cells that partake not only of the general phenomena of lean-tissue catabolism and anabolism but also of the special properties and responses of the blood tissue, including oxygen demand, which is in part itself determined by the size of the lean-tissue mass.

(2) The plasma volume is a division of the extracellular fluid and partakes of its changes. In extracellular fluid reduction, the plasma volume is reduced; only in the obligatory-sequestration effect (burns, crush, peritonitis) do we see extracellular fluid expansion with plasma volume contraction, and even here the general normal uninvolved extracellular

fluid is being restricted *pari passu* with the plasma volume. When the extracellular fluid is expanded, as in congestive heart failure, the plasma volume is likewise expanded.

B. SYMBOLS FOR EXPRESSIONS

The following symbols are used:

    BV = blood volume
    RV = red cell volume
    PV = plasma volume
    LVH = large vessel hematocrit
    WBH = whole body hematocrit. (The whole body hematocrit does not appear in any of the clinical expressions in this book since its relation to the large vessel hematocrit remains constant under most circumstances and, as a correction factor, cancels out in calculation ratios.)
    WBT = whole blood transfused
    PVT = plasma volume transfused
    RVT = red cell volume transfused

C. THE PLASMA VOLUME: THE DILUTION PRINCIPLE

If a known weight of table salt is dissolved in a beaker full of distilled water, it is possible to stir the contents of the beaker around a bit and then take out a sample and analyze it for the concentration of sodium chloride. The concentration found is a function of the weight of salt originally added and the volume of water in the beaker. Since the weight of salt added was known to start with, we are left with only one unknown in our equation, and we can solve the expression for the unknown volume of the beaker according to the following calculation:

Let C_1 and V_1 represent the concentration and volume of the salt before mixing, and C_2 and V_2 the concentration and volume after mixing. Then:

$$C_1 V_1 = C_2 V_2$$

The product of concentration and volume has the dimension of mass or weight. This first expression merely states that the same amount of salt is in the beaker before and after mixing.

Then, solving for the unknown volume of the beaker:

$$V_2 = \frac{C_1 V_1}{C_2}$$

Let us take an example. Suppose we add 5.2 gm. of salt to a beaker. After stirring it around until everything is well mixed up, we then take out a sample and find that it has 0.26 gm. of salt per ml. We can then solve our equation as follows:

$$V_2 = \frac{5.2}{0.26}$$

$$V_2 = 200 \text{ ml.}$$

This tells us that there is 200 ml. of fluid in the beaker.

This is the dilution principle. This simple relation is basic to all the dilution studies of body composition carried out today. It was first applied to the blood volume by Keith, Rowntree, and Geraghty in 1915, and since that time it has been applied to measurements of plasma volume, red cell volume, extracellular fluid, total body water, and, by extension, to the measurement of certain other body constituents such as the total sodium, potassium, and chloride. By calculation, such derivations as total amounts of body fat and intracellular water are obtained. These compositional aspects are dealt with in Part IV. We are here concerned with their meaning in relation to the blood volume.

1. The Dye-Plasma-Hematocrit (DPH) Method

Application of this method of measurement to the blood volume depended originally upon the injection of some substance whose distribution was supposedly confined to the plasma volume, letting it mix around until it was distributed evenly, and then taking out a sample to measure the concentration. From this the plasma volume was calculated and the blood volume derived from the large vessel hematocrit.

Because of the fact that blood is an inhomogeneous system, it is impossible to measure both the water phase and the erythrocyte phase by the dilution of a single substance; for the first twenty years of blood volume study, the thing that was being measured was thus the plasma volume alone. It was measured most commonly by the injection of a dye whose concentration after mixing could be read colorimetrically, and the blood volume was then calculated from the hematocrit. We

call this the dye-plasma-hematocrit (DPH) method.

Unlike the beaker of our salt-water analogy, the plasma unfortunately does not hold the dye securely within it. The capillaries are far from watertight. The dye, like other plasma colloids, leaks across the capillary into the interstitial phase. The dye is taken up by the Kupffer cells of the liver, excreted into the bile, and also taken up diffusely by macrophages. Therefore, the physiologic "beaker" has a leak in it, the final concentration of dye is not constant, and mathematical corrections must be used to compensate for this "leak." This introduces some minor technical differences in plasma volume technology according to the dilution substance used (dye, radioalbumin, etc.). But more important, the size of the leak is not constant. When the patient has sustained a burn or peritonitis, this leak is increased by the diffuse capillary injury. When more dye leaks out, the concentration remaining is lower and there is yielded on calculation an apparently large plasma volume. Therefore, when capillary permeability is diffusely increased (which is the case in many acutely ill surgical patients), methods of measuring plasma volume may produce false high values unless short equilibrium-times are used. These will reduce the magnitude of the biologic error but they will bring the zero-time extrapolation back to the steep portion of the disappearance slope, and enlarge the analytic error.

The dyes used are ones that truly dye the plasma protein; by this we mean that they make a stoichiometric bond with plasma protein. In the case of Evans blue dye or T-1824, the bonding is almost wholly with albumin, at the low concentrations ordinarily used. We therefore are really measuring the "quickly available albumin" and this would be a more accurate term than "plasma volume."

Other methods of measuring plasma volume, based on the dilution of some substance such as radioactive albumin, measure exactly the same space as the blue dye and give results that have the same interpretation and about the same value. There is no theoretical reason why either one is better than the other. There are practical differences that may make one simpler or more readily applicable to a certain laboratory or hospital. The ideal substance for measurement of the plasma volume would be a large protein molecule that circulates in the plasma but does not leak out at all. Some sort of a tagged globulin or polysaccharide, such as high-molecular-weight dextran, might be ideal. New methods of tagging plasma protein will doubtless be developed in the future.

The plasma volume having been measured by such a method, the blood volume has then been calculated on the basis of the fraction of peripheral blood occupied by the plasma. This latter has been determined by taking a sample of blood from a large vein (as for example the antecubital vein) and spinning it down in the centrifuge to determine the cell fraction. Because this sample is taken from a vessel such as an arm vein or a jugular vein or femoral vein, the result is referred to as the "large vessel hematocrit" (LVH). The blood volume can then be calculated by the formula:

$$BV = \frac{PV}{100 - LVH} \times 100$$

Note that in the calculation of the blood volume from a measured plasma volume alone the large vessel hematocrit is an integral part of the calculation, whose value will affect the final result.

The validity of this formula and of this derivation is based on two suppositions relative to the large vessel hematocrit.

(1) The fraction of blood occupied by red blood cells in the centrifuge tube represents the true volume of cells in that tube.

(2) The fraction of blood occupied by red cells in that tube is representative of the red cell fraction in the whole body.

Neither of these contentions is accurate, but despite the faults in this method much good has come of blood volume measurements by using it, and later refinements have introduced only minor improvement. As to the first assumption, it has been shown that there is trapped in among the red cells in a centrifuge tube a "packing fraction" of plasma amounting to approximately 1 to 3 per cent of the packed cell volume.

The second assumption has been the one that causes the difficulty with any blood volume method based on calculation from the plasma volume alone. Throughout the body as a whole the percentage of the total blood volume occupied by red cells varies and in general is somewhat smaller than it is in an isolated sample taken from a large blood vessel. There are many theoretical reasons for this, the most obvious being that in the small blood vessels there must be some extra plasma lining the wall of the blood vessels so that the red cells can get in a line and slip through easily. It is also conceivable that there are other areas of the body (the spleen and bone marrow, for example) where the red cell fraction is greater than it is in large vessels. But there is now solid evidence—based on the dye method and other albumin-dilution techniques—that throughout the body as a whole the percentage of blood volume occupied by red blood cells is somewhat smaller than it is in a large vessel. The percentage of the whole blood volume occupied by red cells, when one considers the entire body as a unit, is called the "whole body hematocrit."

2. The WBH:LVH Ratio

In the normal person the whole body hematocrit is 88 to 92 per cent of the large vessel hematocrit. This relation is fairly constant in normal health and in many chronic disorders; it is often distorted in acute surgical disease. The distortion need not worry the surgeon therapeutically; his guiding concepts and clinical data are not affected significantly by it. But quantitative blood volume measurements are distorted by it unless they are based on simple summation of plasma and red cell volume as described below. Such simple summation also avoids the hematocrit-dependence of the classic dye-plasma-hematocrit method and indeed is the basis for our current data on the whole body hematocrit. Any plasma volume method yielding a slightly lower result than dye or radioalbumin (such as macrodextran) would of necessity also yield a WBH:LVH ratio nearer unity.

3. Hematocrit-Dependence of the Classic DPH Method

The extent of dependence on the large vessel hematocrit of this classic blood volume method (calculated from a plasma volume measurement and the observed large vessel hematocrit) is not generally appreciated. Let us take as an example a plasma volume directly measured at 2400 ml. What blood volume figures does one get with hematocrits of 40, 45, and 50?

$$BV = \frac{PV}{100 - LVH} \times 100$$

$$BV = \frac{2400}{100 - 40} \times 100 = 4000$$

$$BV = \frac{2400}{100 - 45} \times 100 = 4360$$

$$BV = \frac{2400}{100 - 50} \times 100 = 4800$$

It is therefore clear that errors in determination of the large vessel hematocrit, or variations only slightly beyond the normal range, will introduce variability in the blood volume of as much as 800 ml. (25 per cent).

D. THE RED BLOOD CELL VOLUME

The further development of dilution methods, with an increasing appreciation of these problems raised by the dye-plasma-hematocrit methods for blood volume, led naturally to the development of methods for the measurement of the red cell volume. Initially this was done by the dilution of carbonmonoxide–tagged red cells, and was later carried out, during World War II, by using radioactive-iron–tagged red cells. Since that time, methods for using radioactive phosphorus and radioactive chromium have come into general use. The principle involved is the same with all these tags, and the dilution principle exactly the same as that mentioned previously. Tagged red cells of known volume and known radioactivity are injected into the body. They are allowed to circulate. After they are well mixed by the circulation, their concentration is measured, and from this the total volume of red cells is determined by the same dilution equation.

them sharp contrast to the plasma volume

Body, the red cell volume method is almost

perfect from a theoretical point of view. The "beaker" truly has no "leak." After red cells are placed in the circulation, the time course of concentration reaches a plateau that is flat. The red cell volume, as mentioned above, is not fuzzy around the edges but is finite. Of all the dilution methods used in the study of body composition, the red cell volume methods are the most perfect both from a technical and theoretical point of view. Furthermore, although the blood may be spun down to take off the plasma, the final red cell mass calculation is independent of the large vessel hematocrit. If 1.5×10^6 counts-per-minute (CPM) of chromated cells is injected, for example, and the final concentration is 0.0015×10^6 CPM per ml. of cells, the red cell volume measured is 1000 ml., whether the large vessel hematocrit is 20 or 80.

1. Blood Volume by Calculation from Red Blood Cell Volume and Large Vessel Hematocrit (RVH Method)

If the blood volume is calculated from a measurement of the red cell volume alone. the following formula must be used:

$$BV = \frac{RV}{LVH} \times 100$$

This means that if we calculate the whole blood volume by measuring the red cell volume alone and calculating it from the large vessel hematocrit, we are up against exactly the same mathematical impasse that we were with the plasma volume and we are no better off. We are still dependent upon the large vessel hematocrit and upon a relationship between the large vessel hematocrit and the whole body hematocrit which may not be justified by the facts.

The problem may be stated like this:

(1) The red cell volume method in itself is very reliable and is in itself, like the plasma volume alone, independent of large vessel hematocrit errors;

(2) however, *a calculation of blood volume from red cell volume alone is absolutely as hematocrit-dependent as a calculation of blood volume from plasma volume alone; both of these derived calculation of blood volume are equally dependent on the large vessel hematocrit.*

E. MODERN BLOOD VOLUME TECHNOLOGY: PV + RV = BV; SUMMATION

This leads us to our current concept of blood volume technology: that a proper measurement of the blood volume for research purposes, and for the accumulation of data as a basis for surgical care, must be based on the simultaneous measurement of the plasma volume and the red cell volume by two separate but simultaneous dilutions. We then measure the plasma volume and the red cell volume separately and directly. The blood volume is not calculated from the large vessel hematocrit by any formula, ratio, or relationship, but is merely the simple arithmetic sum of the two measurements as follows:

$$BV = RV + PV$$

This is the "PV + RV" or "summation" method.

We may now calculate the whole body hematocrit directly by this expression:

$$WBH = \frac{RV}{BV} \times 100$$

Current knowledge of the whole body hematocrit is based entirely on this method.

For our own purposes in surgical patients we have used the blue dye for the plasma volume and radiochromate for the red cell volume. Any other valid combination would give equally good results. For the rest of this chapter we are referring to the blood volume as based on simultaneous direct measurements of the red cell volume and the plasma volume; the normal values are slightly lower than the old DPH data. From such measurements, reliable generalizations are possible.

Although this book does not describe laboratory or analytic procedures in detail, we have gone to this length to make abundantly clear the meaning of blood volume, plasma volume, red cell volume, large vessel hematocrit, whole body hematocrit, and the DPH, RVH, and PV + RV methods, for it is on a realistic view of these concepts and methods that accurate blood volume replacement therapy is based.

F. THE BLOOD VOLUME: NORMAL VALUES AND TERMS

Normal values for the blood volume are shown in Table I. The mean is 6.5 per cent of body weight for women, 7 per cent for men. Note that a range of values is expressed for each type and sex. In general, the short, obese female has a smaller blood volume than the lean, muscular, "physically fit" male. This relates to the difference in muscle mass in the two types.

To iron out differences in body size, various relative expressions can be used. We prefer to use "per cent of body weight" (% B.Wt.) as a basis for expression. This is a simplification for ease of clinical use: specific gravity of blood is not considered. One ml. of blood is considered to weigh 1.0 gm., 500 ml., 500 gm., and so on. Thus, a plethoric man of 75 kg. with an estimated normal blood volume at 8 per cent of body weight has an estimated 6000 ml. blood volume, or an obese female weighing 50 kg. (estimated blood volume = 6 per cent of body weight) has an estimated normal blood volume of 3000 ml. This basis (percentage of body weight) has the same integer as "cc. per kilo":

$$\% \text{ B.Wt.} = \frac{\text{cc. per kg.}}{10}$$

In either event the exact gravimetric composition of blood has no significance in volume replacement.

The fact that normal blood volumes vary a good deal (as much as 15 per cent in a single sex and age group) has led to the concept that blood volume information is of no value. This is not true. There are many other physiologic entities whose normal values are variable but for which quantitative knowledge is still very useful. Examples are to be found in the normal pulse rate, the normal urine output, the normal blood urea nitrogen, or the basal metabolic rate. It is in analogy to such measurements, rather than to precision values such as the normal plasma sodium concentration (which varies only 1 or 2 per cent), that the blood volume should be used. Looking at a heavily built, rather muscular man weighing 80 kg. it is possible to calculate quickly by mental arithmetic that a normal blood volume (7 per cent of body weight) for him is somewhere around 5600 ml. The variation around this predicted mean is admittedly considerable, but the important thing is that it should be around

Table I. The Blood Volume in Health (in ml.)

BODY BUILD		MALE				FEMALE			
		Normal	Obese	Thin	Muscular	Normal	Obese	Thin	Muscular
BASIS % B. WT.		7.0%	6.0%	6.5%	7.5%	6.5%	5.5%	6.0%	7.0%
WEIGHT									
kg.	lb.								
40	88	2800	2400	2600	3150	2600	2200	2400	2800
45	99	3150	2700	2920	3370	2920	2470	2700	3150
50	110	3500	3000	3250	3750	3250	2750	3000	3500
55	121	3850	3300	3570	4120	3570	3020	3300	3850
60	132	4200	3600	3900	4500	3900	3300	3600	4200
65	143	4550	3900	4220	4870	4220	3570	3900	4550
70	154	4900	4200	4550	5220	4550	3850	4200	4900
75	165	5250	4500	4870	5620	4870	4120	4500	5250
80	176	5600	4800	5200	6000	5200	4400	4800	5600
85	187	5950	5100	5520	6380	5520	4670	5100	5950
90	198	6300	5400	5850	6740	5850	4950	5400	6300
95	209	6640	5700	6170	7120	6170	5220	5700	6640
100	220	7000	6000	6500	7500	6500	5500	6000	7000

5600 ml. and not 3600, 4500, 9000, or 14,000 ml. Faulty use of blood and plasma transfusion stems more frequently from lack of appreciation of normal blood volume values than from any other single consideration.

G. WHAT IS "ANEMIA"? WHAT IS "HEMOCONCENTRATION"? DEFINITION OF TERMS

"Anemia" is an almost indefinable term. It refers usually to a low erythrocyte concentration, but to some signifies a low blood volume. A working definition of this and other terms used here follows.

Oligemia: an acutely low blood volume. A synonymous term is "hypovolemia."

Oligemic shock: shock associated with a low blood volume, regardless of other factors in etiology or deterioration.

Anemia: a low concentration of red cells in the blood without reference to other concentration factors or volume.

Hypervolemia: a high blood volume. A synonymous term is "plethora."

Polycythemia: a high concentration of red cells without reference to cause, concentration factors, or volume.

Compensated Anemia: an acute or chronic

situation following blood loss, in which plasma volume expansion has restored the blood volume to or near normal with a low hematocrit.

Hemodilution: a lowering of concentration of some blood constituents due to the inflow of additional aqueous phase. Hemodilution may be of red cells, protein, or electrolyte, or all three, depending on the circumstances. The particular entity diluted should be specified. Most commonly the reference is to red cell dilution.

Hemoconcentration: strictly speaking, an increase in any fraction of the blood; water loss can cause hemoconcentration of protein, electrolyte, and cells. But as ordinarily used in this book, "hemoconcentration" signifies a rise in erythrocyte concentration (as measured by hemoglobin, red cell count, or hematocrit) because of loss of some or all of the fractions of the plasma phase. If the plasma loss is fractional (i.e., water loss with hypertonicity) the moiety lost must be specified for the term "hemoconcentration" to be specific.

Text continues on page 160.

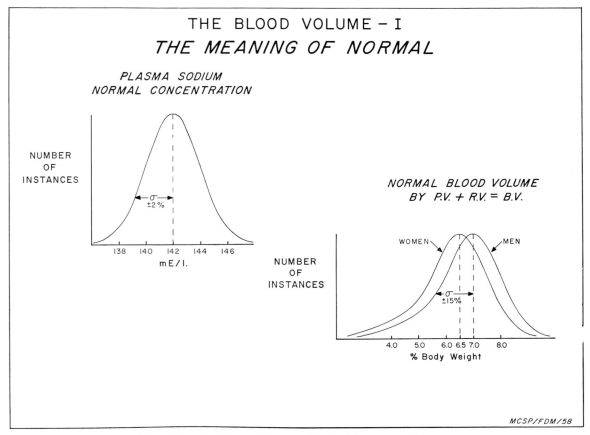

Figure 29. THE BLOOD VOLUME. I. THE MEANING OF NORMAL

It has been alleged that there is no such thing as a normal value for the blood volume. This is erroneous, as shown by blood volume data gathered in many laboratories in this country and abroad. These data permit characterization of the normal blood volume for the two sexes and various body builds. It is important to realize that in statistical terms this is a normal range with a mean, but with a standard deviation that is about 15 per cent of the mean (coefficient of variation) and with a long tail or skew distribution on the low side.

In this chart, above and to the left is shown the frequency distribution curve of the normal serum sodium concentration, as a basis for comparison. This remarkably constant biochemical parameter of the human body has a mean of about 142.5 mE./l. with a standard deviation that is less than 2 per cent of this mean. This is an example of a very "tight" frequency distribution curve.

By contrast, below and to the right are shown the approximate frequency distribution plots for the blood volumes in adult men and women. There is considerable overlap for values in the two sexes. Despite this variability it is possible to state the approximate normal predicted blood volume. The ranges outside this are due to variations in body build. Within this range blood volume therapy can be planned and accurately managed.

Errors in clinical blood volume therapy virtually never arise within the limits of tolerance imposed by these frequency distribution curves. The errors are made when the surgeon mistreats blood volume replacement by errors in the ± 50 per cent or ± 100 per cent range.

Thus, although the frequency distribution plots of normal blood volume data are not as tightly grouped as those of some other biologic parameters, they permit accurate therapy if properly appreciated. The normal blood volume in normally built adult men is 7.0 per cent body weight and in women 6.5 per cent body weight.

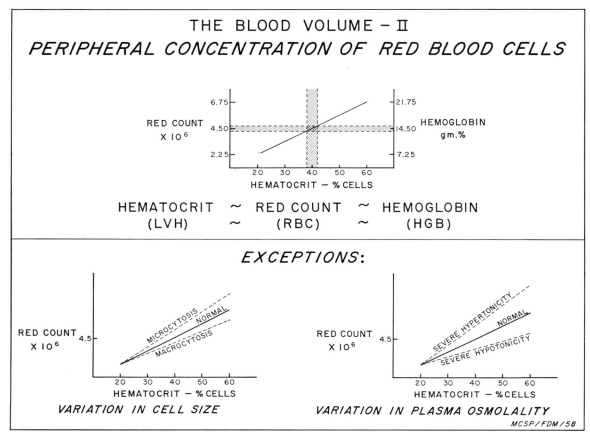

Figure 30.   THE BLOOD VOLUME. II. PERIPHERAL CONCENTRATION OF RED BLOOD CELLS

See facing page for detailed legend.

Figure 30. THE BLOOD VOLUME. II. PERIPHERAL CONCENTRATION OF RED BLOOD CELLS

The concentration of red blood cells in the peripheral blood can be measured by three techniques currently available: the red blood cell count, the hemoglobin concentration, and the hematocrit or spun cell volume. These three indices all measure fundamentally the same thing—namely, how many red cells there are per unit whole blood in the periphery. The hematocrit as used throughout this book refers to a simple centrifuged sedimentation of red blood cells, spun at approximately 3000 rpm until the meniscus is constant. This usually takes from 15 to 25 minutes, depending upon the sedimentation rate of the blood. This hematocrit we refer to as the "large vessel hematocrit" or, abbreviated, LVH.

The concentration of red blood cells in the peripheral blood is of great importance in the care of surgical patients, because it acts as an index of the relative expansion and contraction of the plasma volume over the short term, and of the activity of red blood cell regenerating powers over the long term, and, in certain circumstances, provides a loose index of volume changes of the blood.

It is important to emphasize that these three indices are all linear functions of each other in most acute surgical circumstances. This three-way linearity is grapically demonstrated in the upper chart. The shaded areas are normal ranges: the sloping line shows the usual range of varying values in disease. Below this is indicated the expression that the large vessel hematocrit is proportional to the red blood cell count which is in turn proportional to the hemoglobin concentration.

In the lower part of the chart are shown the two most common circumstances which do give rise to exceptions in this linear relationship. Neither of these circumstances is of particular importance in day-to-day surgical care, although they do enter into one's interpretation of the long-term hematocrit change resulting from hemorrhage or transfusion. *Variation in cell size* (of marrow origin) introduces a variation by which, as the cells grow larger, there are fewer cells (i.e., a lower red blood cell count) per unit spun hematocrit. Macrocytosis and microcytosis in various chronic anemias introduce this nonlinearity between the three indices.

To the right is shown the change produced by *sudden alteration in osmolality* as a cause of change in cell size. These latter data are taken from studies in our laboratory, and demonstrate that when the plasma changes from severely hypotonic (240 mO. per liter) to severely hypertonic (340 mO. per liter) there is produced a change in cell size which produces changes in the linear relationship. Such an extreme variation in osmolality changes a normal-range hematocrit only about 10 per cent of four points.

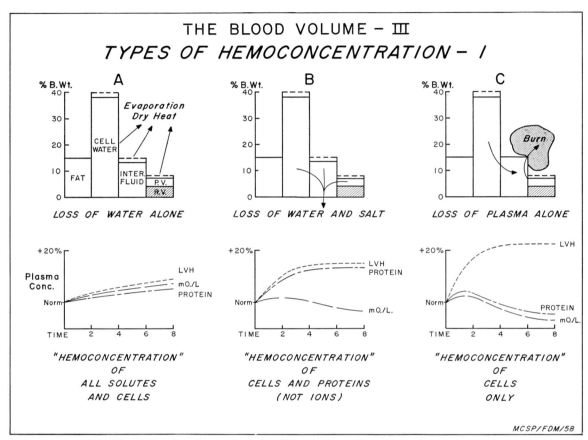

Figure 31. The Blood Volume. III. Types of Hemoconcentration. 1.

See facing page for detailed legend.

Figure 31. THE BLOOD VOLUME. III. TYPES OF HEMOCONCENTRATION. 1.

Increased concentrations of substances in the blood may be produced by three mechanisms and any one of these is referred to as "hemoconcentration." In this book we most commonly use the term "hemoconcentration" to refer to one of these, namely hemoconcentration involving an increase in the cellular fraction of blood as measured by hematocrit, red cell count, or hemoglobin concentration.

In this chart are shown the three distinct types of situation in which components of the blood may be found to be at increased concentration.

To the left (A) is shown the situation that exists with increased pulmonary water loss as an example of loss of pure water from the body, or desiccation-dehydration. It is seen that all the suspended and dissolved elements of the blood are concentrated slowly and proportionately (as shown in the graph below). The hematocrit rises and the concentration of electrolytes in the plasma rises (as measured by total osmolality, sodium concentration, or chloride concentration). The concentration of plasma protein also rises. The rise of these elements is neither very rapid nor very high. A rise of the LVH due to insensible pulmonary water loss and dehydration-desiccation to the extent of only 15 per cent (six points), for example, represents massive (about 6 liters) and potentially fatal loss of water from the body.

In the center (B) is shown the effect produced by loss of water and salt as in acute extracellular desalting water loss. Here the hemoconcentration involves the cells and the proteins but not the electrolytes. The salt concentration of the extracellular phase is not altered until new sodium-free water is added to the system, at which time it is diluted. This type of hemoconcentration occurs more rapidly and to higher levels than the hemoconcentration of desiccation-dehydration. Given a hematocrit level of 55 to 60 in acute desalting water loss, this also indicates a severe loss of water and salt from the body (about 5 liters in a normal-sized adult), but the contribution of cell water is, in the short term (under twelve hours), very small.

By contrast (C) are shown the events with loss of plasma alone. The classic example is the burn. Here the large vessel hematocrit rises very rapidly to very high levels whereas the protein and the total salt concentrations stay the same or fall after a transient rise. In this instance the increase in concentration of red blood cells indicates the loss primarily of plasma and it therefore rises rapidly to very high levels. A hematocrit level of, say, 55 in a burn indicates severe loss of plasma into the burned area (about 600 ml.) but it does not indicate as critical a situation as would the same hematocrit elevation resulting from pure water loss. Treatment is needed but the situation is not hazardous as it stands.

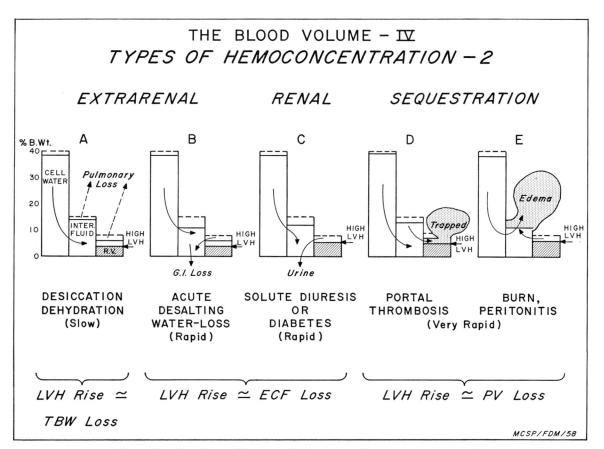

Figure 32. THE BLOOD VOLUME. IV. TYPES OF HEMOCONCENTRATION. 2.

See facing page for detailed legend.

Figure 32. The Blood Volume. IV. Types of Hemoconcentration. 2.

In this chart are shown five situations which represent elaboration of the data from the previous chart. Here are shown extrarenal, renal, and sequestration causes of hemoconcentration, using this term to mean increase in concentration of the red blood cells. Again we observe that there is a rate spectrum. Desiccation-dehydration is slow, acute desalting water loss is rapid, solute diuresis (as in diabetes) is rapid and the plasma loss of portal thrombosis, burns, or peritonitis is very rapid.

Below are indicated the bases for calculating the deficit produced by hemoconcentration. It will be noted that in the case of desiccation-dehydration the total body water lost may be estimated on the basis of the LVH rise. In the case of desalting water loss and rapid solute diuresis, the degree of LVH rise is proportional to the loss of extracellular fluid volume, whereas in the plasma-losing states the LVH rise is proportional to the plasma volume loss. These facts are responsible for the establishment of simple expressions for the calculation of static debt on the basis of LVH rise, described in the text.

The solute diuresis mechanism which is active in diabetes mellitus proceeds at a rate determined largely by the severity of the glycosuria. The loss is of mixed intra- and extracellular electrolyte and the rise in hematocrit produced represents a loss of total body water and salt. It is therefore of very ominous significance, particularly if acidosis is severe.

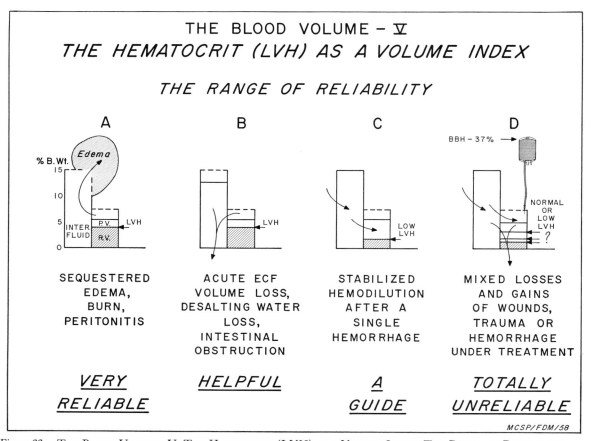

Figure 33.   THE BLOOD VOLUME. V. THE HEMATOCRIT (LVH) AS A VOLUME INDEX. THE RANGE OF RELIABILITY

See facing page for detailed legend.

Figure 33. THE BLOOD VOLUME. V. THE HEMATOCRIT (LVH) AS A VOLUME INDEX. THE RANGE OF RELIABILITY

The surgical patient indicates, by changes in his peripheral blood, alterations in the effective volume of cells, salts, or whole blood. None of these indices is simple to use and all require an understanding of the dynamics of body water. The hematocrit, for example, is an accurate index of volume needs *only under certain circumstances*, whereas under other circumstances it is wholly inaccurate and totally unreliable. It is the purpose of this chart to demonstrate the range of reliability of the large vessel hematocrit (LVH) in indicating volume changes in the patient.

To the left (A) is shown the situation with acute sequestered edema, as in a burn, peritonitis, or portal thrombosis. Here the LVH rise is an accurate index of the plasma volume lost. If one knows the patient's age, sex, and body build, the normal blood volume can be predicted. From this, assuming that the red cell volume is essentially unchanged (a justified assumption in early cases), one may estimate the plasma volume loss on the basis of the elevation of the hematocrit.

In B is shown the somewhat more confusing situation involved in acute extracellular volume loss. Here the rise in hematocrit can be used as an index of extracellular volume reduction. Its accuracy is variable, however, and depends largely upon the acuteness of the process. If a patient has had dysentery, ileostomy diarrhea, or intestinal obstruction (as example) for twelve to twenty-four hours and has an elevated hematocrit, this then becomes an accurate index of total extracellular volume lost. The volume lost may be based on the assumption that the extracellular fluid is 20 per cent of the body weight, and from the increase in hematocrit (and decrease in plasmacrit) one may estimate the volume lost with reasonable accuracy. But if this desalting process is slow and gradual, and there is maximum opportunity for the migration of water from within the cell and oxidation of fat, the hematocrit rise becomes less reliable as a volume index but nonetheless indicates a minimum figure for the static deficit.

In C is shown the situation of stabilized hemodilution after a single hemorrhage. If one could reliably count on hemodilution to a normal blood volume—the usual situation after 24 hours—this would be a quantitative guide to the volume *previously* lost and it would indicate the reexpansion of the plasma volume. Unfortunately, the completeness of transcapillary refilling is not wholly reliable, and for this reason we have adopted the "rule of 15 per cent" which assumes that in acute stabilized hemodilution after hemorrhage the volume is still 15 per cent low. This introduces a safety factor. As described in the text, the stabilized low hematocrit of hemodilution after a single venous hemorrhage may thus be used to estimate the blood volume lost previously.

Finally, at the right (D) is shown the situation, by far the commonest of the four, in which the hematocrit is totally unreliable as a volume index. This is the situation of continuing or intermittent hemorrhage, tissue trauma, or surgical operation, with or without sequestration of traumatic edema and with continuing replacement with banked blood transfusions, dextran, or plasma. In this condition, as long as the injury continues and replacement continues, the hematocrit tells one virtually nothing save the relative proportion of peripheral cells and plasma. If, during such an episode as this, the hematocrit suddenly starts to rise above 42 without additional therapy, one may confidently assume that selective plasma loss is occurring in some area. If, on stopping therapy, the hematocrit suddenly falls, one may confidently assume that blood loss and transcapillary refilling are continuing.

In this most complex situation, it is also important to recognize that the more bank blood is given, the closer the patient's hematocrit will approximate that of banked blood. Blood bank hematocrit (BBH) is 35 to 37 per cent cells, depending upon the nature of the diluent and the bank procedure locally. A patient who has lost his entire blood volume and has been retransfused two or three times will therefore inevitably show up with an hematocrit of about 35. This is the "indeterminate" hematocrit of the severely injured and transfused patient. Most patients in this category carry hematocrits in this range and such a hematocrit is meaningless with respect to the effect of circulating blood volume. It may coexist with severe volume restriction, a normal volume, or a dangerously high overtransfused volume.

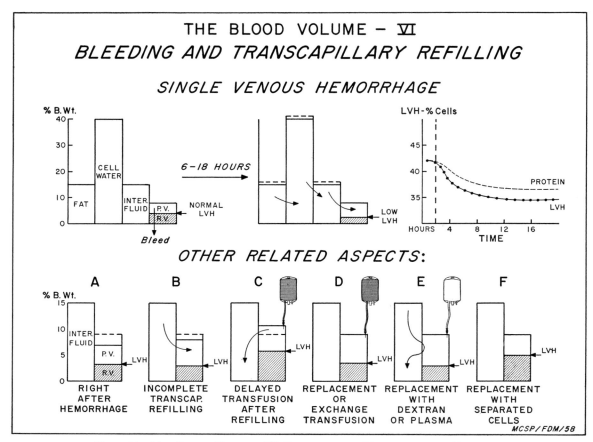

Figure 34. The Blood Volume. VI. Bleeding and Transcapillary Refilling

See facing page for detailed legend.

Figure 34. THE BLOOD VOLUME. VI. BLEEDING AND TRANSCAPILLARY REFILLING

In this chart are shown some of the factors involved in the transcapillary movement of water, salt, and protein that is responsible for refilling of the plasma volume after hemorrhage.

Above are shown in some detail the events that transpire after a single venous hemorrhage of 20 per cent of the blood volume. Over the course of six to eighteen hours, interstitial fluid moves into the plasma volume, cell water moves into the interstitial fluid and, if the patient has nothing to eat, fat oxidation proceeds at the rate of about 250 gm. per day (depending upon the severity of trauma, running as high as 500 gm. per day), also contributing water to the system.

The result is the transcapillary movement of water into the plasma volume. This water, while not wholly free of protein, is low in protein so that as the hematocrit falls, the protein concentration also falls but not quite as much as the concentration of red blood cells. These events are shown in the chart to the right.

This sequence is the fundamental dynamic alteration in the distribution of body water that occurs after hemorrhage. The kidney at the same time conserves water and salt. Below are shown a series of six variations on this theme which may occur under various circumstances.

At the left (A) is shown the situation immediately after the hemorrhage. At this time, prior to the onset of transcapillary refilling, the hematocrit is quite normal despite perilously low volume.

Next (B) is shown the situation should transcapillary refilling be incomplete. As noted in the previous chart, we assume that in the acute stabilized hemodilution the transcapillary refilling is 15 per cent shy of restoring a normal total blood volume. This provides a "safety factor" in calculating previous blood loss on the basis of a stabilized, hemodiluted hematocrit.

In C is shown the situation that obtains if transcapillary refilling of the blood volume is permitted to reach completeness, following which large blood transfusions are given. This is the situation of delayed or procrastinated blood transfusion. A marked hypervolemia is produced if the full volume of previously shed blood is now added to a fully hemodiluted system. This can be dangerous in elderly people or in individuals with heart failure. The hypervolemia is disposed of only slowly by plasma dispersal (see Figure 35). This mechanism takes time and when it is complete, the hematocrit is left high.

In D is shown the situation which occurs if the entire blood volume is bled out and retransfused with blood bank blood. Here, as indicated in the previous chart, the hematocrit stabilizes at about 35 to 37, this being the hematocrit of blood bank blood.

In E is shown the situation that obtains if lost blood is replaced by dextran or plasma. It will be observed that transcapillary refilling of the blood volume no longer has to take place, this being taken care of by the infused material, but a very low hematocrit is the result. If dextran and plasma therapy is pursued over a long period of time with continuing hemorrhage, the hematocrit of course will fall to values as low as 5 to 10. It is generally agreed that a hematocrit below 20 imposes a distinct deficit in terms of peripheral oxygen-carrying capacity; the use of more than 1500 ml. of dextran in any one 24-hour period is apt to be followed by bleeding defects.

Finally, in F is shown the situation that obtains if a single hemorrhage is replaced with separated blood cells. Such preparations carry a hematocrit of about 80 per cent. Here the hematocrit of the patient is raised to an extent that is a function of the amount of blood lost and the amount of separated cells infused.

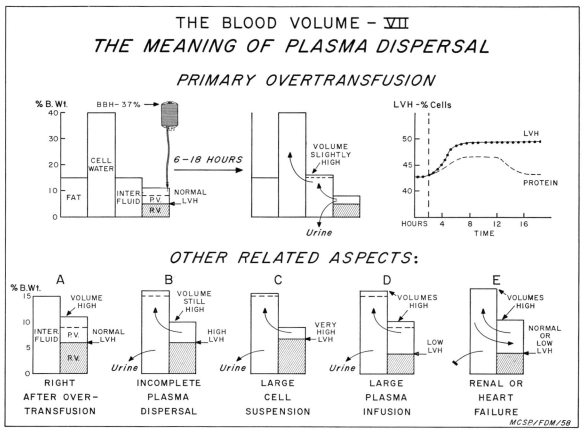

Figure 35. THE BLOOD VOLUME. VII. THE MEANING OF PLASMA DISPERSAL

See facing page for detailed legend.

Figure 35. THE BLOOD VOLUME. VII. THE MEANING OF PLASMA DISPERSAL

In this chart are shown some of the events related to the dispersal of plasma from the plasma volume in hypervolemic states. In many ways, this chart is the exact inverse of the previous chart on blood loss.

Above are shown the events that occur in primary overtransfusion, as the classic example of simple hypervolemia. Clinically this occurs when an operation is attended by excessive blood transfusion. In our experience, this is most prone to occur in those operations where some member of the staff has considered a certain amount of blood as "routinely" employed for an operation and gives this amount of blood without reference to the actual amount of blood lost.

In any event, the situation immediately after this overtransfusion is that of hypervolemia. Such hypervolemia is dangerous if the patient has heart, lung, or liver disease. Then, over a period of six to eighteen hours, the body goes to work on the excess, and plasma dispersal takes place. This takes the form of the increased urinary excretion of water and salt, the distribution of the extra water throughout the total body water, and the metabolic degradation of the protein. This latter is the slowest to occur. The cells are not disposed of at all, save by the expiration of their own natural biologic lifetime and by the inhibition of marrow activity.

The result, shown in the chart at the right, is that after overtransfusion there is a gradual rise in the hematocrit, reaching a stabilized value as plasma dispersal is completed. There is an increase in protein concentration which is not as well maintained, as this protein is degraded in the metabolic mill. Below are shown five situations which represent variations on this theme.

To the left, at A, is shown the situation immediately after overtransfusion where the uncorrected hypervolemia is present. The hematocrit is not remarkable.

In B is shown the situation that obtains when plasma dispersal is not complete. In individuals with heart failure or with disease of liver and kidneys, this is virtually inevitable because such patients carry a high plasma volume normally and seem to be unable to restore their blood volume and extracellular fluid volume downward to normal. While the mechanism of this is unknown, it seems to relate to inhibited urinary excretion of water and salt. Whatever the mechanism, the net result is incomplete plasma dispersal. If a cardiac patient is overtransfused, one cannot rely on normal mechanism to get rid of the overtransfusion and venesection is indicated if venous pressure is high.

In C is shown the situation which obtains if a very large cell suspension is given. Hypervolemia is produced and the cells cannot be disposed of save by the expiration of their natural lifetime; therefore the only mechanism that the body has for restoration of this volume toward normal is that of plasma dispersal. The result is a normal blood volume with a very high hematocrit.

In D is shown the situation that obtains when a large plasma infusion is given. The hematocrit is lowered. If the volume produced is above "normal," plasma dispersal then occurs. Renal mechanisms are called into play and over a period of hours or days the hematocrit gradually rises to normal again as plasma dispersal occurs.

Finally, in E is shown the situation which occurs in the presence of renal or heart failure. A similar change has sometimes been seen in liver disease and chronic pulmonary disease. Here, as mentioned previously, the mechanisms for plasma dispersal are dampened, either because of poor metabolism of protein (liver disease) or because of inadequate renal excretion of water and salt (heart disease and kidney disease). Plasma dispersal is incomplete, hypervolemia is maintained, and the situation is potentially dangerous for the patient.

H. THE PERIPHERAL CONCENTRATION OF RED CELLS: HEMATOCRIT, RED CELL COUNT, AND HEMOGLOBIN MEASUREMENTS

It is a valid clinical simplification to consider that the erythrocyte count, the hemoglobin concentration, and the hematocrit are all linear functions of each other in most acute surgical situations. Any one of the three may be determined clinically and may be considered as changing as a direct function of any of the others. A burned patient's therapy can be managed equally well if one is guided by his hemoglobin concentration, his red blood cell count, or his hematocrit. Whether the blood, taken by venipuncture, is spun down in a centrifuge (hematocrit), hemolyzed and read in a colorimeter (hemoglobin assay), or smeared out on a hemocytometer (red blood cell count), one is measuring the same thing: the concentration of erythrocytes in peripheral venous blood. The same three may be measured on microsamples from finger or ear lobe.*

The above statement is so generally true and so widely significant in surgical care that it seems a carping detraction to mention the exceptions. There are two, however, and they should be brought out, as they may play an important role in isolated surgical cases.

The *first exception* relates to the effect of plasma osmolality changes on red cell size. The normal plasma osmolality is 285 to 295 mO. per l. Were the effective plasma osmolality to rise from 290 to 330, the cells would shrink. Were the hematocrit of that tube to be 45 per cent cells at the start of such a change (290 mO. per l.) it would be about 42 per cent at the end (330 mO. per l.) with no change in the number of cells per unit volume whole blood or in the hemoglobin concentration per unit whole blood.

Large changes in osmolality thus produce small but measurable changes in hematocrit without commensurate change in hemoglobin concentration or red cell count, and thus the ordinarily linear relation of the three is distorted. Sudden swings of osmolality of this magnitude are very rare but do account for occasional anomalies, particularly of the hematocrit response to transfusion in very ill patients.

As a *second exception* to the linearity of erythrocyte indices, in microcytic and macrocytic anemias there may be important loss of linearity among the three indices, as evident in expression of the mean corpuscular volume and hemoglobin concentration. These distortions do not develop acutely and in surgical practice do not interfere with the usefulness of the hematocrit, red count, or hemoglobin in following the plasma volume: erythrocyte volume relationship, particularly in compensated whole blood loss and plasma loss.

The hematocrit (LVH) or spun cell volume is becoming progressively more widely used as the simplest measure of the peripheral concentration of red cells. It is a measure which has some faults and failings. It is a measure of concentration, not total volume, but as will become evident in the next section, there are many situations where it is a reliable guide to the intravascular volume (as is also the red corpuscle count or hemoglobin measurement). In many other situations it is less useful as a volume guide. But in either event its proper use depends on an understanding of its nature and limitations.

For accuracy of hematocrit any blood sample should be spun in the centrifuge until constant. No reasonable figure for revolutions per minute or time will always work. A short respin after the first reading will assure constancy. Errors in sampling produce false low hematocrits; errors in clotting or spinning produce false high hematocrits.

I. THE DISTRIBUTION OF THE BLOOD VOLUME

The distribution of the blood volume within the body is a matter of prime importance in the treatment of trauma, injury, and surgical shock. Although the capillary bed represents the area in which the red cell gives up its oxygen and takes on carbon dioxide, and the area in which water, elec-

---

* If there is stasis of the circulation, as is the case in shock and burns, peripheral values from finger puncture may be unreliable; in finger-puncture blood the hematocrit is slightly lower and the plasma potassium concentration slightly higher than in venous blood.

trolyte, crystalloids, and proteins leave the plasma and exchange across the capillary, it is actually rather small. Estimates based on tracer techniques identify the capillary bed as being approximately 15 per cent of the blood volume. The heart, aorta, vena cava, and the great vessels of the central circulatory bed are tremendous reservoirs containing very large volumes of blood, moving relatively slowly. Somewhere around 70 to 75 per cent of the body's total blood volume is contained in these vessels. The remainder is in transit through the smaller branches that connect the terminal major vessels to the capillary bed.

Although the normal periphery (the capillary bed) is rather small, there seem to be situations in which it can suddenly become greatly enlarged. These situations are divided into three types.

First are those where there is direct injury to the capillary bed, the commonest classic example being a burn. Here there is an accumulation of plasma, water, and red cells in the burned area due to opening up of some capillaries, injury to others, and peripheral stasis. A crush injury or spreading infection, peritonitis, or intestinal obstruction accomplishes the same result in the immediate area of the disease.

Second are those situations where there is obstruction to flow. Venous obstruction to the return from a limb or from the mesenteric vessels produces an increase in the amount of blood in that local area. Whether this blood is in large veins, small veins, or capillaries is for the moment immaterial; it is trapped in that area and represents an expansion of the "periphery" which robs the central circulation of its pressure-supporting mass, producing hypotensive shock.

The third group in which the periphery enlarges are those rare instances of late shock or severe injury where the "appetite" of the vascular bed for blood seems to be expanded. This change has been referred to as an increase in capacity of the vascular bed, and further on is dealt with in detail as the "clinical phenomenon of taking up." It may consist in an opening up of capillary channels that were previously not available, in relaxation of arterioles, in the establishment of arteriovenous shunts over a wide area of muscle after severe injury and shock, or in the accumulation of closely packed red cells (sludging, agglutination) in such areas as the liver or splanchnic bed. Under such circumstances increased avidity or capacity does indeed occur, as evidenced by the fact that a blood volume above normal is required to restore pressure in the arterial tree.

CHAPTER 8

Acute Hemorrhage without Shock

Section I.   The Effects of a Small Venous Hemorrhage (Loss of 10 to 15 Per Cent of the Blood Volume)

A venous hemorrhage of 10 to 15 per cent of the normal blood volume produces easily discernible hematologic effects, the understanding of which is basic to the care of all hemorrhage. There are also minor hemodynamic, metabolic, and renal effects.

A. DEFINITION

In a 70 kg. normal male with a blood volume at 7 per cent of body weight the total volume is about 4900 ml. Such a hemorrhage (10 to 15 per cent of the blood volume) is therefore the loss of 490 to 735 ml. In a short (40 kg.) female with a blood volume of 6.0 per cent of body weight, or 2400 ml., this is a loss of 240 to 360 ml.

B. HEMATOLOGIC EFFECTS

The hematologic effects are:
(1) initially, no change in the hematocrit;
(2) a gradual hemodilution by transcapillary refilling of the plasma volume, occupying a duration of eight to twenty-four hours, and producing
(3) a stabilized secondary anemia, the fully hemodiluted volume of compensated hemorrhage. This is followed by
(4) gradual hematopoietic restoration of the red blood cell volume.

1. Hemodilution

Immediately after the brisk bleeding, the hematocrit (or the hemoglobin concentration or the erythrocyte count, whichever is measured) is quite normal. Whole blood has been removed, and this mixture has contained plasma and red blood cells in the same proportion in which they exist in the blood stream. Therefore, right after bleeding, these concentrations are not altered. In order to alter these relative concentrations, something new that is free of cells must be added to the blood stream. The "something new" that is added after hemorrhage is the inflow of water, salt, crystalloids, and proteins from the interstitial space to the plasma volume.

This hemodilution takes time, and it results in the anemia or lowered erythrocyte concentration that follows hemorrhage. The time course of hematocrit change after a single, non–shock-producing hemorrhage is a very accurate reflection of the rate at which transcapillary passage of water, protein, and solutes can accomplish the filling of the plasma volume.

In a multicameral system containing permeable membranes, there is a rapid equalization of level and hydrostatic pressure after fluid is removed from one chamber. The restoration of fluid to the plasma volume after hemorrhage resembles this type of redistribution. More subtle forces are probably at work, including first a slight lowering of hydrostatic pressure in the distal capillary beyond the point where the arteriole is constricted, permitting some fluid ingress even if systolic pressure in the arterial tree is not lowered, and second, the action of endocrine forces sensitive to change in effective volume.

2. Volume Regulation and Hemodilution

After a hemorrhage, there occur endocrine and metabolic changes whose effect is the conservation of extracellular water and salt, and transcapillary refilling of the blood volume. The central mechanism appears to arise from stimulation of some area (brain? right heart?) sensitive to some parameter of volume, pressure, flow, or oxygenation. This mechanism then acts in the periphery by affecting resorption of sodium and water by the renal tubular epithelium. The chief mediators from the central stimulus to the end organ are antidiuretic hormone and aldosterone. In more severe blood loss the secretion of catechol amines is also stimulated by volume reduction. This volume-conserving mechanism is importantly involved in hemodilution, since it saves for the body the substances whose transcapillary movement tends to refill the plasma volume. Furthermore, water from cells is added to the extracellular fluid and the hemodiluting fluid.

The response to a single small venous hemorrhage is thus one of the classic evidences for the existence of mechanisms for volume regulation.

3. The Nature of the Hemodiluting Fluid

When systolic blood pressure is lowered, the ingress of fluid into the plasma volume is hastened by the resultant imbalance between tissue pressure and capillary pressure. If capillary pressure and tissue flow are further decreased to a critical level, as in shock, transcapillary refilling finally ceases because circulation is failing.

The interstitial space contains salt and water in about the same concentrations as are found in the plasma; correction for the Gibbs-Donnan effect is of practically no importance in the body as a whole because there are large areas of interstitial fluid (such as the liver lymph, lung lymph, cardiac lymph, and mesenteric lymph) in which the albumin concentration is almost the same as it is in the plasma.

Although it is in salt-equilibrium with plasma, the interstitial fluid is relatively protein-poor; as regards red cells it is absolutely poverty-stricken, since it has none. The protein concentration varies, ranging from the aforementioned areas, in which the albumin concentration is as high as 5 per cent, to the peripheral lymph, where it is less than 1 per cent. As posthemorrhage hemodilution occurs, therefore, the erythrocyte concentration falls abruptly, the protein concentration falls somewhat more slowly; potassium is called forth from cells and is excreted.

The time required for the hematocrit again to reach stability at its new lower level after a single, small, non–shock-producing hemorrhage is remarkably variable. We have been unable to determine any single factor that can be relied upon to predict this rate. In some healthy young men hemodilution will have been completed in six hours and in others twelve to eighteen hours will be required.

The tendency of the body is to restore the blood volume toward normal by this hemodilution. With hemorrhage of this size (and even somewhat larger), starting with normal hydration and with kidneys that can respond normally by reduction in the excretion of water and salt, the plasma volume is finally brought to a value distinctly higher than normal, with the result that the blood volume has been returned to normal.

4. The Fully Hemodiluted State: Its Meaning

Under conditions of restored hemostasis and homeostasis, with stable hemodilution, after a single brisk hemorrhage of about 10 to 15 per cent of blood volume, the absolute change in hematocrit is proportional to the amount of blood lost and is a useful guide in treatment. It should not be neglected merely because it is not absolutely precise.

As will be made clear below, the hematocrit is totally misleading as a guide to treatment when kidney, heart, or liver disease is present or when the acute loss involves tissue trauma, multiple bleedings, or mixed replacement, all of which are very common. Despite these exceptions and variations, we have here an important first principle: a stabilized low hematocrit after hemorrhage indicates a compensated plasma volume and a blood volume that has been restored toward normal. The hematocrit change is an index of the magnitude of the initial blood loss and of the degree of transcapillary refilling.

There can be derived for this relationship an expression that is useful in mental arithmetic for the care of the patient. This figure for blood loss, so derived, is a minimal figure since any further transcapillary refilling of the plasma volume will further increase the calculated loss. At the risk of repetition, it must be re-emphasized that massive hemorrhage can occur with no immediate change in hematocrit; the hemodiluted state which lowers the hematocrit requires the passage of time.

The following expression is therefore valid only when that time has passed, hemodilution has been brought to completion, and hemorrhage has ceased.

Where

BV_1 = estimated normal blood volume for this patient
BV_2 = blood volume after hemorrhage and hemodilution
BVL = blood lost at bleeding
LVH_1 = normal hematocrit for the patient
LVH_2 = observed hematocrit after hemorrhage

Then

$$BVL = BV_1 \times \frac{(LVH_1 - LVH_2)}{LVH_i}$$

The above equation merely states that in the fully hemodiluted posthemorrhage state the change in hematocrit is proportional to the amount of blood lost; this relation does not obtain in massive or chronic hemorrhage, in which instance hemodilution is not complete. This expression is based on complete plasma volume refilling and therefore represents a minimum figure for loss.

Example:

An 80 kg. man, athletically built (blood volume equal to 7.5 per cent of body weight), has a melena with hematemesis from ulcer. The next day all signs of bleeding have ceased. He has a hematocrit of 35.

Here

BV_1 = 0.075 × 80 kg. = 6000 ml.
LVH_1 = 44
LVH_2 = 35

Then

$$BVL = 6000 \times \frac{(44 - 35)}{44} = 1230 \text{ ml.}$$

A *minimum* figure for the initial hemorrhage was therefore 1200 ml., or about 20 per cent of the normal starting blood volume. Any further hemodilution will only enlarge the figure for former blood loss, derived from this calculation.

When or whether this much blood should be given back to the patient rests on judgment based on the balance of other clinical data; it is not indicated by this calculation. If the situation requires blood replacement then or later, *this calculation merely states a minimum figure for the previous losses; it is not a transfusion budget.*

The sudden replacement of all the loss, when stabilized hemodilution has occurred, will produce a temporary plethora. In our example, a hypervolemia of about 1000 ml. would be produced by sudden replacement, before plasma dispersal could occur. In a young person, this should do no harm. In elderly people or those with disease of heart, liver, lungs, or kidneys, such hypervolemia is dangerous. Therefore, in elderly or chronically ill patients, there should be caution in blood replacement in the face of a stable hemodiluted posthemorrhagic state when blood pressure is normal.

C. HEMODYNAMIC, RENAL, AND CARDIAC EFFECTS

Following brisk venous hemorrhage in the range of 10 to 15 per cent of the blood volume, few effects are easily seen. There are:
(1) minimal change in pulse or blood pressure,
(2) minor change in glomerular filtration rate, minor decrease in urine flow depending on intake, and
(3) slight peripheral vasoconstriction.

If such things as apprehension and pain are not a part of the picture, there is scarcely any change in the pulse rate. It may actually fall. Syncope, rather than vasoconstricted hypotension, may result. There is a slight increase in the diastolic pressure in most cases, interpreted as vasoconstriction and increased peripheral resistance, the purpose of which is considered to be the maintenance of arterial pressure under conditions of diminished blood volume. None of these changes is striking. If one is dealing with acute blood loss of unknown amount and if there are few hemodynamic effects, it is reasonable to assume that the blood loss is less than 15 per cent of the blood volume. If any hemodynamic effects are present (such as fall in pressure, rise in pulse) a loss of 25 per cent of blood volume should be assumed.

If the hemorrhage were from an open large artery it would—even at this small volume—produce a sudden fall in systolic pressure while the artery was open. Hemodynamic and renal effects would be more marked, hemodilutional and metabolic effects about the same as the venous loss.

The renal effects of a venous hemorrhage of this magnitude are reflected principally in the transport of water and salt. Glomerular filtration rate appears to be unaffected, yet there is a decrease in water excretion, a diminution of urine flow with the increased resorption of sodium, and an increased excretion of potassium. This pattern suggests endocrine (antidiuretic, aldosterone) rather than vascular (vasoconstrictor) effects on the kidney.

D. METABOLIC AND ELECTROLYTE EFFECTS

The metabolic effects of a hemorrhage of 10 to 15 per cent of the total blood volume are:

(1) decreased renal free water clearance (the so-called "ADH effect"),
(2) decreased renal sodium and increased potassium excretion ("aldosterone effect"), and
(3) little detectable change in 17-hydroxycorticoid secretion.

The metabolic and electrolyte effects of such a hemorrhage are not striking, but they indicate a widespread homeostatic adjustment. The decreased renal excretion of water and sodium may be followed by a subsequent period of positive balance of water and sodium. The positive sodium balance lasts for two or three days, depending upon the intake. There is a transient increase in potassium excretion. Blood steroids, urine steroids, and blood eosinophils often remain essentially normal through such a hemorrhage. Any effect on nitrogen balance is so small as to escape measurement by ordinary methods. The effect on potassium excretion is immediate and consists in an increase in the absolute potassium excretion rate, the relative potassium excretion rate (by which we mean the percentage of total urine electrolyte occupied by potassium), and a decrease in the urine sodium:potassium ratio. The expected change in aldosterone secretion has been demonstrated.

E. TREATMENT

The most important aspect of treatment in hemorrhage of this small magnitude is the question of whether or not it should be treated (that is, transfused) at all. Certainly it is inadvisable to do so during operation if homeostasis, tissue perfusion, and circulatory dynamics are normal and well-maintained. An example of such loss when replacement under anesthesia is inadvisable is to be found in the course of an uneventful abdominal operation.

In an adult weighing 50 kg. or more this is blood loss carrying in itself so little hazard that the dangers of transfusion, however slight, contraindicate it under anesthesia when a severe incompatibility reaction may be masked.

If the loss of 300 to 500 ml. of blood is a part of a clinical situation in which further loss may be rightfully expected, then replacement is of course essential. Other than this special example (in early operative blood loss or bleeding ulcer) it is rarely advisable to give an elective transfusion of a single unit (500 ml.) of blood. Most certainly is this true if the patient is anesthetized.

Section II. The Effects of a Moderate Venous Hemorrhage (Loss of 20 to 30 Per Cent of the Blood Volume) without Shock

A hemorrhage of 20 to 30 per cent of the blood volume produces major hematologic, hemodynamic, renal, endocrine, and metabolic effects; these can occur without shock.

A. DEFINITION

The exact definition of such a hemorrhage as is indicated in the title of this section is to some extent dependent upon what one calls shock. We are discussing here the acute loss of approximately 1000 to 1500 ml. of blood in a 70 kg. lean male, 20 to 30 per cent of the normal blood volume of 7.0 per cent of body weight, or 4900 ml., and the effects when that blood is suddenly removed from the venous side of the vascular tree, again bearing in mind the fact that sudden loss of such an amount from an open large artery would produce a very low blood pressure during the period of acute loss, because of the almost complete loss of peripheral resistance.

This is the type of hemorrhage seen in surgical operations that result in unexpectedly large blood loss. This is major hemorrhage, which, if continued, endangers the patient's life, but which in itself does not produce shock. The rate of loss is critical in the nature of the response; the slower the loss, the more easily it is borne by the body. If this loss is spaced out over a long period of time, the effects are quite different from those mentioned here. If rapid and continuing, it progresses on to shock.

B. HEMATOLOGIC EFFECTS

The hematologic effects are four.

(1) Initially, there is no change in the hematocrit.

(2) A gradual hemodilution takes place during twenty-four to thirty-six hours. It cannot restore blood volume to normal.

(3) A stabilized secondary anemia occurs, with a volume about 15 per cent lower than normal.

(4) Gradual hematopoietic restoration of volume takes place through the elaboration of red cells (in the marrow) and the synthesis of albumin (in the liver).

1. Hemodilution

The hematologic response to this type of hemorrhage represents nicely the balance that determines survival in untreated hemorrhage. If compensatory mechanisms (tachycardia with increased cardiac output, vasoconstriction) are adequate, blood pressure and circulation are maintained long enough to permit hemodilution to occur. As this occurs, the plasma volume is gradually increased by transcapillary refilling, the hematocrit falls, and the blood volume is returned in the direction of normal. Unlike the situation in a small hemorrhage, where a stabilized hemodiluted anemia means a nearly normal blood volume, the compensation to a hemorrhage of this magnitude usually fails to restore the blood volume to normal. The body is evidently incapable of moving that much fluid across the capillary without producing hypoproteinemia to such a degree that it then fails to hold water and electrolyte on the plasma side of the capillary. The progressively hemodiluted intravascular mass presents progressively less resistance to flow as cells are diluted below a hematocrit of 30.

Despite these limitations, the transcapillary hemodilution that occurs starts sooner and is much more abrupt than with a small hemorrhage. It may similarly take a long time (twelve to twenty-four hours) to reach completion. When it reaches completion, the circulation has been restored sufficiently to yield a blood pressure in the neighborhood of 100 to 110 mm. Hg, but the patient is still sick, he feels ill, he may be febrile, there is pallor and persistent tachycardia, continued evidence of increased endocrine and autonomic activity as well as increased peripheral vascular resistance. This must have been the characteristic postoperative picture in the first day or so after operation during many centuries of surgery, when almost any major operation was associated with a hemorrhage of this magnitude (whether or not infection subsequently occurred) and transfusion was unknown. Still today, uncompensated reduction of volume is a most potent primary underlying stimulus to endocrine and metabolic change after surgical injury.

Estimation of approximate former loss from the lowered hematocrit is the same as that discussed above, save for the fact the blood volume is not restored by the initial hemodilution. The calculation is meaningless if hemorrhage and transfusion are continuing. The greater the hemorrhage the less complete is the compensatory transcapillary refilling of the plasma volume. The calculation of the blood volume deficit therefore represents a minimal figure; more blood was lost than is now shown by hemodilution of red cells and any further hemodilution will raise the figure for former loss.

2. Effects of Aging and Disease

Visceral diseases (the most important of which are cardiovascular and renal disease) reduce the ability of the individual to compensate for hemorrhage. Compensation depends on adaptability of cardiac output, vascular resilience with increased peripheral resistance, and flexibility in performance of the renal tubule. Cardiovascular-renal disease, especially common in the aged, interferes with these responses. As the average age of surgical patients gradually increases in civilian practice, one encounters more patients who cannot compensate for hemorrhage of this magnitude. A normal, healthy young person compensates effectively.

In older people, restrictions on renal tubular function diminish the extent to which the kidney can conserve salt and water, a mechanism essential to normal hemodilution. Inadequate elasticity of vessels, diminished coronary flow, and, of course, any degree of congestive heart failure, liver failure, or renal failure will hamper the ability of the organism to compensate for hemorrhage.

Dehydration or desalting water loss limits the rate of transcapillary refilling of the blood vessels in any age group.

C. HEMODYNAMIC, RENAL, AND CARDIAC EFFECTS

Following brisk venous hemorrhage of 20 to 30 per cent of blood volume the following are seen:

(1) hypotension, tachycardia, and vasoconstriction;

(2) oliguria.

1. Hemodynamic Effects

The hemodynamic effects of this hemorrhage are obvious. A rise in pulse rate is universally produced except in those occasional situations where the sudden loss of blood produces syncope. This occurrence in clinical surgery is not uncommon in the immediate instance (ruptured ectopic pregnancy, for instance). Arousal from syncope is followed by the other changes.

A rise in pulse rate and a rise in diastolic pressure with a narrowed pulse pressure are the characteristic hemodynamic changes here, and they are associated with peripheral vasoconstriction, decrease in blanching reflexes to skin pressure, and some increase in sweating. Whether or not the systolic blood pressure falls in this hemorrhage depends on the precise balance between cardiac output and compensatory hemodynamic and hematologic changes. If 20 to 30 per cent of the blood volume is lost acutely from a vein, there is usually a reduction in systolic pressure to the level of approximately 80 mm. Hg.

The position of the patient makes a difference in the pressure change seen in this hemorrhage. If he is in the erect posture there is an immediate drop (with syncope) to very low levels. In the supine position there is less fall.

This change in pressure is of key importance in assessing the blood loss in the initial examination of a patient who is in early hemorrhagic hypotension. If hemodynamic changes (hypotension) are of this order of magnitude, one can assume that the amount of blood loss is at least 20 to 30 per cent of the blood volume. Immediate blood replacement must be undertaken to restore this volume regardless of the observed hematocrit.

This is an excellent example of the usefulness of blood volume information. During or after hemorrhage, for example, in a well-built, big, 80 kg. man, hemodynamic effects of this magnitude (hypotension, tachycardia) require the immediate infusion of 1200 to 1800 ml. of blood. Nothing short of this should be considered adequate; a single unit (500 ml.) of blood will have little effect.

The mental arithmetic:

> 80 kg. lean male, athletic build
> BV = 7.5% B.Wt.
> 80 kg. × 0.075 = 6000 ml.
> Acute hemorrhage with hemodynamic effects but not deep shock = 20 to 30% BV
> 0.20 to 0.30 × 6000 = 1200 to 1800 ml.

If homeostatic regulations fail, hemorrhage persists, or other components enter the scene and the blood pressure drops to persistent low values, there is then a persistent deficiency of peripheral flow. This is hemorrhagic shock, and this persistent deficiency of flow produces anoxia of vital organs and ultimately leads to death. Short of this lethal sequence, a lesser deficiency of flow may persist for many hours or even days and its most marked immediate result is that urine output is low and hemodilution is delayed because normal hemodilution requires good peripheral flow.

Here is a vicious circle; as hemorrhage progresses, flow decreases, transcapillary movement of water, protein, and electrolyte decreases, and those very mechanisms destined to restore the blood volume (and therefore the circulation) to normal are inhibited as to rate and volume.

2. Renal Effects: The Relation of Renal Blood Flow to Urine Output in Acute Volume Reduction

The renal effects of a hemorrhage of this size (20 to 30 per cent of the blood volume) are both quantitatively and qualitatively different from those of the small hemorrhage. There are readily demonstrable alterations in renal blood flow: a decreased glomerular filtration rate with efferent arteriolar vasoconstriction and an increased filtration fraction.

Whatever endocrine or biochemical forces are brought to bear on the renal tubule, they are quite ineffective unless there is a normal volume of glomerular filtrate to be processed by these cells. When glomerular filtration rate is reduced, all kidney functions that depend on processing the filtrate are diminished accordingly.

In hemorrhage of this size, one sees a diminution in renal blood flow out of proportion to the vasoconstriction in the rest of the body. This phenomenon was first studied by Cournand *et al.* (1943) and was termed "differential renal vasoconstriction." Understanding it is of central importance in managing patients who are in or near shock due to such causes as hemorrhage, wounds, peritonitis, or burns. There is no evidence, in man, for the opening of juxtamedullary renal shunts in this type of situation.

This differential renal vasoconstriction consists in the restriction of the caliber of the blood vessels in the kidney so that less glomerular filtrate is formed. Such filtrate as is formed is then processed by a tubule that is strongly under the influence of steroids and antidiuretic hormone.* Water resorption is increased and sodium excretion diminished both in absolute and relative terms. Potassium excretion is increased. Since the amount of filtrate formed is very small, the significance of these latter changes is minor.

If differential renal vasoconstriction is pronounced and systolic blood pressure falls to levels below 80 mm. Hg for any length of time (over five minutes), glomerular filtration falls to very low levels and the formation of urine may, to all intents and purposes, cease. The differentiation between a "beneficial" reduction in the loss of water from the body and a death-dealing renal anoxia with failure to excrete intracellular products (heme, potassium) is determined by the duration of this response and the structural changes that ensue in the kidney parenchyma. In this situation, then, urine output is a measure of

---

* It is important to emphasize that the operation of maximal steroid (aldosterone) and antidiuretic hormone (ADH) forces on a large volume of tubular urine does *not* result in oliguria. They are compatible with urine flow up to 1000 to 1500 ml. per day; only when glomerular filtration rate is also reduced does oliguria result from the maximum operation of these endocrine forces.

renal blood flow. It is renal anoxia (not oliguria) that produces renal cell disease.

For short periods of time, complete loss of renal perfusion and urine flow is not deleterious to the organism providing certain other threatening changes (chiefly pigment excretion) do not occur; the transient renal anoxia and oliguria of acute hemorrhage is undesirable because it threatens tubular necrosis; short of this it is entirely reversible.

The prevention of serious damage rests on prompt restoration of volume:flow relationships. Because differential renal vasoconstriction is a sensitive index of effective blood volume, the measurement of the urine output over short periods of time becomes of great help in guiding the care of patients in acute oligemic states. This is done by measuring the urine output from an inlying catheter. These figures are charted at the bedside on an hourly or tri-hourly basis. The measurement of the specific gravity and the benzidine reaction of such urine is also of use, as will be mentioned in greater detail later. But it must be emphasized repeatedly that in surgery, hemorrhage, shock, and acute disease, gross reduction in urine volume is hemodynamic in origin, not tubular, and that altered tubular function is primarily reflected in the character rather than in the volume of the urine.

D. ENDOCRINE-METABOLIC AND ELECTROLYTIC EFFECTS

The following changes occur in moderate venous hemorrhage:

(1) increase in all adrenocortical indices: blood and urine 17-hydroxycorticoid response;

(2) marked decrease in glomerular filtration rate; oliguria;

(3) "ADH effect" (decreased free water clearance) and "aldosterone effect" (decreased urinary sodium:potassium ratio) manifest in what little urine is formed.

Experimental production of hemorrhage of this magnitude in man has rarely been recorded in the literature. From what is known of blood loss in the course of surgery and from comparable information in animals we can reconstruct some of the pattern.

The adrenocortical response is now clear-cut: a fall in eosinophils, a rise in blood and urine steroids, and an increase in the secretion of aldosterone. The effect on electrolyte metabolism is more marked than in the lesser hemorrhage. Alterations in renal function as described produce a marked reduction in urine flow and in sodium excretion in absolute terms. There is markedly negative free water clearance. The increased potassium excretion would be noted by concentration alone and quantitatively significant only when urine flow is re-established. It signifies the mobilization of cell water. When urine flow is low there is a rise in plasma potassium concentration. Tubular cation exchange continues very actively, acting on a very small volume of filtrate until such time as tubular blood flow is so reduced as to compromise the oxygen supply required to support the enzymatic transfer of solutes. Change in nitrogen balance is readily demonstrable, consisting most clearly in a positive nitrogen balance during the subsequent days and weeks when, if diet is adequate, body stores of red blood cells are being resynthesized.

E. TREATMENT

Treatment of acute hemorrhage of this magnitude should be prompt in time and realistic in rate and volume. Pressure infusion or multiple infusion should be used. If blood pressure is still low or if hemodilution is not yet complete, the target should be blood volume restoration in one hour. In the 80 kg. man of our example, infusion of 2000 ml. in an hour requires a rate of 33.3 ml. per minute. This can only be accomplished by the use of pressure apparatus or multiple, simultaneous large-dose infusions. Calcium gluconate (1.0 gm. per 1500 ml. blood) should be given in this situation to neutralize excess citrate.

Re-establishment of volume is quickly followed by restoration of renal blood flow (as shown by the hourly urine output), tissue perfusion, blood pressure, and color of skin. Adrenal medullary activity quickly abates, resulting (if we may extrapolate from the dog) in a return of catechol amine output to normal within minutes. It is this endocrine change that is related to restoration of pulse to normal, reopening of skin vessels, relaxation of the renal arterioles, and diuresis.

As renal function returns, the potassium mobilized with cell water is excreted in an increasing volume of urine of very low sodium:potassium ratio, and the other changes run their course, gradually returning to normal.

Section III.　Operative Blood Loss

A. MAGNITUDE

Unexpected or unreplaced operative blood loss (the two terms are often synonymous) becomes hazardous at the level of 20 to 30 per cent of blood volume. A few special aspects of operative blood loss are described here before we move on to the discussion of shock.

The loss of blood at operations may be measured by one of three commonly-used methods:

(1) hemoglobin or acid hematin measurements on eluates of sponges, drapes, and the like;

(2) nitrogen determination on the same;

(3) weight determination on the same.

Of the three, the nitrogen method is the most accurate, the weight method the most practical; hemoglobin methods are valuable when other fluids (for example, amniotic fluid or saline solution) invalidate the weight method and the nitrogen technique is not available.

By any technique, one finds that surgical procedures cover a graded scale of blood loss ranging from the 50 to 75 ml. lost in an appendectomy to 2500 ml. (or more) lost in a difficult pelvic node dissection, cardiotomy, or craniotomy or where operative control has inadvertently been lost in dealing with a large vessel.

The ideal treatment of operative blood loss is immediate accurate replacement of any loss over 500 ml. Replacement of large losses should always occur before hemodilution takes place. This objective is not always attainable; all too frequently the surgeon finds himself transfusing an anesthetized hemodiluted patient—a very confusing situation to assess.

Two important points should be made about operative loss.

1. Transfusion under Anesthesia

There is a small but clear hazard, as mentioned before, in the transfusion of the anesthetized patient who cannot complain of the early symptoms of an incompatible transfusion reaction and who therefore may receive dangerous amounts of blood before his surgeon becomes aware of the situation. For this reason, where operative blood loss has been low (500 ml. or less), and circulatory changes absent, transfusion is postponed until the patient is awake, and then given only if the clinical situation demands. This delay invites hemodilution by transcapillary refilling, and it may appear inconsistent. But where lost volumes are low, and blood pressure not affected, the hazard of transfusing the unconscious patient is greater than the hazard of delay. When blood loss has been greater than this, has prospects of so being, or where there are changes in blood pressure or pulse, one must of course accept the very small hazard involved and maintain the circulation by accurate transfusion therapy. Here the hazard of delay so outweighs the danger of transfusion that the course is clear.

2. Increased "Avidity" for Blood; Increased Vascular Capacity

Deeper planes of anesthesia lower the tolerance of the patient to blood loss, particularly to blood loss incurred prior to anesthesia. Anesthetics may produce hypotension by themselves. When blood loss has occurred under anesthesia and shock has been pronounced, one may expect to see less defensive resiliency or compensatory vasoconstriction.

A special consideration in operative blood loss is therefore the effect of anesthesia on vascular capacity or the "clinical phenomenon of taking up." To restore the circulation there may be required a volume of blood significantly larger than the volume lost. This condition is described in detail in the next chapter.

CHAPTER 9

Acute Hemorrhage and Shock

Section I. Kinds of Shock: The Essential Reversibility of Shock

In this chapter, it is our purpose to describe the problems of shock as they relate particularly to changes in blood volume, to hemodynamic, hematologic, and metabolic alterations. The management of severe wounds and multiple injury is reserved for discussion in Part VI (Fractures, Wounds, and Burns). We are here considering oligemic shock as a clinical entity—a syndrome of acute reduction in effective volume. In Part VI we shall consider the care of the injured man as a patient—as an individual problem in treatment.

A. DEFINITIONS

The term "shock" refers to a clinical picture. Here is its historic origin, and this is the most sensible way to use the term. The clinical picture of shock includes hypotension as a very characteristic feature. As an arbitrary limit, a systolic pressure below 70 mm. Hg* is observed under most circumstances in which the diagnosis of shock is made. There is initially a high diastolic pressure and a very narrow pulse pressure as vasoconstriction occurs. The patient, once in shock, is not referred to as "out of shocklike state" until his blood pressure has been restored to a level of 100 mm. Hg and so maintains itself. The rest of the clinical picture is just as important as the absolute blood pressure levels and consists in an ashen pallor, a

sweaty skin that does not blanch on pressure, and a rapid pulse which, as the picture progresses, becomes weak and thready. Heart sounds are rapid and weak. There is little thrust to the cardiac impulse. The patient may initially be alert and apprehensive, but as shock progresses he becomes disturbed, disoriented, and restless to an extreme degree, often requiring restraints to maintain position for treatment. The urine flow is below 10 ml. per hour.

There are other hypotensive states, in which the patient may be warm, dry, and pink, which clearly are not shock or anything approaching it. Hypotension alone does not make a diagnosis of shock. Decreased tissue perfusion and prolonged deficiency of flow are the central features of shock. Where there is hypotension but normal tissue flow there is not shock.

The pathogenesis of shock is as multiple as there are vital organs in the body or ways of dying; it is the pathway to death for many diseases and injuries. In clinical care the treatment of shock cannot be divorced from the treatment of the proximate cause. For our purposes here, shock is considered as the mechanism by which peripheral injury to nonvital organs (a leg, for example) is converted into vital organ damage and death.

1. Kinds of Shock

In surgical care, it is helpful to differentiate among four sorts of shock according to their clinical settings. Because volume reduction is

---

* In patients previously hypertensive, severe shock may be present at higher absolute levels of pressure.

a common denominator they are all included in the term "oligemic shock."

a. *Hemorrhagic Shock* is shock due to hemorrhage, with other factors held at a minimum. Examples of situations in which it occurs are ruptured spleen, ruptured ectopic pregnancy, acute massive hemorrhage from duodenal ulcer or esophageal varices, arterial laceration.

The early effects are rather different according to whether the loss is from a large artery (rapid loss of blood pressure), capillary "ooze" (more interstitial fluid is lost with the blood), or venous bleeding (vasoconstrictive mechanisms remain effective for a time).*

b. *Operative Shock* is shock occurring during surgical operation, carried out under anesthesia. Blood loss is the primary cause, but anesthetic effects on the peripheral vascular bed and tissue trauma play a role not found in hemorrhagic shock.

c. *Wound Shock* is shock due to trauma in the unanesthetized individual. The wounded soldier is an example. Pain, fear, muscle damage, tissue necrosis, contamination, and infection all play important roles but blood loss remains the principal initiating factor.

d. *Septic Shock* is shock due to invasion by virulent organisms, particularly gram-negative bacilli. Sequestration of fluid in septic edema and toxic effects on the cardiovascular system both play a role. Primary volume reduction is less prominent.

The effect of all four in producing anoxia of vital tissues and the final common pathway which leads to death is essentially the same. The differentiation among these four types of shock is important in treatment.

Shock due to simple venous hemorrhage in young people is the easiest to treat; in its early phases adequate blood replacement is sufficient. Shock in conjunction with civilian anesthetized surgery is not difficult to treat

if promptly recognized, but the effects of anesthesia and open operation on the vascular bed complicate the picture. Patients have been lost from poor treatment in this deceptively simple situation of oligemic shock under anesthesia in elective operation. Shock in elderly people who have suffered massive hemorrhage in the face of advanced cardiovascular disease is extremely difficult to manage. Shock in the wounded soldier, however, may defy all modes of treatment available at this time. In addition to blood loss and replacement, long delay in treatment, anesthesia, and the blood loss incident to definitive surgical care of open wounds, sepsis, and changes in the central nervous system, the myocardium, lungs, liver, and kidneys enter the equation and any one factor alone may become an apparently insuperable obstacle to recovery. There is thus a wide range in the susceptibility of shock to treatment.

2. Common Pathways of Shock

The initial common pathway in all oligemic shock is a decreased effective blood volume with decreased tissue perfusion. There then ensue a variety of intermediate patterns, depending on the exact nature of injury, the tissues involved, the degree of actual volume reduction, and the presence, nature, and anatomy of sepsis. The final common pathway downward is a prolonged deficiency of blood flow to vital organs. The passage of time is of the essence: the early process is completely reversible. There is scarcely a tissue in the body which is not damaged by prolonged anoxia and metabolic acidosis, carbon dioxide narcosis, cation transfer across the cells, and cessation of oxidative metabolism. In the liver, the effects involve alterations in intermediary metabolism of fat, carbohydrate, and protein. In the liver and in muscle the accumulation of acids from anaerobic glycolysis ("hypoxic acidosis") occurs. In the central nervous system there is a diminution in function more readily appreciated by the clinician than quantitated by the scientist.

The myocardium is itself a peripheral vascular bed; the cardiac muscle is nourished

---

* The loss of effective extracellular and circulating blood volume that produces shock by burns, peritonitis, venous obstruction, intestinal obstruction, and desalting water loss may be considered as belonging in this primary category of volume reduction, although compositional events are quite different, as described in a later section.

by capillaries fed through the coronary vessels. The effects of prolonged shock on the myocardial peripheral vascular bed are like those effects on other muscles. In certain circumstances cardiac decompensation with elevated venous pressure may become a part of the picture of shock. This is rarely seen in early shock in young people and is more characteristic of prolonged shock in elderly people, particularly those who have coronary disease, clinical or subclinical. The occurrence of a cardiac component in shock is readily demonstrated by the electrocardiogram even if venous pressure is low; with oligemia and vasoconstriction, venous pressure may be low despite severe myocardial insufficiency resulting from low coronary inflow pressure.

The effects of shock on the kidney consist at first in differential renal vasoconstriction, decreased glomerular filtration, and anuria. These things are quickly reversible. The damaging renal change (producing tubular necrosis and failure) is associated with prolonged renal anoxia and appears to be potentiated by the simultaneous presentation to the kidney for excretion of a heme pigment, hemoglobin breakdown product, or the products of cell death.

Quantitative studies on adrenal function have shown that the minute output of 17-hydroxysteroids in adrenal blood is tremendously increased. There is evidently no stimulus to adrenal steroid output which equals that of severe hemorrhagic shock. Whether or not prolonged shock finally produces some form of adrenal failure is not known, but there is little evidence for it. Histologic changes of round-cell infiltration and lipid depletion suggest some structural change. Hemorrhagic shock in obstetrical circumstances is evidently capable of damaging the pituitary. Severe hemorrhage and shock are the strongest stimuli to the outpouring of epinephrine and norepinephrine from nervous tissue and the adrenal medulla.

All of these things are the tissue changes of late flow-deficiency in the body tissues. They are, in a sense, nonspecific. There is no treatment for them other than restoration of the circulation. It is to this object that all

therapy is directed. Early in shock the success of intelligent treatment is unique in all medical experience: the dead may indeed be brought to life, and this is due to the essential reversibility of early oligemic shock. This property is progressively and irretrievably lost with the passage of time.

3. Vicious Cycles of Shock

As shock progresses, many changes take place which further aggravate the downward trend.

(1) *Decreased peripheral blood flow* permits the development of invasive sepsis, particularly anaerobic, and inhibits normal transcapillary filling which would otherwise help restore the circulating blood volume toward normal.

(2) *Decreased pulmonary blood flow* is a late phenomenon that produces a further decrease in tissue oxygenation and an increase in acidosis.

(3) *Decreased liver blood flow* permits the accumulation of toxic metabolites and depressor substances.

(4) *Acidosis*, both metabolic and respiratory, interferes with tissue reactions to steroids and catechol amines, and with muscular function, particularly cardiac.

(5) *Decreased coronary flow* (in the elderly) further reduces pressure and tissue perfusion.

(6) *Abnormal intermediates* of the metabolism of fat, protein, and carbohydrates accumulate in the blood.

(7) *Decreased kidney function* is in itself initially harmful to the patient, through the accumulation of unexcreted metabolic acids and intracellular electrolytes.

It is of historical interest that many of these by-products of prolonged deficiency of flow have been singled out in the laboratory and held up as the cause of shock, in the never-ending search for a "unified field theory of shock." Though all of them are important and are often a key to treatment, they are not primary or initiating causes. If the stem of a vine is cut the whole plant withers; but the loss of circulation is the primary cause. Similarly, with shock, the decreased effective extracellular or circulating blood volume is the primary cause; the many other features are secondary even though they, as vicious cycles, perpetuate the flow-deficiency or make the restoration of flow difficult.

4. The "Young and Early" versus the "Old and Late"

Early shock in young people poses no severe problem as long as the surgeon strictly obeys the dictates of early volume restoration.

As time in shock passes, or the age of the patient in shock grows older, complexities multiply and survival is progressively jeopardized. These two times, the one measured in hours the other in years, introduce the factors of prolonged deficiency of flow and chronic vascular disease, respectively. Volume restoration remains the first and most important step in both settings but may not, alone, win out in the "old and late." Treatment of sepsis, of biochemical disorders (acidosis hypotonicity), of heart failure and of hypoventilation may be critical adjuncts to volume restoration in the "old and late." It is this sort of shock—the "old and late"—that constitutes the problem in civilian surgery today.

B. ESSENTIAL REVERSIBILITY OF THE EARLY SHOCK STATE

The essential reversibility of early shock is its most important attribute. The term "irreversible shock" has been coined to cover certain laboratory phenomena; it is a term which should not be used in clinical surgery because it connotes an attitude of hopelessness which may cost the patient's life. A more aggressive approach will uncover the proper diagnosis—often something quite distinct—and effective treatment can be instituted.

Of the four types of shock mentioned above, the favorable period for effective treatment decreases down the scale as the complexity of pathogenesis increases. In *simple hemorrhage*, easy reversibility is a prime characteristic. It is a commonplace to observe a patient, suffering from hemorrhage alone, who is virtually dead by measurable indices such as heart-beat rate, blood pressure, and vital responses. Yet, with securing of a bleeding vessel and adequate transfusion, not only may life be restored but, as early as forty-eight hours later, no measurable sequelae can be discovered.

In *operative shock*, where shock has supervened after a long and difficult operation and is compounded by the use of drugs and anesthetic agents, reversibility is not quite so ready. Treatment must be more extensive. In older people, reversal may take hours of intensive therapy and careful diagnostic study. But reversibility is always a potential occurrence and should never be denied by the diagnosis of irreversible shock.

In the third type, *wound shock*, that of unanesthetized and contaminated massive trauma, treatment may be extremely difficult and, as mentioned above, may on occasion appear to be totally ineffective. The stage in development of the process at which reversibility can no longer be produced is impossible to determine clinically during the passing moments of treatment in crisis.

The use of the term or concept of irreversible shock is therefore clinically unacceptable because it is dangerous to the patient. Common conditions associated with wound shock, which may give the appearance of irreversibility but which are susceptible to specific treatment, are, for example: gross underreplacement of the blood volume, hemopericardium, pneumothorax, mediastinal emphysema, flail chest, mediastinitis, invasive retroperitoneal sepsis, anaerobic sepsis, intraperitoneal hemorrhage, aspiration of gastric contents, pulmonary embolism, and coronary occlusion. Diagnostic search for such phenomena, and their correction if present, are essential to success; they are overlooked if the term "irreversible shock" is used.

In *septic shock* the presence of virulent organisms in the blood stream is the cause of deterioration of the circulation; effective control by drainage of a seeding source or by effective antibacterial treatment is essential to restoration of the circulation; a blood volume larger than normal is needed to support pressure.

Text continues on page 193.

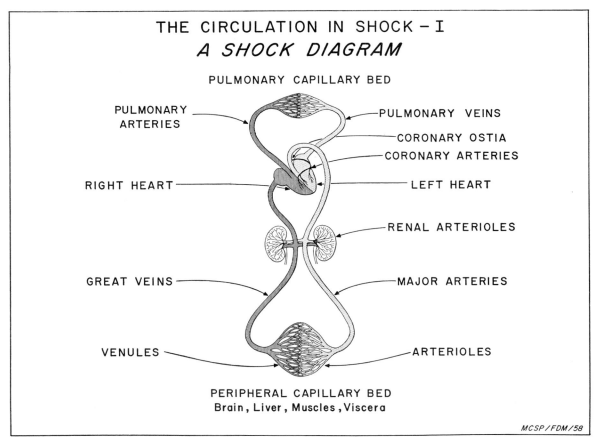

Figure 36. The Circulation in Shock. I. A Shock Diagram

In this and the succeeding five figures is shown a standardized diagram used to depict graphically the location of some of the alterations seen in various circumstances of surgical shock.

Centrally is the heart, showing the right and left heart, and in sufficient detail to show the coronary ostia take-off from the aorta, leading to the coronary blood supply of the myocardium. Above this is shown the pulmonary circulation, arising from the right ven-tricle and terminating in the left atrium. Below the heart is shown the major circulation, the aorta leading to the renal arteries. The kidneys are shown separately because of their particular importance in relation to the circulation in shock. Below is shown the major arteriolar-capillary-venular bed in which peripheral metabolic exchange occurs. The venous system then, in turn, returns peripheral blood to the right atrium.

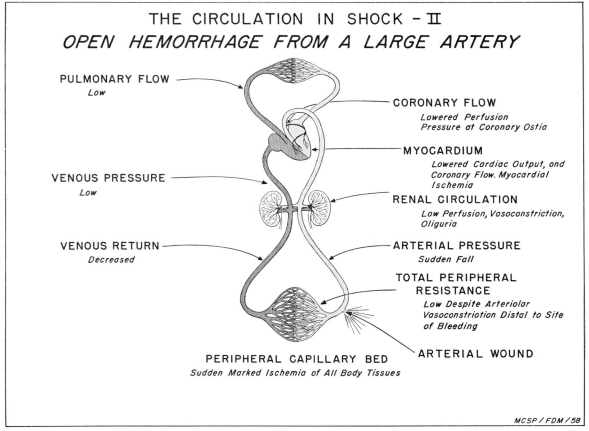

THE CIRCULATION IN SHOCK – II
OPEN HEMORRHAGE FROM A LARGE ARTERY

PULMONARY FLOW
Low

CORONARY FLOW
*Lowered Perfusion
Pressure at Coronary Ostia*

MYOCARDIUM
*Lowered Cardiac Output, and
Coronary Flow. Myocardial
Ischemia*

VENOUS PRESSURE
Low

RENAL CIRCULATION
*Low Perfusion, Vasoconstriction,
Oliguria*

VENOUS RETURN
Decreased

ARTERIAL PRESSURE
Sudden Fall

TOTAL PERIPHERAL
RESISTANCE
*Low Despite Arteriolar
Vasoconstriction Distal to Site
of Bleeding*

ARTERIAL WOUND

PERIPHERAL CAPILLARY BED
Sudden Marked Ischemia of All Body Tissues

MCSP / FDM / 58

Figure 37. THE CIRCULATION IN SHOCK. II. OPEN HEMORRHAGE FROM A LARGE ARTERY

In this chart are depicted some of the events that occur when there is open hemorrhage from an artery the size of the superficial femoral artery, or larger. The wound in the arterial tree is so large that total peripheral resistance immediately drops to a low value. Even though cardiac output may be maintained for a few minutes, pressure drops drastically. Thus, regardless of other events, there is a decreased coronary inflow pressure and decreased coronary circulation, and decreased cerebral blood flow. In older people, even a transient fall in the pressure at the coronary ostia will produce severe myocardial ischemia because of the arteriosclerotic narrowing of the coronary vessels. Electrocardiographic signs of myocardial ischemia occur early. Renal vasoconstriction occurs immediately, with oliguria. Total peripheral resistance, as mentioned above, is low, despite the presence of widespread arteriolar vasoconstriction that reduces tissue perfusion to the danger point.

The significant fact here is that the loss from the blood volume is from the arterial tree *proximal* to the site of peripheral resistance. Blood pressure therefore cannot be developed. Peripheral tissues are ischemic, there is decreased venous return, markedly decreased cardiac output, and decreased pulmonary perfusion and effective ventilation. These events may be rapidly fatal with death primarily due to anoxia of myocardium and brain. Survival depends upon control of the hemorrhage itself so that peripheral resistance and hence pressure may be restored. It is in this situation *par excellence* that operation is a part of resuscitation; control of the bleeding vessel itself is a prerequisite to survival and to further surgical care of the wound.

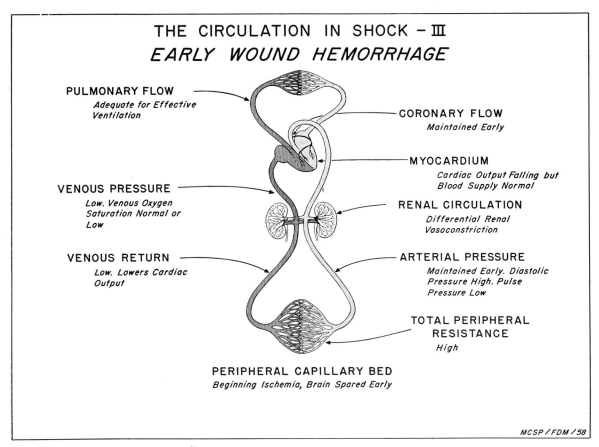

THE CIRCULATION IN SHOCK – III
EARLY WOUND HEMORRHAGE

PULMONARY FLOW
Adequate for Effective Ventilation

CORONARY FLOW
Maintained Early

MYOCARDIUM
Cardiac Output Falling but Blood Supply Normal

VENOUS PRESSURE
Low. Venous Oxygen Saturation Normal or Low

RENAL CIRCULATION
Differential Renal Vasoconstriction

VENOUS RETURN
Low. Lowers Cardiac Output

ARTERIAL PRESSURE
Maintained Early. Diastolic Pressure High. Pulse Pressure Low

TOTAL PERIPHERAL RESISTANCE
High

PERIPHERAL CAPILLARY BED
Beginning Ischemia, Brain Spared Early

MCSP / FDM / 58

Figure 38.   THE CIRCULATION IN SHOCK. III. EARLY WOUND HEMORRHAGE
See facing page for detailed legend.

Figure 38. THE CIRCULATION IN SHOCK. III. EARLY WOUND HEMORRHAGE

By contrast with the preceding figure, here is shown the situation in the much more characteristic mixed peripheral hemorrhage, wherein the site of arteriolar vasoconstriction (and total peripheral resistance) is proximal to or unaffected by the site of blood loss. Venous hemorrhage, or the hemorrhage from injured tissues which involve veins, venules, arterioles, small arteries, and capillaries, falls into this category. This is the commonest type of mixed blood loss in operations and wounds.

In the early phases, coronary inflow pressure is well maintained because, although cardiac output falls, there is a marked increase in peripheral resistance and thus the maintenance of coronary inflow pressure. This situation obtains for some minutes or hours, depending upon the balance of other clinical factors. Renal vaso-constriction occurs early and prior to diffuse vasoconstriction, hence the term "differential renal vasoconstriction."

Tissue ischemia occurs as a result of the widespread peripheral tissue vasoconstriction. There is decreased venous return to the heart and decreased cardiac output. In most patients effective ventilation is normal because of the large reserve factor present in pulmonary blood flow.

This situation is readily restored to normal by blood transfusion, which permits relaxation of the arteriolar vasoconstriction, and restoration of tissue perfusion. In this situation the restoration of blood volume should precede anesthesia; the circulation should be stable before operation.

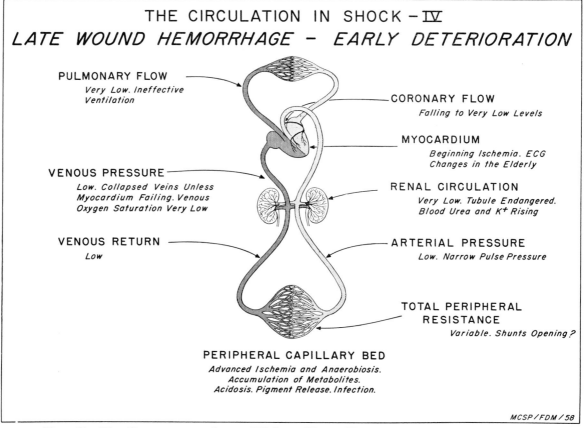

Figure 39.   THE CIRCULATION IN SHOCK. IV. LATE WOUND HEMORRHAGE, EARLY DETERIORATION

See facing page for detailed legend.

Figure 39. THE CIRCULATION IN SHOCK. IV. **LATE** WOUND HEMORRHAGE, EARLY DETERIORATION

In this chart are depicted the events associated with early but severe shock. These changes are more advanced than those shown in the previous chart, yet they have not yet advanced to the point of severe tissue damage. These are the changes of established shock.

Coronary inflow pressure and perfusion are falling as systolic pressure falls and remains low. Cardiac output is low. In elderly people, electrocardiographic changes are often demonstrated at this point and are usually described as those of subendocardial ischemia. Systolic blood pressure is low, renal perfusion is very low, urine output is low, and the renal tubular cell is now extremely vulnerable to nephrotoxic damage. Urea and potassium concentrations begin to rise in the blood.

Peripheral resistance is variable. Usually it appears to be high: the skin is cold, the capillaries empty. The pooling of blood in some segments of the circulation, suggested by the clinical phenomenon of "taking up," indicates that there may be areas in which the balance between inflow and outflow resistance is such as to permit accumulation ("pooling") of some blood. The opening up of arteriovenous shunts and the accumulation of red cells in small vessels ("sludging") may occur in the periphery in this stage.*

---

* Both "pooling" and "sludging" are more regularly seen in the dog than in man. In the dog, this is the phase at which splanchnic pooling with hepatic outflow obstruction and hemorrhage into the gut are manifest. Evidence for splanchnic pooling in man is much less convincing.

Peripheral tissues are ischemic and there is beginning accumulation of metabolites in the periphery. These metabolites take the form of lactic acid, pyruvic acid, amino acids, inorganic acids, and carbon dioxide. The venous oxygen saturation is now very low (20 to 40 per cent) as the sluggish circulation through the tissue permits almost complete removal of oxygen. Acidosis hyperkalemia, and circulating pigments are characteristic of this phase of shock.

The venous circulation shows collapsed veins unless the coronary inflow stasis and coronary caliber are so limited as to produce myocardial failure, in which case one may see some elevation of venous pressure here, particularly if venous transfusion is being pursued very actively. At this stage of shock pulmonary perfusion becomes inadequate. Diaphragmatic muscle function is poor. Effective ventilation is unsatisfactory and, although the pulmonary arterial oxygen saturation may be normal, the peripheral arterial carbon dioxide tension is elevated and respiratory acidosis is beginning to be added to the metabolic acidosis of peripheral hypoxia.

Treatment still centers on volume restoration by the venous route. It is in this setting that the volume transfused must be grossly in excess of the volume lost and is in excess of the normal blood volume in many instances.

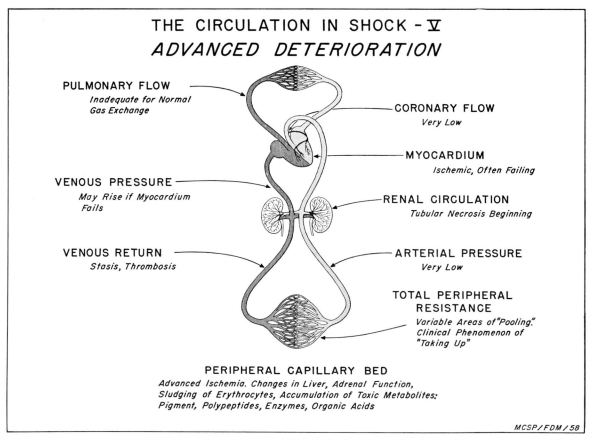

THE CIRCULATION IN SHOCK - V
ADVANCED DETERIORATION

PULMONARY FLOW
*Inadequate for Normal
Gas Exchange*

CORONARY FLOW
Very Low

MYOCARDIUM
Ischemic, Often Failing

VENOUS PRESSURE
*May Rise if Myocardium
Fails*

RENAL CIRCULATION
Tubular Necrosis Beginning

VENOUS RETURN
Stasis, Thrombosis

ARTERIAL PRESSURE
Very Low

**TOTAL PERIPHERAL
RESISTANCE**
*Variable Areas of "Pooling."
Clinical Phenomenon of
"Taking Up"*

PERIPHERAL CAPILLARY BED
*Advanced Ischemia. Changes in Liver, Adrenal Function,
Sludging of Erythrocytes, Accumulation of Toxic Metabolites:
Pigment, Polypeptides, Enzymes, Organic Acids*

MCSP/FDM/58

Figure 40.   THE CIRCULATION IN SHOCK. V. ADVANCED DETERIORATION

See facing page for detailed legend.

Figure 40. THE CIRCULATION IN SHOCK. V. ADVANCED DETERIORATION

In this chart are depicted some of the events seen in very late shock in man. One should not term this "irreversible" since many patients have recovered from such a state with adequate, energetic, and well-planned treatment. Nonetheless, this is the phase of shock where survival hangs in the balance.

Coronary perfusion is now very low. In elderly people with narrowed coronaries, severe myocardial ischemia is inevitable. Even in young people, electrocardiographic changes are now seen and one occasionally observes elevated venous pressure.

Arterial pressure is very low. The kidney has by now almost surely been damaged; whether or not prolonged post-traumatic renal insufficiency will result is still uncertain. At the least the urine will show granular and red cell casts, large amounts of protein, and evidence of severe parenchymatous renal damage.

Peripheral resistance may now fail in the sense of permitting the accumulation of large amounts of blood in areas of the circulation. In the peripheral tissues there are advanced ischemic changes. The liver begins to show histologic alteration.*

The accumulation of abnormal metabolites in the periphery is now very marked and almost any chemical determination carried out on peripheral blood will show abnormalities. These abnormalities are secondary to prolonged tissue hypoxia and for the most part can

not be regarded as primary in the pathogenesis of shock. There are clear changes in gas metabolism, electrolytes, water, and in the intermediary metabolism of fats, proteins, and carbohydrates.

Venous oxygen saturation is variable at this stage. It is usually low but in some instances and in some areas it may be found to be paradoxically high, suggesting that the opening up of arteriovenous shunts is a feature of this phase of shock in some tissues.

Venous pressure is variable, depending on the balance between myocardial function and venous return. In untreated shock, elevated venous pressure is quite rare. In shock at this stage in elderly people being treated by rapid venous infusions of large amounts of blood, an elevated venous pressure may be observed, and the use of digitalis may be important. It is in this setting that intra-arterial transfusion, by perfusing the coronary circulation for a few minutes at high pressure, may help restore myocardial oxygenation and cardiac output.

Here again, as in the previous setting, pulmonary perfusion is inadequate to maintain carbon dioxide clearance. Respiratory acidosis is severe. In addition, the circulation is now so deteriorated that oxygenation of the blood is inadequate, and at this stage of shock the administration of oxygen may have some significance, although it rarely has significance prior to this.

Volume restoration is still the key to treatment; here, in late deterioration, the other "echelons" of treatment must be considered, including massive doses of antibiotics, as well as digitalis and corticosteroids. This is not a setting wherein vasoconstrictors would be expected to be helpful.

---

* In the dog it is at this stage that the animal shows the spontaneous anaerobic septic process or the endotoxemia so characteristic of that animal in late shock. This is rare in man unless anaerobes have been introduced in the wound, or florid sepsis is itself a primary cause of the shock state.

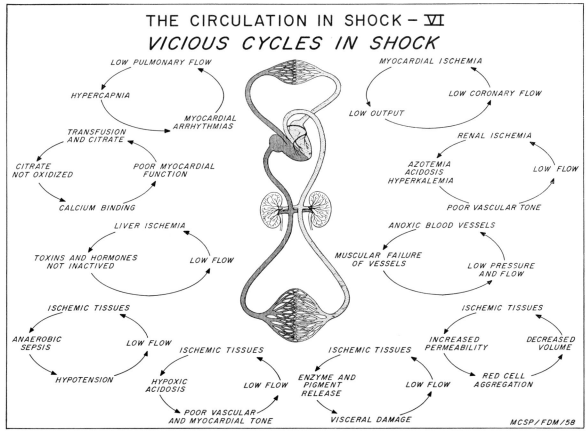

Figure 41. THE CIRCULATION IN SHOCK. VI. VICIOUS CYCLES IN SHOCK

See facing page for detailed legend.

Figure 41. The Circulation in Shock. VI. Vicious Cycles in Shock

Prolonged deficiency of blood flow to the tissues brings in its wake a whole series of events which in themselves speed the downward spiral of deterioration. These are, in a sense, a series of vicious cycles or sustaining factors which come about because of shock and which in themselves make the shock much more profound and make its treatment more difficult. In this chart are shown some of these vicious cycles.

Myocardial ischemia results from low inflow pressure at the coronary ostia together with decreased coronary arterial caliber (most prominent in elderly people suffering some degree of coronary atherosclerosis). This produces further low output which in turn adds to the myocardial ischemia.

Renal ischemia results initially from differential renal vasoconstriction. It contributes to azotemia, acidosis, and hyperkalemia, in turn leading to further lowering of the flow to the kidney.

Anoxic blood vessels in the periphery result from prolonged vasoconstriction proximal to the peripheral capillary.

Ischemic tissues involve increased permeability of the capillary with loss of aqueous components of blood from the capillary, leaving behind an elevated hematocrit within the blood vessels. This "sludging" is one of the vicious cycles of shock but quantitatively not of great importance in man.

These ischemic tissues also release *intracellular enzymes, pigments, and electrolytes* into the circulation (particularly if they have been traumatized directly) and these lead to further deterioration of renal and cardiovascular function.

These ischemic tissues likewise release into the circulation the products of *incomplete oxidation of organic substrates*. The accumulation of lactic acid, pyruvic acid, and citrate is associated with these changes. Inability to oxidize citrate is a feature of both peripheral ischemia and hepatic ischemia.

Hepatic ischemia results in failure to inactivate toxic materials, organic acids, and hormones. Very abnormal levels of these substances are therefore seen in shock and in some cases (catechol amines) may lead to further peripheral deterioration.

If the patient is given citrated whole blood at this time, *failure to oxidize the citrate* results in calcium binding. This diminishes the effectiveness of the heart beat by diminishing ionized calcium in the blood. If the patient has been digitalized, the effect of digitalis is lost by this citrate effect, leading to further myocardial deterioration.

Poor pulmonary blood flow leads to respiratory acidosis which in turn produces hypotension when blood volume is low. This mechanism does not start early in shock because of the easy diffusibility of carbon dioxide and the large reserve or safety factor in pulmonary circulation. However, late in shock both anoxia and respiratory acidosis result from poor pulmonary perfusion and poor diaphragmatic function.

Finally, ischemic tissues in the periphery set the stage for the *growth of anaerobic organisms*. In man this factor is important when there have been breaks in the skin and mucosal barriers to the bacterial environment. One does not see spontaneous anaerobic infection in man in shock; there must be a wound or break for it to occur. However, in such events as compound fracture, bullet wounds, automobile accidents, crushing injuries, traumatic amputations, the presence of a prolonged phase of shock greatly increases the incidence of severe gram-negative bacteremia, anaerobic cellulitis, and anaerobic myositis. Any one of the three of these may in and of themselves produce severe hypotension and shock. When they are superimposed on the organism already in shock, the outlook is very poor; recovery has occurred in such cases after accurate, energetic, and well-conceived treatment. The term "irreversible shock" should never be used in man.

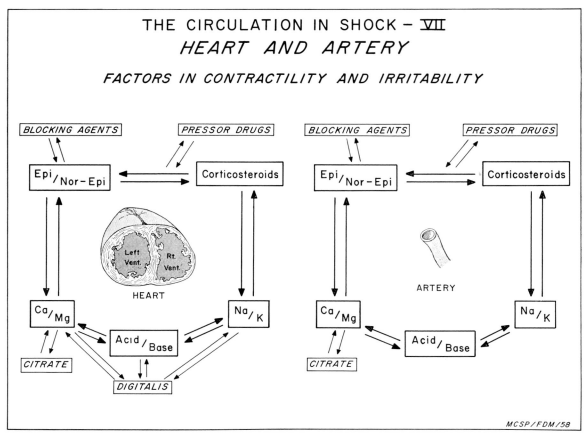

Figure 42.   THE CIRCULATION IN SHOCK. VII. THE HEART AND ARTERY.
FACTORS IN CONTRACTILITY AND IRRITABILITY

See facing page for detailed legend.

Figure 42. THE CIRCULATION IN SHOCK. VII. THE HEART AND ARTERY.
FACTORS IN CONTRACTILITY AND IRRITABILITY

The blood is enclosed and propelled in a system of muscles, ranging on the one hand from the thick, specialized muscle tissue of the heart, through the very muscular large arteries to the arterioles, then the capillaries, essentially free of muscle, and finally the veins wherein muscle is not prominent but some contractile and muscular function is evident.

This vascular muscle is responsive to many alterations in its chemical environment. Seemingly the most important areas at which this muscular responsiveness is manifest are three: the heart, the major arteries, and the arterioles. The heart must maintain normal irritability, contractility, and the normal neuromuscular function required for integration of the heart beat. The major vessels are important with respect to elasticity. If their pulsatile property and elastic function are lost, they become the reservoirs wherein large amounts of blood are circulating more slowly than normal. The arteriole, least frequently seen but most intensively studied, is the site at which peripheral resistance develops so that blood pressure may be exhibited with a given cardiac output.

In this chart are shown some of the interlocking factors which seem to affect the contractility and irritability of vascular muscle. This chart depicts many areas in which the questions loom larger than the facts at this time. Yet a realization of some of the factors which may be involved is helpful in the care of the patient.

The corticosteroids are essential for normal vascular function. Their lack is not a common factor in human shock. In the isolated vasculature of the experimental animal, it can be demonstrated that, after adrenalectomy, response to catechol amines is subnormal until corticosteroids are given. In man, adrenal failure is associated with a shock-like state; and even in patients in shock but without adrenal failure one occasionally sees a favorable response to corticosteroids.

The catechol amines are essential to produce an increase in the total resistance of the peripheral circulation. As mentioned above, they require normal steroids for their activity and their activity is likewise altered by the acid-base balance of the tissue and the presence or absence of pressor drugs, blocking agents, or cholinergic drugs. Without peripheral resistance, cardiac output cannot develop pressure; with too much resistance, there is inadequate tissue perfusion with any given inflow pressure.

These vascular responses are profoundly altered by the cation distribution in the tissues. As a general rule, "high-sodium" states are pressor and "high-potassium" states are depressor. The administration of catechol amines results in the expulsion of potassium and taking up of sodium in the arterial wall. The administration of digitalis to the heart results in the same chemical change. Acidosis is associated with hyperkalemia and hyponatremia, and poor blood pressure maintenance. Alkalosis *per contra* is associated with hypokalemia and hypernatremia and good blood pressure maintenance. These same biochemical factors alter the response of the myocardium, with or without digitalis. If the myocardium has been digitalized, these acid-base-electrolyte changes are most easily seen. As a general phenomenon, acidosis, hyponatremia, and hyperkalemia diminish the ability of the peripheral vessel to respond normally to epinephrine and norepinephrine, diminish the ability of the heart to respond to epinephrine, diminish the effectiveness of digitalis, and diminish the effectiveness of myocardial function.

Finally, the calcium-magnesium complex is essential to normal vascular muscle activity. Hypocalcemia and hypermagnesemia (the latter clinically rare) result in decreased effectiveness of myocardial contraction, and decreased effect of digitalization. The presence of excess citrate has the same effect.

We thus find many factors involving the activity of vascular muscle. These range all the way from the corticosteroids on the one hand to pharmacologic agents, digitalis, and electrolytes on the other. These factors affect the response of the vascular and cardiac muscle to its environment; in the balance between these various factors lies success or failure in the response to volume-restoration in shock.

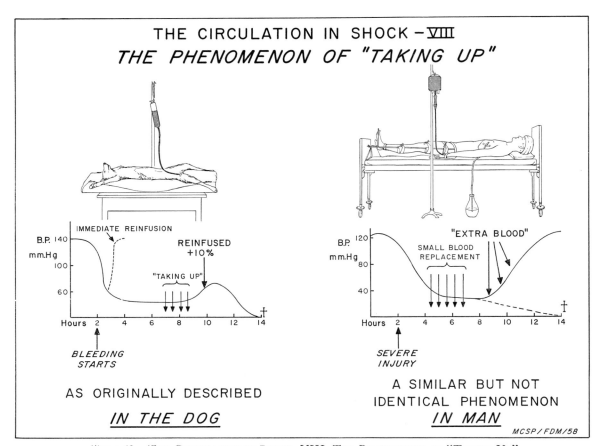

Figure 43.   The Circulation in Shock. VIII. The Phenomenon of "Taking Up"

See facing page for detailed legend.

Figure 43. THE CIRCULATION IN SHOCK. VIII. IS THERE A CLINICAL PHENOMENON OF "TAKING UP"?

This phenomenon has played a key role in experimental work on shock in the dog and appears to be paralleled by some of the phenomena seen clinically in man, although the mechanisms are quite different in the two species.

In this chart are depicted what is meant by the phenomenon of "taking up" in the dog, and our interpretation of its significance in the treatment of shock in man.

To the left is shown the characteristic experiment in the animal. Under sedative anesthesia, the animal is bled upward from an artery into a self-regulating flask so that the blood pressure is held at a fixed low figure (40 mm. Hg, for example). If, early in the experiment (dotted line in the graph below), the amount of blood in the bottle is reinfused, the animal's circulation quickly is restored to normal. If this is not done, and the animal is observed for a time, it is noted after a number of hours that the blood runs spontaneously back into the animal's arterial tree from the elevated bag or bottle. Hence the term "taking up." Some element of the blood vascular tree appears to be dilating, to permit the inflow of blood. Yet, despite this inflow of blood, the peripheral circulation is not improved. This suggests that the blood is pooling in some nonfunctional area.

In the dog, the evidence is overwhelming that this area of "pooling" is the splanchnic bed, between the gastrointestinal arteriole on the one hand (which remains open) and the hepatic outflow tract on the other (which apparently becomes constricted). The result is a large, purplish black, turgid liver, almost twice its normal size, with dilated splanchnic veins, increased portal blood pressure, and massive gastrointestinal ulceration and bleeding. Anaerobic infection soon begins; endotoxins of aerobes may play a role.

If what little then remains in the bottle is reinfused, plus considerable additional blood, the blood pressure rises but transiently and despite this the dog dies. Some deteriorative change has occurred; in certain experiments this can be shown to be associated with infection. Such infection may begin in the liver, in the muscles, or in the gastrointestinal tract. The events in this animal preparation are altered by treatment with vasodilating drugs, vasoconstricting drugs, and antibiotics, or by altering the hepatic blood supply or the mesenteric blood supply.

To the right are shown the sort of events that occur in man and which suggest that some similar change is occurring in late untreated shock. The patient has been traumatized initially. Blood pressure falls. After a number of hours, transfusion is begun. In the instances where this phenomenon is most clearly seen in man there is a dangerous lag period between the trauma and the onset of transfusion; this period is one of tissue anoxia of the type shown in the previous charts of this series. If after this lag period transfusion is commenced and the patient transfused vigorously until his circulation again stabilizes, one finds repeatedly that the amount of blood required is much greater than the measurable blood lost. The patient's blood vascular tree appears to "take up" more blood than it has lost, or very large amounts are infused without restoration of the circulation. Hence the term "the clinical phenomenon of taking up." Days or weeks after the trauma, this blood is still not easily found. It seems to be in tissue planes near the wound, rather than "trapped" in some special area of the circulation. There is evidence to suggest that it is gradually destroyed and the pigment excreted. One to four days after the episode, one may on occasion find measurably high blood volumes, yet this high blood volume seems necessary for the maintenance of the patient's circulation.

By using the term "clinical phenomenon of taking up" we do not mean to imply that in man the site of taking up or the mechanism is the same as in the dog. In the dog the site appears to be the portal circulation. In man the evidence for this is scanty, if present at all; the tissue planes around the wound are the sites of blood-accumulation. In the dog an insidious spontaneous anaerobic infection is a very important factor (even without a wound). This is not seen in man aside from clear clinical sepsis arising with a portal of entry. In the dog a characteristic "endotoxemia" is seen with portal hypertension and massive gastrointestinal hemorrhage. This is not seen in man. But, despite these very important differences, the fact is that in man after a period of shock there is a circulatory deterioration that imposes a demand for blood transfusion considerably larger in amount than any blood that has been lost, and this "taking up of blood" resembles the situaiton seen in the dog. The analogy may be helpful in understanding the necessities of clinical treatment.

In the dog the term "irreversible shock" has been coined to describe this situation; such a term is never justified in man.

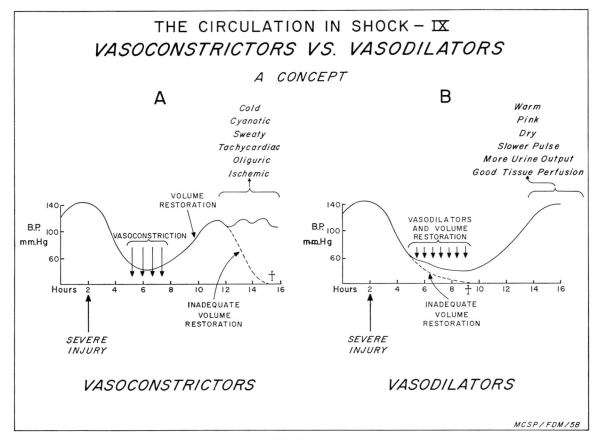

Figure 44.   THE CIRCULATION IN SHOCK. IX. VASOACTIVE DRUGS IN SHOCK—A CONCEPT

See facing page for detailed legend.

Figure 44. THE CIRCULATION IN SHOCK. IX. VASOACTIVE DRUGS IN SHOCK—A CONCEPT

The use of vasoconstricting drugs in shock has been explored since adrenaline was first prepared. However, as early as 1916 it was demonstrated that prolonged administration of adrenaline, epinephrine, or norepinephrine would in itself result in a shock-like state, tissue ischemia, and death. Clearly, the patient in shock is exhibiting some sort of a balance between beneficial peripheral vasoconstriction (with a maintenance of pressure) and severe tissue ischemia resulting from too prolonged or too severe vasoconstriction. In this chart are shown some concepts relative to this matter.

To the left is shown the sort of situation one sees when volume loss is produced and is followed by the use of vasoconstrictors in man. One finds that with the vasoconstrictors there is a tendency for pressure restoration, even before volume restoration is commenced, suggesting increased peripheral resistance. And then, when the lost volume is only partly restored, there may be a considerable restoration of pressure precariously maintained by continuance of the vasoconstrictors. This patient looks cyanotic, cold, sweaty, his tissues look ischemic, and he is often oliguric. In some instances (dotted line) his pressure will fall off and he will succumb despite the continuance of vasoconstrictors. One may theorize that this is an individual with an inadequate blood volume in whom some semblance of blood pressure is being maintained by excessive peripheral vasoconstriction, yet without the benefits of free tissue perfusion. When tissue anoxia finally becomes intolerable there is rapid deterioration. This is a good example of the fact that blood pressure is not to be equated

with tissue perfusion. It is tissue perfusion which is the objective, not blood pressure alone.

To the right is shown the sort of situations which obtain when vasodilating drugs are used.

The initial volume loss in our example is the same. Then, if early in the situation, *before volume has been restored*, vasodilating drugs are used, the pressure will fall off drastically. If the patient is elderly, with atherosclerosis and poor cerebral and coronary circulation, this fall in inflow pressure may result in thrombosis and death.

However, if adequate volume is restored and then vasodilators are given, one sees several interesting changes. First, there is transient fall in blood pressure of little moment, resulting from the opening up of a constricted periphery. Then, the blood pressure continues to rise of itself as, with volume restoration, there is now more complete tissue perfusion and oxidative metabolism in the periphery and, above all, better muscle function. Now we have a volume-restored, vasodilated patient who, in contrast to his vasoconstricted brother, is pink, warm, dry, has good tissue perfusion and good renal function.

Inadequate experience with the widespread use of these methods of treatment has been gained at this time to justify their careless application to patients without very considerable study. The concept, however, is of great help in understanding the occasionally harmful effect of vasoconstricting drugs and the occasionally beneficial effect, either of stopping vasoconstrictors or initiating vasodilators. We are indebted to Nickerson for recent reemphasis of this concept.

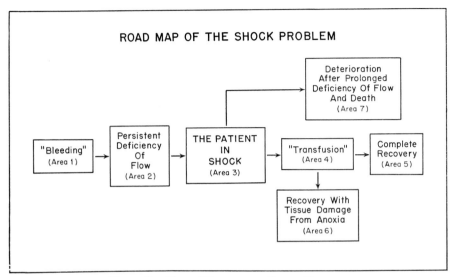

Figure 45.   ROAD MAP OF THE SHOCK PROBLEM

Study of shock in the laboratory, and the treatment of shock in man, involve a number of different areas of observation and study, shown in this chart. The phenomenon of bleeding itself includes study of the magnitude of blood loss required to produce hypotension, as well as the wide variety of other stimuli including tissue trauma, bacterial toxins and anesthetics that produce a similar deficiency of flow.

"Persistent deficiency of blood flow" is the physiologic state associated with shock and involves secondary alterations in the function of many different organs and tissues.

The patient in shock may deteriorate after prolonged deficiency of flow and die of shock. Or, with replacement (marked here as "transfusion" to indicate that this replacement may take many different forms) the patient may recover with persistent tissue damage from the anoxia suffered during a period of deficiency of flow. The most characteristic residual tissue damage seen clinically is that affecting the kidneys. Occasionally one sees prolonged cerebral damage from shock. Anaerobic growth of microorganisms and necrosis of skin and muscle are also examples of this area of change.

Finally, adequate volume replacement may lead to complete recovery. In this situation, if the patient is studied a year or so later, no residual is visible save for the scars of the original injury.

In evaluating the literature on shock, it is important to discern which areas of this dynamic progression are under study.

C. IS THERE A "CLINICAL PHENOMENON OF TAKING UP"?

One more matter remains to be mentioned before describing the volume changes and physiologic alterations of shock. This relates to content and capacity of the vascular bed, and the degeneration of normal pressure-resistance-flow relationships, which occurs in shock.

The work of Fine and his group (1954) on the subject of shock has covered many aspects of the problem in the laboratory animal. Through this work a phenomenon has been extensively documented, known as "taking up." We believe that a clinical counterpart of this laboratory observation is found in certain aspects of late shock in man, but that there is no common relation as to cause, *the dog's problem being bacteriologic, whereas in man this septic factor is much less prominent.*

To understand this, one must relate briefly a typical experiment. An unanesthetized dog, lying quietly on the table, is bled from an artery, the blood from the artery being permitted to pump itself upward into a reservoir. This reservoir is so situated that it exerts a hydrostatic pressure downward into the artery which is equal to a level of about 40 to 60 mm. Hg. During the course of a few minutes the dog bleeds upward into the reservoir until a good deal of blood is present in the bottle. This would rapidly produce a pressure drop, but because of the height of the bottle, the blood pressure of the dog is artificially maintained at a hydrostatic pressure equal to the height of the limb of blood in the tubing from the artery to the bottle.

The arterial chamber of the animal now has two outlets, the capillaries and the elevated bottle, and the bled volume in the bottle artificially supports blood pressure at a set level. When cardiac output meets resistance, pressure develops; the elevated bottle constitutes a fixed resistance which, for a time, permits pressure to be maintained.

After a time, the circulation of the dog appears to undergo a degenerative change. The vascular tree "relaxes" and the blood spontaneously starts to run back into the dog from the bottle. This is the phenomenon of "taking up." The amount of blood in the bottle may now run into the dog's artery and indeed considerable further blood will then easily be accepted by the dog but without the restoration of his blood pressure and tissue perfusion. Some sort of degenerative change has occurred in the peripheral circulation. In most canine experiments this "lost blood" will be found in the hepato-splanchnic area, with a swollen, turgid liver, portal hypertension, and sloughing of the mucosa of the gastrointestinal tract. Such changes are not seen in man.

The significance of this observation is better realized when we consider that only an hour or so previously the infusion of any extra volume of blood into the dog would have produced a slight plethora and even hypertension. Yet, here we have an animal which has in essence lost no blood from a closed system. He has accepted all the blood that has run out of his vascular tree initially. He "takes it up" into his vascular tree without restoring his pressure:flow relationships to normal and will indeed accept a considerably greater quantity of blood without restoring his pressure. According to the time relationships, the outcome may now be fatal. Deterioration evidently involves many factors in the dog, including sepsis, decreased liver oxygenation, increased gastrointestinal vascular permeability, depressor substances, and elevated portal blood pressure. Some of these factors (anaerobic sepsis, endotoxemia, portal hypertension) are less important in man. But an evident loss of effective blood volume is the important degenerative change; the vascular tree suddenly requires tremendous amounts of blood for the maintenance of pressure and flow.

In severely wounded men or in difficult (and prolonged) surgical operations (after shock has been established for some time) an analogous degenerative change occurs that makes it necessary to infuse much more blood than was originally lost, in order to restore an adequate peripheral flow with normal pressure and tissue oxygenation, carbon dioxide transport, removal of metabolites, and renal function. *In man "taking up" does not mean sepsis or irreversibility. Patients still get well but their lives are in jeopardy unless they are given more blood than they lost.*

The blood volume transfusion data from severe injury indicate that some such change as this is occurring. Since the acute loss of 50 per cent of the blood volume is on the borderline of fatality, it would appear surprising that some patients in shock (but still alive) may require from 1.5 to 2.5 blood volumes for their resuscitation. The result is often referred to as an increased capacity of the vascular system. Possibly it could better be called an increased requirement of the circulatory system for blood volume to maintain blood pressure and flow. There is evidence to suggest, in man, that the "lost blood" is in tissue planes around the wound, rather than in a special area of the vascular tree, and that it is later degraded and excreted.

How does one determine the amount of blood that must be infused when it is grossly in excess of any measurable loss and even of the patient's normal blood volume? As a practical rule, if the patient has been hypotensive (meaning that his systolic blood pressure has been lower than 70 mm. Hg) for one hour or more in the presence of severe wounds or a surgical operation, one should assume that the restoration of blood volume must not only be immediate, massive, and fresh but also grossly in excess of any measurable loss; one blood volume is a first approximation of the need.

Section II.   The Blood Volume in Shock

A. ROUTES OF BLOOD LOSS IN SHOCK

1. Venous and Capillary Loss

In oligemic shock of any kind, the route of blood volume loss is of first importance in determining treatment. If the blood is lost by expansion of extracellular fluid (as in crush or traumatic edema) or from the venous side of the circulation (bleeding esophageal varices), the lowering of blood pressure occurs gradually, and one rarely sees an elevated venous pressure. Large volumes are bled out before pressure drops to a low level. In venous bleeding, the restoration of some semblance of circulatory adequacy by transfusion is essential prior to surgery. Venous transfusion is effective. The bleeding is distal to the area of protective vasoconstriction (the arteriole), flow:resistance relations in the arterial tree are not distorted, and pressure is precariously maintained until the venous return to the right heart drops so low that cardiac output drops. The bodily defenses against shock are well attuned to the problem of venous bleeding, but anesthesia and operation distort these defenses and should not be imposed until volume is restored by transfusion and some period of equilibration, however brief, allowed to ensue.

2. Arterial Loss

When the bleeding occurs from an open artery (examples are arterial wounds, aortic rupture) a different sequence follows. A break in the unicameral hemodynamic system of the large arteries has suddenly lowered peripheral resistance so much that the circulation rapidly reaches a point where no effective blood pressure can be produced, and myocardial blood supply is reduced to the point of acute ischemia.

When the bleeding occurs from a somewhat smaller artery, like the gastroduodenal artery or the uterine artery, this change is less dramatic, but the same need applies in lesser degree. Of the total peripheral resistance, the severed small artery constitutes only a small fraction. The open hemorrhage has a less drastic immediate effect on pressure: flow relationships. The same mechanism obtains, however, and its clearest demonstration lies in the fact that a surgical operation that closes the bleeding vessel is followed immediately by a rise in blood pressure quite aside from the rate of blood infusion. This is commonly seen in ruptured spleen and ruptured ectopic pregnancy.

For these reasons, then, open arterial hemorrhage should be treated by early operation without awaiting restoration of blood pressure by transfusion. In ruptured viscera and wounds of large arteries, this diagnosis and this decision are quite simple. In bleeding duodenal ulcer, they are more complex since the surgery involved is more difficult, the continuation of bleeding harder to gauge, and the probability of spontaneous cessation of the hemorrhage greater.

In wound shock associated with unanesthetized injury, where there is tissue trauma as well as blood loss, the question of open arterial hemorrhage and its effects on vascular hemodynamics is of central importance. Where there is open arterial hemorrhage from the severed end of an artery, whether it be in a limb, where it is easily reached, or in the abdomen, control of this hemorrhage will have to precede the rest of the resuscitative procedures. For this reason, surgery (ranging from the application of a tourniquet to a full major operation) is in itself a part of the resuscitation. In major arterial bleeding, hemostasis and resuscitation are inseparable; continued bleeding requires surgical control; as mentioned in the introductory propositions, homeostasis requires hemostasis. In a mixed limb injury immobilization, splinting, pressure, and/or tourniquet may achieve the same result.

A cleanly divided major artery can summon hemostatic mechanisms (retraction and constriction) of remarkable effectiveness and may be completely dry and free of hemorrhage in a few minutes. The patient may have been blood-pressureless in these few minutes, but some degree of flow recovery occurs as peripheral resistance is restored. A side wound or tear in an artery, on the other hand, which impedes retraction and constriction, is more apt to produce a fatal hemorrhage. In traumatic amputation of both lower limbs the wound has cut across several large arteries, hemorrhage from any one of which could readily be fatal. Immediate fatality from hemorrhage alone may not occur from this wound because the hemostatic mechanism of the open-ended artery can operate effectively.

Therefore, even in considering the loss of whole blood alone, either in the body cavities or the gut lumen or to the outside world, the route of blood loss is important in determining the bodily response and the treatment required.

B. VOLUMES INVOLVED IN HEMORRHAGIC SHOCK

The sudden loss, from the venous side, of a portion of the blood volume approximating 30 to 50 per cent produces the hemodynamic effects of shock. We have already seen that in individuals with normal heart and normal elastic blood vessels, the acute loss of 25 per cent of the blood volume produces a hypotension in the range of 70 to 90 mm. Hg, a pulse rate between 110 and 130, and the early picture of hypotension due to acute blood loss. The sudden loss of 50 per cent of the blood volume produces a systolic blood pressure between zero and 50, essentially "no blood pressure." In this setting, peripheral flow is markedly impaired and urine flow is universally reduced to an oliguric level (5 ml. per hour or less).

It is thus possible to make a first approximation of the amount of blood initially lost in hemorrhagic shock. This "first approximation" is crude but its realistic estimate may be of lifesaving significance. For instance, for a 50 kg. woman with a ruptured ectopic pregnancy, whose blood pressure is in the "unobtainable range" (meaning that it is zero to 50 mm. Hg) one may calculate her blood requirement as follows: being female, short, and weighing 50 kg. means that her blood volume (at 6 per cent of body weight) would be about 3000 ml. The patient has therefore lost between 1000 and 1500 ml. of blood.

Replacement of this amount immediately is mandatory. Starting one blood transfusion and permitting it to drip in a leisurely way is as ineffective in such a setting as treating severe diabetic acidosis with a tentative subcutaneous injection of 5 units of insulin. Both therapeutic agents are exactly specific but the doses and rates of administration are so far wide of the mark that virtually no response will be seen. Lack of response to transfusion has to be viewed skeptically and realistically in the light of the volume needs of the patient.

The treatment in such a situation should consist in the simultaneous infusion of blood into two veins, and through one of these veins the blood should be administered under pressure. The required amount of blood should be administered in an hour or less. In early cases hemodilution will be incomplete and the hematocrit no index of need whatsoever. In the particular setting referred to (ruptured ectopic pregnancy) operation should proceed without awaiting the completion of the blood administration, since securing an open-ended artery may also be essential to stop hemorrhage and restore blood pressure, as mentioned above.

By the same token, a strapping athlete of 85 kg. (blood volume at 8.0 per cent of body weight, equaling 6800 ml.) with a bleeding duodenal ulcer may require an amount of blood somewhat closer to 3400 ml. in the initial transfusion (0.5 blood volume). The administration of blood beyond the 50 per cent blood volume mark may of course be necessary. This volume is only a minimum budget in patients in frank shock from hemorrhage alone.

C. OPERATIVE AND WOUND SHOCK, VOLUMES INVOLVED

In the more complex setting of shock during anesthetized operation or of shock in unanesthetized massive tissue trauma, severe shock may be accompanied by a lesser volume loss because of the action of other factors, chiefly anesthesia and sepsis. If all known bleeding points have been secured and the patient is in profound shock, administration of an amount of blood approximating one-half the starting normal blood volume is required immediately. Over a period of time much greater volumes of blood may have to be administered than were originally lost, in order to restore the circulation. Vascular

resiliency is progressively lost either because of anesthesia or because of the pathologic changes of late wound shock; as time passes the "clinical phenomena of taking up" occurs. Restoration of the circulation may start bleeding points again after wound closure. For all these reasons an initial transfusion budget in the vicinity of 0.5 to 1.0 blood volume is essential.

If evacuation of the patient from the site of wounding to the hospital has been very rapid, and the total duration of the bleeding time therefore short, one may see patients still alive in whom the estimated total initial blood loss is as great as 75 per cent of the initial blood volume. This loss is of course not compatible with life for more than a few minutes. In the severely shocked individual, where large areas of muscle trauma are involved and much time has passed since the injury, there may be a smaller measurable blood loss, in the range of 30 to 50 per cent of starting estimated volume. But here, as in the instance mentioned above, the administration of blood will have to be far in excess of the measurable loss in order to restore the circulation. The use of 1.0 to 1.5 blood volume is not unusual.

When the injured, resuscitated patient undergoes definitive operation, the anesthetic agent relaxes the peripheral bed. There is a further loss of blood in the process of debridement, laparotomy, craniotomy, or whatever procedure is necessary. Blood losses in this latter category may run as high as 3000 ml. during a two-hour operation. Because of these two factors, the further infusion of blood becomes vitally important. The final result of transfusion and surgery in such individuals often includes the infusion of quantities of blood up to one to three times the normal estimated starting blood volume.

Section III.   The Effects of Oligemic Shock

A. HEMATOLOGIC EFFECTS

The hematologic effects of oligemic shock are:

(1) volume reduction (reduction in func-

tional extracellular and circulating blood volume) with no systematic change in the hematocrit;

(2) with extensive transfusion, a gradual

approach of the patient's hematocrit to that of the transfused blood, regardless of the total amount lost or replaced.

In shock, changes in the peripheral blood are not a guide to volume needs. The circulatory vitality of the patient is the guide: pulse, blood pressure, skin color, mentation, and urine flow. The prolonged vasoconstriction, anoxia, and deficiency of flow prevent the completion of normal hemodilution; a further factor to diminish any small usefulness the hematocrit may have in early wound shock is the mixed nature of the volume loss. In compound fracture of long bones and in crushing injury to the thighs, buttocks, and other muscular areas of the body, the fluid lost is predominantly whole blood. In lesser tissue damage, the loss is a mixture of whole blood and plasma exudation. Where there is infection or irritation of serous cavities, as in peritonitis due to perforated ulcer or in perforating injury with spillage of gastrointestinal contents, plasma is predominantly lost and an elevated hematocrit is produced early. For this reason one must evaluate the nature of the injury, whether or not a serous cavity is involved, the injury's duration and the presence or absence of infection, in order to understand the volume significance of the peripheral blood. Clinical examination of the circulation and measurement of urine output are the best guides to effective circulatory volume.

As the volume of transfusion approaches the blood volume, the hematocrit within the patient must inevitably approach the hematocrit of the bank blood infused. Bank blood has a hematocrit between 37 and 40. With or without continuing whole blood loss, as transfusion volume approaches 1.0 blood volume, the hematocrit necessarily approaches that in the bank blood. Any continuing plasma loss will raise the patient's hematocrit over that in the infused blood, and any effective transcapillary hemodilution will lower it. But, in hemorrhage, further transfusion of whole blood will not raise it further. Just as in early hemorrhage before hemodilution, so also in massive transfusion therapy, a fatal low blood volume may coexist with a low-normal hematocrit, red count, or hemoglobin concentration.

B. HEMODYNAMIC, RENAL, AND CARDIAC EFFECTS

The physiologic effects of shock have been extensively investigated in the dog. Quantitative data on man are not wholly lacking but are relatively scarce. They have been greatly amplified by the studies of the past fifteen years, including those of World War II and the Korean conflict. Information on the effects of pure shock-producing hemorrhage in man without trauma is very scarce. There are not many sources of hemorrhage which are unassociated with wounds or with blood in the gastrointestinal tract or serous cavities, conditions all of which alter the clinical and metabolic picture.

In this section are described the hemodynamic, renal, and cardiac and the endocrine, metabolic, and electrolyte effects of oligemic shock in which hemorrhage has played a major role.

1. Hemodynamic and Cardiac Effects

The hemodynamic and cardiac effects of shock are:

(1) arteriolar vasoconstriction, with rise in peripheral resistance, and a relative rise in diastolic pressure, with narrow pulse pressure;
(2) fall in systolic blood pressure;
(3) decreased venous return to the right heart;
(4) tachycardia with diminished stroke volume;
(5) decreased cardiac output with fall in arterial pressure, a narrow pulse pressure, and a low venous pressure;
(6) decreased coronary blood flow; the myocardium shares late in the generalized flow deficiency, tissue anoxia, and acidosis.

When acute volume loss is from a large opening in major arteries a different picture supervenes, as described previously.

a. Hemodynamics. When the blood is lost from the venous side of the circuit, arteriolar vasoconstriction maintains the blood pressure initially. As venous return to the right heart is lowered, the cardiac output is diminished. As this sequence progresses, deficiency of peripheral flow ensues, with tissue anoxia, local respiratory and metabolic acidosis, and, ultimately, death.

Loss of mixtures of whole blood and plasma, of plasma alone, or of extracellular fluid, proceeding from large and small veins or from the capillary bed, produces this picture. The rate at which flow deficiency develops is primarily a function of the rate and site of the fluid lost, of the rate of transcapillary refilling, and of the vascular resiliency of the organism—the physiologic age of the patient.

As mentioned previously, when the blood loss occurs from an open large artery, the hemodynamic effects are more drastic because peripheral resistance is distal to the site of loss and cannot restore blood pressure initially. Blood pressure loss and diminution in flow to peripheral organs occur prior to other hemodynamic or hematologic effects. The heart shares dangerously in this immediate flow deficiency in open arterial hemorrhage.

b. Cardiac Effects and Arterial Transfusion. We have no reason to suppose that the reactions of the myocardium to deficiency of flow are any different from those of any other peripheral vascular bed, save for the fact that significant anoxia or acidosis resulting in arrhythmia is rapidly fatal.

With loss of blood volume from the venous side or from the capillaries and with effective peripheral arteriolar vasoconstriction, inflow pressure at the coronary arteries is maintained as long as blood pressure is supported. Cardiac function, as judged by ability to vary cardiac work and by electrocardiographic appearances, appears to remain intact initially. This vital compensation is lost later on in the shock state. By sharp contrast, hemorrhage from a large artery produces an immediate fall of coronary perfusion pressure, which robs the coronary arteries of flow toward the myocardium. The early effect of the catechol amines on the coronary vessels is that of vasodilatation and, given arterial resiliency, there is probably increased

coronary flow in man. But as right heart inflow is reduced cardiac output necessarily falls, stroke volume falls precipitously (there being a progressive tachycardia), and coronary inflow pressure is lost. Regardless of coronary dilatation, no flow results if inflow pressure is lost; myocardial ischemia then results.

Thus, with either venous or arterial loss there comes a time in prolonged shock when decreased myocardial blood supply and function enters as an important factor in the patient's deterioration. If coronary caliber is reduced by disease this eventuality occurs earlier and at a time when digitalization may be effective. Were "heart failure"—in the sense of decreased ability of the myocardium to propel its inflow—to become an important factor in shock, we should expect to see an elevated venous pressure. Elevated venous pressure is seen in human shock only when the shock is of long duration and blood transfusion has been extensive. Severe shock of long duration in man must necessarily involve multiple transfusions, since without them the duration would not be long. These transfusions are given into the venous side of the circulation, and venous pressure ultimately rises as blood volume returns in the face of a failing myocardium. But cardiac anoxia can and does occur before venous pressure is elevated, and its earliest signs may be the electrocardiographic changes of subendocardial ischemia.

Thus, where shock is prolonged (twenty-four to forty-eight hours), decreased peripheral blood flow of the myocardium prolonged, and intravenous blood transfusion large in volume, patients occasionally develop elevated venous pressure. This is often associated with profuse venous bleeding (which may be severe intraoperatively), as well as the electrocardiographic changes of subendocardial ischemia, and evidence of myocardial damage. If arterial pressure is still low while venous pressure is high, intra-arterial transfusion is indicated after digitalization, so that perfusion and pressure at the circle of Willis and the coronary ostia may be increased. This combination—shock with hypotension, a digitalized heart, and elevated venous pressure after "adequate venous transfusion" —is a clear indication for arterial transfusion.

Although animal experimentation has not lent support to arterial transfusion, it is very difficult to reproduce in the dog the situation seen in an elderly man after shock of twenty-four to forty-eight hours' duration, with multiple intravenous transfusions, underlying chronic coronary disease, and elevated venous pressure. Until some such chronic experiment has been carefully studied in the dog, we prefer not to abandon our view that intra-arterial transfusion has a place and that its place lies in those individuals in whom prolonged deficiency of blood flow to the myocardium is the chief factor in decreased cardiac function. The heart cannot restore inflow pressure to the coronary artery ostia when the left ventricle itself is anoxic. This vicious circle may be broken by arterial transfusion.

Myocardial occlusion occurs during or after shock, especially in older people, and is a common cause of death, due to thrombosis under conditions of decreased flow.

Tachycardia, in itself, may so reduce stroke volume as seriously to embarrass forward output. In normal persons this borderline lies at pulse rates between 140 and 160 beats per minute, above which the decreased diastolic filling time is in itself a factor in deterioration. In chronic heart disease, especially of the coronary arteries and of the mitral valves, this "dangerous tachycardia" may supervene at much slower pulse rates.

2. Renal Effects of Oligemic Shock; The Hourly Urine Output

The renal effects of oligemic shock are due to the coincident activity of at least four factors:

(1) local specific and differential hemodynamic changes, consisting initially of afferent and efferent arteriolar vasoconstriction with increased filtration fraction and tubular ischemia;

(2) ischemia shared by other organs and due to the prolonged deficiency of flow in all the periphery;

(3) endocrine effects acting primarily on the tubule;

(4) the nephrotoxic action of certain chemical compounds on the renal epithelium.

Prolonged oligemic shock with absence of urine output for many hours may be associated with the complete return of normal renal function if there are not present other deleterious factors, the most ominous of which are pigment excretion, pre-existent renal disease as in elderly people, and desalting water loss or dehydration.

Very early in shock there is a decreased renal blood flow greater than (i.e., differential to) that observed elsewhere. At the same time, the tubule is coming under very strong endocrine influences favoring resorption of sodium and water from the glomerular filtrate. It is not clinically possible to separate these two influences (hemodynamic and endocrine) in evaluating renal function. But as a general rule, *hemodynamic effects are reflected in gross changes in urine volume, while endocrine effects are reflected in urine composition.*

It is for this reason that an increase in urine flow in response to increased blood volume is so significant. The action of salt resorption and antidiuresis acting on a large solute output (as in shock) will not grossly reduce volume, whereas decreased renal blood flow will reduce volume drastically and immediately. An increased urine volume, after treatment of shock, represents increased blood flow more importantly than decreased endocrine activity, although both may result.

Decreased urine output persists as the patient passes from hemorrhage or wounding into a state of hypotension and shock. The only distinguishing feature of this continued progression is that larger amounts of restorative therapy (whole blood, plasma fractions, or non–colloid-containing solutions) are required to restore renal blood flow and function, which are measured in terms of hourly urine output. A normal hourly urine output varies from 25 to 50 ml. per hour. Under the conditions of oligemia passing on to oligemic shock this is reduced to a level of from 2 to 10 ml. per hour. At such low values bladder washout is a factor making for variability, and the observations can only be made with an inlying catheter. Its insertion is an important initial step in treating any threat to the effective blood volume.

With sudden massive hemorrhage, the urine output is essentially zero. When blood has been infused and volume partially or fully restored (as evidenced by the clinical examination of the patient), yet hourly urine outputs remain in the low range, one is dealing with the possibilities either that severe renal damage has been produced or that volume has not been restored. In such an enigma the infusion test is of basic importance.

a. Infusion Test. Urine flow is nicely restored by adequate infusion when it is given early in the treatment of patients who have a low blood volume with decreased glomerular filtration rate and some continuing renal vasoconstriction. This restoration is decreasingly likely to occur with the increasing passage of time. Therefore, early in the course of oliguria due to a blood-volume-reducing process, some sort of infusion test is very useful. *

This test infusion to discover the nature of continuing oliguria is used *after* the restoration of effective volume has been accomplished, as judged by other clinical indices. These infusions are not to be considered as a part of initial replacement, for the volumes are much too small for this; they represent added extra volume used in a short period of time to differentiate the cause of the continuing oliguria.

The type of infusion used must depend on the clinical setting. One of the following types is used: (1) whole blood, (2) plasma or dextran, (3) saline or lactate, or (4) dextrose in water. The first two (colloids) are given as 500 ml. in thirty minutes; the latter two (colloid-free) as 1000 ml. in forty minutes. The first two are selected for infusion tests in hemorrhage or burns, the latter two in cases of desalting water loss or desiccation-dehydration. Only one such infusion test is given; its performance is a planned and carefully executed study of the response of the kidney to increased perfusion and blood flow.

---

* This is in sharp contrast to the later situation where, in the established oliguria known to be due to parenchymatous damage, sudden infusion may be lethal.

The test infusion should be preceded and followed by accurate measures of the hourly urine output. The only result which is capable of clear interpretation is a definite increase in output with infusion. This signifies that effective volume was previously low, that this was an important factor in reducing kidney function, and that infusion volume should be increased. When such an infusion is not followed by a clear increase in urine volume, one is dealing either with parenchymatous renal damage or a situation in which other factors, such as pre-existent renal disease, are modifying renal function.

C. ENDOCRINE-METABOLIC AND ELECTROLYTIC EFFECTS OF SHOCK

These effects are:
(1) increase in adrenomedullary secretion;
(2) increase in pituitary and adrenocortical secretion;
(3) maximal influences of the following metabolic changes:
    (a) mobilization of nitrogen, potassium, and cell water; increased urinary excretion of nitrogen, depending upon urine volume; where urine volume is low, an early increase in blood urea nitrogen and uremia;
    (b) depletion of liver glycogen and tendency to increase blood sugar levels;
    (c) decreased excretion of water and sodium by the kidney, accompanied by a relative increase in potassium excretion, the absolute magnitude of the latter depending entirely on total urine volume; decreased urinary sodium:potassium ratio;
(4) increasing acidosis in the anoxic tissues (hypoxic acidosis), accompanied or followed by respiratory acidosis (decreased pulmonary perfusion), oliguria, hepatic failure, cerebral anoxia, and myocardial failure.

The evidence available from bioassay in animals and from chemical studies of urine and blood in man suggests that oligemic shock is a most potent stimulus to increased secretion of epinephrine, hydrocortisone, and norepinephrine. Peripheral vasoconstriction and tachycardia seem readily accountable on the basis of these endocrine changes.

The metabolic phenomena produced in shock are not qualitatively different from those seen in other types of trauma, although their magnitude is greater and they start earlier.

The metabolic changes seen early are those of the first phase of surgical convalescence, greatly magnified and in the face of decreased urine output. A mixed hypoxic and respiratory acidosis, uremia, hepatic failure, lack of gastrointestinal function, cerebral anoxia, and myocardial failure may all be mixed in varying degrees in late shock. Many observations in man have delineated the secondary metabolic changes that occur as organ function decreases and death draws near: accumulation of carbon dioxide, fixed acid metabolites, polypeptides, and toxic substances. A complete review of these additional changes will not be entered here. Studies of blood-sludging, liver-trapping, splanchnic stasis, and many related phenomena of late shock in the laboratory are discussed in the section on the literature.

D. THE ROLE OF INFECTION

In the dog a severe infectious process ensues after prolonged shock, as shown by Aub and Fine and their coworkers. Both muscle and gastrointestinal ischemia play a role. The work of Aub is centered on anaerobic infection in the muscle of dogs, that of Fine on aerobic endotoxins largely of gastrointestinal origin. It is further an implication of the many researches of Fine and his group that infection of gastrointestinal origin may play a much earlier role in death from shock than was formerly suspected (in the dog) and can apparently be prevented in part by the administration of antibiotics. There is little evidence to support such a basically septic element in most cases of clinical shock in man.

When there are injuries and wounds in man involving gross contamination, and particularly when they occur under anaerobic conditions and involve the bowel, infection plays a role very early and even during the first eight hours. An invasive infectious process may take hold and push the patient down the path to demise even though blood volume is restored.

The fact that sepsis does occasionally occur as a complication of shock should not lead us to the conclusion that infection is always an important initiating or sustaining factor in early oligemic shock in man, as it is in the dog. All of the evidence, bacteriologic and clinical, is against this conclusion. While the surgeon treating early shock must keep an eye out for infection and should remove devitalized tissues, close or exteriorize injured viscera, and use antibiotics intelligently, he should not delude himself that downward progress in the early hours is due to infection if other factors, most particularly inadequate blood volume restoration, are present.

The prominence of sepsis in the deterioration of the dog in shock has led to an overemphasis of bacterial factors in human shock, and an oversimplified view of those that are truly operative. Clinically there are at least three distinct types of relationship between sepsis and shock in man. Any one of these three might loosely be termed "septic shock" although they are quite distinct. These three relationships are as follows.

1. Sepsis developing as a complication of the same wound that caused the oligemic shock. Such sepsis may be aerobic or anaerobic; its toxemia and the fluid dislocation caused by the sepsis naturally worsen the shock state of the patient.

2. Oligemic shock developing as a result of massive fluid dislocation (edema sequestration) in an area primarily involved with sepsis. The shock of peritonitis and of streptococcal cellulitis are examples.

3. Hypotension in bacteremia. This is particularly prominent in gram-negative bacillary infections of the blood stream. Loss of blood volume is not prominent and a primary "toxemia" appears to be at fault, reducing either cardiac output or peripheral resistance, or both. A shocklike state with oliguria and anuria commonly results.

If shock is due primarily to infection, as in bacteremia, control of the bacterial process is the only route to success in treatment.

E. THE VOLUME EFFECTS OF IMMEDIATE VERSUS DELAYED REPLACEMENT OF WHOLE BLOOD

1. Immediate Replacement

The treatment of shock is based on the immediate quantitative re-establishment of effective circulation. A careful examination of the patient, estimate of his normal blood volume, and an educated guess as to the loss (as indicated by his clinical condition and as modified by his age, vascular elasticity, and organ function) should be followed by prompt infusion of an adequate amount of whole blood. This is the ideal but it is not always obtainable.

The treatment of the individual in shock involves many other matters which are inseparable from the particular disease process or injury which has resulted in shock. These are dealt with in Part VI.

2. Problems in Delayed Replacement

When blood loss has occurred (with or without shock) and blood replacement has been delayed, impossible, or inadequate, hemodilution will have commenced by transcapillary refilling of the plasma volume from the interstitial phase. This, as already described, produces the secondary anemia of hemodilution, characterized by a low erythrocyte volume, a partially restored plasma volume, and a low hematocrit. If shock has occurred, the blood volume is still low despite the partially restored plasma volume. If to this stable hemodiluted system whole blood is then added in large quantities (whose calculation is based often on a delayed appreciation of the magnitude of the initial loss), an acute hypervolemia is produced. If the patient's cardiovascular system can handle the hypervolemia, the blood volume is in due course restored to normal by catabolism of the extra protein and by excretion of the water and electrolyte (plasma dispersal). The patient then passes through a long phase of elevated hematocrit with bone marrow suppression, a phase that lasts until the extra erythrocytes have died off. If the cardiovascular system cannot handle this sudden hypervolemia, a commonplace in the elderly,

all the appearances of congestive heart failure ensue: dyspnea, tachycardia, elevated venous pressure, and pulmonary edema. Nevertheless where hypotension persists in the elderly it is better to replace blood loss just to the point of early congestion than it is to under-replace the loss.

Three general rules apply to late replacement of blood in shock.

(1) It is preferable to transfuse the patient to the point of a beginning elevation in venous pressure (and venesect later if arterial pressure is maintained) than it is to undertransfuse. In elderly patients receiving massive replacement the venous pressure should be measured. If there is elevated venous pressure while hypotension still persists, digitalization and arterial transfusion are indicated.

(2) If hypotension and oliguria still exist and other causes for these changes have been excluded, volume is still severely restricted and whole blood should be used initially. In the late situation, remember: the lower the hematocrit, the higher the plasma volume—proceed with caution after the initial infusion.

(3) If the patient's vital signs are stabilized so that the situation is not quite so pressing, use separated red cells and bring the hematocrit up to normal by slower stages.

The use of separated erythrocytes is especially important in the elderly. In military surgery and in most civilian industrial accidents, the hazard of overtransfusion in an acute stabilized hemodilution is so small that it may be neglected for all practical purposes. In the cancer surgery of the elderly, in heart disease, liver disease, and kidney disease this hazard is great; it must be avoided by accurate volume replacement and measurement of venous pressure.

F. LATE SEQUELAE: KIDNEY DAMAGE

With the development of blood transfusion and modern surgical care, increasing numbers of patients who have been in severe shock for prolonged periods of time now survive. Late effects on the liver have not been recorded; the same is true of lungs, gastrointestinal tract, and endocrine glands. Prolonged effects on the central nervous system are occasionally seen, but the tragedy of a patient who has been in oligemic shock for a day or two and who, when recovered, shows either decerebration or a prolonged mental deficiency is fortunately rare in contrast to the frequency of late mental change and cerebral damage following acute cerebral anoxia produced by cardiac arrest, ventricular fibrillation, or other disorders characterized by periods of total circulatory standstill.

The most common late sequelae of shock have to do with renal function. These changes are associated with prolonged periods of renal anoxia in the presence of nephrotoxins such as the heme pigments. The result of this combination is acute renal insufficiency. Clinically, it is rare to see post-traumatic renal insufficiency without the combination of anoxia and pigment; in the laboratory the two are markedly synergistic in their nephrotoxic effects. Despite the suggestive nature of these two lines of evidence, the precise etiologic role of pigment remains controversial. We may summarize the matter here.

(1) Porphyrin (heme) pigments are dangerous to the kidney in shock. Their presence should be prevented when it is possible to do so, and renal ischemia should be avoided in their presence. Such pigments may arise from dying muscle, from blood destruction, or as a result of liver disease; they include hemoglobin, methemoglobin, myoglobin, methemalbumin, and the bilirubin-biliverdin series.

(2) The combination of shock and hemoglobinemia with pigment release bodes ill, much worse than shock alone, for the future of the kidney.

Since the replacement of whole blood is vital to the treatment of shock, and since transfusion of whole blood is one of the commonest sources of free hemoglobin pigments in the course of oligemic shock, there is here another potentially vicious cycle: the very therapy most essential in the treatment of shock may become most dangerous to the kidney if the blood used is overage, poorly banked, or incompatible. It is for this reason (among many others) that the treatment of the patient in shock should be prompt, accurate, and effective, and should involve the freshest available blood. Central to the effectiveness of such treatment is a clear concept on the part of the surgeon of the absolute volumes of blood needed for restoration of the circulation.

G. VOLUME SUMMARY

The emphasis in this section on shock in relation to the circulation has been on the volumes of lost blood that produce clinical syndromes and on the bodily changes that result from this loss. In recapitulation, the clinical pictures associated with approximate blood losses are as follows:

(1) Bleeding without hemodynamic changes:

Less than 15 per cent of the blood volume has been lost.

(2) Bleeding with early hemodynamic changes and lowered blood pressure, but not shock:

20 to 30 per cent of blood volume has been lost.

(3) After either of the above, if signs of bleeding have stopped and there is a stable hemodiluted hematocrit:

Transfuse with caution; separated cells are useful in elderly or in visceral disease; the extent of hematocrit lowering is a rough measure of previous loss.

(4) Early acute shock with open arterial bleeding:

The extent of blood volume lost cannot be assessed until the open arterial hemorrhage has been secured.

(5) Early acute shock from venous, capillary, surgical, or wound losses:

50 to 100 per cent of blood volume has been lost.

(6) Shock with maintained flow deficiency for over an hour, particularly in wounds:

Assume that the "clinical phenomenon of taking up" has occurred; 100 to 150 per cent blood volume will be needed in replacement.

(7) Shock with an elevated hematocrit:

Plasma loss plays a significant role; the total volume of blood and plasma lost falls into the above categories of loss and response (see Chapter 11).

CHAPTER 10

The Blood Volume, Hemorrhage, and Shock: Notes from the Literature

Section I. Blood Volume

A. NORMAL BLOOD VOLUME

Hicks *et al.* (1956) present various formula for predicting normal blood volume. Their own control series, based on RV + PV methods, is admittedly small (fifteen subjects). In addition they studied sixty-five normal students by DPH methods, correcting to a standard WBH:LVH ratio of 92:100. While very critical of other workers for omitting consideration of obese patients, these authors have accepted as representative of the whole population a group very homogeneous in age. In their study there are only four patients over thirty-five years of age. They measured fat-fold thickness, height, weight, and girth, and confirm very nicely the conclusion of so many compositional studies that the fat factor is sex-linked. They conclude that a blood volume measured by a DPH method and corrected for WBH:LVH ratio is satisfactorily accurate, but they include no studies of sick patients. Their nomograms are developed in an interesting way; the results are not significantly different from our "clinical basis": sex, weight, and body build. Were one to measure fat-fold thickness and use these nomograms, normal values could be predicted much more closely than by simpler means.

Brady *et al.* (1953) studied plasma volume methods and showed again that multiple sampling was to be preferred for accuracy. This simple message seems to need repeated confirmation. Little confidence should be placed in short-cut, one-sample methods. Williams' study also showed that dye and radioactive iodinated albumin (RIHSA) check out well, as of course they should since both are albumin tags. The authors show again that calculating blood volumes from the red cell volume (RVH method) has the same intrinsic fault as DPH methods; that is, they are hematocrit-dependent. They conclude very appropriately that the best method is based on use of the formula RV + PV = BV, by some double tracer. These tracers can be dye and P^{32}, RIHSA and Cr^{51}, or any other convenient pair. Their article has data from which normal predictions and WBH: LVH ratio can be calculated. All data are on young vigorous males and the volume means are rather high.

Verel *et al.* (1956) measured the blood volume in pregnancy by simultaneous DPH and RVH methods. The WBH:LVH ratio showed a wider range than in the controls; the data indicate that a simultaneous PV + RV technique should be used. The increase in plasma volume in normal pregnancy was confirmed; in most instances there was no increase in red cell volume. The increase in plasma volume may be 500 to 1500 ml. (1 to 3 per cent of body weight) over predicted normal. The operative blood loss (direct) at delivery ranged from 200 to 1400 ml. and large amounts of "missing" whole blood were recorded when the blood volume was again measured postpartum. The cause of this large variation gave rise to speculation; the authors did not consider it technical in origin. Uterine thrombus and some sort of mysterious cell removal were entertained as possible causes of the seeming disappearance of erythrocytes at or after delivery. The authors were evidently unaware of the analogous finding of unaccountable whole blood loss after severe injury. Caton *et al.* (1951) and Dieckman and Wegner (1934) have also measured the blood volume in pregnancy.

Blood volume in the aged has been studied by Schmidt *et al.* (1956). Schmidt's study was done by a DPH method, corrected by 0.96 for plasma trapping in the hematocrit tube and 0.91 (as an arbitrary finding) for the WBH: LVH ratio. The study includes thirty-six men and fifty-six women, with many over seventy years of age, and several over ninety. The results are expressed in terms of liters per square meter, and show a very slightly lower red cell volume in men with the same plasma volume as in the Gibson and Evans (1937) young normals. In women, even these small differences were not noted.

Beling *et al.* (1952) report briefly on the results of blood volume data on elderly patients, using a DPH method. Their "normal" values with which comparisons are made are definitely higher than current data (8.5 per cent of body weight for both sexes). The original data are not presented nor are the clinical diagnoses. Their data for patients under sixty years of age closely approximate our norm (about 7.2 per cent of body weight), though here again there is no allowance for sex difference. The older patients were found to have blood volumes in the neighborhood of 6.7 per cent of body weight. The authors state that the patients were better clinically with "restoration of deficits" and withstood surgery more satisfactorily. One would like to see more data to support either the extent of the "deficits" or the contention about "restoration."

Cohn and Shock (1949) studied the changes in blood volume with aging, using a DPH method and a 4 per cent correction for trapped plasma. They found no significant changes from the reported figures in younger people.

In children (Brines *et al.*, 1941) there is a nice linear relation between surface area and blood volume. In older people this precise relation is lost and there is more blood per unit area than in children. Schmidt believes that beyond puberty any sort of prediction is apt to be wide of the mark. But here again what one seeks from blood volume prediction must be defined. Using Schmidt's very precise index (liters per square meter), the blood volume can be predicted from his own data, to within 500 ml. (roughly 10 per cent) for 66 per cent of individuals. This is certainly as good as any compositional or anthropometric prediction and is excellent for clinical use. Our simple sex-weight-body-build basis, as applied to his data, also permits close prediction, to about 650 ml., for 75 per cent of the individuals.

B. TRAPPED PLASMA IN THE HEMATOCRIT TUBE

Chaplin and Mollison (1952) studied the degree of trapping in the measurement of the cellular fraction of centrifuged peripheral blood. They found that even under standard conditions of centrifugation there was some scatter but that, generally speaking, the speed and duration of centrifugation was the sole critical factor after simple sedimentation had been overcome. The correction varied (at thirty minutes of centrifugation) from 2.0 per cent (of the packed red cell column) at a venous hematocrit of 15, to 5 per cent at 85. The nature of the tube used was not critical; the time of spinning (over thirty minutes) introduced a further potential correction of only 1 to 1.5 per cent. Stated otherwise, the decrement in packing fraction after thirty minutes was negligible. For a thirty-minute, 3000-revolution-per-minute, 15 cm. radius centrifugation with hematocrits between 30 and 50, an approximate correction of about 1 to 3 per cent is valid. This means that an apparent hematocrit of 42 is actually (at the lowest) 40.8, and that longer spinning might reduce it at the most to 39.7. When one considers that this degree of precision is rarely attained in clinical work and that random variation is at the level of ± 2 per cent, it is apparent that this correction, while an essential refinement in research, is clinically unimportant. It is also apparent that it accounts for approximately one-third of the WBH:LVH ratio. In other words, the whole body hematocrit is about 10 per cent less than the large vessel hematocrit; correction of the large vessel hematocrit for trapped plasma makes the WBH only about 7 to 8 per cent lower than the LVH.

Chapin and Ross (1942) had indicated about the same conclusions as a result of studies by tracer methods.

C. WBH:LVH RATIO—THE WHOLE BODY HEMATOCRIT RATIO

Chaplin *et al.* (1953) made an extensive study of the WBH:LVH ratio, using dye plus P^{32} for a PV + RV method. They found the ratio to be 0.910 ± 0.026 in twenty-eight patients with venous hematocrits ranging from 9 to 82 per cent; the hematocrit changes were due to a wide range of pathologic conditions. The large vessel hematocrit was corrected for trapped plasma by the method of Chaplin and Mollison (1952). They re-emphasize, as we have pointed out, that this ratio correction (for WBH:LVH) is of theoretical interest but that its constancy renders it applicable to DPH methods or RVH methods without using PV + RV. They did not study patients with burns or in shock. They tabulate WBH:LVH values from five other authors. These values range from 0.895

(± 0.067) to 0.915 (± 0.012). If we take the value of 0.910 as a mean, we find that this range of WBH:LVH ratios, applied to DPH or RVH methods, introduces a range of corrections lying within the error of the initial determination (± 3 per cent). They conclude, as have many before them, that the early steep-slope extrapolation gives a smaller and more "valid" plasma volume value. They do not entertain the possibility that dextran of high molecular weight might dilute in an even smaller volume than Evans blue dye, and thus yield WBH:LVH ratios near unity.

The WBH:LVH ratio is an artifact of the plasma volume measurement. There is no doubt that blood in small vessels has a lower hematocrit than does the periphery; but areas of high hematocrit (bone marrow and spleen, for example) balance out this distribution factor. This is suggested by the data of Craig and Waterhouse (1955) who, using dextran of average molecular weight of 195,000, found plasma volume of 3.68 per cent of body weight in normal men. There are many reasons to suspect that this is a "truer" value than the dye or radioalbumin methods based on dilution of smaller particles; in the long run one may find that the WBH:LVH ratio is closer to 1.00 than is now considered to be the case.

Cominskey *et al.* (1955) have shown that the splanchnic hematocrit is 80 per cent of the venous hematocrit in dogs. Based on data for hepatic sinusoid hematocrit at 69 per cent of LVH (Allen and Reeve, 1953) they conclude that 77 per cent of splanchnic blood is in the sinusoids.

Section II. Blood Loss

A. OPERATIVE BLOOD LOSS

Ditzler and Eckenhoff (1956) studied operative blood loss in relation to operative time and the use of controlled hypotension. Blood loss was measured by sponge weight; the operations were mostly radical procedures done for malignancy. The data are nicely presented and show that normotensive losses are, as examples, as follows:

OPERATION	BLOOD LOST (ml.)	
	Mean	Range
Radical neck dissection	1400	500–1500
Radical pelvic dissection	2750	1000–6000

There was a slight reduction in operative blood loss, using hypotensive anesthesia. The reduction in operative blood loss by the use of controlled hypotension is not a certainty, and the authors question its value when based on this single consideration; they had three deaths under hypotensive anesthesia. The time factor was not clear-cut: larger operations did not necessarily produce more blood loss; the operations took a little longer using controlled hypotension. The authors report three deaths from uncontrollable oozing after operations involving multiple transfusions.

Rains (1955) compared various methods of measuring operative blood loss. He found iron analysis on sponge rinses too laborious but did not try total nitrogen on the same; he preferred sponge weights. By weighing the patient simultaneously he was able to estimate the insensible loss during operation (30 to 120 ml.) and approximate the fluid loss in the wound (120 to 600 ml.). He also made a try at multiple dye-plasma-hematocrit blood-volume determinations but found that, without extensive experience with the method, it was unreliable. The operative blood-loss figures which he finally achieves with sponge weights are far below those of most other observers, for he rarely finds a loss of over 500 ml. even in coarctation surgery. The article points up nicely the pitfalls for the unwary in this well-plowed field.

Albritten *et al.* (1950) showed that in patients with tuberculosis there was a decrease in blood volume and a need for replacement between stages, suggesting continued loss, possibly in the tissue planes of the thoracoplasty.

B. BLOOD LOSS SHORT OF SHOCK; OTHER HYPOVOLEMIAS

Fine *et al.* (1958) have shown that in normal adult human subjects, bleeds of 8 ml. per kg. produced a brisk rise in urinary aldosterone excretion; there was no change in creatinine clearance. Other urinary steroids were unchanged. Hemodilution occurred in twenty-four to forty-eight hours. Nonetheless, restoration of volume in two hours by concentrated albumin failed to decrease or prevent the aldosterone rise. This aldosterone rise was not associated with extremely low sodium concentrations, nor with significant alteration in plasma concentration of electrolytes.

Joergenson *et al.* (1956) studied the blood volume in acute abdominal conditions using a DPH method and a WBH:LVH correction factor of 0.915. They used surface area reference and a figure of 42.5 as their normal basal hematocrit. In most cases the blood volume measurements were done before fluids were given. The authors do not generally distinguish sex or body build in their tabulations or normal values. Many rather large increases in both plasma volume and erythrocyte volume were seen, even in perforations, obstructions, peritonitis, and pancreatitis. In some, but not all, of those cases with increases, fluids had been given. The volume of the peritoneal fluid was measured in some patients by aspiration.

This type of study is sorely needed and these data are of great interest. It is unfortunate that a PV + RV method was not used. The very random results doubtless trace back to the random nature of the cases. The occasional huge red cell volume increases must be methodologic; the increase in plasma volume can of course be real (with transcapillary refilling or after therapy), so long as dye penetrates a large area of increased permeability. The latter cannot be excluded merely by the low dye concentration of the free peritoneal fluid, as found by these authors.

The authors show nicely that shock may coexist with only small reduction in blood volume in certain instances, but in most where hypotension was present there were blood volume deficits of 500 to 4000 ml. Their conclusion that acute abdominal conditions frequently merit blood transfusion of course is borne out by a wealth of clinical data and experience. There is no tabulation of plasma volume as an inverse function of hematocrit in these cases.

C. BLOOD VOLUME IN WOUNDS AND SHOCK

The study of Prentice *et al.* (1954) on blood volume changes in the wounded of the Korean War is of basic importance in this field. Much of the literature on the study of blood volume in surgery has been confused by researches evidently motivated by a desire to "run off a few blood volumes" on a group of patients and carried out by those inexperienced in dilution techniques and unaware of the fact that in this apparently simple area of study reside some of the most complex and inexplicable phenomena of surgical metabolism and biochemistry.

The Korean study group avoided such pitfalls, used both dye and chromate (but not always simultaneously), brought out clearly the internal contradictions in their data, and present the raw information in tabular form, clearly set out for the close scrutiny it deserves.

They studied the severely wounded after initial resuscitative transfusion and surgery. Remarkably large volumes of blood were given to these patients: thirty-one of the fifty-three patients received over 5000 ml., and nine over 10,000 ml. There was little evidence of overtransfusion. Indeed, in about 60 per cent of the cases there was a "static deficit" of 15 per cent of the estimated normal blood volume (or more) after resuscitation, and only three of these twenty-eight patients were in shock at the time of measurement. In general, the more blood given (usually muscle-mass injury required the most blood), the greater the tendency to show a substantial continuing deficit after transfusion. Not infrequently the blood given was substantially greater in amount than that remaining in the circulation after transfusion.

The significance of the static deficits of 15 per cent or less is doubtful, as in several of the normal controls (see their Table 6) the volumes are low in relation to predicted values, another evidence that prediction of normal blood volumes involves a range rather than a closely-grouped mean. But the very large discrepancies observed in many instances are far beyond this range and suggest other mechanisms.

This tendency to "missing blood" was further documented in a remarkable series of eight patients in whom two volume measurements were carried out. The second determination showed a blood volume increase of 600 ml. or less in all instances, despite the fact that from 3500 to 10,500 ml. had been given in the interim! This tendency is shared by both plasma volume and red cell volume.

Significant hemolysis was nicely ruled out by appropriate study of hemoglobin in blood and excreta.

In addition to initial losses, the continued oozing, operative loss (often 3000 to 5000 ml. where multiple wounds are debrided), and postoperative bleeding are all factors in such severely wounded men. Even with such allowances the amounts of lost blood remain very large.

A slowly falling hematocrit was the rule after the initial transfusion episode. This was usually due to a rising plasma volume with constant erythrocyte volume—a continuing hemodilution. The authors point out that previous dextran therapy may play some unexplained role here. But in our experience this is not an uncommon finding in civilian surgery where no dextran is used. The authors ruled out "delayed mixing" as a cause for error; only in abdominal wounds were clear-cut technical factors seen, and here the dye leakage into the peritoneum gave "false high" values for the plasma volume, a small relative error.

Unfortunately, in those instances where both dye and chromate were used, the authors calculated the blood volume from both instead of adding them together to express the blood volume on a "PV + RV" basis and from this a whole body hematocrit: large vessel hematocrit ratio. The latter can be done from their data which, as presented, show the "blood volume by dye" to be larger than the "blood volume by chromate." This is merely an expression of a WBH:LVH ratio of less than 1:0. Determinations usually showed a difference of about 16 per cent, the dye method yielding the larger figure. But in severe abdominal wounds, with liver involvement, the dye volume was 30 to 40 per cent larger, suggesting a large area of increased permeability, possibly in the peritoneal cavity.

Taken as a whole, this work points up, as few other published studies do, the large volumes of blood needed in severe wounds, and the fact that much of the blood given is difficult to account for in or out of the circulation. This brings to mind the "clinical phenomenon of taking up" previously menioned, or some similar explanation for the blood volume phenomena of the severely injured who have been or are in shock. The explanation is probably physiologic, and not methodologic.

In the extensively wounded man much of this lost blood may reside in tissue planes and areolar areas extending over large areas about the wound and up and down the trunk. This blood ultimately represents an increased heme pigment excretion when it is finally broken down, but the process is very slow indeed. Remarkably prolonged and accurate measurements of fecal urobilinogen (or some other measure of heme excretion) would be required to reveal the porphyrins. Nitrogen: phosphorus ratios reveal this blood as a factor in the early balance changes.

Crosby (Howard, BCK, II) continued, expanded, and further refined the work of Prentice *et al.* (1954). Crosby concluded that the wholesale use of stored group O, Rh-negative blood, often in very large amounts, involved very few problems for the patient. The loss of nonviable elements (platelets, white cells, a portion of the erythrocytes) was neither excessive nor deleterious. The remarkable delayed loss of red cells was again observed, particularly in musculoskeletal wounds. In the abdominal wound there was an urgent need for blood, but requirements, once met, might be followed later by evidences of polycythemia and congestion. There was some evidence of a late hemolytic process. Although there were no transfusion reactions, there was difficulty in crossmatching after multiple group O, Rh-negative transfusions, there were demonstrable antibodies against the native red cells of the donor, and delayed recipient type-specific transfusions were somewhat hazardous or at best a source of hemolysis. A period of two weeks was specified after the massive universal-donor transfusions as being the interval after which type-specific blood could again be used.

There were no reactions attributable to the "dangerous universal donor" (Ervin *et al.*, 1950, a, b) in Korea, according to Crosby. The division of the group O blood into "high titer" beyond 1:256 proved to be safe in practice. Neutralizing type-specific substance

can be used in such blood. Crosby's data on coagulation (Howard, BCK, II) further corroborate the data already reviewed. An early hypocoagulability was often noted in the Korean casualties while there was a transfusion hypoprothrombinemia. Lack of labile factor was blamed. Early wound ooze was often noted.

Artz *et al.* (1955) use the figure 70 cc. per kg. (7.0 per cent of body weight) as the normal blood volume as based on his dilution studies (Cr^{51}). He reports a series of extensive injuries with blood volumes after operation in the range of 48 to 107 per cent normal; most were in the range of 65 to 85 per cent normal. Two patients who later died, one of peritonitis and one of shock, had high blood volumes at the close of operation, indicating the obvious fact that further postoperative events can be fatal even though volume is restored. It is of interest that the twenty deaths in the 138 "most severely wounded" in this particular study, all of whom received massive whole-blood transfusion, four died of uncontrolled postoperative oozing, three of shock, three of uncontrolled hemorrhage, and two of cardiac arrest. All twelve of these deaths were potentially related to the amount or nature of the resuscitative blood volume replacement. Of this same group, those that were admitted with unobtainable blood pressure due to abdominal wounds, 65 per cent died; in extremity wounds, a lesser mortality was observed, suggesting that the peritoneal sepsis of the critical and neglected abdominal wound greatly complicates resuscitation. Of those casualties in this series who required 15 or more pints of blood (sixty cases), 35 per cent developed clinically significant post-traumatic renal insufficiency, 14 per cent outright anuria.

Artz (1955) reports an ingenious effort to judge adequacy of preoperative blood volume replacement by the use of a tilt table. Green and Metheny (1947) had used such a method and related a syncopal or severe hypotensive reaction on tilting to the deficiency of about 1500 ml. of blood. Duncan *et al.* (1944) observed the same phenomenon and postulated its clinical usefulness. Artz considered it a possible test of the functional readiness of the circulation for the relaxing and vaso-dilating effects of deep anesthesia. The series was not large but the concept deserves further clinical exploration.

D. OTHER STUDIES IN MAN

Studies on shock in man are very limited in number. Cannon (1918, a, b, c), Cannon and Bayliss (1919), Coonse et al. (1935), Cournand et al. (1943), Beecher (1945, 1947, 1949, 1951), Beecher et al. (1947), and Burnett (1947) had practically covered the field prior to the recent studies reported from Korea. The appealing thing about the study of shock in the dog is its controllability; in man a host of variables interplay. Yet, only by a realistic view toward man can the care of surgical shock be advanced.

Data on shock in man have been derived from the two World Wars, from the Korean experience, and from civilian research in times of peace.

Cannon, in World War I, studied the interrelationships of toxic and oligemic factors. His data from the cat showed that duration of hypotension was related to fatality, and this concept, greatly magnified and decorated over the next forty years, has become rooted in the medical mind as "irreversibility" whether or not there is special pathologic or nosologic justification for such a term.

He also became interested in the biochemical environment of the tissues in shock (Cannon, 1918, a, b; Cannon et al., 1918). Cannon and his collaborators found that the lower the blood pressure, the greater the acidosis (as measured by carbon dioxide combining power). They noticed that with hemorrhage alone (without as much tissue trauma) the change was less marked. They tried giving sodium bicarbonate and got a good clinical and blood pressure response in some cases. They reasoned that acidosis produced vasodilatation and weakened the cardiac contraction. Dr. Cannon was enthusiastic, for a time, about the prophylactic use of oral sodium bicarbonate in the wounded.

To place these observations in their proper framework one must recall that lavish blood transfusion was twenty-five years away and that detailed knowledge of extracellular chemistry and hypoxic acidosis was yet to come. We can only look back and emphasize again that well-documented clinical experience is the basic datum of human biology and that the benefit from the sodium ion or from alkalinization remains of interest today in isolated cases.

In 1942, sensing the new wave of shock research that was about to break in the physiologic and surgical literature, Wiggers (1942) reviewed the then available data with particular reference to animal work. He concluded that some change occurred late in shock that led to changes from and rupture of capillaries. This line of thought was the genesis of the work of Fine and his group, originally oriented towards the "lost plasma" and later toward the liver and sepsis, all in the dog. This concern also led to the studies of "blood sludging," the studies of Zweifach and Knisely and, later, Shorr and his group, with the identification of VEM and VDM as agencies in late animal shock. A present-day extension of these concepts is found in the work of Gelin and the school in Sweden, on aggregation of erythrocytes, and the effects of micro- and macrocolloids.

Cournand (1943), using the most advanced technique open to him at the time, including cardiac catheterization, studied a group of patients in shock on entry to a civilian hospital. He found the venous oxygen saturation elevated, with a raised blood lactate. Both these are evidence of poor peripheral perfusion and best explained by tissue anoxia in the presence of arteriovenous shunts. He found that after about three hours there was a mild acidosis, with pH at 7.28. There was a lowered blood volume and cardiac output, with normal venous pressure. The arteriovenous pCO_2 difference was increased, suggesting slow or poor pulmonary perfusion. Both Beecher (1947) and Burnett (1947), describing studies on the wounded of World War II, found elevated lactates (up to 20 to 40 mg. per 100 ml., with the normal near 20 mg. per 100 ml.) and a mild metabolic acidosis.

On the civilian front the work of Cournand and his group must rank as outstanding

(Cournand *et al.*, 1943). The study was of man, and no unitary concept or "gimmick" was held in mind as the observations were made. The cardiac catheter was used in shock for the first time, and the total peripheral resistance calculated. They documented the fall in cardiac output in shock, and the clear primacy of volume reduction in shock. By their data, blood volume was about 40 per cent reduced in the severe cases. There was decreased venous return to the right heart. Peripheral resistance was not always increased; in fact it was sometimes reduced in traumatic (as opposed to hemorrhagic) shock. They documented the lacticacidemia of low-perfusion acidosis in shock, and the decrease in renal blood flow.

In his Harvey Lecture (Richards, 1944) Richards reviews these data and related observations in man. He summarizes observations on almost 100 patients. The hemodilution of transcapillary refilling was documented, together with its converse, the high resistance and high hematocrit in the plasma-losing traumata such as burns. He describes a hypertensive, hyperthermic, hyperventilatory state in head injury. In all cases of hypotension there was decrease in venous return to the heart. He states ". . . . reduction in the volume of blood returned to the heart is the keystone. . . ." In most of his cases peripheral resistance was high, blood pressure was often maintained precariously at the expense of tissue perfusion, a concept finding rich confirmation in the work of the next fifteen years. Richards describes the failure of vasopressors and re-emphasizes the therapeutic primacy of volume restoration.

The biochemical data in Richards' work are of interest. In only a few cases was pH below 7.20 (arterial) but a few cases were below 7.00. Lactate was elevated, and was obviously a feature only of late shock.

Lauson *et al.* (1944), reporting on the work of this same group, described for the first time the differential renal vasoconstriction as a feature of early shock. This may be regarded as the keystone both of our view of the use of the interval urine output as a measure of renal perfusion in hypovolemic-hypotensive states, and of the concept of the ischemic renal tubule in acute volume reduction, even though the blood pressure is but transiently lowered.

At the time of these studies, the group in the Mediterranean theater under Churchill were carrying out quantitative studies on shock in the field. Summary may be found in BSSW (Beecher, ed., 1952). Changes in nitrogen intermediates, phosphorus, and magnesium, with acidosis and lacticacidemia, were shown. Hyperglycemia was prominent. The concept of "irreversible shock" was then gaining momentum, as based on studies in the dog and invoking some mystical "X factor" producing an ominous and relentless deterioration. These workers adopted a sophisticated view relative to the actual human shock they saw and wrote ". . . . in short, if 'irreversible shock' in the accepted sense was present, we missed it. If toxins caused any of the shock we saw, with the exception of that due to overwhelming and clinically apparent bacterial infections, we failed to recognize it. The shock we saw was caused by loss of blood . . . it was relieved by the administration of whole blood."

More detailed studies by members of this group were published separately. Stewart and Warner (1945) described many of the findings in greater detail. Beecher *et al.* (1947) also analyzed the data on the early findings in severe injury. They documented the narrowing of pulse pressure presumed to be a manifestation of increasing peripheral resistance. Their figures suggest mild shock with a loss of 15 to 20 per cent of the blood volume, and severe changes with losses of 50 per cent of the blood volume or more.

Emerson and Ebert (1945) reported a similar series of studies on the wounded. They again found a reasonable correlation between blood pressure reduction and blood volume deficit. Those patients with a pressure below 85 mm. Hg had lost 25 per cent of volume or more. The mean volume reduction on entry was near 63 per cent of starting value. Severe volume reduction was found to coexist with normal hematocrit prior to transcapillary refilling. They emphasize elevated venous pressure as the only sign of overtransfusion. Refractory cases involved infection, brain injury, anoxia, and long-standing shock with signs of myocardial insufficiency.

Grant and Reeve (1951) summarized clinical data on the British casualties, developed their concept of the "fist" of trauma, described traumatic hypertension, but did not present any quantitative data.

The Korean data are summarized in BCK (Howard, ed., 1955) and have been referred to in many places herein. Artz *et al.* (1955) report a separate analysis of 138 consecutive severe wounds. The average transfusion volume in these patients was 7500 ml. The mortality in this group was 21 per cent. The abdominal injuries were the most ominous, having a mortality of 80 per cent as opposed to 17 per cent for the extremity group. Of the 43 cases living three days or longer, 35 per cent developed renal insufficiency. "Diffuse ooze" occurred after multiple transfusions.

Howard *et al.* (BCK, I) reported the plasma electrolyte changes and found a characteristic post-traumatic sodium lowering and potassium elevation. They felt that most of the hyponatremia was dilutional, the hyperkalemia being due to diffuse "release from cells." There were no arterial acid-base data.

Because of the severe hepatic outflow obstruction seen in the shocked dog, with portal hypertension and massive gastrointestinal hemorrhage, one looks with interest at data from man relative to the liver in shock. Studies have been reported from World War II (BSSW) and Korea (Chute, 1951) and Scott *et al.* (BCK, I). These workers report a decrease in most functional parameters, an exhaustion of liver glycogen, and mild bilirubinemia. *Thus far no one has reported in human shock the characteristic canine tetrad that has so dominated the laboratory literature on this subject.* This combination of four hepatic changes in the dog, unreported in man, includes:

(1) purple turgid swelling of the liver with outflow obstruction and portal hypertension;

(2) mucosal slough and massive gastrointestinal hemorrhage;

(3) severe pooling of venous blood in the splanchnic area;

(4) early spontaneous anaerobic sepsis in the liver and muscle, responding to appropriate antibiotics.

Vasoconstriction as a possible sustaining factor in shock, and the logical sequela, use of vasodilators, has been studied by Engel *et al.* (1942), Converse and Boba (1956), and Converse *et al.* (1957). While the concept is easily embraced and is very appealing, as furthered by Nickerson (1956), there is still a lack of guide lines for use. Clearly blood volume must be restored before vasodilatation. When this is done, vasoconstriction often abates spontaneously.

Recent studies from our laboratory suggest (Smith, unpublished) that acidosis affects cardiac output more adversely than it does the reactivity of the peripheral vessel; also that in surgical shock as we now see it, the use of any significant blood transfusion (citrated) leads to a fairly marked metabolic alkalosis as the citrate is oxidized. Mol for mol, sodium citrate is as effective in moving the extracellular fluid toward alkalosis as is sodium lactate or bicarbonate. The 16.8 mE. of sodium as citrate in each unit of blood quickly mounts to a very significant load. If the citrate is not normally oxidized, then the citrate ion itself may reach troublesome concentrations, as described in detail in Chapter 15.

As to coronary flow in shock in man, data are few. When other hydrodynamic factors are held constant, flow varies as the fourth power of the diameter of a blood vessel. Howard has shown a marked fall in coronary flow in late shock in dogs and a very poor response to norepinephrine in this regard. He has shown that there is a decreased myocardial vascular resistance in shock, possibly associated with the coronary vasodilating action of the catechol amines. The heart in shock cannot metabolize carbohydrate normally, as is indicated by its inability to burn pyruvate. Norepinephrine does not restore this ability. Salisbury (1955) reports a marked increase in the force of right ventricular contraction in low-flow states, after an increase in coronary artery pressure.

The Birmingham Accident Hospital provides a continuing site for the study of injury.

The writings of the Birmingham group have concentrated particularly on the extent of blood loss, its measurement, and its replacement, in compound civilian trauma. The observation that blood transfusion promotes sodium excretion (Flear and Clarke, 1955) is borne out by the work of Bartter (1956) showing the alteration in aldosterone and urinary sodium:potassium ratio produced by bleeding and replacement, and interpretable in terms of the primacy of volume regulation in aldosterone secretion.

Clarke *et al.* (1955) review the extent of blood loss in a variety of random injuries. Their colored photographs of the patients and the wounds are of interest and could well be emulated by others teaching in the field. They base clinical estimates on the "fist-mass" of a wound (Grant and Reeve, 1951). Actual blood requirement is documented. Circumferential volume increments for various degrees of tissue hemorrhage are documented and photographed, indicating graphically the large extent of blood which can be housed in tissue despite a seemingly small increment in circumference. Their clinical data indicate that no one sign was an infallible guide to the volume deficit. Such things as pallor, cold extremities, and sweating were unreliable. The systolic blood pressure and pulse rate, together with wound "mass," nature of fractures, organs injured, and vascular damage, were all of greater value. Stated otherwise, the nature of the wound and the hemodynamic state were best indices.

Topley and Clarke (1956) again conclude that undertransfusion is commoner and more dangerous than overtransfusion; the conclusion is again advanced that hypovolemia brings in its wake a variety of metabolic, endocrine, and bacteriologic consequences.

Davies (1956) summarizes some of the blood volume data gathered by the Birmingham group. Most of their data are based on red cell dilution data, using an arbitrary correction for the WBH:LVH ratio. Their conclusion from many studies of this type is very similar to that of our group, namely, that the data developed by careful volume studies in expert hands are of great importance in the management of trauma, but that the "bedside" or "midnight" application of these methods is more apt to be misleading than helpful; neither the time nor the spot-analytic techniques are available for the latter.

Flear (1956) presents data on sixty-three patients following thoracic operations. He used the stabilized postoperative hemoglobin concentration as his primary index of the adequacy of previous transfusion. Granting that this may lead to confusion due to the fact that complications may cause anemia as well as vice versa, he finds that a major factor in determining the detailed routine of postoperative convalescence is the adequacy of blood replacement. Recalling the nature of surgical illness prior to the advent of transfusion one would scarcely appear to require quantitative proof of Flear's thesis. Nonetheless, the point is an important one and needs constant re-emphasis. With blood freely available there is no excuse for undertransfusion.

The group at the Birmingham Accident Hospital have given especial attention to the reduction in sodium retention which may result from the maintenance of volume during and after surgical trauma. Such a concept finds its theoretical basis in the volume-receptor phenomenon; maintenance of volume obviates the physiologic necessity for the volume restoration that results from sodium retention. Actually, the proof of such a contention is difficult because the normal measured blood volume and that required for support of flow may not always be the same, as mentioned previously. They have described the erythrocyte requirement of the burned patient (Clarke *et al.*, 1955) and feel they can equate the basic requirement for red cells with the extent of full-thickness burn. Their volume data corroborate the work of many other laboratories in this regard.

They have used the hematocrit as the principal laboratory guide to fluid therapy in burns for some years. Results are good, the methods being based merely on the maintenance of the hematocrit at a safe level, usually between 45 and 50. The colloid-crystalloid-salt mixture used depends on age and extent of burn, and ability to take and retain oral fluids. For the early patient with no hematocrit change, a primary dose of colloid is given on an arbitrary basis.

E. SHOCK INTERMEDIATES AND LABORATORY DATA

Many abnormal metabolic products and septic processes have been implicated in experimental traumatic shock in dogs and rodents. Relevance to man is often questionable. Two of the most persistent of these concepts are those of the VDM/VEM systems on the one hand and spontaneous infection on the other, as primary factors in circulatory degeneration in shock.

Vasodepressor material (VDM) was discovered by injecting body fluids from a shocked animal into a very special biologic preparation in which the microscopic circulation could be observed functionally and morphologically. One of the end-points was the secondary response of these vessels to epinephrine. This is a bioassay of the most complex type and quantitation was difficult at best. VDM was later found to be ferritin and its origin presumably hepatic. The "opposite number" was said to be a vasoexcitatory material (VEM) and was presumably renal in origin and similar in some respects to epinephrine itself, or at least it sensitized tissues to epinephrine. These analyses, concepts, and methods were the outcome of a long series of brilliant researches by Shorr et al. (1945, 1947, 1948, 1951), Zweifach et al. (1944, 1945, 1948, 1950), and their coworkers. We are indebted to these workers for a remarkable range of data on the character of the microscopic circulation, but data relative to man are scarce. Howard (BCK, I) and Scott et al. (1955) applied these methods to the Korean wounded in collaboration with Dr. Shorr. In a group of twenty patients, VDM (ferritin) was often found to be present, VEM but rarely. This was the hepatic ferritin rather than the muscle VDM (less specific chemically). The muscle VDM is uniformly present in experimental traumatic shock but was never seen in the wounded. No correlations could be made between VEM:VDM titers and the clinical parameters of severity, resuscitative units, or post-traumatic renal insufficiency. Three patients with intractable and fatal postoperative shock had variable VDM titers, two being of low or neutral value.

Although we have made no attempt to give references to the extensive animal work in many areas of surgical metabolism, special mention should be made of the contributions to the study of shock in the laboratory made by the groups working under Aub, Fine, and Shorr in the past fifteen years.

The studies of Fine and his group include Fine et al. (1943), Fine and Seligman (1943, 1944), Frank et al. (1946), Seligman et al. (1946, 1947), Fine et al. (1947), Frank et al. (1951), Fine et al. (1952), Fine (1954, a, b), Frank et al. (1955), and Fine (1955).

The work of Shorr and his group include Chambers et al. (1944), Zweifach et al. (1944), Shorr et al. (1945), Zweifach et al. (1945), Chambers and Zweifach (1947), Baez et al. (1947), Shorr et al. (1947), Mazur and Shorr (1948), Shorr et al. (1948), Furchgott et al. (1949), Mazur and Shorr (1950), Zweifach (1950), Shorr et al. (1951), Akers et al. (1954), Zweifach and Metz (1955), and Scott et al. (1955).

A summarizing article from Aub's group may be found in Kety et al. (1945).

Other studies on septic shock and bacterial factors include Nelson and Noyes (1953), Hardy et al. (1954), and Altemeier and Cole (1956).

Studies of the vasoactive drugs and steroids in shock include Crawford and Haynes (1953), Moyer et al. (1953), Uricchio et al. (1953), Eckenhoff and Dripps (1954), and Catchpole et al. (1955).

CHAPTER 11

Acute Plasma Loss and Its Repair

Section I. Causes of Acute Plasma Loss

A. TRAUMATIC EDEMA: BURNS, PERITONITIS, CRUSH

Thermal burns produce a large area in which capillary permeability to protein is increased. There is formed an obligatory sequestered edema which pulls water, salt, and protein out of the plasma volume, out of the uninjured interstitial phase, and out of the rest of body water, into the injured area.

Acute peritonitis, due either to the initial widespread irritation of the peritoneal cavity by such fluids as bile or gastrointestinal juice, or to the multiplication of microorganisms, produces a profuse outpouring of protein-rich fluid, creating a situation analogous to a burn: an obligatory accumulation of sequestered edema fluid at the expense of the remaining interstitial space and plasma volume. Pancreatitis and spreading cellulitis are further examples of obligatory sequestered edema as a cause of plasma loss. Crushed tissue and operative dissection do the same, but with an additional loss of red cells.

B. VENOUS OBSTRUCTION WITH PLASMA LOSS

Acute increase in mesenteric venous pressure produces an outpouring into the lumen of the gut of a fluid which is high in protein. The loss of water and electrolyte is sudden and massive. A rapid rise in the hematocrit is produced as plasma volume is compromised by this loss. Massive mesenteric venous occlusion, due either to thrombosis of major radicles of the portal system or to such a

process as midgut volvulus, thus produces a very rapid decrease in plasma volume, and oligemic shock. Thrombosis of the iliofemoral system can do the same, with loss of fluid into a swollen leg, in rare instances.

C. GASTROINTESTINAL MECHANISMS OF PLASMA LOSS; DESALTING WATER LOSS

Acute mechanical obstruction of the small bowel can, at a certain stage in its development, constitute a venous obstruction of the small vessels of the gut as the intramural pressure (due in turn to increasing intraluminal pressure) rises to the point where venous return is obstructed but arterial inflow can continue. At this phase of intestinal obstruction, large amounts of water, salt, and protein are lost into the lumen of the gut, as mentioned above. This desalting water loss with fluid accumulation takes place at the expense of the entire extracellular fluid, including the plasma volume. The hematocrit rises and oligemic shock ensues.

Loss of gastrointestinal juice to the outside, as in diarrhea, cholera, dysentery, and enterocolitis, can produce a deficit in plasma volume with an elevated hematocrit and oligemic shock. Here the biochemical mechanism is acute desalting water loss. The loss of plasma volume that occurs in acute desalting water loss is of central importance in clinical deterioration. Initial steps in treatment during the shock phase should include support of the plasma volume by colloid replacement as well as the restoration of the deficits of water and salt (see Part III).

In all of these instances (burn, crush, peritonitis, venous thrombosis, intestinal obstruction) plasma is lost within the body. The new edematous area can be called traumatic edema, obligatory or sequestered edema, or a new "space" of body fluid, a "third space."

In all, the hematocrit tends to rise as plasma is lost, and in most, body weight will rise as the pathologic condition develops, so long as treatment keeps pace with the accumulation. In all, the total volume of the extracellular phase is enlarged but the functional extracellular and circulating blood volumes are reduced in size.

Section II.   Hematologic Effects and Their Meaning

A. THE ELEVATED HEMATOCRIT: A PRECISE INDEX OF STATIC PLASMA VOLUME NEEDS

When plasma is lost from the circulation, the fluid that is left behind contains a relatively higher proportion of erythrocytes than is found in normal blood. The hematocrit, erythrocyte count, and hemoglobin concentration all rise together and in a linear relation to each other.

We have seen that in hemorrhage the estimation of volume changes from the hematocrit is variable and uncertain in all but a few instances. In sharp contrast to this uncertainty is the elevated hematocrit of plasma loss; it is a precise guide to treatment. Sudden loss of plasma is therefore a situation the recognition of which can lead to one of the most precise forms of volume replacement available in surgical therapy.

Burns, crush, peritoneal irritation, peritonitis, obstruction to drainage of the mesenteric veins, and an occasional case of peripheral venous obstruction produce a loss of plasma from the circulation, the duration of which depends upon the nature of the abnormality. In the case of burns, this usually occupies a period of forty-eight to seventy-two hours; in mesenteric thrombosis, six to twelve hours. In all the duration is variable.

Under most of these circumstances, the erythrocyte volume remains virtually constant. There is bleeding but it is minor. In a burn there is some early hemolysis due to the heat-induced fragility of the red cells. This hemolysis may be the source of heme pigments, potentially damaging to the kidney, and over the long run these red cells should

be replaced. But the magnitude of this loss is not sufficient to alter the quantitative usefulness of the hematocrit elevation in gauging the plasma need. By a variety of measures based on tracer techniques we know that even in massive burns the early erythrocyte loss rarely exceeds 200 ml. the first day. For this reason erythrocyte loss is quantitatively negligible in calculating the early plasma volume need, and we have the basic rule that:

when the erythrocyte volume remains constant and plasma is lost, the absolute magnitude of the hematocrit rise is directly and quantitatively related to the volume of plasma lost.

This tells us that an acute plasma deficit may be accurately estimated quantitatively by the hematocrit change if that change is properly related to the starting normal blood volume.

An illustrative example may help to clarify. If we have an 80 kg., normally built male, we may calculate his expected normal blood volume near 5600 ml., or 7.0 per cent of body weight. With a normal large vessel hematocrit of 45, we may calculate that his erythrocyte volume is normally 2520 ml.*

Our patient has a perforated duodenal ulcer of twelve hours' duration and he is admitted to the hospital in shock, with an

---

* The relationship between the large vessel hematocrit and the whole body hematocrit does not enter into this calculation because the WBH:LVH ratio cancels out as we proceed. It need not be a part of the mental arithmetic, just as we can neglect it in the hematocrit calculation for a single whole blood loss with a stabilized hemodiluted hematocrit.

hematocrit of 55. To the unwary observer, an hematocrit of 55 may not appear very abnormal; it might be regarded merely as the high hematocrit of a red-faced and healthy person with slight polycythemia. Actually it bespeaks a very dangerous plasma deficit in such a situation as this.

We assume that the red cell volume has remained constant. The 2520 ml. of red corpuscles, instead of representing 45 per cent, now represent 55 per cent of the blood volume. We then can calculate the blood volume by the formula $BV = \dfrac{RV}{LVH}$

or, in this instance:

$$BV = \frac{2520}{0.55}$$

and we find that it is 4600 ml. The difference between this value and the assumed starting value of 5600 ml. represents the plasma deficit: 1000 ml. A plasma infusion of this amount should be given immediately and should be considered as an urgent emergency measure, exactly analogous to the urgency of transfusion in hemorrhagic shock.

The total volume of plasma needed for this patient over the course of time is determined, not by this calculation of static deficit, but by the dynamic evolution of his pathologic status, by the balance between vasodilation and vasoconstriction in the area of injury, and by the nature of the developing bacterial infection. The total volume of plasma needed in the treatment of the patient is therefore indicated in clinical terms and not by the hematocrit. This leads us to a second basic rule:

> *while the hematocrit elevation after acute plasma loss provides a precise index of immediate plasma need ("static debt"), the total plasma need—the continuing need or "dynamic debt"—is quite independent of a single observed hematocrit and is determined by the pathologic state, the clinical picture, and the continuing transudation of plasma outward from the circulation.*

1. General Expressions

The expression for the initial calculation of static debt in cases of plasma loss may be derived from the hematocrit as follows:

Where

BV_1 = normal blood volume for the patient as estimated from body weight, build, and sex

LVH_1 = normal large vessel hematocrit for this individual*

LVH_2 = observed large vessel hematocrit

$$PV \text{ deficit} = BV_1 - \frac{(BV_1 \times LVH_1)}{LVH_2}$$

Or, in our example:

$$1000 = 5600 - \frac{(5600 \times 0.45)}{0.55}$$

In the presence of such plasma-losing diseases as perforated duodenal ulcer or a burn, the loss of plasma is not a static affair. The mental arithmetic above is merely a way of calculating the static deficit of plasma at the time of the observation. As the fluid loss progresses, more plasma than this will be required to maintain the blood volume. This is not a formula for the early treatment of burns. It is only an expression of the static debt in established plasma loss. †

One may criticize this approximation of plasma need shown in this formula; after all, we really do not know what the patient's starting (normal) blood volume is. One cannot but accept that criticism. We might not know whether the initial blood volume, for example, is 5600, 5700, or even 5300 ml. But if one carries out the calculation on any of these bases, one arrives at a plasma deficit that is in the same therapeutic order of magnitude. Fatal errors in treating this type of patient do not arise from such small errors in the initial assumption of his blood volume! They arise from a totally unrealistic view of the plasma deficit involved in the original hematocrit elevation.

In this example plasma is used; the same calculation is used for the static need for

---

* In these expressions the hematocrit is indicated as a decimal: an hematocrit of 45 per cent is indicated as 0.45, etc.

† Note that the expression for the new blood volume after plasma loss is based on the *hematocrit* (i.e., the red cell fraction), *not* the plasmacrit (i.e., the plasma fraction) of peripheral blood. Plasmacrit calculations yield a falsely low value.

dextran, albumin, or other colloids. The response of the hematocrit to a rapid infusion of plasma, or dextran, constitutes in itself a rough measurement of the blood volume. After the first dose of plasma has been given, it is possible to remeasure the hematocrit to carry out this second calculation as a check on the patient's actual blood volume, which will make further therapy more accurate; if plasma loss is continuing rapidly such a calculation is useless.

When the effect of large plasma transfusions is measured by serial closely-spaced hematocrits, one may approximate the starting blood volume by the magnitude of the response: the fall in hematocrit in response to a measured plasma infusion is itself a measure of the total blood volume. This expression is based on the fact that in a small blood volume a given amount of plasma will produce a much more profound hematocrit drop than in a large blood volume. Using similar nomenclature,

$$BV_1 = \frac{LVH_2 \times PVT}{LVH_1 - LVH_2}$$

Where

BV_1 = starting blood volume
PVT = plasma infused
LVH_1 = hematocrit before infusion
LVH_2 = hematocrit after infusion

As in our other similar expressions of this category, this is presented to call attention to the fact that such a relation does exist, rather than to suggest that it be used quantitatively in all instances. While a guide, it is not a substitute for clinical judgment.

2. Use of Whole Blood in Treatment of Plasma Loss

The treatment of acute plasma deficit by the infusion of whole blood is effective and makes perfectly good sense, because the objective of treatment is the restoration of the total blood volume, not merely the lowering of the hematocrit. The erythrocyte, by virtue of its space-occupying function, is very effective in the maintenance of blood volume in plasma-losing situations even though most plasma-losing processes do not cost the body red blood cells. It is therefore reasonable to treat peritonitis or burns with whole blood

to restore the circulation. But three facts must be carefully considered if red cells are included in the treatment of acute plasma loss.

First, the calculation of the hematocrit response loses its significance when whole blood is used. A much more complex situation obtains for the estimate of further need. If the hematocrit of the infused blood is known, this calculation can be carried out, but it becomes vastly more difficult to follow the progress of the patient's blood volume relationships. By using whole blood one has lost his most accurate measure of need.

Second, whole blood treatment of plasma loss results in a higher final hematocrit than if plasma is used. With a hematocrit over 65, viscosity effects are encountered which may be adverse.

Third, any deterioration of the blood or subgroup incompatibility presents the kidney with potentially nephrotoxic pigment quite unnecessarily.

B. THE EFFECTS OF PLASMA LOSS

Plasma loss results in oligemia. This, in turn, produces all of the changes previously described as occurring in oligemia from blood loss. When severe enough it interferes with venous return to the right heart, cardiac output, and peripheral oxygenation. Initial changes consist of peripheral vasoconstriction, renal conservation of water and salt, going on to renal vasoconstriction with oliguria, and progressing finally to hypotension, prolonged deficiency of flow, tissue acidosis, shock, and death, just as in oligemic shock from any other cause.

The area into which plasma is lost takes fluid not only from the plasma volume but also from the remaining or uninvolved interstitial fluid. The transcapillary refilling that occurs after hemorrhage therefore cannot occur to restore the plasma volume in such diseases as burns, peritonitis, or intestinal obstruction. The reservoir from which such transcapillary refilling might occur—the interstitial fluid—is itself involved in a loss of fluid into this new parasitic edema compartment of body fluid. Not until this fluid is resorbed do we see transcapillary refilling with a rise in plasma volume and a spontaneous fall in the hematocrit.

The movement of cell water into the extracellular phase also occurs in plasma loss as it does in blood loss. Again one searches for the mechanism and arrives at hydrostatic pressure or possibly steroidal influences such as that of aldosterone. This cell water moves out into the extracellular fluid, where it becomes distributed in the uninvolved interstitial fluid, the plasma volume, and the new parasitic area of sequestered edema. Potassium leaves the cell with this water and is excreted in the urine if urinary output is sufficient to do so. If not, it piles up in the extracellular fluid as hyperkalemia. But, because the total extracellular fluid is expanding apace, hyperkalemia is not prominent. This cell water is sodium-free and it therefore dilutes the concentration of plasma sodium and with it the tonicity (osmolality) of the extracellular fluid, both of which fall.

With these differences, then, the oligemia of plasma volume loss goes on to produce the same sort of deteriorative changes in circulation and cardiac function as do other forms of oligemia.

The body cannot make erythrocytes fast enough to make any impression whatsoever on the oligemia produced by acute plasma loss, and hematopoiesis can be neglected as a factor in therapy. New protein is synthesized rapidly so long as circulation and liver function are maintained; such protein is made even during a brisk catabolism of striated muscle, and yet it cannot possibly be manufactured fast enough to make any impression on the minutes-and-hours crisis of acute plasma deficit. The only new protein entering the blood stream is that preformed albumin equilibrated across the permeable capillaries of liver, intestines, lungs, and other viscera.

Elevation of the hematocrit over 60 due to acute plasma loss alone represents a life-endangering emergency and involves the loss of volumes of plasma that are beginning to approximate 50 per cent of the normal plasma volume and therefore about 25 per cent of the starting whole blood volume. As the hematocrit rises, there is observed a defect in the circulation greater than might be expected in acute loss of the same volume of whole blood. Whether or not this marked illness is due to viscosity effects is uncertain, yet viscosity change is of minor import (in vitro) below a hematocrit of about 65. It appears much more likely that the greater toxicity seen in many of the plasma-losing situations is due to the rest of the pathologic surroundings, particularly the frequent concomitance of severe invasive infection. Examples are peritonitis, with the systemic effects of infection, burns, with many sources of intoxication (the most important of which is infection), and gastrointestinal venous obstruction, where there is opportunity for the absorption of the toxic products of aerobic and anaerobic bacterial growth from the lumen of the gut.

Section III.   Plasma Volume Support

A. PLASMA

The most rational treatment for acute plasma deficit would be the administration of pure human plasma. This is not readily available. Human plasma, as ordinarily derived by withdrawal from cells in ACD-preserved* bank blood, is irritating to peripheral veins, and its prolonged infusion often

---

* "ACD" is used as abbreviation for the acid-citrate-dextrose coagulant mixture of either formula (see p. 253).

produces an irritative phlebitis; it contains a full ration (143 mE. per l.) of sodium plus the sodium of the ACD; other than these rather minor defects there would be very little objection to it were it not for the possibility of its contamination with the virus of infectious hepatitis. The most dangerous form of plasma is that which is gathered in large pools and then lyophilized. When plasma is administered from single donors, the hazard of homologous serum jaundice is no greater than that attendant upon the administration of whole blood.

The incidence of infectious hepatitis in patients treated with large volumes of plasma that comes from single donors and that has been stored at room temperature is low. The hazard of leaving the patient untreated is clearly greater than the hazards of jaundice from plasma treatment. If plasma cannot be obtained free of virus, other agents that do not contain the virus are of course preferable, provided they can give effective volume support.

Of the plasma fractions, albumin is the safest on this score and can be heat-sterilized at 60° for ten hours; fibrin and fibrinogen contain the virus. Gamma globulin is virus-free. Antihemophiliac globulin is virus-free and can be obtained also in plasma frozen within six hours of donation—the frozen plasma is of course a potential virus source.

B. CONCENTRATED HUMAN SERUM ALBUMIN

Concentrated human serum albumin is the only true plasma expander* known. Some capillaries are not readily permeable to albumin. Therefore, when the albumin concentration is increased in the plasma, it will increase the oncotic pressure in such areas of albumin-impermeability and move water and salt from the extravascular spaces into the plasma volume. The clinical and practical usefulness of concentrated human albumin in the treatment of shocked soldiers was disappointing when tried in World War II, but its value in civilian surgery is great. As a plasma expander it has almost disappeared from the scene because of the ready availability of cheaper substances that are useful in plasma volume restoration; if available, it is useful in acute plasma deficit. The greatest usefulness of concentrated albumin lies in the treatment of hypoproteinemia. So used, it can produce a significant increment

---

* We are basing our definition of "plasma expander" here on the actual meaning of the term: a substance that makes the plasma volume expand *after* infusion in the patient and to an extent greater than the volume infused.

of plasma protein concentration. Transfusion of large amounts brings in its wake some dilution of other proteins, including prothrombin.

C. INTRAVASCULAR COLLOIDS: PLASMA VOLUME SUBSTITUTES

This term refers to materials that hold water and salt in the blood stream as though they were plasma protein. Infused into the plasma volume, they produce a temporary increase in volume equal to the volume infused. They hold water and salt in the plasma because of their colloid content. A detailed pharmacologic discussion of all the substances now available is beyond the scope of this book.

In many ways, gelatin has been the most successful of these substances but suffers the difficulty that it will gel at low temperatures and is therefore useless for field operations. Dextran is now the most widely used. It is a heterogenous mixture of polysaccharides of large molecular weight, ranging in size from about 25,000 to close to 4,000,000. When injected into the blood stream, dextran has five clear-cut effects, listed in the following paragraphs.

1. Plasma Volume Change

Dextran increases the plasma volume. This is associated with dilution of red blood cells and fall in the hematocrit. Since the material is not a protein and most assuredly not a human plasma protein, a dilution of protein also occurs. So the giving of dextran, by definition, produces hypoproteinemia and a relative decrease in the peripheral concentrations of erythrocytes, although oncotic pressure is maintained. This property is a function of molecular size and shape. At low molecular weights (below 50,000) transcapillary loss is so extensive and urinary clearance so complete that effective oncotic pressure is not established. Over molecular weights of 500,000 the oncotic pressure of the solution is very low per unit weight of solute because there are so relatively few molecules per unit of total solute. Effective oncotic pressure is established only when colloids of the approximate size of human albumin (molecular weights of 50,000 to 250,000) are facing a membrane impermeable to them.

2. Destruction and Excretion

The body then goes to work on this foreign material and accomplishes several objectives simultaneously. At first it excretes the complexes of small molecular weight in the urine. They are filtered through the glomerulus and, so far as known, they pass down the renal tubule without further significance save for the water carried with them. In twenty-four hours almost 50 per cent of the infused dextran is lost in the urine. This may stimulate a brisk solute diuresis. These lost fractions are the complexes of low molecular weight. The larger ones remain in the plasma volume for prolonged periods of time, exert some effective oncotic pressure, and will maintain some plasma volume increment over prolonged periods of time. The plasma volume increment is not maintained constant, so the hematocrit gradually creeps up again over a period of days or weeks. The metabolism of the polysaccharide itself is not well understood, but it is finally completely metabolized by the body.

3. Protein Dilution

During the period of hyperdextranemia there is a reciprocal hypoproteinemia, yet the colloid osmotic pressure of the plasma is near normal since the deficit of human albumin has been made up by the excess of another colloid: the dextran. There are other plasma proteins, however, which are diluted down and whose deficit is not made up by any property of the dextran, and of these the most prominent are prothrombin and fibrinogen. For this reason, the administration of large amounts of dextran produces hypoprothrombinemia and hypofibrinogenemia. A tendency toward bleeding may be observed, sometimes greater than one would predict from the degree of protein dilution alone.

4. Osmotic Diuresis

When crystalloids of low molecular weight are lost in the urine, an osmotic (solute) diuresis occurs. This osmotic diuresis is usu-
ally regarded as being due to the presence in the tubular fluid of a high concentration of a crystalloid that cannot be reabsorbed. The crystalloid pulls out water with it, and although the water resorptive mechanisms for the proximal and distal tubules can work against a certain osmotic gradient, the rate of passage of the tubular fluid into the collecting system is hastened beyond the capacity of water reabsorption. The net effect is a decreased resorption of water with the excretion of a large volume of urine of relatively fixed osmolality. Tubular processing is poor and some acidosis may occur during solute diuresis. These effects are observed after the administration of large quantities of dextran in burns and shock. Whether this is good or bad for the patient depends on the circumstances. In most situations it is beneficial, since the excretion of large volumes of urine seems to be in itself helpful in desperately ill patients, quite aside from the mechanism producing the polyuria. There is not space here to go into this matter in greater detail except to point out that in the experimental animal the production of an osmotic diuresis will combat very strong factors (anoxia, heme pigment) tending to produce post-traumatic renal insufficiency.

The effect on plasma electrolyte concentrations of a profuse osmotic diuresis depends on the interplay of a number of factors, the most important of which are water metabolism (antidiuretic effect) and electrolyte intake. It is possible under certain circumstances, using osmotic diuretics, to increase the plasma concentration of sodium and therefore the plasma osmolality. This is clearly accomplished by the excretion of more water than salt. This occasionally occurs in patients treated with large volumes of dextran. Renal acidosis with hyperchloremia can also be produced.

5. Hemodilution

We come finally to this most familiar result of dextran therapy: the resulting hemodilution. Dextran reduces the concentration of blood cells. This is of course an inevitable reciprocal of increase in plasma volume. The same effect would be produced by infusions of plasma, albumin, gelatin, polyvinylpyrrol-idone (P.V.P.), or any cell-free colloid.

At what point does erythrocyte dilution become harmful to the patient by virtue of decreased oxygen-carrying capacity? This hemodilution is a "normovolemic" hemodilution, if we use that term to denote a hemodilution occurring in the presence of a blood volume that is either normal or increasing toward normal. If there is acute plasma loss (caused by a burn, for example) as the reason for dextran infusion, this hemodilution is an inevitable by-product of the very effect one seeks: increased plasma volume.

It is in the treatment of the loss of whole blood that the dextran-induced hemodilution is a serious problem placing a definite ceiling limit on the volume of dextran that can be used: the hematocrit should not fall below 25. Below this level the dilution of erythrocytes and protein becomes dangerous. Although tissue oxygenation is not adversely affected by normal tissue perfusion at this hematocrit, it represents a level below which clinical results have been poor. The combination of low perfusion and low oxygen content is responsible. The buffering capacity of the red cell is also lost. It is a simple matter in a severely wounded soldier to lower the hematocrit as low as 8, 10, or 12 per cent by the restoration of his blood volume entirely with dextran. This means that the use of dextran on a large scale in hemorrhagic shock must always be accompanied by the administration of either whole blood or red cell suspensions. It is important to re-emphasize that transfusion of whole blood is the ideal blood replacement; dextran is used as second best and even then must share the job with some erythrocytes.

In burns, dextran lowers the hematocrit toward normal; excessive erythrocyte dilution is not a problem, but protein dilution is. We therefore use it along with plasma or albumin.

If one considers these various facets of the use of dextran or other like colloids, and avoids the pitfalls of overuse or poorly conceived application, they are most useful substances. The shelf-life of dextran is long and it can be continuously available for emergency infusion pending the procurement of blood. It can save tissues from anoxia through its support of the circulation; despite its artificial and nonphysiologic nature it has earned a secure place in surgery. Should military needs again recur, it will be a key substance for mass application.

D. DEXTRAN: NOTES FROM THE LITERATURE

Haynes and DeBakey (1952) showed that dextran was an effective means of plasma volume support. Knutson et al. (1952) reconfirmed the greater efficacy of dextran, especially in the fractions of larger molecular weight.

Frawley et al. (1955) reported certain aspects of the Korean war experience with dextran. They report studies in 26 severely wounded soldiers treated with low-molecular-weight material. Dextran (av. m.w. 42,000) and gelatin (av. m.w. 34,000) were retained in the plasma to the same degree, about 22 per cent remaining in the vascular compartment after six hours. The fraction leaving the plasma was soon recovered from the urine. The usefulness of this material as an emergency stopgap pending blood administration was reconfirmed. Cumulative curves for plasma retention and urinary excretion are given. Other studies presenting data in this area are to be found in Amspacher and Curreri (1953), Bull et al. (1949), Gray (1953), and Hoffman and Kozoll (1946), among others.

In a clinical study, Artz et al. (1955) reported the surgical effectiveness of dextran. The dilution of erythrocytes inevitably produced by the colloid osmotic effect of the dextran macromolecule remaining in the blood stream necessitated caution after the use of 2000 ml. At hematocrit levels of 20 per cent or below, the oxygen-carrying capacity and erythrocyte buffering were sufficiently reduced to compromise recovery even when blood volume was normal. In one case the hematocrit was lowered to 12 per cent, at which point there were signs of anoxia despite normal blood pressure. Dextran was used most importantly at the divisional level where blood was less readily available. The authors emphasize that it was in the "moderate shock" group with blood volume deficits of 20 to 30 per cent that the material was most effective. Where blood volume deficits were over 35 per cent, blood had of necessity to be used if the hematocrit was to be maintained over 25 per cent. A tendency toward bleeding was noted in a few instances but, in this early report, not as yet identified etiologically. Other clinical experiences are to be found in Gropper *et al.* (1952), Frawley *et al.* (1955), Howard *et al.* (1955).

Harrison *et al.* (1955) report a nicely executed study of the treatment of shock with a dextran derivative known as hydrodextran. The response is essentially the same as seen with dextran; the authors claim no special properties for the "hydro" form save a questionably lower reaction rate. Blood volume increase is at the predicted levels; hematocrit values fell from a pretreatment average of 37.5 to 28.6 after the administration of 1000 ml. About 50 per cent of the material was excreted in the urine during the first twenty-four hours. In three cases with more blood loss (the cases were largely arterial lacerations) in which 1500 ml. were given, the hematocrit fell to a lower value. The plasma volume data are of great interest in showing the ebb and flow of transcapillary hemodilution under these circumstances. The authors conclude, as virtually all workers have, that this material is quite satisfactory for emergency use in moderate quantities; there were no untoward reactions.

Howard *et al.* (1956) have studied the properties of dextrans of various molecular sizes, using solutions of greater homogeneity than those usually available. The Korean experience had shown the usefulness of dextran but at the same time its rapid disappearance (especially of the moiety of low molecular weight) from the circulation (Artz *et al.* 1955; Frawley *et al.*, 1955). Howard's data are of basic importance in this field. They confirm the fact that the larger fractions (over m.w. 135,000) are longer retained in the plasma volume and are more slowly excreted in the urine; that the fractions of low molecular weight act as an osmotic diuretic; that the fractions of high molecular weight (in doses of 1 liter or 60 gm.) produced

a serious increase in the bleeding time, some even requiring a pressure dressing for the test puncture site! The bleeding was most marked from six to twelve hours after the infusion, occurred only with a high blood dextran concentration, but did not necessarily coincide with the highest concentrations. The bleeding did not coincide with the maximum lowering of plasma protein concentration. This bleeding tendency has been studied also by Adelson *et al.* (1955) and Carbone *et al.* (1954). It is not associated with leukopenia or thrombocytopenia but does seem to be associated with retention of the component of high molecular weight in blood and tissues.

Any remaining doubt that intravascular site is related to molecular weight of plasma expanders is dispelled by the elegant study of disappearance rates reported by Metcalf and Rousselot (1956). Here, using the Solomon (1949) method of graphic analysis of complex curves not due to single exponential functions, the authors have derived rates for transcapillary transfer, showing that dextrans of large molecular weight are the ones which are slow to leave the blood stream. The gelatin of 30,000 to 50,000 molecular weight disappeared most rapidly. The authors also derived expressions for the rates of renal excretion of these materials.

Grotte (1956) studied the passage of dextran across the blood-lymph barrier in the dog, using dextran of various molecular weights. His data show a much greater permeability of liver capillaries than leg or neck capillaries, to macromolecules. This is consistent with many other observations. A number of constants and indices for diffusion and permeability were derived. He found that dextran of molecular weight 60,000 to 80,000 was distributed in a volume equivalent to that of the plasma, and left this volume with half-times of eight to twenty-three hours.

Gelin (1956) showed that infusions of pure high-molecular-weight dextran produced erythrocyte aggregation (sludging) and death, in rabbits. This has no bearing on clinical use of dextran; the material used had a much higher average molecular weight than any dextrans used clinically.

In considering such work we should not lose sight of the fact that materials of very high molecular weight will remain in the blood stream very nicely but they will exert very little colloid osmotic pressure. The oncotic pressure of a solution is a function of the total number of colloidal particles per unit volume in a solution facing a membrane imperfectly permeable to those particles. Therefore expanders with very high molecular weights, like globulins, "stay put" very nicely but do not exert the same force as an equal weight of particles the size and shape of albumin.

Studies on the tendency to bleeding after administration of dextran are still inconclusive as to precise mechanism. Weil and Webster (1956) reported that, in vitro, dextran precipitated fibrinogen, reduced the number of platelets, and prolonged coagulation time. Clinically, in one hundred patients receiving 500 to 2000 ml. of dextran there was no tendency to pathologic bleeding.

These authors recommend the use of whole blood whenever 1000 ml. or more of dextran is used and re-emphasize the practical emergency usefulness of dextran despite its theoretical shortcomings. The bleeding tendency with dextran is in part a platelet effect due to platelet coating.

The study of Artz (Howard, BCK, II) and Artz et al. (1955) again confirmed that rapid renal excretion of these plasma substitutes was of course abolished by renal failure, yet these patients demonstrated that extrarenal disposal plays a very large part in the disposal of dextran and gelatin. The dextran could be identified histochemically in all parts of the nephron as its primary site of metabolism and excretion. Other tissues took it up but sparsely.

The demonstration by Allen et al. (1954) that plasma stored six months at room temperature was freed of virus was borne out by Hoxworth and Haesler (1956) and this has become standard practice.

CHAPTER 12

Chronic Blood Loss and the Blood Volume in Chronic Disease

Section I. Chronic Blood Loss

Carcinoma of the stomach and carcinoma of the colon are examples of bleeding diseases that produce a chronic anemia due primarily to the gradual loss of blood. The preoperative treatment of this type of chronic anemia has given rise to controversy. Some surgeons advise indiscriminate use of large transfusions just before operation. Reports are conflicting as to the nature and extent of the defect involved. It is our conviction that the objectives and methods for preoperative transfusion in chronic anemia can be based on facts now available rather than rules of thumb, that the hematocrit (or erythrocyte count or hemoglobin concentration) is far lower than total volume, that indiscriminate transfusion may set the stage for pulmonary complications after operation, and that in all instances a full twenty-four hours should be allowed for equilibration and plasma dispersal before anesthesia and surgery.

Let us consider some examples.

A. CHRONIC ANEMIA WITHOUT WEIGHT LOSS

We may start with the simplest example, the instance of an individual with a carcinoma of the right colon, who has suffered no weight loss and who is observed to enter the hospital with a hematocrit of 20. What are the blood volume relationships here, and what should be done preoperatively about the blood volume?

The available data indicate that the blood volume deficit here is primarily in the erythrocyte fraction. The total blood volume is low but not remarkably so. The situation is best described as a primary red cell deficit with partial restoration of the blood volume toward normal by increase in the volume of a plasma relatively poor in protein. It is the chronic analogue of the compensated secondary hemodiluted anemia of acute hemorrhage. But here in the chronic situation the blood volume as a whole may be surprisingly close to normal. The extent of plasma volume increase is indicated by the depression of the hematocrit itself. In the study of many such patients we have found that the total blood volume is only a small fraction lower than the patient's norm and that the red cell volume and static deficit can be calculated on the basis of this assumption. The hematocrit is much lower than the blood volume.

Let us take as our example an anemic female, who has not lost weight and who is of average build, weighing 60 kg. Her normal blood volume, at 6.5 per cent of her body weight, should be 3900 ml. If her volume is 15 per cent low, standing at 3300 ml., with an hematocrit (LVH) of 20, she thus has an erythrocyte volume of 660 ml. and a plasma volume of 2640 ml. Again, WBH:LVH relationships are constant during replacement in this chronic situation and need not enter the mental arithmetic. Her normal red cell volume should be 0.4 $\times$ 3900 or 1560 ml. With a normal red cell volume of 1560 ml., this patient's normal plasma volume would of course be smaller (2340 ml.) than it now is (2640 ml.).

The assumption that the patient's blood volume is 15 per cent below normal in this situation gives her the benefit of the doubt. In our experience based on an RV + PV method, the total volume is normal in about half such instances. In these one might describe the rate of blood loss as never exceeding the rate of transcapillary refilling. In the others a figure running as low as 15 per cent below normal is occasionally seen. We would like such a patient to come to surgery with a hematocrit of 35 or higher, to give her nearly normal oxygen transport, and with a normal (but not acutely elevated) blood volume. The achievement of this objective should be given careful thought.*

1. Preoperative Transfusion

To bring the hematocrit from 20 to around 35 in this 60 kg. woman with the slight (15 per cent) hypovolemia of chronic blood loss, we can use whole blood. In elderly patients with heart disease and in the normovolemic anemia of chronic starvation, separated red blood cells should be used. But the patient considered here has no disease of heart, liver, or kidneys and will do perfectly well on whole blood. The question is: how much?

As calculated above, we estimate that she starts with a blood volume of 3300 ml., hematocrit of 20, and erythrocyte volume of 660 ml. Each transfusion contains a total of 620 ml., of which 500 is blood, with a hematocrit of 40 (RV = 200–225 ml.). The hematocrit of the blood-ACD mixture is about 37. The first blood infused will remain in the blood volume in toto. The effect on the hematocrit will be very small.

---

* Such further blood replacement as is required to restore operative blood losses is carried out intraoperatively or more slowly in the postoperative period.

Let us calculate the example on the basis of two such units of blood:

Starting:

$$BV_1 = 3300$$
$$RV_1 = 660$$
$$LVH_1 = 20$$

Transfusion: 1000 WB (contains 400 RV)

After Transfusion:

$$BV_2 = 4300$$
$$RV_2 = 1060$$
$$LVH_2 = 24.7$$

So we have given her a slight hypervolemia (a blood volume of 4300 rather than her normal blood volume of 3900) and her hematocrit has only gone from 20 to 25! If we now crowd her with several more transfusions of whole blood to "get that hematocrit up" we will send her to the anesthetist with an acute hypervolemic plethora, and trouble is inevitable. To raise her hematocrit acutely from 20 to 35 by mere infusion of bank blood in one fell swoop would require the impressive total of over 3500 ml. of whole blood.

Many postoperative pulmonary complications entered in the books as "pulmonary edema" or "bronchopneumonia" or "atelectasis" have resulted from anesthetizing patients who were hypervolemic from massive preoperative transfusion based on a desire to raise the hematocrit as rapidly as possible or on a mistaken assumption of severe hypovolemia when none exists.

Much harm has been done by overenthusiastic preoperative transfusion immediately prior to surgery in well-compensated secondary anemia; the term "congestive atelectasis" describes this lesion. The passage of time is essential in the equilibration of multiple preoperative transfusions, for plasma dispersal and for erythrocyte concentration to rise.

So, what can we do? We have two courses open.

We can *transfuse slowly* over a period of from four to six days and give the patient twenty-four hours, without transfusion, to equilibrate prior to anesthesia. This is the best course if she is not acutely bleeding. The time spent need not be excessive nor wasteful and it is well spent. This planned procedure of timed-transfusion-with-equilibration must be differentiated from aimless slow transfusion over a period of weeks with a long lapse before operation; such is wasteful of blood and time. With timed transfusion and equilibration her body will dispose of the excess plasma and her hematocrit will slowly rise. Or, secondly, we can *give separated erythrocytes* in suspensions with hematocrits near 80; this is faster and does not require as much time for equilibration and plasma dispersal.

Let us calculate the results of both:

a. Whole Blood Transfusions, with Metabolism of the Plasma Excess and Time Allowed for Equilibration.

Again, we start with:
$$BV_1 = 3300$$
$$RV_1 = 660$$
$$LVH_1 = 20$$

Transfuse whole blood once a day to a total of four units (2000 ml.) with a day before surgery to equilibrate. What result do we get if plasma dispersal is metabolically complete when the blood volume exceeds 4200 and the erythrocytes (fresh) remain in the blood stream?

Then
$$\text{Blood Volume Transfused (BVT)} = 2000$$
$$RVT = 800$$

After transfusion, assuming complete plasma dispersal with BV at 4200 ml.:
$$BV_2 = 4200$$
$$RV_2 = 1460$$
$$LVH_3 = 35$$

Note that we are relying on metabolic disposal of plasma to rescue the patient from a potential hypervolemia of 5300 ml.!*

Were we to give all four transfusions the afternoon before surgery ("to save time"), the patient would present herself to the anesthetist in the midst of the physiologic disorder of an acute hypervolemic plethora of at least 1400 ml. excess. The disposal of excess plasma involves liver function and

renal excretion; both are compromised by operation; the additional volume load on heart and lungs is dangerous during operation.

b. Separated Red Cells

Again, we start with:
$$BV_1 = 3300$$
$$RV_1 = 660$$
$$LVH_1 = 20$$

Transfuse three cell suspensions, each of 300 ml. volume and hematocrit of 85.

Then
$$CST = 900$$
$$RVT = (3 \times .85 \times 300) = 765$$
and
$$BV_2 = 4200$$
$$RV_2 = 1425$$
$$LVH_2 = 34$$

For rapid accurate preparation this has been the best plan; it threatens hypervolemia the least. A hematocrit of 34 has been attained with an infusion of only 900 ml. But if a few days can be taken (while other studies are in progress) the former course (planned equilibration of whole blood) is the cheapest and easiest. Note that either method achieves our announced objective: a hematocrit of 35 with a normal blood volume. *Note also that plasma dispersal is essential to the hematocrit rise: either the patient does it metabolically, which takes time, or we do it in the blood bank (by separation of cells).*

In effect, the net result of transfusions in the secondary anemia of chronic blood loss is somewhere between the "ideal" calculation for hematocrit increase and the maximal expansion in blood volume produced by the blood. Normal renal and metabolic mechanisms care for the plasma excess; interestingly, these mechanisms are most active in the young person who can handle the excess best anyway. In older or debilitated people, liver impairment, salt retention, and antidiuresis slow down the plasma-disposing mechanisms. In such persons large and dangerous volume increases are often the price of hematocrit rise unless the surgeon plans his campaign carefully.

Many difficulties can be avoided by giving

---

* The mechanisms of plasma dispersal are detailed in Chapter 14, Section II, The Fate of Transfused Blood.

the patient separated erythrocytes. Blood with a hematocrit of 75 to 85 repairs the oligemia and the anemia simultaneously and in a manner which allows more quantitative prediction. Infusions of separated erythrocytes represent additional trouble and expense for the blood bank. It has therefore been our policy to use them only in such situations as this where the patient is older, has renal or hepatic disease, is in borderline cardiac decompensation, or for some other reason cannot tolerate or metabolize the plasma excess.

2. General Statement

This leads us to three general rules for the correction of secondary anemia in cases not attended by significant weight loss.

(1) In acute loss where hemodilution is not complete, assume that the blood volume is about 15 per cent low and estimate the approximate erythrocyte deficit from the hematocrit. In late chronic anemia of slow blood loss, assume that the blood volume is 15 per cent low and plasma volume refilling incomplete and hypotonic. Bedside measurement of blood volume, if carefully done, is useful but certainly not essential in the intelligent management of either situation.

(2) If the patient is able to accept whole blood, whole blood may be used, but it should be used with moderation, allowing sufficient time (twenty-four hours) for the plasma fraction to be metabolized before the patient is operated upon. The procedure of timed transfusion with planned equilibration is to be preferred. This will avoid anesthetizing and operating upon a patient with an acute hypervolemic plethora.

(3) If the patient is elderly, with a poor vascular tree, in borderline cardiac decompensation, or with other visceral disease, the erythrocyte deficit should be made up quantitatively and slowly with separated red cells to a hematocrit of 35 to 40.

3. Hypoproteinemia in Chronic Anemia

The hypoproteinemia of chronic blood loss is much more marked than in situations where cachexia exists without bleeding. This hypoproteinemia results from the loss of plasma protein (in the course of the bleeding) and the retention of salt and water triggered by volume reduction. Only if starvation is late and preterminal is albumin synthesis impaired. The body can make albumin relatively faster than erythrocytes; hypoproteinemia in chronic hemorrhage is therefore less marked than anemia. If retention of water and salt is very marked (a common finding in anemia) the concentrations of both plasma protein and red cells fall farther and faster. If renal disposal of water and salt is active (a situation not true after surgery or in visceral disease), the infusion of bank blood (protein concentration 5.5 to 6.0 gm. per cent at best) will result in but a small passive increment in plasma protein concentration: the result is usually disappointing. Concentrated albumin is much more effective as a means of passively raising the plasma oncotic pressure. It is not usually necessary. The avoidance of salt overloads is of critical importance here.

B. CHRONIC BLOOD LOSS WITH WEIGHT LOSS

Thus far we have dealt with the example of chronic anemia in a patient who has not lost weight. This example was selected for ease of estimation and is a situation not infrequently observed. Equally frequent, however, is the case of a patient with chronic anemia who has lost weight through progress of the disease that caused the blood loss. Here the volume relationships might appear confusing were it not for the fact that we now have sufficient evidence from compositional study so that we can base our treatment on sound data; in the majority of instances the blood volume is to be related to the "normal" (that is, pre-illness) weight for that patient.

When patients lose weight with gastrointestinal carcinoma, their weight loss is primarily due to a caloric deficit. It consists in loss of fat and lean tissue, the proportions of which vary, but fat loss predominates. The result is that certain of the patient's body water fractions, particularly the extracellular phase and the plasma volume, remain relatively high. Yet he needs all this extracellular fluid and blood volume to support the circulation. Most of the blood volume is distributed in the major vessels of the body and only 15 per cent lies in the capillary bed. When a patient loses weight, he loses weight from fat depots and from lean tissue, representing the capillary bed in muscle. His heart, lungs, liver, kidneys, and gastrointestinal tract do not become smaller, although the liver may lose protein and gain fat. Instead, the patient's body shrinks around the central viscera. These viscera, which contain some 85 per cent of the blood volume, become relatively larger. Therefore, if there is chronic weight loss (over a period of one to six months) with bleeding and a secondary anemia, the most effective therapy results from relating the ideal normal blood volume for that patient to the starting body weight rather than to the new body weight.

For example, supposing a normally built man has lost weight, going from 70 kg. to 60 kg. while suffering from a carcinoma of the stomach or right colon, with blood loss. He comes into the hospital with a hematocrit of 20. His therapy will be best carried out if one assumes that his blood volume should be about 7 per cent of his starting body weight of 70 kg., or 4900 ml. Basing calculations on this assumption will lead to a more effective treatment of this patient than assuming that his blood volume should be 4200 ml., this latter figure representing 7 per cent of his weight after the weight loss had occurred. If weight loss is very slow indeed (over a year in course) the blood volume may more properly be related to the observed weight, but this is rare and is seen more frequently in weight loss after dieting than after weight loss in disease.

We again counsel caution about preoperative restoration of blood volume immediately before operation. In young people there is little hazard. In sick or elderly patients with chronic anemia, commence transfusion three or four days before operation, and allow a "day of equilibrium" before operation.

C. CHRONIC NONHEMORRHAGIC DEPLETION AND WEIGHT LOSS WITH ANEMIA

Blood volume alterations in chronic caloric depletion, where hemorrhage has not been prominent, may be considered briefly here by a direct extension of these concepts. This matter is dealt with in detail in Part IV.

When the body shrinks because of chronic disease the "chassis" shrinks around the "engine," as previously mentioned; the engine—the central viscera and great vessels—contains most of the blood volume. This type of depletion, therefore, leaves behind a plasma volume that is larger than predicted normal value for the observed body weight with an erythrocyte volume that is diminished. This has been observed by measurement on so many occasions that there need no longer be any question about it. This large plasma volume results because the plasma volume is in hydrostatic and osmotic equilibrium with the extracellular phase; when the body shrinks because of weight loss the extracellular phase of body weight remains constant or actually enlarges by the operation of strong forces acting to conserve water and salt. The result is that as weight drops, the extracellular phase and plasma volume become relatively increased in proportion to body weight.

The erythrocyte volume does not share this property. As the depleting disease and dietary insufficiency have interfered with protein synthesis, erythrocyte volume falls. The decreasing mass of lean tissue needs less oxygen; this may encourage a decrease in the number of red cells or, equally likely, the loss of lean tissue is shared by the erythropoietic tissues. *We therefore find a relatively high volume of plasma and a relatively low volume of erythrocytes, a chronic secondary anemia with a blood volume near normal for the starting body weight, and a relative expansion of total body water and the extracellular phase.*

The depressions of hematocrit seen in nonhemorrhagic depletion are less than those observed where blood loss has formed a part of the depleting disease. In the latter instance, hematocrits in the twenties are a commonplace. When we are dealing with chronic, nonhemorrhagic depletion, the hematocrit is usually in the middle thirties. It is important to realize that this low hematocrit means a relative increase in the plasma volume with a minor decrease in red cell volume. An extensive and careless transfusion program will bring the patient to the operating room with a greatly expanded blood volume unless precautions are taken analogous to those suggested above for chronic anemia. The preparation of such patients for surgery need not include the use of whole blood at all if visceral disease coexists. If one or two erythrocyte suspensions are given, it is enough.

In extensive studies in our laboratories and a search through the literature for competently observed facts on this subject, we have found nothing whatsoever to support either the idea that such patients are suffering from hypovolemia, or the concept that indiscriminate use of blood transfusion in the immediate preoperative period is necessary or desirable.

We therefore summarize treatment in chronic blood loss before operation.

(1) In chronic blood-loss anemia assume that the blood volume is 15 per cent low; relate the predicted normal blood volume to the patient's pre-illness weight; use whole blood or separated cells in a campaign planned to restore oxygen capacity and effective volume, allowing twenty-four hours for equilibration and plasma dispersal before anesthesia and operation.

(2) In chronically depleted patients in whom bleeding has not occurred, use blood transfusion sparingly and accurately; separated cells are useful.

(3) When acute bleeding is not a problem, always allow the patient twenty-four hours to equilibrate his blood "load" before surgery.

(4) Be aware of the many chronic conditions in which a low hematocrit coexists with a normal or nearly normal blood volume.

(5) If bleeding then occurs (at or after operation, for example), blood replacement should be prompt, energetic, and quantitative—as in any other patient.

States of Expanded Blood Volume

Section I.   The Polycythemias

A. POLYCYTHEMIA VERA

Polycythemia vera is an expansion of the erythrocyte mass of unknown cause. The red cell mass is increased more than the total blood volume, which is not as markedly expanded. The few measurements reported in the literature show that the total blood volume is on the high side of normal (8 to 10 per cent of body weight) but it is not increased to an extent commensurate with the large red cell mass. By corollary, the plasma volume is small (1.5 to 2.5 per cent of body weight). This again raises the question of a receptor mechanism for the blood volume and of the regulatory pathways by which the blood volume is maintained at or near normal despite an expansion of the erythrocyte mass. In this instance the maintenance of a nearly normal blood volume must hinge on an increased rate of plasma disposal and the maintenance thereafter of a small plasma volume.

Polycythemia vera appears to be a disease of the erythropoietic system and is in a sense a neoplastic process. Its importance in surgical care lies chiefly in recognition of the fact that the resting normal hematocrits of these patients often run in the middle fifties. Hemoconcentration and hemodilution in response to plasma loss or hemorrhage arise from a different baseline hematocrit, and this naturally affects their interpretation and treatment. The incidences of duodenal ulcer and venous thrombosis are increased.

B. SECONDARY POLYCYTHEMIA

This condition is much more commonly seen on a surgical service than it was in the days before cardiac surgery. The tetralogy of Fallot, other congenital cardiac abnormalities, and late pulmonary vascular disease of chronic congestive failure are associated with either a secondary polycythemia, or a hypervolemia without elevated hematocrit, or both. The mechanism by which the production of erythrocytes is stepped up in response to chronic anoxia is not known. But if anoxia alone is the stimulus, the tendency for the blood volume to remain near normal is responsible for extremely high hematocrits, as in polycythemia vera. The expansion of body water, extracellular fluid, and plasma volume that is characteristic of cardiac failure naturally impedes the action of normal mechanisms for disposal of plasma, and plasma volume tends to be large, with a high total blood volume, as described below in Section III.

Since the body seems to seek, in anoxia, an increase in the oxygen-carrying capacity per unit of blood, the increase in erythrocyte volume cannot be effective unless there is an increased peripheral concentration of erythrocytes, and this in turn involves disposal of the plasma fraction. In congenital heart disease, hematocrits as high as 80 per cent are observed. This is a concentration of red blood cells which, in burns, has been shown to be associated with viscosity changes. It is remarkable how well these congenital cardiac patients get along as regards renal function; the incidence of thrombosis, however, is increased.

Although the total blood volume is held down by some mechanism that reduces the plasma volume, it remains (as in polycythemia vera) on the high side of normal and quite frequently is abnormally high. The highest blood volume that we have seen was in this condition at 12 per cent of body weight. This was almost twice normal for that age, build, and sex.

The significance of this disorder lies in the situation presented to the body when the cardiac defect is corrected surgically. Removal of erythrocytes and replacement with plasma avoids postoperative overcrowding of a heart that may have been in borderline compensation. Usually the loss of blood at operation takes care of the matter; normal transcapillary refilling lowers the hematocrit satisfactorily.

Section II.   Arteriovenous Fistula

The blood volume is expanded in large arteriovenous fistulas, particularly those occurring in the lower extremities. Total peripheral resistance is reduced; at the site of the fistula it is essentially zero. The extent to which total peripheral resistance is reduced depends upon the ratio between the surface area of the fistula and the total peripheral bed. An obvious compensation for the vascular tree is to increase the blood volume so as to maintain pressure in the face of grossly distorted output:resistance relationships. Cardiac output is increased, blood volume is increased, and the patient starts on a trend towards high-output failure. This might be thought of as the exact hemodynamic reverse of an obstructing vascular lesion such as coarctation of the aorta.

As a general rule in arteriovenous fistula, there is no increase in red cell concentration (hematocrit, red count, hemoglobin). In this respect the hypervolemia is in contrast to that seen in polycythemia vera or in chronic cardiopulmonary disease. The stimulus is not so much anoxia as hypotension. The "purpose" of the compensation appears to be the production of a large total volume to maintain pressure in the face of a lowered peripheral resistance. It would again seem logical for the body to do this by increasing all blood elements proportionally, and this it does. Whatever the teleology or the mechanism, the extent of blood volume increase in large arteriovenous fistulas is not great: in large fistulas of the lower extremities the blood volume in men ranges between 9 and 12 per cent of body weight.

Arteriovenous fistulas in a lower extremity produce greater volume changes and are more apt to be associated with cardiac enlargement and subsequent cardiac failure than are arteriovenous fistulas of the upper extremities. This interesting fact demands explanation and suggests certain basic differences between the volume:flow relationships in the upper as versus the lower extremities. The flow to the lower extremity is involved with a large muscle mass and therefore has a proportionally larger capillary bed in relation to the total volume of the major vessels. The characteristic difference in body composition between the erect walking biped and the quadruped such as the dog is the accumulation of a large amount of muscle mass and blood flow around the muscles of the buttocks and thigh, which are responsible for the upright gait. By contrast, the quadruped may literally support himself on his skeleton and use muscles merely to move the skeleton about. The femoral artery in the dog is tiny; in man it is very large. In man, the volume flow to the legs must therefore be capable of sudden alterations of magnitude in response to muscular exertion. Total flow is so much larger and more variable in the leg than in the arm that it may be these factors that produce a more pronounced effect on central volume-control mechanisms when arteriovenous fistulas involve a lower extremity. The correction of volume excess when a fistula is excised is a matter of some importance to the restoration of cardiac output and size downward to normal.

Section III.   Congestive Heart Failure; Renal Failure

Most patients in chronic congestive heart failure are in a hypervolemic state due primarily to plasma volume expansion as but one aspect of the generalized expansion of extracellular fluid, body water, and body sodium. Along with this there may be a very considerable increase in erythrocyte mass if anoxia has been a feature. Here the body is in a difficult round-robin situation.

(1) Anoxia stimulates hematopoiesis (possibly as a result of a circulating hematopoietic factor) with the objective of raising erythrocyte concentration (i.e., hematocrit, red count, or hemoglobin) in the course of improving oxygen-carrying capacity per unit of blood.

(2) Congestive failure expands the total body water and the extracellular fluid, and with them the plasma volume; this adds to blood volume but dilutes the oxygen-carrying capacity of blood.

(3) This further hypervolemia adds to the peripheral manifestation of congestive failure —including anoxia—and further stimulates erythropoiesis.

The clouding of the literature by poorly executed blood volume studies is more prominent in cardiac disease than in any other in the blood volume field. The relationship between large vessel hematocrit and whole body hematocrit can be grossly distorted in congestive heart failure where there is a high venous pressure. The explanation would appear to be that there is more blood pooled in the large veins, where the hematocrit is higher, than in the capillary bed. Whatever the explanation, in these patients with congestive failure the simultaneous use of plasma and erythrocyte volume methods is of first importance; the blood volume must be measured as a simple additive sum (PV + RV method) rather than on the basis of calculation from the hematocrit.

The changes in blood volume and related defects in body composition occurring in late heart disease depend on the nature of the cardiac lesion and the duration of anoxia and of decompensation. Preterminal patients with aortic stenosis have a different compositional defect from those who are in the late stages of congestive failure with mitral stenosis or in late pericarditis or right heart failure. Patients with hypertensive cardiovascular-renal disease who are in chronic congestive failure with renal impairment present a third compositional defect.

The classic hypervolemic congestive failure is found in late mitral stenosis. In its most pronounced form, its victim is seen to be wasted away, with poor oxygenation of peripheral tissues, wasting of the extremities with edema, ascites, a large liver, increased venous pressure, and some pulmonary edema or pleural fluid, depending upon the extent to which the right heart has failed. The blood volume is found to be above normal; here the increase is largely in the plasma fraction. In some instances an increase in erythrocyte volume is also present. The body water and extracellular fluid volume of these patients is grossly enlarged even in the absence of edema, and this fact underlies the plasma volume increase.

The important point in preoperative evaluation is that a patient with congestive heart failure who has a hematocrit in the middle or low thirties should not be considered to be chronically anemic and in need of blood transfusion. He is doubtless hypervolemic and his congestive failure is worsened by this factor. If the patient needs any volume therapy, it is a phlebotomy followed by the reinfusion of separated erythrocytes. Even in these patients there is tissue anoxia, due to the low fixed cardiac output, and the oxygenation of their tissues is in part governed by the oxygen-carrying capacity of the blood per unit volume. For this reason, patients with chronic congestive failure will get along better after operation if they have an adequate peripheral concentration of red blood cells in a normal blood volume rather than a low erythrocyte concentration in a high total volume.

Where patients have edema and an increased venous pressure, one may assume the blood volume to be above normal just as one may assume the total exchangeable sodium to be markedly elevated. Difficulty arises in evaluating those patients with congestive failure who do not have overt edema and do not have increased venous pressure, yet have the same disturbances of water and electrolyte content in lesser degree. Total exchangeable sodium is high, body water and extracellular volume are expanded, and there is a defect in the renal excretion of water and salt. In such patients the blood volume is also high, and surgical care must be predicated on the proximity of pulmonary edema despite an innocent chest X-ray and normal venous pressure and hematocrit.

Analogous to the extended plasma volume of heart failure but arising by a different pathogenesis is the overexpanded plasma volume of renal failure (and to a lesser extent hepatic failure) when edema and ascites are present. Here, the extracellular fluid is expanded by a combination of excretory impairment and overadministration of water and salt. The plasma volume shares in this expansion of the extracellular fluid; a low hematocrit therefore does not mean a low blood volume. Overtransfusion or overadministration of water and salt is very likely to produce hypertension or pulmonary edema.

In any of these states of expanded blood volume one cannot reason that restoration of blood volume downward to normal will improve the patient. He may develop severe hypotension if this is done either by venesection or by diuretics. The circulation appears to be in need of a large volume to support blood pressure and flow, and shock results from its sudden reduction to normal. Yet, when volume is too far above normal as a result of salt-and-water administration or retention, or of transfusion, the congestive manifestations become much worse. In assessing the patient before operation one should arrive at an estimate of the ideal functional volume for that patient, as based on clinical examination and performance. The venous pressure is the guide: if elevated, venesection is to be considered.

With postoperative recovery of compensation there is diuresis and a fall in body water and extracellular and plasma volumes. The hematocrit therefore rises during recovery.

Section IV.   Expanded Blood Volumes: Notes from the Literature

With the newer knowledge of volume phenomena and particularly those evidences that certain states may be associated with a continuing volume-expanding stimulus (acting on the kidney via endocrine influences), the study of conditions in which blood volume is high has acquired new interest. Polycythemia, arteriovenous fistulas, and heart disease are the three prominent examples just enumerated.

Epstein and Ferguson (1955) produced large arteriovenous fistulas in dogs by aortic-caval anastomosis. The plasma volume promptly (in fourteen to forty-two days) rose as high as 140 per cent of normal. There was no change in the erythrocyte volume. The hematocrit fell and the WBH:LVH ratio fell perceptibly.

Nelson and his coworkers (Nelson *et al.*, 1947) studied seven patients suffering from tetralogy of Fallot and nine instances of other forms of congenital heart disease. In the tetralogy cases the blood volumes were uniformly high, the increase being largely—but not wholly—in the erythrocyte volume. The blood volume figures ranged from 10.3 per cent of body weight to 25.9 per cent of body weight and, in an extreme case, to 42.8 per cent of body weight. As an average the erythrocyte volumes were four times normal (about 14 per cent of body weight) and the plasma volumes 1.3 times normal. The hematocrit went up with the high erythrocyte volume. Pulmonic stenosis also gave a high erythrocyte volume. Patients with mitral stenosis in congestive failure shared a high blood volume with increases in both fractions, and in cases of patent ductus the same was observed. The authors theorize that bone marrow anoxia is the main factor in high erythrocyte volume. Patients with cardiac septal defects not in congestive failure showed no differences from normal. These studies were done with dye and calculations of the erythrocyte volume from the hematocrit (a DPH method).

Schreiber *et al.* (1954) again demonstrated the elevated blood volume of cardiac failure using a satisfactory summation (RV + PV) method. They also showed a rise in the WBH:LVH ratio with return to compensation. The range in this latter connection was not great, the mean WBH:LVH ratio rising from 0.87 to 0.91. But the blood volume changes were large, particularly in the plasma volume moiety, which fell from 5.6 per cent to 4.8 per cent of body weight (normal mean, 4.25 per cent of body weight) with compensa, tion. Despite the well-established sex difference in blood volume data, Schreiber and his coworkers make no distinction between sexes in their tables. The authors point out that in cardiacs one must carry out blood volume measurements by PV + RV method in order to detect the rise in plasma volume in decompensation. The DPH or RVH methods will not yield proper data. This fact they assign to the pathologic WBH:LVH ratio.

Gunton and Paul (1955) measured the blood volume using P^{32} cells (an RVH method with no direct plasma volume) and found that patients in failure usually had a high blood volume. The average increase was from 6.98 per cent of body weight (in male normal controls) to 9.07 per cent of body weight in congestive failure; in females, from 6.06 per cent of body weight in controls to 8.82 per cent of body weight in congestive

failure. In twenty-one of seventy-eight cases the volume fell during recompensation. They emphasize that severe congestive failure can exist without a blood volume increase, but that this is unusual. In the blood volume changes there was no correlation with detectable edema. There was also no correlation between the blood volume elevation and the etiology of the heart disease. The blood volume change was on the part of both plasma volume and red cell volume. With recompensation the falling plasma volume left an inordinately high hematocrit (46 to 48). They point out that WBH:LVH ratios (which they did not measure) would accentuate the changes observed as based on the findings of Schreiber *et al.* (1954). See also Meneely and Kaltrieder (1943).

The studies from our laboratories (Wilson *et al.*, 1954; Moore *et al.*, 1956; Oleson *et al.*, 1957) report certain additional observations.

(1) WBH:LVH ratio changes are not great in heart disease save with acute changes in compensation.

(2) Where pulmonary flow or oxygenation is early compromised there is an early increase in the volume of erythrocytes.

(3) When edema and ascites later form there is an early increase in plasma volume; the extracellular fraction of body water increases *pari passu* with the plasma volume in congestive heart failure. Body water also rises. Total exchangeable sodium is high; total exchangeable potassium low. Extracellular hypotonicity is reflected throughout body water.

(4) In late mitral stenosis, extreme muscular wasting is associated with reduction of erythrocytes in some cases. In others, with anoxia and cyanosis, erythrocyte volume rises despite cellular wasting elsewhere.

(5) In aortic stenosis and coronary disease, compositional changes (edema, muscle wasting, blood volume expansion) are less marked even in the terminal stages.

(6) After surgical correction of the abnormality, there is a gradual return to normal body composition.

CHAPTER 14

Blood Transfusions: Rates, Routes, and Hazards; Effects on Blood Volume and Hematocrit

Clinical and metabolic aspects of blood transfusion will be described briefly in this chapter. For a review of techniques and recent advances in blood preservation, banking, major and minor blood groups, statistical and genetic aspects of blood groups, and Civil Defense aspects the reader is referred elsewhere. This chapter will concentrate primarily on volume effects of transfusion, the condition of the blood in the bank, the fate of the blood in the recipient, transfusion reactions, coagulation effects, and the citrate lesion.

Section I.   Transfusion Logistics

A. BLOOD GROUPS

The ideal blood for transfusion is fresh (less than two hours old) type-specific blood anticoagulated by a substance not present in excess. Such an ideal is often unattainable; modern blood bank practice consists, in essence, of establishing the safest alternative.

Blood from universal donors (Group O, Rh-negative) is quite acceptable for massive emergency transfusion. Some additional safety is provided when the isohemagglutinins in the plasma are neutralized by type-specific substance. This should be done if the antibody titer is above 1:200. If a patient enters the emergency ward with massive hemorrhage and must be treated immediately with blood from universal donors, the use of several such transfusions will not hurt this patient; if a prolonged program of universal-donor blood is embarked upon, neutralized blood should be used. The sooner type-specific blood is used, the safer for the future of that patient, but once an extensive course of Group O blood is begun it is inadvisable to return to the patient's own type for eight to fourteen days.

When Group O transfusion volumes approach 0.5 or 0.75 blood volume, the type found in the patient begins to approach that of the infused blood. Grouping and cross-matching become increasingly difficult; hemolysis, back-agglutination of marrow-produced cells, and increased hemoglobinemia become problems.

According to Walter (1955) the commonest cause of mismatched transfusions is misidentification of either recipient or donor. This in turn arises most often from poor methods of donor identification in the blood bank donor center, from mislabeling of blood or patient, or from the presence in the hospital of two patients with similar or identical names. All these are human errors reduced only by constant vigilance.

The approximate frequency of occurrence of the major groups in a mixed urban population is shown below.

BLOOD GROUP	Rh FACTOR	PERCENTAGE OF INCIDENCE
O	+	39
A	+	35
B	+	9
O	−	6
A	−	5
AB	+	4
B	−	1.5
AB	−	0.5
		100.00

AB patients are "universal recipients," a feature rarely useful in surgery.

The anti-human-globulin serum (Coombs) crossmatch is used in evaluation of new antierythrocyte globulin appearing in the recipient's plasma. This reveals incompatibility not shown by the saline, serum, or albumin-potentiated crossmatch. To carry out the test, the donor cells are incubated with the recipient serum, washed in saline, and then exposed to anti-human-globulin antibodies. Agglutination shows that the recipient's serum is being adsorbed on the donor cells by an immune process which may be hazardous should transfusion then be carried out. The Coombs test identifies antibodies coated on red blood cells which cause agglutination; the indirect Coombs test is used to identify such antibodies in the serum. In blood bank practice, the test is used to identify antibodies against the donor's cells, other than the ABO system. A negative Coombs test implies that there are no nonspecific antibodies in the serum of the recipient.

In massive plasma transfusion, neutralization of hemagglutinins with type-specific substance is unnecessary. Massive plasma treatment of burns may be carried out without developing any measurable titers of agglutinins against the patient's erythrocytes.

B. RATES OF TRANSFUSION

Transfusion should be given through needles of adequate caliber to favor an adequate rate of flow. Incompleted transfusions are more often due to low flow rates with sedimentation of cells, and clots in the needle, than any other single factor (Walter, 1955). A needle of #18 caliber is about the smallest that can be used reliably. A #16 or #14 is better; in treating shock it is essential.

An elective transfusion in a conscious patient should be started slowly and run at 20 to 40 drops per minute for ten minutes as a safety measure. If no reaction is experienced, the transfusion can be speeded up to the rate required by the clinical circumstances.

Drop-size varies, but as a general rule there are 15 drops to one ml. Thus, an infusion rate of 60 drops per minute is 4 ml. per minute; 520 ml. of blood (the volume of one whole blood transfusion, consisting of 450 ml. of blood and 70 of citrate) thus would occupy 130 minutes, or a little over two hours. In elderly people in whom transfusion therapy on an elective basis is proceeding continuously, this is a standard infusion rate. In slower transfusion than this, whole blood will usually become sluggish and come to a stop due to sedimentation, unless carefully watched.

For ordinary purposes in people with no cardiovascular embarrassment, a rate of 125 drops (8 ml.) per minute (eighty minutes for a transfusion) is most reasonable after an initial precautionary slow "test" run.

In Rh-negative male patients it is preferable to transfuse with Rh-positive blood, rather than to risk serious hypovolemia. If Rh-positive blood is used in the emergency hours, the change to Rh-negative blood can be made as it becomes available and the patient warned of sensitization should transfusion be necessary in a subsequent illness.

Where blood volume is acutely lowered, with hemodynamic effects anywhere between tachycardia alone and frank shock, transfusion should be much more rapid. With a #16 needle, using gravity with the usual hydrostatic elevation (the blood three to four feet above the heart), a steady flow "wide open" will infuse one unit of whole blood in about twenty or thirty minutes. This rate is agonizingly slow where the need is great.

Pressure may be used either by inflation of air into the bottle above the blood level or by a blood-pressure cuff around a collapsible blood bag. The plastic bag has many virtues, but this is one of its greatest. One unit may be infused in eight to twelve minutes; the needle caliber then becomes the rate-limiting factor. The insertion of another infusion through a second needle doubles the available rate. Where pressure is used, the infusion site must be repeatedly examined to be sure that the blood is not running into the subcutaneous tissues. Care must be taken to avoid air embolism.* Venospasm and subsequent phlebitis is much commoner when pressure is used.

---

* The use of a pressure cuff on a plastic bag carries no hazard of air embolism whereas the use of air under pressure, above the blood in a glass bottle, is obviously dangerous.

C. ROUTES OF ADMINISTRATION

Transfusion may be given by gravity-drip intravenously, pressure intravenously, pressure intra-arterially, and directly into the bone marrow. In most situations, gravity-drip or pressure intravenous transfusion will suffice. We have had little experience with infusion into the marrow. The use of intra-arterial transfusion should be confined to those patients with persistent hypotension in shock; where blood loss has been massive (particularly if from the arterial tree); where intravenous transfusion has failed, and particularly in pre-existent heart disease, with increased venous pressure. The pump-oxygenator may find a place in shock. If it does, it will play in part the role of a continuous-pressure intra-arterial transfusion.

Section II. The Fate of Transfused Blood

A. EFFECTS ON THE BLOOD VOLUME

The effects of transfusion on the blood volume depend on two major variables, the one related to the recipient and the other to the state of the erythrocyte. These two variables are plasma disposal (or dispersal) and erythrocyte viability.

1. Plasma Dispersal

The rate at which the plasma fraction equilibrates into the extracellular fluid and is then metabolized, excreted, and thus disposed of is a recipient or "host" variable that depends on

(1) the relationship of the blood volume after transfusion to the normal blood volume for that individual;

(2) circulatory adequacy; and

(3) metabolic activity.

2. Red Blood Cell Viability

This is a "blood bank" variable, depending on the method of storage, age of bank blood, diluent, means of transportation, and only in rare cases on compatibility, this being readily controlled in most circumstances.

The fate of the plasma fraction of blood thus depends largely on the recipient, whereas the fate of the erythrocyte fraction is largely a function of the donor blood. Situations in which the recipient destroys the infused cells at a rapid rate, barring frank incompatibility, are rare in surgical practice. The most important factor in erythrocyte volume effects of transfusion of whole blood is therefore the state of health of the red blood cells themselves, and this factor has become the controlling consideration in blood-bank technology.

3. Plasma Metabolism (Dispersal and/or Disposal) in Whole Blood Transfusion

Homeostatic mechanisms that maintain the blood volume at a normal figure and combat increases in the blood volume are not well understood. If a normal person is transfused with three or four units of whole blood, his body gradually disposes of the extra water, protein, and salt. This leaves him with a hematocrit which rises slowly as the plasma is dispersed. Plasma dispersal is essential to the hematocrit rise. The body can excrete water via the kidney, pass salt into the interstitial phase, and put extra protein into the metabolic mill much faster than it can degrade healthy erythrocytes that must live out their normal life span. Indeed, if the infused erythrocytes are healthy, they will live out their life span regardless of severe hypervolemia. Once a good erythrocyte is circulating, the body can control increase in erythrocyte volume only by decreasing hematopoiesis, not by hastening destruction of erythrocytes.

The result—as mentioned before—is that an increase in blood volume produced by preoperative transfusion in chronic compensated anemia may embarrass the patient acutely but will, over the course of several days, restore itself to normal. For this reason, in using whole blood to prepare a chronically anemic patient for surgery, the transfusion should be given gradually over the period of several days and a "rest" of twenty-four to forty-eight hours allowed before surgery. The hematocrit increment from the transfusions will continue to develop over a day or two after the transfusion, as the water-salt-protein of the blood plasma is transported metabolically out of the blood stream. Needless waste of time is not required to permit this.

The use of resuspended red cells, or red-cell concentrates from which most of the plasma has been withdrawn, obviates the problem of plasma dispersal and disposal. As repeatedly emphasized, the use of such suspensions is important where hypervolemia is dangerous.

4. Recipient Factors in Plasma Dispersal

The fate of the infused plasma fraction is determined by the fact that the recipient's metabolic arrangements cannot differentiate between the infused plasma and the recipient's own water, salt, and protein. The entire infusion therefore enters into the metabolic mill. If blood volume is above normal after transfusion, the plasma fraction disappears from the blood volume briskly, so long as cardiac, renal, and hepatic function are normal. If blood volume is below normal at the time of the infusion, it appears that the plasma fraction remains in the blood stream longer and supports volume longer than if it is infused in excess of normal blood volume.

We have here, then, an example of a volume-sensitive mechanism to be included under the volume-regulating phenomena discussed at greater length in Part III. Regulation of the size of the blood volume is one of the most critical of the volume-sensitive regulations of the body composition. One method of its operation in high-volume states is by plasma disposal, and another is by decreased hematopoiesis. Both are important in understanding the fate of transfused blood.

5. Mechanism of Plasma Disposal

Sudden reduction in blood volume results in a sharply decreased excretion of water and sodium salts. By contrast, an excess volume of blood produces an increase in the excretion of water and salt.

The salt-water saving of acute volume reduction is evidently mediated at least in part by antidiuretic hormone and aldosterone and is a typical volume-sensitive response. By the same token, the increased disposal of salt and water that follows transfusion hypervolemia may be implemented by a release of normal volume-conserving forces: a reduction in antidiuretic activity and in aldosterone-induced tubular sodium transport, with diuresis.*

Were this to be the case we would expect to see increased urine output of water and salt after iso-oncotic expansion of the plasma volume, and this indeed occurs. This diuresis is in part responsible for plasma disposal after blood transfusion beyond normal volume. The remainder is handled by equilibration into extravascular areas and by metabolic degradation, some of the protein finding its way into protoplasm, the rest being burned and the nitrogen excreted. To the minor extent that infused human plasma enters the protein metabolic pool, it is a nutritional step, albeit an unimportant one. This normal physiologic process for plasma dispersal and disposal is a basic factor in the volume response to transfusion and must be permitted to ensue before a rise in hematocrit to a figure higher than that of the infused mixture

---

* Note that we refer here to iso-oncotic contraction or expansion of extracellular fluid.

can possibly occur. In the transfusion of all chronic anemias and many acute oligemias, it plays a role.

B. FACTORS IN RED BLOOD CELL VIABILITY

The "blood bank" factors in erythrocyte viability are the central features of blood bank practice and research today. A few aspects are dealt with in the following section.

When bank blood is infused, from 4 to 8 per cent of the erythrocytes are destroyed immediately and the rest live out a life span the duration of which depends on the age of the cells previous to donation. This initial destruction may be in part a "collection lesion" (Gibson *et al.*, 1956), but it is largely due to the fact that some of the cells have lived out their lives by the time they arrive in the recipient. Subsequent erythrocyte survival depends primarily on cell viability and only secondarily on host immunity, barring those situations which arise in incompatibility or hemolytic anemias.

Most of the red cells in bank blood live out a span expressed as their destruction at the rate of 0.83 per cent per day (life span of 120 days). Those that have been injured in collection (often as many as 20 per cent of the cells) are destroyed much more rapidly, having an in-vivo half-time of 2.2 hours. It is the accumulation of the products of large numbers of these fragile cells that is in part responsible for the evident hemolytic process seen in surgical patients who require massive transfusion. Resin-collected blood and heparinized blood do not show this collection lesion to the same extent but will deteriorate in the blood bank as does any cellular system.

Although the red blood cell has no nucleus, it is an active energy-exchanging system, requiring the combustion of a substrate to derive the energy needed for the maintenance of the electrolyte gradient across its membrane. To do this it burns glucose to lactate; as the glucose disappears in stored blood the pH falls and electrolyte shifts become prominent, sodium moving into the red cell in exchange for potassium.

Blood as it ages undergoes several changes simultaneously.

(1) The glucose concentration in the medium drops to or near zero.
(2) The sodium concentration in the medium falls.
(3) The pH in the blood drops; the ACD is strongly acid (pH 5.0). In the blood the mixture has a pH of 7.0. But some blood buffers are taken up by this; as the metabolic lactate is added, the pH falls further.
(4) The sodium concentration in the erythrocyte gradually rises.
(5) As a converse of the above (4), the potassium concentration within the erythrocyte falls and the potassium concentration within the medium rises.
(6) The hemoglobin concentration in the medium slowly rises.
(7) Cell fragility increases.

It is not unusual in fourteen-day-old blood to find plasma potassium concentrations in the general neighborhood of 25 mE. per l. and hemoglobin concentrations around 100 mg. per 100 ml.

The rise in plasma potassium concentration is a linear function of time in stored blood. This occurs at a rate that reaches values of 20 to 35 mE. per l. in twenty to twenty-eight days. Osmotic fragility irregularly increases while glucose falls and hemoglobin rises, the latter curve breaking sharply upward at twenty days both in bottles and plastic containers.

In glass containers these changes have progressed to the point where the blood is unacceptable at fourteen to twenty-one days. In plastic containers the blood is still in acceptable condition at twenty-eight days, but there is much variability, and the use of large amounts of blood over fourteen days old in one patient will almost inevitably produce jaundice and hemoglobinuria, the hazards of which depend upon the rest of the clinical condition of the patient. In decreased renal blood flow such a result is very dangerous to the kidney.

At the time of this writing, Tullis and Haynes have reported their initial and highly successful experience with over 500 transfusions of red cells preserved for several months by freezing in glycerol.

The plastic bag (Walter, 1951) represents

a great advance in blood bank practice, and should completely supplant the use of glass containers. The blood is better preserved, more safely and easily transported, and administered more rapidly, under better control.

C. THE EFFECTS OF OLD, OVERAGE BLOOD

Grossly hemolyzed blood given to a patient. even though the erythrocytes be compatible and bacteria seemingly absent, is much more toxic than the infusion of a similar amount of crystalline hemoglobin. The ensuing hypotension and renal damage resemble those of mismatching. The nature of this toxicity is not well understood; intracellular enzymes and electrolytes are toxic when in the extracellular phase in increased amounts. Recent evidence suggests that bacterial growth even of minor degree may render the hemoglobin especially toxic. Such spoiled blood will result from accidental failure of blood bank refrigeration.

On the other end of the scale are those instances where the blood is merely slightly overage. Here there is the immediate in-vivo destruction of many of the cells (up to 50 per cent), the development of hemoglobinemia, mild jaundice, and hemoglobinuria—often without subjective symptoms. Volume effects are of course disappointing.

The infusion of 50 ml. of quickly hemolyzed blood will produce a peak plasma hemoglobin of 300 mg. per 100 ml. Although such an episode may be harmless in the resting patient, it is not benign after injury. If the patient is in shock, and the cells of his renal tubules anoxic, these small amounts of pigment from such blood may be nephrotoxic and large amounts are even more dangerous, producing a tubular lesion and renal insufficiency. Patients with shock and borderline renal insufficiency tend to be hyperkalemic. If their shock has been accompanied by hemolysis or destruction of muscle, there is some hemoglobinuria and myoglobinuria. The infusion of overage blood adds to the extent of the hyperkalemia, hemoglobinemia, hemoglobinuria, and renal damage.

In military usage or in civilian disaster, constant check should be made on the nature of the blood being dispensed. The simplest method consists in spinning down a sample, examining the supernatant visually for hemoglobin, and carrying out on the supernatant a potassium determination by flame photometer. If it is visibly pink or if the potassium concentration is over 30 mE. per l., the blood should not be dispensed. Although this potassium concentration seems very high the actual potassium load of even 2000 ml. of plasma is still only 60 mE.

D. KINDS OF FRESH BLOOD

Under many circumstances the infusion of very fresh blood provides essentials, particularly platelets and the clotting proteins, not well preserved even under ideal conditions. In using fresh blood, one must determine the objective and select the type of fresh whole blood accordingly.

There are four types of fresh whole blood used in transfusion:

(1) fresh blood given by direct transfusion in silicone-lined tubes,

(2) fresh heparinized whole blood,

(3) fresh citrated whole blood, and

(4) fresh ion-exchanged blood (or blood collected with a chelating agent such as EDTA).*

The term "fresh" in all instances should mean that this blood should be infused into the patient within an hour or less after being drawn from the donor.

By fresh transfusion it is possible to get viable leucocytes or platelets into the recipient. Fresh heparinized blood is of value to patients who have received large amounts of citrated blood and in whom citrate effects are worrisome. The amount of heparin added to the blood should be only enough to prevent coagulation of the particular transfusion given and not enough to heparinize the whole patient. Fresh citrated blood is very useful for a number of additional purposes and is easier to prepare. Its proteins, such as immune bodies, globulin, fibrinogen, and prothrombin, are normal and it is effective in treating hemorrhagic states resulting from a deficiency of these protein fractions. Its erythrocytes are

---

* Ion-exchange blood completely lacks platelets regardless of its age.

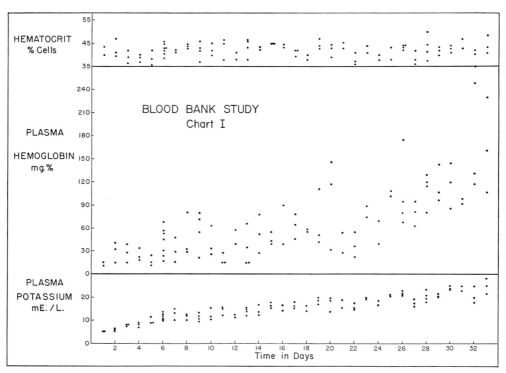

Figure 46. Blood Bank Study. I

In this and the succeeding chart are shown the changes which occur in stored blood over the course of 33 days. This blood was stored in ACD solution by standard blood bank practice.

It will be noticed in this chart that the hematocrit shows no systematic change, indicating that cell destruction is not gross. The plasma hemoglobin concentration gradually rises as some of the cells live out their life span and release their pigment. Associated with this is a gradual increase in the plasma potassium concentration.

As a general rule, bank blood which has visible hemoglobin in the supernatant or a plasma potassium concentration over 15 mE. per liter should be regarded as too old for satisfactory transfusion. Infused in large amounts, such blood is dangerous.

Unpublished studies from our laboratories.

essentially normal but it is virtually devoid of leucocytes and platelets unless collected in a plastic container and rapidly retransfused. In all instances it is the platelet more than any other formed element that is lost in a few minutes of standing. In plastic containers under ideal conditions, the platelets are viable for six to eight hours.

E. COLLECTION AND PRESERVATION

The development of improved blood-storage solutions, the use of plastic containers, and the perfection of blood bank procedures have been major advances in surgical care which have affected all areas of surgery. A detailed discussion of these developments should be left for a work on blood bank practice. It has been shown by Gibson *et al.* (1956) that ACD solution itself is harmful to blood until it has been diluted by a significant quantity of blood to something approaching its final concentration. The first portion of the blood run into the solution is hurt by the raw ACD, and 70 per cent of these cells are destroyed immediately following transfusion. This may account for much of the immediate destruction of erythrocytes seen on transfusion. It is this immediate destruction that accounts for the slight increase in hemoglobin excretion (largely as fecal urobilinogen) seen after multiple closely-spaced transfusions.

Using plastic containers the following procedures are available:

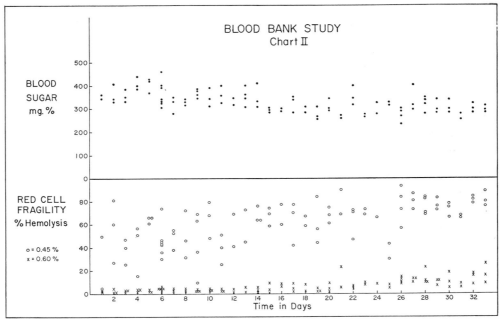

Figure 47. BLOOD BANK STUDY. II.

In this chart are shown other studies on the same samples of blood shown in the previous chart. It will be noted that the blood sugar gradually falls as glucose is oxidized in maintaining the viability of the red blood cell even at the low temperature of blood bank storage.

The change in red cell fragility is most noted in the 0.6 per cent sodium chloride solution. Here, after approximately three weeks, there is a definite increase in osmotic fragility.

(1) *acid-citrate-dextrose* collection, the usual procedure;

(2) *ion-exchange*, the removal of calcium and other divalent cations;

(3) *EDTA* (chelating agent), an anti-coagulant that leaves platelets easily recoverable;

(4) *double pack*, a closed system for separation of plasma and cells;

(5) *triple pack*, a closed system for separation of plasma, platelets, and erythrocytes.

Section III.   The Fate of the Recipient: Reactions

The commonest fault in the use of blood transfusion is "too little and too late." This is chiefly the result of an unrealistic view (or no view at all) of the known facts of blood volumes and their replacement.

A. FREQUENCY OF TRANSFUSION REACTIONS

In civilian practice a well-run blood bank should provide service with a rate of noticeable clinical reactions in the neighborhood of 1 per cent. A reaction rate over 1 per cent should stimulate revision of blood bank procedures. It is estimated that transfusion fatalities rank with anesthesia and appendicitis as causes of death. The national rate is alleged to be about one death in 1000 to 3000 transfusions.

B. NATURE OF TRANSFUSION REACTIONS

There are five general types of transfusion reaction.

1. Reactions to Mismatched or Incompatible Blood

The patient shows chill, fever, pain in the back, with, in severe cases, hypotension. A transfusion of as little as 75 ml. may produce this picture. Lesser degrees of incompatibility produce a milder response. Hemolysis or hemorrhage may result. Renal failure is the hazard.

2. Reactions to Grossly Contaminated Blood

The patient exhibits chill, and fever with less evidence of vascular effect than the above, except in those cases in which gram-negative bacilli are involved, in which case the hypotensive reaction may be extreme or fatal.*

3. Pyrogenic Reactions

The patient has fever with or without chill; this is a lesser clinical response. The symptoms may appear one to three hours after the transfusion is begun.

4. Allergic Reactions

The patient demonstrates itching, leucocytosis, and eosinophilia, sometimes with urticaria and other skin manifestations. This reaction may include a tendency to bleeding, which may be a manifestation of allergy or of incompatibility.

5. Minor Febrile Reactions

The patient may have fever, often delayed, with little else.

Almost all deaths from transfusion have resulted from air embolus,† gross mismatch (error in identification), hypervolemia (especially dangerous in infants, or in adults suffering from heart disease), and hemolytic reaction from mismatch, deterioration, or infection with renal tubular necrosis.

C. DIAGNOSIS

In addition to clinical observation there are two diagnostic methods of special significance in real or suspected transfusion reactions: the immediate re-examination of the infused blood and of the patient's blood

---

* As shown recently by Walter (unpublished), very small doses of certain cryophilic organisms in refrigerated blood will produce renal failure.

† Air embolus is a virtual impossibility with pressure transfusion employing plastic-bag equipment. This feature alone should recommend its adoption in those areas where glass bottles are still used.

(1) for major and minor crossmatch, including recheck of groups; Coombs' crossmatch;
(2) for bacteria, by smear and culture;
(3) for free hemoglobin and potassium concentration; for brown color;
(4) in the patient (in addition to the above), the urine should be examined for heme pigments by benzidine on a spun supernatant.

D. TREATMENT

From the above studies a logical program for the patient is evolved.

(1) If no incompatibility is shown when the blood is rematched and there is no hemoglobinemia or hemoglobinuria in the patient, he should be observed for at least six hours. If no further manifestations arise, the transfusion program may proceed.

(2) If there is hemoglobinemia, hemoglobinuria, or incompatibility on rematch, the patient should be managed on the basis of early renal insufficiency: hourly urine outputs measured, water given only "to balance," and daily weights taken. This management is described in detail in the section on renal insufficiency. If the urine outputs show no persistent decline, vigilance may be relaxed. The effectiveness of alkali, cortisone, and antihistamines is unproven. The latter two, in moderate doses, are probably harmless. A large dose of alkali is dangerous if renal failure is present.

(3) If the evidence points to bacterial contamination, treatment with appropriate antibiotics should be started.

(4) If the symptoms of reaction include hypotension, incompatibility is strongly suggested. Yet, despite the precarious renal function, adequate transfusion must be given to restore pressure and flow. The recent occurrence of even a severe transfusion reaction is not a contraindication to further transfusion. The most careful precautions must of course be taken, but the threat to life is renal failure, and any prolongation of the phase of hypotensive-vasoconstricted renal anoxia greatly increases the potential hazard to the kidneys.

E. TRANSFUSION REACTIONS UNDER ANESTHESIA

As already mentioned, we do not believe there is justification for a single-unit transfusion under anesthesia. If the adult patient's need is limited to 500 ml. of blood, it is better to await his awakening so as to provide the further safety factor of consciousness to assist in determining symptoms of incompatibility. If the patient's need is real he should certainly receive more than 500 ml.; 1000 ml. is a minimum replacement for blood loss showing early hemodynamic changes at the 15 to 25 per cent blood-volume range even in a small person.

If the patient is under anesthesia and receiving transfusion, the two noticeable signs of transfusion incompatibility—severe intractable hypotension and pathologic bleeding—are both very grave. Should either occur this cause should be considered above all others. The steps already enumerated should be taken: re-crossmatch, search for free pigment, check on the age of the blood and potassium content of the plasma. If there is any pathologic finding, steps for the early management of renal failure must be instituted until status can be evaluated at greater leisure.

F. UNDERTRANSFUSION AND OVERTRANSFUSION

In acute hemorrhage and wounds and in surgical shock of less than twelve hours' duration, the commonest cause for transfusion failure is undertransfusion. The correction of this defect is a matter of self-education for all members of the team to be sure that:

(1) the patient's expected normal blood volume is estimated realistically on our clinical age-sex-build basis,

(2) the magnitude of the need is appreciated in the light of the above,

(3) an adequate volume of blood is given at an adequate rate, through adequate equipment,

(4) current losses (e.g., at operation) are replaced *pari passu*,

(5) hidden losses (hemorrhage within the thigh, the belly, the gut) are searched out, evaluated, and replaced, and

(6) the additional need is met if the clinical phenomenon of "taking up" has occurred.

By contrast, overtransfusion is less frequently of grave import. The simplest example of overtransfusion is seen in a normal individual who is electively transfused with two or three units of whole blood. The changes are those of a slowly increasing hematocrit, accompanied by an increased excretion of water and salt. There is a gradual increase in nitrogen excretion over a period of weeks as the extra plasma protein and aging erythrocytes are ground up in the metabolic mill and the end-products excreted. During this time hematopoiesis is markedly inhibited.

When an acutely ill person is overtransfused, these metabolic methods for plasma disposal and for getting rid of this extra volume are slowed down because of the inhibition of water and salt excretion produced by the injury or illness. It is much easier to produce acute hypervolemia with its attendant hazards of increased venous pressure, pulmonary edema, and congestive atelectasis in seriously ill patients or patients suffering from chronic disease of heart or kidneys.

The only reliable sign of overtransfusion in the acute phase is increased venous pressure; this may also evidence myocardial failure; the two may coexist. Venous pressure is monitored via a simple side-arm Y tube during transfusion or infusion.

G. DISEASE TRANSMISSION: DONOR EVALUATION

The diseases transmitted by transfusion are homologous serum jaundice, syphilis, and malaria. Prevention of this transmission is based on history and physical examination of the donor plus luetic serologic test on the blood before its administration. It is usually advisable to reject female donors weighing less than 100 pounds (45 kg.), in whom the donation of 500 ml. would be over 15 per cent of the blood volume. Donors with chronic anemia (hemoglobin below 12.6 gm. per 100 ml.) are rejected. All blood must be cultured and retyped after collection. All contaminated blood is discarded.

When Group O Rh-negative blood is used for transfusion in emergencies, a rapid Kahn or Hinton test is done to exclude syphilis.

With penicillin treatment, transfusion syphilis is very benign and is far preferable to death in oligemic shock.

Section IV. The Volume Effects of the Blood

A. PREDICTION OF VOLUME AND HEMATOCRIT CHANGES RESULTING FROM TRANSFUSION

1. Whole Blood Transfusion

The prediction of the hematocrit increment to be expected from whole blood transfusion is a matter of considerable interest and warrants a further word. The hematocrit response to a transfusion program should always be recorded and interpreted; in some instances it constitutes in itself an estimate of blood volume and of the metabolic state of the patient.

Simple formulas for the calculation of the theoretical maximum and minimum expected hematocrits can be derived. While not a fixed rule, these indicate how blood volume data based on predicted ranges may be helpful in the mental arithmetic of surgical care, and may act as a check on treatment. Such formulas assist in clarity of thinking and help to avoid the pitfalls of totally unrealistic estimates. They are not a substitute for clinical judgment, but a stimulus to "volume-thinking."

A figure for the *maximum* hematocrit that can possibly be expected is based on *complete plasma disposal.*

Where

BV_1 = blood volume as observed before treatment

BV_2 = blood volume after transfusion, assuming complete plasma disposal (that is, no change in plasma volume in the patient as a result of transfusion)

BVT = blood volume transfused

RVT = red cell volume transfused

RV_1 = red cell volume before transfusion

Then

$$BV_2 = BV_1 + RVT$$

and the

$$\frac{\text{maximum expectable}}{\text{hematocrit}} = \frac{RV_1 + RVT}{BV_1 + RVT}$$

This obviously gives a maximum expectable figure. It assumes no plasma volume change—that is, it assumes complete disposal of the infused plasma. This is rarely the case, and indeed such a rise is rarely seen; it **is** the ceiling expectation.

In chronic anemia the plasma volume is high to start with and we expect the disposal of much of the infused plasma as volume exceeds normal during transfusion.

If there is *no plasma disposal,* as in states of low blood volume (where the plasma fraction of the infused blood is retained) or with severe cardio-renal-hepatic disease interfering with plasma disposal, then the expression for the *minimum* expected hematocrit change is

$$\frac{\text{minimum expectable}}{\text{hematocrit}} = \frac{RV_1 + RVT}{BV_1 + BVT}$$

If one estimates the starting volume on the basis of sex and weight, with allowance for pathologic conditions, one will find that *the actual observed hematocrit change from a program of transfusion lies somewhere between these two extremes.* The actual recorded rise is therefore a measure of the extent of plasma disposal.

Plasma disposal is most active when the blood volume is high or near normal. The lower the blood volume is to begin with, the less plasma disposal will occur after transfusion (despite the greater fraction represented by each unit of blood). Hence, a *greater* volume increment and a *lesser* hematocrit increment will be noted when the patient's blood volume is very low before transfusion, as opposed to that situation which obtains when transfusion is given to a large blood volume.

The clinical use of laboratory blood-volume determinations should be expected to be helpful in the management of such situations. It is the rare surgical service which can carry out the multiple "short-order" blood-volume measurements required. More useful than the scattered blood-volume data of an over-worked laboratory is the frequent use of calculations based on what is already known of the blood volume in disease.

2. Transfusion of Separated Cells

It is apparent that the hematocrit response to an erythrocyte suspension (where the plasma disposal problem is minimal) is in itself a measure of the starting blood volume. One may take useful advantage of this fact. In the treatment of hemorrhage from duodenal ulcer—for example, when the bleeding has ceased and we are dealing with a mixture of acute and chronic blood loss with partial transcapillary compensation—some estimate of the blood volume is helpful if not of critical importance. One does not know the extent to which the anemia is compensated by transcapillary transudation of fluid. If the patient is given 400 ml. of packed red cells, and careful hematocrits are taken before and after transfusion, the resulting change in hematocrit constitutes in itself a crude approximation of the blood volume. Although disposal of the patient's own plasma is again a variable, the result has meaning. Where cell suspensions are used or disposal of excess plasma is complete, the volume response is a function of starting volume and infusion volume; the latter is known and therefore the former can be approximated by back-calculation; the lack of absolute precision is not as important as the stimulus to a quantitative approach to volume therapy. The first approximation that this yields is better than no volume data at all. An example of this observation follows.

Suppose the patient is an otherwise healthy male of 80 kg. who has been bleeding, is not yet fully compensated, and has stopped bleeding. His hematocrit increased from 20 to 30 with 400 ml. of separated erythrocytes. We are thus dealing with a very restricted blood volume.

To indicate the nature of this quantitative relationship an expression can be derived, based on addition of the erythrocytes to the blood volume, with increase in red cell volume, hematocrit, and total blood volume but no change in plasma volume. This expression

makes use of the large vessel plasmacrit (LVP) or fraction of blood occupied by plasma, expressed as a decimal.

Then

$$BV_1 = \frac{LVP_2 \times RVT}{LVP_1 - LVP_2}$$

Where

BV_1 = blood volume before red cell infusion
LVP_1 = plasmacrit before red cell infusion
LVP_2 = plasmacrit after red cell infusion
RVT = red cell volume transfused

And, in our example:

$$BV_1 = \frac{0.7 \times 400}{0.8 - 0.7} = 2800$$

Our 80 kg. man had therefore bled down to a volume of 2800 ml., or a little under 4 per cent of body weight, before his infusion—a very low volume. After the transfusion, this patient therefore has a blood volume of about 3200 ml., with a red cell volume of about 960 ml. and a hematocrit of 30. He clearly needs more volume than this and a higher hematocrit, both of them best achieved by further infusions of red cell suspensions.

This estimate yields a *maximum* figure for the starting blood volume. Like all blood-volume equations in this book it is shown to indicate the sort of relationships that exist and that are involved in volume-concentration changes after transfusion; it must be tempered with clinical judgment as to other factors active, if used at the bedside.

3. Multiple Transfusions

When more than five transfusions are given in short order, one discovers that the effect on the blood volume and hematocrit is less than that predicted from their volume. There seem to be several possible explanations.

(1) *Increased Hemolysis.* There appears to be a speeding up of hemolytic processes when many whole-blood transfusions are given close together. This is probably due to the "immediate loss phenomenon" (i.e., the collection lesion) as applied to several units of blood given simultaneously. A slight increase

in the plasma hemoglobin and a very considerable increase in the fecal urobilinogen may be observed.

(2) *Vascular Capacity.* This type of transfusion is usually given to a desperately ill patient, and the clinical phenomenon of "taking up" may have something to do with the apparent disappearance of his blood. Measurements suggest that when multiple, closely placed transfusions are given to severely traumatized oligemic patients, the blood seems to disappear. One cannot find it by hematocrit or hemoglobin elevation but, more important than that, it is difficult to trace by careful measurement of serial volume or pigment excretion. It appears to be lost in tissue planes and retroserous deposits.

(3) *Hematocrit Relations in Massive and Replacement Transfusion.* The hematocrit of banked blood as transfused ranges between 37 and 40. This arises from the facts that the donor may not be in an absolutely ideal state of health and that the preservative fluid has been added. In shock due to loss of whole blood, hematocrit changes are occurring in the recipient only slowly and with the passage of time. A desperately ill oligemic patient with hemorrhagic shock, near death, may have a hematocrit that is no lower than 37 to 40. If one transfuses a large volume of bank blood with a hematocrit of 37 to 40 into a patient who starts with a hematocrit of 37 to 40, there is going to be virtually no change in the concentration of erythrocytes. Indeed, if the patient's entire blood volume were immediately replaced by the bank blood, the final hematocrit would still be 37 to 40, since that is the hematocrit both of his blood and of the infused blood-ACD mixture.

The only factor which can raise that hematocrit is pathologic plasma loss or normal plasma dispersal—the movement of fluid, electrolyte, and protein out of the plasma and back into the interstitial spaces and into the urine after blood volume is restored. As already mentioned, overtransfusion produces a slight diuresis of water and salt. Therefore just as the passage of time is required to observe peripheral hemodilution in untreated hemorrhage, so also *the passage of time is required to observe an erythrocyte concentration increment (i.e., rising hematocrit) when multiple closely-spaced transfusions are given to an individual in shock.*

CHAPTER 15

Blood Transfusions; Special Problems in Massive, Multiple Transfusions: Coagulation and the Citrate Lesion

Section I. Altered Coagulation and Wound Ooze during Multiple Transfusions

During long and difficult operations, patients who have received many blood transfusions are often observed to ooze from open dissected tissue. Treatment must be accurate and realistic to be effective. There are several possible causes, and several considerations should enter into the evaluation of such a situation, not the least of which is the possibility that the coagulation defect antedates the transfusions, is the cause of the bleeding in the first place, and is not caused by the transfusions.

A. VENOUS PRESSURE

The patient may be in a stage of over-transfusion or of decreased cardiac output in which the venous pressure is elevated. This can readily be checked by the anesthetist or by observation in the operative field, and, if it is present, either phlebotomy or intra-arterial transfusion is indicated, depending on the systolic blood pressure. Digitalization is advisable if myocardial function is a factor. The patient may have been overtransfused and may have a high blood volume with plethora, contributing to elevated venous pressure; in that case systolic pressure will be high and phlebotomy should be done. If systolic pressure is low, an elevated venous

pressure suggests myocardial ischemia; digitalization is advisable.

B. VASODILATATION

The degree of vasodilatation produced either by disease or anesthesia may be a factor. If cutaneous vasodilatation is evident, the use of vasoconstricting drugs may be helpful. If the plane of anesthesia is very deep or if spinal anesthesia is being used, vasoconstrictors are useful.

C. COAGULATION DEFECTS

More likely is the probability that the coagulation mechanism has been affected by the process itself or by the multiple transfusions. The mechanisms by which this may occur are six.

1. *Ordinary bank blood has virtually no platelets.* As the patient's blood is progressively diluted with bank blood the platelet count often decreases. This is rare as a cause of bleeding. The decrease in platelet count is not a linear function of the dilution. Platelet production appears to go on, possibly at an increased rate as a result of the procedure itself, yet low platelet counts are occasionally observed after multiple closely-spaced blood transfusions. It is often surprising what a high

platelet count is observed after what amounts to replacement transfusion of platelet-poor blood. Thrombocytopenia can be repaired by transfusion of platelet-rich blood, by direct or very fresh transfusion; it is rare as a cause of surgical bleeding. Platelets in ACD-preserved blood have effectively disappeared in two hours after collection, unless the blood is in plastic bags, in which case they are recoverable for six to eight hours.

2. *An incompatible transfusion reaction* causes a hemorrhagic state which in some instances is more prominent than the hemolytic phenomena. Bleeding that appears abnormal during operation should always excite suspicion of this cause.

3. *Loss of fibrinogen* from the circulating blood occurs rapidly in certain circumstances, particularly in obstetrics and in thoracic surgery, or where there has been bleeding into a body cavity. The fibrinogen is removed by clotting or by bleeding, and a state of hypofibrinogenemia or afibrinogenemia results. This manifests itself by a prolonged clotting time only when fibrinogen is very low, and is specifically repaired by the administration of fibrinogen. The patient's clotting time should therefore be determined in cases of marked abnormal hemorrhage. The administration of fibrinogen is rational if other causes of bleeding are unlikely or the clotting time prolonged. The normal fibrinogen concentration is 200 to 400 mg. per 100 ml.; below 100 mg. per 100 ml. is the critical level. A very simple test for fibrinogen function is the "feel" of the clot. If it is well-structured, firm, and "resistant" to handling, the coagulation proteins are probably normal. If the clot is fragile and fragments easily, one should beware of a dangerous lack of normal fibrinogen.

4. *The presence of abnormal fibrinolysins* in the blood is a manifestation of cell death and is the usual case soon after death and in certain tumors (carcinoma of the prostate), limb gangrene, and in shock. It is observed in surgery under some conditions, including severe injury, liver disease, certain types of obstetrical emergency, and incompatible transfusion reaction. It may be a cause of abnormal bleeding. It is often difficult to distinguish increased fibrinolysins from decreased fibrinogen, on rapid test. Incubation of clotted blood at 37° C. for an hour demonstrates fibrinolysins if the clot dissolves. Such fibrinolysins may arise from cellular breakdown. An increase in "anticlot" factors, including fibrinolysis, may be produced by hypoxia, liver disease, intrathoracic operations (lung trauma), transurethral resection and massive injury. Treatment can consist only in the administration of additional fibrinogen (carrying the hazard of subsequent thrombosis) or the administration of cortisone to neutralize the reaction.

5. *Multiple transfusions of stored blood, dextran, or albumin lower the prothrombin titer.* Liver disease decreases prothrombin synthesis from vitamin K. The rectification of hypoprothrombinemia by the administration of fresh whole blood is readily accomplished. The use of purified vitamin K preparations is slower in its action. A low "prothrombin concentration" often reflects a low concentration of accelerator clotting factors. As a generality, the dextran lesion is due to platelet factors (possibly coating or changing the electrical charge) rather than a simple dilutional hypoprothrombinemia.

6. But finally there is an "*unknown*" group in which the coagulation defect appears to be present but it is not at all clear what feature of this mechanism is at fault. The use of citrated blood naturally raises the possibility that the patient has become "citrated" and therefore his blood cannot clot, because of lack of ionized calcium. Such a supposition has not been confirmed, and the *toxicity of citrate is manifest by cardiac neuromuscular abnormalities rather than clotting defects*, as described in a later section.

Recent studies suggest that citrate may increase wound ooze by an effect on vasoconstriction rather than on coagulation; the giving of calcium is important in multiple citrated transfusion. Salicylates and antibiotics can cause pathologic bleeding.

When multiple transfusions are given over a prolonged period, antibodies against platelets and leucocytes are developed. In treatment, antihistamines are ineffectual; steroids are moderately effective; fresh whole blood is the most effective step.

In pressing cases, one liter of fresh-frozen plasma should be given, as a source of prothrombin and accelerator factors.

Section II. Sequences of Study and Care in Pathologic Bleeding Arising during Operations or Multiple Transfusions

For the reasons just outlined, the treatment of a patient who has received a great many blood transfusions and now seems to be bleeding pathologically should include a careful examination of the patient as to venous pressure and vasodilatation, measurement of the platelet count, bleeding, clotting, and prothrombin time, and, pending the completion of time-consuming laboratory tests, the administration of cortisone, calcium gluconate, and/or fresh whole blood.

The commonest cause of bleeding is poor hemostasis. Hasty and sloppy closure of wounds, particularly in the thorax, produces bleeding not due to any metabolic disorder. When there is an abnormal bleeding tendency in the patient undergoing surgery or in association with multiple transfusions, severe massive injury, or advancing sepsis, the following procedure provides a guide.

A. COMPLETE SEQUENCE OF STUDY

Determine the clotting time.

If clotting time, bleeding time, prothrombin, and platelets are *normal*, consider elevated venous pressure, overtransfusion, or incompatibility as causes of bleeding.

If clotting is *prolonged* more than twelve minutes, consider in order the following steps.

a. Add thrombin.

i. If a *good clot* results, fibrinogen is not deficient. Fresh whole blood, fresh frozen plasma, and/or serum accelerators should be used.

ii. If a *poor clot* forms, which is lysed by incubation in 45 to 90 minutes, excessive fibrinolysis and/or hypofibrinogenemia are suggested. Treatment should include fibrinogen and cortisone.

iii. If *no clot* forms, afibrinogenemia is present. Fibrinogen should be given. The possibility of excessive fibrinolysin cannot be ruled out; cortisone should also be given.

iv. If *poor clot retraction* is evident, platelets are at fault.

b. Determine the bleeding time.

i. If this and other indices are *normal*, as mentioned above, venous pressure, overtransfusion, and incompatibility should be considered.

ii. If bleeding time is *prolonged* over eight minutes:

Do a blood smear and/or platelet count.

If platelets are *sparse* (below 50,000 per cu. mm.) clot retraction will also be poor. The use of platelet transfusion or fresh plastic-collected or direct whole blood transfusion is essential.

If platelets are *normal* one again falls back on treatment with fresh whole blood and cortisone.

c. Determine the prothrombin activity.

i. If it is *low* (i.e., below 15 per cent, depending on method of notation) give fresh whole blood plus intravenous vitamin K_1 oxide (maximum dose is 50 mg.).

d. Miscellaneous

i. Carry out a tourniquet test.

If it is *positive*, vitamin C deficiency, or increased vessel fragility (which occasionally responds to cortisone) is suggested.

The mode of action of cortisone in bleeding states is unknown. It may involve any or all of the following: increased capillary resistance, decreased antiplatelet antibody activity, increased fibrinogen synthesis, decreased fibrinolytic activity, or some other, unknown, mechanism.

B. EXPEDITIOUS SEQUENCE

A certain few therapeutic procedures result from orderly study, such as that just outlined, but in critical situations one must administer the most likely combination expeditiously if blindly, while attending the result of more orderly study based on blood samples taken before treatment was begun. First, check for venous pressure, venous obstruction, and surgical hemostasis. Consider the possibility of an incompatible blood transfusion. Then, the steps to be taken in order of priority for pathologic intraoperative bleeding are:

(1) fresh plastic-citrate transfusion,

(2) platelet transfusion (platelet suspension or very fresh whole blood),

(3) intravenous infusion of 500 mg. of hydrocortisone,

(4) intravenous infusion of 1.0 gm. of calcium gluconate—this should be repeated three times (this is used to forestall cardiovascular problems rather than for coagulation defects),

(5) fibrinogen (fibrinogen carries the virus of hepatitis; the dose is 4 gm. intravenously), and

(6) accelerator factors, best provided by fresh frozen plasma (frozen at −20° within six hours of collection).

C. BONE MARROW DEPRESSION

As a matter of minor importance we should note that the erythropoietic stimulus of hypovolemia or anemia is abolished by restoring the blood volume. There can be no question that transfusion of healthy cells allays the erythropoietic stimulus; overtransfusion of normal individuals reduces the reticulocyte count almost to zero. In most surgical settings, this factor is of no importance as compared with the hemodynamic restoration produced by accurate transfusion therapy.

Section III.   The "Citrate Lesion": A Neuromuscular Defect

The occurrence of florid citrate intoxication as a "pure" syndrome is assuredly rare in surgical practice today, even in infants. But the binding of ionized calcium by citrate, even in small amounts, synergizes with a number of other biochemical components of trauma and surgery to make it a potential hazard under a variety of circumstances. This synergism of calcium-citrate complexing is most marked with respect to hyperkalemia and underdigitalization of the failing heart, and the effects are most likely to be noted as arrhythmias (including ventricular fibrillation) in elderly patients or in patients with heart disease.

When sodium citrate is infused it can follow two paths: the most common is that of citrate oxidation to, effectively, sodium bicarbonate. This is the genesis of transfusion alkalosis. The other pathway is failure of oxidation, with circulation and accumulation of residual citrate. This "oxidation failure" is most apt to occur in shock or in liver disease or where sudden infusion of large amounts of citrate exceeds the normal rather slow rate of oxidation of this substance.

The normal blood citrate level is 2 to 3 mg. per 100 ml. When citrated blood is given in an operation, this may rise to 9 to 12 mg. per 100 ml., or even as high as 20 mg. per 100 ml. In liver disease it may rise to 40 mg. per 100 ml. When up to 50 mg. per 100 ml., it is dangerous as a cause of calcium binding. Fatality has been reported with citrate levels at 120 mg. per 100 ml. Cardiotoxicity is noted and the QT interval is increased in citrate intoxication, as the plasma citrate rises to 40 to 50 mg. per 100 ml. Serial electrocardiograms are helpful in evaluating such situations, but require very expert interpretation. The electrocardiographic changes are those of hypocalcemia. As prophylactic treatment, 2 ml. of a 10 per cent calcium chloride solution can be infused for each unit of ACD-preserved whole blood infused. Blood in the bank under ACD preservation carries a citrate level between 140 mg. per 100 ml. and 165 mg. per 100 ml. This level would be fatal in man, and is tolerated only because of citrate oxidation. This is a level that is about one-third higher than is necessary for anticoagulation of the banked blood; there is about 30 per cent more citrate used than can be taken up by the calcium content of the donor's blood. This "excess citrate" is then free to combine with the recipient's ionized calcium. Measurement of total calcium casts little light on the extent of binding by citrate; lethal citrate effects can exist with a normal total calcium concentration by ordinary analytic methods. The calcium concentration may even be high as new skeletal calcium is mobilized.

The preservative ACD (or acid-citrate-dextrose) comes in two formulas:

Solution A:

    22   gm. sodium citrate
     8   gm. citric acid
    24.5 gm. dextrose
    distilled water to make 1000 ml.
    This contains 27 mM. of citrate and 16.8 mE. of sodium. (70 ml. of this solution per 450 ml. of blood to be transfused.)

Solution B:

    13.2 gm. sodium citrate
     4.8 gm. citric acid
    14.7 gm. dextrose
    distilled water to make 1000 ml.
    (125 ml. of this solution per 500 ml. of blood to be transfused.)

Viewed in the total metabolic situation of the severely injured surgical patient with shock, hypovolemia, and a mixed renal-respiratory acidosis, the citrate ion is "just wrong." In itself it establishes a vicious circle.

(1) Since citrate needs good circulation to be destroyed, the surgical patient in shock is not able to destroy it.

(2) The acid-base effect of its accompanying cation (sodium) is therefore lost, and acidosis progresses.

(3) In acidosis there is hyperkalemia; oliguria and injury hasten its rise. One of its antagonists is calcium, the other sodium and accompanying alkalosis. Citrate binds the calcium that antagonizes hyperkalemia.

(4) Blood banked for prolonged periods shows a progressive rise in plasma potassium concentration to levels of 15 to 30 mE. per l. Such figures seem forbidding, yet the total dose of potassium even in large transfusions (150 to 200 mE. total, for example, in 10 transfusions) is not overwhelming and this is diluted throughout the extracellular fluid. Yet, whatever its magnitude, the potassium dose is undesirable in the presence of shock and a citrate lesion, the latter exerting its myocardial effect in a way resembling potassium toxicity.

(5) Citrate, by binding calcium, increases the cardiotoxic effects of potassium; by failing to be oxidized, citrate minimizes the sodium effect. *Hyperkalemia is thus more pronounced and also more dangerous in the presence of an excess of free citrate.* This decreases cardiac efficiency; if the patient is digitalized, the effect of digitalis may be lost.

(6) Wound ooze is increased; more citrated blood is therefore given to the patient.

(7) Deteriorating cardiac function further impairs the patient's circulation, less citrate is oxidized, and more is given.

(8) The end result is a further trend to hypotension, cyanosis, or ventricular fibrillation.

Citrate toxicity affects the patient by producing a functional hypocalcemia associated with altered neuromuscular irritability, most pronounced in the heart, and by tetany. The antidote is calcium, but this must be given with caution if the patient has been digitalized, since it suddenly boosts the digitalis effect and may precipitate arrhythmias.

The administration of calcium to a hypotensive patient suffering the effects of excess citrate will raise the blood pressure. This effect, however, is also seen in hypotension without citrate.

Section IV.   Notes from the Literature

A. COAGULATION

The use of closely-timed massive transfusion of units of blood from a variety of donors involves several problems that have been studied recently. These arrange themselves into several interrelated groups:

(1) the hemorrhagic state that often ensues,

(2) the—much rarer—thrombophilic state,

(3) the effects of unmetabolized citrate on wound oozing and on calcium binding —and therefore on neuromuscular and myocardial irritability, with particular

reference to cardiac arrhythmias such as ventricular fibrillation.

Friesen and Nelson (1951), in an early study of the problem, reported massive intraoperative bleeding with seven case histories, five of them fatal. "Ooze" was the problem. Hemolytic transfusion reactions were incriminated, as well as thrombocytopenia. Fibrinogen reduction and citrate effects on vasoconstriction were not measured. Calcium was given in some instances, without help. Vitamins C and K, as well as fresh blood, were given. Blood transfusion was large in volume in some cases but in two the oozing reaction began shortly after the first transfusion and in three some kind of "untoward" reaction was noted to a specific transfusion. The authors suggested transfusion incompatibility as a mechanism causing increased bleeding, independent of other factors. Detailed coagulation study was not done.

Jackson and Krevans (1955) studied the hemorrhagic state following multiple transfusions. Of sixteen patients who received more than 5000 ml. in forty-eight hours, twelve developed clinical evidences of abnormal bleeding. Platelet reduction was constant, fourteen patients showing counts below 60,000 per cu. mm. Fibrinogenopenia was rare (one case) and none showed increased fibrinolysis. Various modified transfusion techniques (including direct silicone) did not alter the thrombocytopenic tendency; it is of interest that autotransfusion of comparable quantities did not produce thrombocytopenia, regardless of the mode of collection.

Powers and Brown (1956) studied the proteolytic property of patients with spontaneous fibrinolysis. They found that ether was capable of activating a plasminogen in vitro; they postulate a possible effect of this anesthetic in potentiating fibrinolytic effects after trauma and multiple transfusion.

Scott and Crosby (1954) studied coagulation factors after massive transfusion of the severely wounded in the Korean war. They found in a carefully ordered study of eleven patients a fall in prothrombin which they did not consider as due to the blood diluent (anticoagulant, usually ACD). There was a rise in fibrinogen, as previously reported by Ham and Curtis (1938), seemingly produced by the injury itself. Labile factor deficiency (Fahey et al., 1948) did not seem to be the cause of the apparent prothrombin reduction. Platelet counts were usually high; clotting time (silicone) was usually shortened the first day but occasionally prolonged in the first few days. There was a slight tendency to oozing when more than twenty pints of blood were infused. They considered the possibility that lack of serotonin of platelet origin might help account for the oozing. There was a secondary fall in prothrombin (not clinically evident) starting about the fourth day, which corrected itself gradually. There were no fibrinolytic reactions. This study does not include measurements of citrate levels or ionized calcium as possibly contributory to the oozing. The studies of Warren and Belko (1951) record a somewhat similar "standard sequence" in postoperative patients. Williems et al. (1955) have studied platelet production and megakaryocyte activity in normal surgical convalescence. There was regularly a fall in platelets with a prompt and regular increase in numbers of active platelet-producing megakaryocytes. There were large increases in these latter, yet with a fall in peripheral counts. The conclusion suggested is that there is a block to delivery and a hindrance to maturation of certain phases of megakaryocyte development.

Kiesewetter and Harris (1956) established an experimental method for the measurement of wound oozing. They discovered that citrate ion was capable of producing a severe oozing from the wound despite normalcy of the usual coagulation measurements. The 2.4 per cent sodium citrate solution, alone, could reproduce the wound ooze; citric acid did not seem to do so, in comparable doses. The mechanism here did not seem to be associated with platelet reduction; the possibility of a change in capillary collagen or some other permeability factor was entertained.

It is appealing to consider the sodium citrate effect on oozing as due to an alteration in the relationship of cations (sodium, potassium, and calcium) and acid-base balance such as would interfere with the normal constriction of small vessels essential in wound hemostasis. Kiesewetter and Harris (1956) did not report the reversal of oozing by the administration of calcium.

Cliffton *et al.* (1956) studied a group of patients with special emphasis on fibrinolytic factors. Transfusions were given to all the fifty-five patients studied but only one received more than 6 units. In a group of forty-seven patients without oozing, there were four with abnormal fibrinolytic activity. Of a total of twelve patients found with fibrinolytic activity, eight had clinical oozing. Anoxia and, in one case, a transfusion reaction also played a role. For such factors fresh blood, fresh frozen plasma, or fibrinogen is therapeutic. Cliffton's cases represent a different phenomenon from that seen in the citrate-calcium lesion, where myocardial effects predominate.

Hypofibrinogenemia as a cause of uterine hemorrhage is not uncommon after premature separation of the placenta; the analogy to a surgical wound is not close, however, and there is the possibility of amniotic fluid embolism in the obstetrical cases. Abnormal proteolytic and fibrinolytic activity has been recorded in many types of surgical and traumatic situations, especially in connection with thoracic surgery. As Cliffton points out, both lung and uterus contain enzymes active in the fibrinolytic sequence; the combination of low fibrinogen and fibrinolytic activity is especially significant with reference to oozing. Cliffton, like MacFarlane and Biggs (1946), believes that increased fibrinolytic activity is an intrinsic aspect of traumatic biology, and that this is the initial change.

After a review of this aspect one is left with the impression that the combination of fibrinolysis and hypofibrinogenemia is occasionally (but rarely) a cause of severe hemorrhage in surgery and obstetrics, that its genesis is possibly a mixture of local release of enzymes and trauma itself, that the diagnosis is a specific one, and that multiple transfusions are not etiologic; anoxia, shock, and allergic reactions may often be in the background. Further studies may be found in Coon and Hodgson (1952), who have studied this phenomenon, as have Frank *et al.*

(1950), MacFarlane (1937), and Tagnon *et al.* (1946).

Mason *et al.* (1955) produced transfusion reactions in dogs by infusing human blood. The changes in proteolytic activity of the plasma were not marked even in sensitized animals and did not correlate with other phenomena such as tendency to bleed. Such gross incompatibility resulting from blood heterotransfusion may have little bearing on human incompatibilities and allergic reactions.

The tendency of postoperative patients to bleed is matched only by their tendency to thrombose abnormally. The latter is usually a somewhat later manifestation and leads to thromboembolism as its chief manifestation, occasionally to other consequences including intra-abdominal clotting. Williams *et al.* (1956), Warren *et al.* (1953), and Williams *et al.* (1955) have shown that adrenocorticotropic hormone is capable of reproducing the type of thrombocytopenia seen after injury, accompanied by the same sort of megakaryocytic change. After this downswing (which might, abetted by transfusion, be associated with bleeding), there is a backswing, which in turn might be associated with thrombosis. Implications are clear but proof of clinical significance is as yet lacking in this early study.

Graham *et al.* (1957) report a fatality resulting from the administration of fibrinogen to a patient apparently suffering from hypofibrinogenemia after total hysterectomy for vaginal bleeding. There was abnormal bleeding during and after the operation. The clotting phenomena suggested a reduction of fibrinogen yet with other "thromboplastic substances" possibly increased. The patient received 5 "units" of fraction I, a total of about 15 gm. of fibrinogen. She died suddenly on the third postoperative day. There was a generalized thrombosis in many organs. In this case there were no fibrinolysins and some sort of fibrinogen removal must be postulated, possibly increase in some thromboplastic substance, which not only removed fibrinogen but made its further administration very hazardous.

B. CITRATE

Adams *et al.* (1944), in an early study of the citrate problem, tried to ascertain the lethal level in dogs. They noted an increasing clinical tendency (at that time) to restore all blood lost, quantitatively, often in the 1500 to 3000 ml. range.* They interpreted the earlier work of Ivy *et al.* (1943) in dogs as indicating a large superiority of heparinized over citrated blood in the treatment of acute hemorrhage. Bruneau and Graham (1943) also reported better survivals when citrate was not used. In the study of Adams *et al.* the authors observed the effects, in dogs, of injections of various types of citrate solutions at various rates. When sodium citrate was injected in thirteen to thirty minutes at a dose of 0.29 to 0.40 gm. per kg., all the animals died. These are amounts corresponding to transfusions of 70 to 90 per cent of the blood volume. The mode of death was a sudden cessation of heart action, often at the time of some hyperventilation. Electrocardiographic data are not presented. In the light of evidence ten years later, these studies are of exceptional interest. This "speed effect" was demonstrable with citrated blood as well as with pure sodium citrate. With simulta-

---

* This period of American surgery (1939–1946) was one of change-over from the occasional blood transfusion (considered slightly improper by some authors) to the massive replacement of blood, measured not in milliliters but in blood volumes. While Adams was noting the metabolic effects of transfusion "up to 3000 ml." other authorities (Cutler and Zollinger, 1939) clearly indicated that blood transfusion was to be regarded as a confession of poor surgical technique. They wrote: "If there has been great blood loss, transfusion is obviously the best method of restoring both the fluid and blood reserves; but the surgeon should not habituate himself to this remedy lest he become lax in his attention to hemostasis. It would be wiser if he looked upon postoperative transfusion as a criticism of his technical ability. Certainly transfusion is a useful therapeutic agent, essential in certain disorders, and most valuable in preparing the patient for a major ordeal; but its use following a surgical performance is at least suggestive that a more careful technique would have made this unnecessary."

The experience of World War II, more than any other single factor, changed this viewpoint and established the *pari passu* operative transfusion to replace blood loss in its present perspective and practice.

neous bleeding and retransfusion of the citrated efflux, addition of calcium greatly increased the survival rate, apparently by blocking the "speed effect."

The "human equivalent" (Adams *et al.*) for a dangerous rate is over 0.24 gm. per kg. per hour, corresponding to a citrated transfusion rate greater than 1000 ml. per hour. This is not a high threshold; if this dose is given in twelve to fifteen minutes, it is usually fatal—this would correspond to 4000 ml. in five minutes, a rate that seemed almost inconceivable in the context of 1944. The Korean war and concomitant civilian experience made it more nearly commonplace; cardiac surgery and the pump-oxygenator have made rapid massive blood transfusion, albeit not citrated, a more frequent occurrence.

Adams also showed that citrate tolerance was much more limited in the shocked animal than in the normal. The toxic manifestation was a swing in blood pressure for only a few minutes, then sudden death. Respiratory failure was "never observed" prior to cardiac failure. The term "cardiac arrest" had not yet become fashionable; Adams *et al.* had no electrocardiographic or chemical data. In retrospect it seems a certainty that they were producing classic "cardiac arrest" (possibly ventricular fibrillation) in animals by large doses of citrate. They pointed out the black venous blood at the fatal period, the oxygen desaturation, and the severe acidosis (pH 7.15). They pointed out that the infused blood itself had a pH of 7.25. They employed 4 gm. of calcium gluconate (20 ml. of a 20 per cent solution) for the citrate counteraction in replacement of 0.6 blood volume to 1.0 blood volume in dogs.

Although dogs occasionally had tetanic convulsions, it was neither the report of this nor of bleeding that stood out in Adams' work; it was sudden cessation of the heartbeat, preventable with calcium. *This differentiation points to understanding of the meaning of the "citrate lesion" in modern surgical transfusion and the relation of blood transfusion to what is now called "cardiac arrest." Adams' work stands as the classic in this field.*

Nakasone *et al.* (1954) studied the citrate effect of massive transfusion as employed incidental to the use of an artificial kidney. Their work was done in dogs under Nembutal anesthesia. The electrocardiographic changes (Lead II) were characteristic of hypocalcemia and included prolongation of the QT interval, depression (and later inversion) of the T-wave, and later reduction of P-voltage, and a muscle tremor artifact with pulsus alternans. After the administration of massive amounts (0.357 mM. per kg. per minute) of citrate, death followed quickly after hypotension, which in turn followed the early electrocardiographic changes. There was a marked drop in peripheral resistance as indicated by the pulse contour. Equimolar calcium chloride infusion completely prevented the changes. Similar changes were reported in citrated exchange transfusion for erythroblastosis by Wexler *et al.* (1948) and Ames *et al.* (1950). Ames recorded the lowering of the calcium concentration. Calcium injection quickly restored peripheral resistance in the animal experiments. The rate effect was easily demonstrated. Very rapid infusion of small doses of citrate produced transient changes.

The use of resin-collection for blood banking (Walter, 1951) appeared to solve this problem. Although calcium ion was removed from the blood there is not an excess of "agent" after its removal. Magnesium and potassium are also largely removed from the donor blood by the resin, but they are restored to the blood before infusion. Calcium concentrations are maintained during infusion of the resin-collected blood, probably by mobilization from the skeleton. Citrate levels were not measured. Resin-collected blood is completely devoid of platelets.

This work and other studies of the same type point the way to the avoidance of serious complications from transfusion of citrated blood. The problem is not that of poor coagulation, or tetany, but instead it is one of altered neuromuscular irritability, affecting the heart and arteries and producing the cardiac complex of hypocalcemia with extreme suddenness and severity. Previous anoxia, shock, or underlying visceral disease of heart (particularly with digitalization), lungs, or kidneys may render an otherwise tolerable

"citrate lesion" immediately fatal; the pathologist finds nothing, and one is apt to assign the case as another one of "irreversible" shock or of "cardiac arrest." In the presence of heart disease one need not have "toxic" citrate levels in the blood to produce a serious and dangerous functional hypocalcemia.

The changes in peripheral resistance are of extreme interest. A flabby vasodilated peripheral vasculature would result from calcium binding and might be expected to show the clinical phenomenon of "taking up" (accepting in transfusion large volumes of blood without restoration of pressure or flow); such a vasculature might also respond transiently to large doses of vasoconstrictors and dramatically to calcium. Both of these phenomena are seen in human beings in late shock when there are large citrate transfusions.

A peripheral arterial tree which cannot constrict normally would also be expected to produce a bleeding, oozing wound in which hemostasis is very difficult despite a normal bleeding, clotting, and prothrombin time, platelet counts, and tissue ascorbate. This also is a citrate effect. Further studies in this field are to be found in the work of Ernstene and Proudfit (1949).

Watkins (1955) followed up the results of Nakasone *et al.* (1954) with particular reference to calcium:potassium relationships in the myocardium in shock when massive citrate transfusion is superimposed. He noted the similarity of the electrocardiographic appearance of hypocalcemia to that of hyperkalemia and postulated the "relative hyperkalemia" theory of hypocalcemia to explain the cardiotoxic manifestations of citrate overdosage. In a sense, the distinction is only a play on words, since the potassium effects are antagonized by sodium or calcium and the lowering of one ion can always be likened to the rise of its counterpart. The electrocardiographic changes are very similar.

Watkins showed that the myocardium in shock was very sensitive to citrate transfusion. The sensitization in shock was almost tenfold over the normal, in terms of citrate dosage. There was some evidence of differential sensitivity of the right ventricle. Infusion of small amounts of citrate in the dog in shock quickly produced the so-called "hyperkalemic pattern." The changes were reversible with calcium infusion, but if both calcium and potassium were given together, the changes were not reversed.

Howland *et al.* (1955) studied 253 patients receiving 5 or more pints of blood in the course of radical cancer operations. Two complications were seen: bleeding and "cardiac arrest" (fibrillation or asystole). In total, 43 per cent of the series showed one or another of these complications. Thirty-six patients had a bleeding disorder. The cardiac disorders were very serious, often fatal, and there were three deaths in the operating room in those receiving 5 to 9 pints of blood, and twenty-two deaths (out of 101 patients) in those receiving 10 or more transfusions. There were eleven instances of continuous electrocardiogram tracings; nine showed fibrillation and two asystole. Cyclopropane anesthesia appeared to be an especially poor agent in association with massive citrate dosage.

Wiener and Wexler (1946) calculated that after exchange of one blood volume the circulation is 62 per cent donor blood; after 2 blood volumes, 87 per cent. In Howland's series all the patients who received 18 pints (about 2 blood volumes) or more developed some serious complication (bleeding or myocardial symptoms).

Bunker *et al.* (1953, 1955) measured citrate levels and showed, as suspected from previous metabolic data, that either shock or renal or hepatic disease greatly raised the blood citrate resulting from ACD transfusion. In such patients there was a lowering of ionized calcium.

As Howland pointed out, hypothermia produced inadvertently by massive exchange transfusion in shock may play a role in the vulnerability of the myocardium to the citrate lesion and its accompanying potassium infusion with resulting tendency to neuromuscular disintegration and ventricular fibrillation, both so apt to occur under hypothermia.

While it is not our intent to lay all surgical disaster at the door of citrate, we have pre-sented these data and this review in some detail to emphasize the interesting and subtle, but widespread and serious, effects that can result from accumulations of unmetabolized citrate. In certain settings (particularly those of heart disease, the digitalized heart, shock, and hyperkalemia), small amounts of citrate accumulation, far below the ordinarily "toxic" level, may prove fatal by producing a cardiac arrhythmia or change in extent of digitalization traceable to a sudden reduction in ionized calcium.

Gibson *et al.* (1956) have documented the severe erythrocyte damage (the "collection lesion") that results when the first fraction of the donated blood is run off into a solution as abnormal as the blood preservative-anticoagulant—in this case, the ACD. Although the final concentration of diluent is compatible with good red cell survival, the native solution is very nonphysiologic and initial solute concentrations are very high. As a result, the first 50 to 75 ml. suffers severe osmotic and acidotic damage. These cells then have an in-vivo post-transfusion biological half-life of only 2.2 hours, whereas the remainder of the cells live out a life span that is almost normal.

C. INTRA-ARTERIAL TRANSFUSION

The question of intra-arterial transfusion may be difficult to settle on an experimental basis. When coronary perfusion pressure is low or palpably zero, myocardial function will of course be inadequate for the task of accepting right heart inflow and propelling it through lungs, auricle, and ventricle to the coronary ostia. Clearly such a situation cannot exist for many seconds or minutes. But if, during this time, a brisk pressure infusion is given into aorta or artery, raising the pressure there, the coronary inflow pressure will inevitably be increased. Myocardial function can improve if anoxic changes are not too far advanced. Considering the unicameral hydrostatic nature of the arterial tree, this result (increased arterial pressure producing increased coronary perfusion pressure) is hydrostatically unavoidable, however rare the setting. This is a hydrostatic effect; it does *not* postulate retrograde progress of the infused blood itself to the area of the coronary ostia.

Kohlstaedt and Page (1943) favored intra-arterial transfusion clinically, and Robertson *et al.* (1948) showed that pressure restoration was more rapid. Jones *et al.* (1950) favored the theory that a fall in aortic arch pressure produces widespread vasoconstriction and that intra-arterial transfusion was effective in part because of the improved peripheral perfusion that resulted from the vasodilatation and good aortic pressure; the better coronary filling was clear from their work and that of Leger and Lande (1950).

Very rapid intra-arterial transfusion in the failing, digitalized heart must be approached with awareness of the special hazard presented by the undiluted, unmetabolized citrate. Calcium should be used with the blood.

The study by Artz *et al.* (1955) is one of the very few on record in which rapid intravenous transfusion was studied in comparison to equally rapid intra-arterial transfusion. The two series were small (thirteen cases); intra-arterial transfusion appeared to have no advantage. The data of Kohlstaedt and Page (1943) and Case *et al.* (1953) point to the same conclusion in dogs. Maloney *et al.* (1953) used cardiac output measurements further to substantiate similarity of results by the two routes. Richards and Hansen (1954) report a similar clinical experience.

One must again hedge a little on data based on dogs with normal myocardial function and coronary blood supply. It is in the arteriosclerotic person, over middle age, with poor coronary flow and borderline myocardial function, that the electrocardiogram changes and the venous pressure rises in shock; it is here that intra-arterial transfusion can provide coronary flow unmatched by venous infusion; this is a heart that cannot, of itself, develop effective systolic pressure beyond the aortic valves and at the coronary inflow ostia. If coronary ostia pressure and myocardial blood flow are increased, and cardiac output restored (for even a few minutes) by the increased aortic pressure resulting from intra-arterial transfusion, the heart is then given the opportunity to "take over," reestablish its own coronary flow, and survive. Basic blood-volume restoration must, of course, be via the venous route. Like so many problems in shock and hypotension, this one can probably never be settled in the dog. Observation in man is difficult, and less appealing scientifically, but much more significant.

Any consideration of intra-arterial transfusion involves the matter of coronary flow in shock. An increment in coronary inflow pressure is the immediate objective of intra-arterial transfusion. Studies, largely experimental, of coronary flow in shock include Wiggers and Werle (1942), Kohlstaedt and Page (1944), Kondo and Katz (1945), Wiggers (1947), Opdyke and Foreman (1947), Sarnoff *et al.* (1954), and Edwards *et al.* (1954).

In addition to the studies already mentioned, observations on arterial transfusion may be found in Glasser and Page (1947), Robertson *et al.* (1948), Pierce *et al.* (1949), Wiener (1951), Alrich and Morton (1951), Seeley (1951), Seeley and Nelson (1952), Bingham (1952), Beattie *et al.* (1952), Blakemore *et al.* (1953), Seeley (1954), Richards and Hansen (1954), and Maloney *et al.* (1954).

PART III

Body Fluid and Electrolyte:
Water, Salt, and Acid

Contents of Part III

CHAPTER 16. A GENERAL VIEW OF WATER, SALT, AND ACID

CHAPTER 17. DISORDERS OF HYDRATION: FACTS, CONCEPTS, TERMS

CHAPTER 18. EXTRACELLULAR VOLUME CHANGES: CONTRACTION AND EXPANSION; SEQUESTERED EDEMA; EXTERNAL LOSS; VOLUME REGULATION

CHAPTER 19. INTRACELLULAR VOLUME CHANGES; POTASSIUM THERAPY IN RELATION TO ANABOLISM, CATABOLISM, AND POTASSIUM BALANCE; MAGNESIUM

CHAPTER 20. DISORDERS OF ACID-BASE BALANCE

CHAPTER 21. SOLUTIONS AND PRIORITIES IN THE TREATMENT OF WATER-ELECTROLYTE AND ACID-BASE DISORDERS

CHAPTER 22. COMMON PATTERNS OF WATER AND ELECTROLYTE CHANGE IN INJURY, SURGERY, AND DISEASE

CHAPTER 23. WATER, SALT, AND ACID: NOTES FROM THE LITERATURE

CHAPTER 16

A General View of Water, Salt, and Acid

Section I.   Introduction: Ten Propositions

The organization of this Part of the book is centered around the identification and treatment of the common patterns of water-electrolyte-acid disturbance seen in surgery. These disorders must be characterized as patterns or complexes. The sodium changes, for instance, have meaning only in relation to changes in body weight and water content, pH or blood urea nitrogen; the whole must be seen, understood, and treated together. The disorder must be viewed in its compositional aspects as well as in terms of plasma concentrations. This is a clinically more fruitful view than isolated consideration of one variable ("low

chloride," "hyperkalemia," and so on). Hence the concept of "patterns."

These patterns will be described in Chapter 22. In Chapters 16–21 are briefly outlined the system in which such changes occur, the methods of study by which they can be identified and treated, and the priority list for treatment of complex disorders.

Before turning to the principal discussion one should mention several introductory propositions. These propositions are not in any way new, but by their increasingly evident importance they have replaced many former concepts of the behavior of body water in disease.

A. TEN PROPOSITIONS

1. Renal Retention of Salt and Water Is One of the Body's Primary Responses to Disease.

Trauma, acute illness, and many chronic wasting diseases produce accumulation of water and salt, with water in excess of salt. The result is hypotonicity of the body fluids. Similarly, many drugs and anesthetics, including ether and morphine, are active in producing retention of water or salt, or both. Very minor and transient stimuli, often of a psychologic nature, induce transient water retention.

2. In Patients Observed on a General-Hospital Ward, Expansion of the Extracellular Fluid Is More Common, More Apt to Be Chronic, and More Refractory to Treatment Than Is Contraction.

Page 266

An enlarged volume of hypotonic extracellular fluid with an excess of body sodium and water is found after the treatment of severe injury and in many chronic wasting diseases such as advanced cancer, chronic starvation, heart disease, and liver disease. The lean tissues and fat stores shrink away into a sea of dilute salt water. The volume of total body water is relatively enlarged; it is the intracellular fraction that shrinks. The patient is undernourished and overwatered; he has too much extracellular fluid but not enough intracellular fluid; his total exchangeable sodium is high and his total exchangeable potassium is low; his extracellular fluid is hypotonic. Treatment is complicated and frequently ineffectual.

Contraction of the extracellular fluid is

produced by loss of blood and other body fluids; it is effectively treated by appropriate infusion.

3. Endogenous Water Is Sodium-Free; in Injury and Disease It Is Abnormally Retained.

Endogenous sodium-free water, together with any water administered to the patient, becomes uniformly distributed throughout the body water. It arises from the release of cell water (about 750 ml. per kg. of lean tissue), the oxidation of protein (about 150 ml. per kg. of lean tissue), and the oxidation of fat (about 1070 ml. per kg. of fat). The catabolism of 500 gm. of lean tissue and 500 gm. of fat releases to the extracellular fluid about 1000 ml. of sodium-free water. Catabolism of such amounts of tissue is a daily occurrence after severe injury. In chronic wasting illness, large amounts of water appear within the body from these sources, over long periods.

If this water were promptly excreted, as a normal person excretes it, its presence would be of little note, and it would not produce hypotonicity. But instead of being freely excreted this sodium-free water (either endogenous or exogenous) is largely retained. This is an expression of the strong water-retaining (antidiuretic) tendency of the body after acute injury and in chronic wasting illness. Hypotonicity results. Whether or not this water retention is a direct result of posterior pituitary activation is for the moment unimportant; its behavior resembles that produced by the pituitary antidiuretic hormone. The normal homeostatic "wisdom" of the kidneys appears to have been overruled by strong forces acting to diminish renal water excretion.

4. Most Hypotonicity Is Dilutional.

Loss of renal or gastrointestinal sodium from "available" extracellular fluid or from the body does not, per se, cause hypotonicity. Such salts are lost at isotonic or hypotonic concentrations; loss alone, without other events, would leave the body in a condition of isotonicity or hypertonicity. To produce the observed hypotonicity, sodium-free water must be added to the system and retained. Dilution must occur. As mentioned above, this sodium-free water arises within the body.

The potassium released with cell water is excreted, and hypotonicity ensues.

Transfer of sodium into cells or the skeleton may occur in some circumstances, but this transfer is small in amount and is not as important in producing hypotonicity as is the dilution of that sodium which remains. As sodium concentration falls, the total body water and its extracellular fraction enlarge through the addition of new sodium-free water. Any hypotonic solutions given therapeutically will add further to the total dilution.

5. Current Evidence Suggests That the Body Does Not Tolerate Osmotic Gradients within Itself.

The osmolality of the extracellular fluid is presumably the same as that of the intracellular fluid.

The normal plasma osmolality in milliosmols (mO.) per l. is numerically almost exactly equal to twice the sodium concentration in milliequivalents (mE.) per l.: $143 \times 2 = 286$. The normal plasma osmolality is 285 to 295 mO. per l. This numerical coincidence arises from the fact that some of the ions (whose total equivalence is 310 mE.) are polyvalent (for example, phosphate, sulfate, calcium) and therefore exert less osmotic pressure than electric equivalence, and some (proteins) are so large and heavy that they exert very little total osmotic pressure despite their all-important colloid osmotic pressure.

Any plasma osmolality over and beyond "twice the sodium" may be assumed to be due to abnormal accumulations of crystalloid. Examples of such crystalloids are urea, pyruvate, lactate, or glucose. In the case of urea, 100 mg. per 100 ml. contributes 17.2 mO. per l. to osmolality; in the case of glucose, 100 mg. per 100 ml. contributes 5.5 mO. per l. to osmolality.

Nonelectrolyte solute to which cells are freely permeable, such as urea, contributes to total osmolality but not to water distributional change and does not stimulate the osmoreceptors. By contrast, an acute increase in concentration of solute to which cells are only slowly permeable (such as glucose) effectively increases extracellular osmolality. The same thing is true of an increase in sodium concentration. This can only be compensated for by withdrawing cell water or by the administration of water.

6. After Acute Hemorrhage or Loss of Fluid, the Body Responds by Maintaining Volume at the Expense of Tonicity.

This maintenance of fluid volume is accomplished by the kidney through resorption of water and salt from the glomerular filtrate (as mentioned above) and, when restriction of effective circulatory blood volume is threatened, by renal vasoconstriction. These changes may occur without significant alteration in the plasma concentration of electrolytes or other solutes. This important homeostatic response operating with normal glomerular filtration therefore appears to be activated by some system in the body that is sensitive to alteration in volume, pressure, oxygenation, or adequacy of flow. This receptor system or systems, the location and nature of which are unknown, is called the "volume receptor"; it may represent not one but several interrelated regulatory mechanisms.

This volume-preserving response to reduced pressure or flow is markedly diminished in diabetes insipidus or after adrenalectomy. This, in addition to other evidences from the laboratory, suggests that the "effector arc" involves the response of the renal tubular cell to salt-retaining steroids (such as aldosterone) and water-retaining hormones (such as antidiuretic hormone). Other mechanisms, both endocrine and neurovascular, are also involved.

In addition, there is suggestive evidence that an abnormal or compensatory activation of some such flow-receptor or volume-receptor mechanism may explain the excessive retention of water and salt seen after acute trauma, in chronic wasting diseases, and in disorders of the viscera such as heart and liver. Conclusive evidence on this point is lacking.

7. The Obligatory Sequestration of a Large Area of the Extracellular Fluid Is a Common Cause of Circulatory Failure in Trauma, Surgery, and Acute Infection.

This occurs in burns, peritonitis, venous obstruction, and intestinal obstruction. A rising hematocrit is its trademark. This reduction in effective circulating volume is a strong stimulus to retention of water and salt.

Acute embarrassment of extracellular fluid volume also occurs as a result of the extrarenal loss of water and salt. It is important here to differentiate between desalting water loss (loss of salt and water, leading ultimately to hypotonicity) and true desiccation or dehydration (loss predominantly of water, leading to hypertonicity).

8. The Total Body Content of Ions and Their Concentrations in the Plasma Often Change in Opposite Directions.

Very low sodium concentrations may exist with a very high body sodium; hypokalemia may occur with minimal potassium loss; patients with very large potassium losses may have normal plasma potassium concentrations. Other factors than body content or balance are clearly of prime importance in regulating extracellular concentration of ions.

In the case of sodium, the most important concentration-determining factor is water content. In the case of potassium, the concentration determinant appears to be some parameter of acid-base balance: alkalosis is associated with hypokalemia, and acidosis with hyperkalemia. There is evidence to suggest that the intracellular pCO_2 or pH may be more important than the extracellular pH in determining potassium concentration. Acute disorders produce abnormalities that are more marked than those in chronic equilibrated situations. The concentration of chloride, alone of the ions, seems to respond in a sensitive way to body content.

There is a persistent tendency for plasma sodium and potassium concentrations to move in opposite directions under a wide variety of circumstances. This may not seem surprising in view of their normal position on opposite sides of the cell membrane, their sharply contrasting metabolism in tubular urine, their reverse roles in ion-exchange mechanisms, and the fact that steroid hormones have exactly inverse effects on the transport of the two ions. Despite these several considerations, the exact mechanism by which hyperkalemia usually occurs with hyponatremia (and vice versa) is not entirely clear.

9. The Therapeutic Concept of "Unit Change

Times Total Body Water" Is Rarely Practical or Safe in the Treatment of Electrolyte Abnormalities.

Hypotonicity cannot be treated blindly by the giving of an amount of sodium salts calculated from the unit deficit as multiplied by an assumed figure for the total volume of body water. Such large amounts of sodium are not needed because, as repair proceeds, water excretion occurs and gradually diminishes the need for further salt. If such large amounts of sodium are given rapidly, they are dangerous and may produce pulmonary edema. As an additional consideration, the whole body is hypotonic and needs for its restoration potassium salts just as much as sodium salts. This is particularly evident if desalting has been long continued and has involved the prolonged mobilization of cell water and the loss of potassium.

10. Injury and Surgical Operation Embarrass the Bodily Compensations to Threatened Acid-Base Imbalance.

Acidosis is produced by defective pulmonary ventilation, diabetes mellitus, renal failure, and other visceral diseases. For acidosis the body has many compensations, often rather slow. The pulmonary acid excretion is most rapid. To be effective in dealing with large acid loads, the renal compensation for acidosis requires time to achieve maximum efficiency and a good urine volume processed by normal renal tubular cells. Trauma interferes with these compensations by compromising ventilation and by reducing urine volume, tubular function, and renal blood flow. The tissue buffers are responsible for the acceptance of the major share of an acid load. For this the body needs normal circulation and tissue perfusion, not present in shock or diffuse vasoconstriction.

Alkalosis results from the loss of gastric hydrochloric acid. There are few bodily compensations for this disorder. There appears to be little respiratory compensation. The principal relief is offered by the continued excretion of an alkaline urine, and yet this is compromised by the retention of sodium bicarbonate that occurs after trauma. Injury of itself therefore makes the patient much more vulnerable to alkalosis, in part by the tendency to resorb sodium bicarbonate from the glomerular filtrate (an aldosterone-like effect) and in part by the tendency to develop differential potassium loss (that is, potassium loss at a high potassium:nitrogen ratio). Potassium deficit also interferes with the excretion of an alkaline urine. Trauma and potassium deficit therefore combine to make the urine acid despite extracellular alkalosis. The worsened alkalosis of trauma joins with potassium loss in lowering the plasma potassium concentration when surgery is superimposed on loss of hydrochloric acid. Postoperative hypokalemic alkalosis results from the operaiton of this vicious cycle.

To the ten principles enumerated above should be added one other helpful proposition. It is not a chemical one.

The most important single factor in care of the patient is a concern for his whole pathologic situation and his clinical management: the total problem, not just the chemical aspects, must be solved. The critically ill patient has everything to gain from the care of a well-informed doctor, but he should beware the electrolyte expert who sees his problem only with an eye to the ions.

Section II. Approach to the Patient and Methods of Study

A. CASE SELECTION

The diagnosis and care of surgical patients with disturbances of water and electrolyte balance involve a great deal of extra time, expense, and laboratory work. It is wasteful, in studying an essentially normal individual with uncomplicated cholecystectomy in prospect, to carry out an imposing set of chemical determinations on the blood. But by the same token, it is unfortunate to find patients lying around the wards, not doing well, sallow, somewhat distended, and to find their laboratory data a blank; especially when study the next day reveals azotemia, renal acidosis, hyperkalemia, and hypotonicity. It is doubly so to find a patient in shock or in serious danger because of a false economy in simple laboratory procedures, or stupid neglect of their importance. There is thus a real problem in case selection in this aspect of surgical study and care. How does the surgeon select those cases in which particular study and treatment should be carried out?

B. BASIC STUDY IN THE "NORMAL PATIENT"

No determinations should be carried out on a patient because it is routine. Such determinations soon fall into the same category of organized neglect as the general check-up; much is done but little is learned. When the application of time and thought is devoted to the study of a patient, it should be done with a purpose in mind and with a definite plan to view the results of study critically.

1. Urinalysis, Blood Counts, Occult Blood

In the metabolically normal patient, admitted for elective surgery, the urinalysis is done with the specific purpose of uncovering unsuspected disease of the kidneys or unsuspected diabetes. The examinations of the urinary sediment, the urine sugar (and, if this is positive, the acetone), and the urine protein are the most important items. In elective surgical cases, approximately one in twenty patients over fifty years of age will be found by such study to have a metabolic defect that might lead to some embarrassment of recovery. Measurement of the specific gravity, acid-base reaction, and bile content of the urine is a time-honored procedure that requires little further time or expense.

On the hematologic side, some measurement of peripheral concentration of red blood cells is essential. The hematocrit, red corpuscle count, or hemoglobin assay may be used for this purpose. The white blood cell count is done also.

No patient should be discharged without a search for occult blood in the stool. In seemingly healthy patients, the stool guaiac or benzidine dihydrochloride test must be done. In a year's work on a busy surgical service, two or three unsuspected cases of polyp or cancer of the gastrointestinal tract will be discovered by such a step.

2. Chemical Analyses of the Blood

The age of the patient and the nature of the chief complaint are the important factors in selecting the chemical study of the "well" patient. In patients over forty-five years of age, a determination should be done of either the nonprotein nitrogen or blood urea nitrogen.* This provides a safeguard against elective operation in the face of unsuspected renal disease. In patients with hypertension or disorders of the genitourinary tract, this determination is to be carried out in any instance, regardless of age.

In patients with diseases of the gastrointestinal tract involving loss of weight or appetite, or with extrarenal losses as part of the history, a simple "water and electrolyte profile" should be done. The simplest is the determination of the blood urea nitrogen, plasma protein, and chloride concentrations. In the "well" patient admitted for elective surgery, normalcy of these makes any other serious abnormality of water or electrolyte balance unlikely and further chemical analysis unnecessary unless the picture changes. If the patient appears ill and has suffered extrarenal losses, renal disease, or nutritional difficulty in the recent past, the measurement of the carbon dioxide combining power† (see below under "acid-base study") and the plasma sodium and potassium concentrations is valuable. In most hospitals, these determinations are carried out much more frequently than is necessary on patients admitted for elective surgery. This is a place for the exercise of judgment on the part of the admitting surgeon. Determination of the con-

---

* The blood urea nitrogen (BUN) can be interpreted interchangeably with nonprotein nitrogen (N.P.N.) in the vast majority of instances. The BUN is referred to throughout this book.

† The carbon dioxide combining power (CO_{2p}) is the standard "CO_2" of most clinical laboratories. It is the rare laboratory that routinely determines the true carbon dioxide content, to be done on arterial blood freshly drawn under oil.

centrations of blood urea nitrogen, plasma protein, and chloride suffices for preoperative chemical study in the vast majority of patients entering for elective surgery in whom any blood chemical analyses whatsoever are necessary.

The determination of the blood sugar level after fasting should be carried out for anyone whose urine shows sugar to be present in an ordinary voided specimen. It should be standard procedure in women over forty-five years of age, particularly those whose hair is prematurely gray or white and those who are somewhat overweight—it is in this group that the surgical service will each year uncover a few previously unsuspected cases of diabetes.

There are many other laboratory determinations that are important in the preoperative patient suffering specific visceral disease. For the most part, these do not apply to the seemingly well patient. Such tests include studies of the blood bilirubin, bleeding and clotting factors, blood cholesterol, functional tests, and so on. These will come up for discussion later on in appropriate sections of this book.

In summary, the following is a general plan of study for the seemingly healthy patient admitted for elective surgery.

(1) *On all patients preoperatively:* perform urinalysis (including microscopic examination of the spun sediment); leucocyte count; measure of concentration of erythrocytes (hematocrit, red corpuscle count, or hemoglobin); examine stool for occult blood.

(2) *Patients over forty-five years of age:* measure blood urea nitrogen (BUN). Patients with hypertension or previous renal disease should have this done regardless of age.

(3) *Patients with disorders of the gastrointestinal tract involving loss of appetite, extrarenal loss, or weight loss:* measure blood urea nitrogen, plasma protein, and chloride concentrations.

(4) *Patients in whom chronic or subacute nutritional and metabolic disorder is suggested:* make measurement of acid-base balance as carbon dioxide combining power $(CO_{2\ cp})$; measure sodium and potassium concentrations in plasma.*

(5) *Patients over forty-five (and those with obesity, those with urine sugar, and women prematurely gray):* measure blood sugar after fasting.

C. THE UNSUSPECTED CASE

Having a general plan for the seemingly well patient, we come to a consideration of the clinical groups wherein chemical observations may uncover organ disease or metabolic derangement much more profound than appears on the surface or in relation to the focal complaint.

1. Unsuspected Renal Disease

An elevated blood urea nitrogen concentration should lead to a more precise study of renal function and acid-base balance. When the blood urea nitrogen is normal, but when some metabolic acidosis (carbon dioxide combining power below 20 mE. per l.) is found, a study of renal function by phenolsulfonphthalein test and concentration test may uncover tubular impairment sufficient to embarrass surgical convalescence. This is especially true in the elderly.

2. Unsuspected Diabetes

In elderly patients with vascular disease or in patients with infection, repeated postprandial blood sugar measurements and a glucose tolerance test are necessary to uncover mild diabetes; the glycosuria may be minimal if renal threshold is high.

3. Unsuspected Water Loading and Serum Hypotonicity

This may be found in the chronically ill patient who is on inadequate caloric intake or in whom there is chronic disease of heart, liver, or kidneys. Severe water-loading with hypotonicity can exist without edema.

4. Chronic Unrepaired Anemia

This is especially common in the presence

---

* Plasma concentrations are referred to throughout. In many instances the data are based on serum analyses.

of infection and open wounds. In dealing with peripheral vascular disease and in fractures, as well as in other focal disorders, one encounters patients in whom all attention has been focused on the bone, the dead toe, or the unhealed ulcer. The patient may have hypoproteinemia, anemia, and hyponatremia. Treatment of even a mild systemic disorder of this type will hasten healing of the focal lesion.

5. Retention of Water and Salt

Patients who enter the hospital for cardiac surgery, whether or not they have overt decompensation in the form of elevated venous pressure, tachycardia, pulmonary edema, peripheral edema, and a large liver, may be assumed to be suffering from a defect in the metabolism of water and electrolyte. This involves the retention of water and salt with acidosis. Appropriate studies will reveal the extent of the disorder. Hyponatremia is an indicator of the severity of the process. In occasional cases these findings direct attention to previously undiagnosed heart disease.

6. Chronic Respiratory Acidosis

Patients with borderline asthma-emphysema-bronchiectasis may enter the hospital for surgery on other systems of the body. They should be studied for chronic carbon dioxide narcosis and acidosis. Hypochloremia, elevated carbon dioxide concentrations, and polycythemia are evidences of their poor pulmonary reserve.

7. Unsuspected Polycythemia

This is a not-uncommon finding by hematocrit in the ruddy-faced, slightly obese patient. Chronic pulmonary disease may be in the background; duodenal ulcer may be a result. Both should be looked for.

8. Unsuspected Hypothyroidism

In the overweight woman this diagnosis may be confirmed by basal metabolism rate, or radioiodine studies.

9. Unsuspected Hyperparathyroidism

This condition will be uncovered by insisting on duplicate repeated serum calcium and phosphorus studies on all patients with renal stone, on female patients with duodenal ulcer, and all patients with acute or chronic pancreatitis.

There are many other examples; the above are common ones in which the surgical service uncovers previously unknown disease. In approaching the seemingly well patient for elective surgery, this should always be one objective of laboratory study in preoperative evaluation.

D. THE PROBLEM CASE: SELECTION AND FREQUENCY OF LABORATORY WORK

The need for special laboratory study is quite evident in the care of patients with obvious disorders of water and electrolyte metabolism, such as vomiting, diarrhea, fistula, distention, intestinal obstruction, large open wounds, chronic blood loss, edema, and disease of heart, liver, or kidney. The selection of the laboratory work to be carried out on such patients, however, and the frequency with which it is carried out are matters of fine clinical judgment and considerable economic import. The following are a general guide to frequency of determinations.

(1) Except in the most unusual circumstances analytic measurements of the following are not prone to rapid changes and need not be measured more than once or twice a week: blood urea nitrogen, and plasma concentration of sodium, protein, potassium, chloride, and bilirubin.

(2) The following concentrations can be changed very rapidly by specific treatment (multiple determinations in a single day may at such times be useful, to be followed later by much less frequent determinations): carbon dioxide combining power or other measure of acid-base balance, serum chloride concentration under ammonium chloride therapy.

(3) The following determinations should be done on one or two occasions in the course of the care of patients who have had extrarenal losses: analysis of the fluid loss (vomitus, intestinal tube drainage, et cetera) for sodium and potassium and, in occasional instances, chloride, and analysis of urine for sodium, potassium, and chloride.

The analysis of urine and discharge for

electrolyte should be carried out once or twice during the course of a complicated situation, to provide a basis for subsequent daily care of the patient.

E. THINKING IN TERMS OF BALANCE: CLINICAL BALANCE

Using either established data for electrolyte content of gastrointestinal juice or analyses from the patient, it is possible to carry the patient's management along on a daily basis with the patient reasonably in balance of water, sodium, chloride, and acid-base regulation. A simple record is kept of intake and output by all routes, using approximations where daily analyses would not be justified. This is termed a "clinical balance" method merely to distinguish it from the procedure in a patient in whom accurate daily analyses are done for research.

In setting up clinical balance on an acutely ill surgical patient several important points should be borne in mind. The concept that the patient must be in strict arithmetic zero balance for all measurable items has no basis in fact. Almost all the important body constituents of the acutely ill patient are in negative balance, and premature efforts to restore him to positive nitrogen balance or to zero caloric balance during the acute phase of his illness may be neither practical nor advisable. There comes a time in convalescence from acute disease and injury when these features of his metabolism are of critical importance; but in the acute phase they are not.

In sharp contrast to the nitrogen-calorie complex of macronutrients, it is of outstanding importance to recovery in the acute phase to maintain a reasonable balance of the extracellular complex: water, sodium, and chloride. A record must be kept of the daily extrarenal losses of these three substances. Losses are replaced and negative balance avoided.

Potassium occupies a middle group in respect to the management of clinical balance. So long as a patient is losing lean tissue it is impossible to keep him in zero or positive potassium balance. Yet, his negative potassium balance must not be permitted to exceed that permissible on the basis of tissue loss. A simple rule is to replace all extrarenal losses quantitatively, adding 40 mE. per day for urine loss. If there is no urine secretion, or an abnormal urine volume, this rule must obviously be tempered accordingly.

It is truly a remarkable feature of surgical metabolism that survival can be produced when the balances of water, sodium, chloride, and potassium are cared for accurately from day to day. When they and the blood volume are well managed, disorders of acid-base balance—at least those of metabolic origin—rarely arise, acute volume reduction or excess is avoided, and the human body seems to manage the rest of its homeostasis with ease.

With normal kidneys, the losses in the urine are important chiefly as regards water and potassium. One should not attempt to restore to the patient each day the amounts of sodium and chloride lost in the urine, since these may represent homeostatic discharges of excess extracellular salt. Only by carefully studying the patient's electrolyte flux from day to day is it possible to adjust and interpret all this information accurately.

In order to put such management into effect, some sort of record or chart of the gains and losses should be kept. The exact form of this chart is immaterial.

As a part of the clinical balance procedure the patient's weight should be followed closely.

F. WEIGHT

Frequent measurements of weight are unnecessary for most surgical patients convalescent from injury or surgery. Although but little is known about the weight fluctuations of surgical patients, sufficient research has been done on this subject to indicate what the weight curve may be expected to be after trauma or operation. When the course is complicated by extrarenal losses, or when the trauma imposes unusual alterations in the distribution of body water (as in peritonitis or burns), or when there is severe visceral disease interfering with normal water and salt excretion (as in renal and heart failure and liver disease), the frequent measurement of body weight is of exceptional help in management of the patient.

During acute illness as seen on an active surgical service, gains in weight indicate the overadministration of fluid. In a patient suffering from acute disease or injury, any gain in weight may be assumed to be due to the addition of water and salt to the body. Only under the circumstance of treating established dehydration, desalting water loss, or sequestered edema does one expect weight gain to occur, or accept it with equanimity. Where fluid is rapidly accumulating in the sequestered edema of a burn or obstructed gut, continued administration of fluids has to occur despite a large gain in the patient's weight. Then, when the fluid is remobilized, weight drops again.

By the same token, excessive or sudden losses of weight indicate loss of water. Sudden loss of weight in the region of 500 to 1000 gm. in a twenty-four-hour period usually means gross underadministration of fluid. Whether or not it indicates this depends upon the remaining circumstances and the pathologic processes present. In extrarenal losses, this sudden loss of weight indicates underadministration of fluid. In a recovering phase it means diuresis, as the urine output indicates.

Whereas weight gain due to overtreatment is unacceptable, moderate weight loss is to be expected under most circumstances. A patient with gastric obstruction, for instance, should be expected to lose weight gradually as body fat is burned to support caloric needs during a period of acute illness and through the surgical operation, which restores the functional continuity of his gastrointestinal tract. When this is restored, the patient may lose further weight rather rapidly as he loses some water and salt through diuresis. This delayed weight loss is presumably due to the fact that during the acute phase of his illness, lysis of lean tissue and oxidation of fat have proceeded even faster than the weight curve would suggest.

After a prolonged period of starvation, when the patient starts to eat again, the gain in weight is very slow to begin. When it does occur, it is at a slow rate. Tissue synthesis is a slow process. There is often a period of several days or even weeks when the over-all water change is one of diuresis, the patient gradually losing through diuresis the extra water and salt of the starvation state as the synthesis of lean tissue begins. In such a case, a good beginning of anabolism and tissue resynthesis surprisingly involves no weight gain.

The daily interpretation of the weight changes of an acutely ill patient depends upon a daily evaluation of all the known intake and output and an understanding of the basic pathologic process.

The method by which acutely ill patients are weighed each day is still short of satisfactory. Our experience has been largely based on the use of a bed-type scale to which the patient is moved. After the patient is weighed, the "tare," consisting of the various sheets, pillows, or other impedimenta, is weighed. Other scales have been developed that make it possible to weigh the patient without moving him from the bed. Any scale used for this purpose should be checked for accuracy, using a known standard, and also checked to find out if the exact position of the patient on the scale itself affects the weight reading.

G. A NOTE ON THE INTERPRETATION OF LABORATORY WORK

In a large teaching hospital with a big resident staff, the common tendency is to carry out laboratory work more frequently than thought can be devoted to it and suitable interpretation derived. Oftentimes the attention of the attending staff is more taken by a blank in the lab-sheet than by a significant result. In the community hospital, on the other hand, complicated laboratory procedures are often carried out, but all too frequently there is no framework for interpretation. Both of these difficulties in laboratory management of the patient are somewhat commoner than those of twenty years ago, when most hospitals were unequipped for any laboratory procedures whatsoever.

Just as one may establish procedures for the selection of laboratory work and study, so also a procedure for interpretation should be set up. Two general rules are useful.

1. Consultation Is Essential

Some individual who has had experience in the interpretation of laboratory work and who has given some thought to matters of metabolic care of surgical patients should assist in the interpretation of laboratory results. On the surgical staff of a hospital, it is impossible for every member of the staff to be an expert in all matters. There should be at least one individual on the surgical staff of each hospital who makes it his business to be familiar with the current literature and to be interested in the care of problem patients. As is so frequently emphasized in this book, this individual should be a surgeon, who is competent to judge strategy and tactics in the total situation, not a biochemist or an "electrolyte expert."

2. Tentative Interpretation Is Better Than None

Secondly, it is a good practice to form a tentative interpretation for each abnormality encountered. Such an interpretation may later be found wrong, but at least it has stimulated the surgeon to make up his mind and to form a sensible theory as to the meaning of the abnormality. A classic example of this is the finding of a low plasma sodium concentration. It is a simple matter to keep repeating the plasma sodium determination every couple of days, to find it in the middle 120's. This is recognized as being abnormal, but nothing particular is done about it and no particular interpretive theory is developed. The determination is merely repeated sporadically.

It would be much more suitable if, when this was first discovered, the surgeon in charge of the case made up his mind as to whether this indicated primarily a caloric deficiency, excessive retention of water, loss of sodium-rich fluids, renal disease, or adrenal pathology, or some other cause. Devoting time and thought to this interpretation has the happy result of reducing the number of times that the determination is senselessly repeated and of stimulating those in charge to carry out other determinations that will make interpretation accurate and treatment effective, if needed at all. In this particular instance, such other determinations might be a daily check on the patient's intake, output, weight, and caloric intake, an analysis of the urine for sodium, and a determination of plasma protein concentration. This intentional discipline, that each abnormality discovered by laboratory test must have thought devoted to it and that a tentative interpretation should be developed, has a happy and economical effect on the use of laboratory facilities in a surgical hospital.

CHAPTER 17

Disorders of Hydration: Facts, Concepts, Terms

Section I. Hydration; Osmolality, Tonicity

A. TERMINOLOGY

The water-holding property of salts is a manifestation of the universal tendency to uniform distribution of dissolved substances in solution. Table salt left out in humid air takes up water; if the humidity is high it becomes a moist mass, taking up and holding water out of the surrounding air. If a drop of pure water forms nearby and the two coalesce, the salt takes up the new water also, to become evenly distributed throughout the entire available water. This "water-holding" property of salts is a function of the osmotic pressure of the compound.

Osmotic pressure is a colligative property of solutions. The number of particles (molecules or ions) in solution determines the osmotic pressure, not their weight, valency, or charge: the more molecules of salt or sugar, the greater the total osmotic pressure. Osmotic pressure is the pressure that must be put upon a solution to keep it in equilibrium with the pure solvent when the two are separated by a membrane permeable only to the solvent. The vapor pressure, boiling point, and freezing point are determined by total osmotic pressure, and are other colligative properties. The smaller the molecular weight, the more particles per unit weight and the more osmolar effect per unit solution. Sodium chloride, for example, exerts more osmotic pressure per

unit weight than a very heavy salt like uranyl zinc acetate.

Colloid osmotic pressure is that very tiny fraction of total osmotic pressure in the plasma exerted by colloids. Though quantitatively small (about 3 to 5 mO. per l.) it is of primary importance in maintaining water volume in the plasma because the colloid osmotic pressure on the other side of capillaries is very low. The *total* osmotic pressure is the same on both sides of the membrane. Effective *colloid* osmotic pressure can be exerted only when the solution in question (e.g., plasma) is facing a membrane (e.g., the peripheral capillary) impermeable to the colloid (e.g., albumin). The *total* osmotic pressures of plasma and interstitial fluid (lymph) are the same; the *colloid* osmotic pressure is much greater in plasma.

Osmolarity is a convenient term for the total osmotic pressure of a solution. It is commonly measured by physical methods and is expressed in milliosmols per liter of solution. One millimol of a substance or a monovalent ion exerts one milliosmol of osmotic pressure. For divalent and trivalent ions (and proteins) the milliosmolar figure and milliequivalence are not identical.

Osmolality is a function of the solute concentration per unit of solvent rather than the solute concentration per unit of total volume of the solution. Current methods of measuring total solute by freezing point measure osmolality, not osmolarity. Changes in content of fat or protein do not change the osmolality reading significantly, whereas they change the osmolarity markedly. Body cells also respond to osmolality rather than osmolarity. For this reason the term "osmolality" is generally used in this book. It has the same general significance as "osmolarity," but is more accurate. The numerical difference between the two is very small.

In plasma about 98 per cent of the osmolality consists of electrolyte; one half of this is sodium. In urine about 50 per cent is electrolyte (the sodium being variable and generally proportional to *p*H) and 50 per cent is urea.

Note that the plasma ions total about 310 mE. (approximately 155 each of anion and cation) but only 290 mO. The numerical difference resides in protein, which has much weight and valence but very little total osmotic pressure, and in the polyvalent ions.

Note also that the total plasma osmolality in mO. per l. is numerically twice the sodium concentration in mE. per l. plus a small increment (6 to 8 mO. per l.) due to crystalloid.

The term "milliosmol" (mO.) is defined as being one-thousandth of a mol of a substance in solution, considered as the smallest molecular unit in that solution. The normal plasma osmolality is from 285 to 295 mO. per l. Crystalloids such as urea and glucose exert osmotic pressure according to their molar concentration. The molecular weight of urea is 60. Therefore 1 mO. of urea is 60 mg. In the case of fully ionized salt such as sodium chloride, each ion exerts osmotic pressure separately and therefore 1 mM. of sodium chloride exerts 2 mO. of osmotic pressure (and contains 1 mE. of cation plus 1 mE. of anion). Of the 290 mO. per l. in plasma, approximately 95 per cent of this osmotic pressure is exerted by the extracellular salts, of which sodium is the predominant ion. Of the total osmotic pressure of normal plasma 143 mO. are sodium, 103 chloride, and 27 bicarbonate. The total here is 273, leaving only 17 mO. to be exerted by the crystalloids and other electrolytes in solution. Plasma protein exerts a negligible total osmotic pressure because of its high molecular weight.

Effective osmotic pressure (to be distinguished from "total osmotic pressure" and "colloid osmotic pressure") is a physiologic rather than a chemical term. It refers to the osmotic pressure exerted by substances to which the osmoreceptor cells of the brain are impermeable. An understanding of this point is basic to sound therapy of water abnormalities in surgery. The osmoreceptor is apparently impermeable to extracellular salt (such as sodium, chloride, bicarbonate). Therefore, an increase in sodium concentration stimulates these cells, antidiuretic hormone is elaborated, and water is conserved. This is "effective osmotic pressure." By contrast, the osmoreceptor is evidently freely permeable to urea. So a huge increase in plasma osmolality due to urea (uremia, azotemia) is not an antidiuretic stimulus; the increased osmolality is not "effective"; water output is not reduced.

Specific gravity of a solution is dependent on the weight of dissolved substances. Specific gravity and osmolality of plasma and urine often vary together but not in a linear fashion. Urine with much protein in it has a high specific gravity but may have a low osmolality; hypoproteinemic serum will have a low specific gravity but may have a normal osmolality. Protein is heavy but exerts very small total osmotic pressure.

Osmotic diuresis is an increased urine flow due to the presence in the glomerular filtrate of large quantities of a substance reabsorbed only slightly in the tubules, and requiring water for its solution. Such "tubular water-holding" substances are glucose, urea, peptides, potassium, and mannitol. Infusing them produces an increased flow of urine in the normal kidney. Under certain circumstances sodium does the same. These are solutes whose excretion may dehydrate the body. It is of interest that urea in the plasma does not increase "effective osmotic pressure," as defined above, but its excretion in the urine adds to the solute discharge and thus to urine volume.

The terms "plasma" and "serum" are not synonymous. Plasma is the noncellular fraction of liquid blood as it exists in the body or as studied unclotted. Serum is the liquid left after a clot forms. In this book we refer to "plasma" concentrations. The word "serum" is used but rarely to denote a chemical solvent even though the laboratory analysis is often done on serum.

The terms "cubic centimeter" (cc.) and "milliliter" (ml.) are not synonymous, but the difference for body fluids at body temperature is ultramicroscopic and totally insignificant. Just to adopt a standard practice, we use "ml." here.

Abbreviations used are as follows:
Conventional chemical symbols are used.

For concentrations:
  mE. = milliequivalents.
  mO. = milliosmols.
For acid-base data:
  $CO_{2\,cp}$ = carbon dioxide combining power (in mE. per l.).
  TCO_2 = total carbon dioxide content (in mE. per l.).
  HCO_3 = bicarbonate (as calculated) (in mE. per l.).
  pCO_2 = partial pressure of carbon dioxide (as measured or calculated) (in mm.Hg).
  pH = negative logarithm of the hydrogen ion concentration (in units) as measured.

Section II.   Water Distribution; The Body Osmometer

The distribution of water in the body is governed by the osmolality of the fluids in it. There is good evidence that the body as a whole acts as an "osmometer." By this is meant that an osmolality observed in any one part of the body must be present throughout the entire body; the osmolality of plasma must be presumed to coexist in the cell. There is no evidence that living cells tolerate osmotic gradients across them, with the exception of those particular cells in the renal tubule whose specific job is to do just this in reabsorbing water to elaborate a concentrated urine. If the osmolality of plasma is 295 mO. per l., this same osmolality is presumably found also in the cells.

Acute disturbances in extracellular osmolality are readily produced either by sudden extrarenal desalting water losses (with mobilization of water from cells and fat-oxidation, with dilution), massive pulmonary losses with pure dehydration, or the administration of concentrated salts or excessive amounts of water. We often think of these as affecting concentrations in extracellular fluid and the osmolality of the plasma. It is important to emphasize that such changes are reflected throughout the entire body. For instance, if a patient with severe sepsis (running a high fever and exhibiting dyspnea) is not given adequate water, he will rapidly develop de-

hydration-desiccation due to excessive pulmonary water loss, with a gradually rising concentration of sodium in his plasma and a concomitant rise in the plasma osmolality in the direction of 320 to 340 mO. per l. One might consider that the extent of this water loss was indicated by this osmolality change as multiplied by the volume of his extracellular fluid. In view of the fact that the body as a whole does not tolerate osmotic gradients, the actual amount of water lost is indicated by the change in plasma osmolality considered as a reflection of total body water. The converse of this is seen in water intoxication, where the amount of water required to drive down the plasma osmolality is not a function of the plasma osmolality fall as multiplied by the extracellular fluid but is instead a function of the total body water.

These important facts have been used by some writers to put forth the idea that patients with a low plasma sodium concentration or hypotonicity from a variety of causes should be given an amount of sodium calculated from the unit deficit multiplied by the total body water. This we refer to as the "deficit times total body water" theory of salt replacement. Unfortunately, this further extension of a sound basic concept is invalid.

Text continues on page 286.

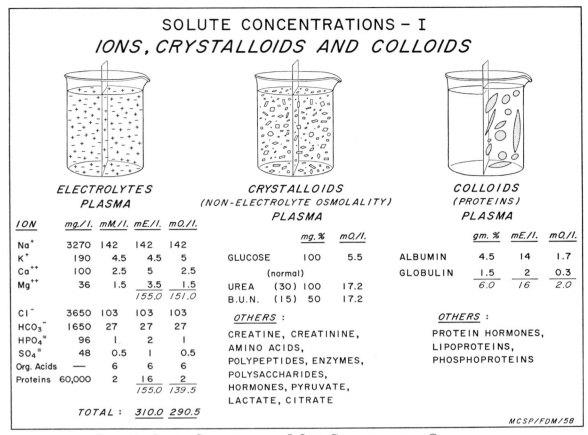

SOLUTE CONCENTRATIONS – I
IONS, CRYSTALLOIDS AND COLLOIDS

ELECTROLYTES PLASMA

ION	mg./l.	mM./l.	mE./l.	mO./l.
Na⁺	3270	142	142	142
K⁺	190	4.5	4.5	5
Ca⁺⁺	100	2.5	5	2.5
Mg⁺⁺	36	1.5	3.5	1.5
			155.0	151.0
Cl⁻	3650	103	103	103
HCO₃⁻	1650	27	27	27
HPO₄⁼	96	1	2	1
SO₄⁼	48	0.5	1	0.5
Org. Acids	—	6	6	6
Proteins	60,000	2	16	2
			155.0	139.5

TOTAL : 310.0 290.5

CRYSTALLOIDS
(NON-ELECTROLYTE OSMOLALITY)
PLASMA

	mg.%	mO./l.
GLUCOSE	100	5.5
(normal)		
UREA (30)	100	17.2
B.U.N. (15)	50	17.2

OTHERS :
CREATINE, CREATININE,
AMINO ACIDS,
POLYPEPTIDES, ENZYMES,
POLYSACCHARIDES,
HORMONES, PYRUVATE,
LACTATE, CITRATE

COLLOIDS
(PROTEINS)
PLASMA

	gm.%	mE./l.	mO./l.
ALBUMIN	4.5	14	1.7
GLOBULIN	1.5	2	0.3
	6.0	16	2.0

OTHERS :
PROTEIN HORMONES,
LIPOPROTEINS,
PHOSPHOPROTEINS

MCSP/FDM/58

Figure 48. SOLUTE CONCENTRATIONS. I. IONS, CRYSTALLOIDS AND COLLOIDS

In this chart are depicted some of the facts relative to the three major categories of solute in the plasma.

To the left are shown the components which, upon dissociation in water, carry an electrical charge and therefore are called electrolytes. Osmolality is a function of the total number of molecules in a solution. The smaller these particles are, the more osmolality is conferred per unit weight. The particle size of the electrolyte solutes is extremely small, and they are therefore responsible for the great majority of the osmolality of the serum. It will be noted from the table beneath the electrolyte diagram that the total milliequivalents of the plasma is 310 but the total (electrolyte) milliosmols is 290.5, this apparent discrepancy resulting from multivalence of certain of the ions and the low osmotic pressure of protein.

In the center are shown crystalloids. These are substances which, generally speaking, do not dissociate in solution or, if they do dissociate (as the amino acids), are amphoteric. The crystalloids of greatest mass in the plasma are glucose and urea. From the table below it is noted that each 100 mg. per cent of glucose represents 5.5 mO. per liter of nonelectrolyte osmolality in the

serum and that for each 50 mg. per cent of blood urea nitrogen, 17.2 mO. per liter are contributed. There are many other crystalloids in the plasma, as indicated below.

To the right are shown the colloids of the plasma. These are principally the proteins. Albumin, being a large molecule as compared with glucose or urea (but at the same time a very small molecule compared to globulin), contributes the major fraction of the colloid osmotic pressure of the serum. This is responsible for the water distribution between the plasma and the interstitial fluid. The albumin contributes an extremely low fraction of total osmolality, somewhat less than one per cent, whereas it contributes about 90 per cent of the oncotic or colloid osmotic pressure. The colloids are diagrammed as unable to pass the membrane they are facing, and thus developing oncotic pressure and holding water in the blood stream with them. Electrolytes and crystalloids can freely pass the capillary membrane, but the cell exercises selective permeability to them. They therefore contribute to water distribution across the cell, but not across the capillary.

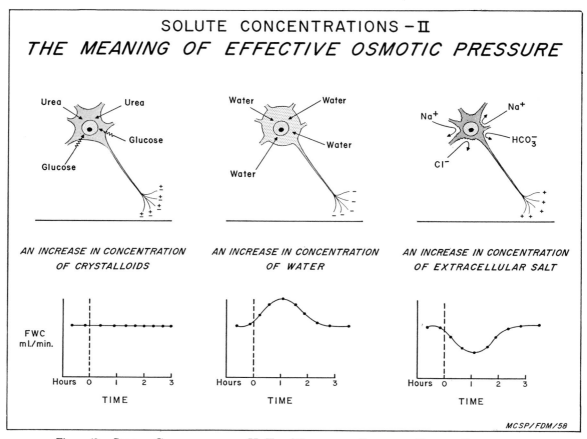

Figure 49. SOLUTE CONCENTRATIONS. II. THE MEANING OF EFFECTIVE OSMOTIC PRESSURE

See facing page for detailed legend.

Figure 49. SOLUTE CONCENTRATIONS. II. THE MEANING OF EFFECTIVE OSMOTIC PRESSURE

As demonstrated by Verney, there are cells in the central nervous system which are responsive to alterations in the osmotic pressure of the fluids bathing them. However, the total osmotic pressure of the fluids bathing these cells is not always effective in inducing changes in water reabsorption in the renal tubule by inducing alterations in secretion of antidiuretic hormone. For instance, a very large increment in concentration of urea produces no decrease in water excretion by the kidney whereas large increases (or decreases) in the sodium concentration of the plasma do produce marked alterations. Hence the meaning of the term "effective osmotic pressure." An "effective osmotic solute" is a solute which is effective in altering the antidiuretic-hormone–producing activity of the osmoreceptor cells in the central nervous system; in general these are solutes which remain outside of cells, such as the extracellular salts.

In this chart are represented, to the left, the events which act upon this cell when there are alterations in the concentration of urea or glucose in the blood. These are ineffective osmotic solutes. Urea penetrates freely into the osmoreceptor cells. Glucose penetrates but not quite so freely, requiring more passage of time to gain entrance to the cell. Thus, large increases in the concentration of urea in the body water have no effect upon the distribution of water between the inside and the outside of the cell. When its concentration increases, there is no change in free water clearance, as shown in the chart below.

In the center are shown the contrasting events which occur when water concentration is markedly increased in the plasma. We now find that water freely penetrates the intracellular environment of the cell. But the electrolytes within the cell cannot get out rapidly, being held within the cell by the cell membrane. The cell therefore swells as the concentration of sodium (an effective osmotic solute) is decreased outside the cell by the increment in water. The result is a marked decrease in antidiuretic hormone secretion with a very marked increase in free water clearance, as shown below. This is the mechanism whereby water loads are normally freely excreted; in post-traumatic situations this mechanism does not operate freely.

Finally, to the right are shown the events which occur when there is a marked increase in the concentration of effective osmotic solute (sodium, chloride, bicarbonate) in the extracellular fluid around the osmoreceptor cell. This is the classic Verney experiment. This withdraws water from the cell, because this solute does not penetrate the cell. The result is that the cell "feels" its relative lack of water, there is a marked increase in antidiuretic hormone secretion, negative free water clearance in the renal tubule, and conservation of water for the extracellular fluid. After trauma this type of "setting" appears to operate for several days, regardless of water or salt concentration or tonicity.

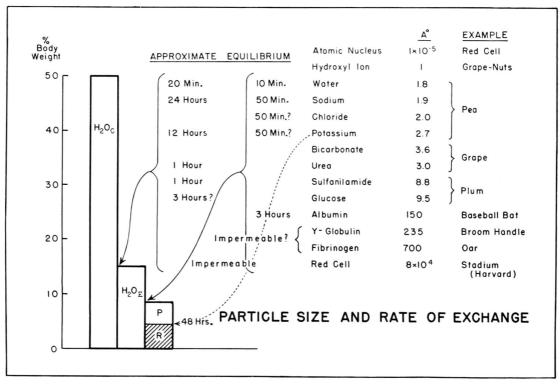

%
Body
Weight

APPROXIMATE EQUILIBRIUM

				A°	EXAMPLE
			Atomic Nucleus	1×10⁻⁵	Red Cell
			Hydroxyl Ion	1	Grape-Nuts
20 Min.	10 Min.		Water	1.8	
24 Hours	50 Min.		Sodium	1.9	Pea
	50 Min.?		Chloride	2.0	
12 Hours	50 Min.?		Potassium	2.7	
			Bicarbonate	3.6	Grape
1 Hour			Urea	3.0	
1 Hour			Sulfanilamide	8.8	Plum
3 Hours?			Glucose	9.5	
	3 Hours		Albumin	150	Baseball Bat
	Impermeable?		Y-Globulin	235	Broom Handle
			Fibrinogen	700	Oar
	Impermeable		Red Cell	8×10⁴	Stadium (Harvard)

H_2O_C

H_2O_E

P

R

◄48 Hrs. **PARTICLE SIZE AND RATE OF EXCHANGE**

Figure 50. PARTICLE SIZE AND RATE OF EXCHANGE

The exchange of water and solutes between the blood, the interstitial fluid, and the cell water is a function of many factors, including the electrical charge, the molecular dimension, and the permeability properties of the cell membrane.

In this chart are shown the relative molecular size (in Ångstroms) of a series of electrolytes, crystalloids, and colloids, as well as the red blood cell. Their approximate equilibrium times across the capillary and cell membrane are also shown.

On the right is shown the relative sizes in terms of objects whose size we can more readily visualize. Using the red cell as a model for the size of the atomic nucleus, we find that electrolytes and most of the crystalloids are quite small, although still many millionfold larger than the atomic nucleus. By contrast, the colloids represent a third magnitude of size, being several feet long on this scale of size. Finally, the red cell itself, on such a scale of size, is to be compared with an old football stadium.

It is clear, then, that when a mixture of red blood cells, water, salts, crystalloids, and colloids are presented to the plasma, the red cells themselves remain in the plasma, occupy space, provide volume, and provide resistance to flow in a way that supports pressure. The red cell is thus unique in not being exchanged between the blood stream and other areas of the body.

Electrolytes are but little more effective than crystalloids when they are infused with the idea of maintaining plasma volume. Their ready equilibrium into the interstitial fluid prevents quantitative intravascular maintenance of the infused volume. However, in the restoration of extracellular fluid volume, they are extremely effective.

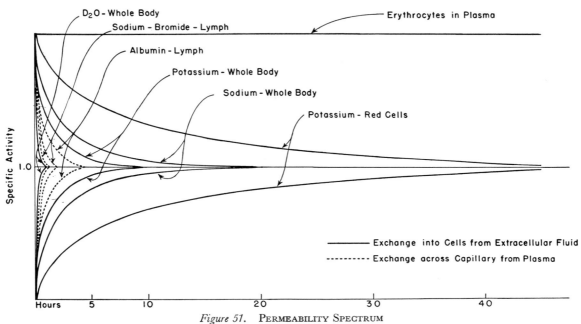

Figure 51. Permeability Spectrum

This chart is to be considered together with the previous one. This merely shows, in another method of presentation, the exchange of substances into cells from the extracellular fluid and across the capillary from the plasma.

These data are based on isotope exchange studies from our laboratories. Above is shown the downsweep of the plasma time-concentration decrement of the isotope; below is shown the upsweep of its appearance in another area as named. Equilibrium is achieved at the various approximate times indicated. Tagged erythrocytes achieve a flat concentration plateau in plasma, which falls slowly over many weeks only as the erythrocyte itself lives out its life span (not shown here).

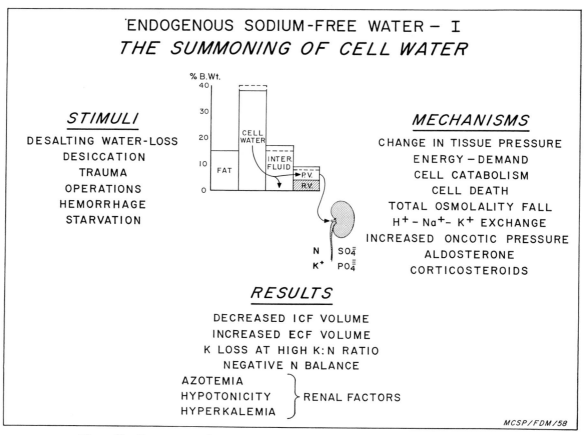

ENDOGENOUS SODIUM-FREE WATER — I
THE SUMMONING OF CELL WATER

STIMULI

DESALTING WATER-LOSS
DESICCATION
TRAUMA
OPERATIONS
HEMORRHAGE
STARVATION

MECHANISMS

CHANGE IN TISSUE PRESSURE
ENERGY — DEMAND
CELL CATABOLISM
CELL DEATH
TOTAL OSMOLALITY FALL
$H^+ - Na^+ - K^+$ EXCHANGE
INCREASED ONCOTIC PRESSURE
ALDOSTERONE
CORTICOSTEROIDS

RESULTS

DECREASED ICF VOLUME
INCREASED ECF VOLUME
K LOSS AT HIGH K:N RATIO
NEGATIVE N BALANCE
AZOTEMIA
HYPOTONICITY } RENAL FACTORS
HYPERKALEMIA

MCSP/FDM/58

Figure 52. ENDOGENOUS SODIUM-FREE WATER. I. THE SUMMONING OF CELL WATER

Water is produced in the body by the oxidation of organic substrates such as fat, glucose, and protein which, at the last stage of oxidation, yield carbon dioxide and water. In addition, water free of sodium is released within the body when cells undergo lysis, destruction, or loss of matrix. In the former event the water is referred to as "water of oxidation" and in the latter case as "preformed water" newly released to the interstitial fluid. In both cases this water is free of sodium and thus available to dilute the extracellular electrolyte of the body if not readily excreted.

In this chart are shown some aspects of the release of cell water to the interstitial fluid and plasma. This is one of the basic responses of the organism to a wide variety of injurious agents. It produces enlargement of the extracellular fluid at the expense of the intracellular fluid; this is the primary compositional change of injury.

This cell water arises both from the oxidation of protein and from the shrinking or death of cells. The stimuli which may produce such a change, the mechanisms, and the results are shown above. The actual mechanisms which call forth this water from the cell to the extracellular fluid are unknown and are of central interest in research at this time.

The most potent of all of these mechanisms may well be the secretion of aldosterone. This material is responsible for the exchange of hydrogen ion for sodium and potassium ion in the renal tubule and may exert a similar effect, with transfer of water, in body cells in general as well as in renal tubular cells.

It will be noted that the results of the summoning of cell water are familiar as the compositional and metabolic sequelae of injury. When renal function is grossly deficient certain additional results are accentuated, as shown below.

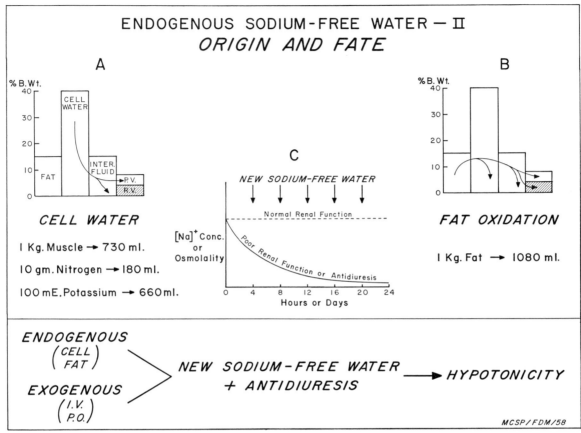

Figure 53. ENDOGENOUS SODIUM-FREE WATER. II. ORIGIN AND FATE

To the left is shown the flow of water out of cells as demonstrated in the previous chart. The figures indicate the amount of water released per unit of various intracellular constituents.

To the right is shown the distribution of water within the body resulting from fat oxidation. The body handles this water exactly as it would an external water load.

Below in the center a chart demonstrates the fact that if this new sodium-free water is added to the extracellular fluid and total body water at a time when renal function is perfectly normal, the water is excreted and there is no change in extracellular osmolality or tonicity. If, however, this water is released in the presence of poor renal function or antidiuresis, then the water is retained and extracellular salt is diluted. This series of events is characteristic after surgical injury and may occur rapidly over a period of hours or slowly over a period of days.

The relation of sodium-free water (added to total body water during a period of antidiuresis) to the production of hypotonicity is shown in the expression below.

In desiccation-dehydration or in pure water intoxication the osmolar change required in treatment must be calculated in terms of the "unit change times total body water." But in sodium deficit and in most complex surgical situations this is not the case.

Were the body a closed system not communicating with the outside world, and were hypotonicity to be wholly due to decrease in the amount of sodium present in the fluid, such a concept based on the total body osmometer concept would be valid as a basis for treatment in most cases of surgical hypotonicity. Neither of these premises is true. The body is not a closed system. As osmolality is restored in treating dilutional hypotonicity, water is excreted. Pure sodium deficits are so rare as to be exceptional, and in nearly all cases of hypotonicity in surgery some degree of water excess is also present. Potassium, also, has been lost. For this reason—even were it possible to do so—filling up this extra body water with new sodium would be deleterious to the patient. Far better to let him get rid of water, adding only enough salt to maintain body content.

While the total osmolality governs the amount of water in the body and the "sodium osmolality" governs the amount of water in the extracellular fluid and outside of cells, the partition of water between the plasma and the extracellular fluid is governed in large part by the colloid osmotic pressure. Those areas of the vascular bed in which the capillary is impermeable to albumin retain their water as a result of the colloid osmotic pressure exerted by the albumin in the plasma. In those large areas of the vascular bed (heart, lungs, liver, gastrointestinal tract) where the albumin concentration on the two sides of the capillary is almost the same, there is very little effective colloid osmotic pressure exerted by albumin. The colloid is facing a membrane permeable to it and therefore its colloid osmotic pressure cannot be exerted to hold water on one side. For this reason the maintenance of water partition on the two sides of the capillary in these areas relates to other factors, not the least of which are the anatomy of the structure itself, body salt content, urine osmolality, and tissue pressure.

Section III.   The Origin and Fate of New Sodium-Free Water: The Cell and Fat

A. INTAKE

In most instances in surgery in which the body becomes hypotonic, as manifested by a low plasma sodium concentration, new sodium-free water has been added to the system. The importance of these mechanisms is generally underrated. The production of hypotonicity by the mechanism of sodium loss alone is quite rare, even in extrarenal loss or adrenal insufficiency. Alterations in water metabolism underlie most changes in sodium concentration.

This new sodium-free water arrives in the body most easily and understandably from external water. A starving patient who cannot eat solids and who has a strong antidiuretic tendency (and free access to water) adds to his hypotonicity by taking in external water in the form of drinking water. The cardiac patient can overhydrate himself in the postoperative period even by free oral access to water during a phase when hypotonicity is readily produced because of the antidiuretic tendency of the disease.

The administration of excessive sodium-free water by vein is obviously another method by which the body may become overhydrated and hypotonic, provided there is some mechanism interfering with the normal excretion of water. The most common circumstances occur in the postoperative or post-traumatic patient who has an antidiuretic tendency interfering with water excretion, or the patient with outright renal failure, where water excretion is inadequate because of persistent oliguria. Patients who become overhydrated owing to the excessive administration of water by the attending surgeon often receive these water infusions over short periods of time; it then becomes immediately clear that the origin of the hypotonicity is misdirected therapy.

By contrast, hypotonicity may "creep up" on the unwary in the form of continuing positive water balances even as small as 200 to 300 ml. a day, becoming cumulative over a period of ten days to two weeks, and failing of excretion through persistent stress-induced antidiuresis.

Over and beyond these obvious sources of new sodium-free water there are two sources within the body which must be described in greater detail. The first of these has to do with the mobilization of water from the cell.

B. LEAN-TISSUE LYSIS AS AN ENDOGENOUS WATER SOURCE

Under conditions in which water and salt metabolism are normal, the lysis of lean tissue that occurs with loss of muscle tissue will not produce any tendency to hyponatremia and bodily hypotonicity. For example, a highly conditioned athlete in the peak of muscular development, breaking training at the end of the season, will lose a good deal of his muscular tissue in the course of a few weeks. This water will pass out of his body. He will be in negative balance of water and potassium as an evidence of this loss of cellular water. He will be in negative nitrogen balance under such circumstances also. Here is an instance where water from cells, containing potassium and other intracellular electrolytes but essentially no sodium, is mobilized into the extracellular fluid and then excreted by the normal route. For each kilogram of muscle tissue lost, the subject would excrete approximately 100 mE. of potassium and approximately 730 ml. of water formerly residing in the muscle cells.

If we now consider the same patient in bed after breaking his femur in a football game, we have a typical situation for the accumulation of sodium-free water in extracellular fluid. Because of the trauma, he is in a strongly antidiuretic phase. If anesthesia and open surgery for the reduction of his fracture are added to his care, the antidiuretic tendency becomes even more marked. The tendency to lysis of lean tissue is also more exaggerated. It is not unusual for such a patient to have his extracellular phase confronted with new cell water at a rate as high as 500 ml. per day (this corresponds to a negative

potassium balance of 75 mE.). If water is not being given in excess by other routes, allowing for this influx of water, hypotonicity does not occur. But if water is freely administered without consideration of this fact, the patient will show dilution of his plasma. The contribution of cell water to this hypotonicity is very real. Sodium concentration quickly drops to 125 mE. per l., osmolality to 250 mO. per l.

C. PROTEIN OXIDATION

In addition, the protein within these cells is oxidized, the carbon chains being thus oxidized to carbon dioxide and water, and the nitrogen excreted in the form of urea. If a kilogram of muscle tissue consists of 73 per cent water, it may be assumed to be approximately 27 per cent protein. In the kilogram of muscle tissue, this 270 gm. of protein, upon full oxidation, will yield 108 ml. of water (0.4 ml. per gm.). Protein does not become as fully oxidized as carbohydrate, however, since urea, the urinary end-product that is responsible for most of the nitrogen excretion, contains one carbon atom that is not fully oxidized.

We are therefore left with the fact that each kilogram of wet lean tissue lysed after trauma releases into the extracellular fluid a total of about 850 ml. of water containing no sodium. If the patient is in an antidiuretic phase at this time and water administration is carried on enthusiastically (intravenously or by mouth) without taking this new cell water into account, the patient's plasma sodium concentration will be diluted as sodium-free water is added to the total amount of body water and dilutes total solute. The potassium also released is excreted. Even were the potassium to be retained within the body and this new water of cellular origin, with its potassium, to be distributed throughout the remaining cellular and extracellular phases, the net effect would still be one of extracellular dilution, with a slight rise in potassium concentration.

It should be re-emphasized that—as far as we know at the present time—the body handles this new cell water just as if it were water from any other source containing the same substances. A very close analogy is the water contained in ingested lean meat, which undergoes dissolution in the gastrointestinal tract, the water being absorbed and metabolized just like any other water entering the body. An ordinary diet containing 2500 to 3000 calories yields 500 to 750 ml. of water.

D. FAT OXIDATION

The third source of sodium-free water, tending to produce hypotonicity in the postoperative patient, is the oxidation of fat. Each kilogram of fat that is completely oxidized yields about 1000 ml. of water and 9000 calories. The carbon is completely oxidized to carbon dioxide and water. Theoretically, some keto-acids may accumulate; this is particularly true in the starving patient, the diabetic, or the patient who is severely dehydrated. These incompletely oxidized carbon fragments, however, are very small in total amount (even in severe ketosis), as compared with the total oxidation that is going on in the background, and under normal conditions are completely oxidized.

The exact caloric equivalent of fat oxidized within the body during starvation or after injury has never been measured, but one may assume that the same equivalence, namely 9 calories per gm., would obtain. The caloric significance of this fat oxidation is critical in considering the starvation that follows injury and operation. The water released by this fat oxidation enters the body water pool just exactly as if it were injected or ingested by other routes. It is fully analogous to the water mobilized from cells or given in an intravenous infusion.

This water from oxidation of body fat is free of any electrolyte whatsoever. Whereas the cell water is released in the extracellular phase with a full load of potassium and other electrolytes (phosphate, calcium, sulfate, and magnesium), this "fat water" comes as pure water of oxidation. Subcutaneous or storage-depot fat does contain a small aqueous extracellular phase, the exact dimension of which is not known, but it is probably less than 3 per cent of the total tissue weight. This large amount of water therefore enters the extracellular fluid without salt.

As a general rule, endogenous water production is at the rate of 10 ml. of water per 100 calories of endogenous caloric production. This general rule can be rationalized in terms of the fact that each 10 gm. of fat oxidized yields about 10 ml. of water and 90 calories. When mixed tissue is burned the ratio of 10 ml. of water per 100 endogenous calories represents a fair average.

Exactly as in the metabolism of water coming from cellular oxidation processes, the water arising from fat oxidation does not in itself produce hypotonicity. It only does so when the total water balance of the individual—including this new water arising from fat—is in excess of his external losses. This situation is especially apt to occur after trauma or operation and is then due to the antidiuretic state induced by injury. In severe illness, wounds, and shock, water retention is intensified by oliguria due to decreased glomerular filtration or by renal failure itself.

In view of the widespread use of intravenous therapy as a routine in postoperative patients it may be a little bit hard to recall that patients can undergo a major trauma or surgery with little or no oral liquid intake for two or three days, yet pull through without severe evidences of dehydration, providing the ambient temperature is not too great and there are no external losses of fluid. Such a program of therapy is not to be recommended and is a hazard should complications arise; the intelligent use of intravenous therapy adds much to the safety and comfort of the postoperative course. However, the survival of injured patients for centuries before the invention of the hollow needle was due not only to the rugged nature of the human frame, but to the fact that it has within it sources of water that are mobilized with especially great rapidity after trauma. These two primary sources of stored water are lean-tissue cells, which undergo lysis and protein oxidation after injury, and fat, which is oxidized.

E. DIURESIS AND ANTIDIURESIS

The constancy of plasma osmolality is an expression of the constancy of plasma water

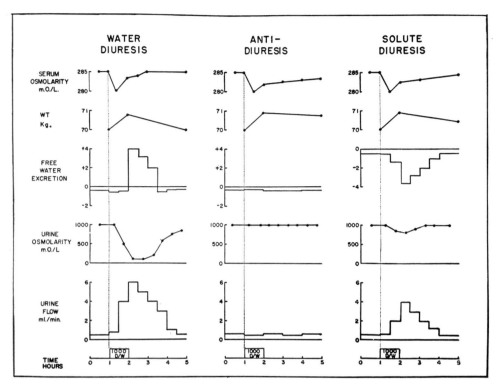

Figure 54. PHENOMENA OF DIURESIS. I. TYPES OF DIURESIS

In this chart are shown the three major categories of renal water excretion: water diuresis, antidiuresis, and solute diuresis. In all three of them, the phenomena are pointed up by administering an infusion of dextrose in water to the subject under study.

It will be noticed, in water diuresis, that the water infusion results in only a transient lowering of serum osmolality, and a transient increase in weight. The free water excretion rises sharply. This means that the urine, as elaborated, has a lower solute concentration than the glomerular filtrate. As a result, urine osmolality falls sharply to a very low value and urine flow increases until the entire water load has been excreted. This is the phenomenon of normal water diuresis.

In the second column are shown the events that would ensue were such an infusion to be given to a patient in a continuing antidiuretic state. This is characteristic after a surgical operation, after severe injury, or with acute disease. It will be noted that the serum osmolality falls and remains at a lower value. The patient's weight gain is maintained. Free water excretion is never achieved and the urine osmolality remains fixed. Urine flow shows no response. The water load is largely retained.

In the third column are shown the events in solute diuresis. These may be demonstrated in a patient who is excreting a large amount of endogenous solutes (such

as urea or glucose) or in a patient being given a large amount of exogenous solute (such as mannitol or the products of a tube feeding). It will be noted that the serum osmolality falls but then rises slowly, and that weight is lost after the infusion but not very rapidly. Most important is the fact that the patient remains in negative free water excretion throughout. By this is meant that the solute concentration in the urine is always higher than in the plasma.

Because of the fact that large amounts of urine are formed when solute diuresis occurs (even in the presence of antidiuresis) negative free water excretion may reach a very high value. Urine flow is increased. This situation is seen after surgical injury or operation when, in the presence of antidiuresis, excessive amounts of solute are presented for excretion; the dextran-treated burn is a good example. Urine flow is high but the water excretion is always negative.

Antidiuresis, alone, does not produce a low urine volume; with a solute load it may involve very large urine volumes. In most surgical and traumatic situations, low urine volumes are a result of low renal blood flow rather than increased renal tubular activity. It is for this reason that the urine volume is such a good index of tissue perfusion in hypotensive-hypovolemic situations.

content. This is guarded by the renal tubule. As glomerular filtrate passes down the tubule, it contains approximately 97 per cent water. In the most proximal tubule isoosmotic reabsorption occurs; farther on salt is abstracted from this water, and acid-base balance is regulated by the exchange of cations and by ammonia secretion. As the water passes into the distal renal tubule, its water resorption is governed by posterior pituitary antidiuretic hormone. Finally, in a most distal site, some additional water is resorbed independent of hormone action.

1. Antidiuretic Hormone

This interesting hormone exerts a unique effect on urine osmolality. If the hormone is virtually absent, urine osmolality drops sharply to 40 to 100 mO. per l. When urine is being secreted in this very dilute form (corresponding in normal individuals to a specific gravity of about 1.004), the urine is as dilute as the blood, and large amounts of water are lost. If water loading has just occurred, as is the case with a large infusion or drink of water, the excretion of such a dilute urine is protecting the plasma osmolality from dilution.

When there is lack of antidiuretic hormone, this diuresis is producing dangerous renal water loss, as in diabetes insipidus. As unregulated water loss proceeds in diabetes insipidus, the plasma sodium concentration and osmolality rise to dangerous levels (350 to 370 mO. per l.), volume is reduced, and finally renal function fails. As glomerular filtration falls the reabsorption of water in the most distal tubular site continues, and osmolality rises despite the lack of antidiuretic hormone. This sequence may be observed in injury or surgery of the brain, where diabetes insipidus is produced by injury to the supraoptic nuclei, and may go unrecognized until severe hypertonicity and oliguria are established.

The antidiuretic hormone can produce maximal distal reabsorption of water in the renal tubule when filtrate volume is normal or low, and the urine osmolality may rise abruptly to 1200 to 1400 mO. per l., which is approximately its maximal concentration. This corresponds roughly to a urine specific gravity of about 1.040. Here the kidney is actively saving water to prevent further dehydration. In individuals working in the hot sun, soldiers fighting in hot or tropical areas, or the sick surgical patient with a high fever and large extrarenal losses of salt and water, the urine osmolality should be in this range between 700 and 1200 mO. per l., providing total outputs are low and the supraoptic-hypophyseal tract uninjured.

In sharp contrast to this highly concentrated urine of low volume in the compensatory antidiuresis of dehydration or desalting, is the copious urine volume produced when there is a large solute discharge even in the face of a marked secretion of antidiuretic hormone. Antidiuretic hormone cannot lower urine volume and raise concentration to maximum figures when glomerular filtrate is very large in volume, high in content of nonresorbed solute, and tubular urine flow very rapid. Characteristic of this state of solute discharge during antidiuresis is urine of fixed osmolality and specific gravity (500 mO. per l., and specific gravity about 1.018), a linear relation between flow and solute, and negative free water clearance despite high urine volume.

2. Post-traumatic Antidiuresis

Throughout a twenty-four-hour period, the water-conserving mechanism goes through a regular cycle. At night, water reabsorption in the distal renal tubule is maximal in healthy individuals; comparatively little urine is formed, and that at rather high osmolality. During the day, this is released and more urine is formed at lower osmolality, presumably as the ingestion of water and solute occurs during meals. This even cycle is interrupted by injury.

The secretion of antidiuretic hormone seems to escape from its normal control and overact in acute and chronic surgical disease, either because of stimulation of the posterior pituitary gland by volume reduction or by trauma or because of failure of the liver to inactivate the hormone. The most characteristic finding is that of continued antidiuretic activity in the face of plasma hypotonicity. As just mentioned, in the normal individual a hypotonic

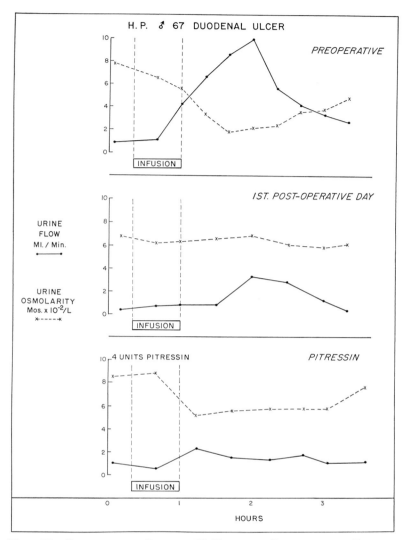

Figure 55. PHENOMENA OF DIURESIS. II. EFFECT OF OPERATION AND PITRESSIN

This patient was studied on three different occasions, once prior to operation, once on the first postoperative day, and once some time later when he was given an injection of Pitressin (vasopressin). Each time he was studied, the urine flow and osmolality were measured, and he was given a standard infusion of 5 per cent dextrose in water.

It will be noted that prior to the operation he excreted the water normally, as one might expect from "water diuresis" in the previous chart. After operation he was unable to excrete the water normally and this was also true when he was given vasopressin.

This type of change is most characteristically produced by dehydration. It is also seen in the normally-hydrated postoperative or post-traumatic patient; it may be triggered off by acute volume reduction, or by some effect of the anesthetic or by the trauma itself.

plasma results in a profuse water diuresis. In surgical disease this is not the case. A hypotonic plasma is inappropriately maintained by antidiuresis.

3. Water Clearance

As the isotonic filtrate passes from glomerulus into proximal tubule, it is isotonically absorbed. Further down, water is resorbed and the osmolality of the urine, which left the glomerulus at about 295 mO. per l., rises. If we know the final solute concentrations in urine and plasma it is a simple matter to calculate the amount of "free" water (water without solute) that has been withdrawn from the distal tubule. This result is called "negative clearance of free water"; it indicates the normal action of antidiuretic hormone. Normal figures are −1 to −2 ml. per minute (1 to 2 ml. of water resorbed per minute over and above solute). In solute diuresis, very large urine outputs may occur with negative

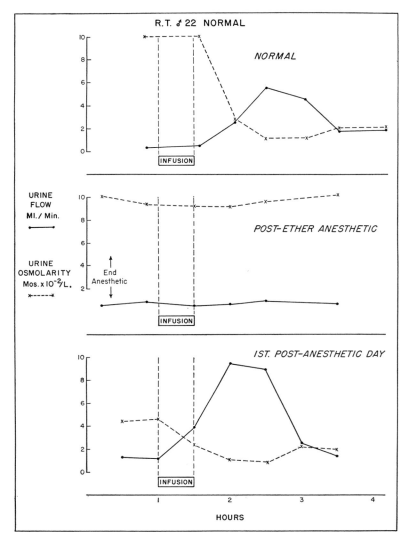

Figure 56.   PHENOMENA OF DIURESIS. III. EFFECTS OF ETHER

Studies similar to that in the previous chart. It will be noted that ether anesthesia alone has an effect similar to that of trauma and vasopressin.

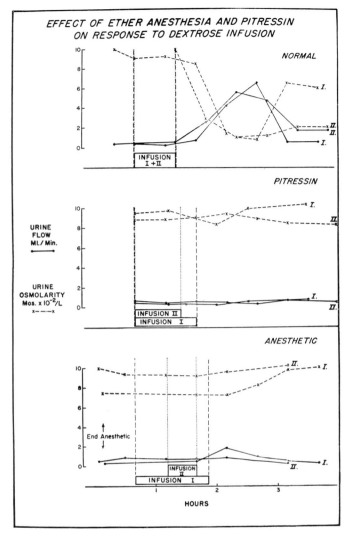

Figure 57. PHENOMENA OF DIURESIS. IV. PITRESSIN AND ANESTHETICS

Study similar to that in the previous two charts. It will be noted that anesthesias resemble Pitressin (vasopressin) in their effect on the ability to produce free water diuresis.

clearance of free water, indicating that large outputs can occur in antidiuresis if there is an obligatory solute (such as urea, mannitol, dextran, or sugar) in the urine in large quantities.

If this same measurement and calculation is made after giving large amounts of water or a large intravenous injection of water (with dextrose), it is found that more salt than water is resorbed from the tubular urine. The urine osmolality thus falls from 295 mO. per l. down to 150 mO. per l., and there is "positive

free water clearance" or "free water diuresis." This condition indicates that there is present no active antidiuretic hormone. This is virtually never seen early after trauma.

An understanding of the solute-diuresis phenomena in relation to tubular function may be aided by the following. A normal diet contains about 1200 mO. of solute for excretion; on pure carbohydrate this solute load falls to 200 mO. In heavy tube feedings this may rise to more than 1600 mO. per day. If the kidney is working very well (concentrat-

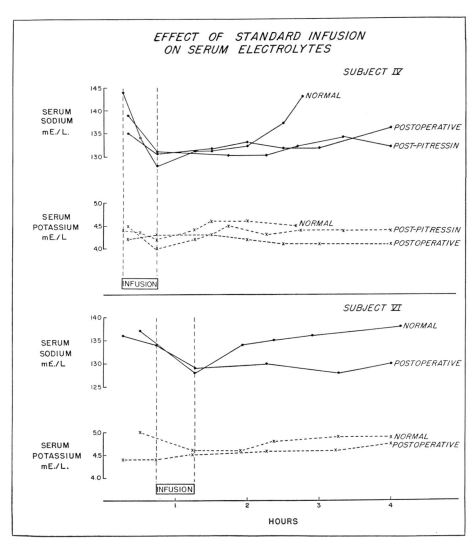

Figure 58.   PHENOMENA OF DIURESIS. V. EFFECT OF STANDARD INFUSION ON SERUM ELECTROLYTES

It will be noted here that, in the normal patient, a standard infusion produces a transient reduction in the serum sodium concentration. There is comparatively little effect on the serum potassium concentration.

In the postoperative or post-Pitressin situation (antidiuresis) the water load is not excreted and the hyponatremia is maintained.

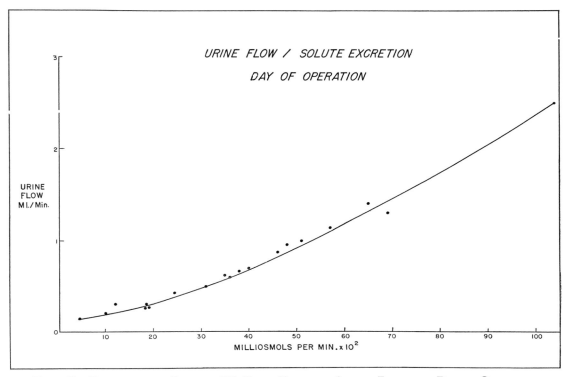

Figure 59. PHENOMENA OF DIURESIS. VI. URINE FLOW AND SOLUTE EXCRETION DAY OF OPERATION

Studies after subtotal gastrectomy.

It will be noticed that the urine flow in milliliters per minute is a linear function of the solute excretion. This is a manifestation of the solute diuresis phenomenon in an antidiuretic state. Were free water diuresis to be established at any time, the urine flow curve would depart sharply above the dots that represent solute excretion.

ing up to 1400 mO. per l.) it can excrete 1600 mO. in 1140 ml. Actually, at such high volumes of urine in solute loading one never sees such concentrated urine. But if the kidney (by loss of some nephrons and disease of the survivors) cannot concentrate over 400 mO. per l., then the 1600 mO. of dietary end-products in a tube feeding will pull out 4000 ml. of water for its excretion, this water loss producing hypernatremia and hypertonicity. Furthermore, the solute load in itself, by presenting very large volumes of urine to the distal tubule, tends to diminish the efficiency of water reabsorption and therefore to dehydrate. It is for this reason that infusions of 10 per cent dextrose are mildly dehydrating

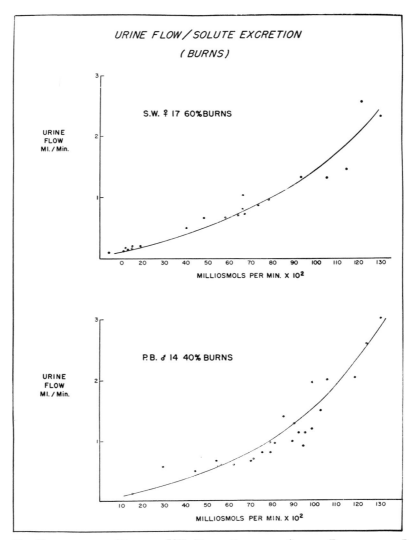

Figure 60. PHENOMENA OF DIURESIS. VII. URINE FLOW AND SOLUTE EXCRETION IN BURNS

Interpretation is the same as in Figure 59.

After burns, over a period of several days, the urine flow-solute relationship is that of solute diuresis in an anti-diuretic state. If one wishes to increase urine flow during this period it can most easily be done by providing extra solute. This can be given as the low molecular-weight fraction of dextran, or as some other crystalloid such as mannitol or urea.

even in normal people, and it is this mechanism that produces the solute-loading hypertonicity of tube feeding.

"Water diuresis" is that produced by copious water ingestion in the normal state; there is a large urine volume of low solute concentration. "Solute diuresis" is that produced by large amounts of unresorbed solute in the tubular urine; there is a moderately high volume of urine of fixed solute concentration.

Such data on water clearance are not needed for the daily care of surgical patients, but the underlying concepts are. An understanding of diuresis, antidiuresis, solute diuresis, free water excretion, and their surgical variations is greatly illuminated by these concepts and is most useful in daily bedside care.

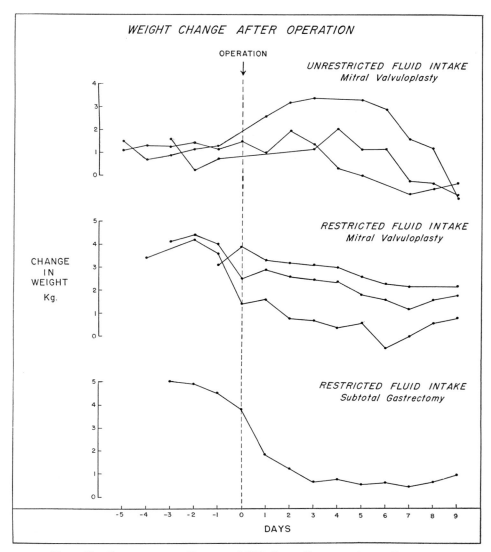

Figure 61. PHENOMENA OF DIURESIS. VIII. FLUID BALANCE AFTER OPERATION

In this chart are shown three types of regimens. Above are shown the effects on body weight of unrestricted fluid intake in patients after mitral valvuloplasty. It will be noticed that in this particular disease, existing with chronic congestive heart failure, there is a very strong tendency to retain water. The patient readily gains weight after operation and this weight gain is associated with profound hyponatremia. Similar findings are noted in pericardial disease, chronic pulmonary disease, severe chronic parenchymatous liver disease, and chronic renal failure. Note that this water loading is on the basis of unrestricted oral intake.

In the middle line is shown the effect, in a similar group of patients, when the fluid intake was restricted.

It will be noticed that weight gain was not as great. The tendency to hyponatremia was also less marked.

Below, for contrast, is shown the effect of subtotal gastrectomy in a healthy young man. This is the typical weight curve after elective, soft-tissue, civilian operation in the absence of chronic visceral disease. The weight loss, as pointed out elsewhere, is due to the lysis of lean tissue and fat. Loss the day of operation is due to removal of the pathologic specimen itself, often weighing 250 to 850 gm. There also is a tendency to water loading here but it is of minor importance as long as the surgeon does not give the patient too much water by vein.

CHAPTER 18

Extracellular Volume Changes: Contraction and Expansion; Sequestered Edema; External Loss; Volume Regulation

Section I. Possible Changes and Range of Values

The normal extracellular phase occupies about 20 per cent of body weight, its true volume, as mentioned in Part I, being virtually indefinable as well as unmeasurable. The fluid phase of the extracellular volume is found in plasma and in lymph and tissue spaces, and a portion of it is in the transcellular water of the joint spaces, spinal fluid, and gastrointestinal tract. This fluid phase can contract and expand over wide limits. In dehydration and desalting water loss it would be expected to contract; in overhydration it must be expected to expand.

Although this important volume of body water can both contract and expand, it much more commonly expands than contracts. The literature on surgical water balance has been largely devoted to its contraction in water-losing states. Although there are few recorded measurements of an actually contracted extracellular fluid, we assume it must contract because of the associated changes, and this is a reasonable assumption, although unproven.

Acute loss of water and salt, with contraction of the extracellular fluid, is an important and potentially lethal event. Expansion of the extracellular fluid is more apt to be chronic
Page 298

and is much commoner because it is produced by a wide variety of conditions, including chronic malnutrition, sepsis, heart failure, liver disease, kidney disease, burns, acute trauma, and most postoperative states. Many writers on this subject persist in an almost compulsive focus on "deficits" when "excesses" are more common, more chronic, and of equal importance.

By inference we observe contraction of the extracellular fluid amounting to about one-half its volume in lethal desalting water loss. Expansion of the extracellular fluid has been measured at twice the normal value in the extreme overhydration of congestive heart failure.

Theoretically, there are six types of change in volume and concentration of the extracellular phase:

contraction of the extracellular fluid—
    (1) hypotonic,
    (2) isotonic, and
    (3) hypertonic;
expansion of the extracellular fluid—
    (4) hypotonic,
    (5) isotonic, and
    (6) hypertonic.

This nicely logical system of description of changes in extracellular fluid is not as useful as one might expect because the *rate* of change is also a very important clinical consideration, as are the degree of participation of cell water (in part a function of rate of change), the area of extracellular fluid involved (tissue water as contrasted with fluid in the gastrointestinal tract), and the possibility of simultaneous expansion in one area and contraction elsewhere (as evidenced, for instance, by hemoconcentration as edema forms in burns).

Section II.   Sequestered Edema; Local Expansion of Extracellular Fluid; Transcellular Expansion of Water

Many types of expansion of extracellular fluid in the surgical patient are due to local processes (such as trauma, burns, or infection), which accumulate extracellular fluid and "rob" the rest of the body of water, protein, and salt, producing a relative dehydration elsewhere. This phenomenon was first described in conjunction with burns but is also found in many other surgical conditions. The total volume of extracellular fluid is large, while the volumes of effective extracellular fluid and plasma are critically reduced.

A. LOSS OF EFFECTIVE BODY WATER WITHIN THE BODY

The effective body water is that portion of the body water actively engaged in exchange (across body membranes) of the solutes that are involved in life processes. In a normal individual in good health, all the water in the body is so involved. In an individual with intestinal obstruction, there may be as much as 5000 ml. of body water within the lumen of large, flabby, distended, edematous loops of bowel. This water contains a large amount of electrolyte, and it is essentially sequestered from the rest of the body water because the normal osmotic gradients across the gut wall have been abolished by distention. The current of flow goes therefore from the plasma to the lumen of the gut instead of vice versa, and we have a new area of body water formed which is lost to the *milieu intérieur*. This is a common example of loss of water and electrolyte from effective body water, occurring within the body as a specialized area of extracellular fluid expansion.

This effect may be observed in the following conditions:

(1) intestinal obstruction;
(2) acute gastric dilatation;
(3) a burn—this being the classic example of the accumulation of extracellular fluid in subcutaneous tissue;
(4) a crush or other massive trauma to a limb;
(5) acute spreading cellulitis;
(6) a large serous effusion, such as peritonitis, ascites, pleural effusion; or
(7) a postoperative area of accumulation after extensive dissection.

There are other examples of local accumulation of fluid. The hydrarthrosis associated with an injured knee and the edema associated with infection represent the same phenomenon. Yet here the amounts of fluid involved are usually so small that they do not significantly alter the total water and electrolyte available for circulation.

Losses occurring within the body have an effect on the remainder of effective body water. Pathologic accumulations of fluid other than whole blood within the body may be graded according to their rate of formation and their protein concentration.

1.   Rate of Accumulation

The protein concentration in the accumulated fluid and the rate at which it forms determine the nature of the defect produced in the remaining body water, its effect on the plasma volume (and therefore on the hematocrit), the blood pressure, and renal function.

Those accumulations of fluid which form rapidly and which are high in protein content will deplete the plasma volume and will produce a rapid rise in the hematocrit, fall in blood volume, and associated circulatory changes ending in shock. Dilution of the extracellular fluid with cell water will be small, and reduction of volume rather than hypotonicity will be the first result.

Those accumulations of fluid which form slowly or which are low in protein will draw their water from all the body water—intra- and extracellular—the size of the fraction drawn from extracellular water being a function of the rate of the accumulation of the parasitic edema. The cell water dilutes the extracellular fluid and sodium concentration falls, the potassium being excreted. The rise in hematocrit is therefore much slower. Effects on plasma volume, blood pressure, and urine flow are more delayed. Hypotonicity is more prominent. Yet, when the hematocrit rise finally does occur, it indicates a very profound alteration in volume of effective body water.

As an example of this differentiation, let us contrast a burn with intestinal obstruction. The burned patient accumulates a considerable protein-rich fluid in the edema fluid under the burn in the first twelve hours. This depletes his plasma volume, and his hematocrit rises rapidly. The volume can quite effectively be restored, however, by giving plasma in adequate amounts. Dislocation of cell water has occurred, but it is small in amount as compared with the plasma shift. The sequestered edema has formed rapidly, is high in protein content, and has largely been at the expense of the plasma volume.

Now consider a patient with ileal obstruction who has (over a period of forty-eight hours) accumulated a large volume of fluid (5000 to 9000 ml.) in the gut, has lost additional fluid as vomitus, and is found now to have a hematocrit of 55. This hematocrit elevation has occurred not merely by the withdrawal of fluid out of the plasma, but also by withdrawal of fluid from the entire extracellular phase and from the total volume of body water. The total amount of fluid lost into this sequestered edema in the gut and to the outside to produce this hematocrit elevation is far greater than that sequestered in an early burn, and the change in plasma volume bespeaks a much greater total dislocation of fluid. Therapy becomes a more complex problem. The maintenance of normal blood volume is compromised by plasma loss; in addition both extracellular and intracellular water have suffered extensive losses the replacement of which is vital. Here, in contrast to the burn, the edema formation and fluid loss have progressed more gradually, low in protein content and at the proportional expense of all phases of total body water, not plasma alone.

2. Classification of Sequestered Edemas

Basing a classification of pathologic accumulations of water within the body on their rate of formation and protein content, one arrives at the following list:

- (a) pathologic accumulations forming rapidly within the body and high in protein content:
  - (1) burn,
  - (2) peritonitis,
  - (3) postoperative effusions and infections,
  - (4) wound collections and crush—also high in erythrocytes,
  - (5) collections proximal to venous obstruction such as portal or iliac thrombosis,
- (b) pathologic accumulations within the body, slower to form and lower in protein content:
  - (1) fluid within the lumen of the gut, as in intestinal obstruction without vascular impairment, in gastric dilatation or obstruction, and
  - (2) accumulations in serous cavities in response to chronic visceral disease, such as cardiac and liver disease.

These fluid accumulations within the body thus produce a lowering of effective body water; plasma volume reduction depends on rate and protein content; hypotonicity depends on the addition of sodium-free water; acid-base changes depend on the nature of the fluid accumulated and are usually minor. The following facts explain the effect of these pathologic accumulations on plasma chemistry.

(1) The loss of protein (which is mostly albumin) comes at the expense of the plasma, lowering the plasma volume and raising the hematocrit rapidly.

(2) Acid-base changes are usually secondary to low blood flow (renal acidosis), though on occasion, as in gastric dilatation, sequestration of fluid can of itself produce a marked acid-base change.

(3) The Gibbs-Donnan effect is inconsequential between plasma water and the fluid in these pathologic fluid accumulations; they are always isosmotic with plasma. For this reason, they do not by themselves produce a lowering of the plasma tonicity or sodium concentrations.*

(4) New sodium-free water must be added to the system in order to lower the salt concentration, a fact basic to the treatment of this phenomenon.

The lowering of electrolyte concentration which is so characteristic of these fluid accumulations thus arises from three causes:

(a) the infusion of salt-free water by the attending surgeon,
(b) the accumulation of cellular water in the extracellular phase, or
(c) the accumulation of salt-free water on the basis of fat oxidation.

An impressive body of evidence supports the concept that in severe illness or after trauma there is a tendency for sodium to move into a new site, probably muscle cells.†

---

* This fact seems to be difficult for many to understand. An analogy would be that of salt water circulating through a hose system: if the hose should suddenly develop a weakness and a large bubble of dilatation (or a leak) that lowered its pressure and diminished its effectiveness, the concentration of salt in the system would not be lowered even though pressure and flow were grossly changed.

† Where muscle is physically crushed or gangrenous, complete sodium-potassium exchange occurs; this is a special case and does not enter the pathologic biochemistry of sequestered edema.

This factor also lowers sodium concentration in the extracellular phase of the body. This is of minor import and not as important in lowering electrolyte concentration as the dilutional factors mentioned above.

The normal manner of release of the pathologic accumulation of fluid has an important effect on the nature of the treatment that should be given. In the case of a burn, the pathologic accumulation in the burn edema is ultimately reabsorbed. This is important in treating the burn, particularly in burns of limited extent in older people. The patient should not be overloaded with fluid, as he must later resorb it all. In sharp contrast, the gut fluid of intestinal obstruction should be removed by intubation to permit the gut to regain its normal caliber, muscular tone, and vascularity. Where there is a large intraluminal accumulation of fluid in intestinal obstruction, a very large amount must therefore be accounted for in treatment. In the case of postoperative effusion, infection, and other such accumulations, resorption also will occur if the patient's circulation is maintained and infection is controlled; it is a more gradual process.

The edema fluid seen in congestive heart failure may not properly be referred to as "loss of effective body water." So far as anybody knows, it is involved in the exchange of water, electrolyte, and metabolites just like any other body fluid, but it has slower exchange rates. However, its great volume and the problems imposed by its disposition, excretion, and resorption do partake of some of the features of the pathologic water accumulations of a post-traumatic type. There is the same tendency for hypotonicity, in this case from water ingestion in the face of the strong antidiuresis of chronic heart disease.

Section III.   External Losses: Dehydration and Desalting

Bearing in mind the importance of these fluid-dislocating processes due to pathologic accumulation and maldistribution of fluid within the body, we turn now to external loss.

A. DEHYDRATION VERSUS DESALTING

Changes in plasma concentrations are rarely due to external loss of fluid alone but are the compound result of losses and dislocations of fluid, the nature of treatment, ingress of cell water, fat oxidation, and pulmonary and renal compensatory mechanisms. It is appropriate therefore to scrutinize the term "dehydration" to find out just what it means. If an orange is allowed to lie in the sun, it loses water and shrivels up. The concentration of its solutes rises abruptly. It is dehydrated. If human plasma is placed in a vacuum distillation outfit in which the pump is then turned on, water is taken off and the plasma becomes dehydrated. If a man lies in the desert sun without water or if he floats on the glassy tropic seas in a life-raft, he becomes dehydrated. In all these situations of true dehydration, concentrations of solutes rise because of the removal of water; true dehydration is desiccation. The best term is "dehydration-desiccation."

At some point in the dehydration of all living things, the level of concentration of solutes in water rises as the volume of the water diminishes. It rises until all the water is gone, at which time the concentration of solute in solid theoretically reaches infinity and the compounds become solid instead of liquid.

True dehydration is therefore characterized by loss of water and a rising concentration of solutes in the system that remains. This is a relatively rare occurrence in surgical practice, and the term "dehydration" should therefore be used with hesitation and respect. The term should be reserved exclusively for a loss predominantly of water followed by a rise in solute concentrations: drying-out or desiccation.

For the much commoner loss of water with salt there is no good single word like the French *déchloruration*, but since one never loses salt without water, these states can be termed "desalting water loss." Where solute protein is also lost in high concentration, the term "plasma loss" is reasonable, since it involves protein, salts, crystalloids, and water in approximately the relationships in which they are found in plasma.

And finally there is blood loss, a special sort of water loss, more rapid than the others, containing red cells, and highly specific in its effects, already discussed in Part II.

B. THE MEANING OF HEMOCONCENTRATION

True dehydration produces a rise in the concentrations of all solutes; desalting water loss may only increase the concentration of erythrocytes. Both results might be called "hemoconcentration." Here again closer definition will help.

(1) *Hemoconcentration with respect to erythrocytes alone:* the situation found in pure plasma loss as in burns or peritonitis. It is best referred to as "erythroconcentration," an unwieldy term.

(2) *Hemoconcentration with respect to red cells and protein:* the situation found in early acute intestinal obstruction, pancreatic fistula, acute gastric obstruction and/or dilatation, or rapid extrarenal salt loss. The hematocrit found here is not as readily elevated as it is in a burn. Protein concentration rises early.

(3) *Hemoconcentration with respect to erythrocytes, protein, and electrolyte:* the situation found in true desiccation-dehydration. Because of the fact that the total osmotic pressure of the plasma (as distinct from the colloid osmotic pressure) is in part a function of the sodium concentration and is determined largely by the total electrolyte concentration, the loss of water alone from the plasma produces an elevation in concentration of any solute one wishes to measure, as already mentioned, and the total osmolality rises. There are linear increases in the concentration of erythrocytes and in plasma protein concentration, but these may not be quite so immediately evident.

Let us consider a plasma sodium concentration of 155 mE. per l. This is a very abnormal and potentially dangerous situation if due to the loss of pure water, as in a starving man in the desert on a hot day, or a burned patient with a tracheotomy. Yet it represents an increase of only 13 mE. per l. in sodium concentration, somewhat less than 10 per cent. In terms of protein concentration, if the norm for the patient is around 6.5 gm. per 100 ml., this would correspond to a protein concentration of only 7.1 gm. per 100 ml. This would not be striking or immediately serious or pathologic; normal protein values are more variable than are those of sodium. On the score of erythroconcentration, assuming a normal hematocrit to be 45, this degree of desiccation would correspond to an hematocrit of only 49. This is high enough to excite suspicion but does not appear as ominous at first glance as it truly is or as a sodium concentration of 155 mE. per l. would. Dehydration of 9 per cent of body water (about 4500 ml.) in normal man therefore produces effects more apparent initially in terms of plasma sodium concentration, or in total osmolality (which in such a case would rise from 290 to 316 mO. per l.). This is the nature of the hemoconcentration in hypertonic contraction of the extracellular fluid, and is typical of dehydration-desiccation.

Stated otherwise, the constancy of the upper limit of plasma electrolyte concentrations is so impressive in the normal individual that loss of pure water is most evident in terms of changes in electrolyte concentrations. Since the osmoreceptors of the central nervous system respond to the effective osmotic pressure of the extracellular water, it is the change in extracellular electrolyte concentration that is not only most evident to the surgeon but also most evident to the patient's cells, and specifically to his osmoreceptor. It is the rise in sodium concentration that stimulates renal tubular water conservation via the osmoreceptors and the posterior pituitary.

If dehydration were the only cause of plasma hypertonicity, it would be a simple matter. Unfortunately, plasma hypertonicity can also be caused by giving the patient large loads of solutes, particularly when he exhibits certain types of renal insufficiency. The hypertonicity of desiccation-dehydration should therefore be distinguished sharply from the hypertonicity associated with the unregulated excretion of solute loads in the presence of renal disease, as described later in this chapter. Both produce hypertonicity, but involve different mechanisms.

Late-stage dehydration with hemoconcentration of protein, cells, and salt is associated with increased blood viscosity.

True dehydration-desiccation, producing plasma hypertonicity, is such a rarity in surgical practice that one may go through a year of work on a busy surgical service, caring for many emergency cases as well as elective surgical cases, and yet treat but a relatively few instances. What then has become of our old familiar antagonist known as "dehydration," which is responsible for such a tonnage of literature, and seemingly occurred so frequently? It is to be found in desalting water loss.

C. DESALTING WATER LOSS; EXTRARENAL LOSSES

The loss of water and electrolyte through channels other than the normal renal regulatory mechanism is responsible for the great majority of deficit abnormalities in surgical patients. The losses may be considered as being losses of the effective body water to the outside as contrasted to those losses (dislocations) within the body, already described as sequestered expansions of extracellular fluid. These losses produce extracellular-fluid contraction which, because of the ingress of sodium-free water from cells and oxidation of fat, is usually or ultimately hypotonic.

1. Losses from the Intestinal Tract

Extrarenal losses comprise the most common group of defects of metabolism of water and electrolyte in surgical patients; losses through the gastrointestinal tract in turn constitute the commonest form of extrarenal loss. The renal response to this extrarenal loss is of importance in its treatment. The classification of these losses depends upon the electrolyte composition of the fluid and the rate at which the fluid is lost. The rate of loss is determined by the nature of the pathologic process, and the composition by the level in the gut or the viscus from which the loss emanates.

Electrolyte composition of intestinal losses may be divided into four general categories; all are isosmotic with plasma (about 290 mO. per l.).

(a) *Highly acid gastric juice.* Sodium and potassium concentrations are low, the hydrogen ion concentration and chloride concentrations are high (*p*H 1.5–2.5).

Average values are:

Sodium	45 mE. per l.
Potassium	30 mE. per l.
Hydrogen ion	70 mE. per l. (pH 1.5)
Chloride	120 mE. per l.
Bicarbonate	25 mE. per l.

(b) *Gastric juice low in acidity* (as found in carcinoma of the stomach). Sodium and potassium concentrations are higher and hydrogen ion concentration much lower (pH 5.0–5.5).

Average values are:

Sodium	100 mE. per l.
Potassium	45 mE. per l.
Hydrogen ion	0.015 mE. per l. (pH 5.5)
Chloride	115 mE. per l.
Bicarbonate	30 mE. per l.

(c) *Losses from the small bowel.* The fluid lost is slightly alkaline in reaction, and with the predominant base sodium (pH 5.0–8.0). In certain instances, particularly low ileal obstruction and ileostomy obstruction, the potassium concentration may be surprisingly high (40–70 mE. per l.).

Average values are:

Sodium	120 mE. per l.
Potassium	20 mE. per l.
Chloride	110 mE. per l.
Bicarbonate	30 mE. per l.

(d) *Loss through the large bowel*, characteristically small. If the losses are increased, as in diarrhea, the chemical characteristics are those of low ileal loss.

In addition, bile and pancreatic juice may be lost in an almost pure state and impose remarkable degrees of abnormality. Bile itself is quite alkaline (pH 8.0) and its loss in any quantity rapidly produces acidosis. Its sodium concentration is rarely higher than 140 mE. per l.

Pancreatic juice is remarkable as being a fluid in which osmotic work has been expended by an organ to concentrate sodium ion more densely than in plasma. The sodium concentration in pancreatic juice sometimes runs as high as 185 mE. per l. Sudden loss of a liter or two of this juice is the most spectacular and classic example of hypertonic sodium loss. This rapidly reduces the plasma sodium concentration, the volume of extracellular fluid, and the pH, and produces a shocklike state with severe subtraction acidosis.

When the body loses fluid that is isosmotic with plasma, the effects on the water left behind depend on the acid-base pattern of the fluid lost, its protein content, the rate of loss, and the ingress of sodium-free water from the cell and fat. Those fluids lost from the body which have a high protein concentration will affect plasma volume sooner and more profoundly as already mentioned, with appropriately severe effects on the hematocrit, blood volume, and glomerular filtrate.

On the basis of these variables we find a spectrum of effects determined in part by the loss and in part by the rate at which sodium-free water arises in the body and is retained there. The chief sources of this water, as mentioned, are body fat, whose oxidation releases slightly over a liter of water for each kilogram burned, and the cell. Sodium-free water may also be added to this system intravenously by the surgeon, furthering the dilution. Finally trauma, by inhibiting water diuresis and increasing both the oxidation of fat and the release of cell water, greatly accentuates this dilutional tendency in extrarenal desalting water loss.

2. The Protein Spectrum

Representative examples of this spectrum of hemoconcentration-dilution factors are seen in three categories.

(1) *Fluid loss high in protein:* hemoconcentration is most evident in the rise in hematocrit and fall in plasma volume; hypotonicity is slow to appear. Profuse purulent discharge, peritonitis, and empyema are examples.

(2) *Protein loss less remarkable; hematocrit rise less pronounced; hypotonicity more evident:* examples are pyloric obstruction, intestinal obstruction, biliary fistula, and malfunctioning ileostomy drainage.

(3) *Hypotonicity much more marked because of traumatic mobilization of cellular water, fat oxidation, and antidiuresis:* examples are operation during gastric or intestinal obstruction, postoperative diarrhea—enterocolitis—and ileus after peritoneal operations.

3. Acid-Base Effects

The pH of the fluid lost is the most important single factor in determining the acid-base disorder left behind in the body as a whole. When strongly acid gastric juice is lost, the patient develops alkalosis. The anion deficit resulting from chloride loss is compensated osmotically by increase in bicarbonate; severe hypochloremia quickly results, before hypotonicity is manifest. When strongly alkaline juices are lost from the gut, the patient develops acidosis. The complicating factors in this otherwise simple picture lie in four areas.

(1) *Starvation* tends to produce ketosis and acidosis by incomplete oxidation of fat. This mechanism is much more marked in young children than it is in adults.

(2) *Dehydration* and *desalting* to the extent of producing reduced glomerular filtration or frank renal failure tend to result in renal acidosis by failure to excrete fixed acids.

(3) *Pulmonary compensatory mechanisms* may fail due to poor ventilation, and may modify the acid-base change; respiratory acidosis is then added.

(4) Where the patient is *postoperative* or *potassium loss* is prominent (or both), the tendency to excrete an *acid urine* greatly exaggerates any alkalotic trend.

The final acid-base change observed in the patient with extrarenal loss is therefore determined by the interplay of these five factors: the nature and rate of the extrarenal loss, the degree of starvation ketosis, the degree of renal acidosis, the nature of the pulmonary compensation, and the postoperative state.

4. The Rate Spectrum

The rates at which extrarenal losses may occur through the gastrointestinal tract are, to some extent, consistent; there seem to be "ceiling loss rates," which are rarely exceeded. In lesser degrees of illness, the loss is less rapid. Starting with the most rapid losses which occur from or into the gastrointestinal tract, we have a diminishing rate scale.

(1) *Acute Gastric Dilatation.* This is a dramatic event which may be lethal unless promptly recognized and treated. The rates at which very strongly acid juice may accumulate in the stomach under these circumstances, some of it expelled by vomiting, may exceed 5000 ml. in five or six hours. There is distention of the upper abdomen with a weak, thready pulse, cyanosis, shocklike state, and retching up small amounts of gastric juice. The picture is rapidly reversed by passage of a nasal tube, which encounters fluid and gas under pressure. Once the tube is inserted and placed on suction, further outpouring at the same rapid rate occurs for a short while, and then for two or three days there may be a continuous negative gastric balance but not at this same spectacular rate. This is one of the most rapid extrarenal losses seen in surgery. Unless it is treated promptly, an alkalotic and isotonic contraction of the extracellular fluid with hemoconcentration occurs, plus shock; in the acute state the loss is too rapid for transcapillary flow to "catch up" and refill the plasma phase of body water.

(2) *Massive Diarrhea.* The cholera-like picture of infantile diarrhea is fortunately a rare situation for the surgeon to treat. The rates of fluid loss can be so rapid as to produce hemoconcentration and death in twelve to eighteen hours, particularly in hot weather. The mechanism of death is almost identical with that described above in gastric dilatation, save that acidosis is the acute pH change. Fall in blood pressure is much more rapid than in gastric dilatation. The loss of fluid is so rapid that it is all at the expense of the extracellular phase despite its relatively low protein concentration. A low plasma volume, high hematocrit, low blood volume, and a shocklike state with renal vasoconstriction, anuria, and death rapidly result. The massive diarrhea seen with pseudomembranous enterocolitis, in untreated ulcerative colitis, and with a malfunctioning ileostomy falls into this same category but is not as rapid. With malfunctioning ileostomy, the loss runs from 1000 to 3000 ml. of fluid per day through the ileostomy or an accumulation of a like amount in the dilated gut proximally. The term "malfunctioning ileostomy" should probably be replaced by the term "terminal obstruction," since the diarrhea-like state with cramps and fluid loss is virtually always due to obstruction at the stoma and can be temporarily relieved by catheterization and placing the ileostomy catheter on siphon-suction. This is one of the few conditions in which extrarenal potassium losses are high, ranging up to 70 mE. per l. In these situations the restoration of plasma

volume is of first priority, and in acute hemo-concentrated oligemic shock from gut losses, the administration of plasma, albumin, or dextran may be an immediate necessity, against the urgent but long-term background therapy of saline solutions.

The treatment of such situations entirely with whole blood may have remarkable deleterious effects on renal function, probably a viscosity effect. Although the restoration of plasma volume is needed, the water:solute relation is clearly such as to require colloid-free water in replacement.

(3) *Intestinal Obstruction.* The rates of loss here are less rapid than those seen in acute gastric dilatation, ileostomy diarrhea, or cholera. As a round figure, mid-gut obstruction with vomiting and rapidly accumulating distention may account for the loss from the body of about 4000 ml. of fluid in the first thirty-six hours. The rate of loss after that is somewhat slower as the circulation fails and gut distention is so great as to interfere with blood supply and further transudation into the lumen.

(4) *Pancreatic, Biliary, and Small-Bowel Fistulas.* Here the loss rates are a good deal lower. A biliary fistula above complete obstruction at the ampulla of Vater rarely produces more than 1500 ml. of bile per day. The figures encountered in the literature as to the total biliary production must be based on some other sort of information, since losses of 2000 ml. and 3000 ml. are simply not seen in these circumstances. A pancreatic fistula rarely puts out more than 1500 ml. of fluid per day. As mentioned above, this is a peculiar fluid and the effects of this loss are quite devastating even though the total volume lost is not great. A fistula of the small bowel, due to necrosis of a loop with exteriorization of the abscess, produces an amount of fluid ranging from 1000 to 3000 ml. per day.

D. PATHOLOGIC RENAL LOSSES

Pathologic renal loss of water and/or salt may exist alone or in combination with other surgical complexities. In the latter instance it may go unrecognized and be a constant source of frustration to the surgeon, who relies so heavily on the homeostatic wisdom of the kidney.

Pathologic renal losses fall into these four groups:

   (a) *acute or chronic tubular disease—*
      (1) recovery from renal failure,
      (2) recovery from urinary obstruction, and
      (3) salt-losing nephritis;
   (b) *solute diuresis, often in combination with the above or due to—*
      (1) diabetes mellitus,
      (2) ureterosigmoidostomy,
      (3) obstructive uropathy, and
      (4) tube feeding;
   (c) *endocrine disorders—*
      (1) diabetes insipidus, and
      (2) insufficiency of the adrenal cortex;
   (d) *inappropriate volume-receptor activity*, with renal salt loss in hypotonic expansion of the extracellular fluid.

The above are dealt with as distinct entities in appropriate sections of the book (Part V dealing with renal and adrenal disease). A few brief comments follow.

Acute post-traumatic renal insufficiency* is associated with marked diminution in renal water loss. During the recovery phase, some patients pass through a period of days or weeks when renal tubular control of water and electrolyte excretion appears to be lost and large amounts of water and solute are excreted in the urine as a more or less continuous osmotic diuresis. This excretion may occur to an extent sufficient to produce dehydration, plasma volume deficit, and an elevation of hematocrit. The solute is urea; the nephrons act as though only a few were functioning and these crowded with a large solute load.

There are in addition some individuals

---

* This term will be used throughout this book to denote the sort of acute anuria seen in surgical and obstetrical patients. The pathologic entity has been referred to as the "crush syndrome," or "lower nephron nephrosis," and there are many other terms, including "acute tubular nephrosis," "ischemic nephrosis," "hemoglobinuric nephrosis." The term "acute post-traumatic renal insufficiency" seems to be the most satisfactory to denote the entire group.

with salt-losing nephritis in whom renal tubular disease, possibly on a vascular basis, is associated with a loss of sodium and other electrolytes far in excess of renal losses. The normal kidney, faced with a plasma sodium concentration of less than 135 mE. per l., will quite efficiently conserve sodium so that loss of sodium in the urine is practically zero. In the presence of abnormal renal loss of salt, such a urine will continue to show sodium concentrations from 30 to 60 mE. per l.

Apparent release from the influence of the aldosterone that is seen with an expanded hypotonic extracellular fluid volume will also result in a high concentration of sodium in the urine with low concentrations in the plasma. This is described below, under volume-receptor phenomena.

Since the normal renal defense of plasma osmolality consists in a very sensitive regulation of the sodium concentration in the urine from the distal tubules, it is to be expected that breakdown of this mechanism results in lowering of plasma concentrations of sodium.

Chronic arteriolar nephrosclerosis can inhibit the ability of the renal tubular cell to respond to a sodium-conserving stimulus. This is manifested by the continued loss of sodium in the urine in the face of a low plasma sodium concentration. Such a diagnosis is suspected when, with the patient's plasma sodium concentration low, a urine sample is found to have a sodium concentration of over 30 mE. per l. This urine sample must be collected under circumstances in which the patient is *not* receiving an intravenous infusion of sodium. If an intravenous infusion is being given at the time the urine is collected, there may be some spillover, which taints the urine with sodium, to an extent great enough to suggest pathologic renal conditions. A good method for studying this is on an overnight sample, providing the patient does not receive an intravenous infusion at night. If, with the patient's plasma sodium concentration low (below 130 mE. per l.), the urine sodium concentration is found to be elevated (above 30 mE.) on a specimen taken when the patient is not receiving intravenous sodium, one should make the diagnosis of

pathologic renal salt loss. The exact cause must await further diagnostic discriminations.

If the patient has adrenal failure, either partial or complete, whether or not he had had previously recognized Addison's disease, the urine sodium concentration is unexpectedly high in the face of a low plasma sodium concentration. Any degree of hypotension further suggests this difficulty. Adrenal failure as a cause of salt loss can be diagnosed by administering desoxycorticosterone or fluorohydrocortisone subcutaneously or intramuscularly, or giving the patient an intravenous infusion of 300 mg. of hydrocortisone over a twenty-four-hour period. Although hydrocortisone and cortisone are much less active in their salt-retaining properties than desoxycorticosterone, they will affect sodium resorption to some extent. If, in response to these hormones, the patient improves and the urinary sodium concentration drops off abruptly, the defect does not lie in the kidney itself but in the production of adrenal hormones which should regulate the function of the tubular cells of the kidney. The treatment of this acute condition is the administration of these hormones. When the crisis is over, one must discover whether or not the patient has chronic adrenal insufficiency requiring further treatment.

The treatment of pathologic renal salt loss in which there is nothing the matter with the adrenal glands (i.e., renal tubular disease) should be based on the intravenous restoration of daily renal salt losses. This is the sole exception to the general rule that renal losses of extracellular salts (sodium, chloride, and bicarbonate) should not be restored quantitatively each day since, with good regulatory diuresis, such replacement therapy would result in perpetuation of an undesirable defect and undo the good work of the kidneys.

E. SALT LOSSES FROM THE SKIN: SWEAT

Large losses of fluid through the skin, by virtue of sweating, are no longer of much importance in the daily management of civilian surgical patients. There was a day, before air conditioning, when operating rooms became extremely hot in the summer.

The unconscious patient could not complain of the heat. The almost universal desire of nurses to keep patients warm resulted in the wrapping of the patient in blankets which had frequently been given a good preliminary warming in the warming closet. This treatment must have produced a very considerable loss from the skin through sweating. It is our impression that this series of events is somewhat less common than it used to be. In military life or the tropics, this type of loss may still be of critical importance.

The sodium concentration in sweat is always hypotonic. Sweat is less concentrated than plasma and therefore its loss in large amounts will tend gradually to increase the sodium concentration in the body if nothing else is done. Stress and trauma tend further to diminish the sodium concentration in sweat, just as they do in the efflux from the renal tubule. This would suggest that the cell in the sweat gland is under somewhat the same steroidal influences as the renal tubule or, more likely, that all body cells respond in the same way and these cells are in a position to respond by diminishing sodium concentration in their exocrine secretion.

Anybody working in a hayfield in the hot sun has had the experience of drinking a lot of nice cold, crystal-clear water in response to a large sweat loss, only to find a few minutes later that he feels waterlogged. The conscious individual's normal compensation to large loss of sweat is the intake of sodium-free water. If this situation progresses further, it produces the hyponatremia seen in tropical workers who are given unlimited amounts of salt-free water. The association of muscular cramps and of prostration, coma, and death has been reported as a result of this sequence. The surgeon is not ordinarily called upon to deal with this problem unless he is in the military service, in which case heavy exercise under tropical conditions may be the cause. If suitable amounts of sodium and chloride are ingested with the water (as enteric coated tablets), dilutional hyponatremia will not occur. Sweat loss is a slow extrarenal desalting water loss; water ingestion and transcapillary flow keep up with it, so that hypotonicity

rather than contraction of volume is the most evident result. It is this secondary dilutional hypotonicity, not volume reduction, which produces the cramps.

The patient's state of consciousness is of signal importance in the management of sweat loss. If a soldier has been wounded under tropical conditions, with a great deal of sweating, and has lost consciousness, he can no longer tell you that he is thirsty. He needs water and salt in large amounts to balance his skin losses, and these cannot be properly compensated without a realistic evaluation of their quantity; if he is conscious, he needs some salt with his drinking water to avoid hypotonicity.

F. PULMONARY LOSSES OF WATER

The loss of water from the lungs is a normal continuing source of extrarenal loss. The normal resting adult male under moderate conditions of temperature and humidity loses about 500 to 750 ml. a day by this route, the female about 250 to 500 ml.

Fever and dyspnea are the factors above all others which increase this rate of pulmonary water loss. A patient with a fever of 104° F., breathing at the rate of 30 to 40 per minute, may lose as much water as 2500 ml. a day through the lungs. This figure is difficult to quantitate daily; it is a matter of clinical judgment to estimate it on the basis of the patient's body build, the fever, and the respiratory exchange. If the patient is being weighed daily, an estimate of total insensible loss may be made and in most circumstances the pulmonary water loss is the predominant feature of the total insensible loss.

The water lost from the lungs is pure distilled water, and it tends to produce hypertonicity of the body fluids unless compensated by appropriate water intake. Under ordinary circumstances in the normal individual and in most surgical situations, this factor is not important as a source of hypertonicity. Fever, dyspnea, heat, and tracheotomy increase this loss, and in patients with disease of the central nervous system who are unconscious, who may have rapid respiratory rates, and who are unable to respond to the normal sensation of thirst, severe degrees of hypertonicity may be produced by pulmonary loss alone. Other mechanisms, particularly heavy solute feedings administered by tube, and diabetes in-sipidus may accentuate the hypertonic trend of the unconscious patient with brain disease or injury.

Section IV. Overhydration and Hypotonicity: "Volume-Sensitive" Phenomena

Thus far we have been dealing with contractions of extracellular fluid: hypertonic (as in pulmonary dehydration-desiccation), isotonic (early change in massive gut losses), or hypotonic (the later compensated phases, or slower losses). We now turn to processes that expand the extracellular fluid diffusely—in contrast to the local pathologic accumulations previously mentioned.

The commonest is the combination of overhydration and antidiuresis, already mentioned. It would seem that the simplest method of producing hypotonic expansion of the extracellular fluid in the human body is to add too much water. This water would then distribute itself throughout the total body water and lower the osmolality of extracellular and intracellular fluids alike as well as the concentration of all solutes. Such a mechanism is easy to understand. The important point is that in the normal individual, this chain of events is very difficult to produce—in fact, almost impossible.

This can be readily proved by simple experiment in a volunteer subject. Give an intravenous injection of water without salt as 5 per cent glucose in water at a rapid rate and you find that it is extremely difficult to drive the plasma sodium concentration down. Instead, urine volume rises to high values and the plasma is unchanged.

Vasopressin alone, likewise, has little activity in producing dilution. If, however, the subject is given 3 units of aqueous vasopressin at the time when the water infusion is begun, severe hypotonicity with alarmingly uncomfortable symptoms and a gain in weight equal to the retained water is readily produced within a matter of minutes: *overhydration plus antidiuresis produces hypotonicity.*

The sources of water in this situation as it is seen in surgery are (as outlined above) exogenous water administered orally or parenterally, mobilization of cellular water, and oxidation of fat. The source of the antidiuretic tendency is not so clear-cut. It probably originates in the hypothalamus or the posterior pituitary, but whatever its origin, it is very prominent in patients suffering from acute disease, immediately after surgical operations or tissue injury, or in chronic disease of heart or liver.

Certain drugs accentuate the antidiuresis. Morphine is at times a strong stimulus to antidiuresis. Ether is the most potent antidiuretic anesthetic agent. Cyclopropane is somewhat less so. Pentothal–nitrous-oxide–curare and spinal anesthesia have virtually no antidiuretic effect.

A. SODIUM LOSS AS A FACTOR IN DILUTIONAL HYPOTONICITY

Sodium loss accentuates dilutional hypotonicity, and this accentuation is more marked the more concentrated the sodium in the solution being lost. Excessive potassium losses have the same effect, acting primarily on the other side of the cellular membrane, but producing hypotonicity as surely as sodium loss plus overhydration. Most significant with respect to sodium metabolism is the fact that hypotonicity due to sodium loss alone is extremely rare in surgery. Change in the volume of body water is a commoner cause of change in sodium concentration than is change in total body sodium. The volume loss incurred with sudden extrarenal losses of fluids containing sodium is initially a loss that leaves the body isotonic in the initial acute phase. The primary loss is one of volume rather than concentration. Yet, there is almost immediately a widespread adjustment in order to conserve volume: the body has appeared to "sense" the change in volume.

B. "VOLUME-SENSITIVE PHENOMENA": THE REGULATION OF THE VOLUME OF BODY FLUIDS

The experiments of Verney demonstrated a mechanism, residing in the central nervous system, by which the body regulated the concentration of effective solute in body water. In its simplest expression this osmoreceptor mechanism, operating through the supra-opticohypophyseal tract, results in alterations in the secretion of antidiuretic hormone, and thus in the concentration of water in the renal tubule, and, by corollary, in the concentration of solute in body water. This mechanism is responsible for the homeostatic regulations of the normal sodium concentration and body tonicity.

Many years ago it became apparent that this was not the only mechanism regulating body fluids. Alterations in volume of certain body fluids produced changes in renal function that regulated the volume of these phases of body fluid. In many instances, as for example a severe hemorrhage, this was accompanied by a decrease in glomerular filtration rate and thus effected an obvious conservation of body water. This was a vascular phenomenon, working through reflexes which provided renal vasoconstriction and reduced glomerular filtration. But further study has since shown that changes in the volume of body fluid produce alterations in the renal excretion of water and salt, *even though there is no change in the concentration of any measurable solutes in body water, and even though the renal blood supply is not grossly reduced.*

In recent years much evidence has come to bear on this phenomenon. It appears that the body senses alterations in volume or flow, and brings influences to bear on the kidney tubule, resulting in alterations in excretion of water and/or sodium. The mechanism is loosely referred to as a "volume receptor," even though the location and mechanism of any single volume-sensitive receptor is unknown.

There is nothing to suggest that there is only a single center sensitive to volume; the sensing areas may be multiple and they may be sensitive to flow, arterial pressure, venous pressure, difference between venous and arterial oxy-genation, or some more subtle physiologic entity. Whatever the afferent arc, it seems clear that the efferent arcs for the regulation of body fluid volume have to do with alterations in renal tubular function in response to the secretion of antidiuretic substances, mineralocorticoids, and possibly other influences, including epinephrine and norepinephrine.

Because of the fact that acute surgical trauma results in reduced volume of body fluid and many chronic surgical diseases result in volume expansion, it is appropriate here to review briefly a few of the evidences for the existence of such volume-regulating mechanisms.

(1) *The Small Hemorrhage.* If a normal human subject is bled a small brisk venous hemorrhage, there is no measurable change in glomerular filtration rate and no immediate change whatever in the extracellular concentration of water or solute. Yet there is an immediate reduction in water excretion, which bears every earmark of being an effect of antidiuretic hormone. There is a marked saving of sodium by resorption of sodium from the glomerular filtrate, a typical aldosterone effect. With this there is a measurable increase in aldosterone excretion. There is a minimal change in the eosinophil count or in the 17-hydroxycorticoids in the blood. In the dog there is a considerable change in the adrenal secretion of epinephrine and norepinephrine measured in blood from the adrenal vein.

(2) *Replacement of Hemorrhage.* Conversely when this small hemorrhage is replaced in the form of retransfusion, there is an immediate release of the renal tubule from these conservational effects. Excretion of free water once again becomes manifest; the excretion of sodium is re-established. The secretion of aldosterone is reduced. The secretion of epinephrine and norepinephrine from the adrenal vein (in the dog) returns to normal.

(3) *Hypernatremia due to Water Loss as Versus That due to Sodium Load.* In dehydration-desiccation there is a rise in plasma sodium concentration (and thus a clear rise in effective osmotic pressure), with a marked reduction of excretion of water and salt through the kidney. This is the classic response to

dehydration, leading to the conclusion that increased osmolality results in decreased water excretion. Yet, volume has also been reduced and the implications must be revised when precisely the same sodium concentration change is produced by a sizable load of concentrated sodium solution. Then, though the brain is exposed to the same osmotic stimulus, some mechanism sensitive to volume appears to be more important and there is a profuse excretion of both water and salt. Here the volume-receptor mechanism seems to outvote the osmoreceptor mechanism.

(4) *Overhydration.* If a patient is intentionally overhydrated with water plus vasopressin until his fluid volume is excessively expanded, there comes a time when the excretion of sodium becomes increased. If aldosterone secretion is being measured at this time, it will be noted that the aldosterone excretion has been reduced. Here the artificial administration of vasopressin plus water has produced an expansion of the extracellular volume. The body can let go its sodium, and this it does. This is a sort of "high-volume release" of sodium.

(5) *Overhydration Treated with Concentrated Sodium.* By the same token, if a patient is overhydrated and reaches a chronic equilibrated state of hypotonicity due to overhydration and is then given a large sodium load, there results a profuse water excretion. This phenomenon has been seen in congestive heart failure and may be considered as the converse of the last experiment listed above. Here, overhydration due to some sort of inappropriate volume phenomenon finally is released and water excretion potentiated when that volume has increased effective osmotic pressure within it.

(6) *Volume Reduction as a Stimulus.* Some evidence appears to demonstrate that acute reduction of effective extracellular or circulating blood volume is the chief stimulus to the production of aldosterone in the body. Aldosterone might be thought of as the "volume hormone"; when volume is reduced, aldosterone secretion is increased and sodium is saved. Under most such circumstances there is a similar increase in production of antidiuretic hormone, although this is much more difficult to demonstrate by bioassay. This results in a restoration of the volume of extracellular fluid and, by corollary, of plasma volume and blood volume.

In addition, acute severe reduction of volume is a strong stimulus to the production of epinephrine and norepinephrine. The adrenal vein is so situated that large increases in catechol amines will be demonstrated there. Since norepinephrine is diffusely produced from neuromuscular endings and neurosynapses, one would not expect to find a large secretion of it in the adrenal vein. With this qualification, then, one may state merely that acute reduction of volume is also a stimulus to the production of epinephrine and norepinephrine.

(7) *Volume Expansion in Disease.* In chronic visceral diseases, such as liver disease and heart disease, there is a persistent conservation of water and salt resembling the conservation that would be produced in response to volume reduction. One may think of the pathologic physiology as an inappropriate volume-expanding phenomenon with conservation of water and salt. The use of the term "inappropriate" in this sense helps to fix the mechanism in one's mind, but there is no way of knowing actually how appropriate it is. If the sensing areas are sensitive to oxygenation, venous pressure, total flow, or difference between venous and arterial pressure, then it is entirely conceivable that in such a disease as late mitral stenosis these centers are constantly stimulated by the inadequacy of circulation, resulting in a conservation of water and salt with a huge expansion of the extracellular fluid.

(8) *Summation of Biologic Components as Volume Stimuli.* Certain biologic components of trauma, such as ether anesthesia, seem to act on the endocrine system by stimulating the production of both antidiuretic hormone and aldosterone. Ether is also a stimulus to the hydrocortisone group, epinephrine, and norepinephrine. It is difficult to relate ether anesthesia to any sort of primary volume reduction. It appears to be a pharmacologic stimulus to these same endocrine organs. By con-

Text continues on page 315.

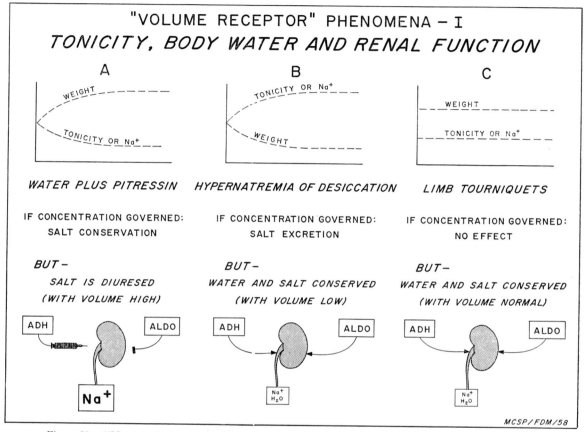

Figure 62. "Volume Receptor" Phenomena. I. Tonicity, Body Water and Renal Function

See facing page for detailed legend.

Figure 62. "Volume Receptor" Phenomena. I. Tonicity, Body Water and Renal Function

There are certain phenomena observed in the renal metabolism of water and salt that suggest an auto-regulatory mechanism for the maintenance of effective extracellular and circulating blood volume. Since this implies some mechanism sensitive to volume change, the concept of "volume receptors" has been established. Such a concept is useful and helpful in surgical care as long as we remind ourselves that no single receptor mechanism has as yet been identified. Indeed, the nature of the stimulus is unknown. Tissue oxygenation, blood flow, venous pressure, arterial pressure, atrial pressure, cerebral blood pressure, and arteriovenous oxygen or pressure differentials have all been considered as possible stimuli to this sensitive mechanism. The effector arc is somewhat less mysterious since there is evidence in some circumstances that the adrenal steroids (particularly aldosterone) and antidiuretic hormone of the posterior pituitary may be involved—together with other hormones or neural mediators (epinephrine and norepinephrine).

In this and the succeeding chart are shown a few of the many evidences suggesting that a mechanism exists wherein volume changes predominate over concentration alterations in determining the course of events.

In A are shown the events that transpire when water loading is carried out in the presence of Pitressin (vasopressin) administration. There is a sharp drop in sodium concentration in the serum. Were this the only factor involved, one would predict that there would be a diminution in sodium excretion in the urine. On the other hand, as total volume is markedly increased (indicated by weight gain) there is instead a marked increase in sodium excretion in the urine.

In B we see the reverse change in which hypernatremia has been produced by extrarenal loss of pure water as in dehydration-desiccation. Here there is a marked increase in sodium concentration in the serum, and if concentration were the only factor involved, one would expect an increased excretion of sodium. On the other hand, volume is sharply reduced and there is a sharp reduction in excretion both of sodium and water.

In C is seen a third situation in which there is no alteration in body weight as an indicator of water volume, tonicity, or sodium concentration but a segment of the circulating volume has been sequestered out of the circulation. This is seen in the application of venous tourniquets to the limbs. Here, if concentration factors were the only governing features of water and salt metabolism, one should see no alteration in renal excretion of water and salt. On the other hand, even though glomerular filtration may not be affected at all, there is an immediate and marked reduction in the excretion of water and salt when limb tourniquets are applied. The "central volume" has been reduced.

In these examples, three of many reported in the literature, volume effects rather than concentration changes appear to determine the renal homeostatic response. The endocrine mechanisms diagrammed here are but one aspect of the renal adjustments involved.

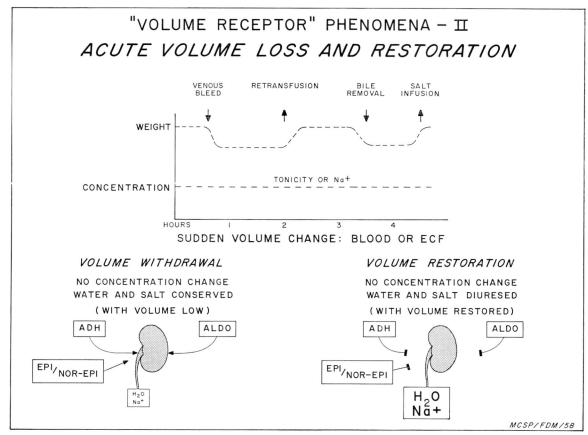

Figure 63. "Volume Receptor" Phenomena. II. Acute Volume Loss and Restoration

In this chart are shown the effects of acute volume removal and restoration on the renal metabolism of water and salt.

We see here the effect on body weight (using this merely as an index of acute changes in over-all fluid volume) of venous bleeding and of sudden removal of a large amount of bile, as through a T-tube. In both instances weight falls but there is no immediate change in tonicity or sodium concentration. It is of course emphasized that were enough time to elapse, sodium concentration would fall in both these situations. However, over the matter of a few minutes or an hour, there is little change. One would consequently expect little alteration in the renal excretion of water and salt, if alteration in concentration of solutes in the plasma were the controlling factor.

However, in both cases water and salt are conserved when volume is extracted and water and salt are then freely excreted when the volume is added.

This change, occurring with loss of effective circulating volume, is basic to the understanding of the dynamics of water and salt excretion after injury and surgery. On the basis of evidence currently available, it would appear that reduction in effective circulating volume is the strongest stimulus to alteration in the renal tubular dynamics of water and salt reabsorption from the glomerular filtrate. It is also very probable that reduc-

tion in effective circulating volume with threatened hypovolemic hypotension constitutes one of the strongest, if not the strongest, stimulus to the adrenal production of aldosterone, the corticosteroids (such as hydrocortisone), and the catechol amines, epinephrine and norepinephrine. All of these profoundly affect the renal excretion of salt and water through an effect either on renal hemodynamics or on renal tubular function.

The location of those receptor mechanisms responsible for sensing this alteration in effective volume is unknown. Whatever the site of receptor sensation and whatever the effective arc, we have here a mechanism that effectively conserves the circulating volume in the surgical patient.

The term "circulating volume" is intentionally vague. This recognizes the fact that the plasma volume is directly supported by the interstitial fluid, that the total available sodium-containing fluid of the body constitutes the effective support of the circulation, and that it is indeed to the conservation of sodium salts and of the fluid volume in which to dissolve those salts that these mechanisms appear to be devoted.

The hormones of the adrenal and posterior pituitary are shown in these charts as being the effector agencies. There is evidence to suggest that other mechanisms are also active.

trast with ether, many of the other biologic components of trauma involve a direct reduction in effective volume, oxygenation, or flow. This is true of even minor tissue trauma where there is accumulation of blood or extracellular fluid. It is true of the effects of sequestered edema, loss of extracellular water, dehydration due to the withholding of water, hemorrhage, desiccation, unregulated urinary water loss as in solute diuresis, infection with accumulation of fluid in an area of infection, and —most potent of all—massive loss of fluid or blood wth oligemia and shock. In all of these instances one would predicate that any volume-cionserving mechanism present in the body would be maximally stimulated.

Three of the most characteristic endocrine-metabolic changes of surgery are those produced by loss of fluid volume and associated with the action of antidiuretic substances, mineralocorticoids, and catechol amines. These three responses are water conservation, salt conservation (with a falling sodium:potassium ratio in the urine), and peripheral vasoconstriction. It is for these reasons, then, that volume-regulating phenomena, for all their ill-defined anatomic nature, are a basic consideration in surgical endocrinology.

C. AVAILABLE ENERGY, STARVATION, AND HYPOTONICITY

Finally in considering overhydration and hypotonicity one must take note of the fact that in late chronic starvation and energy-deficit, hypotonicity is a characteristic occurrence.

If whole blood is placed at room temperature, the glucose in the blood rapidly disappears, and as this happens, sodium begins to leak into the erythrocytes and potassium begins to leak out. Sodium concentration in the plasma falls. This may be too simple an analogy for the whole body but the fact remains that the human body, when exposed to a prolonged energy deficit, exhibits exactly the same phenomenon: a lowering of the extra-cellular concentration of sodium (with consequent hypotonicity) and an increase in the extracellular concentration (and therefore the urinary excretion) of potassium. Evidently energy is required to maintain the normal sodium:potassium gradient across the cell and also to maintain the normal renal excretion of water. In starvation both mechanisms fail and hypotonicity results.

Lack of available dietary energy seems to be a common denominator in many cases of plasma hypotonicity. This leads to the general rule that one should look at the patient's caloric intake and hematocrit level before embarking on the treatment of plasma hypotonicity. Oftentimes, restoring the peripheral concentration of erythrocytes or protein to normal (or improving oxygenation by other methods) or restoring the patient to a normal or nearly normal caloric intake, either by mouth or by vein, has resulted in water diuresis and restoration of normal plasma tonicity without energetic electrolyte therapy.

In starvation, water tolerance is low; large positive water balances are readily accumulated; there is consistent antidiuresis, as if the low-energy state interfered with the inactivation of vasopressin. This latter hypothesis has not been proved.

In starvation there is chronic potassium loss as well as lack of dietary energy. Potassium loss at a high potassium:nitrogen ratio should be expected to produce a low sodium concentration in the extracellular fluid and plasma hypotonicity. This is for the reason that the body tolerates no osmotic gradients. As potassium is lost there is a lowering of total body base in body water just as in loss of concentrated sodium salts; intracellular base concentration falls and extracellular base concentration must also fall.

Until more evidence comes along we would conclude that starvation hypotonicity is due to all three of these mechanisms: insufficient energy for the cellular exclusion of sodium, antidiuresis, and loss of potassium slightly faster than loss of cell matrix and water.

CHAPTER 19

Intracellular Volume Changes: Potassium Therapy in Relation to Anabolism, Catabolism, and Potassium Balance; Magnesium

Section I. The Nature of the Intracellular Fluid; Limits of Change

The intracellular fluid of the body is contained in the cells of liver, spleen, kidneys, gastrointestinal tract, lungs, other parenchymatous and hollow viscera, and smooth and striated muscle. The mass of striated muscle exceeds the others in the adult male. The central nervous system contains a small fraction of intracellular fluid. A tiny fraction of such tissues as bone, skin, tendon, and fascia must also be included in the cellular mass. The body cell mass, taken as a whole, is the "lean body mass" that determines the caloric needs of the body, and it is the cell mass in striated muscle which undergoes the most striking and significant changes in acute and chronic surgical disease. Changes in size of heart, liver, lungs, or gut are small by comparison, although cellular protein is lost from them.

The intracellular fluid is considered to be constant in composition. The intracellular phase is at least 25 per cent solid, and the remaining fluid is an extremely complex system of water, salts, proteins, and enzymes, the

whole encompassed at a total osmolality equal to that of the extracellular fluid, under equilibrium conditions. Because of this osmolar equilibrium, the total solute of intracellular fluid determines its water-holding ability. Since potassium occupies the giant's share of total intracellular cation, the intracellular osmolality may be considered to be proportional to the potassium concentration (exactly as the extracellular fluid osmolality is, under most circumstances, a linear function of the sodium concentration). This potassium exists with other cations such as magnesium, calcium, and with many anions, including phosphate, sulfate, bicarbonate, and those colloids that function as anions at intracellular pH. Potassium is therefore one of the primary determinants of intracellular composition and hydration. It is the cellular ion concerning which we have the most information and the most experience in its use in surgical care.

In a normal adult male, the intracellular

fluid accounts for about 35 per cent of body weight and is thus the largest single fraction of body water. The gross size of the cell mass can be increased only by the active process of anabolism or cellular growth. In this regard it is entirely different from the extracellular fluid, which can be "passively" expanded and contracted. Even with severe intracellular hypotonicity and edema, as represented by a low intracellular concentration of potassium, the gross increase in cell mass is small.

Under conditions of extreme terminal catabolic cachexia, the mass of lean tissue may be reduced to as little as one-fifth of its own starting healthy volume. The patient's entire body weight tends to shrink with this loss, however, so that after such an intracellular contraction (represented, for instance, by terminal starvation) the intracellular water still comprises a fairly large fraction of total body weight, in the neighborhood of 20 per cent or about one-half the normal relative value.

The concentration of potassium in cell water is not accurately known. In muscle, it is probably in the neighborhood of 130 to 160 mE. per l. of cell water. It may be somewhat different in other tissues. Taking the entire body as a whole and dividing the volume of intracellular water by the total amount of intracellular potassium, we find an "average" intracellular potassium concentration of about 150 mE. per l. of cell water.

The actual intracellular environment of lean-tissue cells does not exhibit a very wide range of variation in pathologic situations. This is shown by measurement of body composition. Average intracellular concentration of potassium varies from about 120 to 150 mE. per l., and this is maintained under the widest imaginable circumstances of anabolism, catabolism, acute illness, burns, shock, and premortem sepsis. The cell maintains a certain integrity during life. If this integrity is lost, death ensues. When we consider that the heart itself is a specialized mass of muscular tissue, it is clear that this maintenance of intracellular integrity is a daily concern for survival. Cells, if still alive, are intact biochemical systems. They cannot depart far from this without becoming dead.

A. CATABOLISM: CELL DEATH OR ATROPHY?

Over the course of a few days or a week, a severely injured surgical patient may lose a great deal of the intracellular stuff which formerly resided in his muscle tissue. This acute catabolic phase affects the intracellular fluid profoundly. Does it represent the death of a great many cells, the remainder existing at essentially normal concentrations of protein and salt? Or does it represent "atrophy"? Here we define "atrophy" strictly as "shrinkage" of each individual cell with maintenance of its nuclear integrity but loss of matrix and salts. The whole muscle, of course, atrophies in any case; we are concerned here with a consideration of whether this loss of muscle tissue occurs by death of some cells or by atrophy of all.

Evidences that cast light on this interesting problem are three:

(1) In the acute catabolism of surgical illness, the loss of water and salt from cells outstrips for a few days the loss of matrix, as shown by nitrogen. This is evidence that during an acute catabolic phase there is some degree of "cellular desalting water loss," which must produce some shrinkage of cell mass or some atrophy.

(2) Microscopic appearance of muscles from individuals who have lost large amounts of weight and muscular strength shows that the muscle fibers themselves still appear normal. There may be more of them per unit volume, as the cells have shrunk. A muscle such as the biceps, triceps, or gastrocnemius may shrink to a quarter of its normal, healthy, well-developed size in the course of an acute surgical illness. This is due to the loss of about one-quarter of its cell mass, apparently by the loss of substance from each cell, the cell meanwhile maintaining its myoneural connection and functioning well but fatiguing easily.

(3) In more chronic situations—over a course of months—the loss is almost entirely that of uniform atrophy. The potassium:nitrogen ratios of the negative balance are almost precisely that of tissue composition, and differential loss of potassium is not common although as potassium is lost much of the cell water is retained in the body. Though the cells might die, such an occurrence would

appear neurologically incompatible with the subsequent full recovery of neuromuscular function, a recovery that characteristically occurs after cachectic atrophy.

Thus it appears that catabolic loss of lean tissue is a process of atrophy, not cell death. We are discussing here cachectic atrophy, not actual cellular destruction or removal, as in crush, burn, sepsis, debridement. After destruction, skeletal muscle has virtually no power of cellular regeneration (in the sense of cell multiplication) to produce new cubic tissue such as is seen, for instance, in liver. The areas of cellular loss are replaced by fibrous cicatrix.

B. ANABOLISM: THE BIRTH OF NEW CELLS OR SWELLING OF THE OLD ONES?

Evidence is strong that during initial short-term anabolism after operation, there is some reconstitution of existing cell matrix as evidenced by the loading of water, potassium, and nitrogen at a high potassium:nitrogen ratio. But after this phase—which may be extremely transient, lasting only a day or two—cell growth proceeds in orderly anabolic process, at normal potassium:nitrogen ratios and with normal external and histologic appearances of an increase in total cell mass. If it is "catabolic atrophy," it is now giving way to "anabolic restoration."

C. INTRACELLULAR MOVEMENT OF EXTRACELLULAR IONS

If a muscle is hit with a blunt weapon, some of the cells die and others swell. Such directly traumatized muscle takes up sodium and loses potassium. It seems to be an example in which direct physical injury has produced a diminution in membrane discrimination on the part of the cell. This matter presents no controversy. Where muscles are directly damaged, the cellular contents (electrolyte, protein, enzymes, pigments) leak out into the surrounding fluid, the characteristic components of extracellular fluid (sodium, chloride, bicarbonate) leak into the cell, and the normal gradients across the cell membrane are lost.

The possibility exists that similar changes occur in muscle that has not been directly traumatized, in association with various types of trauma and systemic disease. The evidence is good that shift of sodium into cells occurs in exchange for potassium, that this shift sometimes also involves hydrogen ion, and that it may occur in both chronic and acute disease and be associated with marked acid-base imbalances. This evidence is based in part on observation of balance changes and in part on direct biopsy of muscle. After severe trauma and in certain states of chronic nutritional deficiency with hyponatremia and hypotonicity, some sodium leaks into muscle cells. On the basis of metabolic data, it appears that it is rare for more than 200 mE. of sodium to find its way into the entire muscle mass. In most instances this is clinically unimportant.

Section II. Selective or Differential Potassium Loss in Relation to Plasma Potassium Concentration

As the whole cell mass shrinks or grows, there are large changes in potassium balance. These proceed at normal potassium:nitrogen ratios for the most part. Potassium is not differentially lost. These do not produce, of themselves, any abnormality of plasma potassium concentration, alkalosis, hyperkalemia, or hypokalemia, or any of the disorders discernible by electrocardiogram. Loss of as much as 700 mE. by starvation and catabolism is associated, in most cases, with a normal plasma potassium concentration. "*Potassium deficiency*" *and* "*hypokalemia*" *are therefore not synonymous.* "Potassium deficiency" refers to a low body potassium; "hypokalemia" to a low plasma potassium concentration.

There is evidence that the acute muscle wasting after severe injury is characterized by a very rapid loss of potassium. This latter is loss of potassium at a rate higher than matrix—at a high potassium:nitrogen ratio. This is selective or differential potassium loss and it sets the stage for clinically significant low potassium states. It is the potassium loss with which we are most concerned in evaluating the plasma potassium concentration.

In cases of selective potassium loss in man (differential intracellular potassium deficit such as occurs after operations or injury) there are metabolic changes suggesting the transfer of hydrogen into the cell and lowering of intracellular *p*H. These evidences are the secretion of an acid urine and the refractory nature of the extracellular alkalosis produced by extrarenal losses of hydrogen ion. In man, potassium loss does not seem to produce alkalosis, but it does render him peculiarly vulnerable to alkalosis of other origins; it interferes with his compensations to acid-losing alkalosis because he can no longer secrete an alkaline urine.

In differential potassium loss the sodium bicarbonate is virtually entirely resorbed from the glomerular filtrate; if acid loss is proceeding elsewhere (as in gastric obstruction) the combination will produce severe alkalosis very rapidly.

Rapid differential loss of potassium occurs briefly after trauma; the loss is urinary and its rate is increased by sodium treatment, loss (as in gastric obstruction) of hydrogen ion, or by the renal effects of hormones of the adrenal cortex. This potassium loss alone may be rapid enough to lower the plasma potassium concentration, though this is rare. The aciduria and pernicious alkalosis that occur with loss of gastric acid where potassium loss has occurred or where injury interferes with sodium excretion (aldosterone effect) combines to lower the plasma potassium concentration abruptly. This is hypokalemic alkalosis.

In contrast to these acute situations, slow differential loss of potassium occurs in prolonged diarrheal disease; the urinary loss is at a nearly normal potassium:nitrogen ratio but the bowel loss, while small (10 mE. a day), is at a high potassium:nitrogen ratio (10 mE. per gm.) and gradually lowers the body's potassium:nitrogen rates. A "potassium hole" is being dug in cell composition, and after many weeks plasma potassium concentration falls, usually without alkalosis,

though the patient is very vulnerable to its development should loss of gastric acid then occur. This is chronic potassium-deficiency hypokalemia.

A. ACIDOSIS AND ALKALOSIS IN RELATION TO PLASMA POTASSIUM CONCENTRATION

For the past fifteen years evidence has been accumulating to show that hypokalemia is frequently associated with alkalosis. If one looks back over the accumulated experience with renal failure, it is also apparent that metabolic acidosis is associated with hyperkalemia. For some years it was assumed that the potassium loss itself produced the alkalosis and that the failure of renal function itself produced both the acidosis and the hyperkalemia. There is now evidence to demonstrate that alkalosis of itself—or some aspect of alkalosis, or even a change in the direction of alkalosis—produces a drop in the extracellular concentration of potassium, regardless of external potassium balance or renal function. By the same token, there is good evidence that an acute acidosis, some aspect of acidosis, or a change in the direction of acidosis produces hyperkalemia without change in external balance or renal function.

Many of the phenomena of plasma potassium concentration in surgery have become more understandable when we realize that acidosis and alkalosis can, in themselves, produce alterations in the concentration of potassium in the plasma. Whether this alteration in plasma potassium concentration is a direct function of the *p*H, or whether it is due to some more subtle related alteration, such as the intracellular *p*H, the intracellular *p*CO$_2$, or the secretion of aldosterone, remains uncertain. As will later become clear in the discussion of hypokalemic alkalosis, one of the characteristic features of the syndrome is that the rate of potassium loss is fairly constant; but when the alkalosis suddenly gets much worse, then the plasma potassium concentration falls. Aldosterone tends to produce hypokalemia, aciduria, and alkalosis; surgical injury has a marked aldosterone-like effect. In this particular instance the mineralocorticoid effect of trauma has acted both to increase potassium loss and to make alkalosis worse by blocking excretion of sodium bicarbonate.

By the same token, if a patient with acidosis (for instance, chronic respiratory acidosis or the hyperchloremic acidosis of ureterosigmoidostomy) is treated with a large infusion of sodium bicarbonate, one may be sure that the plasma potassium concentration will fall abruptly. If there is some element of starvation and balanced potassium loss in the background, this base-induced hypokalemia may drop to dangerous levels.

If a patient under anesthesia has a borderline elevated plasma potassium concentration (for instance in a chronic congestive heart failure), an acute respiratory acidosis resulting from insufficient ventilation on the operating table under anesthesia will result in a paroxysmal rise in the plasma potassium concentration, which is, in itself, a major factor in the sudden loss of effectiveness of digitalization and the onset of ventricular fibrillation.

Thus, we find many factors acting on the plasma potassium concentration, of which the simple external balance of the ion is one of the least important. The rate of loss, the potassium:nitrogen ratio of the loss, the occurrence of surgical injury with its strong mineralocorticoid effect, cation exchange across the cell (hydrogen, and sodium for potassium), simultaneous extrarenal chloride loss, and, above all, acidosis or alkalosis of other origin are the controlling factors in plasma potassium concentration.

B. THE MEANING OF POTASSIUM THERAPY

The administration of potassium must be considered in relation to the above facts as well as to the distribution of potassium in the body, which shows that only a small fraction, around 2 per cent, of all the potassium in the body is in the extracellular phase. Every day we eat and excrete more potassium than is in our entire extracellular phase. The exchange of potassium across the cell is very rapid, and it is this exchange which keeps us from killing ourselves with potassium intoxication every time we eat a turkey dinner. Little wonder that the administration by vein of small amounts of potassium may be somewhat disappointing in raising the extracellular potassium concentration!

The addition of potassium to the intravenous flask has been one of the major advances in surgical supportive therapy in the past twelve years. First used during World War II, in about 1943, it has since been used consistently. There is less ileus, patients feel better, renal function is better, there is less edema, and taken all together, the effects of potassium therapy have been excellent. But the exact manner in which this ion exerts its benefit and the best formula for prescribing its administration do not depend solely on potassium balance. The meaning of potassium therapy can be summarized under five broad headings.

(1) *In continuing starvation we cannot produce positive potassium balance by potassium infusion, in the presence of good kidneys.* This is an extremely important point. Prolonged positive potassium balance in regrowth is a manifestation of cellular anabolism requiring calories in excess of requirements for muscular work, a certain "set" of the endocrine system, and the other factors involved in protoplasmic synthesis. It is naive to believe that this series of events may be produced merely by putting potassium salts in the extracellular phase, and indeed it cannot.

(2) *The administration of potassium as potassium chloride has marked effects on extracellular acid-base balance.* Where there has been extrarenal loss of chloride, and with it hydrogen ion, there is a threatened metabolic alkalosis. There is increased urinary potassium loss if operation then occurs. Sodium and hydrogen move into cells in exchange for potassium, intracellular pH falls, extracellular alkalosis is worsened, urine is acid, and the patient has started down the special spiral known as hypokalemic alkalosis. The administration of potassium chloride under this circumstance therefore has several effects: restoring some potassium to cells insofar as it has been lost at high potassium:nitrogen ratio, helping to eject sodium and hydrogen from the cells, assisting to "block" further ingress of sodium and hydrogen into the cell, restoring the ability of the kidney to excrete base, and providing a fixed anion to the

extracellular fluid, which assists in the restoration of extracellular alkalosis to normal.*

(3) *The administration of potassium by vein helps to restore to cells that amount of potassium lost in excess of nitrogen;* it fills up the "potassium hole." It repairs differential intracellular potassium deficit.

(4) *The constant provision of available potassium makes it easier to avoid hypokalemia.* The various situations that produce hypokalemia will naturally tend to be less effective in actually lowering the potassium concentration if there is new potassium continuously available. The plasma potassium concentration fluctuates over a very wide range (2.5 to 6.0 mE. per l., or almost 200 per cent of its lowest value), without any significant change in external balance. It is clear that the administration of potassium is not the sole factor involved, but it helps in avoiding severe hypokalemia.

(5) Potassium has been known for a number of years to be a diuretic; *the kidney defends the extracellular potassium concentration very faithfully, and any tendency to increase it by infusion is accompanied by increased urine flow so long as renal function even approximates normal.*

Rationalized in this way, the giving of potassium is clearly useful even though it does not achieve the announced objective of "restoration of potassium balance."

C. NEUROMUSCULAR IRRITABILITY AFFECTED BY EXTRACELLULAR (NOT INTRACELLULAR) POTASSIUM CONCENTRATION

The changes in neuromuscular function with alterations in potassium metabolism are related more closely to the extracellular concentration of potassium than to the intracel-

---

* Where there is hypokalemia with a high chloride (a rarity), potassium may be administered as the lactate or bicarbonate.

lular concentration. The latter plays a role when differential loss has made a "potassium hole" and plasma concentration falls. But the electrocardiographic changes, ileus, and muscular paralysis seem to be associated most distinctly with the rate and direction of movement of plasma potassium concentration and its associated changes in acid-base balance and state of other ions. Certainly it is true that severe starvation involves huge potassium loss but neither hypokalemia nor electrocardiographic changes. By the same token, in renal failure where long illness has depleted body potassium, an acute hyperkalemia produces the electrocardiographic changes of high, not low, potassium levels.

D. DIABETIC POTASSIUM PROBLEMS

The acidotic dehydrating starvation of prolonged undertreated diabetes is an example of severe differential potassium loss—potassium loss at a high potassium:nitrogen ratio. The acidosis tends to maintain plasma potassium at a deceptively high value. There is a huge differential potassium deficit not accurately reflected in the elevated extracellular fluid concentration of potassium during the acidotic phase.

Then the patient is treated. Large amounts of glucose move into cells and take potassium with them. The acid-base set of the extracellular fluid moves toward alkalosis (i.e., away from acidosis); as a result the potassium concentration in the extracellular fluid is no longer held up by acidosis. Plasma potassium moves into the cell to fill up a tiny part of the "potassium hole" there. Severe hypokalemia results. Treatment with insulin, glucose, and sodium salts (but without potassium salts) greatly accentuates the hypokalemic trend of recovering diabetic acidosis. Potassium in very large amounts must thus form a part of the treatment of diabetic acidosis, whether it occurs alone or in conjunction with trauma.

Section III. Magnesium

A. NORMAL CONTENT AND DISTRIBUTION

Magnesium is a divalent intracellular cation sharing some of the properties of potas-

sium and, in its skeletal location and relation to neuromuscular irritability, some of the properties of calcium. Significant abnormalities of magnesium content or concentration are a rarity in surgical practice, but when they do occur their recognition is a critical factor in recovery.

The normal concentration of magnesium in the plasma is from 1.5 to 2.0 mE. per l., the rather large range being in part a result of the still unsolved problem of an easily reproducible clinical method. The body pool is about 28 gm. This is to be compared with a body pool of 120 gm. of potassium. The normal magnesium requirement is about 220 mg. per day. Approximately 98 per cent of the body magnesium is within cells and in the bones; about one-half the body magnesium is in bone. The ratio of potassium to magnesium per unit of noncollagen nitrogen is always constant, as a manifestation of the constancy of intracellular environment. In the cells of liver and muscle the concentration of magnesium is about 20 mE. per l. of intracellular water; in brain this figure is 13 mE. per l. and in the erythrocyte 5 to 6 mE. per l. From 15 to 50 per cent of plasma magnesium is bound to protein, yet the concentration in cerebrospinal fluid is about 0.4 mE. per l., higher than in plasma.

The magnesium intake is about 20 mE. per day. Excretion is 60 per cent in the feces, 40 per cent (i.e., about 8 mE. per day) in the urine. The ingestion of calcium, phosphorus, and concentrated protein decreases magnesium absorption. The administration of ammonium chloride increases magnesium excretion in the urine. The ratio of magnesium to potassium in the urine is higher than one would predict from body content.

B. EFFECTS OF MAGNESIUM ABNORMALITIES

1. Striated Muscle and Neuromuscular Irritability

For the sake of simplicity one may consider the neuromuscular irritability sequence for striated muscle as involving a complex ratio:

$$\frac{Na^+ \times K^+ \times OH^-}{Ca^{++} \times Mg^{++} \times H^+}$$

If the numerator factors are increased (al-

kalosis) and the denominator decreased (hypocalcemia or hypomagnesemia), the peripheral muscular system passes toward or into a convulsive state or tetany. The numerator factors are the "irritability ions." If the denominator factors (hypercalcemia, hypermagnesemia, acidosis) are increased, muscular paralysis results; they are the "paralysis ions." Clearly, since one is dealing with ion products of unknown coefficients, and ratios of one set of ions to the others, seemingly small changes acting in combination may produce large results. A borderline low magnesium concentration, for example, is greatly accentuated by the transient hyperkalemia of the postoperative state, and under these circumstances a chronic alcoholic may pass into a fatal bout of delirium tremens. Indeed, this is the commonest and most significant magnesium abnormality observed in surgical patients.

In addition, although calcium and magnesium are both factors in the denominator of this ratio as regards skeletal muscle, they antagonize each other in their effects on the central nervous system.

2. Myocardial Muscular Irritability

In contrast to striated muscle, the complex ratio for myocardial irritability is slightly different. In similar oversimplified terms it is:

$$\frac{Na^+ \times Ca^{++} \times OH^-}{K^+ \times Mg^{++} \times H^+}$$

Thus, the alkalosis-hypercalcemia sequence potentiates the digitalis effect, while the hyperkalemia-hypermagnesemia-acidosis sequence produces S-T segment changes in the electrocardiogram, ventricular premature beats, and finally ventricular fibrillation, and antagonizes digitalis strongly. Yet, the cardiac effects of magnesium change are like those of potassium only in certain regards. A high magnesium concentration does not produce the complete cardiac disintegration that potassium does. Auricular flutter has been produced with magnesium. The digitalis toxicity manifested by paroxysmal auricular tachycardia with block, flutter, and fibrillation can be reduced with magnesium as it can with potassium. Two to 4 gm. of magnesium sulfate given as a 25 per cent solution by vein will accomplish this.

In low magnesium states the electrocardiographic changes are not clear-cut, but generally resemble those of hypercalcemia; the two ions are antagonistic in the heart. The cardiac effects of ion changes in surgery are reviewed in detail in Part V.

It is probable, in the light of data on other electrolytes, that the blood level but poorly reflects the state of body stores of magnesium. Yet it is the blood level rather than the body stores that is most concerned with neuromuscular irritability.

C. CLINICAL CONDITIONS OF MAGNESIUM ABNORMALITY

Chronic alcoholism and cirrhosis of the liver most consistently show hypomagnesemia, and the occurrence of delirium tremens can be related to hypomagnesemia and treated effectively by the administration of magnesium salts. If a chronic alcoholic is irritable and hallucinated in conjunction with acute surgical disease a plasma magnesium determination is justified, but magnesium can be given without the chemical determination so long as the dose is properly controlled and the many other sources of mental deterioration in alcoholism are properly sought out. If there is vomiting and alkalosis in such a situation, magnesium should be given along with potassium chloride. When ammonium chloride is used as a diuretic in cirrhosis, magnesium deficiency may be precipitated. The range of plasma magnesium values in symptomatic cirrhotics varies from 1.3 to 1.7 mE. per l.

Hypomagnesemia leads to central nervous irritability, altered cardiac action with electrocardiographic changes, lowered blood pressure, and lowered protein synthesis. The initial stage is one of vasodilatation, hypotension, and irritability, leading then to anorexia, oliguria, and finally convulsions and death. Some of the manifestations of severe hypokalemic alkalosis resemble magnesium deficiency and vice versa; as in so many neuromuscular disorders of chemical origin the result may be achieved by a variety of mechanisms.

Magnesium deficiency of dietary origin is probably rare save for the situation of prolonged parenteral therapy, and even here the magnesium of transfused blood provides intake. In animals it is a conditioned deficiency, made more pronounced by large calcium intakes. The plasma magnesium appears to parallel body content in chronic deficiency.

In malabsorption states the urinary magnesium may fall to very low values (e.g., 4 mE. per day). The administration of magnesium under these circumstances tends to raise the plasma calcium concentration and increase the urinary calcium output as well as the magnesium.

Clinical conditions well proven to involve clinically significant abnormalities of magnesium are not numerous. The concentration may be raised in renal failure and may be lowered by dialysis. In diabetic acidosis the magnesium levels tend to parallel potassium in the plasma, being elevated in the early acidotic phase and falling to subnormal values with energetic treatment. In toxemia of pregnancy the administration of magnesium lowers irritability and prevents or mollifies the convulsive tendency.

Magnesium excess leads to paralysis, as with curare, acting at the neuromuscular junction and antagonized by calcium and neostigmine. At the same time it relaxes smooth muscle, lowers blood pressure and slows conduction in the heart, going on to asystole. In renal failure, the magnesium changes generally parallel those of potassium, but lead to sedation and paralysis. The cardiac effects of the two are different but depend also on pH and the concentration of calcium and sodium. The phosphate transfer enzymes require magnesium.

Fatal hypermagnesemia has resulted from repeated enemas in megacolon, and in epsom salt overdosage in chronic constipation.

CHAPTER 20

Disorders of Acid-Base Balance

Section I.   Concepts, Terms, and Methods

All mammals are acid-producers. The health of cells is closely related to the concentration of hydrogen ion in the surrounding fluids and in the fluids inside the cell. We spend our lives fighting off a metabolic acidosis; renal mechanisms are tuned to this just as they are to warding off dehydration. Urine pH can go far below neutral (down to pH 4.5) and osmolality far above isotonicity (up to 1400 mO. per l.); the range in the other direction is much less (pH 7.8 and 40 mO. per l.). For this subtle reason, while acidosis and dehydration are constant threats, they are ones with which we are physiologically familiar and to which we can compensate. *Per contra*, alkalosis and overhydration may be rarer, but we have a much more limited power of compensation. We live on the alkalotic overhydrated end of our range. Many surgical disorders impair our ability to stay in a healthy range of pH.

A. TERMINOLOGY: "CONVENTIONAL" VERSUS "BRÖNSTED"

The acid-base balance of the patient has meaning to the cells of his tissues in terms of but one concentration: that of the proton or hydrogen ion. This concentration, expressed as its negative logarithm (pH), is the dimension of importance. The surroundings of the hydrogen ion—anions, cations, zwitterions, crystalloids, buffers, protein—are critical in determining its concentration. Nonetheless, it is the pH—the concentration of hydrogen ion—which is of importance to the organism.

There are situations in surgery in which other secondary parameters of acid-base change are of primary importance: the effect of carbon dioxide on cerebral vessels; the effect of intracellular pCO_2 on the exchange of sodium and potassium cations. An understanding of these factors is to be found also in relation to the associated pH changes.

The Brönsted scheme of terminology is based on the hydrogen ion and is merely a way of expressing acid-base facts, findings, or concepts in those terms, to wit:

(1) an acid is a hydrogen donor—something that gives hydrogen ion to solutions and makes them more acid, and

(2) a base is a hydrogen acceptor—something that takes or accepts hydrogen ion out of solutions and makes them less acid.

Specifically, examples of acids and bases under the Brönsted schema are:

Acids (Hydrogen donor)	*Bases* (Hydrogen acceptor)
H_2CO_3	HCO_3^-
NH_4^+	NH_3
$H_2PO_4^-$	$HPO^=$
Lactic acid	Lactate

In this scheme anions and cations are so designated (Na^+, Cl^-, HCO_3^-, NH_4^+) regardless of whether they are acids or bases. Most anions are bases. Hydrogen is a cation (H^+). The basicity of anions depends on pH. This system of nomenclature inevitably focuses attention on the gain or loss of hydrogen ion as the significant entity.

In the conventional framework, cations (Na^+, K^+, Mg^{++}, Ca^{++}, for example) were called "bases" and the anions (such as Cl^-) were called "acids" even though, for example, a very high chloride concentration (3 per cent saline) is not strongly acid. In fact it is neutral; there is no justification for calling chloride an acid.

In this book the terminology used avoids any uncertainty, defining acidity wholly on the basis of pH and referring to the ionized salts in terms of their anions and cations. We believe that the reader will not find this confusing. It is consistent with Brönsted terminology, yet understandable in conventional terms.

The logarithmic nature of the pH scale is best appreciated if re-expressed on a linear basis. The actual concentrations of hydrogen ion for a few pH values are as follows:

pH	H^+ Concentration (mE. per l.)
7.8	0.000019
7.4	0.000039
7.1	0.000079
7.0	0.00010
6.9	0.00013
6.0	0.0010
5.0	0.010
4.5	0.032
4.0	0.10
3.0	1.0
2.0	10.0
1.2	63.0
1.0	100.0

Thus, there is about twice as much H^+ in a solution of pH 7.1 as there is at 7.4; even though the change in pH appears to be only 5 per cent. In urine at pH 4.5 there is about one thousand times as much H^+ as in the blood. In gastric juice at pH 1.2 there is over one million times the concentration of hydrogen ion found in blood bathing the gastric cells.

The H^+ concentration in gastric juice is about that of sodium ion in one-half-normal saline solution. The H^+ concentration of blood would correspond to that of Na^+ in a solution made by adding one drop (0.06 ml.) of normal saline to a large tank containing about 50 liters of water.

These crude estimates call to mind the extreme range of H^+ concentration seen in biological life and the ruggedness of body cells which can live and function between 7.2 and 7.5, a livable range of 400 per cent alteration in H^+ concentration.

B. METHODS OF STUDY

Developed twenty years before electrolyte partition or flame photometry, accurate acid-base methods have been very slow to be applied to routine surgical care. The relationship among blood pH, blood bicarbonate, and blood carbonic acid is such that if any two of these three are known, the third can be calculated. In terms of clinical blood analysis, the total carbon dioxide may be measured, or the pCO$_2$ in alveolar air. There is no direct analytic method for bicarbonate that is completely satisfactory.

This relationship is expressed by the Henderson-Hasselbalch equation as follows:

$$pH = pK + \log \frac{HCO_3^-}{H_2CO_3}$$

or

$$pH = 6.10 + \log \frac{(HCO_3^-)}{.0301\, pCO_2}$$

This equation appears rather surprising. Why is it that the acid-base situation of such a complex system as the blood can be expressed entirely in terms of a single buffer pair? The answer is that the pK of this buffer pair (meaning by that the pH at which the concentrations of the acid and the salt are equal) is closer to the pH of body fluids than is the pK of any of the other important buffer pairs of the body; the phosphate system is the next closest example. Therefore the HCO_3^-: H_2CO_3 ratio is most critical in blood pH regulation and quickly changes if other acids or bases are added or subtracted: it is at once both a determinant and a reflection of pH change.

It should be a simple matter to assess the acid-base situation of surgical patients. All one needs is to measure the pH and the total carbon dioxide content.* One can then read off the tension or partial pressure of carbon

---

* For carbon dioxide, mM. per l. = $\dfrac{\text{Vol.\%}}{2.226}$.

dioxide (pCO_2) from a nomogram and characterize the situation as a metabolic, respiratory, or mixed disorder. When these are taken together with electrolyte partition and renal function, a clear picture should emerge.

This looks simple, but it isn't, for the reason that these measurements, to be significant, should be on fresh arterial blood, collected under oil and analyzed immediately at constant temperature. This is no task for the usual blood chemistry routine.

Methods for determining pH and total carbon dioxide are too complicated for most hospitals to be willing to make them available for all their patients. The pH, for instance, should be determined immediately after withdrawal under oil at constant temperature and usually on arterial blood, as mentioned. Arterial punctures are not a comfort to the patient nor can they be carried out by routine ward personnel. If the venous pH is determined, it is satisfactory for most usual purposes and particularly it is satisfactory in chronic metabolic acid-base imbalances. But it is unsatisfactory in any patient with severe cardiac or pulmonary disease, in shock, or in whom acute respiratory acid-base imbalance is present. One sometimes hears the statement that the "whole blood pH" is measured; it should be re-emphasized that all measurements of pH in the blood are carried out using whole blood as the fluid which is placed in the chamber, but actually the pH determined is that of the plasma around the cells. It is the plasma that makes a layer on the electrode. There is no known method at this time for determining intracellular pH of the red blood cell. Therefore, pH determination carried out on "whole blood" gives plasma pH, although the pH of the plasma will be in part determined by the functions of the red blood cell since, of the total buffering capacity of whole blood, a large fraction resides in the blood cells.

Measurement of the total carbon dioxide is based on a gasometric determination. The problem relates to collecting the blood in such a way that no carbon dioxide escapes, and being assured that the pH of the blood has not been altered during transport. In addition, valid measurements of pH or carbon dioxide must be carried out on blood that has not been exposed to the air and must be carried out immediately, since the passage of time at room temperature involves further oxidation of glucose with resultant accumulation of acid metabolites. Measurement of the alveolar pCO_2 is another way of getting at the arterial pCO_2, since they are normally in equilibrium.

It is readily understandable that all this testing has not as yet been made available to most surgical patients; it is complicated and expensive. Instead, the carbon dioxide combining power ($CO_{2\ cp}$) is measured, and this is the basis for most of the acid-base study available on surgical wards today.

1. Carbon Dioxide Combining Power

From a theoretical point of view, the measurement of the carbon dioxide combining power seems quite inadequate. It measures the total amount of carbon dioxide that can be taken up by blood exposed to a pCO_2 of 40 mm. Hg, this being the normal pCO_2 of the alveolar gas used by the technician.* Patients with a severe metabolic alkalosis can take up a great deal more carbon dioxide than patients with a severe metabolic acidosis. If one thinks of the "anion-cation" differential in the familiar column diagram developed by Gamble, one can then visualize the carbon dioxide combining power as the HCO_3^- portion of the diagram, made up at a predetermined pCO_2 (40 mm. Hg) and regardless of the pH. All it says is: "this is how much carbon dioxide the blood would have in it if respiratory factors were normal and held the pCO_2 at 40 mm. Hg."

Because of the carbonic anhydrase of the erythrocyte and the intracellular buffers that exist there, there is quite a difference in the result, according to whether or not the blood is separated at the time that it is equilibrated with the gas mixture. It should be equilibrated with whole blood, and then the plasma separated for carbon dioxide determination.

---

* The carbon dioxide combining power as reported is the total carbon dioxide minus the dissolved carbon dioxide under these circumstances.

The chief failing of the carbon dioxide combining power is that it demonstrates only metabolic rather than metabolic-plus-respiratory changes. Patients with severe respiratory acid-base imbalance will not show alterations in the carbon dioxide combining power except in so far as the total of fixed anions and cations has been changed by renal and other metabolic compensatory mechanisms. Renal compensation to respiratory acidosis is slow; it takes twelve to eighteen hours or more to manifest itself. A postoperative patient in severe respiratory acidosis (pH 7.1, pCO_2 80) may have a carbon dioxide combining power that is in the normal range, even though the total CO_2 (TCO_2) is very high (35 mE. per l.). When the renal excretion of H_2PO_4, NH_4^+, Cl^-, and titratable acidity has tuned up to compensate, the pH may be back to 7.28 or 7.30 (it rarely comes all the way) and the carbon dioxide combining power will be elevated to 32 to 34 mE. per l. A tendency towards metabolic alkalosis has been created to compensate a respiratory acidosis. The carbon dioxide combining power is thus of interest and help, but alone may give a misleading picture when acute respiratory factors enter the clinical picture.

There is apparently very little respiratory mechanism to compensate for a metabolic alkalosis, so that in metabolic alkalosis a measurement of the carbon dioxide combining power is quite accurate. Metabolic acidosis arouses a marked respiratory compensation consisting of increased frequency and depth of respiration, blowing off H^+ as H_2O and CO_2, lowering the total CO_2, lowering the pCO_2, and raising the pH. Therefore the measurement of the carbon dioxide combining power is inaccurate as an index of net acid-base change.

With all its faults and as long as it is understood, the determination of carbon dioxide combining power in surgical patients is better than nothing. Severe degrees of chronic metabolic acidosis and alkalosis can be very effectively treated, using this as the sole measurement of acid-base balance. It does not adequately characterize the defect; it does not tell the surgeon to what extent his patient has been able to compensate, but it is far more useful than no determination.

2. Determination of Blood pH and Other Measures

If a hospital laboratory is reviewing its procedures, the one that can most profitably be added for the management of sick surgical patients is the determination of the pH of blood, either venous or arterial. The technique of collection under oil, immediate measurement, and constant temperature makes for accuracy and reproducibility.

There are other measurements in the blood that cast light on the acid-base situation. The sum of chloride and carbon dioxide combining power ($Cl^- + CO_{2\ cp}$) is normally 125 to 130 mE. per l. The sodium concentration is normally 140 to 143 mE. per l. The difference between these two sums (10 to 18 mE. per l.) is due to anions other than chloride and bicarbonate. When this "anion-cation spread" is increased above 15 mE. per l. with a fall in carbon dioxide combining power, one may assume that there is a metabolic acidosis, usually due to the accumulation of hydrogen ion from organic or inorganic acids (that is, lactic, pyruvic, or phosphoric). Here the anions (lactate, pyruvate, keto-acids, phosphate) accumulate, and the disparity of measured anions and cations is a crude measure of the extent of pathologic accumulation of new anions. For example, with a sodium concentration of 140 mE. per l., chloride concentration of 100 mE. per l., and carbon dioxide combining power of 10 mE. per l., the expected anion-cation differential of 10 to 18 mE. per l. has become 30 mE. per l. (140 minus 110). One may assume the appearance of new anions totaling 12 to 20 mE. per l., so long as respiratory factors (that is, pCO_2) are about normal. This is characteristic of renal acidosis, diabetic acidosis, and starvation ketosis. When the "anion-cation spread" ($Na^+ - (Cl^- + CO_{2\ cp})$) is more than 20 mE. per l. with a high carbon dioxide combining power and low Cl^-, it suggests metabolic alkalosis due to the loss of hydrogen ion (vomiting of hydrochloric acid, for instance). Knowing the history of the patient and these absolute values, the surgeon may make some reconstruction of events from these simple chemical data. The degree of respiratory compensation and the pH are still elusive by this method.

The relationship between sodium and chloride is also of help in assessing the therapeutic implications of acid-base disturbances. Patients with pyloric obstruction and normal sodium concentrations, with very low concentrations of chloride, are almost invariably alkalotic because hydrogen has been lost with the chloride anion. The steps to correct alkalosis may consist initially in producing an increment of chloride and hydrogen concentrations with a hydrogen donor such as ammonium The response of the chloride and its relation to sodium and carbon dioxide combining power are a very helpful guide in this regard. If the patient is given a large amount of ammonium chloride, the chloride concentration will rise as the sodium concentration falls. As the two approach a more normal relationship to each other, the carbon dioxide combining power falls to normal and the acid-base disturbance seems to be repaired.

The reverse, low sodium concentrations with normal concentrations of chloride, has less significance in indicating acidosis, at least of the uncompensated type. A hypotonic expansion of the extracellular fluid may be present. Enthusiastic treatment with concentrated sodium lactate or bicarbonate may produce a disastrous overloading of the circulation, and, more significant, severe hypokalemia.

At best these makeshift ways of estimating the acid-base situation are inaccurate mental exercises; at worst they are dangerously misleading. The clinical estimate of respiratory compensation may also be very difficult: seemingly increased ventilatory effort (dyspnea, tachypnea) may represent an effort at compensation for metabolic acidosis, or a primary change leading to respiratory alkalosis.

When the pH, pCO_2, and total carbon dioxide (TCO_2) are available, the four basic types of change seen are:

(1) lowered pH
    raised pCO_2 } respiratory acidosis
    raised TCO_2

(2) lowered pH
    normal pCO_2 } metabolic acidosis
    lowered TCO_2

(3) raised pH
    lowered pCO_2 } respiratory alkalosis
    lowered TCO_2

(4) raised pH
    normal pCO_2 } metabolic alkalosis
    raised TCO_2

There are a host of intergrades, variations, electrolyte alterations, and compensations, the understanding of which is the substance of surgical acid-base study, whether in the laboratory or at the bedside.

3. Sodium, Chloride, Osmolality, and pH

If hydrogen and chloride are lost (as in vomiting of hydrochloric acid), regardless of their concentrations, plasma chloride concentration falls and bicarbonate rises. There is no change in osmolality, and a partly compensated metabolic alkalosis has occurred in an isotonic, volume-reduced extracellular fluid.

If sodium is lost at hypertonic concentrations, regardless of the pH of the fluid lost, the plasma sodium concentration starts to fall and osmolality falls with it; there is no new cation that can be expanded (as bicarbonate can in the anion column) to compensate osmotically for base loss. Mobilization of cell potassium, while of great significance in other regards, makes little osmotic contribution; in fact, the water that comes with it only dilutes sodium the more.

Thus, hypotonicity is a prominent feature of sodium loss while of much less significance in chloride loss; it is for this reason that sodium, not chloride, is both the determinant and the indicator of tonicity.

In the sodium-losing situation, pH may change drastically to acidity if the loss has been largely sodium bicarbonate (as in cholera) or it may change but little if the loss has been nearly neutral (as in the obstructed anacid stomach).

4. Study of the Urine

The renal acid excretion in an adult is

about 100 to 225 mE. per day. This takes the form of titratable acidity and ammonia; the anions excreted with hydrogen are bicarbonate, chloride, phosphate, sulfate, and organic anions.

Studies of the urine are helpful in understanding acid-base disorders. Analysis of the urine for titratable acidity, pH, sodium, chloride, potassium, and ammonia may help to reveal the nature of the process producing acid-base disturbances as well as the renal compensation for it. In most instances such extensive study is unnecessary.

The pH of the urine, as measured by nitrazine paper or some other simple index, is very helpful and can be used widely. A patient with a metabolic acidosis should be excreting a urine with a pH of 4.5 to 5.5, this being the lower range of urine pH. A higher pH indicates disease of the tubules, possibly of the carbonic anhydrase system. A patient with a metabolic alkalosis should be expected to excrete a urine with a pH over 6.5. The maximum is 7.8. Departure from this (an acid urine in the presence of alkalosis) is of significance and is especially common in postoperative patients, those on steroids, or those with differential potassium loss.

The presence of renal disease prevents compensations. Therapy must be more accurately tuned to the needs of the extracellular phase of the body since neither the patient nor surgeon can rely on the patient's kidneys for help. In addition, the sort of alkalosis that occurs after stress and in the presence of potassium loss and/or a low plasma potassium concentration is often associated with the paradoxical excretion of an acid urine. The pH of the urine is here an index of the need for potassium in acid-base regulation.

Renal excretion of acid by the phosphate buffer pair is indicated by the fact that the glomerular filtrate at a pH of 7.0 has four times as much $HPO_4^=$ as $H_2PO_4^-$. At pH 4.5 in the final urine, 99 per cent of the phosphate is in the $H_2PO_4^-$ form. In the process, for each 5 mols of phosphate passing down the tubule 4 mols of hydrogen have been excreted and 4 mols of sodium (or potassium) reabsorbed in exchange. Total acid (H^+) removed

is by this process measured by the titratable acidity (in mM. per l.).

The effectiveness of renal compensation in chronic respiratory acidosis is indicated by the fact that it can raise the blood pH from 7.1 to 7.3, but only by increasing blood bicarbonate to 41.8 mM. per l., dropping Cl^- down to 85 mE. per l. (as Cl^- is excreted with H^+ in a highly acid urine). If there were no compensation the pH would be 7.14, the HCO_3^- 29 mE. per l. In either case the pCO_2 (primary defect) is 88 mm. Hg. Complete compensation, not actually achieved, would involve a HCO_3^- concentration of 55 mE. per l. and chloride of 70 mE. per l. These figures are taken from Davenport (1957).

It is clear that oliguria from any cause will impair this renal mechanism, that it takes time (hours or days) to achieve its end, and that such time is not available in acute traumatic or operative respiratory acidosis.

Good excretion of acid by the renal tubules involves excretion of chloride and lowering of plasma chloride concentration. Conversely, in renal tubular acidosis plasma chloride concentration rises. This is the characteristic acidosis (hyperchloremic) of postobstructive uropathy and ureterosigmoidostomy, in both of which tubular function is abnormal.

Where a molecule of ammonia (NH_3) is excreted as ammonium ion (NH_4^+) it has accounted for one atom of H^+. Where two ammonia molecules are excreted as one urea molecule (($NH_2)_2C{=}O$), four hydrogen atoms are excreted, and two hydrogen ions remain to be accounted for by other buffers. It is thus clear that increased ammonium excretion, slow though it is to catch up with an acid load, is important in getting rid of H^+.

The normal daily acid excretion is 15 to 70 mE. by titratable acidity plus 60 to 80 mE. as ammonium. In acidosis this is capable of rising to 700 mE. per day, 75 per cent of the H^+ being carried in NH_4^+. The impact of oliguria (either low glomerular filtration rate or renal insufficiency) on acid disposal is thus clear.

As H^+ is excreted, sodium (as $NaHCO_3$) is resorbed, this process becoming obligatory in the absence of K^+. As urine pH falls the bicarbonate content diminishes until at lower pH ranges there is no bicarbonate and very little sodium. Specifically, at pH 7.5 the urine bicarbonate is about 30 mE. per l., at pH 6.5, 3.0 mE. per l., and below that, negligible. A converse relation holds for the content of $H_2PO_4^-$.

5. Pulmonary Factors

Brief review of carbon dioxide metabolism points up the relative quantitative importance of lungs and kidneys in excretion of total acid.

The total tissue content of carbon dioxide (H_2CO_3, HCO_3, and CO_2) at any one time is about 1100 mM. The resting basal carbon dioxide production is about 13,000 mM. per day, and heavy work will raise this to 30,000 mM. per day. The carbon dioxide content of the blood is about 135 mM. at any one time. Thus, in heavy work, the blood-to-lung route turns over completely about seven times per hour; this is one complete turnover (i.e., transport and excretion of its entire content) every ten minutes.

Thus, the lungs excrete about 12,000 to 30,000 mM. of carbon dioxide per day; the kidneys excrete only about 200 mM. of acid per day, though this can be increased. The minute-to-minute significance of pulmonary function far outweighs renal function in acid excretion. Surgical problems are numerous and pressing in this area: pneumothorax, thoracotomy, airway obstruction, burns, wounds of the face, to mention but a few. In all of these instances, severe respiratory acidosis plays a role should alveolar ventilation be inadequate. This is not repaired by oxygen administration.

It is apparent that the kidneys can excrete hydrogen ion with a variety of fixed anions (Cl^-, $SO_4^=$, $PO_4^=$, pyruvate, lactate), which the lungs cannot exhale; it is equally clear that serious ventilatory impairment will produce severe acidosis much more rapidly than anuria. In twenty-four minutes of severe ventilatory embarrassment pH drops to 7.0 or lower. After twenty-four hours of anuria the acidosis is much less pronounced and, if ventilation is increased, even negligible, although the unexcreted anions (phosphate, sulfate) are beginning to accumulate. In uremia the acid load is about 75 mE. per day; there are 1000 mE. of buffer base to deal with it.

The pulmonary contribution to acid excretion is by virtue of the reaction $H_2CO_3 \rightarrow H_2O + CO_2$, a reaction facilitated by pulmonary carbonic anhydrase. The water and carbon dioxide are then exhaled. Note that the H^+ ion actually leaves the body in the H_2O molecule; the failure to ventilate and exhale these two compounds (H_2O and CO_2) is reflected by a rise in the CO_2 tension of the arterial blood and alveolar air from the normal value of 40 mm. Hg to values as high as 100 mm. Hg.

The extreme diffusibility of carbon dioxide has an interesting corollary here. If the pCO$_2$ of arterial blood is 40 mm. Hg, but the pCO$_2$ of mixed exhaled air from the total bronchial tree is only 20 mm. Hg, it indicates that approximately one-half of the lung is not receiving its normal blood supply. Diffusion defects and circulatory changes in the lung can be studied by such methods, useful in the diagnosis of massive embolus.

Section II.   Range of pH Values and Total Buffering Capacity

A. RANGE OF pH CHANGES

The normal pH of arterial blood is between 7.38 and 7.43 and of venous blood between 7.36 and 7.41. A significant metabolic acidosis is present with a pH of 7.30 or below and similarly a significant degree of alkalosis may be considered to be present with a pH of 7.48 or higher. The extreme ranges ordinarily observed in disease and compatible with life only for short periods of

time are acidosis to the extent of a pH of 6.95 and alkalosis to a pH of 7.8.

It may seem surprising at first glance that a range of only a few tenths of a unit can produce such marked clinical changes. One must recall again that the pH unit is logarithmic in nature and the difference in hydrogen ion concentration between the pH of 7.1 and 7.8 is fourfold.

The normal tension of carbon dioxide

(pCO_2) of the alveolar air and therefore of arterial blood is 40 mm. Hg. Under conditions of underventilation, and retention of carbon dioxide, this pCO_2 may rise to values above 80 mm. Hg, and with overventilation may drop to as low as 15 mm. Hg. The normal relationship between HCO_3^- and H_2CO_3 in blood is such that there is twenty times as much bicarbonate as there is carbonic acid in the blood. Under conditions of severe alkalosis this ratio is increased and in acidosis it is lowered. It is therefore possible to signify the range within which the body works and the significance of changes which might be observed by the use of the pH-bicarbonate diagram shown in Figure 65.

The normal carbon dioxide combining power is about 23 to 27 mE. per l. In surgical patients a significant metabolic alkalosis exists when this rises acutely to values of 29 or 30 mE. per l. or above. This small change may be of considerable portent, particularly in the preoperative state, since alkalosis is much worsened by surgical stress and its resultant effects on the excretion of urine bicarbonate.

Metabolic acidosis as seen in surgery lowers the carbon dioxide combining power to values between 15 and 25 mE. per l. The extremely low values seen in diabetic and renal acidosis, where the carbon dioxide combining power is less than 10 mE. per l., are happily rare in surgical practice. If present they bode ill for survival from any sort of trauma or surgery.

B. THE BODY BUFFERS

A buffer is a chemical substance that takes up hydrogen ion with little change in pH. It takes the H^+ out of ionization and combines it in molecular form so that it cannot exert its corrosive acid effect as a free proton. The buffer with and without hydrogen comprises therefore two different molecules and the two are called a "buffer pair."

If we add hydrochloric acid to distilled water, it immediately becomes very acidic. If we add it to blood, only a small pH change results; blood is well buffered. The buffer capacity is expressed as the hydrogen ion accepted per unit pH change. Familiar buffer pairs are $HCO_3^- - H_2CO_3$, $H_2PO_4^- - HPO_4^=$ and $HHb - HbO_2^-$.

The erythrocyte, by dint of its carbonic anhydrase, hemoglobin-buffer, and carbamino compounds, is responsible for about 83 per cent of carbon dioxide transport and a large fraction of the total buffer capacity of the blood. In severe anemia this property of whole blood is proportionally reduced. Yet, the blood buffers represent only about one-fifth the buffer capacity of the body, the rest residing in the extracellular fluid and cells.

It is difficult to find absolute and readily understandable terms in which to express the buffering capacity of the blood and of the body as a whole. Most surgeons are familiar with the acidity of 0.1 N hydrochloric acid. This is a completely unbuffered acid solution of pH 1.0; the hydrogen ion is associated with an anion (Cl^-) which gives the hydrogen complete dissociation. One-tenth normal hydrochloric acid is a very sour-tasting material and represents the extreme of acidity encountered in the human body, namely, that of the gastric hydrochloric acid as it comes out of the parietal cell. It is therefore a reference point that can be understood in terms of everyday experience.

How much 0.1 N hydrochloric acid can the body take on or lose? If the whole blood volume were simply taken out of the body and stirred around in a beaker, one could add hydrochloric acid to it and make a titration curve for the pH change per unit acid added. This titration curve would show a slope indicating the buffer capacity of whole blood. If the plasma were removed from the whole blood, one would find a somewhat steeper curve since the plasma lacks the buffering mechanisms of the erythrocyte.

Much acid-base chemistry presented in student texts has been conceived of in this "blood in a beaker" fashion. Actually this is quite unrealistic. The entire extracellular fluid contains bicarbonate and carbonic acid in approximately the same concentrations as the plasma and therefore, although it is not associated with the nice buffering mechanisms of the red blood cell, except as transcapillary exchange lets it wash the erythrocyte, the extracellular fluid has a definite buffering capacity (which is also expressed by the Henderson-Hasselbalch equation) but without the additional factors of protein or

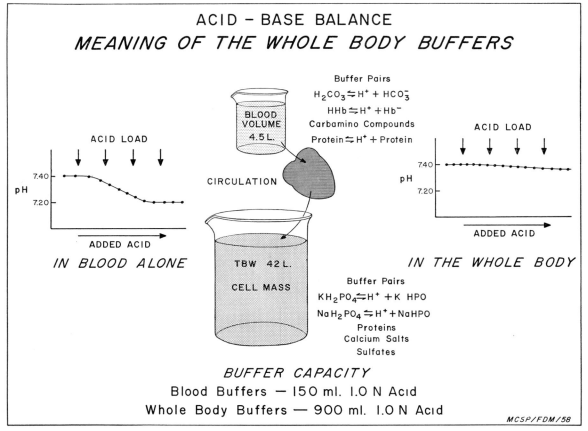

Figure 64. ACID-BASE BALANCE. I. THE MEANING OF THE WHOLE BODY BUFFERS

During the past few years it has become increasingly evident that the blood buffer systems (though carefully studied and well understood for almost forty years) account for but a small fraction of the acid-accepting ability of the body. The buffer capacity of a system is defined in terms of the pH change produced by the acceptance of hydrogen ion. A well-buffered system is one that can take up much hydrogen ion with little change in pH. This is true of almost any biologic system. A poorly buffered system would be one such as distilled water or simple sodium chloride solution in which the addition of acid produces immediate and large changes in pH.

The blood is buffered by a variety of mechanisms shown as the buffer pairs on the chart. Most of the blood buffers also exist in the interstitial fluid, a volume about three times that of the plasma volume. This is true of all of the blood buffers except those that exist within the red cell itself. But beyond the interstitial fluid is the great mass of cell water containing very complicated biologic systems, many of which have the effect of being buffers. The potassium-sodium-phosphate and sulfate systems are salt buffers analogous to those found in the

blood and urine. In addition, calcium salts, protein salts, and many amphoteric ions exist within cells and have the property of buffering acid loads.

To the left is shown the sharp fall in pH which occurs when a large acid load is added to the blood alone. Acute respiratory acidosis occurring in the matter of a minute or less would be an example of this rapid disequilibrated and relatively unbuffered acid load.

To the right is shown the effect when a similar acid load, either endogenous or exogenous, is added to the whole body. A minimal pH change results.

In the center of the chart is shown diagrammatically the difference in volume between the blood and the cell mass, involving the rest of body water. It is seen that merely on the basis of volume alone the cells and body water have about ten times the buffering capacity of the blood. In chemical terms, the buffering capacity of the whole body is about six times that of the blood alone.

The heart is indicated in the center of the diagram to symbolize that normal circulation and the time for its accomplishment are both necessary if the blood is to have the opportunity to present its acid load to the tissue buffers.

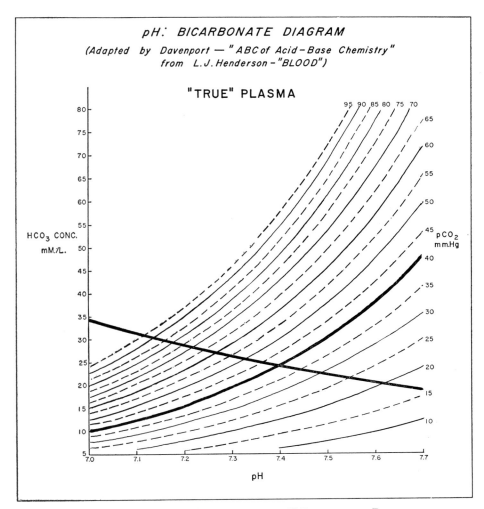

Figure 65. ACID-BASE BALANCE. II. THE *p*H-BICARBONATE DIAGRAM

In this chart (taken from Davenport) is shown the relationship of whole blood *p*H to the plasma bicarbonate concentration.

The heavy line, sloping downward from left to right, is the "blood buffer line" indicating the change in blood *p*H within a narrow range of bicarbonate concentration. The series of lines crossing this horizontal component represents the carbon dioxide tension of blood observed at varying *p*H and bicarbonate concentrations. The heavy line is that of normal *p*CO₂ (40 mm. Hg).

These two heavy lines cross in the middle of the chart, at approximately the area of normal arterial *p*H. The *p*H here is about 7.40, the bicarbonate about 23 mm. per liter, and the carbon dioxide tension 40 mm. Hg.

Values lying above the horizontal line are due to metabolic alkalosis and below the line to metabolic acidosis. Data lying to the left of the normal *p*CO₂ line are associated with respiratory acidosis, and data falling to the right, with respiratory alkalosis.

It is thus possible to take a sample of arterial blood (or, in stable situations, venous blood) and analyze it immediately under anaerobic conditions and constant temperature, for its total carbon dioxide content and its *p*H. From the Henderson-Hasselbalch nomogram, one determines the bicarbonate concentration and the carbon dioxide tension for blood exhibiting the observed *p*H and total carbon dioxide.

Plotting the bicarbonate and the *p*H on this diagram, one can then assess the relative contribution of metabolic and respiratory factors to the acid-base imbalance under consideration.

erythrocyte buffers. Thus, the importance of the circulation and transcapillary exchange lies not only in the transport of oxygen, energy substrates, and metabolites, but also in bringing to the erythrocyte buffers the acids of tissue metabolism. Shock, congestive failure, and arterial injuries are examples of disease processes in which circulatory changes rapidly produce severe local acidosis by dint of failure to bring the acid to the buffer and vice versa. Thus, were an individual to receive 0.1 N hydrochloric acid intravenously, it would be buffered not only by the blood as it circulates but also by the whole extracellular phase, with which it comes into immediate contact by diffusion.

But even this concept of "extracellular-fluid buffers" is too limited. The entire body has a buffering capacity which is due to the additional presence of intracellular buffers. The nature of these buffers and the pK values at which they work is unknown at this time. It is assumed that the monohydrogen–dihydrogen phosphate system is probably the most important intracellular buffer pair in body cells, just as it is in renal tubule cells. Our concept of ranges of buffering capacity cannot be limited to the blood or even the extracellular fluid but must take into consideration the entire body. In addition, anything we do to the living body involves simultaneous respiratory and renal mechanisms.

We can study this whole system as it exists and titrate it to see what sort of a curve we get. To lower the pH from 7.4 to 7.1 in a blood volume of 5000 ml. in a beaker would require 1198 ml. of 0.1 N HCl; if this were added to 5000 ml. of water, the pH of the water would drop from 7.0 to 1.8. But, by contrast, to lower the whole body pH 7.4 to 7.1, assuming all the body buffers are taken up (but not relying on respiratory or renal compensations), would require 6700 ml. of 0.1 N HCl. These figures and general ranges give us an idea of the total acid load accepted within an observed change in pH; it is a load far greater than that required to produce the pH change in blood alone.

The alkalosis mechanisms are much more difficult to understand in terms of total body buffers, and they are more obscure since renal regulation may break down under certain circumstances and the respiratory compensation seems to be practically nil.

In metabolic acidosis the combination of compensations is indicated by the following figures. With a "new" fixed acid level in the extracellular fluid of 27 mM. per l. (an extreme value), the lungs, by lowering the pCO_2 to 24 mm. Hg and the HCO_3^- to 6.2 mE. per l., can yield a pH of 7.02. Without compensation ($pCO_2 = 40$ mm. Hg) the pH would be 6.93. "Complete" compensation (impossible to achieve) would lower the pCO_2 to 5 mm. Hg, HCO_3^- to 2 mE. per l., and even then the pH would be brought back only to 7.20. In surgical patients the respiratory compensation is never complete and often (in open chest operations) totally inactive.

C. "SUBTRACTION" VERSUS "ADDITION"

There is a difference in the effects on acid-base imbalance and pH according to whether changes involve addition or subtraction of hydrogen ion from the body. This terminology has been emphasized by Wynn (1957) and is of great value in surgical disease. Let us consider acidosis. This may be produced by *loss* of alkaline juices (as in pancreatic fistula, ulcerative colitis) or it may be produced by *gain* of acid in the form of hydrochloric, phosphoric, and sulfuric acid in renal insufficiency or as keto-acids in diabetic acidosis. Artificially, it may also be produced by adding acid to the body, as has been done when administering ammonium chloride, this substance being a strong donor of hydrogen ion under the pH conditions of the blood. We therefore have an acidosis caused by loss of base, which might be called "subtraction acidosis," and an acidosis caused by the addition of acid, which might be called "addition acidosis."

Precisely the same distinction may be made in the case of alkalosis. "Subtraction alkalosis" characteristically occurs from the loss of hydrochloric acid in vomiting. "Addition alkalosis" rarely occurs naturally, but it can be produced by the administration of sodium bicarbonate (in ulcer treatment, for example) or sodium lactate. The bicarbonate and lactate ions are bases because they are acceptors of hydrogen ion; the *p*H of the solution is therefore raised.

These distinctions are important and helpful in surgical treatment. Subtraction alkalosis is always associated with loss of water as well as protons and cations. This mixed loss of water and salt produces a contraction of the extracellular fluid, diminished plasma volume, some degree of hemoconcentration, diminished glomerular filtration, and azotemia with renal acidosis. Thus, subtraction alkalosis tends to produce renal changes which, if they go far enough, turn the patient all the way around into a metabolic acidosis of renal origin. A renal event (diminished glomerular filtration rate) follows the initial extrarenal event (acid loss), tending to reverse the *p*H change. It is clearly impossible to equate this alkalosis with one resulting from the infusion of sodium bicarbonate.

By sharp contrast, addition alkalosis, produced by the ingestion of sodium bicarbonate by patients on an ulcer diet, or by the intravenous infusion of sodium bicarbonate, carries none of these threats. An expanded extracellular fluid results; the renal output of water and salt is markedly increased. Indeed, a solute diuresis results. The renal *p*H is uniformly high. The physiologic contrast between the two situations is so great that they cannot be equated simply because they are both a form of alkalosis.

The same factors are present in acidosis. Subtraction acidosis (for example, pancreatic fistula) is associated with loss of base and water, some contraction of the extracellular phase, and, ultimately, diminished renal function, making the acidosis much worse. Fatal worsening of metabolic subtraction acidosis follows this downward spiral, with oliguria adding its insult at the end. Addition acidosis (for example, renal failure) is not associated with these changes; overhydration may instead be the threat. Dehydration, if present (as in diabetic acidosis), is on an entirely different basis: the excretion of a large amount of glucose in the urine with an associated osmotic diuresis.

The terms "acidotic" and "alkalotic" are themselves rather loosely used in clinical work. The *p*H change may be minimal—it may be compensated by renal or respiratory change. This seemingly loose usage is clinically valid, however, and we will stick by it. A burned patient with a *p*CO$_2$ of 60 mm. Hg and TCO$_2$ of 32 mE. per l. should be considered to be in respiratory acidosis even if, by straining to the limit all his buffer and excretory mechanisms, the *p*H has only fallen to 7.32. True, he is worse, and more acidotic, if his *p*H goes down to 7.10; but caution demands that as he *starts* down the path he be considered and called "acidotic."

In summary, then, it is important not only to differentiate between metabolic and pulmonary acid-base changes, but also to differentiate sharply between the addition acid-base changes and the subtraction acid-base changes. The effect of trauma on renal and pulmonary compensation for acid-base imbalance is of central importance in the management of surgical patients.

D. THE EFFECT OF TRAUMA ON ACID-BASE BALANCE

This subject is of recurring importance in surgical care; it is merely summarized here. The effects of surgical trauma on acid-base balance are seven.

(1) Uncomplicated elective surgery produces a slight tendency to alkalosis because the effect on the renal tubule promotes the resorption of sodium bicarbonate.

(2) If a threat of metabolic alkalosis is present (for example, loss of hydrochloric acid by vomiting) or if it is established, surgical injury makes the alkalosis suddenly much worse because of the post-traumatic blockage of compensatory excretion of sodium bicarbonate; concomitant loss of potassium accentuates the defect also by preventing the excretion of an alkaline urine.

(3) Ventilatory difficulty of any sort whatsoever produces respiratory acidosis; it may be very severe, much more severe than the mild tendency to alkalosis mentioned above, in which case severe respiratory acidosis quickly supervenes. Some impairment of ventilation is intrinsic in surgery of the thorax or upper abdomen.

(4) Circulatory difficulty of any sort whatsoever produces metabolic acidosis through

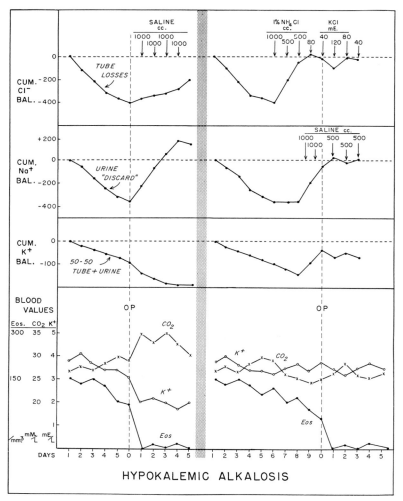

Figure 66. Hypokalemic Alkalosis

In this chart, on the left, are shown the events which transpire when gastric obstruction is improperly treated. The patient is operated on and severe hypokalemic alkalosis results. It will be noticed that tube losses of chloride and urinary "discard" of sodium ion have progressed preoperatively without adequate replacement as shown by their cumulative balances. A considerable amount of potassium is lost, divided about half-and-half between tube and urine. Before operation, the plasma potassium concentration has gradually begun to fall and the carbon dioxide combining power has gradually begun to rise. These minor preoperative changes are important evidences of a dangerous situation. At the time of operation, the patient has been treated entirely with saline, an unfortunate error in this situation because sodium loading accentuates the alkalosis (because of the renal blockade to sodium excretion observed after trauma). The result is that the plasma potassium concentration drops precipitously to dangerously low values and the carbon dioxide combining power climbs. The eosiniphil count is shown as

dropping to zero merely as in indicator of the steroidal aspects of the operation. This is severe hypokalemic alkalosis.

By contrast, on the right is shown a more effective treatment of such a patient. Preoperatively the situation is properly assessed and the cumulative losses of chloride and sodium through tube and urine respectively are replaced by infusions of ammonium chloride, potassium chloride, and sodium chloride. The result is that the patient comes to operation with a body chloride and sodium almost normal. There is still some slight potassium deficit but if alkalosis is avoided, this is of little importance. At operation the eosinophil fall indicates the same steroidal discharge as shown on the left. But, with chloride, sodium, and potassium restored to normal, there is no hypokalemic alkalosis.

The term urine "discard" of sodium is used to indicate an excretion of sodium (and bicarbonate) that is normally compensatory to the alkalosis of acid loss. This compensatory sodium excretion is blocked by trauma or by potassium loss, or both.

failure to mobilize acids from tissues and failure to bring blood buffers to tissue acids.

(5) Anoxia of either ventilatory or circulatory origin produces acidosis (hypoxic acidosis) by the accumulation of lactic and pyruvic acid.

(6) Circulatory occlusion of a part produces severe local metabolic acidosis by the accumulation of carbon dioxide and by hypoxic acidosis.

(7) Decreased urine output produces metabolic acidosis through failure of the kidney to excrete organic and inorganic anions and hydrogen ion.

As a general rule, then, uneventful surgery has a *slight* alkalotic trend, making preexistent alkalosis much worse, while surgical complications, particularly vascular, pulmonary, and renal ones, produce *severe* acidosis.

Section III. A Bird's-Eye View of Acid-Base Changes in Surgery

The many sorts of disorder—gastrointestinal disease, pulmonary disease, shock, diabetes, and many others—that produce acid-base changes in surgery are described in full in various appropriate sections of this book.

A brief outline of typical major acid-base situations with characteristic chemical findings follows.

I. ALKALOSIS

A. *Addition Alkalosis* (very rare)
   1. *Metabolic*. Example—alkali overdosage (as in ulcer therapy).
   Typical findings:

pH	7.48	
pCO_2	40	mm. Hg
TCO_2	30	mE. per l.
CO_2 cp	28.8	mE. per l.
Na	147	mE. per l.
Cl	95	mE. per l.
K	3.0	mE. per l.

   Urine: pH 7.5   Na 75 mE. per l.

   2. *Respiratory*. Respiratory addition alkalosis does not occur.

B. *Subtraction Alkalosis*
   1. *Metabolic* (very common). Example—pyloric obstruction in highly acid stomach.
   Typical findings:

pH	7.52	
pCO_2	40	mm. Hg
TCO_2	32.7	mE. per l.
CO_2 cp	31.5	mE. per l.
Na	146	mE. per l.
Cl	90	mE. per l.
K	2.8	mE. per l.

   Urine: pH 7.5   Na 75 mE. per l. ("normal")
   Postoperatively or in K deficit: pH 5.0 and Na 10 mE. per l.

   2. *Respiratory* (rare). Example—acute hyperventilation tetany.
   Typical findings:

pH	7.54	
pCO_2	20	mm. Hg
TCO_2	17	mE. per l.
CO_2 cp	27	mE. per l.
Na	143	mE. per l.
Cl	103	mE. per l.
K	3.7	mE. per l.

   Urine: pH 7.5   Na 75 mE. per l.

II. ACIDOSIS

A. *Addition Acidosis* (common)
   1. *Metabolic*. Examples—renal failure, diabetes.
   Typical findings in renal failure:

pH	7.25	
pCO_2	30	mm. Hg
TCO_2	14	mE. per l.
CO_2 cp	13.2	mE. per l.
Na	137	mE. per l.
Cl	114	mE. per l.
K	6.5	mE. per l.
P	7	mM. per l.
BUN	150	mg. per 100 ml.

   Urine: scanty; pH 7.0

   2. *Hypoxic* (a special form of metabolic addition acidosis). Example—acute oliguric shock; low pump-oxygenator flow.
   Typical findings:

pH	7.15	
pCO_2	35	mm. Hg
TCO_2	13	mE. per l.
CO_2 cp	12.5	mE. per l.
Na	140	mE. per l.
Cl	100	mE. per l.
K	5.4	mE. per l.
Lactate	90	mg. per 100 ml.
	(10 mE. per l.)	

   Urine: scanty; pH 4.7

3. *Respiratory*. Example—acute ventilatory insufficiency.

Typical findings:

pH	7.05	
pCO$_2$	90	mm. Hg
TCO$_2$	25	mE. per l.
CO$_{2\ cp}$	27	mE. per l.
Na	140	mE. per l.
Cl	100	mE. per l.
K	6.0	mE. per l.

Urine: pH 4.5

B. *Subtraction Acidosis* (common)

1. *Metabolic*. Example—dysentery, biliary or pancreatic fistula.

Typical findings:

pH	7.22	
pCO$_2$	20	mm. Hg
TCO$_2$	12	mE. per l.
CO$_{2\ cp}$	11.5	mE. per l.
Na	120	mE. per l.
Cl	100	mE. per l.
K	5.5	mE. per l.

Urine: scanty; pH 4.5

2. *Respiratory*. Respiratory subtraction acidosis does not occur.

CHAPTER 21

Solutions and Priorities in the Treatment of Water-Electrolyte and Acid-Base Disorders

Section I.   Therapeutic Solutions Available

The pharmacologic classification of intravenous solutions is based on their chemical composition, chief effects, main areas of usefulness, and modes of preparation. A few examples of each are outlined here.

I. Intravascular Volume Replacement
  A. Cells and plasma
    1. Whole blood
      a. Stored, citrated
      b. Fresh, citrated
      c. Fresh, resin-collected
      d. Directly transfused
  B. Cells alone
    1. Sedimented separated cells suspended in their own plasma
    2. Spun cells resuspended in electrolyte solution
  C. Plasma
    1. Single-donor plasma
    2. Room-temperature-stored, single-donor plasma
    3. Pooled, lyophilized plasma
  D. Plasma fractions
    1. Concentrated albumin
    2. Fibrinogen
  E. Plasma-volume substances of non-human origin
    1. Dextran—5% in saline solution
    2. Dextran—5% in dextrose and water

II. Extracellular Salt Mixtures
  A. Hypertonic
    1. 5% NaCl
    2. 3% NaCl
    3. 3% $NaCl–NaHCO_3$
  B. Isotonic
    1. 0.85% NaCl
    2. 0.85% NaCl in 5% glucose
    3. $NaCl–NaHCO_3$ at 0.310 molar
    4. NaCl–Na lactate at 0.310 molar
    5. Ringer's solution, Hartmann's solution
  C. Hypotonic
    1. 0.4% NaCl in 5% glucose
    2. 0.4% NaCl in water for clysis
III. Water and Sugar
  A. 5% dextrose in water
  B. 10% dextrose in water
  C. 35% dextrose in water
  D. 50% dextrose in water
  E. Invert sugar in water
IV. Solutions for Special Acid-Base Effects

When an anion or cation is given that is readily metabolized, converted to a crystalloid, or excreted, the ion is referred to as "disposable." If a cation is thus disposed (ammonia, for example, by conversion to urea), it is replaced by hydrogen ion and the net effect is toward acidosis. It is thus useful in treating subtraction alkalosis. The same in converse is true of bicarbonate or lactate as disposable anions.

A. Cation with disposable anion
   1. 0.150 molar $NaHCO_3$
   2. 0.150 molar Na lactate
   3. Both the above in lower concentration mixed with NaCl
   4. 0.60 molar Na lactate (approximately four times isotonic)
B. Anion with disposable cation
   1. 2% NH_4Cl
   2. 1% NH_4Cl
V. Intracellular Salt Mixtures
   A. KCl, 40 mM./l. in 5% dextrose and water
   B. K lactate, 40 mM./l. in 5% dextrose and water
   C. Magnesium sulfate, 20%
VI. Solutions Useful for Caloric Provision
   A. 5% alcohol
   B. 15% or 30% fat emulsion

Section II.   The Priority List in Treatment of Disorders of Water, Salt, and Acid

There must be an orderly process in treatment. If all the lost substances and water are suddenly returned, or if needless intravenous therapy is given, it may be disastrous: the patient dies either of congestive heart failure, of shock, or of pulmonary edema. Patients compensate in many ways to chemical disorders; and they appear to become adjusted to remarkably askew water distribution. They must be eased, not flooded, in the right direction. Indiscriminate massive treatment is dangerous, and one must discern the most important needs before starting. The surgeon is not dealing with a simple chemical system; he must discriminate among needs and deal with first things first. It is essential to have a realistic priority list of things that should be done for the patient and the order in which they should be done.

The priority list in the parenteral therapy of acute illness involving water and electrolyte losses is as follows (in descending order of urgency):
   (1) blood volume,
   (2) colloid osmotic pressure,
   (3) acid-base balance,
   (4) total osmotic pressure,
   (5) potassium concentration,
   (6) total body water and electrolyte: debt and maintenance, and
   (7) calories.
These therapeutic objectives will be examined in order; in clinical work they are often dealt with practically simultaneously or in combinations.

1. Blood Volume

The first priority in the acutely ill patient is for maintenance of the blood volume. In a patient with acute intestinal obstruction, for example, who has been sick for three or four days, the total deficit of water and sodium may run to several liters of water and several hundred mE. of sodium. But the chief thing that is the matter with the patient when he comes into the hospital in shock with no urine output, a pulse weak and thready, a hematocrit of 55, and no capillary circulation is that his plasma volume has become diminished. The volume of circulating blood must be restored first. This initial priority for blood volume is of first-rank importance; it applies to a wide variety of acute "water and electrolyte" problems where the loss has proceeded at such a rate and volume as to reduce effective extracellular and circulating blood volume. An attempt to deal with the deficit in plasma volume of such patients by sudden massive infusion of water and salt may be successful, but it is less efficient than initial treatment with colloids (plasma, dextran, albumin, and small amounts of whole blood with the foregoing). The basic replacement of water and salt must be given; but during the first six hours the circulation should be restored with solutions aimed at intravascular volume.

Where plasma volume is compromised by pure water deficit (true dehydration or desiccation with hemoconcentration of protein, cells, and salt) it is restored to normal by the energetic administration of water; protein has not been lost and need not be given.

A normal blood volume is the number one priority in acutely ill patients suffering from mixed water-and-salt loss, acid-base imbalance, dehydration, and extrarenal loss of fluid. The restoration of renal function demands filtration pressure. The restoration of the water and salt lost will slowly restore plasma volume—but only at the expense of plasma protein concentration, which will inevitably fall. A colloid solution is far preferable as the initial step, when blood pressure is low, pulse is up, or the hematocrit elevated.

2. Colloid Osmotic Pressure

The second priority in acutely ill, metabolically unbalanced patients is the colloid osmotic pressure. Some might argue as to whether this or total osmotic pressure should come next on the priority list. It is unfortunately easy to lower the colloid osmotic pressure (that is, plasma protein concentration) to critically low levels by giving water and salt rapidly, whereas the total osmotic pressure is unchanged by the giving of large amounts of colloid. For this reason we feel that attention to the colloid should come first. This attention should be maintained throughout treatment, whatever subsequent therapy with water and electrolyte is indicated.

If the colloid osmotic pressure of the plasma is low, the body has a tendency to form edema. For some reason which is not well understood, low colloid osmotic pressure is also associated with hyponatremia. We therefore make it a rule to pay close attention to colloid osmotic pressure (as measured by the concentration of total plasma protein or albumin) in patients who are undergoing extensive therapy with water and electrolyte. If the colloid osmotic pressure is low, there is only one substance that is effective in raising it acutely: concentrated human serum albumin. This substance has a usefulness here probably greater than in any other area of clinical medicine and surgery. In a normal-sized adult individual two or three units of concentrated albumin a day can be relied upon to increase the plasma albumin concentration about 0.2 to 0.5 gm. per 100 ml. per day, and this therapy can be kept up for two or three days, if necessary.

The hazards of administering concentrated albumin, particularly in cardiac patients, have been much emphasized. We believe that they have been overemphasized. The cardiac patient with hypoproteinemia will actually feel better and have better renal function and less edema if the colloid osmotic pressure is raised to normal by the use of concentrated human albumin. If a cardiac patient in congestive failure, with a normal plasma protein concentration, is suddenly loaded down with concentrated albumin, he may go into congestive failure by virtue of the additional fluid called into the plasma from the interstitial spaces by the increased colloid. But this is a situation that is seen in surgery only on most rare occasions, it is far removed from most surgical cardiac problems, and overemphasis on it has given rise to a hesitancy in using albumin which is not justified by the facts. The hypoproteinemic cardiac patient may be induced to diuresis of water and salt by concentrated albumin therapy given slowly and judiciously.

3. Acid-Base Balance

The third priority in the work-list for the acutely ill patient with extrarenal loss, vomiting, intestinal obstruction, or diarrhea, dehydration with changes in the volume of extracellular fluid, or sequestered edema lies in restoration of acid-base balance. The heart of therapy consists in treating subtraction acidosis with a cation accompanied by a disposable anion (sodium accompanied by bicarbonate or lactate) and by treating subtraction alkalosis with an anion accompanied by disposable cation (chloride accompanied by ammonium or potassium, the latter being disposable into the cell mass). The amounts of these unbalanced acid-base solutions to be used rest upon frequent check of the acid-base balance of the patient during the period of therapy. Specifically, if the patient comes in with intestinal obstruction, a hematocrit of 55, a normal plasma protein concentration, and a carbon dioxide combining power of 20 mE. per l., we would commence the treatment by using either plasma or concentrated albumin, and a mixed solution of sodium chloride and sodium bicarbonate, containing 40 mE. per l. of bicarbonate. We would treat the patient with amounts of plasma and of this electrolyte solution, which would be expected to bring his carbon dioxide combining power up within about thirty-six hours of admission.

Acid-base balance is carefully estimated at the start, and one or two checks of carbon dioxide combining power are taken during treatment.

All alkalotic patients should be given liberal amounts of potassium as their metabolic alkalosis is treated. If the patient is acidotic and with established anuria, no potassium should be given initially. If he is acidotic with transient decreased urine output due to loss of blood or extracellular fluid, the use of potassium may assist in restoration of urine output and will avoid a reactive hypokalemia as acidosis is corrected with base in the face of some potassium deficiency. In both cases, his electrocardiograms should be watched during treatment.

It is a fatal error to reconstitute past losses entirely on the first day. Although it cannot always be expressed precisely in scientific terms, there is no question that patients become "adjusted" or "habituated" to very remarkable situations of chemical imbalance. A good example is the mobilization of cell water in chronic desalting water loss. The hyponatremia that results is much more marked than is residual reduction of volume. An hematocrit may be normal despite the loss of much salt water. If to this compensated state a sudden large ration of plasma or saline solution is added, pulmonary edema may result.

If normovolemic patients are suddenly swamped by heroic and ill-advised therapy, they suffer thereby and the therapy becomes more dangerous than the untreated disease. As mentioned, they should be "nudged," not "kicked," in the right direction. If volume reduction is still present, as judged by blood pressure, pulse, or hematocrit, treatment must be vigorous. The clinical guides to circulatory adequacy and glomerular filtration are of first importance in judging urgency.

Acid-base imbalance comes third on our priority list because operation is frequently in the offing. It is essential that acid-base imbalance be restored as near normal as possible before surgery. Acute respiratory acidosis is an acute ventilatory crisis treatable not by fluid therapy, but by improved ventilation; it is a very poor setting for operation.

Uncorrected metabolic alkalosis is also a dangerous preoperative situation.

The first three items on our priority list are, then, the restoration of blood volume, colloid osmotic pressure, and acid-base balance. Measures to correct these will often suffice to restore blood pressure, circulation, and renal function to normal. With restoration of acid-base balance, the plasma potassium concentration will start back to normal; if the patient is hypokalemic, potassium should be given at the rate of 40 to 80 mE. per l.

The question of "rapid preparation" of the extremely sick patient for surgery often comes up for consideration. This is about as far down the priority list as one can work for "rapid preparation" for surgery, by which is meant something in the vicinity of six to twelve hours. It is possible in this time to restore blood volume to normal, start colloid osmotic pressure and acid-base balance toward normal (if not to normal) in fairly short order, and yet avoid drowning the patient with overzealous treatment.

There is something about starting acid-base imbalance back towards normal before surgery that is more valuable than it might appear on the surface. It may have to do with the total body buffering capacity. A patient who has been metabolically alkalotic with a carbon dioxide combining power of 32 mE. per l. is an extremely poor patient for surgery. If operation is necessary in the near future and he has been started back along the road to correction, even though he is only back to 29 mE. per l., he is going to do much better surgically than a patient who has an untreated carbon dioxide combining power of 32 mE. per l. and whose body buffers are giving way under the strain of a subtraction alkalosis.

This priority list indicates which things are most important; they are not mutually exclusive in therapy. In a patient with severe extrarenal loss due to pyloric obstruction, the surgeon may administer his colloid (plasma), concentrated albumin, and ammonium chloride at or about the same time and have the patient ready for surgery in twenty-four hours; such haste is usually not necessary, but if needed can be accomplished.

4. Total Osmotic Pressure

Next on the priority list is total osmotic pressure, by which is meant the restoration of deficit hypotonicity (meaning hypotonicity due in part to salt loss) by concentrated salt. An example is in chronic desalting water loss. Because of the whole-body–osmometer effect, the idea has become current that such treatment should be based on a calculation of the unit deficit multiplied by a presumed figure for the total volume of body water. As mentioned previously, such a concept would be valid were the body a closed system like a beaker, and were deficit hypotonicity to exist with a normal extracellular fluid. The body is not a closed system; the volume of extracellular fluid is usually normal or expanded in chronic desalting water loss with hypotonicity. Therefore, as concentrated salt is given, water is excreted; the enlarged extracellular fluid becomes smaller as normalcy is restored.

For all these reasons the "deficit times total body water" calculation is neither wise nor safe. Deficit hypotonicity should be treated initially with a moderate dose of concentrated salt solution and the effect should be measured. Further treatment is to be based on the findings. Sodium chloride solution at 3 per cent (four times isotonic) in amounts of 200 to 500 ml. is a good starter for the restoration of deficit hypotonicity in chronic desalting. Under circumstances of deficit hypotonicity with subtraction acidosis, concentrated sodium bicarbonate may be used to advantage.

Where hypotonicity is long established, due primarily to water loading and associated with chronic malnutrition (often with edema), the administration of concentrated salt is unwise and unnecessary; restoration of nutrition, colloid osmotic pressure, and normal gastrointestinal function is more important.

5. Potassium Concentration

This comes next in priority. As sodium concentration is restored in chronic desalting, the potassium concentration will often fall; in alkalosis it will be low to start with. In any patient who is acutely ill or not eating, there has been a loss of potassium in the urine, some of which loss is unavoidable with the dissolution of lean tissue and some of which is to be compensated.

The administration of potassium to patients on parenteral management at rates of 40 to 120 mE. per day and 40 to 80 mE. per l. is an empirical and successful step in parenteral therapy. It rarely restores patients to potassium balance, but it restores cellular tonicity, pushes sodium out of cells, restores the ability of the kidney to excrete base, and returns neuromuscular function to normal. The purpose of this treatment is thus to restore differential cell loss of potassium, assist in maintenance of normal plasma potassium, and assist in restoration of normal acid-base balance by its effect on renal tubular function.

Attention to potassium therefore comes high on the list and is here listed fifth; it must often be given early in treatment, particularly in alkalosis. One need not wait for intravascular volume therapy to cause return of urine flow, where renal function has only briefly been jeopardized by loss of blood volume. Where there is oliguria for more than six hours, potassium treatment must await check on the return of renal function.

6. Total Electrolyte

We have now worked down our priority list far enough to start thinking about total body electrolyte, the sixth priority. One is here dealing with both a static debt and daily maintenance requirements. It is our conviction, based on experience rather than experiment, that one should start with the maintenance requirements rather than with the static debt. This may relate to the fact that patients appear to become, to some extent, adjusted to chronic deficits in body salt; skeletal sodium may constitute a partial endogenous electrolyte replacement. When this step in the priority list has been reached, with previous objectives met, it is often surprising that the static "debt" seen on admission seems to have shrunk in importance.

The maintenance requirement can be calculated on the basis of pulmonary loss plus skin loss plus urinary loss plus extrarenal losses. The urinary loss should be assumed to be 40 mE. of sodium, potassium, and chloride each day. One should not try to restore to the patient the next day all the losses analyzed in the urine unless the renal tubule is clearly abnormal. This would initiate a vicious circle since the normal kidney may be compensating for errors of previous treatment.

A ration of 40 mE. per day for each ion to cover renal losses seems to be a successful procedure, barring pathologic losses in renal disease. The loss through lungs and skin has already been mentioned. In order to calculate the daily maintenance requirements of extrarenal losses, these discharges should be analyzed at occasional intervals for sodium, chloride, and potassium. This analysis should form the basis for daily therapy; the patient is managed by clinical balance. All this information should be entered in the record on a daily balance sheet and the patient should be weighed every day or two.

Weighing the patient each day or two provides the closest possible check on the adequacy of therapy. An acutely ill patient who is not eating and has an absolute deficit of caloric intake should be expected to lose weight each day. If there is no stress he should lose from 250 to 500 gm. a day. If he has recently been operated upon or injured, a greater weight loss is understandable, because of the increased rate of fat oxidation and trauma. Overtreatment, especially of compensated salt loss, will produce a gain in weight.

With only one exception the patient should not gain weight under treatment; this one exception is during the restoration of recent losses in the dehydrated, desalted, or volume-reduced patient with sequestered edema (as in a burn). Under such circumstances, a gradual gain of a kilogram or two is permissible as deficits of body water are made up or the demands of sequestered edema satisfied.

Coming on down our priority list, we now have carried out the great majority of the work to be done. Blood volume, colloid osmotic pressure, acid-base balance, osmolality, potassium concentrations, and daily main-

tenance requirements have been met. Theoretically, the next item on the priority list is the static debt that the patient presented in the first place. When the priority list is followed down in this way, one usually finds that the patient has been under care for approximately thirty-six hours and that the static debt which loomed so large at the outset has begun to disappear. The reason for this is that the static debt hurts the patient because of decreased plasma volume, lowered plasma protein concentration, acid-base imbalance, and hypotonicity produced thereby. With these being taken care of and maintenance requirements met, one may find that the patient is well hydrated, and a normal urine output has returned.

7. Calories

The last item on the priority list in treatment of *acute* disorders of salt-water-acid-base imbalance is that of calories. Most of the infusions given the patient up to this point have contained dextrose in concentration of 5 per cent, and this has provided the patient with some caloric intake which may be of significance in preventing an even more rapid breakdown of lean tissue. If the pathologic situation is such that the acute metabolic abnormality of water and electrolyte has been dealt with but the patient still cannot take food by mouth and has no reasonable prospect of doing so in the next few days, one has arrived at a situation where the provision of calories intravenously is necessary and intravenously administered fat or alcohol useful. This is described in greater detail in a subsequent section (Part IV).

Barring this situation, the acutely ill patient with obstruction, diarrhea, fistula, or sepsis must have his homeostasis restored to normal before embarking on an extensive caloric program. Oral feeding is usually impossible in the acute phase, and the interruption of vital intravenous provisions to give fat or alcohol is, at this stage, unwarranted.

CHAPTER 22

Common Patterns of Water and Electrolyte Change in Injury, Surgery, and Disease*

Many of the metabolic disorders seen in the practice of surgery present themselves as patterns, often recurring, that can be recognized and treated as entities. Nineteen of the commonest patterns are presented here, with notes on treatment.

These patterns are arranged as follows:

SECTION I. Patterns of Dilutional Hypotonicity

   A. Mild post-traumatic sodium-potassium shift
   B. Severe post-traumatic sodium-potassium shift
   C. Starvation hyponatremia
   D. Chronic congestive heart failure
   E. Water intoxication

SECTION II. Patterns of Body-Fluid Loss, with Hypotonicity

   A. Acute venous hemorrhage
   B. Acute shocking desalting water loss
   C. Chronic desalting water loss

D. Chronic hypokalemia in differential potassium deficiency

SECTION III. Patterns of Acid-Base Imbalance

   A. Acute hypokalemic alkalosis
   B. Acute respiratory acidosis
   C. Chronic respiratory acidosis and carbon dioxide narcosis

SECTION IV. Patterns of Hypertonicity

   A. Desiccation or true dehydration
   B. Solute-loading hypertonicity

SECTION V. Patterns of Fluid Sequestration with Reduction in Plasma Volume

   A. Sequestered edema—peritonitis, venous obstruction, and analogues
   B. Burns

SECTION VI. Patterns of Disordered Renal Function

   A. Obstructive uropathy with solute diuresis
   B. Uretero-intestinal anastomosis
   C. Acute renal insufficiency

* We are indebted to *The New England Journal of Medicine* for permission to reprint this section in its entirety from N. Eng. J. Med., *258:* 271–285, 325–333, 377–384, 427–432, 1958.

Section I. Five Patterns of Dilutional Hypotonicity

A. MILD POST-TRAUMATIC SODIUM-POTASSIUM SHIFT

1. Clinical Setting and Appearances

This shift occurs after trauma (Fig. 67), with or without anesthesia, and carries no clinical hazard. Greatly magnified, it becomes the severe sodium-potassium shift, which may be life-endangering.

2. Characteristic Plasma Pattern

The plasma potassium concentration gradually rises, reaching a peak in the vicinity of 4.9 to 5.2 mE. per l. from twenty-four to thirty-six hours after the operation. As the potassium concentration rises, the sodium concentration in the plasma gradually falls, and may drop as low as 130 mE. per l. Azotemia and acid-base imbalance are usually absent.

3. Metabolic Background and Genesis

The fall in plasma sodium concentration appears to be typical post-traumatic dilutional hypotonicity; new sodium-free water is added to the extracellular fluid during a period of post-traumatic water retention. The new sodium-free water comes from the lysis of cells and fat and is increased in volume by any sodium-free water that the

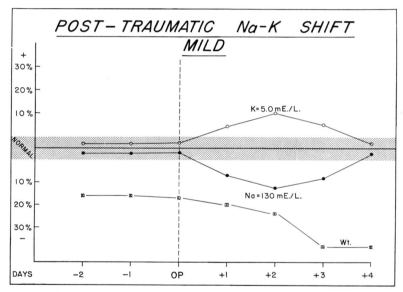

Figure 67. POST-TRAUMATIC SODIUM-POTASSIUM SHIFT—MILD

After operation or injury, with a short period of starvation, lean tissue cells are catabolized, and fat oxidized, releasing new sodium-free water to the extracellular fluid in significant amounts. This water is retained because of the strongly water-retaining (antidiuretic) effect of injury. To this water is added any water given the patient. Since the total water accumulation exceeds water output, a dilutional hyponatremia of mild degree occurs. The slight rise in potassium concentration is less easily susceptible of explanation. The plasma dilution alone might be expected to lower the plasma potassium concentration, and yet a rise characteristically occurs. Alteration in permeability of cells to sodium and potassium has been invoked as an explanation of this phenomenon. Though such an altera-

tion may occur, its importance in this situation is very minor. When diuresis finally occurs, weight drops to its expected post-traumatic level, and sodium concentration rises. The addition of too much water (in excess of metabolic needs) greatly accentuates this defect.

In this and the seventeen remaining figures of this group, the changes in electrolytes (Na, K, Cl) hematocrit, pH, and osmolality are shown in approximate proportion as indicated by the percentiles on the vertical coordinate. Changes in body weight and urea are shown as indications of direction only. Whenever possible, absolute figures are given, merely as typical examples. Time is shown below. (Note that the time scales are quite different for the various patterns.)

doctor gives in excess of the actual requirements of the patient.

The rise in plasma potassium is more difficult to rationalize. The mobilization of potassium from muscle cells seems to be an insufficient explanation. Under most conditions potassium can be excreted readily, and the urinary excretion of potassium is increased after trauma. There may be no acidosis. One is therefore unable to explain this rise in plasma potassium on the basis either of simple cell release or extracellular pH changes, although such explanations would be appealing.

Weight drops but slowly when there is some water loading. Net changes in body composition (total water and electrolyte) are necessarily small during such a brief period.

4. Treatment

No treatment is necessary for this mild hyponatremia and hyperkalemia. It is important to recognize this pattern and be willing to tolerate it if the change does not exceed reasonable limits. Whereas giving the patient too much water makes this change more pronounced, giving him too much isotonic sodium does not seem to make it any less so. Concentrated sodium salts will repair the disorder.

This post-traumatic hyponatremia is a manifestation of the basic tendency of the organism, after injury, to develop water retention and dilutional hypotonicity; the process should be understood rather than treated. It can be prevented by complex maneuvers with mannitol and urea (or other osmotic diuretics) or with concentrated sodium salts. Its endocrine genesis (post-traumatic antidiuresis) is further suggested by the fact that it is not found after hypophysectomy, even when urine outputs are neither excessive nor in the diabetes-insipidus range.

The *normal postoperative patient* (without visceral disease or extrarenal loss) should be given an infusion of water that does not exceed his needs, and a small ration of sodium (about 75 mE.) to balance out the sequestration of extracellular fluid in the site of operative dissection. So treated, his dilutional hypotonicity will be held to a minimum. A small ration of potassium (about 40 mE.) is added daily if it appears that oral intake will be interrupted for three days or more.

B. SEVERE POST-TRAUMATIC SODIUM-POTASSIUM SHIFT

1. Clinical Setting and Appearances

This occurs after operations performed during chronic wasting illness, cachexia, and starvation. Patients undergoing cardiac surgery for advanced mitral stenosis may show life-endangering forms of this pattern (Fig. 68). When surgery is superimposed on starvation hyponatremia, this change may be expected to ensue. Any renal impairment greatly accentuates it. The patient is often hypotensive, is weak and lethargic, and looks "sick"; the clinical picture is entirely nonspecific.

2. Characteristic Plasma Pattern

The characteristic change is a gross exaggeration of mild sodium-potassium shift. The plasma potassium concentration rises, within twenty-four to forty-eight hours, to 6 to 8 mE. per l., and the sodium is reduced to very low concentrations, in the range of 115 to 125 mE. per l. If the patient has shown, before surgery, slightly low plasma sodium and slightly elevated potassium concentrations (characteristic of chronic wasting illness), these move rapidly to dangerous extremes after the operation. Urinary nitrogen output is not usually restricted, although antidiuresis is evident; a rising blood urea nitrogen is not necessarily a part of this picture, although it may occur.

3. Metabolic Background and Genesis

In addition to dilutional hypotonicity and the mobilization of cell potassium, as mentioned in the description of mild post-traumatic sodium-potassium shift, two other factors are active here. One is a chronic energy deficit (due to starvation) with superimposed trauma, a combination that will become more familiar as the discussion proceeds. Low energy levels are often associated with marked disorders of water and salt distribution. Secondly, some of the sodium to be found in the extracellular phase has now

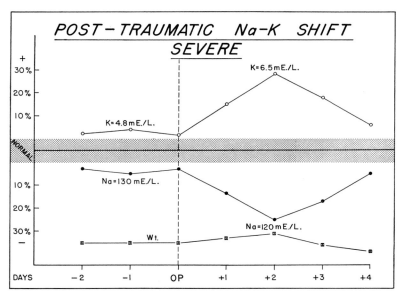

Figure 68.   Post-traumatic Sodium-Potassium Shift—Severe

This more severe form of low sodium–high potassium change occurs after operation in the presence of chronic visceral disease or after very severe injury in healthy persons. In chronic visceral disease there is usually some preoperative alteration of sodium and potassium concentration, as shown here. Under these circumstances the tendency to retain water and dilute the body solute is especially pernicious. Potassium concentration rises abruptly, and the cardiac effects, as indicated by the electrocardiograph, are made more pronounced by the hyponatremia. In the example shown here, there is weight gain as a manifestation of the overadministration of fluid. This markedly accentuates the dilutional hypotonicity and the sodium-potassium shift. In the presence of chronic visceral disease, the intracellular sodium concentration may rise and be of real significance in the hyponatremia observed, in contrast to the milder situation described in the previous figure, in which dilution appears to be wholly responsible.

disappeared into the cells or the skeleton. In the mild form of post-traumatic sodium-potassium shift, there is no evidence of a significant transfer of sodium out of the extracellular phase; in the severe form, there is evidence that this change occurs. If water loading is severe, the patient's weight will rise, and the hypotonicity will become much more marked as the total amount of body water rises, dilution is more severe, and the intracellular fraction of this water contracts.

The electrocardiographic changes that indicate the myocardial toxicity of hyperkalemia are exaggerated by hyponatremia and hypocalcemia. Severe hyperkalemia, with hyponatremia, therefore produces dangerous changes in the heart action. Hypocalcemia may coexist and cause similar electrocardiographic changes. There is a marked reduction in the effectiveness of digitalization during hyperkalemia.

The elevated plasma potassium and low sodium concentrations resemble the electrolyte changes of acute adrenal insufficiency, and yet the concentration of free blood corticosteroids is very high (40 to 80 mg. per 100 ml.) in patients with severe sodium-potassium shift after extensive surgery. One cannot therefore invoke adrenal insufficiency (in its usual meaning) as a cause of severe post-traumatic sodium-potassium shift. Some alteration in relative need for steroids, or in peripheral utilization, might be at fault. There is little evidence on the point except for a clear alteration in intermediary metabolism of steroids after injury.

4. Treatment

Because of its self-limited nature, one would prefer not to treat this situation except by the avoidance of overwatering and oversalting the patient; excessive water intake greatly accentuates the defect. Treatment is sometimes necessitated by the severity of the hyperkalemia, whose hazard is indicated by electrocardiographic changes, or by the depth of the hyponatremia, whose hazard is indicated by semicoma. The administration of concentrated sodium in small amounts, although irrational in terms of total body content (there being already an excess of sodium in the body), is clinically effective. The use of calcium to combat the cardiac effects of hyperkalemia is valuable, but one must beware the marked increase in the toxicity of digitalis that occurs when hyperkalemia under digitalization is treated by means of calcium infusions. This effect is especially noticeable after anesthesia and surgery.

C. STARVATION HYPONATREMIA

1. Clinical Setting and Appearances

Caloric starvation is the clinical setting for this pattern (Fig. 69), encountered after prolonged submaintenance intake of a limited and unbalanced fluid diet, grossly inadequate in calories. Starvation hyponatremia may be expected in patients who have lost over 15 per cent of their body weight. Deficiency of vitamin C is a threat not always clearly evident. The prolonged, quiet, and unstressed starvation associated with carcinoma of the esophagus, stomach, peritoneum, and liver produces this form of hyponatremia and with it a minor degree of hyperkalemia. Characteristic "skin and bones" cachexia is seen in marked cases. Edema is seen in the late stages.

2. Characteristic Plasma Pattern

The plasma sodium is lowered, often to a level in the range of 120 mE. per l. The potassium concentration is slightly elevated, between 4.8 and 5.2 mE. per l. Azotemia is usually absent. Hypoproteinemia is usually present, owing largely to retention of water and salt; interference with albumin synthesis is not seen until late in starvation. Anemia

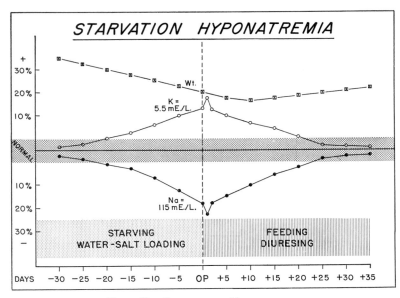

Figure 69. STARVATION HYPONATREMIA

Over a period of a month or two of severe starvation with access only to low-calorie fluids, there is marked loading of water and salt, with a progressive dilutional hypotonicity. A relatively expanded extracellular fluid volume and total exchangeable sodium results, leading ultimately to starvation edema. Differential potassium loss may account in part for the hypotonicity, but for reasons not clearly understood, potassium concentration tends to rise as the mirror image of the sodium fall. Operation at this point may precipitate a severe sodium-potassium shift exactly as it does in congestive heart failure. Beginning caloric nourishment is associated with a rise in the excretion of water and a rise in the plasma sodium concentration. As tissue is synthesized and body weight gradually restored, the extracellular chemical relations return to normal.

(low erythrocyte count) is usually present, but the total blood volume is apt to be normal or high (owing to an expanded plasma volume) if frank hemorrhage has not been a part of the chronic disorder.

3. Metabolic Background and Genesis

Starvation and chronic energy deficit are central mechanisms in this type of hyponatremia, but it is not known why. There is a progressive hypotonicity, with a reduction in sodium excretion and chronic water retention, both of which can be demonstrated in starving patients. Increased amounts of sodium can be shown to be present in the body by isotope dilution and in muscle cells histochemically. There is an enlarged extracellular fluid, with evident dilution.

It is in these patients with starvation and hypotonicity that the compositional change of cachexia is most clearly seen: a high total body water volume, most of which is extracellular, with a high exchangeable sodium and a low exchangeable potassium, a low intracellular water volume, low body fat, and hypotonicity.

Although one does not understand how chronic energy deficit produces hypotonicity, one may consider the matter in evolutionary terms. Vertebrate evolution has developed enzymatic methods of foodstuff conversion to establish energy-exchanging, potassium-rich, lean muscular tissue (and energy-rich fat) in a one-third molar sodium-containing medium. Sodium is excluded from cells and potassium held within, by some sort of pumping mechanism that requires energy. When energy levels drop, the organism appears to "backslide," losing lean tissue and fat and gradually diluting down the solute in its aqueous environment. Starving hypotonic patients often regain their ability to excrete water and salt and return their tonicity to normal when given nothing but caloric energy. This improvement suggests the return toward normal of the inactivation of water-retaining and salt-retaining hormones, or a decrease in activity of some receptor mechanism whose activation increases fluid volume at the expense of tonicity by endocrine influence on tubular function. With returning food intake, sodium is again excluded from cells, both generally and in the renal tubule; this is a factor in the sodium diuresis of recovery.

The normal osmolality of the plasma (as mentioned previously) is approximately 285 mO. per l., or roughly twice the plasma sodium concentration; most of the plasma osmolality is electrolyte-determined. In starving patients with visceral disease, one must ascertain whether or not a low sodium concentration is truly accompanied by hypotonicity. In patients with advanced liver and kidney disease or severe diabetes mellitus, there may be from 20 to 50 mO. per l. of nonelectrolyte solute in the plasma. Urea and related products, sugar, bilirubin, lactate, pyruvate, and other pathologic components account for some of this solute. A determination of the electrolyte-osmolar differential is therefore of help in considering how to treat the patient. If the patient has a low plasma sodium concentration with an isotonic (or even hypertonic) plasma, treatment must depend in part on the nature of the "extra" solute.

4. Treatment

The treatment of starvation hyponatremia is caloric nutrition. It may be necessary to operate upon the patient with obstruction of the upper intestine to enable him to eat. In extreme cases some sort of preliminary step, such as feeding jejunostomy, may be advisable. In our experience this is usually unnecessary. The provision of some caloric intake by vein in the few days before operation may serve to restore liver glycogen to normal; the use of a plastic catheter in the superior vena cava to supply energy in the form of concentrated glucose (with insulin) has been useful. Concentrated glucose also constitutes an osmotic diuretic; mannitol has the same effect. They are both effective in raising the plasma sodium concentration passively, by the removal of water in excess of salt.

Anemia, alone, tends to produce retention of water and salt. The correction of a low hematocrit by infusion of erythrocytes or whole blood may initiate diuresis of water and salt.

Patients with severe hyponatremia, who

have been starving for months, show very few outward evidences of their hypotonicity. The patient seems to be "adapted" to his hyponatremia. Suddenly raising the plasma sodium concentration to new levels by the infusion of large amounts of concentrated salt or mannitol may do the patient more harm than good. Yet he is very vulnerable, after operation, to severe sodium-potassium shift, hypoproteinemia, and edema. As a general rule, in patients with chronic water-electrolyte disturbances, treatment should be gentle and gradual, not violent and sudden. The patient should be starting toward normalcy before operation. It is usually impossible to restore him completely to normal; indeed, such a course may be quite inadvisable. Months of normal convalescent anabolism may be required. Most certainly, the patient with starvation hyponatremia should not be crowded by the infusion of an amount of salt calculated in terms of the "unit deficit times total body water." What he needs is to rid himself of water, not to add salt. Food, whole protein, red cells, and, when needed, definitive surgery (with-

out overadministration of water) are the basic features of treatment.

D. CHRONIC CONGESTIVE HEART FAILURE

1. Clinical Setting and Appearances

Prominent among those exhibiting hypotonic patterns are patients with chronic congestive heart failure (Fig. 70), as in late mitral stenosis, mitral regurgitation, tricuspid stenosis, constrictive pericarditis, and certain congenital heart diseases. In these patients there is wasting of peripheral tissues, and an enlarged heart and liver. There is ascites with edema. The patient is orthopneic, waterlogged, and hemodiluted. The late-stage electrolyte picture is rather different from that seen in aortic stenosis or coronary-artery disease in which angina, syncope, and myocardial infarction are more prominent than maldistribution of water and electrolytes.

2. Characteristic Plasma Pattern

The characteristic finding is hyponatremia with hyperkalemia, a slightly elevated blood

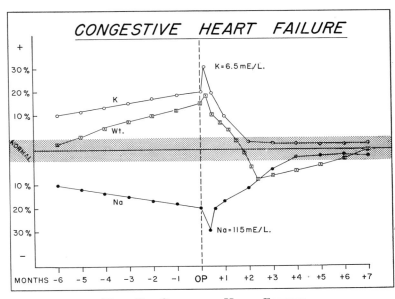

Figure 70. CONGESTIVE HEART FAILURE

As heart failure becomes progressive, there is weight gain due to retention of water and salt (with water in excess) and hypotonicity. The plasma potassium concentration is characteristically elevated. If operation is then successfully performed (as in the example shown here) there may be a severe post-traumatic sodium-potassium shift before diuresis finally occurs. The gradual restoration of body composition and plasma electrolyte concentrations to normal may take as long as a year. The use of diuretics and a low-salt diet with ammonium chloride serves to rid the body of excessive water and salt, but does not alter the basic tendency to accumulation, which rapidly recurs after their use.

urea nitrogen, and hypoproteinemia. The chemical picture resembles that of starvation hyponatremia and cachexia, except that hyperkalemia is more prominent. Edema and ascites are much more marked than in starvation.

3. Metabolic Background and Genesis

Chronic circulatory inadequacy, tissue anoxia, and acidosis appear to be important factors in causing this electrolyte picture. Excessive and abnormal activity of a receptor mechanism sensitive to volume, flow, or oxygenation has been postulated and is appealing but unproved as an explanation of the findings. Retention of water and salt is marked; poor water excretion and increased aldosterone excretion have been shown to exist in these patients, as in those after trauma or with chronic starvation. Although excretion of water loads is poor, there has not been a conclusive demonstration of abnormal antidiuretic activity of the plasma in patients with cardiac disease.

The body sodium level is greatly increased, and the highest exchangeable sodium values seen in clinical medicine and surgery have been observed in such patients. These values run as high as twice normal; yet the extracellular fluid is hypotonic. The magnitude of this water-and-salt maldistribution is unparalleled in other diseases.

Chronic energy deficit is prominent. Most patients with late heart disease are starving, because of insufficient diet, improper absorption, or the failure of transportation of foodstuffs to the tissues.

These patients thus suffer from a combination of all the factors that can be expected to produce dilutional hypotonicity with hyperkalemia. In addition, some have been treated for long periods with a low-sodium diet, ammonium chloride, and mercurial diuretics. As the patient ceases to respond normally to these remedies, they produce a severe chronic, fixed acid acidosis and occasionally a true lowering of the total body sodium. The latter abnormality is rare, is seen only when edema is absent, and requires that the patient follow his low-sodium diet religiously.

4. Treatment

In the long run, the best treatment when feasible is surgical correction of the cardiac lesion. There are few more gratifying sights than that of a patient suffering from late mitral stenosis, with edema, ascites, wasting, hyponatremia, and hyperkalemia, who, over the course of nine to twelve months postoperatively, restores his body composition, vigor, and social effectiveness to normal.

For this recovery to be accomplished, the patient must first be prepared for surgery. Absorbable caloric energy should be provided by mouth if this can be done without overloading the circulation. Total intake of salt and water must be restricted. Ammonium chloride, diuretics, and digitalis must be given, but not blindly. If none of these has been used previously, there is much to gain from their use. If the patient has been receiving all of them under good management by his physician for many months, there is little additional gain to be expected from this source. Lowering of potassium concentration or raising of sodium concentration (for example, by mannitol or concentrated salt) will make digitalis suddenly much more effective, and toxicity may result.

The doctor's objective should be to start the patient moving in the right direction, rid him of as much excess water as possible, provide him with some energy, and then operate, with the patient under ideal digitalization, with adequate oxygenation. Before surgical operation it is virtually impossible to restore to normal the plasma chemical values of patients suffering from severe heart failure. Here, again, the patient must be "nudged," not "kicked," in the right direction during the preoperative period. If biochemical enthusiasm outstrips cardiac capacity, the patient will end his course in the pathology department before he reaches the operating room.

The same general rules hold for the treatment of the patient after operation. Severe sodium-potassium shifts may occur; weight gain means water accumulation and should be avoided; caloric nutrition is important. Adequate ventilation is vital since any degree of respiratory acidosis or anoxia adds to the

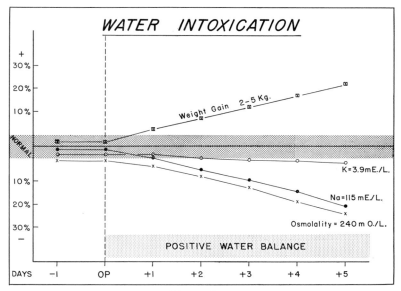

Figure 71. WATER INTOXICATION

The administration of a large amount of salt-free water is ordinarily followed by a profuse water diuresis. In the water-retaining state that follows injury, operation, infection, or acute disease (and is also seen in chronic visceral disease of heart, liver, and kidneys), this free water diuresis does not occur. There is a strong antidiuretic tendency that resembles in many ways the activity of the posterior pituitary antidiuretic hormone. The rate at which dangerous dilution of body solute takes place is dependent on the rate of infusion and the rate of excretion of water. Here, an operation followed by injudicious water administration is used as an example. Serious water intoxication occurs as a result of excessive fluid administration in about four days. Treatment consists of withholding water and giving concentrated salt in moderation.

work of the heart and sets the stage for a potentially fatal arrhythmia. Frequent tracheal suction, careful positioning, and avoidance of pleural-fluid collections are basic steps in convalescent care.

E. WATER INTOXICATION

1. Clinical Setting and Appearances

Acute water intoxication is encountered in postoperative patients who have been given too much water or other hypotonic solutions during their period of post-traumatic antidiuresis (Fig. 71). The route of administration is immaterial; this effect has been produced when the solutions were given by mouth, by vein, by clysis, or by rectal infusion. Drowsiness and weakness are early symptoms, followed by coma and convulsions.

2. Characteristic Plasma Pattern

A rapidly falling plasma sodium concen-

tration, with a proportional change in total osmolality, characteristically coming on after trauma,* is the sign of water intoxication. The patient will be noted to have gained weight rapidly. The plasma potassium concentration will be normal or very slightly lowered, a condition that again indicates the generally persistent tendency of the potassium concentration to change disproportionally to the sodium concentration. Plasma sodium concentration may be as low as 105 to 115 mE. per l., but in general the rate of lowering rather than the absolute level reached is significant symptomatically. Coma and convulsions have occurred with a rapid fall of plasma sodium concentration to 120 mE. per l.

---

* Although considered here as a consequence of water loading after trauma, water intoxication may occur in any setting in which input far exceeds excretion; it is also seen in liver disease, kidney disease, and heart disease.

3. Metabolic Background and Genesis

A normal person given a large excess of water will exhibit, through the production of slight hypotonicity, a complete inhibition of his osmoreceptor activity, with a sudden decrease in secretion of antidiuretic hormone into the circulation. The renal tubule loses its normal antidiuretic "tone," distal tubular water resorption is markedly reduced, positive free water clearance is exhibited to its maximal degree, and there is a profuse water diuresis. Serum tonicity rises again to normal. Anyone who has consumed several flagons of beer in rapid succession has witnessed this phenomenon, whether or not he is aware of its interesting mechanism.

When the patient is in an antidiuretic state, as is true after injury, in acute illness, and in many chronic illnesses, this self-regulatory sequence of changes simply does not occur. There is a continuous and inappropriate antidiuresis seemingly regardless of the volume and tonicity of the extracellular fluid. The water is added to the system, and most of it is held there. All solutes are diluted; the hypotonicity of the extracellular fluid is manifest throughout the whole body.

The brain is sensitive to changes in osmolality, and yet the blood-brain barrier is only slowly permeable to sodium. When the extracellular, electrolyte-determined osmolality suddenly drops in the body as a whole, the brain is left with a relative excess of salt over water. Since it cannot lose the salt, the brain takes up water, producing cerebral edema, coma, and convulsions.

Water intoxication thus starts by a simple mechanism of overwatering: by the addition of hypotonic fluid to a patient in an antidiuretic state. Later on, an interesting secondary mechanism comes into play, apparently resulting from inhibition of the same body receptor-effector mechanism, sensitive to flow or fluid volume, that has already been mentioned. As volume expands excessively, an inhibition of salt retention results; there is an excretion of sodium that lowers sodium content and may further lower sodium concentration. It is as though the body "recognizes" the overexpansion of the extracellular fluid produced by excessive water retention, and then "instructs" the kidneys to start excreting sodium. Sodium retention ceases, but free water diuresis does not occur. In endocrine terms, the changes suggest cessation of aldosterone secretion in the face of continuing antidiuresis, as volume expands excessively. When an overexpansion of the extracellular fluid is due to an excess of sodium, such a "sodium-release" mechanism would clearly be of help to the patient. But when an extracellular-fluid expansion is due to the presence of too much water (as in water intoxication), this increased sodium excretion is inappropriate. It is injurious to the patient and may produce a sudden further deterioration of sodium : water balance, requiring additional sodium in therapy. In this situation, analysis of the urine for sodium may yield important information. If large amounts of sodium are being excreted in spite of hypotonicity, the doctor should consider renal tubular disease, adrenocortical insufficiency, or an inappropriate "volume-receptor" release mechanism in water intoxication as possible cause of the natruresis.

4. Treatment

Ideally, one should withhold the administration of further water and let the patient "blow off steam" by himself. If left to his resources, he will gradually rid himself of water through lungs, skin, and kidneys. If water intoxication has proceeded to the point where there are cerebral symptoms, hypertonic sodium must be given. The amount should *not* be gauged by any standard rule such as "unit deficit multiplied by the total body water." In water intoxication the application of such a rule is especially dangerous and results in the administration of amounts of sodium far in excess of the patient's requirements. As noted above, the body is not a closed system. As sodium is given, the kidneys respond by the excretion of water. It is best to start treatment by giving the patient a test infusion of 300 ml. of 3 per cent sodium chloride. Further infusions are given as repair occurs. Continuing treatment based on progress after an initial infusion is safer and more effective than treatment by rule of thumb.

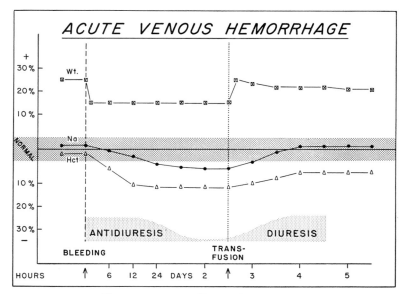

Figure 72. ACUTE VENOUS HEMORRHAGE

The fall in hematocrit is gradual as transcapillary refilling occurs after the hemorrhage. The release of sodium-free water from the cell mass during the antidiuretic state induced by acute volume decrease dilutes the sodium concentration slightly and is responsible for a small loss of potassium. Retransfusion of the lost volume (here shown as about 800 ml.) restores the lost body weight and blood volume, but there is little immediate hematocrit change because the bank blood has about the same hematocrit (36 to 39 per cent cells) as the patient. The volume expansion produced by transfusion permits diuresis of salt and water. As diuresis occurs and a fraction of the infused plasma is thus excreted, the hematocrit gradually rises. In hemorrhage of mild degree without shock, the initial fall in the hematocrit requires for its completion the transcapillary refilling of the blood volume, and the subsequent rise in hematocrit after transfusion requires metabolic and renal disposal of the infused plasma fraction of whole blood.

Section II.   Four Patterns of Body-Fluid Loss, with Hypotonicity

A. ACUTE VENOUS HEMORRHAGE

1. Clinical Setting and Appearances

Under consideration here is simple acute venous hemorrhage (Fig. 72) without shock, sepsis, or coagulation defect. Such hemorrhage may occur in wounds, in bleeding gastrointestinal lesions, in uterine bleeding, in the operative or postoperative state, or in many less common settings.

The normal blood volume averages about 7.0 per cent of body weight in men and 6.5 per cent in women. Obesity lowers this relative figure, whereas muscularity raises it. Acute loss of 10 to 15 per cent of the blood volume from the venous side of the circulation produces minimal hemodynamic change (slight tachycardia, rise in diastolic pressure). Loss of 25 per cent causes early hypotension,

such as that referred to here. Over 30 per cent of the blood volume, lost acutely, results in a shocklike state, the depth and duration of which depend on other factors, especially tissue damage, sepsis, organic disease, and the rate of blood replacement.

An equal amount of blood, lost acutely from a large opening in a major artery, produces a much more profound drop in blood pressure and flow because of the loss of peripheral resistance involved in the arterial wound itself.

2. Characteristic Plasma Pattern

Initially, the plasma chemical findings are normal. Over a period of two to six hours hemodilution begins, gradually lowering the hematocrit as interstitial fluid enters the plasma. The completion of this process requires twelve to thirty-six hours in a normal, healthy, well-hydrated young man.

After a hemorrhage of 750 to 1000 ml., the hematocrit in a young adult stabilizes at a level that indicates virtually complete plasma-volume refilling. The extent of the previous blood loss can therefore be calculated from the stabilized hemodiluted hematocrit; this is not possible in more complex situations. The plasma protein is similarly diluted, but not proportionally. Plasma albumin is rapidly resynthesized, and extravascular stores are called upon; red blood cells are not so easily summoned.

3. Metabolic Background and Genesis

A simple venous hemorrhage is the classic example of an isotonic volume reduction. The widespread changes that take place after even a minor hemorrhage are among the most delicate indexes of the activity of some receptor-effector mechanisms sensitive to volume, flow, or pressure.

Renal excretion of water and solute is sharply reduced. Free water excretion is reduced far beyond any change that may take place in glomerular filtration and is disproportional to reduction in renal plasma flow. Along with this water retention, there is a sharp increase in tubular sodium resorption, and a demonstrable increase in aldosterone excretion, which clearly indicates the mobilization of cellular water. All this occurs without any initial change in the concentration of cells or salts.

Intracellular and extracellular sources of water thus join to replenish the plasma volume by transcapillary refilling, as shown by the falling hematocrit. The extent to which fluids from the two sources participate and the period over which this activity occurs determine its effect on plasma sodium concentration and tonicity. If the contribution of sodium-free cell water is small and transient, plasma sodium concentration is little changed. When hemorrhage is large and prolonged, the contribution of cell water is increased, and plasma sodium concentration falls. The patient is left with a low volume of erythrocytes and a high volume of plasma, a nearly normal blood volume, a stabilized secondary anemia

(repaired slowly by hematopoiesis) and slight hypotonicity.

4. Treatment

The ideal treatment is by transfusion before transcapillary refilling has occurred. In young, healthy persons, a delay in replacement may not be dangerous; resilient blood vessels and youthful tissues readily recover from the insult. In those who are elderly, much harm may result from delay. The acute hypotensive episode may have caused irreversible changes in heart, brain, or kidney. The kidney is rendered vulnerable to other damaging agents. The volume of delayed transfusion (added to the already hemodiluted blood volume) may produce a volume excess that the heart cannot tolerate. Pulmonary edema results.

Treatment with solutions that do not contain colloid is but an inadequate temporizing measure. Cell-free colloids (plasma, dextran) are useful in emergencies as a means of restoring the plasma fraction of blood volume. Whole blood alone will repair the defect quantitatively if given early. In the late hemodiluted state in the elderly patient, there is a place for the use of separated erythrocytes.

As volume is restored, the kidney is released from the restricting influences of vascular and endocrine origin, and a mild diuresis occurs.

B. ACUTE SHOCKING DESALTING WATER LOSS

Having discussed several patterns of biochemical disorder characterized largely by dilutional hypotonicity with normal or high body sodium content, we now consider two in which loss of salt is the predominant factor, although dilution is still important in the hypotonic end-result. The previous dilutional patterns have been partly due to abnormal and seemingly "inappropriate" salt retention and antidiuresis. In acute desalting water loss (Fig. 73), renal salt retention and antidiuresis are not only quite normal and thoroughly appropriate but also essential to survival.

1. Clinical Setting and Appearances

Acute desalting water loss leads to shock when the loss of fluid from the body (usually

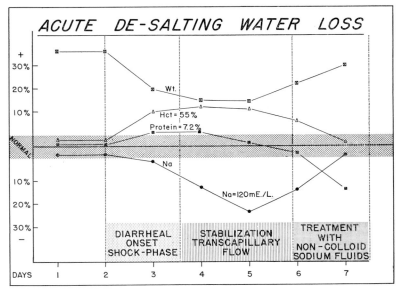

Figure 73. Acute Desalting Water Loss

Loss of weight and loss of extracellular and plasma volume (as shown by the rising hematocrit) are the initial changes during the onset-shock phase of severe desalting as seen in dysentery, ulcerative colitis, and intestinal obstruction. The volume decrease produces a sharp reduction in all renal excretory functions. Protein rise and sodium fall are not marked. During the stabilization phase there is an ingress of sodium-free water from cells and from the oxidation of fat. Because of the strong salt-retaining and antidiuretic effects of

fluid loss, this new extracellular water is retained and lowers the sodium concentration in the depleted extracellular fluid volume. Restoration of volume and concentration by the administration of colloid-free fluid (shown in this example as 3 per cent sodium chloride) restores body weight, sodium concentration and hematocrit but at the expense of plasma protein concentration. Replacement, to avoid hypoproteinemia and hypokalemia, should include protein and potassium.

from the gastrointestinal tract) occurs with such rapidity that a reduction in total body fluid volume (rather than tonicity) is the initial result. Small-bowel obstruction, ulcerative colitis, gastric obstruction fistulas, pseudomembranous colitis, cholera, dysentery, and infantile diarrhea kill by this mechanism. In small-bowel obstruction very large volumes may be lost into the gut, with little or no visible loss by vomiting or nasogastric tube. The clinical appearances are the classic ones of so-called "dehydration" although, as has already been seen, I prefer to reserve that term for true dehydration due to pure water loss in which a hypertonic extracellular fluid is left behind. Acute shocking desalting water loss produces fever, apathy, rapid pulse, oliguria going on to anuria, hypotension, shock, delirium, glassy eyes, soft eyeballs, loss of tissue turgor, and all the rest of the appearances so commonly depicted in the literature.

2. Characteristic Plasma Pattern, Genesis, and Treatment

When desalting water loss is very rapid, producing an initial phase in which the effects are predominantly those of volume loss, it is useful to consider the changes as occurring in three phases.

Phase 1—The Shock Phase. This is the volume-loss phase. The plasma volume partakes of the extracellular fluid loss produced by the extrarenal loss of water and salt. There is a rise in the hematocrit, but other changes in plasma concentrations are minimal; this condition is another example of a change in extracellular fluid volume with little initial change in electrolyte concentrations. Although there is no electrolyte-concentration change, there is a sharp reduction in urine volume and solute excretion. The rise in hematocrit is a quantitative index of the decreasing plasma volume. Here, any bodily mechanism that responds to decreased volume or flow by reduction in renal loss of water and salt is vitally important in survival. If "volume receptors" exist, here is where they are truly needed!

The plasma concentrations of sodium and chloride do not change abruptly because their lowering requires time and the addition of sodium-free water from catabolism of cells or oxidation of fat (or ingestion of water). The actual concentration of these ions in the fluids lost from the gastrointestinal tract is below that of the plasma; the loss alone, therefore, cannot be expected to produce lowering of plasma tonicity.

When volume loss is severe, decreased blood pressure and glomerular filtration occur, with anuria, azotemia, and shock. If desalting is severe, this first phase may be fatal.

Phase 2—Stabilization and Dilution. If, because of a reduction in rate of fluid loss, the patient survives this acute shocking phase, he then passes into a second phase. This phase is characterized by partial refilling of the plasma and extracellular fluid with endogenous sodium-free water. This endogenous water is retained because the volume reduction has stimulated maximal retention of water and salt. In this situation increased salt retention and antidiuretic activity are readily demonstrable. Urine output remains small until the plasma volume is restored.

As this endogenous sodium-free water from cell water and fat oxidation enters the extracellular fluid, there is a gradual reduction in the concentration of the plasma sodium and chloride, and a decrease in plasma osmolality.* There is a gradually increasing urine output, with excretion of potassium, and a slight fall in the hematocrit. The fluid volume of the stabilized patient (after acute desalting water loss) has not returned to normal, but

---

* It should be noted that this reduction in extracellular solute concentration by the mobilization of cell water after desalting water loss is, in a sense, analogous to the reduction in erythrocyte concentration by mobilization of extravascular water that occurs after hemorrhage.

his extracellular fluid is gradually being expanded and diluted. The acid-base effects are determined by the nature of the fluid lost. If the fluid lost is highly acid and the patient has recently been operated upon, a severe metabolic alkalosis (often with attendant hypokalemia) will be produced. In virtually all other situations (and far commoner) is the production of an acidosis due to the combination of starvation, dehydration, ketosis, and loss of alkaline secretions. So long as any urine volume is maintained, the potassium mobilized with cell water is excreted. Potassium is also lost extrarenally.

Phase 3—Treatment. The first need in early therapy is for volume restoration by the infusion of plasma and sodium, chloride, and bicarbonate in liberal amounts. In young adults the use of large quantities of isotonic saline solution is quite satisfactory, despite its disadvantages in many other settings. The use of potassium is essential during this initial resalting and rehydration, because there has been a potassium loss as cell water was mobilized. If the fluid lost has been acid (hydrochloric acid), the addition of potassium will help to prevent hypokalemia and alkalosis. If the patient is oliguric the first six hours of reconstitution may be carried out without potassium.

The patient has lost plasma protein and must be given protein in replacement. This condition is an ideal indication for the use of concentrated albumin; plasma may also be given. It is vitally important, if shock is evident, to use either or both; whole blood may be used in small quantities. If protein is not given, hypoproteinemia will be produced by treatment of severe cases of desalting water loss with salt alone. The more protracted the loss, the greater the tendency to hypoproteinemia when treatment is carried out with salt and water only.

It is a general guide in treatment that the normal extracellular fluid is about 20 per cent and the plasma volume 4 per cent of body weight. If the hematocrit in a normal-sized adult has risen to 55 per cent on the basis of desalting, there has been loss of approximately 40 per cent of the plasma and a like fraction

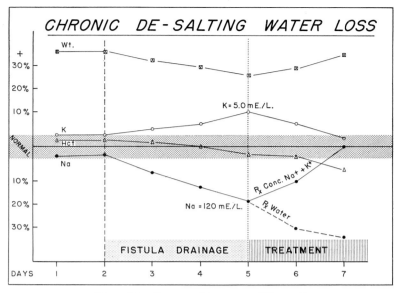

Figure 74. Chronic Desalting Water Loss

This is a slower version of the pattern seen in Figure 73. The extrarenal loss of extracellular fluid is typified here in a gastrointestinal fistula. Renal conservation of water and salt results from the volume threat, preserving volume at the expense of tonicity. As a result, sodium concentration falls progressively as sodium-free water enters the extracellular fluid from cell catabolism, fat oxidation, and treatment. Weight falls slowly whereas hematocrit changes but little. Potassium concentration rises as cell water is mobilized in the face of a restricted urine volume. Treatment with water alone greatly accentuates the dilutional hypotonicity. Treatment with concentrated sodium salts, and later potassium, effectively repairs the defect.

of extracellular fluid volume.* At 70 kg , this would mean about 1100 ml. of plasma and 4000 ml. of salt solution as an urgent initial budget. The rate of hourly urine output, as well as the fall in hematocrit and clinical improvement, is a valuable guide in treatment. Such urgent replacement would cover the "static debt"; to this must be added maintenance rations to cover the continuing needs, carefully tailored to fit the particular pathologic situation.

C. CHRONIC DESALTING WATER LOSS

1. Clinical Setting and Appearances

This (Fig. 74) is merely a slower version of

---

* This calculation is based on the expression for BV reduction with an elevated LVH and no RV loss (see page 217). Here, at 70 kg., the normal RV for such a patient would be expected to be about 2100 ml. (3 per cent of B.Wt.). Therefore, the contracted BV, after plasma loss sufficient to raise the LVH to 55, would be: 2100 ÷ 0.55, or 3800 ml. This yields a plasma loss of 1100 ml. from the predicted normal, or about 39.4 per cent of the starting PV of 2800 ml.

desalting water loss. It is much commoner than shocking, volume-reducing desalting. Examples are to be found in many of the states already mentioned, including ileostomy diarrhea, biliary fistula, gastric obstruction, duodenal obstruction, intestinal obstruction, large-bowel obstruction, and chronic renal salt wasting. The difference is in rate of loss. In this slower desalting, dilutional hypotonicity develops *pari passu* with the loss of salt. Loss of concentration is much more prominent than loss of volume. The patient is found to be feverish, thirsty, enervated, and oliguric.

2. Characteristic Plasma Pattern

A low plasma sodium concentration is characteristic of chronic desalting water loss. Nonelectrolyte osmolality is not elevated. The degree of azotemia is proportional to the interference with glomerular filtration that has been produced in the early phases. The change in plasma potassium concentration is variable and depends upon acid-base balance; if the loss has been largely of acid and has produced a metabolic alkalosis, severe hypokalemia, as described below, may be found at this point. Much commoner is predominant loss of base, producing acidosis, a normal or slightly elevated potassium and a low sodium concentration, a low carbon dioxide combining power, and ketosis. Hypoproteinemia results when protein loss is replaced by the use of electrolyte without protein.

3. Metabolic Background and Genesis

A slow, desalting fluid loss with little reduction in the volume of total body water is accompanied by extracellular dilution through the mobilization of endogenous sodium-free water from the catabolism of muscle cells, from the oxidation of fat, and through the ingestion or injection of water. Increased secretion of aldosterone from the adrenal cortex and antidiuretic hormone from the posterior pituitary gland is demonstrable; these doubtless help the body to recall water and salt from the glomerular filtrate. Decreased glomerular filtration rate further conserves fluid resources, although at the expense of azotemia and acidosis. Thus, even without treatment, there is a gradual dilution of the extracellular fluid. Cell catabolism and fat oxidation proceed because of starvation; they are speeded up after trauma or in the stress of acute extracellular volume reduction.

In rare situations (obstructive uropathy, renal insufficiency, adrenal failure, and osmotic diuresis as in untreated diabetes mellitus), chronic desalting water loss may be renal in route.

4. Treatment

Any therapy modifies the chemical picture and may improve the patient's clinical appearances dramatically. If poorly conceived, "treatment" may produce some remarkable chemical disorders. If the fluids used in treatment are, for the most part, hypotonic, they will produce very severe extracellular dilution.

The hypotonicity of chronic desalting water loss is the indication par excellence for the use of concentrated salt solution. It is in this

situation that the calculation of the salt dosage by multiplying the unit deficit by the total body water is most appealing as a basis for treatment, but even here one should deny the impulse to base treatment on this simple formula. In a patient weighing 70 kg., with established desalting water loss and a plasma sodium concentration of 125 mE. per l. (osmolality, 250 mO. per l.), one finds by this formula of "unit total times total body water" that the deficitamount of sodium needed immediately is around 750 mE. In chronic desalting such amounts of net sodium gain are almost never required because the body is not a closed system. As resalting treatment is begun (and extracellular volume is re-expanded) there is an excretion of water, which hastens repair.

It is in desalting water loss with acidosis that mobilization of skeletal sodium appears, in the laboratory animal, to be most active. Therapy must therefore be approached with discrimination rather than with rules; the sodium need may turn out to be less than the loss. The best way to start is by giving the patient an energetic loading dose of concentrated (3 per cent) sodium chloride or bicarbonate and observing its effect. Further therapy should be guided by this observation.

Potassium must be included in resalting, because it has been lost as cell water was mobilized. One might expect a need for magnesium, sulfate, phosphate, and calcium. Instances of low plasma concentrations of these minerals because of chronic desalting water loss are few, and good therapeutic results are obtained without them. Should severe alkalosis result, hypocalcemic tetany may occur. Potassium problems are also more pressing in alkalosis, as indicated in the next two sections.

D. CHRONIC HYPOKALEMIA IN DIFFERENTIAL POTASSIUM DEFICIENCY

1. Clinical Setting and Appearances

In sharp contrast to acute hypokalemic alkalosis, which most commonly occurs as a complication of disease of the upper gastrointestinal tract, this pattern occurs (Fig. 75) in chronic lower-bowel disease. The lower small intestine or the large bowel is involved. There is persistent loss of colonic secretions

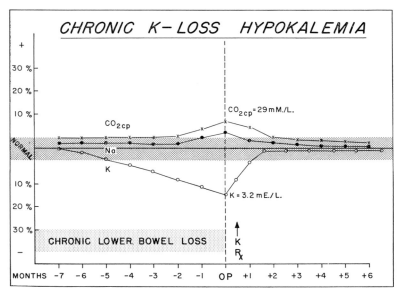

Figure 75. Chronic Potassium-Loss Hypokalemia

In contrast to acute hypokalemic alkalosis, which is an upper-bowel syndrome seen in diseases of the stomach, duodenum, and pancreas, this is a lower-bowel syndrome caused by loss of potassium-rich bowel fluids slowly over a long period and at a high potassium-nitrogen ratio. The plasma potassium concentration gradually falls whereas there is little change in acid-base balance or extracellular tonicity. Associated changes in magnesium and calcium may be observed. The interference with excretion of an alkaline urine caused by potassium deficit renders the patient very vulnerable to severe alkalosis if hydrochloric acid loss is superimposed, or if fluid therapy after surgery involves an excessive load of base. Treatment of this condition involves the administration of very large amounts of potassium.

over a period of months. Chronic ulcerative colitis, chronic large-bowel obstruction, or the overuse of laxatives has been implicated as a cause. The patient looks chronically ill, is usually starved, and shows the electrocardiographic changes accompanying hypokalemia; there is no other special clinical identification.

2. Characteristic Plasma Pattern

The plasma potassium concentration reaches values in the range of 2.5 to 3.0 mE. per l. The plasma sodium concentration is slightly low, 135 mE. per l., for example. Azotemia is variable. The carbon dioxide combining power has been found to be from 23 to 28 mE. per l.; severe alkalosis has been absent in these patients. Weight loss is usually part of the picture.

3. Metabolic Background and Genesis

The potassium:nitrogen ratio of the body is distorted in this disorder. Normal muscular tissue contains about 3 mE. of potassium per gm. of nitrogen. The potassium:nitrogen ratio is 3:1. Prolonged balanced starvation, as in carcinoma of the esophagus, produces large losses of body potassium (up to 750 mE.), but they are proportional to the amount of nitrogen lost. The potassium:nitrogen ratio is still near 3:1. There is no alteration in the potassium:nitrogen ratio of the body, nor of the plasma potassium concentration.

By contrast, loss of lower-bowel juice produces a continuing loss of the fluids that are disproportionately high in potassium (as compared with nitrogen) content. This is "differential" potassium loss. The total amount of potassium in these juices is low, running from 5 to 30 mE. per l., but the amount of nitrogen is proportionally even smaller. The potassium:nitrogen ratio in the juice is as high as 10 mE. per gm. When the patient has prolonged loss of juices from the large intestine, there is therefore a slow, but pernicious, differential potassium loss at high potassium:

nitrogen ratios. The intracellular cation pattern has been disturbed by the slow removal of potassium in excess of other constituents.

Hypokalemia finally results. It is of great interest that alkalosis is not necessarily a part of this picture. This finding seems to be a contradiction of the results of much work done on animals. These studies, upon which is based the concept that potassium loss in itself produces extracellular alkalosis, were done on rats in which a high degree of differential potassium deficiency (along with sodium retention) was produced by the administration of large amounts of sodium salts together with desoxycorticosterone acetate. This highly artificial situation emphasized the importance of steroids and sodium in cellular transfer of cations and hydrogen, and in hypokalemic alkalosis. But its implications cannot be transferred to all potassium-losing situations in man.

Whatever one's convictions on these controversial points, the clinical fact remains that patients with chronic lower-bowel disease develop, after weeks or months, a very refractory hypokalemia that is usually not accompanied by alkalosis. Persistent loss of base in the stool may also be a factor in avoiding alkalosis here.

The occurrence of a potassium-loss nephropathy has been implicated as a feature of the disordered renal function occasionally found in such patients.

4. Treatment

Treatment consists in the provision to the patient of potassium in large excess over the provided nitrogen, so that this differential potassium deficit can be repaired. Very large amounts may be needed. The patient must be cared for with due respect to replacement and maintenance, including water, whole protein, blood volume, dietary nitrogen, calories, vitamins, and such other electrolytes as are needed.

Repair of such a patient by the use of excesses of sodium salts easily produces alkalosis because potassium deficit blocks the urinary excretion of bicarbonate and lowers urinary pH. The sudden superimposition of extracellular hydrogen-ion loss (gastric obstruction) on this lower-bowel hyperkalemic syndrome also rapidly causes a severe alkalosis, because of the interference with normal renal function that is produced by potassium deficiency. Operation has the same effect, and the result closely resembles hypokalemic alkalosis.

Section III.   Three Patterns of Acid-Base Imbalance

A. ACUTE HYPOKALEMIC ALKALOSIS

1. Clinical Setting and Appearances

This is an "upper gastrointestinal" syndrome (Fig. 76). The characteristic setting for this pattern is found in a patient who has suffered acute loss of acid gastric juice (obstructing duodenal ulcer) and is then operated upon. The condition is often, but not always, postoperative. The overadministration of sodium-containing solutions makes the condition worse. In such acute disorders as pancreatitis, in which there is severe stress without surgery, and vomiting of acid gastric juice, hypokalemic alkalosis may occur. The clinical appearances include weakness, distention, and apathy; in severe cases one may see tetany, coma, or convulsions. Changes in

the electrocardiogram, which are due to hypokalemia, are commonplace.

2. Characteristic Plasma Pattern

The plasma chemical changes consist in a high pH and carbon dioxide combining power (7.53 and 32 mE. per l., for example) with low chloride and potassium concentrations (85 and 2.0 mE. per l. or even lower). The sodium concentration is normal or slightly elevated. Desalting water loss may be present in sufficient degree to produce azotemia and some hemoconcentration of erythrocytes, but, generally speaking, urinary volume has been maintained, and this very maintenance of volume is characteristic of this pattern and is in part responsible for pathogenesis. Hypokalemia is not seen in established anuria, in

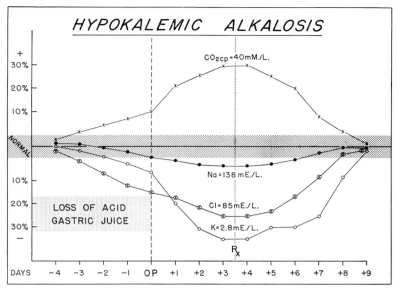

Figure 76. HYPOKALEMIC ALKALOSIS

In the preoperative phase there is loss of acid gastric juice (using here the example of obstructing duodenal ulcer). This threatens the development of alkalosis, initially avoided by the compensatory renal excretion of sodium bicarbonate in an alkaline urine. Serious hypokalemic alkalosis can occur before operation but is commoner in the postoperative period because operation effectively blocks this urinary excretion of base. The loss of this base-excreting mechanism produces a paradoxically acid urine (i.e., an acid urine in the presence of alkalosis). Potassium loss is also increased by surgery; potassium deficit also interferes with base excretion. The alkalosis therefore becomes much worse after operation. The carbon dioxide of the plasma rises abruptly. This alkalosis, together with loss of potassium from the body, produces a sudden and profound lowering of the plasma potassium concentration. Treatment must be directed both at the alkalosis and at the potassium loss.

which azotemia, acidosis, and hyperkalemia quickly dominate the picture.

3. Metabolic Background and Genesis

The complex interplay of factors involved in the production of hypokalemic alkalosis has been clarified by studies made in the past five years. The basic factor is a subtraction alkalosis due to the loss of hydrogen ion, usually in the form of hydrochloric acid from the stomach. In a healthy person, renal excretion of sodium and bicarbonate normally compensates for this loss and effectively prevents alkalosis for some time. It is difficult to produce subtraction alkalosis in normal people. This renal sodium excretion is completely blocked by the sodium-conserving "aldosterone-like effect" of operation, trauma, or acute illness. It is for this reason that metabolic alkalosis becomes much worse after stress or surgery. After trauma this change is manifested by a lessened excretion

of sodium bicarbonate, a paradoxical aciduria, and an increased urinary excretion of potassium. "Potassium deficiency" due to a differential loss of potassium (loss at a high potassium:nitrogen ratio) further interferes with the ability of the kidney to secrete an alkaline urine. All these factors tend to worsen the alkalosis and lower the potassium concentration.

The most important factor lowering the potassium concentration may actually be the sudden worsening of the extracellular alkalosis. It has been shown that metabolic alkalosis (or, possibly, the elevation in total carbon dioxide with a high cellular pCO_2 and intracellular acidosis) in itself tends to lower the plasma potassium concentration. Loss of potassium may not be large but has occurred in all these cases.

In the pathogenesis of hypokalemic alkalosis there is thus a vicious circle.

In the first place, loss of acid threatens the

development of alkalosis, initially abated by renal excretion of sodium bicarbonate.

Secondly, operation* makes alkalosis worse by inhibiting this excretion of base (aldosterone-like effect).

Thirdly, alkalosis lowers potassium concentration.

Fourthly, trauma increases potassium loss.

Fitthly, in potassium loss, sodium bicarbonate excretion is markedly reduced, and the urine is paradoxically acid.

Sixthly, aciduria caused both by trauma and by potassium loss makes alkalosis more pronounced.

Finally, this alkalosis further lowers the potassium concentration.

Hypokalemic alkalosis is not an everyday problem, for two interesting reasons: the fluid loss must be highly acid (this is rare in the elderly patient or in cancer); and anuria (which may result from truly massive fluid loss) quickly superimposes renal acidosis and a rising potassium concentration. The combination of acid loss and trauma must be "just right" for this state to result. Renal function must be maintained throughout the early stages to make the renal factors effectual in pathogenesis of hypokalemic alkalosis.

Electrocardiographic changes are due primarily to the lowered concentrations of potassium in the patient's extracellular fluid. They may be marked even though total body potassium is not very low. In acute situations of hypokalemic alkalosis, one may see dangerously low plasma potassium concentrations (2.0 mE. per l., or a 50 per cent reduction) with as small a reduction in total body potassium as 150 mE. (5 per cent). This is in marked contrast to resting starvation or chronic differential potassium loss from the lower bowel, a condition in which much more drastic reduction in body potassium is asso-

ciated with only a mild hypokalemia and no alkalosis.

4. Treatment

The most effective step in the management of acute hypokalemic alkalosis is prevention, and the most effective prevention is repair of the metabolic alkalosis before surgery. This should be achieved by the administration of potassium chloride and ammonium chloride. Overuse of sodium salts makes the patient much worse, and yet, during the early days of acid loss, there has been considerable urinary sodium loss and its gradual replacement should be considered in the plans for reconstitution.

Repair in acute subtraction alkalosis can be done with potassium chloride, which at one stroke will restore any differential potassium loss, return the extracellular acid-base balance toward normal, and restore the ability of the kidney to excrete base. In acute situations with marked alkalosis, or after operation, additional treatment with ammonium chloride may be lifesaving. The ammonium chloride should be used as a 1 per cent solution, and its administration should be followed very closely by serial determinations of the pH or carbon dioxide combining power or by some other measure of acid-base change. Overdose of ammonium chloride in the acute situation may produce ammonia toxicity or, in excess amounts, overshoot the mark and produce severe acidosis. A patient with obstructing duodenal ulcer should not be operated upon until the carbon dioxide combining power is below 30 mE. per l. and still falling. Here again, the important thing is to start the patient off in the right direction before surgery; complete restoration to normal acid-base balance before operation may be impossible.

B. ACUTE RESPIRATORY ACIDOSIS

1. Clinical Setting and Appearances

Sudden interference with the patient's effective pulmonary ventilation is the clinical setting for acute respiratory acidosis (Fig. 77). Obstruction of the air passages in

---

* This sodium-retaining effect of trauma may have a bearing on experimental work in this field. The production of hypokalemic alkalosis in the rat is best accomplished by a sodium-loading diet and large doses of desoxycorticosterone. This treatment results in a steroid-induced resorption of sodium bicarbonate from the tubular urine as well as in loss of potassium, both of which resemble the post-traumatic situation.

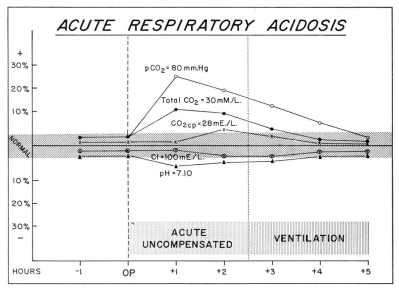

Figure 77. ACUTE RESPIRATORY ACIDOSIS

In the acute respiratory acidosis of operation, shock, and wounds of the airway, there is insufficient time or urine volume for the renal excretion of hydrogen ion to keep pace with the accumulation of carbonic acid that results from insufficient or inefficient ventilation. There is a rapidly mounting acidosis with a falling pH, a rising pCO_2, and a normal or nearly normal carbon dioxide combining power. This acidosis, acting in concert with hyperkalemia, is often associated with a drop in blood pressure (even in its early stages) and later on is capable

of producing ventricular fibrillation. This acidosis may develop in the presence of normal oxygenation.

The only effective treatment is improved ventilation. Bronchoscopy, tracheotomy, or operative reestablishment of normal thoracic mechanics may be necessary for its achievement. The infusion of concentrated sodium bicarbonate may produce temporary improvement but at the price of a large salt load, dangerous at best in the presence of pulmonary disease.

wounds or burns of the upper respiratory tract, pulmonary edema, pulmonary infection, atelectasis, pneumothorax, hemothorax, and the open chest are all settings in which this can be produced. Poliomyelitis, crippling positions on the operating table, abdominal distention, and overdose of opiates may result in acute respiratory acidosis. Severe acidosis can be present even when the patient has normal color and good oxygenation. When ventilation is precarious, respiratory acidosis may be made much worse by oxygen administration.

2. Characteristic Plasma Pattern

The characteristic plasma pattern of acute respiratory acidosis is that of a rising total carbon dioxide, a rising pCO_2, a rapidly falling pH, and little other change. There may be no change initially in carbon dioxide combining power. Hyperkalemia often occurs.

All these are in marked contrast to chronic respiratory acidosis, in which correlative metabolic and electrolyte changes are pronounced, the carbon dioxide combining power markedly elevated, chloride low, and potassium normal, with only a minor fall in pH. The "carbon dioxide combining power" ($CO_{2 cp}$) does not indicate respiratory changes or pH. This well-known fact is often overlooked. On most hospital laboratory sheets the carbon dioxide combining power is indicated as "CO_2." The carbon dioxide combining power is merely a measure of that amount of carbon dioxide which the blood will take up when equilibrated with the technician's alveolar air or a standard mixture of gases. The carbon dioxide combining power is of value, therefore, in the treatment of metabolic acid-base changes in which fixed ion gains and losses are important; it has little value in discerning primary or secondary respiratory alterations. For the study of these the arterial pH and the total carbon dioxide should be measured, and the pCO_2 and HCO_3 calculated.

3. Metabolic Background and Genesis

Acute respiratory acidosis exerts its damage on cellular life and myocardial function. Enzymatic oxidations do not occur in a strongly acid environment. The normal neuromuscular conduction that integrates the heartbeat is altered by acidosis and hyperkalemia. Ventricular fibrillation may occur when respiratory acidosis suddenly appears or is suddenly repaired. Rate of change of pH, associated changes in electrolytes (especially potassium and calcium), and the intracellular pCO_2 may be critical in the onset of fibrillation and other arrhythmias. At very high levels of total carbon dioxide both respiration and vasoconstriction are adversely affected.

The metabolic compensations for respiratory acidosis require three priceless assets: good circulation, adequate renal function, and time. The compensations operate by taking up acid in the body buffers, by the secretion of acid urine (carbonic acid, dihydrogen phosphate, and maximal tubular resorption of sodium bicarbonate), and by the excretion of large amounts of ammonia. By these metabolic compensations, severe pulmonary insufficiency and respiratory acidosis can be tolerated over a period of many months or years.

Consider now the patient in shock with a pressure pneumothorax. He is not perfusing the great masses of muscular tissue in which the whole body buffers reside, he may not be making any urine whatsoever, and, even with urine flow, his normal compensations do not have sufficient time to operate effectively. His blood pH may fall below 7.0 in a matter of minutes. This rapid fall is characteristic of acute respiratory acidosis in surgery. Although the carbon dioxide combining power is no measure of acute respiratory acidosis, the venous pH is also unsatisfactory as a measuring device. The arterial pH alone shows the true magnitude of the acidosis. This lesion is produced by deficient ventilation, but it may exist with only minimal anoxia.

The extrarenal disposal of an acute acid load is much more important than the renal disposal because the latter (even when operating ideally) can excrete acid only at a fixed rate, much slower than its accumulation. When the lungs are primarily at fault, as in respiratory acidosis, this extrarenal disposal is wholly by virtue of the body buffers. The blood buffers are but a part of the chemical mechanism for cushioning the impact of acid; 30 to 60 per cent of the total acid-accepting capacity lies outside the blood stream, in the cell mass.

4. Treatment

The treatment of this condition is easy to describe but difficult to achieve; it consists in providing adequate ventilation. The ventilatory block may occur at all levels, including flow through the pulmonary bed. One must assess the nature of the ventilatory block and take immediate steps to repair it.

Diagnostically, respiratory acidosis should be suspected in any acutely ill or traumatized patient, or intraoperatively, when there appears to be inadequate ventilation or when cardiac action is abnormal or blood pressure poorly maintained. There is not time to wait for chemical confirmation. Active steps— tracheotomy, bronchoscopy, intubation, assisted respiration, or the use of a respirator— must be taken. Many ventilatory situations exist in which cyanosis is absent or minimal but respiratory acidosis is marked; one cannot rely on "good color" as a sign that serious respiratory embarrassment is not present.

The extreme speed with which severe respiratory acidosis may occur is demonstrated by the fact that in volunteer normal subjects with good blood flow and renal function, it is possible to lower the pH to 7.2 in about eight minutes of rebreathing, or breathing a carbon-dioxide-enriched mixture. It is little wonder that the patient in shock on the operating table or in other situations where ventilation is suddenly reduced while urine flow is minimal may develop this condition suddenly and to a lethal extent. Under such circumstances death is often due to acute cardiac arrhythmias.

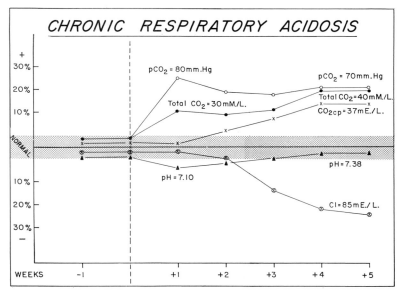

Figure 78. CHRONIC RESPIRATORY ACIDOSIS

With the passage of time and an adequate urine flow with good tubular function, renal compensation catches up with acute respiratory acidosis by the excretion of hydrogen ion as $H_2PO_4^-$, NH_4^+, and H_2CO_3 in a highly acid urine. Bicarbonate reabsorption is at a maximum. A compensatory metabolic change is thus created in the direction of alkalosis. The ultimate result is restoration of pH toward normal, with a very high bicarbonate, high total carbon dioxide, and a low plasma chloride

C. CHRONIC RESPIRATORY ACIDOSIS AND CARBON DIOXIDE NARCOSIS

1. Clinical Setting and Appearances

The characteristic setting here (Fig. 78) is a patient with chronic emphysema, asthma, bronchiectasis, a fixed low diaphragm, barrel chest, some compensatory polycythemia, and a chronic productive cough. He is plethoric, cyanotic, wheezy, and dyspneic, and often he has been a heavy smoker. Such patients do not tolerate superimposed pulmonary infection and are poor subjects for elective surgery, although they may need emergency surgical treatment in the form of bronchoscopy or tracheotomy. With lesser degrees of chronic pulmonary insufficiency, patients of this type may present themselves for abdominal, pulmonary, or prostatic surgery.

2. Characteristic Plasma Pattern

There is a chronic metabolic compensation to chronic respiratory acidosis: hypochlore-

concentration. In chronic pulmonary insufficiency this compensated form of respiratory acidosis may exist over a period of several years.

Although pH is near normal, the total body buffers are completely taken up by hydrogen ion. The acid-accepting ability of the body is strained to the utmost. If surgery, trauma, or acute respiratory infection is now superadded, the patient quickly decompensates, and the acidosis becomes severe and terminal.

mia with a marked elevation of the carbon dioxide combining power. The plasma sodium concentration is normal or slightly low. Some degree of polycythemia may exist, and, if the patient has gone on to develop right-sided heart failure because of cor pulmonale, he will show some dilutional hypotonicity, ascites, and hepatomegaly. The renal compensation for chronic respiratory acidosis is never complete, and the blood pH is at the lower limit of normal. Gastric acidity is often increased.

3. Metabolic Background and Genesis

Chronic respiratory acidosis and carbon dioxide narcosis are produced by chronic pulmonary insufficiency with chronic ventilatory impairment and chronic accumulation of hydrogen ion (as carbonic acid). The renal excretion of hydrogen ion with chloride and phosphate (and other anions), and as ammonium, produces a compensatory metabolic change in the direction of alkalosis. There is a rise in the renal bicarbonate reabsorption: from the normal value of 25 to 28 mE. per l. of glomerular filtrate to values as high as 45 to 60 mE. per l. The very high levels of total carbon dioxide are associated with central nervous system depression (particularly of the respiratory center), and hence the term "carbon dioxide narcosis." In this chronic situation the body buffers have been completely taken up, and excretion of renal acid and ammonia is working at a maximum pitch. The body is at the extreme end of its acid-accepting ability. The ventilatory stimulus is barely maintained by a slight degree of anoxia.

This delicate balance is easily upset. Anything that further interferes with ventilation produces a sudden severe worsening of the respiratory acidosis and a quickly fatal outcome. Bronchopneumonia or surgical operations that interfere with ventilation directly or by abdominal distention have the same effect; advanced carbon dioxide narcosis is indeed a poor setting for trauma or surgery. The administration of oxygen may, by removing the last vestige of central-respiratory stimulus, produce prolonged periods of apnea and a fatal intensification of the respiratory acidosis and carbon dioxide narcosis. The administration of depressant drugs has the same effect.

4. Treatment

Treatment is entirely devoted to improving ventilation: antibiotics, improved diaphragmatic mechanics, postural drainage, positive-pressure-assisted ventilation, and measures ensuring liquefaction of secretions are to be used. In the acute crisis of infection or superimposed secretion, bronchoscopy, tracheotomy, and the use of the respirator may be lifesaving. Most of the pulmonary changes that produce this respiratory acidosis and carbon dioxide narcosis are chronic and irreversible; the outlook is very poor even though the patient may be tided over an acute episode.

Section IV.   Two Patterns of Hypertonicity

A. DESICCATION OR TRUE DEHYDRATION

1. Clinical Setting and Appearances

The clinical setting (Fig. 79) is that of excessive pulmonary water loss. Prolonged exposure to the sun's heat without water intake produces death by this route. In the hospital, dyspnea, hyperventilation, and fever are the most prominent factors predisposing to excessive pulmonary water loss. A tracheotomy accelerates water loss by reducing the dead-air fraction of tidal volume. Because of fever, dyspnea, excessive water loss through the skin (particularly with open treatment), and tracheotomy, severe desiccation may be seen in burns. As water is lost, desiccation produces fever, disorientation, delirium, oliguria, azotemia, coma, convulsions, and death. Shock is not a common feature.

2. Characteristic Plasma Pattern

The characteristic pattern is one of increasing concentration of all the solutes in the plasma. Hematocrit rises, plasma protein rises, the concentration of sodium and chloride rises, and the total osmolality rises. In pure desiccation, osmolality and hematocrit rise together, proportionally. The normal plasma osmolality of 285 to 295 mO. per l. gradually rises to levels of 330 to 350 mO. per l. as the hematocrit rises to about 55. If there is abnormal nonelectrolyte osmolality present (as in diabetes mellitus, or in disease of liver or kidneys), the patient may have dangerous degrees of desiccation with sodium concentrations that are only slightly elevated. Here, again, the sodium-osmolar differential is a helpful figure. The rise in hematocrit occurs as a function of loss of water from the entire body, and a very severe degree of dehydration may therefore coexist with only a moderate rise in the hematocrit. A hematocrit of 55 in a burned patient is a sign of need for additional plasma but is not particularly

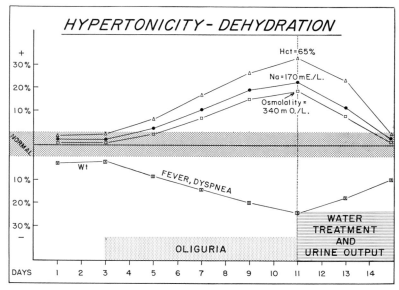

Figure 79. HYPERTONICITY—DEHYDRATION

The two common forms of hypertonicity are due to true dehydration on the one hand and solute loading on the other. True dehydration is shown here. This is desiccation such as that produced by pulmonary water loss, for example. There is a rise in sodium concentration, osmolality, and hematocrit. All three rise in the same general order of magnitude. There is a weight loss as the syndrome develops, with the secretion of a small volume of highly concentrated urine.

Treatment of the syndrome with water results in reestablishment of urine output, a gain in weight, and a restoration of the abnormal chemical values toward normal. If consciousness has been lost by severe dehydration, the initial treatment with water should be quite vigorous; later treatment should be somewhat more cautious, for an element of solute-loading may be present even though unsuspected.

dangerous. In desiccation it bespeaks the loss of 10 to 12 l. of body water and indicates a very dangerous situation.

3. Metabolic Background and Genesis

This lesion is produced by loss of water in gross excess of salt, with increasing concentration of all the water-soluble or water-suspended elements left behind in the body. Because the body appears to tolerate no osmotic gradients within itself or across membranes, when the extracellular osmolality is at 340 mO. per l., one may assume that this is true also of the cell water. There is no justification for referring to this as "intracellular dehydration." Desiccation of this type must necessarily involve the whole body at once, the fluid both inside and outside cells. It is true dehydration.

4. Treatment

Treatment consists in the injection of an

adequate amount of water (in the form of a 5 per cent dextrose solution) intravenously. The amount of water required can be directly calculated by multiplying the unit water deficit by total body water.* This is the only example in the entire water-electrolyte field where the "unit abnormality times total body water" calculation is justified as a basis for therapy. The speed with which the water is given should be gauged entirely by the acuteness of the process. If the patient is extremely ill or comatose, it is important for him to

---

* For example, consider an obese, 60 kg. female with a normal total body water of 40 per cent of body weight (24 l.). She has a plasma sodium concentration of 160 mE. per l. (osmolality, 330 mO. per l.) because of pure water loss. These figures denote an increase of 15 per cent in solute concentration and roughly a 15 per cent deficit of body water—about 3600 ml. This amount of water *must be retained* over and above continuing loss, in order to repair the defect; the first day's ration will therefore be in the neighborhood of 6000 ml.

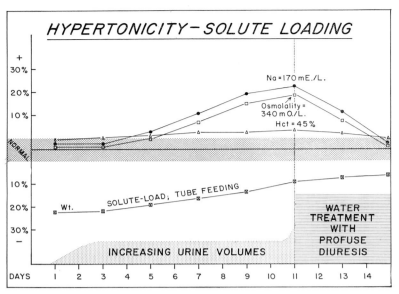

Figure 80. Hypertonicity—Solute Loading

Here is shown the sort of hypertonicity that results from profuse solute loading as exemplified by tube feeding of an unconscious patient who cannot complain of thirst. In contrast to dehydration-desiccation, the electrolyte values in plasma rise much higher, in proportion, than the hematocrit. The body weight rises during the development of the syndrome, and there are large (rather than scanty) urine volumes. The urine concentration is fixed in a mid-range as the profuse solute diuresis persists in the face of strong antidiuretic stimulation. Any degree of tubular dysfunction such as one might see in the arteriosclerotic kidney (or any degree of damage to the supraoptic-hypophyseal tract such as one might see in head injury) renders this sequence much more likely to occur and much more severe because water conservation is impaired.

Treatment with water results in a continued profuse diuresis as the unexcreted backlog of solute in the body is unloaded. There are thus many differences between this syndrome and that of hypertonicity due to true dehydration. The difference in the dynamics of renal excretion may be the most easily identified.

have his water very rapidly. If his desiccation has proceeded somewhat more slowly and is more chronic, it is important not to push fluids too fast during restoration.

B. SOLUTE-LOADING HYPERTONICITY

1. Clinical Setting and Appearances

The typical setting for this syndrome (Fig 80) is in an unconscious patient being given tube feedings. Such a procedure is naturally quite common in disease or injury of the brain. Because certain brain lesions can produce hypertonicity through the production of diabetes insipidus, the assumption has become widespread that hypertonicity itself is due to a specific disorder of the central nervous system. This is true in rare cases, but in the great majority the matter is simply that an unconscious patient is being given more solute than water with which to float it out through the kidneys. Hyperventilation of central origin may add to the water loss. Because the patient is unable to complain of thirst, he assimilates an excessive solute load with inadequate water and develops hypertonicity.* The condition is the exact reverse of water-loading hypotonicity.

2. Characteristic Plasma Pattern

The plasma pattern is characterized by a high concentration of solutes, the solute concentration being out of all proportion to the elevation in hematocrit. In true desiccation,

---

* Though there are many stimuli to thirst, there is none so potent in the conscious patient as hypertonicity. As he slakes his thirst in the presence of the hypertonicity-induced antidiuresis, the water is retained, osmolality returning to normal by dilution, and thirst is satisfied.

all elements of the blood are increased proportionally as water is withdrawn. In solute-loading hypertonicity, the increase in plasma sodium concentration and osmolality is far in excess of the degree of hemoconcentration of red cells, because the concentration here is due largely to solute load, not solely to the abstraction of water. The sodium-osmolar differential is again helpful in determining the state of dehydration and the relative contribution of abnormal crystalloids (urea, lactate, pyruvate, and glucose) to total osmolality.

3. Metabolic Background and Genesis

The patient is given a large load of active solute (salt, foodstuffs, and sugar) over and beyond the water necessary for its excretion. Solute concentration rises.

There are two conditions that complicate this apparently simple disorder: renal tubular disease and osmotic diuresis. If the renal tubule cannot concentrate the urine by water reabsorption, hypertonicity will appear much sooner on a given solute load than when water conservation is maximally efficient.

Osmotic diuresis occurs when the kidney is presented with a crystalloid that is an obligatory tubular solute. This solute carries water out in large volume and at a rapid rate. Even a healthy renal tubule cannot resorb water optimally and exhibit maximum negative free water clearance (or the highest attainable specific gravity) when the flow rate is rapid. In solute diuresis, the flow rate is much too rapid for the distal tubule to exert its maximal concentrating effect on the glomerular filtrate. A continuing solute diuresis is therefore in a sense "renal water wasting." Mannitol is active as a diuretic by this mechanism. Some of the material put in tube feedings, such as glucose and amino acids, has the same diuretic effect. Because these commonly used materials cause glycosuria and continuing solute diuresis, the patient being given large quantities of them loses a great deal of water in the urine. Osmotic diuresis is then, in part, responsible for solute-loading hypertonicity. The renal tubule in age or disease shows the phenomenon of solute diuresis at lower loading rates than the healthy kidney does.

Untreated diabetes mellitus produces hyperglycemic hypertonicity and a continuing solute diuresis that, by a combination of solute loading and osmotic diuresis, results in severe dehydration as well as desalting. A syndrome very much like this has been reported after the feeding of cow's milk to infants, with inadequate water to dilute the solute in the feeding formula. We have seen a similar picture in the treatment of bleeding duodenal ulcer with frequent feedings of milk and cream without water. Here, the absorption of partially digested blood, as well as the milk and cream, provides a severe solute load. Renal function may also be compromised from a recent hypotensive episode. Severe hypertonicity results and may be lethal.

4. Treatment

The contrasts between desiccation hypertonicity and solute-loading hypertonicity illuminate the details of treatment. In solute-loading hypertonicity, the patient gains weight and body water and remains polyuric while hypertonicity is developing, whereas in desiccation the patient is losing weight and body water and is oliguric while he is becoming hypertonic. In solute-loading hypertonicity emergency treatment consists in giving water in large quantities, but the basic management consists in withholding solute while the patient is given adequate water to cover the continuing osmotic diuresis over a period of several days. The patient relies on continuing renal function to help unload the solute. In desiccationed-hydration, the hypertonicity is treated with water alone, and oliguria persists until the water deficit is met. Thus, in solute-loading hypertonicity the entire development, including the treatment phase, may be characterized by remarkably high outputs of urine. In dehydration hypertonicity the patient is initially oliguric or anuric, and regains urine flow only as hydration is accomplished.

In the *burned patient* after the fourth day, one occasionally sees a variant of hypertonicity reminiscent of the solute-loading mechanism and compounded by incipient renal failure or high pulmonary water loss, especially marked where there is a tracheotomy. That burn hypertonicity is dangerous is bespoken by the fact that burn patients rarely survive with plasma sodium concentrations over 165 mE. per l. The most important factors in pathogenesis of burn hypertonicity are the pulmonary and skin losses of water mentioned previously, coupled with a large solute load given in early treatment (particularly if this early treatment has involved tube feedings or large amounts of salt or dextran). The burned patient has necessarily been given a large load of solutes in the form of sodium, because the early phase of treatment may require the administration of as much as 1200 mE. in water and colloid. Dextran has a small-molecular-weight component that acts as an osmotic diuretic. This property is a good feature of dextran when used in moderation, but, used in excess, dextran withdraws water and produces hypernatremia much as mannitol does. If renal failure later supervenes and the only channel for water loss is pulmonary, hypertonicity is inevitable.

Diabetes insipidus should be suspected as a cause of hypertonicity. After head injury or intracranial surgery any tendency to polyuria or hypertonicity, or both, must be assumed to be due to diabetes insipidus until proved otherwise. The defect is not always clearly evident unless sought out by clinical measurement of water balance. Diagnosis rests on continuing free water diuresis in the face of hypertonicity (or water restriction) and response to vasopressin. This water wasting is greatly increased by solute-loading. Treatment is based on the administration of adequate water with small amounts of vasopressin. One must beware the overadministration of water while vasopressin is being given. Severe water intoxication is easily produced by this combination.

Section V.   Two Patterns of Fluid Sequestration with Reduction in Plasma Volume

A. SEQUESTERED EDEMA: PERITONITIS, VENOUS OBSTRUCTION, AND ANALOGUES

1. Clinical Setting and Appearances

This is seen in ruptured ulcer, peritonitis from other causes, and acute spreading cellulitis. A similar mechanism operates in sudden venous obstruction (portal thrombosis) and in the tourniquet lesion with "release edema." Likewise, in intestinal obstruction, as previously mentioned, the major portion of the lost water and salt may reside in the lumen of the distended gut.

Patients with sequestered edema due to inflammatory processes and infection show the systemic effects of the infection, such as fever, rapid pulse, and leukocytosis. In addition, there is evidence of lowered plasma volume: decreased cardiac output, hypotension, oliguria, and a rising hematocrit. Shock may follow. If the infecting organism is a gram-negative bacillus, shock may occur before significant plasma volume reduction has occurred. With this exception, the systemic deterioration is due largely to reduction in effective circulating blood volume.

2. Characteristic Plasma Pattern

In sequestered edema, the most characteristic change from the normal plasma pattern is a rising hematocrit unaccompanied by external desalting water loss adequate to account for it; the relation between salt and protein in the accumulating edema determines whether a rising plasma protein concentration is also found.

3. Metabolic Background and Genesis

Sequestered edema is produced by the obligatory accumulation of a separate and expanding area of extracellular fluid in an area of tissue trauma, infection, or venous obstruction.* This accumulation is parasitic on the remaining extracellular fluid, producing volume reduction in the plasma and interstitial fluid. The accumulation is both within the tissues themselves as inflammatory edema, and free in serous cavities or fascial planes.

---

* A "third space," as termed by Randall.

The subsequent history of this sequestered edema depends upon the cause. In infectious processes the edema is only gradually absorbed. In peritonitis, administration of antibiotics will often control the infection sufficiently to diminish peritoneal signs and muscle spasm without preventing the irritative loss of a plasma-like exudate into the peritoneal cavity. In venous obstruction (as in mesenteric venous thrombosis) the ascites and intraluminal accumulation are rarely resorbed and have to be removed with the needle or the tube. Replacement of fluid must be very active. In direct tissue trauma such as occurs in a crush or fracture, the fluid is resorbed as the capillaries heal and circulation is restored.

4. Treatment

Treatment consists in the administration of adequate colloid, water, and salt to restore the plasma volume—and hence the blood volume and the circulation—to normal. The most sensitive indexes of the restoration of plasma volume to normal are the fall in the hematocrit, the rise in the output of urine, and the restoration of circulatory adequacy, as judged clinically. A rise in glomerular filtration will produce a rising volume output even if maximal salt-and-water retention is still active.

In the presence of an elevated hematocrit, a precise estimate of the amount of plasma required is based on a calculation of the observed as against the expected hematocrit in the light of the patient's expected normal blood volume. Restoration of plasma volume is accompanied by a disappearance of the "toxicity" of the process.

The simplest calculation to give an approximate figure for immediate (as opposed to long-term) plasma needs is based on the change in hematocrit of peripheral blood.

If, at 7 per cent of body weight, the normal blood volume for the patient is estimated to be 5000 ml., and he has lost sufficient plasma into the edema to raise his hematocrit to 62, one may reason as follows (see also page 217). With a normal hematocrit of 42, the red cell volume (RV) would be about 2100 ml. Now, with that same red cell volume occupying 62 per cent of his blood, the total blood volume is 2100 ÷ 0.62 or 3400 ml. There is a 1600 ml. deficit, all in the plasma fraction.* This amount of plasma should be given, as some form of colloid, immediately.

B. BURNS

1. Clinical Setting and Appearances

In a patient with an early untreated burn (Fig. 81), there is a shrinking plasma volume with a rising hematocrit, accompanied by oliguria. This combination produces changes in body water and electrolyte seen most typically in the full-thickness burn not involving the airway and extending over 30 per cent or more of the body surface. Untreated, the patient becomes toxic, febrile, and hypotensive as the metabolic disorder proceeds. Under treatment, the patient is remarkably improved, and a spontaneous diuresis may develop at about the third or fourth day, followed in turn by a prolonged phase of dilutional hypotonicity with hyponatremia and anemia before healing proceeds to anabolism and restoration of tonicity.

2. Metabolic Background and Genesis

In burns, the early biochemical picture is similar to that found in other forms of sequestered edema, except that in burns the edema is larger and accumulates faster and in a very widespread subcutaneous area. The edema continues to accumulate for forty-eight to seventy-two hours, and may be complicated by extrarenal loss of fluid and electrolyte through the burned skin. This extrarenal (skin) loss of salt has been maximal (1000 to 2000 ml. per day) in wet burns and scalds and minimal in dry, charred burns. But in the dry burn treated "open" there may be a considerable water loss by evaporation, particularly as slough begins. As mentioned previously this is one factor in the genesis of burn hypertonicity.

---

* Such a simple estimate assumes constancy of the erythrocyte volume. It yields a useful minimum figure for immediate replacement. When erythrocytes are also lost, the volume deficit is greater than is indicated by the elevation of hematocrit. This estimate cannot be based on the changing plasmacrit alone; it must be based on the estimated erythrocytic volume and the observed hematocrit, as described herein.

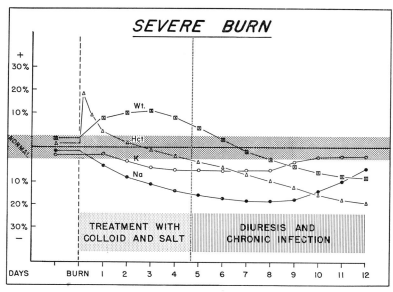

Figure 81. SEVERE BURN

The first two phases of convalescence from a severe burn are shown. In this example there has been some initial hematocrit rise, indicating a decrease in plasma volume which has responded well to treatment with colloid and salt. Body weight rate rises as the infused material partitions itself between the burn edema and the unburned extracellular fluid. This body weight is then lost as normal capillary permeability is restored and diuresis begins. Lowering of the hematocrit, initially therapeutic in origin, is furthered by the destruction of red cells made fragile by the heat (and by infection), leading ultimately to a chronic severe anemia. Transfusion therapy must be vigorous. Potassium values are not remarkable. There is a progressive fall in sodium concentration, largely dilutional in nature. Not shown are the subsequent phases of wound closure and tissue anabolism. Similar early changes are seen in the sequestered edema of peritonitis, venous obstruction, and analogues.

As the edema accumulates under the burn, withdrawing salt, water, and protein from the plasma, and this demand is satisfied by intravenous therapy, the patient must inevitably gain weight. The degree of weight gain provides an interesting and sensitive index of the progress of burn therapy and the extent to which it should be carried. The subsequent development of diuresis, passing on to a long phase of hyponatremia, may be thought of as the release of the renal tubule from the early salt-retaining effects, while at the same time the burned capillary is restoring its normal viability and impermeability to colloid.

If a severe burn involves the respiratory tract, the changes caused by anoxia and acute respiratory acidosis far overshadow those just mentioned, and may be rapidly fatal.

3. Treatment

The fundamental objective of treatment is the same as in other forms of sequestered edema. The plasma deficit should be prevented and if it has developed must be met by the administration of extracellular salt, water, and some form of colloid. Whether one uses dextran, albumin, or plasma, or mixtures of them, seems to make little difference. The amount initially needed for treatment may be budgeted on the basis of the patient's weight and the extent of the burn; the surgeon must be quick to make departures from his preconceived ideas if the occasion demands and developments surprise him.

The estimate of plasma need in the early extensive burn is based on the fact that in burns of 25 per cent of body surface or more the edema accumulation will, in the first forty-eight hours, approximate 10 per cent of body weight; additional water and salt are needed for external losses. The most rapid infusion must be in the first twelve hours. For example, in a 45 kg. woman with a 40 per cent burn of trunk and legs the colloid requirement will approximate 4500 ml. in the first forty-eight hours, of which about 2250 (or half) should be given in the first twelve hours to forestall the plasma deficit. She should have about 2000 ml. a day of noncolloid fluids, depending on fever and dyspnea (pulmonary water loss) and surface burn characteristics (skin loss of water, salt, and protein).

In neglected burns, after the twelfth hour, the static debt may be calculated from the hematocrit as in the foregoing section on sequestered edema, but to this calculation must, of course, be added the considerable further needs of the continuing edema accumulation. Because of the widespread application of sound principles in burn therapy, death from shock within a week of burning has become rare. Yet the over-all survival rate has been little changed owing to the subsequent evolution of other problems, largely those of antibiotic-resistant sepsis. See Part VI for a detailed discussion of burn treatment.

Section VI.   Three Patterns of Disordered Renal Function

A. OBSTRUCTIVE UROPATHY WITH SOLUTE DIURESIS

1. Clinical Setting and Appearances

The setting (Fig. 82) is to be found in an elderly man with hypertrophy of the prostate, suddenly relieved of longstanding partial lower-urinary-tract obstruction. The chronically overdistended bladder has produced ureteral reflux, hydronephrosis, and, when infection is present, pyelonephritis. Relief of the obstruction is followed, in occasional cases, by this characteristic sequence of events.* Renal stones and ureteral obstruction due to injury or tumor may also cause this pattern of disturbance. It is not invariably present; in many cases the relief of obstruction may be followed by uneventful return of normal renal function.

2. Characteristic Plasma Pattern

It is the sequence after relief of obstruction that attracts attention to this situation as being distinct from other urologic disorders. Before catheterization, azotemia and renal acidosis have developed. Yet severe degrees of hyperkalemia are rare, and as a result it is unusual for hyperkalemia to be a cardiac problem in obstructive uropathy. Some degree of desalting and hemoconcentration may be present if vomiting or pulmonary water loss has complicated the developing obstruction. Often, the toxic appearances called "dehydration" are due to uremia, and the patient is grossly waterlogged.

After relief of the obstruction, this "relief diuresis" is marked by large outputs of urine that are seemingly obligatory in nature and by a fall in the blood urea nitrogen (there may be a transient rise). Blood pressure falls from its elevated levels to more nearly normal. As these fall there is a tendency for the plasma chloride concentration to remain high and for the patient to pass through a long period of threatened desalting and dehydration due to solute diuresis, with a chronic "chloride" (that is, fixed acid) acidosis, a markedly elevated plasma chloride concentration, and a low carbon dioxide combining power. The pH is low, and pCO_2 is low as pulmonary compensation is maintained. Urinary sodium loss is massive; total sodium and plasma sodium concentrations both fall, the latter depending largely on water balance. After several days or weeks, the high outputs of urine diminish, and renal function gradually returns to normal as the formerly obstructed tubule regains its ability to recapture water and sodium from the filtrate and to excrete hydrogen ion. The blood urea nitrogen may fall only to a level of 25 to 30 mg. per 100 ml. and remain fixed there, indicating the presence of chronic parenchymatous renal disease in the background of this lesion.

---

* We are not referring here to the urinary suppression resulting from the hurried decompression of an overdistended bladder.

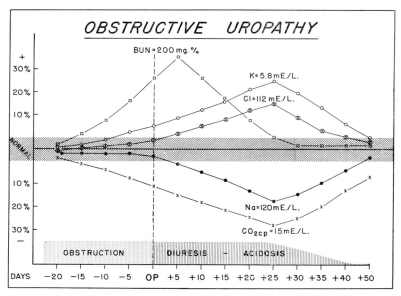

Figure 82. Obstructive Uropathy with Solute Diuresis

As compared with acute renal insufficiency, there is a disproportionate rise of urea over the potassium concentration during the obstructive phase. Renal acidosis and hypotonicity are progressive despite profuse diuresis after relief of obstruction. In some cases a very severe solute diuresis follows relief of obstruction, and there may be a remarkably persistent chloride acidosis. Both require accurate and energetic treatment. Restoration of acid-base balance and tonicity follows the return of normal renal tubular function, a change that may require several weeks.

3. Metabolic Background and Genesis

This polyuria is the result of a continued solute diuresis through a damaged renal tubule. The solute load results from obstructive accumulation of both crystalloid and salt; the tubular damage is produced by the chronic hydronephrosis and pyelonephritis of obstruction. It is more marked in older people suffering from chronic renal vascular disease.

During the obstructive phase, the patient has accumulated an unexcreted backlog of salt and crystalloid, demonstrable in part by edema, a high blood urea nitrogen, and the fact that the total plasma osmolality is 30 to 50 mO. per l. higher than the sum of measurable anions and cations. When obstruction is relieved, the patient begins a diuresis as this backlog of unexcreted solute is filtered into the tubular urine. If renal function were entirely normal, this solute diuresis phase would be transient, and the tubule cell would quickly regain its ability to process the filtrate and concentrate the urine; the tendency to dehydrate and desalt the patient would be minimal. This is the case in young and

healthy people. In older patients with tubular disease aggravated by longstanding renal-tract obstruction, a prolonged diuresis is produced.

This postobstructive diuresis may result in severe desalting water loss, with hemoconcentration and decreased plasma volume. The urine is formed in very large volume, from 5000 to 8000 ml. per day, and is of fixed specific gravity (or osmolality),* as is characteristic of any solute diuresis. The urine contains large amounts of electrolyte and crystalloids and does not respond with a lowered volume to the stimulus of dehydration.

In addition, there is a tendency to acidosis with the accumulation of high plasma chloride concentrations. This suggests that one of the enzymatic processes in the proximal renal tubule is altered in such a way as to inhibit the excretion of hydrogen ion in the course of this solute diuresis. As a feature of this proximal tubular lesion, large amounts of

---

* Specific gravity of approximately 1.010, or about 350 mO. per l.

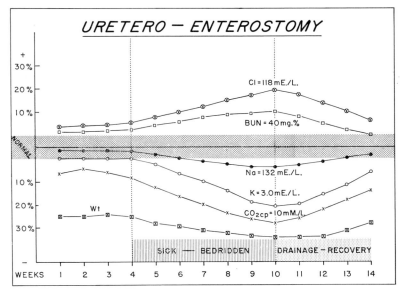

Figure 83. Uretero-Enterostomy

In this example the patient carries a slightly elevated plasma chloride concentration and low plasma carbon dioxide in the resting state as evidence of an underlying trend toward chronic renal disease and hyperchloremic acidosis. With an intercurrent illness, with the patient bedridden, bowel drainage of urine is impaired. Progressively there is the development of severe hyperchloremic acidosis. Urine volumes are high; weight is lost, and potassium falls to a low level. Azotemia is not severe. Plasma sodium concentration is only slightly low. As bowel drainage is restored, and with treatment including both sodium and potassium, there is restoration toward normal both clinically and chemically. In this example a rather slow development and repair is shown; it may be much more rapid, occupying days rather than weeks.

sodium salts are passed down to the distal tubule and contribute to the solute load and water wasting there. Plasma potassium concentration is variable, depending on the balance among bodily depletion, renal impairment, and acidosis. As the acidosis is gradually repaired by infusion of base and by acid excretion, plasma potassium concentration may fall to dangerous levels, and potassium must be given.

4. Treatment

Treatment is based on the maintenance of a reasonable balance of water, sodium, and bicarbonate. This is one of the few situations in surgery where a conscientious attempt should be made each day to repair the urinary loss of sodium salts. Large infusions of sodium bicarbonate or lactate (up to 450 mE. per day) may be required. Clinical judgment must temper this procedure. The presence of pitting edema or other evidences of increase in total body sodium indicate the wisdom of

allowing some sodium loss to proceed for several days after relief of the obstruction, before repair of this loss is begun.

B. URETERO-INTESTINAL ANASTOMOSIS

1. Clinical Setting and Appearances

As with the polyuria of relieved obstructive uropathy, this pattern of electrolyte disorder (Fig. 83) is neither inevitable nor invariable. Many patients with the underlying disturbance, in this case an anastomosis between one or both ureters and some portion of the lower gastrointestinal tract, do very well over a period of years with little abnormality in renal function detectable either by X-ray study or biochemically. Particularly prominent among those who do well are children who have had uretero-intestinal anastomosis for congenital anomalies of the lower urinary tract. Many adults also get along very well if properly managed.

The disordered biochemical pattern associated with uretero-enterostomy is hyperchloremic acidosis, usually with hypokalemia. It is common in older people, often those who have been operated upon for cancer and in whom there is some underlying renal disease. The biochemical disorder of uretero-enterostomy becomes especially marked when the patient must go to bed because of intercurrent illness or when, for other reasons, there is unsatisfactory drainage of urine either from the ureter into the bowel or from the bowel to the outside.

Hyperchloremic acidosis should be suspected in any patient with uretero-intestinal anastomosis who is ill or bedridden. In early cases the volumes of urine recorded from the bowel may be normal or large, in the polyuric range. The clinical appearances are those of a sick, toxic, flushed, feverish patient. He looks desalted and dehydrated. There may be signs of acidosis such as Kussmaul breathing. In later cases there may be oliguria, hypotension, and hypothermia.

2. Characteristic Plasma Pattern

The plasma chloride concentration will be found between 110 and 125 mE. per l., with an appropriate reduction in the carbon dioxide combining power. In the hyperchloremic acidosis of uretero-intestinal anastomosis there is rarely any significant accumulation of organic acids. In renal failure or diabetic acidosis the total of organic anions may be large.

By the same token, the sodium-osmolar differential is usually normal in uretero-enterostomy, indicating (though a mild azotemia may be present) that there is not a large accumulation of crystalloid solute such as one finds in other types of renal (or hepatic) failure.

With severe acidosis one would expect to find an elevated plasma potassium concentration, but the value is usually low (about 3.0 to 3.5 mE. per l.) in uretero-enterostomy because of prolonged potassium loss from both bowel and kidney. In occasional cases the renal acidosis "wins out" over the potassium loss, and hyperkalemia results. The plasma potassium concentration bears little relation to the body potassium here as in many other

situations, and the ratio may actually be inverse. In this disorder a seriously low plasma potassium concentration becomes manifest only when therapy with sodium bicarbonate or glucose has been overused, poorly controlled, or given without any potassium.

Azotemia is usually mild, with a blood urea nitrogen ranging from 30 to 70 mg. per 100 ml. The plasma sodium concentration is usually normal or slightly low.

3. Metabolic Background and Genesis

With a good output of urine, a mild azotemia, and a disorder of the renal regulation of acid-base balance without the accumulation of organic anions, one might reason that this was a disorder of renal tubule rather than glomerulus. It does not suggest the sort of disorder seen when renal blood flow or filtration is impaired.

Current evidence suggests that this is the case. The absorption of urine from the bowel, alone, produces a slight tendency to hyperchloremia that would, of itself, be of little note. There is a slight "chloride acidosis," which is due to the differential absorption of chloride when urine remains in the bowel for several hours. When to this is added some underlying renal tubular disease, a severe defect quickly appears. Like solute-loading hypertonicity, the biochemical challenge alone would produce a mild disorder, but when this is superimposed on underlying renal disease, a marked abnormality results.

The underlying renal disease at fault in uretero-enterostomy is usually that of obstruction, with chronic pyelonephritis. In some cases (especially in older people who have been operated upon for cancer), there may be some underlying renal vascular disease. In any event, it is the combination of selective ion resorption from the large intestine with abnormal tubular function that produces the clinical defect as observed. In addition there is prolonged loss of potassium from kidney and bowel, and a considerable lowering of body potassium. The renal histologic picture resembles potassium-loss nephropathy. This lesion, also, acts to potentiate the tubular dysfunction and the biochemical disorder.

The colon, when not emptied of urine

rapidly or completely (and this is a property particularly of the ascending colon or terminal ileum), resorbs hydrogen ion, and anions, more actively than cations. Chloride is resorbed very actively, as is ammonium, whereas sodium and potassium remain unabsorbed. This reperfuses the kidney with a progressively more acidic blood. The effect is not only that of progressive acidosis but also that of a continuously spiraling solute diuresis as the chloride is repeatedly filtered, reabsorbed, and filtered again. The large volumes of urine that result from this solute diuresis carry out both sodium and potassium, and desalt the patient. Only a renal tubule functioning in top form can constantly maintain large volumes of urine with pH at a low level (pH 4.5 to 5.0) and compensate for this gradually increasing hydrogen ion task. If the kidney is given extra base to work with, body sodium and potassium are restored, and the renal tubule does not have to excrete hydrogen ion against such a gradient to rid the body of the anion abnormally resorbed from the bowel. The hydrogen and chloride can be disposed of at a pH of 6.5 rather than 4.5, an easier task for a sick kidney. This is the basis of treatment.

4. Treatment

The uretero-intestinal anastomosis itself should be done by a technique that permits a free and unimpeded drainage of ureteral urine into the colon. The urine in the gastrointestinal tract should then be drained out completely and as nearly continuously as possible. If a patient with uretero-intestinal anastomosis gets sick or is put to bed, he should have an indwelling rectal catheter. If the anastomosis is to the ascending colon (undesirable) or to the ileum (it should be a very short loop), constant drainage must be provided.

The patient should be given enough water to compensate for the polyuric losses. Finally, and possibly most important in chronic care, the patient should be given extra base (sodium and potassium) so that the renal tubule can excrete the acid load without having to excrete a highly acid urine; the kidney can work at a more "comfortable" pH. A diet low in acid ash is also helpful.

It will be noted that one is here advised to treat "addition acidosis" (that is, an acidosis resulting from the accumulation of hydrogen ion rather than the loss of base) by the administration of fixed base (sodium bicarbonate). The intrinsic fallacy of this mode of treatment is obvious. If one treats the addition acidosis of outright renal failure by the administration of large amounts of base, the patient's life will be in jeopardy because of the load of salt and water. In uretero-intestinal anastomosis, however, one is dealing with an exception that permits this therapy. The exception arises from the fact that urine secretion is voluminous, even though there is selective accumulation of acid. For this reason, one can safely give liberal amounts of sodium and potassium, providing base so that hydrogen ion may be excreted by the kidney without the necessity of elaborating a urine of low pH.

A too-sudden repair of the acidosis with sodium bicarbonate may result in a further marked fall in plasma potassium concentration as acidosis changes toward alkalosis. Potassium has been lost from cells and should be included in treatment unless there is hyperkalemia initially, in which case potassium therapy should be delayed. In the more common situation of hypokalemia, repair of the acute acidosis must be done gradually and must include potassium, to avoid serious hypokalemia. Adequate urinary drainage is the most important single step.

C. ACUTE RENAL INSUFFICIENCY

1. Clinical Setting and Appearances

The majority of patients treated for acute renal insufficiency (Fig. 84) have suffered one of the following five conditions: trauma or surgery (often involving large-muscle bellies) with hypotension, mismatched blood transfusion, obstetric complications with shock, severe desalting water loss, or acute blood stream infection with prolonged hypotension.* There are other clinical backgrounds for acute renal insufficiency, but these are the most common. The output of

---

* The presence of dead tissue ("fourth-degree burn," gangrenous bowel, or ischemic muscle) seems to predispose to the development of renal failure.

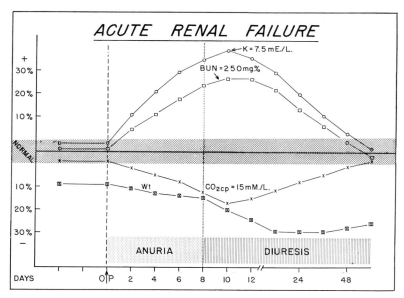

Figure 84. Acute Renal Failure

Trauma and shock have been followed (in this example) by anuria. Diuresis, if it is going to occur, usually starts between 7 and 14 days after the initial insult. Dialysis or other measures to rid the body of potassium are useful in maintaining the patient until diuresis occurs. The continued rise in blood urea nitrogen and potassium concentrations (with worsening of the metabolic acidosis) for a few days after the onset of diuresis is not uncommon. The gradual loss of weight during anuria indicates that fluid intake has not been excessive; a further loss upon diuresis indicates that there has been some water-loading nonetheless. In an occasional case there is a profuse solute diuresis during the recovery phase.

urine, diminished during the hypotensive phase, never returns; it is rare to see the interval of free urinary flow that used to be observed with the crush syndrome. Pre-existing dehydration, with marked abnormalities of electrolyte distribution (as seen, for example, in desalting water loss), leaves the patient more liable to severe renal damage during a shock episode.

The early clinical appearances of acute renal insufficiency are those of its background: trauma, shock, or desalting. There is no specific clinical manifestation of the early renal lesion. If the patient has had in the background any combination of the lesions listed above, and now presents average urinary outputs of 10 ml. per hour or less, he should be considered as suffering from early acute renal insufficiency and should be managed accordingly.

2. Characteristic Plasma Pattern

In the unstressed patient, plasma chemical changes are gradual. Azotemia predominates. In the post-traumatic patient, there are rapidly rising plasma potassium and blood urea nitrogen concentrations. Other electrolyte changes depend largely on therapy or extrarenal complications. Quite characteristically there is mild dilutional hypotonicity, with a low sodium concentration (as fat is burned and cells catabolized with retention of the water) and a mounting renal acidosis, with gradually falling pCO_2 as respiratory mechanisms operate to maintain pH.

3. Metabolic Background and Genesis

As seen in acute trauma, surgery, and obstetrics, the etiology of this lesion appears to involve renal anoxia due to ischemia in a period of decreased renal blood flow, as well as the presence, during the anoxic period, of a nephrotoxin. It is not renal anoxia alone that produces this lesion; it is renal anoxia combined with the action of a nephrotoxin that is so damaging to the kidney. Ischemia and anoxia render the kidney vulnerable to an otherwise tolerable nephrotoxin; dehydration and desalting have a similar potentiating effect on the action of toxic products. The commonest nephrotoxins to be implicated are heme pigments derived from breakdown products of blood. Myoglobin and various bilirubin breakdown products, as well as sulfonamides, mercurials, bacterial products, and allergens, may also be offenders. When nephrotoxins are absent it is not uncommon to see oliguria in severely ill surgical patients for periods up to four days and yet with complete recovery of renal function as blood and body water volumes are returned to normal.

Although the presence of heme pigment in the urine alone does not make this diagnosis a certainty, it strongly suggests that renal damage will result in the hypotensive patient. If the patient is in shock from burns or trauma and there is gross pigment in the blood and urine, the likelihood that this lesion will develop is greatly increased.

The other urinary findings cannot be used diagnostically in this condition. Specific gravity and osmolality appear to be fixed in the middle range of 1.015 to 1.020 and 500 to 750 mO. per l. This has little significance, since virtually all oliguric patients after severe trauma also have fixed specific gravity as a manifestation of solute excretion during antidiuresis and renal vasoconstriction. The presence of tubular epithelium, granular casts, red blood cells, and pigment in the urine is more suggestive, though again not sufficient evidence for positive diagnosis. The characteristic urinary volume in acute renal insufficiency is 150 to 300 ml. per day. Total absence of output is more suggestive of urinary tract obstruction.

4. Treatment

Better than treatment is prevention through the maintenance of normal renal blood flow. It is the surgeon's responsibility to avoid desalting the patient, to maintain the patient's normal blood volume throughout any surgical or obstetric event, and to provide compatible viable red blood cells in transfusion.

Once renal insufficiency has occurred, the kidneys will heal and recover if the patient lives long enough to permit them to do so. Treatment is devoted to keeping the patient alive with a normal circulation until his kidneys heal.

Early Diagnostic Aspects of Management. For most doctors taking care of acutely ill oliguric patients, the difficult period lies in the first day or two of oliguria, when there is uncertainty about the presence of parenchymatous renal damage. If the patient has a low total blood or body water volume and remains hypotensive, his kidneys will suffer. And yet, if the doctor is unrealistic in his attempts to increase these volumes to normal and in so doing overshoots the mark, the patient will suffer from hypertension, cardiac decompensation, and pulmonary edema.

Maintenance of circulation with normal organ perfusion is the first objective. One must use clinical acumen to judge the adequacy of the circulatory volume in the oliguric patient. The performance of blood-volume determinations has not been helpful. The objective is not so much an ideal absolute volume as functional adequacy.

Measurement of venous pressure provides a safety check on transfusion volume; if venous pressure is being measured it is safer to transfuse whole blood or separated cells and bring about a transient rise in venous pressure than it is to leave volume unreplaced.

If the patient has been transfused to the point where he has a strong, slow pulse, good capillary blood flow with normal blanching responses, a normal blood pressure, and a clear sensorium, one must assume that his volume is restored, and should avoid further infusion. An elevated hematocrit in peritonitis or burns may be a quantitative guide to the inadequacy of plasma volume. This deficit should be rectified promptly, and sufficient colloid given to bring down the hematocrit. If the patient's blood and body water volumes, extracellular pH, and electrolyte loss have been returned as close to normal as possible, he should thereafter be cared for by the "in-balance" technique.

There are situations in oliguria after severe operations, shock, and burns in which a cautious trial of "infusion tolerance" is justified. The choice of material for this infusion must depend on the clinical setting. If the test infusion consists of water or salt, amounts approximating 1000 ml. should be given in forty minutes. For plasma we recommend 500 ml. in thirty minutes. The hazard of these tests is so obvious that it should not need to be pointed out again; their value, however, demands that they be used despite hazard. Venous pressure should be measured as well as output of urine. A patient's response to this treatment by increased output (over 20 ml. per hour) suggests lack of colloid, water, or salt as genesis of the oliguria. "No response" signifies parenchymatous damage and calls for the institution of appropriate fluid restriction.

During the acute episode of trauma, shock, or operation an inlying catheter provides an important guide to circulatory status in the kidney. The differential renal vasoconstriction of early volume reduction is corrected with replacement. A carefully placed inlying catheter is greatly to be preferred to repeated interval catheterization, which is almost sure to introduce infection. Whether the volumes are recorded hourly or three-hourly is a matter of little moment.

If the patient is admitted to the hospital in "resting anuria," and the acute episode is past, unnecessary catheterization should be avoided.

Further Management. In terms of water and electrolyte structure, the early threat to the patient is overhydration and oversalting. Patients should be weighed daily and should be expected to lose some weight each day as they oxidize fat. The water requirement is small (500 to 750 ml. a day) unless there are extrarenal losses. The provision of large amounts of carbohydrate or concentrated fat as an energy source is of assistance in preventing cell breakdown and the accumulation of acid metabolites, phosphate, and potassium, but one must be cautious lest the infusion of these substances carry with it an oversupply of water. Testosterone may have the same function.

The ultimate lethal event of acute renal failure is hyperkalemia. After trauma, burn, operation, or shock, the rise of the plasma potassium concentration is more rapid than it is in the resting or unstressed anuric patient. The electrocardiographic changes of hyperkalemia are greatly accentuated by low plasma sodium or calcium concentrations and acidosis.

Despite the fact that it is only symptomatic and temporary, no other form of treatment has been able to match the effectiveness of extracorporeal dialysis as a means of treating acute uremia and dangerous hyperkalemia. After dialysis the plasma potassium concentration may return rapidly to its elevated level. But precious time has been purchased, and the patient has been allowed to survive closer to the point where diuresis can ensue. The return of hyperkalemia suggests that something other than the accumulation of potassium is responsible for it. Recent evidence suggests that this other factor is renal acidosis. During recovery, and after the kidneys begin their urinary flow, there is a tendency for the plasma potassium and blood urea nitrogen concentrations to continue to rise for a day or two. The extracellular acidosis may persist for several days after diuresis begins. The plasma potassium concentration should be measured chemically and electrocardiographically. Its rise may continue to threaten despite diuresis.

If facilities for accurate study and care are not available locally, the patient should be transferred to one of the many renal centers available for care of such patients. This transfer should be carried out before the patient is too ill to tolerate transportation; better an unnecessary transfer early than a fatal transfer late.

Good metabolic management often makes dialysis unnecessary, particularly if diuresis begins before the tenth day of oliguria.

CHAPTER 23

Water, Salt, and Acid: Notes from the Literature

Knowledge of acid-base balance, electrolyte exchange, and renal function has been enriched recently with particular reference to the following areas.

1. Mineralocorticoid activity; aldosterone changes in trauma, volume reduction, and alkalosis.
2. The activity of the entire body as a buffering system.
3. Acidosis, respiratory components, and compensation; anesthesia acidosis.
4. Potassium, aciduria, hypokalemia, and alkalosis.
5. Dehydration, fasting, and desalting.
6. Tissue sodium and potassium: irritability.
7. Bone sodium.
8. Magnesium.
9. Volume-sensitive phenomena.
10. Water distribution: hypotonicity and hypertonicity.

In this section, as in other summaries in this book, some recent literature will be reviewed. This is not an encyclopedic review. Some of the ideas naturally repeat and provide the basis for statements made elsewhere in the book.

Section I.   Aldosterone

The chemical and physiologic characterization of aldosterone as the active "sodium-retaining factor" of amorphous adrenal residues has offered attractive but tentative explanations for many of the metabolic changes seen in surgery. Final evaluation of the complex interplay of endocrine forces on the surgical kidney will require much time-consuming work. The work of Simpson *et al.* (1954) defined the chemical structure and general physiologic actions of this material. It has several unique properties, particularly that its secretion is somewhat independent of adrenocorticotropic hormone or the pituitary gland to an extent not shared by other adrenal hormones. In addition, its action is largely that of regulating electrolyte metabolism by lowering the sodium:potassium ratio in urine, its secretion is very sensitive to changes in extracellular volume, and the material is remarkably potent in this regard. It does possess certain glucocorticoid properties and cannot be regarded merely as a "super 'DOCA.'" Clearly an increased aldosterone effect due either to increased secretion or decreased inactivation might be in the background of the postoperative lowering of the urinary sodium:potassium ratio.

The studies of Bartter and his group (Liddle *et al.*, 1955; Bartter *et al.*, 1956) indicate that restriction of the volume of the extracellular fluid is the prime mover in producing increased secretion of aldosterone; they feel that potassium is a stimulus only when it increases sodium loss. They showed that volume expansion reduces aldosterone production and increases sodium loss despite hyponatremia. They also showed that adrenocorticotropic hormone clearly increases aldosterone production, though the magnitude of the change is small as compared with the production of corticosteroids. These data are further detailed in Bartter *et al.* (1958) and in the work of Fine *et al.* (1958).

Luetscher and Axelrod (1954) have found 1.5 to 3.0 mcg. of aldosterone in the twenty-four-hour urine samples of normal subjects; an increased output of aldosterone on low-sodium diets is the rule. But, as it turns out, it is not the low-sodium diet but volume reduction that is the prime stimulus.

Laragh and Stoerk (1955) have shown, in dogs, that excessive administration of potassium and/or a rise in plasma potassium concentration is a stimulus to the secretion of aldosterone and a much more potent stimulus than changes in plasma sodium concentration. It is conceivable that the post-traumatic discharge of potassium from cells to the extracellular fluid may constitute one of the stimuli to aldosterone production in the patient after trauma. Species differences may make one hesitate to apply these findings to man.

Bartter (1956) reviews the status of aldosterone physiology, and emphasizes that this hormone affects the cellular transport of sodium, potassium, and hydrogen ions; that change in the volume of extracellular fluid is its most potent regulator, but that potassium loads and adrenocorticotropic hormone also can increase the rate of secretion. It was Llaurado (1955) who first found increased aldosterone content in the urine of surgical patients, and who then showed that the sodium:potassium ratio in the patient's urine appeared to be a function of aldosterone secretion. Zimmerman *et al.* (1956) also studied the excretion of aldosterone by the postoperative patient. Zimmerman separated out the aldosterone by chromatography and showed by bioassay on the resulting eluates that there was a clear augmentation of aldosterone excretion after surgical operations.

Zimmerman (1956) showed that pregnanediol excretion was increased after trauma, suggesting mobilization of a salt-active steroid. His data clearly show the drastic alteration in sodium metabolism produced by the total surgical experience; many components are clearly of importance in initiating this change. Randall and Papper (1958) have shown that it requires from 1000 to 3000 ml. of isotonic saline to "normalize" sodium excretion after trauma; once it has been given, sodium dynamics look normal. Rather than indicating that the postoperative patient's sodium metabolism is normal, this appears to demonstrate a drastic alteration in sodium distribution or an acute change in volume sensitivity.

The work of Bartter (1956) is based on bioassay. The method used in Bartter's work consists in an extraction of urine at a low *p*H followed by bioassay based on renal sodium excretion in the adrenalectomized dog. He has found volume effects to be primary in aldosterone regulation; the plasma sodium concentration is inconsequential as a regulator of aldosterone secretion and in many instances the volume change is reciprocal and the change in aldosterone secretion appropriate for volume. The hemorrhage experiments indicate the fine sensitivity of aldosterone secretion to acute changes in blood volume.

Bartter (1956) has shown that normal human subjects bled small volumes show an increase in aldosterone production with salt retention. When this blood is retransfused, there is then a sodium diuresis. ACTH does produce a small but transient increase in aldosterone production.

As mentioned above, the fall in sodium concentration in the plasma is not a potent stimulus to aldosterone production. As a matter of fact, if the subject is water-loaded and given vasopressin so that a high volume is produced, there is a striking fall in plasma sodium concentration (as one would expect from dilution) and coincident with this a marked reduction in aldosterone production and increase in sodium excretion. This is the "aldosterone-release diuresis" of an expanded hypotonic extracellular fluid.

By converse, water deprivation in diabetes insipidus produces a rise in plasma sodium concentration combined with a paradoxical rise in aldosterone production (Bartter, 1956), indicating again the primacy of volume effects in regulating aldosterone production, and the fact that volume effects can overcome inverse concentration changes in sodium.

There is little correlation between aldosterone secretion after operation, and the sodium balance itself. However, the sodium:potassium ratio does indicate a correlation. If, as Bartter indicates, reduction of effective volume is the most important stimulus to aldosterone excretion, we would not necessarily expect to see it after all surgical procedures.

All of these advances in our understanding do not prove either a sole or a linear causation in surgical salt metabolism; they merely establish association.

One must again differentiate among the manifold stimuli of a surgical procedure. Blood loss is clinically a very special (rapid, potent) stimulus to the retention of salt, which is retained with water as in an isosmotic tubular resorbate. The work of Flear and Clarke (1955) and Topley and Clarke (1956) draws special attention to this fact in clinical care. Our studies on metabolic effects of pure hemorrhage indicate that conservation of water and salt is one of the most rapid and reproducible effects of hemorrhage in man. In addition to such volume reduction, the surgical experience may stimulate increased aldosterone excretion by specific anesthetic effects (such as those of ether) by cross-sectional tissue dissection or destruction, or by alterations in renal handling of the steroid itself. There has been little suggestion as yet that the increased salt activity of trauma is an apparent ("permissive") adrenal effect, occurring in the adrenalectomized subject on constant desoxycorticosterone acetate or aldosterone. Yet, such was indeed observed in the work of Ingle (1952). The report of Mason (1955) certainly suggests that this may be the case in man. If so, the search for trauma-induced alterations in the intermediary metabolism of aldosterone, only recently begun for the glucocorticoids, should be initiated.

Finally, mention must again be made of the fact that a low rate of glomerular filtration produces a relatively sodium-poor urine even with basal (that is, normal) adrenal activity. This is because sodium resorption is so nearly complete under normal conditions that even small reductions in the rate of glomerular filtration permit the normal basal resorption to remove essentially all the filtered sodium.

The characteristic reduction in urinary sodium:potassium ratio produced by aldosterone—and the basis of most bioassay methods—is also characteristic of the normal post-traumatic state. The excretion of increased amounts of potassium cannot occur (without reduction in plasma potassium concentration) unless the excreted potassium comes from a source outside the extracellular fluid. This of course it does do, being mobilized from the lean body mass after trauma and also, specifically, after desalting water loss and hemorrhage. This mobilization results in new water (from the cell) becoming available for the maintenance of extracellular fluid and plasma volume. We must therefore include the possibility that aldosterone is the agent that mobilizes cell water after hemorrhage, desalting, or dehydration.

The Korean studies (Howard, BCK, I) showed a very rapid drop in the urinary sodium:potassium ratio within hours after wounding; it is of exceptional interest that some of these patients were seen so early that one could document the drop; by the sixth hour all were down below 1:1. The possible role of decreased glomerular filtration must be considered here, as well as salt-active steroids.

The prolonged nature of lowered urinary sodium:potassium ratios, post-traumatic sodium-potassium shift, water intolerance, and appropriate balance changes (sodium gain, potassium loss) was very striking in some of these wounded men. The eosinophil backswing (with very high counts) persisted through much of this phase, indicating a dissociation of many of the correlations noted in a less complex setting. The tendency for secondary operations to relower the urinary sodium:potassium ratio and reshift the plasma sodium and potassium concentrations was very impressive. In one patient, the cumulative negative potassium balance reached 500 mE. in eight days, with no lowering of plasma potassium concentration, a characteristic sequence so long as alkalosis is absent. In this particular patient the eosinophil count remained low through the potassium-loss phase and came sharply upward as potassium loading was begun.

Where extrarenal loss was noted, sodium balance was less apt to be positive on a low intake, as one might predict. Magnesium changes in plasma were inconsequential in these patients.

The possibility exists that the expanded body sodium content and extracellular volume of visceral disease is actively protected by aldosterone rather than produced by it pathologically. One must then postulate that the "set" of the volume-regulating system has been moved up by the visceral disease: a greater volume is "needed" to maintain the circulation. Of great interest to such a concept are the data showing that the induction of a large sodium diuresis in such a disease as chronic congestive heart failure may be followed by an *increase* in aldosterone production. For example, in a patient with chronic congestive heart failure, the aldosterone excretion rate of 10 mcg. per day (normal for a resting individual) may be increased as high as 90 mcg. per day when there is a large diuresis induced by digitalis and mercurial diuretics. In terms of current volume theory, this would be accounted for by the explanation that in chronic congestive heart failure the body "needs" a large body water and extracellular fluid fraction to maintain circulation. When this becomes reduced, the mechanism for conserving salt (and thus supporting volume) is brought strongly into play.

Section II.   Cellular Buffers

Swan and Pitts (1955) studied the uptake and buffering of acid loads (hydrochloric acid) in nephrectomized dogs. They concluded that 40 per cent of the total buffering was extracellular—10 per cent by the erythrocyte, and 50 per cent by cellular buffers, the latter operating in part by ion exchange and the discharge of Na^+ and K^+ from cells into the extracellular fluid.

The role of the total body buffers was also studied by Schwartz *et al.* (1954). They administered acid loads (ammonium chloride and ammonium sulfate) to sodium-depleted subjects. They found that ammonium excretion was prompt and that the body accepted the hydrogen ion loads largely in the body buffers. Most of the hydrogen load (that is, the acid load) was taken up in tissue or bone; potassium and sodium left the tissues in exchange for hydrogen. During recovery there was potassium retention during the phase of hydrogen discharge.

Schwartz *et al.* (1955) then showed (in dogs) that the infusion of hydrochloric acid produces a loss of cellular potassium and a lowering of extracellular bicarbonate concentration, which reflects accurately the depletion of total body buffers; there is no extracellular:intracellular differential in the degree of acidosis or buffer depletion produced by this type of metabolic acidosis with an exogenous mineral acid. This type of acidosis is rare in surgery, but if the findings can be transferred to the fixed acid acidosis of renal failure in man we may assume that the total body buffers are utilized *pari passu* with extracellular bicarbonate. The study of Schwartz *et al.* (1957) was also based on the infusion of hydrochloric acid in dogs. As one might expect, the extracellular buffer pairs were used up first, and as the infusion was continued the cellular buffers were taken up. In the end, once equilibrium was established, hydrogen ion was distributed pro rata throughout body water. Stated otherwise, the per cent reduction in plasma bicarbonate is an index of reduction in total body buffers.

Elkinton *et al.* (1955) studied the transfer of hydrogen, sodium, and potassium in acute respiratory acidosis and alkalosis in man.

Activity of the buffering mechanism of the body was very rapid and involved transfer chiefly of hydrogen and sodium. Potassium changes were small in these brief experiments. The experimenters estimated that over 90 per cent of the total buffering was extrarenal and the largest portion intracellular in site. Giebisch, Berger, and Pitts (1955) came to the same conclusion on the basis of similar experiments in dogs. Tissue buffering is also indicated by the direct tissue analysis of Darrow and Sarason (1944), Malorny (1948), and Cooke *et al.* (1952).

Elkinton (1956) in a review summarizes his work on whole body buffers. In acute respiratory acidosis and alkalosis, renal adjustments account for only 4 to 6 per cent of the total disposal. Extrarenal adjustments do the rest, and of this extrarenal buffering, 65 to 70 per cent is cellular and achieved by exchange of sodium (only to a minor degree by potassium) with an undetermined anion.

Intracellular buffering is reflected in extracellular buffering processes through the replenishment or exhaustion of extracellular ions from or to cellular stores and by the provision of potassium to the extracellular phase. The two processes cannot be considered as distinct, but their total buffering capacity is far greater than the sum of blood and extracellular fluid. Knowledge of the extent of this cellular contribution has merely extended quantitatively, but not changed qualitatively, the buffering concepts of Henderson, which were the basis of the fundamental clinical work of Van Slyke and Gamble. The extension of buffering capacity to the cellular mass accounts for somewhere around 50 per cent of the total capacity of the body to take up an acid load. In surgical shock or other acute circulatory failures, this buffering is lost because transport of metabolites is impaired.

In alkalosis, hydrogen moves out of the cell into the extracellular fluid in exchange for sodium. In acidosis, hydrogen exchanges in a reverse direction for sodium—largely in bone. The sodium then appears in the extracellular fluid. Potassium transfers are small, but since there are only small amounts of potassium in the extracellular fluid, these transfers result in very considerable and apparent changes in concentration of potassium in the extracellular fluid or excretion in the urine.

The many ion shifts involved in the genesis of metabolic (subtraction) alkalosis, as for instance in vomiting, complicate interpretation of renal and tissue changes. Stanbury and Thomson (1952) studied the effects of acute respiratory alkalosis in normal man and showed that the body defense takes place largely through cellular buffering, organic acids (largely lactate) diffusing into the plasma; a lowered plasma potassium and phosphorus were noted; an increased excretion of sodium and potassium bicarbonate with maximal H^+ conservation was observed. The rate of HCO_3^- excretion was independent of plasma concentration or filtered load, but closely correlated with excretion of Na^+ and K^+. There was no change in plasma concentrations of sodium or chloride in these acute experiments.

Sodium depletion, oddly enough, actually interfered with the renal response to respiratory alkalosis, since the kidney was evidently unable to increase sodium excretion. This is reminiscent of the postoperative aldosterone effect, which blocks sodium excretion and makes the postoperative patient so much more vulnerable to metabolic alkalosis.

Both sodium and potassium ion are required by the kidney in order to effect the ion-exchange mechanisms involved in the renal correction of acid-base disorders including alkalosis; the availability of H^+ for exchange is provided in part by carbonic anhydrase. In the presence of an acid load (ammonium chloride, for example) the use of acetazolamide (Diamox) might be expected to interfere with renal compensation.

Section III.   Other Data on Acid-Base Loads: Anesthesia and Acidosis

Kaufman and Rosen (1956) describe the application of the Brönsted nomenclature to acid-base disorders, particularly as they occur in surgical practice. Schwartz and Relman

(1957) clarify the point relative to renal acidosis. In both instances clinical care is simplified by reference to anions and cations as such, and the reservation of the term "acid" for hydrogen donors: substances that lower the pH of solutions to which they are added.

Bramlitt and Hardy (1956) studied the acid-base response to various infused solutions; the extreme stability of blood pH and the minimal change in pCO$_2$ required to compensate indicate the participation of extravascular buffer systems. In contrast to the findings of Relman *et al.* (1953) these authors found a definite elevation of pCO$_2$ (to 54 mm. Hg), indicating respiratory compensation to the addition metabolic alkalosis due to infusions. Such may not be the case in subtraction metabolic alkalosis, for example in pyloric obstruction. The authors prefer to consider the results as due wholly to blood buffers; the hydrogen ion loads (or OH$^-$ loads) were so large as obviously to involve extravascular buffering.

Dormen *et al.* (1954) showed in dogs that acute respiratory acidosis resulted in the increased reabsorption of sodium and bicarbonate in the tubules. They felt that the pCO$_2$ elevation of body fluids, rather than pH change, was the effective stimulus to bicarbonate resorption. They postulated ionexchange mechanisms involving hydrogen and other cations, depressed by carbonic anhydrase inhibitors, and therefore presumably dependent on the enzymatic hydration of carbon dioxide to provide a source of hydrogen ion. This work is interesting in the light of the data on metabolic alkalosis in the presence of elevated carbon dioxide or with potassium deficiency, wherein resorption of bicarbonate by the renal tubules is also enhanced.

Relman *et al.* (1953) showed (in dogs) that there was a linear relation between plasma pCO$_2$ and renal bicarbonate reabsorption in extracellular alkalosis and that there was no change in pulmonary ventilation in response to extracellular alkalosis. Winkler and Smith (1942) found that the rate of potassium excretion was highest in an alkaline urine with large amounts of bicarbonate and sodium.

The acid-base effects of anesthesia appear to involve a number of variables, the relation between which is not wholly clear. Some of these variables are as follows:

(1) carbon dioxide accumulation with respiratory acidosis as a result of underventilation;

(2) appearance of fixed acid from some source producing a metabolic acidosis, particularly with ether anesthesia;

(3) lacticacidemia as a by-product of ether anesthesia alone, or in combination with respiratory alkalosis due to overventilation, or as a result of tissue hypoxia, or of all three acting in concert;

(4) production of metabolic acids by increased exercise of the respiratory muscles;

(5) concomitance of other factors, particularly changes in adrenocortical function and renal function.

According to Root *et al.* (1940) ether produces an accumulation of lactate as a direct effect. Elkinton *et al.* (1955) have shown that a metabolic alkalosis may occur in man, on breathing of carbon dioxide mixtures. On the other hand, Altschule and Sulzbach (1947) have shown that there is a metabolic component in the acidosis produced by carbon dioxide breathing in curarized patients. Beecher and Murphy (1950), Taylor and Roos (1950), and Gibbon *et al.* (1950) have shown a severe metabolic acidosis to occur when there was interference with normal respiration.

Holaday *et al.* (1957) studied fifty-seven cases anesthetized with a variety of agents. A characteristic change was a mixed respiratory and metabolic acidosis (pCO$_2$ to 80 mm. Hg, buffer base reduced 5 to 7 mE. per l.), coming on early in the procedure with pH values as low as 7.10, and later restoring itself to normal, sometimes during continuance of anesthesia and operation. In general, the metabolic change (acidosis with reduction in buffer base) was proportional to the degree of carbon dioxide retention.

Elevation of plasma potassium concentration is by no means an inevitable sequel to the development of this mixed metabolic and respiratory acidosis.

Peterson *et al.* (Unpub.) found that, in normal persons, acute respiratory acidosis did not increase the plasma potassium concentration whereas respiratory alkalosis did lower it. However, when the hypercapnia of the acidotic group was reduced toward normal there was a transient rise in potassium. In these acidotic patients the pH fell to 7.19 and the pCO$_2$ rose to over 70 mm. Hg. The total carbon dioxide values were near 30 mE. per l.

Winterstein (Dunham Lectures, 1957) has studied the biochemistry and action potentials of the respiratory center and osmoreceptors in relation to oxygen and carbon dioxide. As he re-emphasizes, the extreme diffusibility of carbon dioxide, as against other components of the acid-base complex, introduces special problems. Certain mixtures of carbonic acid with HCO$_3$$^-$ taste acid (i.e., act within cells as an acid) despite a pH of 7.4. Mixtures of sodium bicarbonate and carbonic acid produce intracellular acidosis by carbon dioxide diffusion; sodium bicarbonate may even produce hyperpnea as a result of intracellular acidosis in the respiratory center; intravenous administration of sodium bicarbonate will produce acidity of the cerebrospinal fluid by the same mechanism. In such instances it is the change in intracellular pH that excites the respiratory stimulus. Ammonia (in contradistinction to ammonium ion) is also diffusible, in the sense that carbon dioxide is. Thus, even in the absence of liver disease ammonium chloride produces extracellular acidity and intracellular alkalinity and an analogous blood–cerebrospinal fluid pH gradient. Phrenic nerve action potentials produced by carbon dioxide excess are much decreased by anesthesia; carbon dioxide in high concentration paralyzes nerve conduc-

tion and neurovascular activity. We have here a potential vicious cycle where poor ventilation and anesthesia coexist; the extreme potentiation of mechanisms in such a setting at high carbon dioxide concentrations would not be evident in studies carried out in the normal range of concentrations. It is conceivable that in the anesthetized state there may be effects of carbon dioxide accumulation not indicated by studies under other circumstances.

Literature bearing on the relation of hypercarbia (and its relief) to cardiac arrest and fibrillation is also reviewed in Part V in the section on the heart. Here we are concerned particularly with the genesis of increased tensions of carbon dioxide during operation. Additional references include the following studies describing the effects of anesthesia itself, anesthetic agents, and position: Beecher *et al.* (1950, 1951), Ellison *et al.* (1955), Gabbard *et al.* (1952), Miller *et al.* (1952), Sealy *et al.* (1957), Nealon *et al.* (1956), Taylor and Roos (1950), Ziegler (1948), Seevers *et al.* (1938), Stormont *et al.* (1942), Gibbon *et al.* (1950), Etsten (1953), and Maier *et al.* (1951).

Maier *et al.* (1951) found a high incidence of postoperative hypotension when there was respiratory acidosis, as well as cardiac arrhythmias. Many groups have found similar phenomena and these have provided the basis for the studies of the effects of acidosis and alkalosis on the cardiovascular system, discussed also in Part III and Part VI.

The effect of oxygen therapy on carbon dioxide tensions has been studied by Hickam *et al.* (1952) and Marshall and Rosenfeld (1936).

Section IV.   Potassium Lack, Aciduria, Hypokalemia, "Stress," and Alkalosis

In view of recent interest in the alkaloses of trauma, stress, and the postoperative period, it is noteworthy that as early as 1926 Bothe observed many cases of alkalosis in postoperative patients. He noted the clinical signs of severe alkalosis, particularly as it occurs after operation. Some of his cases went on to

tetany and convulsions, results reminiscent of data from Hardt and Rivers (1923).

At that time both the clinical chemistry and an interpretive framework were in their infancy. The cause of the low plasma chloride concentration was not clear because balance studies had not yet been done, and the relation of extrarenal loss or intraluminal sequestration to total extracellular chloride levels was not understood. Notwithstanding these factors, Bothe correctly deduced the nature and renal significance of postoperative alkalosis. Tileston and Comfort (1914) had postulated that the increased tissue destruction was the cause of the increased tendency to elevate the "blood nitrogen" after injury. Studies of potassium balance in surgery were still twenty years away, but in 1923 Loeb and Gamble, Ross, and Tisdall (1923) published their first studies of potassium balance in patients with diabetic acidosis and in sick children, respectively.

The hesitancy to use intravenous fluids is illustrated by the admonition that "in the more serious cases" the saline solution could be given intravenously and a total of 1500 ml. of saline could be administered intravenously each day (in three doses) in severe alkalosis. As has already been made clear, this treatment is sometimes very hazardous because of sodium loading, yet it was virtually the only electrolyte solution available in 1926. The use of dilute hydrochloric acid and ammonium chloride by rectum was advised but had not been tried extensively. Feeding jejunostomy was also suggested.

In several of the case reports in the paper of Bothe one can discern the characteristic picture now called hypokalemic alkalosis; at postmortem no specific changes were seen; there was a renal lesion, pneumonitis, and ileus, peritonitis, and obstruction.

One of the first to discern the aciduria, seemingly paradoxical, in hypochloremic alkalosis, was Evans, who, with Van Slyke (Van Slyke and Evans, 1947), first described the syndrome. The authors studied hydrochloric acid loss in dogs and found the hypokalemia. They concluded that potassium should be used in replacement. It is noteworthy that in this early work the lesion was produced by hydrogen chloride loss in dogs. The thought of abetting the lesion by using desoxycorticosterone acetate had not yet occurred, to contaminate the literature by reference to steroid-treated animals as primarily "potassium-deficient." The authors noted that sodium chloride infusion was slow in helping and that sodium

bicarbonate caused tetanic convulsions. There have been few studies in the dog that have reproduced so faithfully the clinical and biochemical lesions of acute hypokalemic alkalosis.

Evans (1950) and Randall et al. (1949) review some of the earlier data on potassium deficiency in surgical patients. As was currently the case in most writings, they did not distinguish between potassium lack on the one hand, and hypokalemia or a low potassium concentration on the other. The terms "potassium-deficiency" and "hypokalemia" were used interchangeably, although there is now clear evidence they are not interchangeable. Evans distinguished one group as "the effect of adrenocortical hormones on hypochloremic alkalosis," an interesting expression of the "metabolic alkalosis plus aldosterone" phenomenon, which has formed a central feature of our findings in this field. He also noted that the plasma concentration of potassium rose very rapidly as gastric function returned, and could not reconcile this with the "deficiency" theory of hypokalemia; he saw clearly the contradiction but without data on total body potassium could offer no explanation. He was unaware of the data just being uncovered at that time to show that plasma concentrations of potassium correlated but poorly with body stores.

The data to suggest that acid-base balance alone might alter potassium concentration quite independent of body stores had not yet begun to appear. Evans noted accurately the tendency of hypokalemia to be associated with severe alkalosis. He also noted that in hypokalemia a remarkably hypotensive surgical course may be accompanied by continued good outputs of urine. Data made available since that time have shown that continuous tubular processing of a good volume of filtrate is indeed essential in pathogenesis of hypokalemic alkalosis. Even minor oliguria quickly blots out hypokalemic alkalosis, with the development of renal hyperkalemic acidosis.

Berliner et al. (1950) showed that the renal tubules secreted potassium by cation exchange and that this secretion depended on cellular bicarbonate or possibly intracellular

pCO_2. Berliner *et al.* (1951), in a subsequent study of the urine after the use of carbonic anhydrase inhibitors, showed that when acidification was lost, potassium excretion was increased. They concluded that hydrogen and potassium compete "for some component of the ion exchange mechanism by which both are secreted."

Brazeau and Gilman (1953) showed that bicarbonate reabsorption varied as a function of the extracellular pCO_2 rather than of pH. They concluded that bicarbonate reabsorption was entirely dependent on ion exchange: hydrogen from tubular H_2CO_3 exchanging for sodium ion and potassium ion in the tubular urine, these cations having been excreted with bicarbonate.

Randall and Roberts have made many significant contributions to this field, in a series of studies demonstrating the dependence of the renal tubule on potassium, for the excretion of an alkaline urine containing sodium bicarbonate. Roberts *et al.* in 1953 showed clearly (in dogs) that potassium injection (as potassium chloride) lowered pH and plasma concentrations of bicarbonate and produced secretion of an alkaline urine high in sodium bicarbonate. The implication was that potassium secretion by the tubular cell took place through cation exchange with hydrogen, the increased K^+ load making mandatory a minimal excretion of H^+ and a maximal reabsorption of H^+. As a result, after the injection of potassium the subject excreted a highly alkaline urine with large amounts of sodium bicarbonate rather than an acid urine containing more carbonic acid and $H_2PO_4^-$.

Conversely they showed that infusion of sodium bicarbonate lowers plasma potassium concentration and increases potassium excretion as hydrogen ion is reabsorbed to counteract the extracellular alkalosis. This implies that potassium deficiency causes alkalosis through its paralysis of hydrogen ion reabsorption and by the loss of hydrogen ion into cells. In considering this matter one must weigh in balance the fact that in surgical hypokalemic alkalosis, hydrogen ion loss by vomiting has usually already taken place, that alkalosis per se can lower plasma potassium

concentration (a fact unknown in 1953), and that the adrenocortical discharge of trauma or operation greatly accentuates potassium excretion and sodium bicarbonate reabsorption, probably via aldosterone.

Roberts *et al.* (1953) emphasized the pH gradient across the cell in potassium disorders, an extracellular alkalosis coexisting with intracellular acidosis, and vice versa. Note that this is to be contrasted sharply with the situation in an acid load, where the body buffers are taken up together with the extracellular buffers. Their postulate is therefore that potassium loss leads to intracellular acidosis, this resulting in inability to alkalinize the urine (with failure to reabsorb hydrogen ion and to excrete sodium bicarbonate), the net result being an extracellular alkalosis.

Roberts *et al.* (1956) review the renal mechanisms involved in bicarbonate absorption. This article provides an excellent bibliographic review. They point out that urinary pH is virtually a measure of urinary bicarbonate concentration in the range of 6.8 to 8.0 wherein bicarbonate accordingly ranges from a very low value to 250 mE. per l.; between urinary pH values of 6.8 and 4.4 other buffer systems are more importantly involved; the renal tubules reabsorb 24 to 28 mE. of bicarbonate per l. of filtrate; all beyond this is excreted; normally only 2 or 3 mE. of a daily filtered load of 4700 mE. is excreted; when plasma bicarbonate rises, the rate of excretion rises and pH of blood is maintained.

Roberts brings forth evidence that an elevation of blood pCO_2 or a decrease in cellular potassium enhances the absorption of bicarbonate (and thus favors an acid urine), while respiratory alkalosis (falling pCO_2), carbonic-anhydrase inhibitors, or potassium infusions decrease the absorption of bicarbonate and promote its excretion in a more alkaline urine.

The common denominator seems to be intracellular pH, of which the renal tubule cell is one example. This intracellular pH may fall with loss of potassium or gain of carbon dioxide, either one of which acts to increase bicarbonate absorption and produces an acid urine and extracellular alkalosis. Roberts emphasizes that the carbon dioxide metabolically produced in the tubular cell itself, while small in amount, is essential since, on hydration (requiring carbonic anhydrase), it provides the hydrogen ion involved in cation exchange.

Roberts *et al.* (1955) showed (this time in dogs and man) that the administration of potassium increased excretion of bicarbonate (by diminishing reabsorption in the tubules) both in the potassium-deprivation state with alkalosis and in the presence of a high pCO_2 produced by respiratory acidosis. These workers conclude that intracellular acidosis in the renal tubule cell may well be the stimulus for this shift of potassium into the cell and increased reabsorption of bicarbonate. They also showed that there is no respiratory compensation (by increasing pCO_2) for metabolic alkalosis.

Central to this line of thinking is the concept that potassium deficit *in itself* produces extracellular alkalosis. In this work, criteria for potassium deficit are often very loosely defined. "Potassium deficit" is repeatedly mentioned, without data to support the allegation of its existence. Indeed most of the patients described as deficient in potassium are postoperative and have lost acid gastric juice. For the most part they have had no potassium intake for a few days and potassium deficits must have been small.

The evidence that extracellular alkalosis in man results from potassium loss alone is very slim. But Roberts' evidence that once alkalosis coexists with potassium loss, one cannot correct the dangerous aciduria until potassium is given, is clear, convincing, and very important as a guide in surgical care.

Seldin *et al.* (1956) showed (in rats) that desoxycorticosterone acetate alone did not change acid-base balance, but that the administration of sodium with DOCA to rats on a potassium-deficient diet did produce hypokalemic alkalosis. This finding merely confirms a host of data (not the least of which are the clinical observations on surgical patients) that the post-traumatic or sodium-retaining phase is the dangerous one in alkalosis. Sodium phosphate, they found, was much more "efficient" in producing hypo-

kalemia than was sodium chloride. They found an unidentified anion (citrate?) in hypokalemic alkalosis and emphasized the possible role of dilution, a consideration that seems unlikely in view of the fact that most forms of dilutional hypotonicity (which hypokalemic alkalosis definitely is not) are not accompanied by hypokalemia.

Womersley and Darragh (1955) produced controlled loss of potassium in man, lasting for periods up to eleven days; restricting the intake of sodium assisted the body in conserving potassium. After the pure potassium loss (there was no sodium loading) the alkalosis was very slight (carbon dioxide combining power rose to 29.5 and 30.2 mM. per l.) and the urine, instead of being "paradoxically acid," was very alkaline, with an increase in excretion of sodium bicarbonate. The potassium loss produced sodium retention. Here was pure potassium loss without either steroid hormones or sodium loading; alkalosis and aciduria were absent. The hypokalemia, however, was impressive, with values down to 2.9 and 3.0 mE. per l. Elkinton (1956) also reports very large experimentally-induced potassium deficits in man without extracellular alkalosis, even with sodium loading.

This further amplifies the conclusion expressed in a contribution from our laboratories (Moore *et al.*, 1955) that although potassium loss renders it difficult for the kidneys to alkalinize the urine, it does not by itself produce alkalosis; and by the same token, when alkalosis has been produced by hydrochloric acid loss and there is also a potassium deficit, the potassium lack markedly accentuates the extracellular alkalosis by blocking urine alkalinization. Stress by its aldosterone-like effect adds further to this lesion (that is, lack of sodium excretion), makes alkalosis severe, and results in severe hypokalemia even with little potassium loss deficiency. The reader is referred to Moore *et al.* (1955) for a review of certain pertinent literature not reviewed again here, and showing that:

(1) Plasma concentrations of sodium and potassium rarely reflect body content; indeed the change is often inverse.

(2) Very severe total potassium deficit can

exist with normal plasma concentrations of potassium and sodium.

(3) Severe hypokalemic alkalosis can exist despite minimal potassium loss.

(4) Gastric loss of hydrochloric acid produces a compensatory renal excretion of sodium (as sodium bicarbonate).

(5) Very large sodium losses from this source coexist with normal plasma sodium concentrations.

(6) Adrenocorticotropic hormone or operation blocks this renal sodium loss and makes the alkalosis suddenly worse; then the potassium concentration falls abruptly, producing electrocardiographic changes and a sick patient.

Trauma, operation, or very acute illness superimposed on loss of hydrochloric acid seems to produce hypokalemic alkalosis through this latter sequence. Our early studies in this field were hampered by inadequately accurate measurement of renal acid-base effects, particularly urine pH and bicarbonate. Since that time we have documented in several clinical instances a preoperative high-sodium, alkaline urine in pyloric obstruction suddenly made low-sodium and acid by trauma. This we have interpreted as the mineralocorticoid effect on urinary excretion of sodium (rather than potassium loss alone), producing the paradoxical aciduria.

Scribner and Burnell (1955) showed, in ureter-ligated dogs, that acidosis lowered plasma potassium (to 2.9 mE. per l.) and acidosis raised it (to 7.5 mE. per l.). Here was an experiment totally free of environmental flux of potassium, showing that acid-base factors could be primary in determining extracellular potassium concentration.

Davies *et al.* (1956) measured balances of sodium, potassium, and chloride in patients with peptic ulcer undergoing gastrectomy, both with and without pyloric stenosis. They used postoperative retention as an index of preoperative depletion, and found that about one-third of the obstructed patients were sodium-chloride–depleted, and a few were "potassium-depleted." They noted retention of base in some patients, and observed that it is quite possible for these patients to have a hydrogen-chloride–loss alkalosis as their pri-

mary defect, correctable with positive balance of chloride (and of course hydrogen ion), with little potassium defect. There are only minimal data on plasma potassium concentration. In one patient a clear reduction in urine pH followed operation (7.96 preoperative, 5.84 postoperative), although the stenosis and alkalosis (and "potassium deficit") were present before operation.

Our conviction, based on clinical and laboratory experience, is that extracellular pH (or, by the same token, the buffer state of the total body buffers) may determine the extracellular potassium concentration rather than vice versa. By this interpretation, metabolic acidosis raises the plasma potassium concentration and alkalosis lowers it. The studies of Schwartz *et al.* (1955) clearly show egress of cellular potassium with a mineral acid load. The work of Cotlove *et al.*, (1951) shows that in the nephrectomized rat (eliminating the renal factor) marked alterations in acid-base balance produced by peritoneal dialysis induce hyperkalemia in acidosis, hypokalemia in alkalosis. These concepts find further definitive corroboration in the work, just alluded to, of Scribner and Burnell (1955) where the animal was the ureter-ligated dog. With acute respiratory acidosis (pH 7.0), the plasma potassium rose to 7.5 mE. per l. and with respiratory alkalosis (pH 7.8) it fell to 2.9 mE. per l. without the operation of renal excretion.

One may truly state that *the causes of potassium loss are many; the causes of hypokalemia are few.* The particular combination of acid loss followed by trauma happens to contain all the many keys to the lowering of plasma potassium concentration seen in the surgical care of patients with such diseases as pyloric stenosis and pancreatitis.

Schwartz and Relman (1956) have gathered the data to suggest that potassium loss produces a renal lesion characterized by extensive vacuolization of the proximal convoluted tubules, hydropic degeneration, and a diffuse vacuolar degeneration. In their cases, the potassium loss was due to chronic diarrhea and there was usually a hypokalemia. They would fall into our group of "chronic potassium-loss hypokalemia" as opposed to "acute hypokalemic alkalosis." The authors comment that sodium depletion was not a part of the picture. It is important in this connection to emphasize that when there is differential potassium loss, very large sodium losses may occur with a surprising absence of hyponatremia. This is one of the evidences clinically that the skeleton may act as a sodium reservoir in prolonged losses whereas there is no analogous reservoir for potassium replenishment.

Functionally, these kidneys of "potassium-loss nephropathy" showed vasopressin-resistant hyposthenuria, and diminished glomerular filtration and tubular function. Histologically the glomeruli and tubules are normal.

Schwartz and Relman consider that a wide variety of other syndromes of renal tubular disorder may be associated with and in part due to potassium loss. These include renal lesions in ulcerative colitis, regional enteritis, cholera, dysentery, sprue, Whipple's disease, and malabsorption as well as cortisone treatment, hyperaldosteronism, Fanconi syndrome, renal tubular acidosis, and Versene poisoning in addition to many variants of glomerulonephritis, lower nephron nephrosis, and obstructive uropathy. One might add uretero-enterostomy to this list, as the renal histology closely resembles the cases of Schwartz and Relman.

This contribution will long be felt in evaluating renal lesions in surgical patients; one cannot help but think of the wide variety of other biochemical changes that occur in such patients and which might play as important a role as potassium loss in producing this picture. These include losses of magnesium and other trace minerals, starvation, adrenal stimulation, and infection. Many patients with low body potassium levels are so ill with a complex of factors that one must hesitate before ascribing the renal lesion to a deficit of one ion.

Section V. Dehydration

The study of Yoshimura *et al.* (1953) is one of the comparatively few recent studies of total deprivation (fasting and thirsting) in a normal subject. The period of starvation was incident to Buddhist religious austerities. The subject was a bishop, aged forty-six years. The period of total abstinence was seven and six-tenths days and, as might be predicted, the results of dehydration dominated the rather drastic physiologic effects. The patient lost 8.0 kg., or 15.7 per cent of his body weight, at a steady rate of 1.0 kg. per day. This lost weight all appeared as water, arising from oxidation of tissue and the loss of free body water, more than half of which loss was extrarenal. Renal conservation of water was maximal, with a urine volume falling to 100 ml. per day, specific gravity rising to 1.036. The loss of total body water was 23 per cent (based on an estimate of 70 per cent of body weight; actually the percentage loss of total body water was larger than this as the starting total body water was probably nearer 55 per cent of body weight) and this lost water came proportionally from blood, extracellular fluid, and intracellular fluid. The hematocrit rose from 39.3 to 57.3; plasma protein from 5.8 gm. per 100 ml. to 9.68 gm. per 100 ml. The source of energy was body fat after the second day. During the first two days 437 gm. of carbohydrate was burned and thereafter the respiratory quotient was 0.7. A total of 305 gm. protein was burned at a low potassium:nitrogen ratio.

These results are classic for unstressed total deprivation. They should serve as a "model extreme" to typify the results of total deprivation, and serve to point up by contrast the usual situation in surgery, in which true dehydration and total deprivation are very rare. The extreme rarity of this picture in surgery is traceable to the ease with which fluids can be given, the fact that stress and extrarenal salt loss (absent in Yoshimura's case) produce an entirely different dynamic effect, and that small amounts of carbohydrate have a remarkable sparing action during starvation.

Section VI.   Tissue Sodium and Potassium: Energy and Irritability

The relation of electrolyte metabolism to oxidative energy is seen in the tendency for the starved patient to lose sodium into and potassium out of cells; hyponatremia and mild hyperkalemia are a result. The situation is reversible when adequate calories are provided. The biochemical details by which this occurs are only glimpsed at present; they form one of the most promising areas for research today. The work of Leaf and Renshaw (1956) suggests that 10 to 20 per cent of the total energy produced by the tissue is required for the operation of the sodium "pump," by which sodium is continuously expelled from the tissue cells.

On the other side of the coin is the evidence that potassium is an absolute requirement for intracellular glucose oxidation in vitro; it is this very glucose oxidation that provides the energy to push the sodium back out. Little wonder that the badly injured man, in the midst of a massive substrate conversion from diet to his own fat, loses for a time the cation discrimination of his cell mass.

Ariel (1952) studied tissue electrolytes in a variety of surgical states. In uneventful convalescence he found little change of note. When shock or anoxia was present there was loss of potassium and gain of sodium in muscle. This might be interpreted not so much as the result of oxygen lack as the result of the activity of cellular buffering mechanisms in the face of a mixed metabolic and respiratory acidosis, as seen in shock and anoxia. He also noted that dilutional hyponatremia produced loss of cell potassium consistent with the fact (since clearly established) that in dilutional hyponatremia the plasma potassium concentration is usually normal or high. He also showed that trauma in itself produced cellular potassium loss.

The importance of cellular potassium exchange in tissue metabolism of energy and in neuromuscular activity is well known, and reviewed by Fenn (1941). That it may be difficult with hyponatremia to maintain blood pressure is also familiar. The direct vascular effects of electrolyte changes are less well known. The work of Tobian and Fox (1956), showing that norepinephrine lowers potassium and increases sodium in the artery wall, indicates one path by which marked cation disequilibrium could be associated with hemodynamic disorder.

Dahl (1957) studied norepinephrine responsiveness in hypertensives treated with a low-sodium diet. In general, there was no change in responsiveness, a finding that failed to confirm the results of Raab *et al.* (1952). The pertinence of this special situation to the surgical problems of blood pressure maintenance and cation content or concentration relative to catechol amine response is minimal because of the previous histories of cardiac disease, longstanding sodium restriction, and presumably normal plasma sodium concentrations (though no data are presented on the latter point). Raab's data remain of interest, suggesting that some alteration in cation distribution is capable of interfering with normal vascular responsiveness to pressor amines.

Clowes and Simeone (1957) have been interested in calcium changes in trauma and surgery, and the relation of calcium to other electrolytes, acid-base balance, and cardiac changes. In one group of patients the low calcium concentrations accompanied elevated potassium concentrations and were associated with hypotension responding to calcium. In a small series of patients undergoing thoracotomy to correct cardiac arrest, there was marked lacticacidemia, with hyperphosphatemia and hypocalcemia, with hyperkalemia. In one patient, the potassium concentration was 7.1 mE. per l. Clowes has been measuring the ionized calcium and has found it low in the cases where total calcium was low. Animals in shock with or without acidosis showed a variable calcium curve; acidosis raised calcium concentrations in most but not all instances; late in hypercapnia the calcium will fall. Hypoxia resulted in elevated peripheral resistance and drop in cardiac output in dogs; hypercapnia produced less reliable circulatory changes in dogs.

Section VII. Bone Sodium

The sodium and other mineral contents of the skeleton are described in Nichols and Nichols (1956), Bergstrom (1955), Davies *et al.* (1952), Edelman *et al.* (1954), Forbes and d'Ambroso (1955), Forbes and Lewis (1956), Huggins (1937), and Moore (1954).

Bergstrom (1953) has measured (in rats) the amount of bone sodium which can be mobilized in acidosis both with and without sodium depletion. He found that 29 per cent of the bone sodium can be readily mobilized. This seems to be the "exchangeable" fraction, in terms of isotope exchange. When sodium depletion occurs, large losses can take place without change in plasma sodium concentration. But the obvious corollary does not appear; in sodium repletion the bone losses are not made up. In acute situations bone sodium seems to be a "one-way street" leading to repair of a deficit in extracellular fluid but not in itself requiring acute repair. This may account for the remarkable unimportance of the "static debt" of sodium in so many clinical situations.

The exact identification of the stimulus that leads to the mobilization of bone sodium is still uncertain. Baden, working in our laboratories, showed (thesis, unpublished) that dialysis of rats against ammonium chloride mobilized about 11 mE. of sodium per kg. of dry bone. By contrast, dialysis against dextrose in water alone had no such effect. Certainly the main body of evidence favors acidosis as a major stimulus; it may be that aldosterone is also a stimulus.

Casey and Zimmerman (1956) failed to find evidence of disappearance of sodium *into bone* in ordinary acute dilutional hyponatremia in man. In more prolonged states of sodium loss, the skeletal reservoir may participate more importantly.

Zimmerman (1956) then showed that, while bone sodium may be mobilized in sodium deficiency, there is little to suggest that the nonexchangeable fraction constitutes a ready flux for mobilization or restoration of sodium. Our data corroborate this for acute changes in both sodium and potassium, indicating the chronic nature of bone sodium mobilization. Virtually the only evidence, in man, for bone sodium mobilization is the seeming clinical restoration of functional extracellular fluid volume and concentration with less sodium than has been lost. This is a thin reed of evidence to lean on; it is further diminished by the very considerable amounts of "excess sodium" given with blood: meaning by that term sodium over and beyond that required to maintain tonicity of the plasma in the infused blood.

Certainly the mass of data from our laboratories on the compositional aspects of acute and chronic disease suggests that the major etiologic factor in both acute and chronic hyponatremia is dilutional; even in sodium loss, dilution plays a role in the final concentration change. In acidosis and prolonged cachectic illness there is evidence for skeletal sodium mobilization; we know of no evidence either in animals or man that sodium is quickly or readily replaced into the skeleton.

Section VIII. Magnesium

Flink (1956) reviews the magnesium deficiency syndrome in man. The range of plasma magnesium values seen in symptomatic patients varies from 1.36 to 1.62 mE. per l., depending again on method.

Flink *et al.* (1954) describe the occurrence of low plasma magnesium with muscular tumor and delirium in patients on prolonged parenteral fluid administration. They feel that the tetany of low magnesium is characterized by gross athetoid movements and choreiform manifestations and can be differentiated from hypocalcemic tetany. The same is true of the hypomagnesemia of delirium tremens.

Randall (personal communication) has

documented a case wherein prolonged intravenous feeding was associated with magnesium deficiency. There were electrocardiographic changes that were restored to normal with magnesium. This sort of thing is probably avoided in many instances by the administration of whole blood in the course of an illness, providing enough magnesium to meet daily needs.

In cirrhotics the concentration is apt to be low. The relation to ammonium ion and its effect on magnesium excretion is not clear. In any event, delirium tremens is the clinical condition par excellence in which the plasma magnesium may be low and an almost immediate relief experienced by giving magnesium sulfate intravenously. Considering the very high mortality rate of postoperative patients with delirium tremens, this fact is of importance in surgery.

Fatal hypermagnesemia has been reported from repeated enemata of the material in megacolon (Collins, 1949) and in Epsom salt overdosage (Hirschfelder, 1934; Fawcett, 1943). Additional work on low-magnesium states will be found in Hamersten and Smith (1957) and Suter and Klingman (1955).

Section IX.   Volume-Sensitive Phenomena

Of outstanding interest in any view of surgical metabolism is the wealth of recent evidence suggesting that metabolism of the body fluids in its many dimensions, including the blood volume, is regulated at least in part through some centers sensitive to volume, flow, vascular filling, effective tissue perfusion, or oxygenation. Because no one has yet identified a single sensitive parameter that acts as a receptor stimulus, the generic term "volume receptor" has crept into use to cover a wide variety of phenomena. These are phenomena of regulatory change in body fluids through an alteration in the renal excretion of water and salt. This latter end-organ system gives every appearance of being actuated by aldosterone, antidiuretic hormone, and/or other hormones that affect tubular function.

The work of Borst (1948) on the renal genesis of edema pointed up the importance of volume factors in regulating renal excretion of water and extracellular salts. Borst interpreted his data as indicating a "fundamental regulating mechanism which serves to maintain a normal cardiac output" and interpreted the retention of water and salt as occurring when, for a variety of causes, cardiac output fell below a critical level. At the time, he was seemingly unaware of the fact that a small venous hemorrhage, insufficient to change cardiac output as measured by any of the standard methods, also lowered the excretion of the water-and-salt complex. He showed that in chronic renal disease the rapid infusion of large amounts of blood produced a large increase in the excretion of water and salt. This article will not be reviewed here in detail. The reader is referred to the original for the data, much of which, brought together by Borst for the first time, has led to the "volume receptor" concept, a concept which, however vague as to anatomic detail, rests on physiologic evidence that concentration alone is not the sole activator of change in the body flux of water and salt.

Petersdorf and Welt (1953) showed that rapid infusion of concentrated albumin in man apparently increased antidiuretic hormone secretion, although whether by increased oncotic pressure or by extracellular fluid dehydration was not clear. In either event the change occurred without alteration in electrolyte concentration and was presumably a volume effect. This bit of evidence is troublesome; its suggestion that an expanded plasma volume produces water *retention* is in conflict with much other data. In the dog, we have been unable to substantiate this finding.

Goodyer and Jaeger (1955) studied non-shocking hemorrhage (20 ml. per kg., or about 25 per cent of the blood volume) in dogs and found a reduction in sodium excretion despite lack of any consistent change in sodium filtration or estimated renal plasma flow. Further, with retransfusion the sodium excretion returned, even with a maintained low blood pressure produced by hexamethonium. Renal denervation failed to prevent these changes. The authors conclude that some extraneural pathway is involved; they suspected the response was too fast (and too transient?) to be adrenal-mediated. This bleeding was "nonshocking," the blood pressure being regularly reduced only 20 mm. Hg. It would fall into our category of "hemorrhage with early hemodynamic response" and of course constitutes one of the evidences for the existence of a regulatory homeostatic mechanism dependent on volume or flow (or some related dimension of circulatory adequacy) rather than concentration. The lack of change in renal plasma flow or sodium filtration is especially interesting in the light of the altered tubular function, and the return of sodium excretion with maintained low pressure under hexamethonium.

There is not space here to review all the evidence bearing on the existence of some mechanism in the body which is sensitive, not to concentration alone, but to a parameter of volume. This might be flow, pressure (arterial, capillary, venous), tissue turgidity, cardiac output, oxygenation, or some other entity.

Of the several simple evidences the response to minor hemorrhage is the most easily demonstrated: a sudden change in renal handling of water and salt despite the lack of immediate concentration change following the bleeding. In addition, a high sodium concentration (or osmolality) due to water loss results in a minimal urine flow at high volume concentrations; when due to salt loading it excites a profuse diuresis. Some of these data are reviewed in detail in Section

I of this literature review (aldosterone).

In this connection the sodium diuresis that follows water loading under vasopressin administration in normal subjects is of great interest. Here there is profuse natruresis in the face of remarkably low plasma sodium concentrations. The explanation advanced has been that the expanded volume of vasopressin-plus-water effectively stops the normal secretion of aldosterone. Natruresis results. Wrong (1956) has studied this in detail and believes that the slight lag in sodium release is due to the slow disappearance of aldosterone from body fluids. Leaf *et al.* (1953) and Weston *et al.* (1953) have studied the same phenomenon by different methods, likewise coming to the presumption of some "volume-sensitive" regulatory mechanism. The entire subject is ably reviewed by Grossman (1957).

In the surgical patient one rarely sees the "volume-receptor release" of water loading, because the injury itself establishes an increased aldosterone secretion apparently independent of volume considerations. But the manifold effects of volume reduction are seen in surgical patients, particularly where there has been blood loss, hypotension, or large doses of ether and opiates. These effects—already mentioned so many times in this book—are antidiuresis, a mineralocorticoid effect, loss of cell water into the extracellular fluid, and hypotonicity. All of these are characteristic of the continued operation of a volume-maintaining mechanism.

Epstein (1956) also covers evidence on the volume-receptor hypothesis and reviews the various entities which seem to trigger changes in the excretion of water and salt without respect to concentration. Arterial filling, or pressure, or "vascular volume" seems to be the most critical.

Section X.   Water Distribution and Control: Hypotonicity and Hypertonicity

A. HYPOTONICITY

Robinson *et al.* (1957) describe a blood assay for antidiuretic hormone based on the method of Bisset and Walker (1954). This in turn is based on the water-loaded, alcohol-anesthetized rat (Robinson and MacFarlane,

1956), a method which is sensitive but non-specific. The authors describe a marked rise in antidiuresis during pregnancy over that of normal women; during suckling this activity is almost doubled. They feel that the material they assay is definitely antidiuretic hormone, and that there is failure of enzymatic inactivation in pregnancy and suckling (Hawker, 1952, 1956, 1957).

West *et al.* (1955) compared the effectiveness of vasopressin with that of hydropenia as a stimulus to water economy in dogs and man. Under most circumstances hydropenia was more effective in increasing urine osmolality. Their studies point up again the importance of flow rate and solute diuresis in determining the urine osmolality and the osmolar U:P ratio (urine:plasma ratio) under conditions of maximal water resorption in the tubules. With solute diuresis the urine osmolality rarely rises over 500 to 700 mE. per l. under the stimulus of an antidiuretic hormone, exogenous or endogenous. Tubular resorption of water has a ceiling maximum (in ml. per minute). Under conditions of rapid flow the rate of passage of urine down the tubule is a limiting factor. When tubular rate of flow is low (that is, in absence of solute diuresis) the limiting factor is the osmolar U:P ratio, and very high urine osmolalities (up to 1400 mO. per l., corresponding roughly to a specific gravity of 1.036) are observed. Conversely, when the rate of glomerular filtration is lowered (as in shock), even in the absence of antidiuretic hormone (as in water loading or diabetes insipidus), one observes urine osmolalities far above the theoretical 290 mO. per l. that should be observed were the only mechanisms for processing tubular fluid to a hypertonic urine to be antidiuretic-hormone-linked. This suggests that there is a site in the distal tubules where water resorption is independent of the action of antidiuretic hormone, but takes place at rather low rates of total capacity. When flow from the tubules is markedly reduced (a low glomerular filtration rate), one therefore observes some degree of resorption and conservation of water, even without antidiuretic hormone.

Leaf *et al.* (1954) showed that a large water load is distributed evenly throughout the total volume of body water. This is exactly what one would predict from the distribution of small water loads in the form of deuterium oxide (Schloeb *et al.*, 1950; Dudley *et al.*,

1954). Hetherington (1931), Eggleton (1951), and Wolf and McDowell (1954) showed that a hypertonic salt load is apparently diluted in a volume which approximates total body water. These two findings would appear logically to lead to the "deficit times total body water" theory of treatment of hyponatremia, but they do not. The reasons they do not are many, but the most important is that the vast majority of hyponatremic patients— even those who have suffered some degree of sodium loss—have an excess of body water; as hypertonic saline is administered this water is diuresed, progressively diminishing the "apparent requirement" based on "deficit times total body water."

Edelman (1956) also tangles with this question of hypotonicity. Attracted by the biochemical logic of the matter, he states, "The amount of hypertonic saline to be administered for the correction of hyponatremia must be calculated on a volume of distribution equal to total body water." As we have pointed out so often, this is rarely clinically necessary (and usually positively inadvisable) because there is a dilutional factor present and, as salt is given, possibly owing to a volume-receptor "release" effect, there is a profuse water diuresis. In a 75 kg. man with late heart failure and hyponatremia (120 mE. per l.) the "deficit times total body water" rule would yield a dose of 1000 mE. of sodium, surely lethal. Such a view also neglects the fact that about one-half of the cation deficit is potassium, rather than sodium.

Edelman very appropriately emphasizes the need for restricting the intake of water in dealing with the hyponatremia of late visceral disease, and speaks of the occasional patient with severe hypotonicity (usually due to water intoxication superimposed on late visceral disease) in whom the administration of hypertonic saline is an osmotic emergency despite its compositional irrationality, the patient having an indubitably large body sodium.

To the classification of both Wynn and Edelman should be added "inappropriate volume maintenance" with persistent water retention, volume expansion, and hypotonicity. This has been seen in mediastinal disease, and we have seen it after hypophysectomy with the administration of vasopressin and an overload of water.

Wynn (1956) prefers to use "symptomless hypotonicity" as a term for the hypotonicity and hyponatremia of chronic wasting illness, the group we have termed "starvation hyponatremia." He believes this group has no symptoms traceable to the hypotonicity. One might argue this point in terms of the fact that the patients are uniformly chronically ill, wasted, and weak. Hypotonicity may have something to do with these symptoms of weakness. Wynn also identifies a group of "sodium depletion without water depletion." With the exception of pancreatic disease this is rare. Here again it is merely a matter of semantics; the lesion (our term "chronic established desalting") is due to loss of sodium and water with disproportionate water replacement, either endogenous or exogenous. Salt has been lost, yet dilution is a critical factor in the biochemical result.

Wynn in another work (1955) has shown that in the dog without renal function, water loads are distributed throughout the total volume of body water, as also shown by the deuterium work by these laboratories and by Leaf *et al.* (1954). From this fact he has derived formulas that may be used to calculate the extent of change of extracellular tonicity that will be produced by a measured water load, given the external cation balance.

DeCosse *et al.* (1956) studied post-traumatic hyponatremia with especial reference to the volume of extracellular fluid as measured by inulin or sucrose. They found expansion of the extracellular fluid at expense of the intracellular fluid, and an increase in total fluid volume for sodium—findings similar to those of many other compositional studies. They further postulate that this exit of water from cells may produce intracellular hypertonicity as one stimulus to the continued antidiuresis that follows injury. No evidence is presented to substantiate this establishment of osmotic gradients. This work is strongly reminiscent of the findings of Lyon *et al.* (1949) described in Part I, but the postulate of osmotic gradient certainly has no basis in data from recent biochemical research.

Both our laboratories and those of Edelman *et al.* (1958) have shown by studies based on isotope dilution that the whole body is an osmotically homogenous system. This has shown that the extracellular sodium concentration and effective osmolality are a simple linear function of the concentration of "total exchangeable base" (total exchangeable sodium and total exchangeable potassium) in total body water. This simple demonstration is the culmination of many years of work both in our laboratories and in his. Knowledge simplifies as it progresses; this demonstration clinches the point in understanding and treatment of hypotonicity. Base loss or water excess or both are responsible; there is no chemical mystery in the relation.

Wynn has also reinforced this conclusion (Wynn, 1957; Wynn and Houghton, 1957). Wynn's data on water intoxication in man and dogs (1955) demonstrate that the body does not house any osmotic gradients. The final concentration of electrolyte is a simple product of dilution; where electrolyte gain or loss enters the equation it is again effective in changing concentration only as it adds to or subtracts from the body pool. Wynn emphasizes that lowered cellular osmolality resulting from loss of potassium could be expected to produce hypotonicity. This might help explain the nature of starvation hyponatremia. Unfortunately for such a hypothesis here, the potassium:nitrogen ratio of the loss is usually normal, making it difficult to postulate a primary reduction in intracellular potassium concentration in starvation. In acute hypokalemia, normotonicity or hypertonicity is the rule.

Jenkins *et al.* (1950) describe, in an important contribution, the clinical, pathologic, and physiologic findings in the overadministration of fluids. They use the term "congestive atelectasis" to describe the pulmonary picture; the clinical occurrences of congestive rales, tachypnea, fever, cyanosis, and (often) hypotension are clearly shown. The entire pulmonary appearance closely resembles pulmonocardiac failure. The progressive stiffening of the lung, often with a falling left atrial pressure, was studied experimentally and seemed to be characteristic of the overadministration of saline solution. Maintained pulmonary blood flow, without oxygenation, however, was characteristic. One may presume a simultaneously rising pCO_2.

Zimmerman *et al.* (1956) have shown that giving some sodium the day of operation results in better urine flow and a more normal weight-loss curve, seemingly a solute-diuresis effect in patients in whom aldosterone increases have been held to a minimum by blood replacement. This shows clearly the very delicate balance that exists among the various forces acting on the kidney in the postoperative patient. If large amounts of sodium salts are given while sodium retention is maximal, there is weight gain; if moderate amounts are given when the principal influence on the kidney is antidiuresis, then solute diuresis results and weight loss is greater than if water alone is given.

Hayes *et al.* (1957) showed that reducing the water intake after surgery produces a situation in which there is less reduction in sodium concentration in the plasma and there is then no increase in aldosterone production. These findings of Hayes have not been confirmed by Zimmerman. The explanation is probably to be found in the fact that lowered sodium concentration in the plasma is not a particularly strong stimulus to aldosterone production, whereas reduced volume is a very potent aldosterone stimulus.

Schlegel (1954, a) has studied the provision of large amounts of sodium in various traumatic states (shock, burns, desalting) and the control of sodium administration by the sequential measurement of urinary pH. When sodium was provided in large amounts, the urinary pH fluctuated "normally," whereas there was a fixed urine pH near 5.6 when sodium excretion was minimal. This seems to be reconfirmation of the well-known fact that urinary concentration of bicarbonate is an almost linear function of pH except at the very acid range, that urinary sodium and bicarbonate concentrations fluctuate together, and that normal kidneys require sodium to achieve an alkaline urine, and will achieve it if extra sodium is provided. To reason from this that surgical patients should be given excesses of sodium sufficient to alkalinize the urine at all times requires some sort of clinical, statistical, or physiologic proof; such is not available at present.

In a subsequent study, Schlegel (1954, b) reconfirmed very convincingly the fact that restricting the intake of sodium (or administering ammonium chloride for several days) reduced the excretion ("return") of a measured sodium load administered after the termination of the restriction period. The amount of sodium retained exceeded the measured previous losses, a nice demonstration of a continuing volume effect in the face of sodium replacement. This also points up that sodium retention may occur to an extent disproportionate to previous losses in patients (for example, after surgery) in whom there was some preoperative restriction of sodium and—one might now add—volume of extracellular fluid or blood.

As mentioned previously, during antidiuresis one can produce large urine flows by means of infusion of a crystalloid solute: antidiuresis is compatible with profuse solute diuresis. Free water clearance remains strongly negative, however. On this basis one can rationalize the larger urine outputs seen in burns treated with dextran (the low-molecular-weight fraction of which acts as an osmotic diuretic). The use of mannitol has the same basis. This effect may protect against renal damage (Owen *et al.*, 1954; Dudley, 1957). Schlegel (1957) finds good urine flows after operations and burns when urea is given. This makes use of the same mechanism.

Alcohol acts as a diuretic both by providing solute and by inhibiting the production of antidiuretic hormone. It is appealing to try it as a means of treating low-sodium states. Sealy (1957) has tried this method in conjunction with cardiac surgery. Some of the animal data suggest that the inhibition of antidiuretic hormone release is only evident if the alcohol is given well before the stimulus to water retention.

Monsaingeon (personal communication) calls attention to a situation which may occur after total or subtotal adrenalectomy when the patient receives an adequate dose of cortisone and desoxycorticosterone acetate but insufficient sodium is given. He reports that in this setting there is a urinary desalting water loss characterized by a low sodium:potassium ratio in the urine, a very small drop of sodium concentration in the plasma, acidosis, azotemia, oliguria, a very high concentration of solutes in the urine, loss of body weight, fatigue, but surprisingly enough no thirst. Giving enough sodium restores body weight, strength, urine output, and mental activity.

Edelman and his group (Edelman and Sweet, 1956; Nadell *et al.*, 1956; Sweet *et al.*, 1957; and Gotch *et al.*, 1957) have studied the magnitude and exchangeability of gastrointestinal tract salt. This is a part of the total content of transcellular water—that fraction of extracellular fluid that is formed, at least in part, by active cellular transport mechanisms. He found about 16 per cent of total exchangeable chloride to be within the gastrointestinal tract. In man, at postmortem, much smaller amounts (2 per cent of exchangeable chlorine) were in the gastrointestinal tract. Digestive flux or disease obviously changes these relationships.

The effect of gastric (intubation) fluid losses was observed by Ariel (1954), who documented renal functional changes as well as the alterations in muscle composition. Ariel also showed that the anacid stomach, as one might predict, loses a virtually neutral salt, containing largely sodium, chloride, and potassium. Effects on plasma chemistry were not great and alkalosis did not occur.

B. HYPERTONICITY

The review of Knowles (1956) is especially helpful in the matter of hypertonicity, an aspect often neglected in the literature. He credits Allott (1939) with early identification of hypertonicity in neurologic disease, though dehydration was a possible causative factor. Leutscher and Blackman (1943), Rapoport (1947), and Sweet *et al.* (1948) then identified various components of hypertonicity, including solute excess, dehydration, diabetes insipidus, and specially located basilar brain lesions and solute diuresis. Many of the neurologic cases are suspect. They are often due to diabetes insipidus and the tube-feeding–solute-diuresis syndrome, particularly if there

is some senile renal arteriosclerosis to further compromise distal water resorption.

Danowski *et al.* (1949) noted hypernatremia in some phases of diabetic coma; a mixed effect of pulmonary water loss and solute diuresis seems to account for most of the hypernatremias seen in diabetes mellitus. Where extreme hyperglycemia exists it is of course possible to have severe hypertonicity without hypernatremia. MacCarty and Cooper (1941) found hypernatremia after ligation of the anterior cerebral artery; Higgins *et al.* (1951) described the disorder in head injury; Cooper and Crevier (1952) and Zimmerman and Frier (1952) reported hypertonicity in various clinical and surgical settings where combinations of solute load, unconsciousness (that is, thirst unfelt and unslaked), increased pulmonary water loss, and chronic renal disease lurked behind the allegedly etiologic cerebral lesion. The latter was frequently situated near the supraopticohypophyseal tract, injury to which results in diabetes insipidus.

Finally, in 1954 Engel and Jaeger clearly described the tube-feeding syndrome for the first time, bringing into focus that phase of hypernatremia. Engstrom and Liebman (1953) and Ullman (1953) added further data on the cerebral component. As pointed out by Knowles, it was Welt in 1952 (Welt *et al.*, 1952) who first calculated the amounts of water needed to float out these big solute loads (largely urea) from tube feedings. To this urea load must of course be added the endogenous urea load after injury.

The work of Doolan *et al.* (1955), Schoolman *et al.* (1955), Natelson and Alexander (1955), Cooper *et al.* (1951), and Swann and Merrill (1953) elucidated various aspects of hypernatremia, the last article calling attention to the occurrence of hypernatremia during a "water-losing" phase of recovery from renal failure.

Knowles raises the interesting fact that a degree of dehydration, in itself, compromises renal concentrating ability. The result is a vicious cycle which further reduces the body's stores of solvent with or without a solute load. Knowles feels that the hypertonicity of treated diabetic acidosis is due to shift of water into cells with glucose, as well as to solute diuresis, a concept supported by the work of Peters (1952).

The activity of centers sensitive to volume or flow may also play a role here, the diminished volume associated with dehydration stimulating recall of sodium from the glomerular filtrate (by mineralocorticoid effect), despite the progressive rise in sodium concentration. In fact, the sharply differing renal handling of sodium in the hypernatremia of dehydration as against that of hypertonic administration of salt constitutes one of the prime evidences for the existence of a mechanism active in the regulation of salt and water and governed by a volume parameter rather than tonicity.

Knowles (1956) calls attention to the patient's relative lack of thirst, once hypernatremia has become established. This calls to mind the slow permeability of the blood-brain barrier to sodium as a possible explanation of adaptation to abnormal sodium-dependent tonicity. Once the concentration gradient is obliterated by slow equilibration, the osmoreceptor and thirst mechanisms appear to become less active.

Knowles also calls attention to the hypokalemia of hypertonicity, a most fascinating example of the persistent tendency of concentrations of sodium and potassium in the extracellular fluid to move in opposite effects, and the fact that drastic alteration in sodium concentration due to changes in water content may not be reflected at all in changes in potassium concentration.

In hypernatremia one would expect to find calcium and magnesium concentrations elevated in some instances. Reports are rare (Allott, 1939), but it is noteworthy that large urine volumes and a marked tendency to dehydration occur in hypercalcemia of a variety of causes. The effect of acute calcium loads, in compromising renal concentrating ability (Sanderson, unpublished), calls to mind the similar effect seen in "potassium depletion nephropathy." Calcium and potassium antagonize each other in many regards, including this effect on renal tubular water reabsorption. As emphasized elsewhere herein, the "potassium-loss nephropathy" syndrome is one that may well involve many metabolic and ionic lesions, in addition to that of potassium deficiency.

PART IV

Loss of Body Substance; Body Composition and Clinical Management in Surgical Starvation

Contents of Part IV

CHAPTER 24. SURGICAL STARVATION

CHAPTER 25. THE NATURE OF STARVATION: THE STUDY OF BODY COMPOSITION IN STARVATION AND CACHEXIA

CHAPTER 26. MANAGEMENT OF EARLY STARVATION; THE COMPOSITIONAL DEFECT AS A GUIDE TO TREATMENT

CHAPTER 27. THE NUTRITIONAL MANAGEMENT OF THE NORMAL PATIENT; POSTOPERATIVE CATABOLIC WEIGHT LOSS

CHAPTER 28. LATE POST-TRAUMATIC STARVATION WITHOUT SEPSIS

CHAPTER 29. SEPTIC STARVATION

CHAPTER 30. MISCELLANEOUS SPECIAL PROBLEMS IN SURGICAL NUTRITION

CHAPTER 31. DIETS, ORDERS, AND METHODS IN SURGICAL FEEDING

CHAPTER 32. VITAMINS AND HORMONES

CHAPTER 33. BODY COMPOSITION, STARVATION, AND NUTRITIONAL THERAPY: NOTES FROM THE LITERATURE

Cases

CHAPTER 24

Surgical Starvation

Loss of body tissue is a frequent and often inevitable accompaniment of surgical disease. An understanding of the nature and significance of this loss of body substance is basic to good surgical care. In many instances seen in the practice of surgery, starvation even of marked extent is well tolerated and seemingly innocent of serious consequences; in other instances starvation is the cause of failure of surgical treatment and its avoidance the key to success. Discrimination among the types, causes, and effects of starvation in surgery is therefore important. Our purpose in this part of the book is first to define starvation, to list briefly the sorts of tissue loss seen in surgery, and to describe their biochemical, compositional, and clinical characteristics.

Section I. Definitions and Terms

A. STARVATION

Any person whose absorbed food intake provides less than daily requirements for work, growth, reproduction, and tissue turnover is starving. The change in weight is often confused by concomitant alterations in body water and electrolyte: a starving patient loses weight unless he is in such a salt-and-water-gaining phase as is especially common after injury or in late visceral disease. The degree of weight loss is therefore a function of the interrelationships of loss of water and loss of tissue. Net loss of weight due to water loss alone does not signify starvation.

B. THE FIVE BASIC TYPES OF TISSUE LOSS SEEN IN SURGERY

Five categories include most of the weight-losing states seen in general surgery. The five basic categories are states of starvation in macronutrients (carbohydrate, fat, protein); they vary in their setting and rate, but they all tend to produce similar if not identical compositional changes.

Starvation of micronutrients (vitamins, trace minerals) can occur to varying degree with these five types of starvation; such deficiencies alone (without over-all starvation) are rare in surgical practice (save for scurvy) but are occasionally seen as beriberi, pellagra, night blindness, hypoferremia or other micronutrient-deficiency syndromes.

A brief description of the five basic states of starvation seen in surgical practice follows.

1. Resting Semistarvation

a. Definition. Resting semistarvation is starvation in an unstressed patient whose mixed caloric and protein intake continues but is at an inadequate level.

b. Examples. Examples can be found in carcinoma of the stomach, early carcinoma of the esophagus, obstructing ulcer, advanced carcinoma of the colon, enforced dietary restriction, lack of teeth, lack of desire to eat.

c. Rates and Balances. Weight loss is variable. A rapid rate of weight loss in this category is 150 gm. a day; 1 kg. (about 2 pounds) a week; 50 pounds in six months. An average rate is about one-half this value (25 pounds in six months). This form of starvation may reach an equilibrium state at a lower level of weight and basal metabolic activity; body size and metabolic demand are finally reduced to match the intake and weight loss ceases if disease is not progressive.

The tissue lost is about half-and-half fat and lean tissue, yielding a nitrogen-loss maximum of about 2.5 gm. per day, or an average rate of about 1 gm. per day. It will be appreciated that this small loss is not readily measurable with accuracy by ordinary nitrogen-balance techniques. The fat loss (75 gm. a day) yields about 650 calories and 80 ml. of water a day; protein oxidation about 100 calories; lean-tissue loss about 50 ml. of water. The potassium:nitrogen ratio of the negative balance is about 2.5 to 3.0 mE. per gm. The curve of weight loss is not smooth or constant, even though nitrogen balance and diet are; there are alternating periods of water loading and diuresis associated with wide swings in sodium balance and a subtle but progressive tendency to retain water and salt. The occurrence of chronic hemorrhage adds a special feature to this group, in some carcinomas of colon and stomach.

2. Resting Total Starvation

a. Definition. Resting total starvation is complete lack of intake of caloric nourishment in the unstressed patient, although intake of water and salt continues, by mouth or vein.*

b. Examples. Examples are late carcinoma of stomach or esophagus, late obstructing ulcer, chronic intestinal obstruction. As the lesion progresses, all the evidences of stress and extrarenal loss enter the picture, and the patient is no longer "resting" (that is, unstressed).

c. Rates and Balances. Weight loss is more

---

* Complete fast plus total thirst is rare in the absence of acute disease involving extrarenal loss.

rapid, in the vicinity of 500 gm. a day, 7 to 10 pounds a week. Nitrogen loss is 7 to 10 gm. a day. The potassium:nitrogen ratio is 2.5 to 3.0 mE. per gm. The tissue lost is about half fat and half lean tissue, as in resting semistarvation. The fat loss (250 gm.) provides about 2200 calories and 250 ml. of water each day, the lean tissue (250 gm.) about 200 ml. of water and 300 calories. As in semistarvation, the weight curve is not smooth because of variable periods of diuresis and antidiuresis; as the lesion progresses antidiuresis and retention of salt become very prominent. Edema, hypoproteinemia, and a high relative body water finally result. As weight is lost, the rate of tissue loss progressively diminishes.

In a man weighing 85 kg. (187 pounds) such a process lowers his weight in two weeks to about 160 pounds; as acute illness, operation, or sepsis enters the picture he rapidly develops severe cachexia, even though his weight is not drastically low. By contrast, in resting semistarvation the loss of 50 to 80 pounds may be surprisingly well tolerated, as regards strength, physical appearance, wound healing, and tolerance to surgical trauma.

3. Early Post-traumatic Catabolic Weight Loss

a. Definition. This is the weight loss that follows uncomplicated major surgery or injury.

b. Examples. This is shown in tissue change and weight curve after major surgery or injury, in the absence of visceral disease or overadministration of fluids.

c. Rates and Balances. Weight loss is variable; a brisk rate following major surgery in a male is 500 gm. a day for two days, then 250 to 300 gm. a day for three days, gradually tapering off to a smooth rate like that of resting semistarvation (150 gm. a day), until significant feeding and anabolism begin about the seventh day.

Unlike the situation in simple starvation, feeding is relatively ineffective in reducing the rate of nitrogen loss during the early postoperative period. The more extensive the injury, the more ineffective is nitrogen and calorie provision in altering its early consequences; after severe injury very large intakes are needed to restore balance, and the clinical benefit is doubtful.

The nitrogen loss initially is very rapid, 12 to 15 gm. or more a day. This corresponds to 350 to 450 gm. of lean tissue. By the third or fourth day the nitrogen loss has decreased in disproportion to the weight loss, and the tissue lost is about half-and-half fat and muscle, as in the other categories.

The potassium:nitrogen ratio for the first one to three days is high, in the region of 5.0 to 7.5 mE. per gm., indicating some disproportionate loss of potassium over loss of cell matrix.

The caloric provision of an initial loss (for example, 300 gm. of muscle and 300 gm. of fat) is 300 from protein and 2700 from fat, for a total of 3000 as an approximation. The water arising from these tissues is about 275 ml. from muscle and 300 from fat.

4. Late Post-traumatic Starvation without Sepsis

a. Definition. This type of starvation is defined as the inability to eat or absorb adequate diet in the late phases after major surgery or injury; acute stress is past, anabolism is ready to begin, but diet is not resumed.

b. Examples. This type of starvation is seen in malfunctioning gastroenteric stoma, continuing intestinal obstruction, upper intestinal or esophageal fistula, and failure to regain appetite after trauma.

c. Rates and Balances. The rates and balances are those of resting semistarvation. There are two important differences. First, in resting semistarvation the patient starts from a normal base line, whereas in late posttraumatic starvation the patient's weight continues downward from his early post-traumatic catabolic weight loss. Second, in resting semistarvation there is remarkable maintenance of strength and vigor, while in late post-traumatic starvation, strength and vigor do not return and the dynamic progress of convalescence is stalled. Recovery requires the positive achievement of anabolism and tissue growth. When these do not occur late post-traumatic starvation is present and recovery is not complete.

5. Septic Starvation (Starvation with Continuing Severe Stress)

a. Definition. Septic starvation is defined as inadequate diet during a period—often prolonged—of continuing severe illness usually due to sepsis but occasionally due to repeated trauma or other catabolic stimuli, with fever, tachycardia, and continued challenge to homeostasis.

b. Examples. This occurs, for example, in peritonitis, in an unhealed septic burn, in invasive sepsis in a fracture, in sepsis in the neck or chest, or in fulminating ulcerative colitis.

c. Rates and Balances. This is the most devastating tissue destruction seen. A skin-and-bones, exhausted, avitaminotic cachexia is rapidly produced. Starvation is more prominent as a contributor to lethal outcome here than in any of the other types of surgical starvation.

Weight loss is often as rapid as 1 kg. a day when there is invasive sepsis and high-swinging fever. We have seen weight loss of 1.5 kg. a day in peritonitis. This is the extreme. The tissue lost is high in lean components for a day or two, as in post-traumatic catabolic loss of weight, but it soon settles down to an approximately half-and-half relationship, as in the other groups. With the oxidation of 500 gm. of fat and 500 gm. of muscle the body provides itself with about 5000 calories and a liter of water.

Obvious avitaminosis is more commonly seen and more rapidly produced here than in any of the other groups. The large septic area and the continued severe stress appear to consume vitamins more rapidly. Water-soluble vitamins of the B and C groups are needed in very large quantities even for daily maintenance. Loading of water and salt, antidiuresis, hypoproteinemia, and edema are produced rapidly and to a marked degree. The loss of true tissue may therefore be significantly greater than the loss of weight observed.

CHAPTER 25

The Nature of Starvation: The Study of Body Composition in Starvation and Cachexia

Section I. Methods and Meanings

Starvation produces important changes in the composition of the body: loss of fat and lean tissue and a relative gain in body water, a disproportionately large fraction of which is extracellular.

Increasing knowledge of this defect in body composition produced by starvation has been gained in recent years not only by the measurement of body weight and metabolic balance, but through the characterization of body composition by the dilutional techniques. Only on rare occasions have starving patients been studied by metabolic-balance techniques over long periods of time. Animal work has been done in this field, but because of the different time relationships which obtain in the animal (particularly the laboratory rodent as contrasted with man), the clinical importance of such observations is questionable. In man, the chronically semistarving patient has infrequently been studied by balance techniques, but even were the patient to be so studied, the balance changes seen from day to day or even from week to week would be small (with the exception of those cases with very severe septic starvation).

The chronic nature of many depleting diseases makes their study particularly well adapted to a method that characterizes the body's composition at intervals separated

widely in point of time. In this manner, the composition of the body in terms of fat, water, and lean tissue may be studied over a period of months or years of disease and recovery, a period of time during which the continuous conduct of a metabolic balance study would be impossible. Such a method is provided by the dilutional techniques. The theory and practice of tracer dilution for the study of body composition has been extensively developed over the past fifteen years. These methods and the results in starvation are described fully in the literature (Moore *et al.*, 1952; Moore, 1954; Moore *et al.*, 1954, 1956; McMurrey *et al.*, 1958; Edelman *et al.*, 1951, 1952, 1954).

The principle involved in dilution study and its application to the blood volume have been described in Part II. We are concerned here with its application to areas of the body beyond the blood stream. These areas have been called the "body spaces" or the "body compartments." Neither term is adequate. When one measures the plasma volume, one is measuring a phase of body water which might be called a "space," although it certainly is full of something: plasma. When one

---

* The reader is referred also to the bibliography in Chapter 33.

measures the total volume of body water by diluting deuterium, one is measuring the amount of water in the body by translating the total exchangeable hydrogen into a water equivalent. One is measuring both volume and weight. When one measures the total exchangeable sodium or the total exchangeable potassium by radioisotope dilution based on the equilibrium specific activity, one is measuring a weight. This is not a "space" or a "compartment." It is a "mass" of sodium or potassium, which is measured in terms of kilograms, grams, milligrams, mols, millimols, milliequivalents, or teaspoonfuls, whichever unit one wishes to use. Merely to use a standard terminology we refer to the divisions of body water as "phases," and the isotopically measured solutes as "total exchangeable"; examples are the "extracellular phase" and "total exchangeable sodium."

The studies of body composition that have been most helpful in understanding surgical starvation have been those that have measured the erythrocyte volume, the plasma volume, the extracellular fluid volume, the total body water, the total exchangeable sodium, and the total exchangeable potassium.

Measurement of the volume of the *extracellular phase* (ECF) of body water is the most parlous of all these methods. There is no single ion or crystalloid known at present which confines itself entirely to an area of body water that is exclusively extracellular and at the same time is diluted in the entire extracellular phase. The extracellular phase is poorly defined: it includes water between cells, water in lymphatics, water which has had to pass through cells to get where it is (the transcellular water such as that in the gut and in joint fluid), and it includes also certain special compartments such as the cerebrospinal fluid and the serous fluids. Our own measurements of this phase have, over the past many years, been based on the use of thiocyanate, radiosodium, or radiobromide dilution. All of these yield a normal value of 15 to 20 per cent of body weight.

Measurement of the *total body water* (TBW) is the most satisfactory of all the measurements of body composition. The laboratory technique of measuring deuterium concentration is moderately challenging, but once the method is worked out with good reproducibility, it gives good consistent results. There is a small amount of exchangeable hydrogen in the body, in the hydroxy-, carboxy-, and sulfhydryl groups of proteins and fats. But this is so small that the uncorrected deuterium-dilution figure is used for total body water with negligible error. Other methods for measuring the total body water (such as antipyrine, urea, and sulfonamides) have given information of use in the past, but their interpretation is difficult because of the participation of these agents in metabolic processes and because of selective excretion. Tritium, a radioactive hydrogen isotope of mass 3, is useful in the same way that deuterium is. The mass difference is greater and the detection problems are also complicated.

The *total exchangeable sodium and potassium* (Na_e and K_e) are measured by the dilution of appropriate isotopes of these two ions. The concept here is one of equilibrium of distribution in a mass of dissolved solid, rather than in a mass of dissolving liquid. The final equilibrium is determined as the ratio of radioactive to nonradioactive element, the so-called "specific activity." The measurement of the total exchangeable potassium accounts for virtually all of the potassium in the body. Were one to call this the "total body potassium," one would not be far wrong. There is in the erythrocyte a small amount of potassium which exchanges so slowly that at a twenty-four-hour equilibrium, it is not all measured. But assay of the total exchangeable potassium measures about 95 to 98 per cent of the potassium in the body. There is little evidence that potassium alters in its degree of exchangeability or that there are other mysterious factors operative in this measurement. It is a measurement of the potassium pool, pure and simple.

The same cannot be said of the measurement of total exchangeable sodium. The large amount of sodium in the skeleton which is not exchangeable makes it wholly unjustified to refer to this as "total body sodium." The term "total exchangeable sodium" says just what it indicates: namely, this is the amount of sodium in the body which will exchange with an isotope. The isotope-exchange equilibrium is measured at an interval of about twenty-four hours. For this reason, the interpretation is justified that the total exchangeable sodium is also the "readily available" or "metabolically active" or "physiologically useful" sodium. This measurement is not equivalent to measuring the extracellular phase or an extracellular volume, since some of the nonextracellular sodium in bone exchanges quite readily.

Using these various measures, one can characterize body composition in the starving patient—our immediate concern here—with respect to four important dimensions.

(1) *The intravascular volume:* the blood volume is obtained directly by adding the plasma volume and the erythrocyte volume.

(2) *The extracellular phase* and its most significant cation, sodium, are measured.

(3) *The intracellular phase* is determined by measuring its most significant cation, potassium. The lean body mass is largely composed of skeletal muscle and the viscera; the total exchangeable potassium varies with the amount of skeletal muscle present in the organism. The intracellular water is calculated as total body water minus the extracellular water.

(4) *The total body water:* the measurement of the total liquid in the body is done by deuterium dilution; the relationship of water to lean tissue is fairly constant within the body. Because of this fact, one arrives at an interesting corollary—that is, that the amount of nonaqueous tissue in the body (fat) varies inversely with the total volume of body water. In the normally nourished individual, the relationship between total body water and total body fat is constant and is given by the formula of Pace:

$$\% \text{ fat} = 100 - \frac{\% \text{ water}}{0.732}$$

In a patient with edema and starvation, it is quite apparent that the relationship between water and lean tissue has been distorted, and we have every reason to believe that this formula is unreliable as a means of determining total body fat in states of illness. There is more water per unit lean tissue in chronic disease. For this reason, the factor 0.732, which expresses the amount of water in lean tissue, increases to the range of 0.76 to 0.78. Similarly, in acute dehydration or desalting, this formula factor fails. Calculation will indicate that the change in this Pace formula factor is not great under any circumstances. It probably never rises much over 0.8 or falls below 0.68. For this reason, the measurement of total body water, even in illness, gives us a first approximation of the changes in body fat.

Having carried out such measurements as these, one may carry out a number of other calculations. These include calculation of intracellular water, the average intracellular concentration of potassium, the average amount of sodium outside the extracellular phase, and a number of other interesting points. These will not be dealt with further here. The reader is again referred to the literature.

Using the dilution principle it is possible to measure the body content of many other substances including iron, calcium, magnesium, and urea. Consideration of these measurements is omitted here.

Section II.   Results: The Defect Produced by Starvation

A. FINDINGS: THE "SYNDROME OF DEPLETION"

Using the methods mentioned above, we find that starvation cachexia from a wide variety of causes brings about a central and reproducible change in body composition. We have used the term "syndrome of depletion" to describe this state. This may be a poor term, since it seems to call to mind the loss of water and salt, an event which, as described below, is certainly not characteristic of this state. This is a syndrome so frequently found and so reliably predictable that it is of great importance in surgery. The word "depletion" here refers to loss of body tissue.

The nature of this syndrome may be summarized in the following manner.

(1) As the body loses weight there is a loss of fat, yielding a gradual increase in relative total body water. If this water (and/or salt) is not normally excreted, there is an absolute increase in the volume of body water.

(2) With this there is a loss of lean tissue (identified as loss of muscle mass), measured as loss of total exchangeable potassium. This is manifested also by negative nitrogen balance.

(3) The extracellular aspects of body composition—the total volume of extracellular phase, and the total exchangeable sodium—tend to remain at their starting normal value as the rest of the body changes about them. There is thus a relative increase in extracellular fluid and salt relative to the patient's actual weight, though near normal for his normal weight.

(4) Because the plasma volume is a part of the extracellular phase and in equilibrium with the rest of the extracellular phase, it likewise tends to maintain its starting normal value, producing a relative increase as weight is lost. The erythrocyte volume is an intracellular phase, and it tends to shrink along with the muscle mass as anabolism fails and tissue catabolism proceeds. The result of these two effects is a progressive fall in hematocrit greater than the fall in total blood volume.

(5) These changes bring about the combination of a falling body weight with a drop in the volumes of body fat, lean tissue, and erythrocyte volume, and the maintenance of a relatively normal extracellular volume, plasma volume, and total body water volume. These latter parameters, remaining at their starting normal values in spite of weight loss, come to involve a progressively increasing fraction of total body weight.

(6) The patient therefore terminates the period of starvation with a body composition best described as "too little fat, too little lean tissue, too much sodium, too little potassium, and too much water (too large a fraction of which is extracellular) with a large plasma volume and a small erythrocyte volume."

(7) A tendency to antidiuresis and retention of salt results in disproportionate retention of water (both that ingested and that endogenously produced by the starvation state). Retention of water and salt produces hypoproteinemia, further abetted by decreased albumin synthesis, though this synthetic defect is only a very late manifestation in resting semistarvation. There is thus hyponatremia and hypotonicity.

(8) There is a distortion of cation distribution. Sodium (though low in the extracellular fluid) is found at above-normal concentrations in muscle, and potassium (while low in muscle) is found at above-normal concentrations in the extracellular fluid. The normal ratio between total exchangeable sodium and total exchangeable potassium is distorted in the direction of too much sodium.

The evolution of vertebrate life has consisted in the erection of an edifice of functioning lean tissue high in potassium and low in sodium, in an environment that is rich in sodium and low in potassium. The health of this mass of lean tissue depends upon the maintenance of energy and of osmotic relationships; in the extracellular or "environmental" phase, this osmotic normalcy means normal sodium concentration. At the same time the maintenance of a potassium-rich edifice in an isotonic sodium-rich environment requires energy. This energy is expended not only in protein synthesis and in muscular work but also in that energy required for the maintenance of normal concentrations of certain electrolytes (of which we are concerned with potassium here) within the cell and the exclusion of sodium and chloride from the cell. This is done against high concentration gradients. Whether this mechanism be considered as a "pump" or whether it be considered as some sort of osmotic work carried on at the cell membrane is merely an exercise in semantics until the process is understood. In either event it requires energy, and this energy is best supplied through the provision of glucose. The hypotonicity—"low sodium"—of the starving patient and the tendency to "high potassium" in his extracellular fluid is thus due in part to a lack of sufficient energy to maintain the normal concentration gradients across the cell surface. This lack of energy may act either by stimulating volume-sensitive areas, or by the failure normally to inactivate hormones that inhibit the excretion of water and salt. As mentioned in Part III, differential potassium loss has a tendency to produce hyponatremia by reason of the osmotic equilibrium in body water; this is a minor factor in the genesis of starvation hyponatremia because potassium loss in starvation is usually in proportion to cell matrix and water.

(9) The water-and-electrolyte changes in starvation resemble those produced by aldosterone and antidiuretic hormone in the face of water excess, that is, loading of water and sodium at hypotonic concentrations. Sodium starvation is indeed a stimulus to aldosterone production; the relation of starvation to antidiuresis is not so clear.

(10) We therefore complete our characterization of the starvation state as:

too little fat, too little lean tissue, too much water (too large a fraction of which is extracellular), with a large plasma volume and a small erythrocyte volume, yielding a low hematocrit in a relatively high blood volume, with hyponatremia and bodily hypotonicity, hypoproteinemia, and slight hyperkalemia.

Section III.   Two Examples of Body Composition in Starvation

A. NORMAL VERSUS IDEAL WEIGHT AS A BASIS FOR EXPRESSION

The expression of body composition must relate somehow to body size. Various measures of height, weight, or surface area are used. We prefer to use weight as the simplest reference point. The trouble comes when a patient has lost weight (or—in certain types of visceral disease—gained weight with edema) and the values must now be related to a weight that is not normal. For example, a 75 kg. athletic man has a normal blood volume of 7.0 per cent of body weight, or 5250 ml., with a hematocrit of 44. He then develops carcinoma of the stomach and, without bleeding, loses 15 kg. to drop to 60 kg. Characteristically his plasma volume will stay nearly the same but his erythrocyte volume falls, so that he now has a blood volume of, say, 5000 ml. with a hematocrit of 37. On the basis of his normal weight, this is 6.7 per cent of body weight, or in the low normal range. On the basis of his new body weight it is 8.4 per cent of body weight, or slightly elevated. Clinical experience suggests that this blood volume is not physiologically elevated: he seems to need the blood. His vascular tree is still there to accept it and pump it around. But he will readily develop pulmonary congestion and anesthesia complications if given a large excess of additional blood just before operation on the mistaken theory that his blood volume is low merely because his hematocrit is low. Similarly with any other aspect of body composition: the changing body weight confuses both expression and clinical interpretation of the data.

In Tables II–V, expressions are given for both weights: *normal weight* (the weight of the patient before his illness) and *observed weight* (the weight in illness, at the time of the observation). The changing picture with disease is then appreciated.

B. BODY COMPOSITION IN A NORMAL MALE (TABLE II)

The data in these three tables are based on results from our laboratories. Normal ranges are not shown for all the constituents, nor are variations with age, sex, or visceral disease. For all of these the reader is referred to the literature. In these tables a normal male subject is used as an example, showing in Tables IV and V the changes produced by early (mild) semistarvation and by late severe septic starvation.

For these data the blood phases are measured by summation of red cell volume and plasma volume using radiochromated cells and blue dye, respectively. The body water, extracellular phase, total exchangeable sodium, and total exchangeable potassium are measured respectively by dilution of deu-

Table II.   Normal Body Composition

Male   Age: 30   Weight: 70 kg.

MEASUREMENT	ABSOLUTE		RELATIVE		PER CENT OF NORMAL ON OBS. WT.	COMMENT ON (4)	PER CENT OF NORMAL ON NORM. WT.
1	2		3		4	5	6
Weight	70	kg.					
A. The Intravascular Phase							
Hematocrit (LVH)	45				100	Normal	100
Plasma volume	2800	ml.	4.0%	B.Wt.	100	Normal	100
Red cell volume	2000	ml.	2.9%	B.Wt.	100	Normal	100
Blood volume	4900	ml.	7.0%	B.Wt.	100	Normal	100
Hematocrit (WBH)	40.8				100	Normal	100
WBH:LVH	0.91				100	Normal	100
B. Body Water and the Extracellular Phase							
Total body water	39.8	l.	56.8%	B.Wt.	100	Normal	100
Extracellular water	16.4	l.	23.4%	B.Wt.	100	Normal	100
Total exchangeable chloride	2030	mE.	29	mE./kg.	100	Normal	100
Plasma chloride concentration	103	mE./l.			100	Normal	100
Total exchangeable sodium	2870	mE.	41	mE./kg.	100	Normal	100
Plasma sodium concentration	143	mE./l.			100	Normal	100
Plasma potassium concentration	4.3	mE./l.			100	Normal	100
Plasma osmolality	295	mO./l.			100	Normal	100
Exchangeable sodium:potassium ratio	0.87				100	Normal	100
Plasma protein concentration	7.0	gm.%			100	Normal	100
C. The Intracellular Phase							
Intracellular water	23.4	l.	33.5%	B.Wt.	100	Normal	100
Total exchangeable potassium	3300	mE.	47	mE./kg.	100	Normal	100
D. Derived Values							
Body solids	30.2	kg.	43.2%	B.Wt.	100	Normal	100
Body fat	15.6	kg.	22.3%	B.Wt.	100	Normal	100
Average intracellular K concentration	138	mE./l.			100	Normal	100
Residual sodium	530	mE.	7.6	mE./kg.	100	Normal	100

terium, radiobromide, radiosodium, and radiopotassium.

The measured and derived items (column 1) are self-evident. The "residual sodium" is that portion of the exchangeable sodium that is outside the extracellular phase (in cells and bone).

In column 2 are shown the data as measured, on an absolute basis. In column 3 are shown the data as related to the patient's weight, using the weight observed at the time of the measurement (Obs. Wt.). The units here are "per cent of body weight" (% B.Wt.) and "milliequivalents per kilogram." In col-

umn 4 is shown the relationship of the observed data to normal values for the observed weight. For example, if a blood volume is 4.5% B.Wt. and the normal is 7.0% B.Wt., then the value is 64 per cent of normal as shown in column 4. In column 5 is a comment on the data in column 4. In column 6 are shown the data, as expressed in relation to the *patient's pre-illness weight*, as a per cent of normal. Column 6 therefore indicates the absolute gain or loss.

The data shown in Table II are based on a normal male and show body composition in the middle of the normal range.

Table III.   Body Composition; Normal Ranges and Means

| | MALE | | FEMALE | |
	Range	Mean	Range	Mean
Plasma volume	3.5–4.5	4.0% B.Wt.	3.5–4.5	4.0% B.Wt.
Red cell volume	2.5–3.5	3.0% B.Wt.	2.0–3.0	2.5% B.Wt.
Blood volume	6.0–8.0	7.0% B.Wt.	5.5–7.5	6.5% B.Wt.
Total body water	50–60	55.0% B.Wt.	45–55	50.0% B.Wt.
Extracellular water	18–24	22.0% B.Wt.	18–24	22.0% B.Wt.
Total exchangeable sodium	38–42	40 mE./kg.	38–42	40 mE./kg.
Total exchangeable potassium	45–49	47 mE./kg.	38–42	40 mE./kg.

The approximate normal means and ranges for the primary constituents of adult body composition are shown in Table III.

C. BODY COMPOSITION IN A MALE AFTER A PERIOD OF SEMISTARVATION (TABLE IV)

In Table IV are shown the results when an individual with the body composition detailed in Table II undergoes a mild degree of starvation, as in surgical semistarvation without trauma.

These are typical findings in partially obstructing carcinoma of the gastrointestinal tract with caloric starvation but without major hemorrhage. Such changes are seen in circumstances where there is a loss of about 20 per cent of body weight; here 15 kg. in a 70 kg. man. The table is constructed exactly like Table II.

The *intravascular phase* shows a loss of red cell mass, with a slight increase in plasma volume, resulting in a small drop in total blood volume. Consideration of columns 4 and 6 will illustrate the matter of weight reference. The blood volume at 4400 ml. (column 2) is 8.0 per cent (column 3) of a body weight of 55 kg. In a male of this age and weight the normal blood volume would be (high normal) about 7.0 per cent B.Wt. or 3850 ml. In terms of *observed weight* this blood volume is therefore 114 per cent of normal or slightly high (column 4). When we now consider it in relation to the pre-illness or "normal" weight for this person* we find

*This pre-illness or normal weight is the patient's own normal weight as he has observed it in the past; it is not taken from height-weight tables or other statistical data.

(column 6) that it is reduced, at 4400 ml., to 90 per cent of the normal for this man, at 70 kg., of 4900 ml. The reduction is largely in the red cell fraction, which is only 67 per cent of its former normal value. The plasma volume is essentially maintained (105 per cent of starting value) and is thus of course high for the observed weight (135 per cent of normal).

The question "How much blood does this man need before operation?" is answered as follows. After weight loss, normal vascular homeostasis requires a blood volume higher than normal for the observed weight. Volume here is adequate but the hematocrit, at 32.5, is a little low to provide ideal oxygen transport. One cell suspension would be ideal for transfusion; if in good cardiovascular status, the patient receives the same benefit but more economically from one whole blood transfusion. In either event a period of 12 to 24 hours should pass, after preoperative transfusion, before the induction of anesthesia in an elective situation such as this.

Body water and the extracellular phase show, like the plasma volume, a tendency to maintain their starting sizes, thus being relatively high for the new weight (137 per cent of normal, for extracellular water).

By contrast the *intracellular values* and certain *body solids* are very low. The total exchangeable potassium, about like the red cell volume, is only 60 per cent of its starting size and only 77 per cent of normal for the observed weight. Intracellular water is reduced proportionally, with the result (quite constantly observed) that the average intracellular potassium concentration is nearly normal, despite the loss of cell substance.

Table IV. Body Composition in Semistarvation

Male   Age: 30   Weight (Normal: 70 kg.):Observed: 55 kg.

MEASUREMENT	ABSOLUTE		RELATIVE		PER CENT OF NORMAL ON OBS. WT.	COMMENT ON (4)	PER CENT OF NORMAL ON NORM. WT.
1	2		3		4	5	6
Weight	55 kg.						79
A. The Intravascular Phase							
Hematocrit (LVH)	37.6					Low	85
Plasma volume	2970	ml.	5.4%	B.Wt.	135	High	105
Red cell volume	1430	ml.	2.6%	B.Wt.	87	Very low	67
Blood volume	4400	ml.	8.0%	B.Wt.	114	Slightly high	90
Hematocrit (WBH)	32.6						
WBH:LVH	0.87						
B. Body Water and the Extracellular Phase							
Total body water	33.0	l.	60.0%	B.Wt.	109	Normal	83
Extracellular water	18.0	l.	32.8%	B.Wt.	137	Very high	110
Total exchangeable chloride	2000	mE.	36.3	mE./kg.	125	Very high	100
Plasma chloride concentration	102	mE./l.			97	Normal	97
Total exchangeable sodium	2720	mE.	49.4	mE./kg.	120	Very high	95
Plasma sodium concentration	133	mE./l.			95	Slightly low	95
Plasma potassium concentration	4.3	mE./l.			100	Normal	100
Plasma osmolality	270	mO./l.			95	Slightly low	95
Exchangeable sodium:potassium ratio	1.37					Reversed and high	
Plasma protein concentration	6.5	gm.%			100	Normal	
C. The Intracellular Phase							
Intracellular water	15.0	l.	27.3%	B.Wt.	82	Very low	64
Total exchangeable potassium	1990	mE.	36.2	mE./kg.	77	Very low	60
D. Derived Values							
Body solids	22.0	kg.	40	% B.Wt.	93	Normal	73
Body fat	9.9	kg.	18	% B.Wt.	80	Normal	64
Average intracellular K concentration	127	mE./l.			92	Normal	92
Residual sodium	320	mE.	5.8	mE./kg	76		60

About one-half the body fat has been consumed (about 5.7 kg.), suggesting that weight loss in this particular individual has been about one-half lean tissue.

D. BODY COMPOSITION IN SEVERE SEPTIC STARVATION (TABLE V)

Severe sepsis with starvation, as in peritonitis, colitis, empyema or late malignancy with infection, would be expected to produce such extreme cachexia.

Here, all the changes are much more marked. The tendency of plasma volume and certain extracellular factors to remain high on the basis of observed weight is still noted, but now they are low in relation to normal weight, indicating loss of absolute content. Forty-seven per cent, or almost one-half the starting blood volume, has now disappeared (column 6). Yet, because weight and body substance have been lost to almost the same extent as blood volume, the blood volume relative to body weight (6.5 per cent B.Wt.) is nearly normal. The hematocrit is very low —the anemia of infection. Both blood volume and erythrocyte concentration (hematocrit) should be increased by a carefully planned program of transfusion in such a patient. The extracellular water and total exchangeable sodium are so high (165 per cent and 130

Table V.   Body Composition in Septic Starvation

Male   Age: 30   Weight (Normal: 70 kg.):Observed: 40 kg.

MEASUREMENT	ABSOLUTE		RELATIVE	PER CENT OF NORMAL ON OBS. WT.	COMMENT ON (4)	PER CENT OF NORMAL ON NORM. WT.
1	2		3	4	5	6
Weight	40 kg.					57
A. The Intravascular Phase						
Hematocrit (LVH)	22			45	Very low	
Plasma volume	2080	ml.	5.2% B.Wt.	130	High	75
Red cell volume	520	ml.	1.3% B.Wt.	43	Low	25
Blood volume	2600	ml.	6.5% B.Wt.	93	Slightly low	53
Hematocrit (WBH)	20					
WBH:LVH	0.91					
B. Body Water and the Extracellular Phase						
Total body water	28	l.	70 % B.Wt.	127	High	70
Extracellular water	15	l.	38 % B.Wt.	165	Very high	92
Total exchangeable chloride	1550	mE.	39.0 mE./kg.	135	Slightly low	77
Plasma chloride concentration	94	mE./l.		87	Slightly low	
Total exchangeable sodium	2100	mE.	52.6 mE./kg.	130	Very high	73
Plasma sodium concentration	120	mE./l.		84	Slightly low	
Plasma potassium concentration	5.2	mE./l.		125	High	
Plasma osmolality	250	mO./l.		86	Low	
Exchangeable sodium:potassium ratio	1.3					
Plasma protein concentration	4.5	gm.%			Low	
C. The Intracellular Phase						
Intracellular water	13.0	l.	32.6% B.Wt.	97	Normal	55
Total exchangeable potassium	1630	mE.	41 mE./kg.	87	Low	50
D. Derived Values						
Body solids	12	kg.	30 % B.Wt.	69	Very low	40
Body fat	4	kg.	10 % B.Wt.	45	Very low	27
Average intracellular K concentration	120	mE./l.		86	Slightly low	91
Residual sodium	300	mE.	7.5 mE./kg.	103	Normal	56

per cent of normal for the observed weight, respectively) that one would expect to see some edema.

The extracellular factors, though high for this reduced weight, nonetheless are lower than their absolute starting value, as indicated in column 6.

By contrast, the intracellular factors are low, yet, because weight loss has occurred *pari passu* with intracellular loss, they are not markedly or proportionally reduced in terms of the observed weight (column 4). The true magnitude of intracellular loss can best be seen in column 6 where we find, for example, that a full 50 per cent of the starting body potassium has been lost despite the fact that the relative total exchangeable potassium is still 87 per cent of normal for the observed weight. The plasma potassium concentration is elevated (5.2 mE./l.) despite the low body content (1630 mE.), as is so characteristic in late starvation or in visceral disease.

The ratio of total exchangeable sodium to total exchangeable potassium is high. Loss of fat here has been greater than loss of intracellular water. About 73 per cent of the starting body fat has been burned, leaving 27 per cent still in the body (column 6); 60 per cent of the starting body solids have disappeared. There is extracellular hypotonicity (250 mO. per l.), and the average intracellular potassium concentration is also low.

Section IV. Starvation Debits

A. WHAT GOES FIRST? WHAT HURTS MOST?

As starvation proceeds, certain bodily functions are damped down or reduced in activity. The precise order at which these occur is not a matter for exact analysis; circumstances are too variable. An approximate list of those functions which are impaired by starvation, in order of their occurrence, is given here in three phases: early, severe, and preterminal. The three are not categorically definable, although as a general rule, starting from a normally built individual, loss of 15 per cent of body weight is early starvation, loss of 25 per cent is severe starvation, loss of 40 per cent of body weight is preterminal. Many factors, particularly sepsis and avitaminosis, can bring on the terminal phase with much less net loss of body substance.

1. Deficits in Early Starvation

Reproductive vigor drops; there is amenorrhea, loss of libido, decreased excretion of androgens and 17-ketosteroids. Ability to excrete salt and water loads diminishes; the retention of water and salt after trauma is seen in exaggerated form. Edema of wounds, anastomoses, and lungs is easily produced.

2. Deficits in Severe Starvation

There is decreased work efficiency, due to loss of muscle mass. There is decreased respiratory vigor. Stores of endogenous energy decrease, owing to loss of fat. Production of erythrocytes is decreased; anemia becomes evident. Gastrointestinal function diminishes; the tract becomes atonic. There is loss of appetite and hunger; high gastric residuals and vomiting accompany early efforts at feeding.

3. Deficits in Preterminal Starvation

Albumin synthesis is finally decreased. This occurs earlier if the liver is primarily involved. Decreased protein antibody formation is difficult to demonstrate even in late starvation. Wound healing is less effective, a specific result most noticeable in avitaminosis C and not well correlated with weight loss or caloric deficit alone. Chemical disintegration takes place, owing to deteriorating visceral function: azotemia, acidosis, hypotonicity, hyperkalemia. There is complete loss of muscle power, ambition, and normal mentation. The lack of diaphragmatic effort and lack of cough reflex and tussic effectiveness are the final events producing terminal accumulative bronchopneumonia as the cause of death in most cases of starvation.

4. Malignancy as a Factor

Malignant tumors produce starvation and cachexia according to the viscera involved, gastrointestinal tract, liver, and peritoneum being prominent. Very widespread tumors that do not involve such viscera may coexist with good nutrition, even obesity. The concept of a specific metabolic, biochemical, or toxic lesion to be identified as "malignant cachexia" finds little basis in most sarcomas and carcinomas; there are exceptions, particularly in lymphoma and melanoma.

5. Macronutrients versus Micronutrients

Balanced loss of weight due to decreased intake of carbohydrate, fat, and protein (macronutrients) is much better tolerated than the same starvation when complicated by specific deficiency of vitamins, specific electrolytes, or minerals (micronutrients). The combination of the two, found in severe peritoneal sepsis, is the most destructive. Severe micronutrient deficiency may be seen even in obese people.

Iron deficiency is of special interest in surgical patients, especially those who have bled and now are on subnormal dietary intakes. Determination of the serum iron and appropriate therapy may be of outstanding importance not only in blood formation but also in wound healing and in the gastrointestinal absorptive function.

B. WHY OR WHEN IS STARVATION BAD FOR SURGICAL PATIENTS?

Obese people are poor subjects for injury and surgery. Lean, thin, "thrifty," even wasted patients do well. One can hardly condemn all forms of weight loss as surgical evil, and needed surgery should not be postponed for prolonged preoperative nutritional "build-up," save under most exceptional circumstances. By the same token, complicated postoperative feeding maneuvers are rarely needed in early convalescence.

What then is bad—and when—in surgical starvation? The answers to this question may be listed as five major aspects, and all result from the starvation effects listed above:

(1) *decreased tolerance of water and salt*—tendency to edema, hypoproteinemia, and hypotonicity, all primarily dilutional;

(2) *avitaminosis, especially of C*—a specific lesion with a specific effect on the wound;

(3) *decreased tolerance to overtransfusion*—congestive atelectasis;

(4) *decreased vigor, stamina, drive, decreased desire to eat and get well*—a late effect;

(5) *decreased vital functions late in starvation* as the late debits catch up with the patient; hypoalbuminemia, azotemia, and pulmonary sepsis are the most prominent. Decreased effective cough is found, as alertness, mentation, and diaphragmatic function are progressively impaired—then accumulative bronchopneumonia. Death from starvation is death from bronchopneumonia.

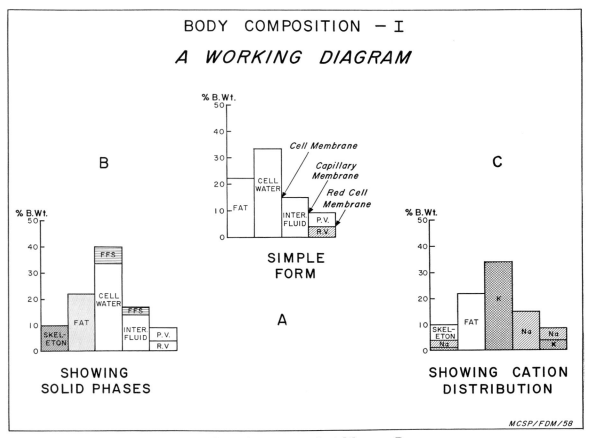

Figure 85. Body Composition. I. A Working Diagram

As is the case with the diagrams relative to shock and the nephron, a working diagram is also useful in considering body composition and the changes imposed therein by acute and chronic disease and injury.

Shown here are three types of diagrams that may be used as a basis for clinical analysis.

To the left, B, is shown a diagram wherein the vertical coordinate represents the fraction of body weight, and along the horizontal coordinate are indicated respectively the skeleton, fat, cell water (with fat-free solids above it as FFS), interstitial fluid (with fat-free solids), and the blood volume divided into the plasma volume and the red cell volume. Here, emphasis is on

the various tissue solids involved.

To the right, at C, is shown a similar diagram in which the emphasis is on the distribution of cations. The "sodium area" is seen to be the interstitial fluid and plasma whereas the potassium area is seen to be the red cell mass and the intracellular environment. There is some sodium and potassium in the skeleton.

In the center, at A, is shown a simple form of diagram which is used throughout this book. The mass of body fat, the cell water, the interstitial fluid, and the components of the blood volume are shown according to the fraction of body weight that they occupy. The location of the significant membranes is shown.

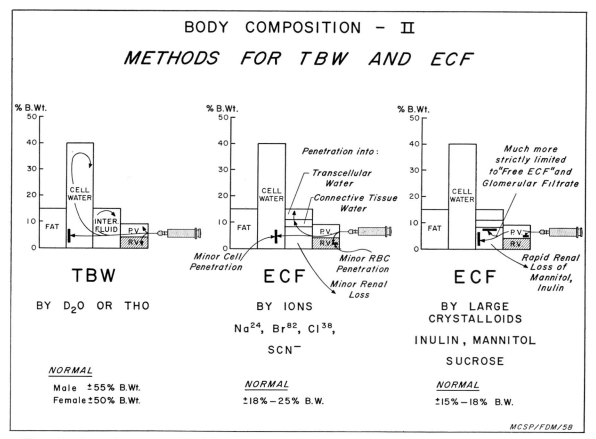

Figure 86. Body Composition. II. Methods for Total Body Water and Extracellular Fluid Volume

Body composition is measured by dilution of tracers that are measured either by their radioactivity, weight, or special chemical and colorimetric properties.

Here (to the left) is shown the principle involved in measurement of the total body water by the dilution of deuterium oxide or tritium oxide (tritiated water). The tracer is injected into the plasma volume and equilibrates throughout the aqueous components of body composition. By the extent of its dilution the total body water is measured. Similar results are given, though with lesser accuracy, by the dilution of such crystalloids as sulfonamides, urea, or antipyrine.

In the center is shown a similar diagram for the measurement of extracellular fluid by the dilution of ions. Radioactive sodium, bromide, and chloride are thus used, as well as thiocyanate, which is measured colorimetrically. The tracer is injected into the plasma volume and equilibrates throughout an area of body water that is largely extracellular. As indicated in the diagram, there is minor penetration into red blood cells, and complete penetration into connective tissue water and transcellular water. For this reason, the "ion methods" give rather large values for extracellular water running from 18 to 25 per cent of body weight.

To the right is shown a similar diagram for the measurement of extracellular fluid volume by the dilution of large crystalloids such as inulin, mannitol, or sucrose. Here, possibly because of larger molecular weight, the tracer distributions are limited strictly to the plasma and to the free extracellular fluid. They do not penetrate as extensively into the connective tissue water or transcellular water. Some of them are very rapidly excreted through the kidney. The normal volume of dilution is therefore somewhat smaller, running from 15 to 18 per cent of body weight.

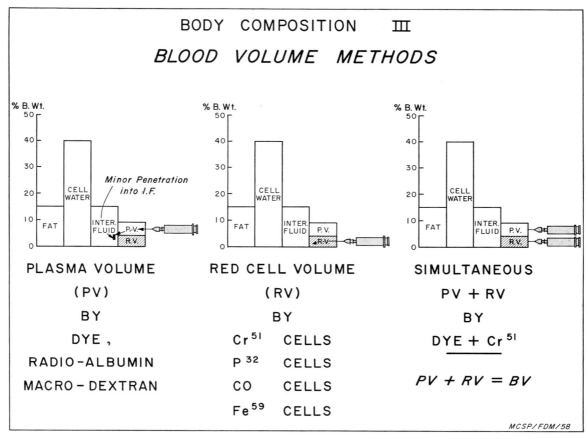

Figure 87. BODY COMPOSITION. III. BLOOD VOLUME METHODS

To the left is represented the measurement of the plasma volume by the dilution of a dye (such as Evans blue), radioactive albumin, or macro-dextran. The material is injected into the plasma volume and dilutes itself throughout the plasma volume with minor penetration into the interstitial fluid. By its dilution, the plasma volume is measured. From this figure, using an equation based on the large vessel hematocrit, one may estimate the blood volume. In such an instance it is important to realize that the blood volume itself has not been measured.

In the center are shown the analogous aspects of the measurement of the red cell volume by the dilution of a tracer such as radioactively tagged red cells or red cells tagged with carbon monoxide. The cells are injected directly into the red cell mass by being injected intravenously. They dilute themselves throughout the red cell mass and, by their equilibrium-specific activity, their dilution in the red cell mass is indicated and the red cell mass is thus measured. As is the case with the plasma volume measurements, one may then carry out

a simple calculation based on the large vessel hematocrit to estimate the blood volume. But, again, the blood volume itself has not been measured. It has been calculated.

To the right is shown the simultaneous measurement of the plasma volume and the red cell volume by double tracer techniques. These are the techniques used in our laboratories and referred to extensively in this book. Here, the measurement of the plasma volume and red cell volume is carried out simultaneously and independently by two different tracers. Examples are the use of the blue dye and chromated red cells. The blood volume is then measured by the simple arithmetic sum of these two, using the formula PV + RV = BV. In this instance the blood volume has actually been measured by dilution and has been derived by an expression independent of chance variations or errors in the measurement of the large vessel hematocrit. It is on the basis of such data that our knowledge of the whole body hematocrit rests $\left(\text{WBH} = \dfrac{\text{RV}}{\text{PV} + \text{RV}} \right)$.

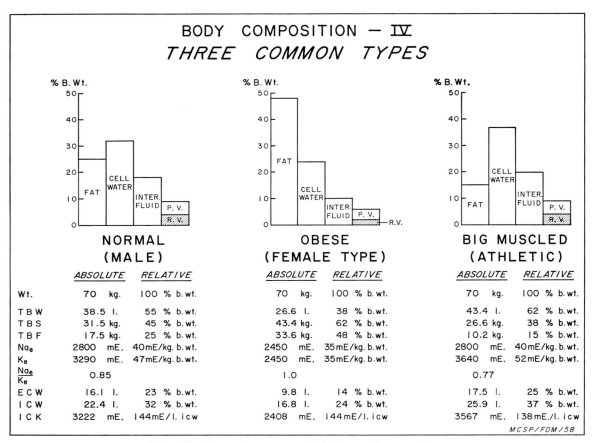

Figure 88.   BODY COMPOSITION. IV. THREE COMMON TYPES

See facing page for detailed legend.

Figure 88. BODY COMPOSITION. IV. THREE COMMON TYPES

In this chart are shown the three major somatotypes or anthropometric types revealed by body compositional study. To the left are shown typical measurements in the normal adult male. Abbreviations are used as follows:

TBW = Total body water
TBS = Total body solids
TBF = Total body fat
Na_e = Total exchangeable sodium
K_e = Total exchangeable potassium
Na_e/K_e = Ratio of total exchangeable sodium to total exchangeable potassium
ECW = Extracellular water
ICW = Intracellular water
ICK = Intracellular potassium

In the center are shown the typical findings seen in obese individuals. Since obesity is much commoner in women, this picture is more characteristic of the female. It will be noted that body water is smaller, body fat arger, and the $Na_e:K_e$ ratio is closer to 1.0, indicating that there is less lean tissue per unit of extracellular material. It will be noted that the average intracellular potassium concentration is the same as in the male, indicating that the lean tissue present in an obese person is actually quite normal in its detailed composition.

To the right are shown the findings in a big-muscled or athletic individual. The principal difference from the normal male is that there is a larger cell mass with less fat. This is associated with a higher total body water and a lower $Na_e:K_e$ ratio. Again it will be noted that the average intracellular potassium concentration is essentially normal.

The values shown in this chart are taken from averages determined in our laboratories.

Both the absolute and relative values are shown. The relative value expresses the body compositional parameter in relation to body weight (b.wt.); in the case of intracellular potassium concentration this is expressed as mE/l. of intracellular water.

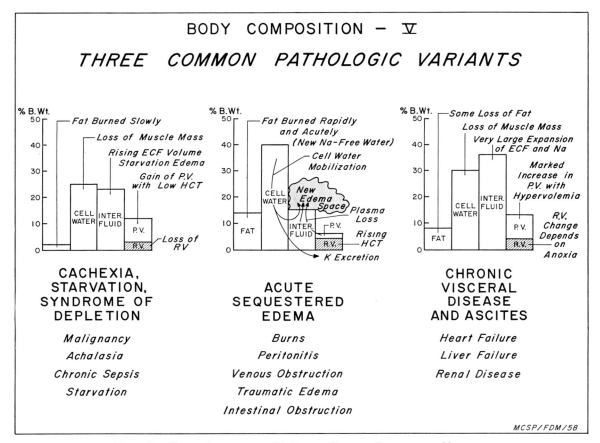

Figure 89.   BODY COMPOSITION. V. THREE COMMON PATHOLOGIC VARIANTS

See facing page for detailed legend.

Figure 89. BODY COMPOSITION. V. THREE COMMON PATHOLOGIC VARIANTS

In this chart are shown the three most common directions in which body composition moves in the face of injury, surgery, acute or chronic disease.

To the left are shown the changes of cachexia or starvation. We have called these body compositional changes the "syndrome of depletion." This distortion is seen in late malignancy, achalasia of the esophagus, chronic infection, or starvation (as examples). Fat has been slowly but completely burned. There has been a loss of muscle mass with accumulation of extracellular water manifested as a rising relative extracellular volume, ultimately producing starvation edema. Associated with this high extracellular fluid volume is a high plasma volume. The red cell mass is small, sharing its diminution in size with the rest of the cell mass. The result is a blood volume which may be normal or relatively high, with an enlarged, diluted plasma volume and a small red cell mass. The hematocrit is low.

In the center is shown the picture typically produced by trauma or acute disease characterized by the formation of acute sequestered edema. This is seen in burns and peritonitis, in venous obstruction and traumatic edema, and spreading cellulitis. An analogous change is observed in intestinal obstruction where there is accumulation of a large amount of extracellular water in the lumen of the gut. Although fat is burned rapidly in such an acute situation, not enough time has elapsed for the fat stores to be exhausted. The same is true of the cells. Cell water is rapidly mobilized but in the course of a day or two only a small impression is made on the total cell mass. By contrast, the extracellular fluid volume grows very rapidly because of the appendage thereto of a parasitic obligatory sequestered edema. This edema is a new edema "space" (often called the "third space," meaning that it is a new space of body composition in addition to that in the cells and in the extracellular fluid). It will be noted in such an instance that the total extracellular fluid volume is grossly increased, but that the actual functional extracellular volume in support of the plasma is quite small. The plasma volume itself becomes severely reduced, giving rise to a small blood volume. The red cell volume is not much changed in the acute phase of such processes as this. For this reason there is a markedly elevated hematocrit.

To the right is shown the situation in chronic visceral disease with ascites, chest fluid, or anasarca. This is the edematous picture seen in heart failure, liver failure and renal disease. There is some loss of fat and some loss of muscle mass over a period of months or years as the disease progresses, as in depletion of any sort. The most spectacular change, however, is a tremendous increase in the volume of the extracellular fluid and in, the total body sodium. This is manifested by edema, ascites, anasarca, and fluid in other body cavities. The change in the red cell volume depends upon a number of other factors, most particularly the presence or absence of chronic anoxia. The blood volume is characteristically enlarged although the hematocrit is usually quite low, owing to a high plasma volume.

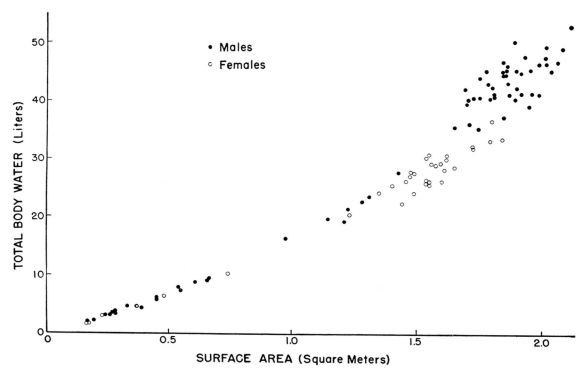

Figure 90.   BODY COMPOSITION. VI. TOTAL BODY WATER AS A FUNCTION OF SURFACE AREA

In this chart are shown the data for total body water over a considerable age span and in the two sexes as measured in normal individuals in our laboratories. It will be noticed that as surface area grows larger (with increasing age) there is a dissociation between men and women, the males developing a higher body water per unit surface area. This has to do with the fact that men have more lean tissue per unit surface area than women. This is correlated also with a higher creatinine excretion, total exchangeable potassium, and basal oxygen consumption in males. This secondary sex character is evidently androgen-linked, is associated with a higher red cell volume in males, and is a manifestation of steroidal growth.

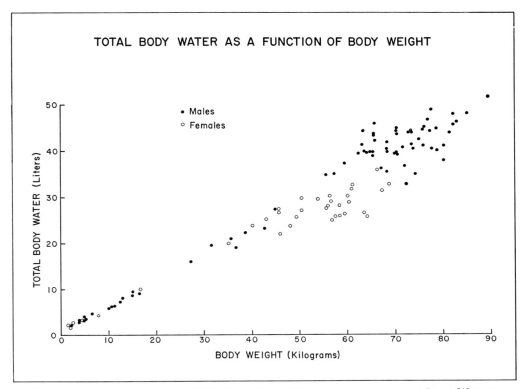

Figure 91. Body Composition. VII. Total Body Water as a Function of Body Weight

This figure is to be contrasted with the previous figure. Here the body water in the same group of subjects is indicated as a function of body weight. It will be noted that as the subject grows larger and reaches puberty (at about 45 to 60 kg.) the female total body water drops off to a lower figure than the male when expressed per unit body weight. This is due to the fact that in the female at puberty the formation of neutral fat deposits in the subcutaneous tissues is a secondary sex characteristic which adds weight but reduces the relative total body water. In the male, *per contra*, the formation of lean tissue and skeletal muscle (a steroidal growth characteristic) produces a larger total body water per unit body weight than in the female.

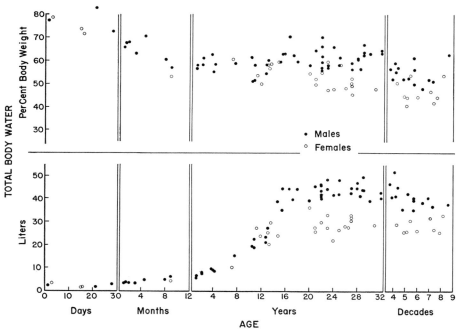

Figure 92. BODY COMPOSITION. VIII. TOTAL BODY WATER AS A FUNCTION OF AGE

In this chart are shown the data from our laboratories on a group of subjects ranging in age from one day to ninety years. It will be noted that there is a rise in total body water (below) with growth in youth and at puberty. There is then a slight falling off of total body water values in the older years.

Above are shown the relative data for the same groups. The infant has a very high body water, the excess being in the extracellular fraction. Some senile people are very "dry" while others are in the normal range for the young adult.

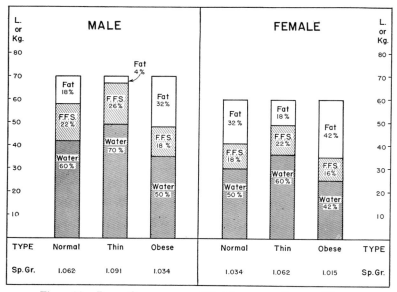

Figure 93. BODY COMPOSITION. IX. MALE AND FEMALE TYPES

In this chart are shown the typical water data for normal, thin, and obese men and women. Water, fat, and fat-free solids (FFS) are shown. Below are shown the total body specific gravities of such subjects. It will be noticed that the figure for an obese male overlaps that for a normally built female. The obese female has more fat than one sees in normal men. Only in severe obesity does one see males with total body fat figures over 40 per cent.

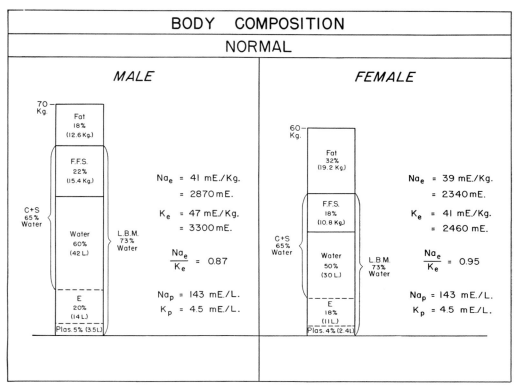

Figure 94. Body Composition. X. Normal

In this chart are shown, in somewhat greater detail, the relations of normal body composition in the male and in the female. Some of the figures are slightly different from those shown in Figure 88. Both of the compositions shown in this chart are based on actual observations in single individuals, rather than being averages as in Figure 88.

It will be noticed that the combination of cells and skeleton (C + S) is 65 per cent water and the lean body mass (LBM) 73 per cent water in both sexes. These rather arbitrary values are not constant in disease. We have every reason to believe that in the presence of ascites, edema, and anasarca (and after severe injury) the water content of lean tissue rises, if for no other reason than that it has a larger extracellular phase.

The total exchangeable potassium is a linear function of the lean body mass and it will be noted that this bears a different relationship to the body weight and to the total exchangeable sodium in the two sexes.

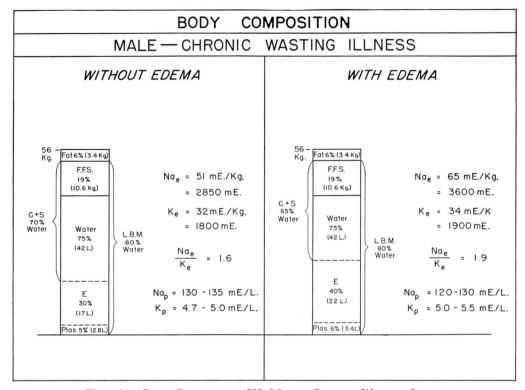

Figure 95. BODY COMPOSITION. XI. MALE—CHRONIC WASTING ILLNESS

In this figure, as in Figure 94, are shown two individual examples of body composition in chronic wasting illness. It will be noticed that the principal difference between the two manifestations (with and without edema) lies in the relative magnitude of the extracellular water and of the total exchangeable sodium. The total exchangeable sodium in the edematous subject (65 mE. per kg.) is about as high a value as one sees for this dimension of body composition. Note also the inversion of the Na_e:K_e ratio, and the tendency to a hypotonic, hyponatremic plasma with slight hyperkalemia.

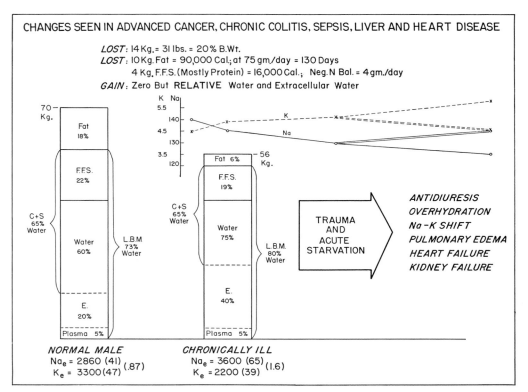

Figure 96. CHANGES SEEN IN ADVANCED CANCER, CHRONIC COLITIS, SEPSIS, LIVER, AND HEART DISEASE

In this chart are shown the progressive changes of a normal male who develops chronic illness which in 130 days is responsible for the loss of 14 kg. The calculation of the dimensions of the loss is shown above. Notice the very large endogenous caloric production involved in such a large fat oxidation.

Note also the relative increase in water content, the increase in the water content of lean tissue, and the disappearance of fat.

When operation or acute illness is then superimposed, such a patient is somewhat more prone to develop anti-diuresis, overhydration, sodium-potassium shift, pulmonary edema, heart failure, or renal failure. If well managed, convalescence is quite normal and wound healing is good.

Above is shown the characteristic sodium-potassium inversion produced by trauma, showing alternatively its return to normal or its progressive widening, a very poor prognostic sign.

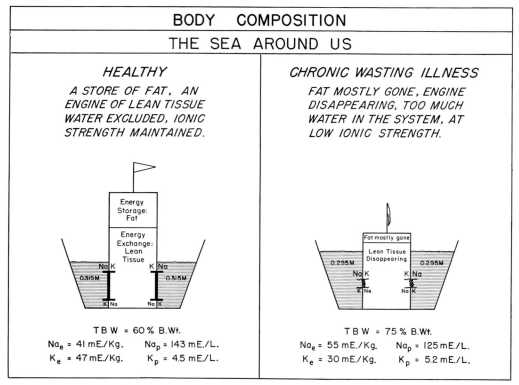

Figure 97. Body Composition—The Sea Around Us

To the left is shown the normal body compositional situation of potassium-rich lean tissue and energy-rich fat being supported in an isotonic saline medium by strong energy forces that maintain the normal electrolyte gradients across the cell. Below are shown typical compositional findings.

To the right is shown the typical finding in chronic wasting illness. Fat has gone, the lean tissue is disappearing, the sodium-potassium "pump" mechanism is breaking down, resulting in hypotonicity of the body with a sodium-potassium "shift" in the extracellular fluid and plasma. Although the total cation involved in the alteration of a plasma sodium concentration of 125 mE. per l. and potassium of 5.2 mE. per l. is actually quite small, it bespeaks a very widespread and fundamental disorder, the pathogenesis of which is to be found in the altered physiology of late or preterminal wasting disease.

CHAPTER 26

Management of Early Starvation;
The Compositional Defect as
a Guide to Treatment

Since resting semistarvation is the commonest starvation state encountered in surgery, such an example is appropriate for analysis as management is arranged on the firm basis of body composition and metabolism.

Section I. Resting Semistarvation; Initial Body Composition

The problem would be typified by a man of fifty-five who has had progressive loss of appetite and weight for four months and is finally discovered to be harboring a scirrhous carcinoma of the stomach without obvious metastatic spread. There is no frank obstruction or hemorrhage, but there is complete loss of normal appetite and desire for food.

He had been slightly obese and his normal weight was 80 kg. He has lost 15 kg., or about 1 kg. a week. He how weighs 65 kg. As a working assumption we may assume that the tissue lost was one-half fat and one-half lean; that he has a relatively expanded volume of body water at this time.

The 15 kg. of lost tissue has provided, from 7.5 kg. of fat, 67,500 (7.5 × 9) calories, or about 550 calories per day, and about 7.7 l. of water (over the four-month period), which he has excreted poorly. Since he was afebrile, his insensible water loss has been small; he has continued to take water and liquids by mouth. His total volume of body water normally would be 44 l. (0.55 × 80); it has fallen only slightly, to 43 l., thus *rising* from a *relative* value of 55 per cent of his body weight to a typical starvation value of 66 per cent of body weight.

He has lost about 7.5 kg. of lean (muscle) tissue. His clothes hang loosely on him and his biceps, gastrocnemii, and other muscle bundles are noticeable because of loss of overlying tissue, but less powerful than before. His face looks drawn. This muscle tissue has disappeared, along with 250 gm. (about 1.9 gm. a day) of nitrogen and 750 mE. of potassium—or one quarter of his total exchangeable potassium. Yet, the remaining tissue has a normal average intracellular potassium concentration and the plasma potassium concentration, at 4.7 mE. per l., is slightly elevated. There is no potassium abnormality that needs treatment here despite the large loss.

Page 437

His retention of water and salt, together with the chronic energy deficit, has increased his exchangeable sodium from a *relative* value of 40 mE. per kg. (3200 mE.) to 45 mE. per kg. (2900 mE.), although the *absolute* total has fallen slightly (300 mE.). He has minimal pretibial edema and a definite hypotonicity—plasma sodium concentration 132 mE. per l., osmolality 275 mO. per l. His plasma protein concentration has been diluted down to 5.8 gm. per 100 ml. Along with these changes his extracellular fluid, normally 16 l. (20 per cent of 80 kg.), has remained at this value while the fat and lean tissue has gone; as a result the extracellular fluid is now almost 25 per cent of his body weight.

His gastric lesion has not bled but his hematocrit, normally 44, is 36. His previous blood volume might be expected to have been about 7 per cent of his body weight.

Plasma volume	= 4% × 80 kg.	= 3200 ml.
Erythrocyte volume	= 3% × 80 kg.	= 2400 ml.
Blood volume	= 7% × 80 kg.	= 5600 ml.
Hematocrit		= 43

The present blood volume would be in this range:

Plasma volume	= 4.9% × 65 kg.	= 3200 ml.
Erythrocyte volume	= 2.8% × 65 kg.	= 1800 ml.
Blood volume	= 7.7% × 65 kg.	= 5000 ml.
Hematocrit		= 36

The blood volume is seen to be normal or slightly high for his observed weight, but there has been a definite reduction in the erythrocyte fraction as a feature of his lean-tissue loss and a relative abundance of salt-poor, protein-poor plasma. The plasma volume has been maintained. The hematocrit is thus reduced much more than the total blood volume.

His activity has been slight and the low daily dietary caloric intake (about 1000) has been made up to thermodynamic requirement by endogenous fat oxidation. He demonstrates no obvious vitamin deficiencies on physical examination, but on study might be expected to show subclinical scurvy.

In this state he is not a poor subject for surgery if the biochemical lesion is understood by his doctor; his wound will heal well if well managed (including the administration of vitamin C), and his body composition is not unfriendly to surgical recovery if he is not abused by the treatment carried out.

Section II. Management of Resting Semistarvation

A. BLOOD TRANSFUSION

If this patient's erythrocyte mass were arbitrarily restored to its former size by transfusion of whole blood the day before operation—which would require 600 ml. of cells, or three transfusions—the patient would come to the anesthetist with a blood volume close to 6500 ml., or 10 per cent of body weight. Little wonder if he should develop some pulmonary complications or congestive atelectasis! He needs time to dispose of the plasma excess. This matter has been discussed in detail in Part II and will not be described again here; the patient should ideally have a larger red cell mass and higher hematocrit than he has. He is slightly hypoproteinemic and anemic, and a proper preoperative intravascular program should be established for him. To devote ten to fourteen days to a protracted preparation of such a patient is equally un-warranted and unwise. The job can be well done in five days.

A sound blood program for him is:

    Day 1: two transfusions of whole blood,
    Day 2: rest while other studies or evaluations are under way,
    Day 3: one transfusion of whole blood,
    Day 4: check blood determinations, and
    Day 5: operation.

In such a case, the use of concentrated albumin will raise the protein concentration much more effectively than would whole blood. Volume is suddenly raised, but, as the water is lost through diuresis, it will drop back toward its starting value, leaving behind an increased protein concentration. Similarly, infused separated erythrocytes will raise the hematocrit more readily and would be used if the patient were more elderly or had heart disease. Many variations of the suggested program will be effective. The important principles are:

(1) the low hematocrit does not denote an equivalent lowering of blood volume;

(2) do not overcrowd the circulation just before operation; let the patient equilibrate before surgery; give him time for plasma disposal, and

(3) bring the patient to operation with a normal colloid osmotic pressure and as nearly normal extracellular chemical relationships as feasible. The hypotonicity will not be reparable in a short course of treatment and the patient should not receive salt infusions.

B. WATER-AND-SALT EQUILIBRIUM

The patient has cancer of the stomach; he has lost a lot of weight; he has a low plasma sodium concentration. All these are apt to suggest a "salt deficit" and lead to the intravenous administration of salt. This reasoning has led more than one patient to severe pulmonary edema. This typical semistarved patient is already "oversalted" and "overwatered"; here there are no pathological extrarenal losses. He is in a salt-retaining, water-retaining phase. His total volume of body water and his exchangeable sodium are relatively high. The best water-and-salt regimen for him is none intravenously until operation and then the minimum required to maintain hydration. If treated energetically with saline fluids, this patient will suffer further expansion of his extracellular fluid, increased edema, lowering of the plasma protein concentration, and all with little change in plasma sodium concentration. If it were felt advisable to raise the plasma sodium concentration passively, it might be done with concentrated salt or by mannitol diuresis. With a sodium concentration at 132 mE. per l., neither measure is necessary.

C. POTASSIUM REPLENISHMENT

Our patient has lost a lot of potassium. This might seem to call for potassium therapy. His total exchangeable potassium has fallen from 3760 mE. to 2900 mE., yet giving him large rations of potassium will not restore his body potassium or the lost muscle tissue.

Potassium therapy will not produce the anabolism required to restore his cell mass and body potassium stores to normal. His plasma potassium concentration is in the high normal range and he needs none intravenously prior to operation.

Adequate intake of food after operation will restore his cell mass to normal; there will be a diuresis; and with these events his plasma potassium concentration will fall and his sodium rise.

D. CALORIC NOURISHMENT AND ORAL FEEDING

Restoring his departed body fat (he has lost 7.5 kg. of fat) is as impossible as restoring muscle tissue prior to surgery. But the patient will do well on calorie-rich potassium-containing egg-and-milk drinks and other enriched drinks, as accepted, preoperatively. Oxidation of endogenous fat can be inhibited and glycogen stores repleted thereby.

E. WEIGHT

Transfusion therapy will add weight; the hoped-for diuresis may remove some of it again. A chart of the weight curve before operation will yield data on the balance between the two. Ideally the patient should come to surgery (on this regimen) at or just below his admission weight. There is not time to await anabolic weight gain (of lean tissue or fat) before surgery.

F. NITROGEN BALANCE

The patient is in negative nitrogen balance. One might allege that his wound could not heal; this might appear as an indication for hormones or the infusion of amino acid solution. Neither is needed.

It is true that he has lost a lot of muscle tissue and its nitrogen. If an adequate intake of calories and nitrogen could be provided, he would start the work of reconstruction. But the five or six days available will hardly alter his cell mass perceptibly; if "nourished extensively" intravenously, he will be further watered down. His negative nitrogen balance will not impair wound healing, but tissue edema might. He therefore does not need intravenous protein hydrolysate supplements, which will not raise his plasma protein concentration anyway. Such protein as he can take and absorb by mouth will be enough. The best things for his wound are good operative technique, vitamin C, and the avoidance of edema.

G. VITAMIN SUPPLEMENTS

He needs vitamin C, and in good quantities (150 to 300 mg. a day). This is another good reason for delaying his operation four or five days, a time required for the restoration of his tissue vitamin C levels in preparation for operation and normal wound healing.

H. OPERATION

The operation may well be a total gastrectomy. Accuracy of concept and meticulous technique are especially important in the starved patient. A caval catheter placed in the superior cava, via an arm vein, the day before operation, and used for quantitative blood replacement then and during the first two days of postoperative care, is a kindly convenience. Operative blood loss must be quantitatively replaced at operation.

I. POSTOPERATIVE CARE

The same principles of avoidance of excess water and salt or premature concern over calories hold during the early postoperative period. The daily provision of 40 to 60 mE. of potassium will help to avoid further potassium loss. The use of 50 to 75 mE. of sodium and chloride a day for the first few days will help avoid further severe dilutional hypotonicity, and will make up for the small losses of fluid through tube and urine which may be expected if recovery is uncomplicated. Some concentrated glucose (25 per cent) may spare excessive further inroads on body stores of fat and muscle more effectively than 5 per cent glucose. Total fluid intake should not, however, exceed total losses and will probably add up to less than 2000 ml. per day, depending on fever and respiratory rate.

As soon as the anastomosis is secure, the nasogastric tube can be removed and feeding begun. As significant intake commences, the patient will start his long uphill climb of convalescent anabolism hampered only by the highly variable digestive effects of total gastrectomy.

Section III.   Resting Semistarvation; Later Course

A. ACUTE COMPOSITIONAL CHANGE AT OPERATION

As described in Part I, acute changes in body composition at the time of operation are not marked, nor are they large in terms of the whole body content. They consist in loss of cellular substance, with conservation of extracellular substance, and a tendency to expand body water and its extracellular components. They are of little account in treatment, save to avoid their misinterpretation.

In our example the patient has started off from a semistarved base line. The only differences from the normal in treatment have been those involved in changes in blood volume described in the preoperative phase, a slightly more accentuated tendency to load salt and water after operation, and a lesser total catabolic weight loss than one might expect in a previously well person. Associated with

the latter is a distinct tendency to pass on to anabolism sooner than would the previously well-nourished patient, and to do this on smaller intakes once the catabolic phase is over.

A normal person would be expected to lose 2 to 4 kg. in the course of the first postoperative week. A man such as this, who has lost 15 kg. just prior to his hospitalization, would not be expected to lose as much weight in terms of nitrogen loss and fat oxidation. His tendency to load water and salt, even on conservative intravenous intakes, will further tend to cover up the underlying tissue change; weight loss may therefore be slight (0.8 to 1.5 kg., for example) and diuresis ill-defined.

B. LATER COMPOSITIONAL CHANGES

The ease with which this patient starts to anabolize new tissue will be demonstrated as soon as intakes become significant. The principal factor acting to the detriment of tissue rebuilding in this man is the effect on digestion of a crippling operation: total gastrectomy.

He has about 15 kg. of tissue to regain, about one-half of which is lean. This 7.5 kg. of muscle and other lean-tissue components represents 250 gm. of nitrogen—his original loss. The potassium content will be reloaded without any difficulty merely as a feature of regrowth, so long as he is on an ordinary mixed diet.

The most rapid consistent nitrogen anabolism we could expect here would be 5 gm. per 70 kg. per day. This would require an intake of 15 gm. of nitrogen and over 2500 calories per day (an intake of over 0.2/30, using our abbreviated notation in terms of grams of nitrogen and calories per kilogram per day). At this rate his synthesis of lean tissue would require somewhat less than fifty days. An average anabolic rate would be 3 gm. of nitrogen per 70 kg. per day, possibly achieved on an intake of 0.1/15, and requiring closer to seventy-five days.

After a total gastrectomy, such a patient will do well to ingest and absorb an intake of 0.08/20, corresponding to about 6 gm. of nitrogen and 1200 calories per day, a calorie: nitrogen ratio of 250:1. A normal person would scarcely hold nitrogen balance on this intake. But a semistarved patient such as this, during postoperative anabolism, can build tissue on this intake: his tissues are more "avid" for nitrogen. The rate of regrowth will be slow, however—near 1 gm. of nitrogen

per day—and it will therefore take over eight months. This is about what one sees clinically if digestive function is reasonably good and no malignancy remains. Furthermore, any physical work, over and beyond a basal existence, will divert caloric energy to other ends than synthesis of protein; any intercurrent illness, bout of diarrhea, or digestive upset will dull this thin edge of anabolic effort. As a result his weight resumption will be slow and intermittent. Should he develop into a continuing digestive cripple, it will never occur. Should his tumor recur, he will quickly slip downward into severe cachexia as food intake falls to zero.

The fat component of his postoperative regrowth will also be slow to appear. Were such studies to be made, he would be found to be burning additional fat during his first few weeks of nitrogen anabolism. Then, should diet be soundly reestablished, fat content would remain constant and reassume its former amount only very late in convalescence. In practice, it is extremely rare to see a patient, after total gastrectomy, regain his full weight and girth. Should this semistarved man have had some other less crippling procedure, his resumption of normal body composition would have occupied two to four months with full return to normal.

The question of anemia following gastrectomy will be discussed in Part V. The vitamin program for this man presents no problem; added orally-administered vitamin supplements should be used throughout recovery.

Parenteral iron and/or liver may later become necessary.

CHAPTER 27

The Nutritional Management of the
Normal Patient; Postoperative
Catabolic Weight Loss

The management of the resting semistarved patient has been described in considerable detail, not only because it is one of the commonest nutritional problems in surgery, but also because it embodies and epitomizes most of the metabolic features of starvation and its

management. Yet, it is a comparatively simple problem and there are surprisingly few functional deficits. With it as background, some of the other categories of nutritional disorder in surgery will be described. First is that of the metabolically normal patient.

Section I. Preoperative Management

The preoperative nutritional management of the unstressed normal patient* is seldom a problem and should not be made complicated. One should be assured that the patient truly is in a metabolically normal state by assessing the history and physical examination and in selected instances making the necessary chemical determinations, as indicated in Part III, so as to exclude those occasional cases of unsuspected azotemia, unsuspected diabetes, chronic respiratory acidosis, or other significant nutritional abnormalities that may occasionally masquerade in a healthy-looking individual. But barring the finding of such unsuspected pathology, the chief matters for nutritional consideration in the resting normal patient preoperatively are as follows.

A collapsed, nondistended bowel is an es-

sential preliminary to extensive peritoneal surgery. It is important for patients who are coming to operation for extensive bowel resection (colectomy, for example) or retroperitoneal procedure, such as aortic grafting, to come to the operating room with well-collapsed, empty intestinal tracts. The preoperative passage of the Miller-Abbott tube was often employed for this purpose. We have largely given this up, and find that by dietary management of the patient the day prior to surgery and the use of a nasogastric tube for the removal of swallowed air, a nicely manageable intestinal tract can readily be produced with much less inconvenience to the patient than by a long tube.

On the day prior to operation, the patient is given his regular breakfast, a "soft-solid" lunch that is practically free of residue, and a very light supper of fluids only. He has no fluids after midnight and comes to the opera-

---
* Our definition of *normal*, however empirical, is as before: "normal weight and strength, at normal occupation, in good health."

Page 442

ting room having had no breakfast, with a nasogastric tube in place. This type of management produces a brief period (of about eighteen hours' duration) prior to surgery when the patient's intake is far less than it has been previously. It is certainly a period of preoperative starvation, but it is of minor nutritional import, and we have not found this to be harmful to the patient. In terms of ease of bowel retraction, the regimen is just as effective as long-tube intubation. There is no bowel residue. One must be careful to see that the patient does not come to the operating room desalted; this short starvation will not hurt him, but desalting will. The withholding of all fluids from midnight to nine or ten in the morning definitely produces mild desalting via the indwelling tube, obviated by a preoperative or intraoperative slow intravenous infusion of 5 per cent glucose in saline. Unless there is some abnormality of bowel motility or a structural lesion in the left colon that prevents emptying, the use of laxatives is unnecessary, as are enemas.

As pointed out in Part I, the nutritional objective of the first phase of convalescence is a scaphoid abdomen; by the same token the nutritional preparation for eighteen hours before operation is aimed at the production of a soft, collapsed, and undistended bowel, not a positive nitrogen balance.

Preoperative colon preparation with sulfonamides or antibiotics occasionally produces avitaminosis K. The administration of the antibiotic interferes with bacterial conversion of vitamin K precursors in the gut and does not interfere with normal oral vitamin K absorption. This avitaminosis should be prevented by the administration of one of the vitamin K preparations by mouth.

Section II. Postoperative Catabolic Weight Loss: Postoperative Management in the Metabolically Normal Patient

The transient period of post-traumatic tissue loss which follows an ordinary midscale trauma in a previously healthy adult is a result both of short-term starvation and of the metabolic effects of trauma. If no complications arise, there is a brisk fall in weight. Following midscale trauma in the adult male, the weight loss in the first few days runs in the general region of 250 to 750 gm. per day. This loss of weight persists for a day or two before a plateau is reached. The relationship of this weight loss to that seen in starvation alone depends largely upon the nature and extent of the trauma and the previous health of the individual, and upon the ability of the individual to excrete water and salt. The latter consideration also accounts for the stepwise and often irregular nature of this weight loss, even in the face of a fairly consistent nitrogen balance. The release of water from the body is irregular, depending upon such factors as the interplay of antidiuretic forces, water: solute relationships, glomerular filtration, and sodium intake.

The role of starvation in this early post-traumatic weight loss is variable. There is evidence that if the patient is given large amounts of intravenous nourishment during this time (3600 ml. of protein hydrolysate and glucose, for example), the rate of weight loss can be reduced. Water accumulation plays a role in this diminished weight loss. The amount of nutrient that must be provided to prevent this weight loss is much greater than is needed to prevent weight loss in resting starvation, if the trauma is severe. These problems in the interpretation of normal postoperative catabolic weight loss, and studies of its meaning to the patient, have been discussed in Part I (pages 123–127) and will not be reviewed again here.

If trauma or operation has not been of major extent and does not involve the peritoneal cavity, the gastrointestinal tract, or its appendages, the resumption of a small oral intake may be virtually immediate, at the latest by the following day. The use of any intravenous supplementation in such a case is a luxury. Patients of this type can tolerate a single day with subnormal fluid intakes, taking small amounts by mouth as postoperative reaction, nausea, or somnolence passes off. It has become virtually a universal practice to give patients an intravenous infusion of some sort on the day of operation even for such surgical procedures as herniorrhaphy. This is unnecessary, but it is not harmful if the amount of fluid given bears some realistic relation to the requirements of the patient and his ability to excrete water.

When the trauma is not of major extent but does involve the gastrointestinal tract, the restoration of feeding should await some signal of readiness, either the passage of swallowed air by anus, audible peristalsis, or the sensation of hunger and desire to eat. It is in this type of setting that the giving of fluids by mouth the first day is quickly followed by advance to soft solids and then solids. Using a gradual advancement of diet, the patient passes from first-stage fluids* in the first two days, followed thereafter by a full diet.

Where stepwise advancement of diet is being pursued subsequent to uneventful major operation, intravenous therapy is advisable only until oral fluid intake approximates one-half to two-thirds normal for that individual. If it is dispensed with, the patient's status becomes increasingly one of dehydration; scanty concentrated urine volumes are seen, with a rising hematocrit and plasma sodium concentration. This is tolerable for a few days, but is a dangerous setting for the patient should atelectasis, embolism, sepsis, or other complications arise; he is much more vulnerable to renal failure than is his well-hydrated counterpart.

The postoperative intravenous infusions for the metabolically normal person are thus based on these six objectives:

(1) replacement of pulmonary and urinary water loss;
(2) replacement of such minor extrarenal loss of water and salt as may occur;
(3) avoidance of gain in weight or dilution of plasma;
(4) provision of 50 to 75 mE. of sodium and, if feeding is not begun in two or

three days, 40 mE. of potassium (in both cases chloride salts are used);
(5) provision of a small amount of carbohydrate calories;
(6) avoidance of inconvenience to the patient. The intravenous therapy is not to be an "all-day affair," but to be discontinued as soon as possible.

Two examples follow.

A. CASE PROCEDURE WITHOUT GASTROINTESTINAL ANASTOMOSIS

Female; weight 60 kg.; hysterectomy; nasogastric tube removed; no fever; no dyspnea.

Day 1: sips of water, broth, tea by mouth; intravenous therapy:

> 1000 ml. 5 per cent dextrose in water
> 500 ml. 5 per cent dextrose in saline

Day 2: first-stage liquids as tolerated; intravenous therapy: 1000 ml. 5 per cent dextrose in water with 40 mM. potassium chloride

Day 3: second-stage liquids as tolerated (intake 1200 ml.). One expects to hear peristalsis.
No intravenous therapy is given.

Day 4: third-stage liquids and soft solids

Day 5: continued dietary advancement

Plan to discharge on Day 8.

B. CASE PROCEDURE WITH UPPER GASTROINTESTINAL ANASTOMOSIS

Male; weight 80 kg.; subtotal gastrectomy; nasogastric tube; fever to 100.6° F.

Day 1: sips of water, broth, tea by mouth; intravenous therapy:

> 1500 ml. 5 per cent dextrose in water with 40 mM. potassium chloride
> 500 ml. 5 per cent dextrose in saline

nasogastric tube removed (450 ml. drainage)

Day 2: same oral intake; same intravenous therapy

Day 3: first-stage liquids up to 30 ml. an hour; same intravenous therapy

Day 4: first-stage liquids as tolerated, not

---

* The terms "first-stage," "second-stage," and so on, refer to the diets outlined in the Appendix and modified from Moore and Ball (1952).

to exceed 100 ml. an hour (800 ml. taken); peristalsis; flatus; same intravenous therapy

Day 5: same oral intake (1800 ml. taken); no intravenous therapy

Day 6: second-stage liquids as tolerated; no intravenous therapy

Day 7: soft solid diet; no intravenous therapy

Day 8: further advancement;

Plan to discharge on Day 10.

Variations on the above are tailored to fit sex, body weight, fever, dyspnea, and extrarenal loss. Detailed measurements of intake and output are dispensable, yet helpful for three days. Detailed measurement of body weight is unnecessary in such cases.

Dietary arrangements of the above type give little cause for concern, and need not be made complex. Most patients, and certainly the elderly, get along better if kept "on the dry side." One need be aware of the approximate intake of his patient during this period only as it bears on the general problem of dietary advancement. A patient who is in the fourth or fifth day of such a program as this, and who then acquires a surgical complication preventing further intake, must be considered as having lost lean-tissue mass during the early postoperative period even though dietary "advancement" was being carried out. With sepsis, obstruction, or reoperation, further tissue loss can no longer be viewed with equanimity. The patient will pay the price of septic starvation (page 452) or late post-traumatic starvation (page 447).

A more detailed example of case procedure for normal convalescence follows.

C. CLINICAL PROCEDURE IN NORMAL CONVALESCENCE

An unstressed, metabolically normal patient is operated upon; his management represents the handling of normal convalescence and post-traumatic catabolic weight loss. Carcinoma of the rectum with combined abdominoperineal resection is used here as an example.

1. *History.* Such a patient might be expected to have had a change in bowel habits with tenesmus and bleeding but no loss of weight. As an example let us consider a man in his fifties who is in excellent general health otherwise.

2. *Physical Examination.* This shows an early low adenocarcinoma of the rectum within easy reach of the examining finger. Proctoscopy shows it to have a broad base; no other lesions. Biopsy is confirmatory. There is no evidence of metastasis.

3. *Admission Data*

> URINE. Urinalysis shows no abnormality.
> HEMATOLOGY. The hematocrit is 42.
> BLOOD CHEMICAL ANALYSES
> > Blood urea nitrogen—15 mg. per 100 ml.
> > Plasma protein—6.8 gm. per 100 ml.
> > Plasma chloride—100 mE. per l.
> STOOL GUAIAC. Strongly positive.
> WEIGHT. 72 kg.

COMMENT. There is no evidence of bladder or ureteral involvement, no anemia, hypoproteinemia, or evidence of metabolic abnormality, corroborating the clinical impression of metabolic normalcy.

4. *Preoperative Study and Care*

> STUDY
> > Chest X-ray—normal.
> > Barium enema—no other lesions.
> > Intravenous pyelogram—normal.
> > Electrocardiogram—normal.

COMMENT. The intravenous pyelogram is necessary in such cases only in the presence of encircling lesions or lesions of the anterior wall. If it is abnormal or if there is hematuria, the patient should be cystoscoped. The barium enema is done in all cases of nonobstructing lesions to rule out the possibility of other tumors or polyps higher in the colon. Blood grouping is done.

DIET AND ORDERS. A soft solid diet is ordered, with plans for operation on the third day. Intestinal antibiotics are not necessary in preparation for combined abdominoperineal resection.

In preparation for the operation, cleansing enemas are given for the two previous days. On the day before the operation, the patient is given a light lunch, and a supper of liquids only. On the morning of the operation, a nasogastric tube is placed, an intravenous needle (a catheter in the superior vena cava may be used) inserted as a channel for anesthesia and transfusion, and an indwelling (Foley) bladder catheter placed.

5. *Operation* (Combined abdominoperineal resection)

PARENTERAL THERAPY. To replace losses, 750 ml. of whole blood is given, and 500 ml. of additional fluid is given intravenously as 5 per cent dextrose in water. Operative blood loss is estimated on the basis of sponge weights. The additional fluid merely covers current losses from skin or tube.

6. *Postoperative Orders*

Measure and record intake and output for three days.

Intravenous therapy:

500 ml. 5 per cent dextrose in normal saline.

1500 ml. 5 per cent dextrose in water.

Vital signs chart.

Nasogastric suction.

COMMENT. Postoperative antibiotics are not indicated if the operation has been uneventful and the bowel not entered. Similarly, hourly urine outputs need not be followed if the procedure has been smooth.

The "salt versus water" controversy is best settled by enough sodium chloride to cover some sequestered edema in the posterior wound, and enough water (here 1500 ml. counting the intraoperative ration) to cover lung and skin losses but to avoid antidiuretic dilutional hypotonicity.

7. *The Postoperative Days.* They should pursue a path somewhat as follows:

FIRST DAY

Colostomy opened. Nasogastric tube removed.

1500 ml. 5 per cent dextrose in water with 40 mE. of potassium chloride.

500 ml. 5 per cent dextrose in saline.

First-stage fluids as tolerated up to 30 ml. an hour.

SECOND, THIRD, AND FOURTH DAYS

Same intravenous ration.

Minimal oral advancement until flatus, hunger, and peristalsis herald returning intestinal function.

FOURTH DAY

Check weight (should be expected at about 69 or 70 kg.).

Blood analysis.

Blood urea nitrogen—normal.
Sodium—135 mE. per l.
Carbon dioxide combining power—
27 mE. per l.
Hematocrit—38.

COMMENT. Intravenous therapy can be simple and conservative in such a case. Caloric provision is minimal, and unimportant here in the first four days. A most important feature is avoidance of significant diet until the gastrointestinal tract is working well. "A scaphoid abdomen is the nutritional objective of the first postoperative days." Air swallowing or cramps dictates resumption of nasogastric suction.

The "check point" on the fourth day shows normal catabolism and no hidden bleeding, hypotonicity, or azotemia. There is no metabolic acid-base disorder of significance. Note the sparsity and simplicity of the laboratory work.

8. *After the Fourth Day.* In such a case one might expect the following:

No further intravenous therapy needed.

Colostomy function established. Oil enema may help initially.

Patient remains in bed until tenth day.*

Catheter out only when patient is up and about.

Diet rapidly advanced to six-meal bland by the tenth day.

Weight: tenth day, about 68 kg. Hematocrit 38.

9. *Discharge*

This should take place about the twelfth day.

The patient should be on 2400 calories per day at discharge.

The patient should not return to work until anabolic weight gain is well established (about four to six weeks).

---

* It is our custom to encourage early ambulation in most patients; here, with a reconstructed pelvic floor, we counsel conservatism.

CHAPTER 28

Late Post-traumatic Starvation
without Sepsis

Section I. The Nature of the Slow Loss of Tissue in the Late Postoperative Period, and the Nature of Intake Required

It is intrinsic to post-traumatic metabolism that the early rapid rate of weight loss, rapid because of the combination of starvation and post-traumatic catabolism, decelerates within a few days and reaches a much slower constant rate. Prior to this time, diet is of comparatively little significance in sparing tissue. It is at this time that exogenous caloric intake becomes the single critical factor in lessening further loss of weight and initiating tissue synthesis and weight gain. In uncomplicated trauma, this corresponds to the phase of the turning point. After more extensive injuries such as multiple wounds, or where sepsis intervenes, this plateau effect is not observed as sharply, and rapid loss of weight continues if intake cannot begin.

After this plateau is reached, the loss of weight is that seen in semistarvation—between 75 and 150 gm. a day. This slow starvation of the later post-traumatic phase will continue until exogenous caloric intake becomes adequate for tissue synthesis.

This dietary intake should ideally be enteral, not parenteral—given into the gas-trointestinal tract, preferably by oral feeding. The ability to reverse *early* weight loss and convert the intake into solid tissue and continuing anabolism by parenterally administered nutrients has never been satisfactorily demonstrated despite the large amount of work which has been done on the subject. This *late*, slow loss of weight can be materially reduced by giving the patient concentrated glucose or parenterally administered fat; the loss of nitrogen can be virtually obliterated by the parenteral administration of protein hydrolysate. *It is in resting starvation or in late post-traumatic starvation that intensive parenteral feeding is most effective and important, yet, despite these favorable factors we have never seen a patient gain solid tissue weight and pass into indubitably significant and lasting convalescent anabolism on the basis of parenteral nutrients alone.**

---

* From a theoretic point of view one should be able to produce anabolic tissue synthesis on parenteral nutrients. Failure to do so is traceable to the rest of the clinical setting as well as to the presentation of nutrients in a peripheral vein rather than in the portal vein.

Section II. Effects of Late Post-Traumatic Starvation

The more protracted this late post-traumatic starvation the more marked become the effects on the organism, yet the appearances of severe cachexia become evident at an early time only if infection or repeated trauma is also present. Remarkable examples of the ability of the body to withstand simple late postoperative starvation used to be provided by the occurrence of malfunctioning stomas after subtotal gastrectomy. This complication, which has virtually vanished from the surgical scene, was an excellent example of the fact that early post-traumatic catabolism later levels off into a more gradual loss of weight, so long as there is no further trauma or infection. The compositional defect produced is that characteristic of any sort of starvation state (see Chapter 25).

It is noteworthy that patients could go from four to six weeks with stomal malfunction, without devastating nutritional effects, provided overhydration was avoided and some glucose given parenterally. Reoperation was usually followed by good healing of the wound. Jejunostomy simplified the provision of water and salt and yielded some absorbable nutrients. It was in these patients that hypoproteinemia was soon found to be due to the overadministration of water and salt. With this avoided and vitamins and potassium provided, a seemingly good state of health and blood chemistry could be maintained. But bodily vigor did not return; the patient did not wish to get up and move around the ward. Weight continued to fall as macronutrients could not be provided adequately. Appetite was lost because of the tendency to vomiting, the presence of an indwelling gastric tube, or jejunostomy feedings. Indefinite continuance of obstruction was incompatible with survival, and after a period of weeks, though the patient's extracellular chemical situation looked reasonably normal and his general state of health appeared good, he was much more vulnerable to the development of complications should secondary operation be necessary. His vulnerability lay largely in the development of loading of water and salt with hypoproteinemia and edema, and in the development of thromboembolism or infection.

A. DURATION OF STARVATION AND INTENSITY OF ATTENDANT CATABOLIC PROCESS

It is in this setting (of late post-traumatic starvation) that the surgeon begins to tread the dividing line between those postoperative interruptions of intake that do not seem to act to the detriment of the patient and those that do. The difference between them lies in their proximity to trauma, in the duration of starvation, and in the intensity of the catabolic process accompanying this starvation. After an extensive operation such as total gastrectomy with partial pancreatectomy and partial colectomy for an extensive carcinoma of the stomach, it is frequently impossible for the patient to receive more than token oral intake prior to the tenth or twelfth day. A characteristic pattern consists in the patient having nothing by mouth for about three or four days, following which he is started on clear liquids, and these are advanced slowly according to his ability to accept them, the state of his lower-bowel anastomosis, and propulsive peristalsis. If the patient is doing well by the eighth or ninth day he will be on an intake of approximately 100 to 120 ml. an hour of stage-three liquids and soft solids. This is an intake in the 0.05/10 range, providing a total of 3 to 5 gm. of nitrogen and less than 1000 calories.

If the patient has not had any infection or abnormal elevation of temperature, he is, some time between the seventh and fourteenth days, passing through the "turning point" with a reduction of urinary nitrogen excretion, indicating that his anabolic processes are ready to begin again. The prolongation of low intake after this turning-point phase appears to "take it out of" the patient in a subtle and ominous way. The patient's strength does not rally, his morale is poor, but—most important—his lack of intake at this time has a vicious-cycle effect on appetite. The less the patient eats the less he wants to eat. For this reason he receives daily intravenous supplements. The glucose in these intravenous infusions further abolishes his own appetite, and yet the glucose itself seems important. The veins begin to become exhausted and likewise the patient. The stomach, long unused to food and accustomed instead to suction, seems to have little of the mechanical activity associated with appetite. Late post-traumatic starvation, without sepsis, has arrived.

B. TREATMENT: APPETITE

The feeding of patients who are suffering late post-traumatic starvation presents a difficult problem. The surgeon would like to provide the patient with the maximum nourishment possible in a small volume. It should also be palatable. Feedings of this type are described in the appendix; they may be useful to tide a patient through a period of small-volume gastric capacity. If the patient is able to take feedings of this type for any number of days, he will usually pass along without much more difficulty to semisolid or solid food.

Glucose kills appetite. If the patient is in the midst of a transition from intravenous to oral feeding, it is important to omit the morning intravenous infusion. This permits the patient some ward activity and permits the development of appetite, damped out by glucose infusion. Intravenous fat and alcohol do the same.

A load of food and fluid in the jejunum decreases gastric peristalsis and emptying. If a patient has had a feeding jejunostomy to reestablish enteral intake, and oral intake is now to be recommenced, the jejunostomy feedings should be discontinued for several days during this period of trial. The small bowel must be hungry for food, not filled up already, if the stomach is to empty well.

An indwelling nasogastric tube is disturbing to appetite at best, and extremely upsetting to the patient at worst. Its use must be tailored to fit the need and the patient. Some patients prefer it indwelling for a long time to the discomfort of repeated passage; others quite the reverse. When the change-over to oral feeding commences, interval aspiration is generally to be preferred to an indwelling tube.

Patients who have weathered a prolonged illness and who are again starting oral intake are frequently offered cold water or strained fruit juices as their initial dietary effort. These things do not stimulate appetite. There are very few situations in surgery in which hot coffee, hot tea, hot meat broth, and thin cream soups are harmful to the patient. They stimulate the gustatory sense and the habit of appetite. The use of whiskey or sherry or other substances designed to increase appetite is helpful. A lifelong habit of cocktails before dinner pays off here, if nowhere else. We have seen patients after a prolonged surgical illness, for whom the preparation of special types of hot foods with stimulating odor was important in again resuming the habit of appetite.

It is in the management of patients at this stage that the true mettle of a surgical dietitian is put to its test. If she attends closely to the patient's desires and dietary habits, it makes a great deal of difference to his recovery. Patients from various national origins may have certain types of foods or flavorings which are important to them and which can be added to their food or brought in by their family. A hot tamale may mean more than a hot dog, shishkabob than a banana split.

If these things fail, or if the patient continues to have a gastrointestinal or peritoneal complicating process that prevents adequate intake, we are then faced with a shift-over to prolonged intravenous feeding or prolonged feeding jejunostomy described in Chapter 31.

C. HORMONES AND APPETITE

Testosterone and cortisone have a helpful effect on appetite in these patients; testosterone-like compounds have anabolic effects of questionable value. Both have disadvantages; the achievement of positive nitrogen balance, alone, is not the objective here. The nutritional use of hormones is discussed in Chapter 32. Testosterone and related compounds are much less hazardous than cortisone and equally stimulating to appetite. Cortisone and its analogues are especially hazardous in this setting because of the danger of gastrointestinal hemorrhage and ulceration when oral intake is small.

An example of the management of such problems is contained in the following clinical procedure.

D. CLINICAL PROCEDURE IN LATE POST-TRAUMATIC STARVATION

If a patient develops stomal obstruction after gastrectomy, his management represents the handling of late post-traumatic starvation with the possible necessity for jejunostomy or, if that fails, reoperation. Large extrarenal losses usually complicate the situation.

1. *History.* Such a patient might be a man in his forties who has had a long history of ulcer intractable to nonoperative measures. He might be expected to have undergone such a procedure as subtotal gastrectomy, the procedure having been uneventful. Postoperative intravenous therapy has been initially simple: 500 ml. of normal saline solution with 1500 of 5 per cent dextrose in water containing 40 mM. of potassium chloride daily. The saline has been given to balance initial tube losses, the potassium because of dietary lack.

The nasogastric tube was removed the day after operation. The first overnight suction volume was 575 ml., a warning sign. Urine outputs were 500 and 750 ml. per day. On the fourth day the patient looked ill, was febrile with an elevated pulse rate. He was nauseated and vomited twice, about 500 ml. Aspiration of the stomach yielded 1200 ml. of bile-free gastric contents.

Physical examination may be expected to show little distention or abnormality in a normal-appearing postoperative abdomen.

COMMENT. In such cases the high volume of suction the first night is often a clue to trouble ahead. Following this large aspiration of 1200 ml., the patient's care should be changed over from simple postoperative measures to a precise metabolic management designed initially to care for extrarenal loss, and thereafter to provide nutrition during late post-traumatic starvation.

2. *Initial Steps (Fifth Postoperative Day)*

> STUDY
>> URINE. Specific gravity 1.028.
>>> Initial average hourly volume: 15 ml.
>> HEMATOLOGY. The hematocrit is 50.
>> WEIGHT. 61 kg. (admission weight: 64 kg.)
>> BLOOD CHEMICAL ANALYSES
>>> Blood urea nitrogen—20 mg. per 100 ml.
>>> Plasma protein—6.5 gm. per 100 ml.
>>> Plasma chloride—90 mE. per l.
>>> Plasma sodium—130 mE. per l.
>>> Plasma potassium—3.8 mE. per l.
>>> Carbon dioxide combining power—30 mE. per l.
>
> CARE
>> Intravenous therapy: 2500 ml. 5 per cent dextrose in saline with 40 mM. potassium

chloride at 150 drops per minute (10 ml. per minute; total time four hours).
> Continuous nasogastric suction.
> Data on analysis of gastric juice:
>> Initial daily volume—1200 ml.
>> Chloride—80 mE. per l.
>> Sodium—80 mE. per l.
>> Potassium—10 mE. per l.
>> Approximate pH—4.5

COMMENT. A weight loss of 3 kg. in four days would be a little high for subtotal gastrectomy alone and corroborates the other evidences of mild desalting water loss; estimated extracellular deficit: 1200 ml. The slight hemoconcentration and azotemia also suggest this. There is no marked acid-base disturbance; the early postoperative gastrectomy stomach does not secrete a highly acid juice; there was no preoperative acid loss. This is an infrequent setting for hypokalemic alkalosis and it is not present here. Hypotonicity is not marked, because the patient has not been overtreated with water. The initial rapid resalting should reestablish urine volume, lower hematocrit, and add weight. One should look with suspicion on its effect on the plasma protein concentration, which may fall.

3. *Continuing Program*
> Measure and record intake and output.
> Weigh two or three times a week.
> Expected daily weight loss—about 300 gm. per day.
> Intermittent nasogastric suction—using six hours of suction twice in twenty-four hours. There is no necessity for reanalysis.
> Daily gastric volume—800 to 1800 ml.
> Daily intravenous program:
>> Dextrose in saline—suction volume plus 500 ml. = 1300 to 2300 ml.
>> 5 per cent dextrose in water—1000 ml. plus 80 mM. potassium chloride.
>> Two units concentrated albumin daily for first four days.
>> One unit of whole blood each week.
>
> Calories:
>> 1000 ml. 15 per cent fat or
>> 1000 ml. 7 per cent alcohol, starting about the second or third day of the program.

COMMENT. For seven to ten days a program of this type is tolerably good. A barium

X-ray of the gastric remnant should be done the third or fourth day to assess the local situation. If patency is not established at about ten days, a jejunostomy for feeding should be done.

The albumin is important here, since edema at the stoma may be a factor. Hypoproteinemia readily occurs during the extensive electrolyte therapy needed for this patient.

The excess of chloride over sodium used here (sodium chloride and potassium chloride) should take care of any tendency for alkalosis to develop if gastric hydrochloric acid secretion tends to return. If check shows a falling carbon dioxide combining power, the program should be changed to sodium bicarbonate and potassium chloride.

Caloric provision here will do much for the patient's strength and vigor. If concentrated glucose is used it will thrombose veins. If a caval catheter is used it must be in the upper extremity, and safety from infection demands that it be removed or changed every three days. The patient should be up and about as much as possible. A nasogastric tube may be left in place or passed intermittently, depending upon the wishes of the patient.

Most important, do not rush into operative correction when the diagnosis of stomal delay or obstruction is first made.

4. *As the Stoma Opens.* In such a situation lowering aspiration volumes indicate opening of the stoma. The nasogastric tube should be placed on gravity drainage, clamped, or re-moved, depending on ease of passage. Intravenous glucose and calories should be stopped for the morning as this occurs. Appetizing hot drinks (broth, tea, coffee, depending on preference) should be given. After twelve hours, recheck aspiration. Repeated periods of aspiration may be necessary.

If jejunostomy has been needed and feedings have been begun, feedings may be instilled into the jejunum after incubation for two hours at 37° with the aspirated gastric juice. This "predigestion" reduces the tendency to diarrhea. As the stoma starts to open, jejunostomy instillations must cease for at least forty-eight hours, since jejunal filling inhibits gastric peristalsis.

A jejunostomy is rarely indicated sooner than ten days after the gastrectomy. Reoperation is rarely indicated under four weeks, or if X-ray findings suggest high jejunal rather than stomal obstruction.

Overzealous intravenous saline therapy is a strong gastric secretagogue; an upward spiral of tube loss and required replacement is easily started. The surgeon must use his judgment here. With high subtotal gastrectomy, complete stomal obstruction usually produces suction volumes in the 2000 to 2500 ml. range; higher values suggest secretagogue effect. An obstructed intact stomach is of course quite capable of losing much higher volumes. The use of hormones is quite unnecessary in such a case as indicated in this procedural example.

CHAPTER 29

Septic Starvation

Infection itself, or acute infectious-inflammatory processes in serous cavities, such as peritonitis, empyema, or ulcerative colitis, drastically alter the dynamics of starvation. The metabolic wheel is speeded up much as it is by trauma itself—only more so and for longer. The loss of body tissue is much more rapid, but it is continuing and devastating. Weight loss—up to 500 gm. per day or more—will occur for long periods, even as corrected for fluid imbalance. Very severe infection, as in peritonitis, produces weight loss as rapid as any seen after trauma: up to 1.5 kg. per day for short periods. The continuing nature of the infectious process produces a much more severe degree of cachexia than is seen after major surgery unless that, too, is followed by sepsis, as in burns or infected wounds. But, like that loss of body substance seen after severe trauma, septic starvation is also very resistant to the efficient utilization of diet; high intakes, beyond the reach of practical achievement, would be essential to obviate body wasting.

Section I.   Dynamics and Energetics

The precise tissue partition of this loss has not been documented as frequently as have the corresponding data after trauma. On the basis of the formula N $\times$ 30, a weight loss of 1.0 kg. per day with a negative nitrogen balance of 15 gm. is a loss of approximately one-half lean tissue and one-half fat, assuming for a moment that all the water of oxidation from both is also lost from the body.

The energetics of such rapid tissue loss merit consideration whether one views the matter as the conversion of potential energy into body work, or from the teleologic view as the endogenous caloric contribution to the patient's welfare during a period of high need. Assuming a weight loss of 1 kg. in a day, on the basis that one-half is lean tissue and one-half fat, we find that the 500 gm. of fat contributes approximately 4500 calories and that the 500 gm. of lean tissue contributes approximately 125 gm. of protein, which would contribute 500 calories if completely burned. In a loss of mixed tissue of this type, the caloric contribution (as well as the water provision) is greater from the fat which is oxidized than from the loss of lean tissue.

There is good evidence that the fat oxidation generally proceeds to completeness, although there is some accumulation of ketone bodies. In renal insufficiency a situation such as this adds to the acidosis. The actual quantity of this incompletely burned fat is small from a caloric viewpoint.

The same cannot be said of protein that is incompletely burned. The excretion of the nitrogenous end-product of protein combustion is carried out largely as urea. The carbon and hydrogen in the urea molecule have not been fully oxidized. The caloric significance of urea is lost as it does its duty in carrying two atoms of nitrogen into the urine in an electrically neutral form.

We have never observed patients who were in negative nitrogen balance who were not at the same time burning some fat. The converse, however, is not always true; that is, patients may be in positive nitrogen balance and still burning some fat.

A. RELEASE OF WATER

The water of combustion of this mixed tissue loss is significant because in septic starvation endogenous water is very rapidly produced. The 500 gm. of fat burned produces slightly more than 500 ml. of water. The 500 gm. of lean tissue burned releases approximately 375 ml. of water by the dissolution of tissue, this being intracellular water. The release of this water into the circulation also contributes potassium (in this instance approximately 70 mE.) as well as phosphate, sulfate, calcium, magnesium, and other intracellular electrolytes. The combustion of this protein, if carried to completeness, will result in the release of about 75 ml. of water. We therefore find that the loss of 1 kg. of tissue of this type has released into the circulation approximately 1 liter of water. If the relation of water to solute in the body is such that this water is all excreted through the kidney or if the total water balance, fever, and dyspnea are such that it is lost through both the lungs and kidneys at the same time, then the full weight loss is observed. If, on the other hand, this much tissue is lost in a setting in which extrarenal loss of water is small, and the renal excretion of water impaired for reasons of renal disease, steroid effects, or antidiuresis, its contribution to body water is not negligible.

In septic starvation "stress" is maximal and water-and-salt excretion is minimal. For example, in three days of such rapid tissue oxidation in the presence of minimal external water loss, a total of 2700 ml. of new sodium-free water is added to total body water. In a normal-sized adult male, this alone would constitute an increment to total body water in the neighborhood of 8 per cent. Assuming equilibrium distribution throughout all phases, we would expect a dilution of plasma constituents of approximately 5 per cent. In the case of sodium, for instance, this would consist in a lowering of the plasma sodium concentration from 140 to 133 mE. per l. Were such oxidation of tissue with retention of the resulting water of oxidation to be the case, the patient would not be observed to lose the full calculated weight and would become severely hypotonic in a few days. Any salt-free water administered in excess of this would only add to the dilutional trend. Such a calculation must be taken into account in the estimate of over-all water needs; if pulmonary and other extrarenal losses are large this endogenous water will contribute but a small amount to total need. But in any event the endogenous water is sodium-free and this removes in large part the necessity for the administration of other salt-free water if pulmonary loss is not large.

B. EFFECT OF SEPTIC STARVATION ON THE PATIENT

It is in septic starvation that "skin and bones" cachexia is most rapidly produced. Hypoproteinemia develops rapidly, owing to the direct loss of whole plasma protein in exudate, as well as to dilution and impaired hepatic synthesis. Edema is soon evident. Repair of this hypoproteinemia can only be carried out passively by the administration of plasma protein in some form.

The development of anemia in septic starvation is accounted for in part by the sequestration of products needed for hematopoiesis, in the area of infection, and by blood loss (direct or hidden) in the septic process itself. The lysis of lean tissue also involves the hematopoietic tissues and with them a reduced formation of the erythrocyte mass.

Avitaminosis B, as manifested by a smooth tongue, cheilosis, and violaceous lips, develops in days. Avitaminosis C is more difficult to diagnose clinically, as the oral changes of scurvy are seen only very late, but may be assumed to be developing unless large amounts of vitamin C are being given.

Loss of appetite and of peristalsis occurs at the peak of fever; as tissue wasting proceeds the septic process tends to spread or become generalized. Although severe starvation does not diminish the formation of antibodies to a single challenge, there is strong clinical suggestion that, once a septic process is established, the advance of tissue wasting interferes with antibody production somewhat as it does with the production of other proteins.

Septic starvation represents the extreme end of the starvation scale in surgery, contrasting maximally with early post-traumatic catabolic weight loss and early semistarvation. Although these latter are well tolerated and bring surprisingly few deficits, *septic starvation takes its toll quickly and leaves in its wake an exhausted, cachectic, avitaminotic patient who can ill tolerate any additional trauma or bronchopulmonary accumulation.*

Under these circumstances acute protein catabolism may proceed faster than renal function can keep pace; a rising blood urea nitrogen concentration with maintained high urine volumes is a sign of continuing sepsis and is characteristic of septic starvation.

Section II. Treatment

The treatment of septic starvation lies primarily in treatment of the septic process itself. Not until fever and acute sepsis have subsided can one make any impression on the disordered metabolism of the septic-starvation state. Again, metabolic and operative care are inseparable.

In utilization of foodstuffs, septic starvation resembles the early post-traumatic state. Catabolism is intense, and very high intakes must be achieved to have any effect on tissue wasting; diet is inefficiently utilized. Every effort must be made to satisfy those needs once the acute peak of fever is over.

During the initial invasive stage of an acute septic process with extreme malaise, oral feeding is as impractical as it is right after severe trauma. Soon thereafter, however, it must be begun. If this is impossible, then here is another situation in which high-caloric intravenous solutions have value.

Whole blood, concentrated albumin, and concentrated electrolyte should be used, respectively, for anemia, hypoproteinemia, and deficit-hypotonicity. To reemphasize: beware of adding more water to dilutional hypotonicity.

A. CLINICAL PROCEDURE

Late peritonitis following colonic surgery illustrates septic starvation and its management.

1. *The Patient.* Such a patient might be a man in his fifties, transferred for care three weeks after colon resection, the operation having been followed by wound sepsis and anastomotic disruption. The latter was exteriorized belatedly, and in the interval (twenty hours) the patient has developed generalized peritonitis and shock. The drainage wound developed local cellulitis and the primary wound dehisced—the patient was judged too sick for resuture. In such a case extensive intravenous therapy—including blood, plasma, and large amounts of saline solution—has usually been carried out. Small amounts of potassium chloride have been given. The patient has had vomiting but not the consistent signs of small-bowel obstruction. A high septic temperature has been developing again. He has been on successive changes of broad-spectrum antibiotics.

2. *Admission Evaluation,* as an example, might reveal the following:

Weight 60 kg.; normal weight 76 kg.; temperature 103.6° F., pulse 120, blood pressure 100/90. There is extreme cachexia with septic wounds, as noted. There is a gaping, partially resutured dehiscence and a fresh colostomy in midepigastrium. Rectal examination shows tender fullness in the cul-de-sac. There is dullness at the right lung base; lower abdomen is soft but with no audible peristalsis. There is slight jaundice. The leucocyte count is 26,800; hematocrit 30. The urinalysis shows bilirubin present, otherwise normal.

BLOOD CHEMICAL ANALYSES
Blood urea nitrogen—45 mg. per 100 ml.
Plasma protein—4.5 gm. per 100 ml.

Plasma chloride—92 mE. per l.
Plasma sodium—128 mE. per l.
Plasma potassium—5.4 mE. per l.
Amylase—350 units (normal = 100 to 150)
Bilirubin—D/I = 4.6/7.8
Carbon dioxide combining power—18 mE. per l.

COMMENT. A patient with such a history, physical findings, and laboratory data would have to be regarded as eminently salvageable, even though critically ill. The findings suggest cul-de-sac and right subphrenic abscesses in need of drainage. He has lost 16 kg. in three weeks, or about 5 kg. a week—a very brisk catabolism characteristic of septic starvation. He is anemic; the azotemia is characteristic of sepsis and does not indicate primary renal disease. He is slightly acidotic, yet the acidosis is supporting his potassium concentration, which may fall precipitously if he is realkalinized with sodium salts. He is hypotonic as a result of dilution and hypotonic replacement. Smoldering pancreatitis, multiple transfusions, and sepsis may account for his jaundice. The bilirubin level is not quite high enough to suggest common-duct obstruction.

3. *General Plan.* Drainage of the abscesses is by far the most important step in treatment of such a case of septic starvation. Preparation for operation can easily be accomplished in twenty-four to thirty-six hours. Operation must not be postponed longer than that. He should make only one trip to the X-ray department. Early management should be devoted to his anemia, hypotonicity, and acidosis. Antibiotics are making little contribution to his welfare at this late stage; they should be changed or stopped pending cultural study.

4. *Procedure*

PARENTERAL THERAPY—first day: slow infusion

    300 ml. 3 per cent saline solution
    300 ml. 2 per cent sodium bicarbonate
  1000 ml. 5 per cent dextrose in water with
           80 mM. potassium chloride
  1000 ml. whole blood
    2 units concentrated albumin

X-RAY FINDINGS

Chest—clear save for fluid at right base.

Abdomen—fluid level under right diaphragm. Diffuse ileus.

LOCAL TREATMENT

Careful wound hygiene; sump suction if needed.

AFTER TWENTY-FOUR HOURS

Checked blood analyses might be expected to show, as a prediction:

Hematocrit	32	
Blood urea nitrogen	40	mg. per 100 ml.
Plasma protein	5.2	gm. per 100 ml.
Plasma chloride	98	mE. per l.
Plasma sodium	134	mE. per l.
Plasma potassium	4.0	mE. per l.
Carbon dioxide combining power	20	mE. per l.

OPERATION

Subcostal drainage of subphrenic abscess (Pentothal–nitrous-oxide anesthesia).
Rectal drainage of the cul-de-sac.
Improved wound drainage.

COMMENT. If operation has provided adequate drainage of all purulent collections, further metabolic care will be a simple but prolonged affair.

Rapid preparation has been based on concentration increment of all solutes. Note the use of concentrated saline, concentrated base, and concentrated albumin. The chemical picture has been started back to normal, but of course cannot be restored in twenty-four hours. With repair of acidosis, the potassium has started to drop despite potassium chloride.

Such caloric lack is critical, yet little can be or should be done in this regard during the first twenty-four hours. With abscesses drained—if no more are present—concentrated nutritional effort can begin: at first parenteral and then enteral.

5. *Further Course.* A program of concentrated salt, albumin, potassium chloride, and blood should be continued but with some caution, gradually (in three to five days) bringing most concentrations to normal. A gratifying diuresis may be expected.

The patient's temperature would be expected to remain slightly elevated until the pancreatic and abdominal wall processes subside. Three days after drainage, caloric provision is begun.

6. *Caloric Program.* An initial attempt to increase oral calories is met by total lack of interest in food and some vomiting although gastric residuals are not high. The decision is therefore made to give intravenous calories for one week before again trying the oral route.

Plan:

(1) Measure and record intake and output.
(2) Intravenous 1000 ml. 5 per cent dextrose in water with 40 mM. potassium chloride daily.
(3) Intravenous 1000 ml. 15 per cent fat *or*
    1000 ml. 25 per cent glucose by caval catheter with insulin and chaser *or*
    1000 ml. 7 per cent alcohol.
(4) Intravenous vitamins.
(5) Intravenous protein hydrolysate to be used if fever has subsided.
(6) Crude liver extract, 3 ml. intramuscularly three times a day.
(7) Whole blood, 500 ml. every four days for three doses.
(8) Weigh daily.

COMMENT. Caloric provision here is far below requirement but after abscess drainage in septic starvation, it spares body substance.

Adequate drainage is followed by gradual resolution of fever. Antibiotics are stopped. There are four wounds to heal, one very large. Vitamin C requirement is large, near 500 mg. a day. Weight loss continues but at a reduced rate, near 250 gm. a day. Anabolism will not be solidly established until the wounds have healed.

7. *Shift to Oral Diet; Anabolism.* After eight days of such an intravenous caloric program, oral intake gradually is increased. Intravenous intake is stopped and a concentrated effort at oral feeding commenced. Early intake is poor, but is not supplemented intravenously because this destroys appetite. Each evening a 500 ml. concentrated tube feeding is given, for four to five days.* Weight would continue to drop, in part due to diuresis, as energy levels rise, fever subsides, and reconstruction begins.

Anabolic weight gain slowly mounts as the wounds heal by granulation. At least ten months will be required to restore body composition in such a case.

_____

* A small soft plastic naso-gastric tube is useful here.

CHAPTER 30

Miscellaneous Special Problems
in Surgical Nutrition

Section I. Starvation with Chronic Hemorrhage

This subject has been described briefly in Part II and is reviewed here again to place it in the broader framework of the body compositional defects of starvation.

When chronic hemorrhage has been a part of the disease process, the reduction of the erythrocyte mass is more marked than it is in nonhemorrhagic depletion. The low hematocrit coexists with a low blood volume, in contrast to the findings in nonhemorrhagic depletion. The extent of the deficit in blood volume can be gauged only very roughly from the degree of erythrocyte dilution. In hemorrhagic depletion the plasma volume, though small, is still relatively large in relation to the erythrocyte volume. This red cell dilution is accompanied by hypoproteinemia, the result both of protein loss in hemorrhage and the retention of water and salt.

The objective of preoperative transfusion in such patients is to restore the blood volume and erythrocyte concentration to normal without overcrowding the circulation, and to restore the erythrocyte volume, plasma protein concentration, and tonicity to correspond to the needs of that patient, although his needs may not correspond to "normal" for his observed body weight. The base-line starting blood volume in depletion (starvation) with hemorrhage should be assumed to be 15 per cent below the norm for that sex and weight.

The use of separated erythrocytes (settled whole blood from which most of the plasma has been removed) is recommended for those patients who are elderly or who have heart disease. They are also patients for whom the use of concentrated albumin is appropriate. The albumin should be used as the concentrate (25 per cent) and the initial infusion should be slow (2 units, or 50 gm., in an hour). A water diuresis is the ideal result and, if it is not achieved as measured by urine output, caution must be used lest the further plasma volume increment overload the circulation. A gradual build-up of plasma albumin concentration toward normal by the use of 2 units every two days for three or four doses has not produced deleterious effects, in our experience, and has a remarkable effect on the sense of well-being and on gastrointestinal function.

If brisk hemorrhage is not continuing, such transfusions can be given over the course of several days and their progress gauged clinically. If the hemorrhage is continuing and operation is imminent, these are patients in whom blood-volume and plasma-protein therapy may have to be completed during and after operation.

Chronic hemorrhagic depletion is classically seen in patients with carcinoma of the right colon, certain types of carcinoma of the stomach, and occasionally in bleeding duodenal ulcer.

Section II.   Chronic Starvation in Visceral Disease

Many of the outward appearances and compositional changes of chronic disease of heart, lungs, liver, and kidney (as well as gastrointestinal tract and pancreas) are those of starvation. The changes in body composition are analogous to those already described, save for a remarkable tendency to gain salt and water far above normal values when heart, liver, or kidney is involved. A very low hematocrit may exist with a high blood volume. These clinical problems are described in greater detail in Part V and will not be dealt with further here.

Section III.   Obesity

Marked obesity is a liability both to the patient and to the surgeon. Efforts to deal with this problem preoperatively have usually been unavailing. On rare occasions one does encounter a female patient, requiring ventral herniorrhaphy, hysterectomy, cholecystectomy, or some other elective operation, who will conscientiously reduce her weight preoperatively by dieting. This is the exception.

In most cases where we have postponed surgery in hopes of significant weight loss, we have not been rewarded. Dieting is no special hazard to those few patients who have dieted conscientiously, since a well-planned and well-balanced diet in the range of 750 to 1000 calories need impose no nutritional liability on the patient so long as protein and vitamin intake is maintained. Postoperative catabolic weight loss may get her down to base weight for the first time in years. Unfortunately it is less rapid in women than in men, and later convalescent fat gain is quite apt to restore the starting situation, a situation of genetic and psychiatric origin not likely to be altered by trauma, and strongly entrenched in habit.

Extreme obesity reduces pulmonary function, producing a chronic carbon dioxide narcosis and polycythemia ("Pickwickian syndrome") with a ruddy face and sleepiness. Like any other pulmonary insufficiency this is not a good setting for anesthesia and operation.

CHAPTER 31

Diets, Orders, and Methods in Surgical Feeding

Section I. Dietary Calculations

The characterization of dietary intake is a simple matter and need not become complicated. Most of the numbers used to describe surgical intake relate to entities that are easily estimated. The important thing is to order diets or infusions or feedings in a way which will help the patient most, with the least complexity to those engaged in his care.

Normal dietary intake is determined by the habits of the individual, his work load, sex, and the genetic factors determining the relative magnitude of fat and lean tissue. The normal-sized, healthy adult male of normal body composition, who is involved in the semisedentary work characteristic of modern urban life, eats a diet characterized about as follows:

Calories	1800–3000
Protein	80–100 gm.
Nitrogen	13–15 gm.
Sodium	100–200 mE.
Potassium	100–150 mE.
Fat	100–150 gm.
Carbohydrate	160–200 gm.

Relative caloric contribution of fat, protein, and carbohydrate—Fat 50 per cent, Protein 20 per cent, Carbohydrate 30 per cent

Calorie:nitrogen ratio—150–200 calories per gram of nitrogen

For a 70 kg. man this diet has about 0.2 gm. nitrogen and 33 calories per kg. per day or 0.2/33, using the shorthand abbreviation previously described.

A. CALCULATION BY BODY WEIGHT OR SURFACE AREA

It is chiefly in the feeding of children that characterization of dietary intake by body weight finds its greatest usefulness. Translation to surface area (in square meters) from height-weight tables makes the definition of dietary needs even more accurate.

The dietary requirements for adults vary according to the patient's weight, and if one is dealing with very small or very large patients, the correction of dietary figures for body weight is important.

B. CALCULATION BY ELECTROLYTE CONTENT

The amount of sodium in a normal diet varies according to the habits of the patient. Individuals who like their food well salted eat as much as 200 mE. of sodium per day. Most of the sodium taken by mouth is in the form of sodium chloride, and for this reason the ingestion of dietary sodium is accompanied by a slight excess of chloride in the body, and the normal sodium:chloride ratio in the urine is relatively low.

The amount of potassium in the diet is the function of the meat and vegetables eaten, since both of these are rich in potassium. The preparation of an oral diet containing no potassium is extremely difficult. It is possible to reduce the potassium intake to low levels by using purified carbohydrate, fat, and cereals. By contrast, a low-sodium diet can be prepared with intakes of sodium in the range of 20 mE. per l. with relative ease though with low palatability. A "no-sodium diet" is extremely difficult to prepare unless one confines the diet wholly to synthetic or crystalized substances.

C. CALCULATION BY POTASSIUM:NITROGEN RATIO

The potassium:nitrogen ratio of the diet is of interest merely because it must control the potassium:nitrogen ratio of the urine in a patient in zero balance, and therefore the potassium:nitrogen ratio of the first few hours of an abrupt starvation. Most normal diets have a high potassium:nitrogen ratio (5 to 10 mE. per gm.).

D. CALCULATION BY RELATIVE CONTRIBUTIONS OF THE CALORIC VALUE OF CARBOHYDRATE, FAT, AND PROTEIN

This type of dietary order is useful in metabolic defects such as diabetes, where there is a differential utilization of the various foodstuffs. The tendency is to increase the carbohydrate contribution over 25 per cent. In surgical patients who are not eating well, it is often valuable to have the dietitian calculate the intake of carbohydrate, fat, protein, and calories for a few days. This dietary check will give the surgeon a realistic picture of the patient's intake, and it is rare that he is pleasantly surprised; much more frequently the reverse. When a patient who has had a prolonged surgical illness begins to eat and is considered by the nurses to be eating well because he is eating at last, check often reveals that his intake is actually rather small.

E. CALCULATION BY CALORIE:NITROGEN RATIO

Calculation of the calorie:nitrogen ratio should properly be based on the ratio of nonprotein calories to protein nitrogen in the intake. The reason for this is that the calorie:nitrogen ratio acquires its significance in relation to the energetics of protein synthesis; it is therefore theoretically inconsistent to include protein calories in the calculation. An amino acid cannot contribute calories by being burned, and at the same time be available for synthesis into protein. As a practical matter the calorie:nitrogen ratio is usually expressed as ratio of total calories to nitrogen in the intake; the numerical difference is not great.

Calculation of dietary intake in terms of the calorie:nitrogen ratio is occasionally of great usefulness. In a patient taking food by mouth (even though this food be a modified soft or surgical diet), the calorie:nitrogen ratio is usually quite high. By this is meant that it is in the neighborhood of 150 to 200 calories per gm. of nitrogen, or higher. This calorie:nitrogen ratio is the normal property of natural food in much the same way that a rather high potassium:nitrogen ratio is the property of a natural diet. When the patient is on parenteral intake for part or all of his nourishment, the calorie:nitrogen ratio falls very low because it is easier to give fairly large amounts of nitrogen (as protein hydrolysate) by vein than it is to give the calories required to cover them. For instance, in 1000 ml. of a 5 per cent protein hydrolysate solution there are about 8.0 gm. of nitrogen. To cover the requirements for this to be synthesized into whole protein, the calories should ideally be at a ratio of approximately 150 calories per gram of nitrogen or higher (a total of 1200 to 1600 calories). This would require very large amounts of carbohydrate (300 to 400 gm. of dextrose). This can be given as concentrated glucose in an intravenous infusion via catheter to the superior vena cava, but it does require special measures and is difficult to provide in the form of the ordinary 5 per cent glucose infusions; there is too much water for daily needs.

One must not gain the impression from this statement that merely providing this number of calories will guarantee that the hydrolysate is synthesized into whole protein! This requires that the patient be out of an early post-traumatic or acutely septic phase, that he have the endocrine situation that leads to protein synthesis, and that he not be suffering from any further surgical complications, acute disease, or sepsis. These factors are all obviously quite beyond the control of the calorie:nitrogen ratio in the diet. Yet, if these factors are all favorable, protein synthesis will occur at its most rapid rates, provided adequate calories are given with the nitrogen in the diet. This means a calorie:nitrogen ratio of 100 or above.*

F. CALCULATION BY CONSISTENCY AND VOLUME

Soft, bland, or low-roughage diets are useful in chronic lower bowel disease and after anastomotic operations. However, if the patient chews well they are rarely necessary and

---

* This calorie:nitrogen ratio is based on enteral (i.e., oral) protein as the source of the nitrogen. When intravenous infusions of protein hydrolysate are used a higher calorie:nitrogen ratio is required for synthesis.

deprive the patient of much dietary pleasure. When used, they need rarely be continued for long. The stepwise dietary advancement using three stages of liquids and soft solids falls into this category and is useful only for short periods of time.

Diets that provide "maximum nourishment in minimum volume" do have a place where gastric capacity is small. This is often achieved by dint of high concentrations of solute per unit water, the precise situation that leads to serious solute-loading hypertonicity if more water is not given by some route.

Diets of these several types are found in the Appendix.

Section II.   Tube Feedings

A certain proportion of patients on intravenous feedings, in whom the change-over to oral alimentation cannot occur, are assisted to more adequate intake through the use of feeding tubes, feeding gastrostomy, or feeding jejunostomy.

If a patient is unable to eat satisfactorily because of a lesion in the gastrointestinal tract which appears to be obstructive or motor in origin, one should not hesitate to introduce barium so as to outline the nature of the fault more accurately. This is particularly true when the obstruction seems to be at the cardia or at the lower portion of the stomach, either in the duodenum or at a gastrojejunal anastomosis.

The hazards of introducing barium in upper gastrointestinal obstruction have been overemphasized. The patient is intubated, and the barium can be readily removed. The inspissation of barium, which is so uncomfortable for the patient in its removal, takes place in those portions of the lower bowel where dehydration of the luminal contents is a normal physiologic process: in the colon, particularly the left colon. This point is mentioned here since patients are frequently kept on parenteral alimentation for long periods of time without a diagnosis as to the nature of the obstructive difficulty. The result is failure to

use other forms of enteral feeding which may be much more effective than the intravenous route.

If the failure is due to lack of interest in food, then the introduction of a gastric feeding tube for tube feedings—a helpful temporary measure to accustom the stomach to food again—is justified. If the patient is semicomatose and unresponsive, tube feedings are dangerous because of the possibility of pulmonary aspiration, and must be cautiously used. A soft vinyl plastic feeding tube may be introduced into the stomach and a feeding mixture run into this tube. Several precautions are essential in initiating this step in any patient; these precautions may be lifesaving in patients who are comatose or semicomatose.

1. First Day

On the first day of such feedings, it is best to use saline solution only, in small amounts. After an interval during which the material is run slowly into the stomach or introduced in injections of 30 to 60 ml. every hour, the patient's stomach should be allowed a period of an hour or two of rest and then the entire gastric contents should be withdrawn. If the material is not going through the stomach and into the lower bowel, this will be evident, and the fatal error of starting with intensive feeding in the face of poor emptying can be avoided. If such precautions are not taken, the patient will vomit and may aspirate the tube feedings within the first two or three days, terminating the illness with aspiration pneumonia. The tragic error of introducing feedings directly into the lungs will also be avoided.

The use of saline solution for these initial "feedings" has some significance since the introduction of tap water will only abstract salt when subsequently withdrawn.

2. Second Day

Assuming that the first day's test run with saline solution is satisfactory, then a mixture consisting of half-and-half boiled skimmed milk with saline solution or lime water may be introduced for the second day. This may be used in somewhat larger quantities, and again the ability of the stomach to transport it into the bowel should be critically tested by withdrawal at least twice during the day.

3. Nutritious Mixture Begun

If the tube feeding procedure then appears to be going satisfactorily, a routine can be commenced in which 500 ml. of a nutritious feeding mixture is given by gastric tube. These formulas are described in the Appendix. This is increased to 1000 ml. the second day, and at this point nutritional maintenance is approximated. It is advisable to keep the patient at this level for about a week before increasing it to any more ambitious amount. The bowel habits of the patient may be affected. Diarrhea occasionally occurs in patients under gastric-tube feedings, but in debilitated patients fecal impaction may be present, and this, rather than the feedings, may be the cause of the diarrhea. It should be watched for by repeated rectal examinations until a regular bowel habit has been established. In gastrostomy or gastric-tube feedings the amounts are given in intermittent feeding loads which stimulate gastric peristalsis, whereas jejunostomy feedings must be given in a constant slow drip.

4. Provision of Adequate Water

In the use of any sort of tube feeding, adequate amounts of water must be provided. The normal osmolar provision of the daily diet is 1200 mO., and this is accompanied by the administration of approximately 2400 ml. of water for an average "intake osmolality" of approximately 500 mO. per l. (or 2 ml. per mO.), an osmolality approximately equivalent to that of normal urine. In the seriously ill patient, the solute discharged from the glomerulus may be further contributed to by the catabolic products of tissue breakdown. If the patient's kidneys are not working well and are unable to respond with a high urine osmolality to an antidiuretic stimulus, or if there is a large solute load, there is the setting for the production of plasma hypertonicity by concentrated tube feedings. This frequently occurs in the unconscious patient, because the individual cannot complain of the telltale symptom: thirst. This is described in detail as the pattern of "solute-loading hypertonicity" on page 370 and is readily avoided by providing extra water, particularly where renal function is poor.

5. Feeding Gastrostomy

If there is benign obstruction at the esophagus or cardia, the performance of a feeding gastrostomy is useful. The simplest possible form of gastrostomy is the best; it consists of concentric pursestring sutures placed around a #18 or #20 F catheter. We have had no trouble with such gastrostomies and have not found any reason or necessity for performing the more complicated valve-type plastic gastrostomies. Some patients have used such gastrostomies as their only form of alimentation for as long as a year.

6. In Uncontrolled Malignancy

If the patient has uncontrolled malignancy, one must question the concept that prolongation of life through gastrostomy feedings is merciful. With benign lesions the feeding gastrostomy can achieve a high degree of usefulness. It is important to observe that patients with terminal carcinoma of the hypopharynx and esophagus do not do well with feeding gastrostomies and that, generally speaking, these are not a good form of palliation. They bring with them a high mortality rate and rarely accomplish much for the patient.

7. Feeding Jejunostomy

Feeding jejunostomy is useful only on rare occasions. The avoidance of continuous intravenous therapy is a blessing to the chronically ill patient. The jejunal site for insertion of the catheter is indicated where the presence of disease makes the stomach unavailable. The jejunal site must be selected with care, and this can be quite difficult under local anesthesia in a sick or distended patient. Every attempt should be made to achieve positive identification of the ligament of Treitz so that the catheter can be introduced as high as possible. A simple Witzel type of jejunostomy catheter insertion is used. The initiation of a feeding jejunostomy is a much more trying and difficult procedure than is the initiation of tube feedings or gastrostomy feedings. The catheter should be left on suction for the first twenty-four hours until there is good sealing around it. At this point, the saline or balanced-salt solution can be introduced in small volumes for the first day, using a continuous drip. This, then, can be followed by a mixture of half-and-half boiled skimmed milk and lime water, shifting gradually over to one of the jejunostomy formulas indicated in the Appendix. The use of paregoric, deodorized tincture of opium, codein, and other such substances, as well as boiled skimmed milk, may help to avoid jejunostomy diarrhea. It has been our experience that when we measure the fecal nitrogen on patients on feeding jejunostomies it is often elevated to 5 or 6 gm. even in the absence of diarrhea. Patients rarely gain weight on a feeding jejunostomy, although their condition may improve remarkably.

The incubation of jejunal feedings with gastric aspirate provides the ideal predigested jejunal feeding. To do this the jejunal feeding and the gastric aspirate are mixed in equal proportions and incubated for thirty to sixty minutes at $37°$, then resuspended and added slowly to the jejunal feeding system.

8. Contraindications to Feeding Jejunostomy

Feeding jejunostomy or gastrostomy obviously should not be introduced in a patient who has continuing intestinal obstruction or ileus. The jejunum and ileum should indicate their readiness to accept food by ability to achieve a normal state of collapse and some evidence of peristaltic activity.

9. Shift to Oral Feedings

In shifting over from tube feedings to oral feedings, it is essential to omit the gastrostomy or jejunostomy feedings for a day or two, since a full jejunum kills appetite and gastric emptying much as continuous intravenous infusions of glucose do.

10. Preoperative Use of Feeding Jejunostomy or Gastrostomy

The preoperative use of feeding jejunostomy or gastrostomy is of limited practical usefulness. One occasionally sees individuals with obstruction of the esophagus and stomach in whom the degree of cachexia is so severe, the extent of weight loss so great, and the chemical imbalance so marked that a period of enteral alimentation through feeding gastrostomy and jejunostomy is advisable. More commonly the objective is to get the patient to the operating room without edema and hypoproteinemia, without significant acid-base disturbance, and with normal colloid osmotic pressure. These steps can often be taken and accomplished by parenteral means more easily than they can by gastrostomy or jejunostomy; the major nutritional damage (starvation) has been done and there is not time to repair it before operation. The more limited objective is usually advisable, and only in rare and special cases is a prolonged tube feeding used as a preliminary to operation. Where, in the exceptional case, preliminary gastrostomy or jejunostomy is performed, one should then rightfully give the patient an adequate period of time to make maximum nutritional use of this step. Four to six weeks should see some change in the patient's body composition, if the material provided in the tube feedings is well designed and well absorbed.

Section III.   Prolonged Total Intravenous Feeding

A. DEFINITION AND OBJECTIVES

If the patient has passed through the early postoperative catabolism and the turning point characterized by a decreasing urine nitrogen excretion and an obvious readiness to accept enteral calories and nitrogen, and yet such cannot be supplied because of the continuance of gastrointestinal, peritoneal, or septic complications, then prolonged total intravenous feeding may become essential.

The shift-over to prolonged intravenous feeding should be a conscious act on the part of the surgeon and not merely a continuance, by default, of the "daily intravenous" which has characterized the previous week or two of postoperative care. Prolonged intravenous feeding is an honest attempt at "intravenous diet"; the "daily intravenous" is largely water and salt.

During the early postinjury period, the purpose of intravenous supplementation is to provide the patient with water and salt necessary to cover renal function and losses of fluid through lungs and skin. He is given some glucose with the hope that it may decrease tissue loss, and he is given salt as required by his losses. This sort of intravenous regimen is not in any sense related to the actual objectives and details of prolonged intravenous feeding.

The terms "total" and "prolonged" intravenous feeding should refer to a conscientious attempt by the surgeon to provide the patient an intake of calories, of nitrogen, and of other substances which at least approximates the maintenance requirements of the body. Patients on prolonged intravenous feeding rarely gain weight by tissue synthesis, yet it is conceivable that this might some day occur as intravenous alimentation is further perfected and concentrated. The immediate objective is rather to avoid significant further destruction of the body's substance by oxidation of fat and protein.

The total volume provided in the daily intravenous feeding is a critical factor because it is an easy matter to exceed volumes of fluid that the patient can readily excrete. In the adult, a total daily volume in the general range of 2000 to 2500 ml. is reasonable. It is permissible to increase this to 3500 ml. in normal-sized adults if close watch of the urine output and patient's weight indicates that water loading is not occurring and if heart, liver, and kidneys are normal.

The carbohydrate provision is best given as concentrated glucose through a catheter to the superior vena cava. Such an intravenous catheter should not remain in a single vein for longer than three days because of the risk of septic thrombophlebitis. This is particularly true if the patient is harboring an infectious process in the body, for in such patients there is an intermittent bacteremia, and the tip of the intravenous catheter becomes the site on which such bacteria lodge in small platelet thrombi.

1. Resting the Gastrointestinal Tract

An additional indication for this therapy lies in the fact that total parenteral alimentation appears to put the gastrointestinal tract and its appendage organs to rest in a way that will minimize gastrointestinal function and secretion. In obstruction and inflammation of the gastrointestinal tract a period of healing is provided by total parenteral alimentation which cannot be provided any other way. Total parenteral alimentation provided in peritonitis also has this function of producing motor and secretory rest of the gastrointestinal tract. It is rare that total parenteral alimentation is required or tolerable for a period longer than one month.

B. WHOLE BLOOD

In patients on prolonged intravenous feeding, it is advisable to give one transfusion of whole fresh blood each week, thus providing a volume of erythrocytes and at least some of the trace minerals and electrolytes found in living tissue and ordinarily ingested in a mixed diet. Such substances include copper, zinc, and magnesium. The provision of calcium and phosphorus in the intake of such patients is still an uncertain point. If the patient is immobilized, the release of these elements from the skeleton is sufficient to cover any reasonable requirement for these ions in other parts of his body composition.

C. CALORIE:NITROGEN RELATIONS; TISSUE SYNTHESIS

The problem in this type of intravenous alimentation is again to provide sufficient calories to cover the proper utilization of the nitrogen. If caloric provision is minimal, nitrogen utilization is also minimal when the nitrogen is provided intravenously as protein hydrolysate.

Many such patients have some elevation of blood urea nitrogen concentrations. It is not altogether logical to present their internal environment with a still greater increase in mixed nitrogen compounds of small molecular weight (of which they already have a surfeit) when they are unable to convert their own nitrogen into protein. Elevated nonprotein nitrogen concentrations in the blood indicate the accumulation of compounds (of which urea is the largest quantity), all representing ultimate breakdown products of the degradation of protein. Such breakdown products are also substrates for synthesis insofar as they include the amino acids, and those amino acids essential for protein synthesis in man. For this reason, more than any toxic effect, it is important not to waste protein hydrolysates in patients with azotemia. Potassium should be provided in prolonged intravenous feeding, at about 40 to 80 mE. per day.

The factor that most commonly interferes with the anabolic efficacy of total parenteral alimentation is the continued presence of infection or the necessity of repeated surgical procedures. Prolonged and unresolved invasive infection, as is seen for example in burns, produces a continuing catabolic intensity which parenteral alimentation can diminish but not abolish.

D. INTRAVENOUS CALORIES: GLUCOSE FRUCTOSE, ALCOHOL, FAT

1. Small Glucose Infusions

Small amounts of calories, in the region of 200 to 500 a day, as are provided by ordinary 5 per cent dextrose in water, are beneficial to the starving patient. In the situation of resting semistarvation as studied in relation to the life-raft rations, it was shown that small amounts of carbohydrate alter the urinary excretion of salt and that they spare body protein and fat, as they do in the preoperative state.

There is no objective evidence in the literature that the 200 to 500 calories a day provided by 5 per cent dextrose in water make any material difference in the postoperative welfare of the patient after elective surgery. On a clinical basis, they appear to help. One must leave this question *sub judice* and consider that the best step is to give the glucose; it apparently does no harm. It is surely not enough calories to make any difference in the other more critical situations, such as late post-traumatic starvation and septic starvation. It is in these situations that extra calories are needed.

2. Concentrated Glucose by Caval Catheter

The use of concentrated glucose has been mentioned in several of the foregoing sections. Used as 25 per cent glucose, it provides 1000 calories per l., which means that without hazard the patient can be given 800 to 1200 calories a day by this route.

This concentrated glucose is irritating to veins in the periphery and has been used as a sclerosing agent. If a small polyvinyl catheter is placed up the brachial vein and into the superior vena cava, this amount of glucose may be run in without difficulty. The superior vena cava is far safer than the inferior vena cava as a site for such a catheter. There is a materially greater hazard of serious thromboembolism in the inferior caval system. The dangers of leaving in the intravenous catheter for longer than three or four days have already been pointed out.

Glucose given in this way will spill into the urine. The actual total fraction of wasted glucose is very small, being in the neighborhood of 1 or 2 per cent. This acts as an osmotic diuretic, combats water loading, and may actually dehydrate if mild diabetes is present and unrecognized.

a. The "Chaser." The severe hyperglycemia produced by concentrated glucose infusions calls forth a production of insulin from the patient's pancreas. If the glucose infusion is suddenly stopped, a reactive hypoglycemia will result which becomes symptomatic; if cardiovascular function is poor, this may be dangerous. Severe hyperglycemia may also be bothersome to the patient symptomatically, and it certainly destroys all vestiges of appetite. It is therefore advisable to follow the 25 per cent glucose with a "chaser" of 5 per cent glucose (250 to 500 ml.) to avoid reactive hypoglycemia.

b. Glucose Plus Insulin. It is logical also to add insulin to this infusion and avoid hyperglycemia. The infusion is better tolerated and possibly better oxidized with less spill in the urine. It will be noted that this mixture involves a great deal of insulin, but one need have no apprehension about this as long as, when the infusion is stopped, it is followed by a 5 per cent glucose "chaser." Without this, a severe and even fatal hypoglycemia might be produced by the prolonged action of the insulin in the absence of the covering carbohydrate.

Combination intravenous infusions of glucose and insulin should never be given during or immediately after operations. If the infusion is accidentally stopped this may not be known to those in charge, no "chaser" will be given, and the patient will have insulin hypoglycemia and may go into shock. Under anesthesia the diagnosis is difficult and the confused clinical picture is seldom unraveled, even by the pathologist.

For intraoperative use, the glucose should be at the 5 per cent level; any insulin given should be regular insulin or crystalline insulin and should be given by the subcutaneous route in small doses unless the patient is a diabetic.

In the conscious patient, adding insulin to the concentrated glucose infusion reduces urinary wastage of calories and avoids wide swings in blood glucose concentration. It is added at a dose of 25 to 50 units of regular insulin per 100 gm. of glucose. This is a large dose, but smaller doses do not materially affect the blood glucose when given in a long slow infusion. A "chaser" of 5 per cent dextrose in water must always be used.

Hyperglycemia lowers plasma sodium concentration drastically. This seems to be a compensatory change maintaining normal osmolality in the presence of high crystalloid concentrations, and is accomplished by the withdrawal of cell water.

3. Fructose and Invert Sugar

Fructose enters the muscle cell without the necessary intermediate action of insulin. It is therefore useful in patients with diabetes, liver disease, and pancreatic insufficiency. Other than these rather rare indications, it has no significant advantages over glucose. It is more expensive.

4. Alcohol

Moving up from the carbohydrate yield of 4 calories per gm. to 7 calories per gm., we come to the intravenous use of alcohol. The material is well tolerated, is apparently burned to completion, and does supply a useful intravenous source of calories. Alcohol is excreted in fairly large quantities in the urine and to some extent through the lungs, but the losses by these routes are not excessive. If the material is run in too fast, the patient gets drunk. This intoxication may be a very bothersome symptom, especially to elderly people who are lying in bed with something dripping in the arm. The rest of the social setting is not present for them to recognize the symptom as one they might possibly welcome. A degree of somnolence and sedation may either precede or follow the intoxicated aspect, and in some patients this is quite useful. In patients with terminal malignancy or patients with apprehension, these side effects of alcohol may be very useful. In an elderly patient whom one is trying to keep moving about in bed to maintain muscular activity so as to avoid thrombophlebitis, the deep sedation produced by intravenously administered alcohol is not welcome.

Alcohol is used intravenously in concentrations of 5 to 10 per cent. We have studied the combination of alcohol with glucose and amino acids so as to provide a solution which in one bottle provided enough calories to cover the synthetic requirement of the conversion of the amino acid into protein. These rather complicated "cocktail mixtures" of nutrients seem to be no more effective than the various nutrients given in sequence. Their use is appealing but they are analogous to the "cocktail mixtures" of electrolytes: interesting but rarely needed.

5. Fat

The perfection of intravenous fat emulsions for use in surgical patients has been an objective sought for at least fifteen years. It is now a realization.

Biologic proof of utilization was settled long before the problems of production and preservation had been worked out. The demonstration that intravenous fat was completely burned, provided useful calories, and was not subjected to some sort of storage or foreign-body reaction came almost ten years before the production of a stable emulsion that could be kept in a bottle on the shelf.

A 15 per cent fat emulsion given intravenously provides about 1350 calories per liter. This begins to approximate caloric requirements through intravenous feeding. In late post-traumatic starvation and in septic starvation, the use of intravenously administered fat is strongly indicated. In occasional patients suffering from such conditions as ulcerative colitis, late sepsis, continuing intestinal obstruction, esophageal obstruction, or unrelieved gastric obstruction, this fat will also be of critical usefulness.

Reactions have been recorded when fat was given daily for thirty days or more to normal volunteers; these reactions consisted of fever and jaundice. They have not been observed in shorter-term treatment in surgical patients.

Section IV.   Clinical Balance

It is occasionally useful to put sick patients on what amounts to a modified metabolic-balance regimen; such a step can be instituted for almost any patient in a well-equipped surgical hospital. The concept of clinical balance was mentioned briefly in the section on extrarenal electrolyte loss (page 303). Such a procedure is of more import as an organizational step and in bringing forward for daily consideration the data on the patient, than it is in any laboratory or analytic complexity. If a hospital is not equipped to carry out such a simple series of measurements as these, it probably should not take care of critically ill surgical patients but should instead transfer them to some other institution that is properly equipped. The following steps are taken in carrying out a clinical balance so as to follow the progress of a seriously ill patient.

(1) *Weight.* The patient is weighed while critically ill, either daily or twice a week, depending on circumstances. During the critical phase, measurement of weight is as important as any other single determination which is carried out. It is difficult to do; the necessary equipment is expensive and cumbersome.

(2) *Fluid Intake and Output.* The patient's fluid intake and output are carefully measured and recorded each day. As a feature of this record, one may calculate the so-called "oral balance," by which is meant the relationship of strictly oral intake to oral output through tube or vomitus. This is an effective way of assessing the patency of gastrointestinal stoma or the relief of obstruction.

(3) *"Total Insensible Factors."* From the weight and the recorded intake-output balance, it is possible to make a first approximation of the "total insensible factors." This term refers to the total unmeasured sources of weight change. These other sources are oxidation of lean tissue and fat, insensible loss of water through skin and lungs, or accumulation of sequestered edema.

(4) *Output Analysis.* The output from tube or fistula is analyzed once or twice for sodium, chloride, and potassium. If, on the basis of one or two analyses, these values are found to be consistent with the values in the litera-

ture, and constant, the analyses may be stopped.

(5) Urinalysis. The urine is analyzed for sodium and potassium, according to the needs of the case. In patients with low plasma sodium concentration, a determination of the urine sodium is important. If elevated, it suggests chronic renal disease, adrenal disease, or volume-release phenomenon producing an unregulated loss of sodium through the kidney. The determination can be carried out on "spot" samples, collected over a period of a few hours, but such samples are not as reliable as an overnight specimen covering a period when no intravenous infusions of sodium are being given.

(6) Fecal Nitrogen Determination. The determination of fecal nitrogen is only rarely useful. With patients who are having infrequent well-formed bowel movements, there is nothing to be gained in terms of ordinary surgical care by analysis of these feces for electrolytes or nitrogen. If there is profuse diarrhea, or large discharges from ileostomy or fistula, analysis should be done. Where the problem is very pressing and the patient is acutely ill, the analyses are most important in terms of sodium, potassium, and chloride. Losses of these minerals should be treated like any other extrarenal losses and replaced quantitatively. Where the problem is a more chronic matter of nutrition rather than imbalance of water and electrolyte, the determination of nitrogen in the feces may be of some significance. For instance, in jejunostomy feedings, determination of the fecal nitrogen will often show that the patient is scarcely in positive nitrogen balance because of a very large fecal loss, despite seemingly good assimilation. Such a fecal nitrogen analysis does not need to be repeated unless the regimen is altered.

(7) Blood Chemistry. Analyses of blood chemistry are carried out at intervals according to the needs of the situation.

(8) Measurement of Dietary Intake. Measurement of the intake on the clinical balance is difficult if one seeks very accurate electrolyte values for oral intake. As clinical balance is usually used, in very critically ill patients who are on intravenous feedings, the electrolyte content of the intake can be determined more accurately than is possible under any other circumstance. If the patient is taking some nourishment by mouth, the dietitian carries out a calculation of the carbohydrate, fat, protein, and total calories of the food as well as a rough approximation of the electrolytes.

(9) Measurement of Urinary Output. Use of the catheter provides the most accurate urine output collections. If available, urine creatinines provide a check on completeness of collection.

In this way, using the analytic facilities commonly available, a crude approximation of the patient's balance may be obtained and plotted from day to day. The data which are gained from this sort of study are rarely accurate to closer tolerance than ± 15 per cent. They form an approximation that is helpful in the care of the patient. The procedure should not be avoided because it smacks on the one hand of too much fancy research, or because of the allegation, on the other, that it is too inaccurate. Data from clinical balance methods permit accurate management of many severe clinical and chemical disrbances and their precise diagnosis.

CHAPTER 32

Vitamins and Hormones

Of the substances used to further the well-being of surgical patients, vitamins are used the most liberally and hormones the most hopefully. In the case of the water-soluble vitamins, little harm is done by their overuse. Money may be wastefully expended, but the patient does not suffer thereby. In the case of hormones, they are often dangerous to the patient and, unlike the vitamins, may seriously upset the patient by destroying his own endocrine mechanisms and defenses.

Section I. Vitamins

A patient who is taking normal amounts of nourishment by mouth on normal, home-cooked foods needs no vitamin supplements to carry him through even the most extensive surgical operation. Were this surgery to become complicated by the development of a septic process, a large open wound, or a prolonged period of late post-traumatic starvation, then the patient would need vitamins badly.

There is little evidence that avitaminosis plays a prominent role in the post-traumatic metabolism of the previously healthy surgical patient undergoing a normal convalescent pattern. If this patient were to await the return of normal oral intake for the provision of vitamins, there is little evidence that this would be harmful provided this interval were no greater than one week. Despite this fact, it has become common practice to administer vitamins to most surgical patients, and these vitamins fall largely into the water-soluble group of B vitamins and vitamin C. The expense of this is relatively small when considered with the remainder of surgical care. The harm to accrue is minimal, and the general view, even among workers in the field, has been to take a complacent attitude toward this common practice of routine overdosage since, though wasteful, it cannot be proved to be harmful.

In sharp contrast, preoperative starvation renders the patient liable to the development of severe avitaminosis C. There is good evidence that most patients with carcinoma in the gastrointestinal tract enter the hospital in borderline states of avitaminosis C. Some have severe scurvy. Minor changes around the oral mucous membrane in such patients additionally suggest some avitaminosis of the B group. There is every reason to believe, though it has never been proved in a controlled series (and probably never will be), that the administration of vitamins to such patients preoperatively, intraoperatively, and postoperatively is beneficial.

Of the nutritional factors that have been related to wound healing over many years of study, ascorbic acid leads all the others in importance and specificity. The most reliable way that experimental animals can be rendered assuredly unable to heal wounds is by

Page 469

producing scurvy in them; one of the few demonstrations of abnormal wound healing in man controllably produced and controllably rectified has been that in avitaminosis C, and virtually the only nutritional defect known which will cause the completely healed wound to reopen is avitaminosis C. Virtually the only phase of wound healing in which avitaminosis does not—as yet—seem to be regularly implicated is the specific lesion of wound dehiscence.

When large amounts of water-soluble vitamins are given in high concentration intravenously, they are poorly retained. The amount of vitamin C given parenterally to surgical patients seems to be in large excess over the actual daily requirement. As long as subclinical scurvy continues to be demonstrated in surgical patients, as long as vitamin C continues to be one of the most critical single factors in wound healing, and as long as the material is as inexpensive and nontoxic as it is, it is difficult to find fault with this procedure despite the waste.

A. VITAMIN THERAPY IN RESTING SEMISTARVATION

In the patient approaching surgery with resting semistarvation with no overt signs of deficiency, and with weight loss, it is standard practice to give blind therapy with vitamins. It is blind merely because there is no ready method, adaptable to daily clinical use, of determining the extent of avitaminosis. Amounts of vitamin C in the range of 100 to 500 mg. per day and of vitamin B should be given from the day of operation until oral intake is renewed. The daily vitamin B dosages for such cases are in the following ranges:

Thiamine	5–15 mg.
Riboflavin	2–20 mg.
Nicotinic acid	50–100 mg.
Pyridoxine	10–25 mg.
Pantothenic acid	10–25 mg.

The vitamin K dosage for parenteral use in such individuals is about 5 mg. per day; with jaundice or other conditions favoring avitaminosis K, 50 mg. is used. For the treatment of established hypoprothrombinemia, 50 to 200 mg. is used.

B. VITAMINS IN SEPTIC STARVATION

Turning from these situations to that of septic starvation and intrinsic disease of the gastrointestinal tract, there is a marked contrast. Patients with peritonitis, empyema, retroperitoneal sepsis, infected wounds, and other causes of septic depletion develop obvious avitaminosis with great rapidity. The large wound and the septic areas appear to consume vitamin C. The increased metabolic activity of these patients (as demonstrated either by measurement of their oxygen consumption or by their rate of weight loss) is associated with an increased requirement, destruction, or excretion of vitamins. In such patients, much larger doses of parenterally-administered vitamins must form a part of daily therapy.

The same is true in patients with certain intrinsic diseases of the gastrointestinal tract, of which regional enteritis and ulcerative colitis are the most prominent. When there is fever and rapid wasting, avitaminosis rapidly develops and is soon evident clinically. Therapy must consist of parenteral administration of vitamins in large doses.

C. VITAMIN K

Avitaminosis K develops when the emulsifying action of the biliary and pancreatic secretions is reduced or absent owing to liver disease, biliary obstruction, or malabsorption from other causes. A strictly dietary (that is, intake) deficiency of vitamin K is difficult to produce aside from total starvation because the vitamin is synthesized by bacteria in the gut.

The synthesis of plasma prothrombin from the absorbed vitamin K is entirely carried out in the liver. When liver function is decreased, hypoprothrombinemia therefore occurs, even though intake and absorption of vitamin K are normal. Therefore the study of blood prothrombin content by appropriate measures of blood coagulation is a test not only of avitaminosis K but, when vitamin K is given parenterally, of the ability of the liver to synthesize this protein.

When liver disease is present, large doses of vitamin K_1 oxide promote prothrombin synthesis when other methods of administration fail. Whenever vitamin K is given, the prothrombin concentration should be measured before and after administration, to assess both the status of the liver and the ability of the patient's blood to clot satisfactorily at operation. A distinct tendency to bleed is present with prothrombin concentration below 20 per cent; at a persistent level between 20 and 70 per cent surgical hemostasis may be normal but liver function is suspect; over 70 per cent there need be no apprehension on either score.

The intestinal use of antibiotics interferes with vitamin K synthesis and absorption and should be covered by giving vitamin K by mouth.

The administration of bishydroxycoumarin (Dicumarol) produces hypoprothrombinemia without producing avitaminosis K and acts by interference with the synthesis of prothrombin rather than the absorption of the vitamin. It is counteracted by vitamin K, vitamin K_1 oxide, or transfusion of fresh blood.

Vitamin K should be given preoperatively to patients who have been semistarved, those in whom biliary obstruction exists (preoperatively or postoperatively) or those in whom postoperative starvation is prolonged, those with defects in liver function and intestinal absorption, and those on intestinal (that is, nonabsorbed or orally administered) antibiotics.

Vitamin K can be given parenterally in two forms, either as vitamin K or as vitamin K_1 oxide. In the presence of hypoprothrombinemia due to extrahepatic biliary block but accompanied by good liver function, small amounts of parenteral vitamin K result in rapid restoration of the prothrombin level to normal. When there is liver disease, when bishydroxycoumarin has been administered, or when there are other factors interfering with the synthesis of prothrombin, then it is justified to use the more expensive vitamin K_1 oxide. This material is a fat and must be completely emulsified before being given. Fat embolization has resulted from the careless use of this material intravenously.

Disorders due to lack of absorption of other fat-soluble vitamins (A, D) are rare in surgical patients. We have seen a patient with chronic liver disease of the cholangiolitic type in whom night blindness developed, a troublesome symptom when the patient was called upon to drive a car. This responded specifically to massive doses of vitamin A given by mouth, even though absorption was poor.

Section II.   Adrenal Hormones and ACTH

In the use of adrenal hormones one must discriminate between those effects that are the result of replacement of a lack of normal function, as in adrenal insufficiency, and those pharmacologic effects that result from the excessive administration of the hormone to persons with normal adrenal glands. For the purposes of this section, we are devoting our attention only to the latter category. This deals with general and "supportive," rather than "replacement," use of hormones. The use of adrenal hormones in hypoadrenalism has clinical significance far greater than any seen in patients with normal adrenals, and is described in Part V.

A. ACUTE ILLNESS, SHOCK, AND HYPOTENSION

Where the patient has little or no adrenal function, shock quickly results from volume reduction or trauma. The use of cortisone is specific. In some patients who are in shock, though their own adrenals are working well, there is a clearly beneficial effect from the administration of additional cortisone, often in large doses.

These are uses of the hormones which should be classified as homeostatic rather than nutritional; a full account is given in the section on the adrenals (Part V) and shock (Part VI).

B. CHRONIC NUTRITIONAL DISORDERS

Patients who have been sick, semistarving, and septic for many weeks might be expected to show some form of adrenal "exhaustion," but this is not the case. These patients show adrenal hypertrophy, more reminiscent of the effects of prolonged administration of adrenocorticotropic hormone, and this appears to be the result of the chronic stress of the illness.

In chronic wasting illness, there is a characteristic reduction in 17-ketosteroid excretion. We have not been able to discern any defect here that demands treatment. Far from requiring "anabolic androgens" these same depleted patients are the very ones who anabolize new tissue most readily, and even on very low intakes, as already described. Normal 17-ketosteroid excretion returns as convalescence is completed.

1. Cortisone

In such patients the administration of cortisone occasionally results in increased appetite, desire for food, and a sense of well-being. The increased catabolic destruction of tissue which cortisone produces does not completely counterbalance these beneficial effects on appetite and emotional outlook, but cortisone, its related derivatives, and adrenocorticotropic hormone are all fundamentally catabolic in their over-all effects.

If the patient is being considered for cortisone therapy on such a basis as this, it is important to give a few initial test doses over the course of a day or two. Amounts of cortisone in the region of 25 mg. twice a day, given by mouth, or 75 mg. a day, intramuscularly, serve to indicate whether or not the patient will receive the emotional and mental support that the surgeon expects. Effects on appetite are usually quite evident. *It has been our unfortunate experience that patients who get the most marked appetite effect from cortisone are also the most prone to gastric hyperacidity and peptic ulceration as a complication of the hormone's action.* For this reason the test doses of the drug should be accompanied by the administration of aluminum hydroxide gel or other gastric antacid, on a prophylactic basis.

The administration of cortisone produces adrenal atrophy, probably through the inhibition of adrenocorticotropic hormone production. The atrophy produced is very real; the glands may become so small that they are hard to find in the perirenal fat. Surgery in the face of this atrophy is very dangerous. This atrophy can be prevented by the simultaneous or subsequent administration of adrenocorticotropic hormone, and this should always be done.

It is wise policy not to continue patients on "nutritional" cortisone therapy for more than four or five days without tapering off with covering doses of adrenocorticotropic hormones to reestablish the patient's own adrenal function. Unfortunately, this is not a general practice, and instances of severe hypoadrenalism have resulted from the careless and continuous use of cortisone in such a setting. The concomitant administration of adrenocorticotropic hormone and cortisone is rational and effective; adrenal atrophy is avoided; mineralocorticoid effects are more marked than with cortisone alone.

Yet, for all its benefits, of the hormones that are used for nutritional purposes in surgery, cortisone is certainly the most dangerous. It will readily produce bleeding peptic ulcer, or serious imbalance of the psyche or the endocrine glands.

Peptic Ulcer. Massive upper gastrointestinal hemorrhage or perforation is the commonest serious and often fatal complication of cortisone therapy in surgical patients. The supportive use of cortisone in debilitated patients (even in small replacement doses where there is adrenal insufficiency) must always be accompanied by alert antiulcer therapy in the form of alkali and atropine. Even with this precaution the hazard is not always obviated and hemorrhage may ensue. In severe burns the hazard of gastrointestinal hemorrhage is always great. The addition of cortisone or adrenocorticotropic hormone increases this hazard. Cortisone administered orally is more dangerous than intramuscular doses in respect to gastric effects.

Should there be massive bleeding, the dosage must be *increased* to tide the patient over the hemorrhage or operation, later to be tapered and stopped under ACTH therapy.

Psychic Disturbances. Nightmare or an unreasonable degree of euphoria is the danger signal. Cortisone should be tapered off, adrenocorticotropic hormone given, and psychiatric assistance sought. A full-blown cortisone psychosis may require prolonged hospitalization; contact with reality is almost totally lost.

Endocrine Complications. Adrenal suppression and atrophy occur as a function of the duration of cortisone treatment. If an operation is performed without cortisone coverage, severe shock results. If performed with cortisone coverage, there is still apt to be difficulty from mineralocorticoid deficiency. The adrenal suppression resulting from cortisone is diffuse. When trauma is superimposed, there may be severe unregulated urinary salt loss even though blood pressure is initially maintained by the cortisone. Desoxycorticosterone should be given in such a case.

These matters are also dealt with in the section on adrenal disease in Part V.

2. Adrenocorticotropic Hormone

There is a limit to the height of blood steroid producible with adrenocorticotropic hormone; with cortisone or hydrocortisone there is no effective limit. Adrenocorticotropic hormone produces a mixed adrenal discharge which cannot exceed the synthetic limit of the gland. Secretion induced by adrenocorticotropic hormone should be better "balanced" than that induced by a single steroid such as cortisone. For these many reasons, adrenocorticotropic hormone is more appealing than cortisone in this general supportive area when the patient has adrenals of his own.

This hormone has the obvious fault that it cannot be taken by mouth. Effects on appetite are usually not quite so striking as those of cortisone. Salt retention is much more prominent with adrenocorticotropic hormone than it is with cortisone. In late unhealed burns (see also page 905), adrenocorticotropic hormone seems to have a helpful effect in furthering the "take" of grafts and healing of the wounds. Its use should always be covered with antiulcer measures. Withdrawal of adrenocorticotropic hormone or cortisone is occasionally followed by venous thrombosis.

Section III. Gonadal Steroids and Anabolic Hormones

The prototype of the male gonadal steroids is testosterone. These hormones as a group are androgenic and can be demonstrated to have a consistent protein-anabolic effect in man. Testosterone propionate and related derivatives are widely used for this purpose.

In this field there are three main questions.
(1) How is this anabolic effect best produced?
(2) What good does it do the patient?
(3) When, where, and in whom should nutritional androgenic-anabolic steroid therapy be used?

A. THE ANABOLIC EFFECT

Testosterone propionate given intramuscularly in doses of 150 mg. two or three times a week produces its maximum anabolic effect. This effect is demonstrable in normal individuals on constant intake of nitrogen and electrolyte, water, calories, and protein, to whom the drug is given. A change in nitrogen balance from zero or weakly negative figures to rather strongly positive figures (that is, 3 to 5 gm. per 70 kg. per day) is readily obtainable. Evidence from the animal laboratories suggests that this nitrogen is almost wholly deposited in skeletal muscle (the development of skeletal muscle being a secondary sex characteristic in the male) and in the secondary sex areas themselves.

For this anabolic effect to be at its maximum, intake must be at a good level—in the region of 0.1/30 (7 gm. of nitrogen and 2100 calories in a 70 kg. man, for example). On lower intakes the hormone still exerts some anabolic effect, and there is less urinary nitrogen excretion. Even on no intake the hormone is thought to exert some sparing effect on body protein, and this is the basis for its use in renal failure. The evidence on this latter point is scanty.

Anabolic tissue synthesis in skeletal muscle is a by-product of gonadal hormone action; the tissue growth is a secondary sex character. In the female, estrogens produce growth of breasts, uterus, and subcutaneous fat. In the male androgens produce growth of larynx, penis, seminal vesicles, and skeletal muscle. To ask what the mechanism of this is, is to restate the basic question "How do steroids affect tissues?" the answer to which is unknown.

The separation of the sex-organ growth factors ("androgenic") from the muscle-growth factors ("anabolic") has appeared chemically possible, commercially appealing, and, if the drug is to be used over a prolonged period, clinically desirable. Yet both aspects ("androgenic" and "anabolic") are secondary sex characteristics and there is no reason to expect them to be completely separable.

There is recent evidence that testosterone given before, during, or after surgery will diminish nitrogen loss on standard regimens. We have not been able to confirm this, but if it is true this suggests that testosterone is not only anabolic in its effect but counteracts the post-traumatic catabolism associated with activity of the corticosteroids.

Further clinical investigation should clear up some of these points.

B. WHAT NUTRITIONAL GOOD DOES STEROID THERAPY DO THE PATIENT?

If the actual data on post-traumatic effects of testosterone are unsettled, the clinical desirability is even more so.

The process of getting well involves a prolonged protein-anabolic phase, identified as the third phase of convalescence—muscular growth. This has led to the assumption that pushing the patient up into anabolism with steroid hormones will, in itself, speed or accomplish recovery. There is no evidence to support such a view. The whole man gets well—not just his protein anabolism.

In the normal course of events no steroid therapy is needed. If the patient is late in convalescence and accepting only borderline intakes, he may make more protein if he is put on testosterone, but there is nothing to suggest that this, in itself, speeds him on his way. What he needs is, first, to be rid of tissue processes—usually complications and usually septic—that are dragging him down by increasing tissue catabolism or interfering with gastrointestinal function and adsorption. Testosterone cannot do this. And, second, he needs to increase his intake by increasing appetite and dietary intake. This, testosterone will occasionally do. Appetite is thus the common denominator, and it is in increasing appetite that the testosterone steroids have their major effect in the later nutritional problems in surgery. This accounts for the seemingly anomalous fact that both cortisone and adrenocorticotropic ("catabolic") and testosterone ("anabolic") hormones are effective in this area. It is not anabolism per se that counts. It is intake. If sepsis, extrarenal loss, and obstruction are gone, anabolism will ensue if intake is good. In fact, this anabolic tendency is strong and urgent. If stress and catabolism are on the wane, anabolism will take care of itself so long as intake is there. Therefore, what we want from a steroid (or for that matter any dietary aid) in late surgical nutrition is not anabolism but appetite; the patient will anabolize when his surgical course and his diet permit it, and without outside stimulus.

C. APPETITE

The appetite effects of the testosterone-like compounds vary. Some of those that are most strongly anabolic in rigid laboratory tests (contrasting growth of levator ani muscle with growth of seminal vesicles in the rat) have the least effects on appetite in man. Testosterone propionate is a very effective appetite agent. It need be used for only a short time, and we have not found trouble from its androgenic effects in this setting.

The concomitant use of the three agents testosterone, cortisone, and adrenocorticotropic hormone, all in small doses, makes perfectly good sense when viewed in this framework. They act synergistically on appetite and help correct ("cancel out") each other's more specific peripheral side effects which are occasionally troublesome. Antacid treatment is essential. The slowly released long-acting testosterone drugs and the oral agents of this group are a useful addition to the armamentarium.

D. BY-PRODUCTS

Mental disturbances and increased libido occur with use of the testosterone drugs. In elderly people the widespread stimulation of the sex steroids, long absent from their bodies, must indeed come as a surprise to the tissues. Small doses should be used at first.

The virilizing effects of testosterone are extremely disturbing and undesirable in women receiving the drugs over a long period of time, for cancer of the breast. This may be the price paid for good palliation in malignancy. In the short-term course needed to assist appetite and intake after trauma, this is not a problem.

E. WHEN AND IN WHOM SHOULD "NUTRITIONAL STEROID THERAPY" BE USED?

There are three principal criteria for patient selection.

(1) The patient should be conscious, alert, cooperative, but with poor appetite and intake.

(2) His complications should be abated or diminishing; he should be essentially afebrile. The presence of large wounds which have yet to complete their healing process is not a contraindication; undrained sepsis is.

(3) A functioning gastrointestinal tract is a prerequisite.

F. PROGRAM SUMMARY

A program for dietary resumption after prolonged illness, then, may include some or all of the following:

(1) A short period of gastric tube feedings to get the gastrointestinal tract accustomed again to food; the tube is then removed.

(2) Whiskey or wine before meals.

(3) Increasing ambulation.

(4) Cessation of intravenous feedings and/or jejunostomy or gastrostomy feedings.

(5) Tasty, hot foods well prepared in a way suiting the patient's habits.

(6) Crude liver extract—3 ml. intramuscularly three times a week.

(7) Testosterone (long-acting)—50 mg. intramuscularly once, or repeat in three weeks.

(8) Adrenocorticotropic hormone gel—10 units intramuscularly every two days for a week; with cortisone—25 mg. by mouth each day (to be stopped in three days); with nonabsorbable antacid—1 tablespoonful between meals.

(9) Calculation and chart of daily intake of protein, carbohydrate, fat, total calories.

(10) Chart of daily weight. When the curve starts upward put the chart on the wall where the patient can see it!

Insulin hypoglycemia has not proved an effective help to appetite in this setting of late post-traumatic starvation. Nutritional aspects of postgastrectomy states and malabsorptive bowel disease are described in Part V.

It should again be reëmphasized that the most important nutritional steps in most surgical patients are the establishment of a patent, unobstructed, functioning gastrointestinal tract and the control of sepsis with the adequate drainage of abscesses. These operative steps are usually the metabolic prelude to normal oral dietary intake and anabolism, without the need for other special measures.

CHAPTER 33

Body Composition, Starvation, and Nutritional Therapy: Notes from the Literature

Section I.   Body Composition

There have been only a few "bedside" applications that have arisen from the body compositional techniques. The importance of the study of body composition has come about instead through an increased understanding of body chemistry, and increased effectiveness of clinical treatment. The extensive discussions of blood and extracellular volume, body water, and electrolyte in such a book as this bear witness to the advances in our therapeutic approach that have arisen from such work.

An extensive review of laboratory methods and analytical details in research on body composition would be out of place here. The reader is referred to the recent review in *Metabolism* (Moore *et al.*, 1956) and to the previous reviews from these and other laboratories.

Hevesy and Hofer described in 1934 some studies on the turnover rate of water in the human body, based on the use of deuterium oxide. In the same volume of this German journal (*Klinische Wochenschrift*) was a review article by Brandt, speculating on some of the tracer possibilities of the newly discovered hydrogen isotope. In the review by Brandt there was, interestingly, no mention of the possibility of measuring total body water by dilution, and no mention of the work of Hevesy and Hofer.

In the article by Hevesy and Hofer studies were described in two adult individuals (presumably the authors) who took 0.46 per cent deuterium oxide by mouth. One of them took a total of about 400 ml. and was found, by dilution, to have a body water of 43 liters, or 63 per cent of his body weight of 69 kg. In the other individual, the total body water was not calculated or measured. The authors were principally interested in the turnover rate, and in the average length of time that a water molecule stayed in the human body. They determined a biological half-time for water as between nine and twelve days, corroborated by several subsequent workers, including ourselves. They also calculated that the average time of a water molecule in the human body under normal circumstances was about fourteen days.

As far as the measurement of body water was concerned, this is where the matter rested until we took it up in 1945. Our original interest in the field arose from our previous experience with radioactive sodium and potassium in the study of body composition by dilution, and from a conviction that deuterium would make an ideal tracer with which to study total body water. In initial correspondence with Dr. Urey, it became evident that this isotope would be available, having recently been released from its wartime and highly restricted use in conjunction with atomic energy development. It was also evident from what little we could find in the literature that the equilibrium ratios of 1.00 were achieved throughout the body within a few hours after injection or ingestion. This fundamental equilibrium characteristic is required of any dilution principle. In our 1946 publication, we described total body water measurements carried out in only one individual. At the time, we did not know of the previous work of Hevesy and Hofer; we used a Linderström-Lang gradient tube for the deuterium determination, our concentrations were very low, and the value we discovered, of 75 per cent of body weight, was unquestionably high for methodologic reasons.

Our laboratories then pursued the problem intensively and soon discovered that the falling drop method was far preferable to the gradient tube. In 1950 we published our first extensive series of total body water data in the adult human being (Schloerb et al., 1950). This was the first well documented series of total body water measurements in man. Subsequently, we have measured the total body water throughout the life's span in the two sexes and under a wide variety of pathologic conditions, as reported briefly in Moore et al. (1952), Moore (1954), Moore et al. (1956), McMurrey et al. (1958), Edelman and Moore (1951), Edelman et al. (1952, 1954, a, b), and Haley et al. (1952). An extensive review of the literature on body composition would be out of place here. The reader is referred to Edelman et al. (1951), Moore et al. (1956), and Hardy and Drabkin (1952) for bibliographic summaries of relevant work in this field.

Starting in 1944 we also attempted to measure the total exchangeable sodium and potassium with appropriate isotopes. In 1946 we described the principle $\left(V_2 = \dfrac{C_1V_1}{C_2}\right)$ embodied in these isotope dilution methods, and our initial data on water, sodium, and potassium (Moore, 1946).

In 1952 (Corsa et al.) we published our initial data on total exchangeable potassium in man.

There have been many contributions to this field of study both from this country and abroad, developing new methods, reporting the laborious work of defining significant values for the normal, or describing aberrations in disease. These include, from our laboratories, those of Schloerb et al. (1950, 1951), Friis-Hansen et al. (1951), Edelman and Moore (1951), Edelman et al. (1952), Moore et al. (1952), all of which set forth data on total body water. Contributions on total electrolyte include Corsa et al. (1950), Edelman et al. (1954, a), Moore (1954), James et al. (1954), Wilson et al. (1954), Moore et al. (1954), Edelman et al. (1954, b). In 1953 a simultaneous method for measurement of a variety of compositional entities was developed, and described in Moore et al. (1956) and McMurrey et al. (1958).

Attention is drawn particularly to the work of Pace and Rathbun (1945) on carcass analysis, Behnke (1941) on fat content, Forbes and Perley (1951) on sodium, and the studies of Cheek (1954), Davies et al. (1952), Ikkos et al. (1954, 1955), and Benson and Yalow (1955).

The foregoing list is by no means complete. The reader is referred to the aforementioned review for more bibliographic background, including historical notes on the blood volume methods. See also Moore (1954) for historical data on early developments of the preisotope era.

Because all dilution methods are indirect, carcass analysis is of great interest. Direct analytic study of body composition is a rarity and therefore worthy of special note, as in the classic contribution of Harrison, Darrow, and Yannet (1936). Nichols et al. (1953) measured the extracellular fluid directly by carcass analysis for chloride and other ions as well as water, inulin, and thiosulfate, the latter two having been injected shortly prior to sacrifice and allowed to equilibrate. They again found that tendon water has a higher chloride space than other tissues. Both inulin and thiosulfate are metabolized and do not constitute "perfect" tracers to determine dilution of extracellular fluid, nor indeed does anything else now known. The authors emphasize the importance of connective-tissue waters a being a slowly penetrated high-chloride area of the extracellular fluid.

Weil and Wallace (1955) have studied the electrolyte composition of connective tissue such as tendon, fascia, and dermis. They find more chloride than sodium; 90 per cent of the chloride was in simple diffusion equilibrium. There is no "reservoir" effect in this area as there is in the skeleton.

Forbes *et al.* (1953, 1956) analyzed two adult cadavers to study body content of ions. Previously, cadaver analyses have been rare and have been made mostly in infants (Forbes, 1955; Shohl, 1939). Widdowson, McCance, and Spray (1951) analyzed three adult cadavers. Forbes, Cooper, and Mitchell (1953) reported other constituents, including protein, in these same cadavers. The analyses of Forbes and Lewis, as well as the others, show the large amount of sodium that is not exchangeable and was previously known to be present largely in bone (Edelman *et al.*, 1954). The total potassium figures for direct analysis are also higher than the exchangeable potassium, but one cannot be certain of the significance level. The location of the small moiety of nonexchangeable potassium needs more study.

Widdowson and McCance (1956) studied body composition in five newborn babies, three fetuses, eleven newborn piglets, and seven litters of pig fetuses. They showed that very early in life there is a minor rise in plasma sodium concentration (going from 126 mE. per l. to 140 mE. per l.) and a remarkable drop in plasma potassium concentration (falling from 10.2 mE. per l. to 4.9 mE. per l.). The fall is responsible for a major redistribution of body potassium, bringing the extracellular fraction of body potassium from a range of 20 to 30 per cent (in the fetus) to 2 per cent (in the adult).

Friis-Hansen *et al.* (1951) measured the total volume of body water in children and found it to be somewhat higher in infants than in adults. Edelman *et al.* (1952) then reported from our laboratories the normal values for the entire life span.

Edelman and Sweet (1956) showed, in man, that only 1.6 per cent of the exchangeable sodium was found in the transcellular water of the gastrointestinal tract, with only 1 per cent of the exchangeable potassium (which is, incidentally, about 33 per cent of the potassium in the entire extracellular fluid). It is of interest that in intestinal obstruction this normally small figure for intraluminal sodium must rise to very large figures, which have never been measured.

Pawan (1956), using urea, found the normal body water to be 62 per cent of the body weight. He did not differentiate between the sexes. In obesity this value fell to 46 per cent with a range of from 25 to 58 per cent of body weight. With rigid dieting the absolute volume of body water fell, but the relative value rose. These data check out fairly well with deuterium and antipyrine data, but the method has neither the theoretical nor practical virtues of the deuterium method.

Skerlj *et al.* (1953) measured subcutaneous fat and studied its distribution, using the skinfold thickness. They found that the human body tends to increase fat as it becomes older. They noted the progressive tendency, on aging, to deposit fat on trunk rather than extremities. Their methods, and the concepts relative to fat distribution on aging, are certainly intriguing for further study and correlation with the dilutional methods for study of body composition.

The correlation of body composition with total body water appears to be closer than with any other comparative index. Boling (unpublished) showed that total exchangeable chloride was a linear function of total body water.

Muldowney (1957) has shown that erythrocyte mass is a linear function of lean body mass in normal man, basing the latter on the total body water and the Keys-Brozek formula. This formula for lean body mass is a derivation from total body water (the "antipyrine space") and the extracellular water—measured in this instance by thiocyanate dilution.

This naturally leads to the possibility that the size of the erythrocyte mass is determined by the oxygen requirement of lean tissue, which is the oxidizing protoplasmic mass of the body. In a later paper, Muldowney *et al.* (1957) showed that there was a significant increase of erythrocyte mass in thyrotoxicosis and a decrease in myxedema; in both conditions the erythrocyte mass was closely related to oxygen consumption. The nature of the communicating-regulating system, by which oxygen requirement makes itself known to the marrow, is still unsettled; simple anoxia is possibly one stimulus, and there may be others.

Recent evidence based on the erythropoietic response of the rat to a variety of test sera from animals after hemorrhage indicates that the kidney may be a key organ in the erythropoietic stimulus, and that it may communicate this stimulus to the marrow by a humoral agent called "erythropoietin." Removal of the kidney abolishes this strong erythropoietic response. This work has been reported by Plzak *et al.* (1955) and Jacobsen *et al.* (1957). Hydronephrosis in man is associated with polycythemia and hypervolemia (Gardner and Freyman, 1958), as is hypernephroma, in occasional cases. Erslev (1953, 1958) discusses the various aspects of this problem. It appears from this important work that some parameter of renal anoxia or decreased renal hematocrit is a stimulus to the marrow by a blood-borne agency. It is of interest that absence of both kidneys in man is not associated with as marked an anemia as is chronic renal disease. There may be other organs (liver, lung) also capable of arousing a marrow response in the presence of anemia or hypoxemia.

Section II.   The Nature of Starvation

A. ADULT STARVATION

The nature and dynamics of starvation have seldom been elucidated with more attention to correlative detail than in the work of Keys *et al.* (1950). In their work, the "Minnesota Experiment," they studied the rates and dynamics of starvation, the change in body composition, and the functional deficit. They include data on starvation obtained from famine areas, particularly in World Wars I and II, from animal and human observation, from clinical problems, chiefly since World War I. Other sources of data are their present work and the 1919 experiment of Benedict, Miles, Roth, and Smith, entitled "Human Vitality and Efficiency under Prolonged Restricted Diet." They found, as we have, that there is little functional disorganization at weight losses of 5 to 10 per cent of body weight. They felt that except for exceptional individuals, human beings do not survive weight losses greater than 35 to 40 per cent. On the basis of our studies of body composition in starvation we would modify this in relation to the pre-illness obesity status: the fatter one is, the more weight one can lose without functional deficit.

As in our laboratories, and others involved in correlative studies of body composition, Keys and Brozek found that whereas the concentration characteristics of the internal environment can vary only within narrow limits, the range of variation in the relative amount of muscles and fat compatible with health (or at least with life) is very great.

From a compositional standpoint, theirs was not an exhaustive work. Only extracellular fluid and plasma volume were measured. They did not include red cell blood volume data, exchangeable electrolytes, or total body water.

They found that during semistarvation, the basal oxygen consumption promptly and steadily declined. At the end of a period of semistarvation, the mean oxygen consumption per man had decreased 38.8 per cent; the metabolic change roughly corresponded to the rate of weight loss, indicating linear lean-tissue loss along with lysis of the obesity tissue.

As the cellular substances diminished in starvation, the cells (muscle) generally diminished in size and eventually began to disintegrate, this being noted only in cases of extremely advanced starvation. In general, the proportional loss of skeletal muscle mass was close to that for the body as a whole.

The morbid anatomy of this muscle loss is of interest. There is agreement in the literature that the individual muscle fibers are decreased in size in undernutrition and, besides reduction in fiber size, there is actual destruction of muscle cells only in extreme emaciation. Cardiac musculature and smooth muscles apparently respond to starvation, much as do the striated muscles. The brain and spinal cord lose very little weight in starvation, but the other soft tissues show larger losses, the liver and intestines, perhaps, suffering to the greatest extent of any of the viscera. The heart and kidneys tend to lose less weight than would be proportional to body weight. The most significant effect of starvation of the blood vessels is an early appearance of changes ordinarily seen at more advanced age. Probably the weight of the skeleton decreases somewhat in starvation, but less than the body weight as a whole, proportionately.

Anemia has been listed as one of the three major causes contributing to death in the severely undernourished. The evidence is overwhelming that anemia develops during prolonged periods of caloric restriction, and the degree of anemia appears to be related to the extent of starvation. As in our data, Keys and Brozek found that the volume aspects of this anemia are quite remarkable. In the Minnesota Experiment, the percentage loss in total hemoglobin concentration was only slightly less than the percentage loss in body weight. Yet, if allowance is made for the increased hydration—increase in plasma volume and extra volume of fluids and edema that occurred during semistarvation—the total body hemoglobin increased in terms of grams per kilogram of body weight.

Mollison's work in 1946 had suggested some reduction in total blood volume in starvation. It was believed that this change was less, in proportion, than the body weight loss in starvation. Perera, in 1946, reported plasma volumes 17.2 per cent above the normal average in starvation. The work of Beady, Herbert, and Bell in 1948 indicated that semistarvation produced little, if any, change in the absolute total plasma volume.

Data on surgical patients from our laboratories virtually always show a relative increase in plasma volume in starvation, with a low erythrocyte volume and a resultant dilutional anemia. Actually, the plasma volume and extracellular fluid volume appear on the basis of our data to maintain constancy while the rest of the body shrinks; the "chassis shrinks around the engine."

In the Minnesota Experiment, after twelve weeks of semistarvation, the body weight declined slightly more than 15 per cent. The blood volume figures (relative) had risen to 53.92 ml. per kg. for plasma and 89.8 ml. of total blood volume per kg. of body weight (5.4 and 8.9 per cent body weight, respectively). Even in absolute terms, the plasma volume increased in starvation an average of 8.3 per cent. The total blood volume, however, diminished by 8.5 per cent, reflecting the fact that there was a considerable degree of erythrocyte volume contraction at this time. At a time when body weight had fallen more than 23 per cent, the plasma volume had risen to a relative value 40.9 per cent greater than in the normal control state. Here again this suggests an absolute as well as a relative increase.

All students of starvation have devoted attention to the nature of the overhydration that is characteristic of late starvation. As described elsewhere, the dilution data indicate that there is a relative increase in total body water and the extracellular fractions as the fat and intracellular fractions decrease. The Minnesota study noted that general causes of famine edema are sheer lack of calories, preexisting cardiac or renal disease, dietary protein deficiencies, vitamin deficiencies, protein lost in the stools from dysentery, anemia, and excessive physical labor. One might add to this list starvation in chronic sepsis, the entity we refer to as septic starvation. This is merely a matter of semantics; both the sepsis and the starvation join to produce the remarkable degrees of tissue wasting often seen.

It is a common observation that nutritional edema may obscure the actual weight reduction, and, during the recovery phase, weight may drop with a difference in the handling of water even as recovery anabolism is beginning. The differences in relative water content of the body present definite complications in the physiologic interpretation of weight changes. There are many indications that all organs of the body are edematous and unduly hydrated in both acute and chronic starvation, except, perhaps, in the terminal stage when dysentery may superimpose some degree of desalting water loss.

In the Minnesota study, the extracellular fluid volume was estimated by the thiocyanate method. The thiocyanate space averaged 33.98 per cent of the body weight after semistarvation, and 23.51 per cent of body weight in the postexperimental control period. Sunderman, in 1947, studied a man who had lost 30 per cent of his prestarvation weight. Plasma volume amounted to 57.5 ml. per kg. (5.75 per cent of body weight) and the thiocyanate space 33.4 per cent of the total body weight. Absolute volumes, however, were not enlarged when expressed in terms of prestarvation weight, being 37.8 ml. per kg. and 23.6 per cent of the original weight, respectively. It is clear that there is a strong tendency for intravascular and extravascular hydration to change in the same direction. Over the whole range of states from normal through starvation to recovery, the correlation was quite good. Stewart and Rourke, in 1938, calculated the correlation coefficient as being strongly positive for the relation between plasma volume and the extravascular fluid volume. In the Minnesota Experiment, the two variables of plasma volume and extracellular fluid volume were closely correlated in all the young men during starvation and in subsequent recovery.

The relation of starvation edema to hypoproteinemia has been the source of much misinformation. There is very little evidence that early starvation produces serious interference with albumin synthesis. The tissue pressure may decrease, but this is a small effect. In the Minnesota Experiment, mean colloid osmotic pressure declined but slightly. There was a trivial decline in the plasma proteins. Cachera and Barbier, in 1943, also found that in famine edema there was relative expansion of the extracellular fluid volume, but not necessarily any absolute abnormality. It was noted in the Minnesota Experiment that the thiocyanate space remained curiously constant in absolute amount. The edematous outcome could be viewed as merely the result of a shrinkage of the cellular components without much change in the absolute amount of interstitial fluid or of the blood volume. The extracellular fraction of body water rose. Except in complicated cases, the venous pressure in famine edema is subnormal according to the Minnesota group. Famine edema frequently develops in the presence of protein concentrations which are well within normal limits. In famine edema the capillary walls ordinarily do not become unduly permeable to colloids, and the colloid osmotic pressure of the tissue fluid (lymph) is no greater. General hydrostatic pressure in the tissues is low in famine edema. Renal function is not grossly abnormal in famine edema. The absolute volumes of both blood and extracellular fluids are at the approximate levels for normal persons of equal height and for edematous persons at their normal prestarvation weight.

The loss of fat in starvation is obvious to any observer. According to Keys and Brozek (1953), from the ordinary anatomic evidence it is clear that much of the fat disappears, the body as a whole becomes more hydrated, and the changes in the bones are relatively small.

As emphasized by Keys and Brozek, the specific gravity method for calculating body fat must presume not only relatively normal hydration, but also a relatively normal relation between the denser skeletal mass and the lighter material of the nonfat tissues. Ideally, then, the proper procedure would be to correct both mass and volume of the total body for this excess skeletal fraction. Since the bony skeleton is normally about 16 per cent of the total body weight, it would seem possible to correct both weight and volume of the body for the excess skeleton in the starved state. Actually, the gross loss of body weight in starvation only slightly underestimates the loss in the active tissues.

Taken as a whole, the data of Keys and Brozek, based on a study of remarkable scope and carried out by a variety of techniques, are entirely consistent with the compositional data gained from the study of surgical starvation by dilutional techniques, outlined at the start of this chapter.

From such work, by whatever method used, come the data upon which a realistic approach to starvation states in surgery may be based.

B. MALNUTRITION IN INFANTS

The malnourished child has been extensively studied in a group of papers by the joint study group of Mexico City and the Boston Children's Hospital (Gomez *et al.*, 1957; Gordillo *et al.*, 1957; and Metcoff *et al.*, 1957).

They describe the intermittent diarrhea that characterizes these infants and that frequently occurs as a late and ominous event. The starved and malnourished infant has very little leeway in matters of desalting and dehydration, and tolerates them very poorly. The terminal event is bronchopneumonia.

Hypotonicity, polyuria, and edema are commonplace in these infants; hypokalemia is occasionally observed. Histochemically, increased water content was noted in muscle and skin; decreased intracellular potassium concentration was noted. Increased intracellular sodium was present in many cases. The potassium:noncollagen-nitrogen ratio was low. Renal function in these infants was most abnormal during dehydration. Intravenous salt infusions were abnormally retained.

These workers interpret the water-and-sodium-loaded cell as an expansion of the intracellular at the expense of the extracellular fluid. This represents a semantic difference from our interpretation of the water-loaded starvation state. In our interpretation the compositional picture is considered to be a loss of cell mass, as indicated by loss of lean tissue proteins (that is, oxidizing protoplasmic cell matrix), and an accumulation of water both endogenous and exogenous. Once this water-loaded stage is reached, a prorated fraction of the water is intracellular (depending on the size of the cell mass) and the hypotonicity is general; the initial step, by our criteria, is loss of cell mass to the extracellular fluid, although the final stage reached finds much water and sodium in the cell. The findings are the same; the descriptive interpretations are different.

The authors have evidence here to support the theorem of Wynn (1956) and Edelman (1956) that differential potassium loss (that is, potassium loss at a high potassium:nitrogen ratio, leaving a low potassium:noncollagen-nitrogen ratio in the muscle cell) must, by simple osmotic behavior, inevitably lead to a low plasma sodium concentration and to body hypotonicity. When this situation exists, potassium infusion may be expected to produce a diuresis of water until such time as normal cell cation concentration is reached.

Section III.   Nutrition and Resistance to Infection

Cannon and his group in a series of experiments (1943, 1944, a, b, 1945) found that protein depletion in rats and rabbits interfered with antibody production. The implication that similar phenomena are readily observable in man has been extensively quoted by the nutritionists but has simply not been borne out by careful observation. The work of Wissler (1947) in rats appears to corroborate Cannon, but the inhibition of antibody production by starvation was not great. Zilva (1919) had previously shown that prolonged protein deprivation did not lower

the level of complement, while Metcoff *et al.* (1948) showed that protein-starved rats were as capable of summoning resistance to a staphylococcus strain as were their controls. Stoerk *et al.* (1947) and Axelrod *et al.* (1947) demonstrated that pantothenic acid, pyridoxine, and riboflavin were needed for antibody production in rats, and inanition without avitaminosis did not seem to impair antibody production.

In man, Krebs (1946) and Wohl *et al.* (1949) brought forth evidence that protein depletion and hypoproteinemia (it is important again to reemphasize that the two terms are not synonymous) only very slightly impaired antibody production against the typhoid organism.

Balch (1950) reviews the above contributions and reports a study of twenty-five patients selected for severe nutritional depletion, with nineteen controls. The causes of depletion were late cancer, cirrhosis, esophageal disease, and pulmonary tuberculosis. He found that, in response to the Schick antigen, "severely ill nutritionally depleted patients were found capable of producing antibody as well as, or better than, the healthy controls." There was no relation between total plasma protein, plasma albumin, or globulin and the antibody response, nor was there distortion of the result by intercurrent infection in either group. Some blood-volume determinations were carried out using the dye-plasma-hematocrit method; the "total circulating" (that is, intravascular) plasma protein was found to be low in the depleted patients, yet antibody production was normal. The total circulating globulin was higher and the total circulating antitoxin increased.

In Balch's group, the weight loss of the patients was around 40 per cent; in the Belsen concentration camp it was 38.8 per cent (Keys, 1948) even though the plasma protein concentrations at Belsen averaged 5.1 gm. per 100 ml. (Mollison, 1946); many of the latter subjects had high globulin concentrations. A weight loss of 40 per cent in starvation has been assigned by Keys (1948) as a lethal level; we have seen several survivals at this level of loss due to surgical disease, especially combinations of obstruction and infection.

Balch reviews some of the populational tragedies which have pointed up the maintenance of resistance against infection despite severe malnutrition. In World War II, where populations were starving with sanitation and hygiene neglected, epidemics arose. In the severely malnourished but clean people of Western Holland and Greece, health was well maintained (Keys, 1948). According to Markowski (1945), the German keepers were worse off than the Russians kept at a prisoner-of-war camp. Gottlieb (1946) found the incidence of postoperative infections to be low among the undernourished American prisoners in a camp in the Far East.

Depression of antibody production is not an important factor in the early stages of peritonitis and other surgical infections where mechanical and physiologic factors (such as poor ventilation, tissue necrosis, undrained pus, obstruction of the gut, abrasion, chemical irritation) are important promoting and sustaining factors in the septic process. As the septic process progresses on to severe septic starvation, "resistance" seems to vanish. By contrast, semistarvation as we ordinarily see it does not have a deleterious effect on resistance to infection.

As contrasted with obesity (with its problems of poor ventilation, high blood pressure, difficulty in anesthesia management, atherosclerosis, and sepsis in subcutaneous fat) it would seem that the spare and thrifty patient is better off surgically, even if he lost some weight (that is, "starved") to get there. It is in lack of muscular strength and vigor, cough, respiration, ambulation, drive, ambition, morale, initiative, and in loss of libido that the starved person suffers most—depending upon the stage of starvation—and it is to the repair of these deficits in late convalescence that his treatment is devoted after a debilitating illness.

Balch and Spencer (1954) further studied this question of nutrition in relation to resistance to infection, noting that there seemed to be a general belief that malnourished patients were more susceptible to infection. Antibody production was normal in emaciated patients. Phagocytosis (staphylococcus) was studied in twenty patients with very advanced wasting, many of whom were preterminal cases. There was no significant difference as compared with seventeen controls; there was no correlation with the erythrocyte mass, age, or plasma protein concentrations.

The latter comparisons (of plasma protein) are of interest in themselves. Despite severe malnutrition the plasma protein concentrations in Balch and Spencer's twenty patients ranged from 4.4 to 7.5 gm. per 100 ml.

(mean = 6.4 gm. per 100 ml.); in the controls the range was 5.3 to 8.1 (mean = 6.9 gm. per 100 ml.). The albumin concentration in the malnourished subjects was lower than in the controls by a larger fraction (the mean was 2.8, as compared with 4.3), but the globulins were significantly higher. The erythrocyte volume differences were very striking. The average erythrocyte volume in the controls was 3200 ml., in the malnourished 1700 ml. Hemorrhage was not prominent in most of the diseases they studied.

It is important to emphasize again that caloric starvation must be differentiated from specific vitamin deficiencies or visceral destruction (as in cirrhosis or renal failure, for example). In the latter, especially with leucopenia or pancytopenia, resistance to infection is markedly reduced.

The recent description of an euglobulin, "properdin" (Pillemer et al., 1954), essential in immune mechanisms, brings to mind the possibility either that trauma in itself might alter the titer of this material or that surgical infections would do so. Benson et al. (1956) report an initial study that did not reveal systematic changes but did show wide swings under circumstances of trauma and infection. As the authors point out, it is too early in this field to draw any conclusions as to significance.

Section IV.   Utilization of Intravenous Supplements

Although there is good agreement that calories are necessary to permit the maximal utilization of intravenously infused protein hydrolysates, the question of how to provide these calories remains less easily solved. Christensen et al. (1955) have demonstrated conclusively in humans that autoclaving glucose with protein hydrolysate increases wastage of both peptide and amino acid when the mixture is subsequently infused. This may be related to the "browning" reaction noted in such solutions. Infusing the glucose first, or adding the glucose in a sterile manner to the hydrolysate immediately prior to infusion, produces the expected decrease in catabolism of the infused material. Alcohol and fat may also be used to cover the energy requirements of protein synthesis, though ideal quantitative relationships to the infused mixture have yet to be worked out; carbohydrate in some quantity is essential to attain a maximum rate of protein synthesis.

The attractions of fructose lie in the fact that insulin is not required for it to achieve access to the cell. Beal and Smith (1954) reported on some fructose studies in man. In their article they present a comprehensive review of the literature up to that time. They found that fructose metabolism did involve a rise in blood glucose, indicating interconversion. They confirmed the finding of a marked accumulation of pyruvate and lactate with a transient metabolic acidosis during fructose metabolism, along with a decrease in phosphate more marked than that accompanying glucose oxidation. In one pair of studies, they appeared to demonstrate with glucose a greater tendency to accumulate nitrogen and potassium (owing to glycogen formation and protein anabolism) and less tendency to lose them in the urine than was observed with fructose. Both Moncrief et al. (1953) and Drucker et al. (1952) felt that fructose was better utilized (that is, metabolized) after operation, a point that Beal and Smith did not feel was settled conclusively by their data. The increased melituria with fructose constitutes a mild osmotic diuresis, a factor that may be active in removing more water and electrolyte than is the case with glucose. The metabolic acidosis may also contribute to loss of fixed base. There is suggestive evidence that some of the utility of fructose depends on its conversion to glucose, possibly via glycogen. Certainly the case for the use of fructose in routine surgical care is not yet established. In special instances, of which liver disease may be an example, it may be justified.

Wilkinson (1955) reviewed the status of alcohol as an intravenous source of calories. One liter of 6 per cent alcohol provides 336 calories. It is well tolerated. At alcohol dose-rates of 10 to 20 ml. per hour, oxidation keeps pace at a sufficient rate to maintain the blood alcohol below 50 mg. per hour, at which level inebriation is not observed. During such infusions most patients sleep. Vein reactions (endophlebitis), surprisingly, were more common with alcohol than after infusions of solutions without alcohol. Wilkinson is not enthusiastic about alcohol as a source of calories, and feels that fructose may be more promising.

Shingleton *et al.* (1956) studied the utilization of intravenous fat. Their reaction rate was near 25 per cent, a rate which is much higher than our current experience with one of the commercial preparations.* They reported, as we had (Moore, 1952), that intravenously injected fat did not reduce early nitrogen loss

---

* Lipomul, Upjohn.

but was very effective in later convalescence in reducing nitrogen loss. The infusions, other than the pyrogens, were harmless.

In a further study Bentley and vanItallie (1956) studied the effect of intravenous fat emulsions on utilization of inadequate diets and showed that the potassium balance was the most sensitive in reflecting a net change in the direction of tissue synthesis. The fat had the same synthesis-promoting effect whether given intravenously or orally.

A recent symposium in *Metabolism* (November, 1957) covers many facets of the use of intravenous fat emulsions. The reader is referred to this account for some of the most recent data available. The occurrence of delayed toxic reactions in patients receiving fat over a prolonged period is reported by Levenson *et al.* (1957). The reactions were characterized by fever and jaundice.

Section V. Steroids in Nutrition

The widespread use of steroids for their anabolic effects, especially in the aged, makes a dispassionate inquiry in this field especially welcome. The concept that the achievement of positive nitrogen balance is, in itself, the ultimate objective of steroid therapy in surgical convalescence needs close scrutiny; the patient's welfare must be the end point. In the study of Freeman *et al.* (1956) a normal control series of men aged seventy-one to ninety were given a placebo and then later a tablet of several hormones (androgens and corticoids) daily over a five-month period. Clinical, psychological, and neuromuscular indices were used. Effects were minimal, but there was a definite increase in the muscular strength of several subjects given steroids. Dietary balances were not measured. These were small doses and given sublingually. The increase in muscular mass and strength may be an explanation of the occasional spectacular improvement in performance seen in older patients on hormone treatment. It may well be correlated with nitrogen accumulation, but if so the functional result, not the nitrogen balance alone, is the significant finding.

Brown and Samuels (1956) studied the effect on nitrogen balance of intravenously administered testosterone. The infusions were short-term (thirty minutes); some were in convalescent patients. There was no alteration in nitrogen balance as judged on a daily basis. When the infusions lasted for twenty-four hours or when the material was given intramuscularly the expected anabolic result was achieved.

Peden and Maxwell (1956) have also observed an anabolic effect from androgenic steroids. They used normethandrolane and, in five patients undergoing hysterectomy, noticed a clear anabolic effect. No comment is made as to the benefits of this nitrogen gain on the welfare of the patients.

Forsyth and Plough (1955) studied the protein-sparing effect of carbohydrate in a variety of circumstances, with and without testosterone. They found, as have others, that increasing carbohydrate intake markedly reduces total nitrogen excretion. One of the most interesting aspects of their work was the observation that testosterone lost its ability to cause nitrogen retention, when the subjects (not severely malnourished) were on a high carbohydrate intake. Stated otherwise, carbohydrate calories seemed to move protein synthesis to a ceiling rate beyond which testosterone could not move it.

The increased nitrogen retention for normal persons on added carbohydrate averages about 0.9 to 1.8 mg. of nitrogen per added carbohydrate calorie. Maintenance calories are most effective where given with the diet; when they are given long after diet, much of the effect is lost. The data of Forsyth and Plough suggest that "obesity tissue" (about 1.1 per cent nitrogen) is being made from the added calories. Lean tissue is 3 to 5 per cent nitrogen. In their subjects the nitrogen gain varied around 1.0 per cent of the weight gained.

Forsyth's data (Forsyth, 1954; Forsyth *et al.*, 1954, 1955) on malnourished patients (in contrast to healthy people) shows that caloric supplementation in no wise reduces the ability to respond anabolically to testosterone; one may think of these patients as below the energy level where nitrogen anabolism is at a ceiling peak and begins to go toward "obesity tissue" (Keys and Brozek, 1953).

From the data shown here one might suspect that once lean tissue mass meets the genetically determined size as modified by exercise needed, testosterone can favor formation of fat.

Prudden *et al.* (1956) considered that bovine growth hormone promoted anabolism after burns, when given in the anabolic phase. Given in the catabolic phase, it seemed to favor some increase in nitrogen loss. The data are on four patients and do not appear to be strongly significant. Extensive statistical treatment of data from four patients result finally in two slopes which are different with $P < 0.001$. The raw data are less convincing. Subsequent study has shown bovine growth hormone to be singularly free of protein-anabolic effects in man; its chief human effects are on carbohydrate metabolism and the growth of cancer of the breast. Prudden's careful studies might well be repeated on a larger series of patients, using human growth hormone.

CASE 1[*]

In Which an Open Esophageal Fistula, in the Face of Pyloric Obstruction, Comes in for Some Special Measures

Case 1. Patient W. B., #9G989.[†] Male. Age 56. Admitted December 3, 1954. Discharged February 16, 1955.

DIAGNOSIS.　Postemetic perforation of esophagus.

OPERATIONS.　Suture of perforated esophagus.
　　　　　　　Empyema drainage.
　　　　　　　Feeding jejunostomy.
　　　　　　　Revision of empyema drainage.

CLINICAL SUMMARY.　This fifty-six-year-old, white,

---

[*] This case, and the other thirty in the book, are presented to exemplify the handling of some very interesting and complex surgical situations. They have been selected for their breadth of surgical interest, and not to argue or discourse on any one point. They should be read as the record of a series of skirmishes between the surgeon and the forces of Nature, skirmishes in which the outcome often was in doubt and turned upon several operative or metabolic issues.

[†] The author is indebted to Dr. J. Shelton Horsley for collecting the data and analyzing the course of this patient.

married business man was taking a refresher course in business administration. Examinations were in the offing. He was suddenly awakened from sleep about midnight with nausea and vomiting. After retching he experienced severe left chest and flank pain with marked shortness of breath. He was seen by a physician who gave him meperidine (Demerol) and sent him to the Emergency Ward with the diagnosis of probable myocardial infarction or severe renal colic.

The patient had been known to harbor a duodenal ulcer, diagnosed by X-ray four years previously. He had only rare symptoms and had been quite well recently.

On admission he was seen to be a well-muscled man of fifty-six years in acute distress with left chest and flank pain and moderate dyspnea. His rectal temperature was 99.4° F., pulse was 100 and regular, respirations were 34 and labored, with splinting of his left chest. The blood pressure was 160/80. There was dullness with absent breath sounds over the lower one-half of the left lung, with a definite "splashing" sound on sudden respiratory effort. The upper abdomen and left flank were rigid and boardlike. His color was slightly ashen and his extremities were cool and clammy, but his pulse was full.

The head of the bed was elevated immediately and nasal oxygen started. An intravenous infusion of 5 per cent dextrose in saline solution was begun through a large-bore needle after blood had been drawn for complete blood count and typing and crossmatching. The patient voided without difficulty. Electrocardiogram was unremarkable.

INITIAL LABORATORY WORK

Urine

Specific gravity	1.020
pH	6.5
Sediment	negative
Sugar	0
Albumin	0

Hematology

Hematocrit	53
Leucocyte count	26,250 per cu. mm.

His condition appeared stable and his color improved on nasal oxygen. At this time he was moved to the X-ray Department where chest film showed a left hydropneumothorax. The patient was given a swallow of methylene blue and five minutes later a thoracentesis obtained bluish fluid from the left chest cavity. The diagnosis of postemetic perforation of esophagus was made. The stomach was aspirated with a Levin tube, which was left in place. Plasma was administered intravenously and the patient taken to the operating room. No time was lost.

When he reached the operating room his tachycardia had increased to 160 and he was hypotensive, despite an intravenous infusion of plasma. Rapid endotracheal intubation and positioning were done and a left eighth intercostal thoracotomy performed. Three liters of gastric content was evacuated from the left chest. A 3 cm. longitudinal tear in the esophagus just superior to the crus of the diaphragm on the left side, slightly posterior, was seen. There was no evidence of any esophagitis or tumor. Primary suture was done with the Levin tube down (past the suture line) into the stomach. The chest was drained. The rapid infusion of plasma and blood then corrected his tachycardia and hypotension.

ARGUMENT. This particular lesion formerly carried a mortality in the range of 80 per cent, due principally to the failure to recognize and treat it early. A good index of the severity of the process here was the fact that the patient was in shock at the time he reached the operating room approximately four and one-half hours after the initial insult, despite his previously good health and a rapid intravenous infusion of plasma. Certainly early recognition and operation were lifesaving here. Whether or not duodenal ulcer with some degree of

obstruction played a role in this case was not yet clear.

The initial hematocrit of 53 provided an index of immediate plasma needs. In a man weighing approximately 70 kg. the expected normal blood volume is 4900 ml., at 7 per cent of body weight. A normal hematocrit of 45 (formerly observed in this patient) gives a red cell volume of 2200 ml. As the hematocrit rises to 53, the red cell volume resides in a blood volume of 4150 ml. (2200 ÷ 0.53). Any loss of red cells further reduces this estimated blood volume. The minimal static deficit of plasma, therefore, was approximately 750 ml. (4900 — 4150). However, with the continuing insult of highly acid gastric juice on the serous surfaces of the pleura a much larger quantity was actually necessary to cover the continuing or "dynamic" debt. This is similar to the treatment of a burn, in which the "static deficit" at any one time is but a fraction of the continuing need. Here again is a demonstration of the importance of having an estimate of the initial need but being ever aware that it is a continuing need as long as the pathologic process is active. The vital signs, urinary output, and hematocrit were all-important landmarks in the estimate of this patient's need for fluid replacement.

Further replacement of electrolyte solution was necessary but not complicated, as his gastric aspirations by constant suction were not large. Active coughing by the patient with occasional endotracheal suctioning of the tracheobronchial tree, plus intramuscularly and intravenously administered antibiotics (penicillin), contributed toward prevention of pneumonitis.

FURTHER COURSE. Although initial recovery indicated the resumption of homeostasis from the shock episode, on the fifth postoperative day the patient developed rapid atrial fibrillation. He was digitalized with digoxin and responded with reversion to normal sinus rhythm at a rate of 110.

Comment. The development of atrial fibrillation in such a case as this is not unusual but suggests some underlying coronary disease. However, the management of digitalis dosage is made more complex because of the possibility of electrolyte aberrations. Fortunately the patient maintained nearly normal electrolyte concentrations and had exhibited his post-traumatic urinary diuresis forty-eight hours previously.

FURTHER COURSE. On the tenth postoperative day a barium study was done of both esophagus and stomach, and showed a large acute duodenal ulcer without obstruction. Having been started on oral feedings gradually since the fifth postoperative day, the patient was placed on an ulcer regimen. There was persistent fever and fluid in the chest. On the eleventh postoperative day a thoracentesis on the left (because of persistent fluid) revealed recently ingested milk. The patient had developed an esophageal fistula and empyema, and this was redrained under local anesthesia. He was placed on gastric suction. An attempt at ulcer feedings through the tube with intermittent clamping was unsuc-

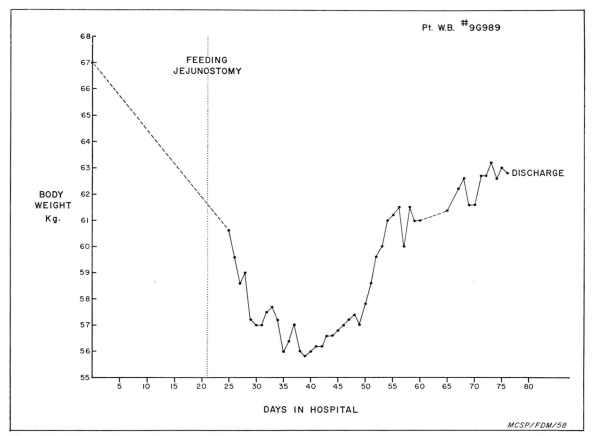

Figure 98.   Weight Curve Following Feeding Jejunostomy in a Patient with Esophageal Fistula (Case 1)

After an initial period of weight loss the patient showed weight gain (5 kg.), not due to water loading, before oral intake was resumed (55th day). This is unusual in jejunostomy; in this instance the feedings were incubated with gastric juice before instillation and the patient tolerated the material unusually well. The reader is referred to the text for details.

cessful, as he began to show obstructive phenomena and spill gastric contents into his chest. He now began to show marked nutritional deterioration, characteristic of septic starvation, with drastic loss of weight.

Comment.   The patient is now a severe nutritional problem. At eighteen days, with most of this period occupied by a septic process waxing and now waning, this patient was at a stage where nourishment not only was essential, but would be utilized. Were sepsis to recrudesce anew, even greater amounts of nourishment would be needed, and utilization would be less satisfactory: septic starvation would soon progress to a threatening stage. With the septic process drained, if not healed, the patient can start the job of reconstruction even though he has lost almost 25 per cent of his body weight. This nourishment could not be given by mouth because of esophageal fistula, nor by gastrostomy because of pyloric obstruction. Prolonged intravenous feeding is uncomfortable, expensive, and inefficient.

Further Course.   On the twentieth postoperative day a feeding jejunostomy was done. Within three days the patient was tolerating a volume of 2000 ml. per day of jejunal feedings. The response to this procedure is best demonstrated by the chart of his weight. At the beginning of his weight stabilization he was taking 3000 to 3500 calories per day. As his weight began to climb his strength increased and his fistula began to close. Within thirty-seven days he gained 7 kg. without edema and was discharged home to continue his jejunostomy feedings there, pending complete patency of the pylorus.

Comment.   This was an unusually good response to a feeding jejunostomy. The patient tolerated large volumes in the range of 3000 ml. with caloric values of 3000 to 3500 calories without difficulty. His weight gain was solid; weight gain and tissue synthesis are rare on feeding jejunostomy.

His jejunostomy feedings were composed of gastric fluid, aspirated by constant suction, and boiled skimmed milk in equal amounts. These were incubated together before instillation into the tube. As his pyloric obstruction subsided the gastric residual became less, finally becoming zero as he "opened up." The Levin tube was removed.

FINAL COURSE. The patient returned home and did very well with spontaneous closure of his fistula in several months. Oral feedings took over the whole burden of his nourishment within a few weeks and the jejunostomy tube was removed. A barium study eighteen months after discharge showed a scarred duodenal cap, with a marked duodenal deformity but no active ulcer, and a small traction diverticulum in the area of esophageal perforation. Nineteen months after his discharge from the hospital, because of ulcer symptoms, he patient returned and underwent a subtotal gastrec-tomy. His recovery was uneventful and he has continued to do well.

SUMMARY. The pathogenesis of this perforation probably involved some degree of pyloric obstruction due to an active duodenal ulcer, reflux esophagitis of highly acid juice, and vomiting. Prompt recognition resulted in salvage despite the combination of pyloric obstruction and esophageal fistula. A feeding jejunostomy was done at about the proper time and produced a nutritional result far better than most; here again incubation of the feedings with gastric contents appeared to improve their utilization.

CASE 2

In Which Ulcerative Colitis Leads to Empyema and Thence to Colectomy, with Some Troublesome Stops Between

Case 2. Patient H. McG., #3K283.* Male. Age 53. Admitted August 4, 1956. Discharged November 6, 1956.

DIAGNOSIS. Ulcerative colitis.

OPERATIONS. Ileostomy and inferior vena cava ligation.

Right rib resection for drainage of empyema.

Total colectomy.

Revision of ileostomy and posterior wound.

CLINICAL SUMMARY. Three months prior to admission this married white timekeeper developed bloody diarrhea and abdominal cramps. He had had loose movements for a short time prior to the onset of bloody diarrhea, but his only episode of melena had been ten years earlier. This was thought to be due to an "ulcer," which had been diagnosed in 1924 by gastrointestinal X-ray. Initially he was on a diet with aluminum hydroxide (Amphojel) and antispasmodics for this, but more recently he had been taking Amphojel symptomatically. In 1951 an appendectomy had been performed. He has consumed three cups of coffee and about ten glasses of beer daily, and smoked two packs of cigarettes daily for fifteen years.

Four days after the onset of the bloody diarrhea, he was admitted to a hospital near his home. Sigmoidoscopic examination revealed a swollen, ulcerated, injected mucosa with a bloody mucous discharge. He remained in the hospital for nine weeks, during which time he became progressively emaciated and "toxic," having up to thirty-five bowel movements a day, and underwent several therapeutic regimens, each with only brief success, and several based on a diagnosis of carcinoma of the sigmoid. He received corticosteroids

---

* The author is indebted to Dr. Richard Wilson for collecting the data and analyzing the course of this patient.

for nine days, with a flare-up of his ulcer symptoms. Aminopyrine, diiodo-hydroxyquinoline (Diodoquin), methantheline (Banthine), propantheline (Probanthine), atropine, vitamin supplements, and oral antibiotics were all tried. He was transfused with 6 units of whole blood and several units of albumin. One month prior to admission here, two days after an intramuscular injection of an analgesic in the buttock, occasioned by a great deal of pain, he began to have swelling of the entire left lower extremity, which was treated with heat and elevation.

He was then transferred to the Brigham Hospital, still having six to twenty bowel movements a day, associated with left lower quadrant pains and anorexia. On admission his temperature was 99° F., pulse 120, respiration 20, and blood pressure 106/72. He was wasted and weak, having lost 25 pounds in the previous four months. The oral mucous membranes were dry and fiery red; his skin had decreased turgor and was pale. There were subcrepitant rales in the right lung base; the abdomen was slightly distended, with tenderness in the periumbilical area. The rectal mucosa was boggy, the stool was light yellow in color, and was positive for occult blood. At 12 cm. in the rectum a polypoid, obstructing lesion could be seen on sigmoidoscopic examination; however, on two occasions biopsies of this tissue demonstrated only chronic inflammatory reaction. The left thigh and calf were swollen to the groin with pitting edema, but no tenderness or pain on flexion of the foot were present. There was a lesser degree of edema on the right.

INITIAL LABORATORY WORK. Electrocardiogram showed sinus tachycardia with some change of electrical activity either due to the tachycardia per se or caused by subendocardial ischemia. An admission chest X-ray revealed no abnormal cardiac or pulmonary findings. A barium enema demonstrated the usual appearance of ulcerative colitis with the possibility of multiple pseudopolyps in the transverse colon.

Urine

    Specific gravity 1.015
    Protein   trace
    *p*H   5.5
    Sediment   6–14 leucocytes per high-
                             power field
    Sugar   0

Hematology

    Hematocrit   38
    Leucocyte count 14,500 per cu. mm.
                   neutrophils   7 per cent
                               —toxic
                               granulations
                lymphocytes 20 per cent
                monocytes   5 per cent
                eosinophils   2 per cent

Blood Chemical Analyses

    Blood urea nitrogen   11   mg. per 100
                                      ml.
    Plasma protein   4.0 gm. with 2.1
                                      gm. of
                                      albumin
    Plasma chloride   97   mE. per l.
    Plasma sodium   131   mE. per l.
    Plasma potassium   2.9 mE. per l.
    Carbon dioxide combining
       power   23.9 mE. per l.
    Prothrombin content   53   per cent
    Thymol turbidity   19   units
    Alkaline phosphatase   10.7 Bodansky
                                      units
    Phosphorus   0.8 mM. per l.
    Bromsulphalein retention   27   per cent

ARGUMENT. This patient presented a complex combination of problems: severe ulcerative colitis which was rapidly progressing, ileofemoral thrombophlebitis, marked body wasting with prolonged negative nitrogen balance, typical of advanced septic starvation, with evidence of expanded total body water and extracellular fluid volume associated with chronic sepsis. In his depleted condition he would not tolerate a major surgical attack upon his colon. It would certainly be desirable and tempting to relieve the source of his sepsis in one procedure, but a planned approach of staged colectomy, to permit some caloric intake and tissue synthesis, appeared essential to a successful outcome.

His acutely and chronically cachectic state might seem to militate against wound healing after any sort of surgical operation and this, more than any other factor, had dissuaded his surgeons at the hospital of admission from operating. In point of fact, given a proper load of ascorbic acid, such patients generally heal their wounds very well. Special surgical hazards here in this patient's weakened state would be found more in the realm of sepsis, pulmonary embolism, perforation of the colon, and accumulative bronchopneumonia.

FURTHER COURSE. Three days after his transfer, the patient developed severe pleuritic pain in the midaxillary region of the right chest. Tachypnea, tachycardia, a pleural friction rub, and fever were all present. The clinical diagnosis of a pulmonary embolism was indisputable. Heparin was given intramuscularly despite colonic bleeding. He received albumin daily from the day of admission as well as 2 units of fresh whole blood in a four-day period, massive parenteral doses of vitamins B and C, and crude liver extract.

Five days after the patient arrived at the Peter Bent Brigham Hospital, an ileostomy and a transperitoneal ligation of the inferior vena cava were performed, using continuous spinal anesthesia supplemented by Pentothal, nitrous oxide, and oxygen. A total of 500 ml. of whole blood was given during the procedure. The appearance of the entire colon was typical of ulcerative colitis and the distal ileum appeared unusually involved as well. There was no clot in the inferior vena cava, which was ligated so that the heparin could be discontinued.

He tolerated this combined operative procedure well. Albumin was administered daily after the operation. He received 1500 ml. of whole blood in the forty-eight hours after the operation. He began taking nourishing warm fluids orally on the first day and received intravenous infusions to replace electrolyte losses. A temporary ileostomy bag was applied on the third day after surgery. There was only a minimal febrile response to this procedure and his abdominal wound healed well as he began to gain weight and become ambulatory.

However, on the eighth day after operation, a nightly elevation of fever was observed and increasing dullness to percussion was noted over the lower right chest. He had received penicillin and streptomycin in large doses for the first four days after his operation, and oral sulfisoxazole (Gantrisin) therapy was initiated one week following operation, because of a low-grade cystourethritis secondary to constant catheter drainage. *Klebsiella pneumoniae* was cultured from the urine.

Twelve days after operation, thoracentesis was performed in the right posterior axillary line. About 125 ml. of serosanguineous fluid was obtained, from which beta-hemolytic enterococci were cultured. Another thoracentesis was repeated the following day and the fluid appeared more cloudy. This also contained a beta-hemolytic enterococcus as well as *Staphylococcus aureus* and *Aerobacter aerogenes*. On the next day watertight intercostal drainage was instituted under local procaine anesthesia. Grossly purulent fluid was aspirated, with the same bacteriologic growth as the previous fluid. These three organisms were most sensitive to chloramphenicol (Chloromycetin), and this was begun at a dose of 2 gm. daily by mouth along with penicillin, 8,000,000 units daily. The diagnosis of empyema after septic pulmonary embolus was established.

The chest tube was maintained on waterseal suction and the size of the empyema cavity gradually decreased. A bronchopleural fistula was demonstrated by Lipiodol instillation, and approximately one month after ileostomy had been performed, right lower rib resections

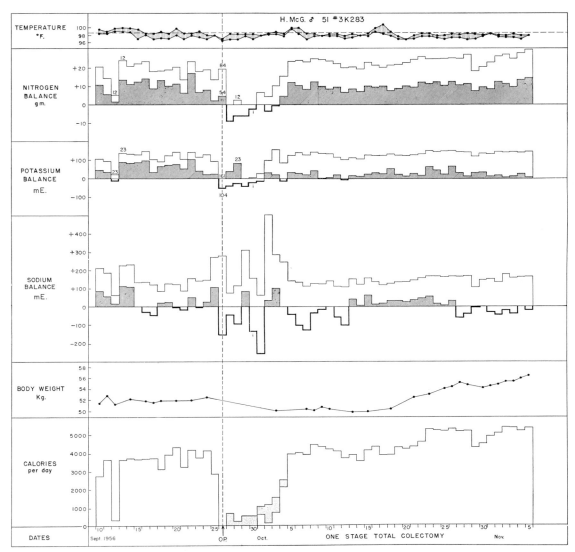

Figure 99. A Fragment of the Metabolic Events Surrounding One-Stage Total Colectomy for Severe Ulcerative Colitis (Case 2)

From the top are shown in order balances of nitrogen, potassium, and sodium; body weight and caloric intake. The reader is referred to the text for details.

This shows a patient at the depth of a catabolic illness, getting the process under control, and making new tissue prior to the final extirpative procedure. Because of his previous loss of body tissue (27 per cent of body weight in three months), there is little catabolic effect even of a one-stage total colectomy. Anabolism is very quickly resumed as soon as intake reaches significant levels. This positive nitrogen balance averages around 10 gm. per 52 kg. (13.5 gm. per 70 kg.) per day. This is about as rapid a synthesis of lean tissue as one sees. Note the lag in weight gain as anabolism commences. Note also that between October 18 and November 6, 6 kg. was gained with 210 gm. of nitrogen. This calculates out to the anabolism of lean tissue almost entirely; fat gain has yet to occur.

were done to provide open drainage for the empyema cavity and fistula. The anesthesia for this operative procedure was Pentothal and endotracheal ether. The fistulous tract was saucerized and the empyema cavity was packed with gauze.

Comment. A pleural effusion progressing to empyema (with a bronchopleural fistula) is a rare complication of pulmonary infarction, but one which might be expected in a patient such as this, with intermittent bacteremia. This emphasizes the danger of doing too much too fast to a severely wasted and depleted individual. By performing an ileostomy initially, and giving this man a chance to eat and become ambulatory, a temporary halt of lean-tissue destruction was achieved. He was able to survive thoracic sepsis. The surgeon should not construe this as anything more than the first stage in his over-all plan to eradicate the septic process in the colon. Now that the source of emboli was controlled, the bronchopleural fistula was no longer a threat, and the ileostomy was functioning well, the proper time to perform the total colectomy was at hand.

FURTHER COURSE. The patient continued to eat well and remained essentially afebrile following drainage of the empyema cavity. The fistulous tract filled in gradually, although it required a month before the air leak was sealed off. His pulse rate continued in the range of 110 to 120. Drainage from the rectum varied, but by mid-September had increased to about 800 ml. of mucopurulent fluid daily. Blood volume studies revealed that with overexpanded extracellular fluid volume, the erythrocyte volume was only 16 per cent low for the patient's pre-illness weight.

On September 26, a one-stage total colectomy with abdominoperineal resection of the rectum was carried out under Pentothal, nitrous oxide, and ether anesthesia with an endotracheal tube in place. The patient received 3500 ml. of whole blood intraoperatively, with a measured blood loss of 2600 ml. There was one period of mild hypotension during the procedure. He made an excellent recovery from this major procedure. After three days of gastric suction, the ileostomy began again to function well and he was placed on oral intake, using intravenous infusions of electrolyte only to repair extrarenal losses. A mild acidosis, on the basis of large sodium loss in early ileostomy diarrhea, was corrected and by the ninth day after surgery he was ambulatory and eating well. The posterior wound required drainage on the ninth day after it had appeared to heal *per primam intentionem*. It is of interest that about two weeks after surgery, the bronchopleural fistula was noted to have sealed off. The only febrile episode after colectomy was on the eighth day after surgery just prior to the institution of drainage for the posterior wound.

The abdominal wound healed per primam but the open granulating posterior wound continued to be a problem. Small pockets of pus recurrently collected, giving low-grade temperature elevations that promptly responded to more adequate drainage. The ileostomy continued to function well but was progressively stenotic; there was some fever and loss of appetite.

Therefore, on October 29, the ileostomy stoma was revised by simple radial incision and the posterior wound was more widely opened, under Pentothal, nitrous oxide, and oxygen anesthesia. The posterior wound filled in rapidly after that, and the patient was discharged eight days after the final operative procedure, still requiring packing of the wound to be performed at home. At the time of discharge his hematocrit was stable at 42. He weighed 56.5 kg. at this time; his estimated weight prior to this illness had been 68 kg., and his lowest point 49.8 kg.

SUMMARY. This is an example in which devastating tissue loss was due to septic starvation. The patient responded to extirpation of the septic colon and drainage of the empyema. As each septic process was controlled, a step toward convalescent anabolism was achieved. In the later stages the revision of ileostomy was a far more important metabolic step than any combination of parenteral measures. Day-to-day management was effective in providing adequate fluid, salt, and blood to replace loss and in supplying the large vitamin doses required. His total weight loss in septic starvation was almost one-third of his starting weight. Then, once anabolism recommenced, lean tissue gain was unusually rapid.

CASE 3

In Which a Complicated Postgastrectomy Situation Is Managed Conservatively, with Later Reoperation, and a Good Result

Case 3.   Patient L. H., #9A191. Female. Age 58. Admitted November 19, 1948. Discharged December 20, 1948.

DIAGNOSIS.   Duodenal ulcer.

OPERATIONS.   Anterior gastrojejunostomy.
              Jejunostomy and entero-enterostomy.

CLINICAL SUMMARY.   This fifty-eight-year-old widow was transferred to the Brigham Hospital with gastric obstruction six days after an abdominal operation for duodenal ulcer.

For approximately ten years the patient has suffered persistent symptoms of duodenal ulcer, with pain, nausea, and vomiting. During the past six months obstructive symptoms had become much more marked and she had lost 15 pounds.

On the strength of these symptoms and with a clear X-ray demonstration of obstruction, an operation had been undertaken, the purpose of which was to have been a subtotal gastrectomy. At operation a very edematous obstructed duodenum was found; it was elected to do an anterior gastroenterostomy. This was done by the unusual procedure of bringing a loop of jejunum up through the transverse mesocolon and then through the proximal greater omentum to the anterior surface of the stomach.

The patient was placed on nasogastric suction and parenteral fluids. The early postoperative course was marked by some degree of obstruction; a blood transfusion was given on the third postoperative day, following which there was a shaking chill and a rise of temperature to 102° F. The question of gross mismatching remained unsettled but it was known that the patient was type A, Rh-negative; she was given type O, Rh-positive blood to which A-B substance had been added. The next day the patient became deeply jaundiced, with deeply pigmented urine. Urine output was 720 ml., then 780 ml., then 450 ml., on successive days. There was no hypotension with this episode. The patient became very weak; vomiting supervened if the tube was clamped. She was transferred to the Brigham Hospital for further care.

Previous history revealed no significant abnormalities other than her ulcer symptoms.

On admission, the patient's temperature was 100.2° F., pulse 110, respirations 25, blood pressure 156/78. There was deep jaundice; her operative incision was healing well. Although a few feedings were tolerated well, she vomited 2300 ml. of bile-stained acid gastric contents. There was 400 ml. of urine in her bladder; hourly outputs ranged around 35 ml.

ARGUMENT. This patient's principal problem appeared to be postoperative gastric obstruction. Her doctors doubtless had a worrisome time over renal function, but by the time of transfer, three days after the transfusion reaction, with urine volumes over 400 ml. a day, renal function was evidently not going to be the main problem. The kidneys were still vulnerable, and should severe desalting or hypotension now be added an acute tubular necrosis might well occur. But as they stood, they were working well.

The transfusion reaction cannot be reconstructed without more information. A Group A–Rh-negative patient received neutralized Group O–Rh-positive blood. This should not cause trouble unless the patient was sensitized to the Rh factor, possible but unproven here. The fact that there were no symptoms until all 500 ml. had run in tends to rule out a gross mismatch incompatibility. The maintained renal function is corroborative, yet the severe jaundice makes some sort of hemolytic process a certainty. The most probable explanation is over-age or poorly preserved blood.

As to the gastric situation, the anastomotic hookup (jejunum brought through the transverse mesocolon to the anterior wall of the stomach) was grossly unsatisfactory. The obstruction was most likely distal to the stoma and a barium study had to be done as soon as possible to gain an initial outline of the local situation. There is little hazard in early barium study of postoperative gastric obstruction, and much is to be gained.

Major reoperation on the obstructed postoperative stomach is rarely indicated, and always dangerous in the early phase. Here, with kidneys recovering well from a hemoglobinuric insult, there was everything to be gained from watchful waiting. A jejunostomy may be very helpful in such cases, not so much for any caloric benefit which might accrue, but because it is a channel for direct replacement of nasogastric tube losses and such other fluids as are needed. Veins are spared.

In obstruction after subtotal gastrectomy, conservative management will often result in opening of the stoma; in any event it gains time for the subsidence of peritoneal reaction. In this case some kind of operation was obviously going to be essential, since the anastomotic hookup is an undesirable definitive measure for a patient of this age, with high acidity, regardless of more immediate considerations.

Alkalosis with hypokalemia is a hazard here, with large gastric losses in the postoperative phase. Were there any significant degree of renal failure, such a change would be progressively minimized by the more serious developing acidosis and hyperkalemia of renal failure.

A reasonable plan, then, would be:

(1) careful metabolic management;
(2) nasogastric drainage with repeated check for possible opening of obstruction;
(3) barium study;
(4) later—reoperation or jejunostomy.

FURTHER COURSE. Laboratory work showed that the urine contained large amounts of bile and protein, a few erythrocytes and leucocytes, and granular casts. It was alkaline.

HEMATOLOGY

    Hematocrit—35
    Leucocyte count—19,300 per cu. mm.

BLOOD CHEMICAL ANALYSES

    Blood urea nitrogen—26 mg. per 100 ml.
    Carbon dioxide combining power—31.6 mE./l.
    Plasma chloride—86 mE./l.
    Plasma sodium—132 mE./l.
    Plasma potassium—4.6 mE./l.
    Bilirubin—3.9 mg. per 100 ml.

It was thus clear that hypochloremic alkalosis was more evident than any changes of renal failure; the general plan could be followed as outlined. Gastric obstruction and jaundice dominate the chemical picture.

Over the next few days the jaundice rapidly decreased; the patient was given intravenous replacement for her gastric losses, which averaged about 1500 ml. per day on an oral intake of 300 to 400 ml. per day. The intravenous ration was about 2500 ml. per day, of which 500 was saline solution, 1000 a potassium-containing mixed electrolyte solution (potassium 40 mE. per l.), and the remainder 5 per cent dextrose in water. On this management she lost weight **gradually**, averaging about 300 gm. per day. Hypochloremic alkalosis was quickly repaired, using additional volumes (about 2000 ml. per day for three days) of KCl and NH₄Cl solutions. As extracellular volume and total body chloride were restored, urine output rose to normal levels, and the hematocrit fell to a range from 35 to 26. This latter revealed an underlying anemia probably due to under-replacement of previous operative losses. Her jaundice subsided rapidly, the bilirubin falling to 7.12 mg. per 100 ml. in four days and to normal in three weeks. A reasonable balance of water, sodium, and chloride was maintained. Some negative potassium balance was permissible on the basis of continuing tissue catabolism. Casts disappeared from the urine in four days.

The stomach allowed the passage of some fluid, as indicated by the drainage figures. Complete gastric obstruction in a well-hydrated person involves a negative "gastric balance" of near 2000 ml. per day, and here it was about 1200 ml. per day. The patient was unable to increase her diet with the tube clamped. Barium study showed no patency of the stoma. Some material passed through the pylorus, but none gained the distal bowel.

The hematocrit persistently fell, despite three additional transfusions. It was thought for a time that she had some additional hemolytic process, but the falling bilirubin was strong evidence against this. There was no evidence of bleeding. Later in convalescence the hematocrit rose from 24 to 33 over a two-week period without further transfusion and during a period when urine outputs were often in excess of intake. This suggests water loading followed by diuresis.

On the tenth day she was operated upon. The two limbs of the gastroenterostomy were easily identified; with an increasingly patent pylorus an enteroenterostomy could be expected to open up the gastrointestinal tract; this was performed, along with a jejunostomy.

Her course thereafter was uneventful; she immediately began taking oral fluids satisfactorily. The jejunostomy was never used save for small fluid infusions. Barium study showed no passage through the gastro-jejunostomy: all was via pylorus and entero-enterostomy.

The patient was discharged on the twenty-second postoperative day, having regained 1 kg. of her lost weight.

Her course at home was satisfactory. The strong likelihood of jejunal ulcer with entero-enterostomy was reviewed; reoperation was not planned. About two and one-half years later, since she showed superficial gastric erosions and symptoms suggestive of jejunal ulcer, a subtotal gastrectomy was carried out. She has been well since.

Comment. Conservative management of the initial situation in the face of jaundice, a questionable renal lesion, and mild alkalosis was successful in moving the patient along in ten days to entero-enterostomy. A subtotal gastrectomy could have been done a few weeks later or postponed for symptoms, as it was. There was little choice here other than the patient's convenience.

CASE 4

In Which Weakness and Blurring of Vision Follow Intravenous Antibiotic Therapy, But Not Due to the Drug Alone

Case 4. Patient M. G., #8H285.* Male. Age 61. Admitted January 22, 1956. Discharged March 11, 1956.

DIAGNOSIS. Subacute bacterial endarteritis following aortic resection with homograft replacement.

OPERATION. None.

CLINICAL SUMMARY. Two months earlier this patient underwent resection and homograft replacement of a slowly leaking abdominal aortic aneurysm manifested initially by abdominal pain and blood-loss anemia. At operation, distal end-to-side anastomosis to the common iliacs left blind iliac pouches proximally. The postoperative course was uneventful save for mild lower urinary tract infection with a moderately antibiotic-resistant *S. aureus*, presumably related to indwelling catheter drainage during the five days immediately after surgery. The patient was discharged on the twelfth postoperative day, but six weeks after operation was readmitted with a forty-eight-hour history of urgency, malaise, nausea and vomiting, chills, and fever to 105° F. *S. aureus* was cultured from blood and *E. coli* from urine. Hematocrit was consistently around 33, having been 43 one month previously. Fever subsided within forty-eight hours after starting erythromycin. Persistent microscopic hematuria and decreasing pyuria continued in the absence of urinary symptoms or related abnormal physical findings. After two weeks' hospitalization, with marked clinical improvement, he went home still on erythromycin therapy.

Four days later the current admission was occa-

---

* The author is indebeted to Dr. William G. Hammond for collecting the data and analyzing the course of this patient.

sioned by nausea, vomiting, chills, and fever beginning shortly after stopping erythromycin forty-eight hours earlier.

Physical examination showed a moderately debilitated, pale, acutely ill man with hot, dry skin, two subungual splinter hemorrhages, fever of 103° F., and pulse rate of 120.

INITIAL LABORATORY WORK

Urine

Specific gravity	1.004
*p*H	4.5
Leucocytes	10–20 per high-power field
Erythrocytes	2–6 high-power field

Hematology

Hematocrit   30.5
Leucocyte count 9850 per cu. mm., with shift to left

Blood Chemical Analyses on Third Day

Blood urea nitrogen	34 mg. per 100 ml.
Plasma protein	7.0 gm. per 100 ml.
Plasma chloride	99 mE. per l.
Plasma sodium	130 mE. per l.
Plasma potassium	4.7 mE. per l.
Carbon dioxide combining power	23.6 mE. per l.
Hematocrit	38

Cultures of blood and urine showed *S. aureus* and *E. coli* as before.

Treatment was begun with massive doses of antibiotics by all routes—orally, intramuscularly, and intravenously. Fever subsided after forty-eight hours and temperature remained normal subsequently. One transfusion was given on the third day. After the patient had done well on continued vigorous intravenous antibiotic therapy for fifteen days, slight intermittent nausea appeared. This became progressively worse and on the seventeenth day the patient vomited four or five times a day. This persisted. There was also semicoma, progressive weakness, and blurring of vision. The patient looked much sicker and became unresponsive. Deterioration was marked. Urinary volume was adequate, but the blood urea nitrogen had been rising. Pyuria, microscopic hematuria, and frequent cylindruria persisted.

Blood Chemical Analyses on the Twentieth Day

Blood urea nitrogen	56	mg. per 100 ml.
Plasma chloride	92	mE. per l.
Plasma sodium	111	mE. per l.
Plasma potassium	4.7	mE. per 1.
Carbon dioxide combining power	16.1	mE. per l.
Hematocrit	41.5	

ARGUMENT. Severe deterioration has occurred in a chronically ill man with blood-stream infection. There is severe hypotonicity, semicoma, and visual disturbance.

Hypotonic water loading in the presence of inability to sustain a diuresis is by far the most common cause of hyponatremia. Progressive weight gain with fluid intake-output discrepancy is the usual picture. The mild vomiting over the past few days has been insufficient to warrant serious consideration as a contributory desalting water loss. Adrenal insufficiency, with the attendant renal sodium loss, may lead to hyponatremia. In this case there was no evidence to incriminate adrenal failure, and the eosinophil count was 56 per cu. mm. The septic process might be blamed, but fever had subsided.

"Salt-losing nephritis" produces hyponatremia without undue extrarenal sodium loss. Many features suggestive of this rare entity were present:

(1) bacteremia and urinary sepsis;
(2) abnormal urinary sediment;
(3) increasing azotemia and acidosis without oliguria;
(4) large volumes of dilute urine.

Further to substantiate the diagnosis, urinary sodium determinations might be expected to reveal negative sodium balance with low sodium intake. With no weight data available, and with urinary volume adequate, a primary renal cause for the hyponatremia (renal salt wasting) was postulated.

FURTHER COURSE. Treatment therefore consisted of intravenous saline plus added sodium bicarbonate, providing a hypertonic sodium solution with bicarbonate to counteract the apparent renal acidosis. During the next four days, a total of 1075 mE. of sodium, 240 mE. of potassium, 676 mE. of chloride, and 357 mE. of bicarbonate was given. Oral intake of the usual house diet continued. Clinically, improvement was marked. Nausea and vomiting disappeared. The patient became more alert and felt stronger. Visual function returned to normal.

There was no change in urine volume or sediment. On the twenty-fourth day, plasma electrolyte values were normal except for a sodium concentration of 129 mE. per l.

ARGUMENT. Urinary electrolyte excretion studies had been started *pari passu* with therapy. On the twenty-first day, 48 mE. of sodium and 34 mE. of potassium were excreted. Sodium output was 54 mE. and potassium output 50 mE. on the twenty-second day. These values were obtained during a period of intensive therapy with concentrated salt solutions and are not compatible with a diagnosis of "salt-losing nephritis."

Since he had been receiving almost continuous intravenous infusions of antibiotics, the intake-output records were then scrutinized more closely. These revealed a cumulative positive sensible water balance of more than 5 l. over the period during which the plasma sodium fell from 130 to 111 mE. per l.

Simple calculations suffice to show the hyponatremic effect of this water load. The theoretical extracellular fluid volume (or volume of distribution of the bulk of body sodium) is 20 per cent of the original body weight of 64 kg., or 12.8 l. (64 × 0.2 = 12.8). Since 40 per

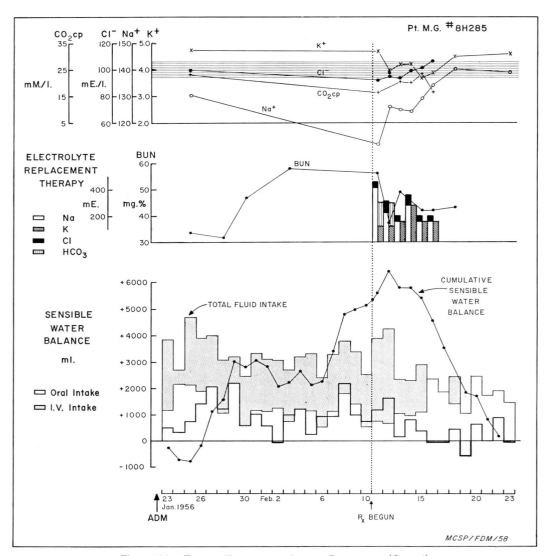

Figure 100.   EVENTS FOLLOWING AORTIC RESECTION (Case 4)

Above are shown the plasma electrolyte findings and blood urea nitrogen in this patient. Below are shown the total fluid intake and output and cumulative sensible water balance. The shaded portion of the total fluid intake below represents the intravenous portion, a very large fraction of which was being required to carry intravenously administered antibiotics.

The fluid intake and output are chartered here as balances, the output being chartered downward from the top of the intake line. The lower fluctuating level (represented by the heavier black line) therefore represents the balance. The cumulative positive water balance is charted as a line, below.

In this patient following aortic resection and homograft with subacute bacterial endarteritis, a severe hyponatremia was produced over a period of approximately 17 days, by a total cumulative positive water balance sufficiently small to escape notice on a day-by-day basis but quite imposing (close to 5000 ml.) when viewed in perspective. This was accompanied by severe clinical deterioration and a semicomatose state.

Treatment consisted in the intravenous infusion of sodium, potassium, chloride, and bicarbonate as shown in the small shaded columns in the middle of the chart. This therapy permitted the patient to restore his plasma sodium concentration to normal, although it was based on the erroneous diagnosis of pathologic renal salt wasting.

It is noteworthy that with this restoration the patient returned to a normal state of orientation and mentation. As the sodium concentration was restored, the potassium concentration fell to levels somewhat below normal and potassium therapy was increased.

The comatose state and hyponatremia were initially blamed on renal salt wasting, whereas it was the water overload, pure and simple, that produced the clinical deterioration.

Subsequent course was uneventful.

cent of the 5 l. water load, or 2 l., remains in the extracellular fluid volume, this volume becomes 14.8 l. (12.8 + 2) after water loading takes place. At the time when plasma sodium was 130 mE. per l. and extracellular fluid volume was 12.8 l., there were 1664 mE. of sodium (130 × 12.8) in this volume. It is reasonable to assume that during water loading no change occurred in the total amount of sodium in the extracellular fluid. Therefore, if 1664 mE. of sodium is present in the enlarged extracellular volume of 14.8 l., the theoretical sodium concentration after water loading is 1664 mE. in 14.8 l., or 112 mE. per l.

The observed value was 111 mE. per l.

Body composition was studied by isotope dilution. The results were as one might anticipate. Although total body water was only 91 per cent of normal, extracellular water was 27 per cent above normal and total exchangeable sodium and total exchangeable chloride were both 18 per cent above normal. The picture was that of lean tissue loss as a result of the prolonged chronic illness after operation, with extracellular fluid expansion due to overhydration. Correction of concentration deficits was accomplished by hypertonic therapy.

FURTHER COURSE. Antibiotics were then given orally instead of by vein and fluid intake was limited. Gradual clinical improvement continued as the patient returned to zero cumulative sensible water balance by the thirty-first day.

With adequate oral intake and no added fluid load he remained normal. Blood and urine cultures revealed no growth following the completion of the antibiotic therapy. The hematocrit persisted in the 30 to 35 range, an anemia similar to that present on admission. Hematologic consultation confirmed the impression that this was secondary to septicemia and would gradually return to normal. Mild azotemia, microscopic hematuria, and pyuria were still present when he was discharged on the fiftieth day.

Comment. Following his aortic surgery, this man developed a renal infection with blood-stream invasion. The ensuing renal impairment prevented him from excreting normally the high water intake accompanying the vigorous intravenous antibiotic regimen. A severe hyponatremia developed insidiously. This was water intoxication of a severe sort. Because of undoubted renal disease, hyponatremia was wrongly attributed to renal salt wasting, and was treated with large amounts of concentrated salt solution. Although the outcome was gratifying, therapy of this sort could well have proved disastrous in a patient whose cardiovascular system was unable to withstand such drastic extracellular fluid expansion. Less hazardous treatment would have consisted in marked restriction of fluid intake and either small volumes of concentrated sodium solution given slowly intravenously, oral salt administration, or osmotic diuresis (with mannitol or urea) to produce large volumes of salt-free urine.

This case reemphasizes the fact that postoperative hyponatremia is often dilutional even in the presence of renal disease. Although the damaged kidney was partially responsible (in that it inhibited diuresis of an excessive water load), it did not produce salt loss. The etiologic clue here was the long-continued administration of intravenous fluids to an ill patient who also took fluids well by mouth. This combination must always be observed closely to prevent water overloading.

LATER COURSE. When this patient was readmitted two years later there was a diastolic aortic murmur, mild hypertension, and blood urea nitrogen of 20 mg. per 100 ml. During the interval between admissions, this mild azotemia and slight hypertension had been noted but had not been progressive. Reconstruction in retrospect suggests the following primary sequence: lower urinary tract infection immediately after aortic surgery, then acute pyelonephritis, bacteremia, and finally aortic endarteritis and mild persistent impairment of renal function followed by water intoxication with weakness, blurring of vision, and clinical deterioration.

The intravenous administration of antibiotics was, in a sense, responsible for the water overload. It must be reemphasized that the antibiotic therapy, as such, was successful in its bacteriologic mission.

The aortic graft has remained patent and the patient has been generally well.

PART V

Visceral Disease in Surgical Patients

Many disorders of metabolism in surgical patients, as well as normal convalescence itself, involve changes in the function of the viscera: gastrointestinal tract, lungs, liver, kidneys, endocrine glands. Any complication—infection, shock, pulmonary edema, desalting water loss—threatens the patient only through its damaging effect on visceral function of heart, brain, lungs, kidney. For these reasons, then, this entire book is concerned with surgical disease in relation to the viscera.

The purpose of this Part of the book is to distinguish and describe those particular situations in surgery in which visceral disease is the primary cause of surgical disease, and a primary consideration in its recognition and in the metabolic aspects of its treatment. In a

summarizing work such as this it is necessary to deal in broad categories, seeking the common denominators in groups of disease entities. This account is by no means complete; such would require a combined text on medicine and surgery. Our intent is rather to concentrate on those conditions most commonly encountered in surgical practice and the salient features of their management.

This Part of the book is neither statistical, pathologic, nosologic, nor a review. It is built around a series of clinical problems related to the viscera, with suggested clinical procedures, and a few case records. The textual accounts are brief, with no attempt at encyclopedic coverage. The emphasis is on the practical application of metabolic principles in surgical care.

Contents of Part V

CHAPTER 34.   THE GASTROINTESTINAL TRACT: OBSTRUCTION

Page 500

CHAPTER 35. THE GASTROINTESTINAL TRACT: PERFORATION, PERITONITIS, AND SEPSIS

CHAPTER 36.   THE GASTROINTESTINAL TRACT: ACUTE MASSIVE HEMORRHAGE

CHAPTER 37. THE GASTROINTESTINAL TRACT: FISTULA, ABSORPTION DEFECTS, AND INFLAMMATORY LESIONS

The Gastrointestinal Tract—Cases

CHAPTER 38. THE LIVER

CHAPTER 39. THE PANCREAS AND DIABETES

CHAPTER 40. THE KIDNEY: RENAL FAILURE AND OBSTRUCTION

CHAPTER 41. THE HEART

CHAPTER 42. THE LUNG: ACCUMULATION, ANOXIA, HYPERCARBIA, AND THE PULMONARY CRIPPLE

CHAPTER 43. THE PITUITARY-ADRENAL AXIS

CHAPTER 34

The Gastrointestinal Tract: Obstruction

Metabolic and operative care of the sick are inseparable; surgical disease of the gastrointestinal tract provides many clear examples of situations in which metabolic care and good operative judgment must be combined under the responsibility of a single individual in order to render the best service to the patient.

Quite frequently the metabolic problems presented by surgical diseases of the gastrointestinal tract are those which fall into the general categories of starvation, enteral and parenteral nutrition, fluid and electrolyte metabolism, and blood loss. These areas of surgical care have already been described in detail and these descriptions will not be repeated.

The surgical diseases of the gastrointestinal tract which produce serious metabolic defects may be divided into those characterized as disorders of propulsion(obstruction and ileus), perforation, absorption, and hemorrhage. These chapters are therefore arranged in this sequence.

The peritoneum covers and envelops the gastrointestinal tract through most of its length. Inflammation and infection of the peritoneum usually arise from the gastrointestinal tract, and whatever their origin, inevitably produce disorders of gastrointestinal propulsion and absorption. Such difficulties are therefore considered in this section also.

The metabolic changes produced by obstruction depend upon the level of the obstructing lesion, its completeness, and its

duration. There are five characteristic patterns:

(1) *Esophageal obstruction:* this leads to lack of intake with caloric starvation.

(2) *Gastric obstruction in the presence of high acidity:* the acute defect produced is one of water and electrolyte metabolism and is characterized by the development of alkalosis and hypokalemia, the latter particularly evident if the patient is operated upon with an uncorrected alkalosis.

(3) *Obstruction in a low-acid stomach:* the defect here is more chronic and is that of semistarvation and caloric loss; some degree of desalting water loss may result, but alkalosis is much less prominent.

(4) *Acute obstruction of the small bowel:* the predominant defect here is the sequestered accumulation in the gut lumen of large amounts of extracellular fluid, some of which is then lost from the gut by vomiting. The effect on the body's fluid environment is one of desalting water loss and sequestered accumulation of fluid, leading to oligemia.

(5) *Obstruction of the large bowel:* obstruction of the large bowel is chronic and singularly free of primary metabolic effects. The spontaneous decrease in oral intake may result in mild semistarvation. Considerable distention of the large bowel may develop, depending upon the location of the lesion and the patency of the ileocecal valve.

Malignant tumors are the cause of most obstructions of the esophagus, obstruction of the low-acid stomach, and the large bowel. One of the characteristics of all these is that even after obstruction has gone on for a long time, physiologic function of the remaining viscus is quite rapidly restored with surgical removal of the obstructing tumor. The patient is in jeopardy not from obstructive residue, but from tumor recurrence.

In sharp contrast are the *benign lesions*— adhesive bands, twists, torsions, internal hernias—which characterize acute obstruction of the small bowel. Here the lesion often lasts for a very short time, but if it is allowed to persist unrelieved, a motor defect is produced in the dilated atonic small bowel, rendering the restoration of normal function very slow and jeopardizing the survival of the patient from this cause.

Section I.   Esophageal Obstruction

Partially obstructing esophageal lesions of a benign sort often present serious problems in metabolic care. Such lesions include strictures at the site of peptic ulceration, hiatus, or diaphragmatic hernias. Cardiospasm and achalasia with more nearly total obstruction produce severe starvation states, indistinguishable, save for their remarkable duration, from malignancy. The principal problem is in malignancy itself.

A. GENERAL PLAN

Where obstruction of the esophagus is due to cancer the patient's weight loss may be among the largest chronic weight losses seen in surgery. The preparation of these patients for operation depends upon a realistic appraisal of their nutritional defects, and a clear understanding of what can and what cannot be achieved in the way of preoperative preparation. Restoration to a state of normal nutrition is unnecessary and impossible. If the patient with a considerable weight loss due to esophageal obstruction comes to operation with a blood volume that is not too large or too small, avoids overhydration, to which these patients are especially vulnerable (and which produces hypoproteinemia so rapidly), and has sufficient energy provision to satisfy the metabolic demands of surgery and its immediate postoperative course, he will do remarkably well despite his starvation. Preparation must include close attention to vitamin C, as such patients have a tissue-depleting lack of ascorbic acid.

Any lingering concept that fully normal bodily nutrition is required for normal wound healing is dispelled by a view through any considerable number of cases of carcinoma of the esophagus. These semistarved, lean, and hungry individuals have a remarkably good tolerance for the extremely extensive surgical dissection required, if they are realistically appraised and managed. They become extremely vulnerable, however, if the general principles outlined in Part IV under "Semistarvation" are not followed.

B. BLOOD VOLUME, WATER, AND ELECTROLYTE

Carcinoma of the esophagus is not a bleeding lesion. Most of these patients present themselves with a low hematocrit and an overextended plasma volume, with a total blood volume nearly normal for their prestarvation weight and thus elevated for their admission weight. The low erythrocyte volume is a nutritional phenomenon allied to their low stores of total exchangeable potassium and the lack of lean tissue throughout the body. Such patients have an elevated total body sodium despite the tendency to hyponatremia: they are en route to starvation edema.

Preoperative preparation of the blood volume consists in giving transfusions of whole blood or cell suspensions designed to restore the red cell volume and hematocrit more nearly to normal. Since the blood volume is high for the observed weight, it is a mistake to overtransfuse these patients, and whatever transfusions are given should not be given the day before operation. There must be a day of equilibration before anesthesia. Hypoproteinemia is best dealt with by withholding unnecessary infusions of water and salt, and giving concentrated albumin. If hyponatremia is severe, it indicates the magnitude and significance of the chronic energy deficit. Three hundred ml. of 3 per cent sodium chloride solution may be given two or three days prior to surgery, with close attention paid to the subsequent concentration changes. Of the three measures (blood transfusion, concentrated albumin, and concentrated salt solution), the concentrated salt is by far the most hazardous to the patient, since it produces an increment that is very slowly dealt with. The red blood cells are the most important.

C. IF THERE ARE AZOTEMIA AND ACIDOSIS, WAIT

These patients usually do not present themselves with acid-base imbalance. If they are acidotic it is because they are starved into ketosis and dehydrated into oliguria. If the patient has gone this far down his starvation pathway, surgery is extremely hazardous, in sharp contradistinction to operations on those semistarved patients who do not show these changes. We therefore regard azotemia and renal acidosis as a positive indication for the postponement of surgery and for a prolonged program of preparation either by oral fluids rich in nourishment or by feeding jejunostomy, over a period of four to eight weeks. While this may jeopardize the patient's chance of recovery from cancer, the latter is sufficiently discouraging so that the increase of surgical survival associated with such preparation is fully justified.

It should be emphasized that even in such a long preparation, one cannot possibly hope to reconstruct all of the body's economy. The purpose is to restore bodily energy levels to an extent that will permit survival after operation and restore renal function as far as possible. With a feeding jejunostomy and the gradual provision of some caloric, protein, and fat requirements, the patient's chronic acidosis and borderline renal function may be expected to improve unless there is intrinsic renal disease such as nephrosclerosis. Jejunostomy is only rarely necessary.

The finding of severe chronic pulmonary disease, especially if aspiration has played a role in its pathogenesis, also dictates delay and the institution of specific therapeutic measures.

D. PROVIDE ENERGY AND VITAMINS

A satisfactory procedure for such patients involves preoperative management in the hospital of from five to seven days. Only rarely (as mentioned above) is a longer time needed. Starting about five or six days before surgery, the blood volume therapy should be given. Adequate parenteral glucose provision the day before, the day of, and for four or five days after surgery is of great significance in these patients. Liver glycogen has been exhausted and body fat stores have been worn thin. The oxidative requirement imposed by surgery must be met, whether or not such provision will alter the adrenal discharge or the nitrogen balance.

A simple method is by the administration for three days (two days before and the day of operation) of 25 per cent glucose through a catheter in the superior vena cava, "covered" with regular insulin. When this is done, one must be sure to follow this intravenous infusion with a "chaser" of 10 per cent glucose in water so as to avoid a reactive hypoglycemia, as described in Part IV. Glucose-insulin infusions should never be given on the day of operation. This may be worked in with the patient's daily routine in such a way that overloading with water can be avoided. All the water-soluble vitamins, plus vitamin K, should be given in generous dosage.

E. CLINICAL PROCEDURE

There follows a detailed schedule for a case exemplifying the metabolic management of carcinoma of the esophagus. This is essentially the pre-and postoperative treatment of resting semistarvation, and reference should be made to the similar procedure discussed in Part IV. In that instance carcinoma of the stomach was selected as an example, and the patient showed every evidence of good visceral function. To give contrast, the example below is that of a somewhat older male patient who has had evidences of congestive heart failure. The reader must be cautioned that any such example as this cannot be considered as applicable to all patients. The reader must approach this and other clinical procedures with the realization that it is an example synthesized from a number of cases, not a general rule applicable to all.

1. *Diagnosis.* Carcinoma of the lower esophagus; arteriosclerotic heart disease.

2. *Admission Data.* A typical example would be a man in his middle seventies, with a four months' history of dysphagia and weight loss, chronic coronary heart disease with failure and edema in the past, well managed on digitalization and low salt diet. There is minimal ankle edema.

WEIGHT. 52 kg. Normal weight is 75 kg.

URINE. Specific gravity 1.012; sediment: some white cells, protein +, otherwise negative.

HEMATOLOGY. Hematocrit 32, white count and smear normal. Blood is typed and crossmatched.

BLOOD CHEMICAL ANALYSES
  Blood urea nitrogen—28 mg. per 100 ml.
  Plasma protein—5.1 gm. per 100 ml.
  Plasma sodium—126 mE. per l.
  Plasma potassium—5.1 mE. per l.
  Carbon dioxide combining power—22 mE. per l.
  Plasma alkaline phosphatase, thymol, bilirubin, cholesterol—normal.
  Prothrombin time—normal.

3. *Interpretation and General Plan.* Such a patient shows the typical findings of chronic semistarvation: anemia, hypoproteinemia, and hypotonicity with mild hyperkalemia. The over-all plan is to devote seven to ten days to preoperative preparation, followed by operation with resection and anastomosis if feasible. There is minimal but significant azotemia.

4. *Preoperative Study and Care.* Physical examination and abdominal and chest X-ray examinations are made for evaluation of neoplasm and the cardiovascular and renal silhouettes. The patient has slight ankle edema; his heart is enlarged; his venous pressure, however, is normal at this time. He has a history of cardiac decompensation in the past and is fully digitalized. Electrocardiogram shows left axis deviation and the heart is slightly enlarged. A test for phenolsulfonphthalein excretion shows only 50 per cent excretion in two hours, and the maximum concentrating ability of the kidney is to specific gravity 1.012.

DIET AND ORDERS. Such a patient should be given esophageal feeding of nourishing liquids six times a day; intake and output are measured and recorded; he is weighed daily. Starting forty-eight hours prior to surgery, the patient is put on oral antibiotics to reduce the intensity of saprophytic growth in the neoplasm itself and in the stomach. In some instances, preoperative or local X-ray therapy may be given, but we are considering here a patient whose primary procedure is going to be exploration for resection. Digitalis is continued, by mouth.

PARENTERAL THERAPY. Initially, the patient needs no intravenous therapy other than the administration of 2 units of separated red cells. These are prepared by gravity or centrifugal sedimentation, and withdrawal of the plasma to an approximate hematocrit of 80 per cent. These are given at least twenty-four hours apart. The patient also receives 4 units of concentrated albumin. One of these is given each day and no intravascular volume replacement therapy is given for twenty-four hours prior to surgery. This period of equilibration of volume therapy is of critical importance to such an individual prior to anesthesia.

Such a patient is given parenteral vitamins daily, including the water-soluble vitamins and vitamin K.

Venous pressure is checked daily during this period when red cell mass and albumin are being restored. Cardiovascular and renal function often improve with such restoration, if it is done with care.

For two days prior to surgery the patient is given a slow intravenous infusion of 1000 ml. of 25 per cent glucose; this is given through a catheter to the superior vena cava, left in for operation. On these days oral water intake is reduced to allow for the infusion, since oral caloric intake has been negligible. Insulin (50 units) is added to the glucose; a short chaser of 5 per cent dextrose in water is given. There is some glycosuria and diuresis with the infusions.

Because of edema, it is felt unwise even to give a trial infusion of concentrated salt; the hyponatremia is improved slightly with the diuresis resulting from albumin and concentrated glucose.

PROGRESS EVALUATION AND INTERPRETATION. The chemical analyses of the blood should be repeated the day prior to surgery.

> Blood urea nitrogen—23 mg. per 100 ml.
> Plasma protein—6.0 gm. per 100 ml.
> Plasma sodium—130 mE. per l.
> Plasma potassium—4.9 mE. per l.
> Carbon dioxide combining power—24 mE. per l.
> Hematocrit—41

With two erythrocyte suspensions, we should expect the patient's hematocrit to rise to about 40. The plasma protein concentration has risen with albumin, and with this rise he has had some diuresis, his edema is less, and he has lost some weight. Hypotonicity is less marked.

The diminished renal function has remained without significant change, although the blood urea nitrogen is slightly lower than it was on admission and the acidosis is inconsequential. The poor renal function together with normal venous pressure contraindicates mercurial diuretics.

The sodium-potassium transposition (126 and 5.1 mE. per l., changing to 130 and 4.9 mE. per l. on initial therapy) is characteristic of the semistarved state. In this man with both starvation and some heart disease, it is largely dilutional. Maintenance of his ordinary cardiac program and the provision of protein, erythrocytes, and energy are its best treatment.

5. Operation

ANESTHESIA. Endotracheal, high oxygen. Because of heart disease the operation is monitored electrocardiographically.

OPERATIVE PROCEDURE. Resection. Low esophagogastric anastomosis.

PARENTERAL THERAPY. Accurate blood replacement is the objective, as based on surgical estimate and sponge weights. Of fluids other than blood, a total of 1000 ml. of 5 per cent dextrose in water is given.

6. Postoperative Study and Care

STUDY. A chemical profile made on the morning after operation would be expected to yield results as follows:

> Blood urea nitrogen—45 mg. per 100 ml.
> Plasma sodium—122 mE. per l.
> Plasma potassium—5.2 mE. per l.
> Plasma bilirubin—2.6 mg. per 100 ml.
>
> Venous pressure—normal.
> Lung bases—dry.

There is an accentuation of azotemia and electrolyte maldistribution. The slight jaundice suggests the use of over-age blood and need not be studied further unless it persists.

DIET AND ORDERS. This patient is given no liquids to swallow for four days, and the intrathoracic stomach is left on suction during this time. The drainage volume is small.

PARENTERAL THERAPY. On the first postoperative day, such a patient is given approximately 1000 ml. of 5 per cent glucose in water with no added salt. Despite the slightly elevated plasma potassium concentration, he is given 40 mM. of potassium chloride. The low sodium concentration expected and discovered is given a small boost the second postoperative day by the administration of 100 ml. of 3 per cent sodium chloride along with the daily infusion of 5 per cent dextrose in saline. He is given large doses of vitamins in his daily intravenous program. Further blood or albumin is avoided in the early postoperative period. Both citrate and calcium are undesirable in this cardiac patient. Chemical profiles should be followed on alternate days for the first four or five days. A rising blood urea nitrogen concentration may be expected for about four or five days. The plasma potassium level is not hazardous unless it goes over 5.5 mE. per l. This patient may be expected to have a persistent sodium-potassium transposition and will recover from this only with completion of his convalescence and resumption of normal caloric intake.

Digitalis is given parenterally for the first few days.

If an unusual amount of blood is lost through the chest tube, or if blood pressure is not well maintained, additional cell suspension or whole blood may be given. Where volume is low, whole blood is indicated. The administration of one erythrocyte suspension and one unit of albumin each day produces the same volume increment as a whole blood transfusion; but the albumin dose is twice as great and the concentration increment of cells more effective.

As the patient stabilizes on the third to fifth postoperative day, the nasogastric tube is removed and feeding begun. Parenteral treatment is dropped, and gradually the patient resumes caloric intake. It is with this caloric resumption that plasma tonicity starts to return to normal. The further use of concentrated salt in such a patient must be based wholly on careful observation of the results of the initial infusion. Extensive use of concentrated salt is both unnecessary and dangerous, yet its cautious use may assist the patient in achieving diuresis and the restoration of plasma sodium concentration and tonicity to normal.

Daily weighing of such a patient is helpful but difficult and may present a hazard to the patient unless carefully done. After the first three or four days, it is spaced out to two or three times a week.

Urine outputs are measured hourly throughout the first twenty-four-hour period until homeostasis has been assured.

PROGRESS EVALUATION AND INTERPRETATION. Further chemical study shows a gradual fall in blood urea nitrogen after its postoperative rise; the sodium-potassium transposition slowly returns, but does not reach normal, as it will take the patient several months to restore his total nutrition. At his age, with heart disease, he may never return wholly to normal in either nitrogen excretion or electrolyte distribution.

Section II. Acute High-Acid Gastric Obstruction

This condition is so commonly produced by duodenal ulcer that it is this lesion that will be considered here.

A. SCAR VERSUS EDEMA

Determination of whether or not the pyloric obstruction is a cicatrix that will require operation, or edema that will subside, is a matter of judgment to rest upon the shoulders of the physician and the surgeon jointly. Obstruction due to "edema" and "pylorospasm" does occur; it is rare to find that these relatively benign causes of obstruction persist as more than a transient episode of twenty-four to forty-eight hours' duration. If the patient has a long ulcer history and X-ray shows a very considerable ulcer deformity, and if he comes into the hospital with a greatly dilated, obstructed stomach and persistent outlet obstruction, one may safely assume that a cicatrix (a hard scar or scars) is at fault. The patient may be "tided over" this acute episode, to go home as a dietary cripple, but study of any series of cases of this type has invariably demonstrated that operative relief is essential. For this reason we have taken the view that early surgery is advisable. From the metabolic point of view, this is of extreme importance. A patient with high-grade gastric obstruction is a progressive problem; as each day or week goes by, the metabolic defects pile up in a pyramid of preoperative metabolic problems: salt loss and alkalosis.

B. GENERAL PLAN

A patient coming into the hospital with a long ulcer history and with acute gastric obstruction for a two- or three-day period should be managed according to a definite plan which schedules the surgical operation (usually subtotal gastrectomy) in three to seven days after admission, according to the detailed circumstances. This is a sufficient time to repair the situation without undue haste, and yet a short enough time to avoid a further downward spiral of the metabolic defect.

The management of the stomach itself is of paramount importance. Such patients should be aspirated completely when they first come in. This may at times require a large-sized lavage tube. The patient should then be kept on continuous nasogastric suction for the first twenty-four to forty-eight hours to allow the stomach to regain its tone and shrink down to normal size. It is at this time that a gastrointestinal X-ray is most profitably performed.

Following this, the procedure of intermittent gastric aspiration is often more rewarding than continuous suction. The pylorus is rarely totally obstructed and such a procedure allows some material to get through, occasionally enough to be of some nutritional significance. The amounts may not be large. This intermittent aspiration may take the form of leaving a tube down all the time and putting it on suction two or three times a day, or, if the patient tolerates the passage of the tube well, he may prefer to have it removed entirely and have a morning and evening aspiration. Were such a procedure to go on for weeks, it would be extremely exhausting to the patient. When operation is scheduled and this type of aspiration is going to persist only for two or three days, it is tolerable, and surely preferable to prolonged continuous twenty-four-hour suction.

The tube should then be inserted and left on suction overnight prior to the operation.

C. FLUID AND ELECTROLYTE

The fluid, electrolyte, metabolic, and nutritional situation is that of threatened or real hypokalemic-hypochloremic alkalosis. This situation has already been described and will not be repeated in detail here*. The important points to reemphasize are two.

1. *The patient should come to operation with acid-base relationships in his extracellular fluid moving toward normal.* The acid-base situation can be judged by the carbon dioxide combining power which, in the absence of pulmonary disease, is significant in this group of patients. Treatment with ammonium chloride (starting with 500 ml. of the 1 per cent solution) has, in our hands, been extremely useful. These patients have always lost large amounts of sodium through their urine, and the use of some sodium salts is essential as long as the patient is not overloaded with sodium and the carbon

dioxide combining power is brought down rapidly. The patient is also given potassium chloride intravenously each day in amounts of from 40 to 80 mE.

The carbon dioxide combining power is determined at close intervals to be sure that it is below 30 and coming down at the time that the patient goes to the operating room.

If these patients come to surgery with alkalosis unrepaired or only partially repaired, the effect of stress on the urinary excretion of sodium is profound, and it is in this setting that severe hypokalemic alkalosis with aciduria may threaten the patient's life. Clinically it becomes manifest in the postoperative period by lethargy, malaise, abdominal distention, oliguria, and by the chemical findings of hypokalemic alkalosis, often with appropriate electrocardiographic changes. The treatment of this condition has been previously outlined in Part III.

With lesser degrees of high-acid gastric obstruction the preparative steps may be less heroic and the use of ammonium chloride, potassium chloride, and other special measures less prominent. We are impressed, however, that a carbon dioxide combining power of 29 mE. per l. in such patients is dangerous if it is rising. A carbon dioxide combining power over 31 mE. per l. and rising is a positive contraindication to surgery, especially since it can be repaired with great accuracy in as short a time as twelve hours if appropriately managed.

2. *The patient should have normal plasma protein and albumin concentrations at operation and may be hypoproteinemic after infusions of water, salt, and acid.* In this case, infusion of concentrated albumin and/or whole blood is indicated. It should be emphasized again that transfusion of whole blood or plasma is a very unsatisfactory way of treating acute hypoproteinemia. The hypoproteinemia in these patients is partly nutritional and partly dilutional.

If the patient comes to operation with his body chloride deficit essentially repaired, with acid-base balance and plasma potassium moving toward normal, with a normal plasma protein concentration and an adequate hematocrit, one need have little apprehension about his postoperative course.

---

* See Part III, page 327.

D. LABORATORY STUDY AN ESSENTIAL

The question comes up as to how these patients may be managed in the absence of "adequate laboratory facilities." What indices are there by which the surgeon may know that surgery is hazardous and hypokalemic alkalosis threatening in such patients, if he does not have these laboratory facilities? There are certain areas of surgery in which operation in the absence of adequate laboratory facilities is in itself unjustified, and this is one. There are very few places in this country from which patients cannot be transported by ambulance or airplane to a hospital where adequate laboratory facilities are obtainable. We know of no crude indices which replace accurate plasma chemical analysis, intelligently interpreted, in the management of acute high-acid gastric obstruction. The measurement of the urine pH, a rough estimate of the urine chloride with silver nitrate, and study of electrocardiographic changes may be useful and helpful, but none of them is an adequate substitute for a good estimation of the acid-base balance and electrolyte metabolism as judged by careful analysis of plasma and of the gastric juice. If a patient with upper gastrointestinal obstruction presents himself where such facilities are not available, he should be treated by means of a nasogastric tube on intermittent suction, given a slow intravenous infusion of 5 per cent glucose in saline solution until some urine output is established, and then transferred to a center where he can be given proper care. If there is a question of obstruction of the large or small bowel he should not be flown, even in a pressurized cabin, unless the distance to the nearest large hospital is excessive.

E. CLINICAL PROCEDURE

A sample program for a patient with obstructing duodenal ulcer follows. As in previous cases used as illustrative examples, the reader is cautioned to avoid generalization from this example to many other patients. It is merely an indication of how the underlying principles of metabolic care may be applied to a single individual.

1. *Diagnosis.* Obstructing duodenal ulcer.
2. *Admission Data.* Such a patient might well be a male in his mid-forties with a ten-year history of ulcer, worse recently. There has been occasional vomiting during the last six months, and severe vomiting of all intake in the two days previous. He looks sick and desalted. The epigastrium is distended. Gastric intubation reveals 750 ml. of bile-free gastric juice with some air under pressure.

URINE. Specific gravity 1.032, otherwise normal. Volume seems to be good (15–20 ml. per hour).

HEMATOLOGY

Hematocrit—52
Leucocyte count—12,000 per cu. mm.
Smear—normal

BLOOD CHEMICAL ANALYSES

Blood urea nitrogen—32 mg. per 100 ml.
Plasma protein—6.8 gm. per 100 ml.
Plasma chloride—82 mE. per l.
Plasma sodium—138 mE. per l.
Plasma potassium—3.0 mE. per l.
Carbon dioxide combining power—38 mE. per l.
Plasma bilirubin—normal
Gastric analysis—highly acid gastric juice with chloride 110 mE. per l.; pH 1.6

WEIGHT. 71 kg. Weight was 74 kg. four days ago.

3. *Interpretation and General Plan.* The patient has been vomiting for four days, and preparations are made for operation within forty-eight hours. The diagnosis has been established by previous history and X-ray. A second X-ray study is not necessary and will not be revealing if carried out before the stomach is decompressed. An X-ray film of the chest is made. An electrocardiograph is made as a base line for possible future use should more severe potassium abnormalities arise. Admission work-up shows this patient to be desalted with a severe subtraction metabolic alkalosis and reduction of extracellular volume, as evidenced by the elevated hematocrit. Hypokalemia is threatening. The objective of preoperative treatment is to restore the patient's acid-base balance toward normal and to reexpand his contracted extracellular volume.

With his hematocrit at 50, his normal red

cell mass of 2220 ml. (3 per cent B.Wt.) now resides in a blood volume of 2220 ÷ 0.5 or 4440 ml. This represents 740 ml. less than his expected normal blood volume of 5180 ml. (7 per cent B.Wt.). This deficit of 740 ml. of plasma is about 25 per cent of his starting plasma volume. We can assume this volume reduction throughout the extracellular fluid. His normal weight is 74 kg. At 20 per cent body weight his extracellular fluid would normally be about 14,800 ml.; a 25 per cent reduction would thus approximate 3700 ml., an amount that checks out with his observed recent weight loss. His chloride deficit is that of the lost volume (about 375 mE.) plus that of the concentration-decrement of 20 mE. per l. in the remaining volume (about 12 l.) for an additional 240 mE. and a total chloride loss of over 600 mE.*

Notice the normal sodium concentration and low potassium concentration so characteristic of this state. The patient was not oliguric on admission (continued normal urine volumes are both characteristic and in part pathogenic in this state), and he will show good urine volumes and ready lowering of blood urea nitrogen with energetic parenteral therapy. A check of the carbon dioxide combining power the afternoon of the first day is vitally important to indicate response to the initial loading dose of ammonium chloride and potassium chloride and the total amount of ammonium chloride which must be given.

The patient should go to operation with carbon dioxide combining power below 30 and moving downward, with good urine outputs and dry lung bases. The complete restoration of this patient to metabolic normalcy prior to surgery is difficult, dangerous, and unnecessarily time-consuming. With ammonium chloride, potassium chloride, and sodium chloride, the patient's plasma chloride concentration may be expected to rise, but

---

* An illustrative calculation of fluid and chloride deficit is given here, as based on the hematocrit increment. In our hands, this has given us the best "first approximation of need"; in any case, the response to initial therapy must provide the ultimate and most critical guide to total needs.

not to normal; a value of 92 to 95 mE. per l. is acceptable before operation.

We expect to spend two days in preparation. Any more time is not only wasteful but hazardous.

4. *Preoperative Steps.* DIET AND ORDERS. The patient is given nothing by mouth. He may rinse his mouth out with mouthwash or chew a stick of gum occasionally to maintain parotid function. Gastric suction is continuous for the first twenty-four hours. After that the patient is on intermittent intubation or intermittent suction.

Intake and output are measured and recorded; gastric juice is sent to the laboratory for sodium, chloride, and potassium measurements. The patient is up and walking around the ward at least twice a day despite indwelling tube and intravenous therapy.

PARENTERAL THERAPY. Treatment is commenced by an intravenous infusion of 500 ml. of 1 per cent ammonium chloride followed by a repeated test of carbon dioxide combining power and the administration of further ammonium chloride and potassium chloride as required, which in this case would total about 1500 ml. of 1 per cent ammonium chloride in the first forty-eight hours; on the first and second day the patient should receive 80 to 120 mM. of potassium chloride; in addition, 2000 ml. of normal saline and 2000 ml. of 5 per cent glucose in water are given the first day and these amounts halved the second day. The patient is placed on water-soluble parenteral vitamins and vitamin K.

PROGRESS EVALUATION AND INTERPRETATION. Under such treatment plasma sodium concentration will be expected to fall slightly; protein concentration may fall slightly from its initial value. The hematocrit should come down to normal, but it would be unusual to expect plasma potassium concentration to rise to normal in forty-eight hours. The carbon dioxide combining power should be below 30 and on its way down at the time of operation, chloride concentration rising.

5. *Operation.* ANESTHESIA. Endotracheal, high oxygen. In hypokalemic alkalosis ether should be avoided if possible because of its further blockade of sodium excretion.

OPERATIVE PROCEDURE. Subtotal gastrectomy.

PARENTERAL THERAPY. Quantitative blood replacement. Subtotal gastrectomy for duodenal ulcer does not ordinarily require blood transfusion at operation, and in most cases it can be avoided. The patient has been dehydrated and resalted, and on this day his rehydration and resalting are further completed. The patient's operative-day therapy should include 1000 ml. of 5 per cent dextrose in water with 80 mM. of potassium chloride, 1000 ml. of sodium chloride solution, and 1000 ml. of 5 per cent dextrose in water. He is young and can tolerate this brisk administration of fluid.

6. *Postoperative Study and Care.* The patient is on measurement of hourly urine output throughout the day. A check of carbon dioxide combining power and plasma potassium concentration the afternoon of the operative day shows no essential change. Chemical analyses the day after operation show:

STUDY
    Blood urea nitrogen—18 mg. per 100 ml.
    Plasma protein—6.2 gm. per 100 ml.
    Plasma chloride—95 mE. per l.
    Plasma sodium—132 mE. per l.
    Plasma potassium—3.2 mE. per l.
    Carbon dioxide combining power—28 mE. per l.

DIET AND DAILY ORDERS. The tube is removed the morning after operation, oral feedings of small amounts of liquids are begun, and, as soon as the patient indicates tolerance and acceptance with audible peristalsis and expulsion of flatus, active feeding is commenced. The patient is weighed daily for two or three days until normal convalescence is established.

PARENTERAL THERAPY. Following operation, administration of potassium chloride is continued at 80 mM. per day, total fluids approximately 2000 to 2500 ml. per day. No further sodium chloride should be given and intravenous infusions are stopped as soon as oral intake is adequate. Any extrarenal loss or complication would of course necessitate realignment of plans.

PROGRESS EVALUATION AND INTERPRETATION. Chemical data on the first postoperative day demonstrate that the patient has shown some reversion of his tendency to hypokalemia. His potassium concentration has not changed markedly; the important thing is that it has not gone any lower. The patient's alkalosis has been repaired and, as the intraoperative effect on his urinary sodium excretion wears off, the patient will return himself to normal. He should be given potassium chloride daily until concentration is restored.

The patient's weight should have increased 1 or 2 kg. during his first two days as he was rehydrated and resalted. For a few more days he should not gain further weight, but with the infusions mentioned above there may be some weight gain the day of operation, depending to some extent on the weight of his stomach in relation to the blood transfusion given. The normal subtotally resected stomach weighs about 350 to 500 gm.

Later care is that given any patient after gastrectomy for ulcer.

The preliminary analysis of ionic concentration of gastric juice is helpful in checking out an approximation of the bodily deficit.

F. ACUTE GASTRIC DILATATION

This complication occurs after peritoneal or retroperitoneal procedures; only rarely is it a preoperative occurrence. Operations that create new "dead space" in the upper quadrants, or interfere with normal gastric motor function, are prone to be in the background. The event can be completely prevented by the presence of a nasogastric tube that is functioning properly.

The picture is that of a patient who is acutely ill, often with tachycardia and an unstable blood pressure. The abdomen looks full, particularly in the upper quadrants; there is retching or vomiting of small amounts.

Passage of a nasogastric tube produces dramatic results. As soon as the tube passes the cardiac sphincter there is an explosive release of swallowed air and a torrent of fluid that is often spring-clear.

This fluid not infrequently has extremely high acid values and a chloride concentration as high as 150 mE. per l. Its massive loss produces severe subtraction alkalosis with hypokalemia (particularly noticeable during the first resalting) and severe extrarenal desalting water loss with reduction in effective extracellular and circulating blood volume, oliguria, and a rising hematocrit.

Treatment follows the principles intrinsic in these metabolic changes and is detailed in Part III. The hydrogen and chloride ions are restored by ammonium chloride, potassium chloride, and smaller amounts of sodium chloride. These are given in volumes sufficient to restore the circulation. The volume of total therapy may run to 8000 to 10,000 ml. the

first day and include as much as 1000 mE. of chloride.

The problem is not solved by the passage of the tube alone. The gastrorrhea continues for two to five days with a continuous outpouring of fluid, which must be balanced in therapy. Then, as gastric motor tone returns, secretion seems to behave itself better, the outpouring subsides, the tube is put on gravity drainage for a day or so, and feeding cautiously begun.

Section III.   Low-Acid Gastric Obstruction

Since low-acid gastric obstruction is due to cancer of the stomach in a majority of cases, malignant obstruction will be dealt with here.

The acid-base disorder imposed by gastric obstruction in the anacid stomach is much less formidable than that produced by obstructing duodenal ulcer. Patients with gastric obstruction due to carcinoma may have a period of low intake with some regurgitation and vomiting, lasting several days or even, intermittently, for several weeks, with no disorder of acid-base balance whatever. Alkalosis, if present, is mild. It is possible on occasion to arrive at a differential diagnosis between benign and malignant obstruction according to the acid-base picture of the patient on admission. If there has been vomiting, little intake, and evidence on physical and X-ray examination of a large distended stomach, but no tendency toward alkalosis, it is reasonable to assume that the patient has an anacid stomach, and this of course favors the diagnosis of malignancy. The reverse, obstruction with severe alkalosis, is strong evidence against malignancy.

The repair of the desalting water loss which accompanies such a situation is a relatively simple matter. Starvation and blood-volume problems are more significant aspects here. Infusions of glucose in normal saline solution will suffice to resalt the patient. If the patient has a concomitant renal lesion, as evidenced by an elevated blood urea nitrogen, renal acidosis, and a high plasma chloride concentration, it is especially important to avoid

overhydrating the patient and to use salt solutions with little or no chloride in them, the anion being replaced as bicarbonate or lactate.

The caloric starvation that these patients have is more prominent than that seen in the duodenal ulcer cases. As previously indicated (Part IV), such caloric starvation is not a contraindication to operation nor does it bode ill for surgical recovery, as long as the patient is given some carbohydrate preoperatively, and is carried through operation with nearly normal extracellular chemical values, blood volume, vitamins, and hydration. If preoperative transfusion and intravenous therapy have been given without a restraining view toward the actual requirements of the patient, the hazard is that of approaching operation with too large a blood volume and too much water in the body.

Patients with carcinoma of the stomach should come to operation with an adequate blood volume and an hematocrit between 35 and 40. If the patient is young and of good cardiovascular reserve, this can be accomplished with whole blood; if elderly or in poor cardiac status, the patient should be given separated cells and, often, digitalis. In either event one basic rule is of vital importance: the patient must have twenty-four hours prior to anesthesia to equilibrate his volume transfusions (blood, cells, plasma, albumin).

Just as in dealing with carcinoma of the esophagus, one will find a rare patient who has become so extremely cachectic that body fat is essentially all gone, whose resources for endogenous calories are so low that preoperative jejunostomy is advisable. This is a rare event, but when it does occur it should be recognized and a preoperative jejunostomy regimen, lasting two to six weeks, should be instituted.

A. CLINICAL PROCEDURE

Management of a resting, semistarved patient is suggested briefly in the following. This clinical procedure is built around the situation of carcinoma of the stomach with loss of weight and is similar in many respects to the first outline of clinical procedure in Part IV. Here there are also heart disease and renal disease to complicate the setting.

As in other clinical procedures in this book, specific data are given as an example; they are selected from a number of cases as being representative of this type of problem.

1. *Diagnosis.* Carcinoma of the stomach.

2. *History.* Such a patient might be a woman in her late sixties with symptoms that are minimal: painless anorexia with weight loss for three months, with some vomiting in the past week. The vomitus has been copious on only two occasions; at other times the recently ingested fluids and food have not been seen in the vomitus; no blood. She has noted some chest pain and shortness of breath.

Physical examination shows no abdominal mass, but she has a few basal rales, an irregular pulse at the wrist, and minimal pretibial pitting edema. Electrocardiograph shows coronary disease, an old infarct, and auricular fibrillation. Chest X-rays show an enlarged heart. Blood pressure is 200/110.

3. *Admission Data*

URINE. Specific gravity 1.028, otherwise negative, sediment clear.

HEMATOLOGY

    Hematocrit—31
    Leucocyte count—8500 per cu. mm.
    Smear—hypochromia
    Platelets—normal
    Stool guaiac—++ to +++

WEIGHT. 45 kg. Normal weight is 60 kg.

BLOOD CHEMICAL ANALYSES

    Blood urea nitrogen—45 mg. per 100 ml.
    Plasma protein—5.5. gm. per 100 ml.
    Plasma sodium—132 mE. per l.
    Plasma potassium—5.2 mE. per l.
    Carbon dioxide combining power—20 mE. per l.
    Plasma alkaline phosphatase—5.0 Bodansky units.
    Plasma bilirubin—1.1 mg. per 100 ml.
    Prothrombin time—normal.

4. *Preoperative Study and Care—First Six Days in Hospital.* STUDY. Study is carried out to determine the presence of metastatic disease; the low values of alkaline phosphatase and bilirubin do not exclude liver metastases. Careful physical examination, particularly of the abdomen, should be done every day. A palpable mass is of great importance. It may be palpable at certain times and not at others. The surgeon should search for liver metastases, Virchow's node, a rectal shelf, or ovarian metastases. Analysis of gastric contents and of urine for uropepsin is done; the former may be expected to show no acid and the latter to show very low uropepsin values; if the X-ray shows obvious carcinoma, these steps are unnecessary.

INTERPRETATION AND GENERAL PLAN. The initial laboratory and clinical evaluations demonstrate slight hypoproteinemia and slight sodium-potassium transposition, corroborating the obvious implication of dietary insufficiency and loss of weight: starvation hyponatremia. The blood volume may be expected to be slightly low for the patient's observed weight, with an overexpanded plasma volume in relation to the contracted erythrocyte mass suggested by the hematocrit of 31; bleeding has not been prominent but has been present, as shown by occult blood in the stool.

From a hematocrit of 31 and a normal weight of 60 kg. one may estimate the missing erythrocyte mass. We assume the normal blood volume at 6.5 per cent of the normal body weight to have been 3900 ml. With the normal hematocrit for a woman at 40, the erythrocyte volume should be about 1500 ml. (2.5 per cent body weight for 60 kg.). Here, with blood in the stools, we assume the blood volume is 15 per cent low for her normal weight, or 3300 ml.; with an hematocrit of 30 she thus has an erythrocyte volume of about 1000 ml. She therefore has a total blood volume deficit of 600 ml. and erythrocyte deficit of 500 ml. The principal volume deficit is in the erythrocyte fraction, as is so characteristic of starvation and depletion with hemorrhage. Note that the volume calculations are based on her normal weight (see Part II).

Three transfusions of whole blood provide about 650 ml. of cells in a total volume of over 1500 ml. The patient has evident heart disease; she is elderly. Such a large volume increment in a chronic compensated anemia would be dangerous. Immediately prior to anesthesia and operation it could be lethal. Here is a clear indication for separated cells, and she should be given a day to equilibrate transfusions before operation. Therefore the plan is to give two transfusions of separated cells and one of whole blood.

Such a patient should be digitalized parenterally (because of the poor gastric emptying) and this should be complete and stable before transfusion is begun. With hypertensive coronary heart disease with auricular fibrillation and early failure, she should do well if managed with care. The possibility of an acute coronary occlusion cannot be ruled out; the best prevention is maintenance of good volume, pressure, flow, and oxygenation throughout the surgical course.

The azotemia (blood urea nitrogen of 45 mg. per 100 ml.) with slight acidosis (carbon dioxide combining power of 20 mE. per l.) is characteristic of early congestive failure in hypertensive cardiovascular disease. Nothing should be done about it initially, pending the results of bed rest, hydration, and digitalization. It is important here that the urine sediment is clear. Neither intravenous nor retrograde pyelography should be done at this time.

Other than this the principal need is for vitamins and the avoidance of oversalting, which will quickly dilute the plasma protein concentration to very low levels. Should she have been more severely hypoproteinemic, concentrated albumin could be used.

DIET AND ORDERS. The patient is given oral feedings of enriched liquids with added vitamins, with one or two evening aspirations, to make sure that obstruction with gastric dilatation does not exist. If obstruction is incomplete, residuals may be expected in the range of 200 to 400 ml. The patient should be up and about, encouraged to exercise by walking every day. She should be weighed two or three times during the first five days. With a large necrotic gastric lesion, an oral antibiotic is used for forty-eight hours preoperatively.

Digitalization is carried out over a forty-eight hour period.

PARENTERAL THERAPY. Two transfusions of separated cells should be given during the next three days. Then after a rest of either one or two days, one additional whole blood transfusion is given. This should precede operation by approximately twenty-four hours. Vitamins B and C should be given parenterally.

After these six days the patient would be hoped to have developed good urine volumes with a loss of edema, and with basal rales less noticeable.

CHECK-UP BLOOD CHEMICAL ANALYSES
Blood urea nitrogen—28 mg. per 100 ml.
Plasma protein—6.2 gm. per 100 ml.
Plasma sodium—134 mE. per l.
Plasma potassium—4.6 mE. per l.
Carbon dioxide combining power—23 mE. per l.

Hematocrit—38

INTERPRETATION. In such a case diuresis is a sign of excellent cardiovascular-renal response to hospitalization and digitalization. Loss of fluid weight will be confused by the weight gain of transfusion. The rise in hematocrit is due in part to the erythrocyte infusions and in part to the diuresis; the rise in plasma protein concentration is largely due to the latter.

The azotemia is less marked but still present. A distinct rise can be expected over the period of the surgical operation.

The move toward normal of the sodium and potassium concentration also bespeaks improvement in water distribution with digitalization and hydration.

Thus, with extracellular fluid chemical findings as near to normal as possible, digitalized, with the avoidance of fluid overloading, with less acid-base imbalance and with a good twenty-four hours to equilibrate her most recent blood infusions, this patient is as good a subject for operation as she can hope to be.

A diuretic program should be instituted if edema is extensive; *at least three days* should pass, after the end of the diuresis, before anesthia and operation.

5. *Intraoperative Period.* Anesthesia should include adequate oxygenation and avoidance of hypotension. Quantitative replacement of blood loss and avoidance of fluid overloading should be the guides. The surgeon's estimate, plus a sponge weight check, is the basis for blood replacement. In such a case radical gastrectomy may be necessary. On the operative day, a patient of this body weight, afebrile, should not receive more than 1500 ml. of 5 per cent glucose in water (with potassium) over and above her blood infusion. Some saline solution may be added to this (for example, 500 ml. of normal saline) without harming the patient. The patient's urine output on the operative day is acceptable if in the 300 to 500 range. Potassium is given early because of the previous starvation. Digitalis is continued without change. The slightly elevated potassium level is a danger sign because its sudden fall would greatly increase the effectiveness of the digitalis; the electrocardiograph is monitored during the operation and frequently thereafter for the first three days.

6. *Early Postoperative Study and Care.* STUDY. Chemical study on the first postoperative day shows the following values:

Blood urea nitrogen—47 mg. per 100 ml.
Plasma sodium—128 mE. per l.
Plasma potassium—4.9 mE. per l.
Plasma bilirubin—2.5 mg. per 100 ml.
Carbon dioxide combining power—26 mE. per l.

Hematocrit—35

INTERPRETATION. Such findings would suggest that blood transfusion has been adequate, although the corroboration of this must be borne out by the patient's clinical appearance, blood pressure, and urine flow.

The elevation of blood urea nitrogen is inevitable following such an operation in the presence of cardiovascular renal disease. The slight elevation of bilirubin is characteristic of patients having abdominal surgery with considerable blood replacement. If this rises any further, one may question its cause with respect to the common duct or intrahepatic changes. If it subsides back to normal, nothing further need be done. The mild sodium-potassium shift indicates merely that severe trauma has been superimposed on starvation hyponatremia and early congestive heart failure; further dilutional hypotonicity would be undesirable.

DIET AND ORDERS. After a high subtotal gastrectomy for carcinoma, the patient is given Stage 1 fluids,* up to an ounce an hour, for the first two or three days, depending upon the results of an abdominal examination and the presence or absence of peristalsis. The nasogastric tube (placed the night before operation) is removed the morning after operation, and by the fourth or fifth day the patient's dietary advancement is rapid. In our experience it is better to wait a few days until the abdomen is obviously clear and gastrointestinal function is good, and then advance diet rapidly, rather than to advance it rapidly initially. By the eighth or tenth day the intake is the same by both methods and the latter is much safer.

The patient should be up out of bed each day. If convalescence is completely clear without complications, weighing the patient is unnecessary after the first few days. Here, with heart disease and renal disease, some early measurements of weight are helpful.

In such a case as this, the postoperative use of antibiotics is unnecessary. If asepsis has been broken during operation, as by spillage of gastric contents in unprotected peritoneal cavity or wound, or if the patient has had any anesthetic complications, prophylactic antibiotic treatment is justified. It should be energetic but of short duration. The spill of anacid and putrid gastric contents in carcinoma is much more hazardous to the patient

---

* The diet stages and related details are to be found in the Appendix.

than is the spillage of a small amount of highly acid gastric juice (often containing but a few organisms) in the course of subtotal gastrectomy for duodenal ulcer. For this reason an oral antibiotic is given before the operation.

PARENTERAL THERAPY. On the first postoperative day, intravenous infusion should include some sodium chloride because of tube losses and the small urine loss. Given as 150 ml. of 3 per cent sodium chloride, this is of some advantage to the patient in terms of concentration increment with minimum volume.

By the fourth postoperative day, such a patient should require no further intravenous therapy. As previously emphasized, overtreatment of this patient with 5 per cent glucose and water will result in a serious lowering of the plasma sodium concentration; overtreatment with salt will dilute the plasma protein dangerously, elevate the venous pressure, and produce pulmonary edema.

PROGRESS EVALUATION AND INTERPRETATION. By the eighth postoperative day, if the patient's convalescence is clearly normal, the chemical profile may be checked. It is expected to show blood urea nitrogen still elevated but lower than the early postoperative value, plasma protein concentration back to normal. The rise of plasma sodium concentration to normal may not occur for some time, but this should be a cause of no concern as long as it is gradually rising and above 132 mE. per l. by the eighth postoperative day.

7. *Discharge and Discharge Orders.* Such a patient should not go home before the twelfth day. Caloric intake should be established before the patient goes home, and she should be instructed as to the special significance of caloric intake. If the gross tumor has been unremovable, these criteria cannot be met before discharge.

Section IV.   Obstruction of the Small Bowel

In dealing with obstruction of the small bowel, the selection of the proper time for operation is the most important single decision the surgeon has to make. With the advent of increasingly safe methods of anesthesia, intestinal intubation, and good supportive therapy, it is the rare patient with obstruction of the small bowel who should not be operated on some time during the first forty-eight hours in the hospital. There are still a few patients who are in the older age group and who have complicating systemic disease or long-established obstruction for whom conservative, nonoperative management is planned as a calculated risk, with the realization that if gangrenous bowel is present or is going to be present, salvage will not be possible in any event. Surgical exploration is possible in 80 to 90 per cent of patients, and in the remainder a tube enterostomy under local anesthesia may be indicated, as described below.

These patients divide themselves naturally into those with early and those with late obstruction. For this reason, they will be described accordingly. The principles of management are the same in both instances, however, and can be broadly described as follows:

(1) accurate diagnosis as to location, etiology, and blood supply;

(2) attempted intubation of the small bowel prior to surgery (surgery is not postponed); in late cases, catheter enterostomy;

(3) maintenance of functional extracellular and circulating blood volume and blood pressure so as to maintain normal perfusion and function of the kidneys, heart, and brain;

(4) gradual restoration of lost fluid and electrolyte.

A. EARLY OBSTRUCTION OF THE SMALL BOWEL

The metabolic management of the patient with acute obstruction of the small bowel of less than twenty-four hours' duration presents few problems; it consists of intubation, an initial period of resalting, followed by definitive operation. This simple program yields such excellent results that there is little justification for departure.

The salt and water whose loss gradually threatens extracellular fluid volume has passed out of the *milieu intérieur* and into the lumen of distended bowel; once there, it is lost from the internal environment whether or not it is vomited or removed by aspiration. Aspiration of this fluid permits distention to subside, normal bowel tone to return, and the vicious circle of fluid loss to cease. The details of biochemical mechanism in desalting water loss and sequestered fluid accumulations have been described in Part III and will not be repeated here.

The initial resalting of such a patient should include 5 per cent glucose in saline solution and 5 per cent glucose in water to which potassium chloride has been added. It is extremely rare, in intestinal obstruction of less than twenty-four hours' duration, to find serious elevation of the hematocrit (above 65) with a shocklike state and oliguria to a degree that would contraindicate the use of potassium.

1. *General Plan.* A program for such a patient might be as follows:

a. Admission to the hospital. The diagnosis of obstruction is suspected on the basis of history and physical findings. Passage of Miller-Abbott tube into the stomach after checking both lumina, thread-windings on the balloon, and balloon capacity. A variety of long tubes is useful; the double-lumen tube has the advantage of control of the extent of balloon distention.

b. Patient goes to the X-ray department for supine and upright films to assess the extent of distention and the possible level of the obstruction. At this time, a single effort under fluoroscopy is made to pass the balloon through the pylorus. A prolonged effort should not be made, as it is very tiring to the acutely ill patient. However, at the completion of this single attempt, the balloon should be left at the pylorus with a single coil in the stomach.

c. The balloon is then half-inflated with water. If the balloon is inflated with air, it will float up to the top of the gastric fluid level and away from the pylorus. If it is partly filled with water, it acts as a small bolus which gastric peristalsis can grasp and it will go much more readily through the pylorus. The addition of a small amount of mercury may add some weight to the balloon and help in this regard but is not as effective as water inflation. A urinary catheter is placed in the bladder and hourly urine output measured.

d. The patient then goes to the ward and has a preliminary period of rehydration and resalting, at the outset of which base-line chemical determinations are carried out. These consist at a minimum of measurements of blood urea nitrogen and hematocrit, erythrocyte count, urinalysis, including measurements of specific gravity and plasma sodium, and determinations of potassium, chloride, and carbon dioxide combining power.

e. An intravenous infusion of 1000 ml. of glucose in normal saline solution and 1000 ml. of glucose in water with 40 mE. of potassium chloride is given over the next three hours. This is a rapid rate of infusion (10 ml. a minute) but this is well tolerated in individuals who have suffered severe desalting water loss. This infusion rate should be reflected by an increase in the hourly urine output.

f. At the end of this three-hour period, urine output should be reestablished, and unless the blood chemical values show some unexpected distortion the patient should go to the operating room.

g. Operation on these patients should be carried out under a satisfactory general anesthetic with endotracheal intubation and high oxygen levels in the inspired gas mixture. Complete relaxation and good oxygenation are a great deal safer for the patient than an attempt to operate under some sort of minimal anesthesia such as local injection of procaine, mistakenly selected because of the patient's illness.

h. Before, during, and after operation the patient should be on a simple clinical balance regimen as described on page 467 to guide his metabolic care until peristalsis and diet are reestablished.

i. Intraoperatively, it is rarely possible or advisable to pass the long tube through the pylorus into the duodenum. We are impressed with the fact that this maneuver is rarely satisfactory, and if sufficient intra-abdominal palpation and manipulation are carried out to push the tube through, it may do the patient more harm than good.

j. If bowel distention is massive, and intubation unsatisfactory, a complementary Witzel enterostomy should be done at the time of surgery. If the reduction of the obstructing process has been satisfactory surgically, gastrointestinal suction should be continued for another day or two until peristalsis is evident. Passage of gas and reduction of distention indicate the resumption of normal peristaltic and absorptive activity. If the Miller-Abbott tube does not function well for gastric suction, it may now be removed and a nasogastric tube replaced.

k. Daily extrarenal losses of water, sodium, potassium, and chloride should be evaluated and replaced but not over-replaced. Acid-base imbalance may go either way in such cases: if the loss of alkaline intestinal juices into the lumen predominates, the patient will develop a subtraction acidosis that is later intensified by renal acidosis. In occasional early cases, the vomiting results in a predominant loss of acid gastric juice, and alkalosis supervenes with the threat of hypokalemia, as in gastric obstruction.

B. LATE OBSTRUCTION OF THE SMALL BOWEL

The dividing point at which the relatively simple problem of "early" obstruction becomes "late" obstruction is difficult to define in precise terms. It is a matter of smooth muscle tone and of infection. For many years there has been the feeling that twenty-four hours was a rather arbitrary dividing line. We see many patients with obstruction of more than twenty-four hours' standing whose early management is essentially that outlined above (i.e. early operation), and who do well. The only indication for procrastination of operation is severe deterioration of the patient. It would therefore appear that a better definition of late obstruction of the small bowel should depend upon the state of the

bowel and of the patient, not the elapsed time in hours.

1. Deterioration of the Bowel

As time passes there develops paresis of the small bowel musculature, in part a result of fatiguing effort to propel its contents against an obstruction. Chemical imbalance, particularly hypokalemia, further detracts from the effective muscular activity. There is massive distention of the proximal bowel. After several days of crampy pain with nausea and vomiting (as evidence of smooth muscle activity), the bowel subsides into a state where there is very little audible or visible peristalsis, distention is large, the loops of bowel appear extremely large by X-ray, and are atonic. Pain is diminished. Obstruction of the small bowel has finally resulted in an atonic, distended small bowel just as obstructive overdistention produces atony and paralysis of other hollow viscera such as the stomach and the bladder. In addition, fluid loss is progressive.

The changes in the bowel wall which favor fluid loss are those of obstruction of the small veins as intramural tension rises. Arterial inflow continues as venous outflow is obstructed. This produces massive accumulation of fluid. When to this is added any factor that occludes arterial supply, bowel viability is quickly lost. The metabolic problem remains much the same in either case. The need for intestinal resection makes little fundamental difference in the management of the patient if peritonitis does not develop.

If gangrene goes on to disruption or perforation, an entirely different sequence is initiated, as described under "leakage peritonitis" (page 546).

2. Deterioration of the Patient

One of the remarkable features of obstruction of the small bowel is the variation in tolerance that one sees from patient to patient in the late cases. Some patients seem to tolerate the late phase of this type of obstruction rather well. A large segment of body fluid has become sequestered in the intestinal lumen; the patient has compensated for this by homeostatic adjustments consisting largely of the withdrawal of cell water, and—a conclusion based on evidence from animals—the mobilization of skeletal sodium. Some patients thus appear to be in fairly good condition, although an elevated blood urea nitrogen and some degree of renal acidosis bespeak lateness of the process, with previous volume reduction (now compensated) and renal vasoconstriction. Such patients often look better than they really are. They are surprisingly brittle, deteriorating rapidly if they are not carefully cared for both metabolically and operatively; azotemia and acidosis are the danger signals here.

In sharp contrast are those patients with late obstruction of the small bowel who show oligemic hypotension on the basis of the loss of functional extracellular and circulating plasma volume into the gut, an elevated hematocrit, markedly elevated blood urea nitrogen concentration with early clinical signs of uremia, severe hyponatremia, oliguria, or anuria, and the appearance of a patient both acutely and chronically ill. Here, volume reduction is the threat and there is nothing illusory about the appearance of illness.

This difference is not to be explained solely on the basis of the level of the obstruction. The level, the ability to decompress into the stomach spontaneously, the bacteriology, and above all the balance between rate of volume reduction and rate of volume compensation are prominent among the unpredictable variables in the deterioration of the patient suffering from obstruction of the small bowel.

In either group of late cases, it is noteworthy that these patients tolerate extensive surgical operation very poorly. In the early case, the release of the obstructing point permits rapid resumption of normal gastrointestinal function because small-bowel tone is still normal. In late cases, an operation that is successful in treating the obstructing point will often be followed by a very prolonged period of immobile bowel, acute illness, or even loss of life. Muscular tone of the bowel wall has been lost, and the mere removal of the obstructing lesion does not restore the patient to normal. For this reason, a full-dress laparotomy with extensive manipulation, exploration, evisceration, and search for points of obstruction is contraindicated in these patients, at least until they have been decompressed and bowel tone has been regained.

3. General Plan

The following policy is used in patients with late obstruction of the small bowel.

a. Early steps on arrival as regards intubation and careful history and physical examination for diagnosis are the same as in the early cases. A Miller-Abbott tube is passed into the stomach as the initial intubation.

b. It is advisable to postpone the trip to the X-ray department until initial fluid therapy has been established. In the late cases very little will be lost by a three- or four-hour period of study of the chemical situation and initial resalting prior to making X-rays. If the hematocrit is elevated and the patient's blood pressure is low and his pulse rapid, initial parenteral therapy should be devoted to the blood volume. The use of plasma, dextran, albumin, or whole blood is essential. The initial defect bothering the patient's renal function, cerebral function, and cardiac output is decreased blood volume. While this has come about through the gradual loss of water and electrolyte from the functional extracellular phase, rapid restoration of blood volume is best accomplished by the use of substances which efficiently enlarge the volume inside the blood stream. Whole blood, alone, is inadvisable in this particular situation, but can be used in conjunction with other solutions.

c. An initial dose of plasma, based on calculation from the hematocrit, will produce a rapid restoration of the patient's vital signs to normal. In such cases the trend of pulse downward, blood pressure and urine volume upward with accurate plasma therapy is most gratifying.

d. Following this, attention to acid-base imbalance and to the partial replacement of total electrolyte loss should be given as outlined in the priority list in Part III. After three to six hours of this program, the final accomplishment of which may take two or three days, the patient goes for X-ray study and for an initial attempt to pass the tube into the small intestine.

4. Special Metabolic Steps in the Late Case

The patient with late intestinal obstruction has lost a great deal of fluid from his physiologic interior. This fluid has only in part been lost to the outside world through vomiting, and the great majority still resides within the lumen of the bowel. The total process has taken many days, and compensation has been massive, though incomplete and hypotonic. The restoration of the patient's lost fluid volume should not be done too rapidly because patients with this type of physiologic deficit become adjusted to new levels of plasma tonicity, total body water, and distribution of body water. If they are too rapidly pushed in the direction of restoration, they will not tolerate it well. The extracellular volume has been in part restored by ingress of cell water; it will be grossly overexpanded if all losses are suddenly returned.

It is for this reason that we emphasize the "priority list" described in Part III. After attention to the plasma volume and colloid osmotic pressure (concentrated albumin is useful in these patients), one should treat the chronic subtraction acidosis that is often present. The use of sodium lactate or bicarbonate is effective and much more so than in the addition acidosis that is found in renal disease. The use of sodium lactate and bicarbonate should be entered into with a wary eye toward the plasma potassium concentration because the use of large amounts of base tends to lower the plasma potassium concentration. Because of the mobilization of cell water and the loss of potassium, these patients are especially vulnerable to this change. If acidotic to begin with, they usually will have a normal or slightly elevated plasma potassium concentration, which falls very rapidly on resalting with base. Potassium must be given.

If the patient is alkalotic to begin with (which may be the case when vomiting of high-acid gastric juice predominates) the plasma potassium concentration will tend to be low, and the initial steps in hydration should consist in the administration of potassium chloride and ammonium chloride as well as sodium chloride, as in gastric obstruction.

With the plasma volume restored, acid-base balance returning toward normal, and a normal colloid osmotic pressure established, one will often be impressed with how well the patient looks, despite the fact that, according to his history, there appears to be a large deficit of water and sodium that has not yet been made up. The gradual restoration of the total body water and sodium volumes toward normal by intravenous therapy over a period of two or three days is advisable. The patient's apparent water deficit has in part been corrected by the movement of cellular water into the extracellular fluid and by the oxidation of fat, and his sodium deficit by the mobilization of bone sodium. Past losses should not be replaced too rapidly, as previously emphasized.

As bowel tone returns to normal, the osmotic gradient across the mucous membrane also returns to normal, and the mucous membrane of the bowel becomes an absorbing rather than an exuding surface. As the patient recovers, some of the fluid within the lumen of the bowel will thus be reabsorbed. These two factors—mobilization of endogenous water and sodium, and resorption of luminal fluid—make it possible to manage these patients without replacing the full total amounts of water and salt previously lost. Over-replacement often results in severe hypoproteinemia and pulmonary edema.

This view—that it is very easy to overtreat cases of late intestinal obstruction with water and salt—should not be misinterpreted to mean that there is no place for intelligent intravenous therapy. Instead, it is our intent to emphasize that a watchful view toward the patient's tolerance and a realistic view of the objectives of therapy will avoid overtreatment. If the surgeon approaches the patient with the compulsive intent of restoring the 600 to 700 mE. of sodium he has lost, and it is all given at once, a very ill or dying patient will result. By the same token, if the surgeon carries out the "sodium deficit" calculation based on multiplication of the "unit deficit times the total body water," he will arrive at an equally unrealistic view of the actual needs of the patient. If, instead, he treats the patient's blood volume, acid-base balance, and lowered volume of extracellular fluid, following the results of treatment by simple indices (blood pressure, urine flow, acid-base data, weight, and hematocrit), and finds, after a day or two, that he has a patient with a slow pulse and little fever, alert, well-oriented, with a good urine output, he should realize that his objectives have been met and that further intensive restoration of large sodium deficits will gain him little and may cost him much.

5. Intubation

If the small intestine can be intubated successfully in the late case of small-bowel obstruction, this will be the most important single step in treatment. As previously mentioned, it has been our experience that the double-lumen tube passes the pylorus best when the balloon is about one-half (15 to 30 ml.) inflated with water. The small bowel can then be completely intubated in six to ten hours if the surgeon in charge will take the proper steps with a long tube that has passed the pylorus. The balloon should be alternately blown up and completely emptied. As this is done the small bowel should be repeatedly irrigated and aspirated. Large quantities of gas and fluid material may in this way be removed from the bowel and the tube quite rapidly advanced. Decrease in abdominal distention and rapid improvement of the patient are the rewards. If, instead of such active steps, the patient's tube is merely blown up, the patient left in bed with a siphon suction in place, and the nurses instructed to irrigate the tube every few hours, very little progress will have been made through this first critical twelve to eighteen hours after pyloric passage, which may often be at night.

In late cases, if the small intestine can be satisfactorily intubated, operation should then be carried out. A median time for this would be from two to four days after admission. This allows plenty of time for restoration of the circulation and renal function. It is important to accept the calculated risk of some gangrenous bowel so as to operate on the patient with a fairly well decompressed small bowel, the smooth muscle tone of which is being restored. This is far preferable to a hasty operation done in the mistaken idea that if there is some gangrenous bowel present, the patient's life will be saved by immediate operation.

If, on the other hand, the small bowel cannot be intubated in the course of thirty-six to seventy-two hours of gentle attempts, a quite different course must be taken. Unfortunately, the patient with very large abdominal distention and tremendous atonic loops of small bowel is the very patient in whom Miller-Abbott intubation may be the most difficult because there is insufficient peristaltic activity. Attempts at passage of the tube must be gentle; if the patient spends all day on a hard fluoroscopic table, rolling from side to side with intermittent massage of his abdomen under darkened lights, he will be a much sicker patient when the ordeal is over.

6. The Operation of Catheter Enterostomy

If a long tube cannot be passed through the pylorus in a late case of obstruction of the small bowel, there is a clear indication for a catheter enterostomy. This operation, all too often neglected despite its technical simplicity, has been responsible for the saving of many lives. The purpose of the operation is unitary: to decompress the small intestine. It has no other object, but through this object the metabolic consequences of bowel distention are obviated, fluid loss gradually ceases, and homeostasis is easily restored. If the operation is inadvertently or wishfully extended into an exploratory laparotomy, it will make the patient worse.

Under local anesthesia, with barbiturate or nitrous oxide supplementation, a small incision is made in the midabdomen, selecting the site according to the location of the dilated loops by X-ray. The first dilated loop that presents in the wound is very gently walled off and a sizeable whistle-tipped catheter (#18 to #22 F) is placed in the lumen of the bowel, making a serosal tunnel about two or three inches long. The catheter is then brought out through the wound, which is closed around it. The catheter is placed on siphon suction. One will often be disappointed in the amount of material that comes out of this catheter in the first few hours. The reason for this is that the loss of tone prevents the atonic bowel from propelling new material to the region of the tip of the catheter. In the second and third twenty-four-hour periods decompression will occur.

Under no circumstances should multiple needle punctures of the bowel be undertaken; even in experienced hands this archaic procedure will almost inevitably result in at least one fistula of the small bowel. It is irrational because the nature of the intraluminal content is such as to prevent its passage out through a needle, and unless steps are taken to decompress the bowel permanently it will rapidly reaccumulate the fluid. The object is not merely the removal of fluid—it is the resumption of tone and normal mucosal blood supply so that absorption may supplant exudation.

After the catheter has been inserted, it is essential that it be irrigated about every two or three hours with sterile saline solution so as to prevent mucus plugs from occluding the lumen. This irrigation should be done only by a doctor, and using gravity rather than forceful instillation.

The patient with late intestinal obstruction now is on the way to control, with a gastric tube in place and on suction, and an enterostomy. He will gradually decompress, regain his intestinal tone, and prepare himself for definitive surgery.

7. Late Definitive Operation

If, after several days of enterostomy or intubation drainage, distention of the small bowel has disappeared but the patient has still passed nothing by rectum, or if there are signs of increasing localized inflammation, a full-dress exploration is then carried out exactly as if he had been successfully decompressed by intubation on the first attempt.

It should be emphasized that in late obstruction, with the use of antibiotics, delay of two or three days in operative treatment of devitalized bowel is not nearly as likely to cause death as is hasty surgery on an ill-prepared patient, or inadequate metabolic care. Treatment with penicillin and streptomycin should be maintained at high doses throughout the first seven days.

In the patient with late intestinal obstruction, who has been treated by intubation or catheter enterostomy and in whom the problem of advisability of full laparotomy arises five to seven days after admission, there is a place for contrast study of the small bowel. Some X-ray departments are resistant to the use of contrast media, particularly barium, above an obstruction. Yet, when the obstruction is in the small bowel, inspissation of the barium above the obstruction is rare. There is so much fluid above the obstruction that there is no mechanism for inspissating the barium. If there is obstruction of the large bowel, that is quite another matter, and barium removal can be difficult. Either barium or one of the iodinated dyes may be used. A small amount introduced through the tube may indicate to the surgeon the point of the obstruction and make his operation much more efficient and accurate, and much less of a burden to the critically ill patient. Its utility to the patient far outweighs the possible hazards. If barium is unrevealing, operation must be undertaken with localizing evidences only from the history and physical examination.

8. Clinical Procedure in Advanced Obstruction of the Small Bowel

The following case procedure is based on the care of an elderly patient very ill with late, advanced obstruction of the small bowel. A calculated risk is accepted in avoiding early operation, in this procedural example based on several representative cases.

a. Diagnosis. Acute mechanical obstruction of the small bowel.

b. Admission Data. This problem is typified by a male in his eighties who has been getting along moderately well save for the infirmities of his age until five days before admission, when abdominal pain began. Those with him did not observe the fact that he failed to pass anything by rectum. He became progressively more distended. There was only a small amount of vomiting. It was noted in the twenty-four hours before admission that there was virtually no urine output. Such a patient arrives in very poor condition, semicomatose and markedly distended. Blood pressure may be expected to be low, but the patient is not in typical clinical oligemic shock. The heart is somewhat enlarged. The blood vessels are arteriosclerotic. The abdomen is distended with occasional small waves of peristalsis visible through a thin abdominal wall. X-ray shows marked dilatation of the small bowel with many fluid levels. There is no gas in the large bowel. Peristalsis is infrequent. There is no mass and no tenderness. Rectal examination is negative. There are no feces for guaiac test.

Chest X-ray shows a large heart, some increased pulmonary markings in translucent lungs, suggesting congestion in chronic emphysema.

Proctoscopy is negative.

URINE. There is a small amount of urine in the bladder.

Specific gravity—1.028
Protein—3+
pH—7.2
Sediment—erythrocytes and leucocytes

HEMATOLOGY

Hematocrit—60
Leucocyte count—18,000 per cu. mm.
Smear—hypochromia

BLOOD CHEMICAL ANALYSES

Blood urea nitrogen—115 mg. per 100 ml.
Plasma protein—7.5 gm. per 100 ml.
Plasma chloride—90 mE. per l.
Plasma sodium—130 mE. per l.
Plasma potassium—5.2 mE. per l.
Carbon dioxide combining power—16 mE. per l.
Plasma bilirubin—2 mg. per 100 ml.

c. Interpretation and General Plan. Immediate operation is contraindicated in such a patient. He is elderly, his process is late, and his renal status is that of virtually complete anuria. Further observation will be necessary before one can distinguish this as being due to desalting and decreased glomerular filtration with maximum water resorption or to an early tubular necrosis. Anesthesia and operation are extremely hazardous to the kidneys

under these circumstances. Intubation should be given every opportunity. If the patient cannot be intubated satisfactorily, catheter enterostomy should be considered. If there is gangrenous bowel present, there are very few signs of it at this time, and, after five days of obstruction, an additional day or two is going to make little difference in the prognosis on that score.

This elderly man shows evidence of marked reduction in plasma volume, as witnessed by his hematocrit of 60. The hypochromia on the smear suggests that his pre-illness hematocrit may have been low. He has a low sodium and an elevated potassium concentration, but none of these situations is as severe as one might rightfully expect them to be after five days of obstruction of the small bowel. The balance between blood supply, distention, increased venous pressure in the mesentery, and the other factors that produce fluid loss in intestinal obstruction have been such as to spare this man from maximal desalting water loss. Otherwise he would have been in shock and nearly dead by this time. This suggests that the obstruction may have been incomplete or that it is sufficiently high so that there is not a long length of bowel involved.

Azotemia, acidosis, and hyperkalemia bear witness to the severity of his renal insufficiency.

d. Preoperative Study and Care. I. INTUBATION. Such a patient should be taken to the X-ray department, where a long tube is passed into the stomach after giving his parenteral therapy a good start. Prior to passage, the tube is soaked in salt water and checked for patency of both lumina. The thread windings are permitted to shrink to be sure that the balloon lumen will not be occluded. This intubation should be performed with the same attention to detail that should accompany any other surgical procedure.

Once the tube is in the stomach, the stomach is aspirated. This material is tested for occult blood, and in this example is found to be negative; the balloon will not pass the pylorus on gentle manipulation. It is therefore left in the stomach with a primary coil, with the tip pointing toward the pylorus and the balloon one-half inflated with water.

The patient is then returned to the ward to continue his parenteral therapy.

II. PARENTERAL THERAPY. It is in this elderly man with the large heart and arteriosclerotic vessels that one may easily overdo the volume of water and salt replacement. This is late, equilibrated, desalting water loss. Treatment is commenced with plasma and sodium-chloride–lactate solution, 1000 ml. of each given at 60 drops per minute. The patient has been catheterized. Hourly urine output and vital signs are measured. In such a patient, with stabilized late obstruction, this initial parenteral therapy should be commenced before the patient is taken to the X-ray department for films and fluoroscopic passage of his long tube.

In this instance, one greets an increasing urine output as evidence of the release of vasoconstriction in the presence of good parenchymatous renal function. The fact that the urine found in the bladder had a specific gravity of 1.028 was of course a good omen in relation to tubular function.

Fluid therapy is continued after this, following the priority list. The patient has mild subtraction acidosis due to loss of alkaline secretion. For this reason, sodium lactate and bicarbonate should predominate in therapy.

Any sort of opiates or sedation is assiduously avoided. The patient is kept up and alert, and some attempt is made to give him some muscular exercise. In the first day the total sodium replacement should not exceed 300 mE., and total fluids 3000 ml., in this old man.

e. Preoperative Progress Evaluation and Interpretation. A brisk flow of urine should follow initial parenteral replacement, and does in this procedural example. This is a most favorable prognostic sign in such a case and indicates more than any other factor the wisdom of conservatism in this setting. With this return of renal function, the expenditure of another twenty-four to forty-eight hours will produce remarkable rewards in terms of improving the general condition of the patient.

An electrocardiogram shows an old infarct and bundle branch block. He is not in failure or fibrillating, but a cardiac consultant should see such a patient.

On the initial infusion of plasma and electrolyte, the hematocrit is lowered to 52. It is felt wiser to continue this elderly patient with a slightly elevated hematocrit rather than to over-replace his blood volume with colloid.

Serial measurements of venous pressure fail to indicate any evidence of congestive heart failure even with fluid replacement. This is also a good prognostic sign. Digitalis is withheld. The electrocardiogram is checked. Should venous pressure rise, digitalization would be carried out.

The tube may not pass the pylorus in the first twenty-four hours, but the patient will usually be improved by his initial treatment. During the second twenty-four hours the tube does pass into the small bowel. Steps are then actively taken to intubate the bowel. A physician remains with the patient for several hours at a time two or three times during that day. He alternately inflates and deflates the balloon, advances the tube gently, and irrigates the bowel. An X-ray is taken, using portable apparatus, on the afternoon of the day that the tube first passes the pylorus, to check its progress. It is progressing down the bowel and the patient's distention is decreasing. His physical and mental states improve.

Recheck of chemical values on the third day would be expected to show that the hematocrit has fallen to about 50 and the carbon dioxide combining power risen to 23 mE. per l. The sodium is still at 130 mE. per l., but the potassium is somewhat lower: 4.7 mE. per l. Such findings demonstrate that the plasma deficit and acid-base imbalance have been repaired by the infusion. A rise in carbon dioxide combining power is accompanied by fall in plasma potassium concentration. The blood urea nitrogen has decreased to 90 mg. per 100 ml., but it will take many days for this to return to normal—if ever, at the age of eighty-two. The slight elevation of bilirubin present on admission has not risen any higher. The patient has been given no antibiotics.

After four days the patient has been completely decompressed but has passed nothing by rectum. Insertion of a small amount of contrast material through the tube shows a point of obstruction beyond the balloon. The patient should therefore be operated upon.

f. Operation. Preparation for operation in

such an elderly person should consist of minimal sedation. The operation is carried out under an inhalation anesthetic with endotracheal intubation. Spinal anesthesia could be used but would have to be extended to T6 and might be accompanied by considerable fall in blood pressure in this elderly man.

The operative procedure would most likely consist in release of an adhesive band obstruction or midgut volvulus, with resection if necessary. Although the bowel above the obstruction has been decompressed, it would still be boggy and with very poor muscular tone.

The patient is returned to the ward on continuing long-tube suction, and parenteral maintenance.

g. Postoperative Study and Care. DIET AND ORDERS. Such a patient should be given something by mouth as soon as possible—tasty hot fluids in small amounts. The purpose is to stimulate peristalsis and parotid function rather than to provide bulk intake. With the return of peristalsis and passage of gas by rectum, diet is advanced as rapidly as possible. The stimulus of familiar tastes and smells of food is essential to beginning gastrointestinal rehabilitation.

PARENTERAL THERAPY. Parenteral maintenance is at the minimum level. The patient is given 750 to 1000 ml. of water each day and minimal electrolyte during the postoperative period. Preoperatively, electrolyte replacement has been active; continuing it postoperatively is unnecessary.

Had this patient shown a seriously depressed sodium concentration at any time, he would have been given some concentrated electrolyte; he was not overloaded with electrolyte-free water and for this reason has not shown further dilutional hypotonicity.

PROGRESS EVALUATION AND INTERPRETATION. The return of such a patient's effective peristalsis is apt to be slow. If X-rays are taken frequently, they will show continued dilated loops and abnormalities of the gas pattern. Such X-rays need not be taken and will often be misleading; clinical progress is the important thing at this time. If the patient does not become distended, if he continues to put out material by rectum, and if he has increasing appetite and ambulation, one should not be misled by the continuing appearance of the X-ray film, which may be very abnormal for days, showing many dilated loops and fluid levels until tone returns. Clinical signs (peristaltic sound, appetite) are the guides.

In older people, the final restoration to normal of bowel tone and appetite is quite slow. The patient may go through a period of refusing food. If he vomits, his intake should be cut back and he should be started again with appetizing small quantities. This is the sort of a dietary situation where quality rather than quantity counts. It is also a situation in which the various factors involved in the "shift-over" from intravenous to oral intake are of critical importance. If a patient such as this is kept on daily morning intravenous rations of carbohydrate and fat or other nutrient, and on gastric suction, his own peristaltic activity will remain indefinitely inhibited. Stop the intravenous therapy, take out the tube, and give him some hot food.

Analysis of intestinal tube returns is helpful as a guide in the treatment of such patients. The results are sufficiently predictable so that the analyses are not absolutely essential.

Analysis of the urine for electrolyte also provides somewhat of a guide. The early urine specimens in this man would be expected to be sodium-free until sodium is given in replacement. Serial measurements of urinary electrolyte have not been an important clinical guide in such cases. When hypotonicity is excessive and blood-pressure maintenance poorly achieved, renal salt wasting should be sought out.

Section V.   Obstruction of the Large Bowel

In contrast to obstruction of the small bowel, the metabolic deficit suffered by patients with obstruction of the large bowel is slight. Distention of the large bowel does not produce an alteration in its osmotic function with outpouring into the lumen of large quantities of water and salt, as it does in the small intestine. The large bowel responds to dilatation by maintaining its tone and blood supply until very late in the process. It may become gas-filled, and the right colon may become fluid-filled with foul-smelling fecal material which threatens to rupture, yet there will be little evidence of acute desalting water loss or reduction in effective volume or renal function. Obstruction of the large bowel often presents itself in a patient with a rather protracted history, over a period of several months, of alternating constipation and diarrhea with some abdominal cramps, and now appearing before the surgeon with considerable abdominal distention and an X-ray picture of a dilated, gas-and-feces-filled transverse colon and cecum.

If the ileocecal valve remains competent, there will be very little reflux up into the small bowel, and the patient will present himself to the surgeon early, with a large cecum. If the ileocecal valve is incompetent, the reflux into the small bowel will be quite considerable. Distention of the small bowel will be shown by X-ray, and some effort must often be used to discern that the lesion is actually in the large bowel rather than in the small bowel. In such a case, more fluid is lost because of this distention of the small bowel.

A. GENERAL PLAN

In patients entering with obstruction of the large bowel, X-ray localization of the lesion should be done early. Some time during the first six to twelve hours of hospitalization, a barium enema should be gently carried out. The X-ray department should be instructed that the objective is not to get a perfect photograph of the entire bowel, but instead to localize the obstructing point. This is particularly important because one commonly sees individuals who appear to have obstruction of the large bowel but in whom there is no obstructing lesion—particularly those with liver disease, in the form of either acute hepatitis or cirrhosis. In advanced peritoneal malignancy, also, a sort of "large-bowel atony" may supervene, resembling malignant obstruction. In those with a widely patent ileocecal valve the initial films may be confusing, as mentioned, and a barium enema essential to the diagnosis.

If an obstructing point is found, the patient is treated conservatively by the use of such parenteral fluids and electrolytes as are required to maintain the patient, expecting a small daily weight loss by oxidation of body fat until diet is resumed. Such needed amounts of fluid and electrolyte are not large.

A long tube is not advisable in most such cases; only when reflux distention of the small bowel is present is it needed. An indwelling nasogastric tube is used to prevent the further passage of swallowed air.

Patients who come into the hospital with the colon obstructed by cancer of the left colon, on going to bed and with fluid therapy, will often start passing flatus and fluid by rectum and decompress themselves sufficiently so that emergency surgery is avoided; the preparation of the bowel for definitive operation is then accomplished either by elective transverse colostomy or by nonoperative measures, depending on the degree of deflation achieved spontaneously.

B. PROXIMAL COLOSTOMY OR CECOSTOMY

If the cecum is extremely distended on admission, decompression must be brought about as an emergency. Under other circumstances—the usual situation—colostomy is not an emergency. The choice lies between cecostomy and transverse colostomy. If the lesion is low in the left colon, a transverse colostomy is a safer and surer method of preparation and will result in a completely defunctioned left colon. If, on the other hand, the lesion is in the upper left colon, the splenic flexure, or the transverse colon, transverse colostomy will compromise the adequacy of the subsequent extirpative operation, and cecostomy is preferable. In extremely ill patients or patients with giant distention of the large bowel, the more extensive manipulation involved in a transverse colostomy is inadvisable and a cecostomy is far preferable. Occasionally, where an emergency cecostomy has been done in the presence of giant distention, a subsequent elective transverse colostomy is an advisable preliminary to left colectomy.

A transverse colostomy should be done so as to bring both limbs fully out of the abdomen as a double-barreled procedure. A partial opening over a glass rod is unsatisfactory for defunctioning. If left colectomy is contemplated the transverse colostomy should be well to the right. A sigmoid colostomy has but few remaining indications in obstructing lesion of the left colon favorable for resection.

Where no obstruction exists, there is no need for preliminary or proximal decompression unless an anastomosis is to be very low or somehow insecure, in which case the proximal vent can be supplementary to the resection.

After cecostomy or transverse colostomy the brief period of starvation until peristalsis is resumed can readily be weathered by the use of very moderate intravenous rations of fluid. The use of 5 per cent dextrose in water with some potassium will suffice, since the loss of sodium chloride in these cases is minimal; only with diarrhea or distention of the small bowel does sodium loss become a problem. Feeding by mouth may soon be resumed. Frequently the patient can pass through a two or three weeks' preparation of the left colon and resumption of caloric intake, wholly on the basis of oral feeding. The overadministration of water-and-salt infusions is a common fault here. When anemia and hypovolemia are present, as they often are, whole blood is to be used, or, in the elderly or infirm, separated cells.

Cases of villous papilloma of the colon have been reported in which the exudation from the redundant surface of the tumor produced significant desalting of the patient.

C. CLINICAL PROCEDURE IN OBSTRUCTION OF THE LARGE BOWEL

The following procedure is based on the occurrence of obstruction of the left colon due to an annular carcinoma of the sigmoid. This example brings together features from several representative cases.

1. *Diagnosis.* Carcinoma of the sigmoid with obstruction of the large bowel.

2. *Admission Data.* This procedure involves a woman in her sixties with a history of intermittent constipation and diarrhea over the past several months. Weight loss has not been marked. The patient's normal weight has been 62 kg., and she has lost 7 kg. to her present weight of 55 kg. She was of obese habitus. She has had no frank bleeding by rectum and no vomiting. Examination shows the abdomen to be diffusely distended and nontender. Typically, in early cases, there is no mass. Rectal and pelvic examination are essentially negative. Proctoscopy fails to reveal pathology, but the mucus seen is grossly bloody.

There is no evidence of collateral system disease.

X-rays show a tremendously distended cecum but no other evidence of pathology. Barium introduced gently by rectum shows a constricting lesion at the lower end of the descending colon. No further films are taken.

URINE.   Normal.

HEMATOLOGY

Hematocrit—32
Leucocyte count—9200 per cu. mm.
Blood smear—normal.

BLOOD CHEMICAL ANALYSES

Blood urea nitrogen—20 mg. per 100 ml.
Plasma protein—7 gm. per 100 ml.
Plasma sodium—135 mE. per l.
Plasma potassium—4.5 mE. per l.
Carbon dioxide combining power—26 mE. per l.

3. *Interpretation and General Plan.* Such a problem appears to center entirely around the election of the initial operative procedure. The patient has tolerated her obstruction quite well. The ileocecal valve is evidently competent, which results in a very distended cecum, with no distended loops of small bowel to be seen proximally. The cecum is so large as to present a threat of rupture. The transverse colon is so large that exteriorization in an adequate transverse colostomy will be difficult. "What's hard for the surgeon is hard on the patient." Cecostomy is the simplest and most direct first step.

The patient's biochemical situation is one of a very mild disturbance, as is characteristically seen in such patients; there is slight azotemia and a slight tendency to dilutional hypotonicity. Neither of these calls for complicated steps or parenteral therapy.

The operation of cecostomy is elected here and need not be delayed.

4. *Preoperative Study and Care.* Such a patient should be given nothing by mouth for the first day or two, or sips only. A nasogastric tube is inserted on suction to avoid further accumulation of swallowed air. There is no use in passing a long tube in such cases. The patient is given a slow intravenous provision of 5 per cent glucose in saline solution, totaling 1500 ml. because she has had very little oral intake in the past twenty-four hours. After six hours she is taken to the operating room.

5. *Operation.* ANESTHESIA. Local infiltration of procaine and field block, supplemented by inhalation agents if there is discomfort.

OPERATIVE PROCEDURE. A sloping, right-sided oblique muscle-splitting incision is made at a right angle to the McBurney incision but in that location. The cecum is gently lifted up. It is so distended that it cannot be delivered in the wound until it is aspirated with a trocar. After it has been partly emptied, it is delivered into the wound and a soft rubber cecostomy tube is inserted with rigorous aseptic precautions. A carefully constructed serosal tunnel is made around this tube for a distance of an inch and a half. The tube is left in place. There is initially a considerable egress of fluid and air. The wound is closed loosely around the tube. The patient is returned to the ward with the cecum on gravity drainage.

6. *Postoperative Study and Care.* PARENTERAL THERAPY. The patient is given one additional intravenous infusion (1500 ml. of 5 per cent dextrose in water) after operation. The following day she is given two slow transfusions of whole blood because of the decreased erythrocyte mass indicated by her hematocrit on admission, and her low-grade bowel hemorrhage. Other than this no parenteral therapy is given.

The patient is started on small amounts of fluid by mouth immediately after operation, and this diet is increased as soon as possible. The nasogastric tube is left in place only over the first night. Rechecked chemical values two days later show little change save for a return of the blood urea nitrogen level to normal.

PROGRESS EVALUATION AND INTERPRETATION. Within three days such a patient often starts to pass some gas by rectum and has a bowel movement. This is characteristic of proximal decompression in left colonic cancer. It suggests that alterations in peristalsis and edema, as well as the neoplasm itself, have something to do with the obstruction.

With the cecostomy functioning well, there is not a great deal to be gained by prolonged procrastination of operation. The cecostomy will not be completely defunctioning. Intestinal antibiotics may be given by mouth and instilled into the cecostomy. One must therefore consider a transverse colostomy to be done at the time of resection, if more complete defunctioning becomes necessary.

The patient's nutritional management prior to operation need not be complicated. Extensive vitamin supplements should be given because avitaminosis is the rule here. The diet is reduced markedly the day before definitive operation, with no solids the evening before; the small bowel will then be well collapsed at the time of surgery.

One hopes to find a favorable lesion of the left colon without hepatic metastases, in which case an extensive left colectomy should be done, taking the inferior mesenteric artery at its source. The splenic flexure is mobilized, the transverse colon is brought downward, and anastomosed to the rectosigmoid.

If the cecostomy tube is removed forcibly, the mucous membrane will be everted, which prevents spontaneous closure and makes operative closure necessary. If, when it is ready to come easily, it is gently removed, and if a satisfactory serosal tunnel has been made, the cecostomy wound will close itself.

It is possible to pass a ballooned double-lumen tube into a cecostomy and thread it down the large bowel to irrigate the large bowel, remove inspissated feces, and infuse antibiotics. If the bowel is large and sluggish and does not decompress well, this is advisable. If the large bowel is not being satisfactorily decompressed, a transverse colostomy should be done as a preliminary to surgery. It should be done well to the right so as not to compromise mobilization of the splenic flexure.

Section VI.   Ileus

A. ADYNAMIC ILEUS

Ileus arising independent of intrinsic disease of the bowel or its serous coverings and manifesting itself as a distended atonic small bowel without propulsive peristalsis can present a serious problem in pain, distention, and starvation. Fractures of the lumbar vertebrae, the passage of ureteral stones, or the other acute diseases of the urinary tract are causes of this state. Acute processes at the root of the mesentery, such as acute pancreatitis, and mesenteric embolus or thrombosis are accompanied by severe ileus. In pneumonia and pulmonary embolism, remarkable degrees of intestinal atony are found. In bleeding ulcer ileus is often bothersome, and is due in part to fecal impaction, a common complication of the nonoperative management of acute bleeding duodenal ulcer. In all of these situations a successful outcome depends largely upon the subsidence of the underlying process, although the ileus *per se* threatens survival.

Fermentation of intestinal contents doubtless produces some gas and is responsible for the odor of the gastrointestinal gas, but the gas so produced would be largely diffusible carbon dioxide. The diffusibility of this gas (as opposed to oxygen and nitrogen) would be such as to militate against its accumulation in the bowel. The gaseous distention of a patient with adynamic ileus is instead due to the accumulation of swallowed air in a partially paralyzed small intestine. Effective intubation and suction are vitally important in treatment. Whether this intubation should be by way of a nasogastric or a long tube must depend upon the circumstances. The difficulty of passing a Miller-Abbott tube in such patients is not surprising in view of the fact that smooth muscle tone is required for the passage of such a tube. Nasogastric suction, if it is functioning well and if the tube is frequently irrigated, suffices to remove the swallowed air, and prevents further distention. It is of interest that the liquid material passed from the stomach into the small bowel does such patients no harm and is ultimately reabsorbed either in the small bowel or in the large bowel. If the patient is placed on continuous gastric suction in the treatment of ileus, a considerable desalting will result from the tube suction, with a tendency toward subtraction alkalosis and volume reduction. At the present time, we have no way of avoiding such a problem other than by intravenous replacement of the lost salts. A suction device that removes swallowed air and reinjects the comparatively small amounts of fluid aspirate would be helpful here.

Distention of the small bowel increases intra-abdominal pressure, diminishes diaphragmatic excursion, and increases the hazard of venous thrombosis and embolism. If long-tube intubation is successful, the highest area of intestine containing the tube will be deflated and regain its tone, develop propulsive motion, and the tube will gradually pass down the intestine. To treat such a patient by operative catheter enterostomy is rational only if one is dealing with extreme degrees of distention. It is most unusual to have to resort to such a step in adynamic ileus associated with retroperitoneal inflammation or disease of other viscera. As X-rays show increasing amounts of gas passing into the large intestine, the use of gentle enemas or an indwelling rectal tube may start the patient around the corner to normal gastrointestinal function.

Too-frequent X-raying of these patients should not become a part of their care. Patients with adynamic ileus do not need to be X-rayed over and over; one is treating the patient and not the X-ray appearances. Patients who are recovering clinically with effective peristalsis and passage of gas and flatus, and who are beginning to take food and fluids by mouth, may show residual areas of dilatation in the small bowel for many days. Frequent X-raying in an attempt to deal with these residual loops of bowel in a recovering patient will lead the patient into much more extensive therapy than is necessary, and often to an unnecessary surgical operation.

In a patient with adynamic ileus, daily parenteral fluid therapy is necessary. The maxim of "in-balance therapy" as regards water, sodium, and chloride again applies. Any attempt to put such patients into nitrogen and calorie balance will be unrewarding in relation to the tremendous effort required. The patient will be overloaded with fluid for little real gain. Daily restoration of losses of fluid and salt is essential. Some accumulation of fluid may occur within the gut lumen in adynamic ileus, but it is not in the order of magnitude found in organic obstruction. Potassium must be given daily in amounts of 40 to 100 mE., depending on circumstances.

B. POSTOPERATIVE "ILEUS-OBSTRUCTION"

The seemingly redundant term "postoperative ileus-obstruction" is used intentionally to describe the situation seen in postoperative patients who have dilated loops of small bowel, cramps, ineffective peristalsis, and fever after an abdominal procedure. It is difficult at first to discern the extent to which organic obstruction plays a role and to what extent ileus due to trauma to the bowel, some degree of contamination, or infection, peritonitis, or pancreatitis is the cause. In such patients it is possible to demonstrate some sort of fibrous adhesions somewhere in the peritoneal cavity, and one readily falls into the conclusion that they are causing the difficulty. They rarely are. The situation is not in any way analogous to acute *de novo* obstruction of the small bowel, and the principles that underlie its treatment are entirely different.

Although postoperative ileus-obstruction is no longer as common a complication of intraperitoneal surgery as it formerly was, it may be seen after a wide variety of surgical procedures. It occurs after such procedures as presacral neurectomy, hysterectomy, oophorectomy, colectomy, combined abdominoperineal resection, cholecystectomy, and subtotal gastrectomy. When this situation arises after subtotal gastrectomy, the surgeon has a difficult differential diagnosis between simple ileus-obstruction, focal sepsis (duodenal stump), and postoperative pancreatitis. The level of blood amylase may be somewhat elevated in postoperative ileus-obstruction and in early focal sepsis; values greater than four times normal are rarely seen except in pancreatitis.

There are four guiding principles.

(1) *In postoperative ileus-obstruction, it is virtually impossible to distinguish the adhesive-band obstructive element from the adynamic feature;* segmental areas of ileus may produce obstruction of neighboring normal areas, giving rise to cramps in a generally quiet abdomen.

(2) *Hasty reoperation on these patients prior to the fourteenth postoperative day invariably makes the patient much sicker* and the recovery of bowel tone must start all over again. Again, it is impossible to tell the obstructive from the motor component, the restoration of bowel tone takes time, and the patient suffers a severe setback from the reoperation.

(3) *Therefore, the treatment of this condition should be basically nonoperative.* Intestinal intubation and therapy with fluid and electrolytes, avoiding hypokalemia or fluid overloading, should take precedence over all other measures. The distended, quiet abdomen is a part of the clinical picture of hypokalemic alkalosis as well as postoperative ileus-obstruction; peristaltic activity is often regained with the help of potassium salts intravenously administered.

(4) *On such conservative measures the picture will often clarify itself* by complete subsidence, or by the gradual revelation of a focal area of sepsis that has previously escaped notice in the distended abdomen; an early rectal abscess or early subphrenic or subhepatic abscess will become evident, and draining it will take care of the intestinal disorder.

If, on two or three days of conservative management, distention is still very considerable, so much as to interfere with diaphragmatic excursion and venous return; and if it is impossible to intubate the small bowel either because of upper abdominal surgery or for other reasons, catheter enterostomy also has a place here. The physiologic situation is rather analogous to late obstruction of the small bowel. The surgeon is aiming his therapy at relief of distention and its deleterious physiologic consequences, and not at a futile and hasty attempt to restore the patency of the entire intestinal tract to normal.

It is a characteristic of patients suffering desalting water loss in the postoperative period that they develop hypotonicity and mild acidosis. Both desalting and dilution play a role in the pathogenesis. With this there is hypotension varying all the way from an unstable blood pressure to a frankly shocklike state. Blood transfusion and concentrated salt (sodium chloride and sodium bicarbonate) are both important in the treatment of such hypotension.

In postoperative ileus-obstruction, full-dress laparotomy before the fourteenth postoperative day results in either a fatal outcome, a shocklike state from which it is extremely difficult to rally the patient, or the development of intraperitoneal sepsis. Attempts to resect or "strip" portions of the intestine or to use multiple needle punctures when dealing with this condition are foolhardy. The defect is physiologic and motor, not anatomic.

If the patient has been treated so that distention has been abated, either by intubation or by tube enterostomy, but he is still obstructed, or if he had had a prolonged period of seven to twelve days of normal postoperative convalescence before becoming obstructed, an organic lesion may be predominant and laparotomy is to be carried out after suitable preparation.

Even in those cases in which the diagnosis is extremely obscure, hasty reoperation for distention without focal signs is inadvisable. Where there are explosive onset and clear localizing signs to suggest bleeding or leak after peritoneal surgery, early reexploration is essential. This is described in the next chapter. In any event, the possibility of acute pancreatitis must be considered.

C. CLINICAL PROCEDURE IN POSTOPERATIVE ILEUS-OBSTRUCTION

The following clinical procedure is based on representative examples of ileus-obstruction coming on after laparotomy, in this example an anastomotic operation in the left colon.

1. *Diagnosis.* Postoperative ileus-obstruction after operative anastomosis for carcinoma of the sigmoid flexure.

2. *History.* Such a patient might be expected to have been admitted to a hospital with carcinoma of the left colon, where a primary resection and anastomosis were carried out. Nasogastric suction was used through the operative period and the operation itself appeared to be uneventful, although there was some inadvertent contamination of the peritoneal cavity with fecal material. Antibiotics had been used in the bowel before operation and the patient has been on postoperative antibiotics in very large doses.

The nasogastric tube was removed the second morning after operation. The patient did not pass anything by rectum. He was apprehensive, swallowing air. Distention was progressive. The patient's temperature did not return to normal. There was evidence of some atelectasis at the lower lobe of the left lung. Such a patient appears to become progressively sicker. His blood pressure is unstable. On the seventh day the nasogastric tube was reinserted. X-ray films showed diffuse abdominal distention. When the patient was seen in consultation, physical examination displayed no focal signs of infection or inflammation in the peritoneal cavity. At this point, a portion of the wound is often openeb and no evidence of wound sepsis found.

LABORATORY FINDINGS

URINE. Normal.

HEMATOLOGY

Hematocrit—32
Leucocyte count—16,000 per cu. mm.

BLOOD CHEMICAL ANALYSES

Blood urea nitrogen—55 mg. per 100 ml.
Plasma protein—5.5 gm. per 100 ml.
Plasma sodium—126 mE. per l.
Plasma potassium—5.3 mE. per l.

Plasma chloride—92 mE. per l.
Carbon dioxide combining power—18 mE. per l.
Plasma bilirubin—2 mg. per 100 ml.
Amylase—Normal

3. *Interpretation and General Plan.* Here is a patient, now a week after operation, whose abdomen is diffusely distended. The patient is febrile. The surgeon is worried about intra-peritoneal sepsis. He is also concerned that there is present obstruction of the small bowel. One school of thought strongly favors re-operation.

The metabolic picture is that of a patient harboring a febrile illness, probably pulmonary in nature. He is hypotensive and weak. There is azotemia, dilutional hyponatremia, slight elevation of bilirubin, and slight elevation of plasma potassium concentration, all characteristic of a sick postoperative patient with ileus-obstruction, desalting, and oliguria.

The lack of signs of peritoneal inflammation is very difficult to evaluate because the patient is on multiple broad-spectrum antibiotics. Peritonitis could be present. There is no tenderness; the leucocyte count is only 16,000. With the exception of this suspicion of peritonitis, which must be watched for with care, the rest of the picture is characteristic of postoperative ileus-obstruction, and an initial program of conservative management should be followed, to be abandoned should new evidences develop.

The X-ray does not show distention of the large bowel. If there were a distended cecum or transverse colon, a cecostomy or transverse colostomy should be done in any patient with this sort of picture after a left colonic anastomosis.

4. *Further Care.* INTUBATION. A ballooned long tube, preferably a Miller-Abbott tube, is passed. It will be very difficult to get this through the pylorus. If it cannot pass the pylorus, it is left in the stomach on continuous suction.

PARENTERAL FLUID THERAPY. The plan of parenteral administration of fluids is arranged so as to restore extracellular chemistry to normal without expanding total volume. Because of the severe hyponatremia with slight hyperkalemia and metabolic acidosis and hypotension, the patient should be started with concentrated sodium bicarbonate or lactate. In the first day, approximately 200 mE. of sodium are given at a sodium concentration of 600 mE. per l. (This corresponds approximately to the sodium concentration of 3 per cent sodium chloride solution.) As sodium is given, the potassium concentration will fall. The patient should be given potassium after the first infusion and reestablishment of urine output.

TRANSFUSION OF WHOLE BLOOD. This patient needs transfusion, but it should come on the second day of management rather than on the first day with the sodium load. On the second day, two transfusions of whole blood are given.

PROTEIN THERAPY. This patient's plasma protein concentration is low to begin with and will fall even lower with sodium administration. Urine output should be watched with interest because we would expect this patient, given concentrated sodium salts, to have a good diuresis. In either event, extra protein is needed and concentrated albumin should be used. Some element of edema may play a role in the ileus-obstruction, and albumin may have a specific effect. Two units of albumin are given daily for the first four days.

ADMINISTRATION OF ANTIBIOTICS. Such a patient is apt to have been put on multiple broad-spectrum antibiotics. There are very few signs of peritonitis. His temperature ranges each day from 100 to 102° F. It is suggested that the antibiotics be stopped completely. It is unlikely that they are making any contribution whatsoever to the patient's welfare. They can be started up again or shifted if clinical signs of sepsis demand. In most instances little change will be noted with their discontinuance and the clinical management will have been clarified and simplified.

5. *Progress Evaluation and Interpretation.* No patient is quickly going to rectify this situation, which is due to a mixture of ileus following intra-abdominal trauma, contamination, infection above the diaphragm, and gaseous distention, in part from swallowing air. The patient's leucocyte count is not sufficiently elevated to support the diagnosis of peritonitis; stopping the antibiotics permits better

evaluation of the physical signs. Rectal examination continues to be negative—an extremely important bit of evidence against peritoneal infection.

The initial block of time for conservative handling is mapped out at three days. During an initial three-day period of intubation and good metabolic management, such a patient should improve enough to indicate that one is dealing with postoperative ileus-obstruction and not some more ominous process.

Careful attention should be given to the bronchopulmonary situation in all such cases. Tracheal suction is often useful; bronchoscopy is occasionally necessary.

Parenteral fluid therapy must be very carefully tailored to the needs of the patient. After the initial period of concentrated salt administration, the patient should be managed on a clinical balance with frequent weighings and allowance for daily weight loss of about 350 to 500 gm.

If distention persists or focal peritoneal signs develop, operation is considered, its chief objective being drainage of any abscess that has formed, or, if distention alone remains the problem, catheter enterostomy. Exploratory laparotomy with rehandling of the intestinal tract will further impair its motor function. As mentioned, if such a patient as this is subjected to full-dress laparotomy there will be discovered, within the peritoneal cavity, various adhesions and fibrinous and fibrous bands, some of which are held accountable for the defect. But after the operation is over the same motor disorder is found to remain, now exaggerated by the new trauma.

If, at the end of three days, the patient is somewhat better, conservatism continues. The long tube is withdrawn as peristalsis returns or there is material passed by rectum. Attention should be given to maintenance of the patient's parotid secretory flow during this long period of dietary interruption. Some candy or chewing gum is used. As peristalsis is resumed, material is passed by rectum, and the long tube removed, dietary advancement should be carried out, using the principles previously mentioned for the shift over from parenteral to oral intake.

The plasma concentration of potassium may fall abruptly upon the administration of basic sodium salt. After the first or second day, daily administration of potassium will be necessary until diet is resumed.

In such a patient with hyponatremia and hyperkalemia the electrocardiogram should be checked periodically; if digitalis is used, the dosage and effects will be affected by this metabolic disorder; if anesthesia and operation become necessary, blood-pressure maintenance will be difficult until plasma tonicity and normal alkalinity are restored.

CHAPTER 35

The Gastrointestinal Tract: Perfora-tion, Peritonitis, and Sepsis

Section I. Esophageal Perforation and Mediastinitis

Perforation of the esophagus with mediasti-nitis is rapidly fatal if not treated promptly and accurately. If the perforation involves the free pleural cavity, there is an acute hy-dropneumothorax, and the diagnosis is not difficult. When the perforation does not in-volve the free pleural cavity and there is no hydropneumothorax, it is initially difficult to differentiate among perforation of the esopha-gus, perforation of an upper abdominal vis-cus, and acute cardiopulmonary events. Whether the perforation is a true hydrostatic rupture of the esophagus or involves a pene-trating ulcer or (most commonly) a combina-tion of the two, the problem in management of the patient is essentially the same: urgent operation, closure of the defect, drainage, and some method for feeding if the patient cannot eat by about the seventh day.

The cause of the rapid fatality in mediasti-nitis is not entirely clear. Infection in a vulner-able areolar space with plasma loss is one aspect. But the shock-producing potential is so great as to suggest that the sepsis around the heart, great vessels, and lung roots or the alteration in intrathoracic pressure and dy-namics also contributes to the rapid deteriora-tion of the patient. The localization of "vol-ume-receptor" areas near the right heart might be invoked to explain hypotension when mediastinal pressure is increased. If

shock is present, intensive treatment with whole blood or plasma is essential; peripheral pressure and flow are guides.

After operation the patient may go through a prolonged period when eating is impossible. In some instances an acute esophageal per-foration will yield to a chronic esophageal leak into the pleural cavity and from there to the outside world. With careful metabolic care and the avoidance of hasty reoperation, such a situation is quite compatible with life. The perforation will heal if gastric drainage is normal, if gastric reflux is not too prominent a feature, and if nutrition is maintained. If the initial rupture has been caused by ob-structing duodenal ulcer, attention must be given to pyloric patency at this early stage. If the gastric outlet is obstructed and there is regurgitation of gastric juice into the esoph-agus, a gastroenterostomy may be necessary to procure healing of the esophageal lesion.

If an esophageal fistula is established, the pa-tient must be fed distal to this. Jejunostomy is more appropriate than gastrostomy because of the hazard of reflux in the latter. An indwell-ing soft nasogastric tube may be satisfactory for feeding but leaves a foreign body at the fistula site and may produce reflux through the fistula. It should be tried, with X-ray study, before jejunostomy is done.

Section II. Early Peritonitis

In the adult, peritonitis is almost always due to perforation of the gastrointestinal tract or its appendages. Metabolic measures are

vitally important in care, as is the proper tim-ing and execution of whatever operative measures are indicated. We can divide these cases into three general groups: first, those early cases due to a process primarily septic; second, those early cases due primarily to leakage of normal gastrointestinal contents into the peritoneal cavity; and third, late peritonitis from whatever cause.

A. EARLY SEPTIC PERITONITIS

Septic peritonitis is a peritonitis resulting from peritoneal dissemination of a body fluid already involved by an invasive bacterial infection. This is most commonly seen in dissemination of sepsis from acute appendicitis and from acute diverticulitis.

The threat to the patient's life initially lies in three areas.

(1) The balance between bacterial invasion and host resistance may be so distorted that an overwhelming infection results, with blood-stream invasion, hypotension, and death.

(2) Unnecessarily extensive or meddlesome operation may be performed at a time when the balance between invasion and resistance is just moving in the patient's favor. Such a favorable change is the result of an unimpeded systemic immune process and local anatomic walling-off; careless or unnecessarily meddlesome operation destroys these defenses.

(3) Acute plasma loss into the peritoneal cavity plays a role that may be critical, depending upon the degree to which the total peritoneal surface has become irritated by the the offending organism. The plasma loss in these cases is not as impressive nor as important in early care as it is in leakage peritonitis, to be described below, but it is definitely a factor.

B. MANAGEMENT OF EARLY SEPTIC PERITONITIS

The management of early septic peritonitis rests on three principles.

1. Antibiotic Therapy

In patients with early septic peritonitis from appendicitis or diverticulitis with rupture, it is impossible when the patient is first seen to gain an accurate idea of the pathogenic flora and their antibiotic sensitivities. The infection is usually a foul purulent collection of organisms from the gastrointestinal tract, together with some gram-positive cocci, presumably of respiratory origin. Such patients are apt to enter the hospital with organisms sensitive to simple antibiotic therapy, and for this reason administration of penicillin and streptomycin in large doses is given initially. The value of such antibiotic therapy in early septic peritonitis is unquestioned, in contrast to the later manifestations of peritonitis, in which the choice of antibiotics is difficult, their value open to question, and other steps much more important. *In early septic peritonitis, antibiotics must be used aggressively and at very high dosage.*

2. Metabolic Management

Metabolic management should be devoted toward maintaining a normal blood volume and a normal volume of body water with normal electrolyte concentrations. Calorie and nitrogen balance cannot possibly be achieved in the early cases. The patient should be placed quietly in bed, a step that may assist in the localization of the peritoneal process. The frequent use of opiate medication is unwise. Nasogastric suction helps to avoid distention; its value consists in the removal of swallowed air. The removal of the normal gastrointestinal secretions accompanying this removal of air is not important and imposes an obligation in fluid and salt therapy.

Parenteral treatment must include sufficient water to cover the insensible losses of a patient with high fever and dyspnea. Insensible losses in the range of 2000 to 4000 ml. a day or more may be encountered in large male patients with early septic peritonitis. The only way to check the adequacy of fluid therapy in covering these losses is by weighing the patient. This should not be done too frequently. In the acutely ill patient with septic peritonitis, frequent measurements of body weight are extremely difficult to carry out and involve some hazard to the patient; daily weighing is seldom possible, but weighing two or three times a week is feasible.

Electrolyte therapy should consist of sufficient sodium, chloride, and potassium to balance the loss of gastrointestinal juices. The simple rule of "volume-for-volume" replacement of gastrointestinal suction losses by 5 per cent glucose in saline solution yields good results in young people with good kidneys. The more accurate quantitative estimate based on electrolyte content of the discharge is superior, but not an absolute necessity in most cases of septic peritonitis. *In older patients a balanced salt solution must be used.*

The loss of potassium in the aspirated gastric juice is not great. There may be some refluxed intestinal content, but, as a general rule, this mixed upper intestinal fluid will not average more than 10 to 30 mE. per l. of potassium. The loss of potassium in the urine may be in the range of 30 to 50 mE. per day, and for this reason potassium replacement as potassium chloride in amounts of 40 to 100 mM. per day is adequate to maintain such patients and is of assistance in avoiding alkalosis. If the loss of gastric juice is excessive and the juice is very highly acid, some replacement with ammonium chloride is indicated.

Periodic checks of the chemical values of the plasma in such patients should be made. An initial measurement of blood urea nitrogen, carbon dioxide combining power, and chloride, sodium, potassium, and protein concentrations should provide a base line against which the therapy may be followed. This series of analyses need not be repeated oftener than twice or three times a week unless there is hypotension or oliguria. If there is, the hourly urine output should be measured as a guide to treatment.

In the abdominal distention that accompanies septic peritonitis, there is a sequestration of fluid and gas in the gastrointestinal tract resembling that seen in ileus and obstruction. It is rarely as large in amount or as significant physiologically as that lost into the lumen above a fixed obstruction. There is also plasma loss into the peritoneum; any hematocrit elevation should be treated quantitatively by infusions of plasma or albumin.

The body wasting produced by an acute septic process is extremely rapid, as described in Part IV. For this reason, after the first five to ten days of most acute illness, it is important to supplement the intravenous water-and-electrolyte therapy with some form of caloric material. The infusions of 5 per cent glucose have provided a small caloric ration; these can be supplemented with 10 per cent or 25 per cent glucose in a catheter to the superior vena cava. As the patient rounds out his first week or two, if he is less ill and afebrile, and if the localized abscesses are drained, but he is still unable to eat, the nutritional program may be furthered by the use of intravenous fat or intravenous alcohol. If it is possible to supply the patient with 600 to 1000 calories per day, the rapidity of body wasting will be lessened.

3. Operative Intervention in Early Septic Peritonitis

The most important of the three factors in the early metabolic management of septic peritonitis is proper choice of the surgical operation and its appropriate timing.

In appendiceal peritonitis, operation during the first twenty-four hours of hospitalization is almost always advisable. Only in those patients who show absolutely no sign of walling off, in whom under medication or anesthesia no mass is found, and who are toxic with high fever, rapid pulse rate, and low leucocyte count should surgery be avoided. In these cases the gamble must be accepted that with antibiotic therapy and good support the infection will localize. It is in these very toxic cases that rooting around in the peritoneal cavity in an attempt to remove a difficult appendix will be fatal despite all other measures. Due consideration should be given to this group of cases in which early surgery is inadvisable, although they are increasingly rare.

Much more typical is the patient with appendiceal peritonitis tracing back to an onset three to six days prior to admission, who has a peritoneal infection with some evidence of localization. In such a case, a preliminary period of hydration, antibiotic therapy, and rest of twelve to eighteen hours should be followed by operation. If the hematocrit is found on admission to be elevated, treatment with plasma or a plasma expander is indicated, exactly as in leakage peritonitis, to be described below.

The choice of anesthesia is critical in the patient's management. A general anesthetic, with the patient showing good oxygenation and relaxation, is far to be preferred over some compromise attempted under local anesthesia. Such local anesthesia is often much more tiring and a much greater trial to the patient than is a general anesthetic.

Under anesthesia, assessment as to the presence of a drainable mass can be made. Oftentimes a wadded omentum around a perforated appendix will be palpable. Gentle approach to the mass by an incision immediately over it will reveal whether this is a drainable collection of pus or a removable appendix. When in doubt it is much better to insert a drain than it is to attempt an extensive dissection for removal of the appendix.

The inexperienced surgeon is all too apt to feel a sense of remorse if, in operating on such a patient, he does not achieve the removal of a specimen which can be sent to the pathology laboratory. He should recall that if this area is drained it can produce very little further deficit to the patient, even though the appendix remains *in situ*. If there is a purulent collection of creamy, foul-smelling pus around the appendix, draining it should be the only objective of the operation. No one ever died from a cecal fistula.

After operation, the antibiotic management of the peritonitis may be based on the antibiotic sensitivity of the organism cultured from the peritoneal cavity.

If the peritonitis arises from ruptured diverticulitis—another common cause of acute septic peritonitis—the early surgical operation should consist merely of a transverse colostomy. The genesis of perforated sigmoid diverticulitis is that of the secondary perforation of a small diverticular abscess; there is usually little drainage of free feces into the peritoneum. It is for this reason that the picture resembles that of acute septic peritonitis rather than acute leakage peritonitis. It is rare that one can make a positive diagnosis of ruptured sigmoid diverticulitis preoperatively. A gentle exploration to determine the source may be necessary, and in some cases the perforated diverticulum may be walled off by packing a piece of omental fat over it. Whether or not this is accomplished, a defunctioning transverse colostomy should be carried out. A double-barreled colostomy with interposition of a skin bridge between the two loops achieves complete defunctioning of the distal segment.

If the patient with ruptured diverticulitis is extremely ill and toxic with high fever, rapid pulse, and a low leucocyte count (analogous to the very toxic appendicitis case), it may be necessary to do a simple loop transverse colostomy.

Other causes of acute septic peritonitis are acute gonorrheal peritonitis in association with salpingitis, idiopathic peritonitis, particularly in association with advanced hepatic or renal disease, and perforated acute cholecystitis. In all of these, the metabolic steps to be taken are very similar to those described above for appendiceal peritonitis, although the indications for surgical intervention are quite different. In all of them, a surgical operation should be accurately timed to coincide with the initial maximal benefit derived from metabolic management, hydration, restoration of blood volume, and renal flow during the first twenty-four hours.

4. Clinical Procedure in Early Septic Peritonitis

This clinical procedure is built around the case of a young man with appendiceal peritonitis. It contains elements from several representative cases.

a. Diagnosis.   Acute appendicitis with perforation.

b. Admission Data.   This is a male in his teens with appendicitis of about six days' duration. Such a history often suggests that perforation had been present for one or two days, occasionally longer. The patient on admission shows a tense, spastic, diffusely tender abdomen. There is no mass. The patient's fever is 103° F., his pulse 120; he looks toxic and ill.

URINE. Specific gravity 1.028, protein is present, the sediment clear, otherwise negative.

HEMATOLOGY

Hematocrit—52.
Leucocyte count—27,000

BLOOD CHEMICAL ANALYSES

Blood urea nitrogen—40 mg. per 100 ml.
Plasma protein—6.8 gm. per 100 ml.
Plasma chloride—98 mE. per l.
Plasma sodium—135 mE. per l.
Plasma potassium—3.6 mE. per l.
Plasma bilirubin—2.1 mg. per 100 ml.

NORMAL WEIGHT. 78 kg.

c. Interpretation and General Plan. Such a patient is toxic; his pulse is elevated in relation to his fever and the duration of his disease. The high leucocyte count corroborates this impression but also indicates that the patient's resistance has been effectively mobilized to meet the challenge of infection. The elevated hematocrit, plasma protein concentration, and blood urea nitrogen together show that he is suffering from oligemia due to loss of plasma-rich exudate into the peritoneal cavity and has some renal vasoconstriction as a result of volume reduction. The high specific gravity of the urine indicates good function of the renal tubules despite hypovolemia and decreased glomerular filtration. The patient's proteinuria merely indicates the extent of his systemic disease. The slightly elevated bilirubin is worrisome. It suggests the possibility of bacterial invasion of the portal vein, but for the moment does not alter treatment. There have been no chills.

The purpose in such a case is to prepare this patient for operation in about twelve to eighteen hours and then to remove his appendix. The balance between indications for operation and indications for conservative therapy is settled in favor of operation by the patient's age and the relatively short duration of his story. There is no rush to the operating room.

d. Preoperative Study and Care. STUDY. Chest film and abdominal films are taken on admission. It is the rare patient for whom acute appendicitis is a 100 per cent certain preoperative diagnosis. The patient's abdominal and rectal examination are carried out ac-

curately, gently, and without repetition. Blood for culture is taken.

DIET AND ORDERS. The patient is given nothing by mouth, and a nasogastric tube is placed on suction. A Miller-Abbott tube may be used in such cases, but a well-functioning nasogastric tube is simpler and equally effective in the face of peritonitis.

The patient is started out on massive antibiotic therapy with intravenous penicillin, to total 20,000,000 units in the first twenty-four hours, and intramuscular streptomycin, 2 gm. per day.

PARENTERAL THERAPY. The patient's primary need is for blood volume at this time. The restoration of his blood volume and, secondarily, the volume of his extracellular fluid should be expected to improve his appearance, lower his pulse rate, and improve his urine output. We would commence this therapy with 1000 ml. of plasma, this calculation being based on his elevated hematocrit.

In a muscular male teen-ager weighing 78 kg., we would expect a normal blood volume to be 7.5 per cent of body weight (or slightly more) or 5800 to 6000 ml. With a normal hematocrit of 44, his expected normal erythrocyte volume would be 2500 to 2700 ml. With the same erythrocyte volume and a hematocrit of 52, we calculate his current blood volume at 4900 to 5100 ml. (2600 ÷ 0.52), a static deficit of about 900 to 1000 ml.

The administration of ordinary pooled refrigerated plasma to this patient has obvious hazards. Room-temperature–stored material may be effective; concentrated albumin can be used. In a young man such as this, blood volume may be restored with transfusion of whole blood if desired. In addition he has lost extracellular fluid volume; he is desalted by the collection in the bowel lumen. The remaining intravenous infusion is 1000 ml. of 5 per cent dextrose in water and 3000 ml. of 5 per cent dextrose in saline solution in the first twenty-four hours.

PROGRESS EVALUATION AND INTERPRETATION. The results of the first twelve hours' treatment of this patient are evaluated in simple terms, the more important for their simplicity. The patient's pulse drops to 110, his urine output picks up to 20 ml. an hour, and he appears less toxic. His leucocyte count might drop as evidence of rehydration, but with a continuing peritonitis one cannot expect it to be much altered. Other than the fall in hematocrit to 44 with refilling of the plasma volume, there are few laboratory evidences by which progress can be gauged in this patient. There is nothing to be gained by further repetition of other early chemical analyses after the twelve-hour interval.

After twelve hours, the patient should appear stronger, somewhat less toxic, and ready for operation. If he is operated upon prior to this restoration of effective volume, there is a serious hazard of irreversible renal damage should he become hypotensive at operation. Although he is dyspneic there appears to be no pulmonary process as a complication.

e. Operation. ANESTHESIA. In such a case thiopental, nitrous oxide, and curare anesthesia with endotracheal intubation would be appropriate.

OPERATIVE PROCEDURE. In such a case operation would consist first in careful palpation of the right lower quadrant under anesthesia. If no mass is found, exploration is carried out. Let us assume that a gangrenous appendix with perforation at its tip is found. There is diffuse peritonitis with no localization. The stump is buried and the peritoneal cavity is not drained. The subcutaneous tissues are not sutured, but sutures are laid in for a delayed primary closure, to be carried out forty-eight hours postoperatively. Culture and smear are made of the exudate.

PARENTERAL THERAPY. Supportive treatment with whole blood and albumin is continued, giving the patient one unit of whole blood immediately after operation and one unit of albumin the next day. This patient has been desalted, in part through his peritoneal loss and in part into the bowel. His pulmonary water loss is high.

After the initial rehydration, fluid therapy is continued on an "in-balance" basis, balancing total losses with intake. With fever and dyspnea, this patient's insensible pulmonary loss is much higher than in other situations; 2500 ml. of 5 per cent dextrose in water and 1000 ml. of 5 per cent dextrose in saline solution are given the day after operation. The patient is kept on short-term urine output records for twenty-four to forty-eight hours.

f. Postoperative Study and Care. STUDY. The next day, the following studies are made with the following results, as typical of such a situation.

URINE. Proteinuria, otherwise negative.

HEMATOLOGY. Hematocrit 45.

BLOOD CHEMICAL ANALYSES

Blood urea nitrogen—80 mg. per 100 ml.
Plasma chloride—90 mE. per l.
Plasma sodium—130 mE. per l.
Plasma potassium—4.2 mE. per l.
Carbon dioxide combining power—18 mE. per l.
Osmolality—285 mO. per l.

PROGRESS EVALUATION AND INTERPRETATION. The patient's hematocrit has evidently stabilized well. He shows hypoproteinemia and hyponatremia, characteristic of the extremely ill, severely stressed, dehydrated, desalted patient who has been rehydrated. These values have fallen despite the use of some saline solution and some concentrated albumin. The severity of the azotemia bespeaks the duration of his low glomerular filtration rate and the severity of the infection; lean-tissue catabolism outstrips urea clearance. The sodium-osmolar differential is 15 mO. per l., indicating minimal accumulation of pathologic crystalloids.

DIET AND ORDERS. Such a patient should be maintained on nasogastric suction with little or nothing by mouth until peristalsis is recommenced and the expulsion of gas by rectum is evident. In appendiceal peritonitis, this may take several days or a week. The patient is allowed to remain quietly in bed, and efforts at early ambulation are avoided. The patient should keep up some quadriceps-setting and flexion-extension exercises of the legs and feet. Examination by rectum to check for pelvic abscess is carried out the third or fourth day. A check film of the chest for early subphrenic abscess need not be taken unless the temperature fails to subside. Antibiotics are continued at reduced dosage for seven to ten days. A positive blood culture would demand higher dosage and possibly a change in drug. Culture of the exudate and study of antibiotic sensitivity improves the accuracy of antibiotic treatment as these data become available.

PARENTERAL THERAPY. The "in-balance" management of this patient is accomplished by covering estimated water loss (1500 to 3000 ml. per day) intravenously. Salt loss in peritoneal exudate and nasogastric tube suction is estimated to require an additional 1000 ml. of normal saline and 80 mE. of potassium per day. Such figures are examples only and are adjusted in relation to the patient's fever and the volume of the gastrointestinal drainage.

Parenteral in-balance management of a patient with septic peritonitis may be continued for as much as two weeks without incurring irrevocable physiologic deficit, so long as water, sodium, chloride, and potassium are provided in accurate consonance with needs. One transfusion of whole blood every five to seven days is essential. Water-soluble vitamins must be given in liberal quantities. Vitamin K is usually not necessary.

In a patient of this type, one may expect subsidence of the peritonitis and resumption of normal gastrointestinal activity by the end of five to seven days. If this does not occur, secondary localizations are presumed to be present. When the patient is well enough again to be weighed, it will be found that he has had an extremely marked weight loss during this period of septic starvation, a weight loss which in such an example as this might total 5 to 15 kg.

C. EARLY LEAKAGE PERITONITIS

Acute septic peritonitis is rarely a surgical emergency in which minutes count; withholding immediate surgery for a few hours and awaiting the ideal moment for operation is of first-rank importance. The few hours spent in preparation are lifesaving. *By contrast, acute leakage peritonitis is, in the early stage, a pressing surgical emergency.* The performance of an operation within one to two hours of the patient's admission to the hospital is far safer than a delay of even six to twelve hours.

1. Definition, Sources, and General Plan

Leakage peritonitis is defined as peritonitis resulting from the dissemination into the peritoneal cavity of a body fluid that is not involved in a septic process at the time of its initial peritoneal dissemination. The term "leakage peritonitis" is thus used to denote those cases in which the peritoneal insult is initially chemical rather than bacteriologic. Although the gastrointestinal tract throughout its length contains an active flora, the initial virulence of this flora from the small bowel and stomach (except in the anacid cancer stomach) is low. Indeed, culture of the open small bowel or of the open stomach (in subtotal gastrectomy for duodenal ulcer, for example) will frequently reveal few significant pathogens.

a. Chemical Irritation. On the other hand, the chemical nature of this fluid is extremely irritating to the peritoneal cavity, and the protein exudate called forth is an ideal culture medium in which the few pathogens initially present multiply rapidly to produce a septic process. The loss of this protein compromises the blood volume. If it is acid gastric juice initially, it is easy to explain the irritation of the peritoneum on the basis of the pH. However, free leakage of the contents of the small bowel is equally irritating to the peritoneal cavity even though the pH is not far from neutrality. The osmolality of all gastrointestinal fluids is close to isotonic, and we must therefore assign their irritating nature either to their detailed ionic composition, which departs from plasma in many ways, or to the fact that they contain active digestive enzymes. The initial features are peritoneal irritation, as evidenced by very severe pain (occasionally pain in the shoulder tip), and a rigid abdominal musculature.

b. Sources. There are many forms of leakage peritonitis, all presenting fundamentally the same problem. Perforated duodenal ulcer is the archetype. Spontaneous perforation of the small intestine is rare below the level of the duodenum. Nonpenetrating abdominal trauma is capable of perforating the small bowel at or about the ligament of Treitz. Because of the possibility of perforation of the small bowel or ruptures of solid viscera such as liver and spleen, the abdomens of patients with nonpenetrating abdominal traumas should be explored on the slightest shades of evidence of intraperitoneal irritation. The surgeon in charge of a patient who has suffered a severe abdominal trauma should feel no sense of error if he explores such a patient for slight abdominal signs and finds no perforation. Preliminary diagnostic tap in the four abdominal quadrants is useful. If negative, it must be regarded with suspicion as being wrong; other evidences must continue to control. If the aspiration is positive, it is clearly of great significance.

Penetrating abdominal traumas, as produced by knife and bullet wounds, will penetrate the intestine and its vascular supply, and urgently demand repair. The peritoneal contamination problem is essentially the same in all, namely that early leakage peritonitis is extremely well handled by the peritoneum if the source of leak is soon closed and continuity of viable intestine restored within a reasonable time.

Leakage peritonitis has resulted from a variety of accidents to the intestine: from the use of a retractor on the duodenum during cholecystectomy, from inadvertent rupture of the cecum in the course of a cesarean section, from the perforation of all parts of the gastrointestinal tract after swallowing sharp foreign objects, ranging in size from the toothpick used on hors d'oeuvres to the transverse process of a lambchop.

c. The Large Bowel as Source. Leakage peritonitis from the large intestine is a different problem. As mentioned in the section on septic peritonitis, perforated diverticulum of the left colon does not represent true leakage peritonitis, since the initial peritoneal insult is from purulent material rather than a quantity of intestinal contents. By contrast, perforated carcinomas of the mid- and left colon occasionally do produce a widespread peritonitis, in which liquid fecal matter, not initially purulent, is the material at fault. Here, proximal defunctioning colostomy or exteriorization is mandatory, and the immediate results are good. The long-term prognosis for perforated carcinoma of the colon is

very poor, however, because of the peritoneal dissemination of the neoplastic cells.

Occasionally carcinoma of the left colon will produce a cecum that becomes tremendously distended and then perforates. This accident is often lethal because of the truly massive extent of the peritoneal contamination with putrid and septic liquid feces harboring many organisms. Aspiration of the peritoneal contents and appropriate exteriorization of the bowel are urgently needed if there is to be a chance of salvage.

d. The Bladder as Source. Leakage peritonitis can occur from other hollow viscera. Intraperitoneal rupture of the bladder is an example. The urine may be quite sterile to begin with, but infection will ultimately supervene and a very severe process result unless the bladder is closed, with suitable urinary drainage by catheter or suprapubic cystotomy. Diagnosis is not always easy and may depend upon the intracystic injection of a contrast medium. Where lower abdominal trauma has been followed by peritoneal signs, study, by contrast medium, of the kidneys and bladder for rupture should be carried out without hesitation.

e. Bile Peritonitis. Bile peritonitis is an example of leakage peritonitis. This may result from the rupture of a duodenal stump after subtotal gastrectomy, in which instance it is merely an exercise in semantics as to whether this is bile peritonitis or peritonitis from contents of the small bowel. A poorly placed common-duct catheter or the slipping of a tie on a cystic duct may produce bile peritonitis. Like urine peritonitis, bile peritonitis is initially uninfected. The changes in body fluid, electrolyte, and plasma volume are essentially the same as in any other form of leakage peritonitis: plasma loss predominates, with a low plasma volume and a high hematocrit. If the disease is promptly recognized and the source of the bile leakage exteriorized by catheter, T-tube, or simply a drain, the prognosis is excellent. Here the pH is high and the sodium concentration is high. Chemical irritation is responsible for the initial signs and systemic disturbance. Coliform bacteria soon predominate.

Bile peritonitis may result from rupture of the liver or from bile leakage from the cut or injured liver surface, as after partial hepatectomy. It is for this reason that drainage of such suture lines is essential. Long-continuing leakage of bile into the peritoneal cavity, even in fairly small amounts, ultimately produces a widespread peritonitis that is extremely difficult to manage; many secondary localizations and septic pockets develop. Late bile peritonitis, undrained, has a very poor prognosis.

2. Management

Early management of all these types of leakage peritonitis departs from that of acute septic peritonitis because, early in the process, the bacterial-invasion:host-resistance relationship is not nearly as important as in a septic process, while the acute loss of plasma-like fluid into the peritoneal cavity is much more prominent. Early operation to stop the leak is critical, and in early cases preoperative resuscitative steps are unnecessary.

Preparation for surgery should consist in the accurate use of plasma, plasma extender, or whole blood if the patient has a thready pulse, an insecure or falling blood pressure, or an hematocrit elevation over 48. Such signs of circulatory failure are exceptional in early cases (that is, under six hours). These aggressive steps, along with conservative use of water and electrolyte, will suffice to restore blood volume and urine flow prior to operation. Rapid infusion is used; operation need not be long postponed. The measurement of the hourly urine output should be commenced by catheterization soon after admission.

3. Operation

Operation consists of an initial diagnostic exploration, since the differential diagnosis may not be clear. If a duodenal perforation has stopped leaking and has resulted in local adherence of the liver capsule, lower portion of the gallbladder, or other neighboring structures, it is not advisable to disrupt this for the purpose of placing one or two sutures in the hole. In most other visceral leaks, or if a duodenal perforation is clearly leaking, sutures and an omental pad should be placed.

In early perforated ulcer, the excellent results and low mortality from simple operative closure render more extensive operations (such as subtotal gastrectomy) inadvisable except in those isolated cases where there is a long ulcer history, concomitant hemorrhage, or obstruction. The good results gained from early operation render the routine use of nonoperative management equally unwise.

If the patient has a long history of duodenal ulcer, particularly if he has had sufficient symptoms in the past to justify serious consideration of subtotal gastrectomy, then a subtotal gastrectomy carried out at the time of perforation is justified if the operation is performed twelve hours or less after the initial event. In most instances it is advisable to carry out the gastrectomy six to eight weeks later, electively.

4. Postoperative Care

The postoperative management of early leakage peritonitis represents a continuation of the same concepts as those that govern the initial therapy. The maintenance of a normal plasma volume, total volume of body water, and extracellular-fluid electrolyte should be the objectives, remembering that the fluid losses in such patients arise from suction drainage of gastric contents and sequestration of fluid (high in protein) in the peritoneum and small intestine, the latter depending upon the extent of distention. Any tendency for the hematocrit to rise after operation indicates an advancing peritonitis and a relatively poor prognosis. Therapy should be very active and aggressive, directed toward the restoration of the plasma volume.

When the perforation has been closed early, restoration of oral intake may often begin by the second or third postoperative day.

D. POSTOPERATIVE LEAKAGE PERITONITIS

Leakage peritonitis, occurring after anastomotic gastrointestinal operations, has been the bugbear of the surgeon for generations.

If a leak occurs, it is usually a manifestation of an anastomosis having been carried out in an area of poor blood supply or with grossly deficient technique, rather than a primarily septic process in the bowel wall. Leakage of the closed duodenal stump after gastrectomy still occurs occasionally, and, again, the blood supply factor is much more important than is generally recognized. The exact anatomic location of the sutures in relation to the blood supply and the "tacking over" of peritoneal surfaces to help retroperitonealize the duodenum are important. Leakage of gastrojejunal anastomoses is extremely rare, which bespeaks the excellent blood supply of those two viscera. Esophagojejunal and esophagogastric anastomoses are prone to leak unless constructed with care.

Free leak from gastrointestinal suture-sites rarely occurs sooner than thirty-six hours after operation or later than five days. Any sudden pain near the site of gastrointestinal sutures, with local tenderness and progressive systemic signs (tachycardia, leucocytosis, hypotension), should excite suspicion and set in motion readiness for operation. Further detailed diagnostic steps, depending on the anatomic site, include plain films, barium study, and diagnostic tap. If suspicion is high, time should not be wasted on these steps. Fever is not an early manifestation in many cases, and should not be set up as a diagnostic criterion.

Differential diagnosis lies between acute cardiopulmonary complications (atelectasis, embolus, coronary infarction), acute pancreatitis, and the relatively benign and chronic situation termed "postoperative ileus-obstruction," in which persistent local tenderness is not found and sudden systemic deterioration a rarity.

In all of these instances, the most important step in treatment is early realistic recognition of the lesion and its immediate exteriorization or drainage. Operative repair should not be attempted. If there is a leak from the large bowel, proximal colostomy is essential. In other settings, drainage is established. A fistula will form, and this fistula will almost invariably close if the patient is well managed metabolically. If there is no obstruction distal to the point of the fistula formation, and if a spherical abscess is not allowed to persist, spontaneous closure is the rule.

The purpose of drainage is to avoid the formation of a spherical abscess around the point of leakage. The very gradual withdrawal of sump, drain, or catheter is of great importance. If this abscess is converted into a linear tract around a drain, and this drain is gradually withdrawn, the tract will cicatrize and close. If the drain is withdrawn while a spherical abscess is still present, and inadequately drained, fever will persist, and the fistula will not close.

In profuse leakage peritonitis (for example from a duodenal turn-in or gastrointestinal anastomoses) the use of a sump-suction drain is useful. This will avoid digestion of the skin and will permit accurate quantitation not only of the amounts of the material drained but of its chemical composition. Such a sump drain should be placed on suction with a negative pressure of 10 to 30 cm. of water. With the use of sump drainage for this type of intestinal or pancreatic fistula, skin irritation and digestion have become a rarity.

E. ANTIBIOTICS IN EARLY LEAKAGE PERITONITIS

In early leakage peritonitis, antibiotics are used because of widespread contamination of the peritoneum with virulent organisms, both local inhabitants and those swallowed from the respiratory tract. Although sepsis has not yet developed, there is a large interface where it will, and where the antibiotic may reach the infecting organism.

The drainage of sterile urine or bile into the peritoneum might not seem to require the use of antibiotics; this is not the case. Though such processes start as sterile chemical inflammation, they rapidly degenerate into a septic process, the pathogenesis of which (in the sense of bacterial origin) is not always clear. It may result from transmigration of colonic flora into the peritoneum. The use of peritoneal dialysis in the treatment of anuria has been of interest here. It was found that although the irrigating fluid was sterile, the formation of a coliform peritonitis was a common complication. The bowel itself, though undamaged, was the source. Whether these organisms pass into the peritoneum through the lymphatics or directly through the wall remains uncertain. In the case of bowel leakage with contaminated—even though not septic—material the pathogenesis is obvious.

The antibiotic management of leakage peritonitis depends upon the fact that the peritoneum can easily handle short-term (but not continuing) contamination with ordinary intestinal flora. Perforations closed under twelve hours have had a low mortality rate, essentially unchanged by the advent of the antibiotics. In older people, or those with late perforations, the mortality rate continues to be impressive even with the antibiotics, and the effect of the antibiotics on mortality in this lesion is not as clear-cut as it is with septic peritonitis. The management of bacterial peritonitis depends also on the maintenance of the circulation, since the detoxification of the products of bacterial growth can be accomplished by the liver if its own metabolism can be supported. Hypotension is a common manifestation of leakage peritonitis, owing in part to plasma loss and in part to the nature of the gram-negative bacilli, their toxic products, and intermittent bacteremia; circulatory failure brings in its train a whole series of deteriorative changes referred to as the "vicious cycles" of shock (Part II). This must be avoided at all costs, if leakage peritonitis has developed. The use of blood transfusion, often in large quantities, has a significant role in the treatment of infection here, as elsewhere.

In leakage peritonitis, whether bowel contents, bile, or urine, one must proceed with early and energetic antibiotic treatment, using penicillin between 8 and 20 million units a day and streptomycin 1.0 to 2.0 grams per day. If the leak is closed early (under twelve hours after onset) and the early postoperative course is good, the use of the antibiotic may soon be stopped. The purpose has been to prevent an invasive infection; the peritoneum can handle the rest of the problem. A culture taken at operation may be of assistance in subsequent antibiotic management.

Thus, leakage peritonitis in its early stages is not so much a problem in sepsis as it is a problem in the prevention of sepsis by early closure and in the establishment of adequate drainage or proximal decompression. As time passes and the two diseases progress, they merge into one and we find an entirely different problem: late peritonitis.

The management of early leakage peritonitis is not complicated. The problems, and the instances of mismanagement, arise in the in-between cases where early leakage peritonitis is undergoing a subtle transition to a much more threatening late septic process. The following procedural example is therefore centered around a case of duodenal ulcer with perforation of eighteen hours' duration.

1. Clinical Procedure in Leakage Peritonitis

There follows as an example the detailed treatment of a man with a perforated ulcer of eighteen hours' duration. This procedure is based on representative features from several cases.

a. Diagnosis.   Perforated ulcer.

b. Admission Data.   Such a patient is most apt to be a male in his mid-thirties or early forties. He has had a known duodenal ulcer for several years. He vomited several times, and then his ulcer perforated, at 9:00 P.M. following a banquet. He was not admitted to the hospital until eighteen hours later. The patient has a boardlike abdomen, his temperature is slightly below normal, his blood pressure is 90/80, his pulse rate is 140. He is in a circulatory state bordering on shock.

URINE.   There is no urine available for analysis until rehydration is commenced.

HEMATOLOGY

> Hematocrit—62
> Leucocyte count—28,000 per cu. mm.
> Smear—normal

BLOOD CHEMICAL ANALYSES.   No chemical analyses are available prior to surgery, but blood taken at the time of admission later shows the following values:

> Blood urea nitrogen—42 mg. per 100 ml.
> Plasma chloride—88 mE. per l.
> Plasma sodium—138 mE. per l.
> Plasma potassium—3.1 mE. per l.
> Carbon dioxide combining power—29 mE. per l.

WEIGHT. The patient is not weighed, as he is too ill. He states his normal weight was 176 lb. (80 kg.).

c. Interpretation and General Plan. Although this process began as leakage peritonitis, the eighteen hours that have passed have seen its unquestionable transition to septic peritonitis. The minutes-urgency of operation, felt in the first hours, has likewise given way to the absolute necessity of careful metabolic resuscitation before anesthesia and operation; if this step is not taken, operation will result in intractable hypotension and renal insufficiency and bring in its wake a series of complications that seriously jeopardize recovery.

The hematocrit of 62 indicates a severely restricted plasma volume. Initial calculation of the plasma requirement is carried out as follows.

A young male weighing 80 kg. should be expected to have a blood volume at 7.0 per cent of body weight or more (5600 ml. or slightly more). With a normal hematocrit at 44, the erythrocyte volume would be about 2460 ml. This erythrocyte volume, with an hematocrit of 62, now resides in a blood volume of 2460 ÷ 0.62, or 3970 ml. This represents a volume deficit of about 1700 ml., a deficit almost wholly in the plasma fraction. This dose of plasma (about 7 units of 250 ml. each) must be given immediately; there is virtually no ceiling or upper limit on its acceptable rate for infusion.

The azotemia is a result of oligemia with severe renal vasoconstriction and decreased glomerular filtration. The renal tubule is extremely vulnerable to any further insult or circulating nephrotoxin at this stage. Both the "toxicity" and the oliguria are compatible with the marked reduction in plasma volume, and one need not invoke other mechanisms. Peritonitis has transposed itself into a septic process (or is in the process of so doing) at the time the patient is seen. The chemical analyses, though not available at the time of surgery, indicate a mild alkalosis, with a tendency to hypokalemia, suggesting that this patient may have had some element of obstruction with his perforation. In another few hours of anuria this would be completely covered by a mounting renal acidosis and hyperkalemia.

The low temperature and low-normal blood pressure indicate the extent of the patient's illness; he is maintaining blood pressure by severe vasoconstriction in the face of a restricted plasma volume and blood volume of increasing viscosity. In a short while compensation may be expected to break, with profound shock.

The plan is to restore blood volume rapidly and, if resuscitation is then adequate, to carry out operation as soon as possible. The estimated duration of this resuscitative delay is from three to six hours. Operation is "the sooner the better" but the disease is already of eighteen hours' duration, and the small delay adds little increment. These eighteen hours have lost the patient the benefits to be gained from immediate operation and have imposed an obligation to restore the circulation first. *Operation during a period of oligemia due to plasma loss, with marked decrease in glomerular filtration rate, represents an unjustified hazard to the patient's kidneys, and has been the setting for many fatal cases of post-traumatic renal insufficiency.* Anesthesia and operation in the face of this preshock state would be extremely dangerous, also, because of the drastic lowering of blood pressure with loss of vasoconstriction that follows anesthetization.

The previous history of duodenal ulcer and the low-grade obstruction might entice one to tarry for a moment with the idea of subtotal gastrectomy. But such an idea should be put aside completely for a patient with this degree of septic peritonitis. There must be no compromise with the safest possible program of treatment. Gastrectomy in the face of established peritonitis is wholly unjustified.

d. Preoperative Study and Care. The patient's plasma volume deficit is first restored. Two simultaneous intravenous infusions are necessary to do this fast enough. The substance used can be plasma, albumin, or dextran. There is reason to suspect that whole blood may not be as satisfactory for entire replacement in this situation; renal function is slower to return. In such an instance, 1500 ml. of plasma is given in the first three hours and after this the patient's hematocrit should fall to about 45.

A nasogastric tube should be placed on suction and X-rays of the abdomen and chest taken. One would expect free air with fluid levels beneath one or both diaphragms in such a late case. The patient is started on antibiotics: 20,000,000 units of penicillin per twenty-four hours administered intravenously and 2 gm. of streptomycin given intramuscularly.

Blood grouping and crossmatching are carried out.

The patient is placed on hourly measurements of urine output. During the period of intensive plasma replacement, urine flow again returns and on analysis demonstrates protein, erythrocytes, and leucocytes in the urine, but no free pigment, and a high specific gravity (1.036). This is encouraging as it indicates a good renal tubular response to acute volume reduction.

The patient's pulse now falls to 100, his blood pressure rises to 110/70, he looks less "toxic," and, with this resuscitative progress, operation is carried out.

e. Operation. ANESTHESIA. Pentothal, nitrous oxide, and curare anesthesia with endotracheal intubation and high oxygen.

PROCEDURE. If a freely leaking duodenal ulcer is found, the ulcer is closed. A large amount of food and gastrointestinal contents may be present in the peritoneal cavity, with a considerable exudate, and is gently aspirated clear. There is some putrid odor. Usually there are few adhesions or other evidences of localization, save at the immediate site itself.

f. Postoperative Study and Care. An interval-output record of urine secretion is maintained for the next three days. Sips of water, broth, or tea are given by mouth.

PARENTERAL THERAPY. The patient is given one transfusion of whole blood during operation, and 2000 ml. of 5 per cent dextrose in water with 80 mM. of potassium chloride and 1000 ml. of 5 per cent dextrose in saline solution during the twenty-four hours following operation. This would be liberally increased were fever, dyspnea, or salt loss to be excessive. If renal function had not returned the management should be changed drastically to that of early renal failure (q.v.).

Culture of the peritoneal fluid, taken at this time, later shows *E. coli* and *Staphylococcus aureus*, the latter sensitive to penicillin. Antibiotics are continued unchanged.

Nasogastric suction should be maintained for about three days, at the end of which time the patient should be expected to appear improved clinically. Although he has no audible peristalsis, if he has passed a small amount of gas by rectum the tube is removed.

Daily intravenous therapy is handled on an "in-balance" basis, with the additional consideration that two units of albumin are given each day for the first two days because of presumed continued loss into the peritoneal cavity of protein-rich exudate.

The daily ration must allow for the increased pulmonary loss in a man of this age with fever, and the quantitative replacement of gastrointestinal suction losses. About 40 mE. per day of potassium is provided. Water and salt are allowed for kidney function on the basis of 1200 ml. of urine per day and 40 mE. each of sodium and chloride. On this basis, the following calculation is carried out, for example, on the second day, with fever 101° F.; tube losses 1400 ml. strongly acid gastric juice; urine output 1000 ml. Intravenous provision: 1200 ml. normal saline, 1500 ml. of 5 per cent dextrose in water with 80 mM. of potassium chloride, 1000 ml. of 5 per cent dextrose in water with vitamins. No attempt at adequate calorie or nitrogen provision is made at this early time.

By about the seventh postoperative day the patient should begin to show appetite and audible peristalsis. Feedings of clear fluids are increased and soon shifted over to soft solids and an ulcer diet.

Before discharge the patient should be checked by gastrointestinal X-ray to study the extent of the obstruction which may have been a factor. In such an individual the duration following perforation and the toxicity of the patient were too great for primary subtotal gastrectomy, although the history certainly made it look tempting. The past symptoms, perforation, and slight obstruction are positive indication for future subtotal gastrectomy, to be carried out in three to six months.

Section III. Late Peritonitis

The early management of septic peritonitis and of leakage peritonitis are quite different; as the process passes into late peritonitis, the two types merge and become indistinguishable. Treatment is the same for both.

Late peritonitis is a disease which is seen relatively more frequently today than it was twenty years ago. Many patients now survive the early insult to the peritoneum by dint of antibiotics and effective metabolic measures, particularly replenishment of the diminished plasma volume. These permit survival into a late phase characterized by chronic sepsis (if seeding of the contaminant continues), or of secondary localization (if it stops). The management of late peritonitis depends upon the facts set forth below.

A. GASTROINTESTINAL ACTIVITY

The gastrointestinal tract functions poorly, intermittently, or not at all in late peritonitis. If it is not functioning, feeding will result only in vomiting and distention, with further clinical deterioration. Intermittent or continuous nasogastric suction or Miller-Abbott intubation is essential to maintain an undistended bowel when the gut is not functional, but it is the worst enemy of returning appetite and it should be discontinued as soon as possible, once peristaltic and absorptive function are ready to return. The recognition of this return of function is based on intermittent closing off of the suction, or removal of the tube and test-feeding the patient small amounts of appetizing liquids. Hunger and passage of flatus are the usual signals of the return of gut function after short-term starvation. After peritonitis one may not be able to wait for them; they may not come until feeding is reestablished. Judgment, curiosity, and patient repeated trials are essential.

The tendency to intestinal distention is very marked when secondary abscesses form and develop pus under pressure. A secondary recurrence of ileus or distention often signalizes the development of drainable pus even though other signs are masked by anti-biotics. Drainage of abscesses and control of the peritoneal process itself is followed by restoration of gastrointestinal function to normal.

B. INTRAVENOUS MAINTENANCE

Patients with late peritonitis are among the most acute nutritional problems seen in surgery. These are the archetype of septic starvation. *It is in these patients, late after onset of sepsis, that continued maintenance of some semblance of normal caloric intake, intravenously administered, becomes critical.* Intravenous infusions of fat and alcohol, and concentrated glucose with insulin and amino acids or protein hydrolysate by caval catheter, are useful and of the greatest importance in the attempt to compensate for starvation. If the patient is running a high fever, these infusions will be poorly retained and utilized, just as they are early after trauma. If the patient is in a chronic phase without high fever, with draining or open wounds and without oral diet, intravenous caloric supplements are effective in preventing further wastage of the patient's body composition by lysis of lean tissue, degradation of protein, and oxidation of fat. The provision of calories and nitrogen is more important than in almost any other situation in surgery, since the wasting of the body which otherwise results is so severe as to interfere with the patient's diaphragmatic excursion, cough-effectiveness, muscular vigor, and peristaltic activity. Survival itself is endangered by the rapid, extreme cachexia.

The patient's daily metabolism of water and salt should be treated "in balance," again with the admonition against quantitative replacement of urinary salt losses if tubular function is good. Extremely accurate correction of extrarenal loss is necessary, since any error made daily will soon become cumulative and pile up to a massive extent when long periods are involved. In such patients the procedure of clinical balance should be instituted and effective parenteral feeding given its most effective opportunity.

C. RESPIRATORY FUNCTION

Death in late peritonitis, like death from severe starvation of any form, is usually a respiratory death. The maintenance of normal respiratory function and bronchopulmonary patency depend upon the avoidance of opiates and the use of tracheal aspiration, bronchoscopy, or tracheotomy if the patient is so desperately ill that the cough reflex is abolished or ineffective. The abatement of abdominal distention, and the avoidance of overwatering and oversalting, all of which increase pulmonary transudation or decrease diaphragmatic excursion, are also respiratory essentials. If there is an expiratory wheeze the patient may benefit from aminophylline or adrenergic drugs. If he is cyanotic, oxygen should be given; otherwise it merely acts to reduce the stimulus to adequate ventilation.

D. DRAINAGE OF ABSCESSES

A most important step is the accurate localization of secondary abscesses and their drainage. An aggressive approach to loculated pus will yield remarkable results, even in extremely ill patients. The patient who looks "too sick to operate on" will blossom if such a collection as a large subdiaphragmatic abscess is cleanly drained. *As in so many other settings, the most important metabolic step is an accurate, effective surgical operation.*

The commonest sites for localization of intraperitoneal pus after either septic or leakage peritonitis, depending somewhat on the intial source, are

    (1) the cul-de-sac of Douglas,
    (2) the right subphrenic space,
    (3) the right subhepatic space,
    (4) the left subphrenic space,
    (5) the right gutter, and
    (6) multiple abscesses among the small-
        bowel loops.

Search for these by physical examination should be carried out carefully and gently each day. Antibiotics will promote localization to these areas and in occasional cases will actually abort an early abscess. Formerly, this was extremely rare; now, one occasionally feels an early cul-de-sac abscess which, under effective antibiotics, melts away. What such

a lesion constitutes pathologically at that time is not certain. It is probably edematous tissue with some fluid in it rather than a loculated sac of exudate. One seldom sees a large well-formed abscess (particularly one containing sufficient gas to be seen by X-ray as a fluid level) resolve spontaneously without drainage. If resolution occurs, one may postulate that the abscess has ruptured into a hollow viscus and drained itself in this way.

When secondary abscesses occur in late peritonitis, they may be watched for a day or two and checked by appropriate X-ray or contrast studies. Draining them is a seemingly minor operation of truly major significance to the patient, and it should be accomplished with good lighting, adequate exposure, adequate assistance, and adequate anesthesia. Great harm is done by approaching secondary peritoneal localizations with inadequate operative preparation or skill.

In all cases except when the subphrenic space is involved, it is advisable to make the initial incision over the presumed area of purulent material, usually over the point of tenderness, and then explore and aspirate with a needle. When the needle finds the pus, drainage can be carried out down the needle tract, the needle being held in place by an assistant's forceps. In the case of cul-de-sac abscess, aspiration should always be carried out after sphincter dilatation and before drainage.

In the case of the subphrenic space, opinion is divided as to the place of preliminary aspiration. If a fluid level is shown by X-ray, such aspiration would seem quite unnecessary. It is our opinion that aspiration is hazardous since it may contaminate the pleura, and it is to be avoided. If carried out carefully by a surgeon who is familiar with the anatomic limits of the pleural space, it may be done either posteriorly, or anteriorly under the costal margin. Approach to the abscess either anteriorly or posteriorly may be followed by aspiration just before the abscess cavity itself is opened, this being merely an added precaution at the time of open operative dissection.

Because of the significance of abscess drainage in recovery, vigilance must be constant.

It is better to make a false approach to a suspected site than it is to leave undrained a collection that is pressing for release and seeding the blood stream, with a daily spike of temperature.

E. AZOTEMIA AND JAUNDICE

Patients with late peritonitis often have some degree of azotemia and jaundice. The azotemia is either the residual of an initial period of shock and dehydration, when there was decreased renal function bordering on acute tubular necrosis, or is the continued manifestation of lean-tissue catabolism proceeding at a rate greater than urea clearance can keep pace; azotemia may rise, with normal or high urine outputs, and is itself a sign of continued sepsis. This situation is often compounded by continued high extrarenal losses and a mixed renal and respiratory acidosis. Azotemia, acidosis, and bilirubinemia are all signs of the ravages of systemic sepsis and they will restore themselves to normal with recovery of the patient, and not separately.

The mild degrees of jaundice seen in such patients are a manifestation of chronic peritoneal infection, which loads the portal system with live bacteria, bacterial bodies, and bacterial toxins even if frank pylephlebitis is not produced. The use of multiple banked-blood transfusions is often required and this, too, adds to the bilirubinemia. At postmortem examination some toxic degeneration and fatty infiltration will be seen in the liver; often there is little else. Multiple liver abscesses and suppurative cholangitis are rare occurrences in late peritonitis.

F. ANTIBIOTICS IN LATE PERITONITIS

As a general rule in surgical infections, the longer the infection has been present in the patient, the less effective the antibiotics are in its management. The use of antibiotics in late infections is therefore quite rightly coming in for extensive re-evaluation. The enthusiasts still believe that massive sensitivity-guided therapy is the best; others believe that this is a somewhat different disease from the acute process, and one in which detailed bacteriologic study is unimportant. The blood stream often carries drug-resistant, low-virulence organisms or the staphylococcus; anatomic site of localization and host resistance seem to be the critical factors. Whatever view one adopts, the following points are evident.

(1) *Ideally, such patients should be managed by accurate surgical attack on any localized abscess and by use of an effective antibiotic in adequate dosage.* In a patient with late peritonitis, it is difficult to deny the use of an antibiotic to which at least some of the organisms are sensitive, although one has great difficulty proving that the antibiotic helps the patient. On stopping all antibiotics some patients improve remarkably.

(2) *The intial favorable response to antibiotics exhibited by the patient early in his course has long since been spent.* In early peritoneal contamination, blood-stream infection may be avoided and excessive toxicity may be abated by the use of antibiotics. This favorable phase of the disease has now passed, and the patient is now in a stage where localized abscesses and alterations in host metabolism are much more important in determining the outcome; a clear drug-response is exceptional.

(3) *In patients with late peritonitis, it is difficult to distinguish clinically whether they are on or off antibiotics.* Frequent changes of antibiotics in an attempt to match the "bacterial sensitivity" show little reflection in the patient's temperature or clinical appearance. Favorable results from antibiotics are difficult to demonstrate.

(4) *Intermittent bacteremia is characteristic and will be found if looked for with sufficient frequency by blood culture.* The organisms involved are frequently of the proteus and pyocyaneus groups, and are resistant to antibiotics. It is not uncommon to see such patients being treated with one, two, or even three broad-spectrum antibiotics. The multitude of flora which have been cultured from the patient over a period of time have shown changing sensitivities. The actual effectiveness of any single antibiotic or combination is questionable in terms of the patient's clinical course.

(5) *The development of pseudomembranous en-*

terocolitis, often traceable at least in part to the antibiotic-induced distortion of normal colonic floral balance, is a terminal event in late peritonitis. The balance of compensation to multiple threats and deficits is too delicate to withstand the massive colonic fluid loss and desalting. Death quickly follows.

(6) *Laboratory sensitivity methods are not infallible; they may not be corroborated by the clinical response.* One should not abandon formerly effective antibiotic therapy simply because of a new finding by in-vitro sensitivity tests.

For all these reasons, then, the antibiotic program in late peritonitis, and indeed in all late surgical infections, should be approached with healthy and inquiring skepticism. Do not hesitate to stop all antibiotics if benefit of the drugs is not clear; use any antibiotics that are being given, in adequate dosage; do not be influenced to pursue an endless round of drug changes by the changing nature of the in-vitro sensitivities.

G. LETHAL EVENTS

Patients with late peritonitis who pass either into shock or semicoma are suffering from one or more of three complications:

(1) continued flooding of the peritoneal cavity with septic material or leakage of visceral contents, with deterioration due to sepsis and loss of sequestered fluid with oligemia;

(2) blood-stream invasion, particularly with gram-negative bacilli; secondary localization of bacteria and sepsis in lethal areas such as the meninges, heart valves, adrenals;

(3) the late effects of secondary pulmonary involvement: pulmonary edema, accumulative bronchopneumonia, or pulmonary embolism.

The therapeutic approach to patients who have started a late downward course days or weeks after the initial insult is very challenging and the results are poor. In occasional instances an attempt to close the site of continued peritoneal contamination—for example, resection of an area of late gangrene of the gastrointestinal tract—has been successful. If the moribund condition of the patient is due to continued peritoneal flooding from a colonic lesion, previously unrecognized, the response of the patient to diversion of the fecal stream may still be favorable. If the moribund state of the patient is due to blood-stream infection or overwhelming pulmonary complications in the face of continued antibiotic treatment, therapy is much more difficult and most therapeutic measures unrewarding. The use of gamma globulin or immune sera deserves consideration and trial in such a situation.

H. CONVALESCENCE FROM LATE PERITONITIS

As the septic process is brought under control, by drainage of secondary localizations or by the gradual closure of any fistulas that may have formed, the patient rounds the corner. The metabolic and clinical appearances here are in many ways strikingly similar to the turning-point phase after a surgical operation. The difference relates to time. After an uneventful major abdominal operation, this turning point occurs about the third to fifth day. In late peritoneal sepsis, it may not occur for three to five weeks after the initial insult. In normal surgical convalescence this phase is discernible only for a day or so; after peritonitis it is a period lasting as much as a week. The patient begins to prepare himself for exogenous intake by increasing gastrointestinal function; his metabolic state is one of avidity for nitrogen and calories. Urinary nitrogen loss is lowered rapidly during this period. Remarkably small intakes result in a clearly anabolic balance.

It is during this time that persistent attempts gradually to increase the patient's oral intake are clinically rewarding. The patient should be given tasty hot foods. It is unavailing in a patient who has not been eating for over a month to start him out with some sort of mixture of water, cold skimmed milk, and strained fruit juices while an intravenous infusion of concentrated glucose is running. These are scarcely appetizing to a normal person and are anathema to the ill. But a hot cup of coffee, hot broth, or some cooked chopped meat that has a good odor of the kitchen about it, and comes unaccompanied by an intravenous needle, may stimulate the patient's peristalsis. Other details on the shift-over from intravenous to oral intake are mentioned in Part IV.

Intravenous glucose infusions should be stopped during the daytime hours at the time when oral intake is being recommenced. Even small amounts of glucose (as little as 1000 ml. of 5 per cent glucose in water) will deaden the hunger sensation for an entire twenty-four-hour period. If the patient will not maintain a normal fluid intake, he can be given an intravenous infusion later in the evening with the hope that he will eat during the daylight hours.

The use of drugs should be avoided as soon as possible. Opiates will deaden the patient's gastrointestinal function, as will salicylates and barbiturates. Chlorpromazine, Benzedrine, and insulin are all unavailing in restoring gastrointestinal function. One exception is alcohol by mouth. The use of a little brandy or sherry or a dry martini will often stimulate the patient's appetite, particularly if he is an individual who has used alcohol before meals while in good health. A lifelong habit of cocktails before dinner pays off handsomely in terms of conditioned reflexes here.

The gastrointestinal tract that has not been working for many weeks contains within itself the seeds of its recovery. At first these patients have no appetite and dislike the sight of food. As they begin to take some food, avidity for more food increases. For this reason, we have occasionally started out such patients with evening tube feedings, even though they were quite able to swallow. After some intragastric nourishment for a day or two, followed with appetizing hot drinks and hot food, they began to relish the normal food intake essential for convalescent anabolism.

It is in this setting that increasing foods by "quality" rather than "quantity" is important. In terms of staged surgical diet, a rapid advancement to the third or fourth stage, or the "maximum benefit, minimum volume of diet," is much more important than loading the patient's rather sluggish gastrointestinal tract with large amounts of watery and mushy white mixtures.

Just as the patient in normal surgical convalescence comes around the corner, demands intake, and then, if he gets the intake, passes into anabolism—so also the patient after prolonged sepsis rounds the corner and passes into a prolonged anabolic phase. The care of such a patient during this anabolic period is a gratifying reward for all the difficulties which both the patient and the doctor have weathered previously. The restoration of weight, strength, morale, and body tissues is among the most spectacular seen anywhere in the field of medicine. Nature takes over and sets about reconstruction with real vigor; after arduous weeks patient and surgeon alike can sit back and enjoy these glories of nature.

I. CLINICAL PROCEDURE IN LATE PERITONITIS

This clinical procedure is based on data from several representative examples of late or neglected infection originating in the lower abdomen. The reader is cautioned against generalization from a single clinical procedure; as in others used in this book, the clinical procedure merely demonstrates an example of the application of metabolic principles in sequence.

1. *Diagnosis.* Late peritonitis such as one might see from a perforated appendix or diverticulitis.

2. *Admission Data.* This procedure is based, as an example, on a male in his forties. The patient has been ill for ten days from a peritoneal perforation, unrecognized and treated initially as intestinal grippe, with penicillin and streptomycin. He now presents a distended, silent abdomen, high swinging fever with periods of disorientation, marked body wasting, and evidences of severe toxicity. Rectal examination shows fullness and tenderness in the cul-de-sac—an abscess not quite ready for drainage. Physical examination shows fluid at the base of the right lung field.

URINE.   Proteinuria, specific gravity 1.012, otherwise negative.

STOOL GUAIAC.   Strongly positive.

HEMATOLOGY

Hematocrit—32
Smear—normal
Leucocyte count—45,000 cu. mm.

BLOOD CHEMICAL ANALYSES

Blood urea nitrogen—70 mg. per 100 ml.
Plasma protein—4.5 gm. per 100 ml.
Plasma chloride—92 mE. per l.
Plasma sodium—120 mE. per l.
Plasma potassium—6.2 mE. per l.
Carbon dioxide combining power—14 mE. per l.
Plasma bilirubin—4.8 mg. per 100 ml.

WEIGHT. Such a patient as this can be weighed on his way to bed on the ward and such data may prove useful as a base line. Frequent weighing early in the course of his disease will be inadvisable.

3. *Interpretation and General Plan.* This patient is as ill clinically as he is chemically. He is jaundiced. While, in itself, this does not indicate pylephlebitis, it is a measure of severe systemic toxicity. He has received no transfusions to provide a ready explanation of his jaundice. The urinary findings are inconsequential; the blood urea nitrogen and metabolic acidosis are a much more accurate reflection of the extent of this patient's failure of renal function. This is due primarily to infection and the products of lean-tissue catabolism presenting themselves to a kidney showing the late effects of intermittent oligemia and oliguria, these resulting in turn from desalting water loss and sequestered edema in the peritoneal cavity during the acute phase. These have produced repeated episodes of renal anoxia with decreased glomerular filtration and renal plasma flow, the tubules vulnerable to pigments and bacterial toxins in the patient's blood. In many cases this sequence results in acute tubular necrosis and death. In this example, urinary volume output has been maintained but with insufficient total nephron function to normalize azotemia or acid-base balance; this is solute diuresis, with azotemia, occurring via a few remaining functional nephrons.

The plan for this man is to stabilize him as best one can and to drain the secondary localizations as soon as possible. The drainage of these is far more important than accurate diagnosis as to their source. Even if his peritonitis results from perforated diverticulitis, it is now so late in the course that transverse colostomy is not urgent and should not be done until further diagnostic evidence can become available.

4. *Preoperative Study and Care.* STUDY. A chest film and an upright film of the abdomen are the only X-ray studies justified early in such a patient's course. Barium enema or any other form of gastrointestinal X-ray procedure is absolutely contraindicated at this time because of distention and ileus. Any extensive manipulation and positioning, particularly that involving an enema, would be hazardous.

DIET AND ORDERS. The patient is placed on nasogastric suction and given nothing by mouth. In our example there are occasional tinkles of peristalsis and cramps, so a long tube is preferable to a nasogastric tube.

In such a patient long-tube intubation may in itself result in dramatic improvement. The tube is inserted into the stomach and the balloon half inflated with water. With good fortune, it will pass through the pylorus within the first eighteen hours, as shown by the sudden change in the character of the drainage. The patient is actively decompressed with it. In the face of peritonitis of this duration, there may be areas of the peritoneal cavity whose infection may have abated. The remaining changes may be due entirely to the secondary localizations, with the result that long-tube intubation is possible. In earlier peritonitis with diffuse ileus, this is rarely possible, and nasogastric aspiration is preferable.

Chemical analysis of the patient's blood is to be repeated approximately every three days, depending on events.

PARENTERAL THERAPY. Such a patient is given two or three transfusions of fresh whole blood the first day, following the reasoning that his low hematocrit indicates a severe degree of erythrocyte wastage after ten days of sepsis and that with his bowel bleeding he has a continued hypovolemia. The blood urea, acidosis, and hypoproteinemia evidence the residual effect of his previous oligemic episodes on renal function.

The severe hyponatremia combines de-salting water loss with dilution (by intra-venous and endogenous water) in its patho-genesis. The intravenous program should include some concentrated sodium salts, but because of the plan to give 1500 ml. of blood the first day, this can be procrastinated twenty-four hours. The hyperkalemia reflects the borderline renal function, the acidosis, and the low sodium. No specific measures should be taken in its behalf other than the avoidance of potassium in treatment. The patient's total body potassium is unquestion-ably low after an acute wasting illness; the plasma level is high because of the factors mentioned above.

He has been on penicillin and streptomycin for ten days and this treatment is therefore arbitrarily shifted to an alternative intra-venous broad-spectrum antibiotic.

The daily fluid regimen of such a patient should be handled on an "in-balance" basis, using the clinical balance technique. Tube losses, urine losses, and insensible pulmonary losses are taken into account. Extensive re-salting and rehydration are avoided because his low hematocrit and hyponatremia indi-cate that, although there may have been de-salting in the past, there is now no element of true dehydration, but instead overhydra-tion. This estimate is further reinforced by his low plasma protein concentration.

For these reasons, he is undertreated rather than overtreated with parenteral water and salt. The administration of salt is initially hypertonic and then is restricted strictly to a balancing-out of current extrarenal losses.

FURTHER COURSE. The febrile course con-tinues but the patient may be expected to look less "toxic" because of his decompression and blood transfusion. Check of blood chemi-cal values would be expected to show a restoration of the hematocrit to about 36, the sodium to about 128 mE. per l., and a fall in potassium to the vicinity of 5.2 mE. per l. Little change in azotemia would be expected this early in his new program.

X-rays, repeated on his third day in the hospital and with better technique, might be expected to show a clearer air bubble under the right diaphragm. Therefore, on the third or fourth day the patient is taken to the operating room for drainage of his right sub-phrenic abscess and of the abscess in the cul-de-sac.

5. *Operation.* Because it is the most criti-cal area, the right subphrenic space is drained first. This is best done with the patient in the sitting position, using the posterior approach through the bed of the twelfth rib. With such a story one would expect an extensive, foul-smelling abscess to be encountered, with pus under pressure. If the patient stabilizes well under observation for half an hour after this procedure and is more comfortable, he is then lightly anesthetized and the cul-de-sac abscess is drained via the rectum after needle aspiration.

6. *Postoperative Study and Care.* The pa-tient's response to his drainage should be very clear-cut. As fever subsides and pulse becomes lower, he looks less toxic and within twenty-four hours complains of hunger.

The long tube is allowed to drain by gravity for twenty-four hours more before taking it out. If the patient has no cramps and com-plains of no discomfort, the tube is clamped for an additional twenty-four hours. Again the patient is asymptomatic (indicating gas-trointestinal competence), so that the tube is removed.

Feedings are begun, but slowly, permitting the patient three to four days before signifi-cant caloric intakes are given. There has been a period of septic starvation for ten days, and caloric intake is needed to achieve convales-cence. One or two days' difference in the timing of this intake is unimportant. Until oral intake is adequate, such a patient is maintained on a simple "in-balance" regimen of water, salt, and glucose. He is expected to lose weight until intake reaches significant levels, but less rapidly than at the height of fever.

Antibiotics might well be stopped by the fourth postoperative day if clinical response is good. Secondary localizations that have not been drained will be unmasked by stop-ping antibiotics without hazard to the pa-tient. The patient's care is much simplified by the cessation of antibiotics. Following drainage of the principal localizations, antibiotics have little effect on such a late, localized purulent process.

Such a patient as this has been fortunate. Two major secondary localizations have been his only serious problems; in other cases the balance is tipped in the direction of bloodstream invasion, accumulative bronchopneumonia, or renal failure as terminal events.

In the patient of our example the diagnosis has not been firmly established even during a week or two of very effective treatment of the secondary localizations. Later, as sepsis clears, the barium enema or other X-ray studies may be done. Then, at an elective time, reparative or extirpative operation is carried out as insurance against another bout of trouble.

CHAPTER 36

The Gastrointestinal Tract: Acute Massive Hemorrhage

Section I.   The Problem

A. THE PROBLEM: TO OPERATE OR NOT TO OPERATE

In *chronic* gastrointestinal hemorrhage, metabolic management depends on the understanding of the changes in the blood volume which result, and on the effects of transfusion. These have been described in Part II and will not be repeated here.

In *acute* massive exsanguinating hemorrhage the essential decision is whether to devote attention wholly to diagnosis and blood replacement, on the one hand, or to operative intervention and positive control of the bleeding site, on the other. This in turn depends on whether or not the natural forces of hemostasis will put an end to the bleeding.

The problem in acute gastrointestinal hemorrhage is: will it require urgent operation? There is no form of gastrointestinal hemorrhage that is not better dealt with electively at a later time than in the acute stage. This is in sharp contrast to the hemorrhage of ectopic pregnancy, ruptured spleen, or arterial wound, in which early operation is the desired course. Therefore, while the principal or strategic diagnosis is pathologic (ulcer, cancer, varix?) the immediate or tactical diagnosis is: will it stop?

Initial treatment is devoted toward helping the hemorrhage stop. If it shows its nature as not inclined to cease, then operation should not be further delayed. If bleeding will end on simple measures, then operation should be avoided until a later time. Upon these simple and obvious rules hangs a large volume of detailed procedure and clinical experience.

In our experience the critical time comes during the second twenty-four hours of hospitalization; the question "Will it stop?" and the discernment as to whether or not the natural forces of hemostasis and homeostasis will hold the patient over a free interval for study and definitive care are best resolved in the second day in the hospital.

B. CAUSES

The common causes of gastrointestinal hemorrhage are varices, gastric ulcer or cancer, duodenal ulcer, colonic cancer, and ulcerative colitis. There are many less common causes.

If red blood is vomited freely, the site is duodenal or above; if the stools are black tar with no red component, it is right colon or higher. Bleeding from any level can produce bright red blood *per anum*. Physical examination, with special attention to spider angiomas, liver enlargement, ascites, abdominal

561

or rectal mass, and proctoscopy, is of course basic. But the most important single consideration in diagnosis is the history. The majority of patients with bleeding duodenal ulcer or varix have an appropriate history. Unfortunately, patients with chronic cirrhosis occasionally bleed from duodenal ulcer, so clear separation is not always possible. There is a small group of patients with massive bleeding for which no demonstrable cause is ever found.

C. CROSS REFERENCES

The relation of hemorrhage and its physiologic result to the blood volume (Part II) is a prime consideration here, as is blood transfusion (Part II). Liver failure (Part V), ammonia intoxication (Part V), solute loading (Part III), shock (Parts II and VI), and renal failure (Part V) enter the equation in various cases. These matters will not be reviewed again here.

Section II.   Strategy and Tactics in Gastrointestinal Bleeding

A. STRATEGY

The basic strategy in gastrointestinal hemorrhage is made up of four considerations.

(1) *Diagnosis.*   Make the diagnosis reasonably certain. Do not hurt the patient through a compulsive desire for absolute diagnostic certainty.

(2) *Blood Volume.*   Maintain the blood volume as near normal as possible, starting as soon as possible. There is no virtue in a low volume or pressure; only harm can result, chiefly to the kidneys.

(3) *Coagulation.*   Be assured that there is not a coagulation defect underlying the process.

(4) *Operation.*   Operate if bleeding will not meet rigid specifications for early cessation.

B. TACTICS

The tactical steps involved depend initially on volume of the hemorrhage and probable diagnosis. If the hemorrhage is massive and shock is present, immediate replacement and physiologic stabilization take precedence over all other steps. The volumes to be replaced and critical rates are indicated in Part II. If varix is suspect, tamponade is done immediately.

If the hemorrhage is less massive and stabilization more readily achieved, then other early steps are taken, directed both at diagnosis—where is the bleeding from and will it stop?—and treatment. Some of these aspects are covered in the following.

1. *Sex and Age.*   Males are more frequently,

proportionally, operated upon in the acute phase than are females. The extremes of age are the most dangerous: when the patient is under twenty or over sixty-five the likelihood of the hemorrhage stopping is significantly less.

2. *Duration.*   Bleeding "off and on" for several days is more apt to stop with the immobilization and other steps of hospitalization than is sudden exsanguination, which is apt to start up again when blood pressure is restored.

3. *Intubation.*   If the patient has recently vomited blood, immediate intubation should not be done.* In all other cases the benefit of intubation far outweighs the hazard. The finding of guaiac-negative gastric contents immediately localizes the bleeding as beyond the ligament of Treitz. Fear of nasogastric intubation has often confused diagnosis.

4. *Early Chemical Methods for Diagnosis.* Early in the hemorrhage one may gain diagnostic help in differentiating ulcer from varix. Bromsulfalein retention is unfortunately rather nonspecific as a test of liver involvement because shock also interferes with hepatic clearance; but markedly elevated retention (over 30 per cent) favors varix. Determination of the blood ammonia level is helpful. Although shock favors ammonia accumulation, this is much less pronounced than that seen when bleeding supervenes in advanced cirrhosis and presents a large am-

---

* If varix is suspect, early tamponade is of diagnostic significance.

monia load to a sick liver. Thus, markedly elevated ammonia level signifies the greater likelihood of a varix bleed.

5. *Early X-Ray.* When history makes the diagnosis of either duodenal ulcer or varix virtually certain, X-ray need not be done in the acute stage. In other cases it should be done, looking only for varices. Detailed fluoroscopy below this level is unsatisfactory and dangerous; make a few spot films for what they may show, then return the patient to the ward. In cases of bleeding from the colon, barium enema should be done early in all cases.

6. *Endoscopy.* In the acute stage there is only one indication for peroral endoscopy: esophagoscopy when the diagnosis of varices is crucial and cannot be made in any other way. Otherwise, endoscopy at the upper end of the tract should be omitted until all signs of acute hemorrhage have abated.

As to the lower end, proctoscopy is essential in all cases in which the colon is suspect. If diffuse ulcerative colitis is found, nonoperative management should hold the field no longer than twenty-four hours. If this does not bring clear signs of control, total colectomy is essential if salvage is to be achieved.

7. *Coagulation.* Tests of bleeding, clotting, and prothrombin times, platelet count, and tourniquet test should be done early. At the same time, base-line blood chemical analyses are carried out. If abnormalities of clotting are found, a sequence similar to that outlined in Part II should be pursued.

C. CRITERIA FOR OPERATIVE INTERVENTION IN ESOPHAGO-GASTRO-DUODENAL HEMORRHAGE

The criteria are rate of bleeding and response to therapy. In a normal adult, if replacement of more than 2000 ml. of blood is needed to maintain blood pressure and flow in the second twenty-four-hour period, operation should be undertaken. This may otherwise be stated:

If the maintenance of blood pressure and urine flow requires replacement of 30 to 50 per cent of the blood volume per day in the second twenty-four hours of hospitaliza-

tion, there is an overriding indication for operation.

During the first twenty-four hours in the hospital there are many factors to confuse discrimination as to the immediate prognosis for cessation: transportation, early transfusion, studies for other systemic disease, trip to X-ray department, chemical study, repeated physical examination. It is the exceptional patient who bleeds so much that operation is needed during the first twenty-four hours of hospitalization.

During the second twenty-four hours in the hospital, the confusion of admission as well as the immediate benefits of bed rest have worn off or the patient has become acclimated; his course can now be observed with reference to the single most important variable: maintenance of effective blood volume in relation to rate of transfusion.

As to response indicating effective volume, the important parameters are pulse, blood pressure, and urine flow. If these are easily maintained at good performance levels with low transfusion rates, one can afford further conservative measures; if they are poorly maintained at any time from the second day onward, the infusion of blood should be doubled in rate and a move toward the operating room initiated.

If varix bleeding has been held likely and tamponade has been effective, blood must be cleansed from the gut and a trial of balloon deflation must be begun between forty-eight and seventy-two hours after admission.

1. Is There a Point of No Return?

It is on this point that the physician often finds himself in error. Our emphasis is on the second twenty-four hours and the early operation, because it is after forty-eight hours of massive blood replacement that the hazards of conservative management become progressively greater, and include:

   (1) oliguria and anuria;
   (2) multiple-transfusion disorders, including pathologic bleeding tendency and citrate toxicity;
   (3) pulmonary complications: aspiration, atelectasis;

(4) hypertonicity, solute loading, acidosis; and

(5) in liver disease: exogenous ammonia intoxication due to digestion of blood.

The physician cannot take the easy course of day-to-day maintenance. At forty-eight hours, a solid commitment must be made. If surgery is vetoed and bleeding continues, then responsibility must be pinpointed on those managing the nonoperative care; the operative opportunity for salvage has begun to wane, if it has not disappeared altogether. As this moment passes, operation becomes progressively less likely to be followed by recovery.

D. CAUSES OF DEATH

Causes of death in acute hemorrhage from the upper gastrointestinal tract, in cases in which the liver is not primarily involved, are as follows:

(1) *Pulmonary.* Aspiration pneumonitis, accumulative bronchopneumonia, and respiratory failure are very prone to develop.

(2) *Renal.* Renal failure occurs commonly if shock has long been present.

(3) *Bleeding.* Continued bleeding, intraoperative or postoperative bleeding, and "multiple transfusion" disorders are common late manifestations in gastrointestinal hemorrhage.

The management of the patient before, during, and after operation is pointed toward the prevention of these three lethal complications.

The *pulmonary* threat is best avoided by preoperative gastric aspiration (using a large tube if necessary), keeping the stomach empty at all times, and bronchoscopy at the end of anesthesia and soon again later as needed. A high-humidity atmosphere (fog room) is very helpful should bronchitis, wheezing, bronchorrhea, or "wet lung" develop. Postoperative bronchoscopy should not await crises; any evidence of incomplete cough-clearing requires it. In elderly patients with massive hemorrhage, bronchopulmonary accumulation is very common and can only be managed by aggressive measures. Tracheotomy is to be avoided in these cases if possible; bronchopulmonary involvement is not due to local disease, and the patient needs an effective cough effort, lost by tracheotomy.

The *renal* threat can be abated, if not obviated, by three admonitions.

(1) Operate only with blood pressure and urine flow near normal even if it takes two simultaneous transfusion channels to do it. Operation on an hypovolemic anuric patient is often followed by renal failure.

(2) Use fresh blood. A small amount of pigment (in poorly preserved or matched blood) does a lot of damage in patients who have been in shock due to bleeding.

(3) Do not dehydrate or overhydrate the patient.

Pathologic bleeding is prevented and treated by using fresh blood in one transfusion out of every four, and by a vigil on the coagulation data and their rectification, if abnormal. The best preventive of postoperative bleeding is solid control of all bleeding points at operation; even this is not infallible if several blood volumes of transfusion have been necessary. Calcium should be given because of citrate infusion.

Miscellaneous Instructions

In varix bleeding the tamponade tube is to be preferred above all else; if urgent operation is needed, a wide portacaval shunt is to be preferred to a local attack on the esophagus.

The nonoperative treatment of gastroduodenal bleeding often involves the use of frequent milk-and-cream feedings with little water. This involves the minor nuisance of fecal impaction and a major hazard: solute-loading hypertonicity. Although minor in most instances, unrecognized fecal impaction leads to severe discomfort, distention, and even sigmoid perforation.

The plasma sodium concentration may rise to 150 to 165 mE. per l. as the crippled kidney struggles to rid itself of the solute load imposed by digested blood, milk, cream, and alkali, floating it out on body water badly needed elsewhere. The kidney is unable to concentrate maximally because of the very solute load itself plus the renal tubular residue of recent hypotension. For this reason adequate water must be provided during all phases, particularly the nonoperative period.

E. CLINICAL PROCEDURE IN BLEEDING DUODENAL ULCER

The following procedure is postulated on the care of an elderly man with massive hemorrhage from a bleeding duodenal ulcer. This example includes procedures and sequences from several representative cases. As in other procedures, the bare outline of a typical hospital course is given, to demonstrate, in the patient's care, the application of underlying principles.

1. *Diagnosis.* Bleeding duodenal ulcer.

2. *Admission Data.* Such a patient might be a male in his seventies, whose bleeding episode commenced eighteen hours prior to admission. The patient felt full and sweaty; he went to the toilet to have a bowel movement; he passed a large black and bloody movement, vomited bright red blood, and then fainted in the bathroom. Several hours often pass before the physician arrives, and additional time is expended before the decision is made to bring the patient to the hospital. X-rays taken five years previously showed an active duodenal ulcer; management has been inconstant.

On physical examination such a patient is found to be in shock, with a pulse near 120 and blood pressure as low as 70/50 or lower. If he is clear in his mind and is cooperative, these two features are of great prognostic importance, as they are in any older patient with severe illness, and especially in one with bleeding.

Catheterization reveals only a small volume of urine, and no further flow in the first thirty minutes. Transfusion is immediately begun.

Physical examination in our example shows a heart that is within normal limits as to size, some peripheral arteriosclerosis, but otherwise an individual in moderately good shape for a man of his years. There is no evidence of liver enlargement. Rectal examination is negative save for the blood. Proctoscopy is negative. Laboratory work might characteristically show the following, but only the hematocrit and urinalysis would be immediately available.

URINE. A small amount of urine. Specific gravity 1.014. No cells in the sediment.

HEMATOLOGY
Hematocrit—20
Leucocyte count—18,000 per cu. mm.

BLOOD CHEMICAL ANALYSES
Blood urea nitrogen—80 mg. per 100 ml.
Plasma protein—5.5 gm. per 100 ml.
Plasma sodium—130 mE. per l.
Plasma potassium—6.2 mE. per l.
Carbon dioxide combining power—18 mE. per l.
Bleeding, clotting, and prothrombin time, platelet count—normal.

WEIGHT. 62 kg.

3. *Interpretation and General Plan.* The lack of liver enlargement in such a case plus the specific history of duodenal ulcer renders a varix hemorrhage entirely unlikely. While it is possible that this patient might be bleeding from carcinoma of the stomach or some other upper abdominal lesion, the initial management will be the same; early gastrointestinal X-rays are unnecessary. The diagnosis of duodenal ulcer is about 85 per cent certain.

Intubation is withheld for the first twelve hours. If he vomits further blood, a tube should be put down; the stomach is emptied and irrigated. If he is found to have over 40 units of free acid or more in a blood-free specimen, this virtually clinches the diagnosis of bleeding duodenal ulcer in a patient with such a history as this. The initial management is therefore devoted largely to restoration of effective circulating blood volume, and vascular homeostasis.

With recent severe hemorrhage (possibly continuing) and an hematocrit of only 20 now, one may assume that transcapillary refilling of the blood volume is well advanced, but not complete in the sense of restoration. In a man of this age, body build, and weight, the expected volume, at 7.0 per cent of body weight, would be 4340 ml. Assuming a blood-volume deficit of between 25 and 50 per cent and an hematocrit of 20, we come up with the following approximate intravascular composition:

Plasma volume—1940–2780 ml.
Erythrocyte volume—480–700 ml.
Total blood volume—2420–3480 ml.

It is clearly important to start with whole blood for up to 1500 ml. to restore volume, thereafter using separated erythrocytes, the entire program to depend upon the presence or absence of continued bleeding. Other intravenously administered fluids should be held to maintenance requirements on the first day.

This blood program should be pushed to completion in six to twelve hours. Elderly people tolerate transfusion perfectly well when they are hypovolemic, and they tolerate hypovolemia much less well than their younger counterparts. *It is overtransfusion, not rapid transfusion, that is poorly tolerated in the older age group.*

The patient should be given ulcer management with feedings every hour, bearing in mind the potential of such feedings to produce hypertonicity, solute diuresis, and fecal impaction.

The blood chemical data, available several hours after treatment has begun, indicate the azotemia of gastrointestinal hemorrhage, the sodium-potassium concentration-inversion characteristic of severe acute illness with poor renal function, and a metabolic acidosis traceable to shock and oliguria.

A chest X-ray is taken. It is normal.

An electrocardiogram shows tachycardia and early signs of acidosis or hyperkalemia (tenting of the T waves).

4. *Initial Treatment.* The first 1500 ml. of blood is given in the course of four hours, or close to 400 ml. per hour. This is about 7 ml. per minute, or a maintained rate of about 100 drops a minute. The separated cells are given more slowly.

Intravenous fluid other than blood totals 1000 ml. of 5 per cent dextrose in water each day for the first two days. The patient is given ulcer feedings every hour and is kept quietly in bed. Urine outputs are observed hourly, via the urethral catheter.

5. *Progress Evaluation and Interpretation.* This example depicts a patient typical of the group in whom the course during the second twenty-four hours dictates the surgical tactics.

During his first twenty-four hours such a patient may become stabilized in the hospital. Although exsanguinating hemorrhage during this time would require immediate operation, it is unusual to observe this in such cases. It is during the second twenty-four hours that the patient must show us, by satisfactory stabilization and maintenance of stabilization without excessive blood replacement, that he is ceasing to bleed actively. For this reason, the course of the hourly urine output, the vital signs, and certain of the biochemical changes are critical in the decision.

In this case, as an example, urine volume has returned rapidly, with replacement of blood volume, to volumes of 15 to 30 ml. per hour. Blood pressure rises initially, pulse drops, and the situation looks favorable. Initial coagulation studies have shown no abnormality, and, after twenty-four hours of care, the patient is well stabilized, with a blood pressure over 100, producing over 15 ml. of urine per hour, and looking much better. His pulse, however, does not come down below 110, and, late the afternoon of the second day, the patient's pulse tends to rise, his blood pressure tends to slip. Up to this time he has received 5 units of whole blood and 3 units of separated cells. In twenty-four hours this totals approximately 3000 ml. of blood. His hematocrit, formerly having risen from 20 to 30, again starts to fall, and urine volume shrinks to zero.

In such a case the second twenty-four hours' maintenance has not been satisfactory. Operation must be definitively planned. Delay now, at the patient's age of seventy, will bring about an irretrievable situation.

6. *Preoperative Steps*

Oral feedings are stopped. A nasogastric tube is reinserted and put on suction.

There is minimal preoperative sedation.

The patient is given 10 gm. of calcium gluconate slowly, intravenously. Two walking donors are prepared, so that fresh blood may be given during or immediately at the close of the procedure.

7. *Operation.* ANESTHESIA. Endotracheal high-oxygen inhalation anesthesia is used, with careful bronchial toilet and bronchoscopy if necessary at the end of the procedure.

OPERATIVE PROCEDURE. Subtotal gastrectomy. At operation the stomach is found filled with clotted blood, which has not been removed through the tube. The stomach is opened and this blood carefully evacuated, but contamination is inevitable in such a circumstance.

The ulcer itself is difficult to deal with. Good duodenal closure cannot be obtained. An indwelling duodenal catheter is therefore left in place, placed on suction, and the omentum is channelized along any exposed portion of the catheter tract.

8. *Postoperative Study and Care.* The hazards to this patient, as mentioned previously, are bronchopulmonary, renal, and hemorrhagic.

Preventive pulmonary steps consist of high-humidity atmosphere, careful bronchial toilet, and bronchoscopy as needed.

The renal hazards can be fended off best by adequate blood volume replacement. The patient lost 1500 ml. of blood during the operation, as monitored by sponge weights. It is replaced quantitatively, including one transfusion of fresh whole blood and two of bank blood. He is given one transfusion of fresh whole blood postoperatively.

Rechecked coagulation data are normal.

The first two postoperative days are the critical ones. If the patient can weather these with satisfactory renal function, pulmonary ventilation, and avoidance of additional hemorrhage, his outlook is excellent.

Should this patient develop acute tubular necrosis with oliguria unresponsive to infusion, his outlook is virtually hopeless. One hates to make such a statement in nonmalignant disease, yet we have not seen a patient in this age group who has developed acute tubular necrosis after gastrointestinal bleeding, and who has then recovered.

Tracheotomy should be avoided if possible. This is an example in which repeated bronchoscopy is to be favored over tracheotomy. The patient can then talk and maintain his cough mechanics.

Should massive hemorrhage reappear with any one of a variety of disorders of coagulation, the stepwise procedure for evaluation of clotting disorders mentioned on pages 251–253 should be used.

CHAPTER 37

The Gastrointestinal Tract: Fistula, Absorption Defects, and Inflammatory Lesions

Section I.   Fistula

The management of gastrointestinal fistula above the colon, and resultant extrarenal loss, depends on four steps.

(1) *Adequate Exteriorization, Drainage of Abscess, and Suction-Sump Drainage.* This avoids skin damage, abates infection, permits measurement of the extrarenal output, and, most important, allows spontaneous closure by cicatrization of the tract.

(2) *Accurate Chemical Control of Extrarenal Loss, and Nutritional Management.* This is described in Part III.

(3) *Patience.* If there is no tumor in the tract, if drainage is adequate so that a tract can form, and if there is no distal obstruction, most fistulas will close. Do not rush into operative closure or bypassing procedures. Occasionally, diversion or feeding jejunostomy is useful.

(4) *In Rare Cases, Operative Closure.* This must involve a clean dissection, anatomic closure, and interposition of normal tissues over the closure.

The nature of the metabolic defect depends wholly on the volume and nature of the loss; accurate replacement is therefore essential. Severe acid-base disorders may arise and must be repaired promptly. All these matters are dealt with in Part III and will not be reviewed again here.

568

Inadequate drainage of the initial abscess is a common cause for failure. The fistula must be a linear tract, not a spherical abscess with a small external opening. Most fistulas will close spontaneously by a cicatrization, but they cannot do so until they are linear tracts; and this in turn requires adequate exteriorization and drainage.

Premature attempt at operative closure is a real hazard here. To the individual who has not dealt with many fistulas of the small bowel, there is a constant invitation to try to close it. In its early phases this is almost universally unsuccessful.

A bypass of the fistula may be helpful where it is feasible, but here again, premature operation is most unfortunate. Attention should be devoted to adequate drainage, sump suction, skin care, and parenteral maintenance. Calories are not important early on; the "priority list" (Part III) is exemplified in the management of these patients.

If mucous membrane protrudes or commences healing to skin, operative closure will be necessary. This is a late phenomenon.

If the fistula is from the large bowel, the same general rules hold; if complex (as in diverticulitis) and in the left colon, proximal colostomy is essential.

Section II. Absorption Defects and Nonspecific Inflammatory Processes

The absorption defects commonly treated by the surgeon fall into three general categories. There is no unitary "malabsorption syndrome."

1. *Anatomic shortening of the gastrointestinal tract:* this includes those cases of massive intestinal resection necessitated by trauma, mesenteric thrombosis, or embolus, and operative freaks produced by the inadvertent anastomosis of the stomach to some portion of the gastrointestinal tract lower down than the high jejunum, to which the anastomosis was intended.

2. *Motor and absorptive defects:* diseases characterized by rapid passage through the small intestine and deficient digestive and enzymatic function; this includes chronic pancreatitis with steatorrhea, and the postgastrectomy states.

3. *Inflammatory lesions:* ulcerative colitis, pseudomembraneous enterocolitis, and regional enteritis.

A. SHORTENING AND RAPID PASSAGE

The normal length of the gastrointestinal tract is involved with mastication, mixing, acid hydrolysis, enzymatic hydrolysis, and then absorption, in that order. The absorption proceeds by absorption of crystalloids (sugars, hydrolyzed protein) in the small bowel, salts and other ionic complexes in the right colon, and water in the left colon.

When normal gastrointestinal tissue is working with a decreased absorptive surface, the nutritional defect produced seems to be more severe if the only remaining tissue is in the high jejunum than if it is in the low ileum. The lower portion of the ileum is a more actively absorbing surface for crystalloids than the upper jejunum, and if it is intact some degree of nutritional competency may be maintained.

When the gastrointestinal tract is shortened, caloric starvation results. This may be mitigated by the use of feeding mixtures or drugs.

1. Food Mixtures

The use of a feeding mixture which makes further hydrolysis unnecessary merely saves time in the completion of normal gastrointestinal function. Instead of starches, polysaccharides, and disaccharides such as sucrose, the carbohydrate should consist of glucose or fructose, which can be absorbed without further processing in the gastrointestinal wall. Instead of whole proteins, complexes of small molecular weight, such as the amino acids and protein hydrolysate mixtures, are used. In this way, carbohydrate and protein can be absorbed with a minimum of time and luminal distance being involved in the hydrolytic process.

Such "predigested" food mixtures have the disadvantage of very high osmotic concentration because the components have been broken down to very low molecular weight. If not well diluted they act as an osmotic laxative, a "dose of salts." They also lead to solute-loading hypertonicity if absorbed with inadequate water. They should be given by mouth, at low concentrations of total solids.

It is impossible without preliminary emulsification, a process which requires time, to prepare hydrolyzed mixtures of fat that contain caloric value and yet are easily absorbed. Alcohol would be extremely useful as a caloric supplement in such instances were it not for the intoxicating effect produced even when amounts are taken which are of little caloric significance. Whatever is given, it should be used in the form of frequent small feedings.

Fat emulsions, by mouth, would appear to be useful here, and they are worth a try. Some sort of crude measure of stool fat should be used before and after such an attempt to judge its effectiveness. In most instances there is an intensification of the diarrhea, inadequate time for hydrolysis and absorption, and little caloric advance. Such mixtures as fat emulsions are not particularly palatable and they do not find the patient in a very receptive mood. They therefore should be given after the day's feedings have been accomplished by more conventional or palatable food. They may be used as a single tube feeding at night. Frequent feedings of normal-tasting fats, such as butter and homogenized milk, seem to be more effective.

In patients such as this the daily measurement of the fecal nitrogen output in relation to the nitrogen intake is the most accurate method of determining the daily adequacy of absorption. Such patients will be found to have elevated stool nitrogen concentrations ranging from 3 to 8 gm. of nitrogen per day, depending upon the mixture used. By carefully regulating the ingested mixture, giving frequent small feedings, and measuring the stool nitrogen concentration, it is possible to improve absorption.

One often encounters patients of this type to whom carefully prepared tube feedings are being given, the tube feeding material being merely a homogenized oral diet—dried milk or a mixture of dried whole proteins in solution. Merely mixing this material up in a blending machine and running it through a tube accomplishes very little for the patient. It is the chemical hydrolysis of this material down to amino acids and dipeptides and monosaccharides which is useful in bowel shortening.

Frequent small feedings even of a rather normal diet low in roughage will accomplish a lot for such patients, just as in the post-gastrectomy group. The mechanism may well be that of reducing the gastrocolic propulsive reflex inherent in large feedings. One often finds that this simple measure is the most effective.

A joint approach is best, using several steps—predigested (evening) tube feeding, frequent oral feeding, and careful measurements of intake and body weight.

Specific vitamin deficiencies (particularly of vitamins B, C, and K) develop rapidly in patients with bowel shortening. Supplements must always be used parenterally.

2. Drugs

A second basic step is to slow down the rate of gastrointestinal passage. In our experience, the most useful measures are:

a. Boiled skimmed milk two or three times a day.

b. Drugs such as paregoric or deodorized tincture of opium in liberal amounts.

c. Codeine administered orally. This is an effective constipating agent and seems to affect the entire range of gastrointestinal motility. The recommended dosage is 30 mg. two or three times a day. This large amount of codeine cannot be administered steadily for long periods of time because of the danger of sedation and addiction, but it can be used to tide the patient over intermittent periods of diarrhea.

Diseases of poor absorption and rapid passage, such as chronic pancreatitis and regional enteritis, present extremely difficult problems. If a patient with chronic pancreatitis and calcification fibrosis has reached the point of steatorrhea, he probably has diabetes also and the pancreas has been essentially destroyed. Low-fat diets, hydrolyzed mixtures, and materials that reduce the time of gastrointestinal passage all find a place in treatment. The patient may be one of those unfortunate individuals who in addition has periodic bouts of severe pain. We have not seen patients in this group who were rehabilitated to good nutritional status by methods now available. The treatment of the pancreatic pain by splanchnicectomy, pancreatectomy, choledochojejunostomy, or sphincterotomy may have a beneficial role in reducing the patient's need for heavy analgesic medication or his tendency to become addicted to drugs or alcohol.

In late regional enteritis, the lesion is partly obstructive. The disorder of gastrointestinal passage is the result of hyperperistalsis proximal to obstruction, analogous to that seen in a malfunctioning ileostomy. In such patients, the performance of an ileotransverse colostomy may in itself reduce intestinal passage rate and improve the patient's nutrition, despite the seemingly paradoxical fact that it has resulted in further shortening of the gastrointestinal tract; it has provided an adequate stoma through which the small bowel may empty into the large without distention.

As a general rule applicable to ileostomy

and ileocolostomy, subacute or incomplete obstruction produces diarrhea. In patients with chronic diarrhea, not only should the usual measures be taken relative to search for undigested fat and fibers but, in addition, partial obstruction higher up should be sought and relieved.

Parenteral high-calorie feedings (fat, alcohol, glucose) and amino acids have an obvious usefulness in short-term management of foreshortening or rapid passage. Over the long term they are but little help.

3. Cortisone

In regional enteritis, cortisone and its analogues may slow down peristaltic activity, presumably by reducing inflammation and irritation. In early cases or those without sepsis or obstruction their use is a wise step, either as a prolonged clinical trial or as a preliminary to operation. One effect of such treatment is to suppress adrenal activity. Should a perforation ensue or operation become necessary, appropriate steps should be taken to increase the cortisone dosage, or add adrenocorticotropic hormone, according to circumstances.

B. THE POSTGASTRECTOMY STATES

Of the disorders coming on after subtotal gastrectomy for duodenal ulcer, the dumping syndrome is the most irksome and failure to gain or maintain weight the most dangerous. The combination—although rare in a severe form—is so imposing as to have driven successive generations of surgeons into a protracted search for a better operation.

1. The Dumping Syndrome

This is so named because it was thought to result from rapid emptying of food from a small gastric cuff into the jejunum. This syndrome is not seen in many patients who empty very rapidly as viewed by X-ray. Yet, despite this fact, a small or slowly emptying stoma does indeed seem to be protective, at least to some extent.

The symptoms are characteristic: flushing, palpitation, sweating, faintness, a desire to move the bowels, a desire to lie down, and "blackout." They come but a few moments after eating and are usually worst after breakfast. Whatever the mechanism there can be little question that the filling of the jejunum with food unprocessed by a normal stomach is somehow at fault. Balloon distention of the jejunum produces similar symptoms. An injection of a large (and dangerous) dose of a cholinergic drug (such as acetyl-beta-methylcholine) reproduces the symptoms almost exactly, and their cholinergic nature is further suggested by the fact that atropine abates, if not obviates, the complex. Yet, despite this parasympathomimetic nature of the dumping syndrome, the vagi are not the effector pathway, nor are they the afferent pathway, since the typical syndrome can occur after complete vagotomy.

Changes in blood sugar, jejunal distention, and a reduction in plasma volume brought about by a transient osmotic segregation of fluid in the jejunum have all been blamed. In our view all three mechanisms play a role. In addition there are psychologic factors, and there may be a basic "neurocirculatory asthenia," as evidenced by postural hypotension.

The symptom-complex of the dumping syndrome occurs "in miniature" and transiently in nearly all patients who have had a subtotal gastrectomy with gastrojejunal anastomosis. If questioned closely (which is not a good idea) they will recognize the complex as having occurred several times in their first month.

In those who have it in worse form (5 to 12 per cent of patients) the following directions are helpful.

(1) For a few weeks have the patient eat the morning meal while still in bed. He should drink warm water and take an atropine preparation orally about twenty minutes before breakfast.

(2) Check the blood for anemia and if it is present, or if the hypotension is prominent, give the patient 1 or 2 units of whole blood.

(3) Give frequent small feedings, trying to

avoid large amounts of osmotically active crystalloid, especially dextrose or sucrose. Proteins, fat, and starches are to be preferred.

The fashioning of a small stoma to avoid sudden emptying of the stomach into the jejunum may turn out to be a helpful step in prevention. In some cases conversion to a gastroduodenostomy will abate the symptoms.

2. Failure To Gain Weight

This complication appears to be related to the extent of the gastrectomy and the preoperative dietary habits of the patient. The heavy eater seems to remain a good trencherman even with most of his stomach elsewhere. But the small-appetite, underweight patient will have this habit accentuated and, unless he is watched and guided, his weight and strength will fall off to hazardous levels. It is in this group that pulmonary tuberculosis has not infrequently occurred as the terminal event.

This picture is seen after total gastrectomy, but because of the relatively short survival of most patients operated on for gastric malignancy, it is not a common problem. Both anemia and weight failure are a greater hazard in total than in subtotal gastrectomy, if the patient survives long enough to develop them in florid form.

The complex interplay of digestive disorders in subtotal gastrectomy does not regularly result in nutritional disorder, although fecal loss of nitrogen and fat is increased. The intake is the primary fault and this in turn is traceable to habit and lost appetite. The cure lies in increasing the intake by multiple small nutritious feedings so that, despite the lesser absorption, the net gain is adequate to maintain body composition. The diet providing most nourishment in minimum volume is best here, but to get the patient to eat it requires the joint skills of cuisine and persuasion.

If the patient is sliding downward with dumping syndrome, weight failure, or both, in spite of simple measures, he should be hospitalized. Study of actual food intake and of urinary and fecal outputs of macronutrients, tests of absorption, avitaminosis, and

blood volume should be undertaken as the basis for further therapy.

C. ULCERATIVE COLITIS

Ulcerative colitis is included in a separate category here because it presents manifestations and problems in metabolic care found to a unique extent in that disease and to a lesser extent in the other enteritides.

1. The Early Untreated Disease

In the untreated disease, the diarrhea is not solely a function of disease in the large bowel. Measurements of mouth-to-anus clearance time and X-ray study of the jejunoileum in such patients will show that the entire gastrointestinal tract is involved in a hyperperistaltic state and has many signs of abnormal bowel pattern.

This hypermotility produces starvation and avitaminosis, both of which are hastened by any sepsis present. The septic factor is variable, ranging from an afebrile, nontender, nonbleeding diarrhea all the way to high fever, abdominal tenderness, and hemorrhagic diarrhea. In the latter category are patients who demonstrate examples of septic starvation, marked avitaminosis, and severe anemia.

Management in the afebrile type may take the form of a prolonged clinical trial with nonoperative care, steroids, and, if needed, antibiotics. Ileostomy is a question of socioeconomic rehabilitation balanced against problems in personal hygiene. Metabolic steps are of little importance in the mild disease.

In those more fulminating cases, ranging up to the severe septic and hemorrhagic forms of the disease, treatment should be aimed initially at ileostomy. The date for operation should be set, allowing about a week for preparation. In this time blood volume should be restored aggressively, cortisone should be used in high dosage, with the physician well aware of its deleterious adrenal suppression and prepared to allow for this at the time of operation, using adrenocorticotropic hormone later, and antibiotics given in large quantities. Some form of parenteral feeding should be given, though the intravenous needle is often being used for the more urgent matter of blood volume replacement. Overwatering is a real hazard; extrarenal loss of salt is large, and severe hyponatremia is readily produced. Concentrated salt and large doses of potassium are both important in the parenteral regimen.

During this initial period, perforation of the colon may occur and, with steroids and antibiotics, be remarkably silent. It must be watched for with care.

In most cases, sufficient improvement has been gained to permit operation after seven to ten days. In a few patients the response will be so dramatically good that a more prolonged trial of nonoperative means may be urged by the physician. Long-range prospects for relief are poor, however, and the need for ileostomy great if the patient is to return to his place in society. In young unmarried women, there exists some additional urge to conservatism; an ileostomy is peculiarly damaging to morale and marriage prospects.

2. One-Stage Operation?

Whether or not ileostomy should be accompanied at one operation by total colectomy depends entirely on the metabolic state of the patient as he approaches surgery. Four groups are discernible:

(1) *Very mild chronic disease of two to three years' duration.* Avoid colectomy. It may be unnecessary.

(2) *Very longstanding disease (seven to ten years or more).* Colectomy should be done as cancer prophylaxis. One-stage operation is convenient but not essential.

(3) *Fulminating destructive and hemorrhagic disease, life-endangering, with continued colonic activity and hemorrhage.* Colectomy is essential to avoid perforation and sepsis; with early perforation it is lifesaving. One-stage operation is essential.

(4) *Fulminating disease with severe debility, but initially well controlled and without hemorrhage, no longer life-endangering.* Here, the patient will gain so much from ileostomy that

a dated second-stage operation for colectomy six to eight weeks later is the wiser course.

3. After Ileostomy: Is Malfunction Inevitable?

After ileostomy has been established, patients often show a remarkable restoration of their nutritional status with rapid gain in weight. The motility of the upper small intestine seems to return to normal when the large bowel is defunctioned, as if irritation of the large bowel, infection, and hyperperistalsis triggered the peristaltic activity in the rest of the small bowel.

One major deterrent to a good result here is the malfunctioning ileostomy. Understanding of malfunctioning ileostomy has improved in the past fifteen years. It was formerly assumed that all ileostomies resulted for the patient in a period of diarrhea, dehydration, loss of fluid and electrolyte, and general deterioration before the stoma "settled down" to good function. It is now clear that a well-made ileostomy that is loose to finger palpation may function well with moderately well-formed movements right from the start, and may require intravenous therapy for no longer than a day or two.

The key here lies in the fact that ileostomy diarrhea and so-called malfunction is, in the majority of instances, a manifestation of partial stomal obstruction. Obstruction at the ileostomy stoma occurs over the point where the mucous membrane is healing to the skin. This site becomes the seat of a prolonged granulating and cicatrizing process that begins soon after the ileostomy is made. Or it may occur, in occasional cases, quite late.

Gastrointestinal obstruction results from a disparity between the effective propulsive effort proximal to a point of stenosis and the degree of stenosis. If the two are well balanced, the patient may have remarkably normal function despite an extremely stenotic ileostomy. If they are poorly balanced, the patient will show the diarrhea, foul discharge, systemic illness, and desalting water loss characteristic of obstruction.

A patient with malfunctioning ileostomy and profuse diarrhea should therefore be assumed to have partial stomal obstruction until proven otherwise. The initial step consists in putting a soft rubber catheter of moderately large lumen (#18 to #22 F) into the ileostomy and leaving it there for two or three days while the obstruction, irritation, hyperperistalsis, and proximal putrefaction subside. Then a small plastic operation can be carried out in which the cicatricial tissue around the ileostomy is incised radially at two or three points.

A most important advance in this field, and one reducing the metabolic disturbance in ileostomy, has been the description by Turnbull of an ileostomy sutured primarily to the skin. When the ileum is brought out through the abdominal wall and is simply left in that position, the serosal surface starts to granulate, as does any mesenchymal surface when exposed to the outside world. The mucous membrane starts to creep down the side to join the skin and when it has finally joined it, healing is complete, the granulating or cicatricial process stops, but a fibrous ring has been formed. This takes from three to five weeks, and a period of diarrhea often occurs. Turnbull's contribution lies in a demonstration of the fact that the mucosa can be turned back and sutured primarily to the skin with immediate healing. This avoids a prolonged cicatricial reaction on the serosa and results in a soft, freely patent ileostomy which produces semiformed, dehydrated material which is relatively nonodorous and does not result in any metabolic defect. The patient leaves the hospital with a healed, stabilized ileostomy on the seventh to tenth day. Attempts to accomplish this by skin grafting and other complex maneuvers are no longer necessary.

Digital dilatation of the ileostomy has been recommended as a maneuver to be carried out by the patient. Although this may be useful in rare cases, we are convinced that in the great majority of cases it should not be done. If the ileostomy is tight enough to produce copious, watery diarrhea, it should be repaired by operation. This is a procedure which will delay the patient in the hospital for only two or three days. If the ileostomy is not stenotic and is functioning well, there is no indication for dilatation. Repeated force-

ful and painful dilatation will only tear the submucosal tissues and stimulate further cicatricial contraction.

The early dietary management of the ileostomy patient can be planned along the lines made possible by the new ileostomy technique. The patient's diet can rapidly be increased to one of good quality. Large quantities of food should not be given until the patient is used to his ileostomy and to ileostomy hygiene. Early on, quality is more important than quantity. After this time, his diet can be rapidly increased. We do not impose artificial restrictions on the patient, but instead instruct him to study the nature of the ileostomy function in relation to the diet eaten and to omit foods which produce gaseousness or excessive quantities of watery ileal contents. We find that patients so instructed, within a few months, are experts on their ileostomy diet to an extent that the physician or surgeon can never attain.

4. Colectomy and the One-Stage Operation of Ileostomy and Colectomy

Preparation and postoperative management of patients with ulcerative colitis for the extirpative procedures depend on general principles which will not again be detailed here. If these patients are acutely ill, their vulnerable points are diminished effective extracellular and circulating blood volume, extrarenal desalting water loss, and infection. In the acute, fulminating, and hemorrhagic disease it is rarely necessary to operate in the midst of an untreated flare-up; massive hemorrhage and perforation are the only indications. With transfusion, antibiotics, and corticosteroids, it is nearly always possible to quiet the local process and bolster the patient sufficiently so that he is a proper subject for operation and not in a desperate state for anesthesia and blood loss. But too long a time should not be expended once the disease has declared itself unfit for nonoperative care. As in so many other severe metabolic disorders discussed in this book, neither the surgeon nor the physician must seek compulsively a patient ideally restored before operation. Instead, a dated period (here about a week) should be expended, with special attention devoted to extracellular volume, blood volume, acid-base balance, and infection, so that the patient is moving toward correction as he proceeds to the operation.

Section III.   The Gastrointestinal Tract; Postgastrectomy States and Absorption Defects: Notes from the Literature

A. ABSORPTION AND DUMPING

Kelly *et al.* (1954), in reviewing twenty-two patients after total and subtotal gastrectomy, concluded that wasting was out of proportion to the moderate fecal fat loss, and ascribed it to poor appetite and small meals traceable in turn to decreased gastric reservoir function. This certainly coincides with the opinion of Randall (1955) that total intake level (achieved by frequent small feedings) is the most important factor in producing weight gain in postsurgical malabsorption syndromes. The anemia observed in Kelly's cases was not severe, iron absorption was only slightly reduced, and the long survivors after total gastrectomy developed megaloblastic anemia, easily responsive to the therapy usually employed for pernicious anemia.

The possibility that low plasma iron concentrations ("sideropenia") might in some way be a primary factor in postgastrectomy digestive disorders has been pursued with especial vigor by the Scandinavian workers (Bruusgaard, 1946; Jasinski, 1945; Lyngar, 1950) and by Drablos *et al.* (1951). The matter is reviewed by Wallenstein (1955), who again reaches this conclusion and finds very encouraging reduction in postcibal symptoms by the intravenous administration of iron. He hypothesizes mucosal changes as the functional factor altered by iron therapy. Sideropenia was considered definite when plasma iron concentrations were below 60 mg. per 100 ml.; a hypochromic anemia was also present in such cases. These data may have a bearing on the observation that blood transfusion or overtransfusion occasionally helps patients with postprandial symptoms after gastrectomy, though the latter finding is also interpretable in terms of the hypovolemic theory of the dumping syndrome.

The appearance of hypochromic anemia is not common after partial gastrectomy. When it occurs it responds readily to oral iron (Owren, 1952), so long as the iron is in the pulverized form, permitting easy access during the very short phase of gastric emptying.

Smith and Mallett (1957) compared iron absorption before and after partial gastrectomy, in patients with duodenal ulcer. They found (using radioiron) that absorption was unchanged when iron was administered as ferrous sulfate.

The so-called "iron-deficiency anemia" after partial gastrectomy needs better definition. It is not clear that there is any such lesion in the specific sense. When total intake of macronutrients is poor and weight is lots grossly, the anemia is doubtless similar to that seen in cachexia: some decreased erythrocyte volume with a tendency to a high plasma volume, making the peripheral concentration of cells proportionally lower than the actual erythrocyte volume itself.

Everson (1954) reported an extensive series of absorption studies on dogs in whom various ablative and anastomotic procedures had been done. The Billroth I and segmental gastrectomies seemed to leave the dog with the most complete nitrogen and fat absorption of any studied, but still slightly short of normal.

The utility of postgastrectomy absorption studies can be questioned when they are carried out on the dog, an animal whose posture, dietary habits, digestive accommodations, and natural food predilections are quite different from those of man.

Everson *et al.* (1957) later reported on similar studies in man and found that although gastrectomy tended to produce more weight loss than vagotomy plus posterior gastroenterostomy, the differences were not great. Indeed, there was no significant difference between the two operations as regards that fraction of patients later found to be below ideal weight. They did feel that preoperatively underweight patients lost more weight following gastrectomy than following vagotomy plus posterior gastroenterostomy, but they were unable to prove this statistically with enough conviction to advocate this operation in the "light-thin" patient.

The study of Robins *et al.* (1957) was carried out in patients after various types of gastric operations, with attention devoted particularly to fecal fat and nitrogen. They used the criteria of Wollaeger *et al.* (1946, a) to indicate the normal range of fecal fat; excretion of more than 10 per cent of the ingested fat is abnormal. For nitrogen, they used 2 gm. per day as a ceiling normal value. These values checked out in control, nonoperated duodenal ulcer patients. In this study the patients were at least three years postoperative and were studied for a single marked fecal period of four days. There was a sizeable group (about a third of the twenty) who were below (28 per cent or more) their normal weight. The investigators found a tendency to elevated amounts of fecal fat and nitrogen, usually in the "borderline" ranges of 5 to 10 per cent ingested fat in the stools, or just over 2.0 gm. of nitrogen. Only a few cases (three or four) showed definitely abnormal values. There was no correlation between elevations of these values and degree of weight loss. Vagotomy appeared (in five cases) to increase fecal losses. The Billroth I and II groups showed little difference. Grossly defective absorption is the chief cause of postgastrectomy weight loss in only the rare and very severe case, at least as judged in terms of fat and total nitrogen.

Abbott *et al.* (1958), by careful feeding experiments, has shown that the slowly emptying small gastroduodenostomy or gastrojejunostomy stoma is far less prone to produce dumping symptoms than is the large one with rapid emptying. He has gathered evidence confirming the low-plasma-volume hypothesis to explain the symptoms of the dumping syndrome, showing a 26 per cent decrease in plasma volume with oral hypertonic glucose. The work of Abbott *et al.* (1958)

represents a logical extension of the studies of Porter and Claman (1949) on the small stoma as a means of preventing dumping.

Roberts *et al.* (1954) presented data showing a reduction in plasma volume with the dumping symptoms. Problems of interpretation are clouded by the lack of a commensurate hematocrit change (difficult to conceive as due to an exactly equal erythrocyte segregation, in view of the lack of bleeding into the lumen) and the evaluation of dye-dilution curves followed for long periods. Certainly the theory is appealing and many of the appearances fit hypovolemic syncope. The studies of Randall's group are to be found in Roberts *et al.* (1953, 1954, 1955) and Medwid *et al.* (1956).

Additional studies of interest relative to the dumping syndrome are to be found in Perman (1947), Culver (1949), Custer *et al.* (1946), Fisher *et al.* (1955), Hayes (1955), Longmire and Beal (1952), Machella (1949), McSwiney and Spurrell (1933), and Muir (1949).

Schwartz *et al.* (1956, a) contributed an exceptionally full and critical research on absorption after resections of the small bowel. They studied five patients. Fecal losses of nitrogen and fat were massive, the former running from 4 gm. to as high as 20 gm. a day, depending on diet and stool volume, the latter from 20 to 120 gm. per day, depending largely on fat intake. Frequent feedings of a high-protein, moderate-fat diet seemed to be more important than various pharmacologic and endocrine aids. The fat losses were very considerably larger than those following total gastrectomy.

Schwartz *et al.* (1956, a, b) also studied absorption after total gastrectomy. There were nine patients in their group. Stool nitrogen losses (2 to 4 gm. a day) and fat losses (10 to 50 gm. a day) were not excessive and were only poorly reduced by 8 gm. (or more) of USP pancreatin. Other pharmacologic aids were also ineffective. Frequent feedings, as in the small-bowel–shortening cases, seemed to be most effective.

In the studies of Schwartz *et al.* it was found that fecal nitrogen was a function of nitrogen intake and that the amount of dietary nitrogen required to maintain balance was greater after total gastrectomy than in normal individuals. Their work leads to the conclusion that a supernormal intake of macronutrients is essential to well-being after total gastrectomy. Unfortunately, such a plan is often very difficult to carry out because of problems of appetite and food capacity. The findings relative to fat were essentially the same; after total gastrectomy a much higher intake was required in order to achieve a satisfactory total absorption. By contrast, the absorption of calcium, phosphorus, magnesium, and potassium was found to be normal.

Additional studies of postgastrectomy states include Goldhamer (1933), Meyer *et al.* (1941), Church and Hinton (1942), Farris *et al.* (1943), Inglefinger (1944), Wollaeger *et al.* (1946, a, b; 1950), MacDonald *et al.* (1947), Beebe and Menelley (1949), Lyngare (1950), Wells and Welbourn (1951), Brain and Stammers (1951), and Everson (1951, 1952).

Additional data helpful in study and clinical management of the postgastrectomy situation include Gordon-Taylor *et al.* (1929), Lublin (1931), Mecray *et al.* (1937), Strauss *et al.* (1937), Rekers *et al.* (1943), Waddell and Wang (1952), Babb *et al.* (1953), MacLean *et al.* (1954), Zollinger and Ellison (1954), Javid (1955), and Schwartz *et al.* (1956).

Several other studies are based on the use of selective absorption studies employing isotopically labelled materials. These include Malm *et al.* (1956), Shoemaker and Wase (1957), and Shingleton *et al.* (1957).

B. GASTROINTESTINAL TRACT: MISCELLANEOUS RECENT STUDIES

Poth has been a major contributor to the development and study of intestinal antibiotics. Much of his work is reviewed in Poth (1953).

Pseudomembranous enterocolitis results in part from the suppression of normal intestinal flora, by either oral or parenteral antibiotics. Studies of bacteriologic and clinical aspects include those of Dixon and Weisman (1948), Reiner *et al.* (1952), Dearing and Heilman (1953), Prohaska *et al.* (1954), Pettet *et al.*

(1954), Dack (1956), Turnbull (1956), and Weismann and Twitchell (1956).

Cope and his group have documented in detail the metabolic changes in perforated ulcer. Many of these alterations are found in early leakage peritonitis of any source. An understanding of them provides the basis for effective care. These studies include Cope *et al.* (1955), Wight *et al.* (1955, 1956), Hopkirk *et al.* (1956), and Cope and Wight (1956).

Ebert *et al.* (1949) have described certain aspects of the mechanism of shock in peritonitis. Welch (1955) has been interested in the operative approach to late peritonitis with obstruction, such "refunctionalization" being possible with good replacement therapy and bacterial control. Operation would be contraindicated in the early phases when bacterial defenses are shaky and invasive sepsis more of a hazard. Here, the conservatism needed is analogous to that we have counseled in "postoperative ileus-obstruction," where early reoperation is so rarely crowned with success. Related studies include Noble (1952) and Schatten (1956).

Smith and Lee (1956) have documented the replacement management of duodenal fistula.

There have been several studies of early surgical operation in bleeding from the upper gastrointestinal tract. Of particular note are those of Stewart *et al.* (1956) and Enquist *et al.* (1957).

Intestinal distention arises from many mechanical, vascular, and biochemical factors. There is a gas phase in the intraluminal material which often dominates the X-ray picture and the crampy pain of the patient. This gas is largely swallowed air, there being only a small increment (CO_2, H_2, and others) from intestinal putrefaction and fermentation. The prophylactic removal of this swallowed air by appropriate intubation is of primary importance in many surgical situations, as described in various sections of this book. The removal of normal quantities of gastric juice that accompanies such air-removing suction is not beneficial and means little to the patient in terms of avoidance of postoperative distention. Studies of this subject include particularly those of Maddock *et al.* (1949) and Bedell *et al.* (1956).

There is evidence to suggest that the distal small bowel may be of greater significance than the proximal portion, if only a small portion is to be left after resection (Kremen *et al.*, 1954). Additional data on massive resection are to be found in Althausen *et al.* (1949), Haymond (1935), and Jackson *et al.* (1951).

The production of 5-hydroxytryptamine (serotonin) by gastrointestinal carcinoid neo-plasms has been the basis of a syndrome re-sulting from the peripheral effects of this compound. The syndrome includes attacks of fiery-red skin, flushing of the face, edema and fullness of the face, vomiting, diarrhea, asthma, hyperperistalsis, and, in late cases, pulmonary stenosis and tricuspid insufficiency. The syndrome is only seen when large masses of the tumor are present—usually as liver metastases—and therefore it is surgically late and therapeutically unpromising in terms of removal.

GASTROINTESTINAL TRACT CASES

CASE 5

A Fifty-Two-Year-Old Man Develops Acute Intestinal Obstruction with Interesting and Typically Minimal Signs of Early Desalting and Volume Reduction

Case 5. Patient E. B., #6B187. Male. Age 52. Admitted February 27, 1957. Discharged March 10, 1957.

DIAGNOSIS. Acute small-bowel obstruction.

OPERATION. Lysis of adhesions.

CLINICAL SUMMARY. This patient was admitted because for two days he had suffered intermittent cramping midabdominal pain with occasional long periods of spontaneous relief. During the eighteen hours just before admission this pain had been more severe, and had been unrelieved. It was periumbilical in location. There had been no passage of gas or feces by rectum. He had vomited several times, never in very large amounts.

Past history included two laparotomies, one for cholecystectomy and one for removal of colonic polyp, six and two years previously.

Physical examination showed the patient to be slightly toxic in appearance; he was flushed, his tongue was dry, and there were evidences of mild desalting water loss. Blood pressure was 120/80, pulse 85. The abdomen was neither tender nor distended; peristaltic sounds were tense, "hollow," high-pitched, and painful. Catheterization revealed a small amount of highly concentrated urine in the bladder; there was no further urinary output until treatment was begun.

X-rays showed dilated loops of small bowel. There was no gas in the large bowel. There were no fluid levels. Normal body weight was 78 kg.

INITIAL LABORATORY WORK

Urine

Specific gravity	1.036	
Protein	4+	
*p*H	5.5	
Otherwise negative		

Hematology

Hematocrit	49
Leucocyte count	9800 per cu. mm.

Blood Chemical Analyses

Blood urea nitrogen	35	mg. per 100 ml.
Plasma chloride	98	mE. per l.
Plasma sodium	136	mE. per l.
Plasma potassium	4.2 mE. per l.	
Carbon dioxide combining power	22.0 mE. per l.	
Serum amylase	131	units

ARGUMENT. The diagnosis of intestinal obstruction is reasonably secure. Operation should be undertaken as soon as possible. Intubation is indicated but should not postpone operation.

The patient is anuric and toxic. His blood chemical values are for the most part deceptively normal. The three laboratory findings which indicate the extent of his volume-reducing desalting are the hematocrit of 49, the concentrated low-volume urine, and the minimal but significant azotemia.

The administration of an anesthetic and performance of operation in a patient under these circumstances is dangerous should a hypotensive episode occur. The oligemic patient with renal vasoconstriction and marked antidiuresis is especially prone to develop acute renal insufficiency should shock supervene; the existing oligemia makes hypotension more liable to occur. All these hazards are present despite the deceptively normal pulse, blood pressure, and plasma chemical values. In the acute episode of the past eighteen hours there has not yet been time for the mobilization of sufficient cell water to lower the sodium concentration in the extracellular fluid.

The extent of the extracellular fluid volume reduction can be calculated as follows. At a normal blood volume (7 per cent of body weight) and a hematocrit value of 40 (recorded on his previous admission), the red cell volume is estimated at 2180 ml. (0.4 × 0.07 × 78). With a rise in hematocrit to 49, this red cell volume now resides in a blood volume of 4460 ml. (2180 ÷ 0.49), 1000 ml. less than the estimated normal value of 5460 ml. This 1000 ml. is the plasma deficit.*

This 30 per cent fall in plasma volume is here shared proportionally by the whole extracellular fluid. It has been lost into the bowel lumen or by vomiting or both; the lack of fluid levels and distention merely indicates that it is moderate, not excessive in amount. A man at 78 kg. would have a normal extracellular fluid volume (20 per cent body weight) of about 15,600 ml. At 30 per cent, this net volume reduction is therefore about .030 × 15,600, or 4650 ml., equivalent to about 650 mE. of sodium. † This is the static net deficit, a minimal figure. Therapeutically, this amount represents basic restoration of extracellular fluid. To this should be added 1000 ml. of salt solution for continuing loss, 1500 of water for lung and urine needs in twenty-four hours, and 40 to 80 mE. of potassium to cover the beginning cell-water mobilization and potassium loss in the gut. A starting ration could therefore be:

4600 ml.	5% dextrose in saline	
1500 ml.	5% dextrose in water, with	
60 mE.	potassium chloride.	

It would be reasonable to include some protein or colloid in early restoration; *should the patient be hypotensive such would be essential.* Some surgeons might await returning urine volume before adding potassium. With a normal plasma potassium concentration it is not dangerous to use potassium early.

An alternative calculation of needs could be based on the clinical appearance of mild volume reduction and desalting, the lack of distention or fluid levels, and the relatively short duration of the recent episode: about 300 to 500 mE. of sodium equivalent is usually sufficient in such circumstances. Note the magnitude of this sodium requirement despite the normal plasma sodium concentration.

The use of saline solution rather than lactate (or other modified extracellular-fluid replacement solution) is open to criticism; such solutions are especially important for use in older people, those with renal disease, or in acidosis. In those settings, excess chloride infusion leads to severe hyperchloremia. Here the use

---

* The relation of whole-body hematocrit to large-vessel hematocrit is not significant here and need not confuse the mental arithmetic.

† This calculation reveals a net water and sodium deficit, including that in the plasma. An estimate based on 15 per cent of body weight would give the analogous figures for interstitial fluid only (i.e., extracellular fluid exclusive of plasma). Any colloid given would be counted as part of the 4650 ml. replacement envisioned here.

of saline is safe and simple. The patient is fifty-two years old; there is little evidence of chronic disease. His ability to concentrate his urine to 1.036 under volume reduction is good evidence of normal renal tubular function; a transient hyperchloremia may result, but should be disposed of in due time. The azotemia bears witness to decreased glomerular filtration during extracellular volume reduction.

FURTHER COURSE. The patient was given, over a four-hour period:

2000 ml. 5% dextrose in saline with 20 mE. of potassium chloride,
2000 ml. 5% dextrose in water with 40 mE. of potassium chloride.

There was an immediate and brisk renal response with hourly outputs in the range of 40 to 60 ml. per hour. The hematocrit fell to 40 in about ten hours, by which time he had received about 3500 ml. of isotonic saline solution.

Operation was then carried out uneventfully, using barbiturate, nitrous oxide, and a relaxant for anesthesia. An adhesive band obstruction was relieved. Convalescence was smooth.

Fluid administration in the first twenty-four hours totaled:

4,250 ml. 5% dextrose in saline with 60 mE. potassium chloride,
2,700 ml. 5% dextrose in water.

The next morning the hematocrit was 39; the blood urea nitrogen fell to normal in forty-eight hours. The only additional metabolic events of note were a mild sodium-potassium shift with the lowest sodium at 132 mE. per l. and highest potassium at 5.0 mE. per l., and a mild diuresis totaling 2,800 to 3,150 ml. per day for three days during the recovery phase as the azotemia was cleared and the gut fluid reabsorbed. At the height of this the patient had a plasma chloride concentration of 111 mE. per l. and carbon dioxide combining power of 15.0 mE. per l.: a tendency to renal acidosis during the solute diuresis of recovery. His clinical appearance during this time was excellent. The administration of less chloride would have diminished this tendency. In renal vascular disease or pyelonephritis, such an acidosis could be of serious import, and the use of a balanced salt solution mandatory.

Comment. This was a simple case of intestinal obstruction with no difficult or outstanding features, yet demonstrating in miniature the following classic features:

(1) acute volume-reducing desalting water loss with no change in plasma sodium concentration, and with a hematocrit rise as its chief laboratory manifestations;

(2) renal response to isotonic volume reduction, with vasoconstriction, antidiuresis, and early azotemia;

(3) the calculation and results of therapy;

(4) mild sodium-potassium shift;

(5) a solute diuresis of renal functional recovery with transient chloride acidosis, following treatment with saline rather than a balanced salt solution.

CASE 6

In Which Volume Replacement in Intestinal Obstruction Is Not Well Planned, But, Thanks to Resilient Kidneys, Success Is Achieved

Case 6. Patient D. M., #6K428.* Female. Age 79. Admitted December 20, 1957. Discharged January 11, 1958.

DIAGNOSIS. Intestinal obstruction secondary to left femoral hernia.

OPERATION. Repair of left femoral hernia.

CLINICAL SUMMARY. This elderly widow was brought to the emergency ward with a history of progressive low abdominal cramps, nausea, and vomiting, beginning five days before entry. She had passed no gas or feces per rectum during this time, and two enemas gave no relief. Over the past two days her vomiting had become brownish with a feculent odor.

Past history involved no previous surgery nor major illness, but the patient had been constipated for many years, and had lost about 12 pounds over the past year despite a good appetite.

On admission, her oral temperature was 98.6° F., pulse 100, respiration 20, blood pressure 110/80. The patient was a moderately obese, acutely ill but alert elderly female with dry skin and mucous membranes. The abdomen showed no localized spasm or tenderness but had a doughy consistency.

X-rays showed numerous loops of dilated small intestine, particularly in the pelvis and lower abdomen. Several of these films were interpreted as showing gas and fluid levels in the proximal colon. Sigmoidoscopy to ten inches was entirely negative, with no stool blood by benzidine test.

INITIAL LABORATORY WORK

Urine

Specific gravity	1.015
Protein	1
*p*H	4.5
Leucocytes	5–10

Hematology

Hematocrit	52
Leucocyte count	3600 per cu. mm.

Blood Chemical Analyses

Blood urea nitrogen	118 mg. per 100 ml.
Plasma chloride	96 mE. per l.
Plasma sodium	135 mE. per l.
Plasma potassium	4.8 mE. per l.
Carbon dioxide combining power	19.6 mE. per l.

ARGUMENT. The patient was admitted with a diagnosis of intestinal obstruction probably secondary to a carcinoma of the colon, with an incompetent ileocecal valve. Evidence for carcinoma was not prominent. The patient obviously had a surgical problem, but operation

---

* The author is indebted to Dr. John M. Kinney for collecting the data and analyzing the course of this patient.

was delayed, both in order to make a more definite diagnosis and to correct her metabolic disorder as completely as possible before subjecting her to anesthesia and operation. As in the previous patient, any hypotensive episode or pulmonary complication will carry a prohibitive mortality if superimposed on this severe acidosis and azotemia, both of which bear witness to the extent of her volume reduction and desalting.

An electrocardiogram on entry showed precordial changes in the S-T waves, suggesting subendocardial ischemia, with occasional ventricular premature beats. The patient had no history of cardiac failure or hypertension, but the electrocardiographic findings suggested that her coronary artery perfusion might have been adjusted to a higher-than-normal blood pressure in the past, and was now suffering a moderate ischemia. The patient's cardiac situation did not limit the amount of fluid which was planned for her over the following eight hours. A plastic infusion set was used which had a side arm for serial measurements of venous pressure. In this way, frequent venous pressure measurements were used to confirm any clinical impression of fluid at the lung bases or neck-vein distention, which would warn against too rapid fluid replacement.

The high blood urea nitrogen concentration and the absence of a concentrated urine (despite considerable desalting water loss) raised the question of primary renal disease. The patient was catheterized, and hourly urine volumes were followed as she was given her initial fluids. Her urine output reached satisfactory levels about two hours after therapy began.

Extracellular-volume depletion could be calculated on the following basis. Assuming that this patient had a normal hematocrit value of 40 and a blood volume of 6.5 per cent of her body weight of 68 kg., we can calculate her estimated normal red cell volume as 1770 ml. with a blood volume of 4420 ml. With the hematocrit now at 52, this red cell volume resides in a blood volume of 3400 ml. (1770 ÷ 0.52). This is a plasma deficit of 1020 ml. (4420 − 3400), or 38 per cent of her starting plasma volume of 2650 ml. Assuming this 38 per cent reduction is shared alike by the remaining interstitial fluid (15 per cent of body weight) we find a deficit of 3880 ml. over and beyond the plasma deficit. These are minimal figures for the *net positive balance* that must be achieved to result and rehydrate. A reasonable plan of intravenous fluids over the first eight hours might be:

1000 ml. 5 per cent dextrose in saline, solution followed by
500 ml. of plasma, followed by another
2000 ml. 5 per cent dextrose in saline solution with potassium chloride.

This plan should be limited immediately if it becomes

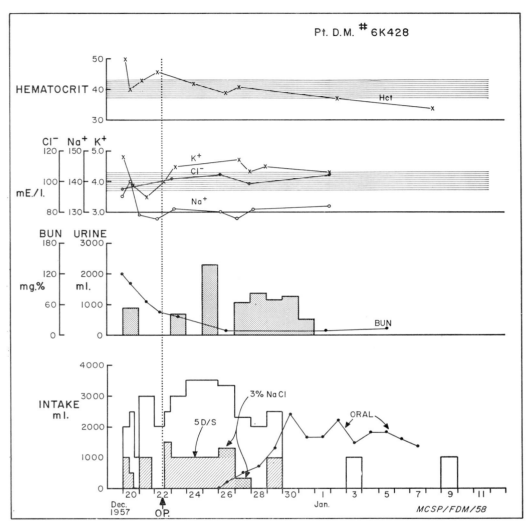

Figure 101. Events in Intestinal Obstruction (Case 6)

Above are shown hematocrit and plasma chemical values in this patient. In the middle and lower portion of the chart are shown the blood urea nitrogen, the urine volume, and the total intake. The intravenous fraction of the intake is shown in the block diagram. The blank portion represents 5 per cent dextrose in water and the shaded portions salt-containing solution. The oral intake is shown by the line to the right. The reader is referred to the text for details.

In this patient with acute intestinal obstruction, it will be noted that a lowering of hematocrit and restoration of circulatory homeostasis were readily produced. Although her therapy included plasma, there were excessively large amounts of water relative to the total salt given. For a patient with intestinal obstruction (essentially a desalting process) the replacement given was more than half salt-free solution (5 per cent dextrose in water). As a result of this imbalance in restorative fluids the patient developed a dilutional hyponatremia acutely on the first day of therapy, which was uncorrected throughout the period shown.

Fortunately, the patient's operative course and postoperative condition were satisfactory despite this unbalanced therapy. Had her urine volume been less easily restored, a more serious defect would have resulted from this excess of water in her replacement.

evident that the patient's urine output is not responding to fluid replacement or if venous pressure should rise. The patient undoubtedly had suffered depletion of her total body potassium, and an effort should be made to treat this during the early hours of therapy, though one must stop potassium treatment if urine volume output is not resumed.

FURTHER COURSE. The patient received 1000 ml. of dextrose in saline solution, followed by 500 ml. of plasma and 1000 ml. of dextrose in water, over her first eight hours in the hospital. During this time, her hematocrit dropped from 52 to 40, and her blood urea nitrogen had begun to drop at the time when she was making urine between 20 to 30 ml. an hour. A Miller-Abbott tube was advanced through the duodenum during this time and the suction losses were noted in order to guide further intravenous therapy. The patient received a total of 3000 ml. of 5 per cent dextrose in water, 1500 ml. of 5 per cent dextrose in saline solution, and 1000 ml. of plasma during her first twenty-four hours in the hospital. This fluid therapy was probably satisfactory in amount, but would have corrected this patient's losses more effectively if there had been more saline solution and less water, and some potassium. Both sodium and potassium concentrations fell (128 and 3.6 mE. per l.) during repletion.

The day after the patient's entry a barium enema revealed no lesion in the colon, but a tender mass became evident in the left femoral area, and an incarcerated femoral hernia was repaired thirty-six hours after entry. Nitrous oxide, cyclopropane, and curare were used as anesthesia. No bowel was found in the hernial sac, but a loop of ileum was kinked around fibrous strands running from the hernial sac to the omentum. At the time of operation, the patient's hematocrit was in the low 40's and her plasma electrolytes were satisfactory, except for the plasma sodium concentration, which had dropped from 140 to around 128 mE. per l. This was accentuated by the patient's receiving a total of 2000 ml. of dextrose in water and only 1000 ml. of dextrose in saline solution on her second hospital day.

Her postoperative course was marked by a slow but steady drop in her hematocrit over the following twelve days. It was felt that this patient probably carried an

hematocrit in the upper 30's before operation. The patient's sodium level remained from 130 to 133 during the rest of her hospital stay and was refractory to concentrated saline therapy on her third and fourth postoperative days, doubtless due to the 2000 to 2500 ml. she was receiving of dextrose in water each day. She had a satisfactory diuresis on her third postoperative day, and urine outputs remained in the low normal range thereafter. Her blood urea nitrogen concentration fell satisfactorily and from the fourth day postoperatively was entirely normal. The patient had a normal plasma potassium level from the time of operation throughout her postoperative course. It was recognized that this undoubtedly masked some body potassium depletion, and potassium was administered in amounts of 60 mE. per day, beginning with the second hospital day, after it was evident that her urine output would be satisfactory.

COMMENT. This patient went home with an unrepaired anemia and hyponatremia, both of them evidences of the basic errors of her replacement. She received too much water in relation to salt, and not enough erythrocytes. Despite this unbalance, the patient did have reasonably effective volume restoration, weathered operation at about the right time, and was able to have a postoperative diuresis, bringing her azotemia back down to normal.

In hyponatremic patients, under most circumstances, no salt-free solutions should be used until tonicity is restored. Each liter given only serves to increase the burden of water excretion in a patient who obviously is not going to excrete it well.

One or two erythrocyte suspensions, plus an earlier turn to concentrated salt, would have been far more sagacious. It would also be wise in an elderly patient with extracellular volume reduction to use some balanced salt (sodium chloride or sodium bicarbonate) for a part of the resalting. This avoids the possibility of hyperchloremic acidosis, which, thanks to good renal function in this patient, did not develop.

The resilience of her seventy-nine-year-old kidneys was bespoken by their homeostatic wisdom even after a five-day period of desalting water loss serious enough to produce severe azotemia and renal acidosis on admission.

CASE 7

In Which Intestinal Obstruction in a Bartender Is Followed by an Unusual But Highly Specific Form of Delirium, Responding Promptly to Treatment

Case 7. Patient F. N., #5D332.* Male. Age 36. Admitted November 28, 1957. Discharged December 15, 1957.

---

* The author is indebted to Dr. Richard Wilson for collecting the data and analyzing the course of this patient.

DIAGNOSIS. Acute intestinal obstruction; delirium tremens.

OPERATION. Resection of small intestine and end-to-end anastomosis.

CLINICAL SUMMARY. This patient was admitted on November 28, 1957, with crampy, severe epigastric pain. A few hours after the onset of symptoms, he vomited some bile-stained material. He had had no bowel movements for twenty-four hours. The crampy pain continued to occur, with shorter and shorter intervals between the bouts, increasing in severity, and at the time he came to the hospital (ten hours after onset) the pain was almost continuous with severe, cramplike exacerbations.

He had had appendicitis with an appendectomy in June, 1956. He was a bartender, with a heavy alcoholic history.

Physical examination showed a temperature of 101.2° F., pulse 100, respiration rate of 26, blood pressure 150/70. The patient was slightly disoriented, and doubling up in pain intermittently. His circulatory status looked good, but he was very apprehensive and there was some tremor. Bowel sounds were obstructive, with peristalsis high-pitched and "hollow." Findings on rectal examination were normal. A neurologic examination did not reveal any further abnormality.

INITIAL LABORATORY WORK

Hinton Test.   Negative

Urine

Specific gravity	1.026
Protein	0
pH	7.6
Sediment	3–5 leucocytes per high-power field
Sugar	+++*

Hematology

Hematocrit	44.5
Leucocyte count	10,600 per cu. mm.
	neutrophils 82 per cent
	lymphocytes 12 per cent
	monocytes 1 per cent
	band forms 5 per cent

Blood Chemical Analyses

Blood urea nitrogen	15	mg. per 100 ml.
Plasma chloride	102	mE. per l.
Plasma sodium	142	mE. per l.
Plasma potassium	4.5	mE. per l.
Serum amylase	46	units
Blood sugar	157	mg. per 100 ml. (during an intravenous infusion)

* Dextrose was being given intravenously at the time of this voided specimen.

FURTHER COURSE. His short course and minimal biochemical disarrangement (normal urine volume, hematocrit and blood urea nitrogen) made operation feasible with minimum time expended on preparation —in contrast to Cases 5 and 6. The night of admission an exploratory laparotomy was performed with a diagnosis of acute intestinal obstruction. There was satisfactory general anesthesia, using Pentothal induction and ether. A Meckel's diverticulum was found attached to

the umbilicus by two fibrous bands at its base. There was occlusion of the proximal ileum, which was pathologically dilated. Because of borderline blood supply in the region of the diverticulum, six inches of small intestine were resected and an end-to-end anastomosis performed. The mesenteric defect was closed and some right-lower-quadrant adhesions were divided.

Immediately following operation the patient appeared to be much sicker than he should have been expected to be. He was completely disoriented, despite the use of sedatives and paraldehyde in large doses. By the second postoperative day his rectal temperature had risen to 104° F. Tracheal suction was necessary for the removal of secretion. He was maintained on nasogastric suction for three days following operation, replacing measured fluid losses quantitatively with water, sugar, sodium chloride, and potassium chloride. He was given massive doses of vitamins, including all of the vitamin B complex. He was on parenterally administered streptomycin for four days and penicillin for seven days. Hydration and urine output appeared to be normal. The patient became increasingly disoriented and apprehensive, breathing rapidly, shouting and screaming, calling for his friends and cronies, thrashing around the bed, seeking protection and help from an ever-changing series of frightening microzoologic hallucinations.

On the seventh postoperative day he was in frank carpopedal spasm with a positive Chvostek sign and a borderline Trousseau sign. He was hyperventilating at a rapid rate. At this time the plasma calcium concentration was 4.7 mE. per l.

ARGUMENT. At this time the patient was critically ill and his survival was in doubt. The diagnosis of delirium tremens was made. Postoperative delirium tremens carries a very high mortality. Hyperventilation alkalosis certainly contributed to the neuromuscular irritability. The suspicion of delirium tremens might well have been aroused earlier, but microzoologic hallucinations had been absent until this time and the very large doses of sedation seemed at times, in an illusory way, to help the patient.

Blood chemical determinations at this time were as follows:

Plasma calcium	4.7	mE. per l.
Plasma magnesium	1.38	mE. per l.
(Normal magnesium by this method:	2.0 ± 0.18 mE. per l.)	

The patient was promptly given magnesium sulfate in a 50 per cent solution, intramuscularly. After receiving only the first 3 gm. over a twelve-hour period, he became completely oriented, less restless, and fully cooperative. He was a changed man. The carpopedal spasm, Chvostek's sign, and hyperventilation completely disappeared. The plasma magnesium level rose to 2.06 mE. per l. He received magnesium replacement over a period of four days for a total of 32 gm. (2 gm. every six hours). There were no more hallucinations.

The plasma magnesium values were as follows:

12-6 1.38 mE. per l. (postoperative day 7)
 7 2.06   "   " " ("   " 8)
 9 1.88   "   " " ("   " 10)
10 2.16   "   " " ("   " 11)
12 1.85   "   " " ("   " 13)

FURTHER COURSE. The remainder of his postoperative course was uneventful, and he was discharged on the eighteenth day following operation. He is now well and alleges that he has completely given up drinking.

COMMENT. This patient may or may not have had magnesium deficiency in the sense of low body magnesium. This cannot be ascertained without more elaborate information. Certainly he had hypomagnesemia and he responded dramatically and clearly to the administration of magnesium at a time when he had marked delirium tremens.

The patient did not have cirrhosis of the liver, at least to a symptomatic extent or an extent indicated by physical signs.

The marked hyperventilation alkalosis with carpopedal spasm and tetany may well have exacerbated the central and peripheral manifestations of low magnesium levels. Rebreathing carbon dioxide might have been helpful.

It is noteworthy that the increase in the patient's plasma magnesium concentration was not particularly spectacular on treatment and that this value was still low even at the time of discharge.

This calls to mind the important fact that patients with chronic alcoholism, cirrhosis of the liver, delirium tremens, or any combination of these three will often have a remarkably favorable neuromuscular response to the administration of magnesium salts, whether or not chemical abnormalities of plasma magnesium are always clearly demonstrable.

CASE 8

Appendiceal Peritonitis Finally Leads to Deep Coma and Severe Hypertonicity, by Reason of a Special Regimen Instituted for Therapeutic Reasons

Case 8. Patient B. M., #0B363. Male. Age 60. Admitted February 22, 1955. Discharged March 22, 1955.

DIAGNOSIS. Appendiceal peritonitis; intestinal obstruction.

OPERATION. Tracheotomy.

CLINICAL SUMMARY. This sixty-year-old patient was admitted in deep coma, one month following the removal of a gangrenous perforated appendix.

His initial attack of appendicitis was characteristic as to symptoms and signs, but the story (eighteen hours from first symptom to hospitalization) was brief in relation to the findings of gangrene and perforation.

On the fourth postoperative day he had developed acute gastric dilatation, which in turn resulted in hypokalemic alkalosis. This then progressed on to volume reduction, hypotension, and azotemia (nonprotein nitrogen = 204 mg. per 100 ml.). Intensive intravenous therapy with water, electrolyte, and blood had been followed by gradual improvement over a ten-day period. About one week later he developed intestinal obstruction and was reexplored. Some kinking of the ileum was found and an attempt was made at correction. Thereafter his course was septic; there was improvement on erythromycin and continuous replacement, by vein, of large fluid losses by nasogastric drainage and intermittent diarrhea.

About twenty-six days after the appendectomy, the patient had improved considerably and there was some peristalsis. He was started on oral and gavage feedings of a very concentrated food mixture in amounts of 750 to 3000 ml. per day. Within twenty-four hours he began to have very large urine outputs (3000 to 5000 ml. per day) and became unresponsive. Despite the large urine volumes there was a mounting uremia and acidosis with a rising sodium concentration. He was transferred to the Brigham Hospital for further care.

Past history included duodenal ulcer, but little else of significance.

On admission the patient's temperature was 101.6° F., pulse 110, blood pressure 130/80. He was semicomatose, restless, and responsive only to strong stimuli. There were a few dry rales heard in both lungs. The abdomen was distended, tympanitic, with peristalsis active and high-pitched. The wounds were free of gross infection. A rectal examination was negative. The tongue and mucosae did not show the signs of dehydration. Electrocardiogram suggested acute hypokalemia. He was increasingly cyanotic.

INITIAL LABORATORY WORK

Urine

Specific gravity 1.011
pH   4.5
Osmolality   465   mO. per l.
Occasional erythrocytes and leucocytes and granular casts
Sugar negative

Hematology

Hematocrit   41
Leucocyte count 13,000 per cu. mm.
Eosinophils   14   per cu. mm.

Blood Chemical Analyses

Blood urea nitrogen   62   mg. per 100 ml.
Plasma protein   5.2 gm. per 100 ml.
Plasma chloride   136 mE. per l.

Plasma sodium	169	mE. per l.
Plasma potassium	4.4	mE. per l.
Carbon dioxide com-		
bining power	16.8	mE. per l.
Plasma osmolality	370	mO. per l.
Blood sugar (intrave-		
nous running)	166	mg. per 100 ml.

ARGUMENT. The first tendency is to term this situation "dehydration." The high sodium and chloride concentrations and osmolality lend credence to such a view and are the most spectacular findings, on a cursory inspection.

The high urine volumes (and, indeed, the massive intravenous therapy being given) are evidence against extrarenal dehydration unless one predicates a primary renal lesion with tubular unresponsiveness to antidiuretic hormone. In a formerly healthy man whose kidneys have battled their way through a stormy postoperative course and, at one time two weeks ago, reduced his nonprotein nitrogen from 204 mg. per 100 ml. to normal, serious parenchymatous renal disease seems unlikely, although a renal factor is doubtless active in the solute diuresis. The high urine outputs are also suggestive of diabetes (either mellitus or insipidus), but there is no supporting evidence.

The normal hematocrit is also against dehydration sufficient to raise the sodium concentration to 169 mE. per l., unless we assume a resting value of about 28 per cent cells. His multiple transfusions and previous hematocrit values around 40 per cent within a few days are conclusive on this point.

The plasma osmolality of 370 mO. per l. is about 30 mO. per l. more than twice the sodium concentration of 169 mE. per l. This suggests the presence of approximately 30 mO. per l. of nonelectrolyte solute; the elevated blood urea nitrogen accounts for a fraction of this. This finding alone is definitely in favor of excessive solute load as opposed to desiccation-dehydration. It is somewhat against severe diabetes or primary renal or hepatic disease, in all of which the nonelectrolyte solute is apt to be from 50 to 70 mO. per l.

The outstanding features therefore are coma, severe hypertonicity, profuse urine outputs, and a normal hematocrit. This is classic for solute-loading hypertonicity, with solute diuresis, probably due to the oral and gavage feeding of an enriched food mixture with inadequate water supply.

The treatment of solute-loading hypertonicity is to withhold further solute and provide water enough for the continued excretion of solute already in the body. But in giving this water, caution must be used. If enough water is given promptly to dilute the solute where it lies, pulmonary edema is inevitable.

The electrocardiographic appearances of severe hypernatremia resemble those of hypokalemia even though plasma potassium concentration is normal, and even though differential potassium loss is missing. It was hypernatremia, then, which gave rise to the electrocardiographic changes termed "hypokalemia."

FURTHER COURSE. On the day prior to admission there was a urine volume of 4000 ml. with an intake of 3700 ml. by vein and 2700 gavage. The patient's temperature was 104° F. Cyanosis was severe and pulmonary embolus was suspected.

Coma had deepened soon after admission. There were no signs of tetany. The first day's program included 5500 ml. of 5 per cent dextrose in water, by vein, with 80 mM. of potassium chloride and 2 gm. of calcium gluconate. Urine output was 2600 ml. Plasma sodium concentration fell from 169 mE. per l. to 147 mE. per l.; there was no change in potassium concentration. But the patient's respirations became labored, cyanosis progressive, and basal rales increased. There was upper respiratory tract obstruction, related to his coma and fat short neck, as well as some degree of pulmonary edema. Within a few hours his condition deteriorated very rapidly; his pulse rose precipitously, his blood pressure fell.

A tracheotomy was promptly done. No anesthesia was required. Within an hour his clinical condition had improved remarkably. Pulse and blood pressure stabilized, and, although still comatose, the patient was clearly better. During the first four days in the hospital he gradually lost weight with his continuing diuresis. Because of tremendous urine outputs there was no weight gain on water administration, a further characteristic feature of solute-loading hypertonicity as opposed to the course in desiccation.

The response to tracheotomy and the rapid subsidence of lower pulmonary signs indicated that his respiratory obstruction was in the upper airway and possibly related to the long-indwelling nasogastric tube. The apprehension that there was serious water overloading in the treatment of this dangerous hypertonicity was not borne out by subsequent events, although it is always a threat in rehydrating such a large solute load.

In the second full day of hospitalization he received 6650 ml. 5 per cent dextrose in water intravenously and his urine output was 5580 ml. He had some diarrhea, with bowel losses estimated at 500 ml.

This day was the turning point, his plasma sodium concentration fell to 134 mE. per l., blood urea nitrogen to 29 mg. per 100 ml. Potassium remained at 4.0 mE. per l.; the hematocrit and plasma protein were unchanged. The patient's clinical appearance continued to improve.

During these first days the urine osmolality was fixed near 500 mO. per l., with a sodium concentration near 40 mE. per l. This suggests a very large quantity of crystalloid solute in the urine. The first day the total urine solute was 1850 mO. in twenty-four hours, of which sodium accounted for 102 mO., potassium 66 mO., and total electrolyte (estimated) 350 mO. The urine sugar was negative. Thus the patient excreted about 1500 mO. of crystalloid solute, on no oral intake. This high solute excretion continued, gradually falling, during six days, to normal. The magnitude of this "solute backlog excretion" is appreciated in contrast to the later total solute excretion of about 700 mO. per day on an oral diet of 3100 calories (100 gm. protein,

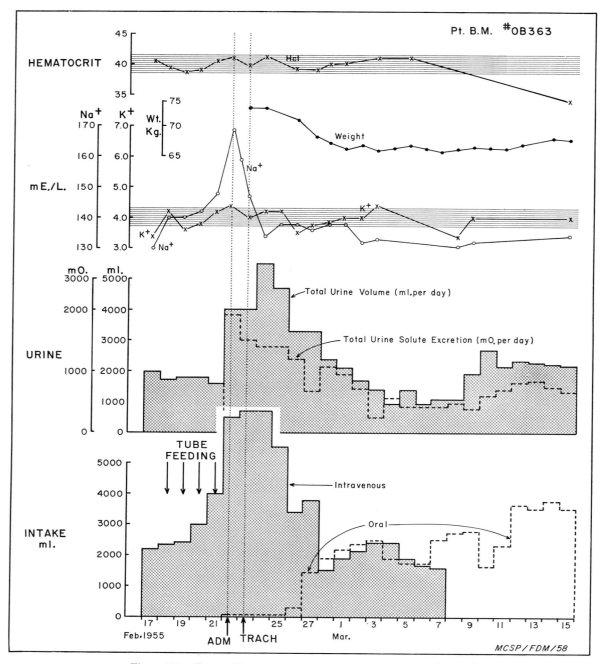

Figure 102. Events Following Appendiceal Peritonitis (Case 8)

In the above three ordinates are shown hematocrit, body weight, and plasma chemical values. Below these are shown urine output and solute excretion, and total intake, both intravenous and oral. The reader is referred to the text for details.

It will be noted that the hypernatremia was unaccompanied by a commensurate elevation of hemato-crit, that it was preceded by tube feedings and followed by large urinary excretions of water and solute, and that body weight fell as hypertonicity was corrected. All these are characteristic of solute-loading hypertonicity, with solute diuresis, and in sharp contrast to desiccation-dehydration with its attendant oliguria.

350 gm. carbohydrate, 150 gm. fat) and 3000 ml. of water. This is a ratio of about 4 ml. of water intake per mO. of solute excreted in the urine. The patient's tube feedings were far more concentrated than this, probably running as high as 2 mO. of solute per ml. of water.

By the third day urine volume began to parallel intake; sodium concentration rose and osmolality fell. The urine was diluted to 100 mO. per l. on occasion. The patient woke up, regained possession of all his faculties, and wanted food. Recovery was progressive and he was discharged one month after entry.

On two occasions during his diuresis he was given vasopressin so that its effect on urine volume and concentration might be observed. There was none. Alone, in the face of a solute diuresis, this does not establish the presence of a diseased tubular cell. Only with a free water diuresis is unresponsiveness to vasopressin significant.

The suspicion of underlying chronic renal disease lurked in the background; subsequent study failed to disclose any. To reassure ourselves on this point, the patient was readmitted six months later for renal study. At this time his renal functions were normal as judged by urinalysis, phenolsulfonphthalein, vasopressin test, acetozolamide (Diamox) test, and creatinine clearance.

COMMENT. This patient's course was typical of solute-loading hypertonicity. Primary renal disease was minimal, as it turned out, but some acute tubular failure to resorb water from the filtrate would potentiate the lesion. Such a minor tubular lesion might well have been a residual from the shock of the septic episodes, and was probably present, even though proof is lacking. The pathogenic sequence in this case was probably as follows. First, a hypertonic solute load was presented by gavage; crystalloid solute initiated solute diuresis and constituted the principal urinary solute during the acute phase. Some tubular disease prevented ideal water absorption, so the solute diuresis soon came to involve huge volumes of urine. Marked hypernatremia resulted, with coma. Tracheotomy was an essential step.

Thereafter it was merely a matter of supplying enough water to accomplish progressive excretion of "excess solute," totaling about 9000 mO. in seven days, before urine volumes and intravenous therapy could return to normal ranges, and then, in due course, oral intake could take over.

In considering the urinary solute load of a tube feeding it is well to remember that the solute presented to the kidney depends on the total metabolic situation of the patient. Early in the postoperative period a patient will tend to deaminate the protein of the feeding and present a large urea load to the kidney; if he is in an anabolic phase the same protein would involve little urea excretion. Similarly with sugar: the urinary solute per unit ingested sugar depends on trauma, diabetes mellitus, and steroid therapy.

CASE 9

A Simple Case of Appendiceal Peritonitis in a Mild Diabetic Demonstrates Typical Secondary Localization and Its Management

Case 9. Patient C. M., #2O174. Male. Age 44. Admitted October 10, 1949. Discharged November 4, 1949.

DIAGNOSIS. Perforated appendicitis, with peritonitis and abscess; diabetes mellitus (mild).

OPERATIONS. Appendectomy. Drainage of pelvic abscess.

CLINICAL SUMMARY. This forty-four-year-old street-car motorman was admitted with a story that twenty-four hours previously a dull steady ache commenced in his epigastrium and then settled in his lower abdomen. There was no sudden worsening. There was nausea and vomiting but no diarrhea. On driving to the hospital, he stated that his belly hurt when the car jounced.

On admission, his temperature was 103.6° F., pulse 84, respirations 18, blood pressure 138/70. The patient looked acutely ill. The abdomen was boardlike with local tenderness in the right lower quadrant, rebound tenderness, and cough tenderness. Psoas function was normal. Peristalsis was diminished. By rectum there was found to be very marked tenderness in the right vault area. There were no masses. X-rays were not significantly abnormal.

INITIAL LABORATORY WORK

Urine

Specific gravity	1.030
pH	6.5
Otherwise normal	

Hematology

Hematocrit	43
Leucocyte count	11,900 per cu. mm.

Blood Chemical Analyses

Blood urea nitrogen	15	mg. per 100 ml.
Plasma protein	5.9	gm. 100 ml.
Plasma chloride	100	mE. per l.
Carbon dioxide combining power	27.8	mE. per l.
Sugar	177	mg. per 100 ml.

ARGUMENT. The salient features are the short story (which favors early operation), the abdominal signs (peritonitis), the low pulse (good control of the situation), and the mid-range white count (sepsis not severe, response adequate). Operation here should not be postponed even for initial antibiotic dose. Urine volume was good; there was no evidence of reduction of extra-cellular fluid volume. The chemical data were not available preoperatively; they were within the normal range save for the blood sugar. There were no signs of acidosis (ketonuria).

The diagnosis of appendicitis is rarely certain; this is as close to certainty as the surgeon can ever hope to attain.

FURTHER COURSE. Under ether anesthesia the appendix was removed about three hours after admission. There was perforation at the tip, free odorous fluid (*Escherichia coli* and beta-hemolytic streptococcus on culture), but no diffuse fibrinopurulent process or abscess. The subcutaneous tissue of the wound were carefully protected during operation, and the wound was irrigated before closure. The skin was closed tight.

The postoperative orders included: constant bladder drainage; an intravenous infusion of 2000 ml. of 5 per cent dextrose in water; nasogastric suction; antibiotics —penicillin 100,000 units every three hours and streptomycin 0.5 gm. every six hours.

Because of the high blood sugar, the report of which returned at this time, the urine was tested for sugar at six-hourly intervals. Occasional glycosuria was observed and small doses of insulin given. A subsequent glucose tolerance test was essentially normal. The patient was judged to have very mild diabetes, of little clinical importance.

By the third postoperative day a moderate fever was persistent, and the leucocyte count had risen to 14,000 per cu. mm. The patient felt well; peristalsis was returning. By rectal examination there was found exquisite tenderness in the cul-de-sac, above the vesicles, bilaterally.

In another two days the leucocyte count had returned to normal; a pelvic abscess had formed and was soft, bulging into the rectum at the height of a fingertip. The patient began to have a few abdominal cramps with some distention.

Antibiotics had been stopped on the tenth postoperative day as the patient's sepsis was localizing well. It was hoped that the lesion would be ready for drainage sooner on such a plan.

On the thirteenth day, a rectal abscess was drained under spinal anesthesia. To do this, the anal sphincter was gently dilated and the abscess was aspirated by long needle precisely in the midline; incision in the mucosa and seromuscular layers was made along the needle as it was held firmly in place. About 200 ml. of very foul pus was evacuated; a drain was inserted, and led out the anus. The patient was placed on penicillin and streptomycin just before the drainage and kept on this medication for two days. He was kept in the hospital until rectal induration was decreasing; discharge was on the eighteenth day after drainage. The organisms recovered from the abscesses were the same as those found initially in the peritoneal fluid.

After the initial procedure the patient's diet had been increased as tolerated. The nasogastric tube was removed on the second day when peristalsis returned.

He passed flatus by the third day. He was on full liquids by the fourth day, soft solids the sixth day. At the time of rectal drainage he was again cut back to intravenous fluids for one day.

COMMENT. With beta-hemolytic streptococcus in the peritoneal fluid, one is forced to concede that the use of penicillin may have had some significance, and is justified in such cases. The careful wound hygiene at operation was successful in avoiding one of the commonest complications of this sort of appendicitis: wound sepsis. The rectal abscess might have been drained a day or two earlier; but with sepsis well localized there is little hazard to waiting until it is soft and well pointed. If one waits too long, secondary intestinal obstruction and ileus may arise from adherence of bowel to the edematous mass. This patient had a few cramps just before drainage.

The relation of water to saline in the intravenous fluids given was in the ratio of from 1.5:1 to 3:1. He was given no potassium or intravenous vitamins, as oral intake was quickly resumed. In general his water needs were met with 5 per cent dextrose in water, and tube losses replaced volume for volume with saline. In a young man with good heart and kidneys this simple procedure is perfectly satisfactory. Where cardiovascular-renal, liver, or lung disease complicates the picture the patient may develop on this regimen either chloride acidosis or, if acid loss is excessive and potassium replacement zero, hypokalemic alkalosis. The surgeon must therefore discriminate those patients (as here) in whom simple procedures are followed (and the patient's visceral function corrects any happenchance errors) from those patients in whom absolutely precise replacement is essential. The time and expense involved in the analytic background for the latter is not justified in simple cases.

The patient lost 7 kg. in twenty days, and gained it back slowly. This loss is to be expected in an acute septic illness. By ninety days after the operation, he had regained all his lost weight and was now 5 kg. above his pre-illness weight.

There was a brisk catabolic process despite the rapid resumption of intake at low caloric levels. This catabolism was intensified by the infection. During the early days weight loss was about 500 gm. per day; later on, it took place at a slower rate. Although this catabolic weight loss was surely abnormal and probably undesirable, it left no harmful mark and was far to be preferred over the abdominal distention or aspiration pneumonitis which might have resulted from premature oral feedings. A complex parenteral caloric regimen is not justified early in the course of such a case.

This patient's case was selected as being a simple and classic example of early septic peritonitis managed by straightforward measures, with secondary abscess formation and expeditious drainage. Clinical management was based on simple surgical principles, and recovery good.

In Which a Patient with Perforated Duodenal Ulcer, Admitted in Deep Coma, Points Up the Multifaceted Challenge of Late Peritonitis

Case 10. Patient G. S., #9B339. Male. Age 38. Admitted September 15, 1951. Discharged November 21, 1951.

DIAGNOSIS. Perforated duodenal ulcer.
OPERATIONS. Drainage of subphrenic and subhepatic abscesses.
Bronchoscopy (multiple).
Feeding jejunostomy.

CLINICAL SUMMARY. This thirty-eight-year-old lawyer-politician, somewhat given to heavy social drinking, was running for local office. He had suffered some upper gastrointestinal symptoms but had had no previous ulcer pain. For five days he had felt poorly; two nights prior to entry, after a political banquet, there was sudden severe midepigastric pain, which either subsided or was tolerated under the extreme pressure of the campaign. Twenty-four hours prior to admission there was a severe recurrence of this pain. During the night there was also pain in both shoulders and the dorsum of the penis. The patient was given meperidine (Demerol) on three occasions by a friend. There was rapid deterioration of mentation and circulation. With onset of shock and coma he was brought to the hospital.

On admission, the patient's temperature was 101.4° F., pulse 132, respirations 32, blood pressure 90/60. He was in deep coma, not responsive to the most painful stimuli. His color was dusky-ashen, nail beds bluish. The abdomen was spastic but not boardlike; there was no peristalsis; his eyes were staring and fixed; the reflexes were normal.

The diagnosis of perforated viscus was a virtual certainty. A superimposed cerebrovascular accident was also considered. Blood was drawn, an intravenous infusion was started, nasal oxygen was given, a nasogastric tube was passed, and a catheter placed in the bladder. There may have been some aspiration of gastric contents on passage of the tube.

X-rays were taken on the way to the ward. Psoas shadows were blurred and indistinct. There was free air beneath both diaphragms, with atelectasis and fluid at the right base, and pneumonitis at the left base.

INITIAL LABORATORY WORK

Urine

Specific gravity	1.019	
*p*H	5.5	
Sediment	clear	

Stool

Guaiac negative

Gastric contents

Guaiac +++

Hematology

Hematocrit	67
Leucocyte count	3500 per cu. mm.

Blood Chemical Analyses

Blood urea nitrogen	14 mg. per 100 ml.
Plasma chloride	107 mE. per l.
Carbon dioxide combining power	21 mE. per l.
Serum amylase	153 units

ARGUMENT. The late and essentially preterminal nature of this man's appearance suggested that he had perforated a viscus three days before entry. This of course could not be proved. The shock, coma, and above all the leukopenia suggested an overwhelming septic process now resulting in late peritonitis after the early leakage episode.

The hematocrit of 67 provided an index of immediate plasma needs. In a man weighing 80 kg. the expected normal blood volume, at 7 per cent of body weight, is 5600 and the red cell volume 2350 ml. With a hematocrit of 67 (normal hematocrit of 42), this red cell volume resides in a blood volume of 3520 ml. (2350 ÷ 0.67). There is thus a *minimum* reduction of plasma volume of 2080 ml. or 64 per cent. The predicted normal plasma volume is 0.58 × 5600 ml. or 3240 ml. The static plasma debt is therefore 64 per cent of the starting plasma volume. More will be lost as time passes.

Immediate therapy must be devoted to the improvement of pulmonary ventilation and the restoration of blood volume. Plasma must be given energetically, knowing that the "static plasma deficit" is only a fraction of the continuing need. The peritonitis is still active and continuing, as in a burn. Were this a 35 per cent body burn the plasma need would total about 8000 ml., or 10 per cent body weight in the first forty-eight hours. As it turned out, this was about the final dose of colloid needed here, for vascular homeostasis in this case of late peritonitis.

The patient is much too sick for a major operation. His leukopenia and his hypovolemia are strong contraindications.

His normal blood urea nitrogen is remarkable, indicating very youthful and adaptable renal function in the face of severe volume reduction.

FURTHER COURSE. An abdominal tap was immediately done, yielding 2700 ml. of gray, thin, slightly odorous fluid not conclusively of gastrointestinal origin. This material yielded *Escherichia coli* in pure culture, sensitive to streptomycin. Its removal greatly improved diaphragmatic excursion and respiratory exchange.

Plasma infusion was begun almost immediately after admission, and following the infusion of 3000 ml. the hematocrit was 45. The patient was bronchoscoped

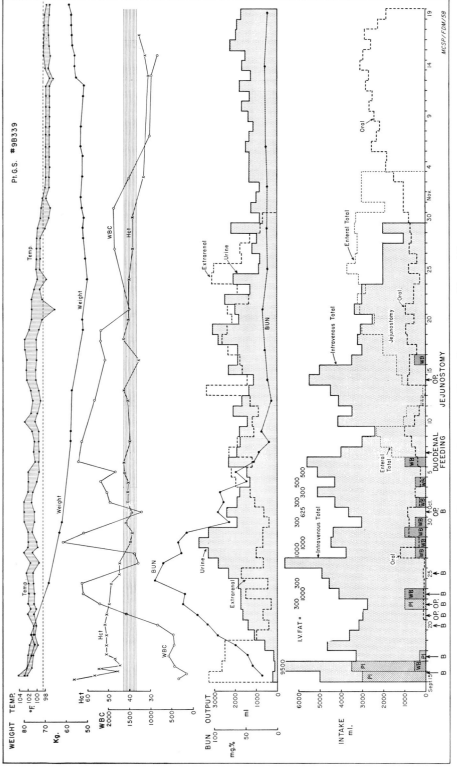

Figure 103. EVENTS IN LATE PERITONITIS (Case 10)

Above are shown temperature and body weight, hematocrit and leucocyte count. Below this is shown the course of the blood urea nitrogen, superimposed on the extrarenal and urine outputs. On the bottom ordinate are shown the intakes by vein, jejunostomy, and mouth, together with plasma and whole blood. Below are shown bronchoscopies (B) and operations. The reader is referred to the text for details.

The elevated hematocrit and depressed leucocyte count are noteworthy in the early course, together with the very large amount of fluid required in early parenteral treatment. The rising blood urea nitrogen with maintained urine output is noted during the first two weeks, a change often seen in very severe invasive infection. The cessation of weight loss coincides with subsidence of fever and this in turn with resumed oral intake. Note the very slow resumption of weight gain.

within three hours of admission. Mucoid gastric aspirate was obtained from the lungs. Alveolar ventilation was then quite good and there was no upper-airway obstruction, so tracheotomy was withheld.

Improvement was now marked. The patient roused, regained consciousness, and his blood pressure returned to 100/70.

The leucocyte count, with rehydration, fell to 1600 per cu. mm., indicating the true extent of his toxic leukopenia. There were no eosinophils in the smear, which contained many band-form polymorphonuclear leucocytes. During the first six hours, the patient excreted 250 ml. of urine.

Comment. The hematocrit drop following the administration of 3000 ml. of plasma indicates, as in a burn, that the area of capillary permeability is still leaking albumin, and that the calculation of static debt yields a minimal figure that must be evaluated clinically and increased to meet needs as indicated by clinical appearance, hematocrit, and urine flow.

The rapid and spectacular clinical response to fluid therapy illustrates that the "toxic" nature of septic processes is often explainable on clear physiologic bases either of reduced blood volume or poor ventilation. It is also a tribute to the resilience of a young man.

The pulmonary process was an immediate threat to survival. Had ventilation not been improved tracheotomy should have been done. The continued leukopenia was most worrisome.

FURTHER COURSE. The patient was given penicillin,

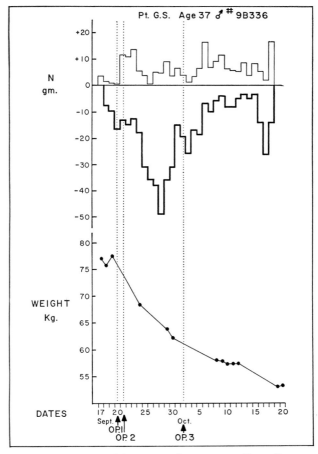

Figure 104. A FRAGMENT OF THE METABOLIC SEQUENCE IN LATE PERITONITIS (Case 10)

Nitrogen balance and weight change are shown during the first month of the patient's course.

The patient did not lose weight during the early phase of fluid sequestration and plasma therapy. He might be expected to have gained weight as in a burn, but this was not noted because his accumulating sequestered septic ascites was being drawn off by paracentesis.

After this he developed an extreme catabolism, characteristic of severe septic starvation. He lost 22 kg. in 33 days over this particular period, or 0.67 kg. per day. Nitrogen loss ranged from 10 to 50 gm. a day. The calculation shows, as an approximation, that about one-half tissue lost was fat and the other half lean tissue.

streptomycin, and Aureomycin intramuscularly and by vein. He received intrabronchial penicillin, and both penicillin and streptomycin intraperitoneally.

During the next twenty-four hours the patient appeared to improve slightly; he was given a fresh ion-exchange plastic-collected blood transfusion; yet his hematocrit tended to rise again and the reaccumulation of peritoneal fluid was obvious. Plasma therapy had to be pushed again; another abdominal tap was done, yielding 1700 ml. Urine output was low (350 to 450 ml. per day), but not in the renal-failure range (100 to 350 ml. per day).

A blood volume determination was done on the second day showing a blood volume of 7180 ml. (On the ninth day it was 5600 ml.)

Over the next two days the patient gradually gained strength and stated that he was hungry. A profuse diuresis commenced, with outputs as high as 55 ml. per hour; the blood urea nitrogen continued to rise.

By the fifth day localization of sepsis was clearly pressing for drainage. A posterior right subphrenic drainage (under local anesthesia) was done, with the release of 400 ml. of foul bilious pus under pressure. Improvement was definite, but limited. The hematocrit was still elevated. Most encouraging was the sudden rise of the leucocyte count to 16,000. Marked azotemia (blood urea nitrogen was 100 mg. per 100 ml.), acidosis (carbon dioxide combining power was 20.3 mE. per l.), and hypotonicity (chloride concentration of 88 mE. per l., sodium of 127 mE. per l.) indicated the severe nature of the visceral disease resulting from his peritonitis.

On the sixth day he was again bronchoscoped, and operative drainage of purulent material in the lower right gutter and subhepatic areas released 1500 ml. of septic material. The blood urea nitrogen rose to 159 mg. per 100 ml. despite high urine outputs. There was profuse gastrointestinal drainage from all operative tracts. Weight loss was extremely rapid (10 kg. in seven days).

The patient now entered a phase where the azotemia and acute febrile illness persisted and there was a pernicious tendency to accumulate bronchial secretion. Tracheotomy was not done. The patient continued to cough well, and this effective cough would have been lost by tracheotomy. He was bronchoscoped repeatedly, which he tolerated well. Had this not been so simple and effective, tracheotomy would have been done forthwith.

On the eighth day he showed thick duodenal secretion, obvious for the first time, in the right upper quadrant drainage site. A day-by-day "balance" regimen was facilitated by daily weighing and analysis of discharges. The peritoneal fluid protein was 1.5 gm. per 100 ml. with a total nitrogen concentration of 2.2 gm. per l.

A typical day's calculation for treatment at this time would run as shown in the table below.

It will be noted that urine sodium loss was not completely replaced; also that chloride was overreplaced relative to sodium. This was because of a slight tendency to alkalosis which the patient occasionally showed. The above allows for only 1200 ml. daily pulmonary loss, a low figure for him.

With continuing fever the patient returned to a disoriented state; the duodenal drainage became massive, by sump suction totaling 500 to 1500 ml. per day. Gastrointestinal bleeding became evident. He was taken off antibiotics, as their frequent changes made little difference in his condition. Their cessation made no immediately discernible difference and his regimen was much simplified thereby.

If nasogastric suction was stopped even for a few hours there was marked increase in duodenal drainage. A feeding jejunostomy was contemplated; he was given fat emulsion intravenously.

On the fifteenth day he became much sicker, more "toxic," more febrile. Again he appeared to be in a terminal phase. A bilateral redrainage of the lower

OUTPUT	VOLUME	SODIUM		POTASSIUM		CHLORIDE		NITROGEN
		Concentration	Total	Concentration	Total	Concentration	Total	Total
	(ml.)	(mE/l.)	(mE/l.)	(mE/l.)	(mE.)	(mE/l.)	(mE.)	(gm.)
Urine	2000	128	256	40	80	60	120	24.0
Nasogastric tube and fistula	1800	98	176	13	24	130	240	3.0
Totals	3800		432		104		360	27.0
INTAKE								
Oral								
Sips of Water								
Intravenous								
5% dextrose in saline	2000	310		0		310		0
5% dextrose in water	1000	0		80		80		0
5% dextrose in water	2000	0		0		0		0
Totals	5000	310		80		390		0

abdomen released still more pus, especially on the left, which had not been directly drained before. For a few days his condition held in the balance without change.

Then, on the twentieth day, he showed a clear turn for the better, which continued unremittingly to complete recovery eight months later. His temperature fell, his blood urea nitrogen fell rapidly to 48 mg. per 100 ml., and the gastrointestinal drainage was much less. A small amount of barium given by mouth lost about 50 per cent of its volume by fistula. The sump drainage tube in the upper abdominal wound could now be insinuated into the duodenum; it was possible to start slow feedings by this route. The intravenous fat program could be discontinued.

A considerable tachycardia continued; the drip feedings directly into the duodenum were not wholly retained, and oral feedings quickly appeared at the duodenal site. His tachycardia seemed to increase with these attempts.

Accordingly on the twenty-seventh day a feeding jejunostomy was done. Extrarenal losses remained high, but after twenty-four hours of suction the jejunostomy tube was used for feeding. At first this was difficult and he had some diarrhea until the feeding (boiled skimmed milk) was incubated with the duodenal drainage and the resulting semidigested mixture instilled into the jejunum. Jejunostomy feedings were continued for about twenty days.

Superficial phlebitis, some nausea, and continued fistula drainage now rapidly subsided. On the forty-sixth day the duodenal fistula closed.

His weight had now fallen from 80 to 51 kg., a total of 29 kg., or 35 per cent of his starting weight. As he began to eat, he was placed on testosterone. He gained weight slowly (8 kg. in a month). By the fifty-seventh day a barium meal showed only a scarred duodenal cap; he was discharged home on the sixty-sixth day.

Repeated visits to the Out-Patient Department demonstrated return to normal weight without recrudescence of his ulcer.

COMMENT. *A. Metabolism, Body Composition, and Nutrition.* Throughout his illness this patient was maintained on a modified metabolic balance regimen ("clinical balance") and body compositional study. Certain of these data deserve mention here.

At the height of his illness over a three-weeks' period, weight loss reached 670 gm. per day. At the most rapid, this rate was 8 kg. in five days, or 1600 gm. per day, with nitrogen loss in the urine about 30 gm. per day. This catabolism therefore approximated 900 gm. of lean tissue and 700 gm. of fat per day. This is an extreme example of septic starvation; acute febrile illness and its attendant stress produced a catabolism of body tissue

at a rate approximately five times that of starvation alone. This fat loss contributed approximately 6300 calories per day; there was high fever.

Blood volume determinations were done during the acute peritonitis and showed a high value at 7180 ml., or 9 per cent of body weight. This high value suggests leakage of the colloid-dye complex into the peritoneal cavity; such an occurrence may introduce an error of 7 to 10 per cent. But more important, it indicates that with falling weight due to catabolism the relative blood volume (like the body water) rises; this "high" volume is apparently needed by the body for maintenance of pressure and flow. With a young heart there is a wide margin between circulatory adequacy and congestive failure at this high-volume level. The heart with myocardial disease narrows this margin to the point where venous pressure rises as soon as volume is restored to provide a normal peripheral flow. The margin of safety is small. One week later the volume at 5600 ml. was still slightly elevated for observed weight (8.3 per cent body weight) but was nearer the expected value.

Extrarenal loss (and its replacement) was a problem through the first month of this patient's illness. He was provided with enough replacement of water and extracellular salt to meet volume maintenance needs plus net losses. He was given potassium, and evidently in adequate quantity to prevent differential potassium loss to the extent of hypokalemia. He was given no magnesium, calcium, phosphate, sulfate, iron, or cobalt except for that contained in whole blood or plasma.

Caloric provision was wholly inadequate until enteral feeding was begun. Glucose was used in low concentrations. Intravenous fat was given for eleven days at the height of his acute catabolism. Once the catabolic forces of sepsis, fever, and acute illness had subsided and he began to eat, he then gained weight rapidly. He was given testosterone at this time, though we would be unable to document a clearly beneficial effect.

The intravenous fat emulsion used in the period of days seven to twenty-two totaled 6200 ml. As a 15 per cent emulsion this provided 8360 calories, or an average of about 560 per day.

From the available data it is possible to calculate the insensible water loss at the height of illness and again later, well on in recovery. This calculation is based on the principle that the total insensible water loss (IWL) is equal to the total intake minus measured output, plus the weight lost for the period. The lost weight represents tissue lost, a fraction of which (about 10 per cent of the mixed tissue) does not appear as water, but as urinary nitrogen and exhaled carbon dioxide. The figure is therefore only an approximation. When weight is constant it is reasonably accurate.

For the two periods:

	TOTAL INTAKE	MEASURED OUTPUT	WEIGHT	IWL	IWL PER DAY
Days 10–15 inclusive	33,900	22,800	−7 kg.	18,100	3,015
Days 48–53 inclusive	18,700	7,600	0	11,100	1,850

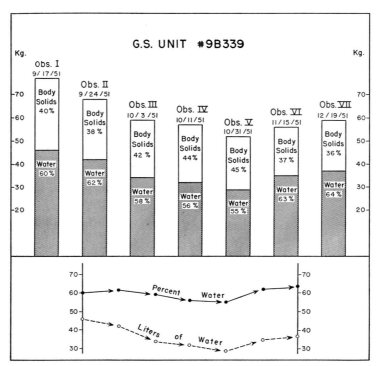

Figure 105. BODY COMPOSITION THROUGH THE PERIOD OF CATABOLISM AND THE TURN TO ANABOLISM (Case 10)

The body water determinations were carried out with deuterium. The first five determinations cover approximately the period of the nitrogen balance shown in the previous figures. The loss of body tissue is so rapid that the relative increase in body water, so characteristic of late starvation, is not seen until the last two observations; prior to that the large extrarenal losses and the relatively high fraction of lean tissue (a high-water tissue) in the loss account for a large weight loss with a reduction in relative water.

These figures indicate a reduction in insensible water loss with subsidence of fever and slowing of the toal catabolic process. Neither figure is excessive: in burns or pulmonary lesion (or with tracheotomy) such figures are much higher.

The release of nitrogen from cells to extracellular fluid can also be approximated during the period of maximum rate of climb of blood urea nitrogen. For example in days four through nine the blood urea nitrogen rose from 45 mg. per 100 ml. to 184 mg. per 100 ml., a rise of 139 mg. per 100 ml. If we assume that the urea is equally partitioned throughout body water and that it constitutes two-thirds of the nonprotein nitrogen in body water, we find that, during this period of six days, 88 gm. of nitrogen accumulated in body water, unexcreted. This is at the rate of 14.5 gm. per day. This is a significant additional "negative nitrogen balance" over and beyond the daily urinary nitrogen of about 20 gm. in this period.

B. Management. When the outcome is successful it is difficult to be critical of the management of such an ill patient. The following points come up for discussion.

Should tracheotomy have been done? Tracheobron-chial aspiration was vital in this man's recovery. As long as bronchoscopy was easily tolerated and skillfully done, the pulmonary tree could be kept clear without the loss of effective cough mechanics and the psychologic price involved in tracheotomy.

Should operative drainage of the abdomen have been done sooner? Had abdominal tap been unsuccessful in relieving pressure, the first surgical drainage should have been done twenty-four to thirty-six hours sooner. Early laparotomy for primary closure on admission was out of the question in a comatose man in shock with advanced peritonitis. Aggressive continuing attack on undrained pus was another factor in success here, and the repeated redrainages were important. The lower abdominal drainage done as the final procedure might well have been carried out a day or two sooner. When drainage of pus from an established abscess will confer physiologic relief (as it almost always does) there is virtually no degree of illness which contraindicates it.

Was the jejunostomy wise? The feeding jejunostomy served a good purpose and provided a good enteral intake during the long transitional phase to oral intake. Had fistula closure failed to occur, jejunostomy might have been a lifeline for the reinstillation of duodenal drainage. The predigestion of the jejunostomy feedings with duodenal drainage seemed to aid in their assimilation. Many other aids were used which have not been detailed here, including vitamins (with vitamin K) and aminophylline (for a wheezy respiration late in his course).

Should extensive operation for fistula closure have been undertaken? Radical fistula closure by gastrectomy, antral exclusion, or direct assault on the duodenum would have been unnecessary, rash, inadvisable, and probably lethal. If there is no obstruction distal to a gastrointestinal fistula, if a tract (rather than a poorly drained spherical abscess cavity) forms, and if mucosa does not heal to skin, the fistula will close as this one did. Heroic surgery for fistula closure confers no immediate physiologic benefit; it is merely difficult major surgery under the most unfavorable of conditions for the patient.

The use of fresh whole blood may have been far more important than antibiotics in treating infection in this leukopenic man.

Finally, the element of capitalizing on luck and "will power" must be emphasized. The surgeon often achieves his best in this type of metabolic problem if he sees the lucky break and capitalizes on it. The most fortunate things here were that the initial abdominal tap decompressed the abdomen and early operative drainage could be avoided, and the patient never developed a blood stream infection. Blood cultures were always sterile. The drainages, the blood, the care he received, all contributed to the sterility of his blood stream. But the rest was bacteriologic good fortune, and a young strong patient with a *will to get well*, the latter of particular importance in his alertness, maintenance of effective cough, cooperation, and tolerance of many uncomfortable procedures including eight bronchoscopies, four abdominal taps, and five operations.

CASE 11

Obstructing Duodenal Ulcer Can Produce a Remarkably Persistent Challenge to Preoperative Preparation, Especially When an Unusual Syndrome Is Present

Case 11. Patient M. A., #9E132. Male. Age 57. Admitted May 10, 1956. Discharged June 3, 1956.

DIAGNOSIS. Obstructing duodenal ulcer.*

OPERATION. First-stage gastrectomy.

CLINICAL SUMMARY. This patient gave a history of duodenal ulcer with intermittent activity for several years, and a major hemorrhage four years previously.

Two months previously he had been in the hospital for about a month with obstruction and bleeding. On conservative measures he resumed a status that was considered satisfactory for discharge. He had received three units of blood, and at one point on this first admission he showed a plasma carbon dioxide combining power of 35.2 mE. per l., potassium concentration of 3.0 mE. per l., and chloride of 90 mE. per l., a foretaste of problems ahead.

During his three weeks at home clinical evidences of obstruction became much more prominent, with pain, vomiting, and upper abdominal swelling.

Physical examination on admission showed a man in distress, hiccoughing and belching. Blood pressure was 160/90, pulse 74. Initially there was upper abdominal swelling, relieved by the nasogastric aspiration of 1500 ml. of guaiac-negative, highly acid gastric contents.

X-rays confirmed the obvious diagnosis of gastric obstruction.

---

* The reader is advised to review Part III and the section on hypokalemic alkalosis before studying this case.

INITIAL LABORATORY WORK

Urine

Specific gravity	1.023	
Protein	+	
pH	7.5	
Sodium	115 mE./l.	

Stool

Guaiac-negative

Hematology

Hematocrit	45
Leucocyte count	16,500 per cu mm

Blood Chemical Analyses

Blood urea nitrogen	7	mg. per 100 ml.
Plasma protein	5.9	gm. per 100 ml.
Plasma chloride	87	mE. per l.
Plasma sodium	140	mE. per l.
Plasma potassium	2.5	mE. per l.
Carbon dioxide combining power	35.4	mE. per l.

ARGUMENT. This patient clearly has an obstruction and needs operation. It is unfortunate that he was not operated upon at the previous admission. It has repeatedly been shown that obstruction, once present, demands operative relief. As he stands now he is a poor subject for operation because of severe hypokalemic alkalosis. The magnitude of the chemical insult may be gauged from the fact that the patient is comparatively "unstressed," he is preoperative, and he is still secreting an alkaline urine containing a large amount (115 mE. per l.) of sodium. Stated otherwise, he is severely alkalotic and hypokalemic despite the fact that his urinary compensation (by sodium excretion) is still active, not having been closed off either by trauma or by body potassium deficit (despite his severe hypokalemia).

A program of treatment should include:

(1) nasogastric suction, continuous at first and later intermittent;

(2) vigorous attack, by intravenous infusion, on his alkalosis and hypokalemia, for example:

First 24 hours: 2000 ml. 1% ammonium chloride,
3000 ml. 5% dextrose in saline with 160 mM. potassium chloride,
2000 ml. 5% dextrose in water with 40 mM. potassium chloride.

The above program should be followed by close check on the plasma carbon dioxide combining power and chloride and potassium concentrations. Further treatment should be based on the results.

His sodium concentration is deceptively normal; there has been extensive urinary sodium loss. Treatment with sodium alone will be disastrous, but some sodium should be given.

The calculation of extracellular-fluid chloride deficit (or hydrogen-ion-equivalent deficit) yields a minimum figure which can satisfactorily be used as a guide to therapy in subtraction alkalosis. Such a calculation must be balanced against the plasma sodium concentration because the acid-base imbalance suggested by a low chloride is less in actuality, in the face of a low sodium concentration and dilutional hypotonicity. Dilution does not, *per se*, alter the carbon dioxide combining power, total carbon dioxide, carbon dioxide tension, or pH, all of which are a function of ionic interrelationships rather than tonicity. The taking up of body buffers (in alkalosis) naturally will increase (rather than decrease) the hydrogen ion needed for repair, over any figure based on the changes in the extracellular fluid alone.

This estimate of his chloride requirement may be approximated on the basis of the extracellular fluid deficit. Such a calculation is valid for chloride where it is not for sodium. Body weight—64 kg.—yields an estimated normal extracellular fluid volume (20 per cent) of 12,800 ml. With a chloride of 87 mE. per l. there is a static net deficit of $12.8 \times 16 = 205$ mE. This is "net static debt" over and above any salt given, and subject to increase hourly as gastric drainage continues.

This is the "excess chloride" (or H^+ equivalent)* which he must receive (*and retain*) to move toward normal. A similar calculation for potassium is meaningless, yielding a deficit of about 35 mE., whereas the patient has probably lost at least 150 to 300 mE., of potassium and may have lost much more. Yet, on the other hand, to assume that the 50 per cent reduction in plasma potassium concentration is shared by the potassium content of the cell mass would yield a deficit of 1500 mE.—equally erroneous.

The continued urine output despite severe illness is of interest, and is characteristic of this condition.

The objective of therapy should be to give ammonium chloride and potassium chloride vigorously as indicated by the chloride ion needs, follow progress clinically and chemically, and operate as soon as the hypokalemic alkalosis is coming under control.

FURTHER COURSE. The further course of this patient was of remarkable interest. For the first day his physicians gave the patient intravenously:

1000 ml. 1% ammonium chloride,
2000 ml. 5% dextrose in saline solution,
3000 ml. 5% dextrose in water with 80 mM. potassium chloride.

Such a program is open to criticism on the basis of the large amount of water as compared to salt, and the comparatively small dose of "uncovered or excess chloride" (that is, chloride with disposable cation such as ammonium chloride and potassium chloride) destined to restore hydrogen ion concentration to normal. Also the amount of potassium (80 mE.) was very small in relation to the sodium given (310 mE.). This is notoriously dangerous in hypokalemia.

The beneficial effect was virtually nil. One reason for this was the treatment, another the large gastric losses. The patient showed certain characteristics of acute gastric dilatation as well as obstruction. On his first day the gastric drainage was 4000 ml. and in the first three days it totaled 12,700 ml., with an average chloride concentration of 150 mE. per l. This acute loss reduced extracellular fluid volume, raised the hematocrit from 40 to 47, and constituted the greatest single challenge to acid-base balance.

For the next thirty-six hours no forward progress was made; the patient was transferred to the surgical service but neither group appreciated adequately the magnitude of the therapeutic problem of static debt plus continuing loss. In this period his intake-output figures totaled:

OUTPUT		INTAKE	
Gastric	9700 ml.	NH₄Cl (1%)	2250 ml.
Urine	3700 ml.	5% dextrose in saline	5500 ml.
		5% dextrose in H₂O	7100 ml. with 200 mM. KCl
Total	13400 ml.	Total	14850 ml.

---

* The term "excess chloride (H^+ equivalent)" refers to the use of potassium chloride and ammonium chloride in the treatment of subtraction alkalosis. In both instances Cl^- ion is given with a disposable cation—that is, one which does not remain in the extracellular fluid as a cation. By the law of electroneutrality this therefore adds H^+ to replace the H^+ lost as vomitus. NH_4^+ is itself an acid because it acts as a hydrogen donor. Therefore the sum of the total chloride given as potassium chloride or ammonium chloride may be referred to as the "chloride excess or H^+ equivalent." This figure is the *effective* added acid.

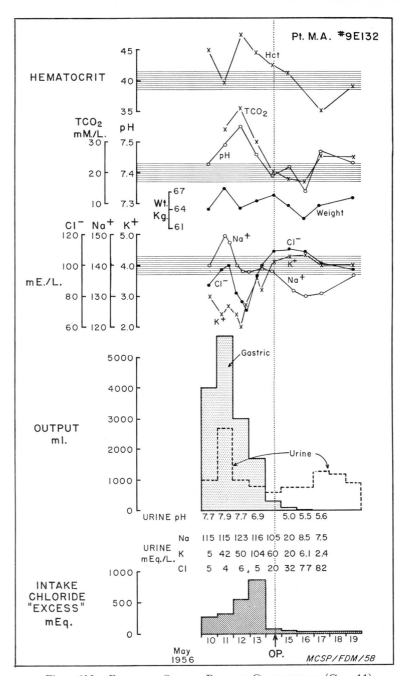

Figure 106. EVENTS IN SEVERE PYLORIC OBSTRUCTION (Case 11)

In the four ordinates above are shown the blood and plasma values and body weight. Below are shown the output volumes, the urine *p*H, and in the bottom line the "chloride excess or H+ equivalent" given in therapy. The reader is referred to the text for details.

It will be noted that the initial therapy rehydrated and resalted the patient as indicated by a rise in weight with a fall in hematocrit. But the nature of the therapy was wrong; the hypokalemic alkalosis became worse. It was not until the very large gastric losses were restored by a very large "chloride excess or H+ equivalent," totaling almost 1000 mE. in one day, that acid-base and potassium values were restored and operation possible.

Note that in the preoperative phase urine *p*H was alkaline and sodium excretion high. It was only with anesthesia and operation that the urine became acid with a low sodium concentration. The concept that hypokalemic alkalosis is of itself always associated with paradoxical aciduria does not find support from such cases; the endocrine response to operation is important in the genesis of aciduria, and thus in worsening the alkalosis. Here therapy could be reduced as obstruction was relieved, and the course was smooth thereafter.

Treatment was energetic but not properly balanced; too much sodium was being given, and the plasma sodium concentration rose to 150 mE. per l., the alkalosis worsened, and the potassium concentration fell further. The hypokalemic alkalosis became more severe. Inadequate potassium had been given. Urine sodium excretion continued and the urine continued to be alkaline; potassium loss in the urine continued unabated (104 mE. per l.). Potassium loss in the gastric juice was always small (10 to 15 mE. per l.).

Finally, two days after admission, the following values were found:

Blood

pH	7.55	
pCO₂	47	mm. Hg
Total carbon dioxide	41	mM. per l.
Plasma chloride	73	mE. per l.
Plasma sodium	138	mE. per l.
Plasma potassium	2.0	mE. per l.
Carbon dioxide combining power	46.5	mE. per l.

Here, *p*H is high but there is little respiratory compensation; there is spectacular hypochloremia, hypokalemia, and alkalosis; sodium is characteristically normal despite the large losses.

Electrocardiographic changes were marked. Note the normal sodium concentration characteristic of hypokalemic alkalosis. This patient became disoriented and then unresponsive at this point.

ARGUMENT. After forty-eight hours of such a poor response in hypokalemic alkalosis, one wonders where to turn. The answer is usually the same in hypokalemic alkalosis: "more H⁺, but faster." The subtraction alkalosis basically due to loss of H⁺ (as hydrochloric acid) can only be combated by giving H⁺ (as ammonium chloride and effectively as potassium chloride) much faster than it is being lost so as to "mend the present and repair the past."

FURTHER COURSE. This was finally done on the third hospital day. On that day the totals were as shown below.

The effects were gratifying. The carbon dioxide combining power fell to 27.7 mE. per l., while the chloride rose to 91 mE. per l. and the potassium to 3.1 mE. per l. The patient was given two units of concentrated albumin. In this day he gained only 800 gm. body weight, indicating that it was not the total quantity but rather the nature of his body fluids which was being altered by treatment. The patient's clinical appearance improved remarkably. He became rational and cooperative. Without further ado he was operated upon.

A considerable duodenal reaction was present; a first-

stage gastrectomy was carried out. Convalescence was smooth.

COMMENT. It is of interest—and we have seen this in other such cases—that we "overshot" the mark on the day of surgery when his obstruction was finally relieved. His chloride concentration rose to 108 mE. per l. and his carbon dioxide combining power fell to 18.5 mE. per l. His potassium concentration rose to 4.1 mE. per l. The "addition metabolic acidosis" we had been trying to create to balance his "subtraction metabolic alkalosis" finally occurred. In a few days of normal renal function this repaired itself. At no time was the patient hypotonic or azotemic.

A careful series of arterial acid-base measurements were carried out in this patient. They demonstrate nicely the worsening of his alkalosis to *p*H 7.55 on the second day, the fall to *p*H 7.47 with more intensive treatment, and the absence of any significant compensatory respiratory acidosis (the highest *p*CO₂ was 50 mm. Hg). The urine was alkaline initially (*p*H 7.8), became acid just after operation (*p*H 5.0), and was acid thereafter. The urine sodium concentration, ranging from 110 to 123 mE. per l. before operation, fell abruptly to 20 mE. per l. after operation. These two changes demonstrate clearly that it was not potassium loss *alone* that produced the "paradoxical aciduria," but, instead, the effect of anesthesia and operation on the renal tubule. The urinary excretion data indicate the changing pattern of loss during treatment and after operation, as shown in the table on page 599.

Note in the table that a low-sodium aciduria was not present until after operation, a nice demonstration of the effect of trauma on urine *p*H in this disorder.

One additional point was the development of minimal signs of ammonium toxicity at the height of his preoperative ammonium chloride infusion.

SUMMARY. This was a remarkably challenging case of preoperative hypokalemic alkalosis with an initially alkaline urine; treatment was complicated by large continuing gastric losses in the range of volumes seen in acute gastric dilatation. The situation was finally repaired sufficiently to permit safe operation, by very vigorous treatment with ammonium chloride and potassium chloride, totaling 4500 ml. of 1 per cent ammonium chloride (chloride concentration equaled 185 mE. per l.) and 320 mM. of potassium chloride during the thirty-six hours prior to operation.

An earlier favorable result would have been achieved if, in the first or second twenty-four-hour period the patient had received sufficient chloride, potassium, and sodium to cover tube losses plus about 300 mM. of potassium chloride "excess" (H⁺ equivalent). Such an endeavor would have involved about the same therapy

Third Day

OUT		IN	
Gastric	7350	NH₄CL (1%)	4500
Urine	2000	5% dextrose in saline	1000
		5% dextrose in H₂O	6000 with 320 mM. KCl
Total	9350	Total	11500

Urine Data

DATE	VOLUME (ml.)	pH	TOTAL mE. PER DAY		
			Sodium	Potassium	Chloride
5/10/56	1000	7.7	123	35	5
5/11/56	2700	7.9	31	115	11
5/12/56	1000	7.7	123	50	6
5/13/56	800	6.9	93	82	4
5/14/56	555		60	35	11
OPERATION					
5/15/56	735	5.0	15	15	24
5/16/56	740	5.5	6	5	52
5/17/56	1300	5.6	11	4	104

that was finally given on the fourth and fifth days of his course.

LATER COURSE. About six months after an uneventful second-stage gastrectomy this patient died of a perforation. Postmortem examination showed multiple fejunal ulcers, one of which had perforated. A reexam-ination of this pancreas in the light of his remarkable gastric acid output showed multiple islet-cell tumors. In retrospect, then, his was a case of the Ellison-Zollinger syndrome with an unusually intractable hypokalemic alkalosis traceable to the unusually profuse gastric secretion.

CASE 12

Diverticulitis, with the Use of Laxatives and Enemas, Produces a Classic Instance of Chronic Potassium Loss, Hypokalemia, and Nephropathy, But without Alkalosis

Case 12. Patient N. S., #39252.* Female. Age 72. Admitted January 24, 1958. Discharged February 25, 1958.

DIAGNOSIS. Chronic diverticulitis with perforation of the colon.

OPERATION. Transverse colostomy.

CLINICAL SUMMARY. The patient was a seventy-two-year-old white female first seen at the hospital seventeen years before with symptoms of left lower quadrant pain. X-rays at that time showed a diverticulum of the sigmoid colon. She refused further follow-up. She was chronically constipated and continued to have sharp, nonradiating, intermittent, crampy, left lower quadrant pain every two to three months, accompanied by a 30-pound weight loss during the one year prior to admission. For three months before admission her pain had been much more severe and more frequent. For two months she had vomited three to five times per day and had many soft stools that consisted mostly of mucus. She had taken mineral oil and numerous enemas during this time.

In her past history she had had a hysterectomy, bilateral salpingo-oophorectomy, appendectomy, and cholecystectomy thirty to thirty-five years prior to admission. Her appetite had generally been good.

Physical examination showed her to be an obese white female in considerable abdominal distress. Her blood pressure was 210/82, pulse 76, temperature (oral) 99.6° F. Her tongue was dry and skin turgor restricted. The heartbeat was irregular; there was a soft systolic murmur heard at the apex. The abdomen was very obese. A tender 8 × 7 cm. mass could be felt in the left lower quadrant just below the umbilicus. Cough tenderness was referred to this area.

X-rays showed a dilated loop of small bowel in the area of the tender mass. Electrocardiogram showed multiple atrial premature beats with a sagging S-T segment, inverted T-waves, and prominent U-waves, all suggestive of potassium depletion.

INITIAL LABORATORY WORK
Urine
    Specific gravity   1.007
    Protein   1+
    Sugar—negative
    pH   6.5
    Leucocytes—loaded on voided specimen
    Otherwise negative
Stool
    Benzidine—negative

---

* The author is indebted to Dr. Martin Litwin for collecting the data and analyzing the course of this patient.

Hematology

    Hematocrit   37
    Leucocyte count   6300 per cu. mm.

Blood Chemical Analyses

    Blood urea nitrogen   5   mg. per 100 ml.
    Plasma chloride   88   mE. per l.
    Plasma sodium   141   mE. per l.
    Plasma potassium   2.2 mE. per l.
    Carbon dioxide
      combining power 27.2 mE. per l.

ARGUMENT. The history is typically that of chronic diverticulitis with perforation of a diverticulum and a local abscess of very low-grade type. The recent 30-pound weight loss certainly would make one suspect the presence of a colonic carcinoma. The absence of high fever and elevated leucocyte count is not uncommon in the geriatric patient with well-localized peritoneal infection.

The biochemical picture is that of severe hypokalemia and a mild hypochloremia. The carbon dioxide combining power is at the upper normal limit.

In this instance hypokalemia is due to long-continuing loss of potassium from the large bowel. The potassium loss per day is not great, but the bowel component is at a very high potassium:nitrogen ratio (10 to 15 mE. per gm.), producing a gradual and insidious differential loss of potassium. The result is that lowering of body potassium content (to a degree no greater than that seen in starvation states where the potassium:nitrogen ratio is normal) produces a severe lowering of plasma potassium, whereas starvation does not. "The causes of potassium loss are many while the causes of hypokalemia are few."

The inability to concentrate the urine is a characteristic feature of the nephropathy of potassium loss.

This furnishes an excellent example of the fact that potassium loss in man may proceed to a severe degree without the production of alkalosis.

The problem, however, remains one of reconstituting a differential potassium loss, and providing the very large amounts of potassium needed to do so.

The electrocardiographic abnormalities indicate that potassium replacement is of the utmost importance prior to operation. Surgery done in the face of this severe degree of hypokalemia would lead to further sodium retention and potassium loss. Ileus, muscular disorders, or death from cardiac arrhythmia might readily result; very severe alkalosis would readily be produced.

The very dilute urine of 1.007 in the face of some desalting represents the tubular lesion of hyposthenuria in the face of dehydration, which will be corrected by potassium replacement.

A starting ration of potassium for the first twenty-four hours should include a minimum of 220 mE. of potassium ion, preferably in the form of the chloride, since this will correct any tendency to alkalosis that may be present. Patients of this type are severely depleted of body stores of potassium and require at least 650 to 700 mE. for replacement over a five-day period. Close check should be kept on the plasma potassium concentration and the electrocardiogram, since potassium toxicity tends to ensue. The deficit is repaired much more readily in a patient like this one than in an alkalotic person.

Electrolyte therapy should be supplemented by adequate antibiotic treatment of the pericolonic infection.

Only after restoration of fluid, electrolyte and acid-base equilibrium should exploratory laparotomy be performed in this case.

FURTHER COURSE. Over the next four days the patient received a total of 414 mM. of potassium chloride intravenously and orally in addition to small amounts of tea and fruit juices. At the end of that time urinary potassium output for twenty-four hours was only 16 mE. in 1100 ml. of urine. Urine osmolality was 250 mO. per l. and plasma potassium concentration was 3.0 mE. per l.

Comment. These latter data are of remarkable interest. The urinary "potassium conservation" (possibly a manifestation of tubular disease) still remains despite high potassium dosage and positive potassium balance. Urinary concentrating ability is still low.

This brings to mind the possibility that the nephropathy seen in chronic potassium loss (from the large bowel) may actually be due to absence of some other entity (such as magnesium or zinc) also lost via the colon; the potassium might be an unimportant fellow traveler in the pathogenesis of the nephropathy.

FURTHER COURSE. Massive potassium replacement was started and continued through the sixth hospital day, the patient receiving 642 mE. of potassium in three days. At that time the plasma potassium concentration had risen to 6.8 mE. per l., urinary osmolality was 925 mO. per l., and urinary potassium output was 37 mE. in 310 ml. of urine. Potassium therapy was then discontinued. Plasma potassium concentration was allowed to drop off to normal levels while the bowel was being sterilized with neomycin.

On the eleventh hospital day abdominal exploration was carried out. A pelvic abscess adhering to the dome of the urinary bladder and communicating with a perforation of the rectum and sigmoid was drained. There was no evidence of carcinoma. A few sigmoid diverticula were noted. Transverse colostomy was performed.

Postoperative course was uneventful. The patient was discharged on the twentieth postoperative day with a well-functioning colostomy, to be followed in the surgical outpatient department. She later returned for sigmoid resection. Her course has been smooth and recovery complete.

COMMENT. This patient demonstrated severe hypokalemia and potassium depletion with little tendency to alkalosis, the syndrome resulting from chronic use of enemas and laxatives with chronic loss of colonic secretion in large amounts. The initial potassium replacement was done rather gingerly, probably too much so,

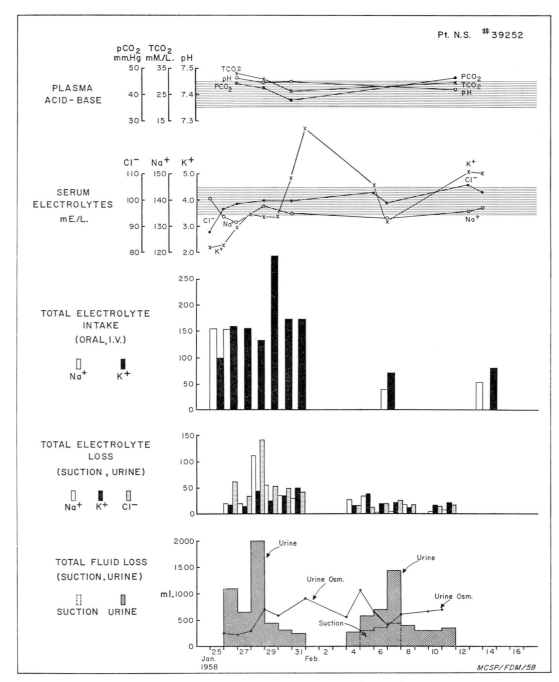

Figure 107. EVENTS IN DIVERTICULITIS (Case 12)

In the ordinates above are shown blood acid-base data, and plasma chemical values. Below are shown intake, losses, and fluid balance data. The reader is referred to the text for details.

On entry the patient had marked hypokalemia (2.2 mE. per l.) due to chronic large bowel loss, with essentially normal acid-base data. This is "chronic potassium loss hypokalemia" and is due to colonic loss at a high potassium:nitrogen ratio, but without differential loss of hydrogen ion over other cations (unlike gastric obstruction with hydrochloric acid loss). On energetic potassium therapy (fifth day) the reloading "overshot the mark" (very difficult to do in hypokalemic alkalosis) and a transient hyperkalemia resulted. Losses were negligible in the hospital.

and later on when a large amount of potassium had been replaced, hyperkalemia occurred with great readiness. Since renal function was good this was of no consequence. The patient then weathered her operations smoothly.

CASE 13

In Which Operation for Ulcerative Colitis Is Followed by a Severe Bleeding Tendency That Responds Rapidly to Specific Therapy

Case 13. Patient M. K., #5G432.* Female. Age 34. Admitted August 31, 1955. Discharged November 25, 1955.

DIAGNOSIS. Recurrent acute ulcerative colitis, with ileostomy.

OPERATIONS. Subtotal colectomy.
Combined abdominoperineal resection.

CLINICAL SUMMARY. This thirty-four-year-old white childless female eighteen months ago first developed diarrhea, which did not respond to diet, antispasmodics, or psychiatric therapy. One year after onset an ileostomy was performed, at which time a carbuncle was also excised from her back. She had been hospitalized twice within the past six months because of recurrent furunculosis and intermittent low-grade symptoms of colitis despite cortisone therapy. One month before, she had been hospitalized elsewhere and received 1000 ml. of blood because of bloody diarrhea. This was her first blood loss serious enough to require transfusions, and on her six previous hospitalizations she had remained afebrile despite recurrent skin infections. Because of progressive intermittent abdominal pain associated with diarrhea she was advised to have a colon resection.

Physical examination on entry revealed her to be an youthful, well-nourished female with a single furuncle of her left axilla and diffuse tenderness in her lower abdomen, particularly overlying the descending colon. A normal-appearing ileostomy was in the right lower quadrant. Her temperature and other vital signs were normal. Results of pelvic and rectal examinations were negative.

X-rays of the abdomen showed some fluid-containing nondilated small bowel in the left midabdomen, but was otherwise unremarkable.

INITIAL LABORATORY WORK

Urine

Normal except for 8 to 10 wbc/hpf.

Hematology

Hematocrit	40
Leucocyte count	5700 per cu. mm.
Eosinophil count	119 per cu. mm.

Blood Chemical Analyses

Blood urea nitrogen	5 mg. per 100 ml.
Plasma protein	6.6 mg. per 100 ml.
Plasma chloride	111 mE. per l.

---

* The author is indebted to Dr. John M. Kinney for collecting the data and analyzing the course of this patient.

Plasma sodium	136	mE. per l.
Plasma potassium	4.0	mE. per l.
Carbon dioxide combining power	19.6	mE. per l.
Prothrombin time	46	per cent

Adrenocorticotropin infusion test dropped the eosinophils from 225 to 54 during eight hours.

ARGUMENT. The patient had an unsatisfactory response to conservative treatment. Steroid therapy had produced temporary improvement with doses too high for prolonged therapy. Her ileostomy had been performed in an attempt to get the patient off cortisone. For the following six months her bowel symptoms were troublesome but not as bad as before. During the previous year the patient had remained afebrile throughout her acute episodes and had experienced no serious bleeding until she required 2 units of blood prior to ileostomy. The decision to perform the subtotal colectomy seemed thoroughly justified in view of the patient's prolonged course and the fact that her mental reaction to the disease was becoming a crippling factor in her convalescence. In addition it was felt that her diseased colon might be a focus of origin for her recurrent skin infections, which did not respond to antibiotic therapy.

Despite her nine-month course of cortisone (75 mg. per day), the patient showed no clinical evidence of adrenal insufficiency during the next eight months. Therefore the patient seemed in reasonably good health, without anemia, and a suitable candidate for colon resection.

FURTHER COURSE. After three weeks of stabilization and high-dose vitamin therapy in the hospital, a subtotal colectomy was performed. On the patient's third postoperative day, chills, flank pain, and pyuria indicated bilateral acute pyelonephritis. After a heavy course of antibiotic therapy, the renal infection slowly subsided. Three weeks after the subtotal colectomy an abdominoperineal resection of the remaining bowel was performed. Because of contamination the posterior wound was packed open rather than closed primarily, as is our custom. The patient's postoperative response was satisfactory until the fourth day after this second operation, when the posterior wound pack was removed without difficulty. The patient was discovered in shock one hour later, with a steady ooze of blood from the sides of the posterior wound. This was repacked on the ward and the patient taken to the operating room after 1000 ml. of blood had restored her blood pressure. Under anesthesia no discrete bleeding points could be identified, and the wound was tightly packed with a layer of oxidized gauze against the wound surfaces. The oozing continued through and around the pack during the night, with a total of 3500 ml. of whole blood required to maintain a stable chart. This had included 500 ml. of fresh blood and 100 mg. of vitamin K_1 oxide given intravenously without effect.

On review it was found that the clotting time, clot retraction, and platelet count were normal, without fibrinolysins. The bleeding time was prolonged to eight minutes (the normal time is two minutes).

ARGUMENT. Although complete characterization is impossible, these data suggest a tissue defect rather than a disorder of the coagulation mechanism, as cause of the bleeding. Fresh whole blood has been tried but without avail. Vitamin C has previously been given in large amounts, and scurvy is unlikely as a cause. One may as well move directly to the most effective (though by an unknown mode of action) therapy. This is high-dose corticosteroid treatment.

FURTHER COURSE. The patient appeared to be bleeding from an endothelial defect, in the presence of normal proteins and formed elements of the blood. The patient was given 100 mg. of hydrocortisone intravenously over ten minutes, and an additional 100 mg. was run in over the following five hours. Within two hours of starting the administration, the bleeding time, as determined by ear puncture, had returned to normal and the blood loss from the posterior wound was sharply reduced.

The patient made a satisfactory convalescence from that time on, except for drainage of a small abscess in the abdominal wall eight days later. The posterior wound pack was removed at that time and the wound healed promptly without sepsis. The steroid therapy was shifted to oral cortisone, which was tapered to 25 mg. per day and stopped after coverage with adreno-corticotropic hormone for three days.

SUMMARY. A case of ulcerative colitis in a young female is presented, in which surgery was complicated by an unusual form of hemorrhage which was felt to be due to an endothelial defect. Prompt improvement occurred after the intravenous administration of hydro-cortisone.

One may speculate that the permeability defect was related either to the ulcerative colitis or to the discontinued steroid therapy, and had been responsible for the metastatic skin sepsis. Whatever the validity of such considerations, the bleeding ceased promptly with corticosteroid therapy.

CHAPTER 38

The Liver

In evaluating patients with liver disease, for operation, it is important to emphasize four general facts.

(1) *Bile-duct obstruction is a relatively harmless process.* A purely obstructive lesion of the liver without proximal infection produces a histologic and functional impairment that is readily and often completely reversible. The pathology and biochemistry of early hepatic obstruction are easily restored to normal. Obstruction *alone* as a cause of cholangitis or biliary cirrhosis is very rare and has been overrated in most texts. For this reason, the patient should be approached with the concept of relieving this obstruction so that reversion may take place, rather than postponing operation in an illusory fear of postoperative hepatic dysfunction.

(2) *Liver cell disease bodes ill for operative survival.* Although the altered function of the obstructed liver is easily reversible, the liver with diffuse hepatocellular disease is extremely vulnerable to trauma. Mistaken operation on early acute hepatic necrosis and extensive elective surgery in the face of cirrhosis both result in a high mortality, due primarily to liver failure.

(3) *Carbohydrate helps.* The administration of carbohydrate has a protective effect on the liver in the face of trauma. An increased liver glycogen appears to protect the liver against damage and can be demonstrated to improve liver function. The use of an anesthetic mixture that presents the patient with normal or high oxygen concentrations is important in protecting the liver just as it is the kidney. The most seriously jeopardized liver in the

Page 604

previously normal surgical patient is that which is depleted of glycogen and then exposed to prolonged anoxia, due either to defects in the airway and the gas mixture, or to prolonged hypotension, shock, and deficiency of blood flow.

(4) *Elaborate or compulsive diagnostic work-up is often inadvisable in obstructive jaundice.* There are many cases of jaundice in which the expenditure of many days or weeks in diagnostic steps is inconclusive, expensive, and hazardous to the patient. Aggressive diagnostic steps—biopsy and exploration—should be carried out after one has ascertained by physiologic study whether or not the danger signs of hepatic necrosis are present. If so, the diagnostic exploration carries an ominous mortality; but even so it may be essential.

On these four facts is based most of the surgical strategy in obstructive liver disease. The physiologic activities of the liver are essential to the continued life of the organism, as evidenced by the rapid demise in the face of widespread hepatic necrosis. Any severe trauma imposes a load on the liver and is deleterious to the performance of certain functions of the liver. In the dog, if not in man, liver anoxia and infection seem to be important factors in the downward spiral of severe shock. Despite all this, the liver is not the viscus whose failure most commonly jeopardizes the welfare of the previously healthy surgical patient. The gastrointestinal tract, the kidneys, the lungs, the brain, and the heart are all much more commonly than the liver the seat of difficulty whose solution is critical for survival. The situations in which liver failure predominates in the metabolic predicament of the surgical patient are those of the liver primarily intoxicated or virus- infected at the time of operation or long affected by hepatocellular disease.

Section I. Liver Function Tests

Most tests of liver function are related to a single biochemical reaction and do not display an adequate picture of total liver capacity. Only in serious liver deterioration do the tests move together, and even here, for example, one may see hepatic coma in the absence of deep jaundice, demonstrating a dissociation of discrete functional capacities even in the terminal state.

It is therefore worthwhile on a surgical ward to divide liver studies into several groups according to their functional meaning. A brief account follows.

1. Excretory Capacity

The excretory capacity of the liver is best studied by measuring the plasma bilirubin concentration. If it is elevated, in the absence of hemolysis, one may assume that excretion of this pigment is impaired. Significant amounts of urobilinogen in the feces or urine indicate that overproduction of bile pigment, rather than underexcretion, plays a role in the jaundice.

Study of the Bromsulphalein excretion also measures pigment excretory capacity and may show abnormal retention in the absence of significant jaundice; for this reason the test is useful in the absence of jaundice and is more subtle than gross accumulation of bilirubin in the blood. One rarely sees diagnosis or treatment altered by the result of Bromsulphalein test in surgical lesions of the liver.

Direct-reacting bilirubin is that fraction of bile pigment which has been processed in the liver itself and freed for water-soluble reaction. It may therefore be assumed to result from the "regurgitation" of processed bilirubin back into the blood stream from the canaliculi. In extrahepatic biliary obstruction or intrahepatic obstruction of the small bile ducts (cholangiolitis) the direct-reacting fraction predominates. This determination is therefore of some value. If the direct-reacting fraction is more than 80 per cent of the total bilirubin, this strongly suggests an obstructive process. At lesser degrees of predominance, this differentiation is unreliable until the direct-reacting fraction drops to 30 per cent or less, when hemolysis is a more likely cause of the jaundice. The fractionation of the plasma bilirubin is probably of no value whatsoever when the total plasma bilirubin is 4 mg. per 100 ml., or less.

The alkaline phosphatase concentration in the plasma rises in extrahepatic block and in some instances of intrahepatic block of the small bile ducts (cholangiolitis and early hepatitis). The alkaline phosphatase concentration is also found to be elevated in patients with metastatic malignancy in the liver. It reaches its highest values (40 to 60 Bodansky units per 100 ml.) in longstanding partial obstruction with inflammation, as in cholangitis or in cholangiolitis.

2. Protein Synthesis

The protein-synthetic functions of the liver are most importantly involved with the synthesis of albumin. According to present evidence, the liver is the sole site of albumin production in the body; liver capillaries are almost perfectly permeable to albumin, and this albumin accounts for the colloid osmotic pressure of the plasma elsewhere in the body, which maintains plasma volume intact. As previously pointed out, hypoproteinemia is readily produced by the overadministration of water and salt, particularly where there is antidiuresis or where there is a defect in the capillary wall (diffuse infection, inflammation, peritonitis, burns) which permits leakage of albumin out into interstitial spaces and hence robs it of its oncotic effectiveness.

In the absence of such conditions, hypo-albuminemia results from an important defect in a certain function of the liver and is of extreme importance in the patient who is approaching surgery or has recently been operated upon.

The absolute albumin concentration is probably the most important consideration in this regard as it is this which determines the colloid osmotic pressure of the plasma. The relationship of the albumin to the globulin, expressed as the "A:G ratio," is of secondary interest. Elevated plasma globulin concentration is found in a number of disease entities, such as sarcoid and certain types of chronic infections. An inverse albumin:globulin ratio due to a process primarily elevating the globulin is not of as great importance to surgical convalescence as an absolute reduction in plasma albumin concentration.

The production of abnormal protein by the liver (or by the reticuloendothelial system in general) is characteristic in certain types of liver disease, and this is typified by finding elevated thymol turbidity, cephalin flocculation, and globulin. These tests may give abnormal results in the presence of normal albumin synthesis. They are evidences of hepatocellular disease, but they are not as ominous surgically as hypoalbuminemia.

The concentration of prothrombin in the blood is another synthetic activity of the liver which depends on (1) the absorption of the prothrombin precursor, vitamin K, from the intestine, and (2) the hepatic synthesis of this absorbed material into prothrombin. Absorption may be inhibited by lack of bile in the intestinal tract, and for this reason is found disturbed in obstructive liver disease. In most cases of simple obstruction, prothrombin is quickly synthesized when vitamin K is administered parenterally. In severe

cellular disease of the liver, such as acute and chronic hepatitis and cirrhosis, this synthesis is impaired. For this reason, the study of prothrombin synthesis in response to an administered parenteral dose of vitamin K is an important liver function test; it also guides the patient to operation only when coagulation mechanisms are intact. Normal prothrombin synthesis can also be impaired by the use of intestinal antibiotics which interfere with the production of vitamin K by intestinal bacteria, and by the use of Dicumarol, an anticoagulant which acts by inhibiting prothrombin synthesis.

3. Carbohydrate Metabolic Functions

Carbohydrate metabolic functions of the liver and the ability to conjugate certain lipids are of considerable interest but of much less practical value in clinical evaluation. None of the tests is clinically convenient. The normal store of liver glycogen is very quickly depleted in response to starvation or certain stimuli such as ether or epinephrine. It is possible to study the carbohydrate storage in the liver by administering epinephrine and observing the peripheral change in blood glucose. Since this test requires multiple blood samples, and involves many uncontrolled variables, it is not widely used. The galactose tolerance test—ability of the liver to convert galactose—is likewise not as useful as it might appear. The study of the fraction of cholesterol which is esterified is indicative of the lipid conjugatory function of the liver but is of surprisingly little importance in selecting or evaluating patients for surgery. The level of plasma cholinesterase is a measure of hepatic cellular "reserve" that has prognostic meaning.

Section II.   Effects of Trauma on the Liver

Other than a transient hyperglycemia thought to be due to the mobilization of liver glycogen by epinephrine and the anti-insulin effects of adrenal steroids, mild to moderate injury has little serious effect on the liver. If

the liver is normal to begin with, it is virtually never the seat of difficulty that becomes critical in the patient's management.

Very severe injury has effects upon the liver most readily seen in the intermediary metabolism of carbohydrates and porphyrin pigments. Hyperglycemia is marked, and there is a transient bilirubinemia. Excretion of Bromsulphalein is impaired. Since most severely injured patients receive blood transfusion, or have hematomas or intraserous hemorrhages which may be the source of bilirubin, this transient jaundice represents increased bilirubin production as well as a defect in liver function. The latter is indicated by the fact that similar amounts of hemolysis in patients who have not been traumatized do not produce as marked an elevation of plasma bilirubin concentration as they do in the patient after severe trauma. This is analogous to the transient azotemia of severe trauma with renal anoxia, observed even though renal function was initially normal.

Chronic semistarvation may occur alone for prolonged periods of time without readily demonstrable alterations in liver function. The liver cell appears to be resilient, and restores itself rapidly to normal with refeeding, just as it restores itself to normal after the relief of obstruction. If prolonged starvation has been accompanied by sepsis, there is fatty degeneration of the liver, seen on either gross or microscopic examination but not readily diagnosed clinically. Injections or infusions at the time of trauma may produce subsequent hepatitis by virus inoculation. Such an unhappy accident should not be laid at the door of the trauma per se.

If there is an increased load of bilirubin to be excreted, any sort of trauma or anesthesia will be followed by a rise in the concentration of bilirubin in the blood. This is usually transient and has no ominous significance. If the trauma is severe the rise may be prolonged, as evidence either of functional damage to the liver or of an increased pigment load, or both. There is at all times a "resting," or basal, load of porphyrin pigments (bilirubin and its precursors) presenting itself for hepatic excretion. If liver function in cirrhosis deteriorates to the point where this resting load is not excreted in the resting state, prognosis after trauma is poor; any sort of trauma in cirrhosis will be followed by a marked increase in severity of the jaundice, this being merely a barometer of the extent of liver failure. It is for this reason that jaundice in cirrhosis bodes ill for surgical recovery should a shunt be attempted.

There is again an analogy to the kidney here. The azotemia (elevated blood urea) is not in itself harmful. The urea in kidney disease, like bilirubin in liver disease, merely constitutes an easily measured index of functional capacity. Neither compound is toxic and both are normally presented in large quantities for excretion. In the case of both the liver and the kidney, obstructive elevations are of little prognostic significance, rises after trauma indicate the cellular repercussions of that trauma, and rises in the resting state without trauma or obstruction are portents of severe cellular degeneration which are ominous should operation be necessary.

Section III.   The Liver Spectrum

It is well to think of the liver disorders involving jaundice as occupying a "spectrum." At the far "right-hand" end of the spectrum is the picture of pure obstruction and at the "left-hand" end the picture of pure hepatocellular disease. In between are many puzzling intergrades where cell disease is present but of variable extent in relation to obstruction or other factors. The differential diagnosis of jaundice is frequently impossible without biopsy or exploration.

Features favoring diagnosis of *purely obstructive* elements are as follows:

(1) lack of systemic manifestations in the nature of malaise, or chronic illness; maintenance of appetite;

(2) a history of pain characteristic of colic;

(3) acholic stools with increased bile in the urine; and

(4) an increased proportion of direct-reacting bilirubin with an elevated alkaline phosphatase level, a normal prothrombin

response to administered vitamin K, a normal or nearly normal albumin concentration, with normal thymol turbidity and cephalin flocculation, stool and urine urobilinogen low or zero.

Crystals of bile acids or cholesterol in the duodenum favor the diagnosis of stone. By sharp contrast at the left-hand end of the spectrum in *hepatocellular disease* of the type associated with acute or chronic hepatitis or cirrhosis, we find as favoring diagnostic factors:

(1) considerable malaise, fever, nausea, vomiting (especially marked in acute hepatitis or homologous serum jaundice); total loss of appetite;

(2) no pain, except in severe hepatic necrosis; and

(3) the preponderance of direct-reacting bilirubin not so great, usually below 70 per cent. Alkaline phosphatase elevation is less marked and appears only in the early stages of acute hepatitis. The prothrombin response to administered vitamin K is sluggish. If the albumin concentration is low, it is significant only if there is no overloading of water or salt. It then indicates severe cell disease.

Between these two ends of the spectrum there are a whole series of gradations and a large intermediate group in which differential diagnosis cannot successfully be based on clinical tests. Splenomegaly and increased hemolysis are strong evidences against obstructive jaundice although patients with longstanding hemolytic processes may later develop gallstones and acute cholecystitis or choledocholithiasis with obstruction.

The group described as cholangiolitis occupies a midposition in this spectrum with signs of both obstructive and intrahepatic disease. This syndrome is discussed in detail in a subsequent section of this chapter.

The liver containing a tumor presents metabolic changes depending on the extent of the tumor and its obstruction of biliary ducts. An elevation of the alkaline phosphatase concentration and anemia disproportional to external blood loss are characteristic. Signs of hepatic cell failure are only seen late, or in hepatoma.

When the differential diagnosis by clinical and chemical means remains dubious, two steps remain.

(1) *Needle biopsy* of the liver. If the liver is easily palpable anteriorly under the costal margin or in the epigastrium, biopsy is best done in the operating room with a tiny anterior skin incision, taking two or three cones of tissue out of the liver for histologic diagnosis. The patient is kept under observation for two or three hours to be sure that bleeding is not troublesome. Hepatic biopsy through the back or axilla involves the hazard of injury to the lungs or pleura. When metastatic disease is feared, peritoneoscopy may be helpful and save the patient a few days in the hospital, but in our experience it has only rarely been useful, and is employed much less frequently than needle biopsy.

(2) *Exploration.* This will yield a definitive result and, frequently, with less inconvenience to the patient than a long series of less conclusive but more time-consuming tests. The hazard lies in exposing a patient with acute hepatocellular disease to the dangers of exploration and anesthesia. The surgeon should therefore seek out these signs, and if they are less prominent than those of obstruction, or if obstruction appears to play an aggravating role, exploration is undertaken. In this situation, unlike many others involving critically ill patients, local anesthesia has a positive indication, as it involves less depletion of liver glycogen and less hepatic inactivation than most other agents.

Section IV.   Treatment of the Patient with Obstructive Jaundice

A. GENERAL PLAN

When the evidence favors an obstructive process, data can be gathered to assist in the differential diagnosis between stone and tumor. The accurate employment of X-rays, duodenal cytologic studies, repeated physical examination of the patient for palpable mass, the presence or absence of a large gallbladder, and the other detailed steps in the differential diagnosis of hepatic obstruction are beyond the scope of this book. From the point of view of metabolic management, several points are worth emphasis.

1. No Delay

Once the patient has been in the hospital for study for a few days or a week with severe jaundice of an obstructive type, we favor moving on fairly rapidly to definitive surgery. The number of X-ray and other diagnostic studies which can be stacked up for the patient's record is quite impressive. But the final answer will come only from laparotomy, and this should not be postponed too long. The metabolic gain of relieving the obstruction far outweighs the benefits of slightly more precise diagnosis gained only at the expense of long delay.

In the differential diagnosis between cell disease and obstruction, needle biopsy is vitally important; exploratory laparotomy occupies the same key position in the differential diagnosis of stone versus tumor where obstruction is present as the predominant process.

2. Preparation of the Liver

It is better to spend those few extra days preparing the patient's liver for operation by good diet or carbohydrate rather than in further exhausting him with innumerable diagnostic tests, many of which require fasting and further depletion of his liver glycogen.

3. Operative Evaluation

When laparotomy itself is undertaken, evaluation must always include liver biopsy, careful exploration of the common duct, and, whenever the surgeon is in doubt, opening the duodenum. In those patients who have been erroneously subjected to pancreatectomy when the lesion was either a benign ulcer of the second portion of the duodenum or some complication of stone, the error could usually have been prevented by simple open duodenotomy with inspection of the ulcerating lesion and biopsy thereof. Biopsy of the pancreas itself through its capsule, and particularly of the head, is notoriously unsatisfactory, but this is not true of duodenotomy. If the lesion is ulcerating in the duodenum, it will show malignant tissue at the edge of the ulcer. We therefore favor open duodenotomy rather early in the operation before extensive instrumentation, cholangiography, or biopsy of the pancreas.

4. X-Ray Study

In most cases, particularly the problem cases, in which cholangiolitis appears to be the most likely explanation, careful X-ray study of the extrahepatic biliary tree should be undertaken as part of operative definition of a problem which is often to be treated medically.

B. OPERATIVE STUDY AND CARE

The preoperative preparation of the patient harboring extrahepatic biliary obstruction is not complicated and need not become so. The important items in operative management are three.

(1) *Avoid excessive use of intravenous salt.* Hypoproteinemia is readily produced in these patients. Their liver disease favors antidiuresis and salt retention.

(2) *The use of concentrated carbohydrate*, either 10 per cent in peripheral vein or 25 per cent in caval catheter, with insulin, appears to favor the laying down of liver glycogen and is a good preoperative maneuver. It need not be carried on for more than a day or two. The volume of water given should be included in the calculation of the rest of the patient's intake to avoid overloading the patient with water. The use of concentrated glucose is in itself a mildly dehydrating procedure; such drying may be beneficial in the patient with liver disease if he has been overhydrated in the past.

(3) *Gentle operation with adequate exposure and good anesthesia with adequate oxygenation* are the

most important metabolic steps in management of these patients. Spinal anesthesia has been recommended for biliary surgery because it allegedly does not involve the epinephrine-like effect and "exhaustion of liver glycogen" associated with ether anesthesia. Spinal anesthesia, for good relaxation and adequate analgesia in the patient undergoing exploration of the upper abdomen, must be at a high level, at least D4 or higher. Unsatisfactory spinal anesthesia in this area has been responsible for many damaging accidents, particularly involving the hepatic duct and artery. It has therefore been our custom to use inhalation anesthesia with endotracheal intubation and a high oxygen concentration, in preference to spinal anesthesia.

The postoperative management of the obstructed liver must include adequate drainage of the extrahepatic biliary tree. The route of egress of the bile from the tube should be free and unobstructed. The subsidence of jaundice after drainage may be rather slow. The relief of itching is immediate and complete.

C. BILIARY DRAINAGE

Staging of operation on the extrahepatic biliary tree has a helpful metabolic effect only where obstruction has been complete and very prolonged. Increasing limitations in the indications for radical pancreaticoduodenectomy have made the staged operation less and less frequent. Its ideal indication lies in those patients who have had a very high degree of hepatic obstruction with high plasma bilirubin concentrations for a period of eight weeks or longer. In such patients a preliminary "breathing spell" for the liver, consisting in extrahepatic biliary drainage for three to four weeks, is a very worth-while preliminary to the long and traumatizing procedure of pancreaticoduodenectomy. At the first operation, the operability of the lesion is tentatively assessed as regards hepatic metastases or spread of growth to the peritoneal cavity. The extensive manipulation, freeing of the duodenum, and exploration of the region of the pancreas and the porta hepatis necessary to make a final decision as to operability

should not be undertaken at this time. The initial biliary decompression is carried out by cholecystostomy if the gallbladder is grossly enlarged, contains bile under pressure, and drains bile freely after it is opened. This can be ascertained further by carrying out a cholangiogram at the time of operation to be sure of the patency of the upper system. If the gallbladder is not enlarged, a choledochostomy can be carried out as a first-stage operation. This does not complicate the second stage if it is done without dissection in the plane behind the duodenum and pancreas.

The relatively poor results from radical pancreaticoduodenectomy have led surgeons increasingly to abandon this operation unless the lesion is favorable by all criteria and shows no evidence of metastases whatsoever. In very early lesions staging is unnecessary. In late obstruction with metastases biliary bypass is to be used.

The hemorrhagic diathesis which used to be such a hazard in the surgery of obstructing liver disease can be completely controlled by the use of parenteral vitamin K preoperatively, liver cell function being assessed simultaneously by study of the prothrombin response.

D. CHOLANGITIS

The characteristic sequences of cholangitis are intermittent shaking chills with fever, deepening of jaundice, and pain in the back. In relation to the severity of the chills and the height of the fever, the malaise is not particularly severe; the analogy with the obstructed urinary tract is interesting here. There is always a bout of jaundice with this episode of chills and fever, and there may be pain around the costal margin, or girdle-type pains. Only rarely is the pain felt high in the scapula, a point of reference associated with disease of the gallbladder.

Spontaneous suppurative cholangitis is rare. Considering the likelihood that the bile contains organisms intermittently as does the urine, it is surprising that prolonged extrahepatic biliary tract obstruction does not more often lead spontaneously to a septic process as urinary tract obstruction leads to suppurative pyelonephritis. The fact is that it does not. The process is usually secondary to operative anastomosis.

A widely patent stoma between the biliary tree and the gastrointestinal tract, as for instance in a choledochojejunostomy, may permit ready reflux into the biliary tree of air and of food or contrast materials taken by mouth. Despite these disturbing findings, cholangitis does not occur unless there is partial obstruction so that drainage out of the bile ducts is inadequate. The commonest cause of suppuration in the biliary tree is an abnormal stoma between the biliary tree and the gastrointestinal tract, which permits inadequate drainage of the contents of the biliary tree into the gastrointestinal tract, but with some communication so as to admit putrid organisms.

E. CLINICAL PROCEDURE IN OBSTRUCTIVE JAUNDICE

The following case combines several features that typify problems in obstructive jaundice. Undue generalization from a single example is unwise; this merely indicates how principles are applied to an individual.

1. *Diagnosis.* Painless jaundice—cause unknown.

2. *Admission Data.* Such a patient might well be a female in her fifties with a history of deepening jaundice without pain, thought to be hepatitis, of three months' duration. Physical examination might characteristically show a mass in the right upper quadrant, possibly liver, possibly tumor. It does not resemble gallbladder. She has formerly been obese.

URINE. Bilirubin strongly positive. Otherwise negative.

HEMATOLOGY

Hematocrit—36
Leucocyte count and smear—normal
Stool guaiac—+

BLOOD CHEMICAL ANALYSES

Blood urea nitrogen—15 mg. per 100 ml.
Plasma protein—6.5 gm. per 100 ml.
A/G = 5.2/1.3
Plasma chloride—100 mE. per l.
Plasma sodium—140 mE. per l.

Plasma potassium—4.3 mE. per l.
Cholesterol—225 mg. per 100 ml.
Carbon dioxide combining power—28 mE. per l.
Bilirubin—14 mg. per 100 ml. total, 12 mg. per 100 ml. direct
Thymol—normal
Alkaline phosphatase—18 B.U.
Prothrombin time—60 per cent normal
Bleeding and clotting times—normal
Blood is grouped and crossmatched.

WEIGHT. 62 kg. Normal weight 70 kg.

3. *Interpretation and General Plan.* In such a case all signs point to obstruction, and both the clinical and chemical data favor this interpretation. The patient's condition would seem to be good: weight loss is only 8 kg. from obesity, renal function evidently normal, coagulation normal. X-rays might show external duodenal pressure but little else. Duodenal drainage is not done in such a case. The choice of peritoneoscopy, liver biopsy or exploration is considered. It is felt that exploration offers the most information, but should an operable pancreatic neoplasm be found, the patient must be able to withstand pancreaticoduodenectomy. Therefore an exploration is not to be approached lightly.

The high proportion of direct-reacting bilirubin strongly suggests obstruction but is of no help in the differential diagnosis of stone versus tumor. The prothrombin is not remarkably or dangerously low; nonetheless its response to vitamin K will be of interest. The mid-range alkaline phosphatase also fits uninfected obstruction.

The normalcy of the acid-base and electrolyte profile in such a case is eloquent evidence of lack of serious systemic repercussion from the obstructed liver.

4. *Preoperative Study and Care.* Studies and care occupy four days.

DIET AND ORDERS. Vitamin K, 50 mg. subcutaneously, is given daily. Diet with supplementary feedings as tolerated is ordered.

PARENTERAL THERAPY. None is given until the day before operation, when she receives 1000 ml. of 10 per cent glucose by vein.

PROGRESS EVALUATION. Her prothrombin rises to 85 per cent. Repeated stool examinations show a trace of blood. There is little other change. A nasogastric tube is inserted the morning of the operation.

5. *Operation.* ANESTHESIA. In such a case we favor a high-oxygen endotracheal-inhalation anesthesia.

OPERATIVE PROCEDURE. A small sloping subcostal incision might well reveal a favorable pancreatic neoplasm. If, as the incision is extended, a positive node, metastasis, or other spread is found, a cholecystojejunostomy only should be done; otherwise a resection.

PARENTERAL THERAPY. Quantitative blood replacement is carried out. On the day of operation, 1500 ml. of 5 per cent dextrose in water and 500 ml. of normal saline solution are given to cover tube losses.

6. *Postoperative Study and Care.* "In-balance" treatment is given intravenously for a few days. The patient's oral intake may be adequate by the third day, and no further intravenous therapy is given if resection is not done. Oral intake is pushed with the social objective of discharge as soon as possible for this patient if inoperable malignancy has been found.

After pancreaticoduodenectomy the course is so variable that no single pattern is identifiable; as in other anastomotic operations there is nothing to be gained from premature forcing of oral intake.

In either event a transient worsening of the jaundice may occur, but there will be little evidence of hepatic cell failure in this purely obstructive complex. If the biliary anastomosis functions well, the jaundice will gradually clear, the depigmentation of the skin taking somewhat longer to reach normal than the blood bilirubin concentration.

Section V.   Surgery in the Face of Parenchymatous Liver Disease

Although liver failure is not a common primary cause of death in surgical illness arising from other sources, even including shock and peritonitis, it always plays some role. By contrast, the occurrence of surgical trauma in the presence of severe parenchymatous liver cell disease is a life-endangering event. Such surgery is undertaken either under a questioning diagnosis of partial obstruction, or specifically to treat the sequelae of the liver lesion itself.

A. NOMENCLATURE, CLASSIFICATION, AND SALIENT SURGICAL FEATURES OF LIVER CELL DISEASE

In the acute phase, the terms "hepatitis" and "hepatic necrosis" are broad enough to include the many types of pathology covered by the terms "catarrhal jaundice," "infectious hepatitis," and "homologous serum jaundice." "Acute" or "subacute" "yellow atrophy" falls into this group also. Despite repeated attempts, no completely satisfactory standard nomenclature has been developed which can be applied clinically. The term "acute hepatitis" will have to do.

In chronic liver disease the term "cirrhosis" is ancient, honorable, and nonspecific; recently it has been possible in some cases to differentiate, by history or his tology between postnecrotic cirrhosis and thegroup, of cirrhoses that are alcoholic or nutritional in origin. Surgically, their effects on convalescence are about the same.

Within this group of chronic liver disorders there is an important clinical distinction between the "dry-yellow" ones and the "wet-white" ones. By this is meant that the superimposition of acute cellular deterioration on chronic cirrhosis produces jaundice, may not be accompanied by so much ascites, and is a very poor setting for surgery: hepatic coma is near. Liver biopsy shows fibrosis, fatty changes, hyaline degeneration, and necrosis. These are the "dry-yellow" ones. By contrast, those patients with stabilized chronic disease have some anemia, may have ascites and edema, but will tolerate anesthesia and trauma moderately well. There is more histologic fibrosis, and less necrosis. These are the "wet-white" ones.* It may seem paradoxical that, in obstruction, marked jaundice even of long standing does not bode ill for operative recovery, while in chronic liver cell disease it is a very ominous sign. It is protoplasmic function of good liver cells that the surgical patient needs for recovery; a moment's reflection indicates no paradox, since in obstruction the jaundice is not due to cell failure, while in cirrhosis it is.

B. PATHOLOGIC BIOCHEMISTRY

A patient dying of liver cell failure after operation shows readily demonstrable alterations in the metabolism of fat, carbohydrate, protein, pigment, hormones, drugs, water, and electrolyte. A detailed description of the terminal events in liver failure is beyond the scope of this book. The clinical surgical defects of this state are:

(1) hypoalbuminemia and hyperglobulinemia;
(2) an inability to oxidize glucose normally, with resulting lactic acid accumulation;
(3) marked intolerance to opiates, barbiturates, and anesthesia;
(4) antidiuresis, water loading, and hyponatremia;
(5) salt retention;
(6) an inability to conjugate and oxidize fat (for example, cholesterol) and
(7) abnormal metabolism of protein, hormones, and pigments.

An understanding of this widespread disorder is helpful in treatment; acidosis, hypoproteinemia, and water-logging may be avoided. But unfortunately we have no lever on these factors that lets us pry them upward toward normal; their enumeration is singularly unrewarding in the positive sense, though they must all be given respect in treatment. They are limiting factors, not pathways to success. They will return to normal only with return of cell function. They are danger signs.

---

* We are indebted to Dr. C. S. Davidson for this helpful terminology.

The interest that attaches to ammonia concentrations in liver disease arises from the fact that their elevation constitutes not only a danger sign but also a guide-mark to success—success at least in the limited sense of abatement of some of the signs and symptoms of liver failure, particularly coma when it is "exogenous," that is, resulting from a large load of ammonia and ammonia precursors (as when there is blood being digested in the gut and the products absorbed).

1. Ammonia Metabolism

Normally, the kidney is the site of ammonia formation from glutamine; yet the majority of urinary excretion of ammonia occurs only after hepatic synthesis to urea. The ammonia concentration in the renal vein is normally about twice that of peripheral arterial blood. After a heavy meal the portal blood ammonia rises to 1000 to 2000 mg. per 100 ml. because of ammonia formed by bacterial action in the gut, a process outside the physiologic interior of the body.

There is a very sharp gradient of ammonia clearance across the liver, the portal vein concentration being 1200 mcg. per 100 ml. and the peripheral concentration about 100 mcg. per 100 ml. The normal pathway for inactivation of ammonia is through synthesis of urea in the liver.

The normal cycle has a secondary pathway involving the formation of glutamine from ammonia and glutamic acid, the deamination and excretion of ammonia by the kidney, and recirculation of the glutamate. High ammonia levels therefore deplete tissue of glutamic acid; this is a mechanism by which symptoms are produced in the central nervous system. Brain tissue needs glutamic acid for a number of functions including potassium transport. Glutamic acid is also the source of the intermediary known as alpha-keto-glutarate, which acts as an important link in the Krebs cycle by which carbohydrate is taken from citrate to acetate, yielding energy, carbon dioxide, and water. Thus, when ammonia concentrations are high and glutamic acid "pre-empted" as glutamine, there is disturbance in cellular energy production.

The brain is impermeable to alpha-keto-glutarate and glutamate, but ammonia and glutamic acid can enter; there is therefore a selective interference with brain function as ammonia enters and binds metabolites present in the brain.

Muscle tissue can take out about 40 per cent of the ammonia presented to it. Diamox (acetazolamide) evidently impairs the capacity of muscle to clear ammonia. When portal concentrations are high, liver urea synthesis cannot keep pace; if the patient is sick, the resulting high peripheral level is more than muscle can deal with, particularly in a catabolic period.

In the colon, protein-plus-bacteria leads to the formation of ammonia. Blood itself is a greater and more potent producer of ammonia than the same weight of lean meat. In a ureteroenterostomy, ammonia production is very prominent because of bacterial action on urea. Production of ammonia in the colon thus results from the action of proteolytic bacteria on protein in the gut, and of urea-splitting organisms on the urea in the urine. When urine is in the gut the two processes are combined in the same site.

Antibiotics block the growth of gut organisms active in forming ammonia from protein; enemas or cathartics can be used to remove the blood that acts as a precursor.

At the normal *p*H of blood, about 1 per cent is present as ammonia and 99 per cent present as ammonium. In alkalosis, the ammonia concentration is relatively increased. Alkalosis thus makes coma worse. Sodium glutamate increases alkalosis and there is therefore a potentially vicious cycle when glutamate is used. Yet ammonia intoxication produces an electrocardiographic change resembling hyperkalemia and acidosis, which are additive in producing these changes.

The correlation of ammonia levels with coma is uncertain at best, and more reliable in exogenous (gastrointestinal bleeding) than endogenous (liver failure) ammonia intoxication. When coma is associated with ammonia concentrations as high as 300 to 400 mcg. per 100 ml., survival is rare.

If sodium glutamate is to be used, it must be used liberally, giving 80 to 120 gm. as a 6 per cent solution over twenty-four to thirty-six hours. This involves almost 1000 mE. of sodium; the effect on acid-base balance, as the glutamate is consumed, is obvious. Any rise in *p*H makes the symptoms of ammonia intoxication worse. Arginine, in doses up to 25 gm., can be used; it speeds up urea synthesis. Arginine glutamate is appealing, as it accomplishes these ends without a base load.

Under certain circumstances, as in acute yellow atrophy, glutamate treatment results in a rise in ammonia and, as a general rule, it is not effective in endogenous coma.

Ammonia is freely dialyzable and can be removed by dialysis on an artificial kidney. Unfortunately, the heparinization incident to hemodialysis is not easily controllable in patients with liver disease and is dangerous if the patient is bleeding. This mode of treatment has therefore not been widely used.

In the "resting" cirrhotic (that is, not bleeding or postoperative) a low-protein diet is the most effective way of avoiding ammonia intoxication; orally administered antibiotics permit the maintenance of a higher protein content in the diet.

Whatever the mechanism, clear abatement of ammonia intoxication is brought about by the administration of glutamic acid as sodium glutamate. Yet, one cannot expect all the other diffuse chemical changes of liver coma to improve on glutamate; it is specific for ammonia intoxication and therefore most effective in those cases in which ammonia is the sole or predominant cause of the symptoms. This (as mentioned) is characteristic of exogenous (that is, shunt or hemorrhage) coma as versus endogenous (that is, resting cirrhotic deterioration) coma.

In summary, from the recent interest in ammonia metabolism has come the following practical points:

a. *Ammonia intoxication* is seen in three settings:
   (1) hepatocellular deterioration, either resting or after trauma;
   (2) portocaval shunt, with protein digestion in the gut, or
   (3) in either of the above, with blood in the gut.

b. *Glutamate therapy* must be very energetic

(80 to 120 gm. of sodium glutamate per day) in order to affect the signs of ammonia intoxication.

c. *Blood in the gut* is a rich source of ammonia and should be removed by aspiration or laxative, as soon as possible. Blood is a more fertile source of ammonia than is the same weight of protein as meat.

d. *The clinical determination of blood ammonia* and its quantitative downward titration with glutamate is most useful in exogenous ammonia intoxication (from blood or shunt surgery) and least useful in endogenous coma (from hepatitis, hepatic necrosis, cirrhosis).

e. *Alkalosis makes ammonia intoxication worse* and results either from hyperventilation in liver coma or the use of large amounts of sodium glutamate, sodium citrate, and other bicarbonate precursors.

f. *Meat feeding* must be considered as a source of symptoms in certain cases of severe liver disease, or after shunt surgery.

g. In certain cases of *massive gastrointestinal bleeding* the blood ammonia may be useful in differential diagnosis, an elevation pointing to liver disease (a varix hemorrhage) rather than ulcer.

h. Ammonia does not *hurt the liver;* it merely reflects liver cell disease.

i. *Intestinal antibiotics* reduce the formation of ammonia in the gut, when blood is present or threatened.

j. *Arginine* speeds urea synthesis and is therefore an ammonia antagonist.

The serum cholinesterase activity is held by some to be of value in the management of chronic liver disease and in the selection of patients and timing of procedures in shunt surgery. The method is a simple colorimetric measurement of pH change following the addition of acetylcholine to the serum. The decreased serum cholinesterase activity seems to correlate with the level of circulating albumin. The cholinesterase activity falls but slowly after the onset of acute hepatic necrosis, but reflects nicely the slow changes of liver cell function in chronic liver disease. A normal or rising value in the cirrhotic suggests a good prognosis both for operative survival and long-term functional result. The normal value is 0.5 delta pH unit per hour;

if below 0.2, outlook is very poor. If it is over 0.35 unit, surgical outlook is good. Moderate lowering is also seen in a variety of nutritional and hematologic diseases; the serial changes in a single patient are the most significant.

C. EMERGENCY OPERATION IN THE PRESENCE OF LIVER CELL DISEASE, CARRIED OUT UNDER A QUESTIONABLE DIAGNOSIS

Acute hepatic processes that stretch Glisson's capsule may give many of the symptoms, physical findings, and laboratory results associated with acute cholecystitis. Hepatocellular jaundice may masquerade as obstruction. It is the rare surgeon who has not at some time explored one of these patients to find to his sorrow an acutely edematous liver stretching its capsule with a rounded edge, a very yellow appearance, and in some instances this superimposed on an obviously ancient process involving considerable regeneration. The finding of any suspicion of liver disease at all is usually an absolute indication for liver biopsy. In the setting of acute or subacute yellow atrophy, the prognosis for the patient is serious enough without compounding it by the further time required for open liver biopsy; a needle biopsy is sufficient. A quick inspection is made to assure oneself as to whether or not there is actually a superimposed element of obstruction of the common duct, after which the wound is closed and the patient is returned to the ward. Several simple steps are taken.

(1) *Provide the liver with plenty of utilizable glucose.* This is an indication for the use of a caval catheter, and glucose alone or glucose "covered" with insulin, again remembering that the sudden cessation of such an infusion will produce a hypoglycemic reaction unless it is "covered" with further glucose.

(2) *Give antibiotics generously.* The diseased and anoxic edematous liver makes the patient particularly vulnerable to the development of sepsis.

(3) *Watch for ammonia intoxication.* If the patient subsides into a disoriented or semicomatose condition with a flapping tremor and a mousy odor on his breath, ammonia intoxication is probable. The measures to

take are cleansing of blood and feces from the gastrointestinal tract by enema or laxative, avoidance of meat in the diet, and the administration of sodium glutamate intravenously. In acute liver failure after exploration, one cannot expect too much of glutamate; this is endogenous hepatic cell failure exacerbated by surgery, leading to coma and not due to ammonia alone.

(4) *If the patient becomes distended, with vomiting*, indwelling gastric suction tube and the avoidance of feeding, particularly of protein, are important.

(5) *Serial observation of blood ammonia and bilirubin* indicates the success or failure of therapy, as crude chemical indices of a complex clinical state.

(6) *Concentrated albumin should be used* to maintain the plasma albumin concentration; without this step, recovery is highly unlikely.

(7) *Vitamin K_1 oxide should be used* if hypoprothrombinemia develops.

(8) *Cortisone* has a remarkably helpful effect* in some instances of acute liver disease, in promoting detoxification and pigment excretion. It should be used without hesitation in this acute and critical situation. The dose is 150 mg. per day intravenously or 100 mg. by mouth. Intramuscular cortisone is less effective. The poor conjugation seen in liver disease makes for higher blood levels; despite this abnormal metabolism the steroids appear to be helpful. Their later tapering and coverage with adrenocorticotropic hormone should follow standard procedure (see Chapter 43).

D. ELECTIVE OPERATION IN THE PRESENCE OF KNOWN CHRONIC LIVER DISEASE

The diagnostic uncertainty which has mistakenly led to laparotomy in the type of case just described does not extend to the performance of elective surgery in the face of chronic liver disease. A common situation is that of the patient with mild or moderately severe cirrhosis, who also has gallstones and

---

* The term "cortisone" here covers the use of either cortisone or related compounds by mouth, or hydrocortisone by vein.

requires cholecystectomy. Patients with cirrhosis develop duodenal ulcer, carcinoma of the stomach, carcinoma of the colon, and other diseases that require elective operation. Patients with heart disease may need definitive surgery for heart disease in the presence of severe cardiac or alcoholic cirrhosis.

In these instances, the measures taken are similar to those already described. They are rarely as urgent as in the jaundiced patient with liver failure who has undergone exploration.

(1) *Avoid excessive infusions* of water and salt. Daily or triweekly weighing of the patient is essential in management.

(2) *Provide carbohydrate* intravenously or by mouth in suitable quantities. Avoid giving the patient meat or high-protein feedings during the period of the acute surgical episode.

(3) *Study the coagulation mechanism* so as to avoid operation in the face of an excessive bleeding tendency, on the basis of either hypoprothrombinemia or other defects. Preliminary study of the patient's bleeding time, clotting time, platelet count, and prothrombin concentration is essential. Defects in prothrombin concentration may be dealt with by the parenteral administration of vitamin K. Abnormalities of clotting time suggest a fibrinogen defect, and of platelet count, hypersplenism. Patients with chronic congestive liver disease who also have splenomegaly may suffer from hypersplenism, as indicated by a pancytopenia or by a relative absence of certain formed elements of the blood while others remain almost normal.

(4) *Correct hypoalbuminemia* by the administration of albumin. In chronic liver disease this should be done gradually and should not be postponed until the day before surgery; a period of approximately four days should be used to build up plasma albumin concentration to normal. This will often result in diuresis. The patient should be allowed to complete his diuresis and become stabilized before surgery.

(5) *Provide for adequate incision, good exposure, and adequate oxygenation* under endotracheal anesthesia with relaxation; these factors loom

large as particularly important factors in the surgical care of the patient with chronic liver disease.

(6) *Remember, as in the previous situation, that cortisone is helpful;* it may be used preoperatively here. It is particularly important if there is an element of viral hepatitis or postnecrotic cirrhosis in the liver lesion. The course of cortisone should be limited to five to seven days unless cholangiolitis is found, in which case a very prolonged course may be helpful. Antacid therapy must be given.

Section VI. Shunt Surgery

A. ELECTIVE SHUNT SURGERY

The metabolic care of patients undergoing elective venous anastomotic operations for portal hypertension involves the foregoing principles, modified only to the extent that ascites may be present, multiple paracenteses required, and time for a prolonged preparation available. Nutritional preparation of a sort not available in other instances and in some cases lasting several months may be of value.

The steps just enumerated for immediate care of patients with liver disease will not be reviewed again. Nutritional measures include a diet high in calories, with large amounts of the vitamin B group and a low sodium intake. Protein is not harmful in the diet if there is not an ammonia problem; it is important to reemphasize that ammonia does not hurt the liver—it is merely a reflection of liver cell disease. Avoidance of alcohol, adoption of prolonged rest, and good diet are often followed by a remarkable regeneration of good liver tissue.

Oligemic shock, hypotension, anoxia, or prolonged deficiency of blood flow for any reason produces a severe acute exacerbation of chronic liver cell disease. Blood replacement must therefore be precise and immediate. The effects of anesthesia and trauma alone may be expected to produce a rise in bilirubin levels and an increase in azotemia after such surgery; oligemia greatly accelerates this trend. Anemia will be more severe if blood replacement involves old or poorly preserved blood or minor degrees of incompatibility.

The most favorable patients for shunt surgery are those who have never been in coma, have no ascites, carry an albumin concentration of over 3.2 gm. per 100 ml. and a bilirubin below 1.5 mg. per 100 ml. In such patients dietary management will cause marked improvement, and a test salt load will not result in too drastic a fall in protein concentration.

There is an approximate inverse relation between portal pressure and albumin concentration, and following a good shunt there is a marked decrease in the tendency to retain water and salt. This diuresis is responsible for a considerable fraction of the early rise in plasma albumin concentration after a good shunt.

Where leucopenia, thrombocytopenia, or anemia (or pancytopenia) coexists with a big spleen and portal hypertension, the formation of an adequate shunt will usually result in relief of the hypersplenism.

An example of case preparation in this category is given below.

B. CLINICAL PROCEDURE IN ELECTIVE SHUNT SURGERY

The following procedure typifies many features of elective shunt surgery and includes aspects from several representative cases.

1. *Diagnosis.* Portal cirrhosis, with massive varix bleeding three months previously.

2. *Admission Data.* Such a patient might well be a female in her fifties with a history of alcoholism in the past, and two episodes of hemorrhage, one massive, occurring three months ago. Typically, jaundice has occurred only after bleeding. Liver and spleen are enlarged, and wasting of peripheral tissue, angiomas, smooth tongue, and moderate ascites are characteristic.

WEIGHT.   62 kg. Three months ago, 58 kg.
URINE.   Negative

HEMATOLOGY

Hematocrit—32
Leucocyte count—4500 per cu. mm.
Platelet count—70,000 per cu. mm.

BLOOD CHEMICAL ANALYSES

Blood urea nitrogen—15 mg. per 100 ml.
Plasma protein—4.5 gm. per 100 ml.
$$A/G = 2.0/2.5$$
Plasma sodium—126 mE. per l.
Plasma potassium—4.9 mE. per l.
Blood sugar—100 mg. per 100 ml.
Cholesterol—250 mg. per 100 ml.
Carbon dioxide combining power—18 mE. per l.
Plasma bilirubin—1.5 mg. per 100 ml.
Thymol—elevated
Prothrombin—60 per cent

3. *Interpretation and General Plan.* The lack of jaundice (the bilirubin elevation is so small as to be negligible) and two months of good nutritional regimen (on physician's orders) with low sodium and without alcohol are favorable. The ascites and hypoproteinemia with some sodium-potassium shift and slight acidosis indicate the extent of the patient's metabolic derangement. The plan is to tap her ascites, give albumin, avoid further over-watering, and carry out a portacaval shunt. In such a case, the low sodium concentration is largely of dilutional origin despite the low sodium intake. The antidiuresis of liver disease is present, with an expanded body sodium level, as shown by the ascites. The indications for shunt surgery rest wholly on her past hemorrhage, large varices as shown by X-ray, and her current avoidance of alcohol. Without motivation to self-improvement, the value of shunt surgery is questionable. The large spleen and low leucocyte and platelet counts suggest some degree of hypersplenism.

4. *Preoperative Study and Care.* The patient enters the hospital a week before the date set for operation.

STUDY.   X-rays of chest, esophagus, and stomach are made. Albumin concentration is studied after treatment. The prothrombin responds to parenterally administered vitamin K. The other chemical determinations are repeated once before operation. Paracentesis is 2500 ml. There is 20 per cent re-tention of Bromsulphalein. Bleeding and clotting indices are normal.

DIET AND ORDERS.   A high-calorie, high-protein diet is given with vitamin B complex and crude liver intramuscularly daily, and a low sodium intake is imposed. Vitamin C is given in large amounts.

PARENTERAL THERAPY.   Three units of whole blood are transfused in a week; two units of albumin are administered every other day for three doses. No other fluids are given intravenously, and the total intake of water is restricted to 1200 ml. The patient is weighed daily.

PROGRESS EVALUATION.   She has taken 3000 calories a day, her most important step. Response has been gratifying. In addition to the 2.5 kg. lost on paracentesis, the patient has had a good diuresis on albumin. She has lost an additional kilogram; the albumin concentration is 3.8 gm. per 100 ml., her sodium concentration has risen to 135 mE. per l. and potassium dropped to 4.1 mE. per l. The carbon dioxide combining power is 25 mE. per l. When all the patient's reactions are this favorable, she will never be in better condition for operation.

5. *Operation.* ANESTHESIA.   Endotracheal high-oxygen inhalation.

OPERATIVE PROCEDURE.   Portacaval anastomosis.

PARENTERAL THERAPY.   Quantitative blood replacement is carried out, measured by sponge weights: the amount is 2500 ml. No salt and minimal water (1200 ml.) are given.

6. *Postoperative Study and Care*

STUDY.   The patient is weighed daily. She should lose weight daily (250 to 350 gm.) until oral intake is reestablished. The strong antidiuresis seen in chronic liver disease makes this hard to achieve.

PARENTERAL THERAPY.   Nonetheless, she should be given only 1000 ml. of water daily and 2 units of albumin every two days for three doses. When she starts to eat significantly she is given no more intravenous fluids.

PROGRESS EVALUATION.   The sodium-potassium shift would be expected after operation, the concentrations changing to about

126 and 5.1 mE. per l. respectively. The water restriction and albumin therapy helped to hold this to reasonable limits. The patient's clinical progress, if good, renders ammonia determinations unnecessary. Only with poor response or postoperative bleeding need detailed attention be devoted to raised ammonia levels.

C. EMERGENCY SHUNT SURGERY FOR BLEEDING

Success or failure here depends on two factors. One is the size of the shunt and the rapidity or dexterity with which it can be made. The other is the ability of the liver and the patient to withstand the ultimate challenge in disordered liver function: shock, operation, and a gut full of blood.

Twenty-four hours of control or attempted control by balloon permits restoration of blood volume, assessment of pathologic tendency to bleed, restoration of plasma albumin concentration, and, above all, removal of blood from the gut. This must be done by enema and purging, the latter by magnesium sulfate distal to the balloon if necessary. The effects of treatment on blood ammonia may be assayed by chemical analysis.

Just as in ulcer bleeding, here also in varix bleeding, the second hospital day is the day of decision. If bleeding stops, as judged by the aspiration data and homeostasis, the balloon may be left in with trials of deflation. *Is a well-placed balloon does not stop the bleeding, it casts serious doubt on the diagnosis of bleeding esophageal varices.* The move to operation should begin.

Too long a period of balloon tamponade cannot be tolerated unless bleeding stops. The total stimulus to hepatic degeneration persists from the *onset* of hemorrhage to about twenty-four hours *after* completion of successful operation (or cessation of bleeding). Undue prolongation of this period cannot help but be deleterious.

Fixation of the balloon to the nose under tension invites ulceration. If there is bleeding above the balloon, aspiration is a hazard. The tube demands expert use, continuous professional attention (with gastric lavage and aspiration), and position check by X-ray.

The steps surrounding operation are based on precisely the same principle, as already outlined in the foregoing and summarized as follows:

(1) supply energy (carbohydrate) for the liver cell;

(2) beware of too much water and salt— use small infusion;

(3) follow detailed program for albumin and prothrombin;

(4) use antibiotics—the sick liver is vulnerable;

(5) assure accurate blood volume therapy —pressure and flow are vital;

(6) keep the ammonia down—use glutamate or other antiammonia measures as indicated;

(7) wash blood out of the gut—use enemas.

Experience with glutamate in this acute situation indicates its possible utility, but the sodium load is very considerable.

Cortisone and hypothermia both appear to have a place here. It would be logical to employ hypothermia to spare the liver the effects of anoxia, but it has been used with only moderate success. The hemorrhagic state in hypothermia is especially undesirable in these cases. Cortisone may potentiate the vasoconstrictor activity of norepinephrine and epinephrine and improve the state of the liver cell. A flat recommendation on either score is impossible.

Transesophageal ligature of varices, high gastric ligature, or other operative steps involve virtually the same hazards as a shunt with substantially less prospect of lasting benefit.

If tamponade stops the bleeding, the balloon may be left in for prolonged periods, particularly if traction is not used. This must depend on the details of patient tolerance and site of bleeding. If low gastric varices are at fault, prolonged tamponade is difficult.

Section VII.   Miscellaneous Hepatic Problems

A. CHOLANGIOLITIS

The term "cholangiolitis" refers to an inflammatory process of the small intrahepatic bile ducts (cholangioles). Otherwise known as "primary biliary cirrhosis," this lesion was first clearly described by Watson, whose eponym is often used. The biochemical changes produced are those of obstruction of the biliary tract, though there is no obstructing lesion distal to the porta hepatis. There is "intrahepatic ductal obstruction." The histologic picture is that of bile-duct proliferation, bile stasis, round cell infiltration in the portal areas, and some disorganization of liver cell architecture. The process goes on gradually over a period of years to that of full-blown biliary cirrhosis. Most of the cases of biliary cirrhosis described in the past have been due to this lesion rather than to extrahepatic obstruction of the common duct. In fact, severe cirrhosis due to common-duct obstruction alone is a rarity. Obstruction of the common duct, as already mentioned, is surprisingly free of irreversible or long-term changes in liver cell function and architecture. The liver in cholangiolitis, by contrast, is severely damaged and the outlook is very poor regardless of any measures now available.

1. Diagnosis

The diagnosis of cholangiolitis should be suspected:
  (1) in jaundiced women (it is *very* rare in men);
  (2) when itching is prominent;
  (3) when pain is not severe;
  (4) when the liver is large, smooth, and rounded;
  (5) with "obstructive" chemistry and a high alkaline phosphatase concentration; and
  (6) with a high cholesterol concentration and xanthomas (in late cases).

2. Exploration and Choledochostomy

Extrahepatic biliary drainage often relieves the severe itching that is so charac-

teristic of the disease. Because of the strong superficial resemblance of cholangiolitis to extrahepatic obstruction due to stone or tumor, exploration of the extrahepatic biliary tree and X-ray delineation by cholangiogram are a necessary preliminary to establishment of the diagnosis.

For these reasons, exploratory operation is not only rational and well tolerated by the patient, but absolutely essential. It rules out curable extrahepatic obstruction. The insertion of common-duct drainage is of symptomatic benefit; liver biopsy is important.

The mechanism by which extrahepatic bile drainage relieves the patient's itching is obscure, but the evidence suggests that the balance of bile acids (which normally recirculate from the gut) is sufficiently negative after drainage to lower the level of some biliary-excreted compound which produces itching. Postoperatively these patients receive some symptomatic benefit and further lowering of biliary pigments in the blood by the use of cortisone.

The late manifestations of the disease include diffuse abnormalities of fat metabolism, xanthomatosis, and a downward pathway that is primarily arteriosclerotic. Ascites, splenomegaly, and esophageal varices are rare.

B. PYLEPHLEBITIS

This term means "a phlebitis of the portal vein" and is confined to those conditions in which there is ascending infection of the portal system. Classically this has been produced by appendicitis, and most of the cases reported in the literature are appendiceal in origin. In the days before the use of antibiotics, the occurrence of a shaking chill or any degree of jaundice in the face of appendicitis was regarded as *prima facie* evidence for pylephlebitis. The disease is rarer now but does still occur, and when it occurs in the face of antibiotic therapy it is very ominous. Treatment lies in adequate drainage of the appendiceal area and gentle operation covered by the use of the proper antibiotic in adequate dosage. Excessively traumatic or meddlesome surgery in the region of the appendix is sure to produce additional peritonitis, portal phlebitis, and death. Portal vein ligation is to be avoided.

Portal thrombosis, or thrombosis of the tributaries of the portal vein occurring in the form of mesenteric thrombosis, is a complication of infection in the portal watershed and of tumors growing in the region of the head of the pancreas and the liver porta. It also occurs *de novo* in patients without previous intra-abdominal disease and without any known predisposing factors. In some instances it occurs in patients with a widespread thrombotic tendency.

From the view of metabolic management the most important aspect of mesenteric venous thrombosis is the excessive loss of plasma into the gut. A very rapidly rising hematocrit with abdominal pain and distention is virtually diagnostic of mesenteric venous thrombosis. The patient can be restored to normal pressure and flow by the rapid infusion of large amounts of plasma, dextran, or concentrated albumin, as described in Part II. Unfortunately, the outlook for recovery is so poor that these measures are unavailing. They do prepare the patient for surgical operation and exploration, necessary to salvage those few patients who are capable of recovery after this dangerous vascular accident.

C. THE HEPATORENAL SYNDROME

There are patients with combined hepatic and renal insufficiency; each component makes the other worse and the combination is a dangerous one. Bile pigments may have set the stage for the renal lesion. To this extent, the two are related, but to term this a syndrome is unnecessary. This term was originally used to indicate a specific combination of hepatic and renal failure after severe injury. A high nonprotein nitrogen concentration with low blood urea nitrogen was alleged to occur. Actually, this almost never occurs with a dissociation between the concentration changes of nonprotein nitrogen and urea nitrogen, and, as a rather mystifying term that says more than it means, the name should be dropped.

Patients with severe liver disease are prone to the development of hypotension; they therefore are prone to renal failure. In addition, pigment derived from breakdown of the porphyrin component of hemoglobin is nephrotoxic. Little wonder that the severely jaundiced patient readily goes into renal failure. When he does, we gain no additional knowledge by terming it the "hepatorenal syndrome." "Bile nephrosis" is equally specious as a term. The treatment of the patient rests on the guiding principles in any renal or hepatic failure, both factors being present.

D. METASTATIC CANCER

Patients may have large tumor deposits in the liver without jaundice or liver cell failure. A slightly elevated alkaline phosphatase level may be the only chemical clue. Definitive diagnosis by exploration or needle may be a great service to patient and family even though the news is unhappy. Prolonged hospitalization for repeated X-rays and analysis of the blood chemistry is, by contrast, of little mercy to the patient with only a few months to live. A nice balance between hasty surgery and careful study must be achieved.

With progress of the lesion, liver cell failure occurs with severe jaundice, markedly disordered plasma chemistry, and, in some cases, ammonia intoxication with hepatic coma. Pending the development of effective antitumor therapy we can see little mercy in biochemical heroics that recall the patient to consciousness for a few more hapless days and nights. Hepatic coma is the last friend of the cancer patient; it should not be denied.

Section VIII. The Liver: Notes from the Literature

A. AMMONIA; MANAGEMENT OF CIRRHOTICS

In 1912 Folin and Denis described the origin and significance of the ammonia of portal blood. In 1941 and 1942 Chunn and Harkins studied the fate of gastrointestinal blood, and in 1956 Young *et al.* observed the role of gastrointestinal blood in the nitrogen partition of peripheral blood.

Laws and Johnston (1952) restudied the meat intoxication problem in dogs, believing it to be one of potassium intoxication. McDermott (1954), in a series of papers published initially at about the same time, showed that:

(1) meat intoxication in portacaval shunted dogs was ammonia-linked;

(2) after portacaval shunt in man an "episodic stupor" could similarly be accounted for on the basis of elevated blood ammonia, even in the absence of liver disease, and related to meat ingestion;

(3) liver damage as well as a shunt could account for the elevation of blood ammonia, the latter originating from protein digestion in the gastrointestinal tract from meat, blood, or urea;

(4) glutamate and possibly other ornithine cycle intermediaries could, on occasion, lower the blood ammonia and help the symptom-complex.

This work of McDermott's stimulated a remarkable outpouring of papers on ammonia, both from medical and surgical laboratories, here and abroad. No effort will be made here to review them all. Eiseman *et al.* (1956, a, b, 1957) infused ammonium salts into the carotid artery of dogs and produced changes closely resembling hepatic coma; a period of time with elevated levels was necessary to obtain the effect. They felt the changes were independent of pH, whereas Randall *et al.* (1955) noted that hyperventilation with respiratory alkalosis was one effect of ammonia toxicity, that respiratory acidosis tended to counteract the cerebral effects, and that the dissociation constant of ammonium ion was pH-dependent.

Taking their cue from Randall's finding of severe respiratory alkalosis in ammonia intoxication, Lawrence *et al.* (1957), studied the effect of induced pH change on blood ammonia. They found that lowering pH raised blood ammonia and raising pH lowered blood ammonia. From these data it was possible to calculate the partial pressure of ammonia (pNH$_3$), analogously to the calculation of pCO$_2$ from pH and bicarbonate. The dissociation of NH$_4{}^+$ to NH$_3$ + H$^+$ is favored by alkalinity; this permits a freer permeation of ammonia into the brain tissue, where its harmful effect is manifest. Thus, alkalinity promotes the symptoms of ammonia toxicity as well as increasing the ammonia concentration. The respiratory alkalosis of hepatic coma thus appears, in a sense, as a vicious cycle, the ammonia favoring alkalosis and the alkalosis making the ammonia concentration higher.

Pearlman (1956) depicts a clear fall in blood ammonia levels with glutamate administration (about 25 gm. sodium glutamate in an hour) and a slow but definite correlation between blood ammonia concentration and clinical manifestations. This slow rate of correlation he ascribes to the slow permeability of the brain to ammonia. Pearlman emphasizes that some degree of resilience of liver function must be maintained in order to demonstrate a favorable effect from glutamate.

Welch *et al.* (1956), in a careful review illuminated by considerable personal experience, reemphasize several important aspects of management of the bleeding portal-hypertensive cirrhotic patient. Their own experience included fifty patients with a mortality of 66 per cent, including a 76 per cent mortality in the first hemorrhage. The Sengstaken-Blakemore tube was invariably successful in stopping hemorrhage, but not in producing survival. All who went into coma after hemorrhage died. Intubation, evacuation of intestinal blood, the use of antibiotics, and support of the patient by transfusion and vitamins (especially K) were emphasized. The approach to ammonia determinations (which they suggest carrying out twice a day) and glutamate therapy is enthusiastic. Some good results from cortisone therapy and dialysis are reported. The author concludes his review with a plea for prophylactic shunt surgery, a view with which many would disagree.

The relation of liver disease to the metabolism of this ammonia of gastrointestinal origin (digested meat or blood) has been studied (in addition to those works already discussed) by Phillips *et al.* (1952), Schwartz *et al.* (1954), Traeger *et al.* (1954), Bessman *et al.* (1954), Drapanas *et al.* (1955), Havens and Child (1955), Leffman and Payne (1955), Fisher and Faloon (1956), Patton *et al.* (1956), and Poppell *et al.* (1956).

Relationships of ammonia metabolism to the amino acids and their use in therapy have been reported also by Phear *et al.* (1956), Webster and Davidson (1956), Najarian and Harper (1956), Summerskill *et al.* (1957), and Martin *et al.* (1957).

The elevation of blood ammonia in states of poor hepatic circulation, including shock, and its relation to amino acid metabolism in impaired circulating states has been studied by Horsley *et al.* (1957), Nelson and Seligson (1954), and Svec and Freeman (1939).

The clinical management of patients undergoing shunt surgery, their selection, and the results achieved have been described by many writers. Contributions from these having a large and intensive experience in this field include Whipple (1945, 1946), Sengstaken and Blakemore (1950), Blakemore and Lord (1945), Blakemore (1946, 1947, 1948, a, b), Baronofsky (1949), Blakemore (1951, 1952), Habif *et al.* (1953), Child (1954, 1955), Jahnke *et al.* (1953), Hughes and Jahnke (1955), Dye *et al.* (1957), Linton *et al.* (1947), Linton (1948, 1951, 1953), Linton and Ellis (1956), Lyons and Patton (1956), Cohn and Mathewson (1957), Ebeling *et al.* (1956), Linton (1958), MacPherson *et al.* (1954), Nachlas *et al.* (1955), Rousselot (1949), Welch (1950), Welch *et al.* (1955), Welch and Ramos (1957), Welch (1957), and Large *et al.* (1952).

The problem of shunt surgery in children has been reviewed by Jordan *et al.* (1956) and Hollenberg and Briggs (1955).

Transesophageal ligation was favored for a time by Crile (1950) and Linton and Warren (1953) as an emergency treatment for bleeding varices. A more conservative approach (tamponade and later shunt) has been more satisfactory in most instances.

Catheter studies of portal and hepatic pressures and flows (in man) are to be found in Myers and Taylor (1951), Friedman and Weiner (1951), and Bradley *et al.* (1953).

Ligature of hepatic and/or splenic arteries in portal hypertension and ascites has been reported by Everson and Cole (1948), Rienhoff (1951), Berman *et al.* (1951), Berman and Hull (1952), and Smith *et al.* (1953).

B. THE LIVER; MISCELLANEOUS

Watson and Hoffbauer (1946) described, in a classic article, the entity to which we refer as "cholangiolitic cirrhosis," or "cholangiolitis." The authors point out the former confusion in referring to this as "hypertrophic biliary cirrhosis," and they draw attention to the absence of extrahepatic pathology, as well as the clinical features including severe itching, hypercholesteremia, and the very poor prognosis.

Reviews of the problem of cholangiolitic hepatitis include those by Eliakim and Rachmelewitz (1956) and Lipschitz and Capson (1955).

McSwain *et al.* (1958) present a recent review of the question of the surgical significance of intrahepatic cholangiolitic hepatitis. These workers review eleven cases seen at the Vanderbilt University Hospital and present the clinical and pathologic findings and the results of bile-duct drainage.

The effect of anesthesia and trauma on the liver has been described also by Tagnon *et al.* (1948), Geller and Tagnon (1950), Fairlie *et al.* (1951), and French *et al.* (1952).

The disorder of fluid and electrolyte metabolism seen in cirrhosis of the liver and providing the metabolic background of shunt surgery has been described in detail by the group at New York Hospital (Gilder *et al.*, 1954, a, b) and by Ralli *et al.* (1945), Eisenmenger *et al.* (1949), Faloon *et al.* (1949), Eisenmenger *et al.* (1950), Goodyer *et al.* (1950), Ricketts *et al.* (1951), Chart and

Shipley (1953), Gabuzda *et al.* (1954), Warner *et al.* (1953), and Hyatt and Smith (1954).

The possibility that the water retention is due to abnormalities of secretion or disposal of antidiuretic hormone is studied in the reports of Adlersberg and Fox (1943), White *et al.* (1951), Nelson and Welt (1952), and Schwartz *et al.* (1953).

Van Dyke *et al.* (1950) felt that there was little relationship between abnormal metabolism of antidiuretic hormone and the water retention of hepatic cirrhosis.

The pathogenesis of ascites and the protein abnormalities of liver disease are the subjects of the reports by Myers and Keefer (1935), Butt *et al.* (1939), Post and Patek (1942), and Madden *et al.* (1954).

The effect of paracentesis on cardiac output in patients with tense ascites has been recorded by Kowalski *et al.* (1954).

Iber *et al.* (1957) showed a systematic elevation of amino acids in progressively severe liver disease, but not always in hepatic coma; methionine and tyrosine were those most often elevated; sodium glutamate appeared to be metabolized normally.

Bollman *et al.* (1926) showed that the hepatectomized dog did not form urea from amino acids. The human counterpart of this, allegedly characteristic of severe hepatic disease, is but rarely seen clinically and most particularly is it rare in surgery. Truly massive liver disease must be present with reasonably good urine formation before the blood urea level falls. This is a rare combination. After hepatectomy in the dog, the plasma amino acids rise abruptly, just as they do in hepatic necrosis (Flock *et al.*, 1951, 1953), and the level may be decreased by the administration of glucose (Flock *et al.*, 1952). This suggests that muscle is the most likely source of the compounds, just as it is after severe trauma. Walshe (1953) showed rises in plasma and urine amino acids in parenchymatous liver disease, not shared by obstructive jaundice.

Crowson and More (1955) postulated a combined hepatic and renal lesion where shock was superimposed on prolonged jaundice. They indicated abnormally retained vasopressors, circulating without detoxification in the liver, and producing severe renal ischemia as a possible physiologic relation; additionally, acute hepatic necrosis is a potent source of intracellular pigments. There certainly is excellent clinical evidence to support the concept that the kidney is more vulnerable to hypotensive episodes in the presence of liver disease with jaundice. Boyce (1941) reviews some of these relationships in his monograph. These are the chemical counterparts of the relation postulated in the "hepatorenal" syndrome.

The detailed chemical character of the direct and indirect-reacting bilirubin complexes has been elucidated recently by Billing *et al.* (1957). The direct-reacting bilirubin seems to be a water-soluble mono- or diglucuronide of the quadripyrrole bilirubin nucleus, whereas the indirect reacting material is a hydrolyzed dipyrrole that is lipidsoluble and hence requires alcohol to give the indirect van den Bergh reaction. The preponderance of the direct-reacting moiety, indicating obstruction, remains a useful differential point.

Plough *et al.* (1956) showed that, in chronic liver disease, large intakes of carbohydrate and fat spared endogenous protein catabolism. These data suggest that at low protein intakes, extra calories lead to the formation of fat, whereas at higher protein intakes, the formation of lean tissue is favored.

Bernstein *et al.* (1953) failed to find abnormal secretion, impaired inactivation, or increased sensitivity of renal tubular cells to antidiuretic hormone in cirrhotics. White *et al.* (1951, 1953) found that cardiac patients could not metabolize (that is, excrete) a water load as fast as normal patients, whereas cirrhotic patients could. They also failed to find decreased inactivation of antidiuretic hormone in these patients. They were skeptical of the evidence for overproduction of antidiuretic hormone in these states. Miller and Townsend (1954) showed that cirrhotic liver inactivated antidiuretic hormone as well as normal liver in vitro.

CASE 14.

A Patient with Cirrhosis of the Liver, Ascites, and Bleeding Responds Unusually Well to Shunt Surgery

Case 14. Patient D.G., #H5521. Female. Age 36. Admitted October 18, 1956. Discharged November 19, 1956.

DIAGNOSIS. Laennec's cirrhosis with ascites and esophageal varices; esophageal hemorrhage.

OPERATION. Portacaval shunt.

CLINICAL SUMMARY. This patient had been followed in this hospital since the age of fourteen. As a child her health had been good but during the winters she had not stood up well to the climate and from time to time had been thought to have congenital heart disease; she was prone to rather wide swings of weight; on another occasion she was thought to have hyperthyroidism. These suspicions had never been borne out. Finally at the age of twenty-one she settled down and actually began to gain weight and became mildly obese. She was married at the age of twenty-six to a salesman for a wholesale liquor firm. During the ten years of her marriage up to the time of admission she had no pregnancies despite the fact that she used no birth control, she became habituated to drinking beer in rather large quantities while watching television, her health began to deteriorate, she grew very large in the abdomen and thin in the extremities, and looked increasingly the picture of chronic illness.

In addition to her beer habits, which averaged as much as three quarts a day, she smoked a good deal and led a very sedentary, indolent existence (although she gave her occupation as a waitress).

Three months prior to admission she noticed a further increase in abdominal girth and her weight suddenly increased from 160 to 174 pounds.

On admission she showed spider angiomata over the thorax, palmar erythema, marked ascites, large external hemorrhoids, edema of the lower extremities and flanks. A diagnosis of Laennec's cirrhosis was made. The ascites was too tense to permit feeling the liver.

INITIAL LABORATORY WORK

Urine. Not remarkable

Hematology

Hematocrit	38	
Leucocyte count	23,000 per cu.mm.	

Blood Chemical Analyses

Blood urea nitrogen	2	mg. per 100 ml.
Plasma protein	6.2	gm. per 100 ml.
Albumin	3.8	gm. per 100 ml.
Plasma sodium	130	mE. per l.
Plasma potassium	5.1	mE. per l.
Alkaline phosphatase	6.6	Bodansky units
Bilirubin	0.68	mg. per 100 ml.
Bromsulphalein retention	45 minutes—28 per cent	

ARGUMENT. This is a remarkably continuous follow-up of a woman from early puberty through to the age of thirty-six when, superimposed upon a rather

unhygienic and unhealthy existence, the patient has developed florid cirrhosis with ascites, probably on the basis of chronic alcoholism.

As she first comes in there is no need to consider surgical intervention. Her primary need is for paracentesis and dietary rehabilitation.

FURTHER COURSE. Liver biopsy showed Laennec's cirrhosis with fatty metamorphosis.

A paracentesis of 12.7 l. was carried out. Cell block was negative. The patient was soon discharged on a high-calorie diet, with low sodium intake (approximately 50 mE. of sodium per day). X-rays showed minimal esophageal varices. The outlook was considered to be good.

On this dietary regimen the patient's weight fell first from 174 to 145 (following paracentesis) and from thence to 124½ pounds on low-salt diet and mercurial diuretics.

Seen repeatedly in the outpatient department, the patient appeared to improve very considerably although weight was not gained. She came back for repeated paracenteses and seemed to require withdrawal of fluid approximately once a month, responding poorly to her low-salt diet and diuretics.

Her second admission was three months after the first and was very similar in character.

The patient was placed on a complicated regimen of diuretics rotating through the week on such drugs as Rolicton, Diamox, Mattrox, in repeated sequences. The possibility of surgical management to improve her ascites by the placing of some sort of ascitic fluid shunt was considered; on this admission she was again tapped —this time of 8 l. Varices could not be demonstrated at this time. She now dropped to a "dry" weight of 101 pounds but soon showed evidence of filling up again with fluid and within one month had to have 10 l. removed. This was repeated again in another six weeks, and again in only three weeks. She began to look sicker and develop abdominal cramps. The urgent necessity of some sort of shunt, either an ascitic fluid or a portal vein shunt, was much more actively considered.

She was admitted for the third time because of this possibility. This time 13 l. of ascitic fluid was removed only two weeks after her most recent tap. Laboratory study still showed little remarkable save for a mild anemia with a hematocrit of 36. Her bilirubin was not elevated, nor was her thymol turbidity. The total protein at 5.9 gm. per 100 ml., with albumin of 3.6 gm. per 100 ml., was low but not remarkably so.

The entire situation with respect to the care and planning for this patient was changed when on the second hospital day she vomited coffee-ground material, passed a tarry bowel movement, and showed definite evidence of beginning esophageal hemorrhage.

ARGUMENT. Again this patient has given a remarkable opportunity for continuous study, passing under our eyes from early cirrhosis to a pressing and difficult problem of recurrent ascites, and then, in the hospital, to her first major hemorrhage. With shunt surgery already under consideration because of her ascites, the occurrence of the hemorrhage makes a shunt virtually mandatory.

FURTHER COURSE. Bleeding persisted off and on for a week, never severe until, toward the end of the week, it became urgent enough to require 4000 ml. of blood in one day. The Sengstaken tube was passed, placed on traction with only the gastric balloon blown up. Enemas were used to clear the colon of blood. The patient was given concentrated glucose, and a splenoportogram was carried out.

The splenoportogram showed minimal distortion of the portal circulation, yet with definite portal hypertension, as evidenced by a splenic pulp pressure of 27 cm. of saline.

At this time the patient showed hyponatremia with sodium 120 mE. per l. and a mild acidosis, with chloride 107 mE. per l. and a carbon dioxide combining power of 15.3 mE. per l.

She was given 300 ml. of 3 per cent sodium chloride with additional potassium chloride and sodium bicarbonate. A caval catheter was placed for the infusion of concentrated glucose. A final paracentesis was done, to improve the vital capacity. Bleeding time, coagulation data, and platelet counts were determined to be normal, and a portacaval shunt was carried out.

ARGUMENT. This patient's preoperative management was reasonably simple because of the minimal evidence of progressive liver cell disease. The patient appears to have a stabilized nonprogressive cirrhosis of the "wet-white" type. She is not jaundiced and has severe ascites, yet even with multiple paracentesis is able to maintain a reasonably normal serum albumin concentration. The Sengstaken tube has controlled her

hemorrhage but it has not been felt advisable to continue on tube treatment alone because of her progressive ascites, and the fact that on three occasions in the ten days prior to operation she appeared to stop bleeding only to start up again.

FURTHER COURSE. A wide portacaval shunt was carried out under hypothermia to 29° C. Portal venous pressure in a large omental vein was found to be 29 cm. of water. A wide-open end-to-side shunt was obtained which immediately lowered the portal pressure to 15 cm. of water. Measured blood loss of 2500 ml. was replaced during operation. A liver biopsy specimen was taken. The liver itself was very large, rounded, and appeared to be the seat of extensive fatty degeneration.

The postoperative course of this patient was gratifying in several regards; she got along well without local or general complications, and the operation was uniquely successful in preventing the further formation of ascites. Other than one tap done in the first postoperative week, the patient has required no further paracenteses over a period of three years. Her appetite has been tremendously improved. She has gained solid tissue weight from a postoperative low of 99 pounds to a weight, on her last follow-up, three years' postoperative, of 152 pounds. Her Bromsulphalein retention is only 8 per cent. On physical examination she still shows a large liver and scattered spider angiomata over the chest. The spleen is not palpable.

COMMENT. This is an unusually fine result from end-to-side portacaval shunt carried out essentially for chronic severe ascites and one bout of major hemorrhage, not of massive proportions.

Lack of jaundice, with an essentially normal albumin, and some dilutional hypotonicity as the only chemical abnormality combined to give this patient an uncomplicated metabolic picture and a smooth surgical course.

CHAPTER 39

The Pancreas and Diabetes

Section I. Acute Pancreatitis

Acute pancreatitis presents a challenge to the patient's survival in the following specific regards:

(1) the early phase of plasma loss and shock with its associated specific biochemical disorders;

(2) ileus-obstruction, late septic starvation; and

(3) diabetes mellitus and digestive insufficiency.

These three aspects will be dealt with in order.

The pathologic process involved in acute pancreatitis, like so many other inflammatory lesions, ranges across a broad spectrum. At one extreme is the most transient pancreatic edema, often accompanied by severe pain and an extremely high amylase reading, but quickly subsiding on the simplest conservative measures. On the other is acute pancreatic necrosis with hemorrhage, a disease which in its severer forms is almost invariably fatal. The comments in this chapter concerning the management of this disease necessarily center around the treatment of pancreatic processes with hemorrhage, plasma loss, calcium changes, nutritional changes, and partial destruction of the pancreas, but of a degree that is potentially salvageable.

A. THE ACUTE SHOCK PHASE

The most important step in this phase is to maintain a normal circulating blood volume. The changes in body composition resemble those of a burn or peritonitis. There is massive loss of plasma into the peritoneal and retroperitoneal planes. In addition, there is considerable loss of whole blood into and around the pancreas. There may be some active intravascular hemolysis; the oligemia is due not only to plasma loss but also to extravasation of whole blood. The elevated hematocrit is an index of the blood volume needs; but, because of erythrocyte loss, it underestimates the total need.

Measures taken to treat oligemia include the infusion of plasma, concentrated albumin, whole blood, and non–colloid-containing fluids. The volume given must be based on a realistic estimate of the need. With the loss of 750 ml. of whole blood into the retroperitoneum and additional loss of 1000 ml. of plasma-like fluid into the edematous tissues around the root of the mesentery, a 70 kg. man may present a hematocrit that is elevated to the range of 52 to 57 and yet be in severe shock with loss of 30 per cent of his total blood volume. If the patient enters with a high hematocrit or develops one quickly, it indicates that plasma loss predominates over the loss of red cells, but in pancreatitis it does not exclude erythrocyte loss.

While these steps are under way, other measures are taken to reduce the hazard of bacteriologic growth—ultimately inevitable—and reduce pancreatic secretion. The use of an indwelling nasogastric tube on suction and parasympatholytic drugs may be helpful in reducing pancreatic secretion. Antibiotics are given, initially in very large doses.

There is evidence from the dog, from the

analogous changes in parotitis, and from experience in pancreatitis in man that early administration of X-irradiation in small doses may serve to cut down the enzymate secretion that produces autodigestion of the pancreas. The radiation must be administered very early—within the first twelve hours. If the process is already well started this therapy is unlikely to be of much benefit. A fall in amylase may follow.

The abnormal presence of proteolytic enzymes in the blood may add to the hypotension; the evidence is conflicting. But the same albumin and plasma given to support volume also acts as a substrate and antagonizes the enzyme action.

The use of adrenocorticotropic hormone or cortisone may lower the amylase, improve homeostasis, lessen pain, and in isolated instances produce a transient improvement. Long-continued high-dose cortisone therapy is unavailing in producing survival in severe cases. Combined cortisone and adrenocorticotropic hormone therapy is rational.

In favorable cases the patient will pass out of this shocklike phase early in the course of this disease, usually within the first three to five days. His requirement for intravascular volume replacement will be reduced markedly. During this period of reduction one must avoid pushing the patient over into pulmonary edema by continued aggressive administration of fluids. The analogy with a burn after seventy-two to ninety-six hours is obvious.

By the same token, if these intravascular fluids are not administered in adequate amounts during the early phase, a period of hypotension with renal vasoconstriction, renal anoxia, and acute tubular necrosis is virtually inevitable and becomes a major contributing cause of death. For these reasons, hourly data on urine output are essential in management.

B. SPECIFIC CHEMICAL DISORDERS— AMYLASE, CALCIUM, POTASSIUM

Elevation of blood amylase concentrations over four times normal (over 600 units where the top normal is 150) is virtually diagnostic of pancreatitis. The degree of elevation is probably correlated with the anatomic extent of the ductal obstruction and increased permeability that produces it, rather than the detailed nature of the process. Extreme elevation (over 2500 units) may be associated with widespread pancreatic edema in a very benign form. The only prognostic sign that we have been able to discern in the amylase level itself is in that patient who, with shock and a large intravascular replacement requirement, later shows a marked drop of the amylase to low or near-zero levels. We interpret this as virtual destruction of the entire pancreas; survival is rare.

The hypocalcemic tendency of patients with acute pancreatitis has been considered as being due to the formation of insoluble calcium soaps, the result of fat digestion in the region of the pancreas or in the peritoneal cavity. Whether or not this is the case, the patient readily develops a low plasma calcium concentration and, with this, various factors are operative which tend to produce alkalosis. Alkalosis makes the neuromuscular effects of hypocalcemia more pronounced and in itself produces hypokalemia. These alkalosis-producing factors are both metabolic and respiratory: loss of highly acid gastric juice by vomiting or tube drainage is an inevitable aspect of the disease, while severe pain and apprehension produce dyspnea with hyperventilation. Irritation of the lower surface of the diaphragms increases respiratory rate if not depth.

If the patient is in borderline hypocalcemia, very few evidences of tetany will be manifest so long as the patient has normal acid-base balance or is acidotic. If, however, the patient has alkalosis of either metabolic or respiratory variety, his tendency to develop the clinical signs of tetany is much increased. It is this alkalosis, together with the hypocalcemia, that produces tetany in acute pancreatitis.

The treatment of hypocalcemia in patients with pancreatitis therefore depends not only on the administration of calcium salts in the form of calcium chloride or calcium gluconate by vein but also on the vigorous administration of potassium chloride and ammonium chloride so as to mend the metabolic alkalosis. Serial plasma data on carbon dioxide combining power, chloride, sodium, potassium, and calcium are essential. Serial data on pH and carbon dioxide content are helpful but not essential.

The elevation in concentrations of enzymes other than amylase (proteolytic enzymes) is as characteristic as that of amylase though less frequently measured. They may be harmful, whereas amylase seems to be harmless. A part of the tendency to thrombosis and/or shock may be traceable to trypsin or other enzymes of this group. As mentioned above, the use of albumin appears to neutralize this proteolytic activity, possibly by providing a substrate, but the greatest usefulness of albumin lies in its volume-expanding effect.

The tendency to alkalosis is also associated with hypokalemia. The patient with acute pancreatitis has most of the settings associated with hypokalemic alkalosis, as described in Part III. The patient is starving, is taking in no potassium orally, is severely stressed, and may be given considerable sodium by vein. Some of the most severe and refractory examples of hypokalemic alkalosis that we have seen have been in patients with acute pancreatitis. The treatment consists not only in giving potassium but also in repairing the alkalosis. The vigorous administration of ammonium chloride to these patients is very useful. Concentrated sodium chloride solution has a place when extrarenal salt loss has been large. Although repair with sodium salts alone will make the alkalosis worse, some sodium is essential here.

Measurement of the carbon dioxide combining power, for all its faults, is a great help in following the acid-base balance of these patients. Ideally, during the initial acute phase, they should be carried with a carbon dioxide combining power below 28 mE. per l. and with the potassium, chloride, and sodium concentrations as near normal as is possible.

C. THE ILEUS-OBSTRUCTION PHASE

Very early in the course of pancreatitis, the patient starts to vomit, a reflex peristaltic inhibition. By imperceptible stages, this reflex vomiting passes on to ileus-obstruction, due in part to peritonitis and in part to the presence of an inflamed lesion in the duodenal loop. This may go on to form a pancreatic abscess, which in turn may later degenerate into a pseudocyst.

Again we use the seemingly contradictory term "ileus-obstruction" here, as we did in Chapter 34, to mean a failure to propel the contents, owing to both motor and mechanical factors. Patients with severe forms of necrotizing pancreatitis have diffuse abdominal distention for many weeks, with little ability to take their food. In other patients, the total distention will be less prominent, but both clinically and by X-ray the signs will be those of an atonic stomach and dilated duodenum. Some show a very characteristic X-ray picture of a dilated atonic duodenum about as far as the ligament of Treitz. Hypokalemic alkalosis worsens this adynamic state.

We know of no practical or safe way to induce peristalsis artificially. Parasympathomimetics are dangerous. If ileus is localized, one may feed beyond it by tube or jejunostomy. In any of these events, the problem in management is that of avoiding the metabolic effects of fluid loss and prolonged starvation.

Such problems as these have already been dealt with in the section on ileus-obstruction in Chapter 34 and will not be reviewed again here. Adequate decompression with a tube, intravenously administered fat, and the occasional feeding jejunostomy at that phase in the illness when the need for calories becomes great are important. The intravenous use of alcohol early in pancreatitis would appear to be contraindicated because of pancreatic stimulation. Later on, when the acute process is burned out and has become one of chronic suppuration, or obstruction, intravenously administered alcohol and fat have no contraindication.

D. PANCREATIC INSUFFICIENCY AND DIABETES

Rather early in the course of the disease, a diabetic state may develop. In the cases that are rapidly fatal, one may detect decreased sugar tolerance as early as the third day. In the midstream cases that go on for a much longer time and ultimately slough some of the pancreas, the diabetic state may not be manifested for a longer time. It is a form of diabetes that is not difficult to recognize or treat, and its occurrence is easily identified by the fasting blood sugar or glucose tolerance test. Once it is identified, treating it with insulin will accomplish much for the patient's nutritional state.

The occurrence of exocrine pancreatic insufficiency, as manifested by steatorrhea, is a very distressing late complication of the disease. It rarely occurs early in the process, since the gastrointestinal tract is not functioning well enough to produce the passage of much fecal matter. When a patient late in pancreatitis is found to have steatorrhea and is beginning to enter late-stage convalescence, he should be fed a low-fat diet, with pancreatin by mouth. The dose of pancreatin must be much larger than usually indicated. Doses as high as 45 gm. a day are necessary for the provision of adequate nourishment. Sodium bicarbonate is given with the enzyme. This problem becomes particularly noticeable in those patients who slough out part or all of the pancreas.

E. THE ROLE OF OPERATION IN THE MANAGEMENT OF ACUTE PANCREATITIS

Many patients with acute pancreatitis are operated upon for an "acute abdomen" and with a questioning diagnosis, including perforated viscus, mesenteric thrombosis, or appendiceal peritonitis. Some evidence of fat necrosis is found at laparotomy, and a suspected diagnosis confirmed. If the patient has no jaundice chemically or clinically, it is our conviction that in such patients the abdomen should be closed without drainage.

1. Cholecystostomy

If there is some jaundice, and laparotomy has been done, the patient should have a cholecystostomy. Gentle insertion of a drainage catheter into the gallbladder will decompress the biliary tree in these patients.

Whatever other etiologic factors operate, the importance of biliary reflux is great enough in pancreatitis to justify this step. If pancreatic edema is sufficient to close off the lower end of the common bile duct, biliary drainage is essential. Jaundice becomes the sole indication for early surgery when the plasma bilirubin concentration is over 3.0 mg. per 100 ml. Other than this biliary drainage, we know of no useful operative procedure in the early acute phase of this disease.

2. Drainage—Late

Subsequently, if there develops a palpable mass, a high swinging fever, or other evidences of an abscess in a pseudocyst, drainage is indicated. Such drainage should be followed by placing a suction sump to avoid damage to the skin. If the patient is treated by suction-sump drainage and the application of a glued-on cellophane dressing, it is possible to avoid the massive wound digestion that is sometimes so distressing. In late cases of pseudocyst, internal anastomotic drainage is practical.

The presence of a pseudocyst, alone, is not an indication for drainage. Many will subside and reabsorb; others will drain spontaneously into a hollow viscus. When the cyst becomes the seat of infection, or produces symptoms due to pressure, then it must be drained.

3. Fistula

Once the area of the pancreas has been drained, during or following pancreatitis, a fistula is prone to occur. If properly handled, so that a spherical cavity is well drained and converted into a linear cicatrizing tract, such fistulas regularly close. Their problems are skin digestion (prevented by suction sump and special skin dressing) and sodium loss.

Pancreatic fluid is unique among all body fluids in that it concentrates sodium above the level found in plasma. Any pancreatic juice draining in amounts over 100 ml. a day should be analyzed. If it is high in sodium (which may run as high as 185 mE. per l.), the patient must have very active sodium replacement. If not, a hypovolemic, hyponatremic state of subtraction acidosis will occur with great rapidity. Suction-sump drainage is essential.

4. Jejunostomy

A third indication for operation is in those patients with late pancreatitis who have intestinal peristalsis, who have no abdominal distention, but who have an ileus-like obstruction at the level of stomach and duodenum. In these patients, feeding jejunostomy may help solve their nutritional problem and provide a channel for fluid therapy until such time as their septic and obstructive process has subsided.

5. Paravertebral Block

Sympathetic paravertebral procaine block early in the course of the disease has been reported to lessen pain and shock; some degree of visceral vasodilation can be conceived of as helpful, so long as blood-volume support is energetic. Experience indicates that in early severe pancreatitis this should be done. The severe pain of the retroperitoneal inflammation is lessened thereby, and the associated clinical deterioration is less marked. There is no special hazard in this procedure.

F. CLINICAL PROCEDURE IN ACUTE PANCREATITIS

The following clinical procedure is based on examples in which severe acute pancreatitis went on to produce diabetes, pancreatic insufficiency, and a large pseudocyst.

1. *Diagnosis.* Acute pancreatitis.
2. *Admission Data.* Such a patient might well be a woman, multiparous and overweight, in her forties, given to alcohol, with a history of three hours of very severe acute abdominal pain and vomiting. She is apt to live in poor economic circumstances, and uses alcohol to excess at times. Although she is not intoxicated at the time of admission, one gains the impression that she may have been prior to the onset of the pain.

The pain is typically very severe in the upper abdomen and the back, with radiation to the left shoulder tip. On physical examination she is found to be very ill; the pulse is rapid; her blood pressure precariously maintained at 100/90. Her abdomen is diffusely tender, particularly so in the upper quadrants and most markedly to the left of the midline. There is no jaundice. She exhibits a positive Chvostek's sign.

URINE.   Normal.

HEMATOLOGY

> Hematocrit—58
> Leucocyte count—24,000 per cu. mm.
> Smear. Shift to the left of leucocytes.

BLOOD CHEMICAL ANALYSES

> Blood urea nitrogen—16 mg. per 100 ml.
> Plasma protein—6.8 gm. per 100 ml.
> Plasma chloride—82 mE. per l.
> Plasma sodium—146 mE. per l.
> Plasma potassium—3.2 mE. per l.
> Plasma calcium—4.0 mE. per l.
> Carbon dioxide combining power—34 mE. per l.
> Serum amylase—1800 units (normal 150)
> Plasma bilirubin—3.2 mg. per 100 ml.

NORMAL WEIGHT.   55 kg.

3. *Interpretation and General Plan.* This patient is admitted very early in the course of her disease, and she is extremely sick. She has acute volume reduction, doubtless due to mixed hemorrhage and plasma loss. The hematocrit is an inaccurate guide to the total need for volume because both erythrocyte and plasma are lost though plasma predominates. Here, the elevated hematocrit indicates only a minimal figure for need. An obese female, at 55 kg., is expected to have a blood volume (6.0 per cent of body weight) of 3300 ml.; with a hematocrit normally at 40 she would have a plasma volume of 1980 ml. and erythrocyte volume of 1320 ml. With a hematocrit at 58 her blood volume is reduced to 2280 ml. (1320 ÷ 0.58). This indicates a *minimal* plasma loss of 1020 ml. (3300 − 2280). With the loss of blood also into the pancreatic area, the figure of total volume lost will be increased. One should consider 1500 ml. as her immediate or static requirement, to which must be added any current or continuing losses. This can be given as plasma, albumin, dextran, or whole blood, preferably as a combination of several. It

should not be made up entirely of any one of these four.

The hematocrit elevation also represents sequestration of about 50 per cent of the uninvolved interstitial component of the extracellular fluids in the pancreatitic edema. If we assume a normal extracellular volume of 20 per cent body weight and interstitial volume (extracellular minus plasma) of 16 per cent body weight, these calculate out to 11,000 ml. extracellular and 8800 ml. interstitial as estimated fluid volumes. Thus, her reduction indicates not only a static debt of about 1000 ml. of plasma, but an additional 3000 to 5000 ml. of colloid-free fluid which must be given at an early time. To this is added the maintenance requirement.

Replacement of this lost volume is the first priority.

The patient is in borderline alkalosis. Her potassium concentration is low, her sodium on the high side. This could become a severe problem if it is not dealt with early by potassium chloride infusion. None of these things is threatening to long-term survival if treatment is active. The chief threat to life in such a woman as this will be acute renal insufficiency, which will surely follow if volume replacement is not active.

She is also in borderline hypocalcemic tetany. She has definite signs of tetany at this time. Her tendency to alkalosis will greatly exaggerate the neuromuscular effects of tetany, and she should be given some calcium during early treatment of her alkalosis. She is slightly jaundiced. Although the history is negative, she may have some common-duct disease. This should be watched carefully through the first twenty-four hours; it may become an indication for operation.

The diagnosis itself seems perfectly secure. The history, physical findings, and laboratory work are all compatible with acute hemorrhagic pancreatitis.

4. *Initial Steps in Care.* VOLUME RESTORATION. The patient is given 1000 ml. of plasma and 500 ml. of whole blood in her first two hours in the hospital. Albumin could be used in place of plasma.

TREATMENT OF INTERSTITIAL FLUID LOSS AND ALKALOSIS. The patient is given 80 mM. of potassium chloride and 120 mM. of ammonium chloride in her total parenteral fluid therapy of 7000 ml. in the first twenty-four hours. Her saline ration is thus about 4000 ml., the rest being colloid and the acidifying electrolyte. In such a patient as this, the hematocrit elevation represents a total sequestration of extracellular fluid as well as plasma, although with such a short course the participation of cell water is not yet marked. She is given 20 ml. of 40 per cent calcium gluconate on two occasions, intravenously.

After the first twenty-four hours, sodium and potassium will be included in this patient's replacement in a more normal relationship than during the first day of treatment, with more sodium per unit of potassium.

The patient is started on antibiotics—penicillin and streptomycin. She is put on nasogastric suction and given Banthine. On this program her pain is less and she is somewhat more comfortable, and for this reason paravertebral block is not undertaken. Vitamins are given intravenously.

5. *Progress Evaluation and Interpretation.* Twenty-four hours after admission, the following hematologic results might be expected.

> Hematocrit—47
> Leucocyte count—60,000 per cu. mm.
>
> BLOOD CHEMICAL ANALYSES
>
> Blood urea nitrogen—40 mg. per 100 ml.
> Plasma protein—6.5 gm. per 100 ml.
> Plasma chloride—92 mE. per l.
> Plasma sodium—132 mE. per l.
> Plasma potassium—4.2 mE. per l.
> Plasma calcium—5.0 mE. per l.
> Carbon dioxide combining power—30 mE. per l.
> Serum amylase—750 units
> Plasma bilirubin—5 mg. per 100 ml.

After such treatment the patient should be better clinically, stronger, and less apprehensive. Urine volume has totaled 450 ml. in the first twenty-four hours. Although this is not enough to make one feel completely secure, this volume, considered together with the restoration of blood pressure and drop in pulse, renders it unlikely that tubular necrosis will develop. The hourly urine output is a valuable guide to renal blood flow. The hematocrit is not yet down; there is still some volume restoration to be done.

The fall in amylase is a good sign, particularly when it does not drop down to extremely low values. The plasma calcium concentration has improved somewhat with calcium and potassium therapy. But there is still a borderline tendency to alkalosis, and this may be manifest for several more days. The Chvostek sign should have disappeared, but if not, more calcium should be given. Most important, however, is the fact that the patient's jaundice is a little deeper, she is now clinically jaundiced, and there is suspicion of an upper quadrant mass below the liver.

For this reason, the patient is operated upon.

6. *Operation.* ANESTHESIA. The patient is operated upon under spinal anesthesia, which occasionally has a helpful effect in pancreatitis. The interruption of pain pathways may last for some hours and it is a satisfactory anesthesia for this procedure once blood volume and pressure and urine flow are restored. Local procaine infiltration is also useful.

OPERATIVE PROCEDURE. A small incision is made in the right upper quadrant. A rather edematous, inflamed gallbladder with fat necrosis in the surrounding tissues is typically discovered. A cholecystostomy should be carried out with a minimum of additional trauma. There is sufficient fat necrosis in the area to confirm the diagnosis of pancreatitis. No effort to explore or drain the pancreas is undertaken. No extensive palpation is done. In a case such as this, the common duct should not be explored. But one should be sure that there is free communication between the gallbladder and the common duct, for the egress of bile and for subsequent cholangiography.

7. *Postoperative Study and Care.* During the first three postoperative days, such a patient may be expected to demand continuing intravascular volume therapy, as demonstrated by difficulty in maintaining her blood pressure and a tendency for the hematocrit to rise unless these steps are taken. In addition, she will usually be draining a large amount of high-acid juice from her stomach via the nasogastric tube, sufficient to indicate that the almost inevitable gastroduodenal obstruction has now arrived. She continues to require ammonium chloride and potassium chloride in liberal quantities in order to avoid alkalosis.

After four days she should begin to stabilize in terms of blood pressure and volume maintenance. Her pulse is a little lower, but she may now begin to develop a high spiking fever. Over the course of ten days a mass forms to the left of the midline, which about a week later is drained, put on sump suction, and is a freely draining pancreatic pseudocyst with fistula. Although biliary drainage is not large in amount, the jaundice gradually subsides.

Throughout this time such a patient's gastrointestinal tract is essentially nonfunctional, and after the end of ten days it is deemed advisable to begin total parenteral alimentation.

Thus, at her third week, although the patient is looking and feeling somewhat better and is essentially afebrile, she will have lost considerable weight, 8 to 15 kg., for example, and is now cachectic. She is unable to eat without vomiting, has a draining pancreatic pseudocyst that requires energetic electrolyte replacement at times, and is becoming a critical problem in venous feeding, parenteral care, and macronutrients.

Under such circumstances, if some peristalsis is beginning to be evident and barium study shows no propulsion of barium around the edematous duodenal loop, a feeding jejunostomy should be performed. It is placed below and lateral to the pseudocyst drainage site.

Into this feeding jejunostomy is introduced the patient's gastric suction product, after incubation for one hour at 37° C., with a simple feeding mixture. This gastric predigestion, even though done in vitro, is a factor favoring jejunal acceptance of feedings; the mixture should be alkaline when placed in the jejunum.

In the course of three or four days, stabilization on this jejunal mixture should be satisfactory, although there is some initial tendency to diarrhea. Gastrointestinal motility is gradually regained. The pancreatic fistula continues to drain but puts out progressively smaller quantities. The cholecystostomy is removed after a cholangiogram is carried out, showing no stones but only irregularity of the lower portion of the duct, compatible with pancreatic edema. Some portions of pancreas are apt to slough out through the draining pseudocyst sinus, but survival has been effected.

A typical hospital stay for such a patient may approximate three months, but it will be a year before the patient's abdominal incisions are completely healed and weight has been regained.

Mild diabetes and steatorrhea would be expected to continue in such a case.

G. POSTOPERATIVE PANCREATITIS

Postoperative pancreatitis is usually hemorrhagic and necrotizing; hence its high mortality. The diagnosis is not a problem if there is an acute surgical abdominal catastrophe with blood amylase twice normal or higher. The event is commonest following subtotal gastrectomy for duodenal ulcer, particularly where ulcer removal has been difficult.

1. Prevention

This rests on gentleness and conservatism. It is our conviction—difficult to prove—that one cause of increased incidence lies in the growing tendency of inexperienced operators to dig out deep distal ulcers rather than to content themselves with duodenal turn-in proximal to the ulcer.

2. Treatment

The treatment is that of acute pancreatitis, greatly complicated by recent major abdominal surgery. One has little to offer the patient other than blood volume maintenance, every effort to maintain normal blood pressure and flow, and normal extracellular chemistry, and to avoid aspiration of vomitus. Exploration is often carried out because of the suspicion of leakage; cholecystostomy should be done. If exploration is not undertaken for diagnosis, the elective cholecystostomy should depend on the occurrence of jaundice. Drains may be helpful. Paravertebral block and Banthine may be tried. Early X-ray treatment is usually unavailing. The rest of the course, should the patient survive the early phase, is that of any other case of severe pancreatitis.

Section II.　Chronic Pancreatitis

The problems in chronic pancreatitis are:
(1) *pain;* addiction to morphine and alcohol;
(2) *body wasting;* steatorrhea and poor absorption;
(3) *diabetes.*

A. PAIN AND ADDICTION

The treatment of the pain is complex and often unsuccessful, usually involves multiple operations, and is confused by opiate addiction in late cases. In rare instances internal drainage of a pseudocyst is very effective. In our hands sphincterotomy has been disappointing; choledochojejunal shunt has been more successful.

The treatment of the pain will often result in improved dietary intake, particularly if the pain is associated with pancreatic calcification. The extreme wasting these patients show is in part a result of addiction, the latter being a vicious cycle in which relief of pain on eating is sought, while the alcohol or morphine makes the dietary intake very poor.

Alcohol is an etiologic factor in early acute pancreatitis. In the late case with pain and calcification it is difficult to associate it with any worsening other than poor intake and avitaminosis.

The pain appears to be of three varieties.

(1) The first consists of acute bouts of pain lasting one to three days, sometimes associated with a palpable mass and always associated with an elevation of the amylase concentration. This is truly recurrent acute pancreatitis and will have the best outlook if treated by a choledocho-enteric biliary shunt.

(2) The second type is acute bouts of severe colicky pain lasting a much shorter time: minutes or hours. There is no elevation of amylase concentrations. We have thought of this as pancreatic colic and as more commonly associated with ductal calculi; pancreaticodochostomy should be expected to be more effective if they are present.

(3) The third is pain of a more constant nagging type ("never goes away") with severe exacerbations, but without elevation of amylase concentration.

In the latter two types a variety of procedures have been used, directed either at improving drainage of the pancreatic duct, or at severing afferent nerves. None of these is uniformly effective. The psychiatric and nutritional aspects of the pain, starvation, and addiction are often a critical factor in rehabilitation. They should be given attention from the start.

B. BODY WASTING: STEATORRHEA AND POOR ABSORPTION

Severe starvation is observed in patients with chronic pancreatitis. Treatment is singularly unrewarding in terms of rebuilding normal body composition, yet it must be tried and is essential to survival.

If steatorrhea is not present it is probable that malabsorption is not a critical factor. In any case, absorption studies should be done. The simplest and best is a two- or three-day fecal nitrogen assay taken while the patient is eating his best diet. If the fecal nitrogen averages more than 2.5 gm. per day on an intake of 5 gm. or more, one may assume that an absorption defect is present, either motor or secretory or both, and that its nutritional severity is roughly proportional to the absolute nitrogen wastage. The fecal fat loss is a more difficult determination. It should total less than 10 per cent of ingested fat. More elegant studies include xylose absorption, vitamin A absorption, and absorption of radioiodine-tagged fat or protein.

If the results of these tests are not abnormal, the patient's starvation is due to his pain, addiction, or alcoholism and should respond to general measures, the most important of which are increase in food intake, frequent small feedings, careful caloric guide, and pancreatin.

If steatorrhea is present some absorption studies should be done, as base-line data, but malabsorption must be assumed to be a major factor. Then, very large doses of pancreatin (45 gm. a day), frequent small feedings, a trial of predigested food, vitamin supplements, evening tube feedings, detergents, evening intravenous feeding of fat, and all the other tricks of the trade should be attempted. The progress of orderly trials of this sort can be followed by measurements of body weight, clinical balance of nitrogen, or stool fat. It is a trial-and-error procedure at best. Some one combination may be found to be most effective; the hospital care and dietary concern may in some instances assist the patient to more intelligent self-help, or answer a psychotherapeutic need. Marked weight gain is rare. Parenterally administered vitamins should be used in large doses; if all else fails a gluten-free diet may be tried. Alcohol intake must cease if progress is to be made, and the freedom from pain that occasionally results from local surgical attack may make the break from alcohol to a good diet successful.

C. DIABETES

Diabetes is not a severe problem in pancreatitis; it is the same endocrine lesion as the diabetes of pancreatectomy. The lack of absorption of carbohydrate potentiates the tendency to ketosis and makes the patient very sensitive to insulin. Insulin regulation should be tuned to measured absorption data; major attention should be directed toward absorption and general nutrition rather than the mild hyperglycemia *per se*.

Section III.   The Pancreatitides: Notes from the Literature

Rich and Duff (1936) emphasized the role of vascular occlusion and necrosis in the etiology of pancreatitis, as well as the oft-quoted common channel theory, with bile reflux. Palmer (1952) showed that various autonomic blocking agents had a beneficial effect on experimental pancreatitis in the dog. Thal (1955) showed that hypersensitivity reactions could cause pancreatitis in animals. All four factors are probably operative in various human cases.

Metabolic problems in acute pancreatitis have been brought into focus by a number of workers since 1940. Treatment involves an understanding of these changes. A few representative references follow.

The problem of proteolytic enzymes in the blood and their inhibition as a phase of treatment has been studied by Coffey (1951) and Hoffman et al. (1953).

Electrocardiographic changes have been described by Gottesman et al. (1943) and Pollock (1956). The calcium defect has been reviewed by Hayes (1955), and its significance in relation to the concurrence of hyperparathyroidism by Cope et al. (1957). Of correlated interest because of the syndrome of duodenal ulcer with pancreatic tumor is the review by Rogers et al. (1947) on duodenal ulcer in parathyroid disease.

Hildes et al. (1952) have reviewed the water and electrolyte metabolism of the pancreas; Shingleton et al. (1953) have elaborated the altered coagulability of the blood in pancreatic disease.

Traumatic pancreatitis and the use of resection in its treatment have been reported by Rini (1952) and Hanson and Sprafka (1957).

The problem of postoperative pancreatitis has been reviewed with respect to etiology, diagnosis, and treatment by Cattell and Warren (1951), Warren (1951), Smith et al. (1951), Renner (1951), Dunphy et al. (1953), and Boles (1956).

Of related interest is the occurrence of pancreatitis after fast and surfeit, as reported by McDermott et al. (1956). It is of interest that the patient reported by McDermott had a second severe attack three years later, after a duck dinner.

Studies of acute pancreatitis from the clinical view, involving series of cases, include Taylor (1949), Howard (1949), Zollinger and Boles (1953), Thal et al. (1955), Baker and Boles (1955), and Rosenberg and Akgun (1957).

Trypsin injected intravenously causes shock, there is increased proteolytic activity in the plasma of patients with pancreatitis, and the shock of pancreatitis seems at times to precede a demonstrably oligemic phase; these facts have stimulated interest in trypsin in relation to pancreatitis. Rush and Clifton (1952) studied the trypsin factor in acute pancreatitis. They studied dogs with experimental pancreatitis; there was a marked increase in serum proteolysis. The use of soybean trypsin inhibitor had a marked therapeutic effect in terms of blood pressure The authors felt that serum proteolytic activity was a shock-producing factor. They were intrigued by good results in the use of their soybean preparation in clinical cases. Pollock and Bertrand (1956) reported ability to produce the diffuse lesions of pancreatitis by the injection of trypsin. In addition they were able to produce shock in dogs by intravenous injection of pancreatic juice, and in experimental pancreatitis were able to produce in a few of their dogs the same electrocardiographic changes as were produced by trypsin injections.

Kenwell and Wels (1953) have reported the use of concentrated serum albumin in the treatment of the human disease with "impressive" results. They studied eleven consecutive cases; there was a more rapid clinical improvement, though no change in amylase. The dose was 300 to 500 ml. per day. They do not state whether or not this was the 25 per cent preparation.

Elliott (1954) considered that the restoration of plasma volume was the mechanism of benefit in albumin administration, in pancreatitis. Enzyme (trypsin) inactivation by provision of substrate might also be an explanation. Pollock (1956) reported in dogs the lowering of mortality in acute pancreatitis by the administration of plasma, or by cross-circulation. The implication is that these measures were "antitryptic"; the significance level of the experimental results was low.

Frieden (1956) presented twenty-two cases of postoperative pancreatitis. Pancreatic trauma was preeminent as a cause; in only four of twenty-two cases was the operation elsewhere than the upper quadrant of the abdomen. The mortality was 100 per cent. According to Perryman and Hoerr (1954), 32 per cent of a random group of surgical patients showed a postoperative rise in amylase concentration; after gastric resection, this rose to 47 per cent. Diagnosis is not difficult when this rise is accompanied by the severe symptoms of acute hemorrhagic pancreatitis. Without the symptoms (that is, with amylase rise alone) the diagnosis should not be made. Therapy has often been reviewed but never improved, and the mortality remains almost unique among postoperative complications, almost 100 per cent, and higher than that of pulmonary embolism, coronary occlusion, or bacteremia.

Sinclair (1956) describes careful studies on a case of pancreatic fistula resulting from placement of a drainage tube near the pancreas at the time of an uneventful gastrectomy. The output ranged from 500 to 2400 ml. per day as a general average. The sodium content was high (near 155 mE. per l.), the chloride around 90 mE. per l., with bicarbonate as high as 87 mE. per l. On days of large volume the secretion was even more alkaline, but less active in relation to diastase. The persistent hypernatremia of the juice is remarkable. When expressed in terms of water concentration, the plasma sodium concentration is about 151 to 155 mE. per l. of water; the low protein of the pancreatic juice thus accounts in part for the seeming sodium concentration of the juice; but on five occasions in this case the sodium was over 160 mE. per l., beyond the range of this correction factor. There was a moderate steatorrhea. The reactions of various drugs were observed. Banthine and atropine markedly lowered secretion. Whatever the kinetics of the situation, the remarkable alkalinity of the pancreatic juice (pH 7.9 to 8.5) and its high sodium content and total base (up to 165 to 185 mE. per l.) put it in a class by itself as regards acute volume-reducing desalting with subtraction acidosis, when it is lost by fistula.

Pancreatic fistula inevitably involves serious problems in fluid loss, skin digestion, and management for closure. Accurate replacement, sump suction, and parenteral supplementation are essential. Reviews of this problem will be found in Kahn and Klein (1932), McCaughan and Purcell (1941), Miller and Wiper (1944), Thomas and Ross (1948), Mahaffey and Haynes (1953), and Bartlett and Thorlakson (1956).

Various operative maneuvers have been tried in the treatment of relapsing pancreatitis. These include resection, denervation, choledochojejunostomy, and caudal anastomoses. Clinical results are to be found in DuVal (1954), Shingleton and Anlyan (1954), Poth and Wolma (1954), Bowers (1955), Cannon (1955), Longmire *et al.* (1956), Doubilet and Mulholland (1956), and DuVal (1957 and 1958).

Shwachman's review (Shwachman *et al.*, 1956) describes the pancreatic insufficiency of cystic fibrosis, with an excellent bibliography.

Shingleton *et al.* (1955) showed, using protein and fat labeled with I^{131}, that in patients with pancreatic disease the I^{131} content of the blood was less than normally expected following ingestion. This was an extension into adult surgery of the techniques suggested in children by Lavik *et al.* (1952) and by Chinn *et al.* (1952). Whether pancreatic disease could be differentiated from gastric or liver disease by these techniques remains for further clinical study. The implication was that this might well be possible.

Section IV. Diabetes Mellitus

A. THE METABOLIC DEFECT IN SURGICAL PATIENTS

1. Hyperglycemia and Acidosis

Mild hyperglycemia is a harmless condition, as is glycosuria. They are both produced quite regularly on a surgical service by the infusion of glucose in water, and they are no more harmful in a diabetic than they are in a nondiabetic. A mild degree of dehydration is about the only effect. By contrast, acidosis, cellular wasting, and desalting are extremely dangerous; these three are produced by severe diabetes mellitus.

Although mild hyperglycemia with blood sugar concentrations between 150 and 300 mg. per 100 ml. is in itself harmless, a more severe hyperglycemia ranging up to 500 to 1000 mg. per 100 ml. represents a marked alteration in body osmolality. Quite aside from other changes that may have occurred as the patient became hyperglycemic, and quite independent of other considerations regarding electrolyte metabolism, the blood glucose adds about 5.5 mO. per l. for each 100 mg. per 100 ml. of glucose increment. As a general rule, when the blood sugar level rises acutely, the plasma sodium concentration falls. This withdrawal of cell water is, in a sense, a compensatory change restoring osmolality toward normal in the face of nonelectrolyte solute—glucose—which is present in such excess. A patient with a blood glucose concentration of 750 mg. per 100 ml. and a plasma sodium of 140 mE. per l. may be expected to have an extracellular fluid osmolality of 320 mO. per l. This is in itself a harmful situation, which can be thought of as "dehydration," although it actually represents an increase of the amount of solute per unit of water rather than a primary decrease in the amount of water per unit of solute. It is analogous to solute loading, and the water loss is mainly through the kidneys by the mechanism of solute diuresis. Some of the clinical improvement seen in a diabetic patient treated with large doses of insulin is related to the rapid restoration of body fluid tonicity toward normal by the combustion of the nonelectrolyte solute. At blood sugar levels of 300 mg. per 100 ml. or less, this osmolar effect is so small as to be negligible.

Hyperglycemia produces hyponatremia, while acidosis produces hyperkalemia. The combination produces the characteristic sodium-potassium shift of diabetic acidosis. As the glucose is burned, the plasma sodium concentration rises towards normal but, as is so characteristic in the face of a rising sodium concentration and correction of acidosis, the potassium concentration falls abruptly. This drop in plasma potassium concentration may be due to the rise in sodium, or to acid-base effects, or to the movement of potassium from extracellular fluid into the cells to cover the combustion of glucose (and the laying down of glycogen). Therefore, while mild hyperglycemia is in itself harmless to the surgical diabetic and indicates merely that there is glucose present which is available for combustion, rapid treatment of acidosis and hyperglycemia with insulin will produce certain characteristic electrolyte changes, including those of hypokalemia.

a. Acidosis. Turning from the relatively harmless hyperglycemia to the effects of acidosis, we find a different picture. Metabolic acidosis is harmful under any circumstances and it is certainly harmful in the surgical diabetic. The manner in which acidosis harms the organism probably is related to neuromuscular irritability. The function of the brain, the smooth muscle of the gut, and the heart is altered in acidosis. The body has a considerable ability to take up acid without significant change in pH, an ability described in Part III under the heading of "Total Body Buffers." As the diabetic patient begins to develop acidosis, these buffers are progressively taken up, there is transfer of cell cation, compensatory mechanisms (renal excretion of acid and increased pulmonary ventilation) are called into play, but in the end all are finally fully expended, compensation ceases, and the pH begins to fall sharply. In this setting, the diabetic patient is placed in extreme hazard by any sort of surgical infection, anesthesia, operation, or respiratory embarrassment. The treatment of his acidosis must therefore take precedence over all other considerations. Fortunately it can be accomplished with reasonable efficacy and speed, provided the patient has not passed into terminal acidosis or coma.

b. Blood Studies. It is the unusual surgical situation in which anesthesia or emergency operation is required for the patient with severe untreated diabetic acidosis. Such an event does occur but is happily rare. Much more common is the need for care of surgical infections in patients with diabetes who are in mild acidosis, or who develop mild acidosis while under surgical care. Therefore, the most important determinations of blood chemistry for the surgical diabetic are tests for the presence of ketone bodies, carbon dioxide combining power, sodium, potassium, chloride, and, if possible, pH and pCO_2. The urine sugar and acetone tests are helpful. These, then, are the determinations that are most important in guiding the care of the diabetic. They far outweigh in significance minor fluctuations of the blood sugar between the levels of 100 and 500 mg. per 100 ml.

The elderly diabetic patient is apt to be suffering from severe chronic atherosclerotic vascular disease. This disease involves the kidney. Whether or not the patient has a specific diabetic lesion of the kidney, many diabetics over the age of fifty-five have impaired renal function. As we will see below, this is of importance in the manner in which their bodies respond to the discharge of a solute load of glucose into the glomerular filtrate. It is also a factor impairing the ability to compensate for a real or threatened acidosis. A careful evaluation of renal function is necessary as the diabetic approaches operation and should occupy equal priority along with evaluation of his cardiac status, vital capacity, pulmonary function, acid-base balance, and glucose metabolism.

2. Cellular Wasting, Desalting, and Solute Diuresis

As the diabetic progresses downhill toward severe acidosis and coma, he undergoes a characteristic metabolic change. This consists in breakdown of fat and protein in a quest for energy, with the excretion of large amounts of potassium, phosphate, sulfate, and other intracellular electrolytes. The extracellular fluid becomes hyperglycemic, acidotic (with keto-acids), and hyponatremic.

This deteriorative metabolic change has three characteristic earmarks: accumulation of a high glucose concentration in the extracellular fluid, the progressive development of metabolic acidosis, and a chronic desalting renal water loss. This pattern may occur with considerable rapidity (in three to five days, for example) in the severe diabetic who suddenly is traumatized or develops infection or misuses his insulin. In other cases it may be much slower in developing. Fully developed, it leads to azotemia, metabolic acidosis, hyponatremia, hyperkalemia, hyperglycemia with keto-acids in the blood and urine, and a chronic progressive renal desalting, leading finally to hypovolemia, renal vasoconstriction, anuria, and shock.

When severe desalting and dehydration have occurred in diabetes, with a contracted volume of extracellular fluid and total body water volumes, one must seek at least two causes. First, and easiest to understand, is extrarenal desalting water loss such as vomiting or diarrhea.

The second cause for desalting and dehydration in diabetic acidosis has to do with renal function in the presence of a profuse solute (glucose) diuresis. In a normal person given infusions of glucose, who is spilling glucose in the urine, a mild dehydration is produced. The relatively small fraction of glucose appearing in the urine is extremely active as a nonresorbed tubular solute (nonresorbed, that is, above the renal threshold). But the normal kidney resorbs water as needed to save body water and minimize dehydration. In the diabetic with poor renal function (especially an older person) this effect is magnified because of the inability of the renal tubule to concentrate the urine over a specific gravity of about 1.015. Under these circumstances, the continuing spilling of sugar in the urine produces a pathologic renal loss of water, which takes salt with it and whose effect (depending on the osmolar U:P ratio) may produce either desalting or an elevation of the body osmolality—in other words, true dehydration. In this sense, then, and for these reasons, the severe decompensated diabetic has had desalting water loss from his body cells and may at the same time be truly dehydrated with an hypertonic extracellular fluid. At this point he tolerates neither surgical trauma nor infection, and is headed for coma.

The situation has been referred to as "intracellular dehydration." This is somewhat misleading, and one must specify exactly what is meant by that term. The intracellular portion of body water has been extensively desalted through the chronic loss of potassium at a high potassium:nitrogen ratio. If the extracellular osmolality is elevated, because of the presence of large amounts of glucose there, one may assume that the intracellular osmolality is also elevated, and in this case it is valid to refer to the condition as intracellular hypertonicity. Such a situation usually exists with a net water deficit. There is a lack of water both inside and outside cells, and this is a double need that must be met in treatment. The dehydration is thus indeed intracellular but not exclusively so.

3. The Effect of Trauma and Infection; The Metabolic Significance of Operation

Infection makes diabetes worse and diabetes makes infection worse. Acute trauma makes diabetes worse in part because it constitutes a stimulus to the production of adrenal steroids that antagonize the peripheral effects of insulin. This is an attractive explanation that one can advance for the worsening of diabetes in the face of acute surgical trauma. This explanation also accounts for the worsening of diabetes in the presence of acute sepsis. It is not unusual to see diabetics requiring from 20 to 60 units of insulin per day when they have acute sepsis, who, on discharge from the hospital, can manage on diet alone or with minimal insulin maintenance.

The question of why diabetes makes infection worse is more difficult to unravel. The presence of large amounts of sugar in the tissue might promote the growth of certain types of bacteria; carbon-dioxide–producing organisms are not uncommonly seen in acute diabetic sepsis and produce large amounts of gas in the tissue, which may resemble gas bacillus infection roentgenographically. Additional explanations may be found in the prolonged nutritional illness characteristic of diabetes, poor protein synthesis, and the low activity of cellular systems that produce antibodies.

It is therefore a primary consideration in diabetes to take care of sepsis expeditiously and thoroughly and to minimize or shorten surgical trauma whenever this is possible, at least until the diabetes is well controlled. This is one more example of the many seen in this book in which the surgical operative steps and the metabolic care of the patient are synonymous. The drainage of diabetic sepsis should be accurate and complete. If there is a choice between radicalism and conservatism, radicalism should prevail. Diabetic sepsis must be completely drained with no overhanging shelves and margins, no unseen pockets, completely exteriorized so that clean granulation and healing will occur.

There are two points of importance with respect to the use of antibiotics in diabetic sepsis.

(1) When the sepsis occurs in an area of diabetic ischemia, blood-borne antibiotics are but poorly brought to the interface between the organisms and the host. Radical drainage and/or amputation is more frequently necessary because of this fact. There is an important place here for locally applied antibiotic therapy.

(2) When infection is diffuse and the bloodstream interface broad, antibiotic therapy in the diabetic cannot be casual or random. It must be energetic, precise, and based, whenever possible, on differential study of the microorganism. We can rely on less help from the patient's resistance to infection; fewer errors are forgiven.

B. TREATMENT

1. Keep the Glucose Burning

As stated, mild hyperglycemia is in itself little hazard to the diabetic. Acidosis is the main hazard. We now come to a third basic point: the diabetic, untreated, is in a state of acute energy deficit. He needs to burn glucose so as to produce the oxidative energy on which life is based, to maintain the function of all his cellular systems, and to avoid the accumulation of the acid metabolites of incomplete oxidation that produce acidosis. The basic steps in metabolic care of surgical diabetics who are not acidotic are therefore very simple and two in number: (1) provide glucose to burn, and (2) keep it burning.

These two steps are accomplished by giving the patient exogenous glucose and insulin. He is producing glucose endogenously all the time by breakdown of his tissues, particularly protein. Giving him glucose exogenously spares his tissues and provides a controlled amount of glucose that the patient can combust. This glucose can be given intravenously. The rate of its administration and combustion can be observed by serial measurements of the blood sugar during an operative or infectious episode. Measurement of the blood sugar achieves its chief importance in this regard— as a barometer of the rate in which glucose is being burned, not as index of severity of the diabetes, as based on a single sample.

The glucose is kept burning by the administration of insulin. In surgical patients this insulin is best given subcutaneously, using regular or crystalline insulin, on a six-hourly basis, guided by tests for urine sugar and, when necessary, blood sugar. This simple treatment weathers the patient through his acute episode much more easily than giving long-acting insulin preparations. If the patient has already been stabilized for days, weeks, or years on long-acting insulin preparation, these can be continued and the short-acting material added as a supplement when necessary.

It is very tempting to add glucose to the insulin infusion, and indeed there may be some reason for doing this in certain types of circumstances in the nondiabetic. In the diabetic this has the hazard that if the glucose-insulin infusion is stopped or runs into the tissues, the patient ceases to receive glucose effectively but he has insulin still in his body and active. *The use of insulin intravenously*

in mixtures with glucose is therefore dangerous and unnecessary in the diabetic. Some diabetics are remarkably sensitive to insulin, much more so than normal persons. In such individuals, the sudden cessation of a glucose-insulin infusion, as, for instance, its removal by mistake, its running into tissues, or its being stopped during a surgical operation, will result in profound insulin hypoglycemia and shock. Under anesthesia this is difficult to diagnose and may go rapidly on to shock (misdiagnosed as of operative origin), cerebral thrombosis, coronary thrombosis, and death.

Insulin given subcutaneously is absorbed at a regular rate so long as the patient maintains peripheral circulation. It is absorbed in a manner that permits ready control by giving glucose by mouth or by vein. It will not overact rapidly or dangerously if glucose provision temporarily fails.

2. The Prevention and Treatment of Acidosis

The patient who has developed severe diabetic acidosis (whether this has occurred in the course of twenty-four hours in conjunction with a severe infection or has occurred over the course of several weeks or months) is a patient who has suffered desalting water loss via the kidneys, as mentioned above. The argument as to whether the patient should or should not be given sodium, whether the patient should or should not be given potassium, is in a sense fruitless. The patient should be given both sodium and potassium; both of these ions have been lost. A disposable anion (lactate, bicarbonate) is preferable for part of the cation replacement in metabolic acidosis. In addition the patient should be given water and glucose. If the patient's blood sugar concentration is extremely high there is a large amount of unoxidized glucose in the body, and the administration of glucose need not be done as an immediate emergency. If we assume that glucose partitions itself throughout body water, a blood glucose level of 500 mg. per 100 ml. means that there are 5 gm. in each liter of body water, or, in a 70 kg. man, about 200 gm. of free glucose in the body. This amount of carbohydrate is burned in a matter of hours and with the administration of insulin it is quickly disposed of. Therefore, glucose must soon be given to supply the patient with continuing energy during a period of acute febrile illness, possibly complicated by infection or, in the case of surgical patients, trauma.

The treatment of diabetic acidosis with sodium bicarbonate alone carries the minor hazard that an addition acidosis is being combated by the addition of base; serious overwatering and oversalting can readily result, particularly in older patients with some degree of heart failure. This "oversalting" hazard is minor in most cases because the "added acid" anions (ketones, lactate, pyruvate) are burned and thus are lost to body water. The use of sodium bicarbonate alone also carries the hazard of hypokalemia, as resalting with potassium-free salts proceeds and a shift toward alkalosis occurs with a drop in potassium concentration.

Unless there has been vomiting of high-acid gastric juice (a most exceptional circumstance in the elderly diabetic), the only commonly-used electrolyte solution that can categorically be claimed to be injurious in diabetic acidosis is isotonic saline, since it has such an excess of chloride that it will make the acidosis worse. The patient has lost large amounts of potassium and, as mentioned above, there may be a disproportionate loss of potassium over cell matrix. For this reason the patient must be given potassium. If the plasma potassium concentration is elevated initially, one may wait eight to twelve hours before starting potassium. A reasonable intravenous procedure, therefore, consists in the administration of adequate glucose, subcutaneous insulin, and sodium bicarbonate (or lactate) with potassium chloride (or bicarbonate). The exact amounts of these substances that must be given are to be based on the details of the case and evaluation of the balance between desalting and dehydration. Any set routine or over-all procedure is obviously unrealistic.

After total pancreatectomy the insulin requirement is not great, but the acceptable range of insulin dosage within which carbohydrate metabolism is normal is very low. This may be troublesome. Absorption is as-

sisted in these patients by giving them very large doses of pancreatic enzyme preparations.

3. Clinical Procedures in Diabetic Surgery

The initial treatment of severe diabetic acidosis and coma is not something in which the surgeon is ordinarily called upon to assist or collaborate. The treatment summaries here, therefore, cover two situations. First is that of the moderately severe diabetic on good management who is undergoing elective operation, in this case cholecystectomy for gallstones. The second instance is that of the severe diabetic entering with a severe infection, who must have emergency surgery. Again gallbladder disease is selected, this time acute cholecystitis.

a. Clinical procedure in stabilized diabetes; elective cholecystectomy.

The patient here might well be a sixty-five-year-old woman who has had diabetes for about twenty-five years and has fared well on diet and 20 units of NPH insulin each morning before breakfast. She tests her urine twice during the day and on occasion gives herself an additional 5 units of regular insulin if she is spilling much sugar or showing acetone. She is shown by X-ray to have gallstones and has had several bouts of typical colic. She has several evidences of vascular disease, including major vessel calcification and one attack in the past thought to have been a coronary occlusion. Physical examination findings are usually unremarkable save for slight obesity, white hair, and palpable sclerotic vessels in the periphery.

1. Preoperative Study and Care. An estimate of the patient's cardiac situation by electrocardiography and a seven-foot film of the heart are made; kidney function is studied by concentration tests; her blood urea nitrogen is normal, and for this reason further kidney function tests are deemed unnecessary.

She is started out on a maintenance of her ordinary diabetic regimen and the following laboratory studies are done with the results shown.

URINE. Sugar, protein, no cells in the sediment.

BLOOD CHEMICAL ANALYSES

  Blood urea nitrogen—7 mg. per 100 ml.
  Plasma protein—6.5 gm. per 100 ml.
  Plasma chloride—98 mE. per l.
  Plasma sodium—132 mE. per l.
  Plasma potassium—4.5 mE. per l.
  Carbon dioxide combining power—24 mE. per l.
  Plasma bilirubin—0.8 mg. per 100 ml.
  Fasting blood sugar—175 mg. per 100 ml.

STOOL.   No occult blood.

INTERPRETATION.   The patient is slightly hyperglycemic, has no renal failure. There is a slight hyponatremia, but no acidosis.

After the patient is stabilized in the hospital and these studies have been recorded, suitable X-rays are taken and operation can usually be arranged for her third day in the hospital.

2. Preoperative and Operative Orders. The patient is not given the usual long-acting insulin the morning of the operation. Preoperative medication is otherwise the same. An intravenous infusion of 5 per cent glucose in water is started during the operation and run extremely slowly throughout the operation. Anesthesia might well be Pentothal, nitrous oxide, curare; deep-plane ether anesthesia is to be avoided.

3. Postoperative Study and Care.   At the close of the operation, the patient is given 15 units of regular insulin subcutaneously; a slow intravenous infusion is continued, to give her a total of 1500 ml. of 5 per cent glucose in water during the operative day.

Her urine is tested every six hours by Benedict's test and for acetone and the orders are written approximately as follows:

  For ++++ sugar—15 units regular insulin
                            subcutaneously;
  for   +++ sugar—10 units;
  for   ++ sugar—no insulin;
  for   + or 0 sugar—no insulin.

Give one-half the dose of insulin if an intravenous infusion containing glucose is running. Call doctor if acetone appears in the urine.

On the morning of the first postoperative day, blood sugar should be checked, and may be expected to be about 200 mg. per 100 ml.; carbon dioxide combining power, 20 mE. per l.

By the third postoperative day the patient should commence to eat significant amounts

by mouth and can be returned to half her regular dose of NPH insulin in the morning. On the sixth postoperative day, her regular dose of NPH insulin is given, and the patient is returned to her standard diabetic diet.

In summary, the significant features of such a program are the operation of the patient's diabetic control by periodic tests of the urine, and the policy that it is best for the patient to continue to have enough excess sugar available to spill some in the urine. Urine without any sugar in it is more dangerous since it may be the harbinger of an insulin reaction. Large amounts of sugar in the urine are obviously indicative of inadequate insulin. The object is to keep the patient somewhere between these two, given enough glucose to burn and sufficient insulin to burn it.

b. Clinical procedure when there is infection in a severe diabetic requiring emergency operation.

This might also be the case of a sixty-five-year-old woman with previous diabetic history similar to that indicated in the procedure above. Such a patient often has had increasing right upper quadrant pain for several days with fever and chills. On entry to the hospital she appears acutely and chronically ill, with a fever near 103° F. and pulse around 120. The abdomen may be expected to show marked tenderness throughout the right upper quadrant, and after the patient has been in bed a while, somewhat relaxed, it is possible to feel the tense, tender, rounded smooth mass below the liver edge. She does not have signs of generalized peritonitis, but rebound tenderness from elsewhere in the abdomen may be referred to the right upper quadrant.

She has a leucocyte count near 30,000 per cu. mm. The diagnosis of acute cholecystitis and local peritonitis seems clear.

The general plan is to get such a patient rehydrated and her diabetes under some control in twelve hours, after which time operation is to be undertaken. She is a known diabetic with severe infection; her care makes a contrast with that of the stable surgical diabetic previously described.

1. Preoperative Study and Care.   During this time two diagnostic areas are especially important: the extent of her diabetic acidosis, and her cardiovascular status.

URINE. Urine shows poor concentrating ability with good volume, with strongly positive sugar, protein, and acetone.

BLOOD CHEMICAL ANALYSES
Blood urea nitrogen—45 mg. per 100 ml.
Plasma protein—5.2 gm. per 100 ml.
Plasma sodium—125 mE. per l.
Plasma potassium—5.4 mE. per l.
Carbon dioxide combining power—8 mE. per l.
Plasma bilirubin—3.5 mg. per 100 ml.
Blood sugar—650 mg. per 100 ml.
Osmolality—315 mO. per l.

HEMATOCRIT. 35

INTERPRETATION. The patient is azotemic and severely acidotic with hyperglycemia, and the typical sodium-potassium shift of severe illness. She has some elevation of bilirubin, compatible with acute cholecystitis, but not sufficient to make common-duct exploration mandatory. She is showing solute diuresis, and is slightly hypertonic with a sodium-osmolar differential greater than that accountable on the basis of the glucose alone.*

X-rays of the heart show it to be somewhat enlarged with some basal congestion of the lungs. Electrocardiograph shows left axis deviation. The patient's venous pressure is slightly elevated. The decision is made to digitalize her.

2. *Therapeutic Plan*

(1) HEART. Such a patient should be digitalized, but not too rapidly. Correction of the hyperkalemia by giving base will increase the effectiveness of the digitalization.

(2) HYPERGLYCEMIA. Such a patient's progress should be followed by multiple blood sugar tests until her hyperglycemia has been brought down by insulin in large doses. The important thing is not so much the reduction of hyperglycemia, as it is titration to indicate how much insulin is required to burn sugar in this particular patient. For example, she might be given 50 units of insulin subcu-

taneously on admission, and this followed at four and at eight hours after admission by two doses of 25 units each, at the end of which time the patient's blood sugar may be down to 200 mg. per 100 ml. An intravenous infusion of 5 per cent glucose in water is given to cover the patient's continuing sugar requirements. If the response is less than this, more insulin must be given.

(3) ELECTROLYTE. The patient is given 1000 ml. of sodium bicarbonate solution containing 155 mE. per l. of sodium; this is followed by 1000 ml. of a solution containing 40 mM. of potassium chloride. Note that this potassium is given in the second liter despite the slight hyperkalemia which the patient shows, and despite her borderline renal function. As the patient's acidosis is repaired with glucose and sodium bicarbonate, a severe hypokalemia will occur unless some potassium is given early. If the doctor wishes to wait six hours to assure himself of renal function, little is lost; but potassium should be given.

The above treatment takes an initial six-hour period. With this patient's elevated venous pressure, it is not advisable to crowd fluids too closely.

The patient is started on intravenous penicillin and intramuscular streptomycin in large doses. After six hours the patient's situation is reevaluated for operation.

(4) PROGRESS. She should now look better and feel better, with her pulse lower at 100. This is a most favorable sign of improvement in a cardiac patient. Her fever is slightly lower, but this is usually too soon for fever to show significant lysis. The patient's venous pressure is lower, despite the fluid that she has been given. This is due to her digitalization, the rest in bed, and the improvement in her metabolic situation.

During the second six hours, the same general program is continued, giving the patient additional fluid, which may now total 1500 to 3000 ml. in this second period.

At the end of this time the patient's carbon dioxide combining power should be near 15 mE. per l. and rising. The blood sugar level is still elevated but it is falling. The patient's blood urea nitrogen may not have changed significantly, as this will require a

---

* Calculation here shows a sodium concentration of 125 mE./l., accounting for 250 mO./l. of electrolyte solute; the glucose accounts for 5.5 mO./l. per 100 mg. or, here, 36 mO./l. The unaccountable solute is therefore 315 minus 286 or approximately 29 mO./l., mostly to be sought as keto-acids in this instance.

longer period of time. The patient's plasma sodium concentration will have risen as the nonelectrolyte osmolality of the glucose has been reduced. At the end of twelve to sixteen hours of such preparation the patient is ready for operation. This is carried out under thiopental, nitrous oxide, and curare, or local infiltration with procaine.

4. Operation. The objective of operation is unitary: to achieve drainage. In such a setting, cholecystectomy is usually contraindicated and should be done later as a staged procedure. To achieve drainage, the large single gallstone characteristically lodged in the lower part of the gallbladder must be removed; if clear bile issues forth, a satisfactory if temporary solution has been achieved. Were the patient's bilirubin level to be significantly higher than it is, a cholangiogram could be done through the gallbladder at this time. In a critically ill patient, a common-duct exploration is generally contraindicated even if a stone is present in the lower end of the duct, a total bile fistula through the gallbladder or a common-duct T-tube being short of perfect but acceptable until the patient's diabetic situation can be more satisfactorily repaired. The cholecystostomy is allowed to drain by gravity freely through a half-inch tube into a bottle.

4. Postoperative Study and Care. Such a patient's progress is followed by study of the blood sugar during the first twenty-four hours, checking the blood sugar level and carbon dioxide combining power twice during this time.

After this the management of the patient is similar to that indicated in the previous case, checking the patient's condition by urinalyses at four-hour intervals and less frequent chemical determinations.

This patient's response to operation should be dramatic, with marked lowering of pulse, lowering of fever, and sudden release of the high insulin requirement, with easy repair of the acidosis despite little further parenteral therapy: the metabolic effect of drainage of sepsis in a diabetic has been achieved.

The patient is maintained on antibiotics for seven days and on digitalis permanently. Prior to her discharge, her diabetes is stabilized on a standard insulin routine, similar to that which she has maintained for some years.

The patient's azotemia may be expected to increase during the immediate postoperative period as a result of the added trauma and catabolism of lean tissue; it then very slowly returns to normal, indicating that renal reserve is small and prognosis on this score guarded.

CASE 15

In Which Acute Pancreatitis with Profound Shock Develops under Our Eyes and with an Important Response to Certain Biochemical Derangements

Case 15. Patient A.P., #5J934.* Female. Age 64. Admitted September 27, 1957. Discharged October 21, 1957.

DIAGNOSIS. Acute pancreatitis.

OPERATION. None.

CLINICAL SUMMARY. Because of one month's history of anorexia, nausea, vomiting, and weight loss, this sixty-four-year-old housewife was admitted to the hospital for further evaluation and diagnosis. Review of the patient's past history revealed that two years previously she had developed intestinal obstruction due to a gallstone impacted in the ileum. This was removed surgically with uneventful recovery. One year previously she underwent an uncomplicated cholecystec-

tomy, closure of cholecystoduodenal fistula, and common bile duct exploration.

Physical examination on this entry failed to disclose any remarkable physical abnormalities. Work-up was begun, and disclosed a normal stomach and duodenum on upper gastrointestinal X-ray examination. A barium enema was negative. Since the patient obtained relief of her symptoms with phenobarbital and belladonna, and there was no jaundice, a diagnosis of gastrointestinal functional disorder was advanced.

Plans were in progress to discharge this woman to the outpatient department for further observation and management when she suddenly developed upper abdominal pain with muscle spasm and absent peristalsis. Her temperature rose to 102.6° F. and an amylase determination was reported as 605 units. A diagnosis of acute pancreatitis was made and treatment

---

* The author is indebted to Dr. Louis L. Smith for collecting the data and analyzing the course of this patient.

begun with a nasogastric tube on suction, meperidine (Demerol) analgesia, antibiotics, and intravenously administered fluids.

Twenty-four hours after the onset of this acute episode, the patient had a spiking temperature of 105.6° F. followed by a profound drop in her blood pressure to 40/0. A total of 600 ml. of plasma was administered rapidly, but there was no response in the blood pressure.

At the outset (first data after onset of pancreatitis) the data showed:

Blood

pH (arterial)	7.25	
pCO_2	47	mm. Hg
Total carbon dioxide	30	mM. per l.
Plasma chloride	100	mE. per l.
Plasma sodium	126	mE. per l.
Plasma potassium	2.7	mE. per l.
Hematocrit	47	

ARGUMENT. The continuation of vague abdominal complaints following the removal of a diseased gallbladder should bring to mind the possibility of a smoldering chronic pancreatitis, which in this woman's case flared to acute proportions during her hospitalization. The marked febrile response is indicative of acute retroperitoneal inflammation due to the acute pancreatitis. This process produces the large retroperitoneal fluid collection responsible for the shock episode. If the hematocrit is elevated it provides a reliable guide to minimum plasma needs, but such insidious alterations in circulation are not always associated with hematocrit changes because whole blood may also be lost in the hemorrhagic process.

The aim of treatment in such a patient is not only the maintenance of blood pressure but, of more importance, the maintenance of adequate tissue perfusion. The use of vasoconstrictor drugs involves the loss of blood perfusion in the splanchnic area, in order to support a sagging blood pressure. Since the common denominator in these problem cases is an ineffective blood volume, the first aim in therapy should obviously be the replacement of whole blood or plasma in adequate quantities. If there is concern about cardiac function in elderly patients when large quantities of colloid or blood are being administered, the venous pressure may be monitored, using a simple disposable venous pressure set. This will help in gauging when circulatory overloading or cardiac failure has supervened.

This patient had a severe respiratory and metabolic acidosis with hyponatremia. Despite the acidosis, her potassium was also low, evidence of very severe and acute potassium loss.

FURTHER COURSE. Following the institution of a phenylephrine (Neo-synephrine) drip, her pressure gradually then returned to normal levels. She was given an additional 500 ml. of whole blood, but since her pressure was unstable, the Neo-synephrine drip was continued. On the second day of her acute illness, the amylase rose to 972 units and her hematocrit stabilized

at 42 to 44. Plasma electrolyte determination revealed a sodium concentration of 125 mE. per l., potassium of 3.2 mE. per l., and chloride of 95 mE. per l.

Because of the poor blood pressure response of this patient to a total of 900 ml. of plasma and 500 ml. of whole blood during the first twelve hours of illness, intravenously adminished cortisone was begun in addition to Neo-synephrine on the evening of the first day of acute illness. Concentrated sodium bicarbonate was administered intravenously because of the acidosis and to bolster the low plasma sodium level. The need for Neo-synephrine decreased remarkably as this elderly patient's metabolic acidosis was corrected. On the fifth day of acute illness, she was weaned completely from Neo-synephrine. Adrenocorticotropic hormone was administered in tapering dosages at the completion of the cortisone therapy, and both were discontinued six days following the acute illness. Oral feedings were begun together with ambulation, and the patient was discharged thirteen days following the onset of acute pancreatitis.

COMMENT. The acidosis present at the outset appeared to demonstrate both metabolic and respiratory components. Its improvement cannot be laid wholly at the door of sodium bicarbonate therapy; improved circulation with volume restoration and better ventilation also played a role. Whatever the mechanism, it was only with restoration of acid-base balance and reestablishment of normal sodium concentration that normal blood pressure and flow could be maintained without Neo-synephrine. Volume restoration preceded this entire aspect, thus leaving in clear profile the effects of these "second echelon" agents. There was no evidence at any time that hydrocortisone helped her; her blood hydrocortisone values were high (60 mcg. per 100 ml.) and went even higher (125 mcg. per 100 ml.) on treatment. By contrast, there can be little question that the Neo-synephrine brought her blood pressure and renal (if not splanchnic) perfusion up; the problem was that of getting her weaned off the vasopressor once flow was restored. Concentrated base appeared to be very effective in this regard. The blood levels of catechol amines were not remarkable at any time.

This patient is quite typical of those elderly, chronically debilitated individuals who develop an acute inflammatory process associated with acute blood-volume reduction. Homeostatic mechanisms are sluggish owing to generalized arteriosclerotic vascular changes, and the response to administered colloid and blood is attenuated. As a result of poor tissue oxygenation, metabolic acidosis occurs, owing to the accumulation of tissue metabolites. What role the lowered plasma sodium concentration plays in such an individual is hard to assess; there is evidence that low-sodium states are generally associated with hypotension. It is therefore important to direct therapy not only toward blood volume replacement, but also to the correction of the acidosis and hyponatremia. The latter metabolic defects can best be repaired by the intravenous administration of concentrated sodium bicarbonate. A word of caution should be inserted regarding the use of

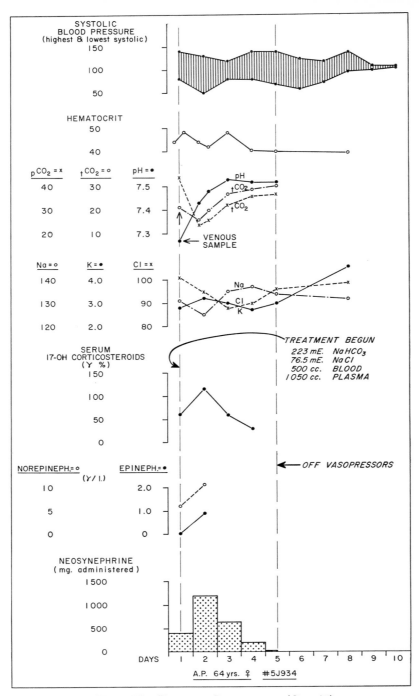

Figure 108. EVENTS IN PANCREATITIS (Case 15)

Above are shown the highest and lowest systolic blood pressures connected by shading. The spread in this shading indicates an unstable blood pressure. Below this are the hematocrit, the plasma chemical findings, and the plasma and urine hormone values, together with Neo-synephrine administered. The reader is referred to the text for details.

It will be noted that this patient with acute hypotension due to acute pancreatitis required large amounts of Neo-synephrine to give her blood pressure any sta-

bility, despite quantitative volume replacement. At this time she was severely acidotic with a marked elevation of the carbon dioxide tension and depression of pH. This acute acidosis responded well to restoration of her circulating blood volume by the administration of plasma and the restoration of acid-base balance by the administration of base. With these steps, her circulation improved, Neo-synephrine could be discontinued and the patient returned to normal vascular homeostasis.

647

vasopressors in such a situation. In a case such as this, further peripheral and splanchnic vasoconstriction only aggravates local tissue anoxia, and the resultant rise in blood pressure is all too frequently bought at the price of tissue perfusion. As a general rule, given a patient in shock due to an acute inflammatory disease, such as pancreatitis, in whom central cardiogenic causes such as coronary occlusion can be excluded, the first line of treatment is the administration of blood or plasma in generous quantities. The correction of a coexisting metabolic acidosis or electrolyte abnormality will enhance the perfusion-restoring effect of volume-replacement therapy. Not until this is done should one resort to catechol-amine pressor agents or corticosteroids.

CHAPTER 40

The Kidney: Renal Failure
and Obstruction

Only rarely does the surgeon become involved in the care of patients with severe chronic glomerulonephritis and chronic nephrosclerosis. The latter complicates surgery for hypertension, but advanced stages of renal disease are generally a contraindication to sympathectomy. The field of renal transplantation opens up new vistas in the treatment of chronic renal disease. But other than these rare occurrences and frontier areas, the surgeon is not concerned with the primary therapy of chronic nonobstructive parenchymatous renal disease.

He is intensively concerned, however, with the effects of acute disease on the kidney, with the effects of obstruction of the urinary tract on the kidney, and of surgery carried out elsewhere in the body but concurrent with chronic parenchymatous renal disease. It is on these areas that this chapter will therefore be focused, with a consideration of the following topics: decreased renal blood flow, acute renal failure, obstruction of the urinary tract, pyelonephritis, uretero-enterostomy, and surgery in chronic renal disease.

Section I. Shock and Other Conditions Associated with a Primary Decrease in Glomerular Filtration Rate

The kidney cannot do its job of regulating acid-base balance, excreting metabolites, and regulating the total volume of body water unless the tubular cells have some glomerular filtrate to process. Glomerular filtration also means renal blood flow and therefore cellular vitality. For this reason, the maintenance of the glomerular filtration rate is the basic renal concern in all of surgical care. This involves first and foremost the maintenance of a normal blood volume, blood pressure, and forward flow with normal tissue perfusion.

In patients with severe hemorrhage, traumatic shock, acute desalting, the oligemia of burns, and peritonitis, there is a marked decrease in the glomerular filtration rate, due

in part to lowered blood pressure itself and in part to vasoconstrictive changes in the renal vasculature, which deny blood to the glomerulus and the tubule and which may accompany very early deficits in volume. This used to be referred to as "prerenal deviation," a devious term for a simple thing, namely, decrease in the filtration of plasma through the glomerulus due to loss of effective volume traceable to disease elsewhere and in the absence of primary renal disease.

The presence or absence of preexistent renal disease in such cases is a primary determining factor in the prognosis. As will be developed repeatedly in this chapter, the presence of preexistent renal disease, no

Page 649

matter how slight, renders the patient especially vulnerable to severe renal damage resulting from acute surgical disease, trauma, or shock.

As effective blood volume is lowered and peripheral vascular constriction begins there is a disproportionate constriction of the renal vessels ("differential renal vasoconstriction"), evidently serving in part to maintain flow elsewhere. To maintain some filtration during such a period of decreased renal perfusion there is a further constriction of the efferent arteriole of the glomerulus, resulting in an increased filtration fraction of the total renal plasma flow. Since it is the efferent arteriole of the glomerulus that carries blood to the tubule, the tubule thus becomes even more anoxic under such circumstances. This is characteristic of severe injury, desalting, traumatic edema, and surgical volume reduction of a variety of causes. It is at this time of tubular anoxia that the tubular cell is so especially vulnerable to nephrotoxins such as the heme pigments.

If decreased glomerular filtration persists for any length of time, the patient begins to pay the price of low urine secretion: metabolic acidosis, a tendency to overhydration (if there is any route by which water intake can be produced), and the accumulation of metabolites that fall into three groups—nitrogen compounds of small molecular weight, intracellular electrolytes (potassium, sulfate, and phosphate), and organic acids. When this is combined with certain other insults, particularly previous kidney disease, renal anoxia, prolonged decreased renal blood flow, and the presence of certain toxic pigments such as hemoglobin and bilirubin, a severe renal lesion develops, known by many names including "acute renal failure" and "tubular necrosis." This will be discussed in the subsequent section on acute renal failure.

Five causes are commonly associated with a decreased glomerular filtration rate in surgery.

(1) *Many anesthetic agents, during the induction stage*, cause a transient decrease in glomerular filtration.

(2) *Extensive surgical operation associated with considerable blood loss*, requiring blood replacement, may be assumed to produce a considerable decrease in the glomerular filtration rate, even though the patient has never been in shock.

(3) *The desalting water losses and sequestered edemas* produce a decreased glomerular filtration rate that seems to be out of proportion to the change in blood volume, even though this latter change may ultimately become marked. Intestinal obstruction, regional enteritis, ulcerative colitis, malfunctioning ileostomy, pancreatic fistula, as examples, are associated with decreased glomerular filtration during the period of acute desalting, particularly if the latter involves a volume-reduction phase (see Part III). Acidosis is associated with (as well as being produced by) renal failure, while alkalosis is associated with a remarkable maintenance of urine output under many circumstances.

(4) *True dehydration* (desiccation) with a rising plasma osmolality is associated with a marked decrease in glomerular filtration rate.

(5) *Frank shock*, whether it occurs from plasma loss, as in burns and peritonitis, or from external blood loss, wounds, or crushed tissue, is associated with a profound and prolonged decrease in glomerular filtration rate.

All of the situations outlined above, occurring transiently and without concomitant complicating effects, are in themselves completely reversible as regards their effect on the kidney, the circulation, and tissue viability.

The therapeutic objective is thus the maintenance of the normal blood volume, pressure, and flow. This, more than any other single factor, will release the kidney from its vasoconstricting influence, restore glomerular filtration to normal, reestablish the blood supply of the tubules, and produce some tubular fluid which the tubular cells can proceed to work on, thus reestablishing the homeostatic efficiency of this organ.

Considerable controversy has turned on the question of whether or not restoration of blood volume should be the first priority in patients with the dehydrating-desalting type of lesion. The renal response is the prime indication for restoring blood volume first. An individual with intestinal obstruction, sick for three or four days, may have lost from

300 to 600 mE. of sodium, with water and other ions to go with it. Yet, when he is first seen, oliguric or anuric, with a high hematocrit and a shocklike state, his first requirement is for restoration of blood volume, and this can be carried out most effectively by the use of plasma (or dextran) or whole blood, or both. The restoration of the blood volume to normal by these steps can be accompanied by the gradual restoration of total body water and sodium to normal. This will result in more rapid improvement of renal function than infusion of water and salt alone. The use of whole blood exclusively has been shown to worsen the renal lesion in dogs after reduction of extracellular fluid; by this token plasma may be preferred, and resalting with rehydration must of course accompany the volume restoration.

Where dehydration and hypertonicity are at fault (as in the solute load or the fever-dyspnea complex) the initial treatment should be water alone, since increased blood viscosity is a factor adversely affecting renal function. Where the initial loss is of intravascular components, as in trauma, hemorrhage, crush, burns, or peritonitis, the initial replacement must be of an intravascular colloidal fluid: blood, plasma, albumin, or dextran.

The placement of an inlying urethral catheter in patients who are acutely ill, to measure the urine output on an interval basis, has a unique usefulness. Its greatest virtue lies in the demonstration of beginning return of filtration pressure and renal output as the blood volume is restored to normal and the kidney released from hypotension and limiting vasoconstriction. The volume of urine output in such a situation reflects renal blood supply, and therein lies its importance.

Study of the urine itself as regards the sediment, specific gravity, and electrolyte content may also be helpful, although the sedimentary findings are usually nonspecific and the other data acquire meaning only with the passage of time. The interval measurement of urine output (hourly or bi-hourly) is quite sensitive in demonstrating gross overreplacement of water and salt under certain circumstances. In the acutely ill patient, the maintenance of hourly urine volumes greater than 100 ml. per hour over a period of several hours suggests overreplacement of fluid.

The apparent limitation of the hourly measurement of urine output due to antidiuresis disappears with an understanding of the antidiuretic effect on urine volume in patients during periods of anesthesia, acute stress, dehydration, trauma, and shock. Under strong antidiuresis, the volume of urine output is a linear function of the discharge of glomerular solute. *In the acutely ill, urine volume is therefore to be equated with blood supply, not tubular activity.* Antidiuresis is not necessarily associated with oliguria. As glomerular filtration rate returns to normal and solutes appear in the renal tubule, water will be extracted from this filtrate according to the capacity of the tubule to exhibit maximal negative free water clearance. If the glomerular filtrate is very small in volume (25 to 30 ml. per minute) the maximal water reabsorptive capacity of the distal tubules can process this urine to a specific gravity of 1.036 to 1.040 (provided the kidney was healthy to begin with), corresponding to an osmolality of 1400 mO. per l. The finding of such urine in the acutely injured or dehydrated individual suggests good function of renal tubules, the need for restoration of bodily hydration, and a generally satisfactory state of affairs for further treatment.

If, however, the body has built up a large "solute backlog" as a result of several hours of oliguria during a catabolic period, the glomerular filtrate will contain a large amount of nonreabsorbable solute, and the mechanism for reabsorbing water in the distal tubules, though acting maximally, may not be able to increase the osmolality much above 700 mO. per l. (corresponding to a specific gravity of about 1.015 to 1.020). Large volumes of urine of this specific gravity may be elaborated.

The volume:concentration relationship of urine has not, in our experience, permitted us to differentiate the patient with some solute diuresis through a responsive renal tubule from the patient starting in renal failure unless a low volume carried a very high concentration; this finding is eloquent evidence of healthy nephrons. Much more important evidence lies in the time course of urine volumes, the presence of benzidine-reacting pigment, and the change in blood urea nitrogen and potassium concentrations. The diagnosis of early renal failure becomes highly suspect with a shrinking urine volume, when there is a rising blood urea nitrogen and a rising potassium concentra-tion in spite of restoration of blood volume and body water to functional normal, as judged by normal tissue perfusion elsewhere, slow pulse, normal blood pressure, good color, and resuscitated clinical status. *Solid clinical evidence of homeostatic resuscitation yet without a corresponding increase in urine flow is the most suggestive evidence of the onset of renal failure*

Section II.   Acute Renal Failure*

A. TERMINOLOGY

The first discrimination of a characteristically acute clinicopathologic entity in surgical patients, leading to renal failure, azotemia, uremia, and death, is probably to be assigned to the description by Bywaters of the "crush syndrome" during World War II. It is historically appealing to suggest that the rather recent description of this lesion depends in large part upon the fact that the seriously injured, seriously wounded, traumatized individual in shock who develops this lesion is a patient who would not have survived the acute phase of the injury prior to the widespread and liberal use of whole blood in transfusion. In all the wars of mankind up to World War II, these patients died before they could develop renal failure. The "crush syndrome" developed in injury with the crush of muscle, and during the later phases of World War II there was a large number of descriptions of lesions of this same general type, usually associated with severe wounds and often with massive transfusion of whole blood, the blood occasionally open to some question as regards its state of preservation.

About 1945 the term "lower nephron nephrosis" was coined to describe this lesion because the histologic appearances were largely confined to the distal tubule. At the present time, it is best to refer to it as "acute renal failure" or "acute post-traumatic renal insufficiency." There is no longer any patho-logic justification for referring to it as "lower nephron nephrosis." It is not different in any important respect from the "crush-syndrome kidney." There is considerable necrosis of renal tubule cells, and for this reason the lesion has also been called "acute tubular necrosis." It can be readily produced in the experimental animal by combinations of renal ischemia and the injection of various pigments, and for this reason the lesion has also been called "ischemic-pigment nephrosis" or just "ischemic nephrosis" or "ischemic renal necrosis." Attempts to discriminate between minor histologic variations of this lesion are not clinically or pathologically rewarding. It is best to group them all together in the one term "acute renal failure."†

B. PATHOGENESIS

As described in the section on shock (Part VI) the kidney is quite tolerant of decreased blood flow. A full forty-five minutes of total ischemia is followed by full recovery. It is also tolerant of pigment loads: hemoglobin, methemoglobin, and bilirubin are excreted without damage in many disease states. The combination, however, is extremely destructive to tubular cells. The pathogenesis of acute post-traumatic renal insufficiency is covered in the axiom: *renal anoxia plus nephrotoxin produces failure.*

This lesion is produced by renal ischemia

---

* Certain of these data are discussed also in the sections on blood volume (Part II) and wound shock (Part VI).

† Despite the multiplicity of terms one must distinguish this lesion from renal cortical necrosis, a rare but very distinct lesion not seen after traumatic shock.

Text continues on page 661.

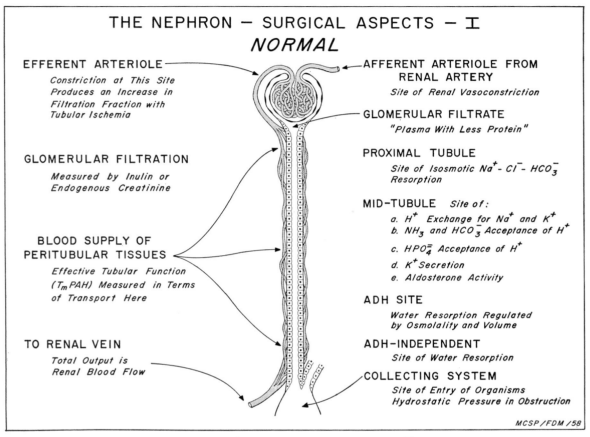

Figure 109. THE NEPHRON—SURGICAL ASPECTS. 1. NORMAL

In this and the succeeding six diagrams are shown a representation of the functioning nephron together with a description of various aspects of function of the nephron in situations commonly seen in surgery.

The nephron is drawn so as to show both the afferent and efferent arterioles, the blood supply of the tubules distal to the efferent arteriole, and the collecting blood and urine systems leading to the renal vein and the renal pelvis respectively.

The detailed functional anatomy shown here is self-explanatory. No attempt at detailed schematic differentiation of portions of the tubule is attempted.

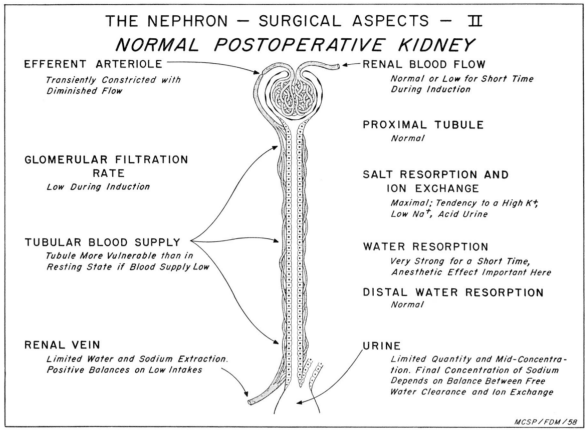

Figure 110.   THE NEPHRON—SURGICAL ASPECTS. II. NORMAL POSTOPERATIVE KIDNEY

In this chart are shown some of the changes in renal function which one observes during the first few hours after an operation not associated with severe blood loss, shock, traumatic edema, desalting water loss, or other marked redistributions of blood or body water. During anesthesia induction glomerular filtration rate is apt to be low, but other than this short episode it will be seen to be normal. Tubular salt and water reabsorption are very active and the net resultant urine, while relatively small in volume, is extremely variable as to precise concentration of any one ion, since this depends upon happenchance balances between the rates of salt reabsorption and water reabsorption. For instance, one may observe a fairly small volume of rather concentrated urine containing sodium in concentrations as high as 120 mE. per liter; yet, because of the small volume, the total sodium excretion may be very small (30 to 50 mE., for example) if volume is low. There is evidence for efferent arteriolar vasoconstriction and diminished tubular blood flow if there is the slightest impairment of the adequacy of extracellular volume. It is probably this factor that renders the tubule more vulnerable to nephrotoxins than in the resting state. Clinical evidence suggests that the intraoperative kidney is more vulnerable to the development of acute renal failure than is the resting kidney.

Negative free water clearance is regularly observed after surgical operation. By this is meant that there is less water in the final urine than there is in the glomerular filtrate. When small amounts of filtrate are formed, this does not require the activity of antidiuretic hormone (ADH) because of the ADH-independent distal tubular site. Negative free water clearance cannot be quantitated without some index of glomerular filtration rate, but if the final urine, as elaborated, has an osmolality higher than 350 mO. per liter, one may assume that negative free water clearance is present.

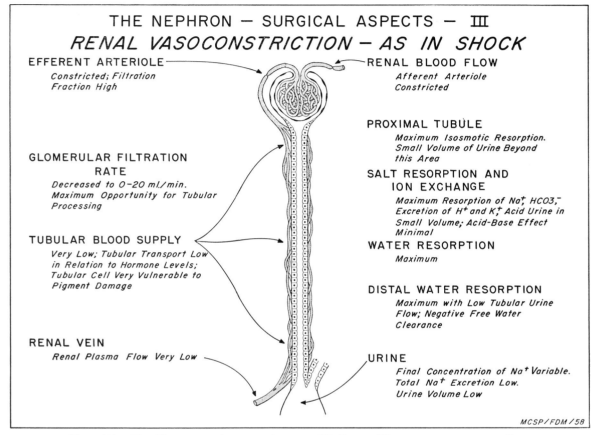

THE NEPHRON — SURGICAL ASPECTS — III
RENAL VASOCONSTRICTION – AS IN SHOCK

EFFERENT ARTERIOLE
*Constricted; Filtration
Fraction High*

RENAL BLOOD FLOW
*Afferent Arteriole
Constricted*

PROXIMAL TUBULE
*Maximum Isosmotic Resorption.
Small Volume of Urine Beyond
this Area*

GLOMERULAR FILTRATION
RATE
*Decreased to 0–20 ml./min.
Maximum Opportunity for Tubular
Processing*

SALT RESORPTION AND
ION EXCHANGE
*Maximum Resorption of Na^+, $HCO3^-$,
Excretion of H^+ and K^+; Acid Urine in
Small Volume; Acid-Base Effect
Minimal*

WATER RESORPTION
Maximum

TUBULAR BLOOD SUPPLY
*Very Low; Tubular Transport Low
in Relation to Hormone Levels;
Tubular Cell Very Vulnerable to
Pigment Damage*

DISTAL WATER RESORPTION
*Maximum with Low Tubular Urine
Flow; Negative Free Water
Clearance*

RENAL VEIN
Renal Plasma Flow Very Low

URINE
*Final Concentration of Na^+ Variable.
Total Na^+ Excretion Low.
Urine Volume Low*

MCSP/FDM/58

Figure 111. THE NEPHRON—SURGICAL ASPECTS. III. RENAL VASOCONSTRICTION AS IN SHOCK

Here one sees the maximum hemodynamic alteration in the functioning kidney. There is severe afferent arteriolar vasoconstriction with diminished renal blood flow and glomerular filtration. The efferent arteriole is also severely constricted, resulting in an increased filtration fraction and a severely ischemic tubule. It is this ischemic tubule that is so vulnerable to nephrotoxins circulating as a result of the trauma, mismatched trans-fusion, crushed muscle or other events leading to pigment release.

Because of the very small volume of glomerular filtrate (and as long as the tubule remains viable) there is maximum opportunity for tubular processing of the filtrate. It is for this reason that early in shock one sees a small volume of acid urine with very high specific gravity. There is negative free water clearance.

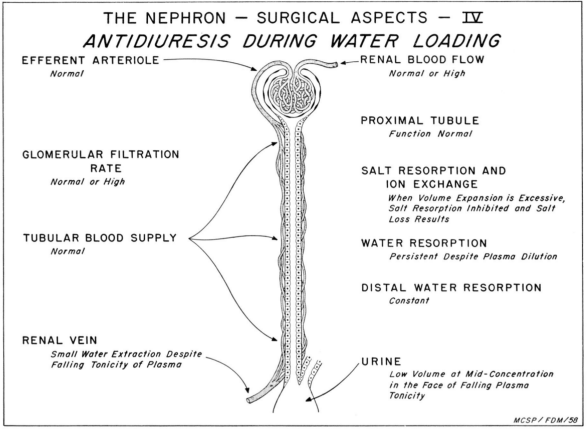

Figure 112. THE NEPHRON—SURGICAL ASPECTS. IV. ANTIDIURESIS DURING WATER LOADING

In this chart is depicted the situation characteristically seen in the postoperative patient who is given too much water. The postanesthesia, post-traumatic patient is in an antidiuretic state for from one to three days as demonstrated by consistently negative free water clearance despite water load. If, in clinical care, these water loads are consistently given in excess of the requirements imposed by renal and extrarenal loss, then this water is retained in the body and hypotonicity results.

The renal mechanisms include normal renal blood flow with normal tubular function and ion exchange, save for the fact that, if extracellular volume is exces-sively expanded by water infusion (as in water intoxication), there may be a sharp cut-off in sodium reabsorption in mid-tubule, with very large sodium excretions despite the hypotonicity. Antidiuretic activity appears to be consistent (as demonstrated by water reabsorption) and there is a low volume of urine at mid-concentration and negative free water clearance, despite falling plasma tonicity. Free water excretion is limited. If, in this situation, a large solute load is presented (glucose, urea, dextran, mannitol, as examples), very large urine volumes are produced but still with negative free water clearance.

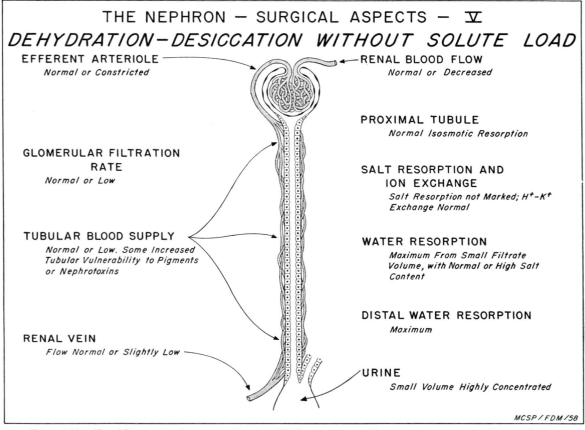

Figure 113. The Nephron—Surgical Aspects. V. Dehydration-Desiccation without Solute Load

In this chart are enumerated the characteristic changes seen in the kidney in the face of dehydration-desiccation as produced by excessive pulmonary water loss. The detailed renal mechanisms in this instance are not different from those seen in acute desalting water loss with the exception of the fact that the acute volume reduction in the latter state (occurring early) produces much more drastic alteration in renal hemodynamics and glomerular filtration than does dehydration-desiccation alone.

Here, renal blood flow is normal or slightly decreased. Glomerular filtration is of low normal volume and there is maximal opportunity for tubular processing of the urine.

This tubular processing is very active and consists primarily of water and salt reabsorption. It is in desiccation-dehydration that one sees the very small urine volume at the highest attainable specific gravity, in the presence of good renal function. Salt reabsorption is also active both in the proximal tubule and in the mid-tubule, particularly if there is over-all volume reduction.

Although tubular transport is very active and tubular blood supply not markedly diminished, the tubular cell appears to be vulnerable to nephrotoxic damage when it is acting on a small volume of glomerular filtrate under maximal antidiuretic stimulation. It is in chronic dehydration that one finds acute renal insufficiency potentiated after wounding. In the experimental animal the same combination can be shown to be dangerous by preparing the animal with dehydration, desalting or vasopressin injections before administering the nephrotoxin.

Clearly, adequate hydration protects the kidney from this vulnerability.

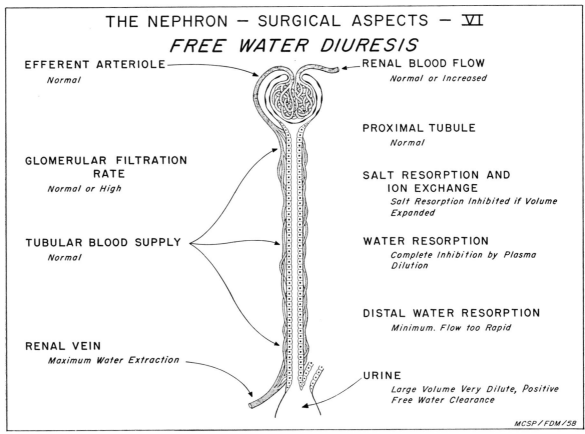

Figure 114. THE NEPHRON—SURGICAL ASPECTS. VI. FREE WATER DIURESIS

In this chart are listed the events of normal free water diuresis. These events occur in a normal person after drinking large volumes of hypotonic fluid such as water, soft drinks, or hard drinks. This is the sort of sequence not seen in the post-traumatic patient, patients suffering from chronic sepsis, burns, congestive heart failure, liver disease, or kidney disease. This normal free water diuresis is the mechanism which is lacking immediately after trauma and inhalation anesthetics.

Normal or increased renal blood flows are seen with normal or increased glomerular filtration rates. Large amounts of filtrate course down the tubule. There is complete inhibition of antidiuretic activity with the resultant formation of a large volume of very dilute urine and positive free water clearance. By this is meant that there is more water in the final urine as excreted than there was in the glomerular filtrate as initially formed. Positive free water clearance may achieve such figures as 12 to 15 ml. per minute. Beyond this the kidney cannot go, and for this reason water loading beyond this rate, from whatever source, will inevitably produce water intoxication.

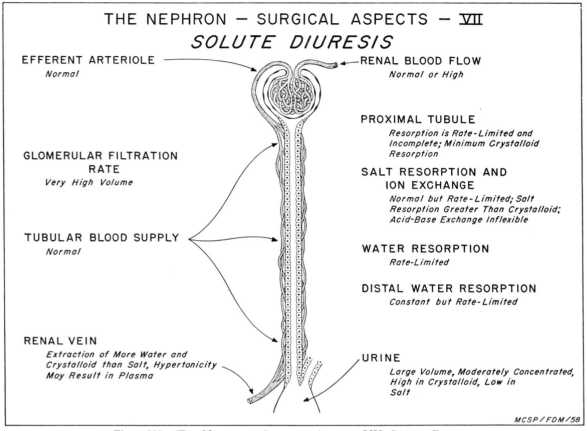

Figure 115.   THE NEPHRON—SURGICAL ASPECTS. VII. SOLUTE DIURESIS

In this chart are depicted the events that occur when the kidney is presented with a large amount of an obligatory tubular solute. Such materials include crystalloids such as glucose or mannitol. Sodium chloride and bicarbonate, however, can constitute obligatory tubular solutes if they get beyond the proximal tubule in large amounts. This may be found in recovering obstructive uropathy, in which case the normal urinary electrolytes are actually the solute diuretic. Furthermore, in the postoperative patient under antidiuretic activity, solute diuresis may still be exhibited and in quite considerable amounts as a result of the infusion of crystalloids or sodium and chloride. Here again the exact balance between solute diuresis, antidiuresis, and salt resorption (aldosterone-like activity) determines the final composition of postoperative urine. It is important to reemphasize that in the normal person, given large amounts of vasopressin, free water diuresis is never demonstrated but profuse solute diuresis is readily demonstrable.

In solute diuresis renal blood flow is normal or high.

Tubular reabsorption is rate-limited, and when glomerular filtrate is formed in very large amounts, no tubular process can reach its ceiling performance value. Antidiuresis is also rate-limited, and in solute diuresis, even though an antidiuretic stimulus may be maximal (as in tube feeding hypertonicity, diabetes mellitus, or recovering mild post-traumatic renal failure), there is still a large volume of urine formed which carries out with it a great deal of water and solute. A very large volume of moderately concentrated urine is formed. It is by these mechanisms that solute diuresis leads to extracellular volume-reduction and desalting water loss.

If the solute diuresis results from the presence of such a solute as glucose, mannitol, or urea, then large amounts of this material will be found in the urine. The low molecular-weight component of commercial dextran acts as a solute diuretic and is found in the urine in very large quantities (up to 50 per cent of the administered dose) in the first 24 hours after dextran treatment.

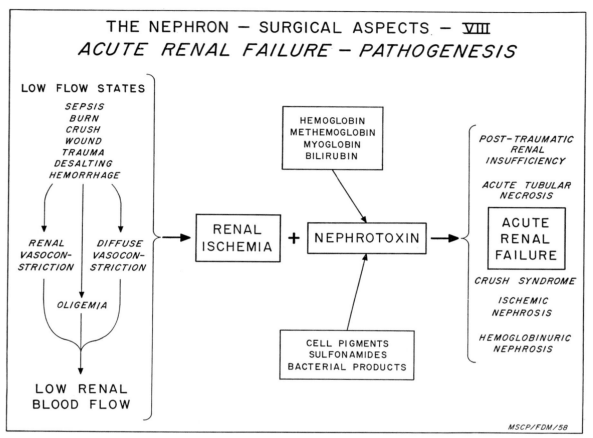

Figure 116. THE NEPHRON—SURGICAL ASPECTS. VIII. ACUTE RENAL FAILURE—PATHOGENESIS

Acute renal failure is produced by renal ischemia and anoxia plus the presentation to the kidney (during the ischemic phase) of nephrotoxic materials. In this chart are shown some of the mechanisms which produce renal vasoconstriction, diffuse vasoconstriction, and oligemia (leading to renal ischemia) as well as some of the types of chemical substances that are toxic to the kidney and whose presence in the anoxic state is followed by acute renal failure.

Synonyms of acute renal failure are shown. These terms are not all absolutely synonymous and some may differ as to their definitions but they cover the same general phenomena and the same clinical and therapeutic implications. The term "crush syndrome," for instance, refers to other clinical features in addition to the renal picture; the term "hemoglobinuric nephrosis" should not be used in a patient who does not have free hemoglobin in blood and urine.

It is the combination of ischemia plus toxin that is so damaging. One often sees long periods of low renal blood flow without serious damage; the same is true of large loads of hemoglobin or bile. But the presentation of these pigment loads in the presence of renal ischemia is very apt to be followed by acute renal failure.

and anoxia caused by decreased blood volume, decreased renal perfusion, or differential renal vasoconstriction and complicated by

(1) the presence of free pigment, either hemoglobin or myoglobin, resulting from blood destruction (in the bottle or in the patient) or muscle crush;
(2) incompatible transfusion reactions, with hypotension and free pigment;
(3) infection with bacteremia, and shock;
(4) preexistent renal disease;
(5) preexistent dehydration or desalting;
(6) the presence of bile pigments, as in hepatic failure;
(7) undue prolongation of decreased renal blood flow, without other nephrotoxic factors; and
(8) other nephrotoxins: sulfonamide allergy, heavy metals.

The majority of patients with acute renal failure trace the origin of their trouble back to severe trauma, surgical operation, obstetrical disaster, or incompatible blood transfusion, and can be analyzed in terms of one of the complications of renal anoxia listed above.

Reduced renal blood flow is of especial significance in producing tissue anoxia because of the fixed capacity for oxygen extraction exhibited by the kidney. In other tissues, as blood flow is reduced a progressively larger fraction of the oxygen is removed from the incoming blood, and oxygenation, however precarious, is maintained for a time with a low venous oxygen saturation. The kidney is unique in its limited and fixed ability to deoxygenate blood; oxygenation of the tissue becomes a linear function of the blood flow. The kidney is accustomed to the hemodynamic wealth of 20 per cent of the cardiac output; the degree of renal anoxia seen in hypotension is suggested by the poverty that follows, as cardiac output is reduced to a small fraction of normal.

C. NATURAL HISTORY AND BIOCHEMICAL LESION

The natural history of this lesion is that of interstitial edema and tubular necrosis going on to healing over a period of one to six weeks. The lesion may heal to an extent that renders either clinical or histologic identification impossible. Although it is highly lethal, it is not the local lesion that kills the patient. His first threat is overhydration, his next is hyperkalemia; infection always threatens him. If these three can be side-stepped or warded off, survival will occur.

1. The Concept of "A Few Good Nephrons"

The kidney of renal failure lacks flexibility and adaptability. It cannot excrete loads of water or salt as fast as normal; it cannot alter urine pH, HCO_3^-, or NH_4^+ as rapidly as normal. It excretes urine that is partially concentrated, in the sense that it is of higher osmolality than plasma. This lack of flexibility is nicely explained by the presence in the damaged kidney of a few normally functioning nephrons in a mass of nonfunctioning nephrons, rather than by a diffuse partial reduction in function. In such a case the remaining nephrons are constantly working at the solute diuresis level and at a maximal rate. They are constantly overloaded. Under such circumstances a relatively fixed urine osmolality, pH, and titratable acidity with tendency toward plasma chloride acidosis are characteristic.

The concept of "a few functioning nephrons" also explains the poor response of *chronic* renal failure to superimposed dehydration or volume reduction in surgical patients. Solute diuresis in the few nephrons is constant. Intake restriction or extrarenal loss is therefore followed by continued solute diuresis with the kidney unable to conserve water. This pathologic renal water loss is continued until blood volume is compromised, glomerular filtration rate reduced, and a sudden reduction in urine output produced. Stated otherwise, the few overloaded nephrons do not conserve salt or water until such time as their blood supply fails completely due to shock and diminished glomerular filtration.

D. EARLY DIAGNOSIS

The trademark of acute renal failure is a falling urine volume despite accurate and adequate restoration of blood and body water volumes to normal.

There is a rising blood urea nitrogen and

plasma potassium concentration, with a specific gravity near 1.015 to 1.020 in the voided urine. The fallacy of this latter criterion or of the urine sediment (fat cells, erythrocytes, pigment casts) as the sole diagnostic feature has already been discussed. The urine volume in acute renal failure is 100 to 350 ml. per day.

The presence of pigment in the urine, found in the supernatant of the spun sediment and reacting postively with guaiac or benzidine, is very strong additional corroborative evidence of the presence of this lesion when other signs are also present; the finding of significant free hemoglobin in the plasma also suggests this lesion. *Both of these findings are not the result of the lesion so much as they are a factor in its cause, of such constancy that their presence acquires diagnostic meaning.*

The complete absence of urine output—truly "zero output," meaning by this only 1 to 5 ml. an hour of material probably arising as transudate from the ureter, bladder, and urethral mucous membranes—is not suggestive of acute renal insufficiency. Patients in shock or with overwhelming infection may have periods of total anuria, but these crises rarely last long, particularly if active volume treatment is undertaken. In the typical situation of post-traumatic renal insufficiency urine volumes of zero are almost never recorded. There is a constant small flow of urine.

If a patient has no urine output over a period of several hours, the first diagnosis which should come to mind is obstruction of the urinary tract. This can be due to stones or tumor, bilateral renal infarction, or occlusion of the aorta. True anuria is excessively rare in acute renal failure of the post-traumatic type. If obstruction is suspected on this or any other basis, retrograde pyelography should be undertaken.

1. Decreased Urine Volume versus Tubular Necrosis

How is one to judge that blood volume and vascular responses have returned to normal, if the patient cannot show a urine-output response because he is passing into a phase of acute renal insufficiency? This question poses one of the most difficult diagnostic problems seen in surgery. Its answer lies in clinical examination of the patient. Renal failure is presumed present if urine volume does not recover when there is restoration of blood pressure to normal, slowing of the pulse, restoration of the hematocrit to normal (if it has previously been elevated), a move in the right direction as regards the concentration of water and solutes in the plasma, return of color, warmth, mentation. All of these things must be considered as the evidences for *accomplishment of mission* as regards homeostatic restoration of the patient with early renal insufficiency. If, as these indices are turned toward normal by appropriate therapy, urine volume does not increase, and blood urea nitrogen and potassium concentrations show a tendency to rise, one should assume that tubular necrosis has occurred and institute steps for the management of this disease.

In instances where shock, fluid sequestration, desalting, or dehydration is in the background, an infusion test is valuable and must be done with care. The hazards of this test, if it is poorly or inappropriately carried out, are obvious. Most of the effective steps in surgery are hazardous, although they must be taken, and the infusion test in early renal insufficiency is no exception.

In general, if a rapid infusion of blood, colloid, crystalloid, or electrolyte produces a significant increase in urine output in early oliguria, this result militates strongly against renal insufficiency as a cause of the oliguria. The response indicates lack of some fraction of body water as the cause and dictates future treatment clearly. If there is no response to appropriate infusion, renal insufficiency is likely, and fluid must be rigidly withheld to "balance."

The selection of the appropriate fluid for infusion test is critical. Blood, plasma (or dextran or albumin), salts, and water have all been used. Each has its proper place. A sharp look at the immediately previous history of fluid imbalance will help in the selection of the infusion fluid; that most likely lacking should be selected.

In general the infusion test volume is about 1.0 to 1.5 per cent of body weight, which is therefore about 20 per cent of the blood volume or—in a 70 kg. man—about 700 to 1000 ml. If colloid is used, 500 to 700 ml. is infused in thirty to forty minutes; if noncolloid, 1000 ml. in forty minutes. Such times of infusion must be regarded as minimal; under many circumstances a longer time is used. Venous pressure should be tested frequently during the infusion in the patient who is elderly, or who has cardiac disease, hypertension, or arteriosclerosis. In early renal ischemia caused by acute loss of blood volume, it is better to transfuse to early elevation of venous pressure than it is to leave the patient in shock. This is not true in later care. Some loose rules of procedure for infusion test in the differential diagnosis of early oliguria are:

(1) *in burns and peritonitis*—use plasma or dextran or 5 per cent albumin;

(2) *in hemorrhage, crush, wounds*—use whole blood;

(3) *in desalting water loss*—use saline and lactate;

(4) *in desalting water loss with subtraction acidosis*—use lactate;

(5) *in desiccation*—use 5 per cent dextrose in water.

E. EARLY MANAGEMENT—SHORT OF DIALYSIS

The early management of acute renal failure depends almost exclusively on the avoidance of therapy that will hurt the patient and hinder the treatment of his surgical disease. Positive steps designed to promote the healing of the parenchymatous lesion in the kidney are unknown. With maintenance of the circulation this occurs as a normal healing process. It is probable that there is no means of accelerating it. The problem is one of keeping the patient alive until the lesion can heal, and avoiding anything that would retard local healing in the kidney itself.

1. Fluids

The causes of death in the early days of post-traumatic renal insufficiency are, first,

the continued overadministration of sodium-containing fluids, second, the overadministration of blood or colloid, and, third, the occurrence of overwhelming infection.

The guide to the use of fluids in this condition is the concept of "thinking in terms of balance." The patient must be managed with a view to restoring to his body those substances that are lost from day to day through his skin, through his lungs, or through his gastrointestinal tract or other discharges. He must be permitted some weight loss each day as he oxidizes body fat to provide caloric energy during a period of low intake. Daily weighing is an important help in treatment.

If continuing hypotension is a part of the oliguric picture after volume restoration, one is left with infection as the most likely cause of the continuing hypotension and oliguria. A constant realistic reevaluation (as often as four times a day) of the fluid and colloid requirements of these patients and of the manner in which they are being met is essential.

Fluid and diet by mouth are of course best, if feasible. In most patients who are in this difficult situation after injury or operation, oral intake is rarely accepted or is positively contraindicated by the occurrence of vomiting and the presence of distention and ileus.

2. Potassium and the Lethal Triad

After the third day, potassium toxicity is the commonest cause of death. The use of exchange resins to get rid of potassium has been found disappointing. The resins cannot be given by mouth to extremely ill patients, and when given by rectum they are not very effective.

Hyperkalemia threatens a lethal outcome when the potassium concentration rises to the region of 7.5 mE. per l. or higher. Metabolic acidosis—so common in renal failure—tends to raise the level of the plasma potassium concentration and to potentiate its cardiotoxic effects. Hyponatremia, often dilutional, aggravates the cardiac toxicity of hyperkalemia. *The three—hyperkalemia, acidosis, and hyponatremia—go together as a lethal triad in renal failure. The fatal event is cardiac arrhythmia.*

Only rarely is the adminstration of sodium bicarbonate useful. The acidotic defect in renal failure is an addition acidosis and the treatment of it by the addition of base threatens the patient with the very overadministration of water and fluid that one seeks to avoid. Only where extrarenal sodium loss has occurred or potassium toxicity is pressing is sodium bicarbonate a valuable adjunct in renal failure.

The time course of potassium concentration must be followed chemically at frequent intervals. Frequent electrocardiograms are important, although the electrocardiogram cannot be considered a substitute for plasma potassium measurement; it is an index of the cardiac toxicity of hyperkalemia.

The rate of rise of plasma potassium concentration in "resting renal failure" is slow— as little as 1.0 mE. per week. After severe injury this rise is much faster—as much as 0.5 mE. per day. This is due to the increased rate of catabolism of lean tissue. This poses a special threat in post-traumatic renal insufficiency.

Concentrated carbohydrate (25 or 50 per cent glucose with insulin) given by caval catheter supplies caloric need and takes potassium into cells for its combustion, but one must beware the caval catheter if left in place too long. It must always be in the superior cava; it should be changed every three days. As a site for the origin of septic emboli it is a hazard.

Intravenously administered fat produces a transient ketosis as the fat is oxidized. Not harmful in other circumstances, this is a hazard in renal failure.

The use of testosterone propionate, 150 mg. three times a week, may hold back destruction of lean tissue, and has become a part of the protocol for most patients. Other steroids are contraindicated.

3. Sodium, Calcium, Tonicity

Because a low plasma sodium concentration accentuates the electrocardiographic effects and cardiac toxicity of high potassium levels, the administration of hypertonic saline solution to patients with hyperkalemia has a place as short-term treatment in a life-endangering hyperkalemic emergency, despite the fact that it threatens the patient with an excessively high body water and salt content with edema, pulmonary edema, and hypertension. The administration of calcium salts will also counteract the hyperkalemic electrocardiogram, even though they do not affect the potassium concentration in itself. They must be given with great caution if the patient is digitalized.

As urea rises, total osmolality rises. In addition, the accumulation of other nonelectrolyte solute (creatinine, purines, polypeptides, keto-acids) adds to total osmolality and tends to lower the sodium concentration. Any increase in water loading adds greatly to this dilutional hypotonicity. There is thus—

(1) An increase in the sodium-osmolar differential—that is, an accumulation of nonelectrolyte solute. As an example, osmolality of plasma may rise to 330 mO. per l., while sodium falls to 130 mE. per l. There are then about 70 mO. per l. of nonelectrolyte solute present in the extracellular fluid.

(2) A tendency to hyponatremia.

(3) A change in effective osmotic pressure, which usually falls despite the rising total osmolality. This disparity is due to the fact that urea and many other "renal-failure solutes" freely permeate body cells and are not "effective" solutes in terms of holding water outside of cells. And finally,

(4) This new crystalloid solute (rising most rapidly after severe injury) promotes the solute-diuresis effect in the few remaining nephrons, and is responsible in part for the dehydration-desiccation seen in some cases of post-traumatic renal failure, especially burns. The adminstration of water quickly repairs this defect.

Hyponatremia and hypotonicity interfere with normal brain function and are important factors in the coma of uremia; they both accentuate the cardiotoxicity of hyperkalemia.

4. The Gastric-Suction Effect

When a patient with renal failure is forming gastric acid and is also on constant gastric suction, a tendency to subtraction alkalosis is produced by the removal of hydrogen ion. This counteracts the addition acidosis of renal failure. Since it is this acidosis which is in part responsible for hyperkalemia, this net effect of gastric suction here is good—if not carried to the extreme of severe desalting. The water may have to be returned quantitatively, and lost salt can be returned as sodium bicarbonate, further reducing the acidosis.

Gastric juice contains an amount of potassium which is, approximately, an inverse function of the pH. Thus, this strongly acid gastric juice is also a good potassium-loser. The net loss per day may be only 15 to 20 mE., but this is a distinct help when the unstressed potassium rise in extracellular fluid is in the vicinity of 0.5 mE. per l. per day.

These factors must be weighed in the balance when considering gastric intubation. One will encounter patients in whom carefully arranged gastric suction and bicarbonate replacement will obviate acidosis and hyperkalemia for many days.

F. INFECTION

The occurrence of infection is a common background factor in patients with renal failure; it is incidental to the original traumatic episode. In addition, renal failure in itself predisposes the patient to severe invasive infection. The very surgical traumas that predispose to acute renal failure (massive trauma, open fractures, large blood loss, burns, and complicated obstetrical situations, for example) also predispose to infection and may in themselves be fatal by sepsis.

Infection that has been of dire significance in these patients includes, as examples: anaerobic cellulitis, gas gangrene, subphrenic abscess, wound sepsis, lung abscess, bowel necrosis, and peritonitis.

Treatment of these infections in patients with renal failure, just as in any surgical setting, depends on an aggressive approach:

(1) accurate anatomic diagnosis,
(2) adequate drainage, amputation, or exteriorization, and
(3) accurate use of antibiotics.

Such treatment should be carried forward precisely as if the renal failure were not present. The dose of certain antibiotics is modified by the lack of a renal excretory pathway. Patients with acute renal failure may be carried through necessary surgical procedures without difficulty and with recovery. Anesthesia, volume support, and fluid therapy must be precisely suited to needs. There is no leeway for overtreatment. In renal failure the maintenance of colloid osmotic pressure and extracellular acid-base balance are supportive objectives that are not always easily met.

G. POST-TRAUMATIC RENAL TUBULAR ACIDOSIS

This syndrome appears to be distinct from acute renal failure. It occurs after hypotensive episodes and it may follow a period of oliguria. It is characterized by a high urine volume with a rising blood urea concentration, and a progressive hyperchloremic acidosis. Sepsis is often present and continuing. In some ways this resembles postobstructive uropathy, but there is no history of obstruction. It is our interpretation that this represents a lesser extent of tubular damage than is seen in renal failure, that the remaining nephrons have inadequate total filtration to remove urea, that proximal back-diffusion further maintains the blood level of urea and other nitrogen metabolites, and that the solute diuresis phenomenon through injured tubules produces the acidification-failure with hyperchloremic acidosis.

Recognition of the syndrome permits intelligent treatment: avoidance of solute loads, avoidance of acid metabolites, avoidance of chloride infusions, and the institution of conservative alkalinization with sodium bicarbonate. Potassium must be provided, as in postobstructive uropathy, after the first few days. Dialysis is never needed with such high urine volumes in this interesting variant of renal failure.*

---

* Sometimes called "high-output failure," a term that is confusing because of its use for a very different form of heart failure.

H. UREMIA AND POTASSIUM INTOXICATION IN ACUTE RENAL FAILURE: DIALYSIS

The fact that many patients with acute renal failure have been dialyzed and have ultimately succumbed to their disease in no way lessens the obligation to make dialysis available to the patient with anuria in acute renal failure. There is very little statistical evidence currently available from large series to support the contention that the artificial kidney is invariably a lifesaving device. The underlying trauma or disease is often overwhelming. Those who have been disinclined to establish or support such units have frequently resorted to such statistical methods to prove that the artificial kidney is of no use. But the fact remains that for the individual patient suffering from acute renal failure after injury, there is no therapeutic device that offers him as much hope for survival as the artificial kidney. He may still die, but, with hyperkalemic acidosis, dialysis is his best chance.

The reason for the statistical failure of the artificial kidney is not hard to find. Patients with renal failure are frequently suffering from many other conditions. Frequently these are related to the surgical, obstetrical, or traumatic episode that produced the renal failure. This episode and its sequelae may be fatal in themselves, and these complications (for example, uncontrolled peritonitis due to an antibiotic-resistant organism) will not be markedly affected by the treatment of renal failure.

The case for the usefulness of the artificial kidney, the validity of the device as an instrument present in the hospital, and the justification for the expenditure of time and money for establishment of such units in each major medical area of the country are to be found, not in a statistical approach based on hundreds of cases, but instead on a close examination and evaluation of individual instances; if one accepts the concept that the purpose of medicine and surgery is to save lives, then one must accept the validity of the artificial kidney as a device in a hospital. If in order to support itself, it has to save 85 per cent of the lives with which it comes in contact, seek some other device and some other disease.

This apologia for the artificial kidney is set forth here because this same philosophy enters into the management of the patient whether or not an artificial kidney is available in the hospital where the patient first resides or is taken. Because dialysis offers these patients the best hope of survival, and because the patients are eminently transportable on the second or third day of their disease, when blood volume and infection have been brought under reasonable control (but before the uremia itself has become threatening), it is incumbent upon the surgeon dealing with these patients to assure their early transfer to a site where there are individuals and equipment available either for dialysis or for the special study and care essential in their management.

Intermittent peritoneal lavage or enteral lavage may be used and may tide the patient through. There are various types of artificial kidneys available, and experience is as yet insufficient to indicate whether any of these alternative models are superior to that with which the greatest experience has been obtained, namely the Kolff-Brigham kidney, now widely available.

The problem of selection of patients for dialysis by the artificial kidney is one that may be discussed under three headings: indications for transfer of the patient, indications for dialysis, and contraindications.

1. Indications for Transfer

The indications for transfer of the surgical patient with acute renal failure to a center where there is a group of doctors with suitable experience and physical equipment to care for him are as follows:

(1) when the patient is in early acute renal failure;

(2) when the restoration of blood volume, body water volume, and acid-base balance has been brought as near normal as is possible without threatening the patient by overadministration of fluids and without restoration of urine volume;

(3) early enough so that transportation itself does not threaten the patient; and

(4) when the surgical infection is either stabilized, under control, or as well-treated as possible for the moment.

Such patients should be moved as rapidly as possible to centers where renal failure can be dealt with. They survive air transport very well. During transfer their care should be continued. If they have ileus, gastrointestinal suction should be maintained and air travel avoided. If they are receiving concentrated carbohydrate by vein, this should be continued. If transportation is delayed too long, salvage becomes impossible.

2. Indications for Dialysis; Diuresis

The prime indication for dialysis is a rising plasma potassium concentration with a threatening electrocardiogram in a patient with acute renal failure and oliguria, in whom other contraindicating complications are absent. Severe acidosis and hyponatremia are additional and accompanying indications.

This dialysis has as its function not only the "washing out" of potassium but the restoration of acid-base balance toward normal. The importance of this latter arises from the fact that acidosis per se tends to raise the plasma potassium concentration, and if acidosis is uncorrected the potassium-lowering effects of dialysis will be transient. The acidosis may quickly recur after dialysis, and the potassium concentration may rise rapidly to dangerous levels again. Multiple dialyses are often necessary.

Although the urea concentration is not of itself harmful, it is a barometer of the rate of accumulation of metabolites, some of which are "toxic" and all of which contribute to total solute concentration. In occasional instances where renal failure has long been established, dialysis is done for "toxicity," a clinical term to describe the net effect of uremia. There is unquestionably an improvement in the patient's symptomatology. It is of interest that in chronic renal failure potassium problems are less pressing and toxicity more so.

If, during the course of treatment and

dialysis, the patient begins to exhibit diuresis, this is a most hopeful sign, but vigilance cannot be relaxed. During the early diuresis phase, not only may the blood urea nitrogen level continue to rise for a few days, but in addition the plasma potassium concentration may also continue to rise; a severely injured or burned patient may be lost for lack of concern over the dangers of the post-diuresis hyperkalemia.

Although the early diuresis phase has as its chief hazard a continued rise of plasma potassium concentration, the solute-diuresis desalting of the diuresis phase may be a problem in isolated cases. As diuresis becomes established, the patient passes into a period where relatively large urine volumes are excreted, these volumes being apparently "obligatory" (that is, independent of intake and therefore potentially dehydrating) and associated with fixed osmolality and specific gravity. This represents a tubular defect. It is additionally the effect of a large solute backlog (nitrogen intermediates, urea, creatinines) being excreted by a kidney that has but a few good nephrons and has not returned functionally or anatomically to normal. Such patients must be given amounts of water and salt that cover a large portion of their renal losses. In so doing, one must be aware of the fact that obligatory high urine output is not always easy to differentiate from compensatory high renal output, in which the kidney is doing its best to unload extra salt and water. In the latter case the administration of volumes of water and solute designed to replace the total renal loss of the previous day is dangerous.

The patient's weight, sodium concentration, hematocrit, and blood pressure are the best indices, indicating respectively the extent of diuresis, the state of hydration, the plasma fraction of blood, and effective circulation.

3. Contraindications to Dialysis

The strongest contraindication to the use of the artificial kidney is the presence of a continuing significant urine output in renal insufficiency. In the early diuresis phase, the artificial kidney may be necessary because of hyperkalemia or acidosis. In instances in which there is a continuing renal output (the patient never truly becoming oliguric) but bizarre electrolyte and water imbalances, dialysis is less effective.

Heparinization of the patient is required for dialysis and if there is recent bleeding from the gastrointestinal tract, or if there are wounds or large open unhealed areas, the dialysis imposes a threat of further hemorrhage. Patients for whom there is danger from hemorrhage should therefore be approached for dialysis with some caution.

Dialysis to get rid of water in cases of overhydration is disappointing. The Kolff artificial kidney has not been a practical means of lowering total body water volumes. The tendency of dialysis is to add water to the body unless there is a very careful balance between the total osmotic pressure on the two sides of the cellophane membrane. Dialysis of a patient against a hypertonic bath will remove water from the patient, but such rapid removal will be largely at the expense of plasma volume and will produce a rising hematocrit, oligemic changes, and hypotension. The pressure-ultrafilter type of dialysis may be more successful here.

I. LONG-TERM MANAGEMENT WITHOUT DIALYSIS: PULMONARY VENTILATION

Many patients saved by the availability of dialysis are never dialyzed. This paradoxical fact is based on their expert management by groups of doctors who have learned, by experiences with dialysis, the natural history and proper treatment of the disease. Some of the most eminent successes are those in whom accurate management was followed by return of renal function: diuresis without dialysis.

The principles are those already enumerated as regards metabolism (glucose, insulin, calcium, resins), with particular emphasis on management of the total surgical problem in terms of normal care—not losing the patient by default of sound surgical or operative procedures.

Further details of the management of chronic renal failure are beyond the scope of this book; the surgeon is primarily concerned with prevention, early diagnosis, and initial treatment of acute post-traumatic renal insufficiency. He must maintain constant vigilance over the pulmonary tissue and the airway because the occurrence of pulmonary infection, atelectasis, or pleural effusion, by reducing effective alveolar ventilation, will quickly superimpose a fatal respiratory acidosis on the mounting renal acidosis. Respiratory compensation, previously effective as indicated by a low pCO_2 and nearly normal pH, suddenly fails and a severe uncompensated acidosis supervenes, with cardiac arrhythmias or hypotension. This is often the terminal event and must be obviated by close attention to ventilation, pulmonary infection, and the airway.

Section III.   Obstructive Uropathy

The course of biochemical changes produced by obstructive uropathy and the nature of the renal and chemical sequences that follow its relief are quite different from those observed in acute renal failure. The effect upon the kidney of renal tract obstruction depends on the degree of obstruction and the nature of the proximal infection. Sudden total obstruction of the urinary tract may exist without pain or infection. The renal parenchyma atrophies. This often occurs, for example, in ligature of the ureter. Renal function effectively ceases despite maintenance of tissue perfusion. It is much commoner, however, for obstruction of the urinary tract to coexist with some degree of infection as the obstructing process develops gradually. This is seen in stone or prostatic disease. If the infection is severe, with fever and pyuria, pyelonephritis dominates the picture and is the most important single determining factor in the ultimate reversibility of the lesion and the ability of the kidney to regain normal function. If infection is not particularly prominent and obstruction not prolonged, the relief of the obstruction is followed by a return to normal by most, if not all, measurable indices of renal function.

Characteristic distinguishing features of the changes in plasma electrolyte concentrations are an elevation of the blood urea nitrogen level, which falls rapidly on relief of the obstruction, and a prolonged defect in the renal tubules, associated with hyperchloremic acidosis and, in some instances, a profuse solute diuresis. The disordered physiology involves impaired proximal tubular resorption of salt as well as impaired exchange of H^+ for Na^+ and K^+; the picture is that of a tubule insensitive to hormonal control by aldosterone and antidiuretic hormone, flooded by unexcreted solute and unable to acidify the urine.

1. Obstructive Phase

In *unilateral ureteral obstruction* (as caused by stone or tumor) the contralateral kidney maintains normal body chemistry while the obstructed side is the cause of pain or infection. After relief the obstructed side may exhibit solute diuresis and tubular acidosis, but this is rarely of clinical significance.

In gradual *bilateral ureteral obstruction* the patient may not notice the decrease in urine output until virtual anuria is present. Symptoms depend almost wholly on the nature of the obstructing process and the degree of proximal infection. In gradual *obstruction of the bladder neck* (as by tumor or enlarged prostate) symptoms are marked, and are those of prostatism, bleeding, infection, or all three. In both bilateral ureteral and bladder-neck obstruction a metabolic disorder develops that is characterized by azotemia and acidosis, with sepsis as a variable.

In the disordered biochemistry of obstruction of the urinary tract, there are three prominent differences from the biochemistry of acute renal failure.

(1) In obstruction, hyperchloremic acidosis is much more prominent; that is, increased hydrogen ion concentration is balanced to electro-neutrality by chloride anion. For hyperchloremic acidosis to develop, urine must be filtered and then processed pathologically. In filtration failure (as in shock and acute renal failure) the acidosis is characterized by a rise in organic acids, phosphate, and sulfate.

(2) In obstruction, the accumulation of unexcreted solute gives the appearance of "dehydration" even though extrarenal desalting and water loss may be minimal prior to relief; there is hypertonicity rather than hypotonicity.

(3) In obstruction, hyperkalemia is rarely a problem and almost never a cause of death.

These differences are in part a function of the rate of development, the obstructive lesion often developing slowly, and in part a result of the fact that the obstructive oliguria, during its many weeks of onset, may be incomplete so as to permit continued significant excretory clearance. It is in this continued formation of urine in a tubule diseased by back-pressure and chronic pyelonephritis that the failure to excrete H^+ and the reabsorption of Cl^- (that is, hyperchloremic acidosis) is so common.

2. Postobstructive Phase

The recovering kidney, opening up after an obstructive episode, may go through a period of profuse solute diuresis, during which time obligatory water outputs as high as 3000 to 10,000 ml. a day are observed.

There is a "load" of solute to be excreted (in the case of obstructive uropathy this is the unexcreted backlog of excretable solute, largely urea), and the renal tubule functions in such a way that it cannot concentrate the solute maximally. This is analogous to the solute diuresis observed during tube feedings in the presence of renal disease. There is a profuse and continuing solute diuresis, which can be both dehydrating and desalting if losses are not replaced accurately.

3. Natural History

The sequence of events following the relief of urinary obstruction runs a natural history occupying a period of two to four weeks. During this interval the patient should be left to complete his renal healing without the problems imposed by additional traumas. Further operation should be delayed until normal renal function is restored, as indicated by the secretion of normal urine volumes and a reasonably normal plasma chemistry. Urinary obstruction is seen in prostatic disease, and in this age group a high incidence of underlying arteriosclerotic renal disease complicates recovery. It is not infrequently that one finds that the pyelonephritis and/or underlying arteriolar nephrosclerosis has produced a mild but irreversible renal lesion with a continuing azotemia in the range of 30 to 40 mg. per 100 ml. of blood urea nitrogen. This situation in itself is not a contraindication to further surgery, provided the acid-base regulating functions of the kidney have returned to near normal and the period of solute diuresis has passed.

The sequence during this postobstructive phase thus includes:

(1) a falling azotemia;

(2) a progressive hyperchloremic acidosis, which may not return toward normal for ten to twenty days (example: chloride 115 mE. per 1.; carbon dioxide combining power 12 mE. per 1.; pH 7.30);

(3) a progressive hyponatremia during the same interval, made worse by excessive administration of water but due in large part to renal sodium loss (replacement is required);

(4) little change in potassium concentration, or a slight rise; and

(5) the whole accompanied by a urine volume which is variable, but which approximates 3000 to 10,000 ml. per day.

4. Management

The patient should be weighed daily and allowed to lose from 1 to 3 kg. in his first three days, as he excretes extra water and solute built up during his oliguric phase. After this the weight change should be controlled to a loss of from zero to 350 gm. per day, depending on oral intake of macronutrients and the phase of convalescence.

Adequate urinary drainage and the maintenance of approximate balance of water and salt are the bases of treatment. Oral intake of food should be begun as soon as possible, but the food should be low in solute ash (that is, high in carbohydrate, low in nitrogen) until the solute diuresis is over. Infection must be controlled by scrupulous attention to urine culture and bacterial sensitivity.

The control of the rate of weight loss is to be found in the rate of administration of water and salt and the balance between intake and output. Intravenous (or oral) intake of water and salt has to be brisk at first. Sodium lactate or bicarbonate is useful, may have to be given in large doses (up to 350 mE. per day), and is of course to be preferred over sodium chloride as long as chloride is elevated and carbon dioxide combining power depressed. The patient should be managed on clinical balance with daily intake and output data, and chemical analysis of the urine at frequent intervals.

Section IV.   Uretero-Intestinal Anastomosis

A special abnormality of renal function develops when the ureters are anastomosed to the intestinal tract. Although this procedure has been carried out over many years in the treatment of such disorders as exstrophy of the bladder in young individuals, its widespread use in the older age group (as applied to malignant disease) is relatively new. The characteristic metabolic defect is not inevitable after ureterosigmoidostomy,

and it is commoner in the older age group than it is in children. This provides a clue to one of the important features of the ureterosigmoidostomy lesion—namely, that underlying low-grade renal disease (arteriosclerotic or pyelonephritic) predisposes to development of the difficulty.

Renal disease in the presence of ureterosigmoidostomy may be due to one of three factors:

(1) chronic obstruction, for which the diversion was initially done;

(2) chronic renal vascular disease in the older age group; or

(3) acute partial obstruction, with or without pyelonephritis as a sequela of the operation itself.

When drainage of urine from the bowel is poor, or when intercurrent disease forces the patient to bed (compromising urine disposal from the bowel by stasis), the disorder is accentuated. This suggests the role of colonic solute absorption in pathogenesis, a suggestion borne out by many other data.

1. The Uretero-Enterostomy Disorder

A chemical lesion is found which is usually characterized by azotemia, hyperchloremic acidosis, and hyperkalemia. Severe degrees of hypokalemia have also been reported. Hypernatremia is occasionally seen, suggesting solute diuresis and renal dehydration. Patients may pass in and out of this chemical disorder apparently without much noticeable change in parenchymatous renal pathology, according to their bowel drainage.

The explanation of this fact lies in selective absorption of ammonia, hydrogen, and chloride from the right colon, chronic renal disease, and ammonia formation. If the ureteral anastomosis has been carried out to the right colon, or if urine reflux is prominent, selective absorption plays a prominent role in the genesis of the lesion. If the anastomosis has been carried out to the lower left colon, the patient may develop this type of disorder when bedridden with an intercurrent illness or when some other such difficulty interferes with normal bowel emptying and produces some reflux of urine up the colon to the right side, where selective electrolyte absorption is more active, or when chronic renal disease exacerbates the defect in the tubules. The syndrome has been reported in isolated left colonic segments, although this is rare. In a short-segment uretero-ileal pouch the lesion rarely develops.

Ammonia is formed by bacterial action on urea in the gut and is resorbed. Since this ammonia is a hydrogen donor at blood pH, it produces acidosis even though the blood ammonia is unchanged, much as in administration of ammonium chloride. In terms of acid-base imbalance, this is an addition acidosis due to absorption of ammonium chloride. Treating it with large amounts of sodium bicarbonate would seem therefore to carry the hazard of salt overloading. Significantly, this is not the case because the renal excretion of sodium is good; it is the tubular ability to secrete urine of low pH that is impaired. Thus, when sodium is given in treatment, hydrogen can be excreted in a urine of higher pH, as sodium bicarbonate and sodium biphosphate. Sodium bicarbonate administration is therefore the keystone of treatment.

The absorbed ammonium chloride is constantly recirculated, refiltered, and reabsorbed. Polyuria results (as in the diuresis of ammonium chloride administration) and this produces the dehydration and hypernatremia observed. Polyuria is not infrequently seen in uretero-intestinal anastomosis during the hyperchloremic phase, with a return to normal volumes as the lesion is repaired and solute diuresis ceases. The provision of sodium lowers the NH_4 content of the urine and helps damp this aspect of pathogenesis.

By contrast with ammonia, chloride, and hydrogen, the potassium excreted in the urine is not absorbed in the bowel. In the polyuric phase potassium loss may therefore be large and body potassium very low. Whether or not the plasma potassium concentration is high or low depends on an almost happenchance balance between acidosis (tending to raise potassium concentration in the blood) and the potassium loss (tending to lower it). But of one thing we can be sure: if the potassium is elevated on admission and energetic sodium bicarbonate therapy begun, a lowering of potassium concentration will occur very rapidly, and severe hypokalemia (potentially fatal) will rapidly result. Therefore potassium must be included in therapy from the start.

In uretero-enterostomy we therefore have two unusual features of electrolyte therapy in surgical metabolism:

(1) sodium is used generously in treatment of an addition acidosis, and

(2) potassium is given despite hyper-kalemia.

The *prevention* of the lesion depends upon a good anastomosis to the ileum or left colon with minimal obstruction, providing an adequate egress of urine from the colon, and, in certain cases, the addition of sodium bicarbonate to the diet.

Section V.   Operation in the Presence of Chronic Renal Disease

One is often called upon to operate on patients with chronic low-grade renal disease, usually of vascular origin. This may escape detection or, if searched out, may manifest itself only in subtle ways. There may be a minor reduction in the excretion of phenolsulfonphthalein or in concentrating ability despite plasma chemical values (blood urea nitrogen level, carbon dioxide combining power) in the normal range and no gross disorder of nitrogen retention. In patients with renal tract disease or essential hypertension there may be more obvious signs of the disorder such as azotemia and renal acidosis.

In either case, there are three effects of trauma in the presence of chronic renal disease.

(1) The blood urea nitrogen level increases to a point above the limits of normal. This transient rise is the result of the accumulation in the extracellular phase of small-molecular-weight nitrogen compounds (resulting from post-traumatic tissue catabolism), accumulating too rapidly to be met by the limited excretory ability of the kidney. These are excreted promptly in individuals with normal renal function. Their appearance either in the extracellular fluid (as azotemia) or in the urine (as negative nitrogen balance) has the same metabolic significance as regards balance of protein synthesis between cells and the extracellular fluid.

(2) The metabolic acidosis becomes worse.

(3) If renal function is badly impaired or acidosis severe, some degree of hyperkalemia may be observed.

If all goes well surgically there is little to fear from this sequence, and there is no established limit of renal impairment beyond which surgery is barred. It depends on the setting and the urgency. If other complica-

tions occur (atelectasis is a good example) the patient with poor renal function will become progressively more azotemic despite good urine volumes; prognosis is poor as compared with the normal. The patient with chronic renal disease can withstand operation but not its complications. He can bear renal acidosis or respiratory acidosis in moderate degree, but not both.

1. Management

In chronic renal disease the kidney has lost its flexibility; oversalting or undersalting is more immediately felt. Whereas normal saline solution is well tolerated in normal man, it may be dangerously unbalanced and acidifying in chronic renal disease; balanced sodium-chloride–lactate solutions should be used. The frequent measurement of body weight is helpful in indicating changes.

Drugs and antibiotics that are excreted via the kidneys may be found to have prolonged action unless dosage is reduced. "Light" anesthetic agents that do not stimulate aldosterone-like and antidiuretic activity are preferable to ether. The staging of operations is important; the patient with chronic renal disease can weather two lesser operations far better than one very massive procedure that tips him over into acidosis and symptomatic uremia.

Chronic renal disease has certain resemblances to chronic liver disease as a setting for major operation. In neither is it always possible to predict which patient will win out easily and which will decompensate. But, in general, if the disease is stabilized, of long standing, and mild, permitting the patient to weather the everyday stresses of life without too much burden—then, with care and accuracy, the needed operation can be accomplished. If, by contrast, the disease of liver or kidney is recent, acute, and with progressive cellular deterioration, *operation will be the last straw in a fatal progression unless in and of itself it contributes to the welfare of the cellular organ.*

Section VI.   The Kidney: Notes from the Literature

A. ACUTE RENAL FAILURE

Bywaters' (1944) review article on the crush syndrome always rewards rereading. The patients he described often had no transfusion, yet had pigment in blood, urine, and kidney tissue; fatal uremia always had a shock episode in the background. The interdependence of shock and pigment excretion in the evolution of the renal lesion was clearly seen. The fact that these patients had crushing injuries was merely a product of the circumstances (the air blitz of 1940), but was of especial interest because of the absence of external hemorrhage and the presence of hemoconcentration and hemoglobinemia. Plasma transfusion was often given in the cases of pure crush. In early cases there was a postshock phase of hypertension and oliguria, retrospectively appreciated as due to overloading of water and salt during early renal failure. Some patients with severe uremia recovered, with a good diuresis around the sixth or seventh day; blood pressure fell during diuresis. About two-thirds of the oliguric patients died, death occurring about the sixth day. Cardiac irregularities and the similarity to potassium intoxication were clearly recognized by Bywaters; doubling of the plasma potassium concentration was noted in some. The crushed muscle was an obvious source of new potassium from intracellular fluid in these patients. Manery and Solandt (1942) had shown in dogs the immediate and massive cation exchange in crushed muscle, and Bywaters confirmed this in man. He also recognized the possible usefulness of glucose and insulin in treating the elevated potassium concentration. The pigment lodged in the kidney was identified as myoglobin, and it was noted that it had a low renal threshold and did not accumulate in the blood stream as readily as hemoglobin.

Bywaters recommended an effort to produce alkaline diuresis, though later experience showed that this sodium loading might in itself be fatal (leading to hypertension and cardiac failure) and did not do much to help the kidney. Duncan and Blalock (1942) quickly checked out these findings of air-raid casualties, in the dog.

Early studies of the post-traumatic renal lesion include those of Van Slyke and his group (Van Slyke, 1944, 1948) and Phillips *et al.* (1946).

Reports on the experiences of the Mediterranean Theater in this field include Mallory (1947) and Burnett *et al.* (1947).

In 1951, Oliver published his classic work on the nephron changes in this disease (Oliver *et al.*, 1951).

Blackburn *et al.* (1954), in Australia, experimented with small infusions of distilled water in patients. Systemic effects were minimal; there were no "transfusion reaction" symptoms. Oliguria developed in seven of the ten patients, was profound but transient. Urine flow fell as a linear function of renal plasma flow; filtration fraction rose. Plasma hemoglobin concentrations rose abruptly to 150 to 300 mg. per 100 ml. Methemalbumin was found in the blood. Infusion of parathyroid hormone produced a prompt diuresis. The mechanism of this was felt to be a nonspecific protein effect. The authors conclude, as presented here several times, that this insult of pigment load alone may do little damage but that if it is prolonged and accompanied by renal ischemia a typical renal insufficiency results.

Balch (1955) reported a study of host-resistance factors in the severely wounded (in Korea), with especial reference to renal failure. Phagocytosis, complement, and antitoxin synthesis were studied. Immediately after wounding there was a decrease in phagocytosis; this soon returned to normal. By the methods studied no alteration or deterioration in resistance to infection was discerned even in those patients in renal failure. Delay in surgical treatment and inadequate debridement were the significant factors in infection, not the antibody and resistance factors. Interestingly, there was significant calorie starvation in these patients, but they showed no reduction in antibacterial defense as a result, confirming the studies of Balch (1950), which showed no alteration in antibody production in pure caloric deficiency.

The fact that severe invasive infection produces progressive azotemia despite urine flows in the low-normal range, coupled with the fact that oliguria may arise from many causes other than tubular necrosis in the post-traumatic stage, have led to false diagnosis of acute tubular necrosis with uremia. Meroney (1955) reviews this problem in relation to battle casualties. It is a situation that is seen also in civilian surgery and has led to neglect of the operative management through mistaken concern for an acute renal failure that does not exist. The typical setting is that of the severely injured patient who shows fever and oliguria with a rapidly rising blood urea nitrogen and some rise in potassium concentration. Here, if an infusion test is done and one finds that the renal output responds to increased glomerular filtration with good flow, attention is properly devoted to the surgical lesion which may be vascular, anaerobic muscle gangrene, or peritonitis. If such a discrimination is not made, operative intervention may be postponed under the impression that renal failure is beginning. Another facet of this diagnostic enigma is the fact, of great clinical importance, that *even were acute renal insufficiency to be in its inception, the surgical and operative indications are not changed in any way*. Were sepsis, myositis, or peritonitis to be present, they must be ideally treated, as they would be in any other patient, although of course suitable steps relative to the renal situation must share the treatment pattern.

The renal insufficiency center of the Korean front admitted and studied fifty-one patients who had survived the first forty-eight hours after wounding and were available for study by the well-equipped and well-staffed unit after the completion of its organizational phases (Howard, BCK, IV).* There were many others in whom renal failure occurred in a nontransportable setting, or was only one phase of an early fatal wound. These were not counted. As vascular-volume resuscitation improved, the incidence of treatable renal failure showed a paradoxical rise. The incidence of renal failure in Korea was low, about 0.5 per cent in one group of 4000 wounded. But of the very severely wounded, renal failure contributed to death in from 20 to 50 per cent of cases both in Korea (Teschan *et al.*, 1955) and in World War II (BSSW, 1952). As one might predict from the frequency of severe wounds, the thoraco-abdominal area was the predominant site of wounding in these cases.

The diagnosis of "renal failure without anuria" was based on severe azotemia with good urine volumes (500 ml. per day minimum, or over). There were eight such cases recorded and a great many others less well studied. Hyperkalemia was never a problem in those cases. Some of these fitted our definition of "post-traumatic renal tubular acidosis."

In oliguric failure, the plasma potassium concentration was often over 7.0 mE. per l. on the first post-wounding day and was far in excess of the "resting accumulation" rate of 0.3 mE. per twenty-four hours. This rapid rise is presumably due to acidosis, direct muscle trauma, and general catabolism as well as erythrocyte breakdown and plasma potassium elevation in stored blood, the latter a minor contributor in most instances. The actual rate of rise averaged 0.7 mE. per twenty-four hours in this group. All patients showed electrocardiographic changes of potassium excess. Hyponatremia and hypocalcemia were often concomitant complicating factors.

The rate of rise of the blood nonprotein nitrogen was also considerably more rapid than the theoretical rate of 12 mg. per 100 ml. per day.

The mean weight loss in Teschan's series

---

* Here, as earlier, BCK refers to Battel Casualties in Korea (Howard, ed., 1955) and BSSW to the report of the Board for the Study of the Severely Wounded (Beecher, ed., 1952).

was 1 kg. per day with a range from 0.5 to 1.6 kg. per day. In eleven days, patients lost 10 to 30 per cent of their body weight. Definite increases of body water with edema formation despite intakes below 400 ml. per day were often seen—a tribute to the rate of endogenous water accumulation from fat oxidation in the seriously wounded.

Infection was the rule, either in lungs or wound. One-third had peritonitis or empyema. Reamputation and redebridement were often needed. Sepsis was a prominent cause of death in those who died after dialysis. There was apparently a tendency to delay fibrotic healing, with wound dehiscence a frequent complication. As was appreciated by Teschan and his group, one cannot unequivocally lay this at the door of renal failure although the incidence was high. Abnormal bleeding was frequent but not always accountable by the usual measures; the heparinization of dialysis was related to this phenomenon only rarely. A progressive anemia was the rule, until diuresis occurred. Hypertension was usually manifest within three days of wounding.

In this group, there were seventy-two dialyses done in thirty-one patients. Clinical and chemical results were good, although the mortality was reduced only from 90 per cent (predialyses) to 53 per cent in the dialysis period of the Center at Wonju. The remaining high mortality was fundamentally traceable to the very extensive nature of wounds in these patients. Without dialysis, uremic death predominated; with dialysis, it was a rarity.

The fall in plasma calcium concentration, relative to the rising phosphate concentration, was marked in the Korean experience (Meroney and Herndon, 1954). As the phosphate rose to the range of 8 to 10 mg. per 100 ml., the calcium fell to 6 to 7.5 mg. per 100 ml. The infusion of 60 to 100 ml. of a 10 per cent solution of calcium gluconate was followed by a marked restoration of electrocardiographic appearances toward normal. In these instances the plasma calcium concentration rose to levels of 12 to 15 mg. per 100 ml. A similar normalization was noted following the administration of 50 to 100 ml. of 7½ per cent sodium bicarbonate. The use of oral and rectal resins was less effective. Salt depletion during diuresis was not a problem.

A standard infusion mixture was developed for use during the oliguric phase, as follows:

10% calcium gluconate	100 ml.
7.5% sodium bicarbonate	50 ml.
25% dextrose in water with 25 units of regular insulin	400 ml.
Isotonic sodium chloride or 1/6 molar sodium lactate	q.s.

The volume was made up to a total ("q.s.") indicated by the total fluid requirement. A caval catheter in the upper extremity is the route of choice. Vitamins are added. One must beware sodium excess in this solution.

Meroney (1955) gave especial attention to the ratio of phosphorus to nonprotein nitrogen in the plasma, as an index of muscle changes in oliguria. He studied twenty-eight of the oliguric patients in the Korean group. The nonprotein nitrogen rise seemed to be independent of the nature of the wound itself and the same was true of potassium. Plasma phosphate rose more rapidly and to higher levels in patients with more extensive muscle damage. He found that a P:NPN (phosphorus to nonprotein nitrogen) ratio of 0.05 indicated muscle damage, while a ratio of 0.06 indicated the presence in the body of a large and potentially lethal mass of muscle necrosis.

Balch (1955) made antibody studies (as mentioned) on this group of the oliguric patients in the Korean experience (BCK, IV). These studies are among the most complete ever accomplished in a group of severely injured surgical patients. Despite the clinical impression of severe liability to infection, this was not borne out by the data. There was an initial depression of polymorphonuclear leucocyte–phagocytic activity early in the course; otherwise the many antibacterial defense parameters studied were normal. Although other indices might indicate deficiency the only possible conclusion was that the nature of the injury and its surgical treatment were the critical factors in sepsis.

The studies of Ladd (Howard, BCK, IV) on the Korean wounded must rank as outstanding in any view of renal function in seriously injured surgical patients. Inulin and para-aminohippuric acid (PAH) clearances were studied as measures of glomerular and tubular function respectively. Ladd showed that under conditions of massive wounding and resuscitation, the endogenous creatinine clearance was unreliable as an index of glomerular filtration, especially when the inulin clearance fell below 90 ml. per minute. The maximal excretory capacity for PAH was also studied, as well as the ability of the tubule to concentrate and dilute the urine. The filtration fraction was calculated from the ratio of inulin to PAH clearance. Osmolality was measured by freezing point. All data were corrected to 1.73 sq. m. surface area. Although based on a small series of the seriously wounded, the work covers studies on a total of forty cases and is unequaled in its thoroughness.*

Ladd's findings are in some ways reminiscent of those of Lauson *et al.* (1944). There was an early depression of inulin clearance, rising with resuscitation and falling again with anesthesia induction. With low glomerular filtration, filtration fraction was often high, indicating efferent arteriolar constriction. Urine volume usually paralleled glomerular filtration rate, but the correlation was not very predictable at very low or very high rates. The same was true for correlation between glomerular function and systolic blood pressure. The maintenance of very low inulin clearance for periods of several hours during or after operation, with low filtration fraction, boded ill for parenchymatous renal recovery.

It was not unusual to observe the restoration of blood pressure by resuscitative measures while the renal indices were still severely depressed, interpretable as the continuance of differential renal vasoconstriction despite functional peripheral adequacy of the circula-

---

* There is no other surgical series, either in civilian or military life, that can offer comparison. This work, including all the analyses, was done by the investigator himself, often under very difficult conditions. Through tragic circumstance the studies could not later be amplified in terms of civilian surgery, as Dr. Ladd had planned, because of his untimely death about a year after his return from the Far East.

tion. This finding supports the doctrine of equilibration and a short period of stabilization after resuscitation and before operation, if the nature of the injury permits it. Restoration of urine flow is evidence for functional restoration of the circulation adequate to permit relaxation of renal vasoconstriction, and is a good omen for response to anesthesia (see Part VI).

The fall in para-aminohippuric acid clearance with anesthesia induction was profound even in some cases where there was normal maintenance of blood pressure, indicating again an efferent arteriolar vasoconstriction with its inevitable tubular ischemia. This is the hazardous and vulnerable period for tubular damage should nephrotoxic substances be present.

The exhibition of a minor diuresis during recovery from anesthesia turned out to be a point of favorable prognostic significance. No recovery-room diuresis was seen in those who went on to renal insufficiency. Lack of urine output after four hours of normal blood pressure marks a dividing line; when anesthesia recovery is part of this setting and there is still no urine output, the diagnosis of renal failure must be strongly suspected.

During the early hours after wounding, during resuscitation, urine flow varied virtually as a linear function of glomerular filtration. When glomerular filtration rate was below 40 ml. per minute, distal tubular reabsorption was very active and the urine volume was very small (1 to 5 ml. per hour). In general, the more severely injured suffered a more severe depression of glomerular filtration and tubular function.

In some cases of less severe injury a period of supernormal glomerular filtration was noted, possibly related to renal hyperemia of pyrogenic origin. With this exception, the more severe injuries on the point scale (40 points or more) had the lowest glomerular filtration rates on admission but many returned to normal with resuscitation at sixty to one hundred fifty hours after wounding. In fact, the glomerular filtration makes a reasonable linear plot with the wound-rating point score. Abdominal and peripheral wounds were associated with transient lowering of the glomerular filtration to levels near 70 ml. per minute.

The elevation of filtration fraction (with lowering of para-aminohippuric acid clearance, thus indicating efferent arteriolar constriction) was a characteristic of the early severe wound in shock; the very severe wound much later in resuscitative effort often showed a decline in filtration fraction. The combination of low clearance and a low filtration fraction was the earmark of the very severe injury, with renal insufficiency ahead. If, in such a setting, the filtration fraction increased and clearance rose, the prognosis was good.

Hexamethonium and spinal anesthesia, in a few cases, appeared to decrease total renal vascular resistance. Again the data suggest that in very severe injury the efferent arteriole passes through a period of increased vascular resistance, then going on to a period when one might conceive the nephron as having very little total blood supply but a low filtration fraction, little filtrate, and ischemic tubules. This appeared to be much more ominous than an equally ischemic tubule with a relatively good volume of filtrate. In the rather lightly wounded, the effective renal blood flow appeared to be a function of blood volume (T-1824); but in very severe wounds the clearances and blood flows were all low despite "apparent" volume restoration. When the glomerular filtration rate was greater than 70 ml. per minute, negative free water clearance was 5.2 ml. per minute, a high value showing good tubular water reabsorption and strong antidiuretic effect. When glomerular filtration was lowered, the free water clearance value fell proportionately, indicating a relatively constant fraction of reabsorbed water. This occurred even in those destined for renal failure later. These studies of free water excretion also showed good distal tubular function in many severely wounded.

In the very severely wounded the osmotic U:P ratio fell toward 1.0 ("fixed specific gravity"), with a rising nonprotein nitrogen. In those patients who developed mild renal insufficiency with maintained outputs, the urine volume settled down at about 10 per cent of the filtrate. This is the pattern of osmotic diuresis in an undamaged nephron and lends credence to the concept of widespread renal destruction with a "few good nephrons" remaining rather than "equal partial damage to all" as the nephron pattern in renal failure. Under these circumstances tubular function approaches a constant, best defined as proximal reabsorption of 4 per cent of the filtered solute, total reabsorption of 90 per cent of the filtered volume, glomerular filtration rate near 10 ml. per minute or lower, and inefficient water reabsorption because of the quantitative limitation inherent in tubular water reabsorption when luminal flow is large. As Ladd states so clearly, "In battle casualties the accelerated accumulation of osmotically active tissue metabolites causes an osmotic diuresis preventing oliguria and masking all but the most extreme grades of renal failure." When this mechanism involves a maximal osmotic diuresis with enough good nephrons left to give urine volumes of 500, 750, or 1000 ml. per day, we have the picture, so common in surgical patients, of hyperchloremic acidosis and a climbing nonprotein nitrogen despite high urine volumes. Or, stated another way, total urine volume in such a case is a very high fraction (10 per cent) of total filtrate volume whereas it should be a very small fraction of filtrate volume (0.5 to 1.0 per cent). This we have mentioned previously as "post-traumatic renal tubular acidosis."

In Ladd's series, as studied by Olney, there was a considerable level of free plasma hemoglobin in those receiving the largest amount of oldest blood. The plasma was quickly cleared, yet the heme-uria persisted; it was never noted in the absence of extensive muscle injury. There was no correlation between maximal plasma hemoglobin and the extent of renal functional impairment. Ladd could see no correlation between heme-uria and renal insufficiency, though it is of interest and possibly significant that he did not plot the combined intensity of prolonged shock plus heme-uria as a function of renal impairment. Many of his data point up the association of very severe injury with renal impairment, and by his own data it is in very severe injury that heme-uria is most marked. In any event, the investigator himself considered the matter of pigment excretion as of purely secondary importance in the pathogenesis of renal failure.

It appears that the lesion in the kidney pathologically is commoner than the clinical syndrome of acute renal failure in the wounded; this is surely accountable at least in part by the early deaths in which the duration and even degree of oliguria is not clearly appreciated in the welter of other more demanding and urgent clinical crises. Some patients still die before they can develop the clinical picture, even though the parenchymatous damage is there.

The nub of Ladd's data lies in the concept that at the depth of shock renal plasma flow and filtration are low, but tubular function returns as clearance returns; the damage is vascular (that is, ischemic), not tubular (that is, not arising primarily from the tubular lumen as by a precipitate, or within the tubular cell). Evidence against a juxtamedullary shunt in man is convincing (Bull, 1950; Bull *et al.*, 1950) and is based largely on normal renal arteriovenous oxygen differences in periods of low nephron function; increased total vascular resistance must therefore be implicated. Ladd felt that the severe-injury picture of low inulin clearance, low para-aminohippuric acid clearance, and very low filtration fraction must be due to increased vascular resistance proximal to the glomerulus even when systolic blood pressure is high. Sheehan and Moore (1951), Sheehan (1950), Sheehan *et al.* (1951), and deWardener and Miles (1952) present evidence to support the concept of afferent arteriolar spasm in serious injury.

Anderson and Steer (BCK, IV) emphasize the pathologic synonymity of "acute renal failure," "lower nephron nephrosis," "acute renal insufficiency," "hemoglobinuric nephrosis," "crush syndrome" and "acute tubular necrosis." They found the pathologic lesion in about one-third of men dying of war wounds. Site and severity of injury, duration and severity of shock were the underlying common denominators. Abdominal wounds and severe extremity wounds were common causes of renal damage; wounds of head,

neck, spine, and thorax showed a low incidence.

Levenson *et al.* (BCK, IV) studied plasma amino acid patterns in the Korean wounded. These were extensive studies carried out in five soldiers. Four were so severely wounded as to become fatalities after several days in the hospital. There was renal failure in four. No plasma amino-nitrogen level rose above 5.8 mg. per 100 ml.; the total free plasma amino-nitrogen remained normal. This is a most significant datum: in renal failure the excretory pathway is inactive and the plasma becomes an appropriate site for study of nitrogen intermediates.

Levenson found that glycine, histidine, threonine, proline, and glutamic acid levels stayed near normal. Leucine, isoleucine, lysine, valine, tyrosine, and alanine concentrations rose inconstantly and then fell. Phenylalanine, aspartic acid, and methionine levels also rose during the first week, but to a greater degree. Taurine was exceptional. It was very high in some instances. In two patients with severe undernutrition, the total plasma amino-nitrogen fell. An amino conjugate was found to be present in all cases; the exact composition varied but was highest in those with the most severe azotemia. Purines were increased, a finding amply confirmed by many studies of renal failure. It was of exceptional interest that, although the plasma amino-conjugates and nonprotein nitrogen were reduced by dialysis on the artificial kidney, the plasma amino acids were unchanged by dialysis.

Herndon *et al.* (BCK, IV) worked out the electrocardiographic changes in relation to plasma concentrations of potassium, calcium, sodium, phosphorus, chloride, bicarbonate, and nonprotein nitrogen in the Korean casualties with renal insufficiency. The most marked effects were noted in relation to potassium and calcium. The QT interval* was prolonged in hypocalcemia and hyperphosphatemia. Normal values range around 0.28 to 0.40 second (0.34 $\pm$ 0.02). In cases where the plasma calcium concentration fell to 3.0 to 3.5 mE. per l., the QT interval was prolonged to 0.50 or longer. Analogous find-

---

* This is the QT interval corrected for rate, or QT_c.

ings were observed when the phosphorus rose to 3.5 to 4.0 mM. per l. The two chemical changes as well as their electrocardiographic effects are obviously related.

The QRS complex was prolonged in hyperkalemia. The normal duration of 0.06 to 0.08 second was spread to 0.12 to 0.16 in severe hyperkalemia (7.0 to 9.0 mE. per l.). This was not an invariable finding in the severely wounded. The T wave was heightened (as measured from the isoelectric line of the precordial T wave) by hyperkalemia. The normal value of 5 to 10 mm. was raised to 15 to 25 mm. as the potassium rose to 8.0 to 9.0 mE. per l. These workers did not measure hydrogen ion concentration. These data were based on 663 electrocardiograms in sixty-one patients.

The plasma concentrations of sodium chloride, bicarbonate, and nonprotein nitrogen appeared to have less electrocardiographic significance.

Looking at the whole electrocardiogram the authors noted that the earliest change indicative of renal failure was seen at potassium values of 6.5 mE. per l. This was peaking of the T wave. The S–ST angle next becomes widened; the ST segment is lost until finally the R–T line is almost direct, approaching a sine wave. This is associated with QRS broadening, which resembles right bundle-branch block. Nodal rhythm may occur. The PR interval is prolonged, often to such a degree that the P wave is lost in the preceding T wave. This is a prefibrillation status.

The authors reemphasize that it is the changing pattern in a patient, rather than the comparison between patients, that is most significant.

Much of the civilian incidence of acute renal failure arises from events in the third trimester of pregnancy, often in association with delivery. Shock, due to either uterine hemorrhage or intravascular hemolysis, is the underlying cause. Ober *et al.* (1956) review some aspects of the pregnancy kidney with relation to acute tubular necrosis. Even with modern methods of treatment, mortality approaches 25 per cent; prevention is clearly possible and, as in acute renal failure throughout civilian surgery, depends on the

totality of good clinical management. The residual kidney changes are inconsequential. Renal cortical necrosis, by contrast, is associated with preexistent arteriosclerotic disease; those rare cases with recovery are associated with residual functional impairment. Severe hyperemesis gravidarum may produce hypokalemia, possibly potassium deficiency, and either a renal lesion of potassium deficiency or fatal hypokalemia or (unlikely) both. In parturition, as in surgical trauma, severe hyperkalemia may develop early in acute renal failure.

Finkenstaedt and Merrill (1956) studied renal function in sixteen patients who had suffered acute renal failure about six months previously. Recovery of function was good unless other pathologic events (obstruction, nephrosclerosis) intervened.

Special aspects of renal insufficiency include discussions of hypercatecholemia (Raab *et al.*, 1956), gastrointestinal hemorrhage (Mason, 1952, and Scaletter *et al.*, 1957), hemopericardium (Guild *et al.*, 1957), and problems of infection (Balch and Evans, 1956). In the latter connection it is of interest that increased susceptibility to infection is generally regarded as a by-product of renal failure, but is not readily demonstrated immunologically. Meroney *et al.* (1956, 1957) have described acute calcification of damaged muscle as a complication of renal insufficiency. Larrain and Adelson (1956) describe the coagulation defect in renal insufficiency.

Clinical data on the course and management of renal failure are given by Swann and Merrill (1953), Kolff (1955), Meroney and Herndon (1954), Balch *et al.* (1955), and Bluemle *et al.* (1956).

Barnes *et al.* (1955) describe a case of oliguria following translumbar aortography.

Renal tubular acidosis may result from an inborn error of metabolism as well as from obstructive uropathy and uretero-enterostomy. Hypercalciuria is often an accompaniment, and, in the childhood form, renal stones. Late-stage muscular weakness and severe electrolyte depletion are not uncommon. When the urine is persistently alkaline with hyperchloremic acidosis, tubular dysfunction is likely; the finding of deficient ammonia excretion and hypercalciuria (often enough to raise question of hyperparathyroidism) suggests the diagnosis of the primary defect. The primary disorder (that is, not related to acute or chronic obstruction, or intestinal absorption) occasionally occurs in the adult (Wilansky *et al.*, 1957).

B. OBSTRUCTIVE UROPATHY

Bricker *et al.* (1957) studied the profuse solute diuresis that occasionally follows the relief of obstruction. They concluded that it was in the nature of a solute diuresis, with most of the solute being sodium chloride, which was abnormally present in large quantities in the distal tubular urine because of a failure of normal resorption by the proximal tubules. The glomerular filtration rate (as tested by inulin) is often low during the diuresis, and the urine is rather concentrated (500 mO. per l.). The latter is characteristic of solute diuresis. Our studies of the same patients (unpublished) also brought out the large weight loss during early diuresis with remarkable clinical improvement, and the very large load of urea excreted during this phase. This solute-and-water "backlog" phenomenon cannot be neglected in evaluating the solute diuresis following relieved obstruction. Persky *et al.* (1956) studied the defect following relief of obstruction of the lower urinary tract. In their group of six patients they did not happen to encounter one of the severe postobstructive diureses, a fact that emphasizes that the spectacular metabolic defect sometimes encountered is by no means a regular occurrence.

C. URETERO-ENTEROSTOMY

Eiseman and Bricker (1952) studied electrolyte absorption in man following ureteroenterostomy into isolated segments of intestine. They found urea and chloride absorption to occur. Concentration, duration of exposure, and area of mucosa involved were all factors obviously influencing the magnitude of the absorption. Their simple and common-sense precautions in postoperative management of uretero-enterostomy resulted in a total lack of metabolic complications in fifty-one patients.

Lapides (1952) supported the concept that the ureterosigmoidostomy lesion is a result of both poor renal function and selective colonic absorption. He rightly points out that hyperchloremic acidosis is characteristic of certain patients with chronic pyelonephritis but without ureterosigmoidostomy. In many of his patients the ureterosigmoidostomy lesion was accompanied by hyperkalemia (5.3 to 7.1 mE. per l.), as one would expect in any form of renal acidosis, along with hyperphosphatemia and with carbon dioxide combining power values in the range of 14 to 20 mE. per l., suggesting that the acidosis is well compensated, the latter supposition borne out by the pH values. His postmortem studies showed the suspected ascending renal infection. Urine enemas in people with good renal function—a most ingenious approach to the study—failed to raise the chloride concentrations, but it is interesting that hyperkalemia (5.3 to 5.5 mE. per l.) was produced. In patients with poor renal function, urine enema resulted in hyperchloremic acidosis in about four days, with borderline hyperkalemia.

Lapides' conclusion that electrolyte imbalance does not follow ureterosigmoidostomy if renal function is good is certainly borne out in children in whom the operation is done for exstrophy of the bladder, in the presence of excellent urinary function.

The additional factors of intercurrent infection, acid loads, and poor colonic emptying must be added to the equation. But the fundamental concept of Lapides remains a valid explanation of the phenomenon: unregulated loss of base, poor excretion of acid, and resorption of chloride produce the lesion.

Persky *et al.* (1955) estimate that 70 per cent of patients with ureterosigmoidostomy develop hyperchloremic acidosis, with an occasional hypokalemia and hypocalcemia. This estimate is surely not valid in children. They studied two patients by balance techniques, a step not taken in previous studies. The factor of preferential absorption of chloride over sodium in the large intestine was confirmed. Diversion seemed to be effective in reducing this factor. Large losses of sodium and water, leading to dehydration, were noted. This led to a more concentrated urine, which in turn led to more absorption of ammonium chloride. The authors feel that the renal factors (in the sense of parenchymatous disease) are secondary and the chloride resorption (and inability to conserve base by excreting ammonium ion) is of primary significance in the genesis of this lesion. Any renal disease present of course potentiates the acidosis. Treatment in the form of adequate water plus sodium bicarbonate and citrate was very effective.

Des Prez *et al.* (1955) studied experimental vesicosigmoidostomy and gathered evidence to show that the typical hyperchloremic acidosis (with, interestingly, both hypo- and hyperkalemia) could be produced or corrected by dietary regulations, regardless of renal damage, and evidently due solely, in this instance, to differential colonic absorption. Dehydration potentiated the sequence. Administration of sodium bicarbonate promoted chloride excretion. As the authors clearly emphasize, any renal damage greatly accentuates the defect, though it is possibly not an essential in the genesis. An excess of fixed bases with metabolized anions (such as lactate, citrate, or bicarbonate) is the key to dietary management. Other studies in this field are to be found in Ferris and Odel (1950), Parsons *et al.* (1952), D'Agostino *et al.* (1953), Mitchell and Volk (1953), Bohne and Rupe (1953), and Stamey (1957).

Perry *et al.* (1956) lend strong support to the concept that decreased renal function plays an important role in the hyperchloremic acidosis of ureteral transplants to the bowel. The occurrence of pyelonephritis decreased renal function, lowered the glomerular filtrate, enhanced chloride resorption, and was associated with an increased tendency to hyperchloremic acidosis.

Joseph *et al.* (1956) report that technical factors associated with certain types of anastomosis lower the incidence of pyelonephritis and metabolic complications. They favor the procedure of Goodwin *et al.* (1953). The dye studies of the former show nicely that even with low implantation there is very considerable reflux of urine proximally in the colon. Their reported experience, however, was short and small (seven cases).

In the case of ureterosigmoidostomy reported by Loughlin (1956) there was severe paralysis as a part of the picture of severe hyperchloremic acidosis, with the plasma chloride concentration at 140 mE. per l. Degree of skeletal muscle paralysis was but poorly correlated with the chemical or electrocardiographic changes.

Visscher and his coworkers have carried out a number of studies of this subject, several using isotopic methods, and including Ingraham and Visscher (1936, 1938), Visscher *et al.* (1944), Visscher and Roepke (1945), and Visscher *et al.* (1945).

Goldschmidt and Dayton have also made a number of important contributions relative to differential electrolyte reabsorption (Goldschmidt and Dayton, 1919, a, b, c, d, e, f), these latter antedating the isotope era.

Additional data on reabsorption of urinary constituents from the colon may be found in Bollman and Mann (1926), Korenberg (1951), Doroshow (1951), Parsons *et al.* (1952), Wilkinson (1952), Boyce and Vest (1952), Creevy and Reiser (1952), Annis and Alexander (1952), Baker and Miller (1952), Rosenberg (1953), Brunschwig and Luscher (1954), Reed and Care (1954), Pyrah *et al.* (1954, 1955) and Care *et al.* (1957).

The loss of potassium in ureterosigmoidostomy may, as mentioned before, result in either hypokalemia (the more common) or hyperkalemia. In either instance a renal histologic lesion resembling potassium-loss nephropathy may be observed. Data here also include Williams and MacMahon (1947), Foster *et al.* (1950), Diefenbach *et al.* (1951), Matern (1954), and Skanse and Widen (1955).

Clinical and operative considerations in ureterosigmoidostomy are described by Howard (1949), Appleby (1950), Leadbetter (1951), Creevy (1953), and Irvine *et al.* (1956).

The acidosis and bone changes associated are described by Boyd (1931), Bohne and Rupe (1953), Schreiner *et al.* (1953) and Sherman (1953).

Reviews of nephrocalcinosis in relation to hyperchloremic acidosis will be found in Baines *et al.* (1945) and Greenspan (1949).

In Which Cesarean Section Is Followed by Oliguria and Renal Insufficiency, the Treatment of Which Teaches Several Important Lessons

Case 16. Patient A.St.H., #5L126.* Female. Age 27. Admitted July 27, 1957. Discharged August 13, 1957.

DIAGNOSIS. Acute tubular necrosis (postpartum).

OPERATION. Cesarean section.

CLINICAL SUMMARY. This twenty-seven-year-old white housewife, previously in excellent health, was admitted to her obstetrical hospital in early labor several days prior to her admission to Peter Bent Brigham Hospital. She had had a seemingly normal full-term pregnancy. This was her first pregnancy. After forty-eight hours of labor, a classic cesarean section was performed under spinal anesthesia because of fetal distress and a question of cephalo-pelvic disproportion. She was delivered of an eight-pound child. The procedure went uneventfully and there were no untoward events or periods of hypotension. However, she was given 500 ml. of Type A whole blood, her blood being Type O.

After operation, she did well for about three days, but then began to have some nausea, occasional vomiting, and abdominal distention. Her urine became grossly bloody after cesarean section and the daily volume fell to 600 to 800 ml. daily for the forty-eight hours preceding transfer. She was treated with nasogastric suction and intravenous fluids, but because of persistent nausea, oliguria, and a plasma nonprotein nitrogen of 116 mg. per 100 ml. she was transferred to the Peter Bent Brigham Hospital for further care.

On physical examination she was found to be a pale, white female, acutely ill, complaining of hiccoughs and nausea. Her blood pressure was 130/80, pulse 80, and temperature 99° F. Her heart and lungs were normal. The abdomen was distended, with diminished peristalsis, but it was nontender. There was slight pitting edema of both ankles.

An X-ray of the chest was not remarkable. Plain abdominal films revealed distention of the large bowel compatible with paralytic ileus. An electrocardiograph showed peaking of the T-waves in the precordial leads, compatible with potassium intoxication.

INITIAL LABORATORY WORK

Urine

Color—smoky	
Specific gravity	1.005
Protein	0
Sugar	0
Sediment	48 erythrocytes
	6–12 leucocytes
	occasional granular and red cell casts

---

* The author is indebted to Dr. Mayo Johnson for collecting the data and analyzing the course of this patient.

Hematology

Hematocrit	31
Leucocyte count	13,600 per cu. mm.

Blood Chemical Analyses

Blood urea nitrogen	190	mg. per 100 ml.
Plasma chloride	102	mE. per l.
Plasma sodium	129	mE. per l.
Plasma potassium	6.2	mE. per l.
Carbon dioxide combining power	11.1	mE. per l.

ARGUMENT. This patient presents a characteristic instance of acute renal failure in an otherwise healthy young woman. The pathogenesis is clearly that of a mismatched transfusion reaction. This occurred during a traumatic episode, namely, cesarean section. The lack of a clear-cut hypotensive episode associated either with the mismatched transfusion or the cesarean section bodes very favorably for the kidney. The lack of a shock episode in the past and the maintenance of urine volume after the episode both suggest that recovery will occur without too much delay.

It is unusual to have the three-day delay before the appearance of heme pigment in the urine and the development of oliguria. This latent period also suggests the mildness of the process.

With the development of oliguria, she has developed a typical chemical disorder characterized by azotemia, hyperkalemia, and hyponatremia with acidosis. The clinical picture of nausea, vomiting, and paralytic ileus is also associated with the uremic state.

The normal urine volumes over a period of two or three days and the admission volumes in the range of 600 ml. a day virtually exclude ureteral obstruction as a source of her oliguria and uremia.

Her initial management has been conservative. A stomach tube had been passed and fluids given parenterally because of nausea, vomiting, and abdominal distention. A more accurate account of the fluid given and the urine output recorded would have been of great help in evaluating her situation on admission, but these were not available.

On admission she did not show hypertension nor was she dehydrated, as her treatment had been very well executed. The slight ankle edema, together with the plasma sodium concentration of 129 mE. per l., suggests a mild degree of overhydration. This hyponatremia may be expected to make the hyperkalemia more pronounced and add to the evidences of cardiotoxicity. There was no evidence of pulmonary edema.

Because renal failure was now established and the question of volume restoration not acute, there was no indication for catheterization. Indeed, catheterization of this patient is contraindicated, as it will add little to the management of the patient and may introduce

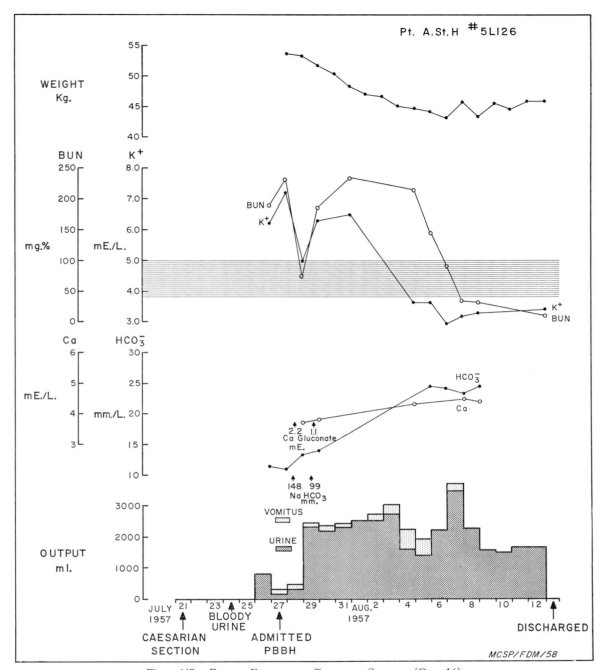

Figure 117. Events Following Cesarean Section (Case 16)

Above are shown body weight and electrolytes. Below is shown output. The reader is referred to the text for details.

It will be noted that the patient's weight fell sharply during diuresis, indicating, as is so typically the case, that some degree of water loading is a virtually inevitable feature of post-traumatic renal insufficiency; some of this is retained water that is endogenously produced.

The rise in calcium and bicarbonate concentrations with treatment using calcium gluconate and sodium bicarbonate is shown; diuresis played an important role in their further rise. The maintenance of azotemia and hyperkalemia for a few days after the onset of diuresis is shown.

infection in an oliguric patient. This is in sharp contrast to the acute phase of volume reduction where the measurement of short-term urine outputs may be vitally important in assessing the adequacy of volume restoration.

The urinary findings of low specific gravity, smoky urine, and red cell casts are consistent with but not pathognomonic of acute tubular necrosis.

The hematocrit at 31 suggests some blood loss in conjunction with previous surgery but, with the sodium concentration of 129 mE. per l., may also partake of overhydration as part of its cause.

The degree of potassium elevation, together with T-wave findings, indicates that the patient must be watched with great care; their appearance within seventy-two hours and with urine outputs alleged to be over 500 ml. per day suggests a rather intense catabolic rate following cesarean section.

As evaluated, then, there are three problems in management.

(1) The patient's prognosis is good if she can be tided over the anuric phase without overhydration, oversalting, or hyperkalemia.

(2) Further water loading must be carefully avoided, cellular catabolism minimized and potassium intoxication avoided.

(3) She need not be dialyzed initially and dialysis may never be necessary.

FURTHER COURSE. The patient's initial management consisted of bed rest and small feedings of Karo syrup and ginger ale to provide a high-calorie, high-carbohydrate, low-volume intake, which might decrease protein breakdown and avoid further water loading. The patient was weighed daily. Very strict records of intake and output were kept. Serial electrocardiographs and electrolyte determinations were undertaken. Chlorpromazine was used to relieve nausea.

In the first twenty-four hours at this hospital the patient voided 340 ml. of urine. The plasma potassium concentration rose slightly further and electrocardiograph showed more intense T-wave peaking. Her fluid intake was limited to 500 ml. a day, rich in carbohydrate, all of which could be given by mouth. Because she had acute renal acidosis, potentiating the hyperkalemic effect, she was given several ampules of sodium bicarbonate intravenously and orally, a measure with less hazard in this young woman with a previously good heart. She was prepared for dialysis with the artificial kidney should potassium intoxication become life-endangering, as suggested by further deterioration of the electrocardiogram.

On the morning of the third hospital day, the plasma calcium concentration was noted to be depressed. Calcium gluconate was given intravenously with a favorable effect upon the electrocardiogram. Her condition soon stabilized on this regimen and diuresis began on the third day of hospitalization, six days after the onset of renal insufficiency. Urine volumes rose precipitously to 2300 ml. a day and remained between 2000 and 3000 ml. daily for the next week.

The patient went on to make an uneventful and complete recovery. As diuresis continued, oral feedings were increased as tolerated, but nausea and vomiting persisted for several more days. Chemical studies showed a gradual return of her concentrations toward normal. Body weight steadily fell as excess water was excreted. Further studies carried out toward the end of the hospital stay showed completely normal renal excretory patterns. She was discharged well on the seventeenth hospital day, almost three weeks after the onset of renal insufficiency.

COMMENT. Although the patient was nauseated, she could still maintain her oral intake and thus avoid the additional hazards of continued intravenous or caval catheters.

It is interesting to note that the blood urea nitrogen and plasma potassium concentration remained elevated for four days after diuresis began.

The cause of the mismatched transfusion was never clearly understood, but it may have been due to misidentification of the patient.

In summary, this was a patient with acute renal insufficiency of the mildest kind, due to a mismatched transfusion reaction, and demonstrating in simple form the essentials of conservative management of this condition.

CASE 17

An Elderly Digitalized Diabetic Comes in with Prostatic Obstruction, and Then Demonstrates Some Truly Remarkable Phenomena, Though They Are Classic for His Particular Syndrome

Case 17. Patient E. Y., #8F842. Male. Age 75. Admitted December 26, 1955. Discharged January 29, 1956. Admitted March 9, 1956. Discharged April 13, 1956.

DIAGNOSIS. Benign prostatic hypertrophy, diabetes mellitus.

OPERATION. Perineal prostatectomy.

CLINICAL SUMMARY. This seventy-five-year-old man was admitted to the emergency ward with a story of pollakiuria and nocturia culminating in five days of progressive weakness, tremor, and overflow incontinence.

Three years previously he had been admitted to the hospital with emphysema, bronchopneumonia, and mild congestive failure. At that time mild diabetes was discovered, as well as prostatic hypertrophy. He was normotensive (blood pressure 140/80). He was digitalized. It gradually became evident that he had significant aortic stenosis as well as some degree of coronary insufficiency. He required no insulin at home. Increasingly his most troublesome symptoms were related to prostatic hypertrophy, with nocturia and pollakiuria.

On admission temperature was 97.6° F., pulse 68, blood pressure 210/88. He was "dehydrated" in appearance, "toxic," with loose skin and soft eyeballs, weak, and acutely ill. The bladder was palpably distended. By rectal examination the prostate was found to be three times normal size. There was minimal edema in the periphery.

He was placed on catheter drainage. The bladder was progressively but slowly decompressed. During decompression (which took eight hours) the blood pressure fell to 160/86 with the removal of 3150 ml. of urine. During this time intake was less than this (2300 ml.), and for the first forty-eight hours intake totaled 11,000 ml., while urine output totaled 12,100 ml. The patient's appearances of "dehydration" were improving rapidly despite this negative water balance.

INITIAL LABORATORY WORK

Urine

Clear, yellow	
Specific gravity	1.008
pH	4.5
Sugar	0
Acetone	0
Sediment—loaded with leucocytes; rare erythrocytes.	

Stool

Guaiac negative

Hematology

Hematocrit	44
Leucocyte count	26,400 per cu. mm.

Blood Chemical Analyses

Blood urea nitrogen	177	mg. per 100 ml.
Plasma protein	5.8	gm. per 100 ml.
Plasma chloride	97	mE. per l.
Plasma sodium	131	mE. per l.
Plasma potassium	3.7	mE. per l.
Carbon dioxide combining power	12.1	mE. per l.
Sugar	154	mg. per 100 ml.

ARGUMENT. The early large urine volumes suggested that the patient was going to show the solute diuresis syndrome following relief of obstructive uropathy. He was dehydrated in appearance (yet he had edema). This so-called "dehydration" improved with negative water balance, a fact that suggested that some of the appearances were due to the nature or amount of solute in the body fluids rather than a scarcity of body water.

The extracellular solute distribution looked like this:

		mO. per l.
Sodium—131 mE. per l.		
Estimated electrolyte solute	=	272
Blood urea nitrogen—170 mg. per 100 ml.	=	29
Blood sugar—150–240 mg. per 100 ml.	=	8
Accountable Osmolality		309
		mO. per l.

There is clearly not enough here to justify the term "hypertonicity." The nonelectrolyte solute is all of the cell-permeating type and therefore does not bias water distribution. None of it (or very little) is adding to the "effective osmotic pressure."

Diabetes of any severity would of course potentiate this diuresis by providing additional solute for excretion; its moderate severity suggests that it was not of major importance in the metabolic situation of this man. The urinary electrolyte loss must be measured and replaced until the diuresis abates. Potassium replacement need not match the loss during the early days.

The metabolic (renal) acidosis (despite evident ability of the kidneys to make an acid urine) also bears tribute to the prolonged accumulation of unexcreted metabolites during the obstructive phase.

Relief of obstruction lowered his blood pressure to a level near normal for him.

FURTHER COURSE. Energetic intravenous therapy was commenced on admission.

Additional laboratory data showed values as tabulated below:

These pH data were interpreted as showing a moderately severe metabolic acid load, compensated by respiratory hyperventilation, lowering the pCO_2 to 31 mm. Hg; pH was about normal.

Oral intakes could be maintained in the range of 2500 to 6000 ml. per day; intravenous supplementation was very vigorous at first, but by the sixth day could be reduced and then discontinued.

Review of electrolyte data from the first few days reveals that sodium replacement was quite accurately

ARTERIAL BLOOD	THIRD DAY		FOURTH DAY	
pH	7.37		7.41	
pCO_2	31	mm. Hg	32.7	mm. Hg
total carbon dioxide	17.7	mM. per l.	19.9	mM. per l.
HCO_3	17	mM. per l.	19	mM. per l.

URINE

(Ranges) (mE. per l.) (First four days)

pH	Volume	Sodium	Potassium	Chloride	Specific Gravity
5.0	4200–9300	28–35	9–18	30–40	1.005–1.012

quantitative. The loss was 1122 mE. in the first four days, replacement 1131 mE. Chloride loss was slightly over-replaced (loss was 1205 mE., replacement 1326 mE.). This is apt to occur when, in cases of this sort, potassium loss is replaced as potassium chloride. It can be avoided by using sodium bicarbonate for a larger fraction of the sodium dose. This chloride overdose was not serious but doubtless did add to the anion load for excretion. Potassium loss (388 mE.) was about two-thirds replaced (240 mE.), an appropriate balance to strike in a patient with poor renal function, not eating and doubtless catabolizing some lean tissue. During these first days the intravenous ration characteristically ran a ratio of water-containing to salt-containing solutions of from 3:1 to 4:3. An excess of water was clearly needed to cover the hypotonic urine plus pulmonary losses.

The situation as regards solute excretion also yielded interesting data as shown at the bottom of this page.

These figures tell us that this urine was as dilute as plasma ultrafiltrate; indeed, it was usually even more dilute than that. The electrolyte data show, however, that it is a heavily processed urine, with a large amount of electrolyte removed relative to the crystalloid solute left in the bladder urine. It is not "just filtrate"; it is a dilute, water-removing urine that has a *relatively* high load of nonelectrolyte solute.

The flow rates approach maximum, which is 8 to 12 ml. per minute.

Electrolyte is only a fraction (estimated here as 50 per cent) of total solute excreted, the remainder being urea and allied compounds. There was usually no sugar in the urine. He was thus getting rid of about 1000 mO. per day of crystalloid solute. If we assume that two-thirds of this was urea (660 mO. or 41.6 gm.) then he was excreting about 40 gm. of urea a day at first, or about 120 gm. in three days. In the first three days his blood urea nitrogen dropped from 177 to 53 mg. per 100 ml. This represented the removal of about 124 mg. per 100 ml. from his body water, or 68.4 gm. of urea. This calculation typically comes out in a way that indicates that more urea is excreted than seems accountable. It is because of continued food ingestion and the production of urea by muscle catabolism, and also suggests that urea may not always be partitioned evenly in body water.

As urine volume was reduced it remained dilute; the total solute load was merely being lowered as the extracellular fluid was cleared.

On the fourteenth day the patient was given a water-load test and vasopressin. His kidneys could increase their flow with water, and when they did so, solute excretion rose slightly. Creatinine clearance was low (25 ml. per minute), suggesting that a relatively few nephrons were functioning, but being swamped with filtrate and unable to concentrate it well.

With vasopressin there was a clear reduction in free water clearance, although other indices changed but little. Previously, on the fourth day, there had been also a minor but definite response to vasopressin. This shows that there was not enough increase in effective osmotic pressure of the blood to trigger maximum water conservation despite the solute present; it also shows that the tubular cell could, under maximum stimulus, resorb more water than it was resorbing despite the very large flow.

Good kidneys excreting 2000 mO. per day find no difficulty in excreting this much solute in four liters, and occasionally in two. This man needed 7 to 9 l. for the job.

Although the patient was slightly febrile at first, infection was never prominent. The urine cultured alpha-hemolytic enterococcus at first and later *Proteus vulgaris.* The patient was treated with tetracycline (Achromycin) for ten days. Cardiac failure and diabetes remained under good control. Ventilatory studies showed a vital capacity of 3.0 l. (predicted normal 3.2 l.) and a maximum breathing capacity of 55.0 l. per minute (predicted normal 78.0 l. per minute). There were also very good functional performances in the supine position.

The patient lost 10 kg. of weight in the first ten days, with urine outputs never below 3300 ml. and several times over 5000 ml. per day. His edema disappeared and his clinical appearance improved considerably. By the fourteenth day his urine volume had fallen to the range of 2000 to 2500 ml. per day.

The blood urea nitrogen concentration fell rapidly from 173 mg. per 100 ml. to 43 mg. per 100 ml. but there was a transient secondary rise at the time intravenous supplementation was reduced. After the tenth day he also tended to regain his weight and to some

	URINE VOLUME (ml.)	URINE CONCENTRATION (mO. per l.)	Specific gravity	URINE FLOW RATE (ml. per min.)	TOTAL SOLUTE (mO.)	PORTION OF TOTAL SOLUTE Na (%)	K (%)
Dec. 27	7400	268	1.008	5.14	1983	13.8	6.0
28	9380	209	1.004	6.51	1960	17.7	4.5
29	7500	296	1.005	5.18	2200	14.2	4.8
30	4580	272	1.008	3.18	1356	11.7	5.1
Jan. 2	4220	373	1.010	2.93	1570	7.5	10.2

extent his edema, but his clinical well-being did not suffer thereby.

Repeat arterial pH study showed (on the twenty-first day):

pH	7.43	
pCO_2	40	mm. Hg
total carbon dioxide	26.2	mM. per l.
HCO_3	25.1	mM. per l.

(Urine pH—8.05)

This is a normal pH profile.

The patient's cardiac compensation was precarious. One transfusion (500 ml.) of whole blood produced a definite increase in congestive manifestations at the time when weight was rising, in part due to accumulation of water and salt.

An intravenous pyelogram showed failure of dye concentration on the thirty-second day. He was discharged home.

During his interval at home he felt well, regained strength, and was readmitted one month later, about two months after his initial obstructive episode, for prostatectomy.

On readmission the vital signs were temperature 98.6° F., pulse 68, blood pressure 120/80. X-ray showed moderate bladder trabeculation. There was marked ankle edema. Eight days after admission a perineal prostatectomy was performed under spinal anesthesia. Convalescence was entirely uneventful. A transient epididymo-orchitis responded well to Achromycin. The patient was sent home on the twenty-eighth postoperative day. The pathology was benign prostatic hyperplasia. He was discharged on a low-salt diet.

The metabolic data on this second admission showed blood urea nitrogen in the region of 37 to 43 mg. per 100 ml. without significant change after operation. Weight was at the "high" level (62.0 kg.) of the previous admission, along with the marked edema. Diabetes was still very mild, metabolic acidosis mild but present (carbon dioxide combining power 22.0 mE. per l.), and urine specific gravity always below 1.012.

Urine culture was consistently positive for *Klebsiella pneumoniae*. The patient was on prolonged low-dose sulfisoxazole (Gantrisin) therapy. He was placed on a two-weeks' course of nitrofurantoin (Furadantin) with little effect. Clinical repercussions of his urinary infection were minor so the drug was stopped. One year postoperative his condition was excellent. There was some dyspnea on exertion; urine sediment still showed white blood cells, blood urea nitrogen was 32 mg. per 100 ml., and the patient's condition was stable on digitalis.

COMMENT. The patient's early response to his illness and therapy had all the earmarks of a profuse solute diuresis in the face of tubular disease. The solute load is due to obstruction, the tubular disease to obstruction, hydronephrosis, and pyelonephritis. The combination produces a severe degree of "water-wasting" as diuresis proceeds, because tubular disease joins with solute discharge to block water reabsorption. These losses were covered in this case by appropriate intravenous and oral fluid therapy. Because of the large urine volumes the total salt loss was considerable; but the concentration (sodium 35 mE. per l.) was very low, indicating that a great deal of sodium was resorbed from the glomerular filtrate, yet the amount of water per unit of solute was excessive in the urine as finally elaborated. This situation, untreated, will eventually lead to hypertonicity, hypernatremia, and renal acidosis. Giving the patient adequate water by mouth and vein avoided these. The renal acidosis initially present was well compensated by respiratory mechanisms (pCO_2 was 31 mm. Hg). By the twenty-first day there was only minimal acidosis.

The sequence suggests that some solutes in the blood (other than sodium-chloride-bicarbonate) or the high total osmolality itself was responsible for the early appearances of "dehydration." As diuresis excreted this toxic solute the clinical appearance improved despite the loss of 10 l. of water. The subsequent reloading with water produced no deterioration. The principal solute identified in the blood was urea and this might well account for a large fraction of the tubular solute producing diuresis in such cases. But many other factors are involved and other crystalloids are present.

It has long been assumed that high concentrations of urea, in themselves, are not responsible for much in the way of clinical appearances. The "toxic," "dry" look of such patients has also been dubbed "intracellular dehydration." Since the body tolerates no osmotic gradients such a term is meaningless. If a patient is hypertonic (from desiccation) or hypotonic (from desalting), the cell mass shares the defect. If he is hypertonic with extra solute the cell mass also shares the defect and indeed shares the same solute if it is one—like urea—to which cells are permeable. So, by no criterion could this patient be referred to as "dehydrated" though he looked it; he might have become severely dehydrated had his renal loss not been replaced or had extrarenal loss (vomiting) supervened. He was solute-loaded, sick, and "toxic." These lead to appearances often erroneously referred to as "dehydration."

Again in this case we can approximate some insensible water loss (IWL) data for his first six days in the hospital, as shown in the tabulation at the bottom of this page.

SUMMARY. This patient typified one of the very special metabolic problems cared for in urologic surgery: namely, postobstructive uropathy with profuse solute diuresis. The result of treatment here was excellent despite heart failure, emphysema, mild diabetes, acute uremia, and chronic renal insufficiency.

TOTAL INTAKE	TOTAL OUTPUT	WEIGHT	IWL	IWL PER DAY
56,335 ml.	40,543 ml.	−2.2 kg.	7,990 ml.	1,330 ml.

CHAPTER 41

The Heart

Each decade since 1880 has witnessed the opening up of a new technical or anatomic area in surgical care. Extirpative abdominal surgery, anastomotic gastrointestinal surgery, neurosurgery, thoracic surgery, vascular surgery, and cardiac surgery have followed in steady march. This book is being written at the close of a decade during which the surgery of the heart has dominated the expanding horizon of operative technique. This growth has been entirely dependent upon the ingenuity and imagination of the new generation of surgical pioneers, and as such has been typical of all surgical advance. While the physician said, "It is inadvisable," and the senile surgical pessimist said, "It's impossible," the cardiac surgeon has gone ahead, to find it feasible, possible, and advisable. Many thousands of patients have been rehabilitated by effective definitive surgical treatment of intracardiac disease.

As the surgeon has found methods of dealing with heart disease in the operating room, the associated metabolic management of the cardiac surgical patient has required a parallel extension. Many of the problems are new. Matters of anesthesia, fluid therapy, and specific medication required solution. In this chapter, a certain few aspects of the metabolic management of patients undergoing cardiac surgery will be described.

The patient with heart disease has been subjected to surgery for extracardiac lesions over the past five decades, and many of the lessons recently learned in cardiac surgery have been applicable to the improvement of his care. Although chronic muscular disease of the heart due to vascular insufficiency is

the commonest cause of death in this country, and although acute arrhythmias are the final common pathway to death in many circumstances (such as hyperkalemia, renal failure, or respiratory acidosis), it is surprising how well the patient with chronic myocardial disease tolerates major operation. If the patient is carefully managed with a clear understanding of the defects in body composition and metabolism accompanying chronic heart disease, he can emerge from his operation successfully. If the operation is done to correct symptomatic or physiologic deficit that adds to his cardiac burdens, the patient emerges far better than he was before.

It is a tragic circumstance for a patient to have necessary operative care postponed, delayed, or compromised because he has heart disease and is considered a "poor risk." Such a patient may be seen months or years later suffering from progression of the original extracardiac disease and still in the same cardiac status. An example was a patient with angina pectoris and two myocardial occlusions in the past, who suffered from a low carcinoma of the rectum. When first seen, the lesion was clearly operable, but because the patient had heart disease and was a "poor risk," the operation was compromised and nothing but a loop colostomy was done. When seen two years later, the patient was suffering the agonies of a massive local growth in the anal area with recurrent tenesmus, pain, and discharge. His heart disease had not changed at all; in fact, his angina was somewhat better. An extensive difficult rectal resection was carried out. The patient survived it well and was immensely relieved of his pain. But the opportunity for cure had passed.

The cardiac patient should therefore be approached as a candidate for extracardiac surgery with optimism as well as realism. The realistic appraisal must include the fact that the patient is "brittle"; he will quickly suffer severe damage from an anoxic anesthesia, hypotension, or the infusion of too much fluid. Even a short period of hypotension or anoxia may be fatal. The surgeon is on his mettle to provide operative care with the most accurate and effective metabolic management possible.

Section I.   Surgery in Chronic Congestive Heart Failure

A. SETTINGS

1. Urgent Extracardiac Surgery

Repair of strangulated hernias, embolectomy, and emergency abdominal surgery for such conditions as appendicitis and acute diverticulitis are examples of circumstances which may require the urgent care of patients in congestive failure. The patient must be managed with only a short period available for preoperative treatment.

2. Elective Extracardiac Surgery

This group includes the entire gamut of elective operations carried out in patients with chronic heart disease: cholecystectomy, prostatectomy, amputation, esophagectomy, and of course many others. An adequate period is available for preparation of the patient.

3. Valvular Cardiac Surgery and Other Intracardiac Procedures

Included in this category is direct operation on the heart and great vessels for intrinsic heart disease. Most such surgical operations are carried out for valvular disease, chronic constrictive pericarditis, and congenital heart disease. In most instances of congenital heart disease, chronic congestive failure is not as prominent as are chronic cyanosis, pulmonary hypertension, and compensated acidosis.

B. MANAGEMENT

1. Emergency Preparation

Rapid (but not too rapid) digitalization, phlebotomy, and thoracentesis are virtually the only positive measures that can be taken in the few minutes or hours available for the rapid preparation for surgery in the patient suffering chronic congestive failure. The previous digitalis history, electrocardiograms, and venous pressure are the guides to these steps. Determination of the carbon dioxide combining power and plasma sodium and potassium concentrations justifies emergency laboratory analysis. The synergism of acid-base disorders and potassium abnormalities in producing alterations in myocardial irritability makes these determinations essential to evaluation of the electrocardiograms and the degree of digitalization. Severe hyponatremia (with edema) usually means dangerous water loading and accentuates the cardiac toxicity of hyperkalemia.

With severe acidosis, hyponatremia, and hyperkalemia in heart failure one usually also finds azotemia. In such instances the outlook for survival is very poor indeed. Where congestive failure, elevated venous pressure, and more nearly normal renal function exist, preparation for surgery by phlebotomy (and often thoracentesis) and digitalization is adequate.

2. Long-Term Preparation

When adequate time is available before operation, real progress can be made in improving the surgical status of the patient in congestive heart failure and in lessening his operative hazards, through attention to the several categories of biochemical and metabolic change produced by his failure. Unless and until the circulatory and hemodynamic defect can be corrected, or at least partially corrected, the patient's body composition and metabolic situation will not return entirely to normal; it is therefore a matter of fine judgment to appreciate that degree of improvement which can be predicted from nonoperative measures, and not to put off the operation any further once the maximum benefit has been attained.

a. Edema and Hyponatremia. The overwatering and oversalting aspect of congestive heart failure represents the extreme exaggeration of a common defect in body composition. The most important steps in its preoperative management consist in adjustment of digitalis dosage, placing the patient on a true low-salt diet (around 15 mE. per day*), the use of diuretic agents, and frequent weighing of the patient so as to follow his progress. Mercurial diuretics and ammonium chloride will produce profuse diuresis with considerable improvement, providing they have not been used extensively in the past. If diuretics are given to digitalized patients, concomitant potassium therapy is advised. Mannitol, used as a long-term slow infusion, will produce a good osmotic diuresis, losing more water than salt. Acetazolamide, chlorthiazide, and other drugs that inhibit the carbonic anhydrase system or interfere with tubular transport will also produce some preferential loss of sodium. If all of these measures have been exercised to the full over a period of weeks or months, little further can be expected. Most commonly the patient has been on a halfhearted or semiregulated routine at home and makes real progress in his first hospital week by assiduous attention to detail. Medical protocols for the use of these pharmaceutical agents in heart disease are beyond the scope of this book.

The patient's water intake should be measured and somewhat limited during this time, although strict limitation is not as important as it is in the postoperative period for the reason that antidiuresis is not as prominent.

b. Acidosis, Azotemia, Hyperkalemia. This is the renal-failure aspect of cardiac failure. The more severe the renal lesion, the more

severe the acidosis and azotemia. A mild hyperkalemia coexists with the hyponatremia of congestive heart failure and starvation; renal disease accentuates the defect. This renal acidosis is an addition acidosis and treating it with sodium bicarbonate or other sodium salts has obvious hazards in a patient who is already in severe congestive failure with a grossly expanded body sodium volume. With diuresis and improved nutrition, the patient's renal function may improve significantly, but if a fixed low renal function persists in the face of heart disease and after a suitable period of hospital preparation, it is one of the most ominous prognostic signs for recovery from cardiac or extracardiac surgery. The use of diuretics is dangerous and ammonium chloride will quickly produce a severe hyperchloremic acidosis.

c. Elevated Blood Volume, Elevated Venous Pressure, Chest or Abdominal Fluid, Diminished Vital Capacity. This complex is related intimately to the rest of the compositional defect: the patient in congestive heart failure has an elevated volume of extracellular fluid and of blood (always in the plasma fraction, sometimes also in the erythrocyte volume). If the heart disease is such as also to produce some compensatory polycythemia, the blood-volume expansion may be very considerable. A diuretic program may be relied upon to reduce the blood volume to only a slight extent; phlebotomy has a place here.

Chest fluid should be removed and abdominal paracentesis performed. The patient's vital capacity should be increasing at the time of surgery. If possible, the patient should be brought to operation with a normal venous pressure. In most instances of mitral stenosis (in Groups II and III) this is possible. In other forms of heart disease, particularly constrictive pericarditis, such an ideal is obviously unattainable until after the operation.

d. Starvation. Patients in chronic congestive failure—particularly those with mitral stenosis—are suffering from starvation for two reasons. The patient's intake of food is poor as he suffers the progressive lassitude and crippling of his disease. Second, the patient with late mitral stenosis has an element of "forward failure," with wasting of the

---

* Fifteen mE. of sodium corresponds to about 800 to 875 mg. of sodium chloride per day. One gm. of sodium chloride contains about 400 mg. of sodium (or 17.3 mE.). One-half gram of sodium chloride or less is a "no-salt" diet.

peripheral muscles, which indicates that with this circulatory defect, nutritional elements are simply not well absorbed or supplied to the periphery. Defective oxygenation in the cyanotic periphery is the most evident nutritional lack. The starvation aspect of this disease is extremely important and often overlooked.

As in most situations where surgery must be performed in starvation, there is no way in which one can reconstruct the starved organism prior to operation. The important requirements are to supply a continuous flow of available energy through and after the surgical operation. Special feedings of highly nutritious foods in small amounts may help to accomplish this objective before the operation. During and immediately after the operation, intravenous glucose must be the source of energy provision. The hazards of using too much water with this glucose are obvious.

e. Chronic Bronchopulmonary Disease. Many patients with chronic heart disease also suffer from chronic bronchopulmonary disease with a productive cough, pulmonary fibrosis, and diminished pulmonary function. The treatment of such patients should include postural drainage, and expectorants in their pre- and postoperative management (see also Chapter 42). For those with bronchopulmonary suppuration, aerosol antibiotics by inhalation are indicated. For those with any degree of bronchospasm (major or mild), bronchodilators should be used freely. These include aminophylline by mouth, vein, or rectum, and the parenteral bronchodilator drugs. Pulmonary vascular disease with pulmonary hypertension is a more ominous feature, for which there is no treatment save repair of the heart disease.

C. DIGITALIZATION PROBLEMS AND ELECTROLYTE CHANGES AND THE ELECTROCARDIOGRAPH

Although the electrocardiograph is rarely an accurate index of precise changes in plasma electrolyte values, it does indicate the electrical activity of the myocardium, its irritability, its total response to the mixed ionic medium in which it works, and its ability to respond to its normal stimuli with an integrated contractile effort. It therefore constitutes an index of the state of the patient's myocardial responses, even though a host of factors (most of which are poorly understood) play upon this neuromuscular system. Before, during, and after operation it must be a principal guide to the threat of overdigitalization and myocardial rhythm and function.

The effectiveness of myocardial effort must be judged in the periphery: by flow, oxygenation of tissues, venous return, and blood pressure.

We wish to present in these paragraphs a simplified view of myocardial neuromuscular irritability that constitutes a useful guide to the complicated interplay of forces seen in the cardiac surgical patient. This view is a "skeleton framework" upon which the surgical reader may construct a further and more detailed interpretation if he wishes to do so. For those who have spent a lifetime in electrocardiography such a scheme as this will offer little save frustration and argument.

Our interpretive scheme rests on the concept that there are two basic and opposing directions in which neuromuscular conditions of irritability and their electrocardiographic changes go, as various forces play upon the heart. Either direction, pursued to its extreme, ends in fatality by arrhythmia.

The first direction, which we have called "the hyperkalemic hypocalcemic hyponatremic acidosis complex," is a direction which, pursued to its ultimate, ends typically in ventricular fibrillation, or occasionally in diastolic arrest.

The opposite direction, which we have called "the hypokalemic hypercalcemic alkalosis complex," is the reverse or inverse of the first and is one which, pursued to its ultimate, results in depression of the ST segment, the development of a single or double contour at the U wave, and, in the end, asystole. Fibrillation may then supervene as a byproduct of anoxia. There follows a brief account of various factors which tend to potentiate moves in either of these two directions.

(1) *Acidosis (metabolic or respiratory), hyperkalemia, hyponatremia, hypocalcemia,* * *citrate overdosage, and digitalis underdosage.* The above factors potentiate each other in moving in this direction up the electrocardiographic scale of myocardial irritability toward a severe and potentially fatal arrhythmia, usually ventricular fibrillation. The acidosis is either respiratory or metabolic in origin. If metabolic (or respiratory) in origin and heavily compensated, this alteration is less important to the heart. As is amply emphasized in the section on acid-base imbalance, the acute respiratory acidosis of the surgical patient is a most threatening event. There are no physiologic compensations possible. Drastic pH changes are produced within a matter of minutes. Acidosis in itself tends to produce hyperkalemia, and the two together potentiate the electrocardiographic changes: peaked T wave, sloping ST, and spread QRS.

Hyponatremia of whatever cause accentuates the electrocardiographic changes of hyperkalemia. Note that severe hyponatremia and hypotonicity often exist with hyperkalemia. Hypocalcemia by the same token is a potentiating factor. Citrate intoxication is analogous because it binds calcium ion; therefore overdosage with citrate ion will produce the electrocardiographic changes of this series.

Citrate overdosage occurs where massive blood transfusion is necessary for a patient who, because of shock, hypothermia, or other factors, cannot oxidize citrate normally. This is not demonstrable by changes in the total plasma calcium concentration, and much more delicate biochemical methods are required to indicate a decrease in ionized calcium, the essential factor in normal neuromuscular irritability. Signs of tetany in the periphery may be manifestations of prolonged citrate intoxication without electrocardiographic alteration. Again we must

---

* In including reciprocal calcium changes in our dual system of interpretation we are taking certain liberties with inadequate data. Hypocalcemia prolongs electrical systole (QT interval) while hyperkalemia shortens it. Nonetheless, the administration of calcium potentiates digitalis effects and can be fatal in heavily digitalized patients exactly as a rapid fall in potassium is; in many ways calcium factors antagonize potassium factors and vary as reciprocals.

note that in the digitalized patient with hyperkalemia even small loads of citrate, far below "citrate toxicity," may be fatal by binding calcium (see Part II).

It is important to emphasize that the series of factors above are potentiating and synergistic. If the patient is otherwise well, overdosage with citrate is not going to alter his situation very much. If, on the other hand, he is underdigitalized, hyperkalemic, acidotic, and hyponatremic, then even borderline amounts of citrate intoxication may produce drastic alterations in cardiac irritability with a fatal outcome, evidently caused by critical lowering of ionized calcium.

It is interesting to recall that all these factors tend to move together as a series in the cardiac patient. Acidosis may be both metabolic and respiratory; hyperkalemia has already been mentioned as part of the body compositional changes of chronic heart disease; and so has hyponatremia. Hypocalcemia in itself is not so common, but is found if renal failure is present, and citrate intoxication may accompany the massive transfusion required in cardiac surgery. On a constant digitalis dose all of these things dampen the effects of digitalis and an extremely threatening cardiac situation may develop in a matter of seconds or minutes and terminate fatally.

(2) *Alkalosis, hypokalemia, hypernatremia, hypercalcemia, digitalis intoxication:* this sequence of changes must also be thought of as potentiating and synergistic. Digitalis alone (in excess) will produce dangerous arrhythmias, but the gradual piling up of any one or more of the factors mentioned above tends to produce severe alterations in myocardial irritability as reflected in the electrocardiograph.

This particular sequence is not so common in surgical heart disease. It is much more common in gastrointestinal disease where hypokalemic alkalosis occurs. However, as mentioned in the section on renal disease, it is interesting that dialysis of the renal failure patient with hyperkalemia may suddenly produce severe degrees of digitalis intoxication as the plasma potassium concentration is lowered. The sudden treatment, with base, of the acidosis of uretero-enterostomy has the same effect. Potassium must be given early. Although the patient is not severely hypokalemic, he has moved in the direction of hypokalemic alkalosis. It is often the duration and rate of electrolyte change which alters neuromuscular irritability rather than the absolute levels attained.

The diagnosis of digitalis intoxication can only be made on the basis of the dosage, recent clinical events, the use of diuretics, the presence of nausea or vomiting, and corroborative electrocardiographic changes; the electrolyte complex accentuates but does not initiate the change. The shortened QT interval of digitalis effect is minimized by hypercalcemia. In *early* digitalis intoxication there is a change in rhythm, usually to an abnormal rhythm (but sometimes a reversion to normal as a nodal rhythm in atrial fibrillation, for example), or ventricular premature beats, "coupling" and A-V dissociation. In *midrange* digitalis intoxication, bigemini and ventricular tachycardia with block are observed, followed by ventricular fibrillation. Progression up this scale is favored by the alkalosis, hypokalemia, hypernatremia, hypercalcemia complex.

Paroxysmal atrial tachycardia with block is most commonly seen in prolonged digitalis dosage complicated by hypokalemia or some cardiac event such as myocardial infarction. It is the trademark of digitalis intoxication and is a dangerous arrhythmia. In surgical patients it is most commonly produced by a high digitalis dose *plus* one of the other members of the potentiating family (hypokalemia, alkalosis, hypercalcemia, and hypernatremia).

All of the changes in rate, rhythm, and conduction are best seen in lead V_4. This lead also suffices to demonstrate the gross irritability changes associated with these two "families" of electrocardiographic alteration.

(3) *Rationalization.* These interrelationships among calcium, sodium, potassium, digitalis, and cardiac function are best rationalized in terms of a tentative schema. There is evidence for the validity of this schema but many details are yet to be elaborated. This is a manner of considering the problem, not a dogmatic rule.

This schema pictures the actin and myosin complexes as being held apart by a cushion of potassium ions. When they are allowed to come together, myocardial contraction is facilitated. Thus, a lowering of intracellular potassium in the heart favors contractility (systole) and a raising favors relaxation (diastole). Actually the disintegrated ventricular beat of ventricular fibrillation may occur at the end of either scale of values, although the prefibrillatory effects as regards electrocardiographic change and myocardial irritability are directly opposed.

Digitalis shortens the refractory period of the ventricle, makes it more irritable, and decreases atrioventricular conduction. Thus, one would expect overdigitalization to be manifest, among other things, by atrial arrhythmias with arteriovenous dissociation. This, in the form of paroxysmal atrial tachycardia with block, is precisely the case. "P.A.T. with block" presages sudden death and must be treated energetically with potassium, by stopping digitalis, and giving Pronestyl.

Thus far in the schema we have not mentioned acid-base balance, sodium, or magnesium. We have mentioned sugar only in passing, indicating that it must be burned to keep potassium in the cell and indeed that whenever it is burned, potassium must enter muscle cells throughout the body, thus lowering the extracellular concentration of potassium around the heart muscle.

Burning glucose lowers the extracellular concentration of potassium; the heart acts like a "low potassium state" when there is change in insulin sensitivity resulting in sudden hypoglycemia. Peripheral muscle robs the heart of potassium in such circumstances.

Acidosis favors hyperkalemia and will in fact produce it *per se* as mentioned previously. The cardiac effect of acidosis potentiates hyperkalemia. Alkalosis favors hypokalemia and potentiates its cardiac effect, as does the sodium ion. Sodium also antagonizes potassium and will antagonize or counteract its myocardial effects. A raised sodium concentration is often associated with alkalosis.

Thus, the "overdigitalization" effect can be produced by:

(1) too much digitalis,

(2) hypokalemia,

(3) alkalosis,

(4) hypercalcemia,

(5) hypernatremia,

(6) hypomagnesemia,

(7) overdosage of insulin, or

(8) any combination of the above.

Of greatest significance for the surgeon, however, is the wide variety of clinical events that can suddenly alter the acid-base balance, sodium:potassium relations, calcium:magnesium relations, or sugar oxidation.

In the digitalized patient these alterations may produce drastic changes in the completeness or toxicity of digitalization with no change in the dose of the drug. If a digitalized patient suddenly drops his potassium concentration, for example, he may be found dead in bed; the pathologist will see nothing to account for the fatality, the internist will defend his digitalis dose as adequate and point to the previously satisfactory state of digitalization. Yet the patient has died of digitalis intoxication owing to the occurrence of hypokalemia while fully digitalized. We have seen such a fatality arising from normal postoperative diuresis in a heavily digitalized patient.

Clinical events that may change the five influencing systems and thus produce hazardous alterations in the degree of digitalization of surgical patients are, among others, as follows:

(1) hypokalemic alkalosis,

(2) vomiting or diarrhea,

(3) postoperative   sodium - potassium shifts,

(4) citrate toxicity with calcium binding,

(5) acute respiratory acidosis,

(6) renal acidosis,

(7) insulin overdosage,

(8) large doses of cortisone (anti-insulin effect),

(9) spontaneous diuresis,

(10) induced diuresis: the action of mercurials or acetazolamide,

(11) calcium intoxication,

(12) parathyroid intoxication,

(13) sodium administration.

In general, the electrocardiograph indicates "presence or absence" of digitalis, or intoxication, but no indication of how *effective* the drug is in improving the contractile effectiveness of the heart. This is reflected in the relationship of arterial pressure to venous pressure, i.e. in the peripheral circulation. The electrocardiograph can give a clue to ionic imbalance, analyze arrhythmias, record digitalis intoxication, and diagnose ischemia of the myocardium—nothing more.

(4) *Electrocardiographic details*. Detailed electrocardiography is beyond the scope of this book. Concern over the nature of myocardial irritability, however, has become as much a part of surgical care as is concern over the state of coagulation or renal function.

The duration of the QT interval (electrical systole) is anomalous as regards our biphasic system, since it is prolonged in hypocalcemia but shortened in hyperkalemia; interrelationships vary the finding. With respect to the T wave, the two (high potassium and low calcium) are additive. In uremia, where potassium is high and calcium low, the QT is characteristically prolonged.

Levine (1954) has systematized some of these findings as shown on the opposite page (as seen in lead V_4). It should be noted that these lists show sequences of progressive effect, progressing down the list with severity.

In the acutely ill surgical patient hypotension and poor tissue perfusion are often prominent. The first electrocardiographic change seen in low myocardial blood flow is depression of the RST segment as a sign of subendocardial ischemia. The frequency of this sign in shock in elderly people is one of the most important evidences of the predominant role of myocardial perfusion in such patients when they are in shock. This is in marked contrast to shock in young people (or in dogs), in whom coronary vascular caliber is normal.

Interestingly, one only rarely sees the electrocardiographic changes of potassium intoxication in diabetic acidosis or adrenal failure. Other factors, having to do with carbohydrate energetics, probably override the electrolyte change; in many instances no electrocardiogram is recorded during the acute phase.

In the high-potassium family one must

TRACING	RHYTHM
"High potassium": progressive findings as follows:	
Peaked T waves	Intraventricular block
Prolonged QRS	Sino-auricular block
RST depressed	Ventricular premature beats
Prolonged P wave	
P wave lost in preceding T wave	
	Irregular ventricular rhythm
Rate slow—atrial standstill or fibrillation	
Smoothed QRS	Ectopic beats
Sine wave	Ventricular flutter
	Rare: Slowing to diastolic standstill
"Low potassium": progressive findings as follows:	
T wave lowered, flattened, or inverted	Nodal rhythm
Prolonged QT interval (digitalis produces short QT interval)	Supraventricular tachycardia
U wave—single or double	
U wave larger than T wave	Atrial and ventricular premature beats
RST depression (like effect of digitalis)	Nodal tachycardia
	P.A.T. with block
"Low calcium"	
Prolonged QT	
Tall T	
"High calcium"	
Short QT	Bradycardia
	Atrial fibrillation
Flattened or inverted P, or T	Atrioventricular block
	Ectopic ventricular beats
Acidosis	
Tall, peaked T—resembles potassium intoxication	
Alkalosis	
Lower T	
Prolonged QT—resembles low potassium	

Of all the electrolyte-induced changes, that for low potassium concentrations, producing the low T wave and increased U wave with depressed RST, is the most characteristic.

expect irregular rhythm only in the middle range; at very high levels there is a regular idioventricular rhythm as A-V conduction is completely blocked—a dangerous sign.

In neither of our two "irritability families" is there a linear correlation between plasma chemistry and electrocardiographic change.

(5) *Rapid digitalization.* The digitalis alkaloids are remarkably potent chemicals. The sudden digitalization of the undigitalized surgical patient by intravenous methods immediately before or after operation is hazardous and only rarely needed. The rapid digitalization of surgical patients has led to fatalities more frequently than is generally admitted by the cardiologist or reported in the literature. It is not surprising that sudden flooding of the extracellular fluid with this material may produce abnormalities of the cardiac cycle other than those predicted by the therapist, especially when one considers that the momentary acid-base balance, electrolyte concentration, available energy, and calcium:magnesium:potassium relationships profoundly affect the myocardial effects of digitalis. It is also not surprising that the medical therapist may not fully appreciate all the factors that play upon the surgical

patient at the time he gives his digitalis intravenously.

For this reason, we are conservative on this point and believe that the additional six to twelve hours required for more leisurely digitalization of the patient rarely compromises the surgical course and is often advisable. The ideal period is twenty-four hours. Digitalis overdosage and toxicity are frequent findings; hypokalemia, alkalosis, and hypercalcemia accentuate them. A diagnosis of digitalis intoxication is not easy to make and its correction and differentiation from other cardiac difficulties by the use of special digitalis tests is a complicated matter that should be entrusted only to the experienced cardiologist.

Surgical operation may, in itself, alter the apparent relationship of digitalis to the heart muscle. Transient respiratory acidosis and hyperkalemia will damp out digitalis effects. If the patient becomes hypokalemic or has a downward change of his plasma potassium concentration (a change characteristic of alkalosis from almost any cause), the patient's digitalis sensitivity will rapidly increase, and on the same dose of digitalis the patient may pass from a state of normal digitalization to one of severe or fatal digitalis toxicity.

For this reason, the progress of the cardiac surgical patient who has had any digitalis problems at all should be followed closely through the operative day and for the next two or three days with electrocardiograms and blood chemical data taken at sufficiently frequent intervals to judge the effects. Measurements of plasma electrolyte and acid-base relationships are helpful in interpretation.

In general, avoidance of complicated combinations of drugs, avoidance of sudden changes in management of the patient, and "moderation in all things" is important in cardiac surgery. The patient is on a knife-edge balance that is easily tipped.

The fully digitalized patient is about two-thirds of the way along the route to digitalis toxicity; the change in plasma potassium concentration then becomes critical and it appears from our experience that this is far more important than the body potassium state in determining digitalis effectiveness. The typical cardiac surgical situation is that of low body potassium and high plasma potassium, as previously mentioned and as shown by Wilson *et al.* (1954). This pattern is associated with decreased digitalis effect (the high plasma potassium effect) rather than any sort of myocardial change of potassium depletion. Hypoxia increases digitalis toxicity. The signs of early digitalis toxicity under these circumstances are ventricular premature beats, bigemini, A-V block (usually 2:1), and an increased atrial rate finally leading to paroxysmal atrial tachycardia with block.

For rapid digitalization parenterally, digoxin is a safe drug because of rapid excretion and short duration of action. It is not too potent; it is given in doses of 0.5 to 1.0 mg. at a time. A wait of forty-five minutes with view of venous pressure and electrocardiogram follows before the next dose. A total dose of 2.5 to 3.0 mg. digitalizes and will hold digitalization at a daily dose of 0.25 to 0.50 mg. By contrast, digitoxin is very long-acting.

D. IATROGENIC DISORDERS IN CARDIAC SURGICAL PATIENTS

Long-term management of heart disease frequently misfires. Common problems are the following.

(1) The low-sodium diet has not been followed. The surgeon has to start all over again.

(2) The low-sodium diet has been rigorously followed, but in the presence of a salt-losing renal lesion plus such drugs as acetazolamide, a remarkable degree of sodium depletion (and occasionally potassium depletion) has been produced. Any sort of trauma or surgery then produces shock. The suggestive clue here is a *low sodium concentration in the absence of edema.* Ironically and paradoxically, sodium must be given the patient.

(3) A long-continued program of ammonium chloride and mercurials has resulted in chloride gain and sodium loss, with the production of a severe acidosis. There may be hyperkalemia, the effectiveness of digitalis is entirely lost, and the patient is then referred to as "refractory." Ammonia intoxication has also been seen, but is rare.

None of the above miscarriages of therapeutic justice was in the surgeon's domain of concern until it became necessary to consider the patient for operation. An awareness of such iatrogenic errors may avoid chirurgenic disaster. A few details follow.

1. "Low-Salt Diet" Not Low Enough

Here, the so-called low-salt diet either has never been adequately prescribed or has not been followed. A normal sodium intake for an adult is about 100 to 200 mE. per day. This figures out to 2.3 gm. of sodium, or approximately 5 gm. of sodium chloride. A low-salt diet is one providing 15 to 20 mE. of sodium per day. Low-salt diets below this figure are extremely difficult to achieve and are almost never followed by patients at home. A 20 mE. sodium diet therefore has one-fifth the amount of sodium of the normal intake, or about 1 gm. of sodium chloride per day. Prescribed diets below this level are unrealistic and represent wishful thinking on the part of either the physician or the patient or both. A quick dietary history will often indicate to the surgeon whether or not the patient actually has been following a low-salt diet. If the patient is water-logged and edematous and has to undergo emergency operation, such a consideration is obviously of purely academic interest. There is not time to repair the damage. But if there is more time to prepare the patient for operation, a knowledge that this sodium restriction has not been followed may be very helpful and indicates that enforcing restriction and the use of mercurial diuretics may be helpful.

Because the various diuretics operate on different phases of the renal tubular excretory processes and affect different enzymatic processes involved in salt excretion, it is reasonable to use them in a rotating or sequential manner.

2. "Low-Salt Diet" Too Low

A much less common iatrogenic difficulty is that the patient has been following his low-salt diet religiously but has severe enough renal disease so that with chronic renal salt loss, the patient is severely hyponatremic and is truly salt-depleted. To understand this, it is well to recall that a normal individual on severe salt restriction will not show salt depletion unless there is loss by an extrarenal route—such as gastrointestinal juice or sweat. The normal adrenal (aldosterone) response to a low-salt diet is a constant increase in aldosterone production and very efficient sodium conservation. But this requires a normal tubule to be effective. If borderline disease of the renal tubules is present, the kidney cannot respond to the aldosterone summoned forth by salt restriction, and the result is that urinary sodium loss goes steadily on (and unrecognized) while the dietary restriction is enforced. This, together with congestive heart failure and continued water intake by mouth with strong antidiuresis, results in severe hyponatremia of a class not seen in other diseases.

It is only rarely that the cardiac patient on low-salt diet has any sort of study of the urinary sodium or plasma sodium concentrations carried out. Physicians frequently do a qualitative urine chloride test. This may have no meaning at all, however, if the patient is receiving ammonium chloride or mercurial diuretics. It is therefore a wise precaution, if time is available, in approaching hyponatremic patients in congestive failure, to carry out some careful studies, particularly the urine sodium determination, to discover whether or not the expected renal salt conservation is active as indicated by a urinary sodium concentration below 10 mE. per l.

If a patient has been on a low-salt diet, has renal salt wasting, and comes in with true sodium depletion, he will not be edematous. This is one of the few rules of thumb that are valid. A series of measurements of total exchangeable sodium in patients with chronic congestive heart failure and with various other renal diseases failed in any instance to reveal total (body) sodium depletion when clinical edema was present. Disaster therefore threatens the severely hyponatremic patient with renal salt wasting, who has been on a low-sodium diet, and who is *not now edematous*, if he is operated upon. The restricted volume of extracellular fluid will make the patient very intolerant of preanesthetic medication, anesthesia, operation, or operative blood loss. He will go into shock and look like a patient with adrenal failure. But he will not respond to adrenal hormones; only sodium salts will restore his vascular tree to normal responsiveness. The preoperative management of such patients includes the cautious administration of concentrated salt solution, gradually "titrating" the extracellular sodium volume and concentration back up to normal.

3. Ammonium Chloride and Mercurials

The injudicious use of ammonium chloride and mercurial diuretics leads ultimately and frequently to a state of severe renal acidosis and in some instances to ammonium intoxication. Ammonium chloride acts by presenting the kidney with an acid load. The kidney goes to work on this chloride by increasing urine volumes to excrete the hydrogen ion and, along with it, chloride; some sodium is lost in the process.* Mercurial diuretics work best on a kidney being presented with an acid load. Ammonium chloride is therefore a mildly effective agent in treating salt excess and edema. It enhances the action of mercurial diuretics and for this reason the two are used together. It will be noted that just as with the use of a low-salt diet, the physician is relying upon normal renal function to help him get on with his painfully slow program. In a patient who is at home, taking pills out of a bottle and occasionally receiving an injection, minor degrees of disordered renal function are not too urgent. When that patient's hernia strangulates, or when he comes into the hospital for a heart operation, these difficulties come sharply into focus as major, life-endangering complications of medical therapy. A typical finding in a patient who is in this difficulty is that he is acidotic with a carbon dioxide combining power of 15 mE. per l. He has an elevated plasma chloride concentration, often as high as 110 to 115 mE. per l. He has a low sodium and high potassium concentration. He is very edematous (remember that when

---

* Interestingly, this is the same ammonium chloride diuresis that we have previously discussed as producing the polyuria and hypertonicity of uretero-enterostomy.

renal function does not handle ammonium chloride properly, the drug only adds to the extracellular salt load and the edema), and he is regarded as being "refractory to diuresis and digitalis."

The best treatment in such a situation, if one has two or three days to prepare the patient for operation, is to leave the patient alone, discontinue all drugs, give him an adequate diet, and let him equilibrate his drugs and excrete some acid and potassium as best he can. Ammonium intoxication has been reported in these patients and it manifests itself just as it does in patients with portacaval shunts—by a semicomatose state and "flapping" tremor. It will clear rapidly with avoidance of ammonium. The chloride acidosis takes much more time to repair itself and obviously should not be treated with sodium bicarbonate!

The cautious use of mannitol as an osmotic diuretic that does not present the patient with a salt load is justified. Mannitol acts by presenting the glomerular filtrate with a nonresorbable solute. It is not necessary to give large amounts of concentrated mannitol, which expand the extracellular volume and threaten the patient in this way. Long, slow infusions of mannitol are of help in removing water.

4. Diagnostic Uncertainty

Finally, in approaching the patient with chronic congestive failure, the surgeon has a right to ask the physician, "What is the diagnosis?"

The course of many patients with congestive heart failure has been followed by their physicians for months or years without a clear diagnosis. Is it truly coronary disease? It is hypertensive vascular disease? Is it thyrotoxicosis? Or is it some peculiar manifestation of heart disease such as cor pulmonale, chronic constrictive pericarditis, myocardial fibrosis, fibroelastosis, chronic right-sided failure with pulmonary hypertension due to multiple emboli, or an atrial tumor? It surely does not seem to be the surgeon's job to sort these out.

But he can create a healthy atmosphere of skepticism about the patient who has been treated at home for months or years and has never had an adequate diagnostic work-up. The surgeon is well aware of the diagnostic difficulties in such a condition as the acute abdomen, and of patients coming to post-mortem without operation, suffering from acute abdominal catastrophes. The clinical diagnosis is just as apt to be wrong as right. The surgeon may not be aware that this also applies to heart disease. Accurate diagnosis is vitally necessary in carrying a patient through his operation, particularly if there is time available to evaluate the cardiac condition and give adequate preoperative treatment, a setting which characteristically exists in the cardiac patient being prepared for elective surgery. The surgeon can be of help in insisting on rediagnosis where needed.

E. ANESTHESIA

The proper use of anesthesia for patients undergoing cardiac surgery in the presence of severe heart disease forms a whole chapter in itself and, as a specific subject in anesthesia practice and pharmacology, is not our primary concern in this book. The surgeon must be aware of certain basic phenomena in this area so that he may appreciate some of the factors considered by the anesthetist in the choice and administration of anesthetic agents.

1. Tachycardia

In the patient with late valvular heart disease, increasing tachycardia means decreasing cardiac output. In the normal individual the "danger area" of pulse rate, where increasing pulse rate ceases to produce increasing cardiac output and further tachycardia results in progressively lowered cardiac output, occurs somewhere around a rate of 120 to 140 beats per minute. In the patient with mitral stenosis, this dividing line may occur at much lower pulse rates, even as low as 100. This is responsible for the decreasing cardiac output observed upon exercise in mitral stenosis and is accounted for by the fact that in this disease the diastolic filling is very slow and the patient must have a prolonged diastole in order to develop an adequate ventricular stroke volume. Premedication and induction of these patients should therefore involve a minimum of "excitement phase" and the use of agents that will not produce tachycardia.

2. Oxygenation

The patient with chronic heart disease has been in a state of borderline oxygenation for many months or years. Any further desaturation will be poorly borne. During his surgical operation it may be possible to provide high oxygen concentrations in the alveolar air and materially improve the patient's ventilation over anything that he has been able to achieve before. Such a step is important. Immediately on extubation the critical time occurs for both anoxia and respiratory acidosis.

3. Depth and Duration of Anesthesia

Patients having surgery for heart disease seem to do better if they can be carried "light" and if their total anesthesia experience is as short as possible, yet haste is just as dangerous here as in other areas of surgery. While unnecessary prolongation of the surgical operation is not warranted, these patients do well on accurate surgery with good hemostasis and careful asepsis. When the surgeon cuts corners in dealing with the cardiac patient, the thing that suffers first is hemostasis. Elevated venous pressure makes hemostasis difficult in these patients. The accumulation of large postoperative hemothoraces is not unusual in cardiac patients. Elevated venous pressure is one cause of postoperative bleeding, but the sense of urgent hurry is another. If the patient's anesthesia is being well managed, the additional ten to twenty minutes required to secure hemostasis is not going to do the patient's heart any harm. The ravages of postoperative hemorrhage jeopardize his survival much more severely. Rapid but effective operation with good hemostasis and resumption of consciousness within a matter of minutes after the incision is closed, rapid return of normal cough reflex, and minimal use of depressing opiates postoperatively are important.

4. Local Anesthesia?

There is a widespread misapprehension that local anesthesia—probably because of its lack of systemic toxicity—is particularly appropriate for these very ill patients. The feeling is that such an anesthetic will be less of a "burden" to the patient.

The fact of the matter is that the acutely ill cardiac patient, usually an elderly person, apprehensive and dyspneic, is placed in a very uncomfortable position for surgery. The patient's breathing may be orthopneic. A supine position on the operating table is in itself uncomfortable and even hazardous. The patient is nervous, and any increased tachycardia, pain, or apprehension further compromises both forward flow and retrograde failure. Local anesthesia presents a hazard in all these departments. Except for the most minor types of surgery, local anesthesia is highly undesirable for the ill patient with heart disease. This is true of most of the "bad anesthesia risks," whose care is further complicated by the use of an inadequate anesthetic. Far preferable is the high oxygen concentration available through an endotracheal tube and the rest, quiet, relaxation, and insensibility to pain that are produced by a light plane of anesthesia such as is obtainable with cyclopropane, thiopental, or nitrous oxide with curare.

F. POSTOPERATIVE MANAGEMENT

The most prominent features are:
(1) careful appraisal of water and salt needs—avoid overadministration;
(2) maintenance of accurate digitalization;
(3) avoidance of oversedation and depression of cough reflex;
(4) tracheal suction as needed to clear secretion;
(5) gradual resumption of diet—avoid early forcing of food and fluids as abdominal distention is hazardous;
(6) check of chemical profile at about two and eight days postoperatively.

If excessive sodium:potassium shift occurs it will diminish the effectiveness of digitalis (see below), and levels at 125/6.0 or beyond

are dangerous. The transient use of calcium or concentrated sodium solutions has a place here, as mentioned previously.

G. CASE PROCEDURE IN MITRAL STENOSIS

As in the other case procedures, the reader is cautioned against undue generalization from a single example. This procedure exemplifies findings from a number of cases of advanced mitral stenosis.

1. *History and Physical Examination.* Such a patient might be a woman in her mid-thirties who has had severe mitral stenosis over the past ten years, much worse recently. There have been few signs of rheumatic activity. She has been progressively crippled until, at this time, she is confined to one floor of her house. She has been on a low-salt diet, digitalis, mercurial diuretics, and ammonium chloride, but with little attempt at close control.

On physical examination the salient features are apt to be dyspnea on exertion, an enlarged heart, pleural effusion, ankle edema, enlarged liver, and wasting of peripheral fat and muscle. The cardiac murmurs are those of mitral stenosis.

2. *Admission Data.* In such a patient one might expect to see the following:

WEIGHT.   38 kg.

URINE.   Protein and casts.

HEMATOLOGY
   Hematocrit—32
   Leucocyte count—4500 per cu. mm.
   Smear—hypochromia.

BLOOD CHEMICAL ANALYSES
   Blood urea nitrogen—40 mg. per 100 ml.
   Plasma protein—5.6 gm. per 100 ml.
   Plasma chloride—95 mE. per l.
   Plasma sodium—128 mE. per l.
   Plasma potassium—5.1 mE. per l.
   Carbon dioxide combining power—15 mE. per l.
   Plasma bilirubin—1.5 mg. per 100 ml.
   Prothrombin—20–30% of normal.

X-RAYS
   Heart enlarged; left atrium prominent.
   Lungs clear.

ELECTROCARDIOGRAM
   Atrial fibrillation.
   Right ventricular hypertrophy.

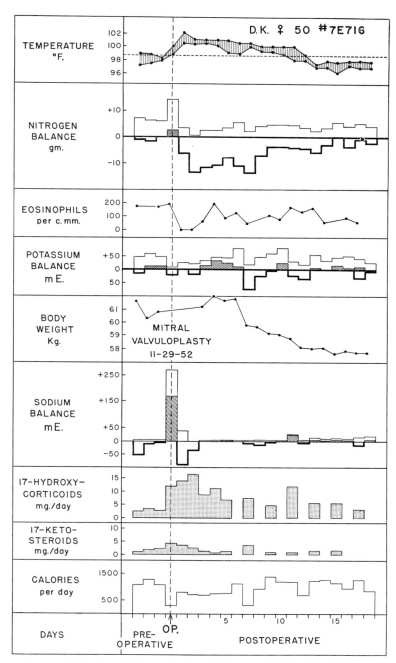

Figure 118. METABOLISM AFTER MITRAL VALVULOPLASTY

This chart shows the events in a fifty-year-old woman undergoing repair of mitral stenosis.

It will be noted that the alterations in nitrogen balance and urinary corticosteroid excretion are not in any way remarkable. Attention is drawn to the sodium balance after the third postoperative day. This type of balance picture is unique, being seen in chronic heart isdease and occasionally in chronic liver disease. It represents "no flux with the environment" and is due to the rigid and persistent sodium conservation exhib-

ited by such patients and its concomitant treatment by the avoidance of sodium intake. Any salt given adds further to the edema, ascites, and elevated venous pressure. This patient later developed sodium diuresis and had a good recovery.

Note also the tendency of the patient to gain weight after operation, such gain being a manifestation of unrestricted fluid intake, and then its later loss here due to a water diuresis (without sodium) and associated with a rise in plasma sodium concentration.

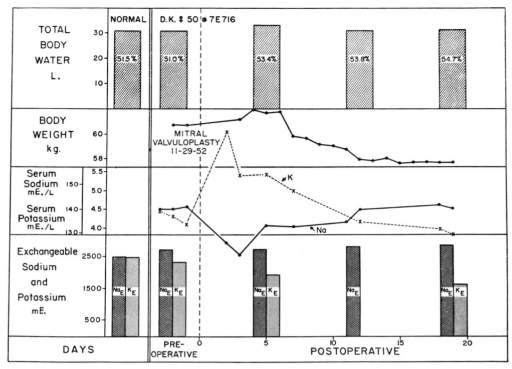

Figure 119. METABOLISM AFTER MITRAL VALVULOPLASTY

Here (same patient as in Figure 118) is shown a very severe sodium-potassium shift after mitral valve repair, together with weight gain. A more moderate fluid regimen after operation will mollify such a change. The rise in sodium concentration during recovery was due to water diuresis (see previous chart).

The body compositional studies here are shown only for a period of three weeks. This is too short a time to permit estimation of the ultimate return to normal composition as cardiac function is fully restored. It is of interest, however, that by three weeks after operation the plasma sodium and potassium concentrations had returned to normal and the patient had a good diuresis and satisfactory weight loss to a basal dry weight. Both of these are good prognostic signs. The body compositional change of a high exchangeable sodium and low exchangeable potassium had shown no tendency to repair itself as yet; indeed it was somewhat exaggerated by the operation itself, which is characteristically the case.

VENOUS PRESSURE.   Elevated.
CIRCULATION TIME.   Prolonged.
VITAL CAPACITY.   Reduced.

3. *Interpretation and General Plan.* This shows us the picture of severe established heart failure of some duration. Desultory treatment in the past leaves a lot of room for improvement with good preoperative management.

The presence of edema and pleural fluids together with the low plasma sodium concentration, the low hematocrit, the moderate elevation of plasma potassium concentration, and the metabolic acidosis is a typical situation in congestive heart failure. The fundamental lesion, as previously outlined, is that of an excess of water in the body with an excess of sodium, an enlarged extracellular phase, and a diffuse energy lack. The elevated blood urea nitrogen is worrisome and is, in itself, the most ominous single finding. The elevated plasma bilirubin with enlarged liver and low prothrombin suggests some degree of early cardiac cirrhosis. The prothrombin response will be sluggish but ultimately satisfactory. The fact that the patient has atrial fibrillation but has had no emboli in the past raises the problem of whether or not reversion of fibrillation should be done prior to operation. This is generally inadvisable.

Therefore, the program would be one of hospital management with frequent diuretics, careful studies of body weight, sequential observation of the chemical and clinical response, and some effort to increase caloric intake.

4. Preoperative Study and Care

ORDERS

(1) Sodium intake is limited to 200 mg. (about 10 mE.) per day.
(2) Fluids are limited to 1500 ml. per day.
(3) Digitalis is continued at same dose.
(4) An electrocardiogram is made daily.
(5) Mercuhydrin, 1 ml. intramuscularly, twice a week. The lack of evidence of digitalis toxicity justifies starting out with more intensive Mercuhydrin. Potassium chloride is given on the days of diuresis: electrocardiographic changes of potassium depletion contraindicate the diuretic.

(6) Ammonium chloride, 1 gm. four times a day for three to four days out of each week. The metabolic acidosis on admission makes intensive ammonium chloride therapy unnecessary. It can be tried for the first week and then stopped, if the acidosis persists or gets worse.

(7) Measure and record intake and output. Weigh the patient daily and record the weight.

(8) Penicillin, 20,000 to 500,000 units per day.

(9) Group and crossmatch blood.

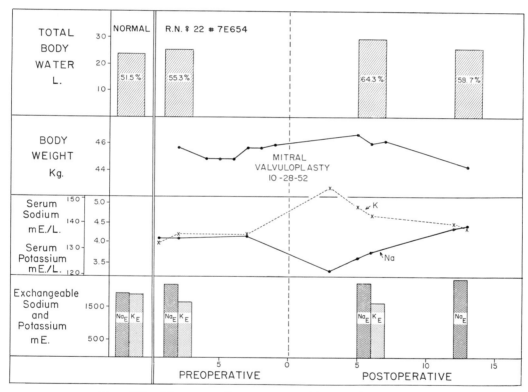

Figure 120. METABOLIC CHANGES AFTER MITRAL VALVULOPLASTY

This chart again shows clearly the early post-traumatic sodium and potassium "shift" that is occasionally observed in severe form after mitral valvuloplasty and other surgical procedures in the presence of chronic visceral disease or chronic starvation.

It will be noted that on the second postoperative day the patient's potassium has risen to a level close to 6 mE. per l. and the sodium has fallen to 122 mE. per l. At this time the patient had clear-cut electrocardio-

graphic changes of potassium toxicity even though urine output was maintained.

Note also that the patient gained weight after operation. Had fluid therapy been more sharply restricted so as to permit loss of weight, the dilutional hyponatremia would not have been as severe, hyperkalemia would not have been as severe, and the patient would not have been threatened so severely by this particular postoperative change.

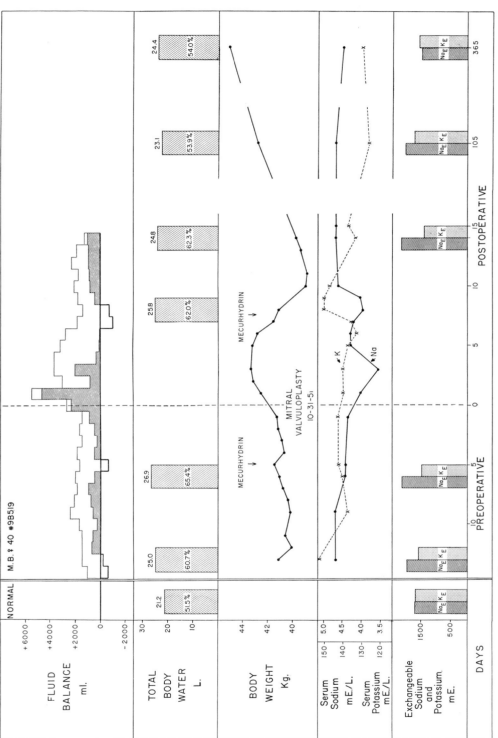

Figure 121. Long-Term Compositional Changes after Mitral Valvuloplasty

In this chart are shown the changes incident to repair of the metabolic defect in chronic congestive heart failure. Preoperatively the patient shows the elevated body water and elevated total exchangeable sodium with low total exchangeable potassium (inverted ratio) characteristic of chronic congestive heart failure.

After operation she showed weight gain, indicating unrestricted fluid therapy and with a severe hyponatremia and a tendency to hyperkalemia. She was given Mercuhydrin both pre- and postoperatively with a better result after operation.

The patient was then followed with multiple body compositional studies up to a full year after operation. It will be noted that at the end of a year the patient's total body water had returned to an approximately normal value, the total exchangeable sodium was reduced to normal and was now smaller than the total exchangeable potassium, indicating a proper restoration of the relationship between lean tissue and extracellular fluid.

5. *Progress Evaluation and Interpretation.* In ten to twenty days on such a program, this patient should be expected to lose from 2 to 5 kg. of edema fluid, with a definite diminution in the extent of ankle edema. Thoracentesis improves the patient's vital capacity and, on a good management program, the fluid will be slow to reaccumulate. In a patient such as this, the maintenance of a high blood urea nitrogen level on diuretics, or with the blood urea nitrogen going even higher, suggests renal tubular disease which will be irreversible. It further suggests that the metabolic acidosis present on admission had a renal component as well as being worsened by the use of acidifying diuretics such as ammonium chloride. If, on the other hand, the blood urea nitrogen falls to normal with hospital management and improved urine output, one may consider the renal prognosis as good.

One would expect and hope that the plasma sodium concentration and plasma protein concentration would rise and the plasma potassium concentration fall slightly on the preoperative regimen. Examples of chemical findings indicating such an improvement after twenty days of preoperative management are as follows:

Blood urea nitrogen—22 mg. per 100 ml.
Plasma protein—6.2 mg. per 100 ml.
Plasma chloride—102 mE. per l.
Plasma sodium—136 mE. per l.
Plasma potassium—4.8 mE. per l.
Carbon dioxide combining power—22 mE. per l.
Plasma bilirubin—0.8 mg. per 100 ml.

The above values have not returned entirely to normal but they have moved in the proper direction, and, if the patient's "dry weight" appears to have been attained, the time for operation has arrived.

During the course of this preparation the patient's digitalization is followed closely by electrocardiogram. With the rising sodium and falling potassium concentrations, the patient may be expected to show increasing clinical evidences of complete digitalization by decreased heart rate and increased diuresis. When this occurs, the digitalis is continued unchanged. If signs of toxicity or unusual arrhythmias develop, one must reevaluate the digitalis dose schedule.

6. *Operation.* ANESTHESIA. Pentothal induction, light ether, with maximum oxygenation. Continuous electrocardiographic monitoring.

OPERATIVE PROCEDURE. Mitral valvuloplasty.

PARENTERAL THERAPY. The patient receives whole blood during operation as quantitative replacement of the blood lost during the procedure. The patient is given 1000 ml. of total fluid the day of operation, increasing this ration in case of dyspnea or fever.

7. *Postoperative Study and Care.* IMMEDIATE POSTOPERATIVE ORDERS. Underwater seal for chest tube. Nasal oxygen. Continued penicillin. Continued digitalis parenterally. Continued low-sodium diet. Blood drainage from the chest replaced.

STUDY. The patient should have repeated determination of plasma chemical values on the second postoperative day in such an instance. Only where the disorder is more marked preoperatively would more frequent chemical determinations be required. Their subsequent timing depends upon the course of the patient.

A chest X-ray should be taken on the first or second postoperative day, depending upon the condition of the patient. Intake and output records should be continued.

PARENTERAL THERAPY. The patient should require intravenous therapy only for a day or two. But the total fluid intake must be carefully and sharply restricted with an eye toward the urinary output and the patient's weight and sodium concentration. This is a small woman. As she comes to surgery, she weighs about 32 kg. Her insensible water loss will be somewhat increased the first day because of dyspnea, coughing, and fever, but her total fluid intake per day for the first few days should rarely exceed 1000 ml., depending on body weight, fever, and dyspnea.

The patient should have tracheal suction and assisted coughing whenever necessary to maintain a good airway.

DIET. The patient should start with soft food, moving along to solid food as soon as peristalsis starts to return. Early feeding in the postoperative mitral patient, if it results in abdominal distention, may be dangerous through the limitation of vital capacity.

8. *Further Course.* With good operative repair, and restoration of normal circulatory hemodynamics, this patient would be expected to have a considerable further diuresis during her first postoperative week. Restoration to weight and strength near normal will occupy the better part of a year. The diuretic program can now be abandoned. Reversion to normal sinus rhythm from atrial fibrillation occasionally occurs spontaneously; it should be tried pharmacologically only if it is of short duration (six months, for example).

Digitalis should be continued for eight to ten months.

During the first three months postoperatively, a characteristic sequence of illness has occasionally been observed, including a febrile period. This is less frequently observed now, and its causation is obscure. Considering the massive medicational therapy used in these patients prior to operation, its cessation after operation, the improvement in circulation, and the pleural process of a healing thoracotomy, it is not surprising that there was some period of physiologic adjustment to be undertaken weeks later.

Section II.   Surgery in Chronic Heart Disease without Failure

A. CORONARY DISEASE

Longstanding angina pectoris and a history of myocardial infarction are most unpredictable threats to the patient undergoing elective extracardiac surgery. Chronic congestive failure, in varying degrees of decompensation in and through the surgical episode, follows an analyzable and reasonably predictable course. This is not the case with sudden coronary accidents.

Every surgical service sees during the year a few patients who succumb during or shortly after surgery to acute myocardial infarction. It is surprising how rarely the pathologist can find the actual site of the clot; not infrequently there is extensive coronary atherosclerosis, multiple myocardial scars suggesting past infarctions, and nothing very acute at the time of death. These patients have died of acute arrhythmias (or *very* early myocardial infarctions), possibly associated with sudden further reduction in coronary flow, increased demand for myocardial oxygenation in the face of diminished flow, or altered conductivity as a result of the acid-base or electrolyte disorders described in the previous section. There are those relatively few patients who die of a myocardial infarction in or about the time of surgery and who have the classical postmortem findings; frequently their previous history is devoid of clue.

A very disturbing variant is the situation wherein the patient succumbs following operation and is found by the pathologist to have a myocardial infarction which occurred several days prior to operation. This is a distressing finding, but it occurs with sufficient frequency to warrant mention. It can be warded off only by careful preoperative electrocardiographic study in patients with a history of coronary heart disease or with unusual symptoms while awaiting operation. Coronary occlusion may be virtually asymptomatic. There is no way of knowing how many of these patients go through operation normally and uneventfully. We do see patients who have urgent operation after coronary occlusion and who weather their major occlusion and their subsequent operation both simultaneously and well.

A history of angina pectoris in the past is a contraindication only to operation of an elective nature that will make little contribution to the patient's physiologic well-being. A history of one or two myocardial occlusions in the past is likewise no contraindication to necessary operation.

But with either of these settings, careful preoperative electrocardiographic study is essential, postoperative management must be accurate, and the most important prophylactic steps against recurrent occlusion must be taken, as described below.

(1) *Adequate oxygenation during surgery.* Diminished blood supply to the myocardium injures the myocardium because of anoxia and the accumulation of local acid metabolites. If generalized anoxia exists, the myocardial anoxia will be, by comparative degree, that much worse. For this reason, the anesthetist must maintain adequate oxygenation throughout the operation. As mentioned above, this is often difficult under local anesthesia or other compromise measures. An endotracheal tube is the best insurance the patient has against further myocardial damage or an acute fatal arrhythmia. Care must be taken at the time of extubation.

(2) *Maintenance of blood pressure and circulatory dynamics.* Transient periods of hypotension or anything that resembles shock is extremely dangerous in patients with coronary disease and may have disastrous results. With some initial reduction in coronary caliber, very small changes in inflow pressure at the coronary ostia will produce disproportionally severe reduction in coronary blood flow. In the patient with atherosclerosis, with coronary and cerebral vascular disease, short periods of hypotension may be followed by coronary or cerebral thrombosis, which marks an end to the surgical episode. The maintenance of blood pressure in these patients may be difficult; norepinephrine is occasionally useful. Overtransfusion is obviously hazardous, but a full oxygen-carrying capacity (hematocrit) is essential. So we come back to our oft-repeated platitude that accurate care with accurate satisfaction of the needs of the patient for fluid or blood, and moderation in all things, are most essential.

B. CHRONIC ARRHYTHMIAS

Atrial fibrillation is such a constant accompaniment of peripheral arterial embolization that the two may be discussed together.

The use of digitalis to control or modify atrial fibrillation at the time of operation is advisable. If the patient has been digitalized preoperatively and is stabilized with a low ventricular rate, it is inadvisable to try to reconvert this fibrillation with quinidine just before or just after operation. Although peripheral embolization has long been considered a hazard of reversion, reversion has not been the setting for the vast majority of peripheral arterial emboli. The hazard of reconversion immediately at or after surgery lies in the fact that anesthesia, changes in water and electrolyte, and endocrine alterations make the selection of quinidine dosage difficult. Patients will occasionally revert to normal rhythm following successful mitral valvuloplasty. If not, they can be readmitted weeks or months later for attempted reversion to normal rhythm. In general a long history of fibrillation makes reversion less likely.

The most effective measure against repeated arterial embolization in mitral disease is surgical repair of the mitral valve. A reduction in the long-range frequency of embolization is one result of this operation.

C. EMBOLECTOMY

Intraoperative or immediate postoperative embolization is not uncommon in patients undergoing mitral surgery; mitral disease forms the most common background for major arterial embolization. From whatever cardiac source, embolization and embolectomy pose certain special problems in surgical care. Often these emboli are small flecks of clot or calcium that lodge in the cerebral vessels; only in the periphery does one have the opportunity to remove them.

The urgency of arterial embolectomy is equally great, whether the patient be middle-aged and suffering from mitral disease or elderly with atrial fibrillation on an arteriosclerotic basis. Although the former patient has more peripheral collaterals and a better outlook for restoration of blood flow, embolization to the bifurcation of the aorta, the femoral region, or the popliteal area presents an equivalent threat to limb. In the older arteriosclerotic group, the threat to life is much greater.

The preparation of the cardiac patient for embolectomy is a common example of the rapid preoperative preparation of the cardiac patient, as previously outlined. The most important items are adequate oxygenation during anesthesia, the maintenance of blood pressure and flow, and the avoidance of excessive fluid intake by mouth or vein. Phlebotomy and rapid digitalization are occasionally useful.

The commonest difficulties encountered after this operation are repeated embolization or local thrombosis or both. The incidence of both may be diminished by the use of anticoagulants. If a patient has one peripheral arterial embolization and within hours to days has another such episode, the indication is just as strong for repeated embolectomy as it was for the first procedure.

Emboli to the brachial artery do not constitute an urgent indication for surgery. The color, temperature, and pulse in the arm are observed. If there is increasing compromise of blood supply, brachial embolectomy may be performed. Most patients will be found to weather this event uneventfully. If the patient has mitral stenosis, it is more advisable to let this embolus pass without special treatment, in the interest of getting on with the important object within the shortest possible time, this being the mitral valvuloplasty. In cases of multiple embolization, mitral surgery is urgent.

Embolization of the superior mesenteric artery or the celiac axis is rarely recognized; the possibility of successful embolectomy always exists, and early recognition by exploration should be encouraged. The use of hypothermia or extracorporeal circulation may make cerebral or celiac embolectomy more practical, though case reports of successful treatment are rare.

Section III.   Cardiac Arrest

A. SETTINGS

Sudden cessation of heart action just before, during, or immediately following surgical operations is known as "cardiac arrest" and seems to be on the increase nationally. Its increasing frequency is not wholly due to increasing recognition. This particular disaster is so spectacular that it is unlikely that a change in recognition alone would account for the apparent rise in frequency. If any single agency is to be blamed, it is the use of multiple anesthetic agents and of the hurried anesthetic induction with overdose of the drugs, followed by anoxia. It is tempting to excuse or mitigate the increasing frequency of this disaster by stating that increasingly large numbers of old, feeble, or seriously ill patients are being operated upon. Unfortunately, it is not in this group that the higher incidence is so clearly noticeable. Instead, it is in the young person seemingly in good health, whose sudden surgical demise is all the more unexpected and tragic. In former years, in infants, this accident was often called "status thymicolymphaticus," a meaningless term.

On the basis of the mechanism involved, there are three distinctly different groups of patients in this complex.

1. Direct Operation on the Heart

Instrumentation, manipulation, endocardial irritation, and preexisting heart disease all combine to produce a high incidence of serious arrhythmias, of which atrial premature beats and fibrillation are by far the most common and ventricular fibrillation the most serious.

2. Prolonged Asystole or Diastolic Arrest in Conjunction with a Surgical Operation

The exact arrhythmia involved in cardiac arrest may be recognizable electrocardiographically or by direct examination of the living heart but by no other means. Peripherally diastolic arrest looks like any other sort of sudden cessation of heart action. The mechanism here may be more neurologic than cytotoxic, it resembles the prolonged asystole of the Stokes-Adams syndrome, and there is less obvious cause in terms of anesthetic dosage, anoxia, cyanosis, or acute acidosis. Some of these patients may have had Stokes-Adams attacks in the past, and some aspect of the surgical experience—as yet unidentified—triggers an attack. "Vasovagal" and "vagovagal" reflexes are accused but not indicted. When a patient who is doing quite well, has good color, and has not received excessive anesthetic agent has a "cardiac arrest" while being intubated or extubated or during the closure of the thoracic incision (all situations in which there is some possibility of afferent autonomic stimulus), the suspicion of diastolic arrest may be especially high. As will be seen in a moment and as has already been mentioned, without electrocardiography this cannot be differentiated from ventricular fibrillation in the acute episode. But treatment is easier and more effective. *The possibility that the event is due to asystolic arrest rather than ventricular fibrillation should in nowise alter the steps in treatment that are outlined below.*

3. Ventricular Fibrillation in Extracardiac Surgery

This arrhythmia often characterizes the later phases of "cardiac arrest" as seen in extracardiac surgery in previously healthy persons, although the initial event may have been diastolic arrest or "standstill." Ventricular fibrillation is an aimless and disintegrated series of contractions of the myocardial fibers. It indicates a complete lack of that integrating mechanism conferred on the myocardium by the bundle of His and its branches, which makes millions of fibers "pull together." It is a degenerative change that takes place as a result of anoxia and respiratory acidosis plus the toxic effect of drugs, particularly anesthetic agents. The exact mechanism by which anoxia, acidosis, and anesthetic agents produce this disintegrative change and the detailed neuropharmacology of the cardiac mechanism is quite beyond the scope of this work. Yet it is important to realize that this is the lethal combination. Anesthetic drugs are depressants of nervous tissue; applied to the heart this action expresses itself as fibrillation, not because of irritation, but because of depression of the normal myoneural mechanism which conducts impulses and integrates the beat.

This may occur during a seemingly smooth surgical operation, though such an event is rare. It may follow a prolonged period of shock, blood loss, or rough manipula-tion in the neck or upper thorax. It may follow multiple transfusions of citrated blood. Although the anesthetist feels the burden of responsibility for ventricular fibrillation in most cases of extracardiac surgery because agent and anoxia are the two most important factors in its genesis, the surgeon can by no means maintain his innocence if uncorrected blood loss, rough manipulation with unsatisfactory exposure, exaggerated bodily position of the patient, or citrate toxicity in digitalized patients and other such factors have been permitted to exist.

Cardiac arrest occurs after the operation in instances in which oxygenation is poor or level of agent high during the recovery phase, particularly at or after the time of removal of an endotracheal tube. The event occurring at this time still falls into our classification of "at or near surgery," a classification that profoundly affects treatment.

B. CAUSATIVE AGENCIES

1. Anesthesia Difficulties: Rapid Induction

A characteristic clinical sequence leading to ventricular fibrillation or diastolic arrest is to be found in a patient in whom anesthesia has been induced too rapidly.

Anesthetic agents have special partition characteristics in the organism, which require time for their achievement. When an attempt is made to anesthetize too quickly, excessive levels of agent are constantly being added to the extracellular fluid in an effort to get the patient "deep." As they later equilibrate into nervous tissue these drugs achieve a much higher concentration than would be needed in a slower induction where the partition is closer to equilibrium as new agents are added during the period of induction. Therefore one of the hazards of hasty induction is very high concentration of agent.

The surgeon should never hurry the anesthetist, and this is one good reason for not doing so. A hasty intubation, misplacing the endotracheal tube, prolonged attempts to intubate with inadequate relaxation, prolonged laryngeal spasm during intubation with repeated Valsalva maneuvers—a sure

mark of hasty attempts to induce the patient
—all of these also set the stage for cardiac
arrest. If the concentration of agent, either
inhalation or intravenous, is then increased,
if the patient has been given some curare, so
that spontaneous respiratory motion is paralyzed, we then have the typical combination
of acute anoxia, high level of agent, and acute
respiratory acidosis.

2. Airway Obstruction

Another characteristic sequence leading to
cardiac arrest is airway obstruction or respiratory embarrassment with anoxia and acute
respiratory acidosis.

In the section on respiratory acidosis in
Part III, it was emphasized that acute respiratory acidosis may occur very rapidly. An
acute respiratory acidosis occurs in conjunction with hypoventilation (and anoxia) in
patients with any sort of acute respiratory
embarrassment. This may be due to spasm or
obstruction of the upper airway, pulmonary
edema, the open chest, and a host of other
causes, all of which may occur under anesthesia and indeed are especially prone to do
so. During or shortly after such an episode of
anoxia, anesthesia, and acidosis, cardiac action is noted to cease. Acid-base changes are
probably less important than anoxia. The
differential diagnosis of diastolic arrest versus
ventricular fibrillation cannot possibly be
made at this point.

3. Extubation or Closure

A third sequence leading to ventricular
fibrillation or diastolic arrest occurs at the
time of chest closure, lung reinflation, or extubation. The opportunity for vagovagal reflexes is great at such times. But more important in our opinion is the "return to room
air" phenomenon in the presence of an unsuspected and unrecognized equilibrated
respiratory acidosis.* Vigilance is apt to be
relaxed at this time, near closure. This may
occur in the recovery room.

---

* See the Notes from the Literature (page 725) for
an explanation of the problem of "return to room air."

4. Ventricular Fibrillation or Diastolic Arrest Unassociated with Operation

In sharp contrast to these situations at or
near surgery are those patients whose hearts
suddenly stop beating while on the ward,
at home, or somewhere far removed from
surgical procedure. Such cessation of heartbeat may be due to asystole, in which case
simple measures (chest percussion or per-
cutaneous needling) may start the heart
again. This is especially true in patients with
known Stokes-Adams attacks. If the patient
is chronically ill with decompensated heart
disease, such an episode is more apt to be
ventricular fibrillation due to additional
coronary occlusion. Finally, the apparent
cessation of cardiac action may or may not
be due to coronary occlusion, pulmonary
embolus, or some cause that leaves the patient
with nothing to gain from the resuscitative
measures employed in cardiac arrest at or
near operation. †

C. TREATMENT AT OR NEAR THE TIME OF OPERATION

At the operating table, great care must be
taken to be sure as to the presence or absence
of heart action before opening the chest in
patients suspected of cardiac arrest. This
"great care" consists largely in previous
mental preparedness, since only a matter of
seconds is expendable. A misplaced blood-
pressure cuff or some change in position of the
head may alter the apparent pulsatile blood
pressure or pulse in a way that leads to false
alarm; to open the chest in such a patient
and initiate cardiac massage may be the
coup de grâce rather than a means of revival.

The following are the steps to undertake
when there is sudden cessation of the heartbeat at or near the time of surgery. Throughout these initial steps four continuing projects
should be under way by other members of the
team: adequate *ventilation* and oxygenation,
which may require intubation; the attach-
ment of an *electrocardiograph;* the fetching of
two drugs (epinephrine and calcium chloride);
and the bringing of a *defibrillator*.

---

† Electric shock or lightning stroke is an exception.
Here, far from operating rooms, heroic resuscitation
may succeed.

(1) *First, assurance of no effective beat is re-affirmed by palpation and auscultation.*

(2) *Second, the thorax is struck several sharp blows; a needle is inserted into the myocardium near the apex.* Neither of these should delay thoracotomy. If asystole with a low threshold of excitability is present, they may initiate the beat again.

(3) *Third, thoracotomy and manual systole with intermittent aortic occlusion are initiated. Elapsed time to here determines brain survival.* If the heart is fibrillating, prolonged manual systole is to be used. Successes have been reported after as long as ninety minutes.

(4) *No drugs are used until the heart is pink as a result of good ventilation and manual systole.* Once myocardial oxygenation is established as a result of the coronary flow of effective manual systole, the following may be undertaken if needed:

(a) electric-shock defibrillation, using 250 volts at 0.05 second;

(b) if electric shock defibrillates the heart to asystolic standstill, calcium or epinephrine may help resume the beat.

A few seconds are spent on those steps which will start the heart going again if asystolic standstill has occurred. After ventricular systole, the threshold of irritability of the ventricle is initially high and becomes lower and lower with the passage of seconds. Stated otherwise: after an initial systole, the ventricle becomes progressively easier to stimulate to a new systole. In asystolic arrest the difficulty arises when conduction down the bundle of His is not communicating to the waiting myocardium an adequate stimulus to initiate systolic contraction. It is in this setting, with a "waiting myocardium," that simple stimuli such as sharp percussion over the heart or insertion of a needle into the heart may be effective. Such steps should be done quickly; inserting the needle through the chest wall may be done despite the hazard of injuring a coronary artery; but preparations for thoracotomy should proceed. As further time passes, the waiting myocardium develops progressive anoxia and acidosis and becomes less and less responsive because it is a dying tissue. Ultimately the threshold of irritability becomes very high; nothing can restore the beat, and the patient is lost. The "*brain time*" for survival in total asystole is around two to five minutes; the "*heart time*," meaning that interval in which the myocardium can remain ischemic with ultimate recovery (at normal body temperature), is much longer, possibly as long as ten minutes.

Fibrillating myocardium requires carbohydrate and oxygen even though it is doing no effective work. The ischemic fibrillating heart will therefore die of ischemia sooner than will the asystolic heart. Resuscitation without electrical defibrillation is of course to be preferred; and the shocks cannot be repeated more than two or three times without serious injury to the myocardium.

The hazards of open thoracotomy without asepsis are not as great as the hazards of waiting to achieve a sterile field when the patient with cardiac arrest is found in the recovery room or off the operating table. This occurrence "near surgery" is an indication for thoracotomy, unlike the condition of most patients on the ward.

D. PREVENTION

The prevention of cardiac arrest depends upon competent anesthesia, unhurried, with adequate oxygenation and avoidance of overdose of agent in a patient who is psychologically and metabolically fit for surgery.

The factor of haste in anesthesia induction has already been mentioned in this connection. A change in American anesthesia in the past 15 years has been not only the introduction of many new agents, of professional anesthetists, and the other well-known factors, but also an increasing tendency to take the patient from full consciousness to deep surgical anesthesia in a matter of minutes. In the 1920's, 1930's, and early 1940's it was customary that anesthesia induction consist of a prolonged period when the patient slowly went down into deeper and deeper phases of anesthesia as ether was added to the extracellular fluid, then entering the brain, and finally permitting the operation to begin. During this time the surgeon, scrubbed and in the operating room, paced up and down muttering imprecations about the passage of time. Possibly that time was not wasted, in view of the tendency today to "snow the patient" within a matter of minutes by a combination of a barbiturate, nitrous oxide, curare, endotracheal intubation, and positive pressure respiration. An anesthetist may on occasion be impatient; whatever occurs, it should not be the impatience of the surgeon that is at fault in an unseemly desire to save time.

When the drug combinations of "sudden-anesthesia" therapy work out well, a patient can be taken from a fully-awake state to a plane where major abdominal surgery can be carried out in a matter of five or ten minutes. Such speed is not necessary. It is our conviction that it is this speed that is the main hazard, and that this hasty induction requires a very high dosage of anesthetic agents because time is not allowed for their equilibration into nervous tissue.

Section IV.   Extracorporeal Circulation*

The metabolic effects of total body perfusion, using a pump oxygenator for extracorporeal circulation during open heart surgery, must be differentiated as between two situations. The ideal situation is *adequate perfusion* that brings in its wake a minimal physiologic and metabolic disturbance. In other instances, either by design or inadvertence, *inadequate perfusion* may be present for minutes or longer, and the metabolic effects are appropriately more rigorous for the patient.

Likewise, in considering the metabolic responses to total body perfusion, one must differentiate between another two categories:

(1) The effects on the patient of the *extracorporeal circulation* and total body perfusion *per se*.

(2) The effects before, during, or after operation of the *pathologic process* in heart or lungs for which the patient is being operated upon.

In this section some of these factors will be reviewed briefly. No attempt will be made to cover the growing literature in this field. The reader is referred to the text on *Extracorporeal Circulation* (Allen, ed., 1958) which sets forth many of these matters in detail.

Initially it is appropriate to consider the biochemical and metabolic aspects of each component of the circuit as blood leaves the patient, passes through the pumps and the oxygenator, and then reenters the arterial

side. This description is based on the disc oxygenator (Kay-Cross) with rotary pump impellers of the deBakey type. Many of the biochemical considerations are basic to any extracorporeal circuit.

A. THE CIRCUIT

1. The Venous Outflow Tract

Venous drainage from the patient is usually achieved via catheters or cannulae which enter the superior and inferior venae cavae through the right atrium. From here the blood has to rise a short distance to get over the side of the patient or operating table and then flows by gravity siphon to the venous reservoir.

In this simple first component—that is, the venous outflow—lies much of the secret of the single most important factor in extracorporeal circulation, namely, total blood flow during perfusion. Clearly, the pump cannot pump nor can the oxygenator oxygenate more blood for return to the patient than comes from the patient through the venous catheters. By the same token the patient's own heart cannot accept or impel more blood than is returned via the same great veins now occupied by the cannulae. Therefore, if the cannulae are freely open, if no venous obstruction or pressure elevation is allowed to occur, and if all the blood accepted by the machine is freely returned to the patient under arterial pressure, the apparatus is able to replace cardiac output. Only a gross distortion of peripheral resistance or the opening

---

* The author is indebted to Dr. Dwight E. Harken and Dr. Robert E. Gross for the privilege of studying and reviewing material based on their large experience in this field.

of A-V shunts will destroy this basic parameter of perfusion; such distortions are in themselves by-products of poor oxygenation or inadequate perfusion due to incomplete venous drainage. Completeness of venous drainage is therefore a first concern and is best monitored by total flow and venous pressure in both upper and lower extremities, which should remain normal.

The negative pressure produced by the siphon system, at about -25 cm. of blood, seems to be about right to maintain complete emptying of the caval return into the reservoir, yet without producing collapse of the cavae. If the cavae are collapsed as, for instance, by using a pump to produce negative pressure at this point, or if the siphon suction is too great, then caval return is poor as the wall of the vessel occludes lumina of the catheters. Blood flow monitoring is ideally placed on this venous side.

If either catheter or cannula is not emptying properly for mechanical reasons, venous hypertension develops in the area drained by that cannula and perfusion immediately suffers. The maintenance of a smooth, large volume flow from these two catheters is therefore critical in pump oxygenator operation.

2. The Oxygenator

Leaving the caval outflow siphon, the blood is collected in one or two reservoirs. Flow can be measured at this point by transient outflow occlusion from one of the reservoirs and a measurement of the rate of its filling. By simple calibration, this produces a direct blood-flow measurement free of the difficulties of electronic instrumentation, or indirect calibration. The blood is admitted to the oxygenator from this gravity feed system in most of the apparatus arrangements that are based on the rotating disc oxygenator. Entering the oxygenator, the blood is exposed to a liquid-gas interface across which is circulated a gas mixture and within which are rotating the discs which permit blood filming and gas exchange.

There are three variables in this system: first, the rate of *blood flow* (determined by the venous return), second, the rate of *gas flow* (determined by appropriate gas control equipment), and third, the rate of *rotation* of the discs (determined by a calibrated rotor).

The interplay of these three factors in the oxygenator is responsible for the degree of oxygenation of the blood as it leaves the oxygenator and the content of carbon dioxide, both appropriately measured as their gas tensions, indicated as pO_2 and pCO_2. Because the only factor affecting the pH of the blood within the oxygenator itself is the tension of CO_2, it is apparent that these factors also determine the pH gradient across the oxygenator. Because the atmosphere to which the blood is exposed elsewhere in the apparatus is essentially supersaturated with water, it is only here in the oxygenator that the blood may be dehydrated if the gas mixture is dry and flows at too high a rate. We thus find that blood flow, gas flow, and disc rate determine, together, the tension of the oxygen and CO_2 in the blood, the pH of the blood, and the humidification. Because of the fact that the blood remains in the oxygenator somewhat longer than it does elsewhere in the circuit, time is also a critical factor in the temperature gradient of the blood across the entire system.

Analyzing in brief these factors, we find the following general principles apply.

a. Disc Rotation Rate. A very slow disc rate will not provide the maximum oxygenating capacity per disc. A disc rotation rate that is too rapid will whip up and froth the blood to a degree that is undesirable. In general, using the 5-inch disc, rates between 70 and 140 rpm. appear to give the blood its maximum oxygenation time while on each disc without untoward effects. The number of discs should be adjusted in relation to the expected blood flow as based on body weight.

b. Blood Flow Rate. This is determined by the total venous drainage of the patient (as described above) which, in turn, is regulated by the blood volume of the patient. The blood volume is related to the total oxygen requirement which, in turn, is regulated by the lean body mass of the patient and the total caloric energy expenditure, as modified by the heart disease present and by the anesthetized situation on the operating table. The blood flow must pass through the oxygenator, and in order to provide ideal oxygenation each portion of blood should remain in the oxygenator from twenty to forty seconds. This provides a smooth flow column without turbulence, but it is sufficiently slow so that there is some inhomogeneity of mixing. Minor oxygen gradients do develop in the blood at the end of the oxygenator before it is again mixed by pumping. In a very slow flow through the oxygenator, the blood will be fully oxygenated early in the oxygenator and will be exposed to the hazard of supersaturation with oxygen before it leaves.

c. Gas Flow Rate. Because of the much greater diffusibility of CO_2 than of oxygen, an oxygenator tends to wash out CO_2 with much greater facility than it oxygenates the blood. Thus, if either air or pure oxygen is used as the gas mixture, one readily finds that the CO_2 tension in the blood falls drastically across the oxygenator from a normal value of approximately 40 mm. Hg. This, in effect, produces respiratory alkalosis in the oxygenator which may have adverse effects as described below.

By the same token, if gas flow is very rapid, this will tend to remove water from the blood because it is very difficult to humidify gases coming from compressed tanks as they expand, and before they enter the oxygenator. For these reasons a mixture is used consisting of 97 or 98 per cent oxygen with 3 or 2 per cent carbon dioxide, and flow rates are maintained that provide 94 to 97 per cent oxygen saturation of the blood at the efflux end of the oxygenator without undue blowing off of water vapor and with an appropriate maintenance of the CO_2 tension close to 40 mm. Hg. Depending somewhat on the size of the patient and the total blood flows involved, gas flow rates between 500 and 1500 ml. per minute are more than adequate for oxygenation, and avoid respiratory alkalosis.

The hazards of overoxygenating the blood are at least two in number. First there is the hazard that blood with high oxygen tension (over 150 mm. Hg) somehow produces diffuse toxic effects. At the present time opinion is divided as to whether or not sufficiently high

oxygen tensions can be produced by extracorporeal oxygenators, working at atmospheric pressure, so as to produce actual oxygen toxicity. Whether or not this is a factor, there can be no doubt that the release of bubbles within the patient is highly undesirable. If blood is maintained below 98 per cent saturation (allowing for errors in oximetry) one can assume that plasma oxygen content, while in normal partition equilibrium with the red cell, is at a very low level. As soon as the red cell saturation reaches 100 per cent, the saturation of the whole blood may pass 100 per cent, indicating a rising amount of oxygen in solution in plasma. If the blood is cooled while it is being oxygenated (often difficult to avoid) or if there are sudden pressure changes as it enters the patient (likewise almost inevitable), the release of this dissolved oxygen may form microbubbles that produce damage in the brain or other organs.

It is for these reasons, then, that gas flow rates must not be too high and oxygenation not too intense: avoidance of drying the blood, avoidance of overoxygenation, and avoidance of respiratory alkalosis (hypocapnia).

d. Temperature. The combination of hypothermia and extracorporeal circulation has sometimes been used intentionally, and often has been used unintentionally. It has been shown by a number of workers that an extracorporeal circuit makes an extremely efficient way of cooling the whole body. If the blood in a circuit is allowed to cool to temperatures in the range of 33 to 35° C. (a relatively small drop), the patient's body temperature will gradually fall to this level. If this is done intentionally because of a desire to lower metabolic requirements in the face of poor perfusion, the process can be measured and controlled. However, if perfusion is adequate, there is every reason to believe that the patient will get along better if body temperature stays near normal. For this a small heating system, consisting of an infrared lamp or other heat source, is placed on, under, or near the oxygenator.

e. Monitoring. If the surgeon wishes to monitor the oxygenator variables (pH, pCO_2, and pO_2), this should be done at the oxygenator efflux point. Total flow is best monitored on the venous side. An operator may control the three variables mentioned above (disc rate, flow rate, and temperature) so as to modify or improve the efflux characteristics of the blood.

Increasing experience has indicated that when perfusion rates are adequate (and data are gained from laboratory study to indicate that the apparatus at hand produces proper oxygenation without respiratory alkalosis), then complex, detailed, or continuous monitoring of the oxygenator efflux becomes less essential.

Certainly for those surgeons who are beginning work in this field, *extensive monitoring of the blood at this point as well as of the patient's vital responses* (see below) *is an essential preliminary to successful operation of the apparatus.* There is no short cut to perfection.

3. Pump

The blood leaving the oxygenator must now climb uphill back to the patient and enter the patient's arterial system at a pressure at or near arterial pressure. This gradient is accomplished by a pump, the characteristics of which will not be reviewed here in detail. A variety of devices have been used. Few seem to have improved on the simple rotor pump wherein the pump output is controlled by rotatory speed and degree of occlusiveness. If the pump is not completely occlusive, it is somewhat less traumatic to the blood and produces a slightly pulsatile high-pressure flow with minimal damage to the blood.

A simple filter and bubble trap is placed between the pump and the patient. If it is placed between the oxygenator and the pump, it will be in an area of the apparatus which is functioning at a slightly negative pressure. This makes it difficult to bleed bubbles out of it. If it is placed between the pump and the patient, the filter trap operates in a high pressure area of the apparatus and bubbles that rise to the top may easily be bled out. A small siliconized screen placed in this filter

permits the screening out of suture material or clots that might form.

Of central importance to the application of the arterial inflow cannulae is the fact that the major arterial tree is a unicameral hydrostatic system. Blood introduced anywhere into the arterial side will maintain the same pressure throughout the tree, whether it be measured at other large arteries, at the coronary inflow ostia, or at the arteriolar outflow tracts of the arterial system. It is often a convenience to introduce this blood into the femoral artery. It can also be introduced into the aorta or into one of the branches of the aorta in the thorax. The important point is that a large amount of blood must be delivered at high pressure to this area. There must therefore be no constriction or bottleneck in the system where it enters the artery, and there should be minimal opportunity for escape turbulence at the point of arteriole inflow jet. It is at this escape turbulence point (greatly accentuated by any bottleneck effect proximal to the escape jet) that trauma is done to the red cell, manifesting itself as hemolysis, or that oxygen in the plasma is released as bubbles. A hydrodynamically smooth inflow jet is therefore of critical importance.

4. Balancing and Monitoring

a. Monitoring. Monitoring the pump efflux for pH, pCO_2, and pO_2 has already been mentioned. This can be done by repeated isolated samples and conventional laboratory and apparatus, or by a variety of refinements culminating in continuous written records, electronically registered from this efflux. The efflux should be close to a pH of 7.35, pO_2 of 110 mm. Hg, and pCO_2 of 40 mm. Hg. These normal physiologic values should be maintained as closely as possible.

Monitoring the patient's responses takes the form of measurement of the patient's systolic and venous blood pressure, mean blood pressure, electrocardiogram, and electroencephalogram as well as the observations of patient's color and capillary flow. It has been the experience of most groups that they started with complicated monitoring of blood and patient and moved on to more simple procedures. This is a natural evolution which is wisely followed by each newcomer to the field. Only by extensive monitoring can he gain experience with this apparatus.

Of the devices for monitoring the patient, the electroencephalogram is most sensitive in determining critically low flows to the brain and can be in a sense a "stop sign." It tells the surgeon when perfusion is dangerously low. If electroencephalographic response is poor, one can be sure that there is something drastically wrong, either with some feature of the apparatus or with the anesthesia. Perfusion should be stopped and the patient's own circulation restored unless the error can be corrected.

The electrocardiogram is possibly of least significance during perfusion itself but is of extreme help after perfusion, particularly if heart block has become a problem.

The patient's blood pressure should be maintained near a systolic pressure of 110 mm. Hg or a mean pressure of between 80 and 100 mm. Hg.

The venous oxygen saturation remains the single most critical measurement of the adequacy of flow. This must of course be measured proximal to the oxygenator and can be carried out either by continuous oximetry or by intermittent sampling. If all of the oxygenator efflux characteristics are normal (pH, pO$_2$, and pCO$_2$) and the venous oxygen saturation is in the range between 70 and 80 per cent, one may assume—quite aside from all other considerations—that perfusion of the patient is adequate as a function of total flow rate, and of oxygen delivery and CO$_2$ removal. Whether or not a flow meter is in the circuit, whether or not the flow meter is working properly, and whether or not venous drainage is adequate, *one may assume that perfusion is imperfect and dangerously so if the venous oxygen saturation falls below 60 per cent.*

The perfusion of ideally oxygenated blood at an inadequate flow rate permits the tissues to extract more oxygen and produce large A-V oxygen differences. This will be manifested within seconds or minutes. Low flow also induces the accumulation of acid metabolites and the beginning of hypoxic acidosis (see below). It is important to recall that as the oxygen dissociation curve descends, it is harder and harder for the tissues to get their share of oxygen out of blood that is progressively desaturated. Low venous oxygen saturation therefore constitutes an important danger signal of low flow rate. Venous oxygen saturation has no regional significance, however. If either cava is improperly draining or obstructed, the venous oxygen saturation will be falsely high as the improperly drained area is not represented in the mixed venous pool. Therefore, despite the overriding importance of this monitoring feature, one must view its results with healthy skepticism if there is any elevation of venous pressure.

The adequacy of caval outflow drainage can be measured only by venous pressure monitoring. In the ideal situation, venous pressure should be monitored in both the upper and lower portions of the body. This is not always possible. It is therefore important for the surgeon and the anesthetist to use clinical observation as well as instrumentation. Elevated venous pressure in the upper portion of the body will be evident by suffused, flushed, plethoric cyanosis of the face. Venous obstruction in the lower part of the body will be manifested by an abrupt and drastic fall in blood flow through the machine, and by the evidence of a turgid cava below the cannula and venous distention of the lower extremities and gut. These latter are often unnoticed during the operation and the surgeon must therefore exert continuous vigilance.

b. Balancing. The balancing of the device refers to the maintenance of an output equal to the inflow rate. Using the type of apparatus envisaged here, balancing presents little problem. The instrument cannot be out of balance more than a few seconds without a visible change of level of the meniscus of blood in the oxygenator. Since there is essentially but one pump in the apparatus, namely that accepting the efflux from the oxygenator and impelling it into the patient's artery, the maintenance of a constant level in the oxygenator by regulating this pump output will effectively achieve balance of the entire apparatus with the patient.

By the same token, a rapid fall in the oxygenator at a time when the pump is operating at constant output indicates a sudden and hazardous reduction in venous blood siphon input.

A low-pressure suction system, permitting removal of blood that is within the heart, or of coronary sinus efflux, also delivers blood to the venous reservoir.

Anticoagulation is achieved by giving the patient heparin. The dose is based on the patient's size, which in turn is a rough determinant of the blood volume. At the close of the procedure, the heparin is neutralized by protamine and this neutralization should be checked by appropriate determination of the clotting time.

B. THE FLOW RATE

As is apparent from the above discussion, the total flow rate through the apparatus is a most important characteristic. The determination of the ideal flow rate for the patient may be based on a number of different measurements.

1. Direct measurement of the patient's resting cardiac output.
2. Estimate of cardiac output from the patient's weight and standard tables.
3. Estimate of the patient's cardiac output from the patient's surface area and other index or standard tables.
4. Some more complex calculation based on the patient's oxygen requirement.

In patients with certain types of heart disease direct preoperative measurement of the cardiac output by the Fick principle or by dye dilution may be helpful in this regard. Again, as has been the case with so many aspects of this problem, progress has been from the complex to the simple.

As experience has been gained, it has been shown that normal flow rates which provide excellent maintenance of the patient with no departure in any important physiologic dimension are in the region between 2300 and 2500 ml. per square meter per minute.

In a 70 kg. man with a surface area of 1.73 square meters, this figures out to a blood flow of about 4000 ml. per minute. For a female the figure would be somewhat lower— around 3500 ml. per minute. Reexpressing this on the basis of weight, these data are in the range of between 50 and 60 ml. per kg. per minute.

The translation of data based on weight in adults to perfusion of very young children cannot be done accurately. The body surface is preferable as an index.

The oxygen requirement of the individual under anesthesia is significantly lower than that of the individual resting and awake. Were the patient to be febrile, the oxygen requirement would be increased. In the normal operative situation, with good anesthesia, the blood flow requirement and oxygen requirement are definitely below that indicated in the "basal" but awake state. It has been found that oxygen requirement ranges very close to 100 ml. per square meter per minute in a variety of patients and with a variety of disease states.

It is interesting in this connection to recall (as mentioned in Part I) that the oxygen requirement of the lean body mass is very inhomogenous. Although the lean body mass is mostly striated muscle, its oxygen requirement at rest is almost wholly determined by the heart, the diaphragm, the liver, and the brain. The requirement of the kidney is important, and the ability of the kidney to abstract oxygen from blood is fixed in such a way that low kidney perfusions produce much more severe local anoxia than do low perfusion rates in brain, liver, or heart. However these variables may arrange themselves, the fact remains that the patient on extracorporeal perfusion is being maintained ideally by flow rates which supply the entire metabolic requirement of his lean body mass, in turn largely determined by the oxygen requirement of brain, heart, diaphragm, liver, and kidneys.

1. Adequate Perfusion

If we define *adequate perfusion* as the performance of a surgical operation on a patient on extracorporeal pump oxygenator flow, at rates in the vicinity of 2300 to 2500 ml. per square meter per minute, of blood entering the body with 95 to 97 per cent saturation, an oxygen tension of approximately 110 mm. Hg, a pH of between 7.30 and 7.40, and a carbon dioxide tension of 40 mm. Hg; if we then additionally define adequate perfusion as including a mixed venous oxygen saturation of between 70 and 80 per cent with normal venous pressure both in the upper and lower parts of the body—if we use these definitions, we can then say that the metabolic response of the patient to total body perfusion of periods up to ninety minutes is only the response to the anesthesia, the operation, and the disease from which the patient suffers.

The achievement of perfect perfusion may be measured in these terms: when, using apparatus currently available, perfusion meets these standards, no additional metabolic or biochemical derangement is discernible in the patient.

One might take exception to this statement by stating that even with perfect devices, a tiny amount of plasma hemoglobin is released by hemolysis, in the range of 15 to 40 mg. per 100 ml. This minor degree of hemolysis may be traceable to the slight trauma that is implicit in blood collection from donors to prime the apparatus, or to the trauma either of the pump, the oxygenator, or the turbulence jet at the arterial inflow site. Whatever its pathogenesis, it is reduced to a minimum by careful handling of the blood before it is put into the machine, by the avoidance of any bottlenecks, kinking, or turbulence areas in the apparatus, by the avoidance of completely occlusive rotary pumps, and by the maintenance of the biochemical parameters intact. Serious departure in any one of these areas may result in severe hemolysis. If the hemolysis can be seen as a faint pink tinge in spun blood during or after the procedure, it is probably over 100 mg. per cent and is potentially dangerous. If darkly tinged with hemoglobin, it indicates gross mechanical fault in the apparatus or the blood collection and a serious threat to the survival of the patient.

2. Inadequate Perfusion

In sharp contrast to the surgically satisfying and biochemically perfect homeostasis of the patient during adequate perfusion are the many disorders that arise from inadequate perfusion.

a. Hypoxic Acidosis. All of these disorders may be analyzed in terms of oxygen want, although they may express themselves in many other ways. One of the most characteristic manifestations is a severe mixed metabolic and respiratory acidosis. We have termed this "hypoxic acidosis." It is found not only in low-perfusion situations on the pump oxygenator but in any other situation in the body where blood flow is low either to the body as a whole or to one limb or organ. For instance, characteristic hypoxic acidosis is seen late in shock. It is seen in tourniquet ischemia. It is seen in distal extremities after wounds of arteries. It is observed in the kidney after prolonged clamping of renal vessels, and in many other situations.

As seen in inadequate perfusion on extracorporeal pump oxygenator apparatus, the defect manifests itself primarily by a low pH, a normal or high pCO$_2$ with elevation of acidic components of both the organic and inorganic moieties. These include lactic acid, pyruvic acid, citric acid, phosphates, and sulfates. All of these accumulating end products are acidic in their effect on the body merely because of the fact (as mentioned in Part I) that the body normally dwells at the alkaline end of its range. Whether this acidosis be regarded as primarily metabolic or respiratory is in a sense academic. If carbon dioxide is not being removed properly by the circulation to a part, one might think of this condition as a respiratory acidosis because the anion (HCO$_3^-$) has a gas phase (dependent upon carbonic anhydrase) as CO$_2$; but the material is of course metabolic in origin and this low-flow acidosis has no primary respiratory component. The factor common to all the features is inadequate oxygenation of the tissue.

Hypoxic acidosis, arising as it does from within the cells, quickly uses up the cellular buffering capacity (see Part III). A patient who has been on low-flow pump oxygenator operation for thirty-five to fifty minutes will have his acid-buffering mechanism as completely taken up as if he had been suffering from chronic asthma, emphysema, and bronchiectasis for years. The essential results of this acidosis will be seen in terms of myocardial arrhythmia, abnormal function of the brain, inability to oxidize carbohydrate, and inability to maintain blood pressure and forward flow after perfusion is removed. A shock-like state with continuing low blood flow, poor cardiac function, hypercapnia, hyperkalemia, hyponatremia, loss of the effect of digitalis with reversion to a high ventricular rate and oliguria—all of these are characteristic of severe hypoxic acidosis.

The only cure for hypoxic acidosis is restoration to good ventilation of the blood and good blood flow. The addition of fixed base (such as sodium bicarbonate) to a patient with hypoxic acidosis is moderately dangerous but can be used in small repeated doses—40 mM. of $NaHCO_3$ at a dose—over a period of approximately twelve to eighteen hours so long as the total dose of base is not excessive. It should be clearly understood that this is a very inadequate and late treatment for a situation most ideally dealt with by prevention. The amount of base that can be given is but a weak antidote for the very large acid loads that have taken up the cellular buffers.

Prevention of hypoxic acidosis in turn depends on the maintenance of adequate flow during perfusion. As mentioned below, hypoxic acidosis can also develop following operation if the cardiac lesion is such as to prevent perfect cardiac function after operation or if heart block or heart failure develops.

b. Hypocapnia: The Effect of Excessive CO_2 Removal. It is a simple matter to remove large amounts of CO_2 from blood as it passes the oxygenator. By high gas flows at low CO_2 tensions, the partial pressure of CO_2 in the blood may be lowered to figures between 15 and 20 mm. Hg. If total flow on the pump is inadequate and the patient is developing hypoxic acidosis, an illusory appearance of normal pH will be produced at the efflux end of the oxygenator if the carbon dioxide wash-out is excessive. An example will illustrate. If, because of low total flow, the venous oxygen saturation is approximately 40 per cent and the venous pH 7.20, it is possible by excessive CO_2 removal—at least over short periods of time—to raise the pH at the oxygenator efflux point to a figure about 7.28 to 7.32. This does not look too bad. But a seemingly normal or close to normal pH is being maintained only by dint of excessive carbon dioxide removal while the nonvolatile acid metabolites continue to accumulate in the blood because of low flow and hypoxia of the tissues.

This has two effects. First, the surgeon is quite unaware of the serious situation developing in the patient. He therefore does not repair it by improving blood flow; everything looks all right while the patient is on the pump. Then when the patient has returned to his own circulation and the ventilation provided by the anesthetist, he seems to deteriorate rapidly. Ordinary anesthesia ventilation aims at the maintenance of CO_2 tensions close to 40 mm. Hg. Therefore, as the patient comes off the pump and returns to a normal CO_2 tension, a very profound acidosis is suddenly produced. The pH falls drastically to 7.10 or lower with myocardial, cerebral, and circulatory defects.

Second, more subtle and more puzzling is the situation in which hypoxic acidosis is developed on the pump, has been masked by hypocapnia due to excessive CO_2 removal, and the anesthetist has then, either intuitively or by design, hyperventilated the patient during the closure of the wound and the completion of the operation. Here again excessive CO_2 removal has artificially supported the pH. Then, as the patient is extubated and returned to the recovery room, collapse occurs. This we have termed the "criss-cross" effect, meaning by this that a severe respiratory alkalosis produced by the oxygenator operation has masked a mounting hypoxic metabolic acidosis; as the patient returns to his own devices $p CO_2$ rises, the pH falls, and we have the uncompensated late hypoxic acidosis of inadequate perfusion now existing in a patient in bed, extubated, off the pump, and much more difficult to control.

One other word about excessive CO_2 removal. For some time it has been habitual for anesthetists to hyperventilate their patients slightly during thoracic operations. This is because of the well-known tendency of these patients to develop respiratory acidosis. Therefore, the patient often comes to the open heart procedure with a slight respiratory alkalosis. It is of interest that respiratory alkalosis of itself, and ether anesthesia also, both result in the accumulation of lactic acid. It is not clear as to why respiratory alkalosis produces lacticacidemia. In the case of ether anesthesia, however, it appears to be a specific effect of ether on the oxidation of carbohydrate, resulting in a diversion of some carbohydrate to the anaerobic glycolytic cycle. Whatever the mechanism is, the fact is that the patient who is hyperventilated prior to perfusion, whether or not he is under ether anesthesia, is already beginning to accumulate some lactic acid. If renal mechanisms are normal and oxygenation adequate, this slight lacticacidemia is of little note. If, however, it is followed by a low perfusion situation and hypoxia, it adds materially to the severity of the ultimate hypoxic acidosis.

For all these reasons, then, these patients are best carried through operation from beginning to end with normal ventilation and a normal tension of carbon dioxide in their blood. If perfusion is adequate there is no reason to consider oxygenator hypocapnia as desirable.

c. Elective Asystole. If the nature of the operative procedure is such that coronary inflow must be occluded, the metabolic damage done to the heart is minimized by elective asystole. It has been estimated that the caloric requirement of the heart is reduced to a large extent when it is arrested at normal temperature. This means that, with essentially no blood supply, there is very little accumulation of acid metabolites in an asystolic heart whereas a heart that is still trying to beat accumulates a very severe and acute hypoxic acidosis that results within a few minutes in anoxic arrest. Elective asystole appears therefore to be less damaging to the heart than is anoxic arrest, but there can be

little question that the maintenance of coronary flow with a normal cardiac beat throughout the procedure—even if the heart is open—is preferable to either elective asystole or anoxic arrest.

d. Carbohydrate. Blood on storage tends to burn sugar (see Part II). The patient under anesthesia burns sugar. One may on occasion therefore find that the blood sugar of a patient on pump oxygenator operation is perilously low toward the end of the perfusion. This is important to mention because it may produce electroencephalographic changes or alterations in blood pressure as does hypoglycemia of any kind. It is readily prevented by the administration of small amounts of carbohydrate to the patient during perfusion; a slowly running intravenous infusion of 5 per cent dextrose in water takes care of this effectively.

C. PROBLEMS AFTER PERFUSION

1. Transfusion Volume

When the pump is properly balanced, the net change in blood volume of the patient traceable to the pump operation alone should be essentially zero. The blood loss incident to the operation, however, may be very considerable. Only a fraction of this has been removed from the field by the low-pressure suction system. In replacing the blood loss, the surgeon should use his customary guides such as sponge weights or other estimates, but considering the large volume of blood constantly being siphoned out of the patient and pumped back again, it is often difficult to keep track of the transfusion adequacy.

By temporarily increasing the pump speed, it is possible to lower the meniscus in the oxygenator, in effect giving the patient a blood transfusion. Transfusion can of course be given the patient through other sites.

The difficulty arises when the patient is taken off the pump. The heart may be regaining normal systolic contraction (if elective asystole has been used) and the adequacy of cardiac output and of blood volume is extremely difficult to judge as based on such familiar evidences as venous pressure. If, as the patient comes off the pump, cardiac function is completely normal and venous pressure low, one may assume that the patient has not been overtransfused; if systolic pressure is likewise low, additional blood should be given.

If, however, cardiac function, rhythm, rate, or integration is poor and venous pressure elevated, one cannot assume that the patient has been overtransfused. One may be dealing with a normal blood volume, but inadequate cardiac output. It is in this aspect of pump oxygenator operation, more than any other, that monitoring devices break down completely and the history of the extent of blood loss and the volume of blood replacement—the simple clinical indices used in any form of surgery—regain their usual important status. The patient's body weight may also be helpful; allowing the loss of approximately 100 gm. per hour on the operating table, one would expect that postoperative weight was approximately equal to preoperative weight. The method is awkward and difficult and cannot be used until the operation is over. Ideally the patient should complete the operation with essentially the same blood volume as he began it unless a hypervolemia due to the cardiac lesion is to be reduced. If cardiac function is poor and venous pressure persistently elevated, with a normal blood volume, venesection has usefulness.

2. Coagulation

The use of heparin and protamine has already been mentioned; careful hemostasis is essential in wound closure. Some hemorrhage into the chest is not unusual despite these precautions. This should be monitored by external water-seal drainage and should be replaced quantitatively if venous pressure is normal. Patients have been observed on occasion to be refractory to protamine and to require excessive amounts in order to neutralize their initial heparin dosage.

3. Fluids

The use of an indwelling urethral catheter and the measurement of hourly urine outputs are helpful in these patients postoperatively. Total fluid ration for the operative day should be determined as it is for any other cardiac patient, by basal water requirement, body weight, and temperature. Unquestionably the tendency is to overhydrate these patients. Severe limitations should be placed on total fluid therapy.

4. Cardiopulmonary Factors

A detailed discussion of cardiac anomalies or diseases and the functional picture after repair is beyond the scope of this book. It should be mentioned that three types of situation can produce chronic hypotension and an uncorrected or mounting hypoxic acidosis. These three situations are characteristically:

(a) left ventricular inadequacy in the face of longstanding congenital or acquired heart disease;

(b) right ventricular inadequacy in the face of prolonged right-to-left shunt or severe chronic pulmonary vascular disease;

(c) heart block or other arrhythmias reducing cardiac output.

Ventricular "inadequacy" is used in the above descriptions rather than ventricular "failure" since the situation may merely be that of a ventricular muscle that, because of a shunt, has never had to bear its full load and, when this load is presented to it, is unable to impel it properly.

The treatment of these difficulties involves the proper use of digitalis, a suitable blood volume, good alveolar ventilation, and the maintenance of an ideal biochemical milieu in the body. Hypoxic acidosis, with or without severe sodium-potassium shift, will make the recovery of such a ventricle extremely unlikely, will rob it of the effect of digitalis, and will be critical as the cause of death. The use of operative devices in the manner of temporary shunts, extracorporeal ventricles, or decompressing apparatus may be important in these disorders.

The preoperative diagnosis of severe chronic pulmonary vascular disease bodes ill for the outcome of surgery. One can hope for very little improvement in such vascular disease with the passage of time; the patient frequently has to face this postoperative hazard without any known palliative step.

Heart block is most apt to occur if a suture has been placed in the bundle of His. If the heart has not been arrested during the placement of these sutures, it is occasionally possible to discern which suture is at fault, and remove it. If heart block has been produced, a pacemaker with an indwelling ventricular electrode can be used to maintain forward output until the block reverts to normal, an event which may require from two to sixteen days. During this entire time the patient is in a hazardous situation and if reversion has taken place, the block may from time to time recur, particularly if there has been direct trauma to the bundle.

In *summary*, perfusion adequacy emerges as the single most critical dimension of extracorporeal circulation. If this is adequate, a normal metabolic situation can be maintained for the patient undergoing open heart surgery. His survival and the adequacy of repair then depend—as they should in any surgical operation—on the anatomic and physiologic defect itself and the skill that can be brought to bear in its correction.

Section V.   The Heart: Notes from the Literature

A. METABOLIC CHANGES IN HEART FAILURE

Barger's classic work (Barger *et al.*, 1955, a, b, c) must be consulted by students of this subject. He has produced by the combination of pulmonary stenosis and tricuspid insufficiency in dogs a "stable" congestive failure that gradually yields a progressive and severe retention of water and salt. A subtle retention of sodium is observed, and this passes on to frank edema and ascites. The early changes precede changes in venous pressure or rate of glomerular filtration. The sodium retention is due to increased tubular resorption of sodium. The early lesion appears characteristic of maintained volume-receptor stimulus, producing increased volume of extracellular fluid (and plasma). Barger (1956) reviews the fact that aldosterone alone is not enough to produce edema. One cannot help but wonder if his preparation also stimulates the output of antidiuretic hormone.

Goodyer and Glenn (1955) studied the operative mitral hyponatremia and concluded, as had Wilson *et al.* (1954), that dilution accounted for the greater part of the lowering of tonicity. Cellular shift was small in amount. The prolonged postoperative activity of an antidiuretic mechanism was also implied by the studies. As in our studies (Wilson *et al.*, 1954), prolonged failure, severe arrhythmia, and rheumatic activity often accompanied or preceded this prolonged dilutional hyponatremia. But prediction on these bases was not possible. There was no correlation between hyponatremia and the alleged "postvalvulotomy" syndrome. Their conclusions regarding salt administration were similar to ours: avoid salt if you can, but if you must, use small volumes of very concentrated sodium chloride.

Friedberg (1957) has also reviewed the fluid and electrolyte disturbances of heart failure and described the use of Diamox (acetazolamide) as a diuretic in its treatment (Friedberg *et al.*, 1953).

Mokotoff *et al.* (1952) found intracellular sodium concentrations to be elevated in skeletal muscle in heart failure. They found almost double the normal value of 11.6 mE. per 100 gm. of fat-free solids, although they did not find potassium reduced, while Iseri *et al.* (1955) did find a marked reduction in muscle potassium (116 as against 151 mE. per l. of intracellular water).

Schwartz and Relman (1954) have reviewed the electrolyte phenomena of congestive heart failure and categorize them as follows:

(1) hypochloremic alkalosis due to mercurial diuretics,
(2) hyponatremia—"low salt syndrome,"

(3) respiratory acidosis and/or metabolic alkalosis,

(4) ammonium chloride poisoning,

(5) potassium depletion,

(6) complications of cation-exchange resins,

(7) acidosis caused by carbonic anhydrase inhibitors.

Many of these are iatrogenic. They complicate anesthesia and surgery, and the response to digitalis. Others are less frequent and relatively unimportant. They all occur on the compositional background of heart failure as described by Wilson *et al.* (1954).

Laragh (1954) studied the effect on edematous hyponatremic cardiac patients of administering potassium chloride. In some there was a gratifying rise in sodium concentration, seemingly a release of sodium from cells—about 60 to 300 mE. becoming available. The changes in external balance were inadequate to account for the change. Some hyperkalemia resulted in certain instances. There was no diuresis.

Rubin and Braveman (1956) present medical aspects of treatment of the low salt syndomes in congestive failure. They point out that hypochloremic alkalosis, as well as hyponatremia, occasionally is seen in mercurial-resistant patients. Mercurial diuretics, especially when presented along with ammonium chloride or in an "acid" setting (that is, urine *p*H 6.0 or below), act primarily on chloride excretion. The authors suggest that water retention rather than salt loss is the cause of hyponatremia. There is of course a large amount of compositional research showing unequivocally that this is the case. The authors report the restoration of responsiveness to mercury by the production of a hyperchloremic acidosis through the liberal use of acetazolamide (Diamox) and ammonium chloride. They found the urine always to have less sodium than plasma has, though they did not measure urine osmolality or free water clearance. The authors reemphasize the fact that by the vigorous use of ammonium chloride, acetazolamide, and mercurial diuretics it is possible to produce large diureses, with a rising sodium concentration, even in hyponatremic cardiacs. The severity of the acidosis produced in some of these cases by

such rugged treatment is truly remarkable with carbon dioxide combining power in the range of 8.0 mE. per l., chloride at 114 mE. per l. There was very strict limitation of fluids. Their emphasis on urine sodium concentrations below those of plasma as indicating the reason for the rise in plasma concentration should be revised in view of the fact that even while patients are becoming hyponatremic, their urine sodium concentrations are virtually never greater than those of plasma. Without measurement of total body water and salt volumes, the rationalization of these measures is difficult. The important thing surgically is that such drastic regimens do lower body sodium totals and raise tonicity, even in the face of late failure. The regimen here discussed includes 10 gm. of ammonium chloride and 750 mg. of acetazolamide by mouth; when urine chloride rises over 40 mE. per l., 2.0 ml. of mercuhydrin is given and the ammonium chloride continued.

Stein *et al.* (1954) assayed the antidiuretic potency of plasma of patients with ascites and edema of various causes, using the intraperitoneal assay in the rat. They did not find significant correlation between water retention and the assay titers. Assay problems beset the many workers who have searched for such correlations.

According to Hanenson *et al.* (1956) and White *et al.* (1953), there is not an abnormality of antidiuretic hormone sensitivity or inactivation in congestive heart failure, even though injection of vasopressin makes the water-and-salt abnormality much worse (Weston *et al.*, 1952, 1953). Evidence of increased antidiuretic activity of human plasma in heart failure is unconvincing, but assay methods are poor.

Luetscher and Johnson (1954) have found excessive quantities of aldosterone in the urine of patients with heart failure; Thorn and Nelson (personal communication) have shown an increase in this hormone after diuresis with digitalis, suggesting that volume reduction, even that toward normal, stimulates a volume-protective reaction in heart failure.

Dexter *et al.* (1954) report on cardiologic aspects of mitral surgery, as have Griffith *et al.* (1953), Dexter *et al.* (1951), Spiegl *et al.* (1952), Spiegl *et al.* (1952), Harken *et al.* (1951, 1952, a, b), Schwartz and Relman (1954), Wasmuth (1953), Wilson *et al.* (1954), and Fox *et al.* (1954). They point out the changing digitalis requirement, the occasional need for quinidine (especially in those with normal sinus rhythm preoperatively), and the importance of the underlying compositional changes and operative response documented by Wilson *et al.* The emotional and psychiatric problems studied by Fox *et al.* may occasionally constitute a serious hazard to life in the postoperative period. Dexter feels that permanent prophylactic antibiotic treatment should be undertaken in all rheumatic cases.

Additional studies of the defects in fluid and electrolyte distribution observed in chronic congestive heart disease, and their meaning in clinical management, include those of Fox *et al.* (1949), Murphy (1950), Miller (1951), Squires *et al.* (1951), Waterhouse *et al.* (1951), Weston *et al.* (1952), Warner *et al.* (1952), Elkinton *et al.* (1952), Uricchio and Calenda (1953), Singer and Wener (1953), Schwartz and Relman (1954), and Farber and Soberman (1956).

The metabolic changes in hypertensive patients are described in Currens *et al.* (1949), and of aortic disease in Gorlin *et al.* (1954).

Further data on the metabolic effects of cardiac operations on the metabolic disorder of heart disease will be found in Deming and Gerbode (1954), Bruce *et al.* (1955), and Goodyer and Glenn (1955).

The safe conduct of patients through cardiac surgery has been described by Black and Harken (1954), Vandam and Burnap (1956) and Johnson *et al.* (1955); all are studies based on careful observation of a large clinical experience.

Representative studies of the effects of mercurials, Diamox, and other medicaments on the metabolic changes of heart disease may be found in Sinclair-Smith *et al.* (1949), Schwartz (1950), Schwartz and Wallace (1950, 1951), Stock *et al.* (1951), Sleisenger and Freedberg (1951), Brown *et al.* (1951), Weston *et al.* (1952), Wesson and Anslow (1952), and Friedberg *et al.* (1953).

Parks (1934) in an early study recorded the fate of patients operated on for various conditions while suffering from organic heart disease.

B ELECTROLYTE AND ACID-BASE BALANCE, FIBRILLATION, AND ARREST*

Stewart *et al.* (1948) reported two cases of potassium intoxication in which atrial standstill appeared, with intraventricular block, when the potassium level was 10 mE. per l. or higher. One was due to the administration of potassium bicarbonate without azotemia, the other was due to advanced renal disease. They used normal saline and hypertonic glucose in treatment. Their article includes a brief review of earlier work in the field, including Winkler *et al.* (1935), the studies of Keith *et al.* (1943), Keith and Osterberg (1946), Keith, Burchell, and Baggenstoss (1944, 1947), Govan and Weiseth (1946), and Martin and Wertman (1947). They characterize the findings of progressive hyperkalemia as:

(1) an increased amplitude of the T-wave; then

(2) a decrease in amplitude of the R-wave with an increase of the S-wave; then

(3) a disappearance of the P-wave, progressive depression of RS-T segments, widening of the QRS complexes to a smooth biphasic curve; then

(4) intraventricular block, and

(5) cardiac arrest in diastole.

Many variants of the above have been described, the most prominent being ventricular fibrillation (Stewart and Smith, 1941). Such changes are seen either with potassium administration or in renal failure. In the latter case, factors of rate of change and concomitant concentration of sodium, calcium, and hydrogen affect the exact details of the final cardiac cessation and the outlook for survival.

Frick *et al.* (1946) studied the use of calcium and sodium in treatment; concentrated (3 per cent) sodium chloride was most effective.

---

* The reader is referred also to the review of citrate effects and myocardial irritability in Part II.

Miller *et al.* (1951, 1952, a, b) showed very clearly that pure carbon dioxide elevation in the inspired air was well tolerated at remarkable concentrations (40 per cent or more), with pH values below 7.0. When death occurred it was caused by a sudden circulatory failure. But, when the stabilized respiratory acidosis was suddenly upset by returning to oxygen (or to "room air"), a severe cardiac arrhythmia occurred, usually ventricular fibrillation, with death. It seems evident that neuromuscular electrical activity depends on cellular pH gradients and electrical potentials that are maintained or initiated under normal conditions. In the Miller experiments one can conceive of the stabilized carbon dioxide toxicity as a severe acidosis, but with gradients maintained as the body buffers are taken up. Then, when the extracellular fluid pH suddenly rises on the patient's again breathing room air, the body buffers respond but slowly and an acute imbalance is established with a very severe cellular acidosis relative to the extracellular fluid. Indeed, the *relative pH gradient* resembles very severe alkalosis. The fact that the potassium rise continues during the return to low carbon dioxide ventilation (Sealy and Young, 1954) is a corroborative suggestion, the passage of potassium from cells to extracellular fluid being a manifestation of a relative excess of H^+ in cells. In any event it was this sudden reversion that produced fibrillation, not the initial carbon dioxide poisoning; sudden "return to room air" was dangerous in equilibrated respiratory acidosis.

Shumacher and Hampton (1951) report clinical cases that correspond to this situation: death near or at the end of surgery when ventilation is restored. The fall in blood pressure that occurs in conjunction with removal of carbon dioxide from the inspired mixture has been noted by Goldstein and duBois (1927) and Dripps (1947). This may be a peripheral vascular manifestation of the same distorted acid-base gradient, as equilibrated and buffered acidotic cells are left with a rapidly rising extracellular pH.

Brown (1956) showed (in dogs) that a return to room air after prolonged breathing of high concentrations of carbon dioxide produced hyperkalemia and death due to ventricular fibrillation. Here during the high carbon dioxide phase the potassium rose to 7.0 mE. per l. and continued to rise on breathing oxygen, whereas with a dose of potassium chloride the level can go to 12 to 14 mE. per l. before death occurs. Speed was a factor. Acute short-term respiratory acidosis, even with the pH at 6.8, seemed to be harmless. This suggests that it is the prolonged load of carbon dioxide, and then its sudden change, possibly due to cellular alteration (in the myocardium?), that does the damage. It would be our interpretation that the long, slow load takes up the body buffers, where the acute load does not; some of this buffering is of course in the myocardium. The sudden relief therefore leaves the muscle cell (or neuromuscular mechanism?) severely acidotic, with a high pCO_2 relative to an extracellular fluid which is rapidly returning to normal. This changes the electrical potential and the conductivity of the bundle as well as the integration of the heartbeat. The high potassium level in the extracellular fluid is a reflection of cellular buffering.

As mentioned previously, the intracellular potassium concentration (or possibly the gradient between intracellular fluid and extracellular fluid) must be lowered to get good myocardial contractility. Digitalis seems to do this, releasing the potassium to the extracellular fluid locally. The sodium changes are reciprocal, and this relation determines the potential. Adding potassium to the extracellular fluid lowers the potential and will produce arrest or fibrillation, depending upon rate and distribution. Under these circumstances, calcium restores this contractility, but, if the calcium concentration is raised progressively and nears 24 mg. per 100 ml., fibrillation again results, as in digitalis toxicity. Norepinephrine is likewise a "fibrillatory" agent. Swan (1958) provides a helpful recent review of myocardial pharmacology.

Beecher and Murphy (1950) reported an extensive study of acid-base changes under anesthesia for thoracic surgery, in forty-three patients. They found that a rather severe combined metabolic and respiratory acidosis occurred, with a rise in alveolar pCO_2 and a fall in pH. This began to develop before the pleura was opened; the agent (nitrous oxide, oxygen, ether) and the apparatus apparently were not responsible; assisted ventilation only occasionally was successful in lowering the pCO_2. Oxygen tensions were satisfactory throughout. Alveolar carbon dioxide rose to 10 to 14 volumes per cent in some instances. In one case an alveolar pCO_2 (arterial blood) of 116 mm. Hg was seen. The authors regard the lateral position as in part responsible, the operated lung being uppermost. It is of interest that this rise, which in a normal person would produce a tremendous increase in ventilation, does not seem to have this effect under anesthesia. There is also an increase in body levels of fixed acids (lactate) with the passage of time.

The sudden decrease in alveolar carbon dioxide that occurs with relief of this condition may be accompanied by a fall in blood pressure, as shown by Goldstein and duBois (1927). Beecher and Murphy suggest that this may be due to the sudden loss of the stimulant action of carbon dioxide and point out its possible relation to the fall in pressure occasionally seen at the conclusion of thoracic procedures.

The authors did not, in this early contribution to an important subject, study cation exchanges which may affect irritability of the arterial wall, response to catechol amines, or myocardial function—any or all of which may be involved in the pressure drop which occurs with sudden release from high carbon dioxide tensions. Dripps (1947) had described an analogous fall in blood pressure after cyclopropane anesthesia.

Miller *et al.* (1951, 1952) noted that the electrocardiographic changes after hypercapnia resembled those of hyperkalemia; elevated potassium was then shown to be the rule in this setting (Young *et al.*, 1951, 1954). The source of this potassium is doubtless diffusely cellular rather than hepatic. As previously noted, such an increase in potassium concentration in the plasma represents but a small shift (about 1 per cent) of total exchangeable potassium. Miller *et al.* have also noted that hypothermia in no wise alters this relation; in fact it appears to make the heart more vulnerable to hypercapnia. The normal dog can endure carbon dioxide concentrations as high as 70 per cent if not too prolonged; it is the later, too sudden, change-over to atmosphere that is dangerous, as already mentioned.

Blakemore *et al.* (1956) found a favorable response to molar (1000 mE. per l.) sodium lactate (500 ml.) in a small group of patients with acute arrhythmias during or following cardiac surgery. This had been proposed by Bellet *et al.* (1955, a, b, c). The patients had a slow ineffective beat at the time. Electric shock was also used in the fibrillators. There was not time to obtain other electrolyte data, but the implication is that a "potassium effect" (hyperkalemia) was counteracted by either the sodium ion or the acid-base effect of the infusion. Although only three out of eight patients responded favorably (at least one having ventricular fibrillation in association with his episode), the data support the addition of this agent to the other agents used.

The injections used in treating cardiac arrhythmias must make sequential sense. It is clearly most advisable to use molar sodium lactate when previous heart or kidney disease or acidosis makes hyperkalemia most likely. The use of sodium lactate plus calcium would be inadvisable in the digitalized patient because of the synergistic action in increasing the digitalis effect.

The studies of Campbell (1955, 1957) are of great interest in this field. He showed (1955) that acidosis of a variety of causes markedly augmented the cardio-inhibitory effects of vagal stimulation, while alkalosis decreased it. Then (1957) he showed that acidosis lowered the responsiveness of the myocardium to epinephrine, and that a change in pH toward alkalosis restored this factor even though normalcy had not yet been reached. Relationships to hypercapnia, ventilation, and the optimal pH range of cholinesterase (pH 7.5 to 8.5) are discussed relative to the findings (1955).

The study of Crowel *et al.* (1955) emphasizes another important feature of the cerebral damage occurring during cardiac arrest. They showed that many small clots form during circulatory arrest and that resuscitation of the heart may fail to produce survival for this reason. In dogs they were able to promote survival by the use of heparin.

There have been several important recent studies of the mechanisms which underlie cardiac arrhythmias at operation, including arrest and fibrillation. Discussion of the citrate effect will be found in Part II. Studies that provide further data on the general problem of alveolar ventilation, carbon dioxide tension, and myocardial effects include the review of Dripps (1955) and the studies of Young *et al.* (1951), Sealy *et al.* (1954), Brown and Miller (1952), Buckley *et al.* (1953), Albritten *et al.* (1954), Clowes *et al.* (1955), Boniface and Brown (1953), and Johnstone (1950).

The studies of Scherf (1945) and Reid and Brace (1940) are of particular interest with regard to cardiac and respiratory reflexes relative to the production of cardiac arrhythmias.

Reviews of clinical problems and management in cardiac arrest include Waters and Gillespie (1922), Howkins *et al.* (1946), Ament *et al.* (1951), Beck (1950), Kay and Blalock (1951), Reid *et al.* (1952), Glenn (1953), Sadove *et al.* (1954), West (1954), and Heckel and Fell (1955).

Stephenson *et al.* (1953) reviewed 1200 instances of cardiac arrest as based on a national survey. Their study supports the concept that there is a true increase in the incidence of this accident as resulting in part from anoxia and overdose of agent.

Schwartz *et al.* (1954) studied potassium and nitrogen balances in nine volunteers in relation to low-potassium state. The potassium depletion was produced with desoxycorticosterone plus ammonium chloride, thus introducing factors of sodium conservation and acid-base disturbance in the experiment. The ammonium chloride acidosis would inevitably minimize the electrocardiographic effects of potassium loss. They classify the electrocardiogram of potassium depletion in progressive stages of severity depending on the degree of T-wave flattening (and finally inversion) with coincident U-wave accentuation. In cases with total potassium losses of 42 to 175 mE. there were few changes; the electrocardiographic change was but poorly correlated with balance, though well correlated with plasma concentration. In some instances, correlation was poor in terms of any measurable index. Interpretation here must be reserved because of the lack of information on concomitant acid-base changes and alterations in metabolism of other pertinent electrolytes. Schwartz's conclusion, however—that the electrocardiogram alone is but a poor index of potassium deficit—has stood the test of time.

Weller *et al.* (1955) removed potassium rapidly from dogs by dialysis; electrocardiographic changes were marked and were correlated with the early fall in plasma potassium concentration. The S–T segment changes were slower to appear, and seemed to correlate most closely with the depletion of body potassium, rather than with the plasma level. In general, however, acute cardiac effects are concentration-linked while chronic effects of a more lasting (but often less dangerous) nature are related to alterations in body content and, by inference, muscle content.

Our studies of the changes and interrelationships of potassium loss, alkalosis, and adrenal stimulation (Moore *et al.*, 1955) point up the remarkably synergistic effect of adrenal stimulation and alkalosis in lowering the extracellular potassium concentration and producing severe electrocardiographic changes despite rather small changes in total body potassium.

Important interrelationships between electrolyte metabolism and the state of digitalization of the heart have already been discussed. Further detailed studies will be found in Amberg and Helmholz (1916), Friedman and Bine (1947), Roberts and Magida (1953), Lown *et al.* (1951), and Regan *et al.* (1956).

CASE 18

In Which Mitral Valvuloplasty Is Followed, on the Seventh Day, by Severe Cardiac Deterioration, Responding Well—and Later, Too Well—to Special Osmotic Therapy

Case 18. Patient A. L., #E9232.* Female. Age 60. Admitted December 1, 1955. Discharged January 5, 1956.

DIAGNOSIS. Rheumatic heart disease with mitral stenosis.

OPERATION. Mitral valvuloplasty.

CLINICAL SUMMARY. This patient entered for consideration of mitral valve surgery because of progressive fatigue, dyspnea on exertion, and palpitation. Although she had had rheumatic fever at the age of fifteen, no cardiac lesion was detected until 1935. Symptoms began in 1945, were markedly relieved by low-salt diet in 1950, but recurred in 1954 while still on this diet. Digitalization four months ago did not relieve symptoms.

Past history was suggestive of mild mental illness.

Physical examination showed a small nervous patient. Blood pressure was 160/84, pulse 80 and regular. Grade II aortic systolic, grade I apical systolic, and grade III apical diastolic murmurs were heard. Lungs were clear. No liver enlargement or leg edema was present.

X-rays revealed right ventricular and left atrial hypertrophy. Electrocardiogram was normal. Initial body weight was 39 kg., height was 56 inches.

INITIAL LABORATORY WORK

Urine
Specific gravity	1.006
pH	5.0
Otherwise negative	

Hematology
Hematocrit	42.5
Leucocyte count	3600 per cu. mm.

Blood Chemical Analyses
Blood urea nitrogen	12	mg. per 100 ml.
Plasma chloride	117	mE. per l.
Plasma sodium	134	mE. per l.
Plasma potassium	4.2	mE. per l.
Carbon dioxide combining power	26.8	mE. per l.

Diuretic therapy was given prior to surgery and the patient lost 1.6 kg. This treatment consisted of ammonium chloride loading (1.0 gm. three times a day) followed by 1.0 ml. of Mercuhydrin intravenously on alternate days. Three such mercurial diureses were needed. Right heart catheterization revealed decreased cardiac output, increased pulmonary vascular resistance, and elevated pulmonary capillary pressure after exercise. Her admission hyperchloremia (presumably

---

*The author is indebted to Dr. William G. Hammond for collecting the data and analyzing the course of this patient.

due to poorly planned ammonium chloride therapy) subsided before operation.

Satisfactory and uneventful mitral valvuloplasty was performed on the fourteenth hospital day. Tight mitral stenosis was noted. Difficulty in voiding postoperatively required continuous catheter drainage.

Laboratory data on the second postoperative day were: hematocrit 37.5, plasma sodium 125 mE. per l., and plasma potassium 5.5 mE. per l.

The patient seemed to be mildly disoriented the first two days after operation, but this cleared. Course was then unremarkable except for mild apathy until electrocardiogram on the seventh day showed a wandering pacemaker with occasional atrial premature beats, intraventricular block, and prolonged Q-T interval and tented T-waves compatible with potassium intoxication. Body weight was 38.8 kg.

LABORATORY DATA ON SEVENTH POSTOPERATIVE DAY
Hematocrit	37.0	
Blood Chemical Analyses		
Plasma sodium	117	mE. per l.
Plasma potassium	6.4	mE. per l.
Plasma osmolality	250	mO. per l.

ARGUMENT. This patient now demonstrates water intoxication, with apathy, marked hyponatremia, and gain in weight. Here, the persistent antidiuretic tendency of congestive heart failure, accentuated after operation, and accompanied by governed, but still excessive, water administration, has been at fault. The patient was very small (about 40 kg.); very small water rations might be expected to produce hypotonicity, if not appropriately excreted. A strong tendency in this direction is demonstrated by her rather marked sodium-potassium inversion right after operation. This has now become grossly exaggerated.

Study of her intake-output records revealed a cumulative positive water balance of 4.4 l. (including in the calculations an estimated 700 ml. per day of insensible loss). From the plasma sodium change, 2.75 l. of water load would suffice to produce the observed fall in concentration. A weight gain of 1.4 kg. is recorded. All these data point to dilution as the genesis of this severe hyponatremia.

In this situation it was not the hyponatremia itself that demands urgent consideration, but rather the associated hyperkalemia with its attendant dangerous cardiac toxicity as manifested by the striking electrocardiographic changes.

A plasma potassium concentration of 6.4 mE. per l. would not, in itself, be expected to produce electrocardiographic changes of any magnitude or severity. The severe hyponatremia, however, greatly potentiates

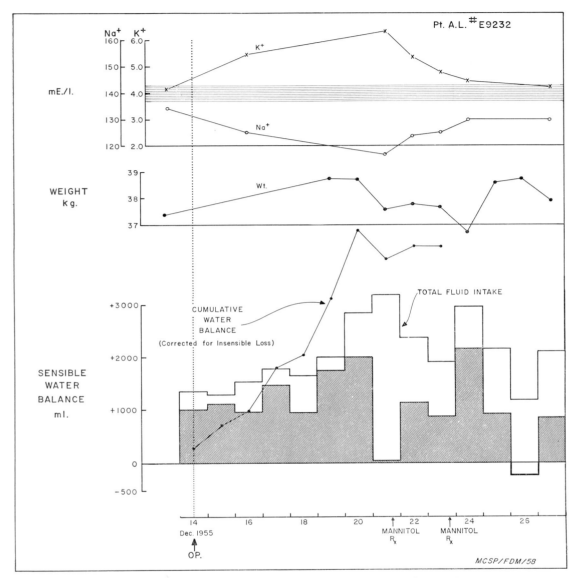

Figure 122. EVENTS FOLLOWING MITRAL VALVULOPLASTY (Case 18)

Above are shown the reciprocal changes in sodium and potassium concentrations and the weight alterations observed in this patient after mitral valvuloplasty. Below is shown the cumulative positive water balance, and the total fluid intake and output. The reader is referred to the text for details.

It will be noted that severe hyponatremia developed approximately five days after cardiac surgery in this patient, together with a gain in weight and a markedly positive cumulative water balance. As is so characteristically the case, the plasma potassium concentration rose while the sodium concentration was falling.

The patient was given slow infusions of mannitol on two occasions. After the first of these a very marked solute diuresis occurred with a loss of considerably more water than salt, and a significant rise in the sodium concentration with a fall in potassium concentration.

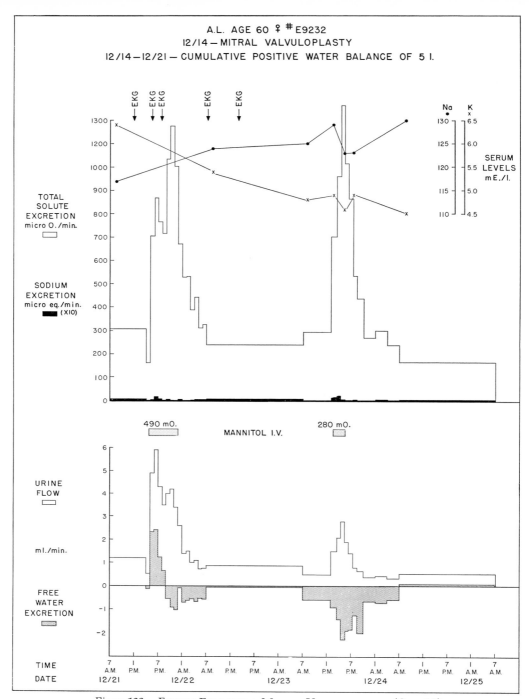

Figure 123. EVENTS FOLLOWING MITRAL VALVULOPLASTY (Case 18)

Same patient as shown in the previous chart. This is a more detailed view of the diuresis produced by slow infusions of mannitol in this patient after mitral surgery.

It will be noted on the left that total solute excretion was increased by the administration of mannitol, but that only a tiny portion of this solute was sodium. This accounts for the "sodium-free solute diuresis" which produces a rise in the plasma sodium concentration as shown.

On the second occasion the total solute and water

removed was considerably less. The fall in sodium concentration resulting from the acute infusion of mannitol itself is shown, together with the restoration to a higher value as solute excretion is completed in the course of the next 12 to 24 hours.

It should be emphasized again that despite the antidiuretic state, very large amounts of water and solute can leave the body when a profuse solute diuresis is established by the presence of an obligatory tubular crystalloid solute in the glomerular filtrate.

Page 730

the cardiotoxic and electrical changes of hyperkalemia. One may see the electrocardiographic changes of "potassium intoxication" in the presence of near-normal potassium concentration, if the sodium concentration is extremely low.

Following operation it is commonplace to note reciprocal changes in plasma sodium and potassium concentrations, although their cause remains obscure. Overadministration of water is an important causative factor. Correction of marked sodium concentration abnormalities is usually accompanied by return of potassium levels toward normal. Oral salt tablets will raise plasma sodium concentration but the forty-eight to seventy-two hours required to produce this effect is too long in this instance. Intravenous hypertonic saline may be used, but carries the danger of overloading an already hypervolemic circulation. Removal of salt-free water is the optimal method of correction here, and may be achieved by effecting an osmotic diuresis with a crystalloid such as mannitol or urea. Mannitol is more predictable in its action and usually more readily available for intravenous use. A sudden single injection of mannitol is dangerous. A 25 per cent solution is therefore given by vein at about 100 ml. per hour, and continued until the desired effect occurs. For maximal benefit, intake of fluid, other than that necessary to contain the mannitol, is restricted drastically. Also, in this instance close electrocardiographic monitoring is essential.

Her osmolality (at 250 mO. per l.) is only 17 mO. per l. greater than the accountable electrolyte solute (estimated as twice the sodium concentration of 117 mE. per l.); she is carrying no excessive load of crystalloid solute spontaneously.

FURTHER COURSE. Upon appraisal of this situation, an intravenous infusion of 20 per cent dextrose in water was started with added crystalline insulin, to decrease the elevated plasma potassium level. Then 87.5 gm. of mannitol was given over an eight-hour period. Oral fluids were not restricted. Nevertheless, a brisk diuresis ensued, its effect being evidenced by a loss of 0.8 kg. at the time of weighing the next day; plasma sodium and potassium were 124 and 5.4 mE. per l. respectively. The electrocardiogram reverted to normal sinus rhythm without significant T-wave elevation.

Clinically, the patient was alert, cheerful, and subjectively much improved. She dressed her hair and applied cosmetics for the first time since operation.

In the hope that this initial successful treatment could be repeated with further elevation of plasma sodium and consequent clinical improvement, another course of 50 gm. of mannitol was given the afternoon of the ninth day after operation. The diuresis was less than before, but another kg. of weight was lost. The plasma sodium rose to 130 mE. per l. and plasma osmolality also rose to 257 mO. per l. the morning of the tenth day. Agitation and disoreintation were present with marked paranoid delusion. As these signs progressed during the day, it was felt that the prompt increase in plasma tonicity had occurred too fast for her brain to become adapted, thus leading to the development of symptoms of hypertonicity. Therefore 1000 ml. of 5 per cent dextrose in 0.45 per cent saline was given intravenously with improvement in mental status. Next morning she was again alert and fully oriented. Plasma sodium remained at 130 mE. per l. and plasma osmolality at 268 mO. per l.

Convalescence continued steadily from this point. A minor superficial wound infection, appearing on the eighth day, cleared promptly when drainage was provided. The patient voided satisfactorily after removal of the catheter. Caloric intake increased, as did her strength and well-being. Plasma sodium was 140 mE. per l. on the twenty-first day and she was discharged on the twenty-second postoperative day.

SUMMARY. This was a typical case of water intoxication due to postoperative water loading in mitral stenosis. The gravity of the problem was increased by hyperkalemia occurring *pari passu* with hyponatremia, a phenomenon peculiar to postoperative hyponatremia that makes the low sodium syndrome more ominous in such a setting than it might otherwise be. Although a gratifying result was obtained initially with mannitol, the untoward consequences of the second diuresis reinforce the concept that these fragile patients must be nudged, not shoved, toward normality. It is also of interest that the sharply rising plasma sodium concentration during the second osmotic diuresis produced some symptoms of hypertonicity, due to its rapidity, even though the absolute tonicity was still low.

At no time was there any significant sodium-osmolar differential to suggest the accumulation of pathologic crystalloid solutes.

The response of the central nervous system to changes in the effective osmotic pressure of the extracellular fluid is one that depends both on the rate of change and the absolute levels reached. The brain is much more permeable to water than it is to sodium and it is less permeable to both than are the other major tissue areas of the body. Therefore, in extracellular hypotonicity, the blood-brain osmotic relation comes to a disequilibrium, the brain being left relatively hypertonic while the extracellular osmolality falls, as occurred in this case of postoperative dilutional hypotonicity. The brain then takes up water faster than it can lose sodium, cerebral edema results and an unresponsive comatose state develops. If this fall is very rapid, coma will become evident at levels of extracellular tonicity near 250 mO./l. (corresponding to a plasma sodium concentration of about 125 mE./l.). If the fall occurs more slowly, then the patient may be alert and evidently "adapted" to the hypotonicity with tonicity as low as 230 mO./l. (sodium about 115 mE./l.).

Exactly reciprocal events occur with hypertonicity, the result of a rapid or high rise in effective osmotic pressure being an irritable, delirious and hallucinated patient.

CASE 19

In Which the Heart Stops—But Starts Again—and Brings Up a Discussion of Cause and Effect

Case 19. Patient B.K., #L6144. Male. Age 57. Admitted November 17, 1958. Discharged December 4, 1958.

DIAGNOSIS. Ruptured intervertebral disc.

OPERATION. Thoracotomy.

CLINICAL SUMMARY. This patient was admitted to the hospital for the sixth time, with a complaint of severe pain in the back. Four days prior to admission he had first experienced this pain, as he bent over to pick a small object off the floor. The pain then became extremely severe, and he was unable to straighten his spine or arise from bed. The pain radiated into the right buttock and down the posterior aspect of the right leg as far as the ankle.

His previous admissions had been surgical in nature, including transurethral resection of multiple bladder tumors, transurethral resection of the prostate, bilateral vasectomy, repair of right indirect inguinal hernia, cystoscopy, left cervical lymph node biopsy, total thyroidectomy, and left radical neck dissection. The latter operations had been done for carcinoma of the thyroid. This remarkable surgical history had been accomplished with the aid of a variety of anesthetic agents and techniques, including spinal anesthesia, nitrous oxide–thiopental anesthesia, nitrous oxide–Surital–curare anesthesia, and thiopental–nitrous oxide–ether anesthesia. In the course of these various operations, and during their pre- and postoperative periods, he had received many different medications including pentobarbital, atropine, morphine, and laxatives. He had also received a topical anesthetic for direct laryngoscopy and the removal of a polyp of the left vocal cord, some years previously.

In the course of these many operations and their attendant anesthetic medications, he had suffered but few complications. He had noted a spinal headache on one occasion and on another there had been a stormy inhalation induction with laryngospasm, respiratory obstruction, and cyanosis. This had occurred at the time of his thyroidectomy. It was not the opinion of those in charge of his case that any of these episodes carried any continuing ominous significance for his future surgical management.

On physical examination he was found to be well developed and healthy in appearance, well nourished and with a blood pressure of 152/80. Heart and lungs were normal. All motions of the back were limited by pain and spasm. Straight leg raising was markedly limited and there was definite hyperalgesia to pinprick over the fifth lumbar dermatone. A diagnosis of herniated intervertebral disc at L4–5 was made. A day or two after admission a myelogram was done, demonstrating a filling defect on the right at L4–5. A laminectomy was scheduled three days later. The electrocardiogram was reported as normal, the hematocrit 40, and the leucocyte count 8000 per cu. mm.

ARGUMENT. It looks like smooth sailing ahead for the removal of a ruptured intervertebral disc. The patient has certainly had his full share of surgical care. He seems to be doing well now two and one-half years after his total thyroidectomy for carcinoma. He requires thyroid for maintenance but shows no other permanent sequelae, or anything to suggest metastatic activity from either the thyroid or the bladder malignancy.

FURTHER COURSE. Operation was scheduled for noon. At 10 A.M. the patient received 100 mg. of pentobarbital by mouth, 0.3 mg. of scopolamine, and 10 mg. of morphine hypodermically. This relatively heavy program of premedication was chosen to avoid the repetition of stormy induction he had previously experienced. He had previously expressed a strong dislike for spinal anesthesia and for ether, dislikes for which he had good enough reason. This time, on arrival in the operating room, he was sleepy but definitely confused, disoriented, and seemingly uncooperative. He overreacted with manifestations of severe pain to anything that was done, including the insertion of an intravenous infusion.

His blood pressure at this time was 130/42, the pulse 72, and the respirations 20 and regular.

Induction of anesthesia was begun at 11:10 A.M. with the injection of 125 mg. of thiopental intravenously. Nitrous oxide and then ether were begun by inhalation. Induction was slow with the production of cough, considerable secretion, and on one occasion transient cyanosis. He seemed to have a remarkable amount of tracheal and bronchial secretions, but there was no change in the vital signs.

Twenty minutes later, because comparatively little progress was being made in achieving relaxation, he was given 15 mg. of *d*-tubocurarine intravenously and his trachea then intubated under direct vision with a straight-blade laryngoscope. The cords were free of papillomata, and the endotracheal cuff was inflated with 12 ml. of air.

Ten minutes later (at 11:40 A.M.) he was placed in a lateral decubitus position and when this was done he showed moderately severe clonus, a manifestation frequently seen under ether anesthesia; in order to position him properly an additional 3 mg. of *d*-tubocurarine was injected. His blood pressure was 140/80. He had received about 60 or 70 ml. of ether although a good deal of this was lost in the atmosphere because of the use of a semi-closed system. His lungs were inflated bilaterally effectively, and the operating table was then moved into position for better illumination. His condition and pulse seemed good and the supervising anesthetist thought his condition satisfactory enough as to indicate that the operation should be begun.

ARGUMENT. This has not been a smooth or desirable anesthetic induction. The patient had quite a large amount of sedative, hypnotic, anesthetic, and paralyzing medications during induction. The heavy premedication may at times lead to a more difficult induction than a less heavy dose of sedatives, for the reason that, with heavy premedication, respiration is not deep and the patient remains for a long time in the second stage of anesthesia, not passing into the deeper planes. He has received 18 mg. of curare, a total dose that is large for a patient who is also going to receive ether anesthesia. A hurried anesthetist might well be anxious to "get the patient down" after the insertion of the endotracheal tube Such a motive may lead, by manual ventilation, to the development of higher blood levels of ether than would be achieved were the patient to be ventilating spontaneously. This is one of the real hazards of an endotracheal tube and manual assistance to respiration—namely, that the normal slight respiratory depression seen under very deep ether anesthesia is lost as a helpful guiding restraint to further ether inhalation and absorption. The anesthetist's manual ventilation may continue to force the patient downward long after spontaneous respiration would have put a stop to further ether inhalation.

As mentioned above, the total dose of curare was especially impressive in a patient under ether anesthesia, because of the synergism between the two drugs. In addition, pentobarbital, scopolamine, and morphine had all been given in the last 90 minutes. As a result we may safely assume that as the patient was being prepared for the operative incision, he was still equilibrating from his blood and subcutaneous sites into his extracellular fluid, and thence into his brain and into the myoneural conduction system of his heart, a number of different agents with disparate actions. This might give no particular cause for concern in itself, though constant vigilance must be exercised; appearances are often deceptive in the anesthetized patient.

FURTHER COURSE. About three minutes later the anesthetist noted that no blood pressure could be obtained. Palpation of the pulse in various locations revealed no effective pulse or pressure. The patient's color was still excellent, however, and the pupils were small.

ARGUMENT. Now the moment for decision has arrived. Although the previous signs, when viewed in retrospect, might give some pause for concern, it should be emphasized that the anesthesia course up to this moment had conformed to standard practice with departures that might seem to be only of minor significance. Save for a rather wet and stormy induction, and a rather large dose of curare, the anesthetist had not, up to this point, anticipated any difficulties or severe complications.

FURTHER COURSE. The surgeon was immediately notified. Fifty mg. of ephedrine was injected intravenously. The patient was placed on his back and ventilated with oxygen. Further attempts to hear a heart beat anteriorly were unrewarding. The chest was struck a vigorous blow twice without result. Thoracotomy was therefore performed using an intercostal incision through unprepared skin at about the sixth or seventh interspace. The blood in the chest and in the chest wall showed good color, suggesting the possibility of some residual circulation still continuing. It was estimated that the heart was palpated within two minutes from the time of noting circulatory standstill.

ARGUMENT. Decision is difficult but time is short, and in this case decision was made with little wasted time. Wishful thinking and aimless diagnostic fumbling can cost precious moments, but did not in this case.

One should not stand on aseptic ceremony in such an instance. The likelihood of sepsis is much less than the likelihood of death from circulatory arrest. Striking the chest is a reasonable procedure and does not take much time. To needle the heart at this point is also reasonable, assuming that the ventricular myocardium may be functional, and waiting for an adequate stimulus. Such a needle should be aimed if possible at the left ventricular apex. Needle puncture of the heart was not used in this case.

During these few minutes an electrocardiograph should be fetched. If available in the hospital an electroencephalograph should also be sought.

FURTHER COURSE. The heart was found to be in standstill. Without opening the pericardium it was gently manipulated with several manual systoles. The heart rapidly assumed a forceful beat with a rise in peripheral blood pressure to 180 mm. mercury.

ARGUMENT. This heart was in asystole, with a low threshold of irritability. Although myocardial depression doubtless played a role in this incident, it was of less significance than a disorder of neuromuscular conduction. For this reason the myocardium was not found to be extensively "poisoned" and started rapidly and easily. The ephedrine given the patient together with continued adequate ventilation, and early resuscitation, all played a role in the ease with which a heart beat was resumed. Although the mechanism producing asystole in such a case as this is quite different from that seen in the Stokes-Adams attack, they nonetheless have one thing in common: the myocardium is responsive and waiting for an impulse rather than being so depressed that it cannot react normally to an impulse it receives.

Had the heart been fibrillating or unresponsive to manual systole it would have been advisable to open the pericardium so as to administer the manual compression more accurately, and to occlude the descending aorta in midthorax from time to time, giving maximal preferential perfusion to the brain. Electrical defibrillation or the use of a pacemaker should be resorted to if necessary.

The injection of drugs directly into the heart should be assiduously avoided until the heart is receiving sufficient coronary circulation by manual systole to make it a well-oxygenated myocardium. With good ventilation and good manual systole, resulting in good coronary perfusion, one can administer drugs into the ventricle without too much hazard. Should such drugs be given while the heart is still anoxic and cyanotic and not being perfused, they will have little effect other than the achievement of further myocardial toxicity. In this instance no drugs were used.

FURTHER COURSE. The patient showed signs of rapid recovery. It was difficult to keep him quiet on the table as the chest wall was being closed. An electroencephalogram had been obtained, as well as an electrocardiogram. The electroencephalogram showed a pattern initially suggesting deep ether anesthesia, and later of waking.

ARGUMENT. This entire course strongly suggests that the sequence was that of an overdosage of drugs, particularly ether and curare, followed by manual forced ventilation into a very deep plane of ether narcosis. Happily, the major effect was on the integrating neuromuscular conduction mechanism of the heart, rather than on myocardial metabolism and function.

FURTHER COURSE. When the patient was extubated he was able to respond to questions logically and intelligently. His subsequent course was marked by a rise in temperature to 100° on one day. He had tracheal suction on one or two occasions. Thoracentesis was attempted on one occasion and on another he showed some slight pleural fluid of little note. He soon aerated his left lung normally and showed no appreciable change. The electrocardiogram taken immediately after the cardiac arrest looked essentially normal and remained so.

SUMMARY. This case typifies many instances of cardiac arrest during operations. In retrospect the sequence looks rather easy to reconstruct, as mentioned above. High dosage of a number of drugs, but particularly ether, was probably responsible. Manual ventilation superimposed on curare-induced paralysis was certainly a factor of importance.

The previous radical thyroidectomy, and need for thyroid replacement, might be of considerable importance in such a case. The marked response to premedication, with confusion, disorientation, and restlessness, might be an abnormal response in a slightly hypothyroid patient; it is further conceivable that tissue sensitivity to anesthetic agents might be unusually great in the hypothyroid condition. These are merely suppositions, since the patient showed no other evidences of hyper- or hypometabolism.

The patient was extremely fortunate in showing a "quiet but waiting" ventricular myocardium at thoracotomy. Had he had a very sluggish heart, one passing into fibrillation, or a myocardium showing other evidence of circulatory or pharmacologic damage the outcome might not have been as fortunate. The anesthetist here was responsible for making the crucial decision that arrest had indeed occurred, for notifying the surgeon, and thus starting in train the events that culminated in survival.

CHAPTER 42

The Lung: Accumulation, Anoxia, Hypercarbia, and the Pulmonary Cripple

Problems in surgical care of patients suffering from bronchopulmonary disease divide themselves into two main groups. First are those matters that pertain to the patient *previously in normal pulmonary status*, who develops bronchopulmonary complications of a surgical operation or of trauma, such as that involving the head, neck, and thorax. These are dealt with in the first section below. Second are those that arise when a patient presents himself for surgical care who is a *long-time sufferer* from asthma, emphysema, bronchiectasis, or severe chronic bronchitis. The study and care of these patients are described in the last section.

Section I.   Bronchopulmonary Accumulation

The terms "accumulation" and "accumulative pneumonostasis"* express better than any others the pulmonary disorder most commonly seen on a surgical service as a complication of surgical injury. The normal cough reflex removes material that has been inhaled and is secreted or exuded from the glands and the mucosa of the respiratory tract. In this regard cough, like urination or defecation, is a means by which the body removes from its interior material produced within the organism, and whose accumulation is deleterious. When removal of endobronchial liquid material is hampered, there follows a whole variety of pathologic states, for which varying terms are used: atelectasis, massive collapse, atelectasis with patchy emphysema,

plate-shaped atelectasis, hypostatic bronchopneumonia, postoperative bronchopneumonia. These are terms that apply to various sequelae of pathologic tracheobronchial accumulation and its secondary clinical, pulmonary, bacteriologic, and pathologic effects. At the least there is fever due to bronchiolar obstruction, at the worst the entire tracheobronchial tree becomes a large undrained abscess.

This endobronchial respiratory-tract liquid arises by any combination of four distinct processes:

(1) irritation and "weeping" of intact mucosa as in smoke inhalation and virus infections;
(2) direct stimulation of the secretion of the bronchial mucus glands, as in the use of neostigmine;

* These terms were proposed by Dr. Walter J. Crandell.

(3) purulent infection of the bronchi and bronchioles with accumulation of pus, often from destroyed and denuded areas; and

(4) pulmonary edema, the accumulation of alveolar transudate that later finds its way upward in the respiratory tree.

In this chapter the term "bronchial secretions" or "endobronchial liquid" refers to any or all of the above, depending on the setting. The first three often go together.

The patient pays the price of tracheobronchial accumulation in terms of three clinical consequences:

(1) *local sepsis:* bronchopneumonia,

(2) *general sepsis:* blood-stream invasion, and

(3) *metabolic deficits:* anoxia and hypercarbia with tachycardia, adrenomedullary phenomena, and, terminally, vascular collapse or cardiac arrest.

A. CAUSES OF ACCUMULATION

Accumulation is due to two factors:

(1) excess production of endobronchial liquids, and

(2) underelimination of bronchial secretion.

In the *excess production* group are included the following conditions:

(a) traumatic wet lung;

(b) overadministration of water and salt;

(c) hypoproteinemia;

(d) starvation;

(e) pulmonary edema, congestive heart failure;

(f) "smoker's lung," chronic bronchitis;

(g) burns, gas, smoke inhalation, and other inhalant-irritant phenomena;

(h) aspiration of gastric contents, and

(i) infection.

The *underexcretion* forms of accumulation are produced by the following difficulties:

(a) diminished cough reflex due to oversedation;

(b) diminished cough due to central nervous disease or peripheral disease of the phrenic-diaphragmatic myoneural mechanism;

(c) distention of the abdomen;

(d) pain in coughing, unstable thorax, "flail chest";

(e) pleural disease—hydrothorax, pneumothorax;

(f) burn of vocal cords, and laryngeal obstruction of any cause, and

(g) atropine drugs or severe dehydration, either of which make the bronchial juices sticky and tenacious.

1. "Overproduction" Causes of Bronchopulmonary Accumulation

a. Traumatic Wet Lung. Severe percussive injury to the chest produces a profuse bronchorrhea lasting many days. The material is watery and frothy. The pathogenesis is not clear. One may liken it to the edema that forms in an area of blunt muscle trauma, caused by some alteration in permeability of capillaries, permitting an increased escape of fluid. This coexists with rib fractures and a very unstable chest, inhibiting normal effectiveness of cough. Thoracic stabilization and tracheotomy are essential. The "death rattle" described in accounts of the fighting of World War I was due to the laryngeal accumulation of unexpelled secretion in the dying wounded.

b. Overadministration of Water and Salt. In the normal young person in otherwise good health, it is very difficult to produce any evidence of increased endobronchial liquid by the administration, alone, of non-colloid-containing fluids. This is not the case where there is chronic disease of the lungs, acute trauma to the lungs or the bronchopulmonary tract, chronic congestive heart failure, or disease of the viscera, such as chronic renal or hepatic failure. In all of these situations, the respiratory tract becomes the Achilles heel; it is the most vulnerable spot to the accumulation of abnormal fluid from the overadministration of water and salt. Infusions of saline fluids, even though insufficient to cause overt increase in plasma volume (as evidenced, for example, by a fall in hematocrit), will be followed by an increase in liquid secretions in the respiratory tract. At what point this increase is to be termed "pulmonary edema" is in a sense academic. The increased respiratory-tract fluid occurs prior to any readily-measured increase in venous pressure. One must therefore carefully distinguish—as we have tried to do throughout this book—those situations in which extreme care in fluid-volume administration must be exercised from those situations in which nature is lenient and provides the therapist with some latitude. In cardiac and bronchopulmonary disease there is no latitude, and nature is very strict and critical.

When the overadministered fluid includes colloid and blood, severe pulmonary vascular congestion is produced, seeming to resemble atelectasis. There is an increase in venous pressure, congestion in the lungs, and in fatal cases evidence of acute failure of the right heart, termed "congestive atelectasis." This is an extreme example of the effects of overadministration of fluid, in this instance manifesting itself primarily by "pulmono-cardiac failure."

c. Hypoproteinemia. Considering the balance between hydrostatic and oncotic forces across the pulmonary capillary, it would not be surprising to find pulmonary edema in clinical hypoproteinemia. As a matter of fact, severe lowering of the plasma albumin concentration, as seen in chronic liver disease, is but rarely associated with pulmonary edema as an initial or prominent manifestation. Patients with severe liver disease and drastic reduction of their plasma albumin concentrations to as low as 1.5 gm. per 100 ml. (levels at which the oncotic pressure has been reduced far below the "edema point") have ascites and peripheral edema but usually they do not have pulmonary edema.

Despite this fact, the hypoproteinemic patient must be considered as a special candidate, like others mentioned above, for the easy production of increased endobronchial liquid and pulmonary transudation by overadministration of water and salt. This is particularly important because the commonest cause of hypoproteinemia in surgical patients is the overadministration of water and salt during the water-and-salt–retaining phases following injury. Pulmonary edema is the end-stage of this sequence.

d. Starvation. The lethal event of advanced starvation is bronchopneumonia. Death from "pure starvation alone" is a respiratory death. The mechanism here is only partly hypoproteinemia. Although hypoproteinemia does not occur until very late in starvation, it does occur then and its occurrence might be expected to favor accumulation and bronchopneumonia if the patient has access to water. Lowered resistance to infection is not a characteristic until very late indeed in the starvation process (see Part IV). The fatal bronchopulmonary accumulation of late starvation probably finds its cause in the altered function of striated muscle that occurs. The patient can no longer be up and about; diaphragmatic and abdominal muscular activity are compromised. He no longer moves or coughs and here, rather than in hypoproteinemia or lower resistance to sepsis, one finds the cause of the respiratory death in starvation: weakness thus causes bronchopulmonary accumulation leading to fatality.

e. Pulmonary Edema in Congestive Heart Failure. Congestive heart failure is associated with pulmonary edema and increased respiratory tract fluid, which may go on to accumulative and obstructive phenomena, including atelectasis and bronchopneumonia—often the terminal events in this disease. The patient with primary left heart disease (as for example mitral stenosis) may go through a prolonged period of pulmonary edema and pulmonic manifestations of congestive heart failure until the right heart in turn fails when he has a "free interval," in which pulmonary function, ventilation, and exercise tolerance are improved while hepatic enlargement, ascites, and peripheral edema gradually become more prominent.

In the patient with borderline compensation one sees the sudden development of pulmonary edema and congestive heart failure after overadministration of water and salt. Patients who are in precarious degrees of compensation and are receiving digitalis in high doses may suddenly develop severe congestive heart failure if the effectiveness of this digitalization is lost through acidosis or hyperkalemia occurring in or about the time of operation.

f. "Smoker's Lung," Chronic Bronchitis. The fingers are a sign of serious pulmonary disease in not one, but two ways—clubbing and to-bacco stains. As one approaches the bedside of a patient and notices five or ten stamped-out cigarette butts in the ash tray, ashes on the bedclothing, and nicotine stains on the fingers, one may also expect to see a half-full sputum cup and a temperature of 102° F. on the second postoperative day.

Chronic bronchitis may occur as a mani-festation of the asthma-emphysema syndrome, quite aside from smoking. But much com-moner is an association with smoking. The chronic use of cigarettes, poor personal hygiene, and chronic productive cough go hand-in-hand with wheeze and emphysema. The exact balance among these various factors varies between patients. Alcoholism is often a part of the picture. The chronic cigarette bronchitis and cough phenomenon is in our experience much commoner in men than women and particularly so in the lower-income groups. Not infrequently there is a trace of alcohol on the breath. X-ray usually fails to show much beyond increased hilar markings, but the hazard of postoperative atelectasis is greatly increased. The surgical deficit is very real although the pathologic changes are not marked.

g. Burns, Gas, Smoke Inhalation, and Other Inhalant Irritant Phenomena. Death from chlo-rine and phosgene gas poisoning in World War I was due to an excessive endobronchial liquid secretion, the most acute form of bronchopulmonary accumulation. The pa-tient "drowned in his own mucus." Fires in closed spaces, particularly where there is smoke, and the products of incomplete com-bustion of paint, organic solvents, and plastic materials produce a similar lesion. Inhalation of flame and smoke creates the same. The aspiration of acid gastric contents has a similar effect but with alveolobronchiolar ob-struction in addition.

h. Aspiration of Gastric Contents. Massive aspiration of the contents of a full stomach is immediately fatal. Short of this, there are many degrees of aspiration. Patients with diminished swallowing reflexes and absent pharyngeal function seem to have an almost continuous channel of material from the stomach to the bronchial tree. It is probable that many such changes are not recognized either clinically or at postmortem examina-tion. The enzymatic and acidic material from the stomach is extremely irritating to the bronchial tree and is the cause not only of the introduction of organisms but also of irrita-tion and excessive production of bronchial secretion. This is prevented primarily by adequate intubation and emptying of the stomach, and is best treated by prompt bronchoscopic aspiration.

i. Infection. Infection is listed last merely because it is usually a result rather than a cause of accumulative phenomena. The nor-mal lower airway is sterile despite the daily oronasal inhalation of many organisms. In primary bronchitis, as in virus pneumonia, and in the very rare development (in an otherwise well person) of a primary broncho-pneumonia, or in the patient with an upper respiratory infection and pneumonic com-plication, the accumulative phenomena are prominent. They are dealt with by atten-tion to the infection rather than by mechani-cal measures.

2. "Underexcretion" Causes of Bronchopul-monary Accumulation

a. Diminished Cough Reflex—Sensory Type. An alert, clear-eyed coughing patient is a patient with a good postoperative pulmonary prognosis. A sleepy, drowsy, uncooperative, irrational, slobbering, disoriented, or heavily sedated patient has a poor pulmonary prog-nosis. This prognosis is often critical in surgi-cal survival. We see here one of the most im-portant parameters by which the mental state of the patient is reflected in his surgical recovery.

The use of sedative drugs is therefore to be avoided in elderly patients, patients with visceral disease, uncooperative, disoriented patients, or patients with emotional or mental problems. The patient must, at times, pay with pain the price of a normal cough reflex. If one is given a choice between the two, the cough reflex is much more important for survival than is the avoidance of discomfort. Atropine and Probanthine lessen volume of secretion but increase its tenacity.

b. Diminished Cough Reflex—Motor Type. This is due to disease of the central nervous system or peripheral disease of the phrenic-diaphragmatic-myoneural mechanism. These patients represent a separate group of diminished-cough-reflex phenomena, since sensation may be normal. The phenomena are not due to readily identified or preventable surgical factors. Patients with disease of the midbrain, or severe trauma to the diaphragm, patients with high spinal cord transection or poliomyelitis, obviously cannot cough actively because of defects at the motor end of the cough arc.

c. Abdominal Distention. The high diaphragm of abdominal distention is associated with accumulative phenomena because of the ineffectiveness of ventilation and of cough mechanics.

d. Pain on Coughing, Unstable Thorax, Flail Chest. The wound-tension of coughing is painful. If a proper dose of analgesic may reduce this pain without excessive reduction in cough reflex, it is permissible and helpful. The age and condition of the patient are the controlling factors. Young, healthy, and vigorous people can develop and maintain effective cough reflexes despite analgesic medication. The older, feeble person, medicated to make his cough less painful, loses his desire to cough at all. In a patient with an unstable thorax and flail chest, as in the crushed chest, every effort at chest stabilization must be made, as well as tracheotomy. This includes external fixation of ribs, traction, or a plaster jacket with traction.

e. Pleural Disease—Hydrothorax, Pneumothorax. These interfere with proper emptying of the bronchial tree by interfering with the expansion of the lung. The chest wall and diaphragm move, but the lung cannot expand. Therapeutic steps are obvious enough once the diagnosis is made.

f. Laryngeal Obstruction. Any sort of neoplastic, traumatic, or mechanical obstruction of the upper airway (including a misplaced endotracheal tube) is obstructive and interferes with proper cough-emptying of the bronchial tree.

g. Burns of the Vocal Cord. Nasopharyngeolaryngeal burns produce exudative lesions, edema, crusting, charring, and membrane formation in the upper airway, and these may be obstructive, quite aside from any bronchial irritation.

B. PREVENTION OF BRONCHOPULMONARY ACCUMULATION

Each of the causes of accumulation implies its own prevention over the long term; the smoker's bronchitis is obviously best prevented by giving up smoking. Given a patient who must face up to the bronchopulmonary hazards of thoracic or abdominal operation, and who suffers from any of the bronchopulmonary liabilities already listed above, prevention of serious postoperative consequences over the short term depends upon the principles given below. Detailed application depends upon the rest of the situation.

Prevention of postoperative complication—prophylaxis—depends on the following steps:

(1) accurate estimate of the functional bronchopulmonary deficit by ventilatory study;

(2) accurate estimate of the bacteriologic situation, both as regards the possibility of tuberculosis, and the antibiotic sensitivity of the nontuberculous pathogens;

(3) preoperative establishment of as clean a lung and bronchial tree as is possible;

(4) expertly administered anesthesia;

(5) accurate colloid, electrolyte, and fluid therapy, and

(6) expeditious surgery, leaving behind a minimal ventilatory and tussive impairment.

In many sections of this book we have seen how tolerant of trauma the healthy organism can be; serious inaccuracies of diagnosis, hydration, anesthetic choice, operative maneuver, volume replacement, and acid-base regulation are borne or corrected by the very patient we treat. Visceral disease removes this tolerant latitude of permissible variety. Renal disease, even minimal renal disease, makes it essential that therapeutic electrolyte or acid-base steps be perfectly diagnosed and executed. Heart disease places a similar premium on accuracy of volume replacement. There are many other examples. Here—in bronchopulmonary disease—we are held strictly accountable for accurate effectiveness in preoperative evaluation, use of anesthetic agents, fluids, and expeditious surgery. Duration of operation exacts a toll where bronchopulmonary disease exists and where, under other circumstances, an added hour is innocent of serious consequences.

The *choice of anesthesia* cannot be generalized. The maintenance of adequate ventilation with high oxygen, expert induction and intubation, and proper bronchial aspiration or bronchoscopy are more important than the anesthetic agent. Postoperative sedation must not be generous. Ether is a strong salivary secretagogue but has not been demonstrated to stimulate gastric secretion.

The prophylactic *use of antibiotics* should be discouraged here. The primary threat is often mechanical or mucosal—not bacteriologic. Preoperative antibiotic administration over the period of several days merely induces resistance and covers up or thwarts attention to the more important factors of hygiene, ventilation, drainage, and bronchial toilet.

If the patient enters with a fever and spotty bronchopneumonia, it is a different matter; therapeutic antibiotics should be added to the other preoperative steps. But there the object is treatment of bronchopneumonia, not its prevention.

Beyond these generalities, the prevention of bronchopneumonia is the treatment of bronchopulmonary accumulation, as discussed in the following section.

C. TREATMENT

The treatment of tracheobronchial accumulation depends upon its etiology. Overproduction and underexcretion often go hand in hand.

1. Simple Measures

Expectorants, particularly potassium iodide and aminophylline, are valuable in the chronic situation. Accumulation produces respiratory acidosis, which in turn moves cardiac irritability in the "hyperkalemic acidosis" direction. Large amounts of potassium iodide may be dangerous in such an instance (particularly if given by vein).

Turning the patient, postural drainage, encouraging cough, and thoracic percussion are essential daily routines in promoting excretion of tracheobronchial secretion in the sick patient.

Local anesthesia and support for chest or abdomen assist in promoting the effectiveness of cough. Intercostal procaine block, even lasting but a few hours, may permit a patient to reestablish normal cough after thoracotomy. Manual pressure or a snug bandage on abdominal wounds, to be released later, may similarly help.

Tracheal suction is the most effective of the simple measures. Tracheal aspiration is done through the nose with a stiff rubber catheter. It is possible in some cases to insert the catheter into the trachea easily and remove large amounts of secretions with marked relief to the patient. In other instances, the patient is so strongly encouraged to cough by the irritation of the procedure that the object is accomplished without actual catheterization of the trachea. This procedure is not without its hazards. It may force the disruption of abdominal incisions. Fatality has been associated with this procedure. Death can be caused by cardiac arrhythmia occurring during the acute anoxia and hypercarbia of a severe coughing effort, with partial obstruction and cyanosis. This suction must be done gently and expertly with maximum opportunity for ventilation between efforts.

2. Bronchoscopy

The effectiveness of bronchoscopy is directly proportional to the promptness with which it is done after the accumulation has begun to be excessive. As each hour passes, the accumulation produces more inflammatory changes in the tissues of the lung, with tissue edema and bronchiolar obstruction. Bronchoscopy removes free luminal secretion, not leucocytes or tissue edema.

In the patient who has had a difficult surgical operation or who has had some pharyngeal mucus or vomiting, bronchoscopy at the end of the procedure starts the patient on a postoperative course of good ventilation. Failure to do this results in a downward spiral of atelectasis, bronchopneumonia, anoxia, and respiratory acidosis. Bronchoscopic irrigation with saline or antibiotic solution is an effective method of clearing the respiratory tract of mucus and exudate.

D. TRACHEOTOMY*

The normal respiratory dead space is 150 ml.; a tracheotomy lowers this to 50 ml. As an example of the meaning of this, one may consider the case of an individual with a crushed chest. The normal tidal volume is 500 ml., of which 150 is dead air volume and 350 ventilatory. With a crushed chest the tidal volume is only 350 ml., dead air is unchanged, leaving only 200 ml. for ventilation. A tracheotomy thus raises the ventilatory volume to 300 ml., a 50 per cent increase.

As a means of improving ventilation and decreasing respiratory dead space, tracheotomy is thus very effective. As a channel for tracheal suction, it is likewise effective. But the tracheotomized patient has lost the closure of his glottis needed for cough.

Tracheotomy in the extremely ill patient doubtless produces some survivals, and every surgical service can point to such cases. This is especially true in acute massive trauma, traumatic wet lung, and burns. But for the chronically ill, debilitated patient with severe tracheobronchial accumulation or congestive heart failure in whom tracheotomy is done, it is all too frequently the final episode. The hospital organisms soon infest both wound and bronchi. The patient can no longer talk or cough; he loses contact, continues his septic process, and dies. This is not an indictment of tracheotomy. It is emphasized merely

---

* Tracheotomy is also discussed in the section on severe injury and burns in Part VI.

to indicate that tracheotomy is not a cure-all. Tracheal aspiration, bronchoscopy, and maintenance of cough reflex often make tracheotomy unnecessary and thus avoid its serious deficits. Moisture, cleanly toilet of the wound and suction tube, and suction as needed are the clinical bases of tracheotomy management.

E. HIGH-HUMIDITY ATMOSPHERE: THE FOG ROOM

Special rooms with approximately 100 per cent humidity have become available for the care of critically ill patients. The inhaled air is completely saturated with water. In individuals with tracheobronchial accumulation, such an atmosphere appears to be effective in increasing liquefaction and the ease of removal of the tracheobronchial material. Such a high-humidity atmosphere is made endurable only by a heavy-duty cooling air conditioner.

In individuals with tracheobronchial secretion and tracheotomy, the insensible water loss through the pulmonary route is increased. This may pose a special task in water ration.

In addition, the vaporization of water from the pulmonary epithelium represents heat loss from the body and requires additional expenditure of caloric energy. A high-humidity atmosphere, by reducing the insensible water loss through this route, thus has an unsuspected systemic significance by reducing endogenous heat production. When patients with tracheobronchial secretory accumulation and tracheotomy are placed in such a room and have a lysis of fever, one may be dealing with either or both of these mechanisms. The patient virtually always has to add water vapor to alveolar air in order to saturate it; he is therefore always expending calories for evaporation. The fog room (or any truly saturated vapor system) permits him to avoid a large fraction of this caloric expenditure.

Section II.   Anoxia: Ventilation versus Blood Flow

Anoxia of pulmonary-ventilatory origin is much less common in surgical practice than is regional or systemic anoxia on a blood-flow–ischemic basis. The latter is not responsive to increased oxygen concentration in the inspired gas mixture.

Anoxia shows itself by cyanosis unless there is such a low peripheral concentration of erythrocytes (hematocrit 20 or lower) that the blue coloration of reduced hemoglobin in the skin arterioles and capillaries is not readily visible. In vasoconstricted persons or in Negroes, cyanosis is hard to see. With a hematocrit above 30, significant anoxia is accompanied by cyanosis and in this regard is much more friendly to diagnosis by physical examination than are hypercarbia and respiratory acidosis, the signs of which are either subtle or nonexistent.

Therefore, the prime indication for the administration of oxygen is cyanosis, but oxygen administration is not effective if the anoxia is due to ischemia rather than ventilatory. A nasal catheter can produce oxygen contents in the inspired air as high as 35 to 40 per cent. Increase beyond this is rarely of significant assistance.

To the ventilatory causes one must add those rare and intractable cases wherein the defect is at the alveolar wall, and the problem is one of diffusion. Lymphangitic carcinoma is one cause seen in surgical care. It is happily rare. It responds for a time to oxygen.

Of the ventilatory causes there are only a few which should be treated by oxygen administration alone. *Ventilatory anoxia should not be treated by oxygen alone; the underlying cause must be sought and corrected.*

The importance of the above rule is most clearly seen in bronchopulmonary accumulation. Here, oxygen administration may keep the patient pink for a while, but at the expense of a mounting respiratory acidosis and a continuing bronchiolar obstruction, which will ultimately lead to bronchopneumonia or massive atelectasis. While oxygen administration may be valuable as an adjunct, the important steps are cough,

tracheal suction bronchoscopy, and tracheotomy—in that order. Carbon dioxide can be removed only by effective ventilation.

A. VENTILATORY ANOXIA

The causes of ventilatory anoxia can be summarized in these headings:
  (1) upper airway obstruction—oro-nasal-laryngeal,
  (2) midairway obstruction—tracheobronchial,
  (3) lower airway obstruction—bronchiolar-alveolar,
  (4) bronchopulmonary accumulation or its results—atelectasis and bronchopneumonia,
  (5) unstable thoracodiaphragmatic respiratory mechanics—flail chest—musculocostal paralysis,
  (6) space-occupation in the chest—tumor, fluid, air,
  (7) neuromuscular—respiratory pain, abdominal distention, and phrenic paralysis at any level.

In the first two categories tracheotomy provides an immediate cure of anoxia, whether used as an ingress for atmosphere or for oxygen. Obstruction of the upper air passages with cyanosis is an absolute indication for tracheotomy unless it can be relieved by simple measures in a matter of minutes. For those experienced in its passage—and providing the equipment is at hand—a peroral endotracheal tube is quicker.

In the last five categories tracheotomy plays a role only as an efficient route for oxygen administration or aspiration of the products of bronchopulmonary accumulation. The other, more important, steps to improve ventilation are intrinsic in the nature of the defect and include:
  (1) tracheal suction—bronchoscopy and treatment of accumulation as previously detailed;
  (2) chest stabilization;
  (3) chest tap; intercostal drainage and suction;

(4) local anesthesia, intestinal intubation;

(5) positive-pressure-assisted respiration, and

(6) use of mechanical respirators.

The importance of seeking and treating the underlying cause rather than resting on the thin reed of oxygen administration is also to be seen in the facts, already mentioned, that oxygen administration may decrease ventilation and actually increase hypercarbia if the latter is primarily ventilatory in origin.

B. OXYGEN ADMINISTRATION

The normal alveolar oxygen concentration is just under 20 per cent. To raise this significantly requires large amounts of oxygen put in the right place. On more than one occasion patients have quietly suffocated in oxygen tents that had imperfect closure, inadequate flow, and no monitoring.

The administration of oxygen is carried out by

(1) nasal catheter, or double plastic catheter,

(2) mask,

(3) tent,

(4) tracheotomy, and

(5) positive pressure.

By *nasal catheter*, oxygen must flow at 6 to 8 l. per minute in the adult to achieve an oxygen concentration in the inspired air of 35 to 40 per cent. If the catheter is inserted too far or if the patient is induced to aerophagia by its presence in the hypopharynx, dilatation of the stomach is produced. A stream of oxygen is very drying to the mucosa. The oxygen stream should be humidified, but even then it tends to produce drying and crusting of secretions.

By *mask*, oxygen concentrations close to 90 per cent may be given. If 90 to 95 per cent oxygen is effectively administered for long periods of time, the arterial pO_2 may be raised to high or even toxic levels. But this is rarely the problem, and mask administration of oxygen is not practical for prolonged periods because of discomfort and the difficulty of perfecting or checking adequacy of closure.

The *oxygen tent* has almost disappeared from the surgical scene. Concentrations of oxygen over 35 per cent are rarely achieved, oxygen flow is wastefully high, and nursing care is difficult. Even the simplest nursing maneuver reduces the oxygen content immediately to that of the atmosphere.

The insertion of a catheter into a *tracheotomy* or the placing of a small tentlike structure over the tracheotomy permits giving oxygen concentrations near 35 per cent into the tracheotomy—a helpful step in some circumstances.

Mechanical assistance to respiration is given either by increasing the endothoracic negative pressure or by increasing the endobronchial positive pressure. The former is done by a mechanical respirator and the latter by self-triggering intermittent positive pressure devices attached to mask or tracheotomy and activated by spontaneous respiratory movement. Positive pressure in the airway reduces venous return to the right heart and may produce hypotension, particularly if blood volume is reduced. In pulmonary edema and bronchopulmonary accumulation, compliance is reduced. This is a cause of ventilatory anoxia.

Compliance is defined in terms of the relation that exists between the change in respiratory volume on inspiration and the force or pressure change required to achieve it. It is the sum of resistant forces against which the respiratory muscles work. This includes the elastic recoil of the lungs themselves and the flow-resistant property of the bronchial lumina. In pulmonary edema, about five times the pressure change is required to achieve a given change in volume. Much more work is expended per unit total ventilation; a vicious cycle is set up since more oxygen is required to do that work and more carbon dioxide produced in its accomplishment, both requiring more ventilation. Yet the ventilation cannot be fully achieved. In mitral stenosis with pulmonary disease, compliance is also decreased. Upward of 10 per cent of total energy utilization may be involved in moving the thoracic bellows.

As compliance is acutely and progressively reduced, and the work of ventilation increased, a vicious cycle is set up that quickly leads to fatality. This situation is one in which the Drinker respirator makes a contribution, particularly if cycling is synergized with the respiratory effort.

C. EXTRAPULMONARY CAUSES OF DECREASED VITAL CAPACITY

Common causes of extrapulmonary reduction of vital capacity in the surgical patient are accumulations of fluid in the pleural cavity, pneumothorax, and severe abdominal distention.

Pleural fluid may accumulate as a result of many processes, including pleural carcinoma, fibroma of the ovary, and congestive heart failure. It is essential to make repeated chest taps.

If the patient has accumulated a small amount of fluid or blood following thoracotomy. a compulsive attempt to remove every last drop of fluid by aspiration, so as to avoid fibrotic adhesion to the parietal pleura, is quite unnecessary. The patient will develop some degree of adherence between the visceral and parietal pleura in any area of trauma, and it does not bother his lung function. A massive hemothorax is quite another matter. It should be tapped as dry as possible as early as possible so as to avoid the formation of an organizing hematoma of fibrothorax with constriction of lung volume. Pleural blood is irritating and summons fluid transudate. This, too, should be removed as it forms.

Acute pneumothorax as a cause of decreased vital capacity need not be discussed further here. It occurs following trauma of a wide variety of types and is a common complication of thoracic trauma if an air leak is produced. This is to be considered first in any patient whose postoperative or posttraumatic pulmonary or ventilatory function is poor.

Severe abdominal distention diminishes vital capacity severely. This has been repeatedly emphasized throughout this book and need not be discussed in detail again here; the nutritional objective of the early postoperative period is indeed a scaphoid abdomen with a freely moving diaphragm. This requires avoidance of food and fluid intake until the patient expels flatus normally; an indwelling gastric tube to remove swallowed air also serves this purpose. If abdominal distention is produced by other causes, such as intestinal obstruction, or sudden accumulation of fluid or blood in the peritoneal cavity, one is influenced toward an aggressive surgical attack by the realization that diaphragmatic excursion is severely compromised.

Incisions in the upper abdomen, as in cholecystectomy, splenectomy, or gastrectomy, produce diminished diaphragmatic excursion because of the pain associated with deep breathing. These often lead to atelectasis and accumulative bronchopneumonia. Procaine block should be used if pain is severe.

Careful peritoneal and pleural irrigation before closure is an important operative step. Blood is irritating. It calls forth fluid and provides a pablum for bacterial growth. It is also painful. The peritoneal cavity should be clean and glistening, free of spilled blood and clots, when closed. This will assist the patient in many ways, not the least of which is in respiratory function.

D. ABLATION OR REPLACEMENT OF PULMONARY TISSUE

By differential bronchospirometry, it is possible to estimate not only the vital capacity of the various segments of the human lung but also their ventilatory efficiency in exchange of oxygen and carbon dioxide. By these methods one can assess the respiratory value of existing segments of pulmonary tissue and predict the possible effects on ventilation of resection of portions of that tissue. A detailed description of these measurements and their interpretation forms a part of pulmonary surgery and will not be given in detail here.

Replacement of pulmonary tissue by tumor is restrictive to the patient's ability to withstand anesthesia, and operation within or outside the chest, depending upon the anatomy of the malignant infiltration. "Snowball," "coin," or focal hematogenous lesions are remarkably free of restricting effect on vital capacity, oxygenation, and the removal of carbon dioxide. By contrast, diffuse lymphogenous spread, which may be rather deceptively difficult to see by X-ray, has a severely crippling effect on the efficacy of ventilation and may constitute a contraindication to surgery.

Section III.   Asthma, Emphysema, and Bronchiectasis; The Pulmonary Cripple

The chronic asthmatic patient with low diaphragm, emphysema, a barrel chest, and a chronic productive cough is a familiar sight on every surgical ward. He is slightly cyanotic and has a compensatory polycythemia with a hematocrit in the low or middle fifties. He is found to have a vital capacity of 50 to 70 per cent of normal, and a very slow expiratory component. Closer study of his respiratory capacity shows a diminished maximal breathing capacity. His tidal air will be only a small fraction of his total vital capacity and his residual air very high. Anoxia and chronic respiratory acidosis are present; administration of oxygen makes his acidosis worse by reducing the drive to alveolar ventilation.

This patient's survival is threatened by this combination of deficits, and it is the development of accumulative bronchopneumonia that does him in. This is a metabolic situation in which any further reduction in pulmonary tissue (as by a small area of pneumonitis), any decreased ventilatory efficiency or dampened sensitivity of the respiratory center, as, for instance, by sedative drugs or opiates, is rapidly lethal. The secondary polycythemia is in itself a factor because of the hazards of venous thrombosis in the extremities, arterial thrombosis in the brain, and the somewhat higher incidence of duodenal ulcer.

The late sequence produced by steady progress of the disease is congestive heart failure with cor pulmonale, cardiac cirrhosis, edema, ascites, congestion of the abdominal viscera, severe acidosis, and death.

This type of disease is a poor setting for any sort of surgical maneuver; in a patient who is going down this pathway over the years there is a place for fine judgment in balancing the hazards of operative as against the hazards of nonoperative treatment of any disease.

A. BACTERIOLOGY

Bacteriologic study of the *afebrile* pulmonary cripple is very unrewarding in terms of preoperative therapy; a variety of organisms will be found; gram-positive cocci and gram-negative bacilli are both dangerous. The use of prophylactic antibiotics is inadvisable.

By contrast, in the patient who is *febrile* because of bronchopulmonary suppuration, selection of the most likely pathogen and treatment according to its sensitivity are of great importance. In either event, sputum culture must be a complete study by culture and sensitivity.

If corticosteroids are to be started four or five days before operation, to improve ventilation and reduce the asthmatic bronchospastic component, it is important to cover with an antibiotic, usually penicillin.

B. ACUTE RESPIRATORY ACIDOSIS

Anoxia, acidosis, and bronchopulmonary accumulation jeopardize surgical survival in chronic emphysema. To be reemphasized here is the rapidity with which acute respiratory acidosis occurs in surgery. Ventilatory changes bring the arterial pH as low as 7.10 in previously normal persons, within a matter of minutes. The normal renal compensations to acidosis are never available to the patient with acute respiratory acidotic disorders. Even if renal function is good, renal H^+ excretion is so slow as to make little impression on the critical events so rapidly occurring in accumulation of carbon dioxide. Blood pressure, elevated at first, is poorly maintained, and the fatality results from changes in cardiac irritability and the occurrence of ventricular arrhythmias. In anesthesia, operation, trauma, or shock, "pure" respiratory acidosis is a rarity; a metabolic component is usually present.

C. CHRONIC RESPIRATORY ACIDOSIS

This situation, otherwise referred to as carbon dioxide narcosis, is most commonly seen as a manifestation of chronic asthma, emphysema, and bronchiectasis (see Part III). The important points to reemphasize are: (1) that the body has produced, by way of compensation, the electrolyte changes of a severe metabolic alkalosis (excretion of hydrogen ion with chloride, phosphate, sulfate, take-up of body buffers) in an attempt to keep the pH somewhere near normal in the face of chronic accumulation of carbon dioxide; (2) that the respiratory center has become insensitive to carbon dioxide accumulation and responds only to the relatively mild stimulus of anoxia; and (3) that anoxia and polycythemia usually coexist. The patient therefore comes to operation with compensation fully extended and body buffers completely taken up. Any further respiratory impairment produces a precipitous drop in pH with a potentially fatal outcome. If the sensitivity of the respiratory center to anoxia is further decreased by the use of opiates, respiration may cease completely.

Patients with chronic carbon dioxide narcosis are very poor subjects for operation. If the patient enters the hospital with carcinoma of the colon, a perforated duodenal ulcer, or other urgent surgical indication, the surgeon must not only balance benefit against "risk" but must reduce the hazards as much as possible by the steps already outlined: bronchoscopy, postural drainage, the use of expectorants, breathing exercises, and, in certain cases, artificial respiration, including the use of the respirator. Tracheotomy often has a place, but the loss of effective cough must be included in considering it.

D. BLOOD STUDY

In stabilized chronic respiratory acidosis, study of venous blood for pH, total carbon dioxide, carbon dioxide combining power, chloride, sodium, potassium, and blood urea nitrogen will accurately estimate the degree of disorder. From the pH and total carbon dioxide the pCO_2 may be calculated; the other data indicate the degree of metabolic compensation. Lowering of the chloride concentration generally parallels the take-up of the body buffers; the lower it is (and the higher the carbon dioxide combining power or bicarbonate) the closer the patient is to the breaking point.

E. PREOPERATIVE STUDY IN CHRONIC BRONCHOPULMONARY DISEASE

1. *History and Physical Examination.* This is taken with particular reference to pulmonary performance, asthmatic components, use of drugs, respiratory mechanics, size and dislocation of heart and liver, and intrathoracic signs.
2. *Bacteriologic Study*
   Complete cultural study of sputum.
   Antibiotic sensitivity of the significant pathogens.
   Examination of sputum for leucocytes.
3. *Ventilatory Study*
   Vital capacity with timed components.
   Maximum breathing capacity. This is a highly artificial procedure testing maximum ability to move air, often with a minimal, but rapid, diaphragmatic excursion; strong motivation is required; despite these limitations the results correlate well with over-all pulmonary performance.
4. *Venous Blood Analyses**
   Smear and hematocrit.
   Blood urea nitrogen, protein.
   Chloride, sodium, potassium, carbon dioxide combining power.
   pH, carbon dioxide content.
5. *Cardiac Evaluation*
   Venous pressure; circulation time.
   Chest X-ray.
   Electrocardiograph.

F. PREOPERATIVE CARE IN SEVERE BRONCHOPULMONARY DISEASE

1. *Tracheal Toilet.* Cough training is instituted, including postural drainage and expiratory movement.

---

* In acute respiratory disorders, arterial blood analyses are necessary; here, venous blood is satisfactory as a basis for analytic data.

2. *Inhalation and Bronchodilators.* No antibiotics are given unless the sputum is purulent. The mouth-vaporizer is used to inhale epinephrine analogues.

Potassium iodide is given by mouth or vein, aminophylline by mouth or rectum.

In severe cases of tenacious sputum, heated aerosols are used: a 125° F. stream run through a mixture of 3 per cent sodium chloride.

3. *Cardiac Problems.* If venous pressure is elevated, digitalis is given to full digitalization, with consideration of phlebotomy.

If there is edema, hepatomegaly, or ascites, diuretics are used.

4. *Medication.* No morphine, Demerol, or barbiturates are used.

If the patient has been on steroids with good effect, they should be maintained and increased (by the intravenous route) during operation.

If not, and the patient is a severe asthmatic with unrelieved bronchospasm, prednisone should be started in large doses (40 to 80 mg. daily) with intensive anti-ulcer measures. During operation intravenous hydrocortisone should be given at the 100 to 400 mg. dose range.

5. *Antibiotics.* Antibiotics are used only if there is fever or if corticosteroids are commenced prior to operation.

G. INTRAOPERATIVE AND POSTOPERATIVE MEASURES IN SEVERE BRONCHOPULMONARY DISEASE

Anesthesia must include maximum ventilation, and frequent tracheobronchial suction. Careful asepsis by the anesthetist is essential. Barbiturates make asthma worse; cyclopropane is contraindicated.

Sudden return to unassisted ventilation with room air after anesthesia may be dangerous if carbon dioxide accumulation occurs. During operation airway and ventilation are assisted and ideal. For this reason a gradual tapering to room air, unassisted, must be made under close supervision and observation.

Oxygen is given only for the indication of cyanosis; ventilation is monitored by arterial or venous pCO_2.

Intermittent positive pressure is used as needed, together with tracheal suction. Tracheotomy is done only in severe cases of bronchopulmonary suppuration, where preoperative management has been inadequate and ventilation with good tracheal toilet cannot be maintained otherwise.

If plasma potassium concentration is high, digitalization falls below optimum levels. Overadministration of water, salt, and blood is carefully avoided.

The hazards of both morphine and oxygen in this situation should be reemphasized. Morphine reduces the sensitivity of the respiratory center, with a resultant reduction in effective ventilation and cerebral anoxia. In some instances, these patients have become insensitive to high levels of total carbon dioxide; anoxia is their only stimulant. The administration of high oxygen concentrations then further reduces their effective pulmonary ventilation by damping out their only effective respiratory stimulus.

The treatment of postoperative pain demands special consideration in any patient who has chronic pulmonary insufficiency. The surgical nurse is alert and sensitive to the pain suffered by her patients; anesthetic agents, opiates, and other analgesics come to hand readily. In patients with chronic respiratory acidosis or in older people with cardiac and pulmonary embarrassment, it may be fatal for the patient to have too much analgesia. It may be advisable for the patient to maintain alertness, an active cough reflex, and ability to move about in bed and ambulate, even though some discomfort is suffered in the process. Local procaine block of a painful wound is preferable to opiates.

Section IV.   Miscellaneous Special Considerations in the Chest

A. SPECIFIC WATER AND ELECTROLYTE FACTORS

There has long been a suspicion that there is a specific volume-concentration defect in pulmonary and mediastinal tumors. It was suggested for some time that pulmonary tumors produce a specific electrolyte defect. There is additional evidence that tumors of the mediastinum have unusual properties with respect to the metabolism of water and electrolyte. In the light of the evidence that pressure-volume-flow receptors may reside in the right heart or in the great veins of the thorax, it is appealing to assign to surgical lesions in this area a special physiologic effect. The occurrence of hypertrophic pulmonary osteoarthropathy certainly suggests that such lesions in this area do produce unusual systemic pathologic and biochemical changes. Recent evidence suggests that tumors of the mediastinum produce a specific systemic biochemical alteration, presumably on the basis of an inappropriate stimulus to the production of antidiuretic hormone, with dilutional hypotonicity.

There have been reports of tumors of the lung associated with chronic adrenal hyperfunction and Cushing's syndrome.

B. CLOTTING DEFECTS

The occurrence of a clotting defect characterized by subnormal fibrinogen levels in the peripheral blood has been observed in thoracic surgery more often than in other forms of surgical trauma. However, it is in obstetrical situations, particularly in premature separation of the placenta with amniotic fluid embolism, that this lesion is most commonly seen.

The occurrence of large pleural blood clots may be a factor in producing hypofibrinogenemia, and in this case the thorax may be unique only in that hemorrhage into the open pleura produces a large monolocular blood clot on a serous surface. The fact that this hypofibrinogenemia is encountered more frequently in thoracic surgery than in other sorts of surgical trauma might suggest that there is some special feature of the lungs or thorax having to do with fibrinogen utilization or the production of fibrinolysins, or both.

Section V.   Pulmonary Embolism

The metabolic problem in pulmonary embolism is an unimportant aspect of management, because we do not know any effective steps to control the coagulation disorder involved nor indeed its cause. In its present status the problem is operative and pharmacologic.

Prevention of embolism rests primarily on good operative and metabolic care. Abdominal distention, sepsis, and a complicated course is often the setting for embolus. Ambulation, early leg motion, and soft lower-leg bandages are all thought to exert a healthy effect. Evidence on the point is scanty but the steps are harmless.

Pharmacal prophylaxis by the use of anticoagulants or *surgical prophylaxis* by vein division is not to be recommended save where prolonged immobilization is required by injury to the lower extremity.

A. TREATMENT

Once embolus has occurred, treatment depends on its magnitude.

(1) If shock and acute cor pulmonale are produced, yet the patient lives, one must consider immediate pulmonary embolectomy, an operation rarely consummated successfully. There is little additional to offer other than oxygen and atropine.

(2) Below this level of magnitude the problem is almost wholly one of prevention of further embolism. This is done, and with

good result, either by the administration of pharmacologic doses of anticoagulants or by operative vein interruption or both. The choice between the two depends on the clinical setting.

Anticoagulants are generally preferable. Heparin is most readily controlled, while oral anticoagulants are most suitable for long-term treatment by mouth.

Contraindications to anticoagulants are:
(1) liver disease;
(2) open wounds;
(3) recent hemorrhage, and
(4) a very prolonged hazard of embolus, as in leg fracture.

Complications of anticoagulants are:

(1) gastrointestinal, uterine, or renal hemorrhage;
(2) hemorrhage into viscera—brain or adrenal;
(3) hemorrhage into the lung at the site of infarction;
(4) widespread thrombosis upon withdrawal of anticoagulant.

Vein division is to be used when embolus has occurred and anticoagulants are contraindicated, or if embolization has occurred on an anticoagulant program which has produced appropriate prolongation of coagulation indices. If there is evidence of thrombosis above the inguinal ligament, ligation of the vena cava is preferable. Otherwise, the common femoral vein is ligated and divided bilaterally.

Section VI.   The Lung: Notes from the Literature

A. PULMONARY FUNCTION IN THE SURGICAL PATIENT*

Recognition of the nature and significance of postoperative pulmonary complications was a product of the period after World War I. In 1925 Scott described postoperative massive collapse, and in 1927 Harrington outlined its treatment by bronchoscopic aspiration. Studies on emphysema, surgical positions, and particular water and electrolyte patterns in pulmonary surgery include Case and Stiles (1946), Sims *et al.* (1950), Aronstam *et al.* (1953), Cohn *et al.* (1954), and Connor *et al.* (1956).

Among the various laboratory advances in the study of pulmonary function during the past two decades has been a more precise evaluation of the mechanical properties of the lungs and thorax. In view of the increasing age of patients undergoing major surgery, careful studies of the mechanical behavior of the lungs in elderly persons achieve special significance. It has been shown that elderly persons have changes in the physical properties of their lungs which are qualitatively similar to, though much less than, those found in clinical emphysema (Frank *et al.*, 1957).

Many reports have emphasized the decreased efficiency of the ventilatory system in a variety of disease conditions. An intriguing part of this work has been the evolving concept of the energy cost of breathing. Such studies are based on measurement of oxygen consumption at rest and when ventilation is increased. If there is no other reason for an increase in oxygen consumption, the excess oxygen required during increased ventilation is assumed to be required by the muscular efforts of moving the thorax (Cournand *et al.*, 1954, Otis, 1954, Cherniack, 1959). This work has shown that, at rest, the respiratory muscles require from 0.25 to 1.0 ml. of oxygen per l. of ventilation, which represents from 1 to 3 per cent of the resting total oxygen consumption. The oxygen cost of hyperventilation normally increases only slightly until the ventilation is increased over 60 l. per minute. However, in patients with reduced ventilatory capacity, the oxygen cost of breathing is increased at rest and may require up to 10 ml. of oxygen per l. of ventilation at rates as low as 20 l. per minute in emphysema. This work has indicated that there is a critical level of ventilation, above which the respiratory muscles use all the additional oxygen provided by further increase in ventilation, and that beyond this the arterial

* The author is indebted to Dr. John M. Kinney for this section of notes.

tension will fall, despite more heroic efforts to breathe. Even at lower ventilation rates, the high proportion of the total oxygen consumption required by the respiratory apparatus greatly decreases the oxygen available to the rest of the body and contributes significantly to a decrease in exercise tolerance and possibly other metabolic functions. The introduction by Gaensler of the timed vital capacity measurement (Gaensler, 1951) has made an important contribution to the bedside evaluation of pulmonary function. Miller and others (Miller et al., 1956, a) have shown that the first 0.5 second portion of the expiratory vital capacity represents the maximum air flow. This is of significance, since it correlates well with maximum breathing capacity in normal people and may be of particular convenience in preoperative screening to uncover decreased pulmonary reserve (Miller et al., 1956, b).

Since the advent of cardiac catheterization procedures, an important body of information has become available regarding pulmonary circulation. This is a much more flexible vascular bed than previously recognized and is normally able to accommodate large increases in pulmonary blood flow with no increase in the pulmonary vascular resistance (Cournand, 1958). Various diseases are characterized by loss of this accommodation to increased flow, so that temporary pressure increases, with increased flow, may progress to permanent and irreversible elevation in pulmonary vascular resistance. It would appear that such individuals are particularly vulnerable to the physiologic disturbances associated with major pulmonary emboli. A measurement of the disturbance in carbon dioxide clearance across the alveolar capillary membrane may aid in the diagnosis and the estimation of severity of acute pulmonary embolism (Robin, 1959).

The association of ventilatory problems with patients undergoing major surgery which is not necessarily located in the thorax has been documented in this country and abroad (Nanson, 1950; Anscombe, 1957; Mastio and Albritten, 1958; and Nunn, 1958). The critical period for the patient with decreased ventilatory reserve under-going surgery is usually not in the operating room but comes in the following forty-eight hours after operation (Kinney, in press). The problems of this period are often centered around alveolar hypoventilation with associated hypoxia and respiratory acidosis (Hood and Beall, 1958).

Hamilton and Devine (1957) studied respiratory insufficiency in 100 patients in the recovery room of a large general hospital. One quarter of these patients had elevated end tidal carbon dioxide tensions. The authors make the point that these patients with respiratory acidosis could be divided into those whose respiratory center was responding to the elevated carbon dioxide tension levels and, therefore, increased ventilation was rapidly clearing the increased tissue carbon dioxide, versus those patients who had depressed respirations and were, therefore, not only acidotic and hypoxic, but lacked the responsiveness to improve the situation spontaneously. The electroencephalogram may be of help in evaluating the narcosis from severe carbon dioxide retention (Clowes et al. 1953).

Two major contributions to the support of the postoperative patient with ventilatory insufficiency have been the introduction of high-humidity therapy in fog chambers and the use of apparatus to provide intermittent positive pressure breathing (Tovell and Little, 1957; Wells, 1959).

In evaluating whether or not the minute ventilation of the patient is adequate to support his needs, a first approximation can be obtained without waiting for blood gas analyses, by the use of a nomogram for basal ventilatory requirements (Radford, 1954). The postoperative use of intermittent positive pressure has been reviewed by Rudy and Crepeau (1958). Many aspects of the application of mechanical devices to assist ventilation have been reviewed by Maloney, Whittenberger and coworkers (Maloney and Whittenberger, 1951; Whittenberger and Ferris, 1957; Maloney et al., 1957). This work emphasizes that introducing intermittent positive pressure into the airway is physiologically combaraple to the same ventilation achieved by exerting a negative pressure around the trunk. In surgical patients, he intermittent positive pressure devices ate preferable to tank respirators in most cares because of the ease of nursing care.

The csinical difficulties associated with the use of thlese instruments are reviewed in the above references. The most important of these have to do with the effect on the circulation. Curiously enough, the *pulmonary* circulation appears to be altered no more by ventilation achieved with a given amount of positive pressure in the airway than by the same tidal volume achieved by conventional normal breathing. However, there is a significant decrease in venous return to the heart and, therefore, a decreased cardiac output, when pressures of 10 to 20 cm. of water are used in the positive pressure phase. The normal individual has compensatory mechanisms which allow maintenance of systemic blood pressure in the face of decreased cardiac output, but a person with inadequately replaced blood loss or compromised vascular reflexes may be thrown into shock by intermittent positive pressures which are barely adequate to achieve routine ventilation. Cathcart and others have reported a group of cardiac output determinations on anesthetized surgical patients. They found a significant depression of the cardiac output could be expected when the mean endotracheal pressure was elevated over 6 cm. of water. This appears to be of greater significance in abdominal operations than in operations where the chest is opened and the endotracheal pressure cannot, therefore, be transmitted against the chambers of the heart and the vena cava.

Relationships of severe obesity to respiratory insufficiency ("Pickwickian syndrome") is covered by Burwell (1956) and by Kaufman *et al.* (1959). The effect of hemorrhage on gas exchange is described in Gerst *et al.* (1959).

Hazards of ventilatory therapy and oxygen administration are described by MacPherson (1958), Smith and Howland (1959), and Marrs *et al.* (1958).

The role of breathing exercises, and other aspects of treatment are covered in Miller (1958) and Sherman (1958).

B. THROMBOEMBOLISM

The use of heparin as the primary anticoagulant therapy of thromboembolism is recommended by many students of the subject. Recent reviews are to be found in de Takats (1955) and Crane (1957). Inadvisable or poorly controlled use is dangerous, but the intrinsic hazard is low.

Flickinger and Henderson (1956) present an experimental and clinical study of the use, in thrombophlebitis, of cortisone, under which the lesion more quickly resorbs and heals to a normal vein. Cortisone may lead to hypersensitivity to anticoagulants. In a small clinical series there was good symptomatic relief. The lack of fibroplasia in the cortisone-treated case might lead to a more severe or more prolonged hazard of embolization. The authors suggest concomitant use of anticoagulants.

Hodgson *et al.* (1955) review contraindications and safety procedures as well as complications of prolonged anticoagulation in such conditions as myocardial infarction. Many of their comments are applicable in the treatment of thromboembolism.

The prophylaxis of thromboembolism is not completely reliable by any one method. Jones, for example (1950), reports 480 cases that were heparinized. In this series there were thirty-five fatal emboli, and recurrent thromboses in 15 per cent. This is, of course, an adversely selected series, in the sense that most of the patients were suspect of a high embolic probability. Most reported series fall into this range.

Crane (1957) reports that 90 per cent of thrombus-containing legs show measurable edema, and 90 per cent of emboli show some pleuritic reaction, whether pain or fluid or a rub. About one-third of thrombotic patients have emboli. These are very helpful data in diagnosis. On heparin, in Crane's series, there were 1.5 per cent fatalities, of which some were due to bleeding, others due to emboli. In some of the latter instances, the trouble came after discontinuing the drug. In the light of the hemorrhagic adrenals produced by severe long-lasting trauma and "stressful" illness, it would appear safer not to use heparin in patients in whom high fever, pain, infection, or repeated operations are part of the situation. A general program which emerges from Crane's work is as follows.

(1) For those with acute illness of short duration who have previously been on bishydroxycoumarin: stay on bishydroxycoumarin.

(2) For those with prothrombotic conditions, such as bed rest, trauma, sepsis, fractures, cardiacs, old thromboses, malignancy: heparin for five to seven days if the signs of embolism appear.

(3) For those with prothrombotic conditions where chronic severe illness or open wounds are involved: femoral vein division or heparin or both.

(4) For those with emboli after adequate heparin, or after femoral vein division, or with septic pelvic phlebitis: vena cava ligation.

C. THE LUNG—MISCELLANEOUS

Templeton et al. (1952) undertook to discover if intrathoracic surgery or disease produced a characteristic fluid:electrolyte imbalance. Their studies were very complete as regards sodium, extracellular fluid volume, pH, and bicarbonate. They noted no characteristic defect, in contrast to a previous study by the same group (Finley et al., 1951) in which hyponatremia (probably dilutional) was a characteristic finding. If there is a sensitive "volume-receptor" area near the caval-atrial junction one might expect to find the dilutional hypotonicity of inappropriate volume-receptor activity when lesions were in that area.

Schwartz et al. (1958) report two cases of bronchiogenic carcinoma in which water loading and sodium excretion suggested the continuous inappropriate secretion of antidiuretic hormone; there was pericardial and mediastinal involvement, as well as pathology in the basal ganglia. In both patients there was a continuous salt loss despite marked plasma hypotonicity. The renal tubule was capable of a good response to desoxycorticosteroid, and water restriction led to sodium conservation, while water administration reestablished the sodium loss; in one patient the administration of hypertonic saline solution resulted in free water diuresis. In the one patient measured, extracellular fluid volume was high. Renal function was normal. These data are best interpreted in the light of consistent volume responses similar to those seen in normal subjects given water plus vasopressin. Whether this was due to mediastinal or cerebral disease is not clear.

CASE 20

Chronic Pulmonary Disease Provides a Complicated Setting for Aneurysm Surgery in a Sixty-Eight-Year-Old Man

Case 20. Patient C. R., #5J936.* Male. Age 68. Admitted January 3, 1956. Discharged January 26, 1956.

DIAGNOSIS. Abdominal aortic aneurysm; bronchial asthma; chronic bronchitis; emphysema.

OPERATION. Resection of abdominal aortic aneurysm.

CLINICAL SUMMARY. This patient was referred to the hospital because of progressive fatigue, exertional dyspnea, and weakness over the previous four months, and the discovery by his local physician of a pulsatile abdominal mass.

He had a history of forty years of wheezing, bronchitis, and asthmatic symptoms thought to be related to allergies to cream and rubber pillows. There had been an episode of pleurisy eleven years before. He smoked two to three packages of cigarettes per day He had been on intermittent corticosteroid therapy for his asthma.

On admission, his temperature was 98.0° F., pulse 92, respiration 24, blood pressure 190/100. The patient appeared young for his age, but had a questionable bluish tint to his lips. There was nasal congestion in the right side. The thorax was increased in diameter and both diaphragms were low but moved well. There were dullness and decreased breath sounds over the left lower lung field. The abdomen was normal except for a large pulsatile midline mass.

X-ray of the chest showed some linear streaky density in both upper lobes, with the left lower lobe appearing

---

* The author is indebted to Dr. John M. Kinney for collecting the data and analyzing the course of this patient.

small and covered with thickened pleura posteriorly. X-rays of the abdomen showed a thin line of calcification along a left bulge in the lower abdominal aorta. Intravenous pyelogram showed good function in both kidneys.

INITIAL LABORATORY WORK

Urine

Specific gravity	1.022
Protein	+
pH	4.5

Hematology

Hematocrit	37
Leucocyte count	6200 per cu. mm.

Blood Chemical Analyses

Blood urea nitrogen	12	mg. per 100 ml.
Plasma chloride	108	mE. per l.
Plasma sodium	133	mE. per l.
Plasma potassium	4.1	mE. per l.
Carbon dioxide combining power	26	mE. per l.
Prothrombin time	100	

Electrocardiogram showed an old posterior myocardial infarct and a suggestion of left ventricular hypertrophy.

ARGUMENT. This patient has a life-threatening lesion amenable to surgery, provided his cardiac reserve is adequate to weather operation, and provided he has a reasonable period of preoperative therapy to improve the ventilatory status of his chronic pulmonary disease.

The patient entered the hospital with no evidence of cardiac failure and he had not been on digitalis. The electrocardiographic evidence of an old myocardial infarct was the same on entry as a tracing taken one year before; therefore, his cardiac status remained essentially unchanged.

The long history of asthmatic symptoms, coupled with history of pleural disease, represents the triple threat of obstructive secretions, infection, and decreased alveolar ventilation. The patient's smoking was eliminated for a ten-day period in the hospital prior to surgery. During this time he was given expectorants and bronchodilator inhalations to treat the low-grade bronchoconstriction which so commonly accompanies mild bronchitis. He was taught breathing exercises and postural drainage with a particular view to more efficient ventilation during the early postoperative period. This is of special importance in this operation, since it is so often followed by severe ileus because of retraction and dissection. This often produces high diaphragms, decreased tidal volume, and pooling of secretions in the lower lung fields.

In the middle of this period of preoperative pulmonary preparation, the patient had a vital capacity of 3.3 l. (predicted value of 3.6 l.) and a maximum breathing capacity of 104 l. (predicted 88 l.) with very little change in either value after Isuprel inhalation. These values confirmed the fact that the patient had reasonably good pulmonary function for his aneurysm surgery. The fact that the vital capacity was a little less

than the predicted value but that the maximum breathing capacity was definitely higher suggests that the extremes of thoracic motion were limited by pleural disease, which the patient's history and X-rays revealed. Efficient rapid air exchange in a mid-range of thoracic motion was evidently very good. The fact that Isuprel made very little difference difference in the test values suggests that whatever asthmatic component was present on entry responded to therapy over the first four days in the hospital and was no longer active. The patient was given two doses of adrenocorticotropic hormone (in gel form), 40 units and 80 units, on the day before surgery, in order to provide maximum adrenal stimulation in a man who had received corticoid therapy intermittently prior to entering the hospital.

FURTHER COURSE. On the tenth hospital day, the patient underwent an uneventful resection of his aortic aneurysm and homograft replacement. He received 8000 ml. of whole blood and had no periods of hypotension during or following the surgical procedure. On the evening of operation his temperature began to climb and it reached 103° F. the following day. His pulse rose to 110 and his respiratory rate to 30. Physical signs were consistent with pneumonitis and atelectasis in both lower lobes. He was vigorously treated with antibiotics, bronchodilators, and repeated tracheal suction. Culture of the bacteria recovered from tracheal suction indicated that the organisms were more sensitive to erythromycin and chloramphenicol (Chloromycetin) than to the large doses of penicillin and streptomycin initially used. The antibiotics were shifted on the third hospital day.

At this time the patient showed some mild distention of the neck veins. Digitalization was performed with digoxin and shifted to digitalis leaf three days later. He had Isuprel inhalations three times a day with a hand nebulizer and his cough loosened, became more productive, and subsided in the five days following surgery. His temperature came down during this interval until it reached normal levels on the sixth postoperative day and remained there until discharge four days later.

The patient received oxygen by nasal catheter for the first forty-eight hours after surgery, but this therapy was not continued beyond this period for two reasons: the patient's pulse and respiration were stabilized without oxygen, and since he had a Miller-Abbott tube in one nostril, ventilation was made more difficult with an oxygen catheter in the other nostril.

COMMENT. Intermittent positive pressure breathing was considered in this case but was not used because the patient had satisfactory thoracic excursion within the limits of his pleural disease. Mechanical assistance would not increase this. Postoperatively he had mechanical problems in clearing secretions, but it was felt that these were largely in damaged areas of the lungs that were not contributing significantly to his ventilation. His vital signs suggested that he was maintaining adequate aeration through the uninvolved portions of his lungs.

This case indicates the importance of careful pre-operative pulmonary therapy for anyone with chronic lung disease undergoing major abdominal surgery, the use of pulmonary function tests preoperatively for abdominal surgery, and the clinical measures used in counteracting postoperative pulmonary sepsis.

CASE 21

In Which Massive Gastric Hemorrhage Almost Carries Away a Man with Severe Chronic Pulmonary Insufficiency; Accurate Care and Adequate Ventilation Keep Him Around

Case 21. Patient G. D., #8G77. Male. Age 66.* Admitted December 27, 1958. Discharged February 9, 1959.

DIAGNOSIS. Massive upper gastrointestinal hemorrhage; duodenal ulcer. Advanced pulmonary emphysema with cor pulmonale. Hypertensive cardiovascular disease. Benign prostatic hypertrophy.

OPERATION. Emergency subtotal gastrectomy.

CLINICAL SUMMARY. This retired telephone lineman had had low-grade bleeding from a duodenal ulcer eight years prior to this entry, and X-ray demonstration of a scarred duodenum two years ago. His ulcer was controlled with diet and antacids until six months prior to this entry. At that time, while being hospitalized for pulmonary study, he had an upper gastrointestinal hemorrhage requiring four transfusions. Ulcer surgery was not advised, because of this man's very marked ventilatory insufficiency. There were no further ulcer symptoms until the evening of this admission, when he suddenly developed melena, weakness and, a few hours later, vomited dark blood. He was seen in the emergency ward with a blood pressure of 80/60, skin pale and cold, with clammy extremities. He was coughing up thick, gray mucus with occasional particles of bloody material. His breath sounds were distant to absent over an expanded, rather immobile chest cage. His ventilation was marked by prolonged expiration, with marked use of abdominal musculature for breathing. Abdomen revealed a liver down three finger-breadths from the right costal margin, and hyperactive bowel sounds.

His past history included intermittent urinary frequency associated with moderate prostatic enlargement.

Most important, there was progressive respiratory impairment. The patient had been a heavy smoker for years, with intermittent episodes of bronchitis for the past ten to fifteen years. Eight years before the present admission, the patient was hospitalized elsewhere for antibiotic treatment of pneumonia. For the past six years, the patient had progressive shortness of breath, substernal discomfort on exertion, and occasional wheezing. The patient noted some benefit from bronchial dilators, expectorants, and breathing exercises. Polycythemia, secondary to his chronic lung disease (hematocrits from 50 to 55), had been noted for the past three years.

* The author is indebted to Dr. John M. Kinney for gathering the data and analyzing the course of this patient.

INITIAL LABORATORY WORK

Urine

Specific gravity	1.017
Protein	0
*p*H	7.0
Acetone	0

Sugar intravenous dextrose running, otherwise normal

Stool reddish black, benzidine $+++$

Hematology

Hematocrit	34
Leucocyte count	10,300 per cu. mm.

Blood Chemical Analyses

Blood urea nitrogen	95	mg. per 100 ml.
Serum amylase	97	units
Blood sugar	167	mg. per 100 ml.

ARGUMENT. This patient is bleeding for the second and, possibly, third time from his upper gastrointestinal tract and the rate of blood loss on this admission is obviously of life-endangering proportions. Duodenal ulcer is the source according to reasonable assumption. Severe acute respiratory insufficiency is superimposed on chronic emphysema. There is good reason to believe that both polycythemia and chronic respiratory acidosis contribute to the severity of the acid-peptic diathesis. The associated hypotension can be expected to be a greater hazard than usual to this patient's coronary and renal circulation, since they have been operating at hypertensive perfusion levels for some years. In addition, a small amount of aspiration pneumonia could easily be lethal, with this man's limited pulmonary reserve.

There are specific and urgent indications for emergency operation. However, this man has had a maximum breathing capacity of under 30 l. demonstrated three times in the past two years. The chance of his surviving major upper abdominal surgery is obviously poor. The decision regarding treatment requires the collaborative thought and judgment of the internist who has been caring for his pulmonary disease, of the anesthetist, and of the surgeon. The problem is one, not only of weighing the magnitude of the risk of operation against the risks without surgery, but also of the wise planning of his emergency circulatory and ventilatory support so that he will be brought into optimum condition within the next few hours, regardless of which form of treatment is decided upon.

Over the past four years the patient has shown progressive ventilatory impairment with a maximum breathing capacity frequently below 40 per cent of predicted normal and a one-second vital capacity as low as 20 per cent of predicted normal.

X-rays now show severe emphysema with bilateral changes of congestion or superimposed infection.

CLINICAL COURSE. The patient was placed on indwelling bladder drainage with hourly urine reports and fifteen-minute recordings of vital signs. A venous cutdown was immediately made and an initial dextran infusion was replaced with whole blood as soon as emergency cross-matching was completed. Over the next two hours, a second venous cutdown was done in another extremity and a total of six transfusions were rapidly given. On occasion, the patient's blood pressure was unobtainable for periods of ten minutes, despite this rapid blood administration. During this interval it was agreed by all that operation, however hazardous, was preferable to this rapid exsanguination.

An emergency subtotal gastrectomy with gastrojejunostomy was performed. A chronic duodenal ulcer deformity was found, but the major hemorrhage appeared to be coming from an arteriosclerotic artery in the gastric wall. During the gastrectomy, the anesthesia (cyclopropane) was conducted with bag breathing to assist the patient's respiration, with special care to achieve adequate oxygenation as judged by the color of the blood in the operative field, but at the same time allow adequate time for prolonged expiration in order to avoid progressive air trapping in the diseased lung parenchyma.

ARGUMENT. This man's hemorrhage had now been satisfactorily controlled by ablation. With further blood transfusions, a stable blood pressure was maintained without vasoconstrictors. Death from hemorrhage had been prevented, but had the operation itself sealed his fate by compromising his small remaining unassisted lung function?

This patient is a dramatic example of the fact that the anesthetist is able, with high flow rates of inspired oxygen in the anesthesia mixture, to offset the depressed respirations and altered lung compliance of chronic lung disease by the use of intermittent positive pressure on the anesthesia bag. The patient's best alveolar ventilation and his safest period is during the operation itself. This man's most critical ventilatory period would come in the hours after leaving the operating room, should he return to breathing room air without mechanical assistance.

Blood gas data would be of importance in following this patient's progress. Although his oxygen saturation would be expected to be below 95 per cent, his pH below 7.42, and his pCO_2 above 40 mm. Hg, one would hope that this trend to anoxic respiratory acidosis would not progress too far.

FURTHER COURSE. At the close of the gastrectomy, a tracheotomy was carried out and a cuffed endotracheal tube was placed in the trachea and immediate positive pressure breathing was begun, using portable apparatus. This apparatus was capable of putting the patient through a respiratory cycle by providing intermittent positive airway pressure at preset timed intervals. This patient had a spontaneous regular respiratory effort, so the apparatus was set to be cycled by the patient's respiratory efforts, which were then rendered much more efficient. The machine was initially set with 100 per cent oxygen inflow, which was later dropped to about 40 per cent oxygen for prolonged use.

The patient's circulation was stabilized with a total of thirteen transfusions from entry until return to the recovery room. He was started on Isuprel in the nebulizer of the positive pressure instrument and intravenous broad-spectrum antibiotics and small doses of morphine as needed. The usual hazard of depressing alveolar ventilation by the use of morphine was offset here by the intermittent positive pressure breathing device. However, the nurse was carefully warned to note whether the morphine slowed the patient's respiratory rate, since the machine was being cycled by the patient. Doses of morphine up to 6 mg. subcutaneously did not alter his respiratory rate. Within three hours after operation, the patient began urine output of around 100 ml. an hour with specific gravity of 1.018. Rectal aminophylline and Isuprel were administered in somewhat smaller doses that evening because of a moderate tachycardia during the night.

The following day the patient was alert and cheerful, with a stable chart and a hematocrit of 44. Breath sounds over both lung fields were very distant, but were heard equally, on and off the respiratory assistor. Therefore, twenty-four hours after surgery, the patient was changed from constant to intermittent use of the I.P.P.B. apparatus, beginning with twenty minutes out of every hour. The resident staff were particularly careful regarding secretions and strict sterile precautions were used in the handling of the tracheostomy fittings and the suction tube. By the second postoperative day the patient's clinical course was satisfactory on the basis of mechanical respiratory assistance for periods of fifteen minutes of each hour. The patient was kept on humidified 100 per cent oxygen by nasal catheter when not connected to the I.P.P.B. machine. Fifteen minutes after the respiratory assistor was shut off, analysis of an arterial blood sample revealed an oxygen saturation of 87 per cent, a carbon dioxide tension of 50 mm. of mercury, and a pH of 7.34. While these values were definitely abnormal, they were considered satisfactory in the light of this man's advanced respiratory disease.

On the third postoperative day the patient developed a temperature of 101.4° F. with some signs of tachycardia. Blood pressure was satisfactory and had never shown serious depression with the use of the I.P.P.B. apparatus, but its inspiratory pressure was never allowed to rise above 12 to 15 cm. of water, so as not to decrease the venous return unduly in a patient whose peripheral circulation had recently been impaired. Electrocardiogram was unremarkable.

Blood gas analysis now revealed that the arterial oxygen saturation *on room air* was 64 per cent with a carbon dioxide tension of 58 mm. of mercury, and a *p*H of 7.36. These values were grossly unsatisfactory, and if the trends progressed, not long compatible with life.

With the patient breathing without assistance, 100 per cent humidified oxygen was then delivered to a perforated plastic fitting over the tracheostomy. On this regimen his blood gases showed improvement to an arterial oxygen saturation of 81.8 per cent, a carbon dioxide tension of 50 mm. of mercury, and a *p*H of 7.4. It was obvious that the patient had had a great deal of help from the I.P.P.B. apparatus, but that even without it, he did surprisingly well so long as he was breathing high oxygen concentrations. However, he showed serious defects in his gas exchange when breathing room air.

The following day, plasma sodium was reported as 150 mE. per l., chloride 115 mE. per l. and carbon dioxide combining power 32.7 mE. per l. The patient's intravenous fluid therapies were modified to add more water and less saline. His respiratory effort had produced mild hypertonicity by increased pulmonary water loss. The carbon dioxide combining power represented metabolic compensation to his chronic respiratory acidosis. On the tenth postoperative day, the patient suddenly showed a drop in his blood pressure to 90 mm. systolic with a pulse of 160. A Levin tube was passed into the gastric remnant and drained 400 ml. of dark red blood. Six thousand units of topical thrombin were installed in the Levin tube, diluted with milk. Bleeding and clotting times were normal at this time. Prothrombin time was in the low normal range and the patient received intravenous vitamin K_1 oxide.

With a transfusion of one pint banked blood and one pint fresh blood, the patient's chart was stable and he showed no evidence of further gastrointestinal bleeding throughout his hospital course.

From the fifth postoperative day onward the patient was slowly weaned from the I.P.P.B. unit, the tracheostomy tube was intermittently closed after the tenth postoperative day, and removed on the fifteenth postoperative day. During this time, the patient had a slowly advancing oral intake which was limited to fluids during the first six days and a steadily increasing solid diet thereafter. Achromycin was discontinued at the end of one week and a combination of Chloromycetin and erythromycin continued for five days, followed by two weeks of Albamycin therapy. His blood urea nitrogen dropped steadily to normal levels as the blood was cleared out of his gastrointestinal tract.

The patient was encouraged to stand beside his bed during the second postoperative week, but any activity produced added strain on his already compromised ventilation. Therefore, it was not until his fourth week that the patient was able to manage ambulation outside his room. The patient was discharged home, ambulatory, with satisfactory blood gas values and eating well, seven weeks after his emergency surgery.

SUMMARY. This severe respiratory cripple suffered an acute hemorrhage from duodenal ulcer; this pathologic process in itself may have been in part the result of his chronic bronchopulmonary disease. He weathered a skilled operation by dint of expert anesthesia and the postoperative use of positive pressure breathing via a cuffed endotracheal tube; blood gas analyses assisted in guiding his later course. Recovery was gratifying.

CHAPTER 43

The Pituitary-Adrenal Axis

Section I. Introduction

As endocrine disorders go, thyrotoxicosis, diabetes mellitus, castration, the menopause, and hyperparathyroidism have a combined frequency of incidence far greater than any combination of disorders of the adrenal cortical tissue. The special interest that attaches to the adrenal glands and their pituitary government lies in the fact that abnormalities affect the general progress of surgical convalescence regardless of the specific disease for which the patient was operated upon, the anesthesia used, or the nature of the injury; these are surgical factors that may be encountered in any patient at any time.

Failure of the adrenal cortex in surgery represents the loss of a basic survival mechanism. The patient dies in hypotensive shock. In contrast to the adrenal medulla, one of whose hormones (norepinephrine) is manufactured widely in other tissues of the body, the adrenal cortex is the only significant site of production of its hormones, hydrocortisone and aldosterone. When the gland is destroyed or atrophic, all of the enzyme systems supported by these steroids sag to inactivity, inadequacy, or complete failure.

The importance of the adrenal cortex in surgical homeostasis has been emphasized during the past twenty years as the endocrinology and biochemistry of the adrenal hormones have been elucidated. The adrenal glands, in relation to surgical convalescence, have had their full share of the swing of the pendulum of surgical fashion. Initial reaction to the description of the role of the adrenal

cortex in surgical recovery was one of enthusiasm. The new knowledge of the adrenals was greeted as that which must surely explain many of the metabolic and physiologic phenomena of convalescence, and the use of cortisone must prevent most surgical catastrophes. There was then a reaction and a denial of the importance of adrenal factors in recovery or adrenal hormones in treatment. Neither of these extreme views has proved correct. While it is true that many other interlocking endocrine and metabolic phenomena are important in surgical convalescence, and overt adrenal failure is quite uncommon, we may now look forward to some backswing of the pendulum as the usefulness of cortisone in pharmacologic excess is more cautiously reexplored.

A. TOO MUCH OR TOO LITTLE; REAL OR APPARENT NEED

In adrenal hormone therapy, one must differentiate between the use of adrenal hormones in pharmacologic excess and their use as replacement therapy of adrenal insufficiency.

No surgical trauma has been identified in which there is a harmful excess secretion of adrenal cortical hormone into the blood. Very complicated surgical illness may be accompanied by a prolonged and massive discharge from the adrenal glands, and in certain instances (as for instance in severe burns or liver disease) the blood concentration of steroids

Page 757

may be elevated for weeks. This elevation may be due in part to failure of normal disposal and in some cases may presage demise. Yet there is no evidence that the extremely elevated endogenous level is, in and of itself, harmful. Acid-peptic disease, with bleeding ulcer, may be exacerbated by the adrenal discharge of prolonged surgical illness, yet this is not a primary disorder of homeostasis. It is, in a sense, a physiologic by-product, albeit a dangerous one.

Prolonged therapy with large amounts of adrenal hormone is harmful in many ways, but most particularly because it favors massive gastrointestinal hemorrhage and produces atrophy of the adrenal gland, preventing the patient from exhibiting a normal response to subsequent trauma. These changes may be seen at dose levels in either the high or low range.

On the other end of the scale, *inadequate adrenal function in trauma and surgery quickly produces a threatening situation and demands immediate treatment.*

It will, therefore, be of importance in the ensuing account to differentiate among the short-term treatment of patients with a large excess of adrenal hormones, the effects on the patient of prolonged treatment with adrenal hormones, and the use of adrenal hormones in replacement therapy. Failure to distinguish among these three distinct categories has been responsible for much confusion in the literature.

Patients who need adrenal hormone to replace a lack of their own secretion may be referred to as having true hypofunction of the adrenal gland. Patients who seem to have quite normal adrenals but who respond favorably when given larger amounts of adrenal hormones might be referred to as having "apparent hypofunction" of the adrenals in conjunction with a surgical illness: they seem to need more hormone than they have, or, as an alternative explanation, they are responding normally to a large pharmacologic excess of a potent drug.

Section II.   Hypofunction of the Adrenals

A. CAUSES: NATURALLY OCCURRING HYPOADRENALISM

1. Absence of Adrenal Tissue

Adrenal tuberculosis, adrenal atrophy, and destruction by localization of bacteria from an acute blood-stream infection or hemorrhage are examples of lesions that can cause adrenal insufficiency and that may operate prior to or in association with a surgical or traumatic episode. In some of these cases adrenal insufficiency (often asymptomatic) is presumed to have been present prior to the surgical episode. True absence of adrenal tissue may also be produced by previous adrenalectomy, by acute trauma with adrenal apoplexy, and by tumors that destroy the adrenal gland. In view of the frequency of metastases of certain forms of carcinoma such as lungs and breast to the adrenal, it is remarkable that hypoadrenalism from this cause is not seen more frequently than it is.

2. Disease of Midbrain, Pituitary, or Other Endocrine Glands

Lesions or operations in the region of the pituitary which themselves involve the pituitary (suprasellar cysts, craniopharyngiomas, acromegaly, pituitary adenomas, tumors in the region of the chiasm, sarcoid of the optic chiasmal area) may all be associated with hypoactivity of the pituitary adrenal axis.

B. CAUSES: IATROGENIC HYPOADRENALISM

1. Cortisone* Treatment

Far commoner as a cause of hypoadrenalism in surgical patients is the use of cortisone in treatment. Prolonged adminis-

---

* The term "cortisone" is used generically throughout. Hydrocortisone is often used for intravenous purposes and has essentially the same effects. Prednisone has many of the same properties in clinical usage, as have many of the new synthetic analogues.

tration of cortisone produces atrophy of the adrenal cortex. The adrenal glands may actually be difficult to find in the perirenal fat. If a patient who has been treated for a long time with cortisone is traumatized without suitable additional hormone, he will show all of the characteristic signs of acute adrenal insufficiency—an Addisonian crisis. In addition to trauma itself, the challenge of salt loss or acute volume reduction is also associated with collapse after prolonged cortisone treatment, quite aside from tissue injury.

Cortisone treatment of five to seven days' duration at dose levels of 50 to 100 mg. a day is sufficient to produce significant functional adrenal atrophy through the inhibition of normal pituitary adrenocorticotropic hormone production. More prolonged courses will produce a more profound functional loss. Once use of the drug has been stopped, the adrenal remains atrophic for a length of time that depends upon the other stresses to which the patient is subject. In the ordinary stresses and strains of life, one would expect the patient to build the adrenal back up to normal strength by repeated release of adrenocorticotropic hormone. We have not seen serious surgical complications from cortisone therapy when it was discontinued six weeks or more prior to the operation, but these have been reported. If a bedridden invalid has had cortisone for a long time, and the cortisone is stopped while the patient continues to be bedridden, it is quite conceivable that four to six months later the patient may still show an atrophic or inhibited adrenal response to surgery because the invalidism provided no stimulus to adrenal build-up.

The administration of adrenocorticotropic hormone throughout a period of cortisone therapy should suffice to maintain the weight of the adrenal gland and render the discontinuance of cortisone less prone to upset the patient's response to trauma. Unfortunately this is an impractical step in most cases. For this reason, the cortisone should be "tapered" when it is stopped and the adrenal weight re-established by injections of adrenocorticotropic hormone, as described below. The management of patients who are on cortisone therapy and who must undergo surgery is also described below.

2. Anticoagulant Therapy and Adrenal Hemorrhage

The adrenal cortices are highly permeable areas of the vascular tree. Tumor cells and bacteria tend to localize in them; blunt trauma to the abdomen and severe burns may produce cellular infiltrates in the adrenals and even gross hemorrhage. It is therefore not surprising that in the face of anticoagulation (brought about by heparin or bishydroxycoumarin) one occasionally encounters patients who suffer hemorrhage into the adrenals with the production, over the course of a day or two, of a hypoadrenal state. Patients on anticoagulants who develop hypotension should be considered suspect of hypoadrenalism and should be studied and treated accordingly.

C. CAUSES: IS THERE SUCH A THING AS "ADRENAL EXHAUSTION"?

Since the description of the role of the adrenal cortex in surgical convalescence, and the description of an exhaustion phase of the "alarm reaction" in rats, there has become rooted in the medical imagination the concept of adrenal exhaustion as a feature of prolonged illness, severe injury, surgery, or chronic infection. There is little or no evidence for the existence of such a state.

There are in the body very few biochemical systems that are exhausted by prolonged chronic disease or infection. Nature seems to have provided a large functional reserve. The thyroid and pituitary glands continue to function, hypoglycemia is not a common complication, glucose or other carbohydrates continue to be oxidized in tissue, nitrogen compounds continue to be produced abundantly from tissue, insulin continues to be produced, and gastric secretion continues. Indeed, in some chronic wasting diseases, the parietal cells of the stomach may function so actively as to produce local disease. The liver is exhausted of glycogen but continues its other functions. It is true that gonadal function ceases, the menses cease, and the urinary excretion of 17-ketosteroids drops. The body's fat stores become exhausted, and this does indeed constitute an ominous milestone in chronic illness—when this endogenous source of calories has ceased to exist. But through it all, most of the essential homeostatic glandular structures in the body continue to function, and often at an increased rate of activity.

It is therefore not surprising to find that in chronic disease the adrenals are not exhausted. Instead, they are markedly hypertrophied. The stress of chronic disease, with repeated episodes of trauma or infection, continues to bombard the adrenal cortex with adrenocorticotropic hormone. There is a clear hypertrophy of the adrenal glands, readily demonstrable by the weight of the adrenals at postmortem after chronic illness, and also suggested by the high blood levels of free steroid found, or by the excessively high blood or urine steroid values produced by standard infusions of adrenocorticotropic hormone after a chronic illness such as a burn.

When a patient with chronic illness is sallow, weak, hypotensive, "washed out," disoriented, and slightly febrile, it is tempting to speak of him as exhibiting "adrenal exhaustion," even though there is no direct evidence for such a state. This temptation is further fortified if the patient appears to take a new interest in life when treated with adrenal hormones. This brings us immediately into that differentiation indicated at the start of this chapter, that one must clearly divide those patients who have true hypofunction of the glands from those who will respond to pharmacologic excess of adrenal hormones despite the presence of functioning glands.

In the patient described above, with a "washed out" and exhausted appearance in chronic illness, it is likely that many things other than exhaustion of the adrenal glands contribute to his appearance. Inadequate blood volume, desalting water loss, hyponatremia, hypokalemia, inadequate caloric energy, hypoproteinemia, and spreading sepsis are all suspect. If the patient does well on adrenal hormones, adrenocorticotropic hormone, or testosterone, it may be from their effect on appetite and psyche or in detoxifying the products of a septic process, rather than replacement of any native lack.

The lowered urinary excretion of 17-ketosteroids in chronic illness has led to the concept of "androgenic exhaustion" and the idea that androgens must be given to such patients to support anabolism. The available evidence is quite the other way. It is the patient depleted after a long illness who most readily shows strong anabolism with minimal intakes. As described in Part IV, the problem is not one of giving androgens or ACTH so much as it is one of controlling the underlying disease (sepsis, for example) and then providing oral intake. The effect on appetite may be one of the rational justifications for the use of gonadal steroids in chronic depleting illness.

D. DIAGNOSIS: IS THE ACUTE SURGICAL CRISIS DUE TO ADRENAL INSUFFICIENCY?

1. Manifestations

Adrenal failure after surgical trauma appears to involve three rather distinct pictures. There may be mixtures of the three in any one patient. They are:

(1) Hypotension and shock very early in the operative experience, often first demonstrated with the induction of anesthesia alone; there is oliguria, disorientation or coma, and fever.

(2) A slower (eight to thirty-six hours) development of some hypotension, with high fever and rapid pulse as the most prominent features, passing along later to mental changes, vascular collapse, shock, and oliguria.

(3) A picture of water-and-salt imbalance —hyponatremia with excessive salt loss in the urine and hyperkalemia. Fever and hypotension may be prominent in this picture when it is advanced. But in its early phases, blood pressure difficulties are not prominent. If blood pressure falls markedly, then oliguria occurs and the renal salt loss ceases.

2. Differential Diagnosis

The differential diagnosis of hypoadrenalism in association with surgical episodes therefore depends upon a careful discrimination among those events in the surgical patient which may be associated with vascular collapse, high fever with rapid pulse, or excessive salt loss with hyponatremia and hyperkalemia. A complete list of these states would include most of the sources of bodily catastrophe. A partial listing of those which must be considered in the patient suspect of adrenal failure is as follows:

(1) external hemorrhage;
(2) hemorrhage into the lumen of a mucosa-lined viscus;
(3) hemorrhage into the tissues;
(4) inadequate blood replacement with any of the above;
(5) peritonitis;
(6) spreading infection, blood-stream infection;
(7) pneumonitis, atelectasis, bronchopneumonia;
(8) mediastinal emphysema, hemopericardium;
(9) pulmonary embolus;
(10) coronary occlusion, cardiac arrhythmia;
(11) acute pancreatitis;
(12) mesenteric infarction or embolus;
(13) anaphylactic reactions to drugs or serums;
(14) mismatched transfusions;
(15) unrecognized salt loss, or overreplacement with water.

Descriptions of the characteristics of the above will be found elsewhere in this book. They will not be repeated here. The surgeon should have this "mental checklist" in mind before embarking on treatment with steroids.

3. Immediate Management

Having considered the above causes of homeostatic failure, hypotension, shock, and oliguria, and taken steps necessary to make a diagnosis, the surgeon is justified in starting adrenal hormone therapy blindly if he cannot reasonably pinpoint one of the above diagnoses or if he is unable to secure one of the rapid diagnostic clues for adrenal hypofunction.

It is in this situation that the eosinophil count achieves its greatest usefulness. A plain blood smear should be expected to show practically no eosinophils in an acutely ill surgical patient. If many eosinophils are present, adrenal failure is strongly suggested. An eosinophil count showing over 150 cells per cu. mm. is likewise very suggestive and a sufficient basis in itself for starting adrenal hormone therapy.

If the patient has had tuberculosis, has infection around the adrenals such as a psoas abscess, or shows adrenal calcification by X-ray, it is of course corroborative evidence.

If the patient has had previous cortisone therapy, one need not stand on ceremony in making the diagnosis but should keep a wary eye out for some of the other items on the above list which may also exist. The measurement of the steroids in the blood or urine is a valuable adjunct here, but the analysis requires from four to six hours and one cannot wait for the result. A blood sample should be drawn, and urine collected for such analyses.

The next diagnostic step is to give the patient hydrocortisone intravenously. This may be done in doses of approximately 100 mg. in a continuous infusion to take eight hours. If this is maintained, it amounts to 300 mg. a day, which is sufficient to produce a favorable response in any individual with hypoadrenalism.

If there is adrenal cortical insufficiency, the patient will respond to this hydrocortisone in an unquestionably specific way. Blood pressure will rise, fever and pulse will fall, mentation will return to normal, and a remarkable improvement will be observed.

If one is dealing with the "water and salt" picture associated with hyponatremia, hyperkalemia, and less prominent vascular phenomena (hypotension and oliguria), then to the cortisone should be added desoxycorticosterone acetate, in dosage of 10 mg. of the rapidly acting material, administered subcutaneously. The administration of concentrated salt solution is also specific in this situation.

The patient with early adrenal failure will show a transient response to both blood transfusion and the administration of salt. This transient improvement on volume restoration will at times confuse the diagnosis. Alternative diagnosis will find considerable support in the temporary nonspecific improvement. Therefore, when hypoadrenalism is suspected, initial steps for diagnosis should be undertaken with vigor, though specific hormone therapy may rightfully be postponed for a few hours of study and trial of other measures. If the patient has hypofunction of the adrenal glands as the major cause of his difficulty, blood transfusion, salt infusion, and the action of antibiotics will fail unless adrenal replacement is also given.

In summary, then, in a patient with suspected adrenal failure after trauma or operation one should carry out the following steps:

(1) History, physical examination, X-ray diagnosis, and rapid laboratory work are carried out so as to rule in or out as quickly as one reasonably can other possible causes for the disorder.

(2) A blood sample is taken for eosinophil count, sodium, potassium, and sugar concentrations, blood urea nitrogen, blood steroid determination if available, and such other studies as are appropriate, including blood culture.

(3) An inlying catheter is placed in the bladder and all urine is collected on a six-hourly basis and analyzed for steroids or sodium concentration, or both.

(4) If the clinical appearances cannot be accounted for on any basis other than adrenal failure, the result of the more time-consuming tests is not awaited. The patient is given an intravenous infusion of hydrocortisone at a dose level of 100 mg. every eight hours. If the salt-and-water-imbalance picture predominates, desoxycorticosterone acetate is added.

E. FURTHER CARE AND DIAGNOSIS

If the favorable turn with steroid therapy suggests adrenal insufficiency, one still does not know whether or not there is a specific or nonspecific ("true" or "apparent") effect. For the first day or two the patient is maintained on hydrocortisone, as outlined above, but in decreasing doses, with desoxycorticosterone acetate if necessary because of salt loss. If the patient's surgical convalescence now rounds the corner with a reasonably normal recovery, the dosage of cortisone can be reduced toward a maintenance dose of 75 mg. a day. This may be taken by mouth if the patient is taking oral nourishment satisfactorily. The general objective is to maintain this dosage for seven to ten days, at the end of which time steps for definitive diagnosis will be undertaken. If the patient has been quite critically ill, it is inadvisable to aim for definitive adrenal study sooner than seven to ten days. Because of this duration of treatment, anti-ulcer steps are vitally important. Alkali gels and atropine are used.

As the time for ceasing hormone therapy draws near, one of two courses may be taken.

(1) An effort to stop the administration of cortisone may be initiated by tapering the dose gradually and covering it with increasing doses of adrenocorticotropic hormone, which are then themselves tapered off. If the patient withstands this procedure well, one may assume that difficulty with the adrenals, if present, was transient.

(2) Generally, it is preferable to undertake a quantitative study of the patient's adrenal function as the support is withdrawn. Only in this way will one know for certain whether the patient had "true" or "apparent" hypoadrenalism—whether he has responded to replacement or pharmacologic excess of corticosteroids. This should partake of the general pattern for elective study of suspected hypoadrenalism. In brief, such steps consist of sequential measurement of the blood or urine steroid values under standard adrenocorticotropic-hormone stimulation. A full account of the differential diagnosis of adrenal functional states may be found in works on endocrinology. The further use of hormone after discharge depends upon the results of these diagnostic studies.

F. COMMENT

Although the two pictures—"true" and "apparent" adrenal lack—do resemble each other, there is one important aspect in which they differ. "True" hypoadrenalism may produce surgical disaster following the most trivial or routine of traumata or operations. The "apparent" hypofunction syndrome, in which the patient responds favorably to moderate doses of cortisone despite normal adrenal function, usually is seen in patients who are passing through a major traumatic experience, usually including severe shock with blood loss, extensive injury, infection, extensive burns, or such toxic episodes as rapidly spreading infection or peritonitis. This sort of differentiation is clearly not mutually exclusive; it merely indicates that *the failure state after a minor challenge more strongly suggests true adrenal hypofunction.*

Such "blind" therapy thus may lead to one of three distinct outcomes.

(1) The patient actually has hypofunction of the adrenals, and the surgeon finds that he is treating an adrenal crisis with gratifying result, as already outlined.

(2) Somewhat more likely, the patient responds favorably to the hydrocortisone but not on a specific replacement basis. He maintains his blood pressure more easily, is more responsive, has a better urine output and lower fever. The explanation is most likely that the cortisone synergizes with catechol amines being given at the same time or secreted by the patient. The cortisone also may interfere with allergenic or antibody responses or toxic effects (of bacterial origin) which are responsible for the toxicity seen in the patient. Whatever the explanation, it is a nonspecific, favorable response.

(3) Or—by far the most common—the patient may show slight transient improvement, but the basic disease process (trauma, shock, sepsis, burn, or renal failure) continues unabated to a long illness or lethal outcome. *This is statistically by far the most common outcome of "blind" cortisone therapy in acute hypotensive surgical illness.*

Section III. Prolonged Cortisone Therapy

A. INDICATIONS FOR GIVING CORTISONE

Treatment with cortisone or related steroids over a period of weeks or months is indicated in a variety of diseases treated by the physician, including ulcerative colitis, rheumatoid arthritis, asthma, skin diseases, and blood dyscrasias. In patients cared for by the surgeon, prolonged cortisone treatment is most frequently required for those who have had adrenalectomy or hypophysectomy, or for the occasional patient who has developed a surgical crisis and has later been shown to be suffering from hypoadrenalism. Occasionally patients with regional enteritis or ulcerative colitis are under cortisone treatment for prolonged periods of time in association with their surgical care. The use of cortisone as an adjunct to splenectomy or in the treatment of cancer of the breast, cancer of the prostate, and other tumors adds another group of patients who may be under prolonged surgical care while receiving cortisone.

The dose level maintained has comparatively little to do with the ultimate development of adrenal inhibition. It is merely a matter of time. Prolonged treatment with even small doses of cortisone (25 to 50 mg. a day) will ultimately produce adrenal inhibition. By contrast, the incidence of complications relating to the gastrointestinal tract is definitely increased by the larger doses, particularly if given by mouth.

In general the dose levels of prolonged cortisone treatment have been as follows:

(1) chronic adrenal replacement therapy, 25 to 50 mg. a day;

(2) cortisone "inhibition," or treatment of inflammatory diseases, 50 to 150 mg. a day; and

(3) massive-dose therapy as used in certain blood dyscrasias, 500 mg. to 1 gm. per day.

B. HAZARDS OF PROLONGED CORTISONE THERAPY

The two chief hazards of prolonged cortisone therapy are adrenal inhibition and gastrointestinal hemorrhage. Adrenal inhibition has already been discussed in the paragraphs above and will not be described further here.

There is the interesting side light discussed below, that patients on cortisone who bleed massively need *more cortisone* (and often desoxycorticosterone acetate), not less, in order to survive the volume-reducing threat of acute blood loss.

Massive gastrointestinal hemorrhage has been responsible for most of the deaths of surgical patients under cortisone treatment, and is seen at times even in patients on prolonged low-dose cortisone therapy, such as sufferers from Addison's disease under lifetime-maintenance cortisone.

The length of therapy required to produce hemorrhage from the gastrointestinal tract varies over a wide range and is the product not only of the cortisone dosage but of the rest of the setting and the patient's history. If a patient is being severely "stressed" by concomitant surgical illness, he may develop an ulcer (the etiology of which may be likened to that of a Curling's ulcer) much sooner than a patient on a low-dose therapy who has no ulcer history and who is not under stress at all. These many variables are impossible to analyze clinically. One cannot predict the latent period. Severe bleeding after less than three days of treatment is a rarity, and this is a helpful guide. Indeed, the critically ill patient treated with cortisone because of its pharmacologic effects is an individual particularly prone to develop gastrointestinal hemorrhage on cortisone therapy. Severe hemorrhage from gastric ulcer has been seen as early as five days after starting high-dose cortisone therapy in the severely ill surgical patient.

Salt retention as a by-product of prolonged cortisone therapy is often bothersome. Its incidence is unpredictable. Some patients on small doses of cortisone will develop swelling of the ankles and evident sodium retention. This is controlled or prevented by the administration of 3 to 5 gm. of potassium chloride per day by mouth in enteric coated pills. Other patients on the same dose of cortisone seem to evince no such tendency.

This is due to individual variations in diet or in renal function.

The production of a round face and other characteristic bodily changes may also result from prolonged cortisone therapy. These changes are prevented by the administration of testosterone if that hormone is not contraindicated by the disease. For this purpose the long-acting testosterone may be used with an injection every three weeks or so.

C. PROTECTION AGAINST GASTRO-INTESTINAL HEMORRHAGE

In the patient who is taking food by mouth and who is treated with cortisone for a long period of time, it is possible to protect against ulcer by the simultaneous administration of alkali and other measures of an "ulcer regimen" type. Frequent small feedings and doses of atropine and nonabsorbable alkali are essential. Although no figures are available to indicate conclusively that this protects against ulcer on cortisone therapy, it is the widespread impression that such a regimen has been successful. The oral use of cortisone is definitely more liable to produce dangerous hyperfunction of gastric digestive activity than will the parenteral use of the drug.

In the critically ill surgical patient recovering from an episode of shock, massive injury, trauma, burns, or sepsis, who is not taking anything by mouth, it is difficult to confer protection against gastric ulceration from cortisone administration. The insertion of an indwelling gastric tube with gastric lavage, antacids, and parenteral medication such as atropine have all been tried. The lack of the neutralizing effect of oral intake in such situations may be one of the many factors that render the surgical patient so vulnerable to gastrointestinal ulceration. If nothing can be given by mouth and cortisone must be continued, one is faced with the likelihood that a complication of the drug which has helped the patient in the past few days will, within the next few days, cause the patient's demise.

A previous history of duodenal or gastric ulcer greatly increases liability to the development of the gastrointestinal complication of cortisone therapy. Whether or not such a history is a contraindication to use of the drug must depend wholly upon the urgency of the positive indication for its use. It is our observation that the patients who derive the greatest appetite stimulus from cortisone are those whose stomachs are most prone to ulcerate.

D. THE SURGICAL MANAGEMENT OF PATIENTS ON PROLONGED CORTISONE THERAPY

When a patient has been on prolonged cortisone therapy and surgical operation is required, two alternative courses of action present themselves:

(1) the cortisone is stopped with appropriate precautions to reestablish adrenal function before the patient is operated upon, or

(2) suitable steps are taken to carry out operation under cortisone therapy, stopping the cortisone under proper precautions several days or weeks after the operation.

Choice between the above two alternatives is clearly determined by other aspects of the patient's care. In most situations the second of the two is advisable because there is not time to stop giving the drug and reestablish endogenous adrenal function prior to surgery.

When there is time to do this, however, the following schedule is maintained.

(1) The cortisone dosage is gradually tapered off over a four-day period.

(2) Starting on the second or third day, adrenocorticotropic hormone is given intramuscularly in doses of 25 units (of the slowly absorbed preparation) twice a day. This is continued for six or seven days, at the end of which the ACTH is gradually stopped.

(3) At some point toward the end of the adrenocorticotropic hormone administration, determinations of steroid values of the blood or urine are helpful in assuring the surgeon that adrenal function has returned.

(4) Four to seven days later the operation is carried out.

On the above program of tapering the dose, one frequently sees a febrile episode and a rather sick-looking patient at the time that the adrenocorticotropic hormone is finally stopped. This is not the time to operate. This "withdrawal fever" is not ominous, and is especially noticeable after long-term cortisone. It is associated with a normally low eosinophil count, normal urine steroid values, and normal blood-pressure maintenance. If the adrenocorticotropic hormone cannot be stopped without a hypotensive episode, further endocrine study should be undertaken to determine whether or not the patient has reestablished normal adrenal function in response to a constant adrenocorticotropic hormone infusion.

If the second of the above two alternatives is to be pursued, and the patient carried through operation on cortisone therapy, the cortisone to be stopped later, the procedure is as given below.

(1) The patient is shifted from oral or intramuscular cortisone to intravenous cortisone at least three hours prior to the induction of anesthesia. For the day of operation and the next one to three days (depending upon the extent of the operation) the patient is given a constant intravenous infusion of hydrocortisone at the rate of 100 mg. every eight hours or 300 mg. per day.

(2) On the day of operation 10 mg. of desoxycorticosterone acetate is given.

(3) This program is then changed to orally or intramuscularly administered cortisone, dropping rapidly down to the previous maintenance dose.

(4) This maintenance dose is continued until the patient's surgical convalescence has reached the point where he may consider returning home in a week or so.

(5) The cortisone is stopped over a four-day period, covering with adrenocorticotropic hormone, which is then stopped according to the procedure for stopping cortisone, indicated above, and as appropriate for the underlying disease process.

Under certain circumstances, as for instance in splenectomy for hemolytic jaundice, it may be advisable to continue the cortisone for a prolonged period of time after operation, in which case the maintenance dose is resumed.

Patients who are on prolonged cortisone therapy should be instructed that, should they receive an injury or require surgical operation or develop an acute infection, their dose of cortisone should be increased through the phase of trauma or acute illness.

E. THE TREATMENT OF GASTROINTESTINAL HEMORRHAGE UNDER CORTISONE DOSAGE

If a patient has been on cortisone (even at low dosage) for a long time, his own adrenals are inactive if not atrophic. If he then bleeds, he suffers one of the most drastic volume-reducing challenges to adrenal secretion; he unquestionably needs and would produce (were he normal) a large amount of adreno-cortical substances as well as medullary amines. He needs this endocrine outpouring to achieve a normal peripheral vasoconstrictive response and renal conservation of salt in response to the challenge of hemorrhage. Lacking it, his shock is profound and compounded as well by renal salt-wasting. Therefore *if a patient on long-duration cortisone bleeds massively he should be given cortisone in even larger doses and desoxycorticosterone acetate to tide his homeostatic needs over the crisis.*

Blood replacement is to be active; antacid measures are taken; the continued secretory stimulus of the cortisone is a minor hazard as contrasted to the fatal collapse that follows if the hormone treatment is stopped and the patient is left to face massive hemorrhage with fully inhibited adrenals.

Although the use of desoxycorticosterone acetate is not always essential, it is a harmless safety measure. If the patient's tubular function is such that he needs the strong stimulus of desoxycorticosterone acetate to conserve salt, its use will provide an extra bulwark against shock. If he is going to save salt adequately on large doses of cortisone, the desoxycorticosterone acetate will not harm him.

With the bleeding controlled—a step often necessitating surgical operation—the procedure for stopping cortisone may be set in motion, days or weeks later.

Section IV.   Adrenalectomy and Hypophysectomy

A. ADRENAL STEROID DOSAGE

Patients undergoing adrenal exploration or adrenalectomy should be carried through operation on a dose schedule essentially identical with that mentioned above for patients undergoing operation on prolonged cortisone therapy.

Intravenous infusions of hydrocortisone at a dose of 100 mg. every eight hours should be started prior to the induction of anesthesia. They should be maintained through the operation and for a day or two afterwards, then shifted over to the intramuscular or oral preparation, depending upon the circumstances. If the patient has had total adrenalectomy, continued maintenance at a level of 25 to 50 mg. per day is satisfactory. Procedure to avoid gastrointestinal ulceration is necessary over the long term.

After total adrenalectomy, most patients can get along satisfactorily on 25 mg. of cortisone a day. They feel better, however, and are more effective citizens on a dosage of 50 to 75 mg. per day.

If the patient becomes hypotensive during surgery on this dose of intravenous hydrocortisone and with adequate blood replacement, it is advisable to give him one of the pressor amines such as norepinephrine or Neosynephrine in small doses. For a patient receiving 300 mg. of hydrocortisone intravenously per day, there is usually little to be gained in terms of blood pressure by increasing the dose to higher levels. If the patient has been on prolonged cortisone therapy, increasing the dose to high levels may be valuable; for the patient on his first cortisone at the time of adrenalectomy, this is unlikely.

Patients undergoing hypophysectomy may be carried on the same management. In most such patients, the shift from intravenous hydrocortisone to oral cortisone may take place on the first or second postoperative day, and the postoperative endocrine management as regards adrenocortical replacement is very simple. The management of diabetes insipidus presents a more complex problem.

In patients undergoing total adrenalectomy for Cushing's disease, the tissues have been accustomed to high levels of hormone, and there has been described so-called "adrenal fever," coming on days or weeks after operation and occasionally associated with a fatal outcome. The postoperative management of such patients is improved by carrying them on high doses of cortisone for quite a long time and only gradually reducing the dose to maintenance level, as the patient's tissues gradually become accustomed to lower levels of hormone.

Under any of these circumstances of cortisone treatment of surgical patients, one may encounter salt retention in the resting state, and, after trauma, serious salt loss. Hydrocortisone and cortisone are not very effective salt-retaining compounds. In large doses, one may observe edema due to salt loading, best avoided by potassium-chloride administration and a low-salt regimen. Yet, paradoxically, the adrenal atrophy produced by prolonged therapy prevents the marked *increase* in salt retention apparently required by the body to weather trauma, surgery, or salt loss.

If there is profuse osmotic diuresis, as in diabetes, or if the epithelium of the renal tubule is not normally responsive to steroids, salt loss may be encountered on long-term cortisone therapy. This will be manifested by greater difficulty in maintaining the patient's blood pressure, a marked tendency to hyponatremia and hyperkalemia and—the most clearly diagnostic finding—the presence of sodium in the urine at concentrations greater than 30 mE. per l., while the plasma sodium concentration is below 130 mE. per l. Under such a circumstance, or after trauma, desoxycorticosterone acetate should be added to the medication.

B. DIABETES INSIPIDUS AND VASOPRESSIN

After hypophysectomy or chiasmal surgery there is often (in 30 to 50 per cent of cases) a transient or persistent diabetes insipidus. This results as much from hypothalamic trauma as from hypophysectomy, and responds specifically to vasopressin (antidiuretic hormone). The problems presented in management result either from neglect due to lack of recognition on the one hand or from overtreatment on the other; these produce, respectively, severe hypertonicity or severe hypotonicity.

Lack of recognition of diabetes insipidus is not unusual. It often is not a part of the doctor's conscience or routine to measure urine output after operation for suprasellar cyst, head trauma, or craniopharyngioma. In forty-eight hours with urine volumes of only 3,000 to 4,000 ml. per day and with no or low intake (because of coma, the patient cannot complain of thirst), the sodium concentration rises to 160 to 170 mE. per l., the osmolality similarly, coma deepens, and a diagnosis of a "specific brain lesion with hypernatremia" is made. If water is given, the output promptly rises to 8,000 to 20,000 ml. per day and the diagnosis becomes obvious. It is indeed a "specific brain lesion with hypernatremia": it is diabetes insipidus.

The confusion here arises from the fact that as volume contracts in diabetes insipidus there is a lowering of glomerular filtration and there is some tubular water resorption in the most distal tubular site. Even in the total lack of antidiuretic hormone there is some water reabsorption as dehydration becomes very severe, and so long as there is no solute load. Urine volumes are therefore not excessive enough to arouse suspicion. Recognition of the condition and careful rehydration of the patient under vasopressin are very effective.

Overtreatment with water is hard to avoid if vasopressin is given on a regular dosage schedule by the clock, with water *ad libitum*, early in the course of diabetes insipidus. Vasopressin alone has no effect on osmolality; given with an excess of water it produces severe hypotonicity. After hypophysectomy an effective standard procedure is as follows.

(1) Measure and record daily urine output and fluid intake. Weigh the patient daily.

(2) Give the patient sufficient fluid to avoid thirst or dry tongue for forty-eight hours. If he is not wide awake this may require intravenous infusion, but it can usually be done by mouth.

(3) During this time avoid vasopressin. Check the patient's plasma sodium concentration daily for the first week.

(4) At the end of forty-eight hours re-evaluate the status. If the patient's urine volume is over 6 l. per day, start vasopressin, 0.5 unit subcutaneously every twelve hours. This serves merely to reduce the total urine output for convenience. Let the patient drink as desired.

(5) If his urine output is less than 6 l., give no vasopressin. Note this high-volume cut-off.

(6) In either event, at the end of one week recheck the urine volume for management status. Attempts to stabilize intake prior to this are rarely successful.

(7) At urine outputs under 5,000 ml. per day, no medication is recommended; between 5,000 and 10,000 ml. per day, the "snuff" or sublingual vasopressin may be sufficient. At outputs over 10,000 ml. per day, the Pitressin tannate in oil is recom-mended. With experience in the management of patients after hypophysectomy, this is rarely necessary.

If, early in the course of the treatment, heavy vasopressin dosage is given and the patient allowed unlimited access to water, the waxing and waning of thirst and its satura-tion are apt to produce serious hypotonicity.

It is gratifying to see severe diabetes in-sipidus subside spontaneously to the point of no vasopressin requirement. This may occur at any time from the fifth day onward with a change from obligatory urine volumes of 16 to 20 l. per day to urine volumes near normal.

By sequential tests of the response of the renal tubule (as measured by free water clearance) to cautious water-deprivation, hy-pertonic salt, nicotine, and vasopressin, it is possible to quantitate the degree of diabetes insipidus and its sensitivity to drug treatment as a basis for long-term management.

Section V.   The Adrenals: Notes from the Literature*

Hayes (1956) reviewed the problems of surgery in patients on previous cortisone treatment. He showed that in such patients an intraoperative eosinophilia was apt to presage a shocklike state; he advised treat-ment with adrenocorticotropic hormone or intravenous hydrocortisone along the lines generally adopted for this purpose.

Troen and Rynearson (1956) studied the use of cortisone in pituitary operations; they showed that postoperative endocrine prob-lems were more frequent in the pituitary in-sufficiency group and that cortisone used prophylactically was effective in avoiding postoperative hypoadrenal states.

The work of Mendelsohn and Pearson (1955) indicates the uncertainty of many of the classical concepts of adrenal physiology. In their studies, patients who were being maintained on cortisone after adrenalectomy for cancer were observed during the with-

_____
* A full review of the literature on adrenal activation in surgery will be found in Part I.

drawal of this hormone. There was lowering of glomerular filtration rate, of blood pres-sure, and (in some) of plasma sodium con-centration without any renal salt wastage whatsoever. Antidiuresis was prominent, with an expansion of the extracellular fluid. Clinical "insufficiency" was marked. We thus find that adrenal insufficiency may not always involve renal salt loss.

It is also of interest that sudden massive doses of cortisone will increase the plasma potassium concentration (Knight et al., 1955). In considering changes in plasma potassium concentration, one should realize that either insufficiency or sudden massive overdosage may produce an increase.

Lewis et al. (1953) report a fatal case of adrenal cortical insufficiency occurring in the course of surgery (knee capsulotomy) after about four months of cortisone therapy for rheumatoid arthritis. Metabolic data are lacking, but there is excellent depiction of gross and histologic appearances of the inhibited adrenal. The initial clinical clue was a shocklike state and then hyperpyrexia, starting about thirty minutes after the end of the operation. It is noteworthy that the patient received 500 ml. of sodium lactate during the procedure and seemed to do well when the infusion was running. She died in shock five hours and forty-five minutes after operation, without benefit of cortisone therapy. Postmortem showed atrophic adrenals with hemorrhage and congestion. The very rapid death is of unusual interest; respiratory failure was the terminating event. Since this report many other examples have been observed and reported.

Fraser et al. (1952) also report irreversible shock after prolonged cortisone therapy, with adrenal atrophy. Harnagel and Kramer (1955) report a case involving joint manipulation only. Hayes (1956) reviews the management of such cases and the prevention of adverse reactions, as do Hills et al. (1956).

Salassa et al. (1953) provide a helpful review of postoperative adrenal cortical insufficiency. Howland (Howland et al., 1956, and Howland, 1957) discusses surgical patients who, at operation, seemed to have better homeostasis when given large doses of cortisone. There is sparse evidence that these patients had adrenal insufficiency. They responded to sizeable doses, as do patients suffering from a variety of toxic or allergic states in which there is no evidence of adrenal disease or lack. The cases reported are of interest, however, in documenting the sorts of intraoperative course that are improved by steroid therapy.

Sevitt (1955) describes "adrenal apoplexy" as an entity occurring after blunt trauma to the abdomen. The two cases he reports were both those involving closed trauma. There was hemorrhage into the adrenals and, presumably, adrenal insufficiency. Evidence for the latter was suggestive clinically but not proven chemically.

Kelly (1931) reported hemorrhage into the adrenal glands following breech extraction; Lewis (1921) had reported adrenal and pancreatic hemorrhage following surgical operations on other parts of the body.

CASE 22

Cholecystectomy Is Followed by High Temperature and Collapse, Due to a Very Specific Cause, Fortunately Recognized in Time and Treated with Vigor and Hormone

Case 22. Patient C. M., #54323. Female. Age 48. Admitted February 6, 1955. Discharged February 28, 1955.

DIAGNOSIS. Gallstones.

OPERATION. Cholecystectomy.

CLINICAL SUMMARY. There was a three months' history of epigastric distress typical of gallstones, the latter confirmed by X-ray; some weight loss in recent months; deliveries six and three years ago of stillborn infants; negative "general check-up" one month previously. Admission blood pressure was 110/80.

Physical examination was generally negative. After suitable preparation which gave no hint of abnormality, the patient underwent cholecystectomy under barbiturate-ether anesthesia.

The intraoperative course was entirely uneventful but within two hours after operation the patient's temperature began to rise, reaching 104° F. within six hours of operation. Blood pressure fell gradually to 60/40, but the patient was warm, dry, and comfortable with a pulse of 90. The possibilities of atelectasis, sensitivity to some drug, or urinary tract infection were considered.

For none was evidence conclusive. The wound was clear.

Through the first night pressure remained low, rising to 100/60 with one blood transfusion. Pulse rose to 110. Fever remained at about 102° F. The patient began to look more toxic; she became profoundly hypotensive, cold, clammy, and the appearances were ominous; the possibility of adrenal insufficiency was entertained. An eosinophil count was carried out, revealing 900 per cu. mm.

ARGUMENT. The elevated eosinophil count, alone, is enough to justify steroid therapy here. It does not establish a diagnosis, but it is a sufficient indication for energetic treatment; even a favorable response does not exclude the coexistence of other complications. The high fever and hypotension are compatible with, but not diagnostic of, adrenal insufficiency.

FURTHER COURSE. An intravenous infusion of hydrocortisone at the rate of 100 mg. every eight hours was begun. The restoration to normal convalescence was immediate; temperature and blood pressure returned to normal. There was a slight diuresis. The eosinophil count fell to near zero.

After two days the patient was shifted to intramuscular cortisone and then to oral cortisone.

Before discharge, tests of adrenal function were carried out as follows:

(1) Adrenal response to adrenocorticotropic hormone (25 units intravenously in eight hours).
    a. Blood steroids ranged rom 7.1 mcg. per 100 ml. to 6.9 mcg. per 100 ml.
    b. Eosinophils rose from 215 per cu. mm. to 550 per cu. mm.
    c. Urine 17-hydroxycorticosteroid was unchanged at 5.2 mg. per day.
(2) X-rays: no adrenal calcification.
(3) Electrolyte data: at the time of her hypotension, plasma sodium concentration was 127 mE. per l., potassium 4.5 mE. per l. These data were not available at the time the cortisone was begun. Her sodium gradually rose on treatment.

COMMENT. These data show adrenal insufficiency. The patient has since required maintenance on about 25 mg. of cortisone per day. Normal weight was regained. A later attempt to withdraw steroid support precipitated clinical insufficiency within forty-eight hours.

A test with adrenocorticotropic hormone repeated three months later again showed no response. Urinary excretion of 17-hydroxycorticosterone was consistently low and unresponsive.

The problem here was etiology. Evidence for adrenal disease prior to operation was meager (weight loss is the only item) and the intraoperative course suggested normal adrenal function. The patient was able to live her everyday existence on her minimal adrenal function, but she had no reserve for "stress." The possibility of postoperative adrenal hemorrhage was appealing but there was no real evidence for this as against any other histologic lesion. No anticoagulants had been used. Blood culture was negative; bacterial destruction of the adrenal seems unlikely.

We are left, therefore, with well-documented adrenal failure coming on immediately following cholecystectomy and of unknown etiology. Had treatment not been prompt and accurate this patient would have died; the immediate event would have taken the form of cardiac "arrest" (probably ventricular fibrillation) and this (or "irreversible shock") might have been the final diagnosis.

CASE 23

A Patient Being Readied for Colectomy in Ulcerative Colitis Goes into Shock before the Operation, Owing to a Special Stimulus

Case 23. Patient F. S., #9G602. Male. Age 29. Admitted June 10, 1956. Discharged July 10, 1956.

DIAGNOSIS. Ulcerative colitis.

OPERATION. Ileostomy and total colectomy.

CLINICAL SUMMARY. For four years this twenty-nine-year-old physician had suffered bouts of diarrhea with bleeding. There had been occasional severe exacerbations but he had been able to remain at work. Two years previously he had required hospitalization for an acute episode, and at this time the diagnosis of ulcerative colitis was established. Four months prior to entering the hospital he had a barium enema which produced a severe and unremitting exacerbation. Nine weeks prior to entry he was started on oral cortisone at the dose level of 100 to 250 mg. per day. This produced a definite improvement in his disease. In preparation for admission he gradually tapered off the cortisone, and took the last dose the day prior to admission. No adrenocorticotropic hormone was given. He continued having frequent bowel movements, but seemed otherwise in good condition.

On admission his blood pressure was 130/70, pulse 96. He did not appear ill; he was slightly obese but did not show the facial changes of prolonged cortisone administration.

In preparation for sugery he was given one injection of adrenocorticotropic hormone gel, 40 units intra-

muscularly. A Miller-Abbott tube was passed the night prior to operation, and placed on suction.

Events then moved rapidly. His diarrhea continued unabated through the night; his tube drainage was 1000 ml. By morning he was in vascular collapse, with blood pressure 80/60, pulse 140, restless, disoriented, and in shock. His hematocrit, 48 on entry, had risen to 56.5.

ARGUMENT. The normal person responds to extracellular fluid volume reduction (here produced by diarrhea and gastrointestinal fluid loss) by a reduction in urine volume and a reduction in the urinary excretion of sodium salts. This normal response to volume reduction requires the effect of aldosterone and antidiuretic hormone on the renal tubule.

Although urine volume was not measured this first night, this patient voided several times up to the point at which he developed hypotension. This suggests failure of the normal stimulus to renal tubular resorption of glomerular filtrate. Other evidence available was the presence of 16 per cent eosinophils on an admission blood smear.

Collapse after fluid loss of this moderate magnitude, together with the history of cortisone dosage, strongly suggests the diagnosis of adrenal insufficiency on the basis of cortisone therapy, now compounded by extra-renal salt loss. The "stress" that unmasks adrenal insufficiency here is not trauma, but salt loss.

The single dose of adrenocorticotropic hormone gel

would not be expected to improve adrenal function after nine weeks of cortisone. From these atrophic glands only a meager corticoid response could be expected, at best.

FURTHER COURSE. The patient was immediately started on intravenous administration of hydrocortisone and fluorohydrocortisone and concentrated (3 per cent) sodium chloride. The Miller-Abbott tube was removed. Within four hours he had changed from a pale, sweating, apprehensive man with a heart rate of 140, thready pulse, blood pressure of 80/60, and oliguria to a warm, pink, dry, smiling, normotensive, slightly euphoric person with a pulse of 85. He voided again in a few hours. The hematocrit fell to 50.

Additional data were obtained at the time of his crisis as follows:

Blood Chemical Analyses

Plasma chloride	103	mE. per l.
Plasma sodium	132	mE. per l.
Plasma potassium	7.8	mE. per l.
Carbon dioxide combining power	20.4	mE. per l.

Electrocardiogram: "acidosis or potassium intoxication" (peaking of T-waves).

On treatment his potassium fell in five hours to 6.3 mE. per l., and overnight to 5.0 mE. per l.

The next day he was given intravenous adrenocorticotropic hormone (25 units in eight hours) to reestablish adrenal structure and function and to test adrenal response. Over the next five days he was given daily adrenocorticotropic hormone (gel). Six days later he was given another intravenous adrenocorticotropic hormone test. This period of adrenocorticotropic hormone testing showed that, the day after the crisis, the patient could summon an essentially normal response with a rise in free blood 17-hydroxycorticosterone (on hydrocortisone) from 14.9 mcg. per 100 ml. to 50 mcg. per 100 ml. in four hours. A week later his response was essentially the same.

He was then operated upon with cortisone coverage at the dose level of 100 mg. every eight hours intravenously (by constant infusion). Postoperatively the cortisone was to be tapered off with adrenocorticotropic hormone coverage.

Even with these precautions, his course was not entirely smooth following his one-stage ileostomy and total colectomy (ether anesthesia). Blood replacement totaled 2000 ml. The operation itself was uneventful, as were the first postoperative twenty-four hours. The patient was given penicillin and streptomycin. Cortisone totaled 300 mg. the day of operation and 150 mg. (plus 20 units adrenocorticotropic hormone gel) the first postoperative day. The eosinophil count fell to 4 per cu. mm. with operation. On the second postoperative day, despite intravenous therapy of 2200 ml. he again complained of weakness and an "all gone" feeling. Measured extrarenal loss was small at first (100 ml. ileostomy, 550 ml. gastric) but soon increased to large losses by tube and ileostomy. Urine volume fell to

20 ml. per hour, and the hematocrit rose to 48.5 and then to 51 in eighteen hours. The patient's abdomen became distended. Urine volume was small and concentration was near maximal at a specific gravity of 1.035. Blood pressure was maintained but pulse rose from 80 to 110.

ARGUMENT. Again the patient is in a critical situation with acute plasma deficit as indicated by the rising hematocrit. But now he has a low urine volume with maximum urine concentration. His abdomen is distended and extrarenal losses are mounting.

There are many features of this picture which differentiate it sharply from the acute adrenal insufficiency of ten days previously. Blood pressure is well maintained, there is no hyperkalemia (whereas the potassium rose to 7.8 mE. per l. during the adrenal crisis). Eosinophil count is very low but, possibly most important, the readily available clinical data indicate an appropriate cause for the situation. The patient has acute desalting water loss by tube and ileostomy and he has two areas of extracellular fluid sequestration: the pelvic dissection and the lumen of atonic bowel.

Hormone therapy was deemed adequate. Indeed, it is a tribute to the homeostatic significance of hydrocortisone that, on moderate dosage, he weathered this volume-reducing threat with little major disturbance of blood pressure or flow.

Treatment was devoted primarily to fluid replacement and blood volume.

FURTHER COURSE. The intravenous administration of hydrocortisone at the level of 150 mg. per day and of adrenocorticotropic hormone gel 20 units twice daily was continued; water, salt, and albumin administration was stepped up to a comfortable excess over the rather considerable extrarenal losses for two days. Total losses ran to about 3600 ml. per day, therapy about 6400. His hematocrit fell to 38.5; urine output picked up, the specific gravity fell to 1.025, and the patient improved clinically. A low-grade fever persisted. He was given 1000 ml. of whole blood over a two-day period.

Electrolyte loss analyses during this phase showed:

	URINE			ILEOSTOMY		
	Na	*K*	*Cl*	*Na*	*K*	*Cl*
Third postoperative day	3	61	89	115	11	106
Fourth postoperative day	45	65		118	50	
Seventh postoperative day	245	14		97	3	

During this period (third and fourth postoperative days) plasma analysis showed a slight tendency to hyponatremia (133 mE. per l.) and hyperkalemia (4.6 mE. per l.), but this was never pronounced. By the sixth day, after large extrarenal losses, the potassium concentration fell to 2.9 mE. per l. (without alkalosis), later returning to normal.

During the next few days large gastrointestinal outputs (up to 5700 ml. via ileostomy plus Levin tube) continued to pose a problem which was met by suitably large infusions.

Six days after the operation, the patient's intravenous ration of hydrocortisone was stopped. Adrenocortico-

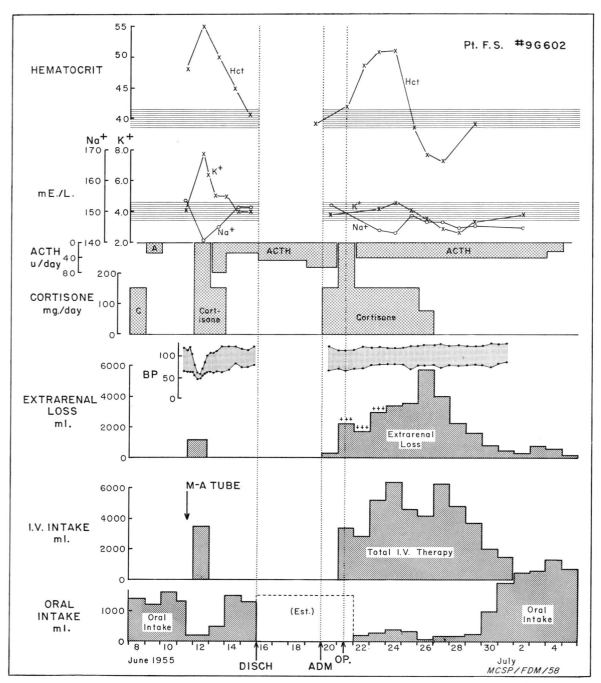

Figure 124. EVENTS IN PREPARATION FOR COLECTOMY (Case 23)

In the two ordinates above are shown the blood and plasma values; below them are shown successively the hormone dosage, extrarenal loss, intravenous intake, and oral intake. The reader is referred to the text for details.

It will be noted that the first episode, that of acute adrenal insufficiency, was accompanied by plasma loss (high hematocrit), marked sodium: potassium shift, and severe hypotension responding to cortisone. The

extrarenal loss required to produce this was minimal.

By contrast, the second episode, though associated with a like reduction in functional extracellular and plasma volume as indicated by hematocrit elevation, was not associated with sodium:potassium shift of any magnitude, nor with hypotension. It required extensive resalting for its repair and responded well to intravenous replacement on constant cortisone (later stopped with adrenocorticotropic hormone coverage).

Page 772

tropic hormone gel was continued at the rate of 20 units twice daily; his gastrointestinal tone gradually returned. A large collection of semipurulent material in the posterior wound was drained on the fourteenth day and the patient was discharged ten days later. Adrenocorticotropic hormone was stopped at the time of discharge.

COMMENT. The postoperative episode showed a marked contrast to the preoperative adrenal crisis. During the postoperative period there was the sequestration of fluid in the area of pelvic dissection and in the lumen of an atonic bowel; very large extrarenal losses added to the acute extracellular fluid reduction signaled by the poor clinical condition and the elevated hematocrit. In response to this challenge there was an appropriate reduction of urine volume and sodium excretion (unlike the adrenal crisis) and good maintenance of blood pressure. Electrolyte concentration changes were minimal, and the entire episode was a clear example of isotonic volume reduction due to mixed extrarenal loss and extracellular fluid sequestra-

tion, responding well to energetic replacement of water, salt, and albumin.

In contrast, the preoperative episode was characterized by renal sodium wasting, failure to maintain blood pressure, severe hyperkalemia, eosinophilia, and a specific response to steroid therapy.

SUMMARY. In one case are shown the contrasting appearances of two responses to extracellular fluid volume reduction. First, the patient developed an episode of adrenal insufficiency resulting from cortisone-induced adrenal atrophy combined with the challenge of rather minor extrarenal salt loss, with profound shock. Second, on apparently adequate adrenal corticosteroid replacement therapy the patient developed a severe postoperative extracellular fluid volume reduction with comparable plasma volume deficit, as indicated by the hematocrit rise, yet underwent an appropriate physiologic response and recovery after adequate resalting, without change in steroid therapy.

CASE 24

In Which Severe Hypertonicity and Volume Reduction Follow Intracranial Surgery; an Important Lesson Is Learned the Hard Way

Case 24. Patient L. S., #5L245.* Female. Age 43. Admitted August 20, 1957. Died September 4, 1957.

DIAGNOSIS. Craniopharyngioma.

OPERATION. Left frontal craniotomy with excision of craniopharyngioma.

CLINICAL SUMMARY. This woman had consulted an ophthalmologist three years ago because of recent headaches and loss of vision in the left eye. Before then she had been well except for appendectomy at the age of nineteen and long-standing menometrorrhagia with infertility. Bitemporal hemianopsia was noted, and confirmed by a neurosurgeon who found no other neurologic deficit. Skull films showed minimal enlargement of the sella turcica and posterior clinoid erosion. At right frontal craniotomy in December of 1955 the bulk of a craniopharyngioma was removed. Vision improved on the right but remained poor on the left.

Nine months following operation progressive loss of visual acuity, early optic nerve atrophy, and progression of nasal visual field defects were halted for a time by external irradiation of 4800 r through bitemporal ports. The patient continued to function domestically, although a two-month period of memory loss and intermittent disorientation occurred in mid-1956. Visual symptoms and headaches recurred again two years after operation, but little if any improvement resulted from external irradiation of 3200 r and headaches continued.

---

* The author is indebted to Dr. William G. Hammond for collecting the data and analyzing the course of this patient.

In June 1957 she could count fingers at twelve feet using the right eye but only at three feet on the left. Since then she had become totally blind on the left and had more frequent memory lapses. Since operation, mild diabetes insipidus had been readily controlled by Pitressin injections biweekly. Maintenance hydrocortisone dosage was 20 mg. per day and thyroid one grain twice a day.

At the time of admission to the Peter Bent Brigham Hospital, physical examination revealed a short plump woman with slightly coarse skin and hair. Blood pressure was 100/70, pulse 70. There was bilateral optic atrophy, total blindness on the left, and only a limited nasal field on the right. Memory deficit was apparent on simple testing. Scars from previous operations were noted.

Skull X-rays showed supra- and retrosellar calcification with posterior clinoid thinning. A pneumoencephalogram revealed only poor filling of the ventricular system. Electrocardiogram was compatible with a deep midline disturbance.

No increase in urinary excretion of 17-hydroxycorticoids or 17-ketosteroids occurred after adrenocorticotropic hormone administration. Plasma protein-bound iodine was 6.6 gamma per 100 ml. Although daily urine volumes were only slightly over 2 l. without Pitressin administration, specific gravity was never above 1.015 and usually around 1.008.

INITIAL LABORATORY WORK

Urine

Specific gravity	1.004–1.015
pH	5.5
Otherwise normal	

Hematology

| Hematocrit | 36 | |
| Leucocyte count | 8800 | per cu. mm. |

Blood Chemical Analyses

Blood urea nitrogen	9	mg. per 100 ml.
Plasma chloride	116	mE. per l.
Plasma sodium	147	mE. per l.
Plasma potassium	3.9	mE. per l.
Carbon dioxide combin- ing power	21.6	mE. per l.
Fasting blood sugar	65	mg. per 100 ml.

OPERATION.   On the ninth hospital day, through a left frontal craniotomy, a large craniopharyngioma was removed from above and behind the sella turcica. The tumor had almost completely destroyed the optic nerves and chiasm and had extended into the anterior hypothalamus. Although the operation was a lengthy and tedious one, the patient withstood it well and responded to simple commands immediately upon arrival in the recovery room.

During the first forty-eight hours a variable right hemiparesis was present. She was totally blind. A tendency toward crowing respiration without abnormal findings in the chest was presumably related to the endotracheal tube, and responded to humidification of the ambient air. Oral intake was tolerated fairly well but not pushed. Daily, 200 mg. of hydrocortisone was being given by vein. Vital signs were stable except for a persistent fever which ranged from 102 to 104° F. rectally and could be lowered only by vigorous cold alcohol sponging. Output (three days) of dilute urine (specific gravity 1.004 to 1.010) totaled 5645 ml. and intake had been 7045 ml. by the morning of the third postoperative day, when these laboratory values were obtained.

Hematocrit	38	

Blood Chemical Analyses on Third Postoperative Day

Blood urea nitrogen	11	mg. per 100 ml.
Plasma chloride	130	mE. per l.
Plasma sodium	162	mE. per l.
Plasma potassium	3.0	mE. per l.
Carbon dioxide combining power	26.8	mE. per l.

COMMENT.   Severe hypertonicity is to be explained and treated. It is not long compatible with life.

Hypophysectomized patients rarely need salt-retaining steroids for sodium homeostasis. In this instance, doses of hydrocortisone were being given during the period when endogenous sodium-conserving forces were maximal. Fever of central origin after brain injury is not usually accompanied by the profuse diaphoresis seen in septic fevers. There were no extrarenal sodium losses. For these reasons, it seemed reasonable to attribute the rise in plasma sodium and chloride concentrations in part to retention of most of the 310 mE. of sodium chloride in the postoperative intravenous infusions and in part to a severe water deficit as evidenced by a positive sensible water balance of only 460 ml. per day for

three days.* Such was the reasoning of those caring for the patient, and an increased water intake was begun. Serial body weights would have been helpful in more surely eliciting the genesis of this hypernatremia, but were not carried out. But of greatest significance— unnoted at the time—were the very low urine specific gravities in the face of severe hypertonicity. This is the trademark of diabetes insipidus.

It was also noteworthy that the patient had made a start in this direction prior to operation (sodium 147 mE. per l., chloride 116 mE. per l.) and was low on water relative to solute even at that time.

FURTHER COURSE.   Blindness, right hemiparesis, and pyrexia persisted. No extracranial cause for the fever was found on physical examination. Mental status varied from stupor to cooperative orientation. Oral intake increased to include soft solids on the fifth postoperative day. Urine continued to be dilute. Intake-output data were:

DAY	IN ml.	OUT ml.	SENSIBLE CUMULATIVE BALANCE ml.
Day of operation	1200	580	+620
First postoperative day	1880	1810	+690
Second postoperative day	3965	3255	+1400
Third postoperative day	3745	4100	+1045
Fourth postoperative day	4930	4825	+1150

Starting around 2:00 A.M. of the fifth day after operation, the patient progressively developed fever to 105° F., coma, mild cyanosis of lips and nails, tachypnea, and tachycardia. A marked cyanosis, with slight mottling, was present over an unusual boot-like distribution involving both feet and ankles but stopping abruptly just above the malleoli. Mild edema was present in the cyanosed area; none elsewhere. The carotids were the only pulses palpable as blood pressure became unobtainable. No oscillations could be detected in any extremity. The chest and abdomen were negative.

Prompt administration of 200 mg. of hydrocortisone intravenously produced no response, although blood pressure could be maintained with rather large doses of intravenous Neo-synephrine. No change in palpability of pulses was noted, however. Neither left paravertebral block nor procaine injections into the left femoral artery produced a significant change in the feet. Electrocardiogram demonstrated the changes of hypokalemia and anterior myocardial ischemia.

By 3:00 P.M. only 220 ml. of urine had been passed since the onset of the acute episode twelve hours earlier. The most recent specimen had a specific gravity of 1.016. During this period 1200 ml. of 5 per cent dextrose in water and 500 mg. of hydrocortisone had

---

* The "positive sensible water balance" is merely the recorded intake-output balance; in a normal resting person it is +500 to +750 ml. a day. With fever it would be expected to be about +1000 ml. per day.

been infused. Results of analyses of blood drawn at 10:00 A.M. were:

Hematocrit	35	
Blood Chemical Analyses		
Blood urea nitrogen	84	mg. per 100 ml.
Plasma chloride	134	mE. per l.
Plasma sodium	187	mE. per l.
Plasma potassium	4.5	mE. per l.
Carbon dioxide combining power	17.7	mE. per l.
Plasma osmolality	412	mO. per l.

ARGUMENT. When a hypotensive catastrophe occurs in a patient with known adrenocortical disease, immediate and massive steroid therapy is paramount. Though the presumption of acute adrenal insufficiency may be later shown to be erroneous, no harm is done. Indeed, in many instances this measure is of great diagnostic help since lack of response strongly suggests that adrenal insufficiency is absent. Such was the case in this patient; time had been wasted on cortisone therapy, no response had been obtained but no other harm had been done.

Having ruled out an Addisonian crisis, another metabolic defect, known in this case to be present, came up for consideration. Diabetes insipidus causes only inconvenience to a conscious and well-oriented patient whose thirst will keep him appraised of his fluid needs for balancing a large urine output. In those insipid diabetics unable to increase their fluid intake voluntarily, the physician must either provide sufficient fluid to meet any increased need or administer vasopressin to lower the need. *Although these intake-output data would not indicate a serious water deficit in a patient with a normal insensible water loss, this patient had been markedly febrile for five days and mildly tachypneic; these urine volumes are large for such a circumstance and the cumulative sensible water balance less than one-third what it should be to cover the pulmonary water losses of this patient.* This history, plus the physical evidences of marked fluid volume reduction—loss of blood pressure with very severe generalized vasoconstriction and oliguria—, provides ample indication for administration of a trial water load. The clinical diagnosis of true desiccation-dehydration was fully confirmed by the blood chemical values.

The role of diabetes insipidus here was deceptive. Because of its apparent mildness, as judged from daily urine volumes, it was not thought to be a proximate cause of this severe desiccation-dehydration. A normal individual, however, undergoing a very large insensible water loss will simultaneously decrease urine output markedly. This compensatory renal water retention in the normal, indicated by neurohypophyseal antidiuretic hormone, is lost in diabetes insipidus. *The only endogenous cutoff mechanism available to an insipid diabetic is cessation of renal blood flow as circulatory collapse develops.* In this instance, oliguria and shock secondary to desiccation-dehydration finally occurred. But prior to that time clear indication of pathologic renal water loss was given by the continuing volume—though low—of low-specific-gravity urine in the face of severe hypertonicity.

The electrocardiogram is of interest in that it shows the pattern of hypokalemia although plasma potassium concentration is at the upper limit of normal. Intracellular osmolality (predominantly potassium) parallels extracellular osmolality (predominantly sodium) when changes occur because of altered bodily hydration. In this instance of desiccation-dehydration, intracellular potassium concentration is estimated to be about 195 mE. per l. Since electrocardiographic evidence regarding potassium status is often dependent upon the ratio of intracellular to extracellular potassium concentration, the present ratio of 195:4.5, or 43, has the same effect upon the electrocardiogram as would a plasma potassium of 3.2 mE. per l. in the presence of the normal intracellular potassium level of 147 mE. per l. The extracellular hypernatremia yields the electrocardiographic appearances of hypokalemia under a wide variety of circumstances.

No adequate evaluation of the level of possible aortic, iliac, or femoral artery occlusion can be made until volume replacement enables blood pressure maintenance without vasopressors. The striking boot-like demarcation of pedal cyanosis rather suggests diffuse distal venous thrombosis, or "venous gangrene," a very rare syndrome for which treatment is expectant at best.

The lack of hematocrit rise in the presence of drastic hypertonicity leads to suspicion of occult blood loss, although there was no external evidence of bleeding. A check of stools and gastric aspirate would not have been amiss.

FURTHER COURSE. About twelve hours after the onset of this catastrophe, a liter of 5 per cent dextrose in water was infused very rapidly. Within 20 minutes of starting the infusion urine flow increased markedly, shortly reaching 300 ml. per hour. Over the next seven hours 3 more liters of 5 per cent dextrose in water was given, resulting in 2500 ml. of urine with specific gravities of from 1.010 to 1.014. As the patient's temperature had remained around 100° F. rectally since early morning, insensible loss should have been much less than before. The net sensible water balance since the catastrophe was then + 2500 ml. As a result, blood studies now revealed:

Hematocrit	25	
Blood Chemical Analyses		
Blood urea nitrogen	44	mg. per 100 ml.
Plasma chloride	109	mE. per l.
Plasma sodium	141	mE. per l.
Plasma potassium	3.9	mE. per l.
Carbon dioxide combining power	14.8	mE. per l.
Plasma osmolality	349	mO. per l.

The hematocrit fall of 10 and the plasma sodium decrease of 46 mE. per l. observed after rehydration are more marked than might be expected from the diluting effect of 2500 ml., since this amount increased extracellular fluid and plasma volumes only about 10 per cent. These changes are, however, compatible with loss of both blood and sodium prior to those determinations (done at the time of maximal dehydration) and again raise the question of concomitant blood loss. Guaiac-positive stool and dark bloody gastric aspirate confirmed this suspicion. A check of clotting parameters showed that the clotting time was fifteen minutes, bleeding time greater than fifteen minutes, and platelets were considered adequate on peripheral blood smear.

Cortisone dosage was decreased to 50 mg. in eight hours, antacids were given via nasogastric tube, and three units of blood were administered during the night. The generalized cyanosis of the feet was noted to decrease and mottling was more pronounced. Cutdown sites and oral mucosa slowly oozed blood. Both radial pulses returned by 7:00 A.M. and the rate of Neo-synephrine drip could be decreased without fall in blood pressure.

Laboratory work done on blood drawn at 8:00 A.M. showed:

Hematology

Hematocrit	25
Platelet count	125,000 per cu. mm.

Blood Chemical Analyses

pH	7.56	
pCo_2	22	mm. Hg
TCO_2	19.9	mM. per l.
HCO_3	19.2	mM. per l.
Plasma chloride	111	mE. per l.
Plasma sodium	141	mE. per l.
Plasma potassium	2.6	mE. per l.
Plasma osmolality	349	mO. per l.

During the interval between sets of laboratory data intravenous intake was 3050 ml. of 5 per cent dextrose and water and urine output was 2700 ml.

By midday femoral and popliteal pulses were palpable bilaterally. The patient now responded slightly, and moved her extremities voluntarily at intervals.

Comment. The remarkable return of blood pressure and pulses after restoration of blood volume and rehydration is of considerable interest in relation to the paralysis of central sympathetic function earlier manifested by marked hyperpyrexia without sweating. It is indeed rare to encounter such prolonged hypotension without apparent myocardial damage or acute tubular necrosis as a consequence.

Massive steroid therapy is a well-known cause for gastrointestinal bleeding; acute gastric ulceration is often associated with brain injury, particulary hypothalamic. The combined effects of steroid therapy and brain damage provided ample reason for upper intestinal bleeding here. Although heparinization was considered early as of possible benefit for the foot condition, the potential hazard of intracranial bleeding was fortunately thought a contraindication. No hematologic cause for the prolonged bleeding time could be ascertained.

There is some discrepancy apparent between the plasma osmolality of 349 mO. per l. and the plasma sodium of 141 mE. per l. Summating the accountable osmolality, sodium, plus other cations (potassium,

calcium, etc.), will total about 150 mO. per l. The demands of electro-neutrality provide another 150 mO. per l. as anion, and the blood urea nitrogen of 44 mg. per 100 ml. is equivalent to 16 mO. per l. of urea. The remainder, 33 mO. per l., would be accounted for were the blood sugar concentration 594 mg. per 100 ml., a level quite compatible with brisk administration of 5 per cent dextrose solution into three different veins simultaneously as was the situation when this blood sample was drawn.

FURTHER COURSE. During the fifth postoperative day, the patient's general condition seemed about the same. She responded to painful stimuli but otherwise remained stuporous. Respirations became slightly labored in the midafternoon but chest was clear. Blood pressure remained stable. Total intravenous intake was 14,250 ml. of 5 per cent dextrose in water from 8:00 A.M. to midnight and urine output was 14,470 ml. over the same period. Pink urine was noted about 8:00 P.M. and this color persisted. Plasma from blood drawn around 10:00 P.M. was noted to be pink also. Blood studies at this time showed:

Hematology

Hematocrit	25	
Clotting time	11	minutes

Blood Chemical Analyses

pH	7.48	
pCo_2	33	mm. Hg
TCO_2	24.6	mM. per l.
HCO_3	23.6	mM. per l
Blood urea nitrogen	23	mg. per 100 ml.
Plasma chloride	90	mE. per l.
Plasma sodium	124	mE. per l.
Plasma potassium	2.2	mE. per l.
Plasma osmolality	328	mO. per l.

A unit of whole blood was given slowly. From midnight until 5:00 A.M. 4850 ml. of fluid was infused, in approximately equal parts as 5 per cent dextrose in saline and 5 per cent dextrose in water. To the fluids was added 80 mE. of potassium chloride. In spite of 2 units of Pitressin given intramuscularly at 1:00 A.M. and 5 units at 4:00 A.M., 3810 ml. of urine was produced with specific gravity never rising above the previous maximum of 1.015.

The patient's clinical condition steadily deteriorated during the night, with less and less effective respirations. Spinal fluid pressure at 1:00 A.M. was 225 mm. of water. Intermittent vomiting of feculent material preceded cessation of respirations and death at 6:15 A.M.

Comment. On clinical grounds it is difficult to specify a single primary cause for death. Certainly an acutely developing plasma potassium of 2.2 mE. per l. is not long compatible with life. The progressive deterioration of respiration in the absence of abnormal auscultatory findings suggests central respiratory involvement. Assignment of a proper role to the acute shock episode is equivocal. More fluid sooner plus more vigorous attempts to combat respiratory alkalosis might have affected the outcome.

It is pertinent to question the wisdom of withholding vasopressin for so long. In our experience with hypophysectomy for metastatic breast carcinoma it has been found that early attempts to regulate water balance, in those patients developing diabetes insipidus, were difficult and fraught with the hazard of water intoxication and consequent cerebral edema. It proved to be both simpler and safer to balance output and intake until needs stabilized some time toward the end of the second week after operation. This patient differed from the usual hypophysectomy patient in that she was unconscious and the hypothalamic damage producing hyperpyrexia led to a greatly increased insensible water loss.

Autopsy findings tended to confirm the clinical diagnosis. The floor of the third ventricle, the infundibulum, and the preoptic structures were not identifiable as such, and most of the hypothalamus was replaced by amorphous hemorrhagic tissue. Diffuse atrophy of the pituitary and thyroid was noted. The zona glomerulosa of the adrenals was hypertrophied, the remainder of the glands was atrophic. These are the endocrine changes of longstanding anterior pituitary insufficiency. Deep and superficial venous thromboses of both legs were present in the perimalleolar areas, while the arteries were patent. A diffuse erosive gastritis proved to be the source of gastrointestinal blood loss.

SUMMARY. In summary, this was a case in which diabetes insipidus was responsible for severe hypertonicity and volume reduction; persistent urine volumes were later masked by shock; the only therapeutic response of significance was obtained by water infusion; earlier recognition and more effective treatment with water and Pitressin might have rescued this patient in whom brain damage (at postmortem) was so massive as to have made rescue unmerciful.

The lesson to be learned is that hypertonicity after cranial trauma should always excite suspicion as to the presence of diabetes insipidus. Unconsciousness hides thirst; urine volumes need not be large; insensible loss is high; urine specific gravity is low despite hypertonicity. It is this type of situation that has been interpreted as indicative of an ill-defined "hypertonicity center" in the brain, damage to which produces a peculiar hypertonic disorder. The "center" involved is the osmoreceptor. The disorder produced is diabetes insipidus. The diagnosis is often obscure and the urine volume low (in shock). Such a lesson may help to rescue others whose outlook is more favorable.

Fractures, Wounds, and Burns

Contents of Part VI

CHAPTER 44. BONE, MUSCLE, AND IMMOBILIZATION; METABOLIC ASPECTS PECULIAR TO FRACTURES AND WOUNDS

CHAPTER 45. TREATMENT OF WOUNDS AND SEVERE MULTIPLE INJURY

CHAPTER 46. FRACTURES IN THE ELDERLY; THE FRACTURED HIP; METABOLISM IN FRACTURES, AND THE USE OF ANABOLIC STEROIDS

Fractures and Trauma: Cases

CHAPTER 47. BURNS

CHAPTER 48. ATOMIC INJURY

CHAPTER 49. CLOSING

CHAPTER 44

Bone, Muscle, and Immobilization; Metabolic Aspects Peculiar to Fractures and Wounds

Section I.   Traumatic Edema

A. THE INITIAL TRAUMA AND TRAUMATIC EDEMA

Bones—healthy bones—do not break easily. It requires the application of a sudden strong force to produce a major fracture in a healthy individual. The amount of force involved is greater than that required for incisions, contusions, or lacerations. Missiles dissipate an even greater energy in tissues. Both, therefore, create an injury much larger than is apparent. The kinetic energy of this impact is absorbed in the tissues, not only of the bone that is broken or the missile track, but also in the muscles and surrounding soft tissues.

In the immediate neighborhood of a fracture, this force (plus the lacerating motion of the bone ends) is responsible for a central zone of necrosing trauma to muscles, fasciae, vessels, and nerves. Equally important, the dissipation of this force is responsible for a much wider zone of hemorrhage and fluid loss in the form of traumatic edema. This loss of fluid brings in its wake a persistent volume reduction, with its inevitable tendency to hypotension and shock. Renal ischemia, hemoglobinemia, and myglobinemia, renal failure, and anaerobic myositis are therefore traceable to the dissipation of this fracturing force and are characteristic of the early fracture, the crushing, contusing wound, or the cavitation of a high-velocity missile.

In addition, the local injury around a wound creates an area of increased vascular and capillary permeability, due not only to the dissipation of the energy of the initial blow through the soft tissues but also to the repeated mechanical trauma of broken bone fragments moving about in the surrounding tissues prior to immobilization. This area is especially large if the surface of the injury is large or if fragmentation of bone is extensive. At the center of this area is a multilocular cavity where there is hemorrhage from many small vessels. Surrounding this central area is a zone where capillary permeability is increased without bleeding, the site of transudation of protein-rich plasma. Finally, in the periphery of the injury there is a borderline rim-zone of lesser injury, in which the tendency to fluid accumulation is limited to salt and water, the peripheral capillary maintaining its normal impermeability to protein.

Because of this area of traumatic edema, fracture patients need the infusion of blood, protein, salt, and water, and show a tendency, both systemic and local in origin, to reduce the excretion of salt and water.

The tendency to retention of salt and water observed after any form of injury pulls sodium salts and water back from the glomerular filtrate. If volume reduction occurs, glomerular filtration is reduced, the tubule is ischemic, and all renal excretory functions are reduced. In addition, and quite independent of such renal phenomena, extracellular fluid is sequestered locally in the area of wound edema and cannot be diuresed until resorbed. Thus, the excretory changes are both renal and peripheral in origin; they are glomerular, tubular, and sequestrational. The analogy of this situation to that of a burn or peritonitis is too close to need further elaboration.

B. DIURESIS

Diuresis of this fluid should occur when the tubule is released from the influence of aldosterone-like and posterior-pituitary-hormone– like influences, but in addition, local healing must have gone far enough to restore capillary permeability to normal, so that the protein on the inside of the capillary may summon the water and salt of the sequestered extracellular fluid back into the blood stream, where it is in turn presented to the glomerulus for excretion. The net result is post-traumatic diuresis, an important and favorable sign after severe injury.

C. TIME RELATIONSHIPS AND BLOOD STREAM FINDINGS

The time relationships of this sequence are variable. The tendency to volume reduction may persist for as long as seventy-two hours. If the area of traumatic edema is very great, as in missile injury to the thigh or buttocks, or an injury such as a crush, then the patient may maintain his weight during initial treatment, or actually gain weight for several days (exactly as in a burn) until diuresis ensues. If the patient is poorly treated and is given large amounts of colloid-free solutions such as saline, so that his plasma protein concentration is lowered by dilution, the onset of diuresis will obviously be delayed. His traumatic edema will last longer because the colloid osmotic pressure differential required to withdraw fluid across the injured capillary is less easily developed.

The hematocrit is a totally unreliable guide to volume needs here in mixed tissue trauma. During the accumulation of traumatic edema, the patient's blood stream shows a mixed loss of cells, protein, and extracellular fluid. If these were all to be lost in the exact proportion that they exist in the blood stream, the hematocrit changes of acute hemorrhage might be expected to ensue: an initial loss of volume without initial change in hematocrit, followed by a subsequent dilutional anemia. If, on the other hand, the nature of the injury is such as to produce a wide area of increased permeability to water, salt, and protein but not to red cells, then the patient becomes hypotensive owing to volume reduction, yet he has an elevated hematocrit as in a burn. Actually all mixtures are observed. It is thus evident that the exact balance among these various types of loss determines changes in blood concentration, and is totally unpredictable in any given injury.

As guides to volume needs one must use the patient's history, physical findings as to color, mentation, blood pressure and flow, pulse, and urine volume.

It should be emphasized again that the usefulness of the hematocrit (or erythrocyte count or hemoglobin concentration) in evaluating and reconstructing previous changes in blood volume is in a descending scale as follows:

1. *Very Useful.* In *burns and peritonitis*, where erythrocyte loss is small and plasma loss is large, the degree of hematocrit elevation is an accurate index of the plasma need at any given moment.

2. *Helpful.* Following *simple, single, massive hemorrhage* with stabilized hemodilution, the fall of the hematocrit provides an accurate index of the amount of blood previously lost, providing the patient has sufficient circulation and body fluid remaining to complete his transcapillary refilling and providing the changes are properly viewed as a function of time.

3. *Very Little Help.* In the *mixed situation of multiple hemorrhages* or repeated hemorrhages treated by the administration of fluids and transfusions, there is a multiplicity of factors bearing on the hematocrit. It is less useful in the equilibrated state, though it may indicate

approximately the amount of the final hemodilution.

4. *No Help.* And finally, in the situation considered here, of peripheral mechanical trauma or other mixed losses of fluid, colloid, and cells, the hematocrit is an entirely unreliable guide to volume changes.

Section II. Catabolic Effects

A. NITROGEN LOSS AND WEIGHT CHANGE

The tendency to lose nitrogen is greater after certain fractures—particularly long-bone fractures—than one might be led to predict on the basis of the magnitude of the readily apparent injury to the soft tissue. This loss of nitrogen from the body pursues its course for ten days to three weeks (in such an injury as a midshaft fracture of the femur) despite intakes of calories and nitrogen well above the normal requirement for the individual. A young man having a fracture of the femur may not have much appetite for a day or two, but quite soon thereafter he will regain his desire to eat, and through a course of two or three weeks he may eat well, with large amounts of calories and nitrogen, and still be in negative nitrogen balance. In this respect, the metabolism of fractures is unlike that of lesser injury to the viscera and the serous cavities, where resumption of the ability to eat (as evidenced by normal peristalsis and gastrointestinal function) seems to occur at or near the time when the body is ready to begin anabolism.

The remarkable wasting of tissue involved in fracture is due to many factors besides cross-sectional tissue injury, including immobilization and disuse atrophy of local muscle groups. As an example, consider the case of a middle-aged man with bilateral compound comminuted femoral fractures incurred in an auto accident. His course initially will be marked by shock requiring several transfusions, though there will be little external bleeding. Operative fixation will stabilize the fractures, and by the end of a week his appetite should be restored and he will be eating a solid diet with gusto. Initial massive swelling of the thigh will subside on about the fourth day with a large diuresis of water and salt. Atrophy of muscle groups and loss of weight will then continue. Quadriceps, abdominal muscles, and gastrocnemii will waste rapidly despite active exercise; fat will gradually disappear for two months and then begin to reaccumulate. The patient will be immobilized in traction for about four months and during that time will lose 5 to 10 kg. of muscle— a sizable fraction of his total muscle mass.

Occurring under these circumstances, and with good diet, normal visceral function, and no avitaminosis, this loss of body tissue and protein is no obstruction to recovery. It is a part (whether good or bad we cannot say) and a seemingly inevitable aspect of severe injury and fracture. Forced feedings have little beneficial effect; vitamins are an essential therapeutic adjunct; dietary intake must be maintained at the highest acceptable level. Were sepsis, starvation, or visceral failure (heart, liver, lungs) to enter the picture, there would be a different course and a different outcome.

Had the patient, through some endocrine-metabolic treatment, now unknown, been able to pass through this long evolution without loss of body tissue, he of course would have had much less "work" to do in bodily reconstruction in late convalescence.

The loss of nitrogen after fracture of long bones (and after complex trauma and wounds) is due partly to the excretion in the urine of the end-products of the destruction of blood that has been diffused through the tissues as a result of the initial trauma. As regards nitrogen, blood is a low-phosphorus, low-calcium tissue in comparison with muscle (higher in phosphorus) and bone (higher in calcium). Thus, the nitrogen loss of blood destruction is relatively high in phosphorus as well as being characterized by large amounts of urobilinogen in the feces (as a prime index of the excretion of the end-products of porphyrin metabolism).

A total of 2000 ml. of blood in the tissues will account, for example, for the excretion of 60 gm. of nitrogen, 760 mg. of phosphorus, and 110 mg. of calcium during the first ten days after a midshaft femoral fracture. This gives blood a nitrogen:phosphorus ratio of 77.6:1, as compared with lean tissue (14.7:1), a calcium:phosphorus ratio of 0.14:1, as compared with bone (2.23:1). The potassium:nitrogen ratio (1.53:1) is low as compared with whole muscle tissue (2.8:1). This excretion of the end-products of blood destruction will be accentuated during a period of generalized tissue breakdown; were the patient to be in an anabolic phase, the nitrogen moieties of the blood could be reutilized for synthesis. The excretion of urobilinogen in the feces remains the most accurate index of the rate of excretion of the end-products of blood destruction.

B. CALCIUM METABOLISM

Contrary to the general impression, major fractures do not result in the urinary excretion of large amounts of calcium and phosphorus.

1. Amount, Rate, and Source

On a 200 mg. calcium diet the normal urinary excretion is from 50 to 150 mg. On a lower intake, it is less. After a fracture of the femur in a young man the urinary calcium excretion rarely runs higher than 200 mg. per day, and the intake is usually 200 mg. or less. There is thus a slight tendency to negative balance but it is not in the same class as metastatic malignancy or hyperparathyroidism, when urinary calcium excretion often runs from 500 to 1000 mg. per day and demineralization of the skeleton is very rapid. If a fracture patient is fed a high-calcium diet during the early period of immobilization, the urinary calcium excretion is increased and the danger of renal stone intensified.

The background of this small loss of calcium in fracture may involve several sources. To begin with, one might suspect that there are some bits of chipped bone around the frac-

ture, of no use where they lie, which should be dissolved for redeposition elsewhere.

Next, one might reasonably predict that there would be loss of calcium from the disrupted bone immediately adjacent to the fracture site, and that this might also appear in the urine, since there is no other place for it to go unless the rest of the skeleton could take it on loan.

When we look at the rest of the skeleton we find a site from whence some of this calcium has come: there is evidence of widespread but mild skeletal decalcification after major fractures.

The studies of Deitrick, *et al.* (1948) show what extensive rigid immobilization in plaster cast does to calcium metabolism. Immobilization resulted in the loss of calcium, but an amount that was still short of the fracture range.

There is no consistently significant change in plasma concentrations of calcium, phosphorus, or alkaline phosphatase in patients after fracture.

2. The Local Wound Changes and Calcium Metabolism

After fracture, the initial sequences in the wound are those of the formation of an amorphous coagulum. In this the fibrillary structure of collagen is formed as a step toward the production of osteoid and final calcification to produce firm callus. The ultimate step, requiring many months or years, is the reorganization of this callus into the stress-conditioned trabecular structure of normal cortical bone.

One might expect the calcium to be "needed" by the local fracture site as soon as four weeks after the injury, when calcification becomes evident by X-ray. Considering the fact that the X-ray appearance of calcification requires the accumulation of large amounts of calcium, one may assume that the tendency of the osteoid to calcify must start several days or a week prior to the initial X-ray evidences of such activity. If this is the case, we would expect the fracture patient to start putting calcium down in his callus about fourteen days after an injury such as a midshaft fracture, providing, of course, that local bacteriologic and mechanical factors were favorable for fracture healing.

It has been postulated that the release of large amounts of nitrogen from the body after soft-tissue injury is a response in part to the need of the wound for raw materials and substrates so as to permit tissue synthesis in the wound to achieve tensile integrity during a period of starvation. The minor calcium release after fracture is subject to the same interpretation. The skeleton is a tremendous calcium reservoir just as striated muscle is a nitrogen reservoir. Many workers have sought to reverse the negative nitrogen balance after soft-tissue injury with the hope that somehow or other this might benefit the patient; up to now we have had no one interested in trying to prevent the hypercalciuria and negative calcium balance after fractures. It is evident enough that the healing of the fracture runs its course and that this minor hypercalciuria is a part of this normal course and not in competition with it; feeding the patient extra calcium is clearly dangerous to his kidneys.

3. Systemic Aspects of Calcium Metabolism

Turning from the local significance of altered calcium metabolism after fractures to the possible effects in other parts of the body, we find several clinically important facts. Most prominent is the tendency to renal calcinosis and the formation of stones. Considering the large number of individuals who suffer fractures and the relative rarity of calcinosis and formation of renal stones, one might assume that severe hypercalciuria was rare in fractures. This, as pointed out above, is indeed the case. Few fracture patients exhibit the persistent severe elevation of urine calcium excretion (over 500 mg. a day) that is characteristic of the stone-former in such a disease as hyperparathyroidism. Yet, if a healthy young man is badly injured and put to bed in a cast or traction for several weeks, and at the end of that time starts ureteral colic, goes through a long phase of renal and ureteral stone formation, obstruction, and retrograde infection, and develops chronic pyelonephritis as one of the complications of

his injury, it is quite evident that this statistically infrequent complication has become a major hazard.

Although the above appears to be a clear-cut pathogenesis, it is not an easy matter to relate increased calcium excretion to stone formation. Many people have hypercalciuria without forming stones. Colloids found in the urine may be of more importance in stone formation than the mere presence of calcium. Given a stone-forming tendency with abnormal urinary colloids, if one floods this kidney with excess calcium, stones are most likely to occur. If a person has a preexistent tendency to form stones, then fracture and immobilization may produce his first stone. It is clearly worth while to try to avoid this complication, whatever its detailed pathogenesis.

(1) *Temper the immobilization* with mobilization, muscular work, exercise of uninjured parts, partial weight bearing, or any other step that will increase the tensile work of the skeleton, thus maintaining its architectural calcium intact. Avoid prolonged recumbency if the fracture will permit it.

(2) *The patient should not be given extra calcium by mouth.* There is no evidence that large calcium intakes do healing fractures any good. The analogy with the futility of nitrogen provision early after soft-tissue wounding is compelling, as already mentioned. The addition of nitrogen to the diet does not alter the early phases of soft-tissue wound healing so far as we know; providing an excess of milk and calcium phosphate similarly has no effect on fracture healing, while the provision of a high calcium intake definitely increases urinary excretion of calcium and the risk of formation of stones.

(3) The patient should be provided with *adequate fluid and adequate urinary drainage* if he is not voiding well. Any infection is prone to alkalinize the urine and promote stone formation. The patient should drink very large amounts of fluid. This, more than any other factor, will tend to maintain the calcium in solution. If he has had previous stones, an acid-ash (ketogenic) diet is advisable. Oral salicylates may help to avoid the formation of stones.

Acute post-traumatic nephrocalcinosis with

renal failure and uremia is a rare complication that must involve, in its pathogenesis, some factor other than mobilization of cal-

cium, since hypercalciuria, alone, is a rare cause of intrarenal calcification.*

Section III.   Traumatized Muscle: A Special Tissue

A. MUSCLE GROUPS IN THE ERECT-WALKING BIPED

Man differs from all other animals, even his fellow primates, in the tremendous development of the musculature of the buttocks and thigh required to keep the "pelvic wheel" rotated to the upright posture. Though the gibbon, chimpanzee, and the gorilla stand and walk, they do not do so except on provocation; man is the only naturally erect-walking biped, and his muscles show it. Wounds in this area show most clearly the toxic manifestations of skeletal muscle trauma. Penetrating wounds in this area, being near the anus, are particularly apt to carry into the damaged muscle colonic organisms, many of them anaerobes. Whether the wound be a blunt crushing injury, a tourniquet type of injury, or a penetrating missile wound, muscle lesions in this area are associated with a high incidence of shock, renal failure, and death. This incidence is high when compared with wounds to the extremity lower down below the knee or with a similar injury to the upper extremity. Wounds of the abdomen, with their attendant incidence of peritoneal transudation, injury to hollow viscera, blood loss, and peritonitis, also have a high incidence of shock and a high fatality rate, but for a somewhat different reason than wounds in the area of the buttocks, pelvic-rectal structures, and upper thigh.

B. CELLULAR INJURY; PIGMENT RELEASE AND CATION EXCHANGE

It is in wounds of skeletal muscle that one finds the wound of the cell mass most significant. Skeletal muscle is a cellular tissue; not more than 8 to 12 per cent of wet muscle is extracellular. A large wound of muscle is therefore unique among wounds in the body in being a massive injury to a lean cellular

tissue. An extensive wound of the tibia and fibula above the ankle involves skin, tendon, periosteum, bone, blood vessels, and nerves. All of these tissues are almost wholly extracellular tissues and in none of them is the total cellular compartment greater than 10 per cent of the wet weight of the tissue. The only other tissue in the body capable of sustaining such a large cellular injury from direct trauma is the liver; and large destructive wounds of the liver, as, for instance, by the passage of a high-velocity missile through that organ are rapidly lethal. Whether this peculiar vulnerability of large masses of cellular tissues arises from the richness of the blood supply or from the leakage of cellular constituents into the extracellular phase remains uncertain.

The clinical types of skeletal muscle damage, any or all of which may combine to present toxic muscle products to the kidney and/or later develop anaerobic myositis, are:

(1) arterial injury with ischemia of the muscle groups supplied by that artery;

(2) venous obstruction with infarction;

(3) arteriovenous obstruction followed by release (tourniquet lesion);

(4) any of the above with crushing, tearing, amputating, or avulsing muscle bellies; cavitation of high-velocity missiles.

Any of the four, alone or in combination, can produce shock, heme pigments in blood and urine, or anaerobic myositis. These are the lesions that, occurring in buttocks and thigh, in the area from navel to knee, accounted for the majority of the cases of anaerobic myositis in World War I and post-traumatic renal failure in World War II and the Korean conflict.

Extensive injury to skeletal muscle thus appears to have an especially dire significance

---

* The section on the literature relative to metabolism in fractures will be found (page 844) following the section on fractures in Chapter 46.

for the organism. This is due to loss of functional extracellular and circulating plasma volume (that is, traumatic edema) into the damaged muscles and to the absorption of materials (that is, pigment and enzymes) from them. The question as to which of these two mechanisms is the active and important one is answered by "both." In addition, ischemic or injured muscle is prone to infection, and if the wound has been a penetrating one, infection is inevitable. Anaerobic myositis in skeletal muscle, unchecked, is rapidly lethal.

Injured muscle releases potassium and takes up sodium. One may assume that the muscle also releases phosphate, sulfate, magnesium, zinc, and calcium, and indeed any other substances that are found in the cells of muscle, including pigments and enzymes. It takes up from the extracellular phase not only sodium but also chloride, bicarbonate, extracellular solute protein, hormones, and other solutes present in the extracellular fluid. These changes occur because the injured cell surface has lost its discriminatory effect, an effect that requires circulation and the expenditure of energy. It is therefore not surprising that when there is extensive muscle damage there is a greater excretion of potassium and pigments in the urine (and a more rapid accumulation of potassium in the extracellular phase if renal function is poor) than in other injury.

Myoglobin or some other product of injured muscle appears to be toxic, quite aside from bacterial contamination or local fluid loss. A long series of experiments carried out during World War II were designed to test this hypothesis in the dog; they culminated in the demonstration that in the dog, ischemic muscle becomes, in a remarkably short period of time, the site of invasive sepsis involving exotoxin-producing anaerobic organisms. This finding of rapidly toxic anaerobiosis applies to man only when anaerobes are introduced by the wound, Man, unlike the dog, does not harbor anaerobic spores in normal muscle. Yet, quite aside from the occurrence of anaerobic sepsis, muscle trauma that produces dead muscle tissue in man is followed by a high incidence of renal failure, suggestively associated with an increased excretion of muscle pigments.

We are therefore left with the fact that injuries to large masses of striated muscle are dangerous, that they occur especially in the buttocks-thigh area, that blood loss, fluid loss, and anaerobic infection all play a role, and that absorption of intracellular materials from dying muscle is harmful, particularly to the kidney or in the presence of renal failure.

It is in this type of wound that surgical debridement must be conscientiously complete to fulfill its objective. The injured muscle must be debrided back to the area at which normal pink bleeding muscle is encountered and viability assured. The "cavitation effect" of high-velocity missiles produces an area of muscle necrosis greater than is apparent from the size, direction, or location of the wounds of entry and exit, or the missile tract. This damaged tissue must be removed.

Section IV.   Immobilization

The healing of long-bone fractures and extremity wounds of muscle requires immobilization of the part. There may be later phases of fracture healing when tensile stress is a stimulus to calcification of callus and architectural change, but malunion and nonunion result from failure adequately to immobilize the extremity. Premature motion threatens non-union and often converts the fracture to a pseudarthrosis.

Whereas it is a simple matter to initiate early ambulation in clean, elective, civilian, soft-tissue surgery, such a procedure is patently impossible in most fractures and in all severe trauma.

The severe and occasionally prolonged immobilization of the fracture patient creates problems, especially in five areas:
   (1) skin necrosis,
   (2) accumulative bronchopneumonia,

(3) thromboembolism,

(4) morale, and

(5) calcium excretion. The latter has already been discussed.

A. SKIN NECROSIS

The prevention and management of decubitus ulcers depend primarily on the vigilance of the doctors in charge. Careful nursing care is essential, but the constant example of concern set by the surgeon is the stimulus to the nurse.

Bedsores are an increased hazard when there is poor vascular supply to the skin, as in older people. Bedsores will not heal in the face of chronic hypovolemia or anemia, hypoproteinemia, or nutritional deficiency, particularly of vitamin C. The mere provision of adequate diet will obviously not insure the healing of the bedsore; the pressure must be removed. In older individuals, almost any position that the patient is left in will result in the formation of a pressure sore. The tips of the ears, the tip of the nose, the back of the head, the back of the heels, the front of the knees, the iliac crests—all of these may ulcerate with pressure in individuals in the older age group in whom vitality is at a low ebb, blood vessels sclerotic, skin flow poor, and motion painful.

Anesthetic areas develop decubitus ulcers because the patient cannot feel pain when pressure becomes excessive; in severe wounds and pelvic fractures pain from other areas, when the patient moves, may be so intense as to drown out the smaller steady warning pain of dangerous skin pressure. After injuries of this type the initial skin break may occur in the first hours. Vigilance must start immediately.

Specific steps that will lower the incidence of decubitus ulcers or assist in their healing are:

(1) cleanliness and dryness;

(2) an inlying catheter;

(3) soft or foam-rubber mattress;

(4) avoidance of oversedation;

(5) care that the patient's position is changed frequently;

(6) overhead trapeze;

(7) optimum nutritional intake in view of age and nature of injury;

(8) normal hematocrit, blood volume, erythrocyte mass, and plasma protein concentration;

(9) proper digitalization and the avoidance of edema.

In special cases such equipment as the alternating sectional-inflated mattress, the Stryker frame, or the oscillating bed is useful. Certain devices, particularly the hard edge of a Bradford frame, are notoriously apt to produce pressure sores, and should be avoided.

The operative closure of large bedsores is often practical, particularly in young people aparaplegics, for example) whose general vit(!ity and vascular resilience has not been lost.

B. ACCUMULATIVE BRONCHOPNEUMONIA

Severely injured or elderly patients confined to bed tend to develop bronchopneumonia. If the patient is in overt congestive heart failure or if fluid is overadministered, the pathogenesis may be circulatory. But in most cases the major pathology arises from failure to maintain sufficient cough drainage of the bronchial tree; this is accumulative bronchopneumonia developing in areas of atelectasis. After severe injury with immobilization, even younger patients are vulnerable to accumulative bronchopulmonary disease. The best preventive is alertness and the avoidance of oversedation, mobilization, encouraging the patient to move about in bed and to practice deep breathing and coughing. Occasionally the patient benefits from the use of antibiotics by inhalation, expectorants, aminophylline, or other special measures, as outlined in the chapter on the Lungs in Part V.

It is not the presence of organisms that is primarily responsible for the development of accumulative bronchopneumonia. The prevention of this lesion is not dependent upon the use of antibiotics, and the systemic administration of prophylactic antibiotics during prolonged immobilization is inadvisable. Antibiotics tend to convert a resting normal flora into one that is antibiotic-resistant. If the local anatomic, vascular, and exudative situation is altered by prolonged immobilization so as to convert the resting flora into an invasive flora, one finds that prophylactic antibiotic treatment has resulted in an accumulative bronchopneumonia due to invasive, antibiotic-resistant organisms. The patient is then much worse off than if no antibiotics had been given. The use of antibiotics early in compound trauma is essential; we warn here against their prolonged use to avoid pulmonic complications in the immobilized patient.

If the patient runs a high fever, with physical and X-ray signs of accumulative bronchopneumonia, antibiotics should be used therapeutically, with vigor and with bacteriologic check on sensitivity. The use of antibiotics for established accumulative bronchopneumonia does not in any way negate the continued importance of postural drainage, mobilization, humidification and liquefaction of secretions, and coughing.

Tracheal suction by the passage of a catheter down the unanesthetized trachea is a rigorous procedure and must be used with some restraint in elderly people. If the patient has an abdominal wound or fractured ribs, such a procedure may introduce strain on the site of the injury, initiating disruption, pneumothorax, or further hemorrhage. The transient cyanosis of breath-holding may also be dangerous in cardiacs. Judgment is essential, but the procedure is effective in improving bronchial drainage. Its helpful effects are the result of the cough stimulated by the passage of the catheter as well as the actual removal of material through the catheter. In addition to tracheal suction, one must consider bronchoscopy and tracheotomy, as described in the section on multiple wounds and bronchopulmonary accumulation.

Aspiration of gastrointestinal contents is a critical and often unsuspected factor in pulmonary deterioration. Gastric stasis, tube feedings, or loss of swallowing reflexes should all be considered as possible causes of aspiration pneumonitis, and dealt with accordingly.

C. THROMBOEMBOLISM

Fatal thromboembolism is commoner in immobilized patients than it is in the general population undergoing elective soft-tissue surgery.

In the immobilized patient after compound trauma there may be:

(1) slowing of the venous return;
(2) damage to the vein intima;
(3) local changes in coagulability of the blood due to release of thromboplastin from damaged tissue;
(4) generalized changes in coagulation as a part of the metabolic effects of injury;
(5) dehydration, alterations in calcium or lipid concentration in the blood;
(6) concomitant degenerative major vessel disease.

From all these theoretical factors we can select only a few commonplace admonitions that provide a practical basis for treatment of the individual patient.

Since fatal thromboembolism is commoner in bedridden people, it is better to get the patient up out of bed. Early mobilization does not prevent fatal thromboembolism, but it has appeared to reduce its incidence. If mobilization cannot be carried out (as in fractures), then exercise of muscle groups, maintenance of muscle tone, avoidance of dehydration, hypotension, or deficit in blood volume, and the maintenance of normal bodily hygiene are of importance in this regard.

If the immobilized, fractured, or elderly patient has pulmonary embolism (as manifest by local or pulmonary symptoms, physical signs, or X-ray) he should be started on heparin, maintaining this treatment for about a week before the drug is gradually tapered off. If the patient is facing a prolonged immobilization of more than four weeks, vein ligation may be advisable, but such a prophylactic division of the superficial femoral vein is occasionally followed by thrombosis and embolization from the profunda system. In most instances of established thromboembolism, any vein division must be bilateral because lateralization of thrombosis is impossible. On one side this is obviously "prophylactic," and may introduce hemodynamic changes which favor subsequent thrombosis.

If veins are to be divided, ligature and division of the common femoral is preferable to the superficial femoral because of the profunda femoris hazards mentioned above. The occurrence of emboli in spite of adequate anticoagulants is the chief indication for caval ligature. Thrombosis above the superficial and profunda femoris areas is evidenced by edema rising up to the upper thigh. This requires caval ligature.

A general policy outline for thromboembolism in fracture patients follows.

(1) *Fracture with Prolonged Immobilization in Prospect.* Neither anticoagulation nor vein division is used routinely. Muscle-setting exercises and constant vigilance are the main safeguards against thromboembolism. Legs are measured and examined daily.

(2) *The Appearance of Signs of Thrombosis in the Leg Veins.* Administration of heparin is begun. A course of at least seven days is contemplated. If immobilization must proceed beyond that time, the use of bishydroxy-coumarin (Dicumarol) should be started.

(3) *Necessity for Late Surgery to the Fracture.* This is an indication for division of the common femoral veins.

(4) *The Appearance of Embolism on Heparin.* Femoral vein division is carried out.

(5) *Further Embolism, on Heparin or after Vein Division.* Ligation of the vena cava is done.

D. MORALE

Morale of the long-immobilized patient depends upon conscientious and solicitous attention paid by the surgeon to the complaints, symptoms, and minor concerns of the patient. A minor discomfort may be the first sign of embolism or of a pressure area under the cast; but if it is neglected by the surgeon, regardless of its organic significance, it will demoralize the patient. Diet, reading, and occupational therapy need not be further elaborated on here. More important than any of these factors is avoidance of apprehension. Painful dressings or cast-changes, debridements, or readjustments of wound drains must be done under anesthesia. The long-immobilized patient has a low threshold for fear and pain. Apprehension over the next day's dressing, based on bitter past experiences, will interfere with diet and sleep, lead to overdosage of sedatives and to demoralization. The administration of a barbiturate anesthesia for a few moments may make morphine unnecessary and is in itself free of injurious effects.

In maintaining the morale of the patient long confined to bed, the future must be explained, the present interpreted, and the habit of pain-free manipulation established.

CHAPTER 45

Treatment of Wounds and Severe Multiple Injury

Section I. Introduction: War and the Automobile

In the severely injured patient and in burns, one encounters a multifaceted challenge to surgical care. Very little written in this book up to this point cannot be applied to the metabolic care of such patients. The purpose of this chapter is to bring together—in many instances only in outline form—some of the important considerations and dynamic procedures used in dealing with injury from physical violence. Wounds of war and of the automobile have much in common, as also do injuries from industrial accidents, farm implements, armed robbery, and attempted suicide. They all fall into the general category of random unregulated unanesthetized physical violence, and most of these injuries include fractures.

From the surgical point of view, automobile injuries are unique because they present to the physician or surgeon practicing in small communities some of the most complicated injuries sustained by the human frame. Prior to the advent of the automobile it is quite true that runaways, kicks from horses, falling off the roof, Fourth-of-July burns, and the other hazards of Victorian life were presented to doctors and surgeons everywhere. The automobile has increased the velocity and severity of the blow, multiplied the total volume of traumatic injury incident to transportation, and scattered the victims widely over the countryside for treatment.

The physician who has for years treated heart disease and diabetes is apt to be ignorant of surgical metabolism and may fail to appreciate that there is such a field of knowledge, of practical importance in clinical care. Let this same individual be presented with a patient three days after an automobile accident, who, oliguric, with accumulative bronchopneumonia starting up, a tracheotomy, a plasma sodium concentration of 120 mE. per l., potassium of 8.3 per l., a pulse of 120, peaking of the T-waves, the question of oligemia and dehydration unsettled as against the possibility that the patient is overhydrated and overtransfused, the question unsettled as to whether he should be operated upon today, tomorrow, or yesterday —let this same physician be faced with such a patient and he will better appreciate the fact that surgical injury presents some remarkably complicated metabolic problems.

An important difference between the war wound and the civilian home, industrial, automobile, or miscellaneous accident lies in the previous health of the patient, his age, and the velocity of the missile producing the injury. The wounded soldier is in the prime of his physical condition and at the stage of his life where recovery comes most naturally. He is injured by missiles with high velocities.

In automobile accidents, the velocity of the missile is slow. The patient may be either an infant or a small child, or an older person in whom diabetes, vascular disease, or kidney disease is prominent and sets the stage for degeneration in function of brain, heart kidneys, or lungs.

Section II. Duration of Injury: The Meaning of Definitive Surgery

A. DURATION AS A CRITICAL FACTOR IN THE EXTENT OF INJURY

When an individual is in shock with anoxic tissues, mortality and morbidity are functions of the length of time that elapses between injury and definitive surgery. Even complete absence of detectable blood pressure and pulse is compatible with survival if it lasts but a short time. By contrast, blood pressures in the range of 70 to 90 mm. Hg over a period of twelve to twenty-four hours, with borderline states of shock and tissue anoxia, may be followed by invasive sepsis or renal changes that are fatal. It is thus clear that in shock and severe trauma, duration before definitive surgery is an important determinant of the final outcome. Tissue trauma in itself, quite aside from hypotension and anoxia, also has an important dependence upon time factors in determining the extent of the total injury inflicted. Time lapse is injurious because of the continuing threat of infection, continuing pain, the presence of dead tissue, and the injurious motion of severed parts (particularly bone), the persistence of which causes further hemorrhage and necrosis.

The purpose of definitive operation in multiple wounds is to put an end to this continuing injury. The injury phase ceases after definitive surgery, and the long upward climb of dynamic convalescence can then ensue, leading finally to anabolism, resynthesis of tissue, and rehabilitation. Definitive operation is therefore a metabolic step of fundamental significance.

Examples are to be found in the penetrating belly wound or open, dirty fracture. If these are sustained near a hospital and quickly given definitive surgery, convalescence from either presents few problems. Consider the opposite end of the time scale. The injured patient lies about in the open, possibly in the heat or numbing cold, for many hours, is then transported crudely or roughly while the fracture is still mobile; there is continued pain, muscle damage, and hemorrhage. In the case of the belly wound, the contents of the hollow viscera establish leakage peritonitis, which the body cannot localize because of the continued soiling. When, six to ten hours later, the patient arrives in the hospital he is hypotensive, anuric, anoxic, and he has established sepsis. He is a much sicker man, but still not beyond recall by effective definitive surgery. In the case of the fracture, careful debridement (removal of dead or dying tissue), immobilization of the fracture, and replacement of lost blood may find the patient still salvageable if renal function is maintained and sepsis controllable. Even in the case of the belly wound with extensive peritoneal contamination, treatment consisting of volume restoration followed by suture of holed hollow viscera, the exteriorization of proximal or injured large bowel, and the aspiration of contaminating gastrointestinal juice from the peritoneal cavity can produce (by the next morning) a patient possibly not as fit as the fracture patient but nonetheless clearly able to make his convalescence.

Extend this duration of injury another twelve hours and the belly wound is virtually beyond hope of recall; the fracture may now involve anaerobic infection in surrounding muscle bellies and require amputation for survival.

The duration of time from injury to definitive surgery is therefore one measure of magnitude of the injury; prolongation greatly adds to the patient's burdens. The most vicious effect of this prolongation is the action of continued tissue anoxia in killing cells, the spread of contamination, and the incubation of invasive infection in devitalized or contaminated tissue. The sensitivity of the patient with restricted blood volume to physical motion may lead to profound shock despite minor blood loss.

B. THE MEANING OF DEFINITIVE SURGERY

The total duration of injury is the time elapsing between injury and the completion of definitive surgery. *Definitive surgery is thus defined as that procedure required to put an end to the continuing injury, abating the deterioration which is progressive in the untreated wound, so that the natural sequences of convalescence can ensue.*

The details of definitive surgical operation in compound injury are described following the section on resuscitation. It is appropriate to consider first the organization required for its establishment.

C. ORGANIZATION FOR DEFINITIVE SURGERY

The objectives of definitive surgical care in compound injury can be met only on the basis of an effective pattern of organization. In civilian life, this pattern of organization includes three sites:

(1) nonprofessional *first aid* at the scene;

(2) the *emergency ward* hospital unit—the first professional site;

(3) the *operating room*—the fully equipped professional site.

In military surgery the same three stages have different names:

(1) the *corpsman*—the *first-aid* man—the first nonprofessional aid;

(2) the *battalion aid station*—the site of first professional help without facilities for definitive surgery;

(3) the *advanced field hospital or mobile army*

surgical hospital—the fully equipped professional site where definitive operation and postoperative care can be carried out.

The site for definitive surgery is characterized by the presence of electric power and other mechanical facilities and a competent professional staff with appropriate equipment.

In naval and air combat the organizational pattern is determined by the peculiar nature of the vessel. In air warfare, the ratio of killed in action to wounded in action is very high, whereas in land warfare, over the course of many centuries, it has remained unchanged at about one to four. Naval warfare occupies a midposition, and in a large naval ship the same three stages of care are, of course, organizationally identical although geographically closer together.

The purposes of care in these three analogous sites are the same, regardless of their location or their names, and they are as follows.

(1) *First Aid—The First Nonprofessional Help.* Control of massive external hemorrhage, establishment of airway, relief of pain, splinting, and transportation are the first requisites

(2) *The First Professional Site—The Battalion Aid Station, Emergency Ward.* Here is given preliminary anatomic evaluation; attention to the airway; restoration of blood volume by infusion; preliminary immobilization of fractures; and further transportation.

(3) *The Equipped Professional Site—Where Definitive Operation Can Be Carried Out.* At this point begins an orderly sequence of accurate diagnosis including X-ray, specialized professional evaluation, resuscitation (including massive transfusion), expert anesthesia and definitive operative care. Convalescence then begins.

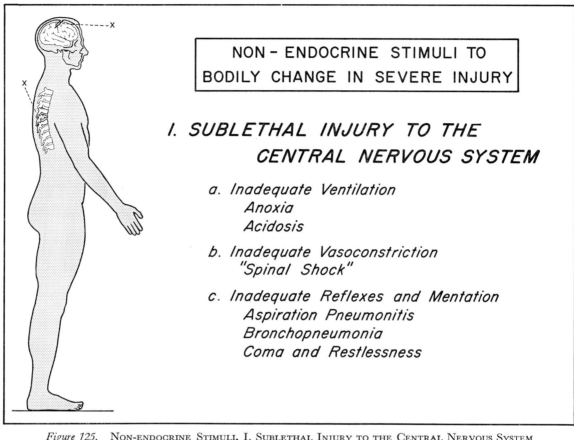

Figure 125.   Non-endocrine Stimuli. I. Sublethal Injury to the Central Nervous System

In this and the subsequent five charts are diagrammed some of the changes occurring in the injured patient that communicate biochemical abnormalities throughout the body without the necessary intermediacy of the endocrine glands. These are changes arising from the wound that produce widespread metabolic alterations; these are non-endocrine "mediators" of the traumatic stimulus; these are factors that are responsible for diffuse metabolic change, factors that *arouse* endocrine alteration, and yet are not primarily hormonal in nature. Most of the non-endocrine stimuli to bodily changes in severe injury are in themselves deleterious. They are factors that challenge homeostasis.

It is the mission of definitive surgery to correct these changes and abate these stimuli so that homeostatic tension may drop back to normal and convalescence ensue. For a fuller discussion of these factors, the reader is referred to Moore, 1958.

It will be noted in this chart that sublethal injury to the central nervous system produces widespread biochemical changes, chiefly by the production of anoxia and respiratory acidosis. Coma and restlessness are also very adverse factors in the seriously injured patient.

Treatment rests on the maintenance of an airway, the removal of pressure, and the control of hemorrhage.

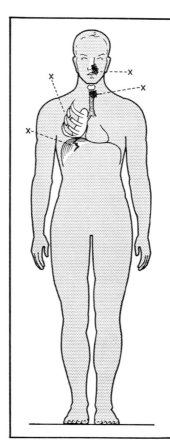

NON-ENDOCRINE STIMULI TO BODILY CHANGE IN SEVERE INJURY

2. WOUNDS OF THE AIRWAY

a. Inadequate Ventilation
1. Anoxia
Cell Death
Cerebral Damage
Renal Insufficiency

2. Respiratory Acidosis
"Too Fast To Compensate"
Hyperkaliemia
Ventricular Fibrillation

Figure 126. NON-ENDOCRINE STIMULI. II. WOUNDS OF THE AIRWAY

Again, as in central nervous system injury, wounds around the airway produce widespread biochemical changes through the production of anoxia and respiratory acidosis.

Both of these agencies are strong stimuli to the secretions of the adrenal medulla and cortex. In addition, they affect the viability of organs and tissues within a matter of minutes. Cardiac arrest and ventricular fibrillation often occur as a result of these changes.

Treatment rests on the restoration not only of the airway but also of the entire respiratory mechanism, so as to achieve an adequate alveolar ventilation with normal pulmonary perfusion.

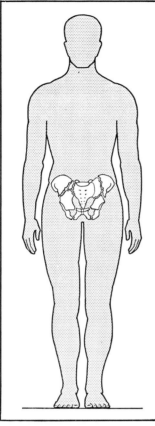

NON - ENDOCRINE STIMULI TO
BODILY CHANGE IN SEVERE INJURY

3. CROSS - SECTIONAL TISSUE INJURY (FRACTURE, MUSCLE CRUSH, BURN, LACERATION)

a. Pain

b. Discontinuity of Structure

c. Necrosis and Anaerobiosis

d. Loss of Skin and Mucosal Barriers
   Contamination ⟶ Infection

e. Metabolic Acidosis and Ion Exchange

f. Accumulation of Muscle Pigment and Enzymes

Figure 127. Non-endocrine Stimuli. III. Cross-sectional Tissue Injury

Tissue injury produces widespread biochemical and metabolic changes through six different agencies, listed in this chart.

Here is represented a crushed pelvis as epitomizing injury to that large mass of striated muscle between knee and navel, injury to which so characteristically releases muscle electrolyte and pigment, develops anaerobic myositis, and results in renal failure.

Treatment rests on restoration of anatomic continuity, immobilization, debridement, adequate drainage, and restoration of normal tissue perfusion.

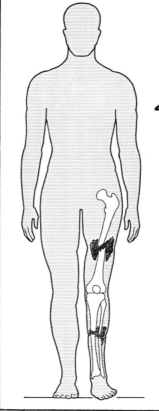

NON - ENDOCRINE STIMULI TO BODILY CHANGE IN SEVERE INJURY

4. WOUND SHOCK
(OLIGEMIA, VASOCONSTRICTION,
PROLONGED DEFICIENCY
OF FLOW)

a. Anoxia and Acidosis
Decreased Responsiveness of Vessels
"Clinical Taking Up"

b. Sepsis – Anaerobic

c. Visceral Damage
Brain – Liver– Kidney

d. Accumulation of Metabolites

Figure 128. NON-ENDOCRINE STIMULI. IV. WOUND SHOCK

Prolonged deficiency of flow in shock produces widespread metabolic and biochemical changes through four distinct mechanisms. Fractures of the leg are here depicted as an example of shocking injury. In late shock these four mechanisms (anoxia, sepsis, visceral deterioration, and accumulation of metabolites) all act together as important "vicious cycles" in sustaining the shock state itself.

Treatment is devoted to the reestablishment of normal tissue perfusion by the restoration of effective blood volume, cardiac output, blood pressure, and blood flow.

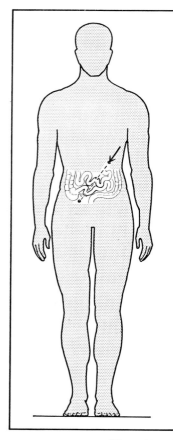

NON - ENDOCRINE STIMULI TO BODILY CHANGE IN SEVERE INJURY

5. CONTAMINATION ⟶ INFECTION

a. Loss of Skin and Mucosal Barriers

b. Devitalized Tissue - Foreign Bodies - Mucosal Leak - Closed Space Pressure

c Special Effects
Gram-Negative Bacilli
Anaerobes
Antibiotic Resistance

d. Hypotension — Tachycardia - Fever - Delirium - Oliguria - Azotemia - Shock - Acidosis - Metastatic Sepsis

Figure 129.   Non-endocrine Stimuli. V. Contamination and Infection

Widespread deterioration in the circulation is produced by infection, particularly if it involves the gram-negative bacilli or anaerobic organisms. Trauma that breaks either the skin or the mucosal barriers of hollow viscera inevitably results in bacterial contamination of previously sterile tissues. If shock is present, decreasing the circulatory efficiency of the immune mechanism and producing anaerobiosis, severe infection is particularly apt to occur.

Theatment rests on anatomic repair, exteriorization of holed hollow viscera, debridement, drainage, restoration of effective blood flow, and the appropriate use of antibiotics.

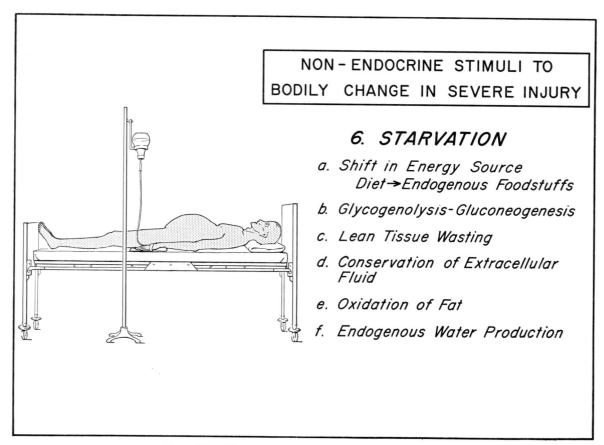

Figure 130. Non-endocrine Stimuli. VI. Starvation

Starvation produces widespread metabolic changes as suggested in the chart. None of these is rapid and none of them is of severe import early in the post-traumatic course.

Treatment rests primarily on restoration of a patent functioning gastrointestinal tract, and the supplying of an oral diet when it can be accepted. Short of this, the use of special intravenous alimentation has a place once the initial catabolic storm has abated and acute sepsis is controlled.

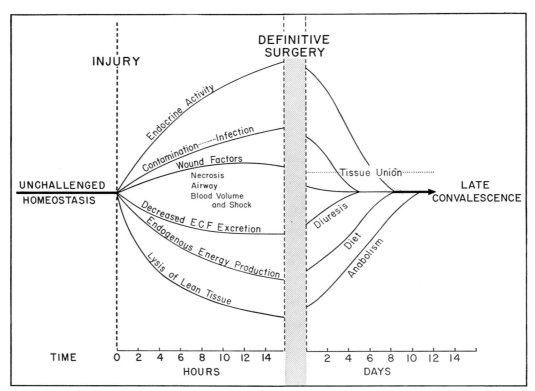

Figure 131.   EFFECT OF DEFINITIVE OPERATION IN SEVERE INJURY

In this chart is shown diagrammatically the developing and continuing injury as seen during a 12- to 16-hour period after severe, unanesthetized trauma such as a war wound or civilian accident. There are increasing evidences of endocrine activity, contamination progressively leads to infection, there is tissue necrosis, there may be airway compromise, and there is decreased blood volume, all of which are progressive. There is decreased renal excretion of extracellular fluid, and falling stores of body fat, carbohydrate, and protein as energy is produced from within the body by the oxidation of fat and the lysis of lean tissue.

Definitive operation puts an end to this continuing injury by surgical repair of the anatomic defects that produce these changes; surgical care ends this cycle by restoring blood volume, and by **operative** treatment of the wound itself. These steps of operative dissection abate the continuing injury and its associated homeostatic tension.

Following the operation the physiologic disturbances of the wound gradually return to normal. Tissue union occurs. There is diuresis of water and salt, resumption of diet, and finally lean tissue anabolism as convalescence is established, strength regained, and normal bodily functional composition restored.

Section III.   The Five Stages of Care in Severe Injury

A strong sense of sequential procedure is essential to the effective care of the severely injured patient. Treatment is dynamic; the patient must move through this sequence in an orderly fashion but, above all else, must be kept moving forward through it unless the force of untoward developments demands a halt or a detour. The next sections will be devoted, in order, to the five basic stages of care in severe injury. These are:

Stage 1. Early Threats to Life; The Base-Line
Stage 2. Wound Shock and Resuscitation
Stage 3. Stabilization and Reevaluation
Stage 4. Definitive Operation
Stage 5. Postoperative Care.

In military surgery, steps must be arranged that permit many surgeons of widely variant backgrounds to achieve similar results using the same tools in many different places. Surgical strategy (the chain of evacuation) and tactics (surgical care) must be standardized but not crystallized; a meaningful sequence must be made available, departures from which are undertaken only on the basis of considered professional judgment. The division of the care of the injured into five phases, outlined here, is such a sequence.

STAGE 1. EARLY THREATS TO LIFE; THE BASE-LINE

This first phase includes:
1. Establishment of the Airway,
2. Control of Massive Hemorrhage,
3. Evaluation of Injury to the Brain and Its Coverings,
4. The First Infusion and the Short-Term Chart,
5. Physical Examination, and
6. Catheterization.

1. The Airway

Difficulties with the airway lead the list of early threats to life in multiple injury. Here, by contrast with purely cerebral injury, simple emergency steps are very effective. In view of the small therapeutic range for head injury in an aid station or emergency ward and the marked effectiveness of airway treatment, *it is damage to the airway which can most threaten life and yet be reparable.* Compromise to the airway may arise by several mechanisms and at several levels.

Damage to the central nervous system itself can prevent adequate motion of the intercostal muscles, the diaphragm, or both. Such damage is often associated with paralysis of the glottis and some degree of upper respiratory obstruction. In such a patient the performance of tracheotomy and establishment of artificial respiration are the only steps that can possibly lead to survival, and even they may be rendered futile by the severity of the head injury. They should be carried out immediately, without question as to their ultimate effectiveness.

Direct trauma, either blunt or penetrating, to the maxilla, the mandible, the nose and throat, or the upper neck, with swelling, edema, local hemorrhage, and aspiration of saliva or blood, will compromise the upper airway. The patient with a wound in this area initially ventilates fairly well but over the course of the next hours, as edema of the injured parts increases, his airway becomes progressively more obstructed. The progressive nature of airway obstruction in this lesion makes it one of the most fruitful for effective recognition and treatment and, at the same time, one of the most deceptive. In a patient with injury to the upper airway, the performance of an early tracheotomy is essential to provide adequate ventilation, to make possible the removal by suction of any aspirated material, and to provide a channel for anesthesia.

Interference with the mechanical effectiveness of the thoracic cage may occur. A flail chest with multiple rib fractures is the common example here. External stabilization of the flail chest and performance of tracheotomy are the essential initial steps. Wounds of the diaphragm also interfere with diaphragmatic ventilation.

Pneumothorax is frequently present and may be at atmospheric pressure or at increased pressure, bilateral or unilateral, and with or without mediastinal emphysema. When sucking wounds of the chest are present, the wound should be sealed by a greased or moist dressing, with the insertion of a small intercostal catheter anteriorly in the second interspace. This catheter is placed on water seal or made airtight with a rubber balloon one-way valve. If there is question of pneumothorax without penetration of the chest wall (as in rib fractures), stabilization of the chest wall, diagnostic aspiration, and establishment of catheter drainage are essential.

Inhalation of toxic substances may have occurred. Interference with normal ventilation through inhalation of smoke irritants is dealt with in the section on burns. Its inclusion here serves to emphasize the fact that problems from inhalation can occur without any surface burn, near areas of smoke, flame, or explosion, and where toxic materials are being used in industry. The injury will be at the pharyngeal-laryngeal area or it may be broncho-alveolar. In either event, tracheotomy will be useful but should not be used indiscriminately.

Aspiration of gastric contents is a frequent complication of orofacial wounds; it is prevented by nasogastric intubation and treated by bronchoscopy.

a. Treatment: Artificial Respiration; Tracheotomy and Bronchoscopy. The details of *artificial respiration* are of critical importance. As the arterial oxygen saturation falls below 70 per cent in the nonrespiring patient, death approaches. The carbon dioxide tension rises, and the combination quickly leads to fatal cardiac arrhythmia or brain damage, or both.

To achieve ventilation the airway must be unobstructed, while effective tidal exchange is achieved. Position of head and neck can spell the difference between success and failure; with the chin up and neck fully extended the posterior oropharyngeal airway can be kept patent. The resistance of the bony thorax to external pressure is a problem with either the prone-pressure or the supine arm-lift chest-pressure method. Neither is an effective way of achieving alveolar ventilation

even if well used, nor will it work effectively with the chin down and neck flexed, a position naturally assumed by the unconscious patient. It has been shown that mouth-to-mouth resuscitation with the head well positioned can bring the oxygen saturation from 80 per cent to 97 per cent in a few moments, even in the fully paralyzed patient, whereas the conventional methods are inadequate. This can be done by direct mouth-to-mouth insufflation, by using a double-ended oropharyngeal tube or with a double mask. In instruction of the beginner, the emphasis must be on tidal exchange achieved, not on pressure applied.

If the patient has aspirated a foreign body, gastric contents, or blood, or has had an acute bout of wet-lung accumulation, such as one may see after trauma to the chest (particularly with overadministration of fluid), then bronchoscopic clearing of the trachea may be required on repeated occasions.

The performance of *tracheotomy* in traumatized patients who have functional or anatomic obstruction at the upper airway is a lifesaving procedure. The performance of tracheotomy solely for suction aspiration of the trachea is a step which must be considered with care. It is not always clearly beneficial for this purpose and it imposes real burdens on the patient that may be out of proportion to the potential benefit.

When a patient coughs, the act of coughing consists in the building up of pressure behind a closed glottis by relaxation of the diaphragms, with contraction of the abdominal and intercostal musculature. Then the glottis is suddenly opened and the explosive decompression of the tracheobronchial tree carries outward a large amount of material. Normal coughing therefore requires not only muscular activity of the abdominal and thoracic wall (which in turn requires normal neuromuscular irritability), but also a period of closure of the upper airway.

Tracheotomy, by making upper airway closure impossible, compromises the effectiveness of cough. The nurse may at times occlude the tracheotomy so as to let the patient develop pressure against it, but the tracheotomy must be airtight for this to be effective, and this is but a poor substitute for closing of the glottis. A patient with a tracheotomy can wheeze and spew the material from his tracheobronchial tree but it is not an effective cough. The performance of tracheotomy as a method of tracheal suction in bronchopulmonary accumulation must therefore be evaluated with realism. Generally speaking, if the patient has a productive bronchial tree—a bronchorrhea, as in traumatic wet lung—then trans-tracheotomy suction will be as effective as the surgeon hopes. If he is unconscious or cannot cough anyway, the same is true. Otherwise, intermittent tracheal suction or bronchoscopic suction is preferable.

Three other deficits of tracheotomy—all minor—must be mentioned.

(1) There often is a *septic process* in the tracheotomy wound, in the upper mediastinum, and up and down the trachea. All tracheotomy wounds become infected just like all other open wounds. The presence of microorganisms with purulent discharge on the surface is inevitable, whether or not invasion takes place. This septic purulent process becomes a considerable nuisance. It is rarely serious.

(2) The presence of a tracheotomy greatly decreases the *respiratory dead space*. This results in increased efficiency of ventilation and an increased tidal air fraction of vital capacity, which will be an important desideratum when tracheotomy is carried out for flail chest or obstruction of the upper airway. When neither has been present, the tracheotomy creates a hazard through greatly increased pulmonary water loss and drying of secretions.

(3) It is a *psychological hazard* to the conscious patient when he can no longer communicate with those in attendance. This can be lessened by appropriate occlusion so as to permit talking.

All of these factors should therefore be taken into consideration in the problem of whether or not a tracheotomy should be done on the injured patient. They should not be a cause for delay when urgency is great. As a general rule tracheotomy is useful; in many cases it should be done as an urgent measure and without question. As generalizations:

(1) *Tracheotomy is lifesaving* where upper airway obstruction exists, as in direct trauma to the mandible, axilla, or throat, in bullet wounds, penetrating wounds, and in many cases of burns. Here tracheotomy is essential. It should be done early rather than late, and its liabilities are but a small price to pay for its benefits.

(2) *Tracheotomy is moderately effective* when it is done for wet bronchus, bronchorrhea, repeated aspiration of gastric contents, traumatic wet lung, and flail chest. It must be done in most cases.

(3) *Tracheotomy is ineffectual* when it is done as partial treatment for accumulative bronchopneumonia; the mortality remains high.

2. Control of Massive Hemorrhage

Massive continuing bleeding has an early priority for treatment. Treatment is often simple when bleeding is open, complex when it is hidden. Massive hemorrhage, as in injuries to the major vessels of arms, legs, and head, constitutes a threat to life that the body handles effectively if the vessel is completely severed so that retraction and coagulation can control the bleeding. Secondary hemorrhage from such injuries may then occur following the restoration of blood pressure by transfusion.

The proper use of a tourniquet saves the patient much loss of blood volume. The details of its use appear to be a cause for controversy among the armed services of the NATO nations. It must be applied above the severed artery in an area where there will not be serious damage to nerves. Once applied, it should not be loosened until the vessel can be secured. The shorter the time it is on, however, the better. Limbs may be lost because a tourniquet has induced damage to muscular branches and collaterals. Its application must represent a balance of judgment between the saving of life versus the saving of limb. This type of fine discrimination is difficult enough for the professional; it is almost impossible for the corpsman or layman involved in first-aid measures.

If, when the patient is first seen, there is continuing rapid hemorrhage, the use of a tourniquet or pressure point is immediately required. If hemorrhage is from multiple sources, as in a crushed or mangled limb, then the immobilization of the limb with the application of firm pressure bandages is as effective as a tourniquet in controlling hemorrhage and will be much safer from the point of view of muscle anaerobiosis.

In either event, whole blood transfusion should be started as soon as possible. Group O, Rh-negative blood may be used without crossmatch; infusions of plasma and dextran are far better than nothing, should blood be unavailable.

If a patient comes to the first professional site with a tourniquet in place, it should be loosened under good illumination and with adequate instruments at hand. If hemorrhage ensues, the vessel is seized and ligated, details depending upon the state of consciousness of the patient and the site of the vessel. External hemorrhage can be considered to have subsided as a threat only when its site has been visualized clearly and adequately controlled with a ligature or sutures.

Hemorrhage of large volume occurring in the abdomen or chest is a much more urgent problem. It is less evident and physiologic hemostasis is less effective. If bleeding is from an end artery, there is necrotic tissue distally. In time, sepsis is added. The accumulation of the blood is in itself irritating to tissues or serous surfaces and compromises other functions (lung volume and diaphragmatic excursion). First-aid measures are of comparatively little value; if hemorrhage continues, surgical closure of the vessel is essential to resuscitation and must occur with, not after, volume-restoring transfusion. *Continuing open arterial hemorrhage (usually in the abdomen) takes surgical priority for open operation over all other traumatic emergencies.*

Bleeding from a large open artery involves, in itself, a loss of that peripheral resistance against which cardiac output develops pressure. For this reason the initial fall in pressure is more sudden and profound than in venous hemorrhage. Venous bleeding, occurring distal to the site of peripheral resistance, is compatible, for a time, with the maintenance of pressure to the left side of the heart, coronary inflow, and renal function. These considerations are of immediate clinical importance in evaluating the status of the injured patient at the first professional site to which he is taken.

If there is massive hemorrhage (particularly if arterial), either externally or in a body cavity, that is not controlled in the first minutes at the first professional site (the emergency ward or the aid station), this is an indication for immediate operative intervention with transfusion in place. Operation becomes an integral step in the restoration of blood pressure and flow.

3. Evaluation of Injury to the Brain and Its Coverings

Survey of the field of an infantry-artillery battle reveals that a large fraction of those killed in action have died of head injuries. The calvarium is virtually the only area of the body silhouette in which the penetration of a small, high-velocity missile is immediately and almost inevitably fatal.

Similarly, in civilian and automobile accidents, injury to the head constitutes the most common cause of immediate death. Just as the skull and its contents are extremely vulnerable to high-velocity missiles, so also is it virtually the only area where forceful blunt trauma may produce an immediately fatal result.

Despite the likelihood of immediate fatality, a patient with very severe head injury may reach the doctor's care from either battle or highway, while still alive. If damage to nervous tissue has already been so extensive as to decerebrate the individual, produce respiratory paralysis or other changes that will lead ultimately to death, the doctor can do little but temporize. The establishment and maintenance of normal ventilation is the first step. Virtually the only form of head injury that is helped by urgent immediate surgery is continued bleeding from the dura or its blood supply, particularly epidural hemorrhage. In most other head injuries, a carefully arranged program of diagnosis by observation is more important than early operative attack.

Observation in Head Injury. The first step is the establishment of a systematic examination and observation. A short-term chart of pulse, respiration, blood pressure, and responses is established, as it is for any severe wound. Emphasis is on pupillary size and equality of reflexes, mentation and responses as well as the vital signs followed in other injury.

The Airway in Head Injury. The patient with a head injury is particularly liable to accumulative bronchopneumonia. Head injury may be associated with effective upper-airway obstruction not amenable to treatment with an oral or oropharyngeal airway or endotracheal tube. This is a positive indication for tracheotomy (see the previous section).

Timing of X-Rays in Head Injury. The desire to obtain X-ray verification of the fractured skull is responsible more than any other single factor for moving the patient prematurely, and subjecting him to unnecessary trauma. There is something about the inability of the examining physician to assess the presence or absence of skull fractures which leads him to seek an X-ray of this area long before he feels a similar compulsion to X-ray the humerus, femur, pelvis, or vertebrae. The presence or absence of skull fracture verified by X-ray does not materially alter the *early* management of head injury. For this reason the patient should be X-rayed only when his general stabilization is adequate to permit one trip to the X-ray department for the completion of all the essential X-ray examinations. If fracture is present, indications for its neurosurgical treatment depend not on its existence but on its clinical effects, as evidenced by an altered state of consciousness, reflex activity, pupillary signs, or intracranial pressure.

The indications for *early* surgical intervention in head and spinal injury are based on the course of the patient as observed above, and are:

(1) progressive lateralization of neurologic signs,
(2) progressive evidence of increasing pressure,
(3) transverse myelitis.

Diagnostic lumbar puncture is rarely indicated in the immediate care of acute head injuries and is positively contraindicated when there are gross evidences of increased intracranial pressure or lateralizing signs.

If a patient is unconscious or in an altered state of consciousness, the consideration of head injury is obvious even to the nonprofessional first-aid worker. It is not so obvious that head injury may be present when consciousness is normal; head injury may still be significant as a cause of hypertension, vomiting, failure of cough reflex, and other peripheral neurologic manifestations.

An initial neurologic examination is performed with particular reference to flexor reflexes, the upgoing toe, the pupillary and extraocular movements, and the state of consciousness. Moderation is important in the use of analgesics, parenterally administered fluids, and blood.

4. The First Infusion and the Short-Term Chart

The evaluation of injuries of the brain, establishment of the airway, and control of open hemorrhage having been completed at the first professional site, the initiation of intravenous infusion of fluids other than blood is next in priority. With the above three high-priority items considered and controlled, it is appropriate to start intravenous therapy. To take time out to start intravenous infusion of fluids other than blood before the prior three are considered and dealt with may be a hazardous time waste, depending on available manpower.

The principles underlying the use of intravenous infusions of fluid and blood have already been dealt with extensively in previous sections of this book. As applied to the early care of severe injury, several points are of special importance: the occasional hazard of infusion, and the selection of the proper solution for the first infusion.

Possible hazards of intravenous infusion therapy in the seriously injured patient are two:

(1) *Closed head injury with intracranial hemorrhage and edema.* This injury, without compromise of the blood volume, represents a hazard to the patient's life which is distinctly increased by infusions of blood, water, and

salt. As intracranial pressure rises, the systemic blood pressure rises, and hemorrhage is promoted. Any tendency to overloading with water and salt increases cerebral edema. In severe head injury of a closed type without external hemorrhage and with suggestive evidences of increased intracranial pressure, there is no indication whatsoever for intravenous therapy unless it be specifically directed toward diminishing brain volume or convulsive activity, as by the use of albumin or sucrose or by specific medication such as barbiturates or magnesium sulfate.

(2) *Injuries to the chest in which hemorrhage does not play a role and blood volume restoration is not a problem.* The same considerations as above hold in these cases. A patient with a flail chest, a crushed chest, or even a severe blow to the chest, as from a steering-wheel injury, tends to develop bronchorrhea and pulmonary accumulation of fluid. The mechanism of production of traumatic wet lung must involve at least three factors: trauma-induced alteration of capillary permeability, inefficiency of cough reflex, and hyperemia in an injured area. The administration of fluid or blood in a manner and dose that increases either the blood volume or the extracellular volume or that decreases osmolality is going to increase the severity of traumatic wet lung. A mistakenly rapid saline infusion may be fatal in traumatic wet lung.

It seems to be a universal medical tendency to start giving an intravenous infusion to anybody who is sick or injured. It is our purpose here merely to emphasize that there are two distinct situations after severe injury in which intravenous therapy is dangerous. An intravenous infusion should always be given for a specific purpose. An individual who has no remarkable losses of fluid, electrolyte, or blood following severe injury should be managed on a strictly "in-balance" basis. By this we assume that he should be expected to lose from 300 to 500 gm. a day as fat and lean tissue are catabolized, and that his fluid requirements are only those of external losses, including loss from tracheotomy. His water balance should not be distorted by needless infusion.

The First Infusion. With the above two exceptions, most injured patients require transfusion as soon as possible. The selection of the material to be used for intravenous therapy depends upon the nature of the injury, the balance between loss of whole blood and of plasma, and the extent of desalting water loss.

In severe multiple injuries loss of blood plays such a major role that in the vast majority of cases the first infusion should be one of whole blood. Under civilian conditions there is rarely any justification for avoiding the ordinary safeguards of blood-bank technology. Grouping, crossmatching, and the infusion of type-specific compatible whole blood are not remarkably time-consuming. In the presence of a normally functioning blood bank, it takes approximately thirty minutes to complete the normal channel procedures for good blood transfusion practice. The patient is often in need of intravascular support during this process. The use of plasma, concentrated albumin, dextran, or group O blood is entirely justified in this interim.

Under circumstances of combat, mass civilian disaster, or extreme pressure on the blood bank of a hospital, particularly a small community hospital, it is justified to cut corners of blood transfusion technique by using group O Rh-negative blood without checking the crossmatch. In military practice this blood has been used in large quantity without crossmatching. Here again one must balance the risk against the gain, a balance intrinsic to any surgical maneuver. For this use, group O Rh-negative blood should be neutralized, meaning that the anti-A and anti-B antibodies in the plasma are neutralized by the addition of type-specific antigen. If but one unit is used, type-specific blood can then be started.

For the initiation of the first intravenous therapy, a needle of adequate caliber should be inserted and an initial blood sample withdrawn before starting the infusion. This blood sample is used to measure the peripheral concentration of red blood cells (hematocrit, erythrocyte count, or hemoglobin) and such other determinations as are appropriate to the case in hand. Since veins will be precious, it is advisable to make the best use of each venipuncture. If it is possible to insert an intravenous catheter at this time and run it up the arm to the superior cava, this may be helpful, but inside caliber is lost thereby and there may be difficulty in running blood as rapidly as needed. A catheter should not be placed in a vein of the lower extremity unless extreme urgency demands it.

In the patient who has had massive bleeding, who is severely injured, or in whom shock is impending or present, the infusion of blood through a single portal will rarely suffice. It is better to use two adequate channels and rely less on excessive pressure than it is to use a single inadequate portal under high pressure.

The initial use of noncolloid saline solutions is almost never called for in severe compound injury; it is a poor and ineffective substitute for colloids or blood.

It is the responsibility of the surgeon starting the first intravenous infusion to note the time and the fluid used, and the amount of blood given initially. This notation should be attached to the record or the patient's person. Under no circumstances should this first infusion contain epinephrine, norepinephrine, or cortisone. Before considering the matter of volume restoration and resuscitation in greater detail, the other initial professional steps in treatment of massive trauma will be described.

The Short-Term Chart. Observation of the patient and evaluation of the status of special systems have begun before this; but it is at about the time of starting the first infusion that a systematic ten- or fifteen-minute chart of pulse, respiration, and blood pressure is established which will be pursued until postoperative stabilization is complete. Other data are gathered as needed: oral responses, pupillary data, reflexes, urine output. The patient is now (fifteen to forty-five minutes after admission) ready for a more detailed physical examination than was previously feasible.

5. Physical Examination

The patient should now be approaching accomplishment of the initial objectives of the emergency ward. Brain injury, airway, hem-orrhage, start of first transfusion have been dealt with. There remains more to be done before moving him, but early in the patient's care he should have a careful physical examination for assessment of extensive injury and he should have the insertion of a catheter into the urinary bladder. Whether this is done before or after the starting of the initial intravenous infusion is immaterial and depends upon the urgency of blood-volume replacement. Here we will consider physical examination first, and then the details of the further treatment of shock by subsequent infusions. This is usually the most advisable clinical sequence.

This physical examination in severe trauma should have the following objectives:

(1) An assessment of *soft-tissue, skeletal, and neurologic injury* with particular reference to frequently-occurring combinations.

(2) The detection of *preexistent disease*—by history as well as physical examination.

(3) The establishment of *base-line observations* for the study of those internal injuries which may become obvious only later through the development of changes in signs. This applies most clearly to abdominal injuries with nonpenetrating trauma, where laceration of the spleen, kidneys, liver, gastrointestinal tract, or bladder may not be immediately evident, but will become increasingly evident as physical examination of the abdomen in the course of the first hour or two is contrasted with the initial observations. The very acutely injured patient, apprehensive, in pain, and in impending circulatory collapse, presents great difficulties in a careful abdominal examination. An hour or two later, when the patient is partially stabilized and better able to make the subjective discriminations required of him in a satisfactory abdominal examination, careful physical evaluation is much more rewarding. Fractures must be kept well immobilized during the motion incident to physical and X-ray examination.

a. Soft-Tissue Injuries to be Considered in the Physical Examination of Patients With Fracture. (1) SKULL FRACTURES—INJURY TO THE BRAIN AND ITS COVERING. Neurologic examination is carried out, with notation of the patient's status to permit evaluation of subsequent changes.

(2) VERTEBRAL FRACTURES—SPINAL CORD INJURY. Careful examination should be made of sensation, reflex changes, and motor power sequentially now, during and after treatment.

(3) FRACTURES OF THE LUMBAR VERTE-BRAE — DISTENTION AND ADYNAMIC ILEUS. Little can be done other than anticipation of the progressive nature of the adynamic ileus produced by hemorrhage under the prever-tebral fascia. Premature feeding is avoided. Suction with a nasogastric tube is an impor-tant prophylactic measure. If the patient is treated early, a well-functioning nasogastric tube will remove swallowed air and prevent distention. If he is not treated until ileus is present, a long tube may be tried. With severe ileus it may be ineffective. In lower dorsal and lumbar vertebral fractures, con-sider rupture of the kidney, liver, or spleen.

(4) FRACTURES OF THE MAXILLA, MANDIBLE, FACIAL BONES, HYOID BONE—AIRWAY OB-STRUCTION. Note the presence or absence of cyanosis, gasping, crowing respiration. "Puff and blow" test against the examiner's palm is useful. Auscultation around the airway and of the chest should be done. Subsequent hemorrhage and edema will produce ob-struction where it did not initially exist.

(5) FRACTURES OF THE RIB—LUNG INJURY WITH PNEUMOTHORAX; RUPTURE OF THE SPLEEN, LIVER, OR DIAPHRAGM; WET LUNG. The surgeon should make careful examina-tion of the thorax and of the abdomen, documentation of the findings to follow their changes, X-ray for pneumothorax or air under the diaphragm, and should look for mediastinal or subcutaneous emphysema.

(6) FRACTURES OF THE PELVIS—INJURY TO THE BLADDER, URETHRA, AND RECTUM. Careful rectal examination should be made. Catheterization should be done. If catheter-ization is difficult, attempts should not be persistent. Where catheterization can be car-ried out and there remains a question of bladder rupture, a cystogram should be done. Urinalysis, if it shows erythrocytes with reasonable evidence that the urethra and bladder are normal, should be followed by

consideration for rupture or contusion of the kidney, such consideration to include either retrograde pyelography or intravenous pye-lography, depending on the setting. If cathe-terization cannot readily be done, cystotomy will be a part of the definitive operation and is an urgent priority.

(7) FRACTURES AROUND THE ELBOW AND KNEE—INJURY TO THE BRACHIAL ARTERY OR POPLITEAL ARTERY. The peripheral pulses should be observed and noted. The surgeon should ask himself: can pulse be restored with traction or simple positioning?

(8) FRACTURES IN MIDSHAFT HUMERUS, AROUND THE ELBOW, WRIST, AND KNEE—IN-JURY TO NERVES AS THEY PASS THE FRACTURE SITE. Peripheral nerve injury may accom-pany any fracture. The above are listed as the most common sites for nerve injury. Careful examination for reflex, motor, and sensory activity in hand and foot is the best insurance here. Examination and documen-tation of neurologic status should be made, whether or not any evidence of damage is seen.

(9) FRACTURES AROUND THE THIGH, PELVIS, BUTTOCKS, FEMUR—INJURY TO LARGE MASSES OF SKELETAL MUSCLE. An estimate of the extent of muscular injury is only a first approximation of the extent of muscular debridement that will be necessary at opera-tion. Under any circumstances, tetanus pro-phylaxis is used as described below.

For the patient in shock these initial steps (airway restoration, physical examination, catheterization) must be taken as resuscita-tion begins. Their interrelationship is deter-mined by the rest of the setting. Whatever the sequence, the continuing treatment of shock and evaluation of the response now takes first priority. Save for those cases of active continuing large-artery hemorrhage, volume restoration precedes surgery.

6. Catheterization

The insertion of a catheter in the bladder has three purposes: first, to study the urine (the initial volume, and the presence or absence of benzidine-reacting pigment and red blood cells); second, to ascertain the hourly urine output, and third, to determine the presence or absence of injury to the urethra or bladder. In fractures around the pelvis and in crushing trauma, the urethra is often lacerated or divided. If catheterization cannot readily be accomplished, it is better to carry out suprapubic cystotomy than it is to jeopardize the patient's survival by inadequate bladder drainage, continued extravasation of urine, or repeated traumatic attempts at catheterization, should the urethra or bladder be injured.

If the urine is grossly bloody, it suggests injury to the bladder or urethra or one or both kidneys. This is a differentiation that requires further study by physical examination, cystogram, retrograde pyelogram, or intravenous pyelogram; these studies are to be postponed until the period of stabilization and reevaluation.

STAGE 2. *WOUND SHOCK AND RESUSCITATION; UNRESPONSIVE SHOCK*

Full attention can now be directed to the re-establishment of blood pressure and flow, and tissue perfusion. This phase will be considered under the following headings:

1. Shock: Frequency and Clinical Appearances,
2. Transfusion,
3. Volume Factors,
4. Signs during Transfusion,
5. Failure to Respond, and
6. Vasoactive Drugs.

1. Shock: Frequency and Clinical Appearances

Virtually all patients with severe multiple injury pass through a period of decreased blood pressure and flow. Only in isolated trauma (to head or arm, or single fracture) is this feature lacking.

In the section on blood volume (Part II) the subject of shock was reviewed in terms of blood-volume loss and support. In that section, it was pointed out that there are four useful terms to describe different settings in which shock appears, though the physiologic mechanisms and sequelae overlap.

(1) *Hemorrhagic shock* is shock due primarily to hemorrhage with a minimum activity of other factors. This is seen, for example, in duodenal ulcer, varix bleeding, and ruptured ectopic pregnancy, as well as in injury to major vessels.

(2) *Operative shock* is shock occurring in the course of a surgical operation and complicated by the by-products of such an operation, particularly anesthesia, with its attendant effects on peripheral vasoconstriction and acid-base balance.

(3) *Wound shock* is shock following unanes-thetized injury where pain, tissue disruption, fluid dislocation, and contamination play a role.

(4) *Septic shock* is shock in which bacterial invasion and host resistance appear in one of several combinations with other etiologic mechanisms.

In this section we are interested primarily in the third of these categories—wound shock—and in its initial recognition, evaluation, and treatment.

Appearances depend on the circumstances in which shock occurs. The surgeon sees the patient for the first time minutes or hours after his injury, in the emergency ward, in the battalion aid station, or in the sick bay. He is lying, covered, on a stretcher. He is still in the clothes in which he was injured. He is usually covered with dirt, grease, grime. The extent of his injury is unknown and all of the steps of initial screening and physical examination mentioned in the foregoing section are yet to be undertaken. The initial objective is to start treatment while an accurate but rapid evaluation is carried out. As we now consider the patient, profuse external bleeding is no longer a problem. If formerly present, it has been secured by tourniquet, ligature, or splinting. Continuing intra-abdominal hemorrhage is sought for: if there is abdominal trauma with peritoneal signs, shock, and no other source of blood loss, staging for immediate surgery is mandatory.

The most characteristic earmarks of wound shock, without which the diagnosis is rarely made, are low systolic blood pressure and a rapid pulse. We expect to find the patient's skin cold and clammy, his cutaneous vessels fully vasoconstricted, with minimal blanching of his skin on pressure and slow return of what little blanching there is. If this is not the case, with hypotension present, and any portion of the patient (either the whole body or the lower extremities) is vasodilated, warm, and dry, one may conclude that the central nervous system is involved in this hypotensive state (injury to brain or spinal cord) and that the patient may respond favorably to pressor drugs such as norepinephrine. In the absence of such findings, the use of such drugs is definitely contraindicated early in the course.

Wound shock is due to a mixed effect of peripheral tissue trauma, muscle damage, blood loss, and transportation with inadequate splinting or in the presence of oligemia. Psychologic factors and pain are not important causes of circulatory failure.

Air hunger is common in shock, but severe cyanosis is rare. Some transcapillary refilling of the plasma volume has been occurring, some anemia is present, and there is not a large enough amount of reduced hemoglobin present to produce cyanosis. Defects in oxygenation of arterial blood are not a characteristic feature of early shock. If the patient is cyanotic, one should be very suspicious that there is something the matter with the airway. Pressure pneumothorax, hemopericardium, and ruptured viscus are sought out immediately by auscultation, percussion, and palpation.

The patient is expected to be moderately depressed and often irrational, but he can be aroused and is able to answer some questions intelligently. If he is in deep coma we cannot blame this on shock alone, and injury to the central nervous system must be sought as the cause.

2. Transfusion

The therapeutic objective is unitary: the restoration of effective tissue flow and perfusion through the restoration of blood volume, cardiac output, and blood pressure.

This patient's veins will be collapsed and will fill but slowly on the application of a tourniquet applied for the withdrawal of blood. If the patient's veins are full and distended and if simple elevation of the arm

shows an elevation of venous pressure, one should suspect a central cardiac aspect in the circulatory failure, as seen in hemopericardium, cardiac tamponade, pressure pneumothorax, coronary sclerosis with hypotension, and coronary occlusion.

Knowing the sex and guessing the weight of our patient, finding him in this state of shock, we assume that the patient is missing at least one-half of his starting normal blood volume. *Our initial transfusion objective should therefore be to give the patient one-half of his assumed normal blood volume as rapidly as possible.* Undertransfusion is the greatest and commonest cause for failure; slow transfusion is just as bad as undertransfusion, and the two are synonymous. Very rapid transfusion has virtually no hazard in this situation, and should not give pause or delay on that account, except for elderly individuals with fully compensated anemias, and with minimal volume loss.

Two #14 or #16 needles or cannulae should be placed in opposite arms. The required blood volume should be infused as rapidly as possible—in sixty to ninety minutes. If the cardiac status is not clear, the venous pressure is measured directly with a sidearm from the infusion tubing, with the assurance that as long as venous pressure remains normal or low, overtransfusion cannot possibly have occurred.

3. Volume Factors

In established wound shock of less than six hours' duration the initial budget for rapid infusion in sixty to ninety minutes is 0.5 blood volume. This amount must be transfused before one worries over unresponsiveness, though careful watch is maintained for the "factors making for unresponsiveness." In most cases the final infusion volume achieved by the end of operation is from 1.0 to 1.5 blood volume.

In established shock after severe injury, failure to respond cannot be claimed until after the infusion of 0.5 blood volume. This is a volume of blood (see Part II) equal to 3.5 per cent of body weight, or about 2500 ml. in an adult male (70 kg.).

During such large transfusion of citrated

blood, calcium should be given at the rate of 1.0 gm. of calcium gluconate for each 1000 ml. of blood transfused.

4. Signs during Transfusion

On admission the patient has been placed on short-term chart observation of pulse, respiration, blood pressure, and vital responses. These observations are continued during resuscitation. In many cases the restoration of blood pressure and circulation from the precarious situation on admission is rapid, gratifying, and complete—although it may take some struggle to maintain it. In others the response is almost nil, for reasons outlined below.

In addition to vital signs, several other things should be watched for. The first is increased bleeding from the wound or into the wound. There may be present an abdominal wound of the open arterial type, which now reopens with additional perfusion pressure, and abdominal signs become evident that demand early surgery. The same is true of limb wounds.

The patient has already been catheterized, as mentioned in the initial section, and his perfused kidneys should now start to make some urine. If this is forthcoming, it should be analyzed, particularly for pigment in the supernatant after centrifugation; the presence of erythrocytes in the sediment is evidence of renal tract injury or of kidney contusion, and may now indicate renal damage formerly hidden by the lack of urine output.

Although infusion of one-half of the patient's normal starting blood volume is the initial transfusion budget, it is by no means the entire amount necessary after severe trauma. Patients in shock after trauma often require transfusion up to their normal blood volume or more, particularly if they have been in shock long enough to show the increased capacity, avidity, or appetite for blood characterized as the clinical phenomenon of taking up, or if there is continued loss during treatment.

As the patient is transfused, careful note should be taken of his transfusion volume in relation to his estimated normal starting blood volume, and this bedside chart should be maintained throughout resuscitation. If the initial transfusion budget is not followed by restoration of blood pressure and normal circulation, energetic transfusion should be continued, but at a somewhat slower rate. Equal concern should continuously be given to possible causes of failure to respond to transfusion therapy and shock, the commonest of which is continuing hemorrhage.

A distinct response should be seen as transfusion volumes equivalent to 0.5 to 1.0 blood volume are approached. If this favorable response is not seen, a further search for "failure to respond" phenomena must be instituted.

5. Failure To Respond: The Evaluation of Unresponsive Shock

Common causes for failure to respond to transfusion in shock will be listed here for review. They fall into five categories:

a. Special Anatomic Sequelae of the Wound,
b. Inadequate Transfusion,
c. Special Visceral Effects: Heart and Lungs,
d. Sepsis, and
e. Biochemical Derangement.

a. Special Anatomic Injuries or Sequelae of the Wound. Events that, in themselves, prevent resuscitation by volume restoration alone are:

Head injury
Hemopericardium
Mediastinal emphysema
Pneumothorax, unilateral or bilateral
Urinary extravasation
Ruptured spleen
Intra-abdominal hemorrhage
Coronary occlusion
Pulmonary embolus
Fat embolus

These must be sought out and, if present, placed in the proper time-sequence for treatment. As mentioned repeatedly, continuing open arterial hemorrhage demands operative intervention without waiting for a preliminary resuscitative response. Several of the others in the above list can be managed by local procedures as a part of resuscitation. Examples of this are cystotomy for injury to the lower urinary tract, pericardiocentesis for hemopericardium, and water-seal pleural drainage for pneumothorax. Such steps are rightly to be considered as a part of resuscitation itself; one cannot consider a patient unresponsive to volume restoration if such steps are left undone.

b. Inadequate Transfusion. In severe traumatic shock the infusion of an amount of compatible blood equivalent to one-half the normal blood volume within ninety minutes must be considered as an adequate initial trial of transfusion so long as continuing blood loss is not occurring; the diagnosis of "failure to respond" is not to be made until this initial criterion has been met. All too often the patient's condition is condemned as "irreversible" without adequate trial of transfusion.

The "clinical phenomenon of taking up" manifests itself by a need for blood infusion greater in amount than that previously lost. This is due to a disorder of peripheral circulation acting via one or more of the following mechanisms:

(1) nonreactivity—failure to vasoconstrict;
(2) opening up of arteriovenous shunts;
(3) changes in the composition of the blood —"sludging" or similar viscosity alterations; or
(4) active trapping or segregation in injured areas.*

Whatever the mechanism, it is in the patient who has long been hypotensive despite seemingly adequate transfusion that one sees irresponsiveness and the clinical phenomenon of taking up. *As a general rule, if the patient has been in shock six hours or more, or there is an element of infection present, do not consider him "unresponsive" until transfusion volume over and beyond continuing loss has exceeded 1.0 blood volume; as large transfusion volumes are approached, watch the venous pressure.*

c. Special Visceral Effects: Heart and Lungs in Unresponsive Shock. I. MYOCARDIAL ISCHEMIA IN UNRESPONSIVE SHOCK. When age and coronary sclerosis have reduced coronary caliber,

blood flow is reduced as the fourth power of the effective radius; when inflow pressure at the coronary ostia is then reduced in shock, the blood supply to the myocardium becomes critical. Low flow here manifests itself in several ways:

(1) *Acute arrhythmias* that may be rapidly fatal or, like supraventricular tachycardia, amenable to precise diagnosis and accurate treatment.

(2) *Outright heart failure* with a rising venous pressure as venous transfusion proceeds, responding to digitalization. This is rare but should be sought out.

(3) *Poor response* to transfusion, with electrocardiographic findings of subendocardial ischemia, but not responding to digitalis. Intra-arterial transfusion at high rates of pressure and flow for short periods has been followed by good recovery in such cases. The mode of action probably involves the establishment of an adequate ostial pressure and myocardial perfusion for long enough to reestablish left ventricular function, which then, as volume is restored, can maintain coronary flow.

(4) *Coronary thrombosis,* presumably a result, at least in part, of low flow. Management here depends primarily on restoring flow by infusion; digitalization is indicated where venous pressure is elevated.

Because these cardiac phenomena are not seen in young men in shock and because they are not easily reproduced in the dog (which is not suffering from coronary sclerosis), the idea has gained currency that they do not occur at all. Clinical and electrocardiographic observation of traumatic shock in people over fifty is recommended for those who still doubt that the myocardium suffers in shock. It is a peripheral vascular bed and will suffer from low rates of pressure and flow, like any other vascular beds; when it suffers, the effects are immediately dangerous to life, whereas ischemia, with its attendant abnormal contractions, can be compatible with life for hours or days when it occurs in other muscle areas.

II. PULMONARY FACTORS IN UNRESPONSIVE SHOCK. The importance of airway patency in early evaluation and resuscitation has already been mentioned. Later on, if resuscita-

---

* Evidence for hepatosplanchnic trapping of blood under high portal venous pressure, so often observed in the dog, is lacking in man.

tion still fails to restore circulation to normal, pulmonary factors remain of equal importance. Here, however (assuming that the airway has been achieved), the pulmonary factors relate to inadequate ventilation of other causes:

(1) diaphragmatic injury or elevation;
(2) pleural blood or air;
(3) parenchymatous pathology due to accumulation or infection; and
(4) inadequate pulmonary perfusion, a rare and late development.

An injured, shocked man, unresponsive to transfusion at 0.5 to 0.75 blood volume range, will immediately restore blood pressure and flow and renal function if a severe ventilatory defect is overcome.

The anoxic patient will not restore his blood pressure after transfusion, nor will the patient with respiratory acidosis. The latter is the more subtle disorder, may exist without cyanosis, and may worsen with the decreased ventilatory effort resulting from the administration of oxygen.

Therefore, if the injured and shocked patient begins to show signs of becoming unresponsive to transfusion, the ventilatory status must again be critically evaluated. The puff of exhaled air, auscultation of the lungs, review of pleural competency and abdominal distention must again be studied. The determination of the arterial oxygen, carbon dioxide, and *p*H is valuable if available. Chest X-ray should be repeated.

d. Sepsis as a Factor in Early Unresponsive Shock. Anaerobic myositis and anaerobic infection in the retroperitoneal or pelvic area may reach a clinical level within six hours after injury, and this septic process will prevent the patient from responding adequately to transfusion. Blood-stream infection with gram-negative bacilli will do the same. In both instances the infection itself will cause shock and may develop as a complication of shock. It is unusual for gram-positive coccal infection to be a problem sooner than twenty-four hours after injury. Contaminated whole-blood transfusions are a source of organisms that produce severe hypotension and renal damage, the manifestation developing within a few hours.

Prevention of these infections rests upon good operative care, including adequate debridement, drainage, exteriorization of holed hollow viscera, and the use of antibiotics. In the neglected patient after compound injury, where such action has not as yet been taken, these infections will become the dominant factor in unresponsive shock. This is particularly true beyond the sixth hour; prior to that time it is most exceptional for sepsis to be a major factor.

In civilian surgery one often sees patients (usually elderly) who are hypotensive twenty-four to thirty-six hours after open injury or operation; at such durations sepsis is very frequently an important part of the pathogenesis of the unresponsive hypotension, must be diagnosed accurately, and dealt with accordingly.

e. Biochemical Factors in Unresponsive Shock. A number of specific biochemical factors, while not a cause of hypotension in themselves, interfere with a normal response to volume restoration. The commonest are: acidosis, hypotonicity (hyponatremia), and hyperkalemia. Less frequent is hypocalcemia.

Acidosis of respiratory origin must be overcome by improving ventilation, as already described. It may produce unresponsiveness in shock by way of a further decrease in cardiac output. Metabolic acidosis of the low-perfusion type (hypoxic acidosis) becomes increasingly evident as time in shock progresses, by the accumulation of lactate and pyruvate as evidences of anaerobic glycolysis in the shock state. Of the two forms of acidosis the former (respiratory) is the more important because it is reparable, while the latter (hypoxic) is in itself a result of shock as well as a factor in unresponsiveness. It is one of the vicious cycles of shock that is repaired only by the restoration of normal tissue-perfusion.

Hypotonicity (hyponatremia) is especially apt to be discovered in the elderly patient in unresponsive shock or in the patient who previously has had visceral disease (liver, kidneys, heart). Overtreatment with water will of course produce hypotonicity very rapidly in the hypotensive, oliguric patient. The sodium ion, for some reason but poorly understood, is essential to vascular homeostasis and the maintenance of blood pressure. When it is present in excess hypertension may result, when in short supply (particularly if at low concentrations) hypotension results, shock is prolonged or is made unresponsive to transfusion. If a patient in shock is hyponatremic (and therefore hypotonic with respect to effective osmolar concentrations), he will respond, often quite dramatically, to the infusion of concentrated sodium salts. If he is hyponatremic and acidotic, concentrated sodium bicarbonate should be used; if not, concentrated sodium chloride. The sodium ion is used here at a concentration four times isotonic, or 600 mE. per l. About 300 ml. of such a solution is used as an initial priming dose to study the response. More is given as needed, chemically and clinically.

Hyperkalemia as a cause of cardiac abnormalities has been discussed in Part V. Its effect in diminishing the pharmacologic action of digitalis is very important in the surgical care of elderly patients. In essence, the heart loses its digitalization within a few hours as the potassium rises. This effect of hyperkalemia is greatly potentiated by hyponatremia and hypocalcemia. Of equal importance is the fact that the adverse contractility effects of hyperkalemia and its electrocardiographic reflections are exhibited by any heart, whether digitalized or not. Hyperkalemia and hyponatremia regularly occur together and have similar and potentiating effects on the heart.

The best treatment for the cardiotoxic effects of the hyperkalemia (that will make a patient in shock unresponsive to volume restoration) is concentrated sodium, as mentioned in the foregoing section. Calcium salts are effective; and they are so effective in the digitalized patient as to be dangerous. *It should be reemphasized that severe hyperkalemia can occur after injury, without any evidence of parenchymatous renal damage.*

Hypocalcemia as a cause of unresponsiveness to volume restoration in shock acts much like hyperkalemia and has similar myocardial effects. It may also affect the peripheral vascular resistance. One will rarely find a gross hypocalcemia in such patients (unless established renal failure is present). It is the slight lowering of the ionized calcium by citrate effects that is significant here. The blood citrate required to reduce the effective beat of the diseased or digitalized heart by calcium-binding is far less than that required to endanger the life of a normal subject. When the additive effects of hyponatremia and hyperkalemia are also present, then very small changes in ionized calcium, resulting from citrate infusion, may become the critical factor in unresponsiveness to volume restoration in shock.

The antidote for hypocalcemia, whether caused by citrate or by renal failure or both, is calcium. One gm. of calcium gluconate contains about 100 mg. of calcium. This dose, repeated once, will usually suffice to indicate whether or not calcium is important in the case under treatment. This should be used with caution and under electrocardiographic control in the patient in shock under digitalis.

6. Vasoactive Drugs

There are three lines of defense in the treatment of shock, three echelons of method. The first is volume restoration. The second is attention to the factors making for unresponsiveness (just described), and the third echelon is the vasoactive drugs. Under no circumstances should the administration of vasoconstrictors or steroids be commenced until the therapeutic resources of the first two echelons have been given a proper application.

If volume restoration has been carried out with a realistic and critical view of actual needs, and if the "factors making for unresponsiveness" have been sought out and dealt with—yet the patient is still hypotensive and not responding well—then administration of the vasoactive materials should be commenced.

Since corticosteroids and vasoconstrictors appear to synergize in their effect on the peripheral vessel and possibly on the heart, they should be used together. One is dealing with a clinical situation where there is little time for elaborate ceremony. A blood sample should be drawn for eosinophil count and blood steroid (if available), and the infusion started. It should contain 100 mg. of hydrocortisone and about 2.0 mg. of norepinephrine (or Neo-synephrine, 2 to 4 mg.) in about 500 ml. of 5 per cent dextrose in water. Of this, 100 ml. is run in rapidly (fifteen minutes) and the rest infused over a period of four hours. If the response is favorable a second similar infusion is given over an eight-hour period.

There are a number of situations, in addition to the nonspecific setting mentioned here, in which the *vasoconstrictors* (norepinephrine and analogues) are specific agents for the treatment of vasodilated hypotension. In these the drug should be used without hesitation. These conditions are:

(1) brain injury or spinal injury with vasodilated hypotension;

(2) spinal anesthesia;

(3) deep planes of ether anesthesia.

There are also a number of situations in which the *corticosteroids* are specific agents that should be used without hesitation. These are, to recapitulate:

(1) natural hypoadrenalism;

(2) hypoadrenalism from steroid therapy;

(3) tumors, injuries, or operations near the pituitary;

(4) anaphylactic reactions or severely toxic states including certain forms of sepsis.

a. Vasodilators. As repeatedly reemphasized here, *the objective of treatment in oligemic shock is not only the restoration of blood pressure but also that of blood flow.* This tissue perfusion may be more effective under vasodilation and low pressure than with vasoconstriction and high pressure.

The application of this principle of vasodilated tissue perfusion in the treatment of shock is important and as yet inadequately explored in man. The basic facts of bodily response to low volume in vasodilated states, upon which such treatment is based, are four.

(1) After full vasodilation a lesser volume loss produces a pressure fall greater than that observed when normal vasoconstriction is active.

(2) When the patient is fully vasoconstricted, a normal or high volume may be associated with poor perfusion, particularly of damaged muscle, liver, and kidney.

(3) If blood loss has occurred, vasoconstriction is naturally present; if blood volume is unreplaced and vasodilation then produced, a fall in pressure results which may be fatal; this sequence is seen when deep ether-curare anesthesia is superimposed on fully vasoconstricted but not fully blood-replaced traumatic shock. Thus we see that vasodilation under this circumstance appears to be a functional test of volume restoration.

(4) Therefore a proper sequence for the use of vasodilators in shock would be:

first, replacement to normovolemia, and control of active hemorrhage;

next, restoration of tissue perfusion by vasodilation. If this produces a transient hypotension, more volume restoration is needed. Should perfusion be improved, a later return to normotension with good perfusion should result.

Our experience with such treatment is small. We have seen several patients in whom cessation of vasoconstrictor treatment (often with a small base load) was followed by improved perfusion, as evidenced by color, urine output, and clinical response. Nickerson has been especially interested in this feature of shock and has recorded the cases of several patients in whom the expected transient "vasodilated hypotension" has been followed by a spontaneous return to normotension.

The most important hazard in this concept hinges on effective blood volume, or lack of it. Measures of transfusion adequacy are poor, although those just noted (the returning urine output, color, and clinical response) are helpful; on the high-volume side, venous pressure is the best index. Thus it is of special interest that the response to vasodilation may in itself provide an index of transfusion adequacy. As currently under investigation it involves the use of a short-acting vasodilator, given when replacement appears adequate. A gradual hypotension followed by normotension indicates good volume restoration. If, by contrast, there is a sudden profound pressure drop, the vasodilator is withdrawn and vasoconstrictor is given, while volume is further built up to an adequacy that might be described as of "vasodilated, flow-supporting" capacity and adequacy.

Although none of these treatments is as

yet explored to the point of routine application, they demonstrate aspects of vasodilation in shock that emphasize the importance of tissue perfusion as opposed to mere pressure-support.

Wounds of the spinal cord produce a hypotensive reaction accompanied by vasodilation in the lower extremity, a situation reminiscent of the hypotension one may see under spinal anesthesia. Injury to the brain produces the same sort of diffuse loss of peripheral resistance for neurovascular reasons. If volume and pressure are both low, treatment is required. If injury to either of these is present it is a positive indication for the use of norepinephrine analogues, and much may be expected from their use in this situation, as already mentioned.

STAGE 3. STABILIZATION AND REEVALUATION; STAGING FOR OPERATION

As we visualize our injured patient, he or she is now returning to normal blood pressure and circulation; the urgent business of definitive operation can now be undertaken. Anesthesia, additional blood loss, and surgical trauma can be tolerated as the price of definitive anatomic dissection. Further postponement loses valuable time in the advance of sepsis, and the ideal moment has come for an expeditious reevaluation of the patient to permit more accurate operation. This precious time—which may be very short (minutes) or may be several hours—depending to some extent on operating-room pressures, also allows the equilibration, in the circulation, of recently infused blood. It is therefore a very important time of pause before operation, and includes the following aspects.

1. Stabilization and Reevaluation,
2. Antibiotics,
3. Tetanus and Gas Prophylaxis, and
4. Surgical Priorities.

1. Stabilization

The patient who has received transfusion and whose blood pressure has been brought to normal is approaching surgery. Resuscitation appears to be a reality and arrangements may move on to definitive operation. Two or three points should be checked before anesthesia is begun; physical examination should also be repeated.

a. Transfusion Equilibration. Has the patient indeed received that additional amount of blood that will permit him to accept general anesthesia without a secondary hypotensive response? The patient should not be taken to the operating room too soon after his blood pressure reaches normal. If there is no evidence of continued bleeding, he should be given about an hour for his vascular status to equilibrate. During this time, blood transfusion should be continued, but at a slower rate. *If an adult patient receives approximately 500 to 1000 ml. of blood after his blood pressure has been restored, he will be a much more solid subject to withstand the vasodilating effects of a general anesthetic and the additional blood loss involved with operation.*

b. The Urinalysis. As already mentioned, urinalysis may be impossible on an anuric shocked patient. With the progress of resuscitation, urine is secreted and available for study, and this study must be done prior to operation. If there are large numbers of red blood cells in the urine, cystoscopy and lateralization of renal injury are essential. Identification of the presence of two kidneys, seemingly a minor detail at this point, may loom later as a major controlling factor in surgical therapy. The presence of sugar has obvious significance. Pigment in the spun supernatant is a danger sign that makes it especially important to avoid hypotension in the forthcoming surgery. All should be sought out.

c. X-Rays. With the patient in shock, it is impossible to X-ray him without further endangering survival. Now that he has been resuscitated, necessary X-rays should be taken. They should be systematically and carefully considered to provide at one trip all of the information that may be needed. They may be taken en route to the operating room.

The nature of the X-rays to be taken and the timing of these X-rays is an important decision. The patient should make but one trip to the X-ray department and have all the X-rays taken that are going to be needed for his early care, as gently and expeditiously as possible. X-rays to search for missiles are helpful because the resting location helps to discern the path taken through the body, and thus the viscera most vulnerable along its track.

Objectives of X-ray examination may in general be included under the following, according to clinical indications:

(1) chest X-ray;
(2) X-ray of suspected fracture sites: skull, spine, extremities;
(3) plain film of abdomen;
(4) bladder and renal films with or without pyelograms as needed;
(5) barium swallow or barium enema for cryptic evidence of perforation; the former more often useful than the latter.

d. Blood Studies. In young people with severe injury it is important to take a blood sample at this time for comparison with the base-line data; the hematocrit, leucocyte count, and blood urea nitrogen concentration should be determined as a minimum. Where multiple transfusions have been needed, the studies at this point should include bleeding, clotting, and prothrombin times.

In the more complex setting of multivisceral injury or of injury in elderly patients or those with preexistent visceral disease, many other studies are needed. No general rules can be drawn; studies to be considered at this stage, which may assist in the hours or days to come, are:

(1) where water imbalance and/or renal abnormalities exist: sodium, potassium, carbon dioxide combining power, protein;
(2) in upper abdominal injury (liver, pancreas, bile ducts): bilirubin, amylase;
(3) in crush injury or massive transfusion: plasma hemoglobin.

e. Medication. Drugs to be used during this period of stabilization and reevaluation depend upon evaluation of the patient's physical status and surgical plans. If serial clinical examination of the abdomen is going to be important, the use of heavy analgesics is inadvisable. The presence of head injury or other lesions affecting the efficiency of respiration is also a contraindication to heavy opiate medication. There is a place for the use of barbiturates to allay anxiety. The pain of limb fractures should be controlled in so far as possible by their temporary immobilization.

2. Antibiotics

Treatment with antibiotics should be started at this time if they have not been given already. If started earlier no harm is done; it is with restoration of the circulation that intramuscular deposits will be accepted and circulated. During an initial hour the absence of antibiotics will be innocent of harm, but should the resuscitative period take longer, they should now be started.

On the basis of data available at this time the best choice in multiple open injury is penicillin in large doses (10 to 20 million units a day), with streptomycin at standard dosage.

The prophylactic use of antibiotics in the first four days is responsible for a lowering of mortality in multiple trauma, in contrast to clean civilian surgery. Severe injury breaks the anatomic barriers that are interposed between the bacterial world at large and the interior of the organism. These are breaks in the skin and in the mucous membranes. If the organisms happen to be of high virulence or if the nature of the anatomic injury is such as to feed these organisms into an area (for example the pelvic retroperitoneum) that is vulnerable to closed-space infection, or if infected material finds ready access to the blood stream, early mortality from infection with septic shock (formerly a commonplace) is always a threat. In clean, elective, civilian soft-tissue surgery antibiotics should rarely be used prophylactically; in multiple trauma they are important.

The usefulness of antibiotics during the early days after trauma is to be contrasted sharply with the deterioration of antibiotic effectiveness that occurs later on. After the sixth day, many patients with massive injury —even burns—seem to get along just as well without unselected antibiotics as with them. This fact is merely another evidence that as time passes, considerations of an anatomic and surgical nature are more important than antibiotics in governing the advance or recession of sepsis in trauma cases. If the patient has an undrained abscess, antibiotics alone will help him little. If he has continued leakage from the bowel, a necrotic area of intestine, a perforation of the liver with bile peritonitis, or if he is developing sepsis in muscle bellies, with anaerobic cellulitis because of inadequate debridement—in all these circumstances antibiotics are but an adjunct to accurate operative treatment, and the latter by far the more important.

3. Tetanus and Gas Bacillus Prophylaxis

a. Tetanus. I. TOXOID VERSUS ANTITOXIN. If the patient has had tetanus toxoid immunization, he will still carry a significant level of antibodies as long as three years, and in some instances as long as ten years, after the last dose; he will show a heightened and accelerated immune response to a booster dosage of toxoid in any case. If the patient has had a previous dose of toxoid within ten years, he should therefore receive toxoid alone. This practice is preferable to any other. However, it should be understood that statistical proof of the validity of this method is lacking and probably will never be forthcoming. This reservation as to the effectiveness of a toxoid booster dose when the last previous dose of toxoid was given up to ten years ago is mentioned here for a specific reason: if the patient has the sort of a wound in which tetanus is extremely likely to be present (a dirty closed puncture wound of muscle, for example, with pyogenic infection), then one may well weigh in the balance the hazard of tetanus (on toxoid) as against the use of antitoxin.

If the patient has not had toxoid before, or has had toxoid more than ten years before and has a wound particularly dangerous from the point of view of tetanus, then antitoxin should be given.

II. ANAPHYLAXIS VERSUS SERUM SICKNESS. The immediate skin wheal reaction which results from skin testing provides the best safety against early and severe anaphylactic reactions to tetanus antitoxin. By the use of skin testing and ordinary precautions such as fractional administration, severe early reactions can be avoided. Cortisone and antihistamines should be used if there is some evidence of sensitivity.

At the present time, serum sickness is the commonest manifestation of sensitivity reaction to antitetanus serum prophylaxis. The early skin-wheal reaction provides no index of likelihood of late serum sickness. If the patient has been given antitoxin and antibiotics, and eight to ten days later has a swinging fever with considerable malaise and leucopenia, the differential diagnosis between serum sensitivity, antibiotic allergy, and septic invasion is quite difficult. A high eosinophil count is helpful as indicating one of the two allergies. Serum sickness is a small price to pay for prophylaxis against tetanus.

b. Gas Bacillus Infection. The use of antitoxin prophylactically against Welch bacillus infection is based on the erroneous concept that it will prevent the growth of the organism in the manner of an antibiotic; this it will not do. The Welch bacillus will grow profusely in a culture medium containing large amounts of antitoxin. The only discernible effect of Welch antitoxin is peripheral neutralization of the exotoxin of the growing organism.

The best prophylaxis against Welch bacillus infection is not antitoxin, but careful debridement of necrotic muscle, leaving wounds open with good circulation, amputation of ischemic members or muscle groups, drainage and exteriorization of contaminated visceral areas, and maintenance of homeostasis. Penicillin is effective prophylactically.

Anaerobic infection of wounds takes two general forms.

(1) ANAEROBIC CELLULITIS. This is a spreading cellulitis of muscle without gas bacillus infection and without its attendant toxicity. It should be dealt with by adequate drainage, antibiotics, and, when necessary, extensive redebridement.

(2) ANAEROBIC MYOSITIS, or gas gangrene. This infection is still seen occasionally and is very dangerous. The Welch bacillus is sensitive to penicillin, and the infection can sometimes be aborted with penicillin. Necrotic muscle is necrotic because it is out of touch with the circulation. Penicillin in the circulation, even in very high dosage, will not reach the organisms in necrotic muscle. For that reason, debridement and redebridement are just as important in the era of antibiotics as they were before their discovery.

Once a Welch bacillus infection is extant, with gas, spreading sepsis, and toxicity, one must then treat the patient with massive doses of penicillin, radical debridement, and excision of the involved muscle groups, transfusion of fresh whole blood, amputation if possible, and antitoxin in large quantities. The mixed antitoxin does not rescue devitalized muscle, it does not do away with gas formation, it does not do away with the organism; it has the sole effect of neutralizing the protein exotoxin of the bacillus in the periphery of the infection.

i. OTHER FORMS OF GAS-FORMING INFECTION. As mentioned in the section on diabetes, a patient with severe diabetes may show gas bubbles in the tissues with infections which are not due to the gas bacillus. This may result from the excessive production of carbon dioxide from tissues containing large amounts of glucose. Whatever the mechanism, the infection should be dealt with by ordinary surgical principles of adequate drainage, maintenance of blood supply, and systemic care of the patient.

Gas in the tissues can also be produced by the widespread emphysema that results from even tiny puncture wounds of the lung or bowel. Emphysema from clavicles to pelvis can be produced by thoracic injuries that have gone almost unnoticed. Patients with fistulas from the bowel into the tissues may show subcutaneous dissection of malodorous large-bowel gas through the subcutaneous spaces of the abdomen and up over the chest. This is apt to be interpreted as a gas-forming infection on the basis of the X-rays, until due weight is given the almost complete lack of any reaction or toxicity on the part of the

patient. Exteriorization of the bowel results in clearing of the process.

4. Staging for Operation: Surgical Priorities

In the initial phase of care, the surgeon has assured himself as to the patient's airway, the nature of central nervous system function, the early control of hemorrhage, intravascular replacement, bladder drainage, and adequate history and physical examination. During the second stage, circulation has been fully restored by transfusion. During the third stage of stabilization and reevaluation, the patient has been given the benefit of X-ray study, medication has been administered, administration of antibiotics has been commenced, and the further physical examination required to evaluate wounds and injuries, particularly to the abdominal and pelvic viscera, has been performed. The patient is now ready for definitive operation.

The duration of time between admission to the hospital and arrival at this phase in the patient's care may be, at its shortest, thirty to forty-five minutes, where intra-abdominal hemorrhage is massive and continuing. An even shorter period may be attainable with excellent organization. The other end of this range is up to about ten or twelve hours.

If definitive operation is planned at all and if there has been a break in the patient's anatomic barrier to the bacterial world around him (as in wounds that break the skin or the hollow viscera), it is highly dangerous when the patient is forced to wait for operation longer than ten to twelve hours. Where there is extreme pressure on the surgical facilities of a hospital, waiting periods of this duration may be necessary. When the waiting period goes beyond this interval, the patient with massive injury begins to pass through that borderline noted in the mortality reports of so many illnesses that involve a break in the barrier against bacterial invasion. The time course of the mortality curve in perforated ulcer, intussusception in childhood, perforated appendicitis, as well as extensive contaminated wounds, shows a deteriorative change when the event precedes definitive operation by more than twelve to eighteen hours. Were it not for this fact, one might procrastinate longer. When the injury is to bone and there is no break in the skin barrier against infection, then there is much less urgency about definitive operation.

The degree of urgency thus varies according to the case at hand. Age of patient, duration of injury, extent of shock, and, most important, nature of the injury are the most critical factors in determining the onus of delay—the price of procrastination.

When all awaiting surgery are of one age and injury pattern (as is so often the case in military surgery), staging for surgery depends wholly on the priority of the injury. In civilian hospitals age enters the equation. In civilian disaster or in nuclear explosion there must be a priority system with a cut-off at both ends: the hopeless on the one hand, and the the minor injuries slated for self-help on the other.

In general, priority factors for admission to the theater of definitive operation may be arranged in order. *Airway obstruction and continuing massive arterial hemorrhage are preeminent priorities*, which not only supersede others but also bypass the phases of nonoperative resuscitation and stabilization—that is, they demand immediate operation before resuscitation can be accomplished or should be attempted.

The priority order for operative care is therefore as follows:

(1) continuing uncontrolled hemorrhage or airway impairment,

(2) progressive signs of increasing intracranial hemorrhage,

(3) mixed abdominal wounds and thoracico-abdominal wounds,

(4) open joints,

(5) open fractures—muscle wounds, neurovascular injuries,

(6) open trauma that has already waited more than ten hours,

(7) other soft-tissue wounds, including those of face and hands, and

(8) simple fractures.

Pulaski (1953) has reviewed the experience of the last two wars in the light of his own experience. The system of priorities to be adopted, in his view, is:

First, immediate threats to life: external hemorrhage, increasing intracranial pressure, internal hemorrhage, airway and respiratory obstruction and/or impairment, cardiac tamponade.

Second, delayed threats to life: mucosal-visceral perforations, cerebral wounds, spinal cord compression, mediastinal wounds, traumatic amputation.

Third, immediate threat to limb or organ, arterial wounds.

Fourth, delayed threat to limb or organ, eye injuries, compound fractures, dislocations and joint injuries.

Fifth, immediate debridement and realignment.

Sixth, delayed closure of soft-tissue wounds and repair of peripheral nerves.

Most classifications of head wounds for surgical priorities and selection of early treatment are based on that proposed by Dr. Cushing in World War I. He described five types in which early definitive operation was indicated (and effective) and three in which neurosurgical treatment was very complex, very extensive, time-consuming, and often unsuccessful. Indications in this latter group must depend on total casualty-pressure on the available facilities.

Head Wounds Amenable to Early Definitive Surgery

(1) Scalp wounds,

(2) Outer table only without penetration,

(3) Fracture of skull, involving dura,

(4) Superficial penetration by bone fragments only,

(5) Minimal penetration by both missile and bone.

Head Wounds More Extensive and Less Amenable

(1) Deep penetration involving ventricles,

(2) Face and brain,

(3) Destructive through-and-through wounds.

It is clear that in staging for surgery it is unwise to tie up personnel and facilities with the latter three categories if serious wounds in the first five are awaiting treatment.

STAGE 4. DEFINITIVE OPERATION

The definitive anatomic dissection of severe traumatic injuries under anesthesia involves orderly consideration of:

1. Anesthesia,
2. Strategy: The End in View,
3. Tactics: Means to That End,
4. The Meaning of Debridement, and
5. Signs during Operation.

Throughout this book we have seen that operative care and metabolic management are entirely synonymous, and inseparable. In definitive operation after massive injury and wounding, the close unity of open operative dissection and metabolic care is again clearly demonstrated. Prior to surgery, the patient is maximally stressed; the restorative phases of convalescence cannot begin. If we think of him in terms of an endocrine-metabolic system, he is at the peak of his homeostatic intensity, an intensity that cannot long be maintained. After definitive surgery, his pulse slows down, his vasoconstriction relaxes, urine flow returns, and his blood hormone levels fall back toward normal; renal conservation of water and salt acts with diminishing intensity. Rest free of pain can occur. The patient will sleep, and an organism which has been tuned to a high pitch of self-preservation, which has been using all its own devices for survival at maximum intensity, can now relax slowly back to the job of bodily reconstitution and rehabilitation in convalescence, even though the ultimate attainment of that object may be weeks or months away. The operative act carried out by the surgeon in this setting is therefore a complex metabolic measure which, when properly applied, terminates the initial stress stimulus of injury, terminates the homeostatic tension that prevents later convalescence, removes the threat of sepsis, and permits convalescence to begin.

1. Anesthesia

In the patient with multiple injuries, the ideal anesthetic involves adequacy in the following respects:

(1) minute volume exchange,
(2) oxygenation,
(3) carbon dioxide removal,
(4) relaxation,
(5) blood pressure maintenance, and
(6) analgesia.

In looking over the above list we note that the original purpose for which the anesthetic was given—to deaden the sensibility to pain—becomes the least important objective once the pharmacologic agent is instituted. This is characteristic of the approach to anesthesia in severe injury. Little further time will be devoted here to the techniques by which an adequate airway for anesthesia is obtained. Skill and experience are needed and no short cuts are permissible. If the patient has an injury around the head and neck, such as a fracture of the facial bones, maxilla, or mandible, or blunt or penetrating trauma to the neck, it may be advisable to insert an endotracheal tube under local anesthesia, while the patient still is conscious and maintains a cough reflex, before doing anything further. Such a patient is easily killed with a small dose of barbiturate; a slight change in the anatomic position of the injured parts produces sudden anoxia and fatal respiratory acidosis with cardiac arrest. Spasm of the glottis readily occurs, and the patient is scarcely salvageable save by emergency tracheotomy. Vomiting and aspiration are extremely dangerous in the early hours, should an anesthetic be given improperly. *

Short of these situations in which preanesthetic endotracheal intubation is advisable, or those in which immediate tracheotomy is required, the more common procedure is to initiate anesthesia and then intubate the trachea.

The maintenance of adequate ventilation thereafter is complicated only if the patient has airway problems lower down or injuries interfering with ventilatory efficiency, in the form of pneumothorax, lung injury, or an open chest. These should be dealt with by the same methods and standards with which one would approach the same problems in

---

* Preliminary gastric aspiration is essential in emergency surgery.

elective civilian surgery. The expenditure of thirty to forty-five minutes in complex measures for the assurance of safe anesthesia is then followed by a brief and simple operation.

Blood-pressure maintenance under anesthesia after severe injury is a particularly difficult problem. The patient whose blood volume has recently been restored by transfusion after a period of hypotension appears to have a fragile homeostatic balance. He is maintaining his pressure to the left of the heart by a low borderline cardiac output against a high peripheral resistance. Since the flow:resistance relationships determine pressure, it is clear here that we have a very dangerous situation when contrasted with its exact opposite—a high cardiac output against a low peripheral resistance in vasodilated warm, pink hypotension.

In the low-output–high-resistance situation of peripheral arteriolar vasoconstriction and threatened blood volume that follows transfused shock, any loss of peripheral vasoconstrictive effectiveness will result in an immediate and drastic lowering of the blood pressure. Deep planes of anesthesia, particularly ether and muscular relaxants, produce this loss of peripheral vascular "tone," which, in the low-output–high-resistance situation, is followed by disastrous loss of perfusion of the tissues and organs of the body. If volume has been restored, as noted above, this effect is harmless; in definitive surgery further blood loss is inevitably superimposed, thus differing from the nonoperative situation where vasodilators are used.

The selection of the anesthetic agent is therefore important, and light planes should be used when possible. There are instances in which the use of combinations of nitrous oxide, cyclopropane, and relaxants will be less dangerous to the maintenance of blood pressure and flow than deep ether.

Although the anesthetic agent itself may be responsible for this loss of blood pressure, it is also important to emphasize that in the low-output–high-resistance phase of transfused shock the patient is very sensitive to further loss of blood volume, particularly if it is from the arterial side. The contrasting physiology of arterial versus venous hemorrhage, in their immediate relationship to peripheral resistance, is clearly seen here. When peripheral resistance is high and cardiac output low, minor degrees of operative arterial hemorrhage (or even arteriolar oozing) represent a further loss of peripheral resistance as well as loss of volume. To the patient who has recently had blood volume restored, in whom volume restoration may not yet be complete or ideal, and who still maintains coronary flow by increase in peripheral resistance, anesthesia is therefore a hazard. Hence the informal rule: "After bringing his pressure up, give him another 1000 ml. of blood; give an hour to equilibrate if possible."

Maintenance of blood pressure under anesthesia is chiefly to be sought by adequate intravascular volume support and by permitting the patient an adequate period of stabilization before operation is commenced. This ideal is unattainable in airway obstruction or arterial hemorrhage (see above). If operation is not of pressing urgency and the patient may be permitted to maintain himself for an hour with normal pressure and some continuing transfusion, he will be a more fit subject for surgery than a patient whose final restoration to normal blood-pressure levels occurs just as the anesthetist commences his induction.

This intentional delay, however, cannot be pursued farther. If the patient is seriously injured and blood-pressure restoration has occurred with transfusion, an ideal moment for operation will be lost if there is undue procrastination.

2. Strategy: The End in View

The objective of operation after severe trauma is to put an end to the continuing injury so that homeostatic tension may subside and convalescence begin. This homeostatic tension is manifested among other things by increased pulse, vasoconstriction, rapid respiration, renal vasoconstriction, increased metabolism, and incidentally an increased blood level of all adrenal hormones. This tension is due to the six nonendocrine agencies that affect bodily processes after injury:

(1) central-nervous-system injury, with inadequate ventilation, mentation, and vasoconstriction;

(2) compromise to the airway or ventilatory mechanics, with anoxia and acidosis;

(3) decreased effective blood volume, due to loss or redistribution of blood or plasma, with shock;

(4) cross-sectional tissue destruction, with pain, fracture, necrosis, anaerobiosis, release of intracellular substances, and loss of continuity of functioning structures;

(5) loss of normal skin and mucosal barriers to contamination of sterile tissues and closed spaces, with sepsis;

(6) starvation, with progressive oxidation of body tissues.

The strategic objective of definitive surgery is to repair these deficits and obviate these threats by open dissection under anesthesia.

3. Tactics: Means to That End

These six causes of systemic deterioration are the basis for the tactics of definitive operation after injury or wounding. The many steps by which these objectives are met form the basis of any text on techniques of operative care in trauma. Their accomplishment is a milestone in the metabolic progress of the patient and their completion is yet another example of the unity of operative surgery and metabolic care. Before definitive operation the patient is maximally stressed, hypotensive, in pain, anoxic, acidotic, and progressively more vulnerable to sepsis. After operation his pulse progressively falls, he rests with proper immobilization and drainage, the injury phase of his wound has now come to a close, and convalescence can begin.

The operative steps of definitive operation will be summarized under the same six headings. Briefly, they are as follows:

(1) *Injury to Central Nervous System.* Control of hemorrhage, removal of foreign bodies, decompression and removal of pressure on brain or spine.

(2) *Compromise to the Airway or Ventilation.* Tracheotomy, repair of thoracic wounds with reestablishment of negative pleural pressure,

lung closure, chest stabilization, repair of diaphragm.

(3) *Decreased Effective Blood Volume.* Transfusion, control of hemorrhage, drainage of serous contamination, amputation.

(4) *Tissue Damage and Discontinuity.* Debridement, immobilization of fractures, restoration of functional continuity of structures, arterial repair, amputation.

(5) *Loss of Skin and Mucosal Barriers to Contamination and Infection.* Closure or exteriorization of holed hollow viscera; debridement; drainage of contaminated closed spaces.

(6) *Starvation.* Repair of gastrointestinal functional integrity and control of infection in surrounding serous surfaces.

4. The Meaning of Debridement

Debridement without primary closure is basic to the management of traumatic wounds in both military and civilian life. Although civilian crushing trauma may be seen earlier and may be cleaner than the war wound, there is no important difference between the two settings, and this step is advisable in both. The term "debridement" means removal of debris (that is, foreign material and dead tissue). If the wound is closed, small amounts of foreign material or devitalized tissue remaining in the wound form a nidus, causing a closed space infection, which becomes invasive and anaerobic. If the wound is left open for either a delayed primary closure (two to four days) or a secondary suture (eight to twelve days) or is drained (depending on anatomic circumstances), any remaining bits of tissue or foreign material are extruded. Bacteria, whose presence is inevitable, will then start their growth under circumstances in which the establishment of increased tissue pressure is impossible because of ready access to the outside world. This open growth will produce less damage than the analogous growth where closed-space tissue pressure develops, seeds the venous drainage with organisms, and produces progressive necrosis. The tissues of certain parts of the face have such a rich blood supply that primary closure is permissible.

Skilful debridement without excessive blood loss, leaving the wound open, immobilizing parts, and dealing with the injuries of the thoracic, abdominal, and pelvic cavity, is very major surgery. One of the purposes of debridement of muscle wounds is to identify the viable tissue; this identification is established by tissue turgor, consistency, color, anatomic continuity, and the occurrence of bleeding. Adequate debridement is therefore incompatible with "no blood loss." Debridement of extensive soft-tissue wounds may involve an operative blood loss of from 2000 to 4000 ml. This is getting close to the level of 0.75 blood volume. It is clear that the transfusion required in support of such definitive operation is very considerable.

The order in which these various tactical objectives of definitive surgery are accomplished must depend on the state of the patient, the duration of the injury, and the number of anatomic areas that have been injured. Thoracic or abdominal exploration with intestinal or visceral repair is best done first. Peripheral debridement and definitive fracture immobilization can come last.

5. Signs During Operation

The short-term chart begun many minutes or hours ago is now perpetuated as the anesthesia chart. In addition, urine volume is measured (as before). But most important are the indices of blood pressure and circulation and tissue perfusion: good heart action with a strong beat, skin and lip color, capillary circulation in fingernail beds and ear lobes. Maintenance of flow in these areas depends on volume, pressure, and vascular patency, as mentioned in the section on vasoconstrictors and vasodilators. Some of the objectives of operation itself, including particularly the airway, ventilation, and the control of hemorrhage, are directed at this same objective.

STAGE 5. POSTOPERATIVE CARE

The early postoperative hours comprise a most important period for the patient after severe injury; many struggles for survival are won or lost then. Vigilance cannot be relaxed and must give a view to the following:
1. Immediate Postoperative Stabilization,
2. Common Complications,
3. Sepsis,
4. Coagulation,
5. Renal Function,
6. X-Rays; Blood Studies, and
7. The Use of Antibiotics.

1. Immediate Stabilization

The short-term observation chart commenced at the time of the patient's admission continues its course in the early postoperative stabilization of a patient with multiple severe injuries who has just undergone definitive operation. Pulse, respiration rate, blood pressure, neurologic behavior, and mentation should be observed and charted at fifteen-minute intervals.

During this time the patient may need considerable further blood transfusion; he must be watched for delayed hemorrhage from his wounds or evidence of hidden hemorrhage. It is at this time, if hypotension persists, that taking up will be seen and huge blood volumes needed to restore flow. Now, with the operation completed, the maintenance of blood pressure, perfusion, and flow spells survival; there is no compromise.

Factors making for unresponsiveness must be considered now, as before, and steps taken for their correction.

2. Common Complications

The most troublesome early postoperative complications in severely injured patients are (approximately in order of frequency):
(1) sepsis,
(2) pulmonary complications,
(3) wound dehiscence,
(4) intestinal obstruction or other gastr-o intestinal abnormalities, and
(5) renal failure.

Later on in convalescence, failure to develop satisfactory nutrient intake with failure of anabolic gain of weight is a troublesome complication. In the early period it can be neglected.

Pulmonary complications of a variety of types are prone to develop. Atelectasis and partial collapse are the commonest. In the young and vigorous person, pulmonary embolus is rare. In older individuals it is more common, especially after injuries to the extremities.

In the patient with prolonged sepsis and extreme inanition due to septic starvation and weakness, the development of accumulative bronchopneumonia is the terminal event (even in the younger patient). This extreme inanition (produced by uncontrolled sepsis) may in itself so interfere with muscular activity as to render accumulative bronchopneumonia inevitable. This is not an early complication.

3. Sepsis

Invasive infection in the early postoperative period is the most dangerous to survival; later infection prolongs convalescence but is less dangerous to life. The most threatening sepsis takes one of four forms:

(1) anaerobic cellulitis or myositis,
(2) blood-stream infection,
(3) closed-space sepsis, and
(4) continued serous soiling.

The first of these, anaerobic infection, should be obviated by careful debridement and open management of wounds. If it develops postoperatively, it must be dealt with by radical incision, excision, and/or amputation.

The second of these, blood-stream infection, is the most common. When it is due to gram-negative bacilli, a protracted and recalcitrant hypotension results, often leading to renal failure. This may develop without a clear focus and with no clear operative shortcomings in the background. Maintenance of blood volume and flow, with the intensive use of antibiotics matched to sensitivity, remains the hope—often forlorn—in invasive blood-stream sepsis after severe trauma.

The third and fourth, closed-space sepsis and continued serous soiling, always mean inadequate drainage (ischiorectal, pelvic, gluteal, or cervical areas, for example), an unrepaired holed viscus (small bowel, liver, or esophagus, as examples), or a broken suture line (as in anastomosis or closure). They are thus evidences of operative failure and must be dealt with precisely as they would be in civilian surgery: recognition with reoperation, exteriorization, or drainage.

4. Coagulation

If the patient's coagulation mechanisms are faulty, it is in this early postoperative period that one first obtains evidences of the hemorrhagic diathesis that may later become a predominant problem in the patient's care. Occasionally these abnormalities become evident during operation. If there is a persistent tendency to bleed, the four studies of most importance are the determination of the prothrombin content, the clotting time, bleeding time, and platelet count (or smear).

Steps to be taken have been outlined in Part II and will not be detailed again here.

5. Renal Function and Infusion Test

It is in this early period of stabilization after definitive surgery that the patient comes under suspicion for the early signs of post-traumatic renal insufficiency. Although there may have been worrisome evidences earlier in the course, and although the patient's definitive operation may have been carried out in spite of threatened renal insufficiency, such evidences are never a contraindication to operative wound management. If surgery is put off because of threatened post-traumatic renal insufficiency, and infection later develops during the azotemic phase, all hope of recovery has been removed by delaying operation.

The relation of definitive operation to renal blood flow is therefore tuned to clinical evaluation of the effective blood volume and simple measures of circulatory adequacy such as color, capillary flow, warmth, mentation, and pulse volume. One cannot wait for clear evidence of lasting normal renal function before carrying out definitive operation. If reestablishment of hourly urine outputs of 15 to 25 ml. occurs with volume restoration, it is a good prognostic sign, but if circulation is restored without reestablishment of urine output, operation must still proceed. If continuing major hemorrhage is a factor, as mentioned previously, neither the blood pressure nor rate of urine flow is significant as a guide to the timing of operation; it must proceed regardless.

After the operation has been performed, the nature of renal function must now be evaluated in detail. If urine volumes maintain themselves at a normal range—from 15 to 50 ml. per hour—one may rest reasonably assured that blood volume is normal or close to normal and that the renal parenchyma is not too severely damaged.

When renal function slowly diminishes, one has a difficult differential diagnosis to accomplish. If dehydration, desalting water loss, or blood-volume deficit has been in the recent background, a test infusion of the most likely missing fluid is justified as a differential diagnostic point. When it is carried on this early in the course of the postoperative period, we have not seen harm result. A day or two later such a test infusion is filled with hazard for the reason that the patient, if in renal failure, may be already overloaded with fluid; transcapillary refilling is complete and the test infusion may itself be harmful. Elevated venous pressure is the paramount guide to infusion excess.

Early in the course such a test infusion involves the choice of water, water and salt, albumin, plasma, dextran, or whole blood. This choice depends on the rest of the clinical situation and the recent history of the patient's care. The substances most likely to be in deficit should be used, as described in Part V. If there is a clear-cut increase in renal output with this infusion, one is justified in assuming that the renal parenchyma is not severely damaged and that the low output was caused primarily by diminished glomerular filtration rate, lack of water, or some component of the ionic composition of blood.

If the output does not increase clearly, one is still dealing with a differential diagnosis that cannot be settled except by the passage of time. Additional signs may be helpful.

(1) The occurrence of *benzidine-reacting pigment* in the urine is a straw of evidence, suggesting that the kidney has been exposed to pigment toxins and that a parenchymatous renal lesion may ultimately develop, if it is not already present.

(2) The presence of *protein and casts* is also evidence, though unreliable, of renal damage.

(3) The finding of a *fixed specific gravity or osmolality* is of little differential diagnostic significance. If one studies the osmolality of the urine in a number of post-traumatic cases with and without renal insufficiency, it will be found that most of them at this stage show an osmolality of 500 to 750 mO. per l., which corresponds to a specific gravity of about 1.015 to 1.020. This is maintained. It is the result of the operation of normal post-traumatic antidiuresis in the face of a solute load. A fixed osmolality below 500 (sp. gr. below 1.010) with low urine volumes strongly suggests renal failure; a very concentrated low volume urine suggests good renal function and a need for additional infusions of fluid or blood.

(4) *Rising blood urea nitrogen and potassium concentrations* are a trademark of renal insufficiency, usually too late to be of help in differential diagnosis. They may also occur in advancing muscle sepsis (myositis) without renal failure, and this must be sought out before assigning "renal failure" to the casualty.

The airway, the central nervous system, the blood volume, renal function—these dominate the early stabilization phase of the patient after definitive surgery just as they did in evaluating the response to volume restoration after the original trauma. Homeostatic tension should now be falling back down toward normal. If not, operation has not accomplished its mission.

6. X-Rays and Blood Studies

Postoperative X-ray study may be needed for one or more of the following, as examples:

(1) gas in the tissues,
(2) reexpansion of the lung and/or hemo-thorax,
(3) position of fracture,
(4) subphrenic gas.

If such studies are needed the same general rules hold as those used before operation: economy of trips to the X-ray department, clarity of purpose, and completeness of accomplishment.

As to blood studies, as soon as possible after operation the hematocrit and blood urea nitrogen concentration should be checked. Other studies may be indicated, as in any surgical patient.

It should be noted again that the most delicate indices of water balance are a good intake-output record, a record of weight, and the plasma sodium concentration. The most delicate blood indices of renal functional adequacy are the carbon dioxide combining power and the level of plasma potassium; for pulmonary function, the patient's color and the carbon dioxide content of arterial blood are most satisfactory.

7. The Use of Antibiotics

The prophylactic use of antibiotics during this early postoperative period assists in the prevention of early invasive sepsis, as already described; antibiotics should be given in adequate doses, and should be administered parenterally. The two questions now are: (1) when should their use be stopped? and (2) should broad-spectrum antibiotics be used early?

It takes considerable courage to stop giving antibiotics to the severely injured man. *It is our conviction that there is little hazard in discontinuing the use of antibiotics on or about the fourth day in a patient whose initial convalescence appears to be satisfactory.* If systemic and metabolic responses are good at this time, the patient will localize any infection he is going to develop, can be more expeditiously cared for, and will have fewer "masked signs" off antibiotics than on. The points to be gained are: diminution in risk or pseudomembranous colitis and avoidance of the development of drug-resistance.

The antibiotic program that follows is advisable for the multiple-injured patient in military or civilian conditions.

(1) Initial antibiotic therapy is given for from four to six days with penicillin and streptomycin at high dosage, administered parenterally. Broad-spectrum antibiotics are not used.

(2) All antibiotics are discontinued at four to six days after operation. Further antibiotics are used only on the basis of invasive infection or the cultural identification of the organism and its sensitivity.

(3) The pulmonary infections (atelectasis, bronchopneumonia), urinary infection, or other local visceral infectious processes are treated by appropriate steps, including antibiotics as needed, as they would be under any other circumstances.

(4) Local wound infection is cared for thereafter by appropriate surgical drainage or exteriorization.

Section IV. The Later Postoperative Period—Anabolism and Rehabilitation

A. THE BEGINNING OF RECOVERY

As the patient stabilizes and regains consciousness after anesthesia, six to twelve hours after definitive operation, with established urine output and good circulation, he starts in the wounded man's version of the first phase of surgical convalescence. He has had a complex course to here, involving five dynamic stages. For several days now he will

tend to be febrile, have little desire for food, lose weight rapidly, demonstrate increased steroid excretion in the urine (even though blood steroid levels may be falling), and will demonstrate the waning of the stress phase (initiated by the wound), which has ceased to operate as a strong stimulus following the completion of definitive operation. In a healthy young man who is severely injured, the intensity of tissue catabolism in this early period is very great indeed. He should be managed "in balance" as regards water and electrolyte; if he is weighed, he should be expected to lose weight briskly for a few days; no effort is made to keep him in perfect balance of macronutrients—fat, protein, calories.

Concerning this early weight loss after trauma, two points are to be made.

(1) It is not necessary to carry out multiple body-weight measurements on every severely injured patient. The weight curve merely illustrates the nature of the catabolic process that follows trauma. The normal loss of weight is due to the oxidation of fat and the lysis of lean tissue. If there is difficulty in managing the patient's fluid balance—as in renal failure or extrarenal loss—multiple body-weight measurements are of practical assistance.

(2) The abolition of this weight loss does not constitute evidence of "improved homeostasis after injury." Instead, in most cases, the abolition of this weight loss means that the patient is being given too much water. After severe trauma, the maintenance of constant body weight on intravenous fluid therapy is *prima facie* evidence of overloading with fluid; after three or four days, if the patient has lost no weight and has been severely injured, one may safely assume that there is from 2000 to 4000 ml. of unnecessary fluid in his body. Under some circumstances this fluid may subsequently be lost by diuresis, and in others—as in renal failure—it may presage the development of severe hypertension, cardiac failure, and death. In still other instances, this loading of water is in a special area of sequestered edema (as in crush or peritonitis) and will be diuresed as capillary permeability is restored.

Considering the frequency of injury to the abdominal cavity, it is not surprising that the effect of taking and absorbing food will be considerably delayed; early forced feeding of such patients is hazardous. Our aphorism that the "nutritional objective of the first phase of convalescence is a scaphoid abdomen" is seldom more true than here. The patient with sutured holes in the bowel, with exteriorized large bowel, with a lacera-

tion of the liver or recently removed spleen, will surely become distended, with cramps, gas pain, vomiting, and aspiration, if he is fed too soon. Acute gastric dilatation and ileus, rather than improved nutrition, are the result. There is no evidence that attempts to feed the patient before he is passing gas freely out the lower end of his gastrointestinal tract make any contribution to his well-being.* Once peristalsis has returned, and the expulsion of flatus through anus or colostomy is established with regularity, then feeding the patient and raising his dietary intake rapidly up to normal or supernormal levels is of unsurpassed importance in his later recovery. This dynamic nature of the changing need for exogenous diet in the injured individual must be repeatedly stressed.

B. LATER NUTRITIONAL PROBLEMS

In patients with chronic peritoneal sepsis, exteriorized bowel, intestinal obstruction, penetrating wounds of the upper gastrointestinal tract, or septic fractures, the subsequent dynamic progress of later convalescence may stall for lack of diet. After two weeks of passing through the catabolic valley of convalescence, an upward climb is expected. In starving patients it does not occur.

A most common difficulty is that the patient is harboring infection that must be abated by appropriate steps. Or, rarely, he simply will not begin to eat. He has no urge for food, no appetite, and seemingly no motive; or, eating, he does not absorb his food as a result of diarrhea, vomiting, or ileus. The use of tube-feedings or total parenteral alimentation occasionally has a place here as a means of tiding the patient over a low-intake phase.

This is a common-sense problem. The patient must take on the nourishment required for convalescence, and he will usually do this

---

* To paraphrase Sir Heneage Ogilvie:
    "Nothing will please as much as
    Sounds that would shock a Duchess;
    They are music of the spheres
    To the belly surgeon's ears."
           Ibid., et al. (1959)

when infection and the functional anatomy of the gastrointestinal tract are restored to normal. Destructive processes, such as pancreatitis, hepatitis, or massive bowel resection, make the resumption of gastrointestinal function difficult. In such cases prolonged parenteral nutriment with high caloric mixtures is important and finds its greatest utility. In the end it is enteral feeding—usually oral—that gets the patient out of the hospital.

A few points of interest in trying to achieve resumption of normal oral intakes in such patients are reviewed here.

The gastrointestinal tract that has not been aeking food for many days or weeks is in itself very trcalcitrant. It does not develop appetite, absorbs food poorly, and seems to suffer an intrinsic functional disorder as a result of the starvation process. It needs food to get started. Initial tube feedings for a day or two may be followed by resumption of normal appetite and gastrointestinal activity, once the functional and anatomic barriers due to obstruction, diarrhea, or fistula no longer exist. Of the micronutrients, iron seems to be one of the most important in promoting normal gastrointestinal function and absorption.

Psychologic factors are important. The presence of an indwelling nasogastric tube or Miller-Abbott tube, sloppy or stinking dressings, irritated skin areas, unattractive food, and disinterested attendants are all deleterious to the patient's resumption of normal food taking. Tubes should be removed, even though they may have to be inserted again at a later time for initial feeding or measurement of residue. The patient should not be fed "slops," but should be given nutritious and appetizing meals of familiar food, tastefully prepared, served hot with full aroma.

Intravenously administered caloric nourishment is a strong inhibitor of gastrointestinal secretion and motility. Intravenously given glucose kills hunger. This is especially true of intravenous feedings of glucose and fat; it is true to some extent of alcohol administered by this route. If the patient is trying to make a shift-over to oral diet, such intravenous feedings must be discontinued or, if they are a necessity,

they should be shifted to an evening time so that the normal morning appetite can be resumed.

Certain types of appetite stimulants such as alcoholic drinks may be useful: sherry, brandy, whiskey, a cocktail. The patient who has not been taking food for some time is extremely sensitive to intoxicating beverages and the dose must be small if it is desirable to have the patient remain conscious. There are other tricks: home cooking, special foods of ethnic association (ravioli, matzos, almond cakes). This is a job for a good dietition, as described in Part IV.

C. THE USE OF HORMONES

Hormones that have been considered potentially useful in late nutritional rehabilitation are:

(1) testosterone,
(2) other "anabolic" (some nonandrogenic) steroids,
(3) adrenocorticotropic hormone,
(4) cortisone.

These are discussed in full in Part IV. It appears that, in a normal person on a fixed caloric and nitrogen intake, it is possible to increase nitrogen anabolism with testosterone. This is occasionally true in this later phase of convalescence. If such therapy avoids unnecessary nitrogen wastage and anabolizes protein in sites and tissues which the body ordinarily would build up at this time, it might be helpful. Increased appetite and sense of well-being, some stimulation of libido, and other side effects of testosterone therapy are much more important in most cases.

We have seen patients in whom such therapy produced systemic benefits, emotional and psychologic assistance. We have no evidence—and we know of none presented in the literature—to indicate that production of nitrogen anabolism *per se* on minimal intake of food is beneficial. The benefit observed is traceable wholly to the increased appetite and total intake.

Testosterone, "anabolic" derivatives, estrogens, and cortisone may all turn out to have a greater area of usefulness in late convalescence after compound trauma than is now generally appreciated, but we can find little evidence for it. Their greatest usefulness may be sought in areas quite aside from the addition of a few grams of nitrogen to muscle. Dose effects, combined usage, reciprocal inhibition, and other aspects of endocrine therapy have yet to be worked out. Of all these drugs by far the most dangerous is cortisone because of its gastrointestinal effects: ulceration and hemorrhage.

The dynamics of late recovery are in nowise different from those of other injury. Caloric output in the form of work must be less than caloric intake until body tissue has been restored by the energy-consuming activity of protein synthesis. In fractures and minor injury this is no problem. In more severe compound injury anabolic convalescence takes a long time.

But, unlike major soft-tissue injury, where this time must be spent over and beyond that seemingly needed for healing the injured tissues themselves, in fracture the two proceed together. The final resumption of full use, as exemplified by weight-bearing after major fracture, may occupy from two to six months, a period during which anabolic restoration of lean tissue and fat is completed. Architectural remodeling of the site may proceed for an additional year on full use—visible evidence of the continued metabolic activity of a wound long after return of tensile integrity. Late bone change or restoration of osteoporosis may consume one to three years.

Active and passive motion of joints, periarticular structures and muscle bellies not only restores the anatomy and range of motion, power, and size of these structures, but also stimulates lean-tissue reconstruction generally, and initiates the stress-determined architectural reorganization of the fracture site itself. The larger role of rehabilitation, physiotherapy, and occupational therapy in recovery is beyond the scope of this book.

Section V.   Wounds and Severe Multiple Injury: Notes from the Literature

A. DATA FROM RECENT MILITARY EXPERIENCE*

Churchill (1944) reviewed the current experience in the surgery of the wounded; he emphasized delayed primary closure of soft-tissue wounds during the "golden period" of four to ten days after wounding. He emphasized the significance of delay in initial treatment as a factor which "increases the loss of life and limbs."

Clinical data on the care of the wounded man, as based on experience in World War II, were gathered together in several reviews by Beecher. These include the official report filed with the Surgeon General (BSSW, Beecher, ed., 1952) and a number of papers in the surgical literature, including Beecher and Burnett (1944), Beecher (1945), Beecher (1945), Beecher et al. (1947), Beecher (1949), and Beecher (1951). Beecher's monograph

(Beecher, 1952, b) summarizes many of these data.

Also emanating from the experiences of the American and British forces in World War II were the reviews of Altemeier (1944), DeBakey and Carter (1945), Baldwin and Reynolds (1945), Forsee (1951), Grant and Reeve (1951), and Beebe and DeBakey (1952).

Much of the Korean experience has already been cited. The work of Howard and his group there was greatly facilitated and strongly oriented by the studies terminated six years previously by Churchill and his group in the Mediterranean Theater. In both instances the presence of an active team of clinical investigators was of prime importance in raising the standard of care in thg area and in providing a focus for the teachind of military surgery to men primarily orienten to the rather different problems of civiliae surgery. Additional Korean data will be

---

* See also Part II for a review of certain aspects of the shock problem.

found in Strawitz *et al.* (1953) and Artz *et al.* (1955).

Despite the short interval between Omaha Beach and Heartbreak Ridge (seven years) the mortality and morbidity data from the experiences of World War II and Korea show striking contrasts. Sako *et al.* (1955) present some of the contrasts. In abdominal and thoracico-abdominal wounds the case mortality rate was reduced by 30 to 50 per cent in the Korean experience as compared to World War II. Some of this was doubtless due to a shorter duration to definitive surgery (6.3 as against 8.9 hours in one series), a more stable front line, helicopter evacuation, and so on. A more limited use of "resuscitative fluids" (averaging 1 liter less in one series) could be discerned in the World War II experience. But the use of antibiotics and the lesser nature of the total operation (permitting more complete concentration of severely wounded in thoroughly competent hands) seem to us to be the most important two factors in the contrast. Barring some important break-through in the treatment of late severe shock, one has no reason to anticipate that the Korean experience would be equaled or surpassed in another general continental war on a large scale, even omitting consideration of irradiation injuries and thermonuclear weapons. In the report of Sako, the abdominal wound (mortality 12.7 per cent) is still among the most lethal, to be contrasted with the over-all mortality in a series of 4711 casualty admissions (mortality 2.4 per cent).

Scully and Hughes (Howard, BCK III) studied the pathology of skeletal muscle after traumatic arterial ischemia, in thirty-one cases. The changes were consistent with previous clinical and experimental reports (Harman, 1947, 1948; Mallory, 1952; Brooks, 1922). Exaggeration of cross-striation, swelling, fiber-separation, and necrosis with patchy regeneration were noted. The post-release swelling was not always explainable histologically. The color change to pale yellow or cream was seen in muscle both with and without total necrosis, indicating that depigmentation is not always a reliable sign of irreversible damage. These changes are very similar to those reported in the crush syndrome in World War II. As an added detail, Scully and Hughes point out that the state of viability of the gastrocnemius is not always a reliable guide to the state of viability of the soleus and other distal groups.

Scully *et al.* (Howard, BCK III) also made a careful evaluation of the clinical criteria for determining muscle viability. Using biopsy control they showed that consistency (firmness, as opposed to mushiness, stringiness, or softness), ability to bleed, and contractility were the reliable guides to viability. Color was unreliable.

Clostridia were cultured with frequency from war wounds of all three recent wars (World Wars I and II and Korea). The percentage of wounded developing clostridial myositis fell from 5.0 per cent to 0.7 per cent to 0.08 per cent in comparable series of the three wars. This declining incidence was due to many factors, of which earlier and more complete debridement and the use of antibiotics must be rated high. The case fatality rates in World Wars I and II were not significantly different—about one in three cases of gas gangrene was fatal. In Korea the cases were few and there were no fatalities (Howard and Invi, 1954). Wound and soil cultures showed that clostridia were often present in the area. The presence of Clostridium perfringens in an infected wound must be regarded as a clostridial infection; this is clearly not synonymous with gas gangrene, an advancing gas-forming myonecrosis due wholly to the clostridium. Once infection is evident, with wine-colored wound fluid, myonecrosis, and gas, the only effective treatment is based on wide excision or amputation, plus antibiotics and antitoxin.

Current work by Lindsay and his group in wounded goats indicates the possibility of fatality from clostridial infection in the absence of gas gangrene. Shock and hypovolemia are also present. Death rate correlates with bacterial abundance and this in turn with blood-volume deficit. The setting is not unlike the experiments of Aub, in which anaerobic infection was fatal without gas gangrene, and Fine, in which a variety of septic processes throve in oligemic shock in the dog. The goat differs from the dog insofar as neither muscle nor liver harbors spores normally as it does in the dog. But the deep skin crypts do, and within hours after a blast injury the wound is overgrown with a variety of pathogenic clostridia. Local antitoxin and systemic antibiotics have a favorable effect. Death occurs after eight to eighteen hours have passed. Clostridial infection in soldiers may be fatal under twelve hours after wounding. Lindberg *et al.* (1955) showed that Aureomycin and terramycin were the most effective antibiotics against the clostridia isolated in Korea.

Blood cultures were positive in about 10 to 12 per cent of severely wounded battle casualties in Korea (Strawitz *et al.*, 1955). Aerobic gram-negative bacilli and staphylococci predominated.

The question of sepsis in battle wounds, its relation to environmental sepsis and renal failure, has recently been reviewed by Howe (1954), Balch (1955), Robertson *et al.* (1956), and Artz and Teschan (1957).

Anaerobic contamination and infections and gas gangrene as occurring in battle wounds of World War II and Korea have been reviewed by MacLennan (1943), Mc-Clean (1943), Cooke *et al.* (1945), Mac-Lennan and Macfarlane (1945), and Lindberg *et al.* (1954 and 1955).

Data from the Korean War on anatomic wound distribution are listed below:

The prominence of the head in all categories is offset only by the later deaths in abdominal wounds after treatment; the two categories together occupy the bulk of morality, both early and late. The late abdominal deaths are due to shock and infection.

Higgins *et al.* (1954) surveyed seventy-six consecutive cases of head injury. There were several cases of dehydration with hypertonicity and several of respiratory alkalosis. Other than these the disorders were those which might be expected after any trauma. There were five cases of what might be called "cerebral salt-wasting," but the biochemical data are too sketchy to reconstruct a possible mechanism; all the patients were elderly and may have had some disease of the renal tubules. Higgins thought the hypertonicity was due to lesions at the base of the frontal lobes; no mention is made of renal tubular findings in these cases.

Studies of head injury by Smolik and his coworkers has been focussed on the blood volume changes. They reported (Smolik *et al.*, 1956) that over half of a group of 21 patients with closed head injury showed an initial increase in blood volume, a change of interest relative to the early hypertension often observed in the wounded by Howard and his group (BCK, I). In some of Smolik's cases the hypervolemia was as much as 60 per cent above normal. Such large changes demand confirmation, but the trend is of great interest relative to transfusion in closed head injury.

Studies on head injury with special reference to mechanisms and physiologic results will be found in Fischer (1952), Gurdjian and Webster (1945), and Gurdjian and Stone (1946).

Levene (1955) reported adrenal hemorrhage after head injury.

Forsee *et al.* (1956) reemphasize the multi-

	LETHAL WOUNDS OF MEN KILLED IN ACTION	TOTAL WOUNDS OF MEN KILLED IN ACTION	WOUNDS IN ACTION	WOUNDS, LATER LETHAL, AFTER TREATMENT
	Per Cent			
Head	41.6	24.1	14.0	28.0
Neck	4.2	6.2	3.0	6.0
Thorax	36.0	27.7	19.0	21.0
Abdomen	9.5	11.0	11.0	22.5
Upper extremity	1.7	14.1	23.0	2.5
Lower extremity	7.0	16.7	29.0	14.0
Buttocks	—	—	—	6.0
Genitalia	—	0.2	1.0	—

ple hazards of closed chest trauma; pulmonary hematoma, lung cavitation, aneurysm, vascular obstruction, and cardiac contusion may all result, even in the absence of fracture. Moerch *et al.* (1956) report on the improved respiratory dynamics, using a forced mechanical hyperventilation in crushing injuries of the chest. The fragmented bony thoracic circumference is then passively conforming to lung expansion rather than attempting to induce pulmonary expansion by muscular effects in a situation where the muscle inserts on broken and unstable bones. The apparatus was used via tracheotomy. Results and respiratory studies seemed to demonstrate the value of the concept. Accurate control of the positive pressure cycle in the airway is essential if reduction in venous return is to be avoided.

Scully (Howard, BCK III) studied postmortem changes with great care in the Korean casualty, and found some evidence of pulmonary fat embolism in 90 per cent of 110 severely wounded patients. In only 19 per cent was the involvement significant in degree. In 4 per cent there was embolization of the kidneys, and in one case there was fatal fat embolus with brain involvement. Pulmonary fat embolism appears to be clinically insignificant.

Air embolus was unfortunately observed in the Korean casualties when transfusion was given under pressure by the air-pump method.

The occasional striking usefulness of 1 to 2 gm. calcium gluconate given intravenously to patients still hypotensive after massive transfusion was demonstrated in Korea (Strawitz, Howard and Artz, 1955). The dose was 10 ml. of a 10 per cent solution of calcium gluconate containing approximately 90 mg. of calcium. The effect was not always lasting. The calcium administered is not inconsiderable, being about one-fifth of the total ionized calcium of the extracellular fluid. These patients had all received large doses of citrate.

In normal individuals a peripheral vasodilatation and slight respiratory stimulus follows the administration of calcium; these

effects may be related to the benefit occasionally observed in severe trauma. The improvement in heart sounds, pulse volume, and blood pressure suggested a role of citrate toxicity in setting the stage for the effectiveness of calcium in these patients.

Vasoconstrictors were most useful (Howard, BCK II) in the postanesthetic and postoperative period after resuscitation of the shocked soldier, when the adrenolytic effect of deep surgical anesthesia could be reversed by the use of vasoconstrictors. As is universally discovered in the care of such patients, vasoconstrictors were limited in usefulness both as to scope and duration. A refractory state appears to develop rapidly; alternative drugs are then only transiently effective. Vasodilators were not used in the Korean experience.

Comments on the protective action of dibenzyline will be found in Remington *et al.* (1950) and Baez *et al.* (1952), of chlorpromazine in Hershey *et al.* (1954, 1956).

Autonomic studies in the Korean casualties (Howard, BCK I) were limited to a series of very ingenious observations of the peripheral circulation made in collaboration with Simeone. Problems of blood volume and environmental temperature obscured results. A few cases of post-traumatic hypertension were observed. The principal conclusion drawn confirmed the impression of a change in sympathetic activity after wounding; degrees of activity were difficult to assess. There was no evidence of obliteration of autonomic activity by the trauma or circulatory disturbances observed. The possibility that high cord lesions might produce a sort of vasodilated hypotension associated with lack of central autonomic connections ("spinal shock") was considered but did not fall into the study categories.

The less severely wounded man who develops hypertension attracted the attention of the investigators. A total of fifty-two patients was observed. The hypertension occurred from thirty minutes to three to four hours after wounding; blood volume loss was in the range of 15 to 25 per cent. Some of the patients had extensive wounds such as traumatic amputation. Transfusion even of 1000 ml. of blood occasionally resulted in marked systolic hypertension. In these cases the administration of an anesthetic, either spinal or thiopental-ether, resulted in a sharp drop in pressure to normal or subnormal levels. The impression is gained that post-traumatic hypertension represents the activity of a pressor mechanism activated by trauma but not entirely volume-linked. When there is trauma with somewhat less than the usual blood volume lost, the result is hypertension. This could be abolished by hexamethonium but not wholly by phentolamine (Regitine); the hypertensive state carried a very good prognosis.

Special studies from the Korean experience include the data of Stahl *et al.* (1954) on the autonomic nervous system, Scott and Howard (1955) on liver function, Scott and Crosby (1955) on coagulation, Levenson *et al.* (1955) on protein intermediates, Howard *et al.* (1955) on adrenal function, and Howard *et al.* (1955) on electrolyte alterations.

The relation of closed abdominal injury to the pancreas, and the special significance of pancreatic injury, have been reviewed by Warren (1951), Popper and Necheles (1951), Estes *et al.* (1952), Joseph (1952), Howard *et al.* (1955), Howard (1955), Howard *et al.* (1955), and Culotta *et al.* (1956).

The Korean experience (BCK II) indicated that the best analgesic combination early in the patient's course is a small dose of morphine (10 mg.) and a barbiturate.

As regards the phenomenon we have termed "clinical taking up," Crosby states that in Korea certain patients were, in a sense, "overtransfused" as *necessary* to support blood pressure and tissue perfusion, and later showed congestive phenomena and then polycythemia (that is, as plasma dispersal could proceed). These were often wounds of the abdomen with considerable bacterial contamination and early sepsis. In the extremity wounds of the muscle-belly type (often involving amputation) the need for blood was great but anemia was observed later. This latter was the prototype of the "disappearing blood" syndrome studied by Prentice *et al.* (see Part II).

Crosby reported no problems from potassium or citrate in his experience, nor from mass use of group O Rh-negative blood. The latter gave trouble only in cross-matching or in return to transfusions of the patient's own type in less than two weeks.

Table VI. Certain relative effects of the sympathomimetic amines, from various sources.

	MUSCLE VESSEL DILATATION	HEART			PERIPHERAL RESISTANCE
		FORCE	RATE	AUTOMATICITY	
Epinephrine	+	+	+	+	0
Norepinephrine	+	+	+	+	+
Ephedrine (slower)	+	+	+	+	+
Methoxamine	0	0	0	0	+
Neo-synephrine	0	0	0	0	+

	CARDIAC EFFECTS	PERIPHERAL VESSELS
Methoxamine	0	++++
Neo-synephrine	±	+++
Norepinephrine	++	++++
Aramine	++	+++
Epinephrine	+++	±
Ephedrine	+++	±
Isopropyl Epinephrine (Isoprel)	+++++	− − (Dilator)
Arfonad	0	− − (Dilator)
Dibenzyline	0	− − − − − (Dilator)

B. DATA FROM CIVILIAN STUDIES

Crash mechanics, decelerative forces, impact velocities, and vehicle design have been studied and analyzed by DeHaven (1946), Woodward (1948), Lombard (1949), Harper (1952), McFarland (1953), Schaefer (1953), Gurdjian *et al.* (1953, 1955) and Campbell (1954).

Giuseffi and Carter (1954) have reported the results of tracheotomy in the crushed chest. Other reports of early care of thoracic trauma include Carter and Giuseffi (1951), King and Harris (1953), Willner (1953), and Webb (1956). Useful reviews of the problem of traumatic wet lung are to be found in Burford and Burbank (1945) and Daniel and Cate (1948).

Noble and Gregerson (1946) reported data on the blood volume in clinical shock, contrasting hemorrhage and trauma with burns. The problem of measurement in such critical and rapidly changing circumstances is always a difficult one.

Burnett *et al.* (1947) discussed the use of alkali in shock. Carryer (1947) described tissue anoxia resulting from the change in oxyhemoglobin dissociation in severe alkalosis. This latter would not be expected in alkali treatment of shock but is a problem in metabolic alkalosis.

Response to vasopressors in shock, and their relation to corticosteroids and acid-base effects, has been studied by Raab *et al.* (1950), Kurland and Freedberg (1951), and Moyer *et al.* (1955).

The controversy concerning intra-arterial transfusion has already been alluded to in Part II. Case *et al.* (1953) state the case against it but, in our opinion, do not consider the situation (elderly, digitalized patients with high venous pressure) in which it is most apt to be useful. Sarnoff (1954) adduces the evidence from the dog that it is useless, evidence that has little bearing on man. Bingham (1952), Seeley and Nelson (1952), Maloney *et al.* (1954), Richards and Hansen (1954), and Alrich and Morton (1951) find evidence favoring intra-arterial transfusion.

Ebert (1955) showed that shock from a bacterial toxin (in dogs) would respond to norepinephrine plus volume support (dextran). It is of interest that the animal in shock has decreased properdin levels and a decreased ability to clear organisms from the blood stream.

Peltier (1954) described a method for detecting fat emboli in the circulating blood, using centrifugation and fluorescence microscopy. In a series of seventy-eight patients following elective bone and joint surgery there were droplets present in forty-three. In only one was there a clinical episode that would suggest fat embolus. There was good correlation between the magnitude of the bony injury and the presence of embolic fat. Peltier at this time advanced the theory that embolic fat was virtually a normal sequel of bony trauma and that its conversion into clinical damage was the result of other factors. In 1955 Peltier reported that dietary lipemia did not affect the fat embolus rate in rabbits after fracture. He interpreted this as further evidence that the local marrow fat is the source of the material at fault in fat embolus.

The same investigator, in a series of articles (Peltier, 1956, a,b; Peltier *et al.*, 1956), has reinvestigated many facets of the problem of fat embolism. He found that human long bones did indeed contain large amounts of fat, especially in the metaphyseal plate, that this fat resembled human subcutaneous fat chemically, and that intravascular toxicity was in part a function of viscosity, with resultant obstruction of the pulmonary vascular bed. He postulates calcium bonding of fat as one toxic feature in capillary endothelium.

The work of Johnson and Svanborg (1956) suggests that fat embolism does not originate from the bone marrow, but results from a qualitative change in the physicochemical state of the serum lipids. The studies of Davis and Musselman (1954) carry the same implication in terms of partial agglomeration.

Peltier (1954) has perfected a method of detecting fat emboli in the peripheral blood and in tissue sections (1954) and has reported (1952) a fatality following intramedullary nailing. In addition to references already cited, the extensive work of Peltier in this field may be found in Peltier (1955, a, b), Peltier (1956), Peltier *et al.* (1956), Peltier (1956), and Peltier (1956).

Reviews of the incidence of fat embolism, its diagnosis and treatment, will be found in Gauss (1916), Lehman and Moore (1927), Wright (1932), Scuderi (1941), Wilson and Salisbury (1944), Newman (1948), Dunphy and Ilfeld (1949), Harman and Ragaz (1950), Rappaport *et al.* (1951), Whiteley (1954),

Swank and Dugger (1954), Saikku (1954), and Nelson and Bowers (1956).

Bryans and Eiseman (1956) studied fat emboli ("globulemia") after a variety of procedures and found that the phenomenon was often observable after soft-tissue procedures, and might be a nonspecific response to trauma rather than a bone-marrow phenomenon. Adrenocorticotropic hormone did not produce the phenomenon.

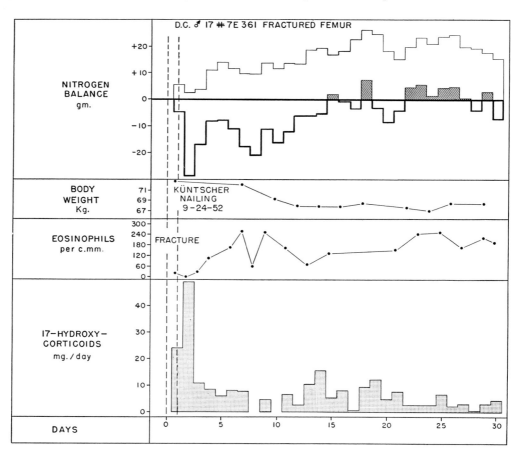

Figure 132. METABOLISM IN FRACTURE OF THE FEMUR

In this chart are shown the nitrogen balance, body weight, eosinophil count, and urinary corticosteroid excretion in a young man with a fracture of the femur incurred on the football field.

The intensity of the nitrogen catabolism will be noted. After the fourth day this catabolism persisted, despite provision of a large caloric intake by mouth.

It will be noted that body weight was maintained for several days before it fell abruptly. This drop was associated with diuresis of water and sodium (not shown here).

The very high urinary hydroxycorticosteroid value bespeaks a maximum traumatic stimulus with a quick restoration to normal.

Studies such as this are eleoquent evidence of the dissociation between corticosteroid excretion and nitrogen metabolism in severe injury. A portion of the nitrogen lost here results from the degradation of blood extravasated into the thigh, and the excretion of the end-products during a catabolic period when they are not used as building blocks for other tissues.

CHAPTER 46

Fractures in the Elderly; the Fractured Hip; Metabolism in Fractures, and the Use of Anabolic Steroids

Section I.   Fractured Hip as a Disease

A. THE MEANING OF THE SEX DIFFERENTIAL

The sex differential of incidence in fractures of the femoral neck and intertrochanteric area suggests one of three explanations. Either

(1) more women live to senility than men, or

(2) more women fall down than men, or

(3) there is a systemic factor—postmenopausal osteoporosis—that favors the occurrence of this injury in women.

All three factors play a role in this disease, but the third is by far the most important. There is a strong likelihood in many fractures of the femoral neck, particularly those with a vertical shear, that the fracture preceded the fall and was due to postmenopausal osteoporosis with weakening of the femoral neck resistance to shear stress. Where the distal fragment is driven in and the fracture impacted, one may postulate that the fall provided the fracturing force; but here again weakness in the skeletal structure plays a role since, of the basic skeletal stresses (torsion, shear, and impaction), it is impaction to which the normal skeleton is most resistant.

There is evidence that the osteoporotic skeleton of the older woman is soft and stress-sensitive. This is one of the few solid facts about the soft bones of older women; very little is known of the actual healing deficit in osteoporosis, if there is any. That this osteoporosis is due to estrogen lack at an age when corticosteroids are still active seems logical. In the male the slightly longer androgenic phase and its greater skeletal effect seem to account for the lower incidence of osteoporosis.

When we turn to fracture healing, however, the story is not so clear. There is little to suggest that osteoporosis interferes with fracture healing; there is little to suggest that the administration of androgens and estrogens hastens bone healing. There are data to suggest that these gonadal steroids will favor calcification (as evidenced by calcium balance) and increased laying down of osteoid (as evidenced by nitrogen balance).

B. THE MEANING OF AGE IN TRAUMA

Quite aside from the role of osteoporosis in the pathogenesis of these fractures, age itself is an important factor in treatment. The effect of age on recovery after trauma, as in surgical care as a whole, is to be interpreted in the light of specific organ function, the latter in turn largely determined by vascular degeneration. Liver and lung function in the elderly are largely independent of atherosclerosis and degenerative vascular disease, whereas heart, brain, and kidney can only work as well as their arteries will let them. Liver and lung are low-pressure areas of the circulation; their vascular diseases are relatively rare problems and not, generally speaking, a function of the age-atherosclerosis-hypertension complex.

The aging traumatized patient should therefore be cared for, as indeed is any other surgical patient, according to a realistic evaluation of visceral function: heart, brain, and kidneys. If viscera still have some youthful functional resilience, the operative care can proceed with little change necessitated by age alone. If one or more of the viscera are doing poorly (as evidenced by renal or heart failure or poor mentation), one must devote attention—often futile—to improving their function. Equally important and, by contrast, always effective is the avoidance of further deterioration by ill-conceived treatment. Aside from minor improvement before operation by close attention to fluids and medication, one cannot expect too much functional improvement in senile heart, brain, or kidneys. But with poorly arranged management the systemic deficit due to poor visceral function is greatly magnified. A tolerable balance is easily tipped to failure.

The elderly patient with senile changes of atherosclerotic disease in kidneys, heart, and brain displays a very narrow margin between good treatment and treatment that is dangerous. As an example, oligemic hypotension is very poorly tolerated and carries in its wake a high incidence of renal failure or vascular thrombosis, yet overtransfusion rapidly results in pulmonary edema. The same narrow range exists in dehydration versus fluid therapy, in pain versus coma, and in the planning of anesthesia and sedation.

Although these factors may be susceptible to leisurely analysis in elective surgery, they permit of only a few hours of leeway in preparing for operation after a fractured hip. Immobilization of the fracture must take precedence over a too-prolonged period of preparation.

C. THE MIND AS A PROGNOSTIC FACTOR IN SURGERY OF THE ELDERLY

The alertness of the elderly patient, her response to surroundings, visitors, and the personalities of those in attendance, and her desire to assist in the petty-nuisance details of convalescence—all these are priceless assets. One may assign the reason for the importance of these qualities of mind, or soul, to some intangibles. The concept of "*élan vital*" may have a place. But the causes for death when these are lacking are to be found in the following very practical terms:

(1) aspiration of food or tube feedings,
(2) starvation,
(3) accumulative pneumonia,
(4) incontinence; decubitus ulcers,
(5) disarrangement of apparatus,
(6) dehydration, and
(7) restlessness, sleeplessness, aimless thrashing, and fatigue.

If the traumatized elderly patient lacks the qualities of mentation there is usually little to be done to recapture the clear-eyed vision of an earlier year. In rare cases, improvement in cardiac compensation or some other contributory factor may "wake up" the drowsy or "tame down" the irrational. In practical terms, the more important step is to be found in recognition of the blessing of good mentation when present and the avoidance of anything (such as oversedation or overhydration) that may unseat the mind of the senile surgical patient. Good lively (but not tiring) visitors, stimulating food, normal conversations and surroundings, a bit of the stimulus of preprandial alcohol may accomplish a good deal in the field of geriatric surgery.

D. AGED BONE: OSTEOPOROSIS AND ISCHEMIA

The young child heals quickly and gains both local and systemic anabolism. His fractures heal solidly with rapidity, he rebuilds muscular strength, and goes ahead with normal skeletal growth very soon after an injury. Whether this rapid and effective turning of the post-traumatic metabolic wheel peters out gradually through the years or whether it goes along at a steady rate, somewhat slower than in childhood, through the years of middle age, and then drops off rapidly with endocrine quiescence is unknown. When soft-tissue operation, such as that for carcinoma of the stomach, carcinoma of the rectum, or cholecystectomy, is carried out in elderly people, convalescence may be slow, but final healing and recovery are surprisingly good. The patient will recover according to his visceral function: kidneys, heart, and brain. The indefinable systemic factors of age seem to be somewhat less important than in fractures.

Fractures in elderly people involve especially difficult problems already alluded to: the osteoporotic fragile bones, the strong tendency to develop decubitus ulcers, cardiovascular disease, and the ravages of immobilization and sedation. Additionally, the aged patient regains ambition, strength, and vigor much more slowly, if at all, and may take a longer time to produce solid union. But more important as a local factor in the aged is the fact that it requires blood supply to heal fractures.

Were one to measure the resiliency of the vasculature by oscillometry, rubor, blanching, or reactive hyperemia, one would find that such patients have the diminished peripheral blood flow characteristic of arteriosclerosis, but, even in the aged, vascular impairment is not critical in visceral healing unless the surgery itself is poorly done. The stomach, for example, has a generous blood supply associated with parietal cell function, which requires such a vast energy expenditure. After operation the same blood supply is devoted to healing.

By sharp contrast, the skeleton exists throughout adult life on a vasculature only barely sufficient to maintain the small cellular mass of bone cortex. The rich blood supply of the marrow would be helpful if the marrow were particularly active. In most bones it is not a high-oxygen–requiring tissue and in many long bones it is inactive, fatty marrow. Therefore, when the bone is broken and the blood vessels disrupted, the healing process must proceed on an interrupted minimal vascular supply. In young and healthy people this seems to be enough. With the vascular impairment of advancing age, it is not sufficient.

It is therefore a first concern, in elderly people with fractures, to support the circulation. The oxygen-carrying capacity per unit of blood becomes of critical importance in individuals with borderline circulation, whereas in young and healthy people it is a matter of much less importance so long as the hematocrit is maintained over 25.

In young adults the vascular supply to the extremities is so much in excess of local tissue requirements that even with a hematocrit of 20, anoxia of peripheral tissues does not readily result. In the elderly, where only a small trickle of blood is passing through the skeletal tissues, the peripheral erythrocyte concentration (as indicated by hematocrit, hemoglobin, or erythrocyte count) is critical. Such a patient should be liberally transfused so as to bring the hematocrit up to normal level, above 40. This transfusion must be carefully done: the patient is elderly, may be digitalized, and may have poor cardiac function. The transfusion must be given slowly. This is one of the many indications in elderly people for the use of erythrocyte suspensions.

The maintenance of adequate colloid osmotic pressure and a normal total osmolality, as well as the maintenance of acid-base balance, are important, as indicated in Part III. These aspects will not be further detailed here. Age reduces the latitude for variation and the tolerable margin of safety.

Section II. Clinical Management

A. TIMING OF OPERATION

If the patient is restless, in pain that can be controlled only by severe immobilization or heavy medication, early operation has compelling virtue. The reduction of the fracture and its fixation by nailing or other internal means constitute definitive operation in the sense that they terminate the period of stress, pain, immobilization, and sedation. A period of six to twenty-four hours is devoted to evaluation and care of visceral abnormalities. The patient is then operated upon.

If she is quite comfortable prior to operation, stabilized and equilibrated, then the expenditure of several days in achieving the best possible systemic status of the patient will be justified. This expenditure is not devoted to getting the patient into positive nitrogen balance or some other ill-directed systemic measure. The purpose of these two or three days is to stabilize the circulation, accomplish adequate digitalization or other specific measures, and then carry out the operation. The weight of evidence in most cases favors early operation. By this is meant operation within twenty-four hours of the fracture.

Adequate oxygenation is essential during the surgical operation. In people of this age, the number of hours spent in the operating room is a factor of real importance. An older person cannot be regarded as having a "long sleep" during the anesthetic. The entire episode is nonphysiologic and it should be carried out with the maximum dispatch compatible with a good surgical job.

B. CARDIAC AND RENAL CARE

The patient's venous pressure, rhythm, and heart rate, and ventilatory function are the guides to cardiopulmonary status. Previous performance and the history of functional capacity are as revealing as most functional tests. If there is cardiac failure, the patient should be digitalized. There is plenty of time for slow digitalization, using digoxin over a period of six to twenty-four hours, as

described in Part V. Patients who have been on digitalis for many years may never have been adequately digitalized. Or they may have given up the drug for some days or weeks and then begun taking it again when the prescription was renewed, without reestablishing digitalization. The consulting physician or cardiologist must evaluate this point.

If the patient has an elevated blood urea nitrogen level after several days of bed rest and good hospital hygiene, it evidences a fixed degree of renal insufficiency. Other tests such as concentration-dilution or phenolsulfonphthalein excretion add little to the clinical evaluation but pyelograms should be taken. If, however, the patient has a normal blood urea nitrogen concentration, it is worth while to do some of the more discriminatory studies of renal function to find out if the patient is close to renal failure. If renal function is poor, very careful attention must be given to acid-base balance of infused fluids, their total volume, and to bladder drainage. Here in the elderly with some degree of renal failure, isotonic saline solution is nearly always contraindicated and will inevitably produce chloride acidosis. A balanced solution such as sodium-chloride-bicarbonate should be used for most electrolyte replacement. Any impairment of ventilatory function will result in a very rapid worsening of any renal acidosis that is present.

Pulmonary insufficiency and ventilatory impairment must be evaluated and treated with special care in the elderly.

These steps in visceral disease have been detailed in Part V and will not be reviewed again here.

C. POSTOPERATIVE CARE

Oversedation and overadministration of fluids are the enemies of recovery in the elderly. In many aspects of surgery the patient must trade some discomfort for the maintenance of lifesaving reflexes. The desires to cough and to change position are lost with too much sedation. Overadministration of fluids is quickly reflected in basal rales. In the elderly patient with renal and heart disease such overwatering may occur by mouth as well as by the more obviously hazardous intravenous route. No fixed rules may be made as to quantity of fluid to be given. The "normal homeostatic limits" of safe fluid therapy have no meaning in an eighty-five-year-old digitalized cardiac patient with a fractured hip and a blood urea nitrogen concentration of 60 mg. per 100 ml. A few possible generalizations in elderly patients such as those with fractured hip follow.

(1) The patient's insensible water loss will be very low—as low as 250 ml. per day if she is afebrile and dyspneic.

(2) Hypoproteinemia is always imminent; loading of water and salt will accentuate it.

(3) Even with good heart and kidney function, post-traumatic antidiuresis necessitates a close watch on intake excesses; any visceral disease promotes this water-retaining tendency.

(4) Catabolic weight loss is minimal in these patients; any short-term weight gain means water loading. Weighing such patients daily is a practical impossibility, but interval weights are essential in care.

D. NUTRITION

Carbohydrate and vitamin C are the important early concerns in fractured hip. Elderly patients, especially those living alone, are often admitted with multiple vitamin deficiencies.

As emphasized in so many other places in this book, the sudden forcing of a patient into positive nitrogen balance soon after trauma has nothing to offer. Most certainly it has no place in the elderly patient with a fractured femur. Early attempts at forced feeding or tube feeding will result in distention, aspiration of stomach contents, pneumonitis, and death.

The patient will take something by mouth, and the important point is to devote some attention to that "something" to be sure that it has the maximum amount of nutrition per unit volume and is easily digested and absorbed. Fecal impaction is inevitable in these

injured elderly people unless special and active vigilance is maintained.

Postoperative management follows the lines that have already been mentioned as regards visceral function. As mentioned above, the patient should be permitted to pay the price of some discomfort in order to achieve alertness and a good cough reflex; avoid opiates. She should move about in bed and use an overhead trapeze, and should receive massage, active and passive motion, quadriceps setting, regular turning and coughing, and occupational therapy. Mental alertness is an important asset that may be assisted through other simple bedside measures in which the family can help.

E. HORMONES

The use of hormones in such patients has been enthusiastically promoted but inadequately explored. There are sparse reports in the literature. Hormone treatment may be considered as having two objectives in fractures of the hip:

(1) improvement of patient's alertness, *joie de vivre* (if any is possible after a femoral fracture!), and appetite, and

(2) the laying down of osteoid and calcium in the skeleton.

In giving older people adrenocorticotropic hormone, cortisone, androgens, or estrogens, the surgeon should be aware that the old analogy "whipping a tired horse" has biologic meaning. The patient's tissues have not been exposed to high levels of these potent and effective steroids for many years. For a patient of eighty-five suddenly to develop all the secondary sex characteristics of a thirty-year-old man or woman involves an unaccustomed diversion of nutritional substrates to special purposes, special purposes not necessarily related to the trauma or sought by the surgeon. The surgeon wants the fracture to heal and the patient to get well; the hormone wants the patient to look like a young person with development of skeletal muscle in the male and with skin changes, circulatory changes, and breast changes in the female. Certain of these objectives of the surgeon and of the hormone may coincide or overlap—such as, for example, positive calcium balance and the improved manufacture of osteoid. When the two objectives do overlap the hormones are useful. But the surgeon should be skeptical of their usefulness.

Hormones are effective only as they reach reactive tissues. If the patient is in congestive heart failure with advanced arteriosclerosis, plasma protein concentration 4.0 gm. per 100 ml., and a hematocrit of 25, it is ridiculous to give hormone treatment. After the patient has been returned to cardiac compensation, the oxygen-carrying capacity of the blood restored with packed cells, and the capacity for water and electrolyte exchange restored by albumin, and the patient's oral intake increasing, then it might make some sense to give him gonadal hormones, hopefully believing that the hormone will reach the tissues and tell them to do something useful—increase appetite and alertness.

The arithmetic of nitrogen balance does the patient no good; only if an increased intake and physical vigor accompanies the nitrogen-loading, is it beneficial These problems are reviewed in Part I.

Section III. Metabolism in Fractures; Osteoporosis; Steroid Therapy: Notes from the Literature

A. BALANCE CHANGES AFTER FRACTURE

The data from the literature on metabolism after fracture are very sparse. Cuthbertson (1944) studied nitrogen balance in twenty-four patients, calcium and phosphorus balance in fourteen patients, and all three in five patients. Howard (BCK) studied nitrogen balance in six patients, with urinary calcium studies in a few. Sachar (1947) studied nitrogen balance in twelve patients. We (Moore, 1955) have studied nitrogen, sodium, and potassium balances and endocrine activity in three fractures and then, in our more recent studies, balances of those three elements plus calcium and phosphorus in a total of twelve, of which six have been prolonged complete studies through to discharge from the hospital.

In all compound multiple injury, a very prolonged negative nitrogen phase has been shown, often maximal six to ten days after the trauma and continuing for three to six weeks, long after caloric intake is restored. An example demonstrating these aspects, particularly the long nitrogen loss with low corticosteroid activity and high caloric intakes, is to be found in Moore *et al.* (1955). By contrast, elderly people with fractures of the hip show a minimal catabolism.

As regards calcium, the findings have generally been consistent. The net loss of calcium is negligible or small and the plasma calcium concentrations are normal. Calcium excretion in the urine may be twice normal (250 mg. rather than 125 mg., for example) but this still represents only a very small urinary loss; balance may be positive. In Howard's cases the maximum excretion came at the second and third months after injury.

It should be emphasized that calcium balance differs from that of nitrogen, sodium, potassium, or phosphorus in that the fecal excretion is larger than the urinary loss. The fecal loss must be regarded as largely exogenous, and in the postoperative patient with few bowel movements one cannot justifiedly "average out" the fecal loss over a period of several days. The absolute urinary calcium excretion on a constant diet is in many ways more significant as regards mechanisms and skeletal changes. But of course the question of extent of demineralization can be settled only by the total balance.

As to demineralization, certain data are of great interest. The total skeletal calcium has been estimated (Reifenstein, 1947) to be 1150 gm. in an adult female. To show a density change on X-ray there must be a loss or gain of 30 per cent, or 345 gm. In osteoporosis the average daily loss is 100 to 200 mg. This is a high figure, and in fracture the loss is even less rapid. Thus, it would take about five to ten years to show an X-ray change in degree of skeletal calcification at this rate. After fracture no change would be visible in weeks or months unless all the loss were localized to one small area.

By the same token, with steroid therapy in osteoporosis, X-ray changes would require from four to ten years to be demonstrable; this of course makes no reference to symptomatic improvement that may occur long before this. The point to be emphasized is that gross changes in general calcification of the skeleton, as measured by X-ray, are slow to occur or to be repaired. Promotional claims based on such data are to be regarded with skepticism.

Actually, these times are borne out by experience; X-ray demineralization of the skeleton does require from five to fifteen years after the menopause to be manifest.

As regards phosphorus, there has been a universal finding of a small increase in phosphorus excretion after fracture. In Cuthbertson's cases there was a loss as great as 950 mg. per day in the second week. These losses have been parallel to and proportional to the nitrogen loss and seem to come from lean-tissue loss, little influenced by the skeleton. Plasma phosphorus values were slightly raised.

The picture that emerges from these studies, then, is certainly not one of massive skeletal reorganization after fracture.

The minor magnitude of calcium loss from the skeleton is indicated by the fact that after fracture a net negative balance of 50 mg. a day is a representative figure. In hyperparathyroidism this may reach 500 mg. a day and in rapidly advancing skeletal carcinoma, 1000 mg. a day.

Stevenson, Schenker, and Brown (1945), Grossman *et al.* (1945), Beattie (1947), Sacher, Walker, and Whittico (1950), and Thomsen (1938) have reported various aspects of fracture metabolism. Dietrich *et al.* (1948) and Wyse and Cattie (1954) have observed effects of immobilization and of paraplegia on skeletal demineralization, as measured by calcium balance.

These studies are not all entirely comparable; variations in intake and fecal excretion make interpretation difficult; but there can be little question that the weight of evidence indicates a minimal mobilization of skeletal salts after trauma. This is borne out by the phosphorus data, which generally parallel the nitrogen (rather than the calcium) changes, indicating a protoplasmic (rather than skeletal) origin when tissue extrusion of blood is of minor import.

Reviews of the special problems of surgery in aged people will be found in Brooks (1937), Welch (1948), Hamilton and Hamilton (1948), Parsons and Purks (1942, 1949), Parsons and Williams (1950), Haug and Dale (1952), Owen and Murphy (1952), Bosch *et al.* (1952), Pincus *et al.* (1954), Stewart and Alfano (1954), Mithoefer and Mithoefer (1954), Johnston and Jordan (1954), Parsons *et al.* (1956), and Limbosch (1956).

In addition to works already cited, data on endocrine and metabolic aspects of fracture healing and bone repair, experimental and clinical, will be found in Armstrong *et al.* (1945), Gillespie (1954, a, b), Haldeman and Moore (1934), Howard *et al.* (1944), Howard *et al.* (1945), Leriche and Policard (1928), McLean and Urist (1955), Moffatt and Francis (1955), Schran and Fosdick (1943), Shands (1937), Starr (1950), Stewart (1934), and Urist and Johnson (1943).

Studies of the blood supply of the femoral head have been supplemented recently by the use of isotopes to measure local exchange rates. Data on these studies, with related data on blood supply (by other methods), will be found in Tucker (1949), Bohr and Sørensen (1950), Boyd (1951), Tucker (1950), Smith (1954), Boyd *et al.* (1955), Judet *et al.* (1955), and Ralston (1956).

B. OSTEOPOROSIS

Reifenstein (1957) has proposed an ingenious theory to explain the occurrence of senile osteoporosis in women and not in men. This relates to the cessation of the production of skeletal-anabolic hormones from the gonads as against the continued activity of skeletal-catabolic hormones from the adrenals. In women the menopause sharply cuts off the former, while the adrenals continue their secretion; the normal balance that maintains skeletal composition is thus lost.

In men there is no sharp gonadopause or climacteric, and no adrenopause. Thus the balance is reasonably well maintained until late in life.

These concepts fit the endocrine and clinical facts and explain why steroids of gonadal origin affect the skeleton in the woman suffering postmenopausal osteoporosis. They also raise the possibility that the wide variation seen in the severity of postmenopausal osteoporosis is due to chance differences in increasing adrenal function or in decreasing gonadal function.

The papers of Black et al. (1941), Burrows and Graham (1945), Cooke (1955), and Reifenstein (1957) review the structural, biochemical, and endocrine aspects of osteoporosis. Few have contributed as much to this field as has Albright. In 1940 Albright et al. reported studies on forty patients with senile osteoporosis, two of whom were men. In a few of the women the condition followed upon surgical oöphorectomy. He proposed his classification of bone diseases (Albright, 1947; Reifenstein and Albright, 1947; Reifenstein, 1957), and pointed out that osteoporotic bone was normal in detail; there was too little of it. It was, in his opinion, a disease characterized by failure to form the protein matrix. The response to estrogens in the postmenopausal form of the disease was shown. The effect appeared to be one on bone proteins (as reflected by nitrogen balance), the calcium change coming secondarily.

Observations of this general type have been reported by Anderson (1950), Shorr and Carter (1950), and Bogdonoff et al. (1954); the subject was later reviewed by Hennemann and Wallach (1957), who treated and studied a much larger group of patients. The question of the effects of androgen as against estrogen or combined therapy is reviewed by these authors as well as by Reifenstein (1947, 1957, 1958). Two of the basic questions in the choice of androgens and estrogens relate to the sex and age of the patient. The strongly nitrogen-anabolic effects of androgen, even in young men, give it a property not shared by estrogen that may bear on differential skeletal effects. Shorr and Carter (1947, 1950) may be consulted for the data on strontium effects in osteoporosis and the apparent differential absorption of mineral versus matrix.

C. OSTEOPOROSIS AND FRACTURE

There is no question about the fact that osteoporosis is a predisposing cause of fractures in elderly women. These are usually fractures of the femoral neck of intertrochanteric area, the vertebral bodies (particularly dorsal), or the upper end of the humerus. In the case of the femoral neck it is not uncommon to elicit the story that the break preceded the fall. In the vertebrae, the trauma is often negligible. There is no evidence, by sharp contrast, that osteoporosis interferes with bone healing.

Burdeaux and Hutchison (1952) studied the osteoporosis that follows fracture. They noted the osteoporosis in the distal fragment, and reasoned that neither disuse nor local chemistry could produce this selective effect. They wondered if circulatory changes resulting in venous and lymphatic stasis might not be at the root of this local effect.

Pearse and Morton (1930) reportedly accelerated fracture healing by producing venous stasis; these authors appeared to show that fractures heal better in osteoporotic bone. In their experiments they differentiated venous stasis from the osteoporosis of disuse. The histologic appearances were distinct. Distal to a fracture, both types of osteoporosis were seen. The authors also concluded that venous stasis promotes fracture healing.

D. STEROID HORMONE EFFECTS IN FRACTURE

The effects of the gonadal steroids on bone formation are nowhere better demonstrated than in birds, where the cyclic tide of calcium mobilization from bone for the eggshell, and its redeposition, involve rates of calcium flux far greater than occur in mammals. This work is reviewed by Williamson (Unpub.), and several new aspects of avian calcium metabolism, as related to estrogens and the problem of osteoporosis, have been worked out by Urist (1956).

Bogdonoff et al. (1954) gave stilbestrol to

elderly men without effect on calcium. Jonston (1941) gave estrogen to young girls with an apparent increase (rather than decrease) in the rate of calcium excretion. Data on effects in normal people are thus extremely sparse.

The effect of steroid hormones on healing of experimental fractures has been studied in the oöphorectomized dog by Marsiglia (1922), in the rat by McKeoun *et al.* (1933), Pollock (1940), Brush (1945), Key *et al.* (1952), in rabbits by Blunt *et al.* (1950), Sissons and Hadfield (1951), and Moffat and Francis (1955), and in cats by Hills and Weinberg (1941). No unitary conclusion is possible, and certainly no clear-cut beneficial effect is discernible. Here again, as in so many other fields of surgical metabolism, the animal is unsuitable not only because of species differences but also because the pathology appearing spontaneously in man (osteoporosis) finds no parallel in the laboratory.

Interestingly, a combination of growth hormone and adrenocorticotropic hormone studied by Shepanek (1953) was the most effective of any in *retarding* healing, leading to nonunion in a few instances.

The gonadal steroids will reduce the degree of osteoporosis in a paralyzed limb (Armstrong *et al.*, 1945).

In many of these studies the doses used were very large, possibly so large as to exhibit effects quite the reverse of those to be expected from more moderate doses.

The lack of any distinct end-point makes study of the effect of gonadal steroids in this field very difficult. Most of the papers report an "impression," with little control data or attempt at quantitative measurements. This applies to the reports of Mosti (1939), Hagenbach (1941), Debrunner (1945), Schmid (1946), Lamarca and Posteroro (1956), and Connolly (1945). Sherman (1948) reported a remarkable effect from estrogen in a young woman with postoöphorectomy osteoporosis and Paget's disease.

Cobey (1949) advocates the effectiveness of estrogen therapy in reducing the incidence of hip fractures in elderly women.

Wolf and Loeser (1954) point out the improvement in muscle tone, skin toughness, and morale that results from testosterone therapy in elderly males.

There are few data currently available to support the concept of a beneficial result from gonadal steroid therapy in fractures, although the effect on osteoporosis is virtually indubitable.

E. BALANCE INTERRELATIONSHIPS IN FRACTURE

The excretion of creatine, and in some instances creatinine, is increased after severe injury. This is evidence of muscle wasting. Normal striated muscle contains 350 to 400 mg. of creatine and 5 to 10 mg. of creatinine per 100 gm. The creatine excretion per kg. body weight has been called the "creatinine coefficient" and in men is 18 to 32 mg. per kg. per day (average 25 mg.). In women this figure is 9 to 26 mg. per kg. per day (average 18 mg.). This figure is considered as representative of the total muscle mass; we showed some years ago that it correlated well with the total exchangeable potassium.

In lean tissue generally and in muscle the ratio of nitrogen to phosphorus (the N:P ratio) is 14.7 gm. of nitrogen per gm. of phosphorus, the potassium:nitrogen ratio is about 2.8 mE. of potassium per gm. of nitrogen. In bone the calcium:phosphorus ratio is 2.23 gm. of calcium per gm. of phosphorus. Blood has a potassium-nitrogen ratio of 1:53, a nitrogen:phosphorus ratio of 77.6, and a calcium:phosphorus ratio of 0.14. It is therefore clear that blood is a very high-nitrogen tissue in relation to phosphorus (as compared to muscle) and that it is a very low-calcium tissue in relation to phosphorus (as compared to bone). Thus if after trauma a patient excretes large amounts of nitrogen that are all out of proportion to phosphorus (in relation to muscle tissue) while the phosphorus rate remains in part accountable on the basis of calcium (as of osseous origin), one sees the balance change characteristic of the degradation and excretion of large amounts of whole blood, presumably destroyed following extravasation into tissue planes.

Such an interpretation would be strengthened were the change in urinary creatinine excretion to be small or negligible, which is usually the case. Only in very severe injury is creatine excretion manifest, and creatinine excretion elevated, after trauma.

We have seen this combination in long-bone fractures and believe that it may account for a part of the "excessive" nitrogen excretion noted after certain fractures reported in the literature. Further work must be done before any consistent interpretation can be worked out on the basis of these ratios for such a complex metabolic event as compound skeletal injury.

CASE 25

In Which an Elderly Man Develops Lethargy, Basal Rales, and Hypotonicity by Reason of a Double Mechanism after a Fractured Hip

Case 25. Patient R. N., #1H432.* Male. Age 87. Admitted November 13, 1956. Discharged December 10, 1956.

DIAGNOSIS.   Fracture, left femoral neck.

OPERATION.   Closed reduction and internal fixation of fracture of left femoral neck.

CLINICAL SUMMARY.   Two years previously, this eighty-seven-year-old ex-musician had sustained a fracture of his right femoral neck, which was treated with internal fixation by means of a Johannsen nail. Healing of the wound was uneventful. His urine specific gravity had been 1.009 and his blood urea nitrogen 20 mg. per 100 ml. at the time of this former admission.

He discarded his crutches completely six weeks after fixation, and on December 31, 1954, he reentered the hospital with right hip pain. This was found to be due to displacement and vascular necrosis of the femoral head. On January 6, 1955, the right femoral head was replaced by a Moore prosthesis. The procedure required five hours of general anesthesia. Blood transfusion total 1500 ml. His preoperative blood urea nitrogen was 23 mg. per 100 ml. The urine specific gravity was 1.025, plasma sodium was 132 mE. per l.

The postoperative period was complicated by disorientation for four days, followed by lethargy for about one week. During this period of lethargy, the blood urea nitrogen rose to 35 mg. per 100 ml. but the plasma sodium remained stable at 131 mE. per l. The patient also developed fever and chills related to acute cystourethritis. However, he made an excellent recovery, and was discharged thirty days after surgery.

Almost two years later, he sustained a subcapital fracture of the left femur, and was readmitted. His general status had changed very little in the interim. He now took digitalis and was on a low sodium (2 gm.) diet. Frequency, nocturia, and some incontinence of urine were noted. His blood pressure was 160/100. His chest was emphysematous with rhonchi in both lung bases. Cardiac rate was 78 in normal sinus rhythm. The prostate was twice normal size and the findings of left hip tenderness and external rotation of the left lower extremity were noted.

---

* The author is indebted to Dr. Richard Wilson for collecting the data and analyzing the course of this patient.

INITIAL LABORATORY WORK

Urine

Specific gravity	1.015
Protein	1+
pH	6.5
Sediment—loaded with leucocytes	

Stool

Benzidine negative

Hematology

Hematrocrit	36
Leucocyte count	11,200 with 72 per cent neutrophils and 14 per cent band forms

Blood Chemical Analyses

Blood urea nitrogen	21 mg. per 100 ml.

Electrocardiogram showed persistent left ventricular hypertrophy and evidence of subendocardial ischemia.

X-rays of the chest revealed bilateral pulmonary emphysema and pleural thickening with no cardiac enlargement. There was a subcapital fracture of the left hip in good alignment.

FURTHER COURSE.   The next day, under spinal anesthesia, reduction of the fracture of the left femoral neck was carried out and internal fixation was accomplished by a Johannsen nail and Thornton plate. The patient received 500 ml. of blood during the operation.

He did very well for the first forty-eight hours. He was taking oral fluids freely. This intake was supplemented by intravenous infusions of 5 per cent dextrose in water. He was able to sit in a chair by the second postoperative day. His urine output was adequate. On the third postoperative day, however, he became semicomatose and began to run a temperature to 100.8° F. Diagnosis of cerebral hemorrhage or cerebral thrombosis was entertained. Moist rales were noted in both lung bases. Chest X-ray revealed some fluid at the left base. The electrocardiogram was unchanged. The plasma sodium concentration was 117 mE. per l., plasma chloride concentration 91 mE. per l., and potassium 4.8 mE.

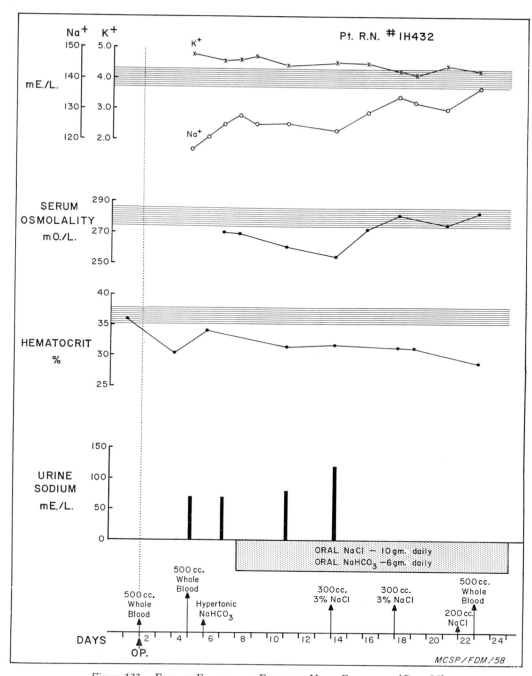

Figure 133. EVENTS FOLLOWING FEMORAL NECK FRACTURE (Case 25)

Above are shown plasma electrolyte values, osmolality, and hematocrit. Below are shown the urine sodium concentrations and the sodium therapy. The reader is referred to the text for details.

It will be noted that there was persistent urinary sodium loss despite low plasma sodium concentrations during the period of semicoma (fourth day). As plasma sodium concentration was increased the patient regained satisfactory clinical convalescence, osmolality returned toward normal, the potassium concentration returned to a normal range—yet the patient required additional oral sodium to compensate for his persistent abnormal urinary sodium loss.

per l., while the urine sodium concentration was 70 mE. per l.

ARGUMENT.   Several factors entered into the production of this patient's severely symptomatic hyponatremia. Here was an elderly man with impaired renal function, as demonstrated by slightly elevated blood urea nitrogen and a (dehydrated) urine specific gravity of 1.015. He then underwent severe surgical trauma and (despite the somewhat protective effect of a spinal anesthesia) his antidiuretic mechanisms were maximally stimulated. His intake for the first forty-eight hours after surgery was 3500 ml. of clear liquids orally and 1600 ml. of intravenously administered 5 per cent dextrose in water. His urine output was 450 ml. and 1200 ml. on the first two postoperative days. His insensible loss was no more than 1500 ml. total for these two days, since he was a small man with poor respiratory exchange. This water balance alone would account for the loading of 2 l. of excess salt-free water in addition to that produced by cell breakdown. This amounts to the initiation of mild water intoxication and dilutional hyponatremia.

In the antidiuretic state following trauma and surgery, the renal regulatory mechanisms for handling dilution could not function properly. Progressive hypotonicity of the extracellular fluid became evident. As further urinary sodium studies will indicate, renal tubular disease with persistent salt losing contributed to the development of hyponatremia in this patient, but the initial impetus was excessive water loading during an antidiuretic state.

His symptomatic picture was that of pallor, lethargy, slight fever, and basal rales. This clinical picture is not quite severe enough to dignify by the term "water intoxication," despite a plasma sodium concentration of 117 mE. per l.

Therapy of this condition should be directed toward getting rid of water and providing hypertonic solute. Once the diagnosis is made, correction should be started immediately but cautiously. A test infusion of 3 per cent sodium chloride to the amount of 200 to 300 ml. will go a long way in an old, debilitated patient, and, as the tonicity is increased, spontaneous diuresis often occurs. It is important to restrict intake of salt-free water sharply and to plan the fluid therapy on a day-to-day basis as correction progresses.

FURTHER COURSE.   On the third postoperative day this patient was given 150 ml. of 3 per cent sodium chloride, 150 ml. of 5 per cent dextrose in water, and 500 ml. of whole blood, with 250 ml. of oral fluids. Within twelve hours of the initiation of this therapy, he became much more alert, and his plasma sodium concentration rose to 121 mE. per l. On the following day, although venous pressure was normal, he was re-digitalized with lanatoside C and received an intravenous infusion of 500 ml. of 5 per cent dextrose in water with 135 mM. of sodium bicarbonate and 40 mM. of potassium chloride. His temperature returned to normal and his urine output was 1650, 1000, and 1525 ml. for the third, fourth, and fifth postoperative days respectively. By the fifth postoperative day his plasma sodium concentration

was 125 mE. per l. and he was alert and back up in a chair. He received daily intravenous infusions of hypertonic sodium bicarbonate, which was used instead of 3 per cent sodium chloride because of the mild acidosis, but during this period the plasma sodium concentration did not rise above 128 mE. per l. On the twelfth postoperative day he again received 3% sodium chloride (300 ml.) because his plasma sodium concentration had reached a level of 123 mE. per l. and his plasma osmolality was 255. This infusion produced a gratifying response, the plasma sodium rising to 134 and plasma osmolality to 281. His clinical state brightened remarkably at this time.

His eosinophil count was low and he showed no evidence of adrenal insufficiency throughout the episode.

Urine sodium determinations were studied throughout this course and they ranged between 70 and 80 mE. per l. However, the day when his plasma sodium concentration reached its recurrent low point of 123 mE. per l. the urinary sodium value was also 123 mE. per l. Following the salutary response to the repeated intravenous 3 per cent sodium chloride, he was placed on 10 gm. of sodium chloride and 6 gm. of sodium bicarbonate daily in oral dosage, and he was able to maintain his plasma sodium concentration in the range of 135 mE./l. with no evidence of congestive failure.

The patient recovered nicely and was discharged on the twenty-eighth postoperative day.

COMMENT.   This patient demonstrates well the extreme fragility of elderly patients undergoing surgery or sustaining trauma. Although he was water-loaded to a mild degree in the face of marked antidiuresis, had his renal tubular function been unimpaired the hypotonicity would not have been so marked nor his disorder so severe. His renal disease, probably arteriosclerotic in origin and associated with aging, was responsible for the salt-loss phase of his hypotonic disorder.

It is of interest that as resalting was established the patient had a marked diuresis, losing 4175 ml. in three days. His basal rales actually disappeared with the administration of sodium, as this facilitated water diuresis.

The increased renal sodium excretion might have been interpreted as an effect of volume expansion in antidiuresis. But it later was shown that this was a renal tubular effect that persisted as both volume and concentration returned to normal. As the story unraveled we see that he required 240 mE. of oral sodium daily as a dietary supplement to maintain his plasma sodium at a respectable level.

SUMMARY.   This was the case of an eighty-seven-year-old man who developed hyponatremia with marked clinical manifestations, following reduction and internal fixation of a fractured hip. The genesis of this hypotonic state appears to be water loading in a post-traumatic antidiuretic state with increased sodium excretion. After recovery from the acute hyponatremic state, marked renal tubular loss of sodium was demonstrated, which had contributed to the development of the abnormal electrolyte pattern.

A Woman of Seventy-One Suffers Severe Multiple Fractures and Demonstrates Certain Interesting and Important Aspects of Her Blood Requirements for Resuscitation

Case 26. Patient H. W., #7L938.* Female. Age 71.

Admitted December 9, 1957. Discharged March 22, 1958.

DIAGNOSIS. Compound fracture of tibia and fibula; fractured pelvis; lacerated scalp; ovarian cysts.

OPERATIONS. Debridement and suture of lacerations.

Reduction and external fixation of tibial fracture.

Laparotomy and bilateral salpingo-oophorectomy.

CLINICAL SUMMARY. This elderly woman was seen in the emergency ward thirty minutes after injuries were received when she was hit by a car while walking. When first examined, she was conscious but confused. She was cold and sweating, with a blood pressure of 100/60 mm. Hg. There was a 10 cm. laceration of her scalp. She complained of lower abdominal pain, and palpation revealed a mass in the left lower quadrant. The mass was tender, firm, and rounded, mobile, and cystic. Findings on pelvic examination were normal. Her right lower leg was deformed and painful, with the tibia protruding through a 7 cm. laceration on the medial side of the lower third. Previous history and physical examination indicated no other disorders.

An intravenous infusion of saline solution was begun while her blood was crossmatched. Her leg was splinted, she was examined radiologically, and then transferred to the ward. X-rays confirmed the presence of multiple comminuted fractures of the right tibia and fibula with marked displacement. Films of the pelvis revealed fractures of the ischial and pubic rami. An intravenous pyelogram showed normal kidneys and collecting systems, but marked displacement of the ureters and bladder was seen in the pelvis, suggesting extensive extraperitoneal hemorrhage. Her urine was grossly blood-stained on admission, but subsequently clear.

Six hours after injury debridement and suture of lacerations, followed by reduction, and Roger Anderson fixation of the leg fracture were performed under general anesthesia. One liter of blood was given before and during operation.

Six hours after operation it was observed that her hematocrit had fallen from a preoperative level of 38 to 30.5. Her blood pressure was steady initially following operation, but could now be maintained only by continuous infusion of blood, and a further 3 liters was given. During this time her abdomen had become a little distended, the left lower quadrant was tender, and the mass in that region was increased in size. Bowel

sounds were normal. It was decided to perform a laparotomy.

ARGUMENT. This patient has minimal external hemorrhage, and yet needs continued transfusion (now over 4000 ml.) to maintain her blood pressure. Estimation of the blood loss is always difficult. On arrival at the hospital she was shocked and hypotensive. This may be taken to indicate a blood loss of 25 to 50 per cent of her blood volume. If the blood volume of this woman is taken as 6.5 per cent of her body weight (60 Kg.), her blood volume would approximate 3900 ml. Her blood loss on admission was thus a minimum of 1500 to 2500 ml.

What blood loss might be anticipated from her injuries? A lower leg fracture may be associated with a 0.5 to 1.0 l. extravasation of blood into the tissues without extreme swelling. A fractured pelvis can incur concealed interstitial hemorrhage of 2 to 3 l. of blood. It was accordingly not surprising that she had required 4 l. of blood, replacement of that loss continuing after admission. It was now significant that her blood pressure could not be maintained without continued transfusion. The falling hematocrit cannot be taken as an indication of the extent of recent hemorrhage, since hemodilution occurs but slowly. With continuing hemorrhage and an abdominal mass, exploration is mandatory.

FURTHER COURSE. At laparotomy the abdominal mass was found to be a left-sided ovarian cyst rising high out of the pelvis, with a smaller cyst on the right. A small amount of free blood was present in the peritoneal cavity, and this had come from a laceration of the pedicle of the cyst. The pubic fracture had caused a hematoma of the rectus sheath, which was evacuated. There was considerable retroperitoneal hematoma. A bilateral salpingo-oophorectomy was performed.

The patient made a good immediate postoperative recovery, her Levin tube being removed on the second day, and she was taking solid food by the fourth day. She gradually developed a very large ecchymotic area over the right buttock and leg.

On the sixth postoperative day she had an episode of right chest pain, which recurred two days later. These symptoms were associated with a rise in temperature and pulse rate. Chest X-ray demonstrated no parenchymal lung lesion. Electrocardiogram showed changes suggestive of acute cor pulmonale.

There was no hemoptysis. Examination of her legs revealed no site of origin for the pulmonary embolus that was provisionally diagnosed. She was treated by the administration of fibrinolysin, 50,000 units intravenously daily over a four-hour period, and four days later she was symptom-free. Following this her recovery was slow but uneventful. She commenced to sit out of

---

* The author is indebted to Dr. A. W. R. Williamson for collecting the data and analyzing the course of this patient.

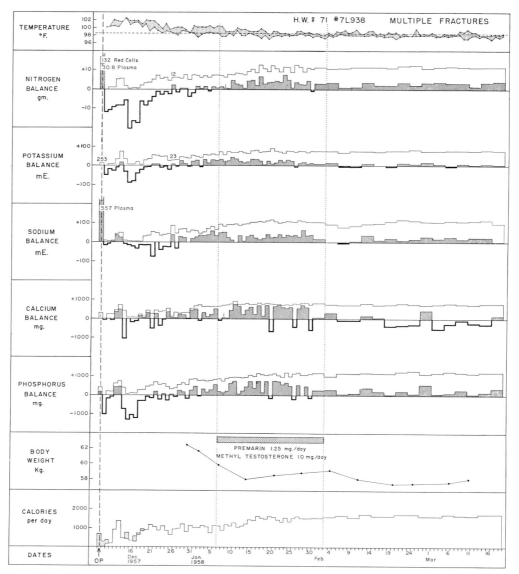

Figure 134. Events after Multiple Fractures in a Seventy-One-Year-Old Woman (Case 26)

In this chart are shown balances of nitrogen, sodium, potassium, calcium, and phosphorus with the body weight and the caloric intake. The reader is referred to the text for details.

Of particular interest is the outpouring of nitrogen, potassium, and phosphorus starting on the 6th post-traumatic day and shown (by its balance ratios) to be due to the digestion of blood in the tissues and the excretion of the products of its degradation. This patient had approximately 2.5 l. of blood in the tissues, known to be required as transfusion to maintain circulation, and in excess of external losses.

The patient achieved anabolism by about the 21st day on caloric intakes in the general range of 1500 per

day. For a period of approximately a month thereafter the patient was given a mixed androgen and estrogen preparation. This resulted in some increased caloric intake, and a definitely increased balance of nitrogen, calcium, and phosphorus. Note that if the gonadal steroids had been started about two weeks sooner one might have been led to the erroneous conclusion that they initiated anabolism. As the hormones were stopped there was a brief weight loss as water, loaded during hormone administration, was excreted.

We have no evidence, either from this case or from other studies, to indicate that such steroidal anabolism is beneficial to the patient. Her recovery continued as favorably, after treatment was stopped.

bed after four weeks and to learn crutch walking eight weeks after injury.

COMMENT. Throughout this patient's stay, she received metabolic study for intake and output of nitrogen, potassium, sodium, calcium, and phosphorus. As a seventy-two-year-old woman with extensive injury and fractures, she represented the changes of fracture metabolism in the postmenopausal subject. Data on such patients are scarce.

During the first fifteen days after injury she was in markedly negative nitrogen balance, reaching its maximum on the eighth day, when she lost over 20 gm. of nitrogen. In evaluating this figure, one must consider her age, her sex, and her weight of only 60 kg. The total loss during this period was 136.2 gm. of nitrogen. As an indication of the extent of this over-all nitrogen loss, 136 gm. of nitrogen may be calculated as representing 850 gm. of protein, or about 9 pounds of wet lean tissue.

As we shall see below, there is evidence to suggest that some of this nitrogen did not come from skeletal muscle.

Calcium intake and output were virtually in balance during this fifteen-day period. This has been characteristic of our findings in fractures. A strongly negative calcium balance is very unusual in such patients, even with extensive immobilization. In this regard, our data have not corroborated the teaching that there is large calcium loss after fracture. There was a small negative phosphorus balance.

If we consider the period of the first fifteen days in the hospital, we find certain interesting facts. First, that the maximum washout of nitrogen occurred a few days after admission and was associated with a marked excretion of phosphorus. However, since the calcium balance was virtually zero during this period, it is very unlikely that this phosphorus came from bone. Furthermore, when one calculates the relation of nitrogen to phosphorus, one finds that there is much more nitrogen than one would predict, were the phosphorus to have come from a combination of skeletal muscle and bone.

Looking to blood in the tissues as a possible source of these anomalous balance changes, we find certain additional facts. Whole blood is a tissue which contains large amounts of nitrogen in relation to both calcium and phosphorus. Compared either with bone or skeletal muscle it is a "high-nitrogen, low-calcium, low-phosphorus tissue."

As a result of her injury, this patient required the transfusion of 5.5 l. of whole blood. The hematocrit changes tell us that she was not overtransfused; she never developed a high hematocrit. In the course of her two operations, she lost approximately 3 l. of blood. We may therefore estimate that approximately 2.5 l. of blood were extravasated into her tissues.

If we assume that the balance change in the first fifteen days involved an amount of tissue nitrogen accountable by the phosphorus in skeletal tissue and bone, plus the amount of nitrogen arising from the catabolism of 2.5 l. of blood, we find that it balances out well with the measured nitrogen loss. Such calculations

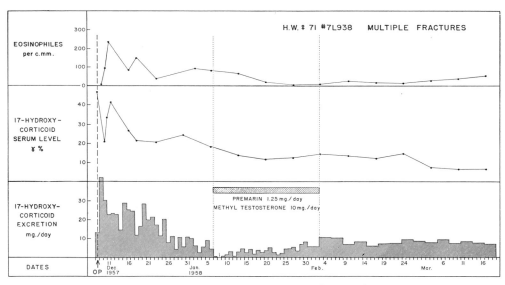

Figure 135. MULTIPLE FRACTURES (Case 26)

This shows the very considerable early increase in corticosteroid excretion in this patient's urine, together with the remarkable inhibition of adrenal steroid output produced when gonadal steroids were given. The anabolic effects of gonadal steroids may lie in the inhibition of endogenous production of catabolic steroids from the adrenal cortex, as well as in peripheral effects of the gonadal steroids. This patient demonstrates such an effect, whether or not it represents the actual mechanism of steroid-induced anabolism.

are admittedly approximate. But, where observed nitrogen balance is much more strongly negative than one may account for by any combination of skeletal and lean-tissue changes (as represented by the sum of calcium and phosphorus balances), one is justified in assuming that the extra nitrogen comes from the breakdown of a tissue very high in nitrogen (relative to calcium or phosphorus) such as blood. In fracture cases, this particular source of nitrogen in the balance is particularly prominent because so much blood is lost into the tissues around the broken bone. It enters the metabolic mill, is catabolized, and much of the nitrogen is excreted. Such measurements indicate the true extent of the blood lost into the tissues. The porphyrin compounds resulting from the breakdown of hemoglobin are excreted in the feces as urobilinogen.

Late in this patient's course, she was placed on mixed androgen and estrogen therapy. This resulted in an increased retention of nitrogen, calcium, and phosphorus, and a marked inhibition of her own adrenal glands, as evidenced by the decreased urinary excretion of 17-hydroxycorticosteroids. The biologic activity of the administered estrogens was confirmed by an increased cornification of the vaginal epithelium during hormone treatment and an appropriate change in the urinary excretion of the follicle-stimulating hormone of the pituitary (FSH).

SUMMARY. This patient represents severe trauma in an elderly, postmenopausal woman. Information on the metabolism of such individuals is scarce and for this reason this patient was selected for an unusually complete series of studies. From the clinical point of view her case was well managed. A laparotomy was carried out because of apprehension about the possibility of continuing free hemorrhage. She showed clinical, chemical, and metabolic evidences of the extravasation of a very large amount of blood in her tissues and, indeed, the metabolic changes observed early in her course can be explained only on the basis of the breakdown of about 2500 ml. of blood in the tissues.

In this particular patient, gonadal steroid therapy resulted in an increased positive balance of nitrogen, potassium, phosphorus, and calcium, and marked adrenal inhibition. We are unable to say that this increased positive balance was beneficial to the patient.

CASE 27

An Elderly Woman Requires Gallbladder Surgery Some Weeks after a Fractured Hip; She Develops Severe Hypotension after This and Responds to Mixed Therapy, Including Rectification of a Specific Metabolic Lesion That Makes for "Unresponsiveness"

Case 27. Patient A. R., #OB732.* Female. Age 81.

Admitted June 29, 1957. Discharged September 5, 1957.

DIAGNOSIS. Intertrochanteric fracture of right hip; chronic cholecystitis with cholelithiasis.

OPERATIONS. Internal fixation of right hip.
Cholecystostomy.

CLINICAL SUMMARY. This eighty-one-year-old woman fell, on the morning of hospital admission, with resulting pain in the right hip beginning shortly after her fall.

Past history revealed a prior admission to the hospital because of nausea and vomiting and abdominal discomfort associated with mental confusion and abdominal tenderness in the right upper quadrant. She was treated at that time with supportive therapy and discharged improved ten days later, with the diagnoses of cerebral arteriosclerosis and cholelithiasis. Operation was avoided because of her age.

Physical examination on entry to the emergency ward revealed her to be an elderly woman in profound shock with an unobtainable blood pressure. There were inspiratory crackling rales in both lung bases posteriorly and the heart tones were distant and associated with a grade III systolic murmur at the apex

---

* The author is indebted to Dr. Louis L. Smith for collecting the data and analyzing the course of this patient.

radiating to the axilla. Results of an abdominal examination were negative. There was a massive hematoma of the right thigh. There was external rotation and flexion of the right lower extremity. Measurements of both thighs at a point 30 cm. above the tibial tubercles were: right thigh circumference—67 cm., left thigh circumference—51 cm. Deep tendon reflexes were intact. X-rays showed intertrochanteric fracture of right hip.

INITIAL LABORATORY WORK

Urine

Specific gravity	1.007
Protein—negative	
Sugar—negative	
Sediment—no cells	

Hematology

Hematocrit	44.5
Leucocyte count	22,100 per cu. mm.

The patient was given 1500 ml. of blood following which her blood pressure was 130/96 and her pulse 100. The decision was made for operative fixation of the fractured hip in order to allow free movement of this elderly patient in bed, and to prevent further hematoma formation. She was anesthetized with Pentothal, cyclopropane, and nitrous oxide, and a Smith-Petersen nailing of the right hip was carried out.

Shortly after anesthesia induction and the beginning of surgery, the patient's blood pressure dropped from 180 to 95 mm. systolic. She responded promptly to the administration of whole blood and received a total of 3000 ml. blood during operation and immediately postoperatively.

ARGUMENT. This woman demonstrates two points worthy of further consideration. The first is the magnitude of blood loss encountered in association with closed fractures. The second is the amount of acute blood-volume reduction necessary to produce profound shock.

When she entered the hospital measurements were made of the diameters of the midportion of both thighs. If one considers the volume of a cylinder 20 cm. in height, and uses these measurements to calculate the volumes of both thighs in this woman, the volume of the right thigh is 7200 ml. and the volume of the left thigh is 4100 ml. The inherent errors of trying to compute the volume of the human thigh are evident to the reader and must be considered in interpreting this result. Since the circumferential measurement was taken at the midpoint of the height of the calculated cylinder, inherent errors are minimized. It was estimated that this elderly woman lost about 2500 ml. of her blood volume in the formation of this huge interstitial hematoma of the thigh.

On admission this woman's blood pressure was unobtainable. She was extremely obese and of medium height; her estimated body weight was 70 kg. Assuming her blood volume at 6 per cent of her body weight, this would give a total blood volume of 4200 ml. It has been estimated that in order to produce profound shock, the blood volume must be reduced by about 50 per cent. From the calculation previously made as to the estimated volume of blood lost in the hematoma of this patient's thigh, the acute blood-volume reduction was indeed over 50 per cent, or 2500 ml.

Initially this patient responded well to the rapid administration of 1500 ml. of blood. However, the fact that she was still hypovolemic is demonstrated by the precipitous drop in blood pressure experienced following anesthesia induction and the start of operation. This is a classic example of precarious resuscitation upset by the vasodilation of anesthesia. Here again she responded well to further blood replacement and during the operation received an additional 3000 ml. of blood. Had she received adequate blood replacement preoperatively, this hypotensive episode could have been avoided, with its attendant hazards of coronary or cerebral thrombosis in an elderly patient.

FURTHER COURSE. One month following the internal fixation of the fractured right hip, this woman developed epigastric pain with vomiting and right upper abdominal tenderness. Her leucocyte count was 12,900 per cu. mm. A diagnosis of acute cholecystitis was made and she was treated by propantheline (Probanthine) and intravenous fluids. Her symptoms and findings did not subside on conservative management. Five days later the patient was operated upon and a cholecystostomy with removal of gallstones carried out.

A total of 500 ml. of blood was administered during the operation, which was carried out with minimal blood loss, under Pentothal, nitrous oxide, and oxygen anesthesia.

When she returned to bed in the recovery room, the patient's blood pressure fell to 0/0; consequently 500 ml. of blood was administered followed by 50 mg. of Neo-synephrine in 500 ml. of 5 per cent dextrose in water. Her hematocrit was 40 postoperatively, and an electrocardiogram revealed a sinus tachycardia. Since she could not be weaned off the vasopressor drug during the ensuing twelve-hour period, intravenous hydrocortisone therapy was begun, without benefit to the patient. Plasma electrolytes at this time were: sodium concentration, 127 mE. per l.; potassium, 3.9 mE. per l.; and chloride, 101 mE. per l. Twenty-four hours after operation she was still being maintained on Neo-synephrine and demonstrated lethargy and fever with marked peripheral vasoconstriction, cold clammy hands and cyanotic nailbeds. Her condition was said to resemble "irreversible shock" in an old woman. An arterial blood sample was taken for an acid-base profile and was reported as:

pH	7.47	
pCO$_2$	30.3	mm. Hg
Total carbon dioxide	22.3	mM. per l.
HCO$_3$	21.4	mM. per l.

These data showed a very mild metabolic acidosis with a strong respiratory alkalotic component to account for the elevated pH. Arterial catechol levels were within normal levels and the plasma corticosteroid concentration was later reported as 14.0 micrograms per cent.

The patient received 88 mM. of sodium bicarbonate and 150 ml. of 3 per cent sodium chloride during the evening and the same amount of bicarbonate and hypertonic saline solution during the early morning hours of the next day. Her hematocrit then dropped to 32.5, at which point 1000 ml. of whole blood was administered, followed by 88 mM. of sodium bicarbonate. Following the adminstration of the first blood, the patient was able to maintain her blood pressure without Neo-synephrine support and made an uneventful recovery from her acute illness. Adrenocorticotropic hormone subsequently demonstrated normal adrenal function by eliciting a normal corticosteroid response.

COMMENT. Here the acidosis was not marked nor the hyponatremia pronounced. Restoration of the two toward normal permitted the cessation of pressor amine therapy, and made the volume restoration more effective.

It is of interest that a total blood volume and a pressor mechanism adequate to maintain circulation before operation were not adequate when anesthesia and operation were superimposed, in the setting of hyponatremic acidosis. After operation, though transfusion more than replaced the loss, blood pressure could not be maintained and the patient's condition became critical.

Elderly debilitated patients not infrequently demon-

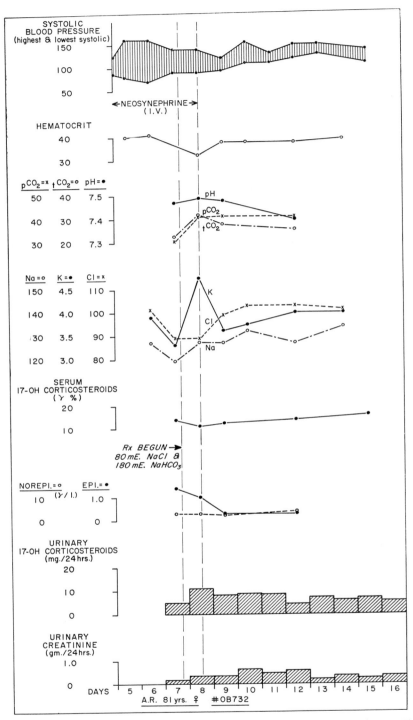

Figure 136.   EVENTS FOLLOWING FRACTURED HIP AND CHOLECYSTITIS (Case 27)

See facing page for detailed legend.

strate difficulty in maintaining their blood pressure following trauma. Their acid-base and electrolyte composition falls within a consistent pattern. They demonstrate some degree of acidosis, and have a low plasma sodium concentration and osmolality. Hematocrit determinations are normal or slightly low. Since there is no readily explainable cause for the hypotensive episode, all too frequently they are treated with vasopressors in increasing amounts (and corticosteroids) with poor results. If, as in this elderly woman, the underlying defect is recognized and vigorously treated, homeostatic mechanisms for the maintenance of blood pressure can be reinstated. The judicious use of sodium bicarbonate to restore a normal acid-base composition and the administration of concentrated sodium chloride to repair the low plasma sodium concentration result in the reestablishment of normal blood pressure. The favorable response of hyponatremic acidotic patients to concentrated base has led to the false impression that such treatment should always be expected to be

effective in shock. Such is clearly not the case; if a lesion is not present, its "repair" will be unavailing. As these elderly patients are often cardiac problems as well, the constant monitoring of the venous pressure is mandatory to prevent overloading the circulation.

This patient needed whole blood; she also needed salt and base. When given these three she did well. The vasopressors and corticosteroids were ineffective and inadvisable. They should not have been tried until the "second echelon" of shock therapy had been explored: repair of coexistent biochemical disorders.

It is also worthy of reemphasis that during her hypotensive crisis after cholecystectomy this patient was stated to be in "irreversible shock"; resemblance to "endotoxemia" was mentioned by several observers. Her recovery was accomplished by volume restoration and biochemical correction without change in bacterial manifestations or antibacterial therapy.

No matter how one chooses to use the term, this patient's shock was certainly not "irreversible."

Figure 136. EVENTS FOLLOWING FRACTURED HIP AND CHOLECYSTITIS (Case 27)

Opposite are shown the blood pressure, hematocrit, and blood chemical findings on this patient. Below are shown the blood and urine corticosteroids, epinephrine, norepinephrine, and the urinary creatinine. The reader is referred to the text for details.

It will be noted that, at the time this patient was first taken under study, she had a very wide range of systolic blood pressures during the day. On some occasions it was very low and on others very high (shown by the shaded area in the upper portion of the chart). This was due to the precarious maintenance of the blood pressure with Neo-synephrine. Whenever it was stopped the patient's blood pressure fell to a level below 50 mm. Hg.

Her condition was very poor; she appeared to be dying. It will be noted that the patient was severely hyponatremic and moderately acidotic at this time. The patient was then given a sodium load consisting of both

sodium chloride and sodium bicarbonate. With this there was a gradual restoration of the sodium concentration to normal and a return of the carbon dioxide tension to normal, indicating restoration of acid-base balance. Following this therapy the patient's hematocrit fell initially (owing to some hemodilution), but later restored itself to normal with transfusion and diuresis. Most important and clear-cut was the fact that it was now possible to discontinue the Neo-synephrine, and blood pressure was well maintained. The patient's course was normal thereafter.

Had the patient succumbed during the hypotensive phase, microorganisms could doubtless have been recovered from the abdominal drainage site. They or their endotoxins might well have been blamed for "irreversible shock," on the basis of increased concentrations or susceptibility to bacterial toxins or endotoxins.

A Fracture of Pelvis and Lower Leg in a Man of Sixty-One. There Is Also Massive Hemorrhage with Transfusion Alkalosis and, Later, Gallbladder Disease

Case 28.   Patient J. M., #8L280.* Male. Age 61. Admitted January 1, 1958. Discharged May 22, 1958.

DIAGNOSIS.   Compound fracture of tibia and fibula; fractured pelvis; acute cholecystitis.

OPERATIONS.   Debridement and suture of laceration.

Reduction and external fixation of tibial fracture.

Laparotomy and ligation of right internal iliac artery.

Cholecystostomy, cholecystectomy, and exploration of common bile duct.

CLINICAL SUMMARY.   At 6:30 P.M. on January 1, 1958, this middle-aged unemployed man was struck down by an automobile. He was brought to the emergency ward within ten minutes. When first seen he was in a state of shock, pale, and sweating, with a blood pressure of 90/50 mm. Hg and a pulse rate of 120 per minute. While his examination was proceeding an intravenous infusion of blood was commenced, and he was catheterized. Physical and radiologic examination revealed a severely comminuted compound fracture of the left tibia and fibula with extensive local soft-tissue damage. Very marked swelling was apparent, involving the right buttock, groin, and iliac fossa, and on X-ray, fractures of the superior and inferior pubic rami were to be seen.

Following the infusion of 2.5 l. of blood, his blood pressure steadied at 105 mM. systolic, but could be maintained at this level only by the continued administration of blood. When transferred to the ward he was warm, with a good color, and fully conscious. The swelling and bruising of his right buttock had, however, increased and it was tense and painful. The scrotum was hugely distended with blood. The left leg was pale and cold, no pulses could be felt in it, but sensation was present.

Seven hours after injury he had received 6.5 l. of blood, and it was still not possible to stop giving blood without his condition deteriorating. The swelling around the right side of his pelvis continued to increase in size. It was decided to transfuse a further 500 ml. of fresh blood rapidly and then to perform a laparotomy. In addition to 4.0 l. more blood, 2 gm. of calcium gluconate and 3 gm. of calcium chloride were given before and during operation. A total of 10.5 l. of blood was transfused into this patient in his first six hours.

ARGUMENT.   This patient was clearly bleeding somewhere and the signs pointed to an arterial hemorrhage into the tissues around his pelvic fracture. Although

---

* The author is indebted to Dr. A. W. R. Williamson for collecting the data and analyzing the course of this patient.

exploration is only rarely needed in pelvic fractures, it was clearly indicated here. An additional intraperitoneal hemorrhage could not be excluded.

If 7 per cent of his body weight is taken as his blood volume, a figure of 6.5 l. is obtained. This may be a little high, since he was obese. In either case the 10.5 l. of blood he received is approaching twice his normal total blood volume, a massive transfusion. It is in this type of case that the "citrate lesion" is a risk. Florid citrate toxicity is rare; but lowering of ionized calcium may synergize with other disorders (particularly hyperkalemia and hyponatremia) so as to produce dangerous cardiac changes. The citrate load given in the anticoagulant solution mixed with the blood would not be too great for the normal liver to metabolize rapidly. In shock the circulation to the liver is impaired and hepatic function thereby diminished. It is this circulatory element that is so difficult to assess accurately, and accordingly it is wise in such a patient requiring massive blood replacement to give calcium intravenously, as was done here. Were he successfully to convert all his citrate to bicarbonate, quite a different result might be observed.

FURTHER COURSE.   At operation the bleeding was found to be from a major artery lacerated by the fracture of the pelvic bones. Bleeding was controlled by packing and ligation of the internal iliac artery on that side. Debridement of the leg laceration and closed reduction with external fixation of the fracture were then performed. Following these procedures evidence of an adequate circulation in the left leg slowly became apparent.

His recovery was slow. He developed severe paralytic ileus, necessitating gastric suction and intravenous fluids for two weeks. During this same period he was jaundiced, having a plasma bilirubin of 5 mg. per 100 ml. five days after operation. The jaundice slowly cleared.

ACID-BASE STUDIES.   On entry to the hospital arterial blood samples were drawn and the following results obtained.

pH	7.44	
pCO_2	25.2	mm. Hg
HCO_3	16.6	mM. per l.

These results indicate a metabolic acidosis masked by a respiratory alkalosis. The latter may either be a compensatory mechanism or result from hyperventilation due to pain. The metabolic acidosis is an indication of inadequate tissue perfusion as a result of shock.

During the next twenty-four hours 10.5 l. of whole blood was transfused, containing 30 mM. of sodium citrate per liter as anticoagulant. As the citrate was metabolized, an excess (315 mE.) of sodium ion remained as the bicarbonate. This is reflected in the de-

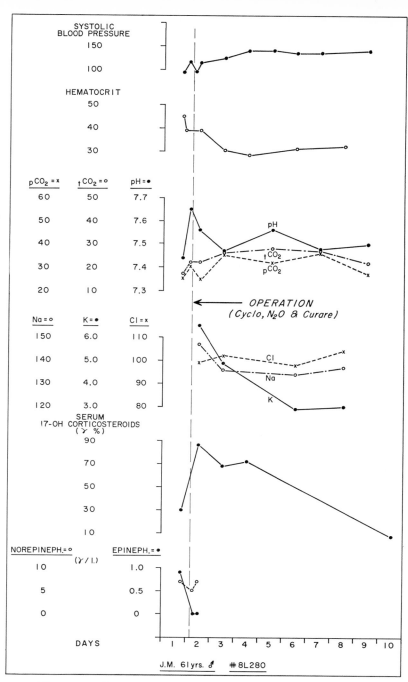

Figure 137. EVENTS FOLLOWING MULTIPLE FRACTURES (Case 28)

Above are shown the systolic blood pressure, hematocrit, and plasma chemical findings in this patient. Below are shown the blood corticosteroid, epinephrine, and norepinephrine values. The reader is referred to the text for details.

The patient was in shock following severe compound trauma. It will be noted that extensive blood replacement (11 liters) resulted in an acute alkalosis during therapy followed later by the development on the third day of a more chronic alkalosis.

In the initial phase, respiratory factors were prominent and the carbon dioxide tension was quite low,

suggesting that hyperventilation in this seriously injured man was a factor in his acute alkalosis. The situation on the third day is much more that of a patient who has been given a large load of sodium (as sodium citrate—effectively sodium bicarbonate). The carbon dioxide tension is close to normal and the total carbon dioxide elevated at the time that the pH is high. The potassium concentration in the plasma is likewise low at this time, the picture of transfusion alkalosis as the citrate ion of the preservative-anticoagulant is metabolized.

Page 859

velopment of a metabolic alkalosis, which reached a maximum on the fourth day after injury:

Arterial Blood

pH	7.56
pCO$_2$	31.8 mm. Hg
HCO$_3$	27.6 mM. per l.

This transfusion alkalosis gradually corrected itself and twelve days later his acid-base studies were normal:

Arterial Blood

pH	7.37
pCO$_2$	41.65 mm. Hg
HCO$_3$	23.4 mM. per l.

FURTHER COURSE.   Clinical improvement continued until seven weeks after his injuries, when the patient developed pain in the right upper abdomen, jaundice, and rigors. Acute cholecystitis was diagnosed. He did not improve on tetracycline (Achromycin), gastric suction, and intravenous fluids, and on February 2 a cholecystostomy was done under local anesthesia. The gallbladder was distended and tense, containing much biliary mud. Culture of the bile grew *Aerobacter aerogenes.* Following operation his temperature fell rapidly and he was much improved.

On March 4, 1958, a split skin graft was taken from his thigh and applied to his granulating leg wound under local anesthesia. Cholecystectomy and exploration of the common duct were carried out on March 24. Recovery from this was uncomplicated apart from some pyrexia and persistence of biliary drainage. The tube was removed on April 7.

He then began for the first time to be mobilized. After several weeks of intensive physiotherapy he was discharged in a long leg cast on May 5, 1958, with crutches to avoid bearing weight. At the time of discharge his leg wound was almost healed, but no callus was yet visible on X-ray. When he was seen in the clinic six weeks later, early callus was present. During the last twenty-nine days in the hospital he had been given combined androgen and estrogen therapy.

COMMENT.   During his stay in the hospital this patient, like that of Case 26, was on balance measurements of nitrogen, sodium, potassium, calcium, and phosphorus.

During the first eight weeks after injury, he was in negative nitrogen balance, totaling 430 gm. In evaluating this, we should realize that he was a muscular man, not in the senile group, being sixty-one years of age. He had also suffered an unusually complicated injury, involving flat-bone injury, long-bone injury, and major hemorrhage. The first four weeks after injury were characterized by the loss of 315 gm. of nitrogen, involving the catabolism of approximately 1970 gm. of protein or 20.8 pounds of wet lean tissue. In this patient, as in Case 26, there is evidence that some of this nitrogen came from other sources than muscle.

He never was in strongly negative calcium balance. This, again, is representative of our findings in fractures. It should be recalled that this patient was completely immobilized as well as having extensive skeletal injury; yet he lost comparatively little calcium.

His phosphorus balance was negative throughout. But the extent of his phosphorus loss was much less than would be predicted from the total of his nitrogen loss (representing lean tissue) added to his calcium loss (representing skeleton). Stated otherwise, this patient also showed evidence in his early postoperative phase of having catabolized a tissue that is very high in nitrogen relative to phosphorus and calcium, a tissue which likewise has very little calcium in it relative to its phosphorus. This is characteristic of whole blood.

It is also of interest that the episode of cholecystectomy and common-duct exploration excited only a minimal nitrogen loss (14.7 gm.). This is very reminiscent of Case 2, in which secondary trauma in a patient already depleted by prolonged illness excited only a minimal additional loss of nitrogen. This has been repeatedly reported in previous studies, both in our laboratories and elsewhere.

For reasons that we do not understand, this patient did not lose calcium strongly until the episode of cholecystitis. At that time he did lose a good deal of calcium. One might assign this to loss in the stools because of poor absorption of calcium; the fact was, however, that he lost this extra calcium in the urine. We have no explanation of this.

Androgen and estrogen therapy had no discernible effect whatsoever on his metabolic balances or on his clinical course; this is in contrast to the patient in Case 26 (a postmenopausal female), in whom these gonadal steroids were quite effective metabolically.

The patient showed a very high level of corticosteroids after admission, in part due to the transient parenteral administration of hydrocortisone. It is of interest that his cholecystectomy gave rise to a brisk adrenocortical response, with a blood corticosteroid level of 30.5 mcg. per 100 ml. Yet, with this brisk adrenal response, he showed very little nitrogen loss. This is another example of the dissociation between the two, so commonly seen in chronic illness.

SUMMARY.   This patient suffered multiple injuries and later developed biliary disease. Very large nitrogen losses resulted from his mixed injury of long-bone fracture, flat-bone fracture, and major hemorrhage, requiring the infusion of approximately 11 l. of blood in his first twenty-four hours. He developed transfusion alkalosis.

Balance changes were noted and again showed the characteristic balance manifestation of blood in the tissues—namely, a nitrogen loss much larger than can be accounted for by the sum of the predicted nitrogen: phosphorus (lean tissue) and calcium (skeleton) balances.

CASE 29

In Which an Industrial Accident Leads to Renal Failure, Treated by an Unusual Means, with Good Result

Case 29. Patient S. S., #5L249.* Male. Age 42. Admitted August 21, 1957. Discharged November 18, 1957.

DIAGNOSIS. Abdominal hemorrhage secondary to traumatic laceration of the mesentery; acute mesenteric thrombosis; acute renal failure.

OPERATIONS. Splenectomy and suture of torn mesentery. Resection of small bowel.

CLINICAL SUMMARY. This patient was a forty-two-year-old businessman who had been crushed between the back of a truck and a loading platform six hours before admission. He lost consciousness and was carried to a nearby hospital, where he received 6 units of citrated whole blood to bring his blood pressure up from 60 mm. Hg systolic to 100 mm. Hg. He was then transferred by ambulance.

Physical examination showed a conscious but acutely ill white male, ashen in color, lying flat in bed. Blood pressure was 100/70, pulse 130. There were no visible marks of trauma. Heart and lungs were normal. The abdomen was distended, with direct and rebound tenderness and spasm most marked in the left lower quadrant.

X-rays showed no air under the diaphragms and no sign of splenic rupture. The diagnosis of ruptured abdominal viscus, possibly spleen, was made.

INITIAL LABORATORY WORK

Urine

Specific gravity	1.040
Protein	±
Sugar—negative	
pH	6.0
Leucocytes—few	
Erythrocytes	0

Stool

Guaiac—negative

Hematology

Hematocrit	40
Leucocyte count	25,900 per cu. mm.

Blood Chemical Analyses

Blood urea nitrogen	21	mg. per 100 ml.
Plasma chloride	103	mE. per l.
Plasma sodium	143	mE. per l.
Plasma potassium	4.0 mE. per l.	
Carbon dioxide combining power	26.0 mE. per l.	

Arterial

pH	7.34	
pCO$_2$	37	mm. Hg
Total carbon dioxide	20.3	mM. per l.

---

* The author is indebted to Dr. Martin Litwin for collecting the data and analyzing the course of this patient.

ARGUMENT. This patient presented the history and physical findings of acute rupture of an abdominal organ or viscus with intra-abdominal hemorrhage. It is impossible in such cases to determine with certainty what organ or organs have been torn. Exploration should be done at the earliest possible time. The laboratory data shown above were of course not all available at the hour of decision.

Over the six hours previous to admission the patient had received 6 units (3000 ml.) of citrated whole blood. On admission to the emergency ward, his blood pressure was 100/70, pulse 130, and his skin color was ashen. With this increased pulse rate, and a slight drop in blood pressure, he was still short 15 to 25 per cent of his blood volume. Since the normal man of this weight has a circulating blood volume of about 5300 ml., he was still at least 1000 ml. short on blood. This should be replaced under pressure and exploratory laparotomy carried out at once. His hematocrit was still normal because sufficient time had not passed to permit transcapillary refilling of the vascular volume.

FURTHER COURSE. The patient was transferred to the recovery room, where he received transfusion of whole blood rapidly. It was evident that complete resuscitation was not attainable by transfusion despite the administration of a total of 6000 ml. He was moved to the operating suite. When the abdomen was opened, approximately 2 l. of fresh arterial blood was aspirated. A resection of a portion of the jejunum with ligature of a torn branch of the superior mesenteric artery and repair of a torn area of the mesentery were performed. The spleen was also removed.

By the end of the first day his blood pressure and pulse rate had stabilized within normal limits. Urine output was good. He received 2500 ml. of blood during this time.

On the second hospital day the patient was on constant gastric suction because of a distended, quiet abdomen. Despite seemingly accurate electrolyte replacement, a moderate metabolic alkalosis was noted; arterial blood pH was 7.50, and total plasma carbon dioxide content 33.2 mE. per l.

Over the next ten days gastric suction was continued and the patient gradually resumed his oral diet and became ambulatory.

ARGUMENT. Adequate blood replacement and immediate operation in this traumatized and still bleeding patient were essential. Resuscitation before operation was clearly impossible. His postoperative course was good. On the second postoperative day a moderate metabolic alkalosis was noted. This was the result of the metabolism of a very considerable amount of sodium citrate present in the transfused blood, with the freeing of base. However, this is an effect to be desired in the acutely ill patient. This excess alkali may serve to neutralize metabolic acids formed as a result of inadequate tissue perfusion during the acute episode.

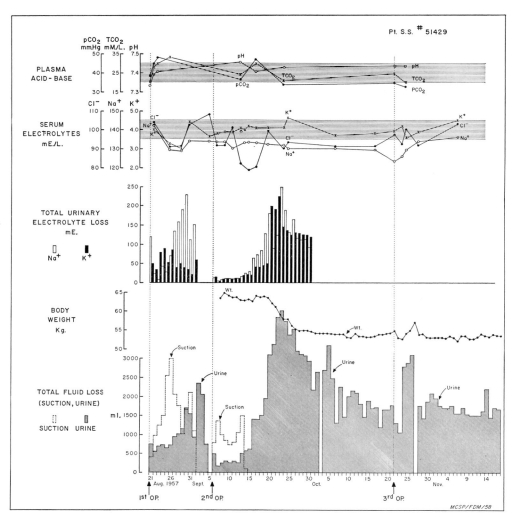

Figure 138. Gangrene of the Bowel with Renal Failure (Case 29)

Above are shown the plasma electrolytes, then the urinary electrolyte excretion. Below are shown body weight and volume losses by tube and urine. The reader is referred to the text for details.

It will be noted that during the oliguric phase there was hypochloremia as a manifestation of the loss of gastric acid by suction. With this there was not as severe an acidosis as one would expect in renal failure, and there was never any hyperkalemia. Electrolyte losses were not measured after the diuretic phase.

The events at diuresis, particularly as regards weight loss and potassium excretion, with very large urine volumes, are of particular interest.

Further Course.   On the sixteenth postoperative day, the patient's abdomen suddenly became distended, tender, and silent. Upright X-ray film of the abdomen showed a moderate amount of free air beneath the diaphragm. A diagnosis of mesenteric thrombosis with perforation of the small bowel was made and the patient again taken to the operating room. During exploratory laparotomy approximately three feet of vascular, necrotic, perforated distal jejunum was resected. A venous thrombosis had occurred, followed by gangrene and arterial thrombosis. There was massive

peritoneal leakage and contamination. Neomycin solution was left in the abdomen and broad-spectrum antibiotics begun. Blood pressure remained good at all times and a total of 7 units of whole blood was administered.

By the first postoperative day the patient's circulation had stabilized, as witnessed by normal blood pressure, pulse, color, and warmth. He was well hydrated, but urine output had dropped off sharply to about 15 ml. per hour; this urine was benzidine-negative. Treatment as a case of acute tubular necrosis, with fluid and electrolyte restriction, was begun. For the next six days urine output remained low and the patient was on constant gastric drainage. His blood urea nitrogen concentration had risen progressively to 205 mg. per 100 ml. His arterial blood pH was 7.46, total arterial plasma carbon dioxide content 24.5 mM. per l., and partial pressure of carbon dioxide in arterial blood 34 mm. Hg at the end of the third day.

His gastric acidity was normal; gastric suction removed large amounts of acid. This—whenever feasible—helps to compensate metabolically for the mounting renal acidosis; the potassium removed by this route is not as impressive as the acid.

On the sixth postoperative day urine output began to climb and diuresis began on the tenth day. Blood chemical data at the start of the diuretic phase were:

Blood urea nitrogen	250	mg. per 100 ml.
Plasma chloride	80	mE. per l.
Plasma sodium	133	mE. per l.
Plasma potassium	4.1	mE. per l.
Plasma osmolality	355	mO. per l.
pH (arterial blood)	7.41	
pCO_2	47	mm. Hg
Total carbon dioxide	30	mM. per l.

Output of urine continued to increase until on the seventeenth day following his second operation it was 4.3. l. His weight decreased during this diuretic phase from 64.3 kg. to about 54 kg. The patient continued to diurese until the thirty-first day after his second operation with a fall in blood urea nitrogen to 15 mg. per 100 ml. The total urinary output of potassium during this first fifteen days of diuresis amounted to 1823 mE.

COMMENT. This patient developed acute renal failure in unusual circumstances and under the eyes of the clinicians who had been watching him closely for two weeks before its onset. Sixteen days previous to his renal difficulties, he had undergone a major abdominal operation because of severe trauma. These events served initially as a stimulus for the conservation of sodium by the kidney. From about the fifth day after his initial operation until about the sixteenth day we may assume that he was losing significant amounts of potassium in the urine as well as smaller amounts in his gastric suction.

Thus, on the sixteenth hospital day, when his renal difficulties began, the patient was in an unusual condition to enter a period of anuria. In patients with renal failure of a prolonged sort the elevation of the plasma potassium concentration becomes progressively less noticeable; it is in the *early period after injury* when its rise is most severe. Here, that period and its "quickly available potassium" had both been spent.

In addition, during the period when renal output was diminished, and when metabolically-produced hydrogen ion could not be excreted, the patient was on constant gastric suction. He put out large amounts of highly acid gastric juice. This removed moderate amounts of hydrogen ion (with chloride) and small amounts of potassium, which were not replaced by intravenous therapy. Thus, we were effectively producing a trend toward a "subtraction hypokalemic alkalosis" in a patient who was metabolically prone to develop an "addition hyperkalemic acidosis." When gastric acid is present in renal failure this becomes a form of treatment that cannot replace dialysis, but can help the patient avoid the ravages of severe acidosis, with hyperkalemia. The removal of hydrogen ion (as hydrochloric acid) via gastric tube would of course produce severe volume reduction were not the volume aspirated also replaced by intravenous salt infusion. This replacement is done on an equimolar basis, using sodium bicarbonate; this further abates renal acidosis. Here, the hypochloremia (80 mE. per l.) bespeaks the extent of the loss of Cl^- (and H^+) from the stomach. The hypochloremia in itself does the patient no harm; the attendant acid-base change is the important thing —here, a tendency to counteract renal acidosis.

During the eight days of oliguria the urinary output averaged around 300 ml. per day, with an average osmolality of 355 mO. per l. The total volume was 2596 ml., with 99 mE. of potassium. The patient's gastric juice loss during this time totaled 8035 ml., with 1127 mE. of chloride and 81 mE. of potassium. The total hydrogen ion lost in the gastric juice may be approximated by subtracting the sum of potassium and sodium from the chloride losses. This indicates the loss of about 300 mE. of H^+. During this time the plasma potassium concentration did not rise over 4.1 mE. per l. although the blood urea nitrogen rose to 250 mg. per 100 ml. He received 180 mM. of sodium bicarbonate during this time. The magnitude of the "excess potassium" present in the cellular mass awaiting excretion during the oliguric phase is indicated by the fact that he excreted 1823 mE. of potassium during diuresis, and lost 10 kg. of weight; this extra potassium did not present itself in the extracellular fluid, because the patient was not permitted to become acidotic.

The pathogenesis of the renal failure was, in itself, of interest. He had gangrenous tissue present in the abdomen, a circumstance that favors the development of renal failure; this occurred with an episode of volume reduction doubtless associated with renal vasoconstriction even though there was no hypotension. The net result was acute renal failure.

FURTHER COURSE. For the next few weeks the patient was sitting up in bed and did well. A daily fever spike to 103° F. pointed to a local wound infection, which was drained. He was discharged from the hospital to be followed as an outpatient, ninety days after admission.

CASE 30

In Which a Bullet Wound of the Lung Leads Finally to Death Due to a Terminal Breakdown in Certain Compensations to Post-traumatic Renal Tubular Acidosis

Case 30. Patient J. H., #8J615. Male. Age 54. Admitted May 13, 1956. Died May 29, 1956.

DIAGNOSIS. Bullet wounds of chest.

OPERATION. Tracheotomy.

CLINICAL SUMMARY. At 2:00 A.M., one hour prior to admission, this patient was shot through the left upper chest in the course of a filling-station holdup. The wound of entry was lateral and high, in the back, and the bullet (0.32 caliber) was palpable under the skin anteriorly, low, at the left costal margin.

On physical examination the patient was in shock, blood pressure 50/0, pulse 130. He was pale, listless, cold, and sweaty with feeble pulses. There were decreased breath sounds over the left chest, with a tympanitic area in the axillary region. The trachea was in the midline. There was no cyanosis or venous distention. Chest tap on the left was unproductive; admission hematocrit was 40. Administration of dextran (250 ml.), plasma (500 ml.), and then blood (1000 ml.) was started, with nasal oxygen. Urinary drainage by catheter was instituted.

The initial clinical response was poor. An additional 1000 ml. of blood was given. Chest tap in another area yielded 1300 ml. of whole blood, with relief of respiratory distress. The hematocrit remained at 40. Blood pressure stabilized at 136/80.

The liver was enlarged. The patient vomited blood on two occasions but there was no abdominal tenderness. Other than chronic alcoholic intake, the past history was not remarkable. There were no spider angiomata or liver palms. Urine output was good. The patient was deemed stable for X-rays in about forty-five minutes. X-rays showed full aeration of both lungs with no residual fluid, but evidence of an anterior pulmonary hematoma.

Within forty-eight hours, however, more ominous signs began to appear. The patient became tremulous, disoriented, combative, and occasionally hypotensive; urine output became reduced. He required restraints. The question of delirium tremens was raised. He developed hallucinations, none of which was colored or microzoological. But most worrisome was a progressive reduction in urine volume to the range of 10 ml. per hour. Temperature began to rise. The patient had been started on erythromycin and chloramphenicol shortly after admission.

INITIAL LABORATORY WORK

Urine

Specific gravity	1.020	
*p*H	4.5	
Sediment	20-30	wbc/hpf
	5-10	rbc/hpf

Bilirubin++++

Stool

    Guaiac-negative

Hematology

Hematocrit	37
Leucocyte count	15,200 per cu. mm.

Blood Chemical Analyses

Blood urea nitrogen	34	mg. per 100 ml.
Plasma protein	7.7	gm. per 100 ml.
Plasma chloride	99	mE. per l.
Plasma sodium	145	mE. per l.
Plasma potassium	4.2	mE. per l.
Carbon dioxide combining power	21.1	mE. per l.
Plasma bilirubin	2.3	mg. per 100 ml.
Osmolality	327	mO. per l.

ARGUMENT. The admission events require little discussion. They are characteristic of a thoracic wound seen early. There was acute volume reduction (hemothorax) seen prior to hemodilution, and, characteristically, with no hematocrit change. There was a good response to adequate transfusion. The hemothorax further embarrassed respiration and this added to the hypotension. After admission chemical and hematologic study were entirely normal save for a bilirubin of 2.3 mg. per 100 ml., possibly due to the pleural blood.

But by the third day clinical deterioration was marked with disorientation, rising fever, and oliguria. Azotemia was not yet pronounced, but there was a moderately severe metabolic acidosis. The plasma osmolality (327 mO./l.) was 37 mO. per l., greater than twice the sodium (145 mE. per l.); this nonelectrolyte solute was partly accounted for by the urea but it suggested a considerable burden of renal or hepatic disease. Blood sugar was normal.

This combination of events could be due to:

(1) beginning post-traumatic renal insufficiency with a "free interval" of maintained output after shock;

(2) mixed metabolic and respiratory acidosis with or without hepatic failure;

(3) advancing or invasive sepsis—in the chest or abdomen;

(4) a new volume reduction with oliguria and azotemia due to unreplaced loss such as gastrointestinal hemorrhage;

(5) delirium tremens; magnesium deficiency; or

(6) dehydration (desiccation) superimposed on any of the above.

There was no obvious source for desalting water loss, but the labored rapid respiratory rate with fever could account for an increased pulmonary water loss needed to raise the sodium to 145 mE. per l. (One would predict a value of about 135 mE. per l., or lower, at this stage.) The high protein (7.7 gm. per 100 ml.) was also evidence for water loss, either desiccation or desalting. With so much hemorrhage and blood replacement the hematocrit is of little help here.

FURTHER COURSE. The thymol turbidity, alkaline phosphatase, and prothrombin time were entirely normal—all evidence against rapid hepatic deterioration.

The patient was given magnesium sulfate without specific effect.

No further bleeding was evident.

He was then given a rapid intravenous infusion of 1500 ml. of 5 per cent dextrose in water. Immediately urine output was restored, and this return lasted until the final day of his illness. *This response to infusion test indicates conclusively that dehydration, probably due to pulmonary loss, in turn increased by dyspnea, played a decisive role in the genesis of the oliguria and hypertonicity.* The lack of potassium elevation at this or any other time was evidence against acute tubular necrosis and is characteristic of desiccation hypertonicity.

Despite the increased volume output the blood urea nitrogen continued to rise and the carbon dioxide combining power to fall as evidences of continuing sepsis and acidosis. This is the picture of rising urine volume with tubular acidosis and azotemia that is characteristic of the post-traumatic state when hypotension and oliguria have previously been present. It suggests tubular damage, not severe enough to present as oliguric renal failure.

By the following day temperature was 105° F. and the patient comatose. Blood cultures, spinal fluid, and chest fluid cultures were all sterile. The local area of the wound cultured *Escherichia coli* and *Staphylococcus aureus*. The lung fields were "remarkably clear" to auscultation but by X-ray showed infiltration along, and spreading out from, the bullet track.

Acid-base profile at this time showed:

Arterial Blood Analysis

pH	7.37	
pCO_2	34	mm. Hg
total carbon dioxide	19.0	mM. per l.
HCO_3	18.0	mM. per l.

Other chemical data confirmed the increasing azotemia (blood urea nitrogen 70 mg. per 100 ml.) and increasing acidosis.

ARGUMENT. Rising blood urea nitrogen with normal plasma potassium concentration and good urine outputs, in our experience, is almost always a sign of advancing sepsis and tissue catabolism in the presence of renal function adequate to provide good volumes, but with low urea clearance, tubular damage, and "chloride acidosis." When the period of oliguria has been as brief as it was here, though such an azotemia and acidosis does signify acute tubular necrosis, it does not suggest an irreparable renal insult. The renal findings are those of solute diuresis through a reduced glomerular mass (i.e., the remaining undamaged neph-

rons) with inadequate tubular cation exchange (K^+ and Na^+ for H^+) to excrete acid properly. The excreted urine represents a high fraction (sometimes as high as 10 per cent) of the total glomerular filtrate. This is solute diuresis through the few remaining nephrons, producing post-traumatic renal tubular acidosis.

The acid-base data are interesting. The arterial profile indicates some respiratory compensation (the pCO_2 at 34 mm. Hg) for a metabolic (HCO_3^-, 18 mM. per l.) acidosis. The arterial HCO_3 and venous carbon dioxide combining power are found to be the same only under well-equilibrated conditions, with normal plasma electrolytes and a carbon dioxide tension near 40 mm. Hg. The abnormal acid-base picture, as it turned out, held the key to the outcome: when respiratory compensation to this mounting renal tubular acidosis finally failed, the patient quickly succumbed.

These findings, with nearly normal sodium, chloride, and potassium concentrations, indicate the accumulation of inorganic acids, and probably sulfate and phosphate. These add to the total osmolality and account for both the evident metabolic acidosis and the nonelectrolyte osmolality—their source having been obscure up to this point.

FURTHER COURSE. The site of the sepsis was almost unquestionably pulmonary. Antibiotics were changed to intravenously administered tetracycline (Achromycin), 1500 mg. per day.

The patient's temperature was lower, but his mental state continued very poor until the ninth day when he became better oriented and his fever was lower. He began to eat. The blood urea nitrogen remained fixed at 75 to 90 mg. per 100 ml.

Plasma potassium levels fell to 3.0 mE. per l.; the oral and intravenous ration included potassium chloride and sodium chloride. On the nineteenth day a plasma chloride concentration of 118 mE. per l. and a carbon dioxide combining power of 12.8 mE. per l. indicated continued impairment of normal tubular function. Urine electrolyte excretion during this period, per day, was: sodium, 7 to 15 mE. per l.; chlorine, 15 to 30 mE. per l.; potassium, 30 to 40 mE. per l.

The urine osmolality was 626 mO. per l., with a sodium-chloride-potassium total of 100 mO. per l. at the highest, indicating that most of the solute was nonelectrolyte. Urine volume was 1700 to 3000 ml. per day; blood urea nitrogen rose to 105 mg. per 100 ml. Sodium bicarbonate (6.0 gm. per day), was added to the oral regimen; the obvious hazard of overloading militated against a larger dose of base.

Brain abscess, meningitis, and lung abscess were added to the differential diagnosis. There was no conclusive evidence for any of them. Clinical management was continued on the basis of pulmonary sepsis superimposed on a renal tubular lesion. Tracheal aspirations cultured *Staphylococcus aureus*.

Tube feedings of skimmed milk were begun. On the thirteenth day the clinical appearances continued to be those of variable semicoma, restlessness, occasional lucid periods, and a discouraging lack of forward progress.

Chemical data on the thirteenth day:

Urine

pH	5.54

Blood

Arterial

pH	7.33	
pCO₂	23	mm. Hg
total carbon dioxide	11.9	mM. per l.
HCO₃	11.2	mM. per l.

Venous

Hematocrit	39	
Leucocyte count	14,600	per cu. mm.
Blood urea nitrogen	90	mg. per 100 ml.
Plasma chloride	124	mE. per l.
Plasma sodium	148	mE. per l.
Plasma potassium	4.6	mE. per l.
Carbon dioxide combining power	12.7	mE. per l.

ARGUMENT. The dilute, copious urine of low pH, yet with slight plasma hypertonicity and severe metabolic acidosis (still well compensated by respiratory mechanisms), continues to indicate an unresponsive renal tubule facing a solute diuresis. Although the tube feedings were small in volume and consisted only of skimmed milk they may have contributed to the solute diuresis and hypertonicity.

As one saw the patient at this time, his fever (101 to 102° F.) and tachycardia (pulse 120) with dyspnea (respirations 40 to 60) were impressive. There were no other localizing signs. Focal sepsis was not evident other than in the chest. The azotemia, severe acidosis with hyperchloremia, and now rising potassium concentration (4.3–4.6–5.2 mE. per l.) on successive days dominated the metabolic scene. Treatment with sodium bicarbonate was continued at about 6.0 gm. (about 60 mM.) per day.

FURTHER COURSE. Antibiotics and careful replacement therapy were continued. Suddenly on the fourteenth day the patient's fever again rose to 105° F., he became hypotensive and oliguric; bloody diarrhea, not profuse, was evident. Replacement of blood and fluid lost was continued, but the patient appeared moribund. A tracheotomy was performed for aspiration; this brought good ventilation to the upper airway but little over-all progress. Sputum was profuse and purulent, though the breath sounds were normal.

Norepinephrine and Neo-synephrine were increasingly ineffective in pressure maintenance. Although the eosinophil count was near zero, hydrocortisone was given, but without avail. Sodium bicarbonate was continued but without effect on the acidosis or blood pressure.

Arterial pH fell now to 7.15, pCO₂ rose to 46 mm. Hg, and total carbon dioxide to 17.4 mM. per l.

There was deep coma. Blood pressure was maintained only with large doses of norepinephrine; bloody diarrhea continued, never profuse. There was no cyanosis. On the sixteenth day, the patient expired in shock and coma, with evidence of pulmonary edema or bronchopneumonia.

COMMENT. This patient apparently died of sepsis. The exact site and anatomic nature of the septic process were not wholly clear; lung abscess and brain abscess were considered. His renal lesion with severe acidosis was the terminating event. When pulmonary compensation ceased, pCO₂ (owing to advancing bronchopneumonia) rose from 23 to 47 mm. Hg, pH fell to 7.15, and he was unable to maintain his blood pressure and circulation. Prior to this he was able to keep going by effective pulmonary compensation (pCO₂ 23 mm. Hg) to his renal acidosis.

Treatment seemed to have two shortcomings. First, some change in antibiotics or massive doses of penicillin might have been more effective. Listed briefly, the antibiotic coverage and dosage were:

DAYS	AGENTS AND DOSAGE PER DAY (GM.)	
1–4	Streptomycin	2.0
	Penicillin	8 × 10⁶ U
4–12	Acromycin	1.5
9–17	Chloromycetin	1.0
12–17	Erythromycin	3.0

Second, there was a persistent tendency to treat the metabolic (that is, renal) acidosis with sodium bicarbonate. The patient's continued high urine output made such a course permissible and certainly less hazardous than in renal shutdown; but the hazard of pulmonary edema was always present. Early in the course too much chloride may have been given as potassium chloride and sodium chloride; but renal acidosis with hyperchloremia is not unusual in such a situation even where there has been no exogenous chloride treatment whatsoever.

The tube feedings started four days before death and maintained for forty-eight hours constituted an additional hazard as a solute load, and as a threat to aspiration of feedings. They could easily have been dispensed with in this acutely ill man: calories are indeed far down on the priority list in such a situation.

The patient never showed weight gain under treatment; but weight loss was not marked. This suggests moderate overadministration of fluids. A man with such extreme stress and febrile illness should be expected to lose weight if body water remains constant. On the day before death, his total intake was 5300 ml. with only 1420 ml. of urine; he was not weighed. This high intake was in part the result of continuous intravenous administration of norepinephrine. It undoubtedly contributed to his death.

There are three aspects of this case which have a familiar ring in terms of present-day hospital practice: effective transfusion in shock, mysterious sepsis with multiple frequently-changed antibiotics of decreasing effectiveness, and finally a pulmonary episode suspiciously traceable to overadministration of water and salt.

There is unusually clear documentation of the breakdown of respiratory compensation to metabolic acidosis, with collapse of blood pressure as pH falls to drastically low levels (pH was 7.15 toward the end).

Postmortem examination showed the lungs to be overweight with a mixed lesion of edema and pneumonitis; there was a lung abscess in the middle of the bullet track. It was not large, but spreading out from it was an area of acute inflammation. The kidneys showed a nephrotic lesion. There was ileus. The other organs and viscera were not significantly abnormal. There were superficial gastric erosions. There was no colitis.

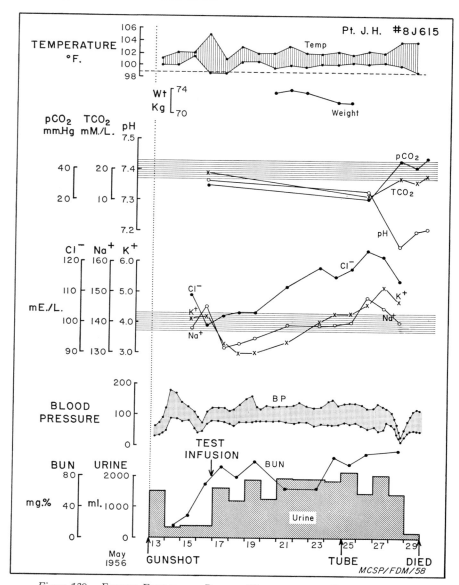

Figure 139. EVENTS FOLLOWING BULLET WOUNDS OF THE LUNG (Case 30)

In the upper ordinates are shown temperature, acid-base data, electrolytes. Below are shown blood pressure, blood urea, nitrogen, and urine output. The reader is referred to the text for details.

It will be noted that the course was febrile throughout. The pH was maintained near normal by hyperventilation producing a low pCO$_2$, until the terminal spread of bronchopneumonia, which produced a sharp rise in pCO$_2$ with a precipitous fall in pH and blood pressure. The continued rise in blood urea nitrogen and chloride bespeaks a progressive renal tubular acidosis despite large urine outputs. This was the result of tubular damage during the hypotensive-oliguric phase after the initial trauma. Tracheotomy was unsuccessful in providing good alveolar ventilation during the final episode.

CHAPTER 47

Burns

Section I.   Introductory Comment and Organization

Medical knowledge appears superficially to grow more complicated each year; but it has long been our conviction that in biology and medicine true knowledge simplifies as it progresses. Increasingly basic, inclusive concepts and truths are developed or discovered which clarify rather than complicate, and permit the understanding of a wide variety of peripheral phenomena in terms of simple central mechanisms. In this sense increasing knowledge simplifies understanding, teaching, and treatment. In the past ten years, this change has occurred in the field of burns. The teaching and understanding of the care of burns need not be nearly as complicated as it formerly was.

A description of the care of extensive thermal burns should always take its place along with that of the rest of the trauma. The particular problems of resuscitation, the special aspects of infection, the extremely prolonged nature of the traumatic illness, and the need for definitive surgery, albeit delayed in most cases, are best understood in terms of the general surgical care of trauma rather than as unique phenomena. Further, the exaggerated disorder of burns illuminates certain aspects of other traumata, an example being traumatic edema.

In most hospitals there are one or two surgeons who have interested themselves in burns and who take over the early care, if not the total management, of the patient.

This centralization of experience should be encouraged and is good for all, not the least being the patient admitted to that hospital's care. Many concepts and techniques that are applicable to surgical metabolism as a whole were first studied *in extenso* as a feature of burn metabolism.* Many of the difficulties and abnormalities seen in burns were not clearly understood until almost ten years of study of other types of trauma had passed. There are many problems yet to be solved.

The severely burned patient represents a remarkably polyvalent challenge to the surgeon. For the physician, pediatrician, or internist who has rarely dealt with such problems, it is difficult to conceive of a massive burn as being a challenge in the understanding of bodily metabolism. However, in magnitude of disorder encountered, complexity of interplay of somatic factors, and salvage to be gained by successful management, the extensive burn has few peers in the whole field of medicine.

It is our objective in this chapter to describe in broad outline those aspects of the natural history of the burn the understanding of which is most helpful to therapy, and the detailed methods by which they can be put

---

* It was in this group of patients that we first attempted a coordinated study of metabolic balances, body composition, and electrolyte abnormalities in the study of surgery.

in practice. This chapter will take the form, first, of a description of the evolution and care of a life-endangering thermal burn in the range of 40 to 50 per cent of body surface, a burn in a young person, and a burn that does not involve complications in the pulmonary or renal area. This type of case is the proto-typal central pattern, the "dangerous but salvageable" burn. It is the burn the surgeon hopes to see when called, as opposed to the seemingly hopeless problems in the infant, the aged or the crippled, so commonly encountered in the treatment of burns in civilian life.

Just as definitive operation in the severely injured has a profound metabolic significance for the patient by terminating the homeostatic tension of the untreated continuing injury, so also definitive operation in burns (by which is meant a lasting wound closure) has a remarkable significance for the metabolism of the burned patient. It so happens that definitive surgery in this injury usually comes after delay, and occurs, not as one event, but as a series of coverage procedures. In our initial example this closure is begun at ten days.

A. GENERAL PLAN

Our treatment of burns as they occur in "mid-scale" (the extensive but salvageable burn) is based on three interlocking basic principles and procedures.

(1) *Fluid therapy* is administered on the basis of the predicted expansion of the extracellular phase, using as the principal replacement fluid, plasma, dextran, and/or albumin, with only a small amount of saline solution or whole blood. This therapy is followed and controlled by hourly urine output, weight change, and hematocrit measurements.

(2) *Open treatment* is given the wound, with our objective a cool, dry, pain-free eschar.

(3) *Early sharp debridement* with total coverage (starting the fifth to tenth day), using cadaver homografts if necessary, is carried out.

The ensuing account traces the course of a patient through such an evolution; thereafter the atypical variants and special problems are described.

B. THE FOUR PHASES OF A BURN

In describing a characteristic case of primary, elective, closed, soft-tissue trauma, we identified four phases of convalescence: the injury period of *initial catabolism,* the *turning point,* the period of *spontaneous nitrogen anabolism* to muscular strength, and finally the period of *fat redeposition.* These four phases of convalescence are clearly discernible in a burn, but superimposed upon them are the alterations in fluid metabolism that characterize the first four to six days, not unique to burns but larger in extent than in any other injuries. Also superimposed on the basic pattern of normal convalescence is the very much later closure of the wound. For this reason, we prefer to describe the burn course in terms of the following phases:

(1) *burn edema:* demand, satisfaction, and diuresis;

(2) *the wound:* sepsis and catabolism;

(3) *the upswing:* completion of closure, beginning anabolism; and

(4) *healing:* maturation of the new skin, and rehabilitation.

The last stage above is analogous to the last described for convalescence after closed soft-tissue trauma and includes fat gain. The surface changes are prominent. The first two phases have an underlying physiology somewhat exaggerated over that seen in nonburn trauma, because of the large size of the sequestered edema and the prolonged septic process. The two of them together go to make up an initial catabolic phase. The "turning-point" phase or "corticoid-withdrawal phase," which is often so clearly seen after extensive soft-tissue trauma without burning, is not sudden in the burn, though it just as surely occurs with diuresis and early wound closure. If successful complete wound closure is accomplished at about the tenth to fourteenth day, an upswing in nitrogen metabolism due to sudden restriction in the urinary excretion rate is visible, looking like the familiar anabolic tendency of the "turning-point." It results not only from post-traumatic metabolic reversion but also from decrease in the extent of infection as closure is accomplished.

In this section we will refer repeatedly to the infection and the septic aspects of the burn between the fifth and about the thirty-fifth day, during operative closure. By this is meant the inevitable growth of flora on the surface, low-grade fever, and tendency to febrile spikes in temperature after wound surgery.

We do not mean to imply by the word "septic" that an uncontrolled, invasive, septic process with blood-stream infection is either inevitable or uncontrollable. Such may indeed occur, and be fatal, yet, it cannot be regarded as inevitable though the surface contamination surely is.

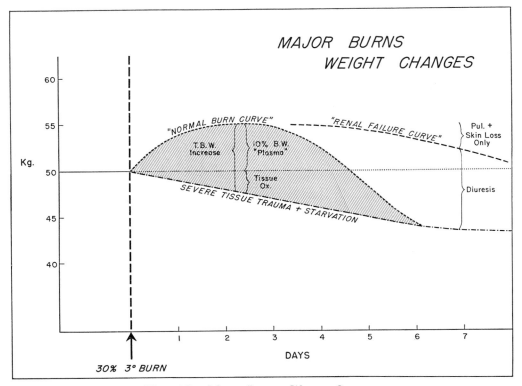

Figure 140. MAJOR BURNS—WEIGHT CHANGES

In this chart is shown a schematic representation of the change in weight observed after major burns when they are treated with salt solutions or plasma in various combinations.

It will be noticed that the patient gains weight abruptly as the obligatory edema forms under the burn and as the demands of this edema are satisfied by therapy, so that it can form without compromising the plasma volume.

Because of tissue trauma and starvation, the "true" (tissue solids) weight (lower line) falls and the cross-hatched area between the actual weight and this "edema-free" weight indicates the extent of the edema. If the patient develops normal postburn diuresis, his weight will start to fall about the second to fourth day

and by approximately one week after the burn he will have lost all this fluid by diuresis and his actual weight will have regained the "edema-free" weight curve well below his normal weight.

If, however, he develops acute renal failure, he then cannot lose water save by the skin and pulmonary routes; these are ineffective routes for the loss of salt. For this reason the patient loses water, not salt, only a small amount of weight, and develops a progressive hypernatremia. The inability to lose the edema weight, together with a rapidly rising plasma sodium concentration, is an ominous manifestation of renal failure in a burn. In our experience this combination (hypernatremia without diuresis) has often been fatal.

Section II. The First Phase: The Burn Edema;
Demand, Satisfaction, and Diuresis

There follows the description of the pattern of recovery to be expected in the case of a 40 per cent body burn in a young man. The burn involves the anterior trunk and the legs and thighs, mostly anteriorly and to some extent circumferentially. His arms are unburned, his back, buttocks, perineum, scrotum, and penis are unburned, and there is no burn of the face, nares, or pulmonary tract. Let the carping critic point out right now that this type of burn is all too rare. Suffice it to say that such burns do occur and that an understanding of this "norm" (free of the complexities of inevitable pressure-maceration, pulmonary lesions, renal failure, accumulative bronchopneumonia, or uncoverable surface without adequate donor sites) provides a basis for the understanding of those very same complexities. To follow this example of a simple, normal, burned patient through his course should teach us something about the clinical evolution of the burn metabolism.

A. CLINICAL APPEARANCES AND EVOLUTION OF THE SKIN BURN

Let us picture this as a burn produced by the ignition of the patient's clothing after he has spilled gasoline on it while cleaning out the carburetor in his garage. This type of flame burn from burning clothing is not infrequently confined to the front or back of the body, and if the undershorts are made of some material slightly less inflammable than the trousers and the patient can strip his clothes off fast enough, he may avoid the burn of buttocks and perineum which is so hard to close.

The patient's discomfort at the outset is not extreme. He is frightened and in some pain. The sudden unexpected conflagration and the stripping off of clothes will frequently stand out in his recollection much more prominently than any sensation of pain. His freedom from pain is doubtless associated, at least in part, with the thermal destruction of pain endings in the skin, a change that pro-duces anesthesia of the skin, one of the characteristic physical manifestations of deep burns.

Full-thickness burns ("third-degree") defy exact anatomic or histologic definition. The term is a functional, surgical one. If the burn is (or becomes) one that will require coverage by new sheets of epithelium, it is (or has become) a full-thickness burn. In small areas the new sheets are home-grown; in large areas they must be grafted. *In essence a third-degree burn is one that requires new epithelial coverage by ingrowth or grafting; a second-degree burn does not.*

The physical appearances of full-thickness burns include anesthesia to cutting and pinching and a variety of surface characteristics, including:

(1) failure to blanch on pressure,
(2) thrombosed skin vessels—purplish-black cords,
(3) parchment-like translucency with thrombosed vessels beneath,
(4) leather-like wrinkling and consistency; "tanned" appearance,
(5) colors: black, brown, cadaverous white, or cherry pink.

Deep partial-thickness burns are very difficult to differentiate from full-thickness burns and may be converted into full-thickness burns by pressure, maceration, or infection.

During the first phase this complex of cutaneous burn and subcutaneous edema undergoes a natural evolution characterized by formation and then diuresis of the edema fluid while the skin burn dries out and separates from its deeper layers, forming an interface between the dead heat-precipitated proteins of the full-thickness burn and the unburned cutaneous and subcutaneous layers. It is along this interface that bacteria grow and epithelial regeneration will occur if it is to do so at all, either from the margins or from the deeper dermal appendages. In the comparatively few days of the first phase this wound evolution proceeds but a small way along its course, and the surface looks much as it did on admission, the lighter areas of full thickness later becoming darker or jet black on exposure to the air, other areas forming a crusted eschar.

B. FIRST STEPS ON ADMISSION; EXAMINATION AND TREATMENT

1. First—Clearing the Airway

As the patient is first seen, initial attention is given the airway. If there is difficulty in ventilation, a tracheotomy should be done; if there is burn of the nasal hair and pharynx, and blackening of the vocal cords, a tracheotomy will be necessary very soon. Excessive delay is dangerous. If there is crowing respiration and hoarseness, tracheotomy will also be needed; steam inhalation may abort the need.

2. Second—Catheterization

The patient is then gently catheterized with careful asepsis; in the female with perineal burn any delay here may make the procedure difficult. This urine is examined for pigment and concentration; its volume is recorded hourly.

3. Third—The Venipuncture

A vein is now carefully entered. A blood sample is taken for base-line values. An indwelling apparatus for infusion is left; a polyethylene catheter is placed in the superior vena cava if possible. This indwelling venous catheter must never be placed in the inferior caval or femoral system because of the prohibitive risk of thromboembolism. In any site, the catheter must be removed and changed after three days because of the virtual certainty of platelet thrombi and septic embolization. Through this indwelling device an infusion is started; saline solution or plasma may be commenced pending crystallization of the plan of therapy.

4. Fourth—Mapping the Wound; History and Physical Examination

It is now appropriate to slow down and assess the damage. The patient's history is important with particular reference to previous illness, psychiatric status, and the actual nature of the burning episode. Physical examination of heart, lungs, liver, abdomen, eyegrounds, airway (including rectal and pelvic examinations), are especially important along with a complete examination of the surface burn. Mapping the wound takes the form of a carefully drawn chart of the burned areas together with a detailed examination for skin consistency, appearance, and sensation. The surgeon makes a definite commitment as to the extent of full-thickness destruction. The "rule of nines" is very helpful for adult surface estimates: 9 per cent each for arms and head; 18 per cent each for legs and trunk surfaces (front and back). The "burn index" is the sum of the third-degree surface extent plus one-half the second-degree extent. With these things accomplished—a task requiring fifteen to thirty minutes—it is now appropriate to sit down and plan the fluid therapy.

C. THE BURN EDEMA

Within minutes after the burn is sustained, edema starts to gather beneath the surface. The formation of this edema is generally regarded as due to destruction by heat of any vascular tone in the area which might produce arteriolar vasoconstriction, and of the integrity of the capillary walls themselves, the two producing an intense vasodilated transudation of protein-rich fluid into the burn. The description of this burn edema, its magnitude, and the timing of its formation was a most important advance in the understanding of burn biochemistry traceable to the work of Cope and his group in the decade of the 1940's. Prior to that time, it was thought that the requirement of the burn for plasma was due to the loss of plasma to the outside world by the "weeping" of the surface. The fact that a burn which was an absolutely bone-dry char still required much plasma in treatment was neglected, or the burn was regarded as "toxic," or the occurrence was simply never brought into focus as a phenomenon at all. It should have been the clue to the nature of the burn fluid-demand.

In considering the magnitude of edema formed under a burn, one must consider for a moment some of the aspects of the volume of a cylinder. We have already mentioned how much blood may be in the thigh after a fractured femur. These same volumetric considerations hold in a burn. A patient with a burn of the anterior thorax and abdomen—as in our hypothetical case—and burns of the legs, may accumulate as much as 8000 ml. of protein-rich plasma filtrate with comparatively little gross distortion in size or shape of the trunk and thigh. Specifically, an increase of thigh diameter of only two inches and of thoracic diameter of only 0.5 inch would be compatible with the total accumulation of about 8000 ml. of protein-rich plasma-like edema fluid in the subcutaneous tissue of a burn such as we are describing in an average-sized adult male (a 70 kg. man who is 5 feet, 8 inches tall).

1. Edema versus the Patient

The accumulation of this edema appears to be parasitic and obligatory; it will accumulate as long as the patient can maintain effective forward flow of blood to the injured part. If the patient is untreated, his hematocrit will progressively rise, and as it approaches the region of 60 to 70, he has a blood-volume reduction of approximately 35 per cent due to the loss of about one-half his plasma into the burn. He then passes into a shocklike state, and may later die. If he is untreated but very fortunate, the exact balance of loss rate and oral fluid intake may permit a precarious survival. As flow is reduced in shock, less edema accumulates.

The systemic illness of a patient in burn shock, suffering from acute plasma loss, is considerably more striking than it is in a patient who has the same volume-deficit through loss of whole blood. We do not understand the reason for this; it may be a viscosity effect or some more subtle alteration in function of the central nervous system as well as the early ravages of invasive infection. As the patient goes into burn-shock, he is febrile, disoriented, anuric, and will show all the characteristics that one would associate with oligemic shock of any cause, but he is much more "toxic." Before the days of plasma treatment there were no doubt many individuals who passed through this phase, went into shock, and then rallied later as they weathered the storm by a small margin, began to reabsorb their edema, and were lucky enough to maintain renal function. One cannot help but wonder about the subsequent course of such patients in the days before skin grafting or the emergence of any concept of how to close the burn wound. Early accounts are very glowing and florid in their description of the various types of ointments and unguents and other medicaments applied to burns, but there are very few descriptions that permit one to visualize what the doctors thought of the late, unhealed, burned patient who had been able to weather this early oligemic phase without treatment. In severe burns without treatment, and without primary pulmonary damage, death occurs around the second to fifth day and is a mixture of the effects of burn-shock and invasive sepsis. Severe burns are not a cause of very rapid or sudden death of themselves—barring a pulmonary component.

The purpose of treatment early in the course of a burn is to provide to the blood stream and to the unburned interstitial fluid those substances (water, protein, salt) that are being lost into the burn. This infusion maintains the circulation and the perfusion of the organs of the body, it maintains or restores the plasma volume and as it does so the hematocrit falls downward toward normal. It provides filtration pressure for renal function, and, because it adds water to the body, it is accompanied by a gain in weight.

2. Quantitative Estimates

Without treatment the disordered renal physiology of a burn is summarized as maximal retention of sodium, chloride, and bicarbonate by tubular resorption; maximal antidiuretic activity with water conservation; increased excretion of potassium nitrogen and other cellular components as cell water is mobilized; and finally, decreased renal blood flow. Any homeostatic tubular responses become meaningless as glomerular filtration rate falls toward zero with the development of oligemia and shock. In the end, the concentrated low-volume urine of effective homeostassi becomes the oliguria and then the anuria of decreased renal perfusion in shock. Whether or not post-traumatic renal insufficiency then eventuates depends on many features, chief among which is the vascular age of the kidney at the outset and the magnitude of the pigment load presented for excretion during the oligemic phase.

With treatment a similar train of events is initiated, but as treatment replaces the plasma lost as transudate into the edema fluid, the patient does not progress to oliguria or shock. The accumulation of the burn edema continues, and this, together with the renal changes, results in the positive balances of the early burn.

(1) The burn edema accumulates (to the amount of about 50 per cent of the volume of the normal extracellular fluid) or approximately 10 per cent of the starting body weight. This includes 1000 mE. of sodium in a large male patient. With this go proportional amounts of chloride (about 750 mE.) and bicarbonate (150 mE.).

(2) Water to suit approximates 7 l., and weighs 7 kg., or about 10 per cent of body weight.

(3) Protein concentration in the burn edema is about 3 to 5 gm. per 100 ml., or 350 gm. This accumulation and its matching replacement account for a considerable nitrogen accumulation (in the form of whole protein), contingent of course on protein administration.

Cell-water mobilization contributes about 500 ml. a day to the satisfying of edema during the first few days. There is thus a negative potassium balance of 70 mE. per day for a short period.

Without treatment none of the positive balances can be exhibited; renal conservation and edema formation alone indicate the nature of the redistribution.

External loss through the skin proceeds according to the nature of the burn. If it is a wet and exuding "weeping" surface, it will lose from 1500 to 3000 ml. a day. This aspect of fluid loss is strictly determined by extent and surface character of the burn. A scald or a steam burn is wet and very exudative; a flame burn tends to be dry; flash burns occupy a mid-position.

The pulmonary water loss is determined by body size, fever, dyspnea, and the presence or absence of a tracheotomy. The range is very large, running from 750 to 5000 ml. per day. If urine output ranges in the vicinity of 30 to 75 ml. an hour, the water needs for this output are accordingly 720 to 1800 ml. per day. Fever, dyspnea, and tracheotomy increase the pulmonary loss. Knowing the nature of these determining pulmonary and renal variables, the surgeon must use his clinical judgment to gauge the total water treatment to cover the external losses (as opposed to the solute needed for the edema satisfaction).

After the first twelve hours the pulmonary water loss can be accurately calculated by the weight change, as shown below. Heat-engendered fragility costs the patient about 250 ml. of red cells in the first forty-eight hours, an entirely unimportant consideration in replacement treatment, although the products of that hemolysis may be very dangerous to the kidney.

3. Weight Gain

The normal extracellular volume is approximately equal to 20 per cent of the body weight. As indicated in Part III, the absolute dimension of this depends upon the method of measurement used, and the results vary from about 14 to about 24 per cent of body weight, the lower figures being found when crystalloids of high molecular weight are used. In any event, the figure of 20 per cent of body weight is a clinically valid approximation to be used as a basis for treatment.

This normal extracellular-fluid volume is capable, following a burn, of a maximal expansion of about one-half its original size or an increase of 10 per cent of body weight to a total volume of 30 per cent of body weight. This figure is the key to our method of treating burns; it is such a basic value that it appears to cut across many of the differences between burned patients and therapeutic formulas, and it provides a basic guide to the fluid therapy that has been remarkably useful.

Its final validity depends not only on use and experience, but also upon the observation of the net weight gain after treatment. This weight gain indicates the extent of the increase in extracellular-fluid-volume in burns. *This weight gain is an index of the volume of the edema, not an objective per se.* We have repeatedly measured the weight gain in burns and found it to check out to a value between 8 and 10 per cent of the patient's body weight, when the therapy was guided by using all of the useful clinical indices: hematocrit, hourly urine output, blood pressure, clinical appearance, and common sense. This empirical result is therefore a reinforcing corroboration that the figure of 10 per cent of body weight for the maximum expected extracellular-fluid expansion is a valid guide to burn therapy.

This gain in weight is due to the accumulation of an obligatory new area of extracellular fluid. If the normal body-fluid phases remain normal and a new edema phase is to form, weight must be gained. Its occurrence merely indicates that the burn edema is being formed, that its needs are being satisfied by the fluid administered rather than wholly at the expense of the patient's plasma volume. In this sense, the gain is analogous to the weight gain of heart failure, liver failure, or renal failure: a gain in weight due to gain in water; a gain in weight which then disappears when the water is lost by diuresis. Yet, obviously, weight cannot be gained without intake.

4. General Outline: The Budget

The method we use might therefore be called "the body-weight burn budget." The term "budget" is more descriptive than the term "formula." A budget is a general scheme or forecast plan that must be changed as conditions vary and according to the needs and circumstances. It is a starting plan; it is a blueprint or a road map; it is not a precise chemical formula or expression that should be pursued with a compulsive desire to avoid change.

In summary the critical data for our case now under consideration are:

Age = 45; Sex = male; Weight = 65 kg.
Estimated normal extracellular fluid = 0.2 × 65 kg. = 13.0 l.
Area of burn = 40 per cent of body—anterior trunk, legs, and thighs. Dry char.
Estimated contents of burn edema (first 48–72 hours):
  Water = 6500 ml. or 10% of body weight
  Sodium = 900 mE.
  Chloride = 600 mE.
  Bicarbonate = 150 mE.
  Protein = 325 gm. = 50 gm. nitrogen
Cell water mobilization into edema (first 48–72 hours):
  Water = 1000 ml.
  Potassium = 150 mE.
Pulmonary water loss (first 48 hours) = 2000 ml.
Renal water loss (first 48 hours) = 2000 ml.
Surface water loss (first 48 hours) = 1000 ml.

Our basic budget therefore consists in giving the patient 10 per cent of his body weight as colloid solution in isotonic electrolyte in the first forty-eight hours, on a descending scale of infusion: he is given one-half of this in the first twelve hours, one-quarter in the second twelve, and one-quarter in the second twenty-four hours.

One-quarter of the colloid is given as dextran, because the low-molecular-weight component acts as an osmotic diuretic. The remainder is given as plasma. Single-donor plasma units, which have been stored at room temperature, are preferred.

In addition he is given about 1000 ml. a day of 5 per cent dextrose in water to cover pulmonary loss, this figure being revised sharply upward if the patient has a tracheotomy, high fever, or severe dyspnea with a pulmonary injury. He is additionally given 1500 ml. of dextrose in saline solution a day to compensate for his urinary and skin water losses. The saline allotment is revised sharply upward if the patient has a very wet burn with much weeping, and it is revised sharply downward if the patient is anuric. These last two allotments—the dextrose in water and the dextrose in saline solution—are given as a constant allowance throughout the first twenty-four hours and are matched to changing clinical circumstances.

The patient is given one transfusion of whole blood in the first forty-eight hours to compensate for the blood cells destroyed by the initial heat.

This, then, is the body-weight burn budget, and we proceed to apply it to the patient as follows:

5. Getting Started

First 12 hours: 3250 ml. total colloid ($\frac{1}{2}$ ration), consisting of
2400 ml. plasma and
850 ml. dextran
Rate: 275 ml. per hour
or: 4.5 ml. per minute
or: 75 drops per minute

Second 12 hours: 1625 ml. total colloid ($\frac{1}{4}$ ration)

Second 24 hours: 1625 ml. total colloid ($\frac{1}{4}$ ration)

This colloid ration is the basic need of the patient. Over and above this he needs noncolloid fluids to cover his urinary and pulmonary losses and losses by transcutaneous exudation (highly variable). The calculation for this is as follows (for the first forty-eight hours):

Five per cent dextrose in saline solution: 3000 ml. at a rate of about 750 ml. each twelve hours, or about 60 ml. an hour.

Five per cent dextrose in water: 2000 ml. at a rate of about 500 ml. each twelve hours.

The two above may be interlarded in the colloid infusion from time to time and at rates therefore greater than is indicated above, but accomplished at the same over-all budgeted volume.

Note that the above noncolloid infusion does not involve the diminishing rate factor demanded by the colloid requirement; the noncolloid fluids are given at a reasonably constant rate to match reasonably constant loss. With fever or a wet burn, they would have to be given at a faster rate and larger volume than indicated here.

D. THE WOUND

After an evolution of many complex treatment patterns for the surface wound, there has been a return to the simplest. Nothing is done to the wound itself in the way of scrubbing or cleansing. It is left open. In a burn such as that described here, the nature of the surface is "made to order" for successful open treatment. The patient can lie on his back and sides without lying on the burn, and it will dry and crust over in pink and light-brown firm crusts, which have a slight flexibility, which are not painful, and which will show dry, scaly wrinkling around the edges as evidence of beginning epithelial ingrowth under the crust, with lack of infection.

There is not space here to discuss all the forms of surface treatment that have been advocated. This simple open treatment seems to be the most effective, either in hospitals where burns are seen singly or in "burn units" that have a constant load of burns in large numbers. If a patient with a burn must be transported, the open treatment can be accomplished merely by wrapping the patient in a sterile half-sheet; there is no need to put on a complete dressing.

The important attributes of the open treatment are coolness and dryness. The normal skin temperature of an exposed extremity is between 75° and 85° F. At this low temperature saprophytic growth is minor, and with a dry outer surface contamination is of less significance. When a large dressing is wrapped around the burn, an insulated cocoon is formed which raises the surface to incubator temperature (98.6° F.). Saprophytes grow, the exudate is increased in amount and cannot evaporate, and this pus is held against the surface, which then macerates and commences autodigestion. Each time the pus-soaked dressing is changed a malodorous sack of exudate is removed and a new receptacle put in place; organisms from the hospital environment find a culture medium ideally suited to their needs.

When the open treatment is successfully pursued this cycle never gets started; when the time for early sharp debridement arrives the burn, although contaminated and infected by growth of organisms in the nonviable pabulum of the burned dermis, is surgically acceptable as a site for grafting.

The nature of the burn surface must be evaluated realistically. Flame burns are usually dry. Burns that can be exposed to the air from the start remain dry in a satisfactory fashion, and it is for this reason that we illustrate treatment by the case of a burn that is predominantly on the anterior surface of the trunk and thighs, the most favorable type for open treatment. If both surfaces are involved, the patient may be put on a Stryker frame or Foster rotating bed for frequent turning. Some patients tolerate this form of immobilization well and others tolerate it poorly. Forceful attempts to restrain them should never be used; if the patient cannot tolerate a turning device he should be moved to a foam rubber mattress and turned by other methods, the back undergoing almost inevitable maceration.

However these details may be worked out, the requirement of salt and water for the weeping surface burn is much greater when the surface is wet, as in scalds, hot-water burns, certain chemical burns, and macerated flame burns. In the dry flame burn it may be almost nil. When the burn is a very wet and weeping one, the material that exudes from the burn will be found to contain approximately 4 gm. per 100 ml. of albumin: it is just like the burn edema fluid. One might therefore expect that it would increase the plasma requirement rather than the salt-and-water requirement. Yet, since it represents the loss to the outside world of burn edema that would otherwise collect under the dermis, it has seemed logical not to alter the colloid requirement on this basis, and this has proved valid by experience.

An open granulating surface is an evaporative one; the water loss increases the endogenous caloric requirement of the patient. But this is not true of the early open burn that is dry to begin with, or that becomes dry on a few hours of exposure, with crusting over.

Here, the dry crust is relatively impermeable to liquid, and sharply limits evaporative loss.

Steps such as pressure bandages and ice packs have been suggested to reduce the accumulation of subcutaneous fluid in burns. Pressure bandages on a burned extremity are dangerous because of the hazard to the arterial circulation as edema forms and increases tissue pressure. A pressure bandage on the trunk or abdomen is meaningless, since respiratory oscillations make the pressure uneven and convert it into a pump. General hypothermia or local application of cold might be expected to reduce the fluid permeation, if the heat damage has left some reactive arterioles that can constrict. Inadequate experience has been gained in either animals or man to make a solid conclusion on this point, but the experience recorded has been generally disappointing save in very localized burns.

Once the eschar is to be removed and a start made on skin replacement, the grafts may be left open if favorably situated, or held in place by circumferential occlusive dressings if the anatomic area is not suitable for open management. But even these should be removed quite early. Donor sites can be left without any dressing whatsoever. The bulky, hot, macerated, smelly, green, pus-soaked dressing of the early burn is a thing of the past.

1. Antibiotics

Just as antibiotics have produced a reduction in the incidence of early invasive sepsis following massive mechanical trauma, so also have they lowered the incidence of early invasive infection with positive blood culture in the first few days after burns.

This infection arises from growth of organisms in the deeper layers of dermis and subcutaneous fat where the heat has destroyed the circulation and made a pabulum for bacteria. Antibiotics are therefore not as effectual in aborting the local process as they are in controlling the blood-stream invasion.

The patient is started on penicillin and streptomycin at a dosage, for example, of 10 to 20 million units and 2 gm. per day, respectively. This is given intramuscularly or intravenously, depending upon circumstances and the availability of sites for intramuscular injection.

E. GUIDES TO PROGRESS

1. Clinical Appearances

Although blood pressure is often very difficult to measure in burned patients, its observation is a helpful minimum guide. Color of unburned skin, warmth of extremities, mentation, pulse, and respiration are the basic clinical guides. To these clinical indices of early progress are added three all-important measurable indices: the hematocrit, urine output, and body weight.

2. The Hematocrit

There is no sequential index of changing plasma volume as sensitive as is the peripheral concentration of red blood cells as measured by hematocrit, hemoglobin, or erythrocyte count, so long as the red-cell volume remains nearly constant. The early blood destruction of burns is so small as to be negligible in the account of volume changes.

Serial determinations of the hematocrit are essential. The fact that the initial fluid requirement has been estimated on the basis of the predicted expansion in the extracellular fluid, and the fact that the weight and hourly urine output are also being used as guides, should in no wise dissuade the surgeon from carrying out multiple hematocrit determinations. The balance between rate of loss of plasma from the blood volume and the effectiveness of infusion in maintaining blood volume can be gauged more accurately by hematocrit measurement than in any other way. The hematocrit provides the "fine control" for the rate of colloid administration; while the "gross control" is based on urine output and body weight.

If the patient enters the hospital with an elevated hematocrit several hours after the burn, the degree of elevation of the hematocrit indicates the immediate need ("static debt") of the patient for plasma. The derivation of this formula and its significance in acute plasma loss are described in Part II,

Chapter 11. It should be reemphasized that the initial hematocrit elevation is not a measure of the total plasma requirement; it is merely a way of estimating the static debt of the patient and the amount of plasma he needs to restore homeostasis within an hour or two. After such an amount of plasma has been given and the hematocrit has dropped down to a level of between 46 and 50, the patient drops back to the continuing budget of fluid administration described above.

When the patient's hematocrit is near normal to begin with, it is determined once every twelve hours throughout the first two or three days, and if it tends to rise, colloid therapy is speeded up. Occasionally one encounters patients in whom the hematocrit falls very easily and seems to be unusually sensitive to plasma infusion, dropping down into the middle or low forties within the first six to eight hours with an excellent clinical response. This is eloquent evidence that the patient's burn edema is not forming in the amount or magnitude that one expected. This, in turn, is evidence that the burn does not involve as extensive an area of third degree as was previously considered. The fluid therapy budget is accordingly revised downward.

By converse, a hematocrit (or red cell count or hemoglobin concentration*) that stubbornly refuses to fall indicates a very massive, continuing plasma loss and treatment budgets must be increased.

3. The Hourly Urine Output

This has been discussed as a measure of homeostasis in a wide variety of acute illnesses. It must be reemphasized that in the oligemic oliguric situation *gross fluctuations in urine volume are a measure of renal blood flow and glomerular filtration.* They are not attributable to the delicate alterations in renal function associated with the endocrine control of tubular function. No amount of aldosterone or antidiuretic hormone will reduce urine volume to 0 to 5 ml. per hour, particularly

---

* Any one of the three may be used as a guide; whichever is selected must then be followed consistently.

in the face of large loads of crystalloid solute emanating from the burned tissue. While release from endocrine influence, or solute loading, will elevate urine volume far above normal, its reduction to oliguric levels early in the course of a burn must be regarded as due to low plasma volume, low blood volume, and renal vasoconstriction with or without frank hypotension and shock.

It was in dealing with burns that the use of the short-term urine volume record was first described (Cope and Moore, 1946), and it is in the care of burns that the hourly urine output provides such an extremely useful criterion of homeostatic normalcy. The hourly urine output should best be maintained between 15 and 50 ml. per hour. Fluctuations from this standard, observed for less than three hours, should not be viewed with too much concern, because difficulties in bladder drainage and adequacy of collection techniques may be the cause. If the urine output remains at a normal volume, one may be confident that glomerular filtration rate is being maintained and that kidney function is good, and one may be reassured as to the adequacy of colloid replacement, the normalcy of the blood volume, the maintenance of blood pressure, and the general state of hydration. When well maintained, the hourly urine output tells the physician a great deal; when it is low, the proximate cause of the poor renal circulation or bodily volume deficit remains to be elucidated.

A persistent lowered output, in the range of 2 to 10 ml. per hour for three hours or more, suggests that blood volume is low, that total hydration is inadequate, or that a renal lesion is developing. An infusion test can then be carried out. If the response to the infusion test is clearly positive, with an increased hourly urine output, such information is useful in indicating the further direction to be taken in care of the patient. If the infusion test is negative (that is, no rise in volume) interpretation is much more difficult and one had best proceed with caution. If pigment has been present in the urine and the patient has had a clear episode of shock, it is most likely that this presages acute renal insufficiency. The interpretation and management

of such findings is dealt with in the section on renal insufficiency in burns.

For an infusion test in burns, plasma or dextran is the best substance to use in most instances; with a high sodium concentration, 5 per cent dextrose in water should be used for the infusion test. The amount must be gauged by the history and findings; in general, about 1000 ml. in thirty minutes is used. *

A continuous excessive hourly urine output is evidence (analogous to the hematocrit that has fallen too far and too fast) of fluid overloading. The high urine volume suggests overloading, especially with water-and-salt solution, while the hematocrit is more sensitive to overloading with plasma. Overloading with water and salt will produce large urine outputs. Consistent outputs for three hours of over 100 ml. or more per hour are evidence of excessive fluid infusion, or, starting at the second to fourth day, when fluid infusion is being sharply restricted, they are evidences of the onset of the postburn diuresis. This calls for further restriction of fluid and, whenever possible, shifting the patient over entirely to oral intake.

4. Body Weight

The patient is weighed near the time of admission, although his stated weight is an adequate guide to the first budget. If the surface is treated "open" it is a very easy matter to weigh the patient, and his weight will be close to a "true weight." As his treatment is begun and the demands of the burn edema met, he naturally gains weight.

The speed and rate at which the patient gains weight will be a combined function of the speed at which the fluid therapy is given and the speed at which it is lost. If the schedule above is followed, it will be found that the weight gain is most rapid in the first twelve hours and tapers off thereafter. *Patients should not be permitted to gain more than 8 to 10 per cent of their body weight.* If they gain more than this, it indicates fluid overloading to a

---

* See Parts II and III for a discussion of infusion tests in oliguria, as well as the differential diagnosis of post-traumatic oliguria in Part V.

dangerous degree. The exact balance between fluid administration and loss is best determined by weight, since it is almost impossible to measure quantitatively the amount of fluid lost into the dressing or onto the bed sheets and the insensible loss by lungs is totally unmeasurable.

When the patient is weighed frequently—once or twice a day—and these weights are taken into consideration together with data on the fluid intake and the urine output, it is possible to guide the fulfillment of his fluid needs very accurately. One must first carry out some simple calculations that lead to the derivation of a figure we have called "total insensible factors." This means the net change in weight due to loss of water from lungs and skin as modified by oxidation of fat and lean tissue. This "total insensible factor" figure is useful in each twelve-hour period as the burn progresses, since it gives one a firm idea of the pulmonary water loss and how much water is needed to compensate for it. It must be emphasized that an accurate figure for "total insensible factors" is unobtainable unless the patient is weighed and the intake and urine output measurements are accurate. In addition, the plasma sodium concentration is a useful guide to total hydration, or the body-water to total-solute ratio. If the plasma sodium falls abruptly it is an index of overhydration; if it rises sharply it is a sign of excessive water loss.

The interpretation of sequential weight changes in burned patients yields helpful data, and involves various problems of arithmetic according to the circumstances. Let us postulate three situations to illustrate the usefulness of weight change as a guide to burn therapy.

Problem A—Early Weight Gain. Let us postulate that the patient gains 1.2 kg. between the twenty-fourth and forty-eighth hours, and that during this time therapy was:

Plasma	1000 ml.
5% dextrose in water	2000 ml.
5% dextrose in saline	500 ml.
Fluid by mouth	300 ml.

This is a total intake of 3800 ml. Urine output during this time was 500 ml. and vomitus 200. The burn is a dry char. Temperature is 102° F. and there is slight dyspnea.

It is clear that the apparent or "intake minus output" balance of body water is (3800 − 700) or +3100 gm., or 3.1 kg. But the patient only gains 1.2 kg., about normal for a burn at this stage in a small person.

There is thus a total "unaccounted" weight that "might have been gained but was not" of (3.1 − 1.2) or 1.9 kg. With fever and dyspnea the total insensible water loss may be assumed to account for this 1900 ml. If the surface is moist this would account for a portion of the total lost. The oxidation of fat has contributed about 400 gm. to the weight and water lost. Insensible factors of loss, therefore, total 1900 ml., of which about 1500 will constitute the ration for pulmonary loss the next day, if fever and dyspnea are unchanged.

Problem B—Small Weight Loss. Let us now postulate that the patient loses 0.45 kg. between the fourth and fifth days. This is an unusually small loss for this period; diuresis should be under way. He had previously gained 7.2 kg. Fever is high at 103° F.; dyspnea at 36. The patient is very sick. The hematocrit is fixed near 37.

Intake for the twenty-four hours under consideration was:

5% dextrose in water	4000 ml.
Fluid by mouth	3000 ml.

Output:

Urine	2000 ml.

With an "intake minus output" fluid balance of +5000 ml. and a weight *loss* of 0.45 kg., we have to account for 5450 gm. of water that has disappeared. It should have appeared as weight, but did not. With fever and dyspnea at this level, insensible loss is increased; the wound is wet and the two factors together could account for the full 5450 ml. under normal circumstances. But during this day the patient's sodium concentration fell from 130 to 122 mE. per l. With urine output at 2000 ml., the combination suggests that with less intake he would have lost more weight and had a better net diuresis; water loading has occurred despite weight loss. This is borne out by the sodium change; on the next day intake should be much less energetic and he should be permitted a greater loss of weight.

Problem C—Large Weight Loss. Let us now

postulate the same intake and output as in Problem B (7000 ml. intake, 2000 ml. output), with a weight loss of 2.3 kg. in a patient with very high fever, dyspnea, and a tracheotomy. We now have 7300 gm. (5000 + 2300) to account for. This has been the net extrarenal loss from the system. Such excessive loss can occur in a febrile wet burn with a tracheotomy. The plasma sodium concentration has risen from 140 to 145 mE. per l. Although this change is small it is an evil portent. This, together with the weight-change, signifies that insensible loss is tremendous and by all factors totals at least 7300 gm. The patient is approaching true desiccation-dehydration. In a burned patient a sodium concentration even as slightly elevated as 145 mE. per l. is a providential early warning that desiccation is starting, whether by tracheotomy, loss through skin, or osmotic diuresis, or all three acting in concert. This must be noted and brisk treatment (water) begun, or the next day the sodium will be 165 mE. per l. and the downward spiral of desiccation will have begun. The following day treatment must be increased so as to maintain or dilute the sodium concentration and avoid such rapid weight loss. On the basis of the insensible loss (as estimated by intake minus output) corrected for weight change, intake will approximate 8500 ml., and on such an intake the next day he should be expected to lose about 0.8 kg. if the other factors are constant.

At this early phase in such a patient, measurements of blood urea nitrogen, plasma potassium, carbon dioxide combining power, chloride, sugar, and protein are helpful largely as a base-line, but there is nothing to be gained by multiple determinations during the first two or three days if all goes well with circulation and urine volume. In some of the burn variants to be discussed later, multiple determinations of these chemical values may lead to the elucidation of a progressive biochemical disorder, a discovery that is of first-rank importance in therapy.

A fourth problem—problem D—might be posed to illustrate the use of the hematocrit change during the course of treatment. An 85-kg. man, on his second day of treatment, poorly and inadequately cared for, enters now by transfer with a hematocrit of 62. Weight is here of less use. The opportunity to use it as a guide has been lost. The urine volume is about zero, as one would expect in such a setting.

How much plasma does the patient need—immediately—to restore his plasma volume and his circulation to normal? This calculation is discussed in detail in Part II, Chapter 11. To recapitulate, it depends on the difference between his normal blood volume (estimated here at 7 per cent of body weight, or 5950 ml.) and his observed blood volume with a hematocrit of 65. His normal erythrocyte volume (hematocrit of 42) is 0.42×5950, or 2500 ml. The present blood volume (hematocrit 62) is therefore $2500 \div 0.62$, or 4030 ml. The difference (5950 − 4030), or about 1900 ml., is the static debt. This large amount of colloid must be infused with the same urgency as blood transfusion in hemorrhagic shock. *This calculation has not indicated the ultimate need (or dynamic debt); it only tells us the static debt at the moment of the hematocrit.*

F. STABILIZATION AND EVALUATION; TRANSPORTATION

Let us visit our patient now. He has been in the hospital for about three hours. He is stabilized, and much of his apprehension and discomfort has disappeared with the use of medication, and by leaving the wound alone. An intravenous infusion, through which his initial colloid infusion is being given rapidly, has been started. If necessary, two intravenous infusions are given simultaneously to meet the rate requirement. The calculation of the rate of infusion must be a realistic one and must be accomplished without fail. The hematocrit and weight have been measured, looking forward to some of the aspects just mentioned. The patient has an indwelling catheter, through which his hourly urine output is being measured.* He has been started on antibiotics. A history and physical examination for other injuries or antecedent

---

*Grouping the output data in three-hourly or six-hourly units is an equally effective device, less sensitive to rapid change.

illnesses have been carried out. A chart of the extent of the burn has been made, with an estimate of those portions of it which are third-degree burns.

The patient is now in the stage of reevaluation and stabilization, exactly analogous to the wounded man after initial resuscitation. He is eminently transportable at this time. He may be surprisingly free of pain and the next day may want to eat some breakfast and talk with visitors. The emotional and physical rehabilitation of the burned patient during this brief respite of two to four days is often quite remarkable and belies the painful dressings, multiple operations, and dangerous valley of infection through which the patient must pass during the next three to eight weeks. On occasion burned patients who are intelligent and inquisitive young people may at this stage be so comfortable that they wonder if they can go home "in a day or two." It is necessary to discuss with such a patient the natural history of the burn course so that, without being frightened, he may realize that there is a rocky road lying ahead.

Thus stabilized, the patient is ready to be moved to the ward or removed to another hospital, if such a course is advisable. It is our conviction that the care of a burned patient, if initially accomplished in an outlying unit, should be entrusted from here on to some individual or group of individuals who have a special interest and competence in this field. This is no place for the "do-it-yourself" or "cookbook" approach. There is no substitute for experience. The burned patient stabilized at this point looks deceptively like a simple problem; fluid management, which has been such a source of so much conflict and query, has been dealt with successfully. The patient doesn't look "too bad"; the usual tendency on the part of the inexperienced is to overestimate the extent but underestimate the depth of a burn. As mentioned before, large areas may be wishfully considered as "second degree that will heal themselves." This type of rationalized inexperience leads in three to five weeks to a tragic situation that may threaten the patient's life when, with surgery still postponed or incompetently performed, burns

and graft sites septic, infection uncontrolled, nutritional decompensation and morale a problem, the patient is not only not transportable but almost unsalvageable. If the patient is to be moved to another hospital, early is the time to do it.

The patient now starts a period of two to four days that mark the completion of his edema formation. Following this we may expect the extremely variable fluid-unloading process that constitutes diuresis. During this time his fluid therapy is continued according to the program already outlined, under the guidance of serial hematocrits and hourly urine outputs. The weight curve indicates the extent of edema accumulation. Antibiotic therapy is maintained.

The patient should be kept moving in bed. Leg exercises and quadriceps setting exercises are useful, and if the feet and legs are unburned the patient may stand up and walk around at this stage. As soon as the patient is able to take fluids by mouth and show—on the basis of twelve hours of cautious administration of clear liquids—that he is able to retain these in his stomach, he can start having food and fluids by mouth. One will encounter occasional young patients who, like our ideal case, will start taking and retaining food at significant caloric intakes even at this early stage. While such early intake may not in itself produce positive nitrogen balance, it will diminish the extent of weight-loss due to the injury and it most certainly permits the patient to swing up into his anabolic resumption of muscular strength at the earliest possible time. It therefore should be encouraged if the intake is retained and therefore safe. Forced feeding or tube feeding of burned patients is both dangerous and useless prior to the end of the first week. In patients who do not wish to or cannot take the material by mouth, in very young children or in babies, or elderly or comatose persons, such tube feeding is attended by hazard and has resulted in fatalities due to vomiting with aspiration of gastric contents.

G. DIURESIS

The patient passes out of this first phase of the burn edema with a diuresis. Edema of eyelids, face, and dependent areas will disappear, sometimes quite suddenly, by a combination of diuresis and gravitational loss.

In some patients this diuresis will announce itself in a spectacular way with a sudden increase of urine output in the face of rapidly diminishing intake, as the "budget" runs out its ration and weight gain stabilizes. In cases in which the onset of the diuresis of burn edema can be identified at a specific hour, one is dealing with a very spectacular change in renal physiology, as effective extracellular volume rises because of edema resorption. Almost simultaneously the hemodynamic and tubular restrictions are released and an outpouring of body fluid results.

Much more often, however, there is a subtle change in balance between fluid intake and output. If the patient is being weighed frequently and the total insensible weight change is being measured, this step in evolution of the burn physiology easily becomes apparent. As the patient comes to the end of forty-eight to seventy-two hours, his intravenous therapy has been markedly cut back as a result of the planned diminishing rate; his weight has risen and is now stable somewhere around 8 to 10 per cent above its starting norm. If at this time the patient's intake-output records are carefully maintained, it will be found that somewhere between two and six days after a burn, the urine volume tends to maintain itself or even to increase, despite diminished intake; weight tends to drop off, and examination of the patient's burn will show that the edema is rapidly diminishing. This is the burn diuresis. It may occur dramatically in twenty-four hours; it may take several days for its accomplishment. At the end, the patient is "dried out again" and has a normal look about him. His facial contours have returned to normal even though there is some burn over the face.

If one calculates daily the "output fraction" (that is, fraction of intake returned as urine output), this diuresis will be evident even though multiple weight measurements cannot be made. During the first two days of the burned patient's treatment, the "output fraction" is around 15 per cent; that is, urine output is about 15 per cent of total output—the rest is cached away as edema or lost via the lungs and skin. A normal person in resting balance in bed has an output fraction of about 85 per cent. A burned patient in diuresis has an "output fraction," that will run from 90 to 115 per cent through transient periods of increased output. A rising "output fraction" denotes the burn diuresis; the absolute output does not change in some cases, but the fraction of total water flux which it represents rises sharply.

The quantitative nature of the burn diuresis depends on its rate. If a brisk diuresis commences on the fourth or fifth day and persists for three or four days until, on normal intake, the output fraction has again reduced itself to a normal value, one might expect a total diuresis of the magnitude of 4 to 6 kg. In many cases the diuresis is more gradual and the weight curve merges imperceptibly into that expected for this rate of tissue catabolism.

As diuresis is established and the patient passes through a borderline between his fourth and sixth days, he passes out of the first phase of his burn and into another phase equally important and equally characteristic, but a phase unfortunately much more complicated and uncomfortable for the patient and much more challenging to the surgeon.

Section III.   The Second Phase: The Wound; Sepsis, Catabolism, and Beginning Closure

A. CLINICAL APPEARANCES AND STRATEGY

The burned patient now passes into a phase, the duration of which is almost entirely a function of the extent of the burn and the skill, judgment, and good fortune of the surgeon who is closing the wound and the patient whose wound is being closed. The tendency to gain weight is gone; the edematous appearance of face and hands is gone. Fluid balance measurements will indicate a high normal "output fraction" of total intake, and metabolic measurements demonstrate that the patient has passed out of his positive sodium balance followed by diuresis and into a phase of sodium metabolism without much significant change over the weeks. Hyponatremia tends to occur because of progressive dilution. Potassium balance has again become positive, frequently becoming so within the first week after a burn (so long as some nourishment is taken by mouth), while nitrogen balance is still negative, a negativity that may persist for many weeks.

This is a period of rising fever. It is not unusual to see burns of moderate extent, under antibiotic treatment, remain virtually afebrile for the first three to five days. This effectiveness of antibiotics in holding down bacterial growth diminishes progressively as the weeks go by and as the flora on the burn becomes progressively more saprophytic and more tolerant of the antibiotics to which it is exposed. This afebrile period gives way to a moderate but unremitting fever as the third-degree areas begin to undergo slough and as the bacteria beneath them begin to multiply in the liquefied tissue. This rising fever starts at about the third to fifth day and often coincides with the completion of the phase of burn edema formation, satisfaction, and diuresis. In the burn that we are considering here as an example, fever of 102° to 103.5° F. would be expected at this time and would remain intermittently present until the wound is essentially closed. A considerable fever and a tachycardia that rises somewhere between the sixth and twelfth days must not be considered as a contraindication to excision and grafting. This is a very important point: do not postpone the operation because the patient is febrile. Removal of the slough will often reduce the fever after an initial operative spike, probably traceable to transient blood-stream infestation.

The operative judgment involved in expeditious coverage of burns is often lost sight of in the welter of information bearing upon the biochemical and metabolic alterations.

The definitive surgical care of a burn, instead of being a single operation, is a whole series of operations and dressings, occupying the space of three to five weeks. The patient at the start of this race for closure is the patient painted in the paragraphs above. In the hands of the incompetent or bungling, after two or three weeks, he is depleted of blood and protein, demoralized, septic, with donor areas converted into septic third-degree areas, febrile, disoriented, and virtually unsalvageable. By contrast, in competent hands—and with skillful management of the use of grafts and donor sites, blood, diet, and protein, avoidance of blood-stream inoculation, careful dressings, use of exposure at the proper time and closed dressings at others—the patient is on a progressively uphill course. He will emerge at the end of this phase with only small unhealed areas, open to the air to close of themselves without maceration. He is eating, mobilized around the ward, and on the way to recovery.

In the section on extensive wounds, it was mentioned that definitive operation has a remarkable metabolic significance because it terminates the period of injury and initiates the period of recovery. The debridement and grafting of an extensive burn has exactly the same sort of significance, save for the fact that it is much more difficult to accomplish and it is several operations, not just one. It terminates the strongly catabolic phase of nitrogen loss and permits the patient to come up into an anabolic phase of later convalescence. Each operation for grafting and closure is a new anesthesia and a new tissue stress and a bacterial threat, yet the reduction in the open area of the burn affected by a successful procedure permits a progressive stepwise reduction in the intensity of the septic catabolism and tissue-wasting, an intensity related at least in part to the amount of open, bacteria-harboring tissue present.

B. METABOLISM

The characteristic metabolism of this second phase in the evolution of a burn is as follows:

(1) prolonged negative nitrogen balance;

(2) progressive increase in extrarenal loss of body fluids and solids through the open, progressively more exudative, septic burn surface;

(3) septic starvation and rapid weight loss;

(4) a diminution of the above changes and a trend toward anabolism as the wound is closed.

This is a period after a burn when the intake profoundly affects the total rate of body wasting. The rate of urinary nitrogen excretion varies from 5 to 15 gm. per day. On intakes of 12 to 15 gm. of nitrogen a day with intakes of 2000 to 3000 calories the patient will not go into strongly or consistently positive nitrogen balance, but he will reduce his net loss from the body and will lose weight much less rapidly. If large intakes are maintained persistently, the patient's weight loss is reduced to a minimum throughout this phase. A common sequence is weight loss of approximately 2 kg. per week, accounted for in part by the lysis of lean tissue (negative nitrogen balance) and the remainder as fat oxidation. For example:

DAYS 6–30:

Average nitrogen intake per day	=	12 gm.
" caloric " " "	=	2000 cal.
" calorie:nitrogen ratio	=	166
" urinary nitrogen loss	=	18 gm.
" nitrogen balance	=	−6 gm.

TOTAL—24 DAYS

Nitrogen balance	=	144	gm.
Lean wet-tissue equivalent (N × 30)	=	4320	gm.
Weight loss	=	6	kg.
Fat oxidation = approximately	=	1.7	kg.

Sodium and potassium metabolism show changes of lesser clinical significance. There is a persistent hyponatremia due largely to water retention and somehow related to the chronic septic illness *per se* (see Part III, Chapter 22). There is a small positive potassium balance with normal plasma level.

Study of the extrarenal fraction of total loss has shown that during this period up to 50 per cent of the total nitrogen and up to 30 per cent of the total potassium and sodium lost from the body may be through the wound. The wound is now inevitably moist and exudative; dressings are required. These factors are important in considering the passive support by dietary intake mentioned below, and the significance of wound closure.

The degree of starvation, weight loss, and cachexia produced in this phase depends upon the balance of three factors: the duration of the phase, the dietary intake, and the extent of the septic process. When this period is long in duration (due to inability to achieve wound closure), diet poor, and sepsis marked, the degree of body wasting produced is extreme. Weight loss up to 5 kg. a week may be observed. Some of the most severe pictures of septic starvation seen in surgery are in the neglected burn after several weeks of this second phase of sepsis and catabolism. Early grafting, good diet, intelligent use of antibiotics, and aseptic techniques can so reduce these deleterious factors that the patient emerges from this most devastating nutritional phase in good if not excellent clinical condition.

The tendency of this phase to be terminated by closure of the wound is a very interesting metabolic phenomenon. The wound itself accounts for considerable nitrogen loss. That this is not the only factor is demonstrated by the reduction in *urinary* excretion of nitrogen as the wound is closed. If closure is commenced on about the twelfth day and completed about the thirtieth or thirty-fifth day (an ideal situation for a massive burn), the achievement of positive nitrogen balance is concomitant with the closure of the wound. The open wound with its attendant sepsis constitutes a continuing stimulus toward nitrogen loss from the muscle mass of the body.

That local loss is not the only negative factor is also suggested by the fact that even it, after many months of low-grade infection, ceases to stimulate wasting. If small amounts of wound remain open, the patient passes into a late phase, eating well, gaining weight. but still with many patchy areas of exuberant granulations not covered by skin. This is the hypermature or "overripe" late unhealed burn, to be discussed in a later section.

It is not the positive nitrogen balance that produces closure of the wound and it is not the closure of the wound, alone, that produces the positive nitrogen balance; the two tend to occur at about the same time and either one—severe nitrogen wastage at low intake or open septic wound—tends to prolong the other, the wound delaying anabolism and the catabolism, here, delaying closure.

The most important step in clinical management of this phase of the burn is therefore to close the wound. The other steps, vastly important in the success of this primary objective of wound closure, are listed in what follows. These measures alone, without effective wound closure, will not rescue the patient.

C. OPERATIVE WOUND CLOSURE

1. Terminology

The term "*primary excision*" should be reserved for the sharp excision of a burn within the first forty-eight hours. This is done as an initial elective procedure in burns of small extent, the plane of dissection carried out as in normal tissue. It is our conviction that in severely burned people with burns covering over 15 per cent of body surface, a complete primary excision takes an unnecessary risk with the patient's life in the hopes of an operative *tour de force*. The identification of third-degree areas is often difficult at this stage.

The term "*sharp debridement and immediate grafting*" describes the procedure that we favor on the basis of the present evidence. This is the removal of eschar between the sixth and fifteenth days by sharp dissection. It should be followed by immediate grafting. When a burn is approached surgically between the sixth and the fifteenth days, some of the eschar lifts off but most of it has to be dissected off, and there is some bleeding encountered which must be carefully secured, either by electrocoagulation or by ligature. The plane of dissection is actually within the burn, but it is at a deep point within the burn tissue, so selected as to involve the minimum of sharp dissection and at the same time to leave behind a viable bed that will take the graft.

The terms "*late debridement*" and "*grafting on granulation tissue*" are synonymous and merely mean the removal of the late macerated, partially digested slough and the placing of grafts on the underlying exuberant granulation tissue after the third or fourth week.

Skin grafts in burns take very kindly on a bed of freshly debrided subcutaneous tissue, a bed that does not look normal and certainly does not have the appearance of "granulation tissue" in the classical sense. It does have microscopic granulations, but anatomically it is subcutaneous fat with areas of white dermal collagenous tissue running through it. When burns undergo sharp debridement between the sixth and fifteenth days and grafts are placed on such an area, one may confidently expect "takes" as high as 90 to 95 per cent. A basic advance in burn therapy of the past fifteen years has been the realization that one does not need to wait for "good granulations" for a graft take: the duration of time after injury is the critical factor. During an interval from the sixth to the fifteenth day, grafts will take well on a seemingly pathologic base; they will even take hold and grow adjacent to unremoved slough.

Because of this high incidence of successful grafts in the early phase of burn care there is a very precious time when the patient has progressed far enough to be well through the upsets of the first phase, when he is metabolically and bacteriologically ready for grafting, yet when the local tissue makes the surface "thirsty for skin," and has not progressed on to chronic purulent infection. This is the golden moment when sharp debridement with skin grafting offers the most extensive burns the benefits of early definitive surgery and a safe-conduct to convalescent rehabilitation. *This moment must be apprehended in advance, perceived when imminent, and seized on arrival.*

2. Early Sharp Debridement

In a patient such as our example under consideration, an early sharp debridement is now the objective; it is the ideal procedure for which we have been seeking the proper moment. The patient has been off antibiotics from his fourth or fifth day on. He has been febrile during this time. His burns have become increasingly painful, and as he moves about in bed they have begun to bother him a good deal. The open areas show a few cracks and interstices, and culture of these shows microorganisms, although grossly purulent material may not yet be present. At some of these cracks and interstices there are little yellow crusts where the exudate evaporates, and under these crusts early purulation may be seen. He looks progressively more "toxic."

Precious time is passing but he has not yet been ready for operation. At the tenth day the patient has been restarted on new antibiotics, now selected on the basis of sensitivity studies. From the sixth to the twelfth day the patient has been given three units of whole blood to bring his hematocrit up to normal. Blood volume measurements at this stage in burns demonstrate that reduction in the hematocrit is associated with reduction in the total volume of blood and an expansion of the plasma volume, although the two are not necessarily a linear function of each other, and the blood volume, as usual in such complex situations, is difficult to predict from the hematocrit. On the basis of these three transfusions of whole blood, the patient's hematocrit has been brought up from 36 to 41. The plasma protein concentration is normal. The plasma sodium concentration is low. The patient is still eating well but not as well as he did on the fourth to seventh day, when his edema had freshly subsided and he was coming out of his early phase.

With these steps in the background, he is taken to the operating room about the fourteenth day and given a general anesthetic with endotracheal intubation and good oxygenation and is held with stable homeostasis and hemostasis throughout.

At this operation, normal donor areas are first prepared and draped and, with careful aseptic precautions, skin grafts are removed to the extent advisable for the extent of the patient's burn and the donor areas available. This will surely not be enough skin to cover the entire burn of 40 per cent of body surface.

These donor sites are then carefully dressed with an occlusive dressing, designed only to prevent gross contamination from the burned areas during the rest of the procedure.

The excision is then carried out. It is slow, long, hard, and exacting. Blood loss is much greater than one would predict; measurements have demonstrated the loss of amounts in excess of 2500 ml. This amount should be gauged during the operation by sponge weights (or any other technique that yields a rough approximation) and should be quantitatively replaced throughout.

Excised areas are then covered with skin grafts, most of which are merely laid on. Preserved or cadaver homografts cover those areas which cannot be autografted. A careful circumferential dressing is applied and the patient returned to his bed. This procedure may take from three to six hours and ties up a large operating team. There is no short cut. Any compromise with maximal operative effort is unforgivable since this is the patient's most important hope for recovery. The success of this first operation has more to do with the date of the patient's discharge than any other single factor; it is a moment and an opportunity never to be regained.

The patient may be returned to an ordinary bed with a foam rubber mattress, or he may be returned to some special bed, such as a Stryker frame or Foster bed, which permits turning. If it is contemplated to use the latter form of bed after skin grafting, it is advisable to have the patient on it some time prior to the operation so that he becomes accustomed to it and is not frightened by the act of turning.

The patient's response to this operation will be expected to have the following features.

(1) He will have quite a high fever the afternoon of the operation or the next day. This is due to cutting and dissecting in an area where there is abundant bacterial growth and where natural anatomic and immune barriers must inevitably be disrupted. This probably means a transient bacteremia.

(2) He will lose his appetite for food for two or three days.

(3) He will be very rigidly immobile for a few days and will not want to move at all.

(4) His endocrine-metabolic response will involve a drop in eosinophils, a rise in blood steroids, an increase in nitrogen excretion, and the other familiar features. The patient has not yet been sick long enough to show the paradoxical eosinophilia of late operation in burns.

(5) If the grafts take, the patient's temperature and pulse will fall to a lower level than before, even prior to the fifth postoperative day when the dressings are changed, his appetite will improve, and the discomfort and apprehension about pain in the wounds will diminish.

3. The Second Operation

On the fourth to sixth day after the first operation, the patient is again taken to the operating room and again anesthetized. Previous to this operation, additional whole blood may be given and the antibiotic again changed, although he has been on his new antibiotic regime for only seven days at this time and it may be continued another four to five days.

This second operation is as important as the first in its clarity of concept. It is not just a dressing. It must be an aggressive operation designed to achieve further closure of the wound despite the apparent expense in terms of trauma, anesthesia, and decreased alimentation.

The donor sites are dressed first, and further skin grafts are taken from areas not touched at the first operation. If skin homografts are to be used, it may be advisable to use them at this time rather than at the first operation. This depends on the extent of the wound and the extent of utilization of the available donor areas. The new donor sites are then dressed, along with the old ones, which should be partly healed at this time. Depending on the anatomic location, some of the donor sites may again be left open to complete their healing without the macerating effect of a dressing.

The burn wounds are then divested of dressings so as not to remove any grafts that are still delicately held to the underlying recipient bed. Grafts that have taken will be pink and clearly viable, those that have not taken will have a whitish rolled appearance and will brush easily off the underlying surface.

In burns of this extent, a 90 per cent take may be expected with the first grafting. As mentioned previously, the expected degree of success diminishes progressively with repeated dressings and graftings and with the passage of time.

At this second procedure, the areas which remain open—many of them odd-shaped corners between the grafts—are covered. In addition, if there are unexcised areas, they are now excised by sharp debridement and grafted.

Donor sites are ideally left open to heal. In a burn of the extent that we visualize here, such a procedure is not always possible, because donor sites may have to be on the back or on the posterior aspect of the thighs.

4. Further Operative Course

It is now seventeen to twenty-one days after our patient's burn, and if the entire burn has been covered with grafts and they have all taken, one is about to witness a very satisfactory result in burn treatment for a burn of the degree and area suggested here. The further course consists of repeated dressings under anesthesia on several more occasions at five-day intervals, then omission of dressings as the areas between the grafts coalesce and heal. The use of tub treatments and beginning mobilization might at the best achieve discharge from the hospital by the thirty-fifth to fortieth day.

Such a triumph—the ideal—is occasionally achieved, but much commoner than this, unfortunately, is the burn which now at the seventeenth to twentieth day is largely covered—approximately two-thirds covered —but which also has areas where grafting has failed, frictional motion has been too great, some local infection has been a problem, or where flexion creases or other surface problems have prevented ideal early grafting. We will assume that our patient falls into this latter, more common category and we will follow his course on that basis.

D. CLOSURE GRADUALLY COMPLETED; THE STRUGGLE TO ACHIEVE ANABOLISM

In the instance described above the patient should be returned to the operating room quite regularly every four or five days. This type of aggressive continual effort pays its dividends in terms of successful accomplishment of surgical closure. If medication, antibiotic, blood transfusion, and anesthesia are well handled, the patient does not dread these repeated trips to the operating room, and if they are studied from the point of view of "stress," one finds that the blood steroid rise and eosinophil fall are progressively less until, at about the twenty-fifth or thirtieth day, one may begin to witness a rise in eosinophils and in some instances an actual fall in blood steroids with repeated dressings, some of which are accompanied by grafting. These anomalous changes are not accompanied by circulatory failure and they do not mean adrenal insufficiency.

At these dressing changes, the wounds are carefully opened and some areas where grafts appear to be taking well and some coalescence seems to be occurring are left open to the air. This is a relief to the patient and permits him to begin some motion of joints and extremities better than he can with a dressing on. The new skin, once open, thickens up and tightens its grip on the underlying tissue.

Donor sites that have healed over can be used for a "second crop." Donor sites that have become infected or converted into third-degree injuries by infection present a problem exactly similar to that of the burns which they were designed to cure. If, at some of these sessions, more skin can be taken from donor sites than the patient's burns require at the moment, one may put these patches in the refrigerator and use them in ten to fourteen days.

Characteristically, this phase of repeated trips to the operating room and progressive closure of the wounds, though with some areas recalcitrant and possibly regressing, lasts for approximately six weeks. During this time the management of the patient becomes progressively more difficult. It is hard for him to eat. Open wounds may be increasingly septic and resistant to combinations of antibiotics. It is an extremely critical period for the patient and there is no substitute for wound closure as a way of bringing this period to an end.

1. Blood Transfusion

The patient now develops a progressive anemia. This is not due to the initial heat injury to the erythrocytes, that phase having passed long since. It finds its cause instead in prolonged sepsis, bone marrow depression, cryptic hemorrhage into dressings, and blood loss at multiple operations. The blood loss is often greater in volume than the surgeon might suspect. Cryptic hemorrhage into dressings and into the tissues around the burns is difficult to measure, but the most important factor in this anemia is chronic sepsis. The biochemical mechanisms by which infection interferes with blood formation are beyond the scope of this book. Suffice it to say that depressed hematopoiesis is easy to demonstrate in burns; it was first demonstrated using radioactive iron and showing that the incorporation of this material in the peripheral red cells is markedly inhibited at this phase after a burn. Later on, hematopoiesis is greatly accelerated. These findings have since been corroborated by a variety of techniques.

Whatever the mechanism and by whatever method one chooses to demonstrate or quantitate it, the important fact is that the burned patient must have his erythrocyte mass supported passively throughout this phase of his care. In emphasizing erythrocyte support, the surgeon must not neglect the other factors in human blood, which the body may be making but poorly at this time. These include particularly the coagulation factors, antibodies, and albumin. The amount of blood to be given cannot be demonstrated by any rule. The hematocrit should remain somewhere between 38 and 45 during this period.

2. Food Intake

During this long and trying phase of sepsis, catabolism, and beginning wound closure the patient's food intake is of importance, just as it is in the turning point and early anabolism of closed trauma. His intake is repeatedly interrupted by operation, skin grafts, and dressings. This is the period of pain and opiate medication, which, taken together, will kill the appetite of the most cooperative. A patient who is not taking a diet cannot exhibit the phenomenon of bodily tissue synthesis required for later recovery. If he is taking a poor diet, he will not exhibit positive nitrogen balance to the same degree as nor as soon as a patient who is taking a very full diet. A patient on full diet will be permitted to swing up into a strongly anabolic phase as the evolution of his wounds, his sepsis, and his endocrinologic recovery proceed. The effect of this diet on reducing oxidation of endogenous fat is important: the late catabolic weight loss of burned patients who are on high dietary intakes is less than in those who are on low intakes.

If the burn wound does not close the patient cannot anabolize; but without diet neither can occur.

Tube feeding of the very early burned patient is quite unnecessary and is dangerous, especially in the elderly or in infants. Tube feeding starting at about the fourth to eighth day may have a place, particularly in children.

The skill of a dietitian is best measured by her ability to get adequate intakes into a burned patient at this phase. Tasty food is needed, palatable, yet not requiring a great deal of effort in chewing and swallowing, a diet that does not produce constipation or diarrhea. If the patient does not eat now he becomes an example of septic starvation and extreme degrees of tissue wasting are readily produced.

There are few other situations in surgery where truly forced feeding has such significance as it does in a burn at this late period. The hazard (aspiration) of forced feeding is now less than it was. The dietitian must have an objective each day. Putting a tube into the stomach in the evening to leave a feeding there overnight, hopeful that it will pass the pyloric barrier, and removing the tube afterward, is more effective than using an indwelling tube. We have used intravenously administered fat emulsions in patients at this time, taking care to give them in the evening so that they do not interfere with diet and normal alimentation during the day.

Hot coffee, sherry, whiskey, and other dietary stimulants are useful and must depend upon the previous dietary habits of the patient. Such liquids are far to be preferred over cold white tasteless drinks. The patient should be pampered and given the foods that seem especially appealing to him. Patients at this stage may turn down all the ordinary food that is provided but have a craving for certain items not ordinarily provided on hospital diet. One young patient stands out in the records because, as she went through this phase, all she wanted was quart after quart of chocolate ice cream. This is good nourishment. There seemed no excuse to give her mashed vegetables, pureed white meat and cold oatmeal gruel if what she really wanted was chocolate ice-cream cones.

An adequate intake of vitamins is essential. Subclinical scurvy is readily produced. Open wounds eat up vitamin C. From the twentieth to the thirty-fifth day the burned patient needs a generous dose of vitamin C (250 to 500 mg. per day). In addition, it has been our practice to give crude liver extract intramuscularly two to three times a week.

3. Protein and Sodium

Patients easily become overwatered and oversalted in this phase, and this is particularly marked if they have not had a good diuresis at the close of the first phase. The patient becomes hypoproteinemic, the result of overexpansion of the extracellular fluid with water and salt, loss of whole protein through the wound, and alterations in protein synthesis due to the prolonged septic process and interference with liver function. In this setting, concentrated albumin is unique in its usefulness, and it is possible to maintain a normal plasma albumin concentration with this material. This is a good step but it should not be overdone, because overadministration of concentrated albumin results in hypoprothrombinemia.

This is a period in the burned patient's

life when his plasma sodium concentration tends to be low. It is also a period of nutritional difficulty, and it is possible that this hyponatremia is on the basis of inadequacies in energy intake. But the patient does lose salt with the plasma-like exudate into the dressing, and sodium loss is considerable. Some patients at this stage profit from an occasional infusion of concentrated salt, which seems to initiate a diuresis—possibly an osmotic diuresis. This is followed by some minor degree of passive support of the plasma sodium concentration, although the effects are neither immediate nor dramatic. This use of salt, like the use of albumin, should not be overdone, and should be followed by observation soon enough to assess the effect.

As an example, two units of albumin per week and one infusion of concentrated salt solution every four or five days, depending upon the plasma albumin and sodium concentrations, would be a feasible plan. A patient in this phase, given much too much salt-free water, will dilute down his plasma sodium concentration more than he otherwise would, and this is especially true if the water is given intravenously. Stated otherwise, the sepsis, catabolism, and starvation produce recurrent antidiuresis. Burned patients at this time do not require a great deal of intravenous therapy and do better without it. Such infusions as they do require—blood, albumin, concentrated salt—should be planned out on a weekly basis so as to conserve veins.

4. Antibiotics

The following general principles are guides to the use of antibiotics in this troublesome phase in burns.

(1) Antibiotics, no matter what agents are used or in what combination, are of diminishing effectiveness as time passes. In the first week they effectively prevent or abort fatal septicemia; in the fourth week it is difficult to discern an effect.

(2) If the patient is started on penicillin and steptomycin and kept on this combination for the first four or five days, it is then advisable to stop antibiotics completely for several days. This permits the patient to make his own antibodies during a period in which he is not being subjected to operative interference with his bodily defenses against infection, and while the burn eschar is still intact. A mixed, sensitive flora rather than a pure, resistant one remains. Excision or sharp debridement threatens the patient with bacteremia. A day or two prior to the beginning of excision the patient's antibiotics are therefore changed or recommenced.

(3) Sensitivity studies may be unrevealing. On occasion they have dictated the use of remarkably effective antibiotics. This unreliability may be due in part to the notorious unreliability and variability of commercial antibiotic filter discs. Unfortunately antibiotics may be changed to a combination more effective against the patient's organisms in the laboratory, yet be followed by no clinical change in the patient's course. This is not to say that sensitivity tests should be discouraged. It is rather to emphasize that the basic change that produces progressively less favorable effects from antibiotics in burns is one that sensitivity tests often cannot overcome. Other factors—resistance, circulation in dead tissue, and surgical trauma—are involved.

(4) The use of local antibiotics in burns is underemphasized in current practice. Burns that are open and infected are wounds in which very high concentrations of extremely effective antibiotics (which may be toxic when used systemically) can be used. Examples of such antibiotics are bacitracin and tyrothricin. Their use is to be encouraged.

During the period of the first two or three operations the patient should be treated with some combination of antibiotics as effective as can be constructed on the basis of sensitivity study. These are periods when bacteremia may occur. After these first two or three excisions systemic antibiotics are less important, and these agents should be used locally as the wound progressively opens an available interface between the dressing and the flora, the tough impenetrable eschar of precipitated protein being removed.

With these steps, and through the repeated adjustments of the dressing and placing of small skin grafts, the wound will gradually heal. The removal of the dressings and re-exposure of the wound to open air often serves it well, apparently by coolness and dryness, just as it did in the initial phases. Occasional trips to the tub for a soak also assist the patient in regaining mobilization and self-confidence. With these steps, the wound finally starts its closure. The last few areas (the size of a postage stamp or more) seem to present more problems than did thousands of square centimeters at the twelfth to fourteenth day. The process of contraction can most effectively assist when all the open areas are spotty and small, not single and large. To achieve this geographical pattern the available skin should be dotted over the larger areas, rather than in an edge-to-edge mosaic that leaves large areas uncovered.

The use of acetic acid dressings and propyl alcohol dressings has been suggested in such cases, particularly where pyocyaneus predominates. Azochloramide and Dakin's solution have been used with good result. The effect of all of these is apparently to change the *p*H or concentration of other ions in the local wound in a way which is inimical to some of the flora there and which converts the surface into one where epithelium can grow.

As wound closure finally moves towards completion, the patient's fever and pulse recede, his appetite increases, sleep is better, and medication less. Anabolism begins and strength and ambition return. The second phase is over.

Section IV. The Third Phase: The Upswing; Completion of Closure, and Beginning Anabolism

A. CLINICAL APPEARANCES

As the temperature chart shows fewer elevations and the portion of closed wound far outweighs the remaining open areas, the appearances are increasingly those of progressive convalescence. Weight stabilizes at a low plateau, and diet increases.

The hazard lies in overestimating the security of the position. With a minor infection by new and virulent organisms, grafts that a few days before seemed securely healed will melt away. The new skin is thin where epithelization is spontaneous, and areas of pressure or maceration quickly destroy it.

B. METABOLISM

The turn to anabolism requires closure of the wound, and diet. As mentioned above, the wound closure and anabolism tend to occur together but failure of either will delay the other. Treatment is devoted toward both.

It is at this phase that reoperation often results in a rise in eosinophils despite an increase in corticosteroid secretion. A test dose of adrenocorticotropic hormone reveals that the long stressful and septic illness has re-sulted in marked functional hypertrophy of the adrenal glands.

As mentioned above, anabolism can occur before the wound has completely closed; this is rare and results in the hypermature late open burn (see below). *A large, open, continually septic wound absolutely prevents the onset of anabolism.*

C. TREATMENT

Treatment during this period of a burned patient's recovery is a continuation of the steps taken in the late second phase as regards diet and general metabolic rehabilitation, but the most important point is that a continually aggressive surgical attack must be made. In the care of the extensive burn one has the sensation of crossing a dividing line seen when all but a few areas of the burn are closed. Prior to this, the closure seems to become progressively more difficult. Each series of graftings is accepted less well until finally most of the burn is closed, and then the rest may close quite easily if the entire event has been completed prior to the thirty-fifth day. But areas that are open after the fortieth day are extremely difficult to close; healing appears to be a less urgent biologic priority for the organism.

In the burn at this phase, there is a place for the use of adrenocorticotropic hormone. This appears to favor the take of late graft. Cortisone is less desirable because of the hazard of gastrointestinal ulceration; testosterone may play a role in stimulating appetite, though its diversion of nitrogen to muscle regrowth prior to healing of the wound is conceivably undesirable.

Mobilization of joints must be started as soon as possible. The use of the tub helps in the performance of dressing changes and in beginning motion of joints long held rigid by pain or dressings. Guided exercise is of increasing importance as the wounds are healed enough to permit motion. Tube feeding occasionally has a place, as mentioned before.

Section V. The Fourth Phase: Maturation of the New Skin, and Rehabilitation

A. CLINICAL APPEARANCES

This period may be said to have begun when the last operation for closure has been done. As the wounds complete their closure, the patient is progressively mobilized, resumption of diet is little problem, and the patient will now consume progressively larger amounts of food with progressively less urging. There may still be areas that need small bits of skin laid on, but they are few and small. The motion of joints must be resumed early. Walking and the upright posture produces hyperemia and a purplish cyanosis of skin grafts over the legs, but with supporting pressure bandages this is borne satisfactorily through the many weeks or months until walking can be resumed without difficulty.

The patient's weight will now have reached a plateau from 15 to 50 pounds below his initial weight, the degree of loss depending on the duration of dietary interruption and the extent of sepsis.

During the next twelve months, the patient will gradually resume his body weight, owing to the regrowth of his skeletal muscle and the redeposition of body fat, a process involving the protein anabolism and fat redeposition of the final two stages of closed soft-tissue trauma. Burned patients of adolescent or young adult age may appear (twelve to eighteen months after the burn) unusually fat and flabby with extremities that show marked vasomotor activity with blanching, cyanosis on dependency, and excessive sweating. This is the result of high intake with inadequate muscular exercise to build muscle, and large areas of skin that do not have normal sudomotor activity.

As the initial weeks of this phase go by, the patient returns home, and this step is often best taken even before the last few little traces of open area have closed. Many patients at this stage have areas of very thin epithelization that open transiently (or on minor trauma) and weep plasma, only to close again, until finally all of the epithelium becomes underlain with an adequate layer of dermis to give it firmness, depth, and protection as a cover to the tissues beneath.

The admonition that the patient should not put out too much caloric energy in the form of physical work during this phase of rehabilitation need scarcely be stressed in a burned patient. The limiting factor with a burn is the physical fitness of the extremities. The caloric intake usually exceeds the work output, and an intensive and aggressive program of exercise and muscle reeducation is essential.

B. METABOLISM

The characteristic metabolic feature of this phase of a burn is positive nitrogen balance and weight gain, although it has been noted by several groups that fat oxidation may persist to some degree during the early weeks of nitrogen anabolism.

As in convalescent anabolism throughout surgical care, it is impossible for the convalescent surgical patient to anabolize unless he is given the necessary substrate and energy in the diet. He must eat more than his ordinary resting diet because he must rebuild tissue (and in the case of the child, grow) in order to resume his former status. In a burn at this phase, one would aim at caloric intakes in the range of from 3000 to 5000 calories per day and 12 to 15 gm. of nitrogen. On a regimen of this type, the anabolic weight gain is in the general range of 3 to 5 gm. of nitrogen per day per 70 kg.

C. TREATMENT

Physiotherapy progresses through active and passive motion to walking, eating, progressive self-help, and return home.

Each new area to achieve even the most tentative healing must be taken out of dressings and given the "open-air treatment" so that, free of the maceration of a dressing, the surface can dry and harden.

Other steps in rehabilitation fall into the realm of physiotherapy and plastic reconstruction. The patient at this time may have wrist drop, foot drop, or flexion or extension deformities from prolonged immobilization. Even under ideal care some degree of deformity is almost unavoidable; severe contracture with syneresis of neighboring structures (jaw, arm, chest) is clearly preventable. These should be brought back slowly by a mixture of active and passive motion, exercises in the tub, and other simple physiotherapeutic measures.

Most patients will lose all these seemingly crippling joint deformities as they themselves become mobilized. Burn contractures under the chin and in the axilla, ectropion due to contractures below the eye, and severe scarring on the dorsum of the hand, with the resultant subluxation of joints and inability of flexion, are common sequelae of deep burns and are dealt with by subsequent plastic procedures.

Our 40 per cent burn in a young man is now healed and the patient has finally returned to work. The physical appearance of the wound changes gradually from skin grafts interlaced with red raised scars to skin grafts interlaced with concave, flat white scars with fine transverse striations. These local changes which occur during the six- to twelve-month period after elective soft-tissue surgery may in a burn take two to five years before they are complete.

With this completed convalescence of the ideal—and all too rare—burn as background, let us turn now to some of the commonest and most troublesome variants and abnormal patterns of burn behavior.

Section VI.   Burns: The Troublesome Variants

In the foregoing account we have considered, for the clarification of general principles and rationale of treatment, a burn that was extensive but otherwise quite favorable for treatment. All the common variants, to be described below, are best considered as departures from the pattern seen in the foregoing. With the exception of the first common variant—the lesser burn—all of these are due to complications of the burn itself or to miscarriages of treatment. They present especially difficult aspects, many of which carry a very high mortality.

Several of these troublesome variants, such as renal failure or Curling's ulcer, bloodstream infection or septic starvation, are often seen in combination.

A. THE LESSER BURN
EARLY EXCISION; ORAL TREATMENT

The small burn of home, kitchen, and workshop can be treated with the simplest possible measures. Second-degree areas are painful for several hours and feel much more comfortable with some sort of a grease dressing. A supporting bandage brings physical and mental comfort to the patient. The only place where the surgeon may go seriously wrong with these small burns is by harmful overtreatment or in misjudging second- and third-degree depth. The appearances of third-degree or full-thickness destruction must be borne strictly in mind in approaching the small burn.

For example, consider a child with an irregular burn 6 or 8 cm. in diameter on the thigh. This burn, if it is first- or second-degree, will be completely healed and the child will have (unfortunately) forgotten about it in about two weeks. If the surgeon believes it is second-degree, but it is in point of fact full-thickness, at two weeks the burn will just be beginning to slough and separate. It will then become an open, painful, granulating surface and may not be healed for one to three months. The surgeon will be more than embarrassed to find that his prediction to the family has been in error.

This sort of small, localized, deep burn is the most favorable for primary sharp excision and grafting, and such a procedure may be carried out within a few hours of the burn. In such a case, primary 100 per cent take of the graft should be expected, and again the patient may be out of dressings and doing well at two weeks. The lesser burn, therefore, presents some problems of discrimination which are important and can be troublesome if underestimated or misunderstood.

"Pure" second-degree burns are almost never seen greater in extent than 7 to 10 per cent of the body surface, except in sunburns. Extensive burns almost invariably involve sizeable areas of third-degree damage. Extensive third-degree burns do have some second-degree areas around them, a fact that is important largely because these superficial burns should not be excised if any primary excision is done. With open treatment they heal very readily. With closed treatment such partial burns may develop a sort of cocoon sepsis and maceration from the heat and liquid under the dressing, and be converted into third-degree burns. The rapid healing of these peripheral second-degree areas is in itself an entirely compelling argument for the use of the open treatment of burns.

Two general rules in reference to the diagnosis of full-thickness burn are helpful.

(1) All *extensive* burns (over 15 per cent of the body) must be assumed to contain some full-thickness areas.

(2) All *flame* burns should be assumed to contain full-thickness areas. An open flame or burning clothing is a thermal agent that rarely spares the deeper layers.

In dealing with burns—mixed second- and third-degree—that cover from 10 to 20 per cent of body surface, we find the sort of burned patient whose systemic care can be carried along on oral treatment; such patients show few of the devastating systemic manifestations of the more extensive burn, but should be hospitalized under any circumstances short of major civilian disaster. This burn might be exemplified by a burn of the back in a patient whose clothing caught fire but could be removed rapidly enough. The burn of the dorsum of both hands, both forearms, and face is a rather characteristic pattern for industrial flash burns and can be cared for with little intravenous therapy. Discrimination between the burn that needs intravenous therapy and the burn that does not is one requiring clinical judgment and an estimate of the total situation of the patient, particularly the ability to take and retain food and fluids. If the burn is bordering on 18 to 22 per cent of body weight and beginning to approach that of maximal extra-cellular-fluid expansion, the patient should receive plasma or some other colloid but will not need the full allotment budgeted for a larger burn.

As a rule the tendency in intravenous therapy is to overtreat rather than undertreat lesser burns. Many lesser burns can get along quite well without this aid. However, any burn of significant size should be treated with antibiotics during the early phase, and tetanus prophylaxis should be given.

It is a universal tendency to overestimate the extent and underestimate the depth of burns when they are first seen.

B. THE VERY EXTENSIVE BURN: HOMOGRAFTING

There are many instances on record in which patients with burns in the range of 70 to 80 per cent of the body surface have recovered. Most of them have been in younger people, and a considerable fraction of the burn has in these cases turned out to be second-degree and has not involved full-thickness slough requiring extensive grafts.

Somewhere, depending upon the patient's age and visceral function, we cross the boundary into the "never-never land," in which no one has ever seen a survival. In people over seventy the line occurs near 70 per cent of body surface. In healthy, vigorous young people, this dividing line may indeed be very high—as high as 85 per cent of the body surface. In older people, this dividing line is much lower, getting down to the general range of 30 to 40 per cent of the body surface.

What does one do with a burn that seems essentially hopeless? In the section on shock, we pointed out that the term "irreversible shock" should never be used in clinical surgery because it connotes a spirit of hopelessness, which tends to deny more accurate diagnosis and which leads to sloppy neglectful treatment or no treatment at all. Surgery can never lower its standard for those seemingly hopeless without endangering the salvageable patient in the next instance. The same truism should be applied to the very extensive burn. In a civilian hospital no burn should be denied the ultimate in therapeutic effort—even the 70–70 burn (age 70, 70 per cent full-thickness).

In military or civilian disaster, however, this is not true. A practical view toward the treatment of the whole group must, at times, involve merciful palliation of single individuals without the full therapeutic effort. Burns of over 70 per cent in people over seventy years of age certainly constitute a borderline beyond which treatment is generally futile by present methods. Below this age and below this percentage, neglect is indefensible under any circumstance.

The impression has become firmly rooted in the literature that the dangerous burn in any age group is in the 70 per cent range. Such a statement implies that the lesser burn than this carries little hazard. It is inadequately appreciated that a very high mortality is found in burns in the 50 per cent range.

Body burns over 50 per cent of the body surface are seriously life-endangering and are always impossible of coverage from the patient's own donor areas at the first few procedures.

In the very extensive burn the initial steps in treatment and all of the general principles already discussed are fully applicable. One of the virtues of the "body-weight burn budget" lies in its restraint to excessive fluid therapy. Those formulas that are based on a certain volume of fluid per surface area burned do not take into consideration the patient's body weight—which is the single most important factor in determining his body water and extracellular fluid volume—and they do not involve any but arbitrary restraints on increased total volume. The so-called "Evans formula," as applied to a 70 per cent burn, becomes "restrained" (by the arbitrary ceiling values set) so soon in its calculation that it would be much simpler to start out simply with giving 10 per cent of the patient's body weight as plasma, a figure that is arrived at after very simple calculation and involves no additional arbitrary ceilings.

In an adolescent or in a child, the prognosis for the extremely extensive burn is still sufficiently good so that we proceed by the regular rules of burn management. The timing of excision at the eighth to twelfth day and the management of fluids and antibiotics are the same as that for a less extensive and more favorable burn.

In the older person, however, over the age of fifty to fifty-five, a burn covering more than 75 per cent of the body surface involves a mortality rate of over 85 per cent, and virtually the only favorable factor lies in the possibility that the estimate of third degree may be in error. In experienced hands the extent of third-degree burn usually is not grossly overestimated. Thus we are up against a prognosis approaching in gravity that of massive coronary occlusion, late diabetic coma with sepsis, portal thrombosis, extensive bowel gangrene, and only a few other selectively ominous situations in nonmalignant disease. To what extent community resources should be devoted to such a situation must be left to the judgment and to the conscience of the surgeon and his associates.

In some instances, we have made a heroic attempt to save such patients by reasoning that the burn must be excised and covered early at all costs and that without this step survival is impossible. Since by standard methods the patient rarely lives long enough to pass into the period of early sharp debridement we have attempted early excision under hypothermia and would not hesitate to do so again, although we have had no survivals. It is at least a chance.

If a patient has a burn of 50 per cent of his body surface, it might appear logical that skin grafts to cover this might readily be obtained from the unburned 50 per cent. It does not take long to demonstrate the fallacy of this point of view. There are many areas of the body, such as the face and scalp, palms and soles, the flexion creases, the scrotum, the perineum, and the buttocks, the anterior surface of the knees, and the shoulder, which serve as poor donor sites. A patient who has a truly third-degree burn of 50 per cent of his body surface cannot possibly have more than one-quarter of this covered at his first skin grafting. It may be advisable to complete the sharp debridement of the rest, nevertheless, since the removal of this devitalized skin may help to avoid the development of invasive infection beneath it.

The remaining debrided portion should be covered immediately with homografts; these take quite well and serve as a remarkably effective and semipermanent dressing.

Skin homografts may be obtained as follows:

(1) fresh skin homografts from a member of the family or other living donor,
(2) fresh cadaver homografts taken and immediately transferred to the patient,
(3) refrigerated skin homografts taken from donors either living or dead, and
(4) refrigerated, lyophilized human skin from a variety of sources.

Our experience is not sufficient to choose among these save to conclude that the fresh cadaver homografts seem to be as good as skin taken from a living donor and much

simpler. The lyophilized skin has not functioned well, in our experience.

The cadaver skin should be taken under sterile precautions as soon as possible after death.

Were the patient to be a child and were the mother to be of the same blood group (blood grouping being unimportant in other skin grafting settings, but here indicating the possibility of tissue identity) we would favor the use of the mother as the skin homograft donor. For an infant the total area is small in terms of the mother's surface. We would further postulate that were this to become a widespread practice, some individuals would be found in whom such maternal homografts would persist indefinitely without rejection. Favorable reports have been made of the use of amniotic membrane.

C. BURNS AT THE EXTREMES OF AGE

As mentioned above, the effect of advancing age on mortality is analogous to that of enlarging extent. There appears to be a boundary of hopelessness, but one never knows quite where it is; our general maxim again must hold here that maximal therapeutic effort must be made. In the very elderly a burn of only 8 to 10 per cent of the body surface, particularly involving the face or upper thorax, may well be fatal.

The colloid dose schedule must be sharply restricted in elderly people. It is advisable to start with a plasma dosage equal to around 8 per cent of body weight in patients over sixty-five. We would prefer to have the patient slightly undertreated, because we can always speed up treatment and catch up as needed; if overtreated, the patient will never unload the therapeutic fluid and may go into pulmonary edema during the diuresis phase as this fluid is reabsorbed into the active extracellular fluid. It is of interest that overtreatment with plasma is much easier to undo (by venesection) than is overtreatment with water and salt.

The care of the elderly here involves many of the considerations mentioned in connection with hip fractures in Chapter 46. Alertness is worth almost any price and overmedication is to be avoided. Digitalization should be considered and controlled with care. The arteriosclerotic kidney is a poor setting for burn trauma, and renal insufficiency is much more common in this age group than in the young.

The feeble-minded or crippled patient is often burned ("can't-get-out-of-the-way-fast-enough" syndrome). One aspect of feeble-mindedness is continued restlessness, failure to understand or cooperate, and a wearing-down process that is very pernicious. The only true examples of post-traumatic exhaustion we have ever seen were in seriously injured or burned patients, unable to understand or unwilling to cooperate, who, struggling against the fetters of their disease, septic and starving, wore themselves out in five to seven days. Heavy sedation to control the aimless motion only brings respiratory problems in its wake.

Children with burns tend to develop burn edema more rapidly and in larger relative quantity than in adults. In patients under twelve, the body-weight burn budget should call for 12 per cent of body weight as colloid. The indices of therapy in children are similar to those in adults. It is well to remember that water turnover is much faster in children and that insensible water loss may occur very rapidly. In children there is no need to carry out a venipuncture on sparse veins to follow the peripheral concentration of red cells. The microhematocrit may be used, and the hemoglobin or erythrocyte count is equally effective. In very young infants, as in the very elderly, the mortality rate even of lesser burns remains high.

D. THE BURNED PATIENT IN SHOCK OR OLIGURIC ON ENTRY

The occurrence of this picture depends on the duration between burning and the arrival of the patient at the hospital. In the absence of other injuries, it is rare for the burned patient to be in oligemic shock under six hours after receiving the injury. The patient will become oliguric long before shock develops, the oliguria initially reflecting the diminished glomerular filtration rate of differential renal vasoconstriction.

Three important questions come up for answer in a patient of this type.

(1) Will the hypotension respond to restoration of the blood volume to normal? And if not, what other factors enter into its pathogenesis?

(2) Will the patient's urine volume respond to blood-volume restoration?

(3) Does the urine contain hemoglobin end-products and are there other evidences of extensive hemolysis as an additional nephrotoxic factor?

The best way to answer these questions is to restore the patient's blood volume as rapidly as possible. The "body-weight burn budget" described in the foregoing section involves rates of plasma infusion starting at the first hour. *The budget is still useful in the later burn, however, if one counts the number of hours elapsed as from the time of burning rather than from the time of admission.* For example, if a patient should have 4000 ml. of plasma in his first twelve hours, according to the burn budget, and he is seen at eight hours, he then must have 4000 ml. in the first four hours after hospital admission. This type of correction has been made in many cases, with good result.

In addition, the initial elevated hematocrit is a direct guide to the blood-volume deficit on admission to a degree not shared by hematocrit indications in the early burn (where the hematocrit is normal despite a large colloid requirement in the hours to come) or in virtually any other situation seen in surgery. The hematocrit elevation on admission—an elevation almost inevitably present if the patient is in shock—provides a direct guide to the amount of plasma that should be given with great rapidity. This checks out remarkably well with the "budget debt." There may be some upper limit of infusion rapidity which should be respected, but it certainly need not be respected when plasma volume or blood volume is reduced. Even in elderly people with heart disease, the hypotensive state with shock and tissue anoxia is far more dangerous to the myocardium, the brain, and the kidneys than is a sudden infusion of plasma that restores volume and flow to normal.

At the risk of repetition, a typical calculation for a fifty-five-year-old man admitted to the hospital eight hours after a burn, hypotensive and oliguric, weighing 82 kg., of normal build, and with an entry hematocrit of 55, would indicate the amount of plasma to be given rapidly as follows:

Normal estimated blood volume	= 7% of 82 kg.	= 5740 ml.
Normal estimated erythrocyte volume	= 0.42 × 5470	= 2410 ml.
Observed blood volume	= 2410 ÷ 0.55	= 4400 ml.
Plasma deficit	= 5740 − 4400	= 1340 ml.

This amount of plasma (1300 ml.) should be given promptly and the response measured; thereafter the patient should return to his "budget" infusion rates. The urine-volume response to this volume-restoring infusion is the most important observation that will be made relative to the prognosis for the kidneys (see below).

In a patient in shock or oliguric on entry, the early analysis of the urine should be carried out just as in any other case. The examination of the urine for protein, for erythrocytes, and for specific gravity is important. The *p*H of the urine may be useful since, if the urine is alkaline with many leucocytes in the sediment, chronic renal infection is probably present. Chronic pyelonephritis leads more rapidly to renal insufficiency after any sort of injury, particularly a burn, than is the case with normal kidneys.

The most important examination of the urine, from a prognostic point of view, has to do with the benzidine dihydrochloride (or guaiac) reaction on the supernatant after centrifugation. The object is to discover whether or not there is hemoglobin-like pigment in the urine arising from the destruction of cells initiated in the area of burn, a destruction which in turn is caused by the effect of heat on erythrocyte fragility. Its importance lies not only in the fact that the products of hemolysis are toxic to the kidney, but also in the observation that post-traumatic renal insufficiency after burns virtually never occurs in individuals who do not show hemoglobinuria. Almost the only circum-

stance in which it occurs is in the extremely rare patient who has been in severe shock for many hours (or even days) after burning and before treatment, or in very elderly people who have severe arteriosclerotic renal disease to begin with.

The presence of pigment in the urine does not signify that renal insufficiency is going to occur; it merely signifies that it is more likely to occur. *The presence of heme pigment in the scanty urine of an oliguric burned patient in shock signifies that the individual has an approximately 80 per cent likelihood of developing severe renal insufficiency.* If it is over eight hours after burning when the patient is first seen for treatment, the likelihood is even greater. If the patient is over seventy-five years of age, has been burned more than eight hours earlier, is in shock and oliguric, with pigment in his urine, it is a certainty—as surely as anything in surgery is a certainty—that he will develop post-traumatic renal insufficiency, and it is likewise a virtual certainty that this will be the primary cause of his death.

If the early burned patient is oliguric but not in shock—a frequent combination—his therapy should be started out in a systematic and orderly way, measuring hourly urine outputs as one goes. No special alteration in the infusion pattern should be introduced because of his initial oliguria. The static debt should be repaired as previously noted, and the "budget" followed thereafter. If, after several hours of treatment, including the restoration of his plasma deficit, the patient is still oliguric or becomes oliguric, then an additional infusion test of the type previously described is carried out. Usually the patient will resume output as therapy is instituted; if he does not, it is a bad sign.

In oliguric burns, as in severe trauma in general, one must distinguish clearly between the renal response to blood-volume restoration and the renal response to an infusion test carried out after blood volume has seemingly been restored to normal. Oliguria is to be expected in the presence of hypotension and oligemia; there is no arbitrary ceiling on the fluid to be administered to restore volume: it should be "enough." Urine volume is usually restored. If, after restoration of blood volume to normal as judged by the usual criteria (pulse, blood pressure, color, mentation), oliguria still persists, an infusion test is justified. This should be carefully planned, and should be done but once. Prolonged continuous forcing of fluid in the presence of oliguria will produce pulmonary edema, and is entirely unjustified. The venous pressure is a helpful guide to the danger point in colloid administration to oliguric patients after burns and other traumas.

The early treatment of the patient who is admitted in shock follows basic principles of trauma; the early restoration of blood volume is a first priority, just as it is in any other type of injury. It is the further development of events in this patient that presents the major challenge. If urine output is resumed and the patient maintains it at reasonable volumes throughout his convalescence, he will show no chronic evidence of renal damage as a result of his transient nephrosis. If, on the other hand, the oliguria is maintained, a situation is introduced into the burned patient's care that becomes the prime determinant in survival: established renal failure.

E. RENAL FAILURE IN BURNS

It has been noted previously that among the chemical determinations to be made early in a burned patient's course is the measurement of the blood urea nitrogen. If the blood urea nitrogen is elevated early (during the first six hours) and if the patient's urine output is maintained and he carries on satisfactorily with his course, the early mild azotemia diminishes in importance and is soon forgotten. Older people may have an azotemia with blood urea nitrogen values of 25 to 50 mg. per 100 ml. for many weeks after a burn and yet do well. This seems to be merely an indication of the fact that the urea clearance is not quite adequate to keep up with the tremendously increased endogenous urea production characteristic of the burned patient.

If, on the other hand, the patient becomes oliguric, fails to undergo diuresis with blood-volume restoration, and appears to be going into post-traumatic renal insufficiency, as judged by clinical course and infusion test, we now look back to the early blood urea nitrogen values with great interest. If the blood urea nitrogen tested ten, twelve, or twenty-four hours previously, at the time of admission, was elevated, and if that time was less than six hours after burning, we have an extremely bad prognostic sign for recovery from the patient's post-traumatic renal insufficiency. *The preexistent renal disease, however slight, greatly decreases the insult required to produce renal failure, as well as the likelihood of recovery.* Treatment must be carried on just as in other cases, but a high blood urea nitrogen level remains an ominous portent.

The high percentage of elderly and debilitated people among the victims of severe burns makes renal insufficiency more common than one might expect following trauma in the population at large. For the patient in post-traumatic renal insufficiency after a burn (whether or not the admission level of blood urea nitrogen showed the presence of preexisting renal disease), the following are basic principles.

Once blood volume has been restored, the care of the burned patient in renal failure should proceed exactly as if he were producing a normal amount of urine, with the sole exception of the total amount of fluid volume to be used in treatment. Attention to maintaining the airway, the use of antibiotics, careful nursing, attention to the detail of fluid administration, and observation of the weight of the patient are the essentials. The patient still needs the fluid required to maintain his normal blood volume, but it becomes additionally important not to overcrowd this requirement—to underadminister rather than overadminister the fluid. When the tissues resorb the burn edema, the patient will not be able to lose extra fluid by diuresis. Yet if his blood volume is allowed to fall below normal, it will add further to his renal insult. The surgeon is therefore walking a line which is not only thin but of which the edges are badly obscured. Clinical appearance, blood pressure, pulse rate, mentation—these must be the common-sense guides to fluid therapy in this situation, closely checked by frequent hematocrits. In elderly patients and patients with visceral disease (including renal disease), it is better to proceed with a slightly high hematocrit (46 to 50) than to overadminister fluid and produce a low hematocrit with the threat of congestive failure.

The presence of renal failure makes one gravitate toward using plasma in relatively larger amounts with relatively less water and salt. The object of fluid therapy is, as mentioned before, a very simple one: to maintain blood volume. Since the oliguric patient is going to have extreme difficulty in excreting extra water, it is clearly better to maintain his blood volume with a substance that involves a lesser total fluid load and which, to a greater extent, remains inside the vascular tree. For this reason, plasma is preferable. The use of whole blood in this situation is equally logical for the preservation of volume without an undue expansion of body water.

The rise in blood urea nitrogen and plasma potassium concentrations will now start in earnest and may be quite abrupt. If the plasma potassium concentration approaches the level of 7 to 9 mE. per l. during the first week, dialysis should be offered the patient, despite its many hazards. The burned patient less than two weeks after his burn does well on dialysis. We have not seen hemorrhage result from the heparinization. Were a patient to be dialyzed immediately during or after surgery, the hemorrhage hazard would be greater. It is the rare occasion when burned individuals with severe renal failure recover, yet we have seen a number of patients improve markedly with dialysis, decrease their plasma potassium concentration, and get a new lease on life. It is this experience that makes us feel that dialysis is worth while in burned patients in renal failure, and that in a large civilian or military experience one will surely save a few young individuals by this step.

Short of dialysis, there is little to suggest. The administration of large amounts of carbohydrate and testosterone, which in other more chronic uremic settings may result in a slower accumulation of blood urea nitrogen and potassium, would be expected to have comparatively little effect on the rate of rise

of these substances in the plasma early after burning. Resin therapy is apt to be disappointing in a patient with poor gastrointestinal function. In older men, the possibility that the oliguria is partially obstructive in origin should not be overlooked. The pulmonary water loss without renal function that occurs in burned patients with renal failure is a potent cause of hypernatremia.

F. HYPERNATREMIA

Occasional burned patients will demonstrate a severe hypernatremia, starting about the third or fourth day after the burn. This occurs in burns under three types of circumstances. It is most often associated with some degree of renal failure, often with complete oliguria. In a second group, fever with tracheotomy is underlying. In a third group, hypernatremia is associated with continuing profuse diuresis of the solute-loading type. Ironically, the three etiologies may be combined.

In the oliguric cases, we have reasoned in the following manner.

(1) During the edema-demand phase, the patient has been treated with large amounts of fluid containing salt.

(2) The protein fraction of this material is gradually degraded. The water fraction is lost through insensible routes, chiefly lungs, and to some extent evaporation from skin.

(3) Lacking renal output to get rid of the salt fraction, the patient has no other way of disposal, and is capable of excreting only water (via lungs) with the inevitable result: hypernatremia, hyperchloremia, and hypertonicity. The fluid lost through the skin is isotonic with plasma and does not act to repair the defect.

In burned patients with or without renal failure there is a large pulmonary water loss. When tracheotomy is added the pulmonary water loss rate may rise to 5000 ml. per day. It is evident that this lack will lead to hypertonicity if the water is unreplaced. If renal function is poor or absent, so that salt excretion is diminished following the salt load of early therapy, hypertonicity will appear the sooner.

The treatment of hypernatremia is the administration of water. Only in this way can the patient be brought down to anything even approaching a normal state of body tonicity, normal consciousness, and the hope of resuming normal visceral function. If renal function is absent, the prognosis is extremely poor, since reloading the patient with water to cover the extra salt when the salt itself cannot be excreted merely replaces hypertonicity with hypervolemia. It is possible that some of the new extracorporeal dialysis mechanisms (such as the pressure kidney) may permit one to carry a patient of this type through prolonged periods of anuria by contracting the total blood volume during dialysis.

Viewed in this framework and in the presence of anuria or oliguria, hypernatremia is a very bad prognostic sign in burns, and one rarely sees a recovery when the plasma sodium concentration is higher than 165 mE. per l.

In burned patients treated with a large amount of dextran, considerable hypernatremia is seen in the presence of high urine outputs and apparently without a disastrous prognosis, though the more severely hypernatremic patients will succumb. Here the mechanism in at least some of the patients seems to involve a profuse solute diuresis initiated by the dextran.

To understand this, one must recall that giving patients sucrose, mannitol, or low-molecular-weight dextran produces a solute diuresis. The available solute fraction of urine at these profuse urine flows is largely occupied by the crystalloid being administered at a urine osmolality of 500 to 750 mO. per l. Therefore, although the urine is not particularly dilute, the ratio of water to electrolyte is very high and, viewed in the terms of water-electrolyte relationships, the effect is one of almost pure water loss. This is exactly the same mechanism seen in severe diabetics with profuse glycosuria and is analogous to tube-feeding hypertonicity. Any minor renal damage, preexisting or burn-induced, potentiates the lesion.

When a burned patient is treated with large amounts of dextran, and the low-molecular-weight fraction is rapidly excreted,

one might therefore expect to see a urine containing a very large amount of water per unit of extracellular salt. *The antidiuretic state does not inhibit solute diuresis.* Initial treatment taking account of this principle is helpful. Prolongation of such a situation results in some degree of hypernatremia, particularly if saline-containing fluids and plasma are also being administered by vein.

In the presence of profuse urine outputs, burn hypernatremia is relatively benign and is readily treated by "covering" the loss with suitable quantities of water and desisting for a time from the excessive administration of solute. This is in contrast to the very poor outlook when severe hypertonicity coexists with oliguria or renal failure.

G. PULMONARY INJURY: TRACHEOTOMY

The nature of injury to the respiratory system in burns cannot be described on a unitary basis. The heat itself may penetrate into the lower tracheobronchial tree and do damage there. Such an injury is rare because this area of the body is efficient in removing heat. It is difficult to burn it directly even with blasts of hot burning gases. Burns of the oropharynx and vocal cords can result, however, from the direct inhalation of hot gases or flame, and these become obstructive and require tracheotomy.

The role of heat (that is, caloric input) below the vocal cords is probably minimal save in the case of the inhalation of steam. Here the temperature of the vapor plus the heat of condensation produces burns of the respiratory system all the way down to the terminal bronchioles and alveoli.

Smoke is finely divided ash (which may produce caustic alkaline compounds when dissolved in the body fluids), mixed with gases which are the product of combustion (for example, phosgene, nitrites) and which, in themselves, may be extremely irritating. In civilian life, the pulmonary lesion one commonly sees in burns seems to be associated most frequently with the inhalation of smoke. Which of these various factors in the smoke causes the particular injury at hand is not always clear.

Whatever noxious mixture causes the injury, it manifests itself initially by dyspnea and cyanosis. Heat injury to the vocal cords produces a crowing respiration which may or may not progress to signs of a lower respiratory injury. As the tracheopulmonary lesion progresses an exudative response is produced, resulting in a "wet lung," which further compromises effective ventilation.

The outward signs of a dangerous tracheopulmonary burn range all the way from findings on history to those seen by direct laryngoscopy. The finding of an unconscious person who has been burned in a closed space, particularly if there are not many surface burns or if the surface burns are out of proportion to the degree of respiratory embarrassment, suggests severe pulmonary injury, quite aside from any other findings. Many persons burned in closed spaces succumb without any surface burns at all, presumably from a mixture of smoke inhalation and acute anoxia. The same may be true of flame-thrower injury in military combat. If the patient has burns around the face, including the nares and the nasal hair, with a sore throat, a burned pharynx, crowing respiration, and smoky or burned vocal cords, one may assume that an injury to the upper airway is present, and it is very rare to see one of any extent that does not involve some injury to the lower respiratory tract.

Hoarse crowing respiration, dyspnea, or cyanosis is an immediate indication for tracheotomy in tracheopulmonary burn. Tracheotomy may be postponed from hour to hour in borderline cases to determine whether oxygenation will remain satisfactory. As pointed out previously, a tracheotomy is not entirely on the credit side of the ledger, as it virtually abolishes an effective cough. It should therefore not be rushed if not needed. If there are extensive burns around the face and neck that will soon produce excessive edema of the neck tissues, tracheotomy should be done early rather than late. If there are no burns around the face and neck, tracheotomy can be postponed with the certainty that when it becomes necessary it can be carried out without increased difficulty. Tracheotomy is occasionally worth while

even in lower respiratory injuries (even though clearly above the area of obstruction), because it lessens the residual air and improves the efficiency of ventilation. The use of tracheotomy suction is essential to replace the lost ability to cough effectively and may additionally remove secretion and exudate from the tracheobronchial tree.

Tracheotomy in burned patients should be carried out with good lighting and exposure under satisfactory conditions of anesthesia and in the operating room whenever possible. The effect on pulmonary water loss has already been mentioned.

Three other steps are helpful to the patient with pulmonary burn injury.

(1) *The Avoidance of Fluid Overloading.* The burn budget already outlined calls for the equal of approximately 10 per cent of the patient's body weight to be given as plasma in the first forty-eight hours. In elderly people, and in patients whose injuries show pulmonary components, this should be reduced to 8 per cent as a starting figure and progressively lowered if severe need is not demonstrated by low urine outputs or elevated hematocrit. A decrease in the amount of salt solution and water used is also advisable in such instances. Patients with pulmonary injury but with little surface burn can be carried along without any parenteral fluid therapy whatsoever.

(2) *The Use of a High-Humidity Atmosphere.* This is an important aspect of the care of pulmonary injuries in general and particularly in patients with tracheotomy. The fog room, which is capable of producing 100 per cent humidity, seems to have a salubrious effect on any sort of exudative inflammatory process in the airway. Just how this works and what the mechanism is by which it produces the defervescence and improved ventilation is not wholly clear, but apparently it has to do with the greater content of water in the exudate as a result of the high humidity of the inhaled air and the lessened caloric demands of decreased vaporization. If a fog room is lacking, the use of steam-kettle inhalations, steaming up the room, and other such steps should be undertaken with vigor.

(3) *The Use of Oxygen.* Additional oxygen,

best used after passing it through a detergent for wetting, may be necessary. The continuous administration of oxygen through a catheter into a tracheotomy is irritating and drying to the secretion. One may therefore use a tracheotomy tent and maintain both oxygenation and humidification. As shown repeatedly and epitomized in many of our cases, the problem with these patients appears to be the ventilatory removal of carbon dioxide rather than the inhalation of adequate oxygen. Severe respiratory acidosis is probably the penultimate cause of death in most patients with severe pulmonary burns, sudden cardiac arrhythmia (cardiac arrest) being the final stroke.

Many patients with pulmonary-component injuries have recovered. It is not nearly as grave a development as is persistent renal insufficiency.

H. BLOOD-STREAM INFECTION

A major contribution of the antibiotics to burn therapy has been the prevention of early death due to invasive blood-stream infection. It is probable that the work of Price (1956) casts more light on the genesis of this infection than does any other recent study. This is not a blood-stream infection that results from the proliferation of exogenously introduced microorganisms. It is instead an unlimited multiplication of the normal organisms in the deeper crypts and dermal appendages of the skin, a multiplication made possible by the virtual obliteration of blood supply and the maintenance of body heat with a perfect culture medium in the destroyed dermal layers. Little wonder that this bacterial multiplication soon breaks through normal barriers into the blood stream and produces a severe infection.

Because the organisms initially present in a burn may be expected to be sensitive to the antibiotics, early demise with positive blood culture followed by widespread metastatic sepsis and toxemia is now relatively rare. Many patients with third-degree burns receiving antibiotics maintain an almost normal temperature for four or five days until lique-faction of the burn in its deeper layers begins and fever is produced, presumably by tissue necrosis and bacterial invasion as resistance to antibiotics becomes established.

The diagnosis of bacteremia is suggested by swinging fever, "unexplained" hypotension, loss of appetite, further sharp rise in blood urea nitrogen levels, and an altered state of consciousness.

The studies of several groups have recently shown the importance of positive blood-stream infection as a cause of delayed death in burns under antibiotic therapy. Such deaths now occur, not in the first five days but in the second to fourth week, and often involve organisms that might previously not have been considered to be particularly pathogenic, such as *B. proteus* and *pyocyaneus*. These organisms become insensitive to the antibiotics used, and they may appear in the blood stream, from the burn, in overwhelming numbers. Blood-stream infection is much commoner in burns than is generally realized; frequent careful blood cultures must be taken to demonstrate the organisms. One would presume that the spike in fever that ordinarily follows sharp debridement under antibiotic coverage is due to transient blood-stream infection.

No single solution to this problem can be offered. If a patient with a burn has massive blood-stream infection, careful selection of antibiotics according to sensitivities is much more important than it is with surface infection. The prevention of blood-stream infection rests on early removal of the burned tissue, early skin grafting, and closure of the wound.

The introduction, from the hospital environment, of virulent organisms resistant to antibiotics is a more prominent problem in burns than in almost any other aspect of surgery. The burn wound is so large and its complete isolation from the hospital environment so difficult that it is almost impossible to avoid the presence in the burn of antibiotic-resistant organisms. The origin of these organisms may be presumed to be the hospital personnel although, after the first ten days, one cannot be certain that these are not organisms which the burned patient originally had and which have become insensitive as a result of antibiotic treatment.

The attending surgeon can protect the patient most effectively by early wound closure, careful ward technique to avoid massive contamination, and the avoidance of indwelling venous catheters in place longer than seventy-two hours (never to be placed in the inferior-caval system). The latter invites septic thrombosis with massive embolism. An indwelling catheter is dangerous enough in any vein, once there over forty-eight hours; in burns, with intermittent bacteremia the inevitable small platelet thrombus soon becomes infected and a constant receding of intravascular sepsis results. If a catheter must be placed, an arm vein should be used to guide the catheter to the superior vena cava and the catheter should be removed or changed in forty-eight to seventy-two hours. Very small amounts of heparin introduced into the catheter periodically are of some service in staving off the septic process.

The use of gamma globulin may have a place here; proof of its effectiveness is lacking.

I. CURLING'S ULCER

A complication of burns that carries a mortality rate second only to that of bacteremia is massive hemorrhage from the gastrointestinal tract. This hemorrhage may occur from duodenal ulcer, gastric ulcer, or hypertrophic gastritis. The presumed pathogenic mechanism is the prolonged effect of a stressful situation in the patient, acting in the face of progressive nutritional depletion which may, through changes in the gastrointestinal mucous membrane, render it additionally vulnerable to acid-peptic digestion. The prevention of such a lesion through the commencement of antiulcer therapy early in the treatment of the burn is important. In young men, or individuals with a previous ulcer history, such steps should be routine, but there is no proof that they are effective.

If ulcer bleeding starts, it can occasionally be controlled by frequent feedings and ant-

acid management such as one might institute for any bleeding ulcer. The severe additional load which this complication places on the blood volume is obvious, and replacement must be rapid and accurate. Burned patients have been subjected to emergency subtotal gastrectomy for this complication, but we know of only a few who have survived.

If a burned patient is treated with cortisone through his early period, the hazard of this complication is greatly increased.

J. THE LATE, UNHEALED, DIRTY, "HYPERMATURE" BURN

Not infrequently the hospital is asked to take over the care of a patient six to twenty-four weeks after the burn, with chronic suppurating granulating surfaces that have refused all grafts. Despite the surgeon's hope that such problems will never arise in his own hospital, such is sadly not the case and he may therefore occasionally recognize the development of this syndrome under his own eyes. The systemic state of such patients fall into two distinct groups.

First, and by far the commonest clinical status, is that of advanced septic starvation. The patient is cachectic, febrile, anemic, hypoproteinemic, and demoralized, and often has severe contractures and bed sores.

The second, alternative, picture is that of a patient whose visceral function and metabolic status have been well maintained but whose surfaces have not been covered, whether because of their extent, the happenchance combination of bacteria, poor technique of attempted closure, or just plain procrastination. It is this burn that we refer to as "hypermature," in the sense that nitrogen balance has been achieved despite unhealed wounds—a rare and late event. It is in this burn that the ACTH-reoperation tactic is especially effective.

Initial steps should be directed at nutritional management when this is needed. An intensive bacteriologic study of the burn wound is undertaken. It is usually advisable to take the patient off antibiotics entirely and institute a simple routine for the surface wounds while nutritional build-up is taking place. The burn wounds may be treated by frequent dressings, exposure, or tubbing. These steps should be simple and gentle and, in so far as possible, free of pain or the necessity of general anesthesia. Patients who present many unhealed areas with well-formed exuberant granulations that refuse to accept skin grafts frequently also have septic donor sites and exist in a delicate immunologic balance with their flora.

If, in the first few days, such a patient is taken down to the operating room and put to sleep, and all his burned surfaces are soundly scrubbed with some sort of an antiseptic, he will promptly die of blood-stream infection. As initially seen, he represents a very delicate balance in a starved patient between invasion and resistance, and initial steps should be almost wholly devoted to improvement in morale, lessening of pain, and restoration of systemic factors. In such instances, antibiotics, introduced locally in wet dressings or through catheters placed in the dressings, plus frequent wet dressings, may control the infection. The use of frequent blood transfusions, gamma globulin, and, as recently recommended, plasma from patients who have recently recovered from burns, will have usefulness here which has not yet been fully explored or reported.

Multiple whole-blood transfusions, tube feedings, concentrated albumin, and massive doses of vitamins all have a place. In occasional instances we have placed an intravenous catheter in the superior vena cava and used concentrated solutions of carbohydrate and fat for a few days in an effort to replenish the exhausted caloric resources of the patient. Septic starvation at this late stage interferes with vigor, digestion, peristalsis, respiration, immunity, and healing. The patient is frightened and demoralized at this time and this should be taken into account in his management.

After an initial period of five to seven days, the patient should be placed on local and systemic antibiotics (those most appropriate for the sensitivity of the organisms found) and, after two days of such therapy, started on adrenocorticotropic hormone (20 units of gel, twice a day). After two or three days of adrenocorticotropic hormone the patient is taken to the operating room, the exuberant granulation tissue is trimmed or excised, and skin grafts are placed. In this situation the patient's own skin is the only graft that can be counted on for acceptance, but temporizing homografts may be necessary if the areas are large. Since the open areas may far outstrip the available donor sites, small postage-stamp grafts laid in mosaic that can later coalesce are advisable. Homografts have usefulness here (as they have in the early burn) in achieving temporary closure while the patient's own donor sites are further developed by healing.

Adrenocorticotropic hormone treatment may be continued for five to ten days and then tapered off and stopped. The increased hazard of spreading infection is acknowledged, but the success of such measures would suggest that the adrenocorticotropic hormone has some other activity in this regard with respect to the relationship of the organism to the wound.

Patients who, eight to twelve months after the burn, have significant unhealed areas are much rarer today than they were. An occasional cause of this development is the failure of an individual, inexperienced with burns, to recognize a third-degree burn, thus letting it pass by (with wishful thinking or ignorant procrastination) through the favorable period for excision and grafting and into a phase when it is too late for grafting. This is particularly true in limited late burns, which, unlike massive late unhealed burns, are not big enough to produce prolonged septic starvation.

As mentioned above, patients may present themselves with local unhealed burns, although they have gone ahead eating and gaining weight, passing into a strongly anabolic phase, and even into a late phase of fat gain, still with the wound unhealed. This represents the metabolic counterpart, in burns, of the nonunited fracture. Reoperation on the lesion itself has always been considered essential. One of the aspects of extensive surgery on the late unhealed burn may be the renewed stress, which again sets the organism back to the stage of an early injury, where the wound has a high biologic priority. The activity of adrenocorticotropic hormone suggests that it may act by somewhat the same mechanism.

K. FOURTH-DEGREE AND ELECTRICAL BURNS; AMPUTATION

Some burns are so penetrating as to amount to coagulation of the muscles and deeper tissues of a portion of the body, usually an extremity. Electrical burns are frequently of this type. There is a nephrotoxic factor from burns of this type that is far more serious than that seen in the ordinary skin burn. This would suggest that the products of dissolution of deeper tissues, particularly muscle, are toxic to the kidney, a suspicion already amply aroused by evidences from other areas of surgery, such as crush and war wounds. Burns of this type, therefore, have an incidence of renal failure out of all proportion to the total extent of the burn or even to the shock phase. We have seen fatal renal failure in fourth- and fifth-degree burns of this type, with total extent of only around 10 per cent of body surface, without any shock phase but with early oliguria as evidence of renal vasoconstriction, then persisting as renal failure.

In burns of this type, where salvage of the extremity is almost hopeless, there is a strong indication for primary amputation. This may save the kidneys (and thus the patient), simplify care, and hasten recovery, by reducing the surface needed for a graft.

In skin burns of the extremely extensive type, amputation, particularly of one or both legs, has occasionally been suggested as a way of reducing the total surface area that is to be grafted. We have had no experience with amputation merely as a means of reducing skin surface, and such a step is not easily forgiven nor is it to be equated with the amputation of a deeply charred extremity with necrotic muscle.

Fat embolus is a rare complication of burns, but should be suspected in comatose cases; examination of urine and sputum for fat is the only available diagnostic test. We know of no clearly effective treatment.

Pulmonary embolus is another rare complication. Its incidence is tremendously increased by the use of intravenous catheters, either in the femoral vein or threaded up into the inferior vena cava. For this reason the use of such catheters is absolutely contraindicated even on a temporary basis; if venous catheterization is to be employed, it must be in the arm and superior vena cava.

Section VII.   Burns: Notes from the Literature

A. ENDOCRINE CHANGES

There are several references to data from burned patients in the literature reviewed in Parts I, II, and III. These will not be mentioned again here.

The adrenocortical response in burns has been studied by several groups, including Cope (1943), Evans and Butterfield (1951), Moore *et al.* (1955), Moore (1957), Wight *et al.* (1952, 1953), Wilson *et al.* (1955), and Hume *et al.* (1956). Hume's paper is based on the burn experience following the fire on the aircraft carrier Bennington. Both blood and urine glucocorticoids were measured. There was no clinical or chemical evidence of adrenal failure. Indeed, elevated levels in the blood were very prolonged.

Adrenocorticotropic hormone tests done at various intervals were not remarkable; two patients who died did show extreme elevations of the free blood corticosteroids (230 mg. per 100 ml. and 104 mg. per 100 ml.) and had received both adrenocorticotropic hormone and cortisone. Others who had received these drugs did not show such high values. The seemingly paradoxical fall in steroids and rise in eosinophils in late grafting procedures (during the second and third month after the burn) was not observed, but studies were not carried on after the fiftieth day in most cases.

Burns, considered in relation to other traumas, are characterized by a very prolonged adrenocortical response, which may be related to the prolonged septic wound, the multiple minor or major operations, or other factors. Wight *et al.* (1953) showed that a prolonged low eosinophil count, failing to return toward normal about the fourteenth day, pointed to a poor prognosis, presumably because it indicates the continued stressful presence of complications later destined to become fatal.

Once the initial enthusiasm for adreno-corticotropic hormone in burns (Whitelaw and Woodman, 1950) had been smothered by the rebuttal (Wight *et al.*, 1952), there was a place for renewed careful evaluation on a more conservative basis. The report of Martin *et al.* (1955) presents observations on twenty-two seriously burned patients. Although the mortality rate was not affected in this small series, the ease of resuscitation and the maintenance of homeostasis seemed to be improved on hormone (cortisone) therapy.

Monsaingeon *et al.* (1957) have studied the course of the eosinophils in twenty-six burned patients. Their findings are similar in many ways to those of Cope and his group (Wight *et al.*, 1953). It is the late changes that are most significant; the late high count does not signify any sort of adrenal failure and appears to coincide with cicatrization; the late low count simply signifies the coexistence of complications.

B. CURLING'S ULCER

Hummel *et al.* (1956) studied the ulcer diathesis in burned patients. Basing their research on the large experience at Brooke Army Hospital (ten cases in 194 burns in a twenty-one-month period), they found that in the moderate burn there was an elevation in uropepsin concentration not found in the more severe burns; correlation with steroid excretion was slight; the development of Curling's ulcer was not predictable on the basis of the data developed.

Gastrointestinal tract ulceration in burns, so rarely followed by survival when there is massive hemorrhage, has been reported and studied by Harkins (1938), Curling (1922), Herbut (1945), Friesen (1950), Lillehei *et al.* (1952), Weigel *et al.* (1953), Fletcher and Harkins (1954), Davis *et al.* (1955), Dragstedt *et al.* (1956), Bogardus and Gustafson (1956) and Derrick *et al.* (1957).

C. ANEMIA

The fragility, early destruction, and decreased volume of erythrocytes, and resulting anemia of burns have all been documented and measured many times by workers studying both burned man and the experimental animal. The marrow response in man appears to be one of depression followed later by hematopoiesis (Moore *et al.*, 1946), the entire sequence profoundly affected by infection and its sequelae (Wintrobe, 1952). The studies of Davis *et al.* (1955) in the rat revealed increased medullary and extra-medullary hematopoiesis early after burning. This may be related to species differences in the time of onset of serious postburn sepsis.

Davies and Topley (1956) again restudied this problem, using different tagging methods and isoagglutinin techniques. They found a gradual fall of erythrocyte volume in seventy-one patients with severe burns, in rare instances amounting to a loss of 30 per cent of starting red cell volume in the first forty-eight hours. They found evidence to suggest that patients' cells and transfused cells participated equally in the disappearance. Without discussing technical features in too great detail, there is nothing to suggest that abnormally fragile cells near the end of a life in vivo take up the tag (Cr^{51}) normally. With the complex situation of cryptic loss into septic burns, sampling, decreased hematopoiesis (Moore *et al.*, 1946), and increased fragility (Shen and Ham, 1943) with splenic destruction, one can not interpret the data so closely. The authors' conclusion is that a part of the loss is "unexplained" at present.

D. ELECTROLYTES, NUTRITION

Hyponatremia is a commonplace finding in the convalescent burn patient after the fourth day. The expected hypotonicity accompanies this hyponatremia unless there is unusual nonelectrolyte osmolar solute (such as sugar or urea) in the blood, as is seen in diabetes and renal failure. This postburn hypotonicity is primarily dilutional, the result of the accumulation (by ingestion, injection, cell lysis, and fat oxidation) of new sodium-free water during a prolonged antidiuretic period, during which positive renal free-water clearance is almost never seen (Dudley *et al.*, 1954). Soroff *et al.* (1956) made an exhaustive survey of these phenomena in twenty-four severe burns and concluded again that this hyponatremia was dilutional. They postulate that osmoregulation is "set" at a new lower level in burns, a finding for which there is no direct evidence without osmolality data and calculation of renal water clearance; they point out quite rightly that within ten days or so after a burn, a patient's serum sodium concentration raised even as little as 145 mE. per l. may indicate a serious dehydration (desiccation) and a need for large volumes of water. The importance of tracheotomy, dyspnea, and fever in occasional cases in which pure water loss has produced desiccation should be emphasized. Soroff and his group reemphasize the need for continuance of accurate fluid therapy after the first critical days, as in any other major trauma.

Recent work of Moyer's group (Morgan *et al.*, 1956) shows that large increases in metabolic turnover and insensible water loss occur after burns, and that some of this metabolic activity (as indicated by metabolic rate) can be reduced by so covering the burn as to reduce the water evaporation from the burn and its attendant caloric output (heat of vaporization). This may open an entirely new vista in understanding the increased oxygen utilization and fat oxidation after burns and trauma, particularly with reference to the use of the high-humidity atmosphere.

The loss of protein from an intravascular to an extravascular, extracellular site has been observed and measured by many workers (among them Cope *et al.*, 1948, and King *et al.*, 1956, have written especially helpful reports). Knowledge of this loss provides the basis for understanding and treating the early plasma-need of the burned patient.

We have become increasingly aware of the fact that, while the great bulk of burned patients show hypovolemic signs, renal changes, and clinical appearances commensurate with the degree of loss of plasma volume, there are atypical marginal cases of great interest. One group is the small deep (electrical) burn, in which renal damage is out of all proportion to the area or hypovolemia. Another is that exceptional patient in whom clinical neglect is rewarded not by death but by weathering of the hypovolemic storm, with final restoration of plasma volume by edema resorption and yet without renal damage. There may be much to learn from these marginal cases and the intergrades.

Cooling, either local or general, might be expected to reduce local fluid loss (Reynolds *et al.*, 1956) as would pressure bandages (Cope *et al.*, 1949). Neither has as yet proved clinically practical, feasible, or free of hazard. Much that has been used under the name of pressure bandage does not warrant the term.

The group at the Surgical Research Unit at Fort Sam Houston have recognized and documented their experiences with 121 inlying venous catheters in burns (Moncrief, 1948). The incidence of complications was highest between twenty-two and thirty days after the burn; cultures of the catheter tip often showed organisms. There were many proven thromboses at the site; and several fatal thromboembolic episodes. All the latter were associated with catheters in the lower extremity.

Experience with the systemic use of bacitracin has also been extensive at the Surgical Research Unit. The patients have been in the younger age groups and have tolerated the systemic application of bacitracin despite elevations in the level of blood nonprotein nitrogen. Using bacitracin (300,000 units per day intramuscularly) plus gamma globulin, they have had a number of survivors from the most dangerous types of burn septicemia: staphylococcal, proteus, and pyocyaneus. Properdin levels were normal in these patients.

DaCosse and Baxter (personal communication) have shown that the blood pH is regularly raised in burned patients who have mild pulmonary damage. They have shown further that this is probably due to the hyperventilation stimulated by chronic hypoxia in such patients.

This chronic hypoxia appears in those patients with chronic open wounds, evidently regardless of whether or not the respiratory tract is burned. Arterial oxygen saturation is reduced to 80 per cent in many of these patients, the normal ranging from 93 to 98.2 per cent. The normal tension of oxygen in blood is (pO_2) 80 to 100 mm. Hg. In these burns this runs as low as 50 to 80 mm. Hg.

In general, DaCosse's studies appeared to show that the more severe burns were associated with the more severe depression of oxygen tension, oxygen saturation, compensatory hyperventilation, and respiratory alkalosis. This situation appeared to exist for many days after the burn.

The nature of the oxygen dissociation curve is such that when alkalosis is present hemoglobin saturation is higher at any given oxygen tension. Thus, the alkalotic patient will oxygenate his blood more easily but release it to the tissues less easily than his normal counterpart. This fact makes the studies of DaCosse and Baxter even more significant; the low oxygen saturations, coexisting with alkalosis, are a much more significant lesion in terms of tissue oxygenation than if pH were normal or low.

Dudley et al. (1957) report a possible prevention of postburn hemoglobinuric nephrosis by the administration of low-molecular-weight crystalloids such as mannitol. They are thus taking advantage of the prevention of renal damage by producing osmotic diuresis, suggested by the work of Rosoff and Walter (1952) and Owen et al. (1954). The principle is fundamental to Schlegel's urea-diuresis method. Both procedures are physiologically appealing; neither can easily be proved effective. In one of Dudley's cases, hypernatremia was observed exactly as in any form of continuing osmotic diuresis; this was also a feature of many of the Bennington burns (Hume, 1956), in which dextran was liberally used.

Schlegel (personal communication) has produced copious urine volumes in burned patients by the administration of urea. In an antidiuretic phase, profuse osmotic diuresis can be produced by any such means, using urea, glucose, mannitol, dextran, or concentrated salt. Such treatment may have some beneficial effect, particularly in the prophylaxis against post-traumatic renal insufficiency and in the avoidance of water overloading. If plasma and blood volumes are reduced, however, and glomerular filtration is low because of diffuse renal vasoconstriction, volume restoration is still urgently needed. Schlegel's idea is a stimulating one to the burn therapist, who welcomes large amounts of renal output with pleasure; more experience is needed before assigning a place to this new addition to the treatment shelf. The patient is producing large amounts of urea from his own muscle—up to 40 gm. a day.

Early fluid therapy, blood-volume changes, and the guides to progress in the first few days have been described and analyzed by Harkins and Long (1945), Evans and Bigger (1945), Fox and Keston (1945), Cope and Moore (1947), Fox and Baer (1947), Moyer (1949), Salzberg and Evans (1950), Evans et al. (1952), Quinby and Cope (1952), Reiss et al. (1953), Hardy et al. (1953), Bluemle et al. (1953), Fogelman and Wilson (1954, 1955), Haynes et al. (1955), Hardy et al. (1955, a, b, c), King et al. (1956), and Markley et al. (1956).

Metabolic changes, protein and nitrogen alterations after burns may be found in Abbott et al. (1945), Levenson et al. (1946), Prendergast et al. (1952), Blocker et al. (1954, 1955), Reiss et al. (1956), and Blocker et al. (1957).

The role of exudate losses was documented by Moore et al. (1950) on the basis of the analysis of dressing eluates.

E. MORTALITY

Barnes (1957) has reviewed the mortality rates of the burned patients admitted to the Massachusetts General Hospital over a fifteen-year period, 1939–1954. There were 785 cases available for analysis. The statistical analysis yields a series of "mortality contours," by which, on the basis of this experience, mortality could be predicted within certain confidence limits. The interdependence of age and burn-area is again pointed up: the older a person is the less burn it takes to kill him. If under twenty he is also more vulnerable, this effect progressing steeply down to childhood. By these approximations, for example, a "50 per cent mortality burn" at the age of twenty is 60 per cent of surface area, at the age of seventy it is only a 30 per cent surface burn, and at the age of ten, it is a 37 per cent burn.

Such a study anchors current experience solidly for future reference; it is interesting that there was no statistically significant improvement in the crude mortalities over the fifteen-year period though there did appear to be a trend ($p > 0.05$). The time of death has been postponed as the early problems have been solved and later problems (especially sepsis) emerge as significant.

Bull and Squire (1949, 1954) and Moyer (1953) also reported on burn mortality, allow-ing in their analyses for the age of the patient as well as the extent of burn.

Clinical reviews of burn therapy are to be found in Wilson *et al.* (1938), Lund and Browder (1944), Colebrook *et al.* (1944), Bettman (1946), Wallace (1951), Artz *et al.* (1953), Artz and Soroff (1955), Hitchcock and Horowitz (1957), and Griswold (1957).

Special problems in burned children have been reviewed by Adams *et al.* (1951), Becker and Artz (1956), and Allen and Day (1956).

The mass therapy of burns has been reviewed by Wakeley (1941), Jackson (1953), Enyart and Miller (1955), and Schenk *et al.* (1955).

The combined radiologic and thermal injury has been studied by Evans (1951), Brooks *et al.* (1952), Pearse and Kingsley (1954), Reid *et al.* (1955), and Davis *et al.* (1955).

CASE 31

In Which a Burn Appears to Require Urgent Respiratory Measures — and Responds Well to Simple Ones

Case 31. Patient J. M., #3L22. Male. Age 74. Admitted May 15, 1957. Discharged July 7, 1957.

DIAGNOSIS. Second and third degree burns of hands, shoulders, and forehead.

OPERATIONS. Debridement and grafting of burns.

CLINICAL SUMMARY. This patient was referred to the hospital from his own community hospital forty-four hours after receiving burns of the hands, face, and neck.

The patient had been found unconscious in a burning building. The fire had evidently started in a kitchen and the patient had tried to put it out with pails of water. The patient, rather senile for his age, was a retired Portuguese fisherman who had a fusion of the right hip producing some limp and making it difficult for him to get around. He had been overcome by smoke inhalation and received the burns either at the time that he became unconscious or shortly thereafter. He remembered little other than the start of the fire.

On admission to the hospital near his home he was diagnosed as having first, second, and third degree burns of the head, neck, shoulders, and both upper extremities. The burns were most marked over the face, the scalp, the back of the neck, the ears, the shoulders, the forearms, and hands. Large sheets of skin were hanging loose, denuded as the result of large blisters. On admission the patient was taken to the operating room and without anesthesia the denuded areas were gently debrided and a thick layer of baci-tracin ointment gauze was applied to the burns. It was estimated that his total burn was 20 per cent of body surface.

During the first twenty-four hours he received 6500 ml. of parenteral fluids including 5000 ml. of glucose solution with 25 gm. of albumin, and 1500 ml. of glucose in saline. He vomited once. He had urine output of 900 mm. His hematocrit (44 on admission) rose to 50 and remained there throughout the day.

On his second day his condition deteriorated seriously. The patient was hoarse and could not breath well. Respirations were crowing and obstructive. The possibility of tracheotomy was considered. There was no burn of the oropharynx but the larynx and vocal cords had not been visualized directly. The urine became dark reddish brown and the volume output steadily declined. The patient vomited every time he was given anything by mouth but he maintained his blood pressure well at 100/70 with a pulse of 100 and good quality. During the second twenty-four hours he received 2000 ml. of 5 per cent glucose in water, 250 ml. of 5 per cent glucose in saline with 6 gm. of albumin. Arrangements were made for transfer. He was loaded into an ambulance with an infusion of dextran in place, and started his trip to town.

ARGUMENT. This patient's management thus far has been energetic and effective. He has received an amount of fluid therapy (9000 ml. total) that might be regarded as slightly enthusiastic for an elderly man with burns of only 20 per cent of body surface. One might also raise the point that this fluid was very short on colloid and long on noncolloid-containing fluids; such a supposition would be supprted by the fact that under this treatment his hematocrit rose from 44 to 50.

None of these points would be of great moment, however, were it not for the pulmonary component. The patient has maintained his blood pressure well. His urine volume, while on the decline at the time of his transfer, has been reasonably good. His burns had been treated with a closed dressing and at the time of transfer the face and neck burns were tightly wrapped with a heavy dressing.

Tracheotomy has been considered but has been withheld pending further evaluation after transfer. The awareness on the part of his own doctors of his need for additional colloid (and less noncolloid fluid) is evidenced by the start of the dextran at the time he was put into the ambulance. It now remains to be seen how he gets along on a fifty mile ambulance trip and what his condition is on arrival.

FURTHER COURSE. During the ride in the ambulance an additional 500 mm. of dextran was given with an increase in urine output (an inlying catheter had previously been placed) to a level of 20 to 30 ml. By telephone call it was learned that his hematocrit at the time he left his home hospital had risen further to 55.

On admission he was found to have a blood pressure of 150/90, temperature 98.8° F., pulse 96, and respirations 26 to 36. He had a very large, tight, occlusive facial dressing with elastic dressings over both shoulders and hands. His inspiration was hoarse and labored with crowing sounds. His mouth and throat were edematous; the pharyngeal mucosa was inflamed. There was no exudate in the pharynx. His eyes were swollen shut and he appeared unresponsive.

Examination of the lungs showed increased AP diameter, suggesting some preexistent emphysema. There were coarse rhonchi and whistling sounds over both lung fields with a retraction at the lower costal margin. There was an occasional productive cough which did not successfuly clear the sounds.

The patient's family spoke English poorly and it was impossible to determine whether or not he had suffered asthma previously.

He had a venous cutdown in the saphenous. There was limitation of the motion of the hip on the left. He was rapidly given an additional infusion of dextran totaling 500 ml. because of the recent evidence of a rising hematocrit.

The patient's lips became somewhat more cyanotic within a few minutes after admission and even before the new dextran infusion. Preparations were made for a tracheotomy.

ARGUMENT. Here is a situation in which tracheotomy would seem essential. The patient has hoarse crowing respirations. He may have had some previous pulmonary disease. He has a smoke-inhalation type of pulmonary injury. Large amounts of fluid have been given and may possibly have some association with his wet lungs. Despite this, his hematocrit is rising and he

has recently been oliguric. One is on the horns of a familiar dilemma—he needs more fluid to maintain blood volume but he already has wet lungs. Such a dilemma is best solved by giving fluids that will give the maximum volume expansion per unit infusion (that is, colloids or blood) and by doing a tracheotomy.

Before doing a tracheotomy, however, one should consider the fact that it is already almost forty-eight hours after his burn, that he has very tight dressings on his face and neck, that he is probably past the maximum period of accumulation of subcutaneous edema, and he is also past the period when one may expect the maximum upper respiratory burn component. The lower respiratory or pulmonary component, however, may not reach its maximum until from seventy-two to ninety-six hours.

Also in considering a tracheotomy one again must be reminded of its deficits, chiefly those of loss of speech (of less importance here in a man who doesn't speak English anyway), loss of cough effort, and the insertion of a new and potentially septic wound.

FURTHER COURSE. Bearing these things in mind, the patient's fluid therapy was maintained using largely colloid. All his dressings were taken off and he was put quietly in bed in a sitting position and moved to the Fog Room where he would be exposed to 100 per cent humidity.

These things were done with the concept of planned and timed trial. If in the course of one or two hours there was not material respiratory improvement, tracheotomy would be done forthwith.

His course, however, was most gratifying and quite spectacular.

Upon removal of the tight and restrictive bandages the patient could look around, open his mouth, move his head into a more comfortable position, move his arms, and open his eyes somewhat. He seemed to arouse from a semicomatose state.

With improved position of his head his respiratory effort was more rewarding in terms of air moved in and out of his mouth and nose.

In the Fog Room he was exposed to supersaturated air at 78° F. Improvement was marked. The stridor and retraction soon subsided and the patient breathed more easily. His color returned to normal without oxygen therapy. The tenacious mucus became thin and watery and was readily coughed up and expelled. No tracheal suction or oxygen therapy was given at any time.

After twenty-four hours in the Fog Room the saturation was reduced to the range of 70 to 90 per cent at 78° F.

His course was febrile through his first few days, with fever running as high as 101° F. even during the period that his chest was clearing. Open treatment of the burns in a Fog Room of course made it impossible to give the burns the sort of drying one might wish. Nonetheless it was felt that the humidification was much more important for the pulmonary tract than any deficit in terms of skin surface burns.

By the third day at the hospital the patient's temperature was settling down, he was beginning to eat well, and he was taken out of the Fog Room.

Review of his biochemical and metabolic situation at this time showed that his hematocrit had been brought down from an admission reading of 51 to a value of 42.5, where it remained. An initial severe leucocytosis as high as 25,000 had returned to 9,900. A slight elevation of blood urea nitrogen at 25 mg. per 100 ml., accompanied by hyponatremia (120 mE. per l.) and some acidosis (carbon dioxide combining power of 18.4 mE. per 1.), had returned to essentially normal values by his sixth day in the hospital.

The burned areas of skin had not made as much progress as one might have expected had he not required the high-humidity atmosphere. They were moist and covered with some liquid exudate. On removing the patient from the Fog Room they were allowed to dry out for a few days and then, when it was observed that there was too much crust accumulation, he was started on soaks.

After three days of soaks the areas on the dorsum of each hand were gently debrided, some sharp excision was done, and split-thickness grafts were placed on these areas, taken from the thigh.

The face burns showed the typical evolutionary sequence, appearing rather forbidding in the edematous phase, then going on to crusting, gradual desiccation of outer layers, and finally complete healing without grafting as the skin of the face, richly supplied with blood, healed its deep partial-thickness injury.

One additional minor operative procedure was required to cover some residual areas over the shoulders and the back of the scalp.

The patient was then discharged home seven weeks after his burn with all areas well healed and with good range of motion of his hands. There was some cicatricial disfiguration over the shoulders. The chest X-ray, initially showing evidence of emphysema, showed no residual peribronchial infiltrate at the time of discharge. Cultural study of the sputum at the time of admission had yielded *Staphylococcus aureus* and *E. coli*.

SUMMARY. This patient exemplifies an elderly man with preexisting pulmonary disease in the form of emphysema. A severe smoke-inhalation injury produced marked respiratory symptoms that were well controlled by a high-humidity atmosphere. Had this not been successful, tracheotomy would have been carried out without further delay.

The effect of the high-humidity atmosphere in this pulmonary burn injury was that of liquefaction of secretion, increased efficiency of cough, and improved alveolar ventilation.

The tight restricting bandages which the patient had on the face and neck were also a component in his respiratory distress on admission.

The skin burns were little problem. Their treatment was somewhat delayed by the pressing urgency of the pulmonary component but they ultimately responded to sharp debridement with small areas of grafting.

CASE 32

A Fifteen-Year-Old Boy with a 47 Per Cent Burn Provides an Example of Many Classic Features of Burn Metabolism and Care, But He Gives Us Some Bad Moments toward the End of His Stay

Case 32. Patient P. B., #5G524. Male. Age 15. Admitted February 23, 1954. Discharged May 22, 1954.

DIAGNOSIS. Second- and third-degree burns.

OPERATIONS. Multiple skin grafts.

CLINICAL SUMMARY. This fifteen-year-old boy was burned at his home when he was cleaning and adjusting a portable pressure gasoline stove that exploded. He was admitted to his community hospital where he was treated by the infusion of 1300 ml. of plasma, 500 ml. of whole blood, 2500 ml. of saline solution, 2000 ml. of 5 per cent dextrose in water, and 1000 ml. of mixed oral fluids. An indwelling catheter was placed. During this time his urine output was 603 ml.; he vomited 300 ml. He was given 1,000,000 units of aqueous penicillin intramuscularly, and tetanus toxoid. A dressing was applied. Approximately sixteen hours after the burn, his hematocrit had risen to 62. He was becoming increasingly drowsy and he was transferred to the Brigham Hospital.

On admission his blood pressure was 138/70, his temperature 103.6° F., and his pulse 130 with respirations of 28. He looked very toxic and much closer to a

state of shock than would have been evident from his blood pressure alone.

His burns were mixed second and third degree, involving the forehead and face, with some on the back of the neck; there was deep burn over the left shoulder, back, arm, and lateral side of trunk. The left leg was circumferentially burned with the deepest burns on the dorsum. There were also scattered third-degree areas over the right knee, the right ankle, and the dorsum of the right hand. It was estimated that 47 per cent of his body was burned, largely third-degree.

The eyelids were edematous but could be opened. The hairs of the nose were burned anteriorly but the mucous membrane of the interior of the nose, the back of the tongue, and the throat were not injured and there was no evidence by physical examination of a burn of the respiratory tract.

INITIAL LABORATORY WORK

Urine
Specific gravity   1.006
Sediment—clear

Hematology
   Hematocrit   62
Blood Chemical Analyses
   Blood urea nitrogen   20   mg. per 100 ml.
   Plasma sodium   128   mE. per l.
   Plasma potassium   4.1 mE. per l.

An indwelling urinary catheter had been placed by the hospital of his first admission and there was a large cannula in the left saphenous vein that was open and functioning well.

ARGUMENT. This patient represents an extensive burn which in a boy of fifteen should be *clearly salvageable if no serious errors are made and if blood-stream infection can be consistently avoided over a period of six to twelve weeks.*

The treatment in his home hospital has been aggressive and effective but despite this the patient now shows evidence of diminished plasma volume, both by hematocrit and physical examination. His urinary output at the hospital of his first admission was good, but has been much smaller in the last two hours. The very low specific gravity is worrisome.

Treatment should be begun on the body-weight burn budget. With a normal weight of 62 kg. it would be estimated that in the first forty-eight hours the patient would need 6200 ml. of plasma (that is, 10 per cent of body weight). In the first twelve hours he should receive half of this or approximately 3100 ml. of plasma, with 1550 ml. in the second twelve hours and 1550 ml. in the second twenty-four hours—a gradually decreasing rate. To this would be added approximately 3000 ml. of saline and 3000 ml. of water in the first forty-eight hours.

Thus, at the end of fifteen to eighteen hours (at the time of his admission to the Brigham) he should have received approximately 3600 ml. of plasma. Actually he had received 1300 ml. of plasma and 500 ml. of whole blood for a total of 1800 ml. of colloid-containing solution. This left him with a theoretical colloid deficit of 1800 ml., a deficit responsible for his increased hematocrit and evidences of blood volume reduction.

The erythrocyte fraction of the whole blood that had been administered, approximately 225 ml., would make a small contribution to his hematocrit, yielding an hematocrit approximately 3 to 5 points higher than it would have been without whole blood administration.

The 5500 ml. of noncolloid-containing solution received at his home hospital had been effective in maintaining body water closer to normal than otherwise would have been the case. There was a slight excess of sodium-free water in this ration (3000 ml. total of sodium-free water and only 2500 of saline). This was responsible for his dilutional hyponatremia of 128 mE. per l.

It was therefore reasoned that his plasma deficit when first seen was in the region of 1500 to 2000 ml. This, plus the estimated needs for the next twelve hours, yielded an initial plasma infusion budget of 3000 ml. to be accomplished within the first eight to twelve hours after admission, reasoning that this infusion should be somewhat faster than normal because

of his age, and because of the fact that he was already quite far behind.

FURTHER COURSE. This procedure was carried out with energy. Twelve hours later (twenty-four hours after burns) his total of plasma administration had reached approximately 4650 ml. and his hematorcit had dropped to 39. His clinical appearance improved markedly and his pulse fell. During this time his urine output picked up and was maintained at a normal to high value with one or two readings as high as 185 ml. per hour. He no longer looked "toxic"; he stated that he felt better, and was hungry.

For this reason, the plasma infusion was reduced in rate and during the third twelve hours following his burn he was given 1000 ml., yielding, together with the noncolloid fluids given at this time, a total of approximately 12,000 ml. of total therapy since his burn. During this time his urine output was well maintained, totaling 2765 ml. In his third twelve hours the hematocrit rose slightly to 47. The patient gained a total of 4.83 kg. during this time.

On the basis of the intake-output discrepancy, it was calculated that an excess of 8580 ml. of fluid of all types had been given over and above output by all routes, including vomitus. But during this time (as mentioned above) he had gained 4.83 kg. This is a typical weight increment with appropriate output discrepancy. It was therefore calculated that his total insensible loss through lungs and skin was 3750 ml. (8580 − 4830), or about 2200 ml. per day. This figure was used as a basis for predicting total insensible loss factors during the next day or two.

Starting at the beginning of his third twenty-four hours in the hospital, therapy was sharply cut back because his weight gain had stabilized at approximately 67 kg. (a gain of about 5 kg.), his hematocrit was stable at 45, and it was felt that the period of edema expansion was over.

Physical examination at this time showed a patient whose fever was somewhat lower than on admission (101° F.). His pulse was much slower, between 90 and 110. The patient's face and burned areas were very edematous but he was reasonably comfortable, breathing well, talking well, eating a good deal, and not in severe pain.

Between forty-eight and sixty hours the patient was given no additional plasma and a total of 2700 ml. of oral and intravenous fluids containing only a small amount of saline. The patient gained some small additional amount of weight (1.64 kg.) and the calculation of total insensible losses showed a marked reduction.

Twenty-four hours later the patient's diuresis became clearly established when, in that twenty-four-hour period, he put out 2345 ml. of urine in the face of only 4390 ml. intake. This is a good example of the "output fraction" as evidence of diuresis. During his first two days in the hospital, with approximately 12 l. of therapy, he put out 2765 ml. of urine, an output fraction of approximately 25 per cent. Likewise, during this period, he gained approximately 5 kg. By contrast, in his fourth twenty-four hours, he put out more than 50 per cent of his intake ration, in the form of urine, and lost 1.5 kg. of weight.

From this time forward, the fluid imbalance presented no additional problems. His weight loss proceeded smoothly and between the 28th of February (his fifth day postburn) and the 9th of March (fourteenth day postburn) the patient lost weight briskly, passing from 67.5 kg. to approximately 59 kg. During this time the plasma sodium concentration rose to 137 mE. per l. and his clinical appearance changed dramatically. The edema departed from his face, he seemed to "wake up." He took an interest in his surroundings and was not in severe pain. His temperature continued to be elevated to between 102 and 104° F. by rectum with a pulse between 90 and 120. During this time he was given three whole blood transfusions and his hematocrit was well maintained between 40 and 43.5. Although his sodium concentration rose with his initial diuresis, it tended to fall off later to the region between 126 and 132 mE. per l. with an appropriate slight elevation of potassium concentration between 4.0 and 4.9 mE. per l.

SURFACE TREATMENT. On admission to the hospital in his home community, his burn therapy had been started with dressings. These dressings were removed and he was maintained on open treatment thereafter. It was possible to keep him in a moderately comfortable position in his bed without lying on dangerous pressure areas.

By the 5th of March (tenth postburn day) his burns were dry and had the appearance of third-degree burned skin with precipitation of the skin protein into a firm blackish eschar but without much exudation or crusting. Over the face there was some evidence of new epithelialization under the yellowish brown crusts of the burn.

Wound cultures were begun and he was changed from penicillin to a broad spectrum antibiotic in preparation for grafting. He was given an additional blood transfusion.

ARGUMENT. The patient is now approaching his fifteenth day postburn. His fever is still elevated to the region of 100 to 102° F. by rectum, slightly lower than it has been previously, but still definitely up. His oral intake is climbing to the region between 2800 and 3600 calories a day, and the patient's diuresis by this time has proceeded downward to a body weight of 60 kg., approximately 2 kg. less than on admission.

Has the time come for his initial procedure in the operating room? Certainly this patient is in the ideal position for early sharp debridement and grafting. If one waits until he is afebrile for such a procedure, the wait will be of indefinite duration. One must accept the fact that operation is to be carried out in the face of a swinging fever and one must also anticipate that immediately after operation the fever will be somewhat higher. Excision and grafting carried out at this time should have every likelihood of good success whereas a further postponement will result in loss of this golden opportunity. It is time to "take the bull by the horns" and start closure. Procrastination or delay here is

responsible more than any other factor for very long hospitalization in burns.

FURTHER COURSE. For this reason, having had a change of antibiotics and an additional blood transfusion, the patient was taken to the operating room and under endotracheal anesthesia, on the fifteenth postburn day, a large operative procedure was done.

This consisted first of using the entire skin circumference of the right thigh for split skin graft donor areas. These grafts were then placed on the left arm and both hands, the right wrist, right knee and right ankle, after sharp debridement of eschar. These critical areas of mobility and potential flexion contracture were covered first. The left arm and a portion of the left leg were placed in a plaster cast to remain in good immobilization. Certain other areas, where the precipitated skin proteins of the eschar had become underlain with purulent material, were opened, gently excised, and left open with a moist dressing.

Following this procedure, the patient's temperature immediately spiked to 103.4° F. and his pulse to 130. But by the next morning his temperature and pulse had returned to the preoperative condition and he continued his diuresis, as mentioned above, his weight falling during the next ten days another 5 to 55.6 kg. This no longer represents fluid diuresis alone, but instead a continued lysis of fat and lean tissue in the face of caloric intakes averaging approximately 2500 calories a day but on some days dropping as low as 700 and on other days approaching 3000.

Exactly five days later the patient was again taken to the operating room and given a general anesthetic. A total of 70 per cent of the grafts on the left arm had taken well but the take was not as high as had been expected or hoped. Grafts taken from donor areas remaining in the left thigh and right calf were now applied to the lower leg and some open areas on the arm. The chest wall burn had not yet been grafted but was further debrided at this time.

His course after this was good. Four days later he had a dressing under anesthesia and on the following day his third skin grafting was carried out. Take of grafts was now excellent. It is of interest that at this time it was felt that 90 per cent of the raw surface was covered with skin and now, only four weeks after his burn, the prospects for early discharge looked good. At this third operation, additional grafts were taken and covered over the remaining areas in postage stamp style. On the 21st of March a progress note in the record stated that no further grafts would be necessary and there was nothing but minor bridging left to be completed. This minor regrafting with small pieces was completed on March 25th, just slightly over a month after the burn.

It was at this time that the patient's surface coverage began to deteriorate. His systemic condition continued to be good, and approximately one month after the burn the patient's temperature was only slightly elevated (around 99 to 100° F. by mouth), though his pulse continued to be elevated. He was beginning to gain strength.

On reviewing his operating room appearances on

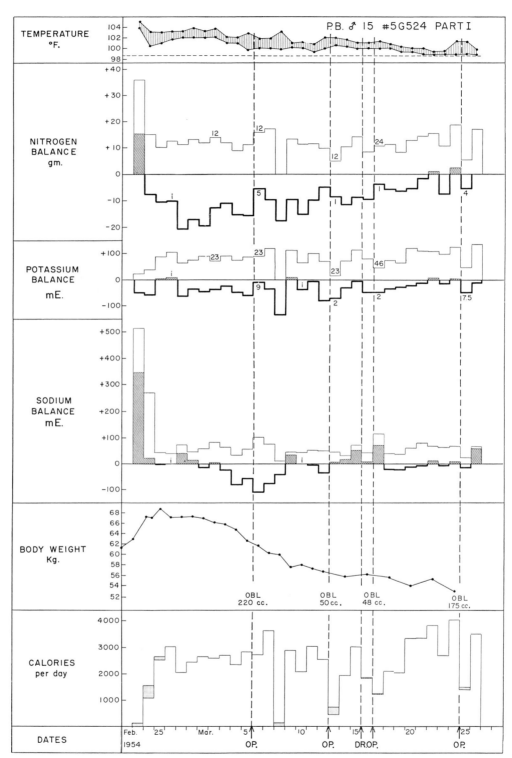

Figure 141. MAJOR BURN. I. (Case 32)
See facing page for detailed legend.

the last two occasions, it became clear that some of the areas of initial take were now melting away. This was particularly noticeable over the sides and back and over the face and forehead. It was also noticed the grafts were not coalescing as they normally would be expected to be. Review of his bacteriology showed that his burns contained a *Staphylococcus aureus*, sensitive to erythromycin and bacitracin.

The patient was eating well, often consuming from 3500 to 4100 calories per day. Weight loss was still proceeding and the patient's weight ultimately fell to 45.6 kg. from his original weight of 62 kg.

ARGUMENT. This patient shows a change not infrequently seen. He has withstood his first month very well. His period of fluid imbalance, his initial phase of edema demand, satisfaction and diuresis has proceeded uneventfully, and the initial operative steps for closure of the wound have appeared to be successful. Now, without developing blood stream infection, urinary tract infection, pulmonary infection, or any of the other hazards of the course, he simply seems to have ceased an active healing process on the surface. Although the signs of invasive sepsis are not present in the burn, recently placed grafts are melting away, and others do not seem to be coalescing. On one or two occasions, merely in the course of twenty-four hours, areas on the forehead as large as a postage stamp that had previously been covered became open granulating surfaces which were exquisitely painful in contrast to his previously moderately comfortable status.

Such a process may be metabolic in origin, but it does not seem likely here. The patient is young and resilient. If intake of food is any factor in such a patient, we have an individual who is cooperatively taking a caloric intake running as high as 3000 to 4100 calories a day with a good mixed intake of minerals and vitamins. Although one might claim that this intake should be nearer 6000 calories a day, such an objective is rarely attained.

It therefore seemed wisest to proceed on the concept that the process on the surface was bacterial in nature and that the biologic priority of the wound was falling from its former high position.

FURTHER COURSE. All antibiotics were therefore stopped for ten days and at the end of this time the patient was started on large doses of a new antibiotic to which his organisms were sensitive, namely, erythro-mycin, and with this a course of adrenocorticotropic hormone.

His response to this combination was most gratifying. One should hesitate to assign a good result in such a complex disease as a burn, to any one combination of therapies. All one can say in reviewing a single case such as this is that a very recalcitrant burn surface, upon which grafts were melting away and others failing to grow or coalesce, became a drier surface on which every evidence of healing rapidly became manifest. Grafts no longer disappeared. Other grafts began to coalesce, and the patient's situation improved markedly. The effect of the adrenocorticotropic hormone on his appetite and food intake was not particularly noticeable. He was given alkali therapy to avoid the complication of a duodenal ulcer and four days after beginning his new antibiotic and adrenocorticotropic hormone he was again taken to the operating room, given 1000 ml. of whole blood and another extensive grafting procedure was undertaken. Following this the patient was given daily dressings on the ward, many of the dressing areas were left open and five days later another operative procedure showed that the new grafts had taken solidly, that there were many areas of new epithelization, and that the burned surface had a much healthier appearance.

From this time forward, the patient's course was gratifying. He soon was sufficiently healed to go to the tub for underwater exercise, flexion of joints, and gentle washing of macerated areas. His last operative procedure was carried out on the 6th of May, at which time a few small residual areas were covered with skin.

Adrenocorticotropic hormone and antibiotics were presently stopped, the patient increased his mobilization and finally was able to leave the hospital on May 22, approximately three months after his burn. At the time of his departure, the patient's weight had returned to 60 kg. In fact, the gain had been steady from the time that the new antibiotic and adrenocorticotropic hormone were started.

METABOLISM. Metabolic and endocrine studies on this patient are shown in Figures 141 and 142. These demonstrate the massive nitrogen loss, the early gain in weight followed by loss of diuresis. Later metabolic changes of anabolism are not shown. The patient passed into a prolonged positive nitrogen balance which was not affected one way or another by the administration

Figure 141. MAJOR BURN. I. (CASE 32)

In this chart are shown the nitrogen, potassium, and sodium balances, body weight, and caloric intake of a boy age 15 with a burn approximating 40 per cent of his body surface (Case 32). Detailed interpretation will not be entered here. This chart shows clearly the extent of the nitrogen loss, the early positive balance of nitrogen and sodium with plasma and electrolyte therapy, the postburn diuresis of sodium, and the characteristic early weight gain of the treated burn.

The figures above and below the metabolic columns indicate the nitrogen and potassium content of red cells either infused or lost. The operative blood loss (OBL) is shown in conjunction with each operative procedure (OP.) and dressing (DR.).

The metabolic findings in this young man are typical of the extensive but salvageable burn in the young male, as described in the text.

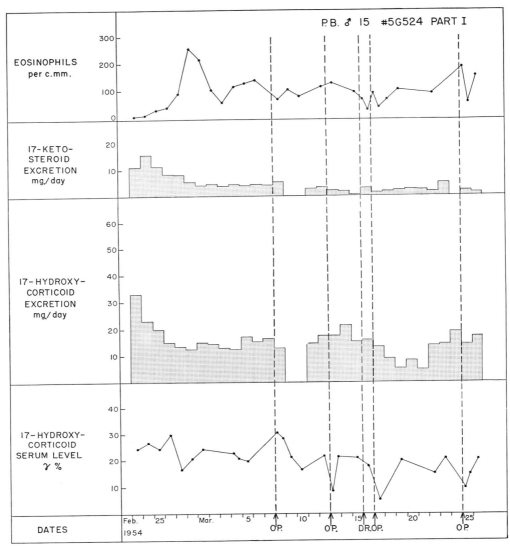

Figure 142.   MAJOR BURN. II. (CASE 32)

Endocrine events in the patient (Case 32) whose metabolism is shown in Figure 141.

It will be noted that the eosinophils are depressed for only a short time, their return upward being a good prognostic sign. The urinary and blood corticosteroid values are somewhat elevated over a period of several weeks and do not show the sharply pointed configuration characteristic of elective soft-tissue trauma.

of adrenocorticotropic hormone, but which became more manifest as his wounds closed. It is of interest that he came into positive nitrogen balance early and before his wounds were all closed; he was starting up into positive nitrogen balance at the time that his wound surface appeared to be most recalcitrant.

The favorable effect of adrenocorticotropic hormone seemed clinically clear but is unproven. It is of interest in this regard that the patient showed no evidences whatsoever of adrenal insufficiency and that, when given test doses of adrenocorticotropic hormone at a later time, he showed a tremendous adrenal response, suggesting that the prolonged septic burn had produced considerable adrenal hypertrophy. This is characteristically the case after prolonged surgical illness.

COMMENT.   In summary, this is a young man with a burn with a very favorable prognosis. His initial operative procedure took place at fifteen days after the burn, an ideal time. Early progress was excellent, and by a month after the burn we felt confident that he would be leaving the hospital in another couple of weeks. At that time, however, deterioration began which was surface in character. It was not associated with any clearly defined metabolic or systemic disturbance and appeared to be bacteriologic in origin. We believe it is significant that this deterioration of the surface occurred at a time when the patient was coming into positive nitrogen balance.

The complete cessation of antibiotics for ten days followed by the recommencement of an antibiotic to which his organism was shown to be sensitive, and the administration of adrenocorticotropic hormone, together proved very effective in giving him coverage. Of these two steps, the antibiotic was clearly the more important.

His dietary intake was at a high level, starting at about his sixth postburn day and never faltering for more than one day thereafter, and often reached levels of 4000 to 4500 calories. Despite this fact, the patient lost a total of 17 kg. (approximately 25 per cent of his body weight). By the time of discharge, anabolic weight gain had replaced much of this loss.

In retrospect, it is hard to know what might have resulted in his leaving the hospital sooner than ninety

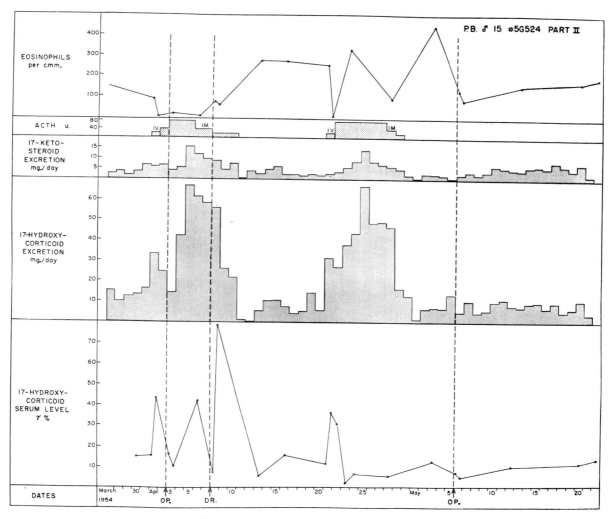

Figure 143. MAJOR BURN. III. (CASE 32)

Here are shown the results of the administration of ACTH late in the course of Case 32. The hormone was given because of lack of skin and graft healing. The clinical results appeared to be good. Here it is seen that the outpouring of corticosteroid in the urine was very great on each of two courses of ACTH. Far from being "exhausted" adrenals, these are very responsive indeed, and possibly hypertrophied.

On the second course of ACTH the blood steroid change is small, suggesting facilitated disposal of the hormone. The very minimal response in 17-ketosteroid excretion is characteristic of chronic illness.

days. A more aggressive program of changing antibiotics between the second and fourth weeks might have been successful in this regard. The patient never developed a blood-stream infection clinically nor were bacteria ever demonstrated on blood culture.

His labor rehabilitation required approximately eight months during which time the leg burns were fragile and often cyanotic, occasionally breaking with minor trauma. They finally thickened up, and, when seen a year later, the patient's skin was mobile, he had no serious flexion contractures, but showed some unsightly scarred areas over the face, arms, and legs.

CHAPTER 48

Atomic Injury

Atomic injury involves three injurious agents: heat, blast, and irradiation.

The *heat input* produces severe thermal injury at the level of 30 calories per square meter per second. This is the level at which clothing burns as a flash burn.

Blast produces severe injury at levels of 10 pounds per square inch (abbreviated "psi"). This is a level of blast pressure that will collapse a flimsy wooden house structure.

Radiation injury may be considered to be severe at levels that deliver from 300 to 800 roentgens to an adult subject. The universal lethal dose (LD_{100}) in man is probably between 600 r and 800 r, delivered in a fraction of a second as a single dose.

Injury perimeters delivering heat, blast, or irradiation at these levels vary in their distance from the center of explosion of an atomic weapon according to the nature of the weapon itself. The size of the ground rings in which injury will be sustained depends also on the geographical location of the blast, chiefly its height above ground.

Near the center of an atomic explosion, all forms of life are immediately destroyed, incinerated, and translated large distances. Far out in the periphery, or with suitable shielding, immediate injury is minimal. Between these two, all ranges of injury may be observed. According to certain test data, it will be unlikely to see significant surgical injury without severe irradiation damage. Significant surgical injury due to direct blast or falling building structures may be observed to occur, however, without much burn. Direct burn will be very unlikely without severe irradiation. But indirect burn, from burning structures, may of course occur under any circumstance.

Protection from direct radiation from an atomic explosion can be achieved by a variety of techniques, including the foxhole, the small shelter, the building cellar, the dugout, et cetera. It is of interest that many inches of steel will not protect against immediately lethal gamma radiation levels near the center of explosion, even though protection against both blast and heat is achieved.

A. PHYSICAL DATA

After an atomic explosion of the now-familiar type, a cloud is lifted above the troposphere to the stratosphere at 35,000 to 40,000 feet. As this cloud ascends, a large amount of radioactivity falls out to the ground nearby. This is the prompt fall-out. In the case of a kiloton or fission weapon, this fall-out is active because of fission products within it, as well as induced radioactivity. In the megaton or fusion weapon, it is largely induced activity.

It is this prompt fall-out that makes areas dangerous for entry, or for the emergence of individuals from protection such as dugouts and cellars. The area of prompt fall-out may be restricted according to the nature of the blast.

Delayed fall-out is that atmospheric component which comes down by the force of gravity at a later time, often in conjunction with atmospheric moisture; whereas the area of prompt fall-out may be measured in yards or miles, the area of delayed fall-out may of course be measured in terms of hundreds of miles or may even be worldwide.

The dangerous irradiation from fall-out is mostly due to the radioactive isotopes of iodine, cesium, strontium, and cerium. All of these isotopes are gamma emitters except strontium-90. They tend to move together geologically, however, so that the detection of fall-out by gamma-sensitive instruments is possible. Strontium is probably the most dangerous of these, once ingested into the body, because of its affinity for bone matrix.

The I^{131} activity is found nearby; with thyroid localization and a half-life of eight days the material could be a serious problem if present in large amounts.

The Cs^{137} activity is in a sense a potassium tracer. The half-life is twenty-eight years and the localization in the body is very widespread.

The Sr^{90} activity constitutes up to $3\frac{1}{2}$ per cent of the yield of certain weapons, has a half-life of twenty-five years, and localizes in bone.

In the case of all three isotopes, the immediate or survival effect is a product of time and dose plus localization. Delayed effects in the sense of late carcinogenesis, cataracts, or genetic modification are less well understood.

From prompt fall-out, activities may range near 500 r per hour for appreciable periods of time. This is near the LD_{50} for man.

Estimates regarding ambient activity and whole body exposure follow.

The safe dose for "lifetime" exposure is about 0.1 r per day, or 0.5 r per week. At the present time urban life involves an over-all dose of 0.3 r per year. The former or "pure" radiation background used to be about 4.3 to 5.5 r in thirty years. Present fall-out adds 0.02 to 0.5 r in thirty years.

In the case of an underwater burst in salt water, the high capture cross-section of sodium would yield very high intensities of Na^{24} in the splash areas, both wet and after drying.

The data from Japan showed that, near the airburst, gamma rays and neutrons did most of the damage. Beyond 2000 meters,

X-rays and gamma rays in the range of 1.5 to 2.0 m.e.v. predominated. The median lethal dose of this radiation given instantaneously was 400 ± 100 r. The body size is one critical factor here as shown by the following (Hempelman, personal communication).

SPECIES	MLD
Virus	10^6 r
Cockroach	10^6 r
Guinea pig	200 to 300 r
Mice	700 r
Rats	900 r
Man	400 ± 100 r

Death in the lower ranges of irradiation is slow and hematopenic; in the higher ranges of dose it is fast and neurologic in nature.

The larger the period over which irradiation is absorbed by the living organism, the larger is the dose required for a given biologic effect, be it local tissue destruction or lethal whole-body irradiation.

Evans *et al.* (1955) studied cutaneous injury in relation to caloric input in the range of 3.2 to 4.8 calories per square centimeter, this representing a range expectable from A-bomb flash under certain circumstances and at distances of 7000 to 9000 feet from the explosion. At the closer range, partial-thickness burns were produced, whereas over 4.8 calories per square centimeter a full-thickness burn was produced in about 50 per cent of instances. At 2.0 calories per square centimeter a small first-degree injury was obtained. The burns were produced in a duration of about 0.54 second. The same energy delivered over a longer time was less injurious. The authors estimated that 70 per cent of the total thermal dose from a 20 kiloton bomb will be effective in producing burns; larger bombs may release thermal energy more slowly and be slightly less effective in producing cutaneous injury per unit of energy release.

B. BIOLOGIC AND CLINICAL DATA

The best method for studying numbers of casualties for extent of ingestion of prompt or delayed fall-out material probably consists in using the whole-body counter or in studying the urinary excretion of total activity, or of separate isotopes, separating them by pulse-height analysis.

From certain of the larger weapons of the so-called "megaton" variety, the thermal and blast effects will probably produce more biologic damage than will irradiation effects, whereas for the smaller weapons, the reverse may be the case.

Metabolic balance studies on total body irradiation have shown (Levenson, personal communication) that the changes are very similar to those seen after surgical injury. There is an increase in the extracellular component at the expense of intracellular mass. This manifests itself by increased urinary nitrogen excretion, loss of nitrogen and potassium, a tendency to retain sodium, and so on. An increase in taurine excretion may be seen just as in battle casualties (Levenson). These metabolic changes may not be so great as to produce large changes in weight. On the basis of present knowledge, they are of comparatively little significance.

McDonald *et al.* (1955) have studied the changes in body composition and tissue electrolytes in dogs subjected to whole-body irradiation. Their articles also include a review of previous knowledge on this little-studied subject. The radiation dose was in the neighborhood of 450 to 550 r, using a 250 kv. X-ray machine. In contrast to Levenson, they found no evidence of gross changes in body composition; there was weight loss and water loss with both intracellular and extracellular phases contributing. Anorexia was prominent, and most of the changes seen were readily accountable on the basis of low intake, vomiting, and diarrhea. The most marked changes in tissue composition were seen in the lymph nodes, which showed cell lysis with inflow of extracellular fluid. In these dogs a hemorrhagic syndrome, fatal in three weeks, was usually produced.

Data on metabolic effects of irradiation in various animals may be found in Bennet *et al.* (1949), Bowers and Scott (1951), Edelman (1949), Furth *et al.* (1951), Goldman (1943), Pohle *et al.* (1930), Soberman (1951), Sprunt (1931), and Swift *et al.* (1948).

Wound healing appears to be a biological parameter that is not easily or readily affected by irradiation. Radakovitch (1954) (working with rats), Raventos (1954) (with mice), and Levenson *et al.* (1958) have studied wound healing following irradiation. They find that there is only a narrow band of time within which a ready effect can be demonstrated on the tensile healing or histologic healing of skin wounds in laboratory rodents; in most cases the wound was made after the irradiation. Normal collagen formation comes quite late in the process of tensile healing and does not seem to be significantly altered by irradiation.

The most significant changes after whole-body irradiation may be considered as involving the central nervous system, the gastrointestinal tract, and the blood-forming organs. Immediately after large doses of whole-body irradiation, the central nervous system is involved, probably by small hemorrhages. The result is altered consciousness with convulsions. This is invariably followed by death. Central-nervous-system manifestations may be seen as late as fourteen days after irradiation. Here they may again be due to delayed hemorrhage or infection.

The effects on the gastrointestinal tract also appear early, if they are severe. Early vomiting and bloody diarrhea are almost invariably followed by death. A period of gastrointestinal dysfunction between the eighth and fourteenth days is a manifestation of irradiation damage to the whole body in the range that is probably survivable, using such methods as bone-marrow transfusion.

The effects on the blood-forming organs become manifest early. There is a rapid fall in leucocyte count that may be judged by the so-called rapid or "pinhead" count (Crosby *et al.*, personal communication). This rapid fall in leucocyte count is later followed by a drop in reticulocyte activity and the number of platelets. The result is a severe hemorrhagic state and one in which the patient is extremely vulnerable to sepsis.

The lower the dose of irradiation the longer is the "lag" period before ominous symptoms become evident. In the normal course of events, after whole-body irradiation that is not immediately fatal, death results from infection or from hemorrhage, or both.

Treatment is largely supportive, in the sense of recognizing the injury and supporting the blood volume with blood transfusion. The provision of coagulation elements requires special steps not available in routine blood banks. These include platelet transfusion and a transfusion of very fresh blood. The possibility of giving bone-marrow transfusion to individuals following whole body irradiation opens new vistas in this field, not yet fully explored at the time of this writing.

The geographical and geometric combinations are such that one will only rarely see survival after the combination of large wound or burn with high radiation dosage acutely. In the "close-in" situation the radiation injury predominates so severely as to make treatment almost totally ineffectual by current methods. In the "far-out" or "fall-out" situation the wound or burn is apt to be of secondary origin and the radiation either no problem or a chronic one with delayed hematologic effects.

Changing radiation patterns of nuclear weapons may make such conclusions invalid; experience has been small. Research and clinical preparedness must therefore continue to be focused on the combined lesion.

The army technical bulletin (TB Med. 246, Dept. of the Army, 12 Oct., 1955) describes the early treatment of mass casualties in nuclear warfare.

In this bulletin (TB Med. 246) the triage precedent is clearly outlined whereby the very severely injured will receive "expectant" (that is, no) treatment. It is estimated that these will comprise no more than 20 per cent of the casualties. The cut-off point for this group seems low (for example, burns of 40 per cent of body surface or greater), but the general principle is sound in terms of the greatest good for the greatest number.

Low-velocity debris (1000 ft. per second or less) will produce much injury in dwelling areas under such circumstances, with an expected over-all wound distribution as follows:

Head–face–neck — 12 per cent
Thorax   15 "   "
Abdomen   14 "   "
Upper extremities   22 "   "
Lower extremities   37 "   "

Early severe radiation may constitute the most hopeless of the extensive or "expectant" group, at least by present standards of treatment. Therefore, the isolation and identification of these becomes very important. The "pinhead white count" is a real contribution here because it permits early definition of severe radiobiologic damage to the hematologic system. In general, the earlier the gastrointestinal and neurologic manifestations of radiation appear, the more severe is the prognosis.

CHAPTER 49

Closing

Looking back over the area of knowledge represented by this entire work a few things stand out as common denominators and as central themes running through the book, sometimes unsaid, often implied, frequently mentioned and always inadequately expressed.

First and foremost is the fact that the responsibility of the surgeon extends into all areas of human biology so as to provide the wise and effective care which is ever the trademark of good surgery. Although many of the data expressed in this book may appear coldly scientific, their application at the bedside is one of the most warm and human aspects of surgical care. The surgical patient in severe or threatening illness who is well cared for by the use of this knowledge and these skills is a patient who rests comfortable and confident in the hands of a competent surgeon. When the act of operation is followed by inadequate thought, ignorant fumbling measures, or a diffusion of responsibility into many hands through default by the surgeon, then metabolic care is ineffective, survival is threatened, and the quality of mercy is lacking.

A second recurring concept is the unity of surgical care. The surgical operation itself is usually the most important single metabolic step in the patient's care. This fact is demonstrated to some extent in elective, clean, soft-tissue civilian surgery, but it is very marked in relation to the care of such emergencies as intestinal obstruction or perforated ulcer. The unity of surgical care and the metabolic significance of the operation itself are perhaps nowhere more clearly seen than in the definitive operative care of unanesthetized accidental trauma, war wounds, or burns. In all these instances the very performance of the operation itself permits the cessation of a series of metabolic processes that impede convalescence. Far from initiating deterioration, the operation itself permits convalescence to ensue. An understanding of the metabolic significance of the operation itself in such cases is one of the most important contributions that metabolic care can make to the practice of surgery.

A third recurring concept is that expressed in the section on burns, namely, that the growth of knowledge simplifies as it progresses. Although there are many areas of thought mentioned in this book that are not ordinarily found in textbooks of surgery, they represent an attempted clarification of vague and ill-defined data. Much that is now still confusing, irrelevant, or impractical will in the future become clear as better insight is developed. The growth of knowledge permits the understanding of many confusing peripheral phenomena in terms of simple central mechanisms. As Bronowski has emphasized, the essence of the scientific process, as is also true of the artistic process, consists in finding unity in the variety of nature. Examples of this unity in surgical biology are to be found in the common factors of post-traumatic tissue change and later anabolic convalescence seen in all trauma, the communal similarities of many events of surgical trauma such as dilutional hyponatremia, post-traumatic renal insufficiency, and the sequestered

Page 925

edemas, the response to volume reduction, and the healing of a tissue wound.

Looking to the future, one can but speculate on the basis of the past growth of surgical knowledge. As surgical skill brings elective open tissue dissection to the treatment of new types of human illness, new areas of surgical care will become defined. As biological science brings new methods to bear on these problems, likewise is the scope of surgical metabolism broadened. Examples of these are to be found in cardiac surgery in the last decade and tissue transplantation in the next. In both of these there are many important new areas of surgical metabolism that must be studied, analyzed, tested, experienced, and written down. One would include hypothermia, extracorporeal circulation, and whole body irradiation as recent examples of new environmental settings for the surgical patient that bring in their train specific new areas of metabolism that must be understood. Were this book to be rewritten a decade hence, it would surely include areas of knowledge of practical importance in the daily bedside care of the sick that are not included at present.

Surgery is an effective area of applied biology—the "specialty of getting patients well"—and in much of its research and scientific development it remains close to the patient. As long as the methods of biological science continue to provide for the student such a rich variety of useful concepts and techniques, the surgical investigator is fortunate. He does not need to get very far away from the patient. Someone else is doing that digging groundwork for him. By contrast, in some of the areas of knowledge represented in this book (particularly those relating to endocrinology, water and electrolyte metabolism, and body composition) the surgical investigator has, on his own necessity and initiative, delved far into the groundwork of science leaving the patient far above him, only to return again to the surface as his study was ready to bear clinical fruit.

Appendix and Bibliography

Surgical Diets and Parenteral Supplements

ORAL DIETS

Surgical diets generally are constructed to achieve one of three objectives:

1. The gradual resumption of diet after injury or surgery, accompanied by minimum complications.

2. Maximum nourishment in minimum volume, in a form that is easily absorbed. This is particularly useful in the patient who is not eating very much or who has some gastrointestinal disorder preventing a normal diet.

3. Special purpose diets. These include the diets for use in gastrectomy, in the presence of pancreatectomy, and so on.

Many of these diets are constructed from simple building blocks. These building blocks are shown in the table below.

SURGICAL DIET I. RESUMPTION OF DIET AFTER INJURY OR SURGERY UNACCOMPANIED BY GASTROINTESTINAL COMPLICATIONS

In the simplest kind of injury and after uneventful minor surgery dietary advancement is best left to the discretion of the dietitian and nurse.

ITEM	WT. OR VOLUME	CARBO-HYDRATE gm.	FAT gm.	PROTEIN gm.	NITROGEN gm.	SODIUM mE.	POTASSIUM mE.	CALORIES
1 cup tea	120 cc.	0	0	0	0	0	1	0
1 lump sugar	5 gm.	5	0	0	0	0	0	20
1 glass milk	240 cc.	12	9	8	1	5	9	166
1 cup bouillon; 1 4 gm. cube	120 cc.	0	0.1	0.2	0.03	42	0.1	2
1 glass orange juice	100 cc.	13	0.1	0.6	0.1	0.1	5	55
1 glass tomato juice	100 cc.	4.3	0.2	1	0.16	10	7	55
1 egg	50 gm.	0.4	6	6	1	2	1	80
1 eggnog*	240 cc.	15	14	13	2	2	9	237
1 milkshake*	240 cc.	31	20	11	2	9	10	350
1 cup custard*	100 gm.	21	8	7	1	4	5	183
1 serving vanilla ice cream	100 gm.	22	12	4	0.7	4	2	212
1 slice bread or toast	25 gm.	13	0.5	2	0.3	7	1	65
1 pat butter	5 gm.	0	4	0	0	2	0	37

*Recipe for eggnog:
1 egg   1 tsp. sugar
1 tsp. vanilla   200 cc. milk

*Recipe for milkshake:
100 gm. vanilla   200 cc. milk
  ice cream

*Recipe for custard:
½ egg   1 tbs. sugar
120 cc. milk   1 tsp. vanilla

* This appendix and the data on diets are modified from the Diet Manual of the Peter Bent Brigham Hospital, and the Appendix to Moore and Ball (1952).

When the gastrointestinal tract has been directly involved, the responsibility for dietary advancement must rest upon the physician because it is he that is best equipped to judge the state of the patient's peristaltic activity, the presence or absence of diaphragmatic elevation, abdominal distention, or the passage of flatus.

For these situations—largely those of peritoneal or anastomotic gastrointestinal surgery—we use a four-stage diet as follows:

First Stage

Order: "First stage liquids; water and tea without sugar as tolerated not to exceed _____ ml. an hour while awake."

Given: In an average waking day, fifteen such rations will be given, one-half of which are tea. The hourly ration may be varied.

Values:

	30 cc. an hour		60 cc. an hour		90 cc. an hour	
Fluid	450 ml.		900 ml.		1350 ml.	
Carbohydrate	0		0		0	
Fat	0		0		0	
Protein	0		0		0	
Nitrogen	0		0		0	
Sodium	0		0		0	
Potassium	2.1 mE.		4.2 mE.		6.3 mE.	
Calories	0		0		0	

Second Stage

Order: "Second stage liquids (with milk) as tolerated, not to exceed _____ ml. an hour while awake."

Given: Water, broth, tea with sugar, coffee with sugar, plain Jello, milk, sherbet, cocoa.

Not included are fruit juices, carbonated beverages, and enriched milk drinks. The amount of the hourly ration is varied according to the situation of the patient; if the patient can take 90 ml. an hour of this he should be advanced. Sixteen such are given. Neither of these "diets" (first- or second-stage liquids) is in any sense adequate nutritionally. The patient should remain on them as short a time as possible, moving along as soon as possible. *It is important for the nurse to avoid forcing these hourly rations.* The sick postoperative patient should be offered his ration, and should accept it only if he feels able to.

Values (Calculated on two rations of each food or liquid listed, a total of 16 rations):

	30 cc. an hour		60 cc. an hour		90 cc. an hour	
Fluid	480	ml.	960	ml.	1440	ml.
Carbohydrate	42	gm.	85	gm.	127	gm.
Fat	6	gm.	12	gm.	17	gm.
Protein	7	gm.	14	gm.	22	gm.
Nitrogen	1.3	gm.	2.3	gm.	3.4	gm.
Sodium	43	mE.	86	mE.	129	mE.
Potassium	13	mE.	26	mE.	39	mE.
Calories	250		490		740	

Third Stage

Order: "Third stage liquids as tolerated, not to exceed 2000 ml., with two-hourly feedings of soft solids."

Given: All liquids as allowed on first stage and second stage *plus* strained fruit juice and enriched milk drinks. In addition, feedings every two hours of soft solids are offered.

Not included are carbonated beverages.

The values are calculated on the basis of the following typical schedule:

LIQUIDS

Water	2 glasses	480 ml.*
Milk	2 glasses	480 ml.
Bouillon	1 cup	120 ml.
Tea with 1 lump sugar	1 cup	120 ml.
Coffee with 1 lump sugar	1 cup	120 ml.
Strained orange juice	2 small glasses	200 ml.
Eggnog	1 glass	240 ml.
Strained cream soup	1 cup	120 ml.
Tomato juice	1 small glass	100 ml.
	Total fluid	1980 ml.

* In this and succeeding diets exact amounts are indicated as a basis upon which the calculations could be made. They are a specific but representative example of what a patient takes on such a regimen. In addition, the exact amounts given herein may be used to run a simple balance study where facilities for diet analysis are not available.

SOFT SOLIDS

Custard	2 servings (100 gm. each serving)
Ice cream	2 servings (100 gm. each serving)
Dry or Melba toast	4 slices

2 poached or coddled eggs
Ground beef (or veal, or lamb; white fish; chicken white meat)—2 servings (60 gm. each serving)

Values (Calculated on the above specific rations):

Fluid	2000	ml.
Carbohydrate	226	gm.
Fat	99	gm.
Protein	104	gm.
Nitrogen	16.6	gm.
Sodium	140	mE.
Potassium	87	mE.
Calories	2210	

The above diet is nutritionally inadequate if it is continued for long periods. It lacks vitamin D and the patient should receive vitamin supplements intravenously or parenterally or by some other route.

As a general rule anastomotic gastrointestinal procedures should permit the patient to progress beyond the third stage by the end of the first week. If not, one may reasonably assume that there has been an anatomic or infectious complication.

Fourth Stage (High Protein House Diet)

Order: "Liquids ad lib.; house diet with added nourishment."

Given: All liquids on first three stages may be included; total fluid intake in neighborhood of 2500 ml. easily obtained. Three meals are given; and on three occasions, between meals, extra nourishing drinks are offered to boost the protein and caloric totals. For this calculation the patient will be assumed to take the following liquids (this includes liquids with meals and between meals):

Water	3 glasses	720 ml.
Milk	1 glass	240 ml.
Bouillon	1 cup	120 ml.
Tea with 1 lump sugar	1 cup	120 ml.
Coffee with 1 lump sugar	1 cup	120 ml.
Orange juice	1 small glass	100 ml.
Tomato juice	1 small glass	100 ml.
Eggnog	3 glasses	720 ml.
	Total fluid	2240 ml.

MEAL PLAN

BREAKFAST

Orange juice (100 ml.)
1 serving cream of wheat (20 gm.) with cream (50 gm.) and sugar (10 gm.)
1 soft boiled egg
2 slices toast
1 pat butter
1 serving jelly (10 gm.)
Coffee (120 ml.), cream, sugar (5 gm.)

LUNCH

Tomato juice (100 ml.)
Chicken (60 gm.)
Baked potato (100 gm.)
Carrots (100 gm.)
1 pat butter
Bread 2 slices
1 serving jelly (10 gm.)
Jello (65 gm.) with whipped cream (15 gm.)
Tea (120 ml.) with sugar (15 gm.)

SUPPER

Broth (120 ml.)
Macaroni (100 gm.) and cheese (60 gm.)
Peas (100 gm.)
Lettuce and tomato salad (100 gm.), mayonnaise (20 gm.)
One-half peach (canned) (100 gm.)
1 glass milk (240 ml.)

The above meal plans account for all the liquid except the water taken between meals, and the eggnog given at 10 A.M., 3 P.M., and 8 P.M. Whiskey or brandy may be added to the afternoon or evening eggnog for those who find it enjoyable; this will add 75 calories to each drink.

Values:

Fluid	2290	ml.
Carbohydrate	297	gm.
Fat	117	gm.
Protein	116	gm.
Nitrogen	18.2	gm.
Sodium	180	mE.
Potassium	97	mE.
Calories	2675	

In none of these diets is the water content of the food or the water of oxidation taken into account. This "house diet" is of course subject to wide variation; the above meal plan is given as a specific example of one day's intake to provide a basis for the values given. In arranging a short balance study on a patient on house diet the above exact diet may be given, and the values used as an approximation of the intake.

The above scale is like a family budget. It is made as a guide; in use it is often honored in the breach as well as the observance. The freshly postoperative ileostomy patient does much better to start on solids than liquids; older people who have had intestinal obstruction, once the obstruction has abated (for example, by cecostomy), often respond better to early feedings of solids which stimulate gastric peristalsis. Such matters are left to the reader's experience in the art of surgery.

SURGICAL DIET II. MAXIMUM NOURISHMENT IN MINIMUM VOLUME EASILY ABSORBED

Order: "High protein soft solids to 3500 calories."

Given: Six meals are given, with the provision of between-meal nourishment and the avoidance of water. An adequate fluid intake (1500 to 2000 ml.) is given largely as nourishing drinks. Milk, not water, should be at the patient's bedside. Citrus juice should be omitted if there is any tendency to diarrhea; substitute boiled milk.

Values (These values are calculated for the following exact diet, plus two glasses water — 480 cc.):

Fluid	2300	ml.
Carbohydrate	326	gm.
Fat	227	gm.
Protein	160	gm.
Nitrogen	25.4	gm.
Sodium	170	mE.
Potassium	132	mE.
Calories	4015	

MEAL PLAN
BREAKFAST

1 glass orange juice (strained) (100 ml.)
2 soft boiled eggs (10 gm. butter)
1 slice buttered toast (50 gm.) and jelly (10 gm.)
Milk (200 ml.)
Coffee (120 ml.), cream (50 gm.), sugar (5 gm.)

MIDMORNING

1 glass tomato juice (100 ml.)
Oatmeal (40 gm.) with cream (50 gm.) and sugar (5 gm.)
Milk (200 ml.)

LUNCH

Cream soup (120 ml.)
Chicken (60 gm.)
Peas (100 gm.) with butter (10 gm.)
Ice cream, vanilla (100 gm.)
Milk (200 ml.)

MIDAFTERNOON

Eggnog (240 ml.)
2 cookies (50 gm.)

SUPPER

Broiled scraped or chopped beef (60 gm.)
Baked potato with butter (10 gm.)
Carrots (100 gm.) with butter (10 gm.)
Custard (100 gm.)
Milk (200 ml.)

EVENING

Milkshake (240 ml.)
American cheese sandwich—butter (10 gm.), cheese (60 gm.)
Chocolate pudding (150 ml.)
2 slices bread

The above diet is described without the addition of artificial enrichment in the form of added glucose, dried milk, fat emulsion, and so on. Such may be added easily to increase the calories to 4500.

This diet is adequate in all respects save that it is high in calcium and should not be adhered to for long periods in immobilized patients in whom the endogenous excretion of calcium is also large. Other foods which may be used for substitution and variety are entered under the six-meal bland diet.

Foods avoided (both here and in six-meal bland diet): Bran cereals, seeds, skins, raisins, nuts, fried foods of any kind, flavored cheese, Welsh rabbit, smoked or cured meats, heavy meats with greasy fat (pork, roast ham), spicy foods, rich gravies, cabbage, onions, peppers, radishes, broccoli, cucumbers, dried beans, raw vegetables and fruits (bananas are acceptable), rich desserts, hot pastries, cakes, carbonated or alcoholic beverages.

SURGICAL DIETS III. SPECIAL PURPOSE DIETS

Six-Meal Bland Diet

This is one of the most widely used diets in surgery. It is designed for the individual with a small gastric or intestinal capacity and it therefore involves *six small feedings* of easily digested material. The commonest abuse is to give three large meals with small in-between-meal nourishments; this completely defeats its purpose in surgical patients. It is similar to the previous diet (maximum nourishment in minimum volume) save that it is less bulky and has less dietary value (protein, calories). It is useful as a "fourth stage" advancement in certain types of gastrointestinal disease.

Order: "Six-meal bland diet."

Given: Six small equally divided meals, with liquids *ad lib.* It is well not to offer milk or other nourishing liquids between the meals as this reduces the appetite of the type of patient for whom this diet is designed. Citrus juices and carbonated beverages are avoided.

MEAL PLAN
BREAKFAST

Bananas (100 gm.) and cream (50 ml.)
1 soft boiled egg
1 slice toast, butter (10 gm.), jelly (10 gm.)
Coffee (120 ml.), cream, sugar (5 gm.)

MIDMORNING

Cream of wheat (20 gm.) with cream (50 ml.) and sugar (5 gm.)
Custard (100 gm.)
Milk (200 ml.)

NOON

Cream soup (120 ml.)
Chicken (60 gm.)
Baked potato (100 gm.) with butter (10 gm.)
Ice cream (100 gm.)
Milk (100 ml.)

MIDAFTERNOON

Eggnog (240 ml.)
Jello (60 gm.) with cream (50 ml.)
Cookies (50 gm.)

SUPPER

Hamburger (90 gm.)
Baked potato (100 gm.)
Buttered peas (100 gm.), butter (10 gm.)
Milk (100 ml.)
Canned peach half (10 gm.)

EVENING

Cream soup (120 ml.)
Milkshake (240 ml.)
Cream cheese-jelly sandwich—2 slices bread, butter (10 gm.), cream cheese (30 gm.), jelly (10 gm.)

Values (Based on an additional 4 glasses (960 ml.) of water):

Fluid	2350 ml.
Carbohydrate	362 gm.
Fat	186 gm.
Protein	133 gm.
Nitrogen	21 gm.
Sodium	160 mE.
Potassium	125 mE.
Calories	3600

Other Foods for Substitution and Variety in six-meal bland diet:

Eggs, poached, scrambled or omelet; tender meats without extra fat; refined cereals; rice; noodles; macaroni; spaghetti; melba toast; rusk; zweibach; well cooked carrots; beets; squash; ripe bananas; cooked or canned pears; applesauce; junket; tapioca; plain cake; milk toast.

Foods avoided on six-meal bland diet are the same as those listed as avoided under "maximum nourishment in minimum volume" diet.

This diet is deficient in vitamin C, containing only 54 mg. A polyvitamin supplement should be given orally.

The secret of success with a six-meal bland diet is to make the "between-meal" feedings large enough to add nourishment but not so large as to destroy appetite for the other three meals.

Low-Fat Diet

Order: "Low-fat diet."

Given: A three-meal diet low in fat and therefore relatively high in protein and carbohydrate. As described here, between-meal nourishments are given to increase the dietary value. Despite this, total caloric value is low. Eggs are allowed if not fried.

MEAL PLAN
BREAKFAST

Sliced orange (100 gm.)
Cream of wheat (20 gm.) with skim milk and sugar (5 gm.)
1 boiled egg
2 slices toast with jelly or jam (10 gm.)
Skim milk (200 ml.)
Coffee and milk, sugar (5 gm.)

LUNCH

Lean beef, ground (60 gm.)
Baked potato (100 gm.)
Carrots (100 gm.)
2 slices bread
½ pat butter
Jelly or jam (10 gm.)
Jello (65 gm.)
Skim milk (200 ml.)
Tea (120 ml.) with sugar (5 gm.)

SUPPER

Fat-free broth (120 ml.)
Chicken (60 gm.)
Peas (100 gm.)
Lettuce (120 gm.), cottage cheese (30 gm.), vinegar (30 ml.)
Bread, 1 slice
½ pat butter
Jam (10 gm.)
Pineapple (canned) (100 gm.)
Skim milk (200 ml.)

Midmorning, midafternoon, and evening nourishments are given of chocolate milk made with skim milk, milkshakes made of skim milk and sugar flavored with vanilla, and orange juice.

Values (Based on above diet plus 960 ml. of water (4 glasses), and 240 ml. each of the above added liquids):

Fluid	2670 ml.
Carbohydrate	318 gm.
Fat	32 gm.
Protein	100 gm.
Nitrogen	16 gm.
Sodium	133 mE.
Potassium	115 mE.
Calories	2000

Other Foods Allowed for Substitution and Variety: rice, macaroni, spaghetti, noodles, prepared without fat; fruits of all kinds; vegetables of all kinds except as listed below; Jello, gelatine, angel cake, fruit whip, junket made with skim milk, sherbet, carbonated beverages; honey, molasses.

Foods Avoided: fried foods of any kind, cream, mayonnaise, butter, margarine, peanut butter, avocado, gravies and rich sauces, ice cream, cake, cookies, rich desserts, muffins, biscuits, hot bread, pickles, spices, nuts, fatty cheese, ham, pork, sausage, frankfurters, canned salmon or tuna fish, onions, cauliflower, broccoli, cabbage, turnips.

SURGICAL DIETS IV.   TUBE FEEDINGS

Tube feedings for surgical use may be divided, for simplicity's sake, into two general groups. First are those for use where a normal gastric digestion phase is carried out in the patient's stomach. Second are the tube feedings which must be introduced directly into the jejunum. These will be taken up in order.

1. Tube Feeding for Gastric Digestion in the Patient

Order: "Gastrostomy (or gastric tube) feeding, 250 ml. every three hours while awake."

Given: A feeding suitable for gastric tube (comatose patients, burns, irrational patients) or gastrostomy. This is a feeding of natural foods best given in intermittent "loads" of about 250 ml. to stimulate gastric peristalsis. Two alternate formulas are given:

FORMULA A. (EVAPORATED MILK)

Evaporated milk	600 ml.
Light cream	120 ml.
Karo	80 ml.
3 eggs	150 ml.
Applesauce	50 gm.
Salt (NaCl)	5 gm.
Elixir ferrous sulfate	8 ml.
Vitamin C	250 mg.
B complex	1 tablet or 4 ml.

Values (Formula A):

Fluid	1000	ml.
Carbohydrate	134	gm.
Fat	88	gm.
Protein	64	gm.
Nitrogen	10.6	gm.
Sodium	123	mE.
Potassium	55	mE.
Calories	1570	

FORMULA B. (CONCENTRATED MILK)

Concentrated milk	600 ml.
Light cream	120 ml.
Karo	80 ml.
3 eggs	150 ml.
Applesauce	50 gm.
Salt (NaCl)	5 gm.
Elixir ferrous sulfate	8 ml.
Vitamin C	250 mg.
B complex	1 tablet or 4 ml.

Values (Formula B):

Fluid	1000	ml.
Carbohydrate	163	gm.
Fat	111	gm.
Protein	85	gm.
Nitrogen	13.7	gm.
Sodium	150	mE.
Potassium	75	mE.
Calories	1970	

Note the significant increase in protein and calories using concentrated milk. Both these are palatable feedings, an important consideration since gastric tube feedings may be regurgitated and will cause nausea and vomiting if they are unpalatable. Two liters a day may be given, once the stomach is habituated to the feedings.

2. Tube Feeding for Use Directly Into the Jejunum

Order: "Jejunostomy feeding in slow drip to ____ ml. total."

Given: A tube feeding which may be utilized without gastric digestion and which is not mechanically or osmotically irritating to the jejunum. It should not be introduced in full quantity until peristalsis is well established, and small quantities have been well tolerated. The fecal nitrogen will be elevated (up to 5 gm. per day) even when bowel habits are good, on such feedings. Nitrogen balance cannot be estimated without fecal nitrogen measurements. This feeding may also be used through a Miller-Abbott tube or into duodenal tube. It is much more dilute than the gastrostomy feeding. Two formulas are given. Formula C is that of Case (1950) with minor modification. Formula D is one of those used for some years by the author.

FORMULA C

Homogenized milk	1000 ml.
Aminoids	50 gm.
Dexin (Burroughs-Wellcome)	60 gm.
Pureed liver	50 gm.
Vi-Syneral	0.6 ml.

Values (Formula C):

Fluid	1150	ml.
Carbohydrate	130	gm.
Fat	40	gm.
Protein	66	gm.
Nitrogen	10	gm.
Sodium	65	mE.
Potassium	50	mE.
Calories	1140	

FORMULA D

Evaporated milk	300 ml.
Lime water (U.S.P.)	480 ml.
Karo	20 ml.
Water	200 ml.
Vitamin C	250 mg.
Elixir Feosol	8 ml.
B Complex	1 tablet or 4 ml.

Values (Formula D):

Fluid	1000	ml.
Carbohydrate	45	gm.
Fat	24	gm.
Protein	21	gm.
Nitrogen	3.5	gm.
Sodium	15	mE.
Potassium	20	mE.
Calories	470	

A slow drip avoids mechanical distention of the jejunum which is the commonest cause of cramps and diarrhea on such a feeding; if diarrhea occurs, reduce volume and remove vitamins for a few days, or give small amounts of "half and half" milk and lime water. The milk should be boiled; if the patient has a tendency to diarrhea, boiled skimmed milk is best tolerated.

Notice that the gastric feeding can be concentrated to 2 calories per ml. whereas the jejunum requires a more dilute solution.

The formula of Dr. Case is twice as concentrated as the author's and is therefore preferable in any patient who can tolerate this added tonicity in the jejunum. Up to 2500 ml. per day may be accepted once the jejunum is accommodated to the feeding. If the patient also is having gastric contents aspirated daily, the aspirated material may be incubated with the jejunostomy feeding before the latter is introduced into the jejunum. This saves electrolyte and gives the patient an in vitro gastric digestion phase.

BIBLIOGRAPHY

Abbott, W. E., Krieger, H. and Levey, S.: Technical surgical factors which enhance or minimize post-gastrectomy abnormalities. Ann. Surg. *148:*567, 1958.

Abbott, W. E., Levey, S., Benson, J. W. and Davis, J. H.: Symposium on parenteral fluids, nutrition and electrolytes; alterations of carbohydrate metabolism following trauma. Minnesota Med. (suppl.) *38:*55, 1955.

Abbott, W. E., Pilling, M. A., Griffin, G. E., Hirshfeld, J. W. and Meyer, F. L.: Metabolic alterations following thermal burns; use of whole blood and electrolyte solution in treatment of burned patients. Ann. Surg. *122:*678, 1945.

Abercrombie, M., Flint, M. H. and James, D. W.: Collagen formation and wound contraction during repair of small excised wounds in the skin of rats. J. Embryol. & Exper. Morph. *2:*264, 1954.

Adams, F. H., Berglund, E. R., Balkin, S. G. and Chisholm, T.: Pituitary adrenocorticotropic hormone in severely burned children. J.A.M.A. *146:*31, 1951.

Adams, W. E., Thornton, T. F., Jr., Allen, J. G. and Gonzalez, D. E.: The danger and prevention of citrate intoxication in massive transfusions of whole blood. Ann. Surg. *120:*656, 1944.

Adelson, E., Crosby, W. H. and Roeder, W. H.: Further studies of a hemostatic defect caused by intravenous dextran. J. Lab. & Clin. Med. *45:*441, 1955.

Adlersberg, D. and Fox, C. L., Jr.: Changes of the water tolerance test in hepatic disease. Ann. Int. Med. *19:*642, 1943.

Aikawa, J. K., Felts, J. H., Jr., Tyor, M. P. and Harrell, G. T.: Exchangeable potassium content in disease states. J. Clin. Invest. *31:*743, 1952.

Akers, H. P., Hershey, S. G. and Zweifach, B. W.: Blood-borne vasoactive substance(s) produced by splanchnic nerve stimulation. Am. J. Physiol. *178:*63, 1954.

Albright, F.: Cushing's syndrome: its pathological physiology, its relationship to the adreno-genital syndrome and its connection with the problem of the reaction of the body to injurious agents ("Alarm Reaction" of Selye). Harvey Lect. Ser. *38:*123, 1943.

Albright, F.: Osteoporosis. John Phillips memorial lecture. Ann. Int. Med. *27:*861, 1947.

Albright, F., Bloomberg, E. and Smith, P. H.: Postmenopausal osteoporosis. Tr. A. Am. Physicians *55:*298, 1940.

Allbritten, F. F., Jr., Haupt, G. J. and Amadeo, J. H.: The changes in pulmonary alveolar ventilation achieved by aiding the deflation phase of respiration during anesthesia for surgical operations. Ann. Surg. *140:*569, 1954.

Allbritten, F. F., Jr., Lipshutz, H., Miller, B. J. and Gibbon, J. H., Jr.: Blood volume changes in tuberculous patients treated by thoracoplasty. J. Thoracic Surg. *7:*71, 1950.

Allen, H. S. and Day, S. W.: Burns in children. A.M.A. Arch. Surg. *72:*288, 1956.

Allen, J. G., (ed.): Extracorporeal Circulation. Springfield, Ill., Charles C Thomas, 1958.

Allen, J. G., Emerson, D. M., Barron, E. S. and Sykes, C.: Pooled plasma with little or no risk of homologous serum jaundice. J.A.M.A. *154:*103, 1954.

Allen, J. G. and Julian, O. C.: Response of plasma prothrombin to vitamin K substitute therapy in cases of hepatic disease. A.M.A. Arch. Surg. *41:*1363, 1940.

Allen, T. H. and Reeve, E. B.: Distribution of "extra plasma" in blood of some tissues in dog as measured with P_{32} and T-1824. Am. J. Physiol. *175:*218, 1953.

Allende, D. A.: The experimental relationship of malnutrition to protein reserve and tolerance to a major operative load. S. Forum *6:*41, 1956.

Allott, E. N.: Sodium and chlorine retention without renal disease. Lancet *1:*1035, 1939.

Almy, T. P. and Laragh, J. H.: Reduction in circulating eosinophils following epinephrine, insulin and surgical operations. Am. J. Med. *6:*507, 1949.

Alrich, E. M. and Morton, C. B.: Intra-arterial transfusion. S. Forum *1:*503, 1951.

Altemeier, W. A.: Treatment of fresh traumatic wounds J.A.M.A. *124:*405, 1944.

Altemeier, W. A. and Cole, W.: Septic shock. Ann. Surg. *143:*600, 1956.

Althausen, T. L., Uyeyama, K. and Simpson, R. G.: Digestion and absorption after massive resection of the small intestine. Gastroenterology *12:*795, 1949.

Altschule, M. D. and Sulzbach, W. M.: Tolerance of the human heart to acidosis; reversible changes in RS-T interval during severe acidosis caused by administration of carbon dioxide. Am. Heart J. *33:*458, 1947.

Amberg, S. and Helmholz, H. F.: The detoxifying action of sodium salts upon potassium salts on intravenous injection. J. Pharmacol. & Exper. Therap. *8:*120, 1916 (Proc.).

Ament, R., Papper, E. M. and Rovenstine, E. A.: Cardiac arrest during anesthesia—a review of cases. Ann. Surg. *134:*220, 1951.

Ames, R., Syllm, I. and Rapoport, S.: Effect of infusions of citrated plasma on the plasma citrate level of infants. Pediatrics *6:*361, 1950.

Amspacher, W. H. and Curreri, A. R.: Use of dextran in control of shock resulting from war wounds. A.M.A. Arch. Surg. *66:*730, 1953.

Anderson, I. A.: Postmenopausal osteoporosis, clinical manifestations and treatment with oestrogens. Quart. J. Med. 19:67, 1950.

Anderson, T. R. and Steer, A.: Renal changes in patients dying of war wounds: Korea, 1950–1952—a preliminary report. In Howard, J. M. (ed.): Battle Casualties in Korea. Volume IV, Post-traumatic Renal Insufficiency. Washington, D. C., U. S. Government Printing Office, 1955.

Andrews, R. P., Morgan, H. C. and Jurkiewicz, M. J.: The relationship of dietary protein to the healing of experimental burns. S. Forum 6:72, 1956.

Annis, D. and Alexander, M. K.: Differential absorption of electrolytes from the large bowel in relation to ureterosigmoid anastomosis. Lancet 2:603, 1952.

Anscombe, A. R.: Pulmonary Complications in Abdominal Surgery. Chicago, Yearbook Publishers, 1957.

Appleby, L. H.: Proctocystectomy—the management of colostomy with ureteral transplants. Am. J. Surg. 79:57, 1950.

Ariel, I. M.: Effects of a water load administered to patients during the immediate postoperative period— the hypotonic syndrome. A.M.A. Arch. Surg. 62:303, 1951.

Ariel, I. M.: Effects of operation, anoxia and the postoperative administration of dextrose and water upon tissue electrolytes as revealed by analyses of muscle biopsies. S. Forum 2:611, 1952.

Ariel, I. M.: Metabolic alterations induced by intraabdominal operations. Ann. Surg. 138:186, 1953.

Ariel, I. M.: The effects of acute hypochloremia on the distribution of body fluid and composition of tissue electrolytes in man. Ann. Surg. 140:150, 1954.

Ariel, I. M.: The effects of gastric anacidity upon the metabolic alterations induced by gastric aspiration. Surg., Gynec. & Obst. 98:213, 1954.

Ariel, I. M. and Miller, F.: The effects of abdominal surgery upon renal clearance. Surgery 28:716. 1950.

Armstrong, W. D., Knowlton, M. and Gouze, M.: Influence of estradiol and testosterone propionates in skeletal atrophy from disuse and on normal bones of mature rats. Endocrinology 36:313, 1945.

Aronow, L. and Howard, F. A.: Improved fluorometric technique to measure changes in adrenal epinephrine-norepinephrine output caused by veratrum alkaloids. Fed. Proc. 14:315, 1955.

Aronow, L., Howard, F. A. and Wolff, D.: Plasma epinephrine and norepinephrine content in mammals. J. Pharmacol. & Exper. Therap. 116:1, 1956.

Artz, C. P.: Evaluation of a standard tilt test for estimation of blood volume deficiency. S. Forum 5:803, 1955.

Artz, C. P., Howard, J. M. and Frawley, J. P.: Clinical observations on the use of dextran and modified fluid gelatin in combat casualties. Surgery 37:612, 1955.

Artz, C. P., Howard, J. M., Sako, Y., Bronwell, A. W. and Prentice, T.: Clinical experiences in the early management of the most severely injured battle casualties. Ann. Surg. 141:285, 1955.

Artz, C. P., Reiss, E., Davis, J. H., Jr. and Amspacher, W. H.: The exposure treatment of burns. Ann. Surg. 137:456, 1953.

Artz, C. P., Sako, Y. and Bronwell, A. W.: Intra-arterial vs. rapid intravenous blood transfusions—experiences in a forward surgical hospital in Korea. U. S. Armed Forces M.J. 6:313, 1955.

Artz, C. P., Sako, Y. and Bronwell, A. W.: Massive transfusion in the severely wounded; report of a patient receiving 23,350 cc. of blood in the first 24 hours. Surgery 37:469, 1955.

Artz, C. P. and Soroff, H. S.: Modern concepts in the treatment of burns. J.A.M.A. 159:411, 1955.

Artz, C. P. and Teschan, P. E.: Infection—a major unsolved problem in severe trauma. Am. J. Surg. 93:647, 1957.

Atchley, D. W., Loeb, R. F., Richards, D. W., Jr., Benedict, E. M. and Driscoll, M. E.: On diabetic acidosis—a detailed study of electrolyte balances following the withdrawal and reestablishment of insulin therapy. J. Clin. Invest. 12:297, 1933.

Axelrod, A. E., Carter, B. B., McCoy, R. H. and Geisinger, R.: Circulating antibodies in vitamin-deficiency states. I. Pyridoxin, riboflavin and pantothenic acid deficiencies. Proc. Soc. Exper. Biol. & Med. 66:137, 1947.

Axelrod, D. R. and Pitts, R. F.: Effects of hypoxia on renal tubular function. J. Appl. Physiol. 4:593, 1952.

Baar, S. and Topley, E.: Haemoglobin metabolism and serum proteins following trauma. Acta med. Scandinav. 153:319, 1956.

Babb, L. I., Chinn, A. B., Stitt, R. M., Lavik, P. S., Levey, S., Krieger, H. and Abbott, W. E.: Evaluation of protein and fat metabolism in postgastrectomy patients. A.M.A. Arch. Surg. 67:462, 1953.

Baez, S., Zweifach, B. W., Mazur, A. and Shorr, E.: Hepato-renal factors in circulatory homeostasis. II. Disappearance of hepatic vasodepressor material following intravenous administration. Proc. Soc. Exper. Biol. & Med. 64:154, 1947.

Baez, S., Zweifach, B. W. and Shorr, E.: Protective action of dibenamine against the fatal outcome of hemorrhagic and traumatic shock in rats. Fed. Proc. 11:7, 1952.

Baines, G. H., Barclay, J. A. and Cooke, W. T.: Nephrocalcinosis associated with hyperchloraemia and low plasma-bicarbonate. Quart. J. Med. 14:113, 1945.

Baird, I. McL., Podmore, D. A. and Wilson, G. M.: Changes in iron metabolism following gastrectomy and other surgical operations. Clin. Sc. 16:463, 1957.

Baker, J. W. and Boles, T.: Observations pertaining to the place of surgery in acute pancreatitis. Gastroenterology 28:536, 1955.

Baker, R. and Miller, G. H., Jr.: The physiology of the uretero-intestinal anastomosis. I. Ureteral reflux. J. Urol. 67:638, 1952.

Balch, H. H.: Relation of nutritional deficiency in man to antibody production. J. Immunol. 64:397, 1950.

Balch, H. H.: The effect of severe battle injury and of post-traumatic renal failure on resistance to infection. Ann. Surg. 142:145, 1955.

Balch, H. H. and Evans, J. R.: The influence of acute renal failure on resistance to infection—an experimental study. Ann. Surg. 144:191, 1956.

Balch, H. H., Meroney, W. H. and Sako, Y.: Observations on the surgical care of patients with post-traumatic renal insufficiency. Surg., Gynec. & Obst. 100:439, 1955.

Balch, H. H. and Spencer, M. T.: Phagocytosis by human leukocytes; effect of fibrin on phagocytosis of staphylococci and of encapsulated pneumococci by normal human leukocytes. J. Clin. Invest. 33:1314, 1954.

Balch, H. H. and Spencer, M. T.: Phagocytosis by human leukocytes; relation of nutritional deficiency in man to phagocytosis. J. Clin. Invest. 33:1321, 1954.

Baldwin, M. and Reynolds, C. W.: The treatment of battle casualties in the initial phases of the operations at Iwo Jima Island. Mil. Surgeon *97:*288, 1945.

Balikov, B., Artz, C. P. and Solometo, D. F.: Serum gamma globulin in the burned patient, with special reference to septicemia. U. S. Armed Forces M. J. *8:*321, 1957.

Barger, A. C.: The pathogenesis of sodium retention in congestive heart failure. Metabolism *5:*480, 1956.

Barger, A. C., Brooks, L. B., Wilson, G. H. and Price, H. L.: Relationships between exchangeable sodium and sodium excretion in dogs with experimental valvular lesions of the heart. Am. J. Physiol. *180:*387, 1955.

Barger, A. C., Richardson, G. S. and Roe, B. B.: A method for producing chronic cardiac failure in dogs. Proc. Soc. Exper. Biol. & Med. *73:*113, 1950.

Barger, A. C., Roe, B. B. and Richardson, G. S.: Relation of valvular lesions of exercise to auricular pressure, work tolerance and to development of chronic, congestive failure in dogs. Am. J. Physiol. *169:*384, 1952.

Barger, A. C., Ross, R. S. and Price, H. L.: Reduced sodium excretion in dogs with mild valvular lesions of the heart, and in dogs with congestive failure. Am. J. Physiol. *180:*249, 1955.

Barger, A. C., Rudolph, A. M. and Yates, F. E.: Sodium excretion and renal hemodynamics in normal dogs, dogs with mild valvular lesions of the heart and dogs in frank congestive heart failure. Am. J. Physiol. *183:*595, 1955 (abstr.).

Barger, A. C., Wilson, G. M., Price, H. L., Ross, R. S., Brooks, L. and Boling, E. A.: Relationship between exchangeable sodium and rate of sodium excretion in dogs with experimental valvular lesions of the heart. Am. J. Physiol. *180:*387, 1955.

Barnes, B. A.: Mortality of burns at the Massachusetts General Hospital, 1939–1954. Ann. Surg. *145:*210, 1957.

Barnes, B. A., Shaw, R. S., Leaf, A. and Linton, R. R.: Oliguria following diagnostic translumbar aortography; report of case. New England J. Med. *252:*1113, 1955.

Baronofsky, I. D.: Portal hypertension, with special reference to acid-peptic factor in the causation of hemorrhage and extensive gastric resection in its treatment. Surgery *25:*135, 1949.

Bartlett, M. K., Jones, C. M. and Ryan, A. E.: Vitamin C studies on surgical patients. Ann. Surg. *111:*1, 1940.

Bartter, F. C.: The role of aldosterone in normal homeostasis and in certain disease states. Metabolism *5:*369, 1956.

Bartter, F. C., Bigheri, E. G., Pronove, P. and Delea, C. S.: The effect of changes in intravascular volume on aldosterone secretion. In an International Symposium on Aldosterone. London, J. A. Churchill, 1958.

Bartter, F. C., Liddle, G. W., Duncan, L. E., Jr., Barber, J. K. and Delea, C.: The regulation of aldosterone secretion in man: the role of fluid volume. J. Clin. Invest. *35:*1306, 1956.

Bartter, F. C., Liddle, G. W., Duncan, L. E. and Delea, C.: The role of extracellular fluid volume in the control of aldosterone secretion in man. J. Clin. Invest. *35:*688, 1956 (Abstr.).

Bartlett, L. C. and Thorlakson, P. H. T.: The etiology and technique of surgical management of pancreatic fistula. Surg., Gynec. & Obst. *102:*413, 1956.

Bass, W. P., Watts, D. J. and Chase, H. F.: Ether hyperglycemia as influenced by premedication and pentothal induction. Anesthesiology *14:*18, 1953.

Battle, R. J. V., Clarkson, P., Mowlem, R., Osborne, R. and Wallace, A. B.: Fluid replacement in burned patients. Lancet *1:*98, 1954.

Beal, J. M., Cornell, G. N. and Gilder, H.: Factors influencing nitrogen metabolism in surgical patients. Surgery *36:*468, 1954.

Beal, J. M. and Smith, J. L.: The metabolism of fructose in man. Surgery *36:*243, 1954.

Beattie, E. J., Jr., Thistlethwaite, J. R., Blades, B. and Wood, O.: Experimental studies with intra-arterial transfusion; overtransfusion of normal dog. Surgery *31:*411, 1952.

Beattie, J.: Metabolic disturbances after injury. Brit. Med. J. *2:*813, 1947.

Beattie, J., Herbert, P. H. and Bell, D. J.: Famine oedema. Brit. J. Nutrition *2:*47, 1948.

Beattie, J., Herbert, P. H. and Bell, D. J.: Nitrogen balances during recovery from severe undernutrition. Brit. J. Nutrition *1:*202, 1948.

Beck, C. S.: Treatment of cardiac arrest. Veterans Admin. Tech. Bull. TB 10–65: 1, 1950.

Becker, J. M. and Artz, C. P.: Treatment of burns in children. A.M.A. Arch. Surg. *73:*207, 1956.

Bedell, G. N., Marshall, R., DuBois, A. B. and Harris, J. H.: Measurement of the volume of gas in the gastrointestinal tract—values in normal subjects and ambulatory patients. J. Clin. Invest. *35:*336, 1956.

Beebe, G. W. and DeBakey, M. E.: Battle casualties: incidence, mortality, and logistic considerations. Springfield, Ill., Charles C Thomas, 1952.

Beebe, R. T. and Meneeley, J. K.: Pernicious anemia following gastrectomy. New York State J. Med. *49:*2437, 1949.

Beecher, H. K.: Anesthesia for men wounded in battle. M. Bull. Mediterranean Theat. Op. *3:*113, 1945; Ann. Surg. *122:*807, 1945.

Beecher, H. K.: Preparation of battle casualties for surgery. Ann. Surg. *121:*769, 1945.

Beecher, H. K.: Timing as factor in treatment of shock. S. Clin. North America *27:*1188, 1947.

Beecher, H. K.: The management of traumatic shock. In Resuscitation and Anesthesia for Wounded Men. Springfield, Ill., Charles C Thomas, 1949.

Beecher, H. K.: Early care of the seriously wounded man. J.A.M.A. *145:*193, 1951.

Beecher, H. K.: Early Care of the Seriously Wounded Man. Springfield, Ill., Charles C Thomas, 1952.

Beecher, H. K. (ed.): Surgery in World War II: The Physiologic Effects of Wounds. By Board for Study of Severely Wounded, North African-Mediterranean Theater of Operations. Washington, D. C., Office of the Surgeon General, Department of the Army, 1952.

Beecher, H. K., Anfinsen, L. F. and Anfinsen, C. B.: Metabolic effects of anesthesia in man. I. Acid-base balance during ether anesthesia. J. Pharmacol. & Exper. Therap. *98:*38, 1950.

Beecher, H. K. and Burnett, C. H.: Field experience in the use of blood and blood substitutes (plasma, albumin) in seriously wounded men. M. Bull. North African Theat. Op. (No. 1) *2:*2, 1944.

Beecher, H. K., Francis, L. and Anfinsen, C. B.: Metabolic effects of anesthesia in man. Acid-base balance during ether anesthesia. J. Pharmacol. & Exper. Therap. *98:*38, 1950.

Beecher, H. K. and Murphy, A. J.: Acidosis during thoracic surgery. J. Thoracic Surg. *19:*50, 1950.

Beecher, H. K., Quinn, T. J., Jr., Bunker, J. B. and

D'Alessandro, G. L.: Effect of position and artificial ventilation on the excretion of carbon dioxide during thoracic surgery. J. Thoracic Surg. *22:*135, 1951.

Beecher, H. K., Simeone, F. A., Burnett, C. H., Shapiro, S. L., Sullivan, E. R. and Mallory, T. B.: The internal state of the severely wounded man on entry to the most forward hospital. Surgery *22:*672, 1947.

Behnke, A. R.: Fat content and composition of the body. Harvey Lect. *37:*198, 1941–42.

Beling, C. A., Bosch, D. T. and Carter, O. B., Jr.: Blood volume in geriatric surgery. Geriatrics *7:*179, 1952.

Bell, E. T.: Renal Diseases. 2d ed. Philadelphia, Lea and Febiger, 1950.

Bellet, S., Wasserman, F. and Brody, J. I.: Effect of molar sodium lactate in increasing cardiac rhythmicity: its use in the treatment of slow heart rates. Stokes-Adams syndrome and episodes of cardiac arrest: a clinical and experimental study. Tr. A. Am. Physicians *69:*161, 1955.

Bellet, S., Wasserman, F. and Brody, J. I.: Molar sodium lactate; its effect in complete atrioventricular heart block and cardiac arrest occuring during Stokes-Adams seizures and in the terminal state. New England J. Med. *253:*891, 1955.

Bellet, S., Wasserman, F. and Brody, J. I.: Treatment of cardiac arrest and slow ventricular rates in complete A-V heart block. Use of molar and half molar sodium lactate: clinical study. Circulation *11:*685, 1955.

Bennett, E. V. and Moore, F. D.: The effect of surgical trauma and exogenous hormone therapy on the urinary excretion of 17-ketosteroids. S. Forum *2:*551, 1952.

Bennett, L. R., Bennett, V. C. and Howland, J. W.: Effect of acute x-irradiation on distribution and excretion of radio sodium in the rat. Fed. Proc. *8:*350, 1949.

Benson, J. W., Abbott, W. E., Holden, W. D. and Levey, S.: The serum properdin titers in surgical patients. S. Forum *6:*49, 1956.

Benson, S. A and Yalow, R. S.: Critique of extracellular space measurement with small ions. Na²⁴, Br⁸² spaces. Science *121:*34, 1955

Bentley, W. B. A. and Van Itallie, T. B.: Metabolic effects of fat emulsions administered intravenously to human subjects. J. Lab. & Clin. Med. *48:*184, 1956.

Bergstrom, W. H.: The participation of bone in total body sodium metabolism in the rat. J. Clin. Invest. *34:*997, 1955.

Bergstrom, W. H. and Wallace, W. W.: Bone as a sodium and potassium reservoir. J. Clin. Invest. *33:*867, 1954.

Berliner, R. W., Kennedy, T. J., Jr. and Hilton, J. G.: Renal mechanisms for excretion of potassium. Am. J. Physiol. *162:*348, 1950.

Berliner, R. W., Kennedy, T. J., Jr. and Orloff, J.: Relationship between acidification of urine and potassium metabolism: effect of carbonic anhydrase inhibition potassium excretion. Am. J. Med. *11:*274, 1951.

Berman, J. K. and Hull, J. E.: Hepatic, splenic and left gastric arterial ligations in advanced portal cirrhosis. A.M.A. Arch. Surg. *65:*37, 1952.

Berman, J. K., Koenig, H. and Müller, L. P.: Ligation of hepatic and splenic arteries in treatment of portal hypertension; ligation in atrophic cirrhosis of the liver. A.M.A. Arch. Surg. *63:*379, 1951.

Berne, R. M.: Hemodynamics and sodium excretion of denervated kidney in anesthetized and unanesthetized dog. Am. J. Physiol. *171:*148, 1952.

Bernhard, W. F., McMurrey, J. D., Ganong, W. F. and Lennihan, R.: The effect of hypothermia on the peripheral serum levels of free 17-hydroxycorticoids in the dog and man. Ann. Surg. *143:*210, 1956.

Bernstein, S. H., Weston, R. E., Ross, G., Grossman, J., Hanenson, I. B. and Leiter, L.: Studies on intravenous water diuresis and nicotine and Pitressin antidiuresis in normal subjects and patients with liver disease. J. Clin. Invest. *32:*422, 1953.

Bessman, S. P., Fazekas, J. F. and Bessman, A. N.: Uptake of ammonia by the brain in hepatic coma. Proc. Soc. Exper. Biol. & Med. *85:*66, 1954.

Bettman, A. G.: Causes of death in burned patients; report of 23 deaths in 744 burned patients. Am. J. Surg. *71:*26, 1946.

Billing, B. H., Cole, P. G. and Lathe, G. H.: The excretion of bilirubin as a diglucuronide, giving the direct van den Bergh reaction. Biochem. J. *65:*774, 1957.

Billing, B. H. and Lathe, G. H.: Excretion of bilirubin as an ester glucoronide, giving the direct van den Bergh reaction. Biochem. J. *63:*6, 1956.

Bingham, D. L. C.: Intra-arterial transfusion. Lancet *2:*157, 1952.

Bisset, G. W. and Walker, J. M.: Assay of oxytocin in blood. J. Physiol. *126:*588, 1954.

Black, H. and Harken, D. E.: Safe conduct of the patient through cardiac surgery with special reference to diseases of mitral and aortic valves. New England J. Med. *251:*45, 1954.

Black, J. R., Ghormley, R. K. and Camp, J. D.: Senile osteoporosis of the spinal column. J.A.M.A. *177:*2144, 1941.

Blackburn, C. R. B., Hensley, W. J., Grant, D. K. and Wright, F. B.: Studies on intravascular hemolysis in man. The pathogenesis of the initial stages of acute renal failure. J. Clin. Invest. *33:*825, 1954.

Blakemore, A. H.: Portacaval anastomosis: a report on 14 cases. Bull. New York Acad. Med. *22:*254, 1946.

Blakemore, A. H.: Indications for portacaval anastomosis —analysis of cases. Surg., Gynec. & Obst. *84:*645, 1947.

Blakemore, A. H.: Portacaval anastomosis. Surgery *24:*480, 1948.

Blakemore, A. H.: The portacaval shunt in the surgical treatment of portal hypertension. Ann. Surg. *128:*825, 1948.

Blakemore, A. H.: Portacaval shunt for portal hypertension, follow-up results in cases of cirrhosis of the liver J.A.M.A. *145:*1335, 1951.

Blakemore, A. H.: Portacaval shunting for portal hypertension. Surg., Gynec. & Obst. *94:*443, 1952.

Blakemore, A. H. and Lord, J. W., Jr.: The technic of using vitallium tubes in establishing portacaval shunts for portal hypertension. Ann. Surg. *122:*476, 1945.

Blakemore, W. S., Dumke, P. R. and Rhoads, J. E.: Gangrene following intra-arterial transfusion; report of 2 cases. J.A.M.A. *151:*988, 1953.

Blakemore, W. S., Zinsser, H. F., Kirby, C. K., Bellet, S. and Johnson, J.: The use of molar sodium lactate in certain arrhythmias complicating intracardiac surgery. Ann. Surg. *144:*511, 1956.

Bliss, E. L., Migeon, C. J., Branch, C. H. H. and Samuels, L. T.: Reaction of the adrenal cortex to emotional stress. Psychosom. Med. *18:*56, 1956.

Bliss, E. L., Rumel, W. R. and Branch, C. H. H.: Psychiatric complications of mitral surgery; report of death after electroshock therapy. A.M.A. Arch. Neurol. & Psychiat. *74:*249, 1955.

Bliss, E. L., Sandberg, A. A., Nelson, D. H. and Eik-Nes, K.: The normal levels of 17-hydroxycorticosteroids in the peripheral blood of man. J. Clin. Invest. *32:*818, 1953.

Blocker, T. G., Jr., Levin, W. C., Lewis, S. R. and Snyder, C. C.: The use of radioactive sulphur labelled methionine in the study of protein catabolism in burn patients. Ann. Surg. *140:*519, 1955.

Blocker, T. G., Jr., Levin, W. C., Nowinski, W. W., Lewis, S. R. and Blocker, V.: Nutrition studies in the severely burned. Ann. Surg. *141:*589, 1955.

Blocker, T. G., Jr., Levin, W. C., Perry, J. E., Lewis, S. R. and Blocker, V.: The influence of the burn state on the turnover of serum proteins in human subjects. A.M.A. Arch. Surg. *74:*792, 1957.

Blocker, T. G., Jr., Levin, W. C., Snyder, C. C., Lewis, S. R. and Hurst, W. R.: Radioactive techniques in the study of protein metabolism of severe burn patients; studies with radioactive iodinated human serum albumin. S. Forum *4:*428, 1954.

Blount, H. C., Jr., and Hardy, J. D.: Thyroid function and surgical trauma, as evaluated by iodine conversion ratio. Am. J. M. Sc. *224:*112, 1952.

Bluemle, L. W., Jr. and Elkinton, J. R.: A stretcher-scale for the accurate weighing of bedridden patients. J. Lab. & Clin. Med. *41:*300, 1953.

Bluemle, L. W., Jr., Potter, H. P. and Elkinton, J. R.: Changes in body composition in acute renal failure. J. Clin. Invest. *35:*1094, 1956.

Bogardus, G. M. and Gustafson, I. J.: Gastroduodenal ulceration complicating other diseases. Surgery *39:*222, 1956.

Bogdonoff, M. D., Shock, N. W. and Parsons, J.: The effect of stilbestrol on the retention of N, Ca, P, and K in aged males with and without osteoporosis. J. Gerontol. *9:*262, 1954.

Bogoroch, R. and Timiras, P.: The response of the thyroid gland of the rat to severe stress. Endocrinol. *49:*548, 1951.

Bohne, A. W. and Rupe, C. E.: Hypochloremic acidosis: a study of the mechanism in ureterosigmoidostomy. Surg., Gynec. & Obst. *96:*541, 1953.

Bohr, H. and Sørensen, A. H.: Study of fracture healing by means of radio-active tracers. J. Bone & Joint Surg. *32–A:*567, 1950.

Boles, E. T., Jr.: Postoperative pancreatitis. A.M.A. Arch. Surg. *73:*710, 1956.

Bollman, J. L. and Mann, F. C.: Nitrogenous constituents of blood following transplantation of ureters into different levels of intestine. Proc. Soc. Exper. Biol. & Med. *24:*923, 1926.

Bollman, J. L., Mann, F. C. and Magath, T. B.: Studies on the physiology of the liver. VIII. Effect of total removal of the liver on the formation of urea. Am. J. Physiol. *69:*371, 1924.

Boniface, K. J. and Brown, J. M.: Effect of carbon dioxide excess on contractile force of heart, in situ. Am. J. Physiol. *172:*752, 1953.

Borst, J. G. G.: The maintenance of an adequate cardiac output by the regulation of the urinary excretion of water and sodium chloride, an essential factor in the genesis of oedema. Acta med. scandinav. suppl. 207(v.130):1, 1948.

Bosch, D. T., Islami, A., Tan, C. T. C., and Beling, C. A.: Elderly surgical patients; analysis of 500 consecutive cases of patients 60 years of age or older. A.M.A. Arch. Surg. *64:*269, 1952.

Bothe, F. A.: Alkalosis. Ann. Surg. *84:*465, 1926.

Bowers, J. Z. and Scott, K. G.: Distribution and excretion of electrolytes after acute whole-body irradiation injury. I. Studies with radiopotassium. Proc. Soc. Exper. Biol. & Med. *78:*645, 1951.

Bowers, R. F.: Choledochojejunostomy: its ability to control chronic recurring pancreatitis. Ann. Surg. *142:*682, 1955.

Bowman, J. R.: Medical care in major pediatric surgery. South. M. J. *43:*720, 1950.

Boyce, F. F.: The Role of the Liver in Surgery. Springfield, Ill., Charles C Thomas, 1941.

Boyce, W. H. and Vest, S. A.: The role of ammonia reabsorption in acid-base imbalance following ureterosigmoidostomy. J. Urol. *67:*169, 1952.

Boyd, J. D.: Chronic acidosis secondary to ureteral transplantation. Am. J. Dis. Child. *42:*366, 1931.

Boyd, H. B., Zilversmit, D. B. and Calandruccio, R. A.: The use of radioactive phosphorus in determining the blood supply to the head of the femur. Fifth Congress, Internat. Orthopedic Soc., Stockholm, 1951.

Boyd, H. B., Zilversmit, D. B. and Calandruccio, R. A.: The use of radio-active phosphorus (P^{32}) to determine the viability of the head of the femur. J. Bone & Joint Surg. *37–A:*260, 1955.

Bradfield, J. R. G. and Kodicek, E.: Abnormal mucopolysaccharide and "precollagen" in vitamin C-deficient skin wounds. Biochem. J. *49:*XVII, 1951 (proc.).

Bradley, S. E., Smythe, C. M., Fitzpatrick, H. F. and Blakemore, H. F.: The effect of a portacaval shunt on estimated hepatic blood flow and oxygen uptake in cirrhosis. J. Clin. Invest. *32:*526, 1953.

Brady, L. W., Cooper, D. Y., Colodein, M., McClenahan, J. E., King, E. R. and Williams, R.: Blood volume studies in normal humans. Surg., Gynec. & Obst. *97:*25, 1953.

Brain, R. H. F. and Stammers, F. A. R.: Sequelae of radical gastric resections—clinical and metabolic findings in 35 cases. Lancet *1:*1137, 1951.

Braithwaite, F. and Moore, F. T.: Some observations on anemia in patients with burns. Brit. J. Plast. Surg. *1:*81, 1948.

Bramlitt, E. E. and Hardy, J. D.: Further studies in body fluid physiology. I. The effect of 3% NaCl, M/6 Na lactate, and M/6 NH₄Cl on plasma carbon dioxide combining power, pCO₂, and blood pH. S. Forum *6:*11, 1956.

Brazeau, P. and Gilman, A.: Effect of plasma CO₂ tension on renal tubular reabsorption of bicarbonate. Am. J. Physiol. *175:*33, 1953.

Breed, S. and Baxter, S. F.: Renal function in surgery. S. Clin. North America *32:*617, 1952.

Brewster, W. R., Isaacs, J. P., and Wainø-Andersen, T.: Depressant effect of ether on myocardium of the dog and its modification by reflex release of epinephrine and nor-epinephrine. Am. J. Physiol. *175:*399, 1953.

Bricker, N. S., Shwayri, E. I., Reardan, J. B., Kellog, D., Merrill, J. P. and Holmes, J. H.: An abnormality in renal function resulting from urinary tract obstruction. Am. J. Med. *23:*554, 1957.

Brines, J. K., Gibson, J. G. and Kunkel, P.: The blood volume in normal infants and children. J. Pediat. *18:*447, 1941.

Brodie, B. B. and Axelrod, J.: The fate of aminopyrine (Pyramidon) in man and methods for the estimation of aminopyrine and its metabolites in biological material. J. Pharmacol. & Exper. Therap. *99:*171, 1950.

Brodie, B. B., Berger, E. Y., Axelrod, J., Dunning, M. F., Porosowska, Y. and Steele, J. M.: Use of N-acetyl

4-aminoantipyrine (NAAP) in measurement of total body water. Proc. Soc. Exper. Biol. & Med. 77:794, 1951.

Bronsted, J. N.: The conception of acids and bases. Rec. de trav. chim. 42:718, 1923.

Brooks, B.: Pathologic changes in muscle as a result of disturbances of circulation. A.M.A. Arch. Surg.5:188, 1922.

Brooks, B.: Surgery in patients of advanced age. Ann. Surg. 105:481, 1937.

Brooks, J. W., Evans, E. I., Ham, W. T., Jr. and Reid, J. D.: The influence of external body radiation on mortality from thermal burns. Ann. Surg.136:533,1952.

Brown, E. B , Jr.: The role of hypotassemia in the production of ventricular fibrillation following hypercapnia. School Av. Med. Report No. 56–20, 1956.

Brown, E. B., Jr. and Miller, F. A.: Ventricular fibrillation following a rapid fall in alveolar carbon dioxide concentration. Am. J. Physiol. 169:56, 1952.

Brown, H., Englert, E., Jr., Wallach, S. and Simons, E. L.: Metabolism of free and conjugated 17-hydroxicorticosteroids in normal subjects. J. Clin. Endocrinol. 17:1191, 1957.

Brown, H. and Samuels, L. T.: Effect of intravenous testosterone on nitrogen balance in man. J. Clin. Endocrinol. 16:775, 1956.

Brown, H., Tanner, G. L. and Hecht, H. H.: The effect of potassium salts in subjects with heart disease. J. Lab. and Clin. Med. 37:506, 1951.

Brown, H., Willardson, D. G., Samuels, L. T. and Tyler, F. H.: 17-Hydroxicorticosteroid metabolism in liver disease. J. Clin. Invest. 33:1524, 1954.

Browne, J. S. L., Johnson, J. C., Schenker, V. and Venning, E. H.: Protein metabolism in acute and chronic disease and the relation of protein metabolism to excretion of glucocorticoids. Proc. First Clinical ACTH Conference. New York, The Blakiston Co., 1950, p. 108.

Browne, J. S. L., Schenker, V. and Stevenson, J. A. F.: Some metabolic aspects of damage and convalescence. J. Clin. Invest. 23:932, 1944.

Bruce, R. A., Merendino, K. A., Dunning, M. F., Scribner, B. H., Donohue, D., Carlsen, E. R. and Cummins, J.: Observations on hyponatremia following mitral valve surgery. Surg., Gynec. & Obst. 100:293, 1955.

Brun, C., Knudsen, E O. E., Petersen, C. S. and Roaschov, F.: Hydrodynamics of semi-permeable tubes with reference to glomerular function of the kidney. Acta. physiol. scand. 12:321, 1946.

Brun, C., Knudsen, E. O. E. and Roaschov, F.: Kidney function and circulatory collapse; postsyncopal oliguria. J. Clin. Invest. 25:568, 1946.

Bruneau, J. and Graham, E. A.: A caution against too liberal use of citrated blood in transfusions. A.M.A. Arch. Surg. 47:319, 1943.

Brunschwig, A. and Lüscher, M.: Hyperchloremic acidosis following anterior partial and complete pelvic exenteration. Surgery 35:197, 1954.

Brush, H. V.: The effect of thyroxin and stilbestrol on healing fractures in the rat. Am. J. Anatomy 76:339, 1945.

Bruusgaard, C.: The operative treatment of gastric and duodenal ulcer; clinical and roentgenologic study. Acta Chir. scandinav. (Supp. 117) 94:1, 1946.

Bryans, W. A. and Eiseman, B.: The incidence of fat globulemia following soft tissue and orthopedic operations. S. Forum 6:28, 1956.

Buckley, E. S., Jr., Gibson, J. G., 2nd and Walter, C. W.: The use of ion-exchange resins to prevent coagulation of whole blood. In proceedings of conference on separation of the formed elements, the protein, carbohydrate, lipid, steroid, peptide and other components of plasma. Harvard University, 1950. Cambridge, Mass. Harvard University Press, 1951.

Buckley, J. J, Van Bergen, F. H., Dobkin, A. B., Brown, E. B., Jr., Miller, F. A. and Varco, R. L.: Postanesthetic hypotension following cyclopropane: its relationship to hypercapnia. Anesthesiology 14:226, 1953.

Bull, G. M.: Acute tubular necrosis—functional pattern. Brit. Med. J. 1:1263, 1950.

Bull, G. M., Joekes, A. M. and Lowe, K. G.: Renal function studies in acute tubular necrosis. Clin. Sc. 9:379, 1950.

Bull, J. P. and Fisher, A. J.: A study of mortality in a burns unit: a revised estimate. Ann. Surg. 139:269, 1954.

Bull, J. P., Ricketts, C., Squire, J. R., Maycock, W. D'A., Spooner, S. J. L., Mollison, P. L. and Patterson, J. C. S.: Dextran as a plasma substitute. Lancet 1:134, 1949.

Bull, J. P. and Squire, J. R.: A study of mortality in a burns unit. Standards for the evaluation of alternative methods of treatment. Ann. Surg. 130:160, 1949.

Bunker, J. P., Brewster, W. R., Jr. and Beecher, H. K.: Citric acid intoxication during the transfusion of banked blood in man. Fed. Proc. 12:306, 1953 (abstr.).

Bunker, J. P., Stetson, J. B., Coe, R. C., Grillo, H. C. and Murphy, A. J.: Citric acid intoxication. J.A.M.A 157:1361, 1955.

Burdeaux, B. D., Jr. and Hutchison, W. J.: Studies in osteoporosis following fractures. S. Forum 2:434, 1952.

Burford, T. H. and Burbank, B.: Traumatic wet lung— observations on certain physiologic fundamentals of thoracic trauma. J. Thoracic Surg. 14:415, 1945.

Burnett, C. H., Bloomberg, E. L., Shatz, G., Compton, D. W. and Beecher, H. K.: A comparison of the effects of ether and cyclopropane anaesthesia on the renal function of man. J. Pharmacol. & Exper. Therap. 96:380, 1949.

Burnett, C. H., Shapiro, S. L., Simeone, F. A., Beecher, H. K., Mallory, T. B. and Sullivan, E. R.: Effects and use of alkalies in traumatic shock. Surgery 22:1029, 1947.

Burnett, C. H., Shapiro, S. L., Simeone, F. A., Beecher, H. K., Mallory, T. B. and Sullivan, E. R.: Post-traumatic renal insufficiency. Surgery 22:994, 1947.

Burnett, C. H., Shapiro, S. L., Simeone, F. A., Beecher, H. K., Mallory, T. B. and Sullivan, E. R.: Recent advances in surgery. III. Post-traumatic renal insufficiency. Surgery 22:994, 1947.

Burnett, C. H., Shapiro, S. L., Simeone, F. A., Beecher, H. K., Mallory, T. B. and Sullivan, E. R.: Renal function studies in the wounded. Surgery 22:856, 1947.

Burns, T. W., Engel, F. L., Vian, A., Scott, J. L., Jr., Hollingsworth, D. R. and Werk, E.: Studies on the interdependent effects of stress and the adrenal cortex on carbohydrate metabolism in man. J. Clin. Invest. 32:781, 1953.

Burrows, B. A., Davis, D. J., Kelly, J. F., Lewis, A. A. G. and Ross, J. F.: The effects of surgical procedures on simultaneously determined radiosodium, radiosulphate and radiopotassium spaces in human subjects. J. Clin. Invest. 34:924, 1955 (abstr.).

Burrows, B. A. and Ross, J. F.: The use of radiosodium and radiopotassium tracer studies in man. Proc. Int. Conf. Peaceful Uses of Atomic Energy *X:*430, 1955.

Burrows, H. J. and Graham, G.: Spinal osteoporosis of unknown origin. Quart. J. Med. *14:*147, 1945.

Burwell, C. S. *et al.:* Extreme obesity associated with alveolar hypoventilation—a Pickwickian syndrome Am. J. Med. *26:*811, 1956.

Butt, H. R., Snell, A. M. and Keys, A.: Plasma protein in hepatic disease; a study of the colloid osmotic pressure of blood serum and of ascitic fluid in various diseases of the liver. A.M.A. Arch. Int. Med. *63:*143, 1939.

Bywaters, E. G. L.: Ischemic muscle necrosis. Crushing injury, traumatic edema, the crush syndrome, traumatic anuria, compression syndrome: a type of injury seen in air raid casualties following burial beneath debris. J.A.M.A. *124:*1103, 1944.

Calloway, D. H., Grossman, M. I., Bowman, J. and Calhoun, W. K.: The effect of previous level of protein feeding on wound healing and on metabolism response to injury. Surgery *37:*935, 1955.

Calman, C., Hershey, F. B., Skaggs, J. O. and Spencer, A.: Serum lactic dehydrogenase in the diagnosis of the acute surgical abdomen. Surgery *44:*43, 1958.

Campbell, G. S.: Cardiac arrest: further studies on the effect of pH changes on vagal inhibition of the heart. Surgery *38:*615, 1955.

Campbell, H. E.: Correspondence: Deceleration and the motor car. J.A.M.A. *154:*1023, 1954.

Campbell, R. M., Sharp, G., Boyne, A. W., and Cuthbertson, D. P.: Cortisone and the metabolic response to injury. Brit. J. Exper. Path. *35:*566, 1954.

Cannon, J. A.: Experience with ligation of the pancreatic ducts in treatment of chronic relapsing pancreatitis. Am. J. Surg. *90:*266, 1955.

Cannon, P. R.: Protein metabolism and resistance to infection. J. Michigan M. Soc. *43:*323, 1944.

Cannon, P. R.: The importance of proteins in resistance to infection. J.A.M.A. *128:*360, 1945.

Cannon, P. R., Chase, W. E. and Wissler, R. W.: The relationship of the protein-reserves to antibody-production. I. The effects of a low protein diet and of plasmapheresis upon the formation of agglutinins. J. Immunol. *47:*133, 1943.

Cannon, P. R., Wissler, R. W., Woolridge, R. L. and Benditt, E. P.: The relationship of protein deficiency to surgical infection. Ann. Surg. *120:*514, 1944.

Cannon, W. B.: A consideration of the nature of wound shock. J.A.M.A. *70:*611, 1918.

Cannon, W. B.: Acidosis in cases of shock, hemorrhage and gas infection. J.A.M.A. *70:*531, 1918.

Cannon, W. B. and Bayliss, W. M.: Note on muscle injury in relation to shock. Special report series, No. 26, Great Britain Medical Research Commission, p. 19. London, H. M. Stationery Office, 1919.

Cannon, W. B., Fraser, J. and Cowell, E. M.: The preventive treatment of wound shock. J.A.M.A. *70:*61, 1918.

Carbone, J. V., Furth, F. W., Scott, R., Jr. and Crosby, W. H.: An hemostatic defect associated with dextran infusion. Proc. Soc. Exper. Biol. & Med. *85:*101, 1954.

Care, A. D., Reed, G. W. and Pyrah, L. N.: Changes in the reabsorption of sodium and chloride ions after ureterocolic anastomosis. Clin. Sc. *16:*95, 1957.

Carryer, H. M.: Tissue anoxia resulting from respiratory alkalosis. Proc. Staff Meet., Mayo Clin. *22:*456, 1947.

Carter, B. N. and Giuseffi, J. Tracheotomy, a useful procedure in thoracic surgery, with particular reference to its employment in crushing injuries of the thorax. J. Thoracic Surg. *21:*495, 1951.

Cartwright, G. E., Hamilton, L. D., Gubler, C. J., Fellows, N. M., Ashenbrucker, H. and Wintrobe, M.M. The anemia of infection. XIII. Studies on experimentally produced acute hypoferremia in dogs and the relationship of the adrenal cortex to hypoferremia. J. Clin. Invest. *30:*161, 1951.

Cartwright, G. E., Lauritsen, M. A., Humphreys, S., Jones, P. J., Merrill, I. M. and Wintrobe, M. M.: The anemia of infection. II. The experimental production of hypoferremia and anemia in dogs. J. Clin. Invest. *25:*81, 1946.

Cartwright, G. E., Lauritsen, M. A., Jones, P. J., Merrill, I. M. and Wintrobe, M. M.: The anemia of infection. I. Hypoferremia, hypercupremia, and alterations in porphyrin metabolism in patients. J. Clin. Invest. *25:*65, 1946.

Case, E. H. and Stiles, J. A.: The effect of various surgical positions on vital capacity. Anesthesiology *7:*29, 1946.

Case, R. B., Sarnoff, S. J., Waithe, P. E. and Sarnoff, L. C.: Intra-arterial and intravenous blood infusion in hemorrhagic shock; comparison of effects on coronary blood flow and arterial pressure. J.A.M.A. *152:*208, 1953.

Casey, J. H., Bickel, E. Y. and Zimmermann, B.: The pattern and significance of aldosterone excretion by the postoperative surgical patient. Surg., Gynec. & Obst. *105:*179, 1957.

Casey, J. H. and Zimmermann, B.: The role of bone sodium in surgery. S. Forum *6:*7, 1956.

Catchpole, B. N., Hackel, D. B. and Simeone, F. A.: Coronary and peripheral blood flow in experimental hemorrhagic hypotension treated with L-nor-epinephrine. Ann. Surg. *142:*372, 1955.

Caton, W. L., Roby, C. C., Reid, D. E., Caswell, R., Maletskos, C. J., Fluharty, R. G. and Gibson, J. G.: The circulating red cell volume and body hematocrit in normal pregnancy and the puerperium. Am. J. Obst. & Gynec. *61:*1207, 1951.

Cattell, R. B. and Warren, K. W.: Medical progress; pancreatic surgery. New England J. Med. *244:*941, 1951.

Chambers, R. and Zweifach, B. W.: Blood-borne. Vasotropic substances in experimental shock. Am. J. Physiol. *150:*239, 1947.

Chambers, R., Zweifach, B. W., Lowenstein, B. E. and Lee, R. E.: Vaso-excitor and -depressor substances as "toxic" factors in experimentally induced shock. Proc. Soc. Exper. Biol. & Med. *56:*127, 1944.

Chanutin, A. and Ludewig, S.: Effects of protein and methionine on nitrogen balance of burned rats. Surgery *21:*593, 1947.

Chapin, M. A. and Ross, J. F.: The determination of the true cell volume by dye dilution, by protein dilution, and with radioactive iron. The error of the centrifuge hematocrit. Am. J. Physiol. *137:*447, 1942.

Chaplin, H. and Mollison, P. L.: Correction for plasma trapped in the red cell column of the hematocrit. Blood *7:*1227, 1952.

Chaplin, H., Mollison, P. L. and Vetter, H.: The body venous hematocrit ratio: its constancy over a wide hematocrit range. J. Clin. Invest. *32:*1309, 1953.

Chart, J. J. and Shipley, E. S.: The mechanism of sodium retention in cirrhosis of the liver. J. Clin. Invest. *32:*560, 1953 (abstr.).

Cheek, D. B.: Observations on total body chloride in children. Pediatrics *14:*5, 1954.

Cherniack, R. N.: The oxygen consumption and efficiency of the respiratory muscles in health and emphysema. J. Clin. Invest. *38:*494, 1959.

Child, C. G.: The Hepatic Circulation and Portal Hypertension. Philadelphia, W. B. Saunders Co., 1954.

Child, C. G.: Portal circulation; the Shattuck lecture. New England J. Med. *252:*837, 1955.

Chinn, A. B., Lavik, P. S., Stitt, R. M. and Buckoloo, G. W.: Use of I^{131} labeled protein in the diagnosis of pancreatic insufficiency. New England J. Med. *247:*877, 1952.

Chirico, M., Bonomo, E. and Bernardi, E.: Serum glycoproteins after operations. Chem. Abstr. *50.5:*14092 i, 1956.

Christensen, H. N., Wilber, P. B., Coyne, B. A. and Fisher, J. H.: Effects of simultaneous or prior infusion of sugars on the fate of infused protein hydrolysates. J. Clin. Invest. *34:*86, 1955.

Christenson, R. M., Shoemaker, W. E. and Moore, F. D.: The effect of surgical trauma on the blood levels of free 17-hydroxycorticosteroids after adrenalectomy in animals receiving a constant infusion of hydrocortisone. (In preparation.)

Chunn, C. F. and Harkins, H. N.: Experimental studies on alimentary azotemia. I. Role of blood absorption from the gastrointestinal tract. Surgery *9:*695, 1941.

Chunn, C. F., Harkins, H. N. and Boals, R. T.: Experimental studies on alimentary azotemia. III. Site of blood absorption. Surgery *11:*56, 1942.

Church, R. E. and Hinton, J. W.: Follow-up results in subtotal gastric resection for ulcer. Am. J. Digest. Dis. *9:*317, 1942.

Churchill, E. D.: The surgical management of the wounded in the Mediterranean Theater at the time of the fall of Rome. Ann. Surg. *120:*268, 1944.

Chute, A. L.: Hepatic function in shock. Symposium on shock. Army Med. Service Graduate School, 1951.

Clarke, E., Evans, B. M., Macintyre, I. and Milne, M. D.: Acidosis in experimental electrolyte depletion. Clin. Sc. *14:*421, 1955.

Clarke, R. and Fisher, M. R.: Assessment of blood loss following injury. Brit. J. Clin. Practice *10:*746, 1956.

Clarke, R., Topley, E. and Flear, C. T. G.: Assessment of blood-loss in civilian trauma. Lancet *1:*629, 1955.

Cliffton, E. E., Grossi, C. and Siegel, M.: Hemorrhage during and after operation secondary to changes in the clotting mechanism; physiology and methods of control. Surgery *40:*37, 1956.

Cline, T. N., Cole, J. W. and Holden, W. D.: Demonstration of an antidiuretic substance in the urine of postoperative patients. Surg., Gynec. & Obst. *96:*674, 1953.

Clowes, G. H. A., Jr., Hopkins, A. L. and Simeone, F. A.: A comparison of the physiological effects of hypercapnia and hypoxia in the production of cardiac arrest. Ann. Surg. *142:*446, 1955.

Clowes, G. H. A., Jr., Kretchmer, H. E., McBurney, R. W. and Simeone, F. A.: The use of the electroencephalogram in the evaluation of the effects of anesthetic agents and carbon dioxide accumulation during surgery. Ann. Surg. *138:*558, 1953.

Clowes, G. H. A., Jr., Neville, W. E., Sabga, G. and Shibota, Y.: The relationship of oxygen consumption perfusion rate, and temperature to the acidosis associated with cardiopulmonary circulatory bypass. Surgery *44:*220, 1958.

Clowes, G. H. A., Jr. and Simeone, F. A.: Acute hypocalcemia in surgical patients. Ann. Surg. *147:*530, 1957.

Cobey, M. C.: Fractures of the neck of the femur due to osteoporosis. M. Ann. District of Columbia *18:*243, 1949.

Coffey, R. J.: Trypsin and antitrypsin in acute pancreatic disease. S. Forum *1:*166, 1951 (abstr.).

Cohn, J. E., Carroll, D. G. and Riley, R. L.: Respiratory acidosis in patients with emphysema. Am. J. Med. *17:*447, 1954.

Cohn, J. E. and Shock, N. W.: Blood volume studies in middle-aged and elderly males. Am. J. M. Sc. *217:*388, 1949.

Cohn, R. and Mathewson, C., Jr.: Observations on patients during the surgical treatment of acute massive hemorrhage from esophageal varices secondary to cirrhosis of the liver. Surgery *41:*94, 1957.

Cole, J. W. and Leuchtenberger, C.: Cellular changes during surgical stress. I. Morphologic alterations in hepatic cells. Surg., Gynec. & Obst. *102:*702, 1956.

Cole, W. H., Schneewind, J. H. and Canham, R.: The role of protein metabolism in surgery. Surgery *37:*683, 1955.

Colebrook, L., Gibson, T., Todd, J. P., Clark, A. M., Brown, A. and Anderson, A. B.: Studies of burns and scalds (reports of the burns unit, Royal Infirmary, Glasgow, 1942–3). Med. Res. Council Spec. Rep. Ser., London No. 249, 1944.

Coleman, W. and Dubois, E. F.: Clinical calorimetry. VII. Calorimetric observations on the metabolism of typhoid patients with or without food. A.M.A. Arch. Int. Med. *15:*887, 1915.

Coller, F. A., Rees, V. I., Campbell, K. N., Iob, V. L. and Moyer, C. A.: Effects of ether and cyclopropane anaesthesia upon renal function in man. Ann. Surg. *118:*717, 1943.

Collins, E. N. and Russell, P. W.: Fatal magnesium poisoning following magnesium sulphate, glycerine, and water enema in primary megacolon. Cleveland Clin. Quart. *16:*162, 1949.

Cominsky, B., Preedy, J. R. K., Hayes, R. and Wheeler, H. O.: The distribution of circulating blood within the splanchnic vasculature. J. Clin. Invest. *34:*927, 1955 (abstr.).

Conn, J. W.: Primary aldosteronism, a new clinical syndrome. J. Lab. & Clin. Med. *45:*6, 1955.

Conn, J. W., Fajans, S. S., Louis, L. H., Seltzer, H. S. and Kaine, H. D.: A comparison of steroidal excretion and metabolic effects induced in man by stress and by ACTH. Rec. Prog. Horm. Res. *10:*471, 1954.

Connolly, P. F.: The effect of oestrogens on wound healing. J. Michigan M. Soc. *44:*377, 1945.

Connor, T. B., Thomas, W. C., Jr. and Howard, J. E.: The etiology of hypercalcemia associated with lung carcinoma. J. Clin. Invest. *35:*697, 1956 (abstr.).

Converse, J. G. and Boba, A.: The use of ganglionic blocking agents in the treatment of hemorrhagic shock. Current Res. Anaesth. & Analg. *35:*644, 1956.

Converse, J. G., McKechnie, F. B. and Boba, A.: Arfonad in hemorrhage. New York J. Med. *57:*731, 1957

Conway, E. J. and McCormack, J. I.: The total intracellular concentration of mammalian tissues compared with that of the extracellular fluid. J. Physiol. *120:*1, 1953.

Cooke, A. M.: Osteoporosis. Lumleian lectures. Lancet *1:*887, 929, 1955.

Cooke, R. E., Coughlin, F. R., Jr. and Segar, W. E.: Muscle composition in respiratory acidosis. J. Clin. Invest. *31:*1006, 1952.

Cooke, W. T. *et al.:* Clostridial infections in war wounds. Lancet *1:*487, 1945

Cookson, B. A., Costas-Durieux, J. and Bailey, C. P.: The toxic effects of citrated blood and the search for a suitable substitute for use in cardiac surgery. Ann. Surg. *139:*430, 1954.

Coon, W. W. and Hodgson, P. E.: Fibrinolysis in surgical patients; possible relationships to hemorrhagic diathesis. Surg., Gynec. & Obst. *95:*717, 1952.

Coonse, G. K., Foisie, P. S., Robertson, H. F. and Aufranc, O. E.: Traumatic and hemorrhagic shock, experimental and clinical study. New England J. Med. *212:*647, 1935.

Cooper, D. R., Iob, V. and Coller, F. A.: Response to parenteral glucose of normal kidneys and of the kidneys of postoperative patients. Ann. Surg. *129:*1, 1949.

Cooper, I. S. and Crevier, P. H.: Neurogenic hypernatremia and hyperchloremia. J. Clin. Endocrinol. *12:*821, 1952.

Cooper, I. S., Rynearson, E. H., MacCarty, C. S. and Power, M. H.: The catabolic effect of craniotomy and its investigative treatment with testosterone propionate. J. Neurosurg. *8:*295, 1951.

Cope, C., Nardi, G. L., Quijano, M., Rovit, R. L., Stanbury, G. B. and Wight, A.: Metabolic rate and thyroid function following acute thermal trauma in man. Ann. Surg. *137:*165, 1953.

Cope, C., Nathanson, I. T., Rourke, G. M. and Wilson, M.: Metabolic observations. Ann. Surg. *177:*937, 1943.

Cope, C. L. and Llaurado, J. G.: The occurrence of electrocortin in human urine. Brit. Med. J. *1:*1290, 1954.

Cope, O.: Care of the victims of the Coconut Grove fire at the Massachusetts General Hospital. New England J. Med. *229:*138, 1943.

Cope, O.: Management of the Coconut Grove burns at the Massachusetts General Hospital. Ann. Surg. *177:*801, 1943.

Cope, O., Culver, P. J., Mixter, C. G. and Nardi, G. L.: Pancreatitis, a diagnostic clue to hyperparathyroidism. Ann. Surg. *145:*857, 1957.

Cope, O., Graham, J. B., Moore, F. D. and Ball, M. R.: The nature of the shift of plasma protein to the extravascular space following thermal trauma. Ann. Surg. *128:*1041, 1948.

Cope, O., Hopkirk, J. F. and Wight, A.: Metabolic derangements imperiling the perforated ulcer patient. I. The dehydration and fluid shifts. A.M.A. Arch. Surg. *71:*669, 1955.

Cope, O. and Moore, F. D.: The redistribution of body water and the fluid therapy of the burned patient. Ann. Surg. *126:*1010, 1947.

Cope, O. and Wight, A.: Metabolic derangements imperiling the perforated ulcer patient. VI. Plan of therapy. A.M.A. Arch. Surg. *72:*571, 1956.

Coppinger, W. R. and Goldner, M. G.: The eosinophil response to surgical trauma. Surgery *28:*75, 1950.

Corcoran, A. C. and Page, I. H.: Effects of anesthesia dosage of pentobarbital sodium on renal function and blood pressure in dogs. Am. J. Physiol. *140:*234, 1943.

Corsa, L., Jr., Olney, J. M., Jr., Steenburg, R. W., Ball, M. R. and Moore, F. D.: The measurement of exchangeable potassium in man by isotope dilution. J. Clin. Invest. *29:*1280, 1950.

Cotlove, E., Holliday, M. A., Schwartz, R. and Wallace, W. M.: Effects of electrolyte depletion and acid-base disturbance on muscle cations. Am. J. Physiol. *167:*665, 1951.

Co Tui, Wright, A. M., Mulholland, J. H., Carabba, V., Barcham, I. and Vinci, V. J.: Studies on surgical convalescence. I. Sources of nitrogen loss postgastrectomy and effect of high amino-acid and high caloric intake on convalescence. Ann. Surg. *120:*99, 1944.

Cournand, A.: Control of the pulmonary circulation in normal man. In Michael, J.: Circulation. Proceedings of the Harvey Tercentenary Congress, Royal College of Surgeons, London. Oxford, Blackwell Scientific Publications, 1958.

Cournand, A. *et al.:* The oxygen cost of breathing. Tr. A. Am. Physicians *67:*162, 1954.

Cournand, A., Riley, R. L., Bradley, S. E., Breed, E. S., Noble, R. P., Lauson, H. D., Gregerson, M. I. and Richards, D. W.: Studies of the circulation in clinical shock. Surgery *13:*964, 1943.

Craig, A. B. and Waterhouse, C.: The volume of distribution of high molecular weight dextran and its relation to plasma volume in man. J. Clin. Invest. *34:*928, 1955.

Craig, F. N., Visscher, F. E. and Houck, C. R.: Renal function in dogs under ether or cyclopropane anesthesia. Am. J. Physiol. *143:*108, 1945.

Crandon, J. H., Lund, C. C. and Dill, D. B.: Experimental human scurvy. New England J. Med. *223:*353, 1940.

Crane, C.: Embolism to the bifurcation of the aorta. New England J. Med. *258:*359, 1958.

Crawford, E. S. and Haynes, B. W., Jr.: Use of norepinephrine in treatment of hypotension associated with common surgical conditions. Am. Surgeon *19:*191, 1953.

Creevy, C. D.: Facts about ureterosigmoidostomy. J.A.M.A. *151:*120, 1953.

Creevy, C. D. and Reiser, M. P.: Observations upon the absorption of urinary constituents after ureterosigmoidostomy: the importance of renal damage. Surg., Gynec. & Obst. *95:*589, 1952.

Crile, G., Jr.: Transesophageal ligation of bleeding esophageal varices: preliminary report of 7 cases. A.M.A. Arch. Surg. *61:*654, 1950.

Crismon, C. A., Hanvey, R. V. and Luck, J. M.: The effects of epinephrine, potassium, pentobarbital and insulin on concentration of amino acid nitrogen in the blood of fasting dogs. Am. J. Physiol. *130:*171, 1940.

Croft, P. B. and Peters, R. A.: Nitrogen loss after thermal burns. Lancet *1:*266, 1945.

Crosby, W. H. and Howard, J. M.: The hematologic response to wounding and to resuscitation accomplished by large transfusions of stored blood. A study of battle casualties in Korea. Blood *9:*439, 1954.

Crowell, J. W., Sharpe, G. P., Lambright, R. L. and Read, W. L.: The mechanism of death after resuscitation following acute circulatory failure. Surgery *38:*696, 1955.

Crowson, C. N. and More, R. H.: Glomerulotubular nephrosis correlated with hepatic lesions. II. Incidence and morphology of associated kidney and liver lesions in human autopsy material. A.M.A. Arch. Path *.60:*73, 1955.

Culotta, R. J., Howard, J. M. and Jordan, G. L.: Traumatic injuries of the pancreas. Surgery 40:320, 1956.

Culver, P. J.: The dumping syndrome. M. Clin. North America 33:1321, 1949.

Curling, T. B.: An acute ulceration of the duodenum in cases of burns. Medico-Chir. Tr., London 25:260, 1942.

Currens, H., Reid, E. A. S., Maclachlan, E. A., Terry, M. L., Butler, A. M. and White, P. D.: Physiologic, metabolic and electrolyte balance studies of hypertensive patients while on the rice diet. J. Clin. Invest. 28:776, 1949 (abstr.).

Currie, A. R. and Symington, T.: An attempt to correlate the histological changes in the anterior hypophysis and adrenal glands in various diseases in man. Ciba Foundation Coll. Endocrinol. 8:396, 1955.

Custer, M. D., Jr., Butt, H. R. and Waugh, J. M.: The so-called "dumping syndrome" after subtotal gastrectomy—a clinical study. Ann. Surg. 123:410, 1946.

Cuthbertson, D. P.: The disturbance of metabolism produced by bony and non-bony injury, with notes on certain abnormal conditions of bone. Biochem. J. 24.2:1244, 1930.

Cuthbertson, D. P.: Certain aspects of metabolic response to injury. Glasgow M. J. 121:41, 1934.

Cuthbertson, D. P.: Post shock metabolic response. Lancet 1:433, 1942.

Cuthbertson, D. P.: Protein intake and metabolism in relation to wound healing. Fifth conference on convalescence, Josiah Macy, Jr., Foundation, Oct. 8–9, 1943, p. 44.

Cuthbertson, D. P.: The physiology of convalescence after injury. Brit. M. Bull. 3:96, 1945.

Cuthbertson, D. P.: Interrelationship of metabolic changes consequent to injury. Brit. M. Bull. 10:33, 1954.

Cuthbertson, D. P. and Tompsett, S. L.: Note on the effect of injury on the level of the plasma proteins. Brit. J. Exper. Path. 76:471, 1935.

Cutler, E. C. and Zollinger, R.: An atlas of surgical operations. New York, The Macmillan Co., 1939.

Dack, G. M.: The role of enterotoxin of *Micrococcus pyogenes* var. *Aureus* in the etiology of pseudomembranous enterocolitis. Am. J. Surg. 92:765, 1956.

D'Agostino, A., Leadbetter, W. F. and Schwartz, W. B.: Alterations in the ionic composition of isotonic saline solution instilled into the colon. J. Clin. Invest. 32:444, 1953.

Dahl, L. K.: Pressor effects of norepinephrine after drastic reduction of sodium intake. Circulation 15:231, 1957.

Dalton, A. J. and Selye, H.: The blood picture during the alarm reaction. Folia haemat. 62:397, 1939.

Daniel, R. A., Jr. and Cate, W. R., Jr.: "Wet lung"—an experimental study; The effects of trauma and hypoxia. Ann. Surg. 127:836, 1948.

Danowski, T. S., Peters, J. H., Rathbun, J. C., Quashnock, J. M. and Greenman, L.: Studies in diabetic acidosis and coma, with particular emphasis on the retention of administered potassium. J. Clin. Invest. 28:1, 1949.

Danziger, A.: Resuscitation from "irreversible" shock by intra-arterial transfusion. Lancet 2:701, 1955.

Darrow, D. C.: Disturbances in electrolyte metabolism in man and their management. Bull. New York Acad. Med. 24:147, 1948.

Darrow, D. C. and Sarason, E. L.: Some effects of low

atmospheric pressure on rats. J. Clin. Invest. 23:11, 1944.

Darrow, D. C., Schwartz, R., Iannucci, J. F. and Coville, F.: The relation of serum bicarbonate concentration to muscle composition. J. Clin. Invest. 27:198, 1948.

Davenport, H. W.: The ABC of Acid-base Chemistry. 3rd ed. Chicago, University of Chicago Press, 1950.

Davies, A. P.: The Meaning of the Dead Sea Scrolls. New York, Mentor Books, 1956.

Davies, H. E. F., Jepson, R. P. and Black, D. A. K.: Some metabolic sequels of gastric surgery in patients with or without pyloric stenosis. Clin. Sc. 15:61, 1956.

Davies, J. W. L.: Blood volume studies in acute injury. Brit. J. Clin. Practice 10:785, 1956.

Davies, J. W. L. and Topley, E.: The disappearance of red cells in patients with burns. Clin. Sc. 15:135, 1956.

Davies, R. E., Kornberg, H. L. and Wilson, G. M.: The determination of sodium in bone. Biochem. J. 52:xv, 1952.

Davies, R. E., Kornberg, H. L. and Wilson, G. M.: Non-exchangeable sodium in the body. Biochem. et Biophys. Acta 9:703, 1952.

Davis, H. L. and Musselman, M. M.: Blood particle agglomeration and fat embolism. Internat. Rec. Med. 167:439, 1954.

Davis, R. A., Wetzel, N. and Davis, L.: Acute upper alimentary tract ulcerations and hemorrhage following neurosurgical operations. Surg., Gynec. & Obst. 100:51, 1955.

Davis, W. M., Alpen, E. L. and Davis, A. K.: Studies of radioiron utilization and erythrocyte life span in rats following thermal injury. J. Clin. Invest. 34:67, 1955.

Davis, W. M., Davis, A. K., Lee, W. and Alpen, E. L.: The combined effects of thermal burns and whole-body X-irradiation. III. Study of blood coagulation. Ann. Surg. 142:66, 1955.

Dearing, W. H. and Heilman, F. R.: Micrococcic (staphylococcic) enteritis as a complication of antibiotic therapy; its response to erythromycin. Proc. Staff Meet. Mayo Clin. 28:121, 1953.

DeBakey, M. and Carter, B. N.: Current considerations of war surgery. Ann. Surg. 121:545, 1945.

DeBodo, R. C.: The antidiuretic action of morphine and its mechanism. J. Pharmacol. & Exper. Therap. 82:74, 1944.

Debrunner, H.: Ueber die Verwendung von Perandren bei Erkrankungen am Skelettsystem. Schweiz. med. Wschr. 75:947, 1945.

DeCosse, J. J., Randall, H. T., Habif, D. V. and Roberts, K. E.: The mechanism of hyponatremia and hypotonicity after surgical trauma. Surgery 40:27, 1956.

DeHaven, H.: Crash research from the point of view of cabin design. Aeronaut. Engineer Rev. 5:1, 1946.

Deitrick, J. E., Whedon, G. D. and Shorr, E.: Effects of immobilization upon various metabolic and physiologic functions of normal men. Am. J. Med. 4:3, 1948.

DeKruif, H. and Baker, N. H.: Early use of ACTH in severe burn; report of case. Minnesota Med. 34:1092, 1951.

Deming, Q. B. and Gerbode, F.: Observations on sodium balance in patients undergoing mitral valvulotomy. S. Forum 4:18, 1954.

de Niord, R. N., Jr. and Hayes, M. A.: Endocrine interrelations concerned with the postoperative renal response to a water load. Surg., Gynec. & Obst. 99:617, 1954.

Derrick, J. R., Wilkinson, A. H. and Howard, J. M.:

Perforation of stress ulcers of the esophagus following thermal burns; report of 2 patients. A.M.A. Arch. Surg. *75:*17, 1957.

DesPrez, J., Persky, L., Levey, S. and Abbott, W. E.: Metabolic alterations following experimental vesicosigmoidostomy. Surgery *37:*369, 1955.

deTakats, G.: The management of venous thrombosis in the lower extremities. Surgery *37:*507, 1955.

Deutsch, H.: Some psychoanalytic observations in surgery. Psychosom. Med. *4:*105, 1942.

DeWardener, H. E. and Miles, B. E.: The effect of haemorrhage on the circulatory autoregulation of the dog's kidney perfused in situ. Clin. Sc. *11:*267, 1952.

Dexter, L., Gorlin, R., Lewis, B. M., Haynes, F. W. and Harken, D. E.: Physiologic evaluation of patients with mitral stenosis before and after mitral valvuloplasty. Tr. Am. Clin. & Climatol. A. *62:*170, 1951.

Dexter, L., McDonald, L., Rabinowitz, M., Saxton, G. A., Jr. and Gaynes, F. W.: Medical aspects of patients undergoing surgery for mitral stenosis. Circulation *9:*758, 1954.

Dieckmann, W. J. and Wegner, C. R.: The blood in normal pregnancy. I. Blood and plasma volumes. A.M.A. Arch. Int. Med. *53:*71, 1934.

Diefenbach, W. C. L., Fisk, S. C. and Gilson, S. B.: Hypopotassemia following bilateral ureterosigmoidostomy. New England J. Med. *244:*326, 1951.

Dingwall, J. A., Heinzen, B. R. and Pifer, M.: The eosinophilic response to surgery. Surgery *36:*87, 1954.

Ditzler, J. W. and Eckenhoff, J. E.: A comparison of blood loss and operative time in certain surgical procedures completed with and without controlled hypotension. Ann. Surg. *143:*289, 1956.

Dixon, C. F. and Weisman, R. E.: Acute pseudomembranous enteritis or enterocolitis, a complication following intestinal surgery. S. Clin. North America *28:*999, 1948.

Doolan, P. D., Shaw, C. C., Shreeve, W. W. and Harper, H. A.: Post-traumatic acute renal insufficiency complicated by hypernatremia. Ann. Int. Med *42:*1101, 1955.

Dorman, P. J., Sullivan, W. J. and Pitts, R. F.: The renal response to acute respiratory acidosis. J. Clin. Invest. *33:*82, 1954.

Doroshow, H. S.: Electrolyte imbalance following bilateral ureterosigmoidostomy. J. Urol. *65:*831, 1951.

Doubilet, H. and Mulholland, J. H.: 8-year study of pancreatitis and sphincterotomy. J.A.M.A. *160:*521, 1956.

Drablos, A., Linden, V. and Skjelbred, P.: The late results of gastric resection for gastro-duodenal ulcer—a follow-up study with special reference to serious late complications, subjective symptoms and anemia. Acta med. scandinav. *140:*327, 1951.

Dragstedt, L. R., Ragins, H., Dragstedt, L. R., II and Evans, S. O., Jr.: Stress and duodenal ulcer. Ann. Surg. *144:*450, 1956.

Drapanas, T., Becker, D. R., Schenk, W. G., Jr., Shaw, W. W., Potter, W. H. and Stewart, J. D.: Ammonia intoxication from portal diversion and hepatic failure. Ann. Surg. *142:*560, 1955.

Dripps, R. D.: The immediate decrease in blood pressure seen at the conclusion of cyclopropane anesthesia; "cyclopropane shock." Anesthesiology *8:*15, 1947.

Dripps, R. D. and Severinghaus, J. W.: General anesthesia and respiration. Physiol. Rev. *35:*741, 1955.

Drucker, W. R., Costley, C., Stults, R., Gross, G., Holden, W., Miller, M., Craig, J. and Woodward, H., Jr.: The effect of anesthesia on intermediary carbohydrate metabolism. Clin. Res. Proc. *4:*202, 1955 (abstr.).

Drucker, W. R., Costley, C., Stults, R., Miller, M., Craig, J. W. and Woodward, H.: The effect of ether anesthesia on pyruvate metabolism. S. Forum *7:*185, 1957.

Drucker, W. R., Krieger, H., Babb, L. I., Levey, S. and Abbott, W. E.: Metabolic alterations in surgical patients. II. The excretion of salt and water postoperatively following the administration of various sodium containing solutions. S. Forum *4:*544, 1954.

Drucker, W. R., Miller, M., Abbott, W. E., Craig, J. W., Jefferies, W. M., Levey, S. and Woodward, H.: The effect of stress on glucose and fructose metabolism. J. Lab. & Clin. Med. *40:*794, 1952 (abstr.).

Drucker, W. R., Miller, M., Craig, J., Jefferies, W. M., Levey, S. and Abbott, W. E.: A comparison of the effect of operation on glucose and fructose metabolism. S. Forum *3:*548, 1953.

Dudley, H. A. F.: Recent advances in the understanding and management of haemorrhagic and wound shock. J. Roy. Coll. Surgeons, Edinburgh *2:*202, 1957.

Dudley, H. A. F., Batchelor, A. D. R. and Sutherland, A. B.: Management of hemoglobinuria in extensive burns. Brit. J. Plast. Surg. *9:*275, 1957.

Dudley, H. A. F., Boling, E. A., LeQuesne, L. P. and Moore, F. D.: Studies on antidiuresis in surgery: effects of anesthesia, surgery and posterior pituitary antidiuretic hormone on water metabolism in man. Ann. Surg. *140:*354, 1954.

Duff, I. F., Gamble, J. R., Willis, P. W., Hodgson, P. E., Wilson, W. S. and Polhemus, J. A.: The control of excessive effect by anticoagulants. Ann. Int. Med. *43:*955, 1955.

Duncan, G. W. and Blalock, A.: Uniform production of experimental shock by crush injury; possible relationship to clinical crush syndrome. Am. Surg. *115:*684, 1942.

Duncan, G. W., Sarnoff, S. J. and Rhode, C. M.: Studies on the effects of posture in shock and injury. Ann. Surg. *120:*24, 1944.

Dunphy, J. E.: Wound healing. Surg., Gynec. & Obst. *102:*750, 1956.

Dunphy, J. E., Brooks, J. R. and Achroyd, F.: Acute postoperative pancreatitis. New England J. Med. *248:*445, 1953.

Dunphy, J. E. and Ilfeld, F. W.: Fat embolism. Am. J. Surg. *77:*737, 1949.

Dunphy, J. E. and Udupa, K. N.: Chemical and histochemical sequences in the normal healing of wounds. New England J. Med. *253:*847, 1955.

Dunphy, J. E., Udupa, K. N. and Edwards, L. C.: Wound healing. A new perspective with particular reference to ascorbic acid deficiency. Ann. Surg. *144:*304, 1956.

Duval, M. K., Jr.: Caudal pancreaticojejunostomy for chronic relapsing pancreatitis. Ann. Surg. *140:*775, 1954.

Duval, M. K., Jr.: The effect of chronic pancreatitis on pressure tolerance in the human pancreatic duct. Surgery *43:*798, 1958.

Duval, M. K., Jr.: Pancreaticojejunostomy for chronic pancreatitis. Surgery *41:*1019, 1957.

Dye, W. S., Capps, R. B., Baker, L. A., Grove, W. J. and Julian, O. C.: Evaluation of venous shunt surgery in portal hypertension. A.M.A. Arch. Surg. *74:*958, 1957.

Ebeling, W. C., Bunker, J. P., Ellis, D. S., French, A. B., Linton, R. R. and Jones, C. M.: Management of patients with portal hypertension undergoing venous-shunt surgery. New England J. Med. *254:*141, 1956.

Ebert, R. V., Borden, C. W., Hall, W. H. and Gold, D.: A study of hypotension (shock) produced by meningococcus toxin. Circulation Res. *3:*378, 1955.

Ebert, R. V., Hagen, P. S. and Borden, C. W.: The mechanism of shock in peritonitis—a study of the hemodynamics of shock occurring in peritonitis experimentally produced in dogs. Surgery *25:*399, 1949.

Ebert, R. V., Stead, E. A., Jr. and Gibson, J. G., II: Response of normal subjects to acute blood loss; with special reference to the mechanism of restoration of blood volume. A.M.A. Arch. Int. Med. *68:*578, 1941.

Eckenhoff, J. E. and Dripps, R. D.: The use of norepinephrine in various stages of shock. Anesthesiology *15:*681, 1954.

Eckenhoff, J. E., Helrich, M., Hege, M. J. D. and Jones, R. E.: Respiratory hazards of opiates and other narcotic analgesics. Surg., Gynec. & Obst. *101:*701, 1955.

Ecker, E. E. and Rees, H. M.: Effect of hemorrhage on complement of blood. J. Infect. Dis. *31:*361, 1922.

Edelman, A.: Effects of x-radiation on water and electrolyte metabolism in the rat. Fed. Proc. *8:*39, 1949.

Edelman, I. S.: The pathogenesis of hyponatremia: physiologic and therapeutic implications. Metabolism *5:*500, 1956.

Edelman, I. S., Haley, H. B., Schloerb, P. R., Sheldon, D. B., Friis-Hansen, B. J., Stoll, G. and Moore, F. D.: Further observations on total body water. I. Normal values throughout the life span. Surg., Gynec. & Obst. *95:*1, 1952.

Edelman, I. S., James, A. H., Baden, H. and Moore, F. D.: Electrolyte composition of bone and the penetration of radiosodium and deuterium oxide into dog and human bone. J. Clin. Invest. *33:*122, 1954.

Edelman, I. S., James, A. H., Brooks, L. and Moore, F. D.: Body sodium and potassium. IV. The normal total exchangeable sodium; its measurement and magnitude. Metabolism *3:*530, 1954.

Edelman, I. S., Leibman, J., O'Meara, M. P. and Birkenfeld, L. W.: Interrelations between serum sodium concentration, serum osmolarity and total exchangeable sodium, total exchangeable potassium and total body water. J. Clin. Invest. *37:*1236, 1958.

Edelman, I. S. and Moore, F. D.: Body water, water distribution and water kinetics as revealed by the use of deuterium oxide. J. Clin. Invest. *30:*628, 1951.

Edelman, I. S., Olney, J. M., James, A. H., Brooks, L. and Moore, F. D.: Body composition: studies in the human being by the dilution principle. Science *115:*447, 1952.

Edelman, I. S. and Sweet, N. J.: Gastrointestinal water and electrolytes; equilibration of radiosodium in gastrointestinal contents and proportion of exchangeable sodium (Na_e) in gastrointestinal tract. J. Clin. Invest. *35:*502, 1956.

Edwards, L. C., Pernokas, L. N. and Dunphy, J. E.: The use of a plastic sponge to sample regenerating tissue in healing wounds. Surg., Gynec. & Obst. *105:*303, 1957.

Edwards, L. C. and Udupa, K. N.: Autoradiographic determination of S^{35} in tissues after injection of methionine-S^{35} and sodium sulphate-S^{35}. J. Biophys. & Biochem. *32:*757, 1957.

Edwards, W. S., Siegel, A. and Bing, R. J.: Studies on myocardial metabolism. III. Coronary blood flow, myocardial oxygen consumption and carbohydrate metabolism in experimental hemorrhagic shock. J. Clin. Invest. *33:*1646, 1954.

Egdahl, R. H., Nelson, D. H. and Hume, D. M.: Adrenal cortical function in hypothermia. Surg., Gynec. & Obst. *101:*715, 1955.

Eggleton, M. G.: The state of body water in the cat. J. Physiol. *115:*482, 1951.

Eik-Nes, K., Sandberg, A. A., Migeon, C. J., Tyler, F. H. and Samuels, L. T.: Changes in plasma levels of 17-hydroxycorticosteroids during the intravenous administration of ACTH. II. Response under various clinical conditions. J. Clin. Endocrinol. *15:*13, 1955.

Eik-Nes, K., Sandberg, A. A., Tyler, F. H. and Samuels, L. T.: Changes in plasma levels of 17-hydroxycorticosteroids during the intravenous administration of ACTH. I. A test of adrenocortical capacity in the human. J. Clin. Invest. *33:*1502, 1954.

Eiseman, B., Bakewell, W. and Clark, G.: Studies in ammonia metabolism. I. Ammonia metabolism and glutamate therapy in hepatic coma. Am. J. Med. *20:*890, 1956.

Eiseman, B. and Bricker, E. M.: Electrolyte absorption following bilateral uretero-enterostomy into an isolated intestinal segment. Ann. Surg. *136:*761, 1952.

Eiseman, B., Fowler, W. G., White, P. J. and Clark, G. M.: The role of ammonia in the production of hepatic coma. S. Forum *6:*369, 1956.

Eiseman, B., Johnson, R. T., Pratt, E. B. and Clark, G. M.: Studies in ammonia metabolism. II. Ammonia metabolism in hemorrhagic shock. Surgery *41:*910, 1957.

Eisen, V. D. and Lewis, A. A. G.: Antidiuretic activity of human urine after surgical operations. Lancet *2:*361, 1954.

Eisenmenger, W. J., Ahrens, E. H., Jr., Blonheim, S. H. and Kunkel, H. G.: The effect of rigid sodium restriction in patients with cirrhosis of the liver and ascites. J. Lab. & Clin. Med. *34:*1029, 1949.

Eisenmenger, W. J., Blondheim, S. H., Bongiovanni, A. M. and Kunkel, H. G.: Electrolyte studies on patients with cirrhosis of the liver. J. Clin. Invest. *29:*1491, 1950.

Eliakim, M. and Rachmilewitz, M.: Cholangiolitic manifestations in virus hepatitis. Gastroenterology *31:*369, 1956.

Eliel, L. P. and Heaney, R. P.: The effects of steroid hormones and anabolism and catabolism of normal tissues and lymphoid tumors in humans on protein—the diets. J. Clin. Invest. *34:*932, 1955 (abstr.).

Elkinton, J. R.: Whole body buffers in the regulation of acid-base equilibrium. Yale J. Biol. & Med. *29:*191, 1956.

Elkinton, J. R., Singer, R. B., Barker, E. S. and Clark, J. K.: Effects in man of acute experimental respiratory alkalosis and acidosis on ionic transfers in the total body fluids. J. Clin. Invest. *34:*1671, 1955.

Elkinton, J. R., Squires, R. D. and Bluemle, L. W., Jr.: The distribution of body fluids in congestive heart failure; exchanges in patients, refractory to mercurial diuretics, treated with sodium and potassium. Circulation *5:*58, 1952.

Elliott, D. W.: The mechanism of benefit derived from

concentrated human serum albumin in experimental acute pancreatitis. S. Forum *5:*384, 1955.

Ellison, R. G., Ellison, L. T. and Hamilton, W. F.: Analysis of respiratory acidosis during anesthesia. Ann. Surg. *141:*375, 1955.

Elman, R. and Weichselbaum, T. E.: Significance of postoperative glycosuria and ketonuria in nondiabetic adults. A.M.A. Arch. Surg. *62:*683, 1951.

Elman, R., Weichselbaum, T. E., Moncrief, J. C. and Margraf, H. W.: Adrenal cortical steroids following elective operations; quantitative studies in the peripheral plasma of 17-hydroxy- and 17-desoxycorticosteroids. A.M.A. Arch. Surg. *71:*697, 1955.

Elmes, P. C. and Jefferson, A. A.: The effect of anesthesia on the adrenalin contents of the suprarenal glands. J. Physiol. *101:*355, 1942.

Emerson, C. P., Jr. and Ebert, R. V.: Study of shock in battle casualties; measurements of blood volume changes occurring in response to therapy. Ann. Surg. *122:*745, 1945.

Emmelin, N and Strömblad, R.: Adrenalin and noradrenalin content of the suprarenals of cats in choralose and morphine-ether anesthesia. Acta physiol. scandinav. *24:*261, 1951.

Engel, F. L.: On the nature of the interdependence of the adrenal cortex, non-specific stress and nutrition in the regulation of nitrogen metabolism. Endocrinology *50:*462, 1952.

Engel, F L.: A consideration of the roles of the adrenal cortex and stress in the regulation of protein metabolism. Recent Progr. Hormone Res. *6:*277, 1955.

Engel, F. L.: Some unexplained metabolic actions of pituitary hormones with a unifying hypothesis concerning their significance. Yale J. Biol. & Med. *30:*201, 1957.

Engel, F. L. and Fredericks, J.: A contribution to the understanding of permissive action of corticoids. Proc. Soc. Exper. Biol. & Med. *94:*593, 1957.

Engel, F. L. and Jaeger, C.: Dehydration of hypernatremia, hyperchloremia and azotemia complicating nasogastric tube feeding. Am. J. Med. *17:*196, 1954.

Engel, F. L., Martin, S. P. and Taylor, H.: On relation of potassium to neurological manifestations of hypocalcemic tetany. Bull. Johns Hopkins Hosp. *84:*285, 1949.

Engel, F. L., Mencher, W. H. and Engel, C. L.: "Epinephrine shock" as a manifestation of a pheochromocytoma of the adrenal medulla. Am. J. Med. Sc. *204:*649, 1942.

Engstrom, W. P. and Liebman, A.: Chronic hyperosmolarity of the body fluids with a cerebral lesion causing diabetes insipidus and anterior pituitary insufficiency. Am. J. Med. *15:*180, 1953.

Engstrom, W. W. and Markardt, B.: The effects of serious illness and surgical stress on the circulating thyroid hormone. J. Clin. Endocrinol. *15:*953, 1955.

Enquist, I. F., Karlson, K. E., Tanaka, A. M., Dennis, C., Fierst, S. and LaVonne, A. Y.: Statistically controlled evaluation of three methods of management of upper gastrointestinal bleeding (a progress report). Gastroenterology *32:*610, 1957.

Enyart, J. L. and Miller, D. W.: Treatment of burns resulting from diaster. J.A.M.A. *158:*95, 1955.

Epstein, F. H.: Renal excretion of sodium and the concept of volume receptor. Yale J. Biol. & Med. *29:*282, 1956.

Epstein, F. H. and Ferguson, T. B.: Effect of formation of arteriovenous fistula upon blood volume. J. Clin. Invest. *34:*434, 1955.

Epstein, F. H., Goodyer, A. V. N., Lawrason, F. D. and Relman, A. S.: Studies of the antidiuresis of quiet standing: the importance of changes in plasma volume and glomerular filtration rate. J. Clin. Invest. *30:*63, 1951.

Epstein, F. H., Kleeman, C. B., Rubini, M. E. and Lamdin, E.: Effect of changes in extracellular fluid volume upon the volumes of distribution of ferrocyanide and inulin. Am. J. Physiol. *182:*553, 1955.

Ernstene, A. C. and Proudfit, W. L.: Differentiation of the changes in the Q-T interval in hypocalcemia and hypopotassemia. Am. Heart J. *38:*260, 1949.

Erslev, A. J.: Humoral regulation of red cell production. Blood *8:*349, 1953.

Erslev, A. J.: Erythropoietic function in uremic rabbits. A.M.A. Arch. Int. Med. *101:*407, 1958.

Ervin, D. M., Christian, R. M. and Young, L. E.: Dangerous universal donors. II. Further observations on in vivo and in vitro behavior of isoantibodies of immune type present in group O blood. Blood *5:*553, 1950.

Ervin, D. M. and Young, L. E.: Dangerous universal donors. I. Observations on destruction of recipient's A cells after transfusion of group O blood containing high titer of A antibodies of immune type not easily neutralizable by soluble A substance. Blood *5:*61, 1950.

Estes, W. L., Jr., Bowman, T. L. and Meilicke, F. F.: Non-penetrating abdominal trauma with special reference to lesions of the duodenum and pancreas. Am. J. Surg. *83:*434, 1952.

Etsten, B. E.: Respiratory acidosis during intrathoracic surgery: the (Overholt) prone position. J. Thoracic Surg. *25:*286, 1953.

Etsten, B. and Li, T. H.: Hemodynamic changes during thiopental anesthesia in humans: cardiac output, stroke volume, total peripheral resistance, and intrathoracic blood volume. J. Clin. Invest. *34:*500, 1955.

Evans, B. M., Macintyre, I., Macpherson, C. R. and Milne, M. D.: Alkalosis in sodium and potassium depletion; with especial reference to organic acid excretion. Clin. Sc. *16:*53, 1957.

Evans, E. I.: Potassium deficiency in surgical patients: its recognition and management. Ann. Surg. *131:*845, 1950.

Evans, E. I.: The treatment of high intensity burns. A.M.A. Arch. Surg. *62:*335, 1951.

Evans, E. I. and Bigger, I. A.: The rationale of whole blood therapy in severe burns; a clinical study. Ann. Surg. *122:*693, 1945.

Evans, E. I., Brooks, J. W., Schmidt, F. H., Williams, R. C. and Ham, W. T.: Flash burn studies on human volunteers. Surgery *37:*280, 1955.

Evans, E. I. and Butterfield, W. J. H.: The stress response in the severely burned. Ann. Surg. *134:*588, 1951.

Evans, E. I., Purnell, O. J., Robinett, P. W., Batchelor, A. and Martin, M.: Fluid and electrolyte requirements in severe burns. Ann. Surg. *135:*804, 1952.

Everson, T. C.: Collective review—nutrition following total gastrectomy, with particular reference to fat and protein assimilation. Surg., Gynec. & Obst. (Internat. Abstr.) *95:*209, 1952.

Everson, T. C.: The effect of esophagojejunostomy on fecal fat and nitrogen loss following total gastrectomy. S. Forum *2:*68, 1952.

Everson, T. C.: Experimental comparison of protein and

fat assimilation after Billroth II, Billroth I, and segmental types of subtotal gastrectomy. Surgery *36:*525, 1954.

Everson, T. C. and Cole, W. H.: Ligation of the splenic artery in patients with portal hypertension. A.M.A. Arch. Surg. *56:*153, 1948.

Everson, T. C. and Fritschel, M. J.: The individual essential amino acids in plasma and urine of surgical patients. Surgery *30:*931, 1951.

Everson, T. C. and Fritschel, M. J.: The effect of surgery on the plasma levels of individual essential amino acids. Surgery *31:*226, 1952.

Fahey, J. L., Ware, A. G. and Seegers, W. H.: Stability of prothrombin and Ac-globulin in stored human plasma as influenced by conditions of storage. Am. J. Physiol. *154:*122, 1948.

Fairlie, C. W., Barss, T. P., French, A. B., Jones, C. M. and Beecher, H. K.: Metabolic effects of anesthesia in man. IV. A comparison of the effects of certain anesthetic agents on the normal liver. New England J. Med. *244:*615, 1951.

Faloon, W. W., Eckhardt, R. D., Cooper, A. M. and Davidson, C. S.: The effect of human serum albumin, mercurial diuretics and a low sodium diet on sodium excretion in patients with cirrhosis of the liver. J. Clin. Invest. *28:*595, 1949.

Farber, S. J., Becker, W. H. and Eichna, L. W.: Electrolyte and water excretions and renal hemodynamics during congestion of the superior and inferior vena cava of man. J. Clin. Invest. *32:*1145, 1953.

Farber, S. J. and Soberman, R. J.: Total body water and total exchangeable sodium in edematous states due to cardiac, renal or hepatic disease. J. Clin. Invest. *35:*779, 1956.

Farr, L. E., MacFadyen, D. A., Taylor, G., Shands, A. R., Jr., Ferguson, W. R., Dunlap, E. B., Jr. and Johnson, C.: Changes in plasma amino acid nitrogen concentration following nitrous oxide and ether anesthesia and surgery. Proc. Soc. Exper. Biol. & Med. *50:*256, 1942.

Farrell, G.: Regulation of aldosterone secretion. Physiol. Rev. *38:*709, 1958.

Farris, J. M., Ransom, H. K. and Coller, F. A.: Total gastrectomy; effects upon nutrition and hematopoiesis. Surgery *13:*823, 1943.

Fawcett, D. W. and Gens, J. P.: Magnesium poisoning following enema of epsom salt solution. J.A.M.A. *123:*1028, 1943.

Fenn, W. O., Bale, W. F. and Mullins, L. J.: Radioactivity of potassium from human sources. J. Gen. Physiol. *25:*345, 1942.

Fenn, W. O., Noonan, T. R., Mullins, L. J. and Haege, L.: The exchange of radio-active potassium with body potassium. Am. J. Physiol. *135:*149, 1941.

Ferris, D. O. and Odel, H. M.: Electrolyte pattern of the blood after bilateral ureterosigmoidostomy. J.A.M.A. *142:*634, 1950.

Finch, C. A. and Marchand, J. F.: Cardiac arrest by action of potassium. Am. J. M. Sc. *206:*507, 1943.

Finch, C. A., Sawyer, C. G. and Flynn, J. M.: Clinical syndrome of potassium intoxication. Am. J. Med. *7:*337, 1946.

Fine, D., Meiselas, L. E. and Auerbach, T.: The relationship of acute reduction in blood volume to the release of "aldosterone." Clin. Res. Proc. *4:*126, 1956 (abstr.).

Fine, D., Meiselas, L. E. and Auerbach, T.: The effect of acute hypovolemia on the release of "aldosterone" and on the renal excretion of sodium. J. Clin. Invest. *37:*232, 1958.

Fine, J.: The bacterial factor in traumatic shock. Springfield, Ill., Charles C Thomas, 1954.

Fine, J.: Relation of bacteria to failure of blood-volume therapy in traumatic shock. New England J. Med. *250:*889, 1954.

Fine, J.: Host resistance to bacteria and to bacterial toxins in traumatic shock. Ann. Surg. *142:*361, 1955.

Fine, J., Frank, E. D., Ravin, H. A., Rutenberg, S. H. and Schweinburg, F. B.: The bacterial factor in traumatic shock. New England J. Med. *260:*214, 1959.

Fine, J., Frank, H., Schweinburg, F., Jacob, S. and Gordon, T.: The bacterial factor in traumatic shock. Ann. New York Acad. Sc. *55:*429, 1952.

Fine, J. and Seligman, A. M.: Traumatic shock: experimental study including evidence against capillary leakage hypothesis. Ann. Surg. *118:*238, 1943.

Fine, J. and Seligman, A. M.: Traumatic shock. VII. A study of the problem of the "lost plasma" in hemorrhagic, tourniquet, and burn shock by the use of radioactive iodo-plasma protein. J. Clin. Invest. *23:*720, 1944.

Fine, J., Seligman, A. M. and Frank, H. A.: A study of the problem of the "lost plasma" in hemorrhagic shock by the use of radioactive plasma protein. J. Clin. Invest. *22:*285, 1943.

Fine, J., Seligman, A. M. and Frank, H. A.: On specific role of liver in hemorrhagic shock; report of progress to date. Ann. Surg. *126:*1002, 1947.

Finkenstaedt, J. T. and Merrill, J. P.: Renal function after recovery from acute renal failure. New England J. Med. *254:*1023, 1956.

Finley, R. K., Jr., Templeton, J. Y., III, Holland, R. H. and Gibbon, J. H., Jr.: Changes in urine and serum electrolyte and plasma volumes after major intrathoracic operations. J. Thoracic Surg. *22:*219, 1951.

Fischer, R.: Disturbances of vegetative function after closed brain injuries with special consideration of venous pressure, eosinophilic leucocytes and blood albumin. Arch. klin. Chir. *274:*88, 1952.

Fisher, C. J. and Faloon, W. W.: Episodic stupor following portacaval shunt. New England J. Med. *255:*589, 1956.

Fisher, J. A., Taylor, W. and Cannon, J. A.: The dumping syndrome: correlations between its experimental production and clinical incidence. Surg., Gynec. & Obst. *100:*559, 1955.

Flear, C. T. G.: The influence of transfusion adequacy on clinical progress in thoracic surgery. Brit. J. Gen. Pract. *10:*787, 1956.

Flear, C. T. G. and Clarke, R.: The influence of blood loss and blood transfusion upon changes in the metabolism of water, electrolytes and nitrogen following civilian trauma. Clin. Sc. *14:*575, 1955.

Fletcher, D. G. and Harkins, H. N.: Acute peptic ulcer as a complication of major surgery, stress or trauma. Surgery *36:*212, 1954.

Flexner, L. B., Wilde, W. S., Proctor, N. K., Cowie, D. B., Vosburgh, G. J. and Hellman, L. M.: The estimation of extracellular and total body water in the newborn human infant with radioactive sodium and deuterium oxide. J. Pediat. *30:*413, 1947.

Flickinger, F. M. and Henderson, I. W. D.: An experimental and clinical study of the prevention of thrombophlebitic sequelae by cortisone acetate (11-dehydro-17-hydroxycorticosterone-21-acetate). Surg., Gynec. & Obst. *102:*66, 1956.

Flink, E. B.: Magnesium deficiency syndrome in man. J.A.M.A. *160:*1406, 1956.

Flink, E. B., Stutzman, F. L., Anderson, A. R., Konig, T. and Fraser, R.: Magnesium deficiency after prolonged parenteral fluid administration and after chronic alcoholism complicated by delirium tremens. J. Lab. & Clin. Med. *43:*169, 1954.

Flock, E. V., Block, M. A., Grindlay, J. H., Mann, F. C. and Bollman, J. L.: Changes in free amino acids of brain and muscle after total hepatectomy. J. Biol. Chem. *200:*529, 1953.

Flock, E. V., Block, M. A., Mann, F. C., Grindlay, J. H. and Bollman, J. L.: The effect of glucose on the amino acids of plasma after total hepatectomy. J. Biol. Chem. *198:*427, 1952.

Flock, E. V., Mann, F. C. and Bollman, J. L.: Free amino acids in plasma and muscle following total removal of the liver. J. Biol. Chem. *192:*293, 1951.

Fogelman, M. J. and Wilson, B. J.: Internal water exchange rates in burns and other forms of trauma. S. Forum *4:*473, 1954.

Fogelman, M. J. and Wilson, B. J.: Blood, extracellular fluid and total body water volume relationships in the early stages of severe burns. S. Forum *5:*762, 1955.

Folin, O. and Denis, W.: The origin and significance of the ammonia in the portal blood. J. Biol. Chem. *11:*161, 1912.

Follis, R. H., Jr., Orent-Keiles, E. and McCollum, E. V.: The production of cardiac and renal lesions in rats by diet extremely deficient in potassium. Am. J. Path. *18:*29, 1942.

Forbes, A. P., Donaldson, E. C., Reifenstein, E. C., Jr. and Albright, F.: The effect of trauma and disease on the urinary 17-ketosteroid excretion in man. J. Clin. Endocrinol. *7:*264, 1947.

Forbes, G. B.: Inorganic chemical heterogony in man and animals. Growth *19:*75, 1955.

Forbes, G. B. and D'Ambruso, M.: Determination of sodium in bone with the aid of cation exchange chromatography. J. Biol. Chem. *212:*655, 1955.

Forbes, G. B. and Lewis, A.: Determination of specific activity of sodium in bone. Proc. Soc. Exper. Biol. & Med. *90:*178, 1955.

Forbes, G. B. and Lewis, A.: Total sodium, potassium and chloride in adult man. J. Clin. Invest. *35:*596, 1956.

Forbes, G. B. and Lewis, A.: Relation of exchangeable sodium, potassium and chloride to total body content in man. J. Clin. Invest. *35:*703, 1956.

Forbes, G. B. and Perley, A.: Estimation of total body sodium by isotopic dilution. I. Studies on young adults. J. Clin. Invest. *30:*558, 1951.

Forbes, R. M., Cooper, A. R. and Mitchell, H. H.: The composition of the adult human body as determined by chemical analysis. J. Biol. Chem. *203:*359, 1953.

Forsee, J. H.: Forward surgery of the severely wounded. Am. Surgeon *17:*508, 1951.

Forsee, J. H., Blake, H. A. and Goyette, E. M.: Chest clinic: "Closed chest injury." Surgery *40:*763, 1956.

Forsham, P. H., Lee, H., Kolb, F. O. and Liddle, G. W.: Metabolic and therapeutic effectiveness of modified ACTH preparations. J. Clin. Endocrinol. *12:*956, 1952.

Forsham, P. H., Renold, A. E. and Frawley, T. F.: The nature of ACTH resistance. J. Clin. Endocrinol. *11:*757, 1951 (abstr.).

Forsyth, B. T.: The effect of testosterone propionate at various protein and calorie intakes in malnutrition after trauma. J. Lab. & Clin. Med. *43:*732, 1954.

Forsyth, B. T. and Plough, I. C.: The protein-sparing effect of carbohydrate with and without testosterone. J. Lab. & Clin. Med. *46:*840, 1955.

Forsyth, B. T., Shipman, M. E. and Plough, I. C.: The variability of fecal nitrogen excretion with liquid and solid diets. J. Lab. & Clin. Med. *43:*440, 1954.

Forsyth, B. T., Shipman, M. E. and Plough, I. C.: The relation of nitrogen retention to nitrogen intake in adults with post-traumatic malnutrition. J. Clin. Invest. *34:*1653, 1955.

Foster, F. P., Drew, D. W. and Wiss, E. J.: Hyperchloremic acidosis and potassium deficiency following total cystectomy and bilateral ureterosigmoidostomy. Lahey Clin. Bull. *6:*231, 1950.

Fox, C. L., Jr. and Baer, H.: Redistribution of potassium, sodium and water in burns and trauma, and its relation to the phenomena of shock. Am. J. Physiol. *151:*155, 1947.

Fox, C. L., Jr., Friedburg, C. K. and White, A. G.: Electrolyte abnormalities in chronic congestive heart failure; effects of administration of potassium and sodium salts. J. Clin. Invest. *28:*781, 1949 (abstr.).

Fox, C. L., Jr. and Keston, A. S.: The mechanism of shock from burns and trauma, traced with radiosodium. Surg., Gynec. & Obst. *80:*561, 1945.

Fox, H. M.: Psychiatric research in a general hospital. Psychosom. Med. *16:*435, 1954 (abstr.).

Fox, H. M., Rizzo, N. D. and Gifford, S.: Psychological observations of patients undergoing mitral surgery. A study of stress. Psychosom. Med. *16:*186, 1954.

Frank, E. D., Fine, J. and Pillener, L.: Serum properdin levels in hemorrhagic shock. Proc. Soc. Exper. Biol. & Med. *89:*223, 1955.

Frank, E. D., Frank, H. A. and Fine, J.: Traumatic shock. XVII. Plasma fibrinogen in hemorrhagic shock in the dog. Am. J. Physiol. *162:*619, 1950.

Frank, E. D., Frank, H. A. and Fine, J.: Traumatic shock; plasma prothrombin activity in hemorrhagic shock in the dog. Am. J. Physiol. *167:*499, 1951.

Frank, H. A., Seligman, A. M. and Fine, J.: Traumatic shock. XIII. The prevention of irreversibility in hemorrhagic shock by vivi-perfusion of the liver. J. Clin. Invest. *25:*22, 1946.

Frank, N. R. *et al.:* Mechanical behavior of the lung in healthy elderly persons. J. Clin. Invest. *26:*1680, 1957.

Franksson, C. and Gemzell, C. A.: Blood levels of 17-hydroxycorticosteroids in surgery and allied conditions. Acta chir. scand. *106:*24, 1954.

Franksson, C., Gemzell, C. A. and von Euler, U.: Cortical and medullary adrenal activity in surgical and allied conditions. J. Clin. Endocrinol. *14:*608, 1954.

Fraser, C. G., Preuss, F. S. and Bigford, W. D.: Clinical notes: adrenal atrophy and irreversible shock associated with cortisone therapy. J.A.M.A. *149:*1542, 1952.

Frawley, J. P., Artz, C. P. and Howard, J. M.: The use of dextran and gelatin as plasma volume expanders in combat casualties. U. S. Department of the Army, Office of the Surgeon General, Med. R. & D. Board Annual Report, 1954.

Frawley, J. P., Artz, C. P. and Howard, J. M.: Muscle metabolism and catabolism in combat casualties; systemic response to injury in combat casualties. A.M.A. Arch. Surg. 71:612, 1955.

Frawley, J. P., Artz, C. P. and Howard, J. M.: Plasma retention and urinary excretion of dextran and modified fluid gelatin in combat casualties; a study in Korea. Surgery 37:384, 1955.

Frawley, J. P., Howard, J. M., Artz, C. P. and Anderson, P.: Investigations of serum protein changes in combat casualties; the systemic response to injury, A.M.A. Arch. Surg. 71:605, 1955.

French, A. B., Barss, T. P., Fairlie, C. S., Bengle, A. L., Jr., Jones, C. M., Linton, R. R. and Beecher, H. K.: Metabolic effects of anesthesia on man. V. Comparison of effects of ether and cyclopropane anesthesia on abnormal liver. Ann. Surg. 135:145, 1952.

Freeman, H. et al.: Steroid replacement in aged men. J. Clin. Endocrinol. 16:779, 1956.

Friedberg, C. K.: Fluid and electrolyte disturbances in heart failure and their treatment. Circulation 16:437, 1957.

Friedberg, C. K., Taymor, R., Minor, J. B. and Halpern, M.: Use of Diamox, a carbonic anhydrase inhibitor, as an oral diuretic in patients with congestive heart failure. New England J. Med. 248:883, 1953.

Friedberg, F. and Greenberg, D. M.: Endocrine regulation of amino acid levels in blood and tissues. J. Biol. Chem. 168:405, 1947.

Frieden, J. H.: Postoperative acute pancreatitis. Surg., Gynec. & Obst. 102:139, 1956.

Frieden, J. H., Rice, L., Elisberg, E. I., Eisenstein, B. and Katz, L. N.: Effects of chronic peripheral venous congestion on renal sodium excretion. Am. J. Physiol. 168:650, 1952.

Friedman, E. W. and Weiner, R. S.: Estimation of hepatic sinusoid pressure by means of venous catheters and estimation of portal pressure by hepatic vein catheterization. Am. J. Physiol. 65:527, 1951.

Friedman, M. and Bine, R., Jr.: Observations concerning influence of potassium upon action of digitalis glycoside (lanatoside C). Am. J. M. Sc. 214:633, 1947.

Friesen, S. R.: The genesis of a gastroduodenal ulcer following burns; experimental study. Surgery 28:123, 1950.

Friesen, S. R. and Nelson, R. M.: The occurrence of massive generalized wound bleeding during operation, with reference to the possible role of blood transfusions in its etiology. Am. Surgeon 17:609, 1951.

Friis-Hansen, B. J., Holiday, M., Stapleton, T. and Wallace, W. H.: Total body water in children. Pediatrics 7:321, 1951.

Fritz, I. and Levine, R.: Action of adrenal cortical steroids and nor-epinephrine on vascular responses of stress in adrenalectomized rats. Am. J. Physiol. 165:456, 1951.

Furchgott, R. F., Zweifach, B. W. and Shorr, E.: Hepatorenal factors in circulatory homeostasis. XXIV. Conditions leading to aerobic formation of VDM by liver. Fed. Proc. 8:201, 1949 (abstr.).

Furth, J., Andrews, G. A., Storey, R. H. and Wish, L.: Effect of x-irradiation on erythrogenesis, plasma and cell volumes. South M. J. 44:85, 1951.

Gabbard, J. G., Roos, A., Eastwood, D. E. and Burford, T. H.: The effect of ether anesthesia upon alveolar ventilation and acid-base balance in man; with particular reference to deficient ventilation and its prevention during intrathoracic procedures. Ann. Surg. 136:680, 1952.

Gabrilove, J. L.: The levels of the circulating eosinophils following trauma. J. Clin. Endocrinol. 10:637, 1950.

Gabuzda, G. J., Traeger, H. S. and Davidson, C. S.: Hepatic cirrhosis: effects of sodium chloride administration and restriction and of abdominal paracentesis on electrolyte and water balance. J. Clin. Invest. 33:780, 1954.

Gaensler, O. E.: Analysis of ventilatory defects by timed vital capacity. Am. Rev. Tuberc. 64:256, 1951.

Gaillard, W. R.: Interaction between tissue cultures of hypothalamus, pituitary and adrenals. Biological workshop conferences, Rockefeller Institute, 1957 (unpublished).

Gamble, J. L.: The Chemical Anatomy, Physiology and Pathology of Extracellular Fluid. 6th ed. Cambridge, Mass., Harvard University Press, 1958.

Gamble, J. L., Ross, G. S. and Tisdall, F. F.: The metabolism of fixed base during fasting. J. Biol. Chem. 57:633, 1923.

Gardner, F. H. and Freymann, J. G.: Erythrocythemia (polycythemia) and hydronephrosis; report of a case with radio-iron studies, with recovery after nephrectomy. New England J. Med. 259:323, 1958.

Gaunt, R., Renzi, A. A. and Chart, J. J.: Aldosterone—a review. J. Clin. Endocrinol. 15:621, 1955.

Gauss, H.: Studies in cerebral fat embolism, with reference to the pathology of delirium and coma. A.M.A. Arch. Int. Med. 18:76, 1916.

Gelin, L. E. and Löfstrom, B.: Preliminary study on peripheral circulation during deep hypothermia; observations on decreased suspension stability of blood and its prevention. Acta chir. scandinav. 108:402, 1955.

Geller, W. and Tagnon, H. J.: Liver dysfunction following abdominal operations; the significance of postoperative hyperbilirubinemia. A.M.A. Arch. Int. Med. 86:908, 1950.

Gemzell, C. A. and Notter, G.: Effect of androgens on plasma levels of 17-hydroxycorticosteroids. J. Clin. Endocrinol. 16:483, 1956.

Gerst, P. H. et al.: The effects of hemorrhage on pulmonary circulation or respiratory gas exchange. J. Clin. Invest. 38:524, 1959.

Gibbon, J. H., Jr., Allbritten, F. F., Jr., Stayman, J. W., Jr. and Judd, J. M.: A clinical study of respiratory exchange during prolonged operations with an open thorax. Ann. Surg. 132:611, 1950.

Gibson, J. G. and Evans, W. A.: Clinical studies of the blood volume. II. The relation of plasma and total blood volume to venous pressure, blood velocity rate, physical measurements, age and sex in ninety normal humans. J. Clin. Invest. 16:317, 1937.

Gibson, J. G., II and Evans, W. A., Jr.: Clinical studies of the blood volume. III. Changes in blood volume, venous pressure and blood velocity rate in chronic congestive heart failure. J. Clin. Invest. 16:851, 1937.

Gibson, J. G., II, Murphy, W. P., Jr., Scheitlin, W. A. and Rees, S. B.: The influence of extracellular factors involved in the collection of blood in ACD on maintenance of red cell viability during refrigerated storage. Am. J. Clin. Path. 26:855, 1956.

Gibson, J. G., II, Seligman, A. M., Peacock, W. C., Aub, J. C., Fine, J. and Evans, R. D.: The distribution of red cells and plasma in large and minute vessels of the normal dog, determined by radioactive isotopes of iron and iodine. J. Clin. Invest. *25:*848, 1946.

Gibson, J. G., II, Weiss, S., Evans, R. D., Peacock, W. C., Irvine, J. W., Jr., Good, W. M. and Kip, A. F.: The measurement of the circulating red cell volume by means of two radioactive isotopes of iron. J. Clin. Invest. *25:*616, 1946.

Giebisch, G., Berger, L. and Pitts, R. F.: The extrarenal response to acute acid-base disturbances of respiratory origin. J. Clin. Invest. *34:*231, 1955.

Gilder, H., Redo, S. F. and Barr, D.: Water distribution in patients with Laennec's cirrhosis using radioactive sodium. S. Forum *4:*578, 1954.

Gilder, H., Redo, S. F., Barr, D. and Child, C. G., III: Water distribution in normal subjects and in patients with Laennec's cirrhosis. J. Clin. Invest. *33:*555, 1954.

Gillespie, J. A.: The influence of sex hormones in the bony changes occurring in paralysed limbs. J. Endocrinol. *11:*66, 1954.

Gillespie, J. A.: The nature of the bone changes associated with nerve injuries and disuse. J. Bone & Joint Surg. *36-B:*464, 1954.

Giuseffi, J. and Carter, B. N.: Further experiences with tracheotomy in the management of crushing injuries of the chest. A.M.A. Arch. Surg. *69:*483, 1954.

Glasser, O. and Page, I. H.: Intra-arterial transfusion in treatment of experimental hemorrhagic shock. Cleveland Clin. Quart. *14:*121, 1947.

Glauser, K. F. and Selkurt, E. E.: Effect of barbiturates on renal function in the dog. Am. J. Physiol. *168:*469, 1952.

Glenn, F.: Cardiac arrest during surgery. Ann. Surg. *137:*920, 1953.

Glendening, M. B., Winter, H. A., Williams, H. H., Abbott, W. E., Hirshfeld, J. W. and Heller, C. G.: Study of the "alarm reaction" in burned human subjects and its possible significance in war injuries. Endocrinology *35:*220, 1944.

Gold, J. J.: Blood corticoids: their measurement and significance—a review. J. Clin. Endocrinol. *17:*296, 1957.

Gold, N. I., Macfarlane, D. A. and Moore, F. D.: Quantitative urinary 17-hydroxycorticoid patterns: effect of ACTH and "operative stress." J. Clin. Endocrinol. *16:*282, 1956.

Gold, N. I., Singleton, E., Macfarlane, D. A. and Moore, F. D.: Quantitative determination of the urinary cortisol metabolites, "tetrahydro F," "allo-tetrahydro F" and "tetrahydro E": effects of adrenocorticotropin and complex trauma in the human. J. Clin. Invest. *37:*813, 1958.

Goldenberg, I. S., Lutwak, L., Rosenbaum, P. J. and Hayes, M. A.: Thyroid-adrenocortical metabolic interrelations. J. Clin. Endocrinol. *15:*227, 1955.

Goldenberg, I. S., Lutwak, L., Rosenbaum, P. J. and Hayes, M. A.: Thyroid activity during operation. Surg., Gynec. & Obst. *102:*129, 1956.

Goldenberg, I. S., Rosenbaum, P. J. and Hayes, M. A.: Patterns of thyroid-adrenocortical response after operation. Ann. Surg. *142:*786, 1955.

Goldhamer, S. M.: The pernicious anemia syndrome in gastrectomized patients. Surg., Gynec. & Obst. *57:*257, 1933.

Goldman, D.: Metabolic changes occurring as the result of deep Roentgen therapy. I. The effect of 200 kilovolt Roentgen therapy. Am. J. Roentgenol. *50:*381, 1943.

Goldschmidt, S. and Binger, C.: Studies in the mechanism of absorption from the intestine. VI. The colon—the influence of calcium salts upon the absorption of sodium chloride in the intestine. Am. J. Physiol. *48:*473, 1919.

Goldschmidt, S. and Dayton, A. B.: Studies in the mechanism of absorption from the intestine. I. The colon—a contribution to the one-sided permeability of the intestinal wall to chlorides. Am. J. Physiol. *48:*419, 1919.

Goldschmidt, S. and Dayton, A. B.: Studies in the mechanism of absorption from the intestine. II. The colon—on the passage of fluid in two directions through the intestinal wall. Am. J. Physiol. *48:*433, 1919.

Goldschmidt, S. and Dayton, A. B.: Studies in the mechanism of absorption from the intestine. IV. The colon—the behavior of sodium and magnesium sulphate solutions. Am. J. Physiol. *48:*450, 1919.

Goldschmidt, S. and Dayton, A. B.: Studies in the mechanism of absorption from the intestine. III. The colon—the osmotic pressure equilibrium between the intestinal contents and the blood. Am. J. Physiol. *48:*440, 1919

Goldschmidt, S. and Dayton, A. B.: Studies in the mechanism of absorption from the intestine. V. The colon—the effect of sodium sulphate upon the absorption of sodium chloride when the salts are introduced simultaneously into the intestine. Am. J. Physiol. *48:*459, 1919.

Goldstein, J. D. and DuBois, E. L.: The effect on the circulation in man of rebreathing different concentrations of carbon dioxide. Am. J. Physiol. *81:*650, 1927.

Goldstein, F., Gibbon, J. H., Jr., Allbritten, F. F., Jr. and Stayman, J. W., Jr.: Combined manometric determination of oxygen and carbon dioxide in blood in presence of low concentrations of ethyl ether. J. Biol. Chem. *182:*815, 1950.

Gomez, F., Ramos-Galvan, R., Cravioto, J., Frenk, S., Janeway, C. A., Gamble, J. L. amd Metcoff, J.: Intracellular composition and homeostatic mechanisms in severe chronic infantile malnutrition. I. General considerations. Pediatrics *20:*101, 1957.

Goodall, M.: Studies of adrenalin and noradrenalin in mammalian heart and suprarenals. Acta physiol. scandinav. *24:* (suppl. 85), 1951.

Goodall, M., Stone, C. and Haynes, B. W., Jr.: Urinary output of adrenalin and noradrenalin in severe thermal burns. Ann. Surg. *145:*479, 1957.

Goodwin, W. E., Harris, A. P., Kaufman, J. J. and Beal, J. M.: Open, transcolonic ureterointestinal anastomosis—a new approach. Surg., Gynec. & Obst. *97:*295, 1953.

Goodyer, A. V. N. and Glenn, W. W. L.: Observations on the hyponatremia following mitral valvulotomy. Circulation *11:*584, 1955.

Goodyer, A. V. N. and Jaeger, C. A.: Renal response to nonshocking hemorrhage—role of the autonomic nervous system and of renal circulation. Am. J. Physiol. *180:*69, 1955.

Goodyer, A. V. N., Relman, A. S., Lawrason, F. D. and Epstein, F. H.: Salt retention in cirrhosis of the liver. J. Clin. Invest. *29:*973, 1950.

Gordillo, G., Soto, R. A., Metcoff, J., Lopez, E. and Antillon, L. G.: Intracellular composition and homeostatic mechanisms in severe chronic infantile malnutrition. III. Renal adjustments. Pediatrics *20:*303, 1957.

Gordon-Taylor, G., Hudson, R. V., Dodds, E. C., Warner, J. L. and Whitby, L. E. H.: The remote results of gastrectomy. Brit. J. Surg. *16:*641, 1929.

Gorlin, R., Mathews, M. B., McMillan, I. K. R., Daley, R. and Medd, W. E.: Physiological and clinical observations in aortic valvular disease. Bull. New England M. Center *16:*13, 1954.

Gotch, F., Nadell, J. and Edelman, I. S.: Gastrointestinal water and electrolytes. IV. The equilibration of deuterium oxide (D_2O) in gastrointestinal contents and the proportion of total body water (T.B.W.) in the gastrointestinal tract. J. Clin. Invest. *36:*289, 1957.

Gottesman, J., Casten, D. and Beller, A. J.: Changes in the electrocardiogram induced by acute pancreatitis; a clinical and experimental study. J.A.M.A. *123:*892, 1943.

Gottlieb, M. L.: Impressions of a POW medical officer in Japanese concentration camps. U. S. Nav. M. Bull. *46:*663, 1946.

Govan, C. D., Jr. and Weiseth, W. M.: Potassium intoxication: report of an infant surviving a serum potassium level of 12.27 millimoles per liter. J. Pediat. *28:*550, 1946.

Graham, J. H., Emerson, C. P. and Anglem, T. J.: Postoperative hypofibrinogenemia—diffuse intravascular thrombosis after fibrinogen administration. New England J. Med. *257:*101, 1957.

Grant, R. T.: Remarks on diagnosis and treatment of "wound shock" in limb injuries. Brit. M. Bull. *10:*13, 1954.

Grant, R. T. and Reeve, E. B.: Observations on the general effects of injury in man, with special reference to wound shock. Medical Research Council Special Report, series 277. London, H. M. Stationery Office, 1951.

Gray, I.: Metabolism of plasma expanders studied with carbon-14-labeled dextran. Am. J. Physiol. *174:*462, 1953.

Green, D. M. and Metheny, D.: Estimation of acute blood loss by tilt test. Surg., Gynec. & Obst. *84:*1045, 1947.

Greenberg, J. and Laszlo, D.: The influence of ionizing radiation on the body fluid compartments of patients with malignant lymphoma. J. Clin. Invest. *34:*405, 1955.

Greenspan, E. M.: Hyperchloremic acidosis and nephrocalcinosis—the syndrome of pure "lower nephron" insufficiency. A.M.A. Arch. Int. Med. *83:*271, 1949.

Greenspan, E. M.: Survey of clinical significance of serum mucoprotein level. A.M.A. Arch. Int. Med. *93:*863, 1954.

Greenspan, E. M., Lehman, I., Graff, M. and Schoenbach, E. B.: A comparative study of the serum glycoproteins in patients with parenchymatous hepatic disease of metastatic neoplasia. Cancer *4:*972, 1951.

Griffith, G. C. *et al.:* The selection and medical management of patients with mitral stenosis treated by mitral comissurotomy. Circulation *7:*30, 1953.

Griswold, M. L., Jr.: Treatment of one hundred forty-eight burn cases in a community hospital. J.A.M.A. *164:*861, 1957.

Gropper, A. L., Raisz, L. G. and Amspacher, W. H.: Plasma expanders. Internat. Abstr. Surg. *95:*521, 1952.

Gross, R. E.: A scale for rapid measurement of blood which is lost in surgical sponges. J. Thoracic Surg. *18:*543, 1949.

Gross, R. E.: Surgery of Infancy and Childhood. Philadelphia, W. B. Saunders Co., 1953.

Gross, R. E. and Ferguson, C. C.: Surgery in premature babies—observations from 159 cases. Surg., Gynec. & Obst. *95:*631, 1952.

Grossman, C. M., Sappington, T. S., Burrows, B. A.,

Lavietes, P. H. and Peters, J. P.: Nitrogen metabolism in acute infections. J. Clin. Invest. *24:*523, 1945.

Grossman, J.: Volume factors in body fluid regulation. A.M.A. Arch. Int. Med. *99:*93, 1957.

Grotte, G.: Passage of dextran molecules across the blood-lymph barrier. Acta chir. scandinav. *112* (Suppl.): 515, 1956.

Guild, W. R., Bray, G. and Merrill, J. P.: Hemopericardium with cardiac tamponade in chronic uremia. New England J. Med. *257:*230, 1957.

Gunton, R. W. and Paul, W.: Blood volume in congestive heart failure. J. Clin. Invest. *34:*879, 1955.

Gurdjian, E. S., Lissner, H. R., Latimer, F. R., Haddad, B. F. and Webster, J. E.: Quantitative determination of acceleration and intracranial pressure in experimental head injury; preliminary report. Neurology *3:*417, 1953.

Gurdjian, E. S. and Stone, W. E.: Cerebral lactic acid and phosphates in concussion. Fed. Proc. *5:*38, 1946 (abstr.).

Gurdjian, E. S. and Webster, J. E.: Experimental and clinical studies on the mechanism of head injury. A. Res. Nerv. & Ment. Dis. Proc. *24:*48, 1945.

Gurdjian, E. S., Webster, J. E. and Lissner, H. R.: Observations on the mechanism of brain concussion, contusion and laceration. Surg., Gynec. & Obst. *101:*680, 1955.

Habif, D. V., Papper, E. M., Fitzpatrick, H. F., Lowrance, P., Smythe, C. M. and Bradley, S. E.: The renal and hepatic blood flow, glomerular filtration rate, and urinary output of electrolytes during cyclopropane, ether and thiopental anesthesia, operation and the immediate postoperative period. Surgery *30:*241, 1951.

Habif, D. V., Randall, H. T. and Soroff, H. S.: The management of cirrhosis of the liver and ascites with particular reference to the portacaval shunt operation. Surgery *34:*580, 1953.

Hagenbach, E.: Perandren bei schlechter Kallusbildung. Schweiz. med. Wchnschr. *71:*1212, 1941.

Haigh, C. P.: An analysis for deuterium based on the photoneutron effect. Nature, London *172:*359, 1953.

Haigh, C. P.: A photoneutron method of measuring deuterium .In Johnston, J. E. *et al.* (eds.): Radioisotope Conference, 1954. Volume II: Physical Sciences and Industrial Applications. New York, Academic Press, 1954.

Haldeman, K. O. and Moore, J. M.: Influence of a local excess of calcium and phosphorus on the healing of fractures—experimental study. A.M.A. Arch. Surg. *29:*385, 1934.

Hall, W. H. and Gold, D.: Shock associated with bacteremia; review of 35 cases. A.M.A. Arch. Int. Med. *96:*403, 1955.

Hallock, P.: Polycythemia of morbus caeruleus (cyanotic type of congenital heart disease). Proc. Soc. Exper. Biol. & Med. *44:*11, 1940.

Halme, A., Pekkarinen, A. and Turonen, M.: On the excretion of noradrenalin, adrenalin, 17-hydroxycorticosteroids and 17-ketosteroids during the postoperative stage. Acta endocrinol. *24:* (suppl. 32), 1957.

Ham, T. H. and Curtis, F. C.: Plasma fibrinogen response in man—influence of the nutritional state, induced hyperpyrexia, infectious disease, and liver damage. Medicine *17:*413, 1938.

Hamerman, D., Reife, A. and Bartz, K. W.: Levels of hexosamine and hexose in plasma and urine in patients with certain diseases or injuries. Med. Nutrition Lab. Project 6-60-11-020, Report No. 179, 1956.

Hamilton, H. B. and Hamilton, J. B.: Ageing in apparently normal men. I. Urinary titers of ketosteroids and of alpha-hydroxy and beta-hydroxy ketosteroids. J. Clin. Endocrinol. 8:433, 1948.

Hamilton, W. K. and Devine, J. C.: The evaluation of respiratory adequacy in the immediate postoperative period. Surg., Gynec. & Obst. 100:229, 1957.

Hammarsten, J. F. and Smith, W. O.: Symptomatic magnesium deficiency in man. New England J. Med. 256:897, 1957.

Hammond, W. G., Aronow, L. and Moore, F. D.: Studies in surgical endocrinology. III. Plasma concentration of epinephrine and nor-epinephrine in anesthesia, trauma and surgery, as measured by a modification of the method of Weil-Malherbe and Bone. Ann. Surg. 144:715, 1956.

Hammond, W. G., Vandam, L. D., Davis, J. M., Carter, R. D., Ball, M. R. and Moore, F. D.: Studies in surgical endocrinology. IV. Anesthetic agents as stimuli to change in corticosteroids and metabolism. Ann. Surg. 148:199, 1958.

Hanenson, I. B., Goluboff, B., Grossman, J., Weston, R. E. and Leiter, L.: Studies on water excretion following intravenous hydration and the administration of Pitressin or nicotine in congestive heart failure. Circulation 13:242, 1956.

Hannon, D. W. and Sprafka, J.: Resection for traumatic pancreatitis. Ann. Surg. 146:136, 1957.

Hardt, L. L. and Rivers, A. B.: Toxic manifestations following the alkaline treatment of peptic ulcers. A.M.A. Arch. Int. Med. 31:171, 1923.

Hardy, E. G., Morris, G. C., Jr., Yow, E. M., Haynes, B. W., Jr. and De Bakey, M. E.: Studies on the role of bacteria in irreversible hemorrhagic shock in dogs. Ann. Surg. 139:282, 1954.

Hardy, J. D.: Role of the adrenal cortex in the postoperative retention of salt and water. Ann. Surg. 132:189, 1950.

Hardy, J. D. and Drabkin, D. L.: Measurement of body water; techniques and practical implications. J.A.M.A. 149:1113, 1952.

Hardy, J. D., Jabbour, E., Lovelace, J. R., Neely, W. A. and Wilson, F. C., Jr.: Thermal burns in man. IV. Body weight changes during therapy. Surgery 38:685, 1955.

Hardy, J. D., Neely, W. A. and Wilson, F. C., Jr.: Thermal burns in man. VII. "Insensible fluid loss." Surgery 38:692, 1955.

Hardy, J. D., Neely, W. A., Wilson, F. C., Jr., Lovelace, J. R. and Jabbour, E.: Thermal burns in man. V. Cardiac output during early therapy. Surg., Gynec. & Obst. 101:94, 1955.

Hardy, J. D., Neely, W. A., Wilson, F. C., Jr., Milnor, E. P. and Wilson, H.: Fluid kinetics following thermal burns in man; a preliminary report. Surgery 34:457, 1953.

Hardy, J. D., Richardson, E. M. and Dohan, F. C.: The urinary excretion of corticoids and 17-ketosteroids following major operations. Surg., Gynec. & Obst. 96:448, 1953.

Hardy, J. D. and Turner, M. D.: Hydrocortisone secretion in man: studies of adrenal vein blood. Surgery 42:194, 1957.

Harken, D. E., Dexter, L., Ellis, L. B., Farrand, R. E. and Dickson, J. F., III: The surgery of mitral stenosis. III. Finger-fracture valvuloplasty. Ann. Surg. 134:722, 1951.

Harken, D. E., Ellis, L. B., Dexter, L., Farrand, R. E. and Dickson, J. F., III: The responsibility of the physician in the selection of patients with mitral stenosis for surgical treatment. Circulation 6:349, 1952.

Harkins, H. N.: Acute ulcer of the duodenum (Curling's ulcer) as a complication of burns; relation to sepsis; report of case with study of 107 cases collected from literature, 94 with necropsy, 13 with recovery; experimental studies. Surgery 3:608, 1938.

Harkins, H. N. and Long, C. N. H.: Metabolic changes in shock after burns. Am. J. Physiol. 144:661, 1945.

Harman, J. W.: A histological study of skeletal muscle in acute ischemia. Am. J. Path. 23:551, 1947.

Harman, J. W.: The significance of local vascular phenomena in the production of ischemic necrosis in skeletal muscle. Am. J. Path. 24:625, 1948.

Harman, J. W. and Ragaz, F. J.: The pathogenesis of experimental fat embolism. Am. J. Path. 26:551, 1950.

Harnagel, E. E. and Kramer, W. G.: Severe adrenocortical insufficiency following joint manipulation; report of patient receiving cortisone orally. J.A.M.A. 158:1518, 1955.

Harper, W. W.: Prevention and reduction of injuries in traffic collision. J. Crim. Law, Criminology & Police Sc. 43:515, 1952.

Harrington, S. W.: Relief of post-operative massive collapse of the lung by bronchoscopic aspirations. Ann. Surg. 85:152, 1927.

Harris, G. W.: Hypothalamic control of the anterior pituitary gland. Ciba Foundation Coll. on Endocrinology, London, 4:106, 1952.

Harrison, H. E., Darrow, D. C. and Yannet, H.: The total electrolyte content of animals and its probable relation to the distribution of body water. J. Biol. Chem. 113:515, 1936.

Harrison, J. H., Durden, W. F. and Kellom, A. S.: Hydrodextran in the treatment of hemorrhagic shock: with plasma volume, blood volume, protein and excretion studies. Ann. Surg. 142:824, 1955.

Harvey, S. C. and Nickerson, M.: Chemical transformations of dibenamine and dibenzyline and biological activity. J. Pharmacol. & Exper. Therap. 109:328, 1953.

Harwood, C. T. and Mason, J. W.: A systematic evaluation of the Nelson-Samuels plasma 17-hydroxycorticosteroid method. J. Clin. Endocrinol. 16:790, 1956.

Haug, C. A. and Dale, W. A.: Major surgery in old people. A.M.A. Arch. Surg. 64:421, 1952.

Havens, L. L. and Child, C. G., III: Recurrent psychosis associated with liver disease and elevated blood ammonia. New England J. Med. 252:756, 1955.

Hayes, M. A.: Adrenocortical function during surgical procedures. Surgery 32:811, 1952.

Hayes, M. A.: Shock and the adrenocortex. Surgery 35:174, 1954.

Hayes, M. A.: The dietary control of the postgastrectomy "dumping syndrome." Surgery 37:785, 1955.

Hayes, M. A.: A disturbance in calcium metabolism leading to tetany occurring early in acute pancreatitis. Ann. Surg. 142:346, 1955.

Hayes, M. A.: Surgical treatment as complicated by prior adrenocortical steroid therapy. Surgery 40:945, 1956.

Hayes, M. A. and Brandt, R. L.: Carbohydrate metabolism

in the immediate postoperative period. Surgery *32:*819, 1952.

Hayes, M. A. and Coller, F. A.: The neuroendocrine control of water and electrolyte excretion during surgical anesthesia. Surg., Gynec. & Obst. *95:*142, 1952.

Hayes, M. A., Williamson, R. J. and Heidenreich, W. F.: Endocrine mechanisms involved in water and sodium metabolism during operation and convalescence. Surgery *41:*353, 1957.

Haymond, H. E.: Massive resection of the small intestine—an analysis of 257 collected cases. Surg., Gynec. & Obst. *61:*693, 1935.

Haynes, B. W., Jr. and DeBakey, M. E.: Evaluation of plasma substitutes in clinical shock: dextran. S. Forum *2:*631, 1952.

Haynes, B. W., Jr., Martin, M. M. and Purnell, O. J.: Fluid colloid and electrolyte requirements in severe burns. I. An analysis of colloid therapy in 158 cases using the Evans formula. Ann. Surg. *142:*674, 1955.

Hawker, R. W.: Antidiuretic substance in human serum. Lancet *2:*1108, 1952.

Hawker, R. W.: Inactivation of antidiuretic hormone and oxytocin during pregnancy. Quart. J. Exper. Physiol. *41:*301, 1956.

Hawker, R. W.: Antidiuretic substance (ADS) in normal pregnancy and preeclamptic toxaemia. J. Endocrinol. (London) *14:*400, 1957.

Heckel, E. and Fell, E. H.: Cardiac arrest during surgical operations—causes, prevention and active management. S. Clin. North America *35:*243, 1955.

Helman, L., Bradlow, H. L., Adesman, J., Fukushima, D. K., Kulp, J. L. and Gallagher, T. F.: The fate of hydrocortisone-4-C14 in man. J. Clin. Invest. *33:*1106, 1954.

Helmreich, M. L., Jenkins, D. and Swan, H.: The adrenal cortical response to surgery. II. Changes in plasma and urinary corticosteroid levels in man. Surgery *41:*895, 1957.

Henneman, P. H. and Wallach, S.: A review of the prolonged use of oestrogen and androgen in postmenopausal and senile osteoporosis. Arch. Int. Med. *100:*715, 1957.

Herbut, P. A.: Acute peptic ulcers following distant operations. Surg., Gynec. & Obst. *80:*410, 1945.

Herndon, R. F., Meroney, W. H., Jr. and Pearson, C. M.: The electrocardiographic effects of alterations in concentration of plasma chemicals. Am. Heart J. *50:*188, 1955.

Hershey, S. G., Zweifach, B. W. and Antopol, W.: Factors associated with protection against experimental shock. Anesthesiology *17:*265, 1956.

Hershey, S. G., Zweifach, B. W. and Metz, D. B.: An evaluation of the protective action of autonomic blocking agents in peripheral circulatory stress. Anesthesiology *15:*589, 1954.

Hetherington, M.: State of water in mammalian tissues. J. Physiol. *73:*184, 1931.

von Hevesy, G. and Hofer, E.: Der Austansch des Wassers in Fischkörper. Ztscht. f. phys. Chim. *225:*28, 1934.

von Hevesy, G. and Hofer, E.: Die Verweilzeit des Wassers in menslichen Körper, untersucht mit Hilfe vom "schwerem" Wasser als Indicator. Klin. Wchnschr. *13:*1524, 1934.

von Hevesy, G. and Hofer, E.: The turnover rate of water in the human body. Nature *134:*879, 1934.

Hickman, J. B., Sieker, H. O., Pryor, W. W. and Ryan,

J. M.: Carbon dioxide retention during oxygen therapy. North Carolina M. J. *13:*35, 1952.

Hicks, D. A., Hope, A., Turnbull, A. L. and Verel, D.: The estimation and prediction of normal blood volume. Clin. Sc. *15:*557, 1956.

Higgins, G., O'Brien, J. R. P., Lewin, W. and Taylor, W. H.: Metabolic disorders in head injury; hyperchloraemia and hypocloruria. Lancet *1:*1295, 1951.

Higgins, G., O'Brien, J. R. P., Lewin, W. and Taylor, W. H.: Metabolic disorders in head injury; survey of 76 consecutive cases. Lancet *1:*61, 1954.

Hildes, J. A., Ferguson, M. H. and Bartlett, L. C.: The water and electrolyte excretion of the human pancreas. Gastroenterology *21:*64, 1952.

Hill, S. R., Jr. *et al.:* Studies on adrenocortical and psychological response to stress in man. A.M.A. Arch. Int. Med. *97:*269, 1956.

Hills, A. G., Forsham, P. H. and Finch, C. A.: Change in circulating leukocytes induced by the administration of pituitary adrenocorticotrophic hormone (ACTH) in man. Blood *3:*755, 1948.

Hills, A. G., Zintel, H. A. and Parsons, D. W.: Degrees of adrenal deficiency and shortcomings of cortisone as replacement therapy observed in patients with spontaneous and iatrogenic adrenal deficiency. Ann. Surg. *144:*733, 1956.

Hills, R. G. and Weinberg, J. A.: Influence of estrin on callus formation. Bull. Johns Hopkins Hosp. *68:*238, 1941.

Hirschfelder, A. D.: Clinical manifestations of high and low plasma magnesium: dangers of epsom salts purgation in nephritis. J.A.M.A. *102:*1138, 1934.

Hitchcock, C. R. and Horowitz, S.: Therapy of severely burned patients; eleven years' study at the University of Minnesota. A.M.A. Arch. Surg. *74:*485, 1957.

Hoar, W. S. and Haist, R. E.: Amino acid nitrogen changes in shock. J. Biol. Chem. *154:*331, 1944.

Hoch-Ligeti, C., Irvine, K. and Sprinkle, E. P.: Investigation of serum protein patterns in patients undergoing operation. Proc. Soc. Exper. Biol. & Med. *84:*707, 1953.

Hoffman, H. L., Jacobs, J. and Freedlander, S. O.: The use of crystalline soybean trypsin inhibitor in acute hemorrhagic pancreatitis in dogs. A.M.A. Arch. Surg. *66:*617, 1953.

Hoffman, W. S. and Kozoll, D. D.: The fate of intravenously injected gelatine in human subjects. J. Clin. Invest. *25:*575, 1946.

Holaday, D. A., Ma, D. and Papper, E. M.: The immediate effects of respiratory depression on acid-base balance in anesthetized man. J. Clin. Invest. *36:*1121, 1957.

Holden, W. D., Cole, J. W. and Portmann, A. F.: Myocardial intolerance to excessive blood transfusion. Surg., Gynec. & Obst. *90:*455, 1950.

Holden, W. D., Krieger, H., Levey, S. and Abbott, W. E.: The effect of nutrition on nitrogen metabolism in the surgical patient. Ann. Surg. *146:*563, 1957.

Hollenberg, H. G. and Briggs, B. P.: Portal caval anastomosis in infants. Ann. Surg. *141:*648, 1955.

Holliday, M. A.: Acute metabolic alkalosis: its effect on potassium and acid excretion. J. Clin. Invest. *34:*428, 1955.

Holman, E.: Vitamin and protein factors in pre-operative and post-operative care of the surgical patient. Surg., Gynec. & Obst. *70:*261, 1940.

Hood, R. M. and Beall, A. C.: Hypoventilation, hypoxia and acidosis occurring in the acute postoperative period. Presented at the Boston meetings of the American Association for Thoracic Surgery, May 17, 1958.

Hopkirk, J. F., Wight, A., Merrington, W. R. and Cope, O.: Metabolic derangements imperiling the perforated ulcer patient. V. Acceleration of metabolic rate and altered endocrine activity. A.M.A. Arch. Surg. 72:439, 1956.

Howard, H. H.: Observations in transplantation of the ureter. J. Urol. 61:735, 1949.

Howard, J. E.: Hypercalcemia and renal injury. Ann. Int. Med. 16:176, 1942 (editorial).

Howard, J. E.: Protein metabolism during convalescence after trauma. A.M.A. Arch. Surg. 50:166, 1945.

Howard, J. E., Bigham, R. S., Eisenberg, H. and Bailey, E.: Studies on convalescence. IV. Nitrogen and mineral balances during starvation and graduated feeding in healthy young males at bed rest. Bull. Johns Hopkins Hosp. 78:282, 1946.

Howard, J. E., Parson, W. and Bigham, R. S., Jr.: Studies on patients convalescent from fracture. III. Urinary excretion of calcium and phosphorus. Bull. Johns Hopkins Hosp. 77:291, 1945.

Howard, J. E., Parson, W., Stein, K. E., Eisenberg, H. and Reidt, V.: Studies on fracture convalescence. I. Nitrogen metabolism after fracture and skeletal operations in healthy males. Bull. Johns Hopkins Hosp. 75:156, 1944.

Howard, J. E., Winternitz, J., Parson, W., Bigham, R. S., Jr. and Eisenberg, H.: Studies on fracture convalescence. II. The influence of diet on post-traumatic nitrogen deficit exhibited by fracture patients. Bull. Johns Hopkins Hosp. 75:209, 1944.

Howard, J. M.: Surgical physiology of pancreatitis. S. Clin. North America 29:1789, 1949.

Howard, J. M.: Experiences with shock in the Korean Theater. In Green, H. D. (ed.): Shock and Circulatory Homeostasis. Transactions of the Third Conference. New York, Josiah Macy, Jr., Foundation, 1953.

Howard, J. M. (ed.): Battle Casualties in Korea: Studies of the Surgical Research Team. Army Medical Service Graduate School, Walter Reed Army Medical Center. Washington, D. C., U. S. Government Printing Office, 1955.

Howard, J. M.: The systemic response to injury: gastric and salivary secretion following injury. Ann. Surg. 141:342, 1955.

Howard, J. M.: The systemic response to injury: studies of the absorption and metabolism of glucose following injury. Ann. Surg. 141:321, 1955.

Howard, J. M., Artz, C. P. and Stahl, R. R.: The systemic response to injury: the hypertensive response to injury. Ann. Surg. 141:327, 1955.

Howard, J. M. et al.: Studies of adrenal function in combat and wounded soldiers; study in the Korean theater. Ann. Surg. 141:314, 1955.

Howard, J. M. and Crosby, W. H. (eds.): Battle Casualties in Korea: Studies of the Surgical Research Team. Vol. II. Tools for Resuscitation. Army Med. Serv. Grad. School, Walter Reed Army Med. Center. Washington, D. C., U. S. Government Printing Office, 1956.

Howard, J. M., Frawley, J. P. and Artz, C. P.: The systemic response to injury: a study of plasma amylase activity in the combat casualty. Ann. Surg. 141:337, 1955.

Howard, J. M., Frawley, J. P. and Artz, C. P.: A survey of plasma electrolyte changes in the seriously injured battle casualty; a study in Korea. A.M.A. Arch. Surg. 71:205, 1955.

Howard, J. M., Frawley, J. P., Artz, C. P. and Sako, Y.: The fate of dextran and modified gelatine in casualties with renal insufficiency. Surg., Gynec. & Obst. 100:207, 1955.

Howard, J. M. and Hughes, C. W. (eds.): Battle Casualties in Korea: Studies of the Surgical Research Team. Vol. I, parts 1, 2, 3, 4. The systemic response to injury. Army Medical Service Graduate School, Walter Reed Army Medical Center. Washington, D. C., U. S. Government Printing Office, 1955.

Howard, J. M. and Inui, F. K.: Clostridial myositis—gas gangrene: observations of battle casualties in Korea. Surgery 36:1115, 1954.

Howard, J. M., Olney, J. M., Frawley, J. P., Peterson, R. E. and Guerra, S.: Adrenal function in the combat casualty. A.M.A. Arch. Surg. 71:47, 1955.

Howard, J. M., Teng, C. T. and Loeffler, R. K.: Studies of dextrans of various molecular sizes. Ann. Surg. 143:369, 1956.

Howe, C. W.: Postoperative wound infections due to Staphylococcus aureus. New England J. Med. 251:411, 1954.

Howes, E. L., Sooy, J. W. and Harvey, S. C.: The healing of wounds as determined by their tensile strength. J.A.M.A. 92:42, 1929.

Howkins, J., McLaughlin, C. R. and Daniel, P.: Neuronal damage from temporary cardiac arrest. Lancet 1:488, 1946.

Howland, W. S.: Adrenal cortical insufficiency occurring during surgery and in the postoperative period Geriatrics 12:147, 1957.

Howland, W. S., Boyan, C. P. and Schweizer, O.: Ventricular fibrillation during massive blood replacement. Am. J. Surg. 92:356, 1956.

Howland, W. S., Schweizer, O., Boyan, C. P. and Dotto, A. C.: Physiologic alterations with massive blood replacement. Surg., Gynec. & Obst. 101:478, 1955.

Howland, W. S., Schweitzer, O., Boyan, C. P. and Dotto, A. C.: Treatment of adrenal cortical insufficiency during surgical procedures. J.A.M.A. 160:1271, 1956.

Hoxworth, P. I. and Haesler, W. E., Jr.: Safety of stored liquid plasma—a clinical study. Ann. Surg. 144:336, 1956.

Huggins, C.: Composition of bone and function of bone cell. Physiol. Rev. 17:119, 1937.

Hughes, C. W. and Jahnke, E. J., Jr.: The surgical aspects of portal decompression. Am. J. Gastroenterology 24:372, 1955.

Hume, D. M.: The role of the hypothalamus in the pituitary-adrenal cortical response to stress. J. Clin. Invest. 28:790, 1949.

Hume, D. M.: The relationship of the hypothalamus to the pituitary secretion of ACTH. Ciba Foundation Coll. on Endocrinol. 4:87, 1952.

Hume, D. M.: The neuro-endocrine response to injury: present status of the problem. Ann. Surg. 138:548, 1953.

Hume, D. M. and Nelson, D. H.: Corticoid output in adrenal venous blood of the intact dog. Fed. Proc. 13:73, 1954.

Hume, D. M. and Nelson, D. H.: Adrenal cortical function in surgical shock. S. Forum 5:568, 1955.

Hume, D. M., Nelson, D. H. and Miller, D. W.: Blood and urinary 17-hydroxycorticosteroids in patients with severe burns. Ann. Surg. 143:316, 1956.

Hume, D. M. and Wittenstein, G. J.: The relationship of the hypothalamus to pituitary-adrenocortical function. Proc. 1st. Clin. Conf. Philadelphia, Blakiston Co., 1950, p. 134.

Hummel, R. P., Balikov, B. and Artz, C. P.: Studies in Curling's ulcers. S. Forum 6:306, 1956.

Hunt, A. H.: The role of vitamin C in wound healing. Brit. J. Surg. 28:436, 1940.

Hurtado, A., Merino, C. and Delgado, E.: Influence of anoxemia on the hemopoietic activity. A.M.A. Arch. Int. Med. 75:284, 1945.

Hutchison, W. J. and Burdeaux, B. D., Jr.: The effect of short-wave diathermy on bone repair. J. Bone & Joint Surg. 33A:155, 1951.

Hyatt, R. E. and Smith, J. R.: The mechanism of ascites; physiologic appraisal. Am. J. Med. 16:434, 1954.

Iber, F. L., Rosen, H., Levenson, S. M. and Chalmers, T. C.: The plasma amino acids in patients with liver failure. J. Lab. & Clin. Med. 50:417, 1957.

Ikkos, D., Ljunggren, H., Luft, R. and Sjögren, B.: Content and distribution of potassium and chloride in adults. Metabolism 4:231, 1955.

Ikkos, D., Luft, R. and Sjögren, B.: Distribution of fluid and sodium in healthy adults. Metabolism 3:400, 1954.

Ingelfinger, F. J.: Medical progress—the late effects of total and subtotal gastrectomy. New England J. Med. 231:321, 1944.

Ingle, D. J.: The role of the adrenal cortex in homeostasis. J. Endocrinol. 8:23, 1952.

Ingle, D. J.: Some further studies on the relationship of the adrenal cortical hormones to experimental diabetes. Diabetes 1:345, 1952.

Ingle, D. J.: Discussion. In Ralli, E. P. (ed.): Adrenal Cortex: Transactions of the Fourth Conference. New York, Josiah Macy, Jr., Foundation, 1953, p. 14.

Ingle, D. J.: The permissive action of hormones. J. Clin. Endocrinol. 14:1272, 1954.

Ingle, D. J., Meeks, R. C. and Thomas, K. E.: The effect of fractures upon urinary electrolytes in non-adrenalectomized rats and in adrenalectomized rats treated with adrenal cortex extract. Endocrinology 49:703, 1951.

Ingle, D. J. and Nezamis, J. E.: Effect of stress upon glycosuria of force-fed depancreatized and adrenalectomized-depancreatized rats. Am. J. Physiol. 162:1, 1950.

Ingle, D. J., Ward, E. O. and Kuizenga, M. H.: The relationship of the adrenal glands to changes in urinary nonprotein nitrogen following multiple fractures in the force-fed rat. Am. J. Physiol. 149:510, 1947.

Ingraham, R. C. and Visscher, M. B.: The production of chloride-free solutions by the action of intestinal epithelium. Am. J. Physiol. 114:676, 1936.

Ingraham, R. C. and Visscher, M. B.: Further studies on intestinal absorption with the performance of osmotic work. Am. J. Physiol. 121:771, 1938.

Irvine, W. T., Allan, C. and Webster, D. R.: Prevention of the late complications of ureterocolostomy by methods of fecal exclusion. Brit. J. Surg. 43:650, 1956.

Iseri, L. T., Boyle, A. J., Chandler, D. E. and Myers, G. B.: Electrolyte studies in heart failure. I. Cellular factors in the pathogenesis of the edema of congestive heart failure. Circulation 11:615, 1955.

Iseri, L. T., Boyle, A. J. and Myers, G. B.: Water and electrolyte balance during recovery from severe congestive failure on a 50 mg. sodium diet. Am. Heart J. 40:706, 1950.

Ivy, A. C., Greengard, H., Stein, I. F., Jr., Grodins, F. S. and Dutton, D. F.: The effect of various blood substitutes in resuscitation after an otherwise fatal hemorrhage. Surg., Gynec. & Obst. 76:85, 1943.

Jabbour, E. and Hardy, J. D.: Adrenocortical reserve in debilitated surgical patients. S. Forum 4:587, 1954.

Jackson, D. M.: Treatment of burns: exercise in emergency surgery; Hunterian lecture. Ann. Roy. Coll. Surgeons, England 13:236, 1953.

Jackson, D. P. and Krevans, J. R.: A hemorrhagic state following multiple whole blood transfusions. J. Clin. Invest. 34:942, 1955.

Jackson, W. P. U., Linder, G. C. and Berman, S.: Small gut insufficiency following intestinal surgery; a clinical and metabolic study of a man surviving with 7 in. of small intestine; with psychiatric report. S. African J. Clin. Sc. 2:70, 1951.

Jacobson, L. O., Goldwasser, E., Fried, W. and Plzak, L.: Role of the kidney in erythropoiesis. Nature 179:633, 1957.

Jahnke, E. J., Jr., Palmer, E. D., Sborov, V. M., Hughes, C. W. and Seeley, S. F.: An evaluation of the shunt operation for portal decompression. Surg., Gynec. & Obst. 97:471, 1953.

Jailer, J. W., Wong, A. S. H. and Engle, E. T.: Pituitary-adrenal relationship in full-term and in premature infants, as evidenced by eosinophil response. J. Clin. Endocrinol. 11:186, 1951.

James, A. H., Brooks, L., Edelman, I. S., Olney, J. M. and Moore, F. D.: Body sodium and potassium. I. The simultaneous measurement of exchangeable sodium and potassium in man by isotope dilution. Metabolism 3:313, 1954.

James, G. W., III, Abbott, L. D., Jr., Brooks, J. W. and Evans, E. I.: The anemia of thermal injury. III. Erythropoiesis and hemoglobin studied with N^{15}-glycine in dog and man. J. Clin. Invest. 33:150, 1954.

Jasinski, B. and Ott, W.: Larvierter Eisenmangel, ein wesentlicher Teilfaktor des Dumping-Syndroms bei Magenresezierten. Schweiz. med. Wchnschr. 81:1141, 1951.

Javid, H.: Nutrition in gastric surgery with particular reference to nitrogen and fat assimilation. Surgery 38:641, 1955.

Jenkins, M. T., Jones, R. F., Wilson, B. and Moyer, C. A.: Congestive atelectasis: a complication of the intravenous infusion of fluids. Ann. Surg. 132:327, 1950.

Jepson, R. P., Edwards, K. M. and Reece, M. W.: Adrenocortical response to corticotrophin and operation. Clin. Sc. 15:603, 1956.

Jepson, R. P., Jordan, A. and Levell, M. J.: Urinary steroid response to operation. Brit. J. Surg. 43:390, 1956.

Jepson, R. P., Jordan, A., Levell, M. J. and Wilson, G. M.: Metabolic response to adrenalectomy. Ann. Surg. 145:1, 1957.

Jessner, L., Blom, G. E. and Waldfogel, S.: Emotional implications of tonsillectomy and adenoidectomy on children. In Eissler, R. S. *et al.* (eds.): The Psychoanalytic Study of the Child. Vol. 7. New York, International University Press, 1952.

Joergenson, E. J., Davis, H. A. and Wooley, M.: Blood and plasma volume studies in patients with acute surgical lesions of the abdomen. Am. J. Surg. *92:*325, 1956.

Johnson, H. T., Conn, J. W., Iob, V. and Coller, F. A.: Postoperative salt retention and its relation to increased adrenal cortical function. Ann. Surg. *132:*374, 1950.

Johnson, J., Kirby, C. K. and Blakemore, W. S.: Symposium on applied physiology in modern surgery; physiologic considerations in cardiac surgery. S. Clin. North America *35:*1729, 1955.

Johnson, S. R. and Svanborg, A.: Investigations with regard to the pathogenesis of so-called fat embolism. (Serum lipids and tissue esterase activity and the frequency of so-called fat embolism in soft tissue trauma and fractures.) Ann. Surg. *144:*145, 1956.

Johnston, C. G. and Jordan, P., Jr.: Cardiovascular surgery in geriatrics. J. Am. Geriatrics Soc. *2:*529, 1954.

Johnston, J. A.: Factors influencing retention of nitrogen in periods of growth Am. J. Dis. Child. *62:*708, 1941.

Johnstone, M.: Cyclopropane anaesthesia and ventricular arrhythmias. Brit. Heart J. *12:*239, 1950.

Jones, P. G., Davis, J. H., Jr., Hubay, C. A. and Holden, W. D.: Physiologic mechanisms of intra-arterial transfusion. Surgery *27:*189, 1950.

Jordan, P. J., Jr., Patton, T. B. and Benson, C. D.: Portal hypertension in infants and children. A.M.A. Arch. Surg. *72:*879, 1956.

Joseph, M.: Pancreas and the steering wheel. West. J. Surg. *60:*129, 1952.

Joseph, E. G., Katz, J. and Barzilay, B.: Ureterosigmoidostomy: experience with the Goodwin procedure. Ann. Surg. *143:*337, 1956.

Judet, J., Judet, R., LaGrange, J. and Dunoyer, J.: A study of the arterial vascularization of the femoral neck in the adult. J. Bone & Joint Surg. *37-A:*663, 1955.

Kahn, J. and Klein, H. M.: Human pancreatic secretion studied from a case of pancreatic cyst with fistula. Am. J. M. Sc. *184:*503, 1932.

Kartin, B. L., Man, E. B., Winkler, A. W. and Peters, J. P.: Blood ketones and serum lipids in starvation and water deprivation. J. Clin. Invest. *23:*824, 1944.

Kaufman, B. J. *et al.:* Hypoventilation and obesity. J. Clin. Invest. *38:*500, 1959.

Kaufman, H. E. and Rosen, S. W.: Clinical acid-base regulation—the Brönsted schema. Surg., Gynec. & Obst. *103:*101, 1956.

Kay, J. H. and Blalock, A.: The use of calcium chloride in the treatment of cardiac arrest in patients. Surg., Gynec. & Obst. *93:*97, 1951.

Kaye, M. and Halpenny, G. W.: Needle biopsy of the kidney. Canad. M. A. J. *75:*480, 1956.

Keeton, R. W., Cole, W. H., Calloway, N., Glickman, N., Mitchell, H. H., Dyniewicz, J. and Howes, D.: Convalescence: a study in the physiological recovery of nitrogen metabolism and liver function. Ann. Int. Med. *28:*521, 1948.

Keith, N. M., Burchell, H. B. and Baggenstoss, A. H.: Electrocardiographic changes in uremia associated with a high concentration of serum potassium: report of 3 cases. Am. Heart J. *27:*817, 1944.

Keith, N. M., King, H. E. and Osterberg, A. E.: Serum concentration and renal clearance of potassium in severe renal insufficiency in man. A.M.A. Arch. Int. Med. *71:*675, 1943.

Keith, N. M. and Osterberg, A. E.: The tolerance for potassium in severe renal insufficiency: a study of 10 cases. Tr. A. Am. Physicians *59:*62, 1946.

Keith, N. M. and Osterberg, A. E.: The tolerance for potassium in severe renal insufficiency: a study of 10 cases. J. Clin. Invest. *26:*773, 1947.

Keith, N. M., Rowntree, L. G. and Geraghty, J. T.: A method for the determination of plasma and blood volume. A.M.A. Arch. Int. Med. *16:*547, 1915.

Kelly, J. F.: Hemorrhage of suprarenal glands following breech extraction. J. Indiana M. A. *24:*135, 1931.

Kelly, W. D., MacLean, L. D., Perry, J. F. and Wangensteen, O. H.: A study of patients following total and near-total gastrectomy. Surgery *35:*964, 1954.

Kenwell, H. N. and Wels, P. B.: Acute hemorrhagic pancreatitis; report of 11 consecutive cases treated with human serum albumin. Surg., Gynec. & Obst. *96:*169, 1953.

Kerrigan, G. A., Talbot, N. B. and Crawford, J. D.: Role of neurohypophyseal-antidiuretic-hormone-renal system in everyday clinical medicine. J. Clin. Endocrinol. *15:*265, 1955.

Kety, S. S. *et al.:* The toxic factors in experimental traumatic shock. III. Shock accompanying muscle ischemia and loss of vascular fluid. J. Clin. Invest. *24:*839, 1945.

Keys, A.: Caloric undernutrition and starvation, with notes on protein deficiency. J.A.M.A. *138:*500, 1948.

Keys, A. and Brozek, J.: Body fat in adult man. Physiol. Rev. *33:*245, 1953.

Keys, A., Brozek, J., Henschel, A., Mickelson, O. and Taylor, H. L.: The Biology of Human Starvation. Minneapolis, University of Minnesota Press, 1950.

Keyser, J. W.: The serum tryptophane-perchloric acid reaction as a measure of tissue destruction. J. Clin. Path. *3:*106, 1950.

Keyser, J. W.: Blood serum protein-bound carbohydrate after injury. J. Clin. Path. *5:*194, 1952.

Kiesewetter, W. B. and Harris, J.: Bleeding after large transfusions of citrated blood. S. Forum *6:*91, 1956.

Kiesewetter, W. B. and Koop, C. E.: The surgeon's role in the management of obstructive jaundice in infancy. Bull. Ayer Clin. Lab. *4:*55, 1952.

King, J. D. and Harris, J. H.: War wounds of the chest among marine and naval casualties in Korea. Surg., Gynec. & Obst. *97:*199, 1953.

King, T. C., Reynolds, L. E. and Price, P. B.: Local edema and capillary permeability associated with burn wounds. S. Forum *6:*80, 1956.

Kinney, J. M. *et al.:* Evaluation and management of ventilatory insufficiency in the surgical patient. In press.

Kinney, J. M. and Moore, F. D.: Carbon balance. A clinical approach to energy exchange. Surgery. *40:*16, 1956.

Klein, R., Papadatos, C., Fortunato, J. and Byers, C.: Acid-hydrolyzable corticoids of serum. J. Clin. Endocrinol. *15:*215, 1955.

Klein, R., Papadatos, C., Fortunato, J., Byers, C. and Puntereri, A.: Serum corticoids in liver disease. J. Clin. Endocrinol. *15:*943, 1955.

Knight, R. P., Jr., Kornfeld, D. S., Glaser, G. H. and Bondy, P. K.: Effects of intravenous hydrocortisone on electrolytes of serum and urine in man. J. Clin. Endocrinol. *15:*176, 1955.

Knowles, H. C.: Hypernatremia. Metabolism *5:*508, 1956.

Knutson, R. C., Bollman, J. L. and Lundy, J. S.: Comparative effectiveness of certain volemic substances in maintaining plasma volume after blood loss. S. Forum *2:*637, 1952.

Kolff, W. J.: Experiences in the treatment of surgical patients having anuria and uremia. Surg., Gynec. & Obst. *101:*563, 1955.

Kohlstaedt, K. G. and Page, I. H.: Hemorrhagic hypotension and its treatment by intra-arterial and intravenous infusion of blood. A.M.A. Arch. Surg. *47:*178, 1943.

Kohlstaedt, K. G. and Page, I. H.: Terminal hemorrhagic shock—circulatory dynamics, recognition, and treatment. Surgery *16:*430, 1944.

Kondo, B. and Katz, L. N.: Heart size in shock produced by venous occlusion of hind limbs of dog. Am. J. Physiol. *143:*77, 1945.

Korenberg, M.: Electrolyte disturbance in ureterocolostomy. J. Urol. *66:*686, 1951.

Kowalski, H. J., Abelmann, W. H. and McNeely, W. F.: The cardiac output in patients with cirrhosis of the liver and tense ascites with observations on the effect of paracentesis. J. Clin. Invest. *33:*768, 1954.

Krebs, E. G.: Depression of gamma globulin in hypoproteinemia due to malnutrition. J. Lab. & Clin. Med. *31:*85, 1946.

Kremen, A. J., Linner, J. H. and Nelson, C. H.: An experimental evaluation of the nutritional importance of proximal and distal small intestine. Ann. Surg. *140:*439, 1954.

Krevans, J. R. and Jackson, D. P.: Hemorrhagic disorder following massive whole blood transfusions. J.A.M.A. *159:*171, 1955.

Krieger, H., Abbott, W. E., Levey, S., Babb, I. L. and Holden, W. D.: Metabolic alterations in surgical patients. III. The influence of peritonitis on nitrogen, carbohydrate, electrolyte, and water balance. Surgery *36:*580, 1954.

Kulka, J. P., Pearson, C. M. and Robbins, S. L.: A distinctive vacuolar nephropathy associated with intestinal disease. Am. J. Path. *26:*349, 1950.

Kurland, G. S. and Freedberg, A. S.: The potentiating effect of ACTH and of cortisone on pressor response to intravenous infusion of L-nor-epinephrine. Proc. Soc. Exper. Biol. & Med. *78:*28, 1951.

Kushner, D. S. *et al.:* Studies of serum mucoprotein (seromucoid). II. Physiologic variations and response to stress. J. Lab. & Clin. Med. *47:*409, 1956.

Ladd, M.: Renal function in the battle casualty. A report to the Army Medical Service Graduate School, 1952.

Ladd, M.: Renal sequelae of war wounds in man. Functional patterns of shock and convalescence. Final Report to the Army Medical Service Graduate School, Washington, D. C., 1954, Chap. 6.

Ladd, M.: Renal sequelae of war wounds in man. In Howard, J. M. (ed.): Battle Casualties in Korea; Studies of the Surgical Research Team. Vol. IV. Army Medical Service Graduate School, Walter Reed Army Medical Center, Washington, D. C., U. S. Government Printing Office, 1955.

Lamarca, V. and Posteraro, G.: Il metilandrostendiolo nella terapia della fratture. Riv. clin. pediat. *58:*89, 1956.

Lanchantin, G. F. and Deadrick, R. E.: Serum protein changes in thermal trauma. I. Electrophoretic analysis at pH 8.6 and pH 4.5. U. S. Army Surgical Research Unit Interim Report, 1957.

Lanchantin, G. F., Morico, J. L. and Tausig, F.: Serum protein changes in thermal trauma. IV. Some quantitative and qualitative aspects of total serum glycoprotein and seromucoid following burns. Report NC 12–56, U. S. Army Surgical Research Unit, Brooke Army Medical Center, Texas, 1957.

Lapides, J.: Mechanism of electrolyte imbalance following ureterosigmoid transplantation. Surg., Gynec. & Obst. *93:*691, 1951.

Lapides, J.: Mode of development of electrolyte imbalance in ureterosigmoid anastomoses. S. Forum *2:*343, 1952.

Lapides, J.: Physiopathology and therapy of fluid disorders in prostatism. Geriatrics *9:*20, 1954.

Laragh, J. H.: The effect of potassium chloride on hyponatremia. J. Clin. Invest. *33:*807, 1954.

Laragh, J. H. and Almy, T. P.: Changes in circulating eosinophils in man following epinephrine, insulin and surgical operations. Proc. Soc. Exper. Biol. & Med. *69:*499, 1948.

Laragh, J. H. and Capeci, N. E.: Effect of administration of potassium chloride on serum sodium and potassium concentration. Am. J. Physiol. *180:*539, 1955.

Laragh, J. H. and Stoerk, H. C.: On the mechanism of secretion of the sodium-retaining hormone (aldosterone) within the body. J. Clin. Invest. *34:*913, 1955 (abstr.).

Large, A. M., Johnston, C. G. and Preshaw, D. E.: The portacaval venous shunt with special reference to side-to-side portacaval anastomosis. Ann. Surg. *135:*22, 1952.

Larrain, C. and Adelson, E.: The hemostatic defect of uremia. I. Clinical investigation of three patients with acute post-traumatic renal insufficiency. Blood *11:*1059, 1956.

Lauson, H. D., Bradley, S. E. and Cournand, A.: Renal circulation in shock. J. Clin. Invest. *23:*381, 1944.

Lavik, P. S.: Use of I[131]-labelled protein in study of protein digestion and absorption in children with and without cystic fibrosis of the pancreas. Pediatrics *10:*667, 1952.

Lawrence, W., Jr., Jacquez, J. A., Dienst, S. G., Poppell, J. W., Randall, H. T. and Roberts, K. E.: The effect of changes in blood pH on the plasma total ammonia level. Surgery *42:*50, 1957.

Laws, J. and Johnston, R.: The significance of the meat intoxication syndrome in Eck fistula dogs. S. Forum *2:*188, 1952 (abstr.).

Lawson, H. C., Rappaport, D. B. and Ramirez, A.: The recovery of injected dye and the yield of blood cells by perfusion of the cardiovascular system in barbitalized dogs. Am. J. Physiol. *147:*412, 1946.

Leadbetter, W. F.: Consideration of problems incident to performance of uretero-enterostomy: report of a technique. J. Urol. *65:*818, 1951.

Leaf, A., Bartter, F. C., Santos, R. F. and Wrong, O.: Evidence in man that urinary electrolyte loss induced by Pitressin is a function of water retention. J. Clin. Invest. *32:*868, 1953.

Leaf, A., Chatillon, J. Y., Wrong, O. and Tuttle, E. P., Jr.: The mechanism of the osmotic adjustment of body cells as determined in vivo by the volume of distribution of a large water load. J. Clin. Invest. *33*:1261, 1954.

Leaf, A. and Renshow, A.: A test of the redox hypothesis of active ion transport. Nature *178*:156, 1956.

Le Femine, A. A., Marks, L. J., Teter, J. G., Leftin, J. H., Leonard, M. P. and Baker, D. V.: The adrenocortical response in surgical patients. Ann. Surg. *146*:26, 1957.

Leffman, H. and Payne, J. T.: Episodic coma due to meat intoxication as a fatal complication of portacaval shunt in the human being. Am. J. Surg. *21*:488, 1955.

Leger, L. and Lande, M.: La transfusion intra-aortique. Presse méd. *58.2*:851, 1950.

Lehman, E. P. and Moore, R. M.: Fat embolism including experimental production without trauma. A.M.A. Arch. Surg. *14*:621, 1927.

Le Quesne, L. P.: Postoperative water retention with report of a case of water intoxication. Lancet *1*:172, 1954.

Le Quesne, L. P. and Lewis, A. A. G.: Postoperative water and sodium retention. Lancet *1*:153, 1953.

Leriche, R. and Policard, A.: The Normal and Pathological Physiology of Bone. St. Louis, C. V. Mosby Co., 1928.

Levene, M.: Concealed traumatic suprarenal haemorrhage. Lancet *2*:321, 1955.

Levenson, S. M. *et al.*: Ascorbic acid, riboflavin, thiamin, and nicotinic acid in relation to severe injury, hemorrhage, and infection in the human. Ann. Surg. *124*:840, 1946.

Levenson, S. M., Adams, M. A., Green, R. W., Lund, C. C. and Taylor, F. H. L.: Plasma alpha amino nitrogen levels in patients with thermal burns. New England J. Med. *235*:467, 1946.

Levenson, S. M., Birkhill, F. R. and Waterman, D. F.: Healing of soft tissue wounds; effects of nutrition, anemia and age. Surgery *28*:905, 1950.

Levenson, S. M., Howard, J. M. and Rosen, H.: Metabolic effects of injury; studies of the plasma non-protein nitrogen components in patients with severe battle wounds. In Howard, J. M. (ed): Battle Casualties in Korea, Vol. IV. Washington, D. C., U. S. Government Printing Office, 1955.

Levenson, S. M., Howard, J. M. and Rosen, H.: Studies of the plasma amino acids and amino conjugates in patients with severe battle wounds. Surg., Gynec. & Obst. *101*:35, 1955.

Levenson, S. M. and Upjohn, H. L.: Effect of irradiation on wound healing. Personal communication.

Levenson, S. M., Upjohn, H. L., Preston, J. A. and Steer, A.: Effect of thermal burns on wound healing. Ann. Surg. *146*:357, 1957.

Levenson, S. M., Upjohn, H. L. and Sheehy, T. W.: Two severe reactions following the long-term infusion of large amounts of intravenous fat emulsion. Metabolism *6*:807, 1957.

Levine, H. D.: Electrolyte imbalance and the electrocardiogram. Mod. Concepts Cardiovas. Dis. *23*:246, 1954.

Lewis, C. J.: Adrenal and pancreatic haemorrhage following operation. Brit. M. J. *2*:706, 1921.

Lewis, L., Robinson, R. F., Yee, J., Hacker, L. A. and Eisen, G.: Fatal cortical adrenal insufficiency precipitated by surgery during prolonged continuous cortisone treatment. Ann. Int. Med. *39*:116, 1953.

Li, C. H., Geschwind, I. and Evans, H. M.: The effect of growth and adrenocorticotropic hormones on the amino acid levels in the plasma. J. Biol. Chem. *177*:91, 1949.

Li, T. H. and Etsten, B.: Effect of cyclopropane on cardiac output and related hemodynamics in man. Anaesthesiology *18*:15, 1957.

Liddle, G. W., Bartter, F. C., Duncan, L. E., Barber, J. K. and Delea, C.: Mechanisms regulating aldosterone. J. Clin. Invest. *34*:949, 1955 (abstr.).

Liedberg, N. C. F., Reiss, E. and Artz, C. P.: Infection in burns. III. Septicemia, a common cause of death. Surg., Gynec. & Obst. *99*:151, 1954.

Lightfoot, L. H. and Coolidge, T. B.: The distribution of collagen in the guinea pig. J. Biol. Chem. *176*:477, 1948.

Lillehei, R. C. and MacLean, L. D.: The intestinal factor in irreversible endotoxin shock. Ann. Surg. *148*:513, 1958.

Lillehei, C. W., Roth, F. E. and Wangensteen, O. H.: The role of stress in the etiology of peptic ulcer; experimental and clinical observations. S. Forum *2*:43, 1952.

Limbosch, J.: Experiences with more than one thousand elderly surgical patients. A.M.A. Arch. Surg. *73*:124, 1956.

Lindberg, R. B., Wetzler, T. F., Marshall, J. D., Newton, A., Strawitz, J. G. and Howard, J. M.: The bacterial flora of battle wounds at the time of primary débridement. Ann. Surg. *141*:369, 1955.

Lindberg, R. B., Wetzler, T., Newton, A., Strawitz, J. G. and Howard, J. M.: The early flora of battle wounds in the Korean war. Preliminary Report to the Army Medical Service Graduate School, Washington, D. C., 1954.

Lindberg, R. B., Wetzler, T., Strawitz, J. G. and Howard, J. M.: The early bacterial flora of wounds in Korean conflict. In Howard, J. M. (ed.): Battle Casualties in Korea. Vol. III, The Battle Wound: Clinical Experiences. Army Medical Service Graduate School, Walter Reed Army Medical Center, Washington, D. C., 1956.

Linton, R. R., Jones, C. M. and Volwiler, W.: Portal hypertension: the treatment by splenectomy and splenorenal anastomosis with preservation of the kidney. S. Clin. North America *27*:1162, 1947.

Linton, R. R.: Portacaval shunts in the treatment of portal hypertension, with special reference to patients previously operated upon. New England J. Med. *238*:723, 1948.

Linton, R. R.: Selection of patients for portacaval shunts with summary of results in 61 cases. Ann. Surg. *134*:433, 1951.

Linton, R. R.: Emergency treatment of bleeding esophageal varices and the results of portacaval shunts in 90 patients. New York J. Med. *53*:2192, 1953.

Linton, R. R.: Bleeding esophageal varices: the emergency and definitive treatment. Am. Surgeon *24*:101, 1958.

Linton, R. R. and Ellis, D. S.: The emergency and definitive treatment of bleeding esophageal varices. J.A.M.A. *160*:1017, 1956.

Linton, R. R. and Warren, R.: Emergency treatment of massive bleeding from esophageal varices by transesophageal suture of these vessels at time of acute hemorrhage. Surgery *33*:243, 1953.

Lipschutz, E. W. and Capson, D.: "Cholangiolitic hepatitis," with special reference to its physiopathologic concept, diagnosis and therapy. Ann. Int. Med. *43*:1037, 1955.

Lipson, C. S.: Blood banking and transfusions: immunohematologic basis and practical applications. J. Maine M. A. *48:*183, 1957.

Llaurado, J. G.: Increased excretion of aldosterone immediately after operation. Lancet *1:*1295, 1955.

Llaurado, J. G.: Aldosterone excretion following hypophysectomy in man: relation to urinary Na/K ratio. Metabolism *6:*556, 1957.

Llaurado, J. G.: Feasibility of the oral route for the bio-assay of aldosterone-like materials in the rat. Proc. Univ. Otago M. School *35:*23, 1957.

Llaurado, J. G.: Postoperative transient aldosterone. Surgery *42:*313, 1957.

Llaurado, J. G. and Woodruff, M. F. A.: The stimulus to post-operative transeint aldosteronism. Proc. Univ. Otago M. School *35:*19, 1957.

Localio, S. A., Chassin, J. L. and Hinton, J. W.: Tissue protein depletion: a factor in wound disruption. Surg., Gynec. & Obst. *86:*107, 1948.

Localio, S. A., Chassin, J. L. and MacKay, M.: The effect of stress, the adrenal and the pituitary on healing. Am. J. Surg. *97:*521, 1956.

Localio, S. A., Gillette, L. and Hinton, J. W.: The biological chemistry of wound healing: the effect of d1-methionine on the healing of surface wounds. Surg., Gynec. & Obst. *89:*69, 1949.

Localio, S. A., Morgan, M. E. and Hinton, J. W.: The biological chemistry of wound healing. I. The effect of d1-methionine on the healing of wounds in protein-depleted animals. Surg., Gynec. & Obst. *86:*582, 1948.

Loeb, R. F.: On the diffusibility of the calcium of blood serum through collodion membranes; the effect of sodium chloride and changes in hydrogen ion concentration. J. Gen. Physiol. *6:*453, 1923.

Lombard, C. F.: How much force can the body withstand? Aviation Week *20:*1949.

Lombardo, T. A., Eisenberg, S., Oliver, B. B., Viar, W. N., Eddleman, E. E., Jr. and Harrison, T. R.: Effects of bleeding on electrolyte excretion and on glomerular filtration. Circulation *3:*260, 1951.

Longmire, W. P., Jr. and Beal, J. M.: Construction of a substitute gastric reservoir following total gastrectomy. Ann. Surg. *135:*637, 1952.

Longmire, W. P., Jr., Jordan, P. H., Jr. and Briggs, J. D.: Experience with resection of the pancreas in the treatment of chronic relapsing pancreatitis. Ann. Surg. *144:*681, 1956.

Loughlin, J. F.: Quadriplegia, hypopotassemia and hyperchloremic acidosis after bilateral ureterosigmoidostomy. New England J. Med. *254:*329, 1956.

Lown, B., Salzberg, H., Enselberg, C. D. and Weston, R. E.: Interrelation between potassium metabolism and digitalis toxicity in heart failure. Proc. Soc. Exper. Biol. & Med. *76:*797, 1951.

Lublin, H.: On late symptoms after gastroenterostomy and resection of stomach (Billroth II) for gastric and duodenal ulcer. Acta med. scandinav. (Suppl. 41): 1, 1931.

Luetscher, J. A., Jr. and Axelrad, B. J.: Increased aldosterone output during sodium deprivation in normal men. Proc. Soc. Exper. Biol. & Med. *87:*650, 1954.

Luetscher, J. A., Jr. and Blackman, S. S., Jr.: Severe injury to kidneys and brain following sulfathiazole administration. High serum sodium and chloride levels and persistent cerebral damage. Ann. Int. Med. *18:*741, 1943.

Luetscher, J. A., Jr. and Curtis, R. H.: Aldosterone: observations on regulation of sodium and potassium balance. Ann. Int. Med. *43:*658, 1955.

Luetscher, J. A., Jr. and Curtis, R. H.: Relationship of aldosterone in urine to sodium balance and to some other endocrine functions. J. Clin. Invest. *34:*951, 1955 (proc.).

Luetscher, J. A., Jr. and Curtis, R. H.: Symposium on biochemistry of disease; observations on aldosterone in human urine. Fed. Proc. *14:*746, 1955.

Luetscher, J. A., Jr. and Johnson, B. B.: Observations of the sodium-retaining corticoid (aldosterone) in the urine of children and adults in relation to sodium balance and edema. J. Clin. Invest. *33:*1441, 1954.

Luetscher, J. A., Jr., Neher, R. and Wettstein, A.: Isolation of crystalline aldosterone from the urine of a nephrotic patient. Experentia *10:*456, 1954.

Luetscher, J. A., Jr., Neher, R. and Wettstein, A.: Isolation of crystalline aldosterone from the urine of patients with congestive heart failure. Experentia *12:*22, 1956.

Luft, R. and von Euler, U. S.: Excretion of catechol amines during administration of ACTH, cortisone and desoxycorticosterone acetate. Metabolism *1:*179, 1952.

Lund, C. C.: The effect of surgical operations on the level of cevitamic acid in the blood plasma. New England J. Med. *221:*123, 1939.

Lund, C. C.: Ascorbic acid and human wound healing. Ann. Surg. *114:*776, 1941.

Lund, C. C.: Ascorbic acid deficiency associated with gastric lesions. New England J. Med. *227:*247, 1942.

Lund, C. C. and Browder, N. C.: The estimation of areas of burns. Surg., Gynec. & Obst. *79:*352, 1944.

Lyngar, E.: Blood changes after partial gastrectomy for ulcer. Acta med. scandinav. (Suppl. 246–250): 1, 1950.

Lyon, R. P., Stanton, J. R., Freis, E. D. and Smithwick, R. H.: Blood and "available fluid" (thiocyanate) volume studies in surgical patients; normal patterns of response of blood volume, available fluid, protein, chloride, and hematocrit in postoperative surgical patient. Surg., Gynec. & Obst. *89:*9, 1949.

Lyons, C. and Patton, T. B.: Bleeding esophageal varices. Surgery *39:*540, 1956.

MacCarty, C. S. and Cooper, I. S.: Neurologic and metabolic effects of bilateral ligation of the anterior cerebral arteries in man. Proc. Staff Meet., Mayo Clin. *26:*185, 1951.

MacDonald, R. M., Inglefinger, F. J. and Belding, H. W.: Late effects of total gastrectomy in man. New England J. Med. *237:*887, 1947.

Macfarlane, R. G.: Fibrinolysis following operation. Lancet *1:*10, 1937.

Machella, T. E.: The mechanism of the post-gastrectomy "dumping" syndrome. Ann. Surg. *130:*145, 1949.

Macfarlane, R. G. and Biggs, R.: Observations on fibrinolysis—spontaneous activity associated with surgical operations, trauma, etc. Lancet *2:*862, 1946.

MacLean, L. D., Perry, J. F., Kelly, W. D., Mosser, D. G., Mannick, A. and Wangensteen, O. H.: Nutrition following subtotal gastrectomy of four types (Billroth I & II, segmental and tubular resections). Surgery *35:*705, 1954.

MacLennan, J. D.: Anaerobic infections of war wounds in the Middle East. Lancet *2:*63, 94, 123, 1943.

MacLennan, J. D. and Macfarlane, R. G.: Toxin and antitoxin studies of gas-grangene in man. Lancet *2:*301, 1945.

Macpherson, A. I. S., Owen, J. A. and Innes, J.: Hepatic function after operations for portal hypertension. Lancet 2:356, 1954.

MacPherson, C. R.: Oxygen therapy—an unsuspected source of hospital infections. J.A.M.A. 167:1083, 1958.

Madden, J. L., Loré, J. M., Jr., Gerold, F. P. and Ravid, J. M.: The pathogenesis of ascites and a consideration of its treatment. Surg., Gynec. & Obst. 99:782, 1954.

Maddock, W. G., Bell, J. L. and Tremaine, M. J.: Gastrointestinal gas; observations on belching during anesthesia, operations and pyelography and rapid passage of gas. Ann. Surg. 130:512, 1949.

Mahaffey, J. H. and Haynes, B. W., Jr.: Observations on pancreatic juice in case of external pancreatic fistula in man. Am. Surgeon 19:174, 1953.

Maier, H. C., Rich, G. W. and Eichen, S.: Clinical significance of respiratory acidosis during operations. Ann. Surg. 134:653, 1951.

Mallory, T. B.: Hemoglobinuric nephrosis in traumatic shock. Am. J. Clin. Path. 17:427, 1947.

Mallory, T. B.: Pathology of the crush syndrome in battle casualties in the physiologic effects of wounds. Washington, D. C., Department of the Army, Office of the Surgeon General, 1952.

Malm, J. R., Reemtsma, K. and Barber, H. G.: Comparative fat and fatty acid intestinal absorption test utilizing radioiodine labeling—results in normal subjects. Proc. Soc. Exper. Biol. & Med. 92:471, 1956.

Maloney, J. V., Jr. et al.: The direct effect of pressure breathing on the pulmonary circulation. Ann. New York Acad. Sc. 66:931, 1957.

Maloney, J. V., Jr., Smythe, C. M., Gilmore, J. P. and Handford, S. W.: Intra-arterial and intravenous transfusion: a controlled study of their effectiveness in the treatment of experimental hemorrhagic shock. Surg., Gynec. & Obst. 97:529, 1953.

Maloney, J. V., Jr., Smythe, C. M., Gilmore, J. P. and Handford, S. W.: A controlled comparison of intra-arterial and intravenous transfusion; effect on blood pooling and survival rate in experimental hemorrhagic shock. S. Forum 4:484, 1954.

Maloney, J. V., Jr. and Whittenberger, J. L.: Clinical implications of pressures used in the body respirator. Am. J. M. Sc. 221:425, 1951.

Malorny, G.: Das Verhalten der Electrolyte im Blut und Gewebe bei erhohten CO₂-spannungen der Atmungssluft. Arch. exper. Path. u. Pharmakol. 205:684, 1948.

Man, E. B., Bettcher, P. G., Cameron, C. M. and Peters, J. P.: Plasma amino acid nitrogen and serum lipids of surgical patients. J. Clin. Invest. 25:701, 1946.

Manery, J. F. and Solandt, D. V.: Studies in experimental traumatic shock with particular reference to plasma potassium changes. Am. J. Physiol. 138:499, 1942.

Manger, W. W. et al.: Chemical quantitation of epinephrine and norepinephrine in thirteen patients with pheochromocytoma. Circulation 10:641, 1954.

Marchand, J. F. and Finch, C. A.: Fatal spontaneous potassium intoxication in patients with uremia. A.M.A. Arch. Int. Med. 73:384, 1944.

Margulis, R. R., Wiseman, M. E., Moyer, E. Z. and Pratt, J. P.: Changes in the electrophoretic pattern of the plasma proteins as induced by surgery. S. Forum 3:571, 1953.

Markley, K. et al.: Clinical evaluation of saline solution therapy in burn shock. J.A.M.A. 167:1465, 1956.

Markowski, B.: Some experiences of a medical prisoner of war. Brit. M. J. 2:361, 1945.

Marks, L. J. and Leftin, J. H.: A note of caution on the lack of specificity of the Porter-Silber reaction for 17, 21-dihydroxy-20-ketosteroids. J. Clin. Endocrinol. 14:1263, 1954.

Marrs, J. W. et al.: Acute gastric dilatation due to nasal oxygen. Ann. Surg. 148:835, 1958.

Marshall, E. K., Jr. and Rosenfeld, M.: Depression of respiration by oxygen. J. Pharmacol. & Exper. Therap. 57:437, 1936.

Marsiglia, G.: Il retardo nella consolidazione della fratture. Arch. ital. chir. 5:197, 1922.

Martin, G. A., Phear, E. A., Ruebner, B. and Sherlock, S.: The bacterial content of the small intestine in normal and cirrhotic subjects: relation to the methionine toxicity. Clin. Sc. 16:35, 1957.

Martin, H. E. and Wertman, M.: Electrolyte changes and electrocardiagram in diabetic acidosis. Am. Heart J. 31:646, 1947.

Martin, J. D., Jr., Garity, W. C. and Smith, F. C.: Evaluation of ACTH and cortisone in the treatment of burns. Surgery 38:543, 1955.

Mason, A. D., Jr., Mueller, C. B. and Stout, D. G.: Plasma proteolytic activity associated with experimental transfusion reaction in dogs. S. Forum 5:549, 1955.

Mason, A. S.: Metabolic response to total adrenalectomy and hypophysectomy. Lancet 2:632, 1955.

Mason, E. E.: Gastrointestinal lesions occurring in uremia. Ann. Int. Med. 37:96, 1952.

Mastio, G. J. and Albritten, F. F.: The respiratory function of the postoperative patient. A.M.A. Arch. Surg. 76:732, 1958.

Matern, D. I.: Hypokalemia accompanying hyperchloremic acidosis after ureterosigmoidostomy. New England J. Med. 250:941, 1954.

Mazur, A. and Shorr, E.: Hepatorenal factors in circulatory homeostasis. IX. The identification of the hepatic vasodepressor substance, VDM, with Ferritin. J. Biol. Chem. 176:771, 1948.

Mazur, A. and Shorr, E.: Quantitative immunochemical study of Ferritin and its relation to hepatic vasodepressor material. J. Biol. Chem. 182:607, 1950.

McCaughan, J. M. and Purcell, H. K.: Pancreatic fistula, clinical and experimental observations. A.M.A. Arch. Surg. 43:269, 1941.

McClean, D., Rogers, H. J., Williams, B. W. and Hale, C. W.: Early diagnosis of wound infection with special reference to gas-gangrene. Lancet 1:355, 1943.

McDermott, W. V., Jr., Adams, R. D. and Riddell, A. G.: Ammonia metabolism in man. Ann. Surg. 140:539, 1954.

McDermott, W. V., Jr., Bartlett, M. K. and Culver, P. J.: Acute pancreatitis after prolonged fast and subsequent surfeit. New England J. Med. 254:379, 1956.

McDermott, W. V., Jr., Wareham, J. and Riddell, A. G.: The treatment of "hepatic coma" with L-glutamic acid. New England J. Med. 253:1093, 1955.

McDermott, W. V., Jr., Wareham, J. and Riddell, A. G.: Bleeding esophageal varices—a study of the cause of the associated "hepatic coma." Ann. Surg. 144:318, 1956.

McDonald, R. E., Jensen, R. E., Urry, H. C., Bolin, V. S. and Price, P. B.: A study of the irradiation syndrome I. Water, electrolyte and nitrogen balances. Am. J. Roentgenol. 74:701, 1955.

McDonald, R. E., Jensen, R. E., Urry, H. C. and Price, P. B.: A study of the irradiation syndrome. II. Tissue water and tissue electrolytes. Am. J. Roentgenol. *74:*889, 1955.

McFarland, R. A.: Human Factors in Air Transportation. New York, McGraw-Hill Book Co., Inc., 1953.

McGovern, J. J., Jones, A. R. and Steinberg, A. G.: The hematocrit of capillary blood. New England J. Med. *253:*308, 1955.

McKeown, R. M., Harvey, S. C. and Lumsden, R. W.: Breaking strength of healing fractured fibulae in rats. Arch. Surg. *26:*430, 1933.

McLean, F. C. and Urist, M. R.: Bone; an Introduction to the Physiology of Skeletal Tissue. Chicago, University of Chicago Press, 1955.

McMurrey, J. D. *et al.:* Body composition: simultaneous determination of several aspects by the dilution principle. Metabolism *7:*651, 1958.

McSwain, B. J., Herrington, J. L., Edwards, W. H., Sawyers, J. L. and Cate, W. R.: Intrahepatic cholangiolitic hepatitis; its surgical significance. Am. Surg. *147:*805, 1958.

McSwiney, B. A. and Spurrell, W. R.: Influence of osmotic pressure upon the emptying time of the stomach. J. Physiol. *79:*437, 1933.

Mecray, P. M., Jr., Barden, R. P. and Ravdin, I. S.: Nutritional edema: its effect on gastric emptying time before and after gastric operations. Surgery *1:*53, 1957.

Medwid, A., Weissman, J., Randall, H. T., Bane, H. N., Vanamee, P. and Roberts, K. E.: Physiologic alterations resulting from carbohydrate, protein and fat meals in patients following gastrectomy: the relationship of these changes to the "dumping syndrome." Ann. Surg. *144:*953, 1956.

Mendelsohn, M. L. and Pearson, O. H.: Alterations in water and salt metabolism after bilateral adrenalectomy in man. J. Clin. Endocrinol. *15:*409, 1955.

Meneely, G. R. and Kaltreider, N. L.: A study of the volume of the blood in congestive heart failure. Relation to other measurements in fifteen patients. J. Clin. Invest. *22:*521, 1943.

Meroney, W. H.: The phosphorus to nonprotein nitrogen ratio in plasma as an index of muscle divitalization during oliguria. Surg., Gynec. & Obst. *100:*309, 1955.

Meroney, W. H.: Uremia-like symptoms not due to uremia in battle casualties. J.A.M.A. *158:*1513, 1955.

Meroney, W. H., Arney, G. K., Segar, W. E. and Balch, H. H.: The acute calcification of damaged muscle with particular reference to acute post-traumatic renal insufficiency. J. Lab. & Clin. Med. *48:*925, 1956.

Meroney, W. H., Arney, G. K., Segar, W. E. and Balch, H. H.: The acute calcification of traumatized muscle with particular reference to acute post-traumatic renal insufficiency. J. Clin. Invest. *36:*825, 1957.

Meroney, W. H. and Herndon, R. F., Jr.: The management of acute renal insufficiency. J.A.M.A. *155:*877, 1954.

Merrill, J. P., Murray, J. E., Harrison, J. H. and Guild, W. R.: Successful homotransplantation of the human kidney between identical twins. J.A.M.A. *160:*277, 1956.

Metcalf, W. and Rousselot, L. M.: The kinetics of expander transfer and distribution from the plasma disappearance curves. S. Forum *6:*32, 1956.

Metcoff, J., Darling, D. B., Scanlon, M. H. and Stare, F. J.: Nutritional status and infection response. I. Electrophoretic, circulating plasma protein, hematologic, hematopoietic, and immunologic responses to *Salmo-*

nella typhimurium (Bacillus aertrycke) infection in the protein-deficient rat. J. Lab. & Clin. Med. *33:*47, 1948.

Metcoff, J. *et al.:* Intracellular composition and homeostatic mechanisms in severe chronic infantile malnutrition. IV. Development and repair of the biochemical lesion. Pediatrics *20:*317, 1957.

Meyer, F. L., Hirshfeld, J. W. and Abbott, W. E.: Metabolic alterations following thermal burns. VII. Effect of force-feeding, methionine, and testosterone propionate on nitrogen balance in experimental burns. J. Clin. Invest. *26:*796, 1947.

Meyer, K. A., Schwartz, S. O. and Weissman, L. H.: Pernicious anemia following total gastrectomy. A.M.A. Arch. Surg. *42:*18, 1941.

Miles, B. E. and DeWardener, H. E.: Renal vasoconstriction produced by ether and cyclopropane anesthesia. J. Physiol. *118:*140, 1952.

Miles, B. E., DeWardener, H. E., Churchill-Davidson, H. C. and Wylie, W. D.: The effect on the renal circulation of pentamethonium bromide during anesthesia. Clin. Sc. *12:*73, 1952.

Miller, F. A. *et al.:* The evaluation of carbon dioxide toxicity in man and experimental animals. S. Forum *2:*35, 1952.

Miller, F. A., Brown, E. B., Jr., Buckley, J. J., VanBergen, F. H. and Varco, R. L.: Respiratory acidosis: its relationship to cardiac function and other physiologic mechanisms. Surgery *32:*171, 1952.

Miller, F. A., Hemingway, A., Brown, E. B., Jr., Nier, A. O., Knight, R. and Varco, R. L.: Evaluation of carbon dioxide accumulation in anesthetized patients utilizing a portable mass spectrometer to analyze exhaled gaseous concentrations. S. Forum *1:*602, 1951.

Miller, G. E.: Water and electrolyte metabolism in congestive heart failure. Circulation *4:*270, 1951.

Miller, G. E. and Townsend, C. E.: The in vitro inactivation of Pitressin by normal and cirrhotic human liver. J. Clin. Invest. *33:*549, 1954.

Miller, J. M. and Wiper, T. B.: Physiologic observations on patients with external pancreatic fistula. Ann. Surg. *120:*852, 1944.

Miller, R. A.: Observations on the gastric acidity during the first month of life. Arch. Dis. Child. *16:*22, 1941.

Miller, W. F.: Physical therapeutic measures in the treatment of broncho-pulmonary disorders. Am. J. Med. *24:*929, 1958.

Miller, W. F. *et al.:* A convenient method of evaluating pulmonary ventilatory function with single breath test. Anesthesiology *17:*480, 1956.

Miller, W. F., Johnson, R. L. and Wu, N.: Half-second expiratory capacity test: a convenient means of evaluating nature and extent of pulmonary ventilatory insufficiency. Dis. Chest. *30:*33, 1956.

Mitchell, A. D. and Volk, W. L.: Hyperchloremic acidosis of ureterosigmoidostomies. J. Urol. *69:*82, 1953.

Mithoefer, J. and Mithoefer, J. C.: Studies of the aged—surgical mortality. A.M.A. Arch. Surg. *69:*58, 1954.

Moffatt, W. L. and Francis, W. C.: Estrogen in bone repair. Surg., Gynec. & Obst. *101:*311, 1955.

Mokotoff, R., Ross, G. and Leiter, L.: The electrolyte content of skeletal muscle in congestive heart failure; a comparison of results with inulin and chloride as reference standards for extracellular water. J. Clin. Invest. *31:*291, 1952.

Mollison, P. L.: Observations on cases of starvation at Belsen. Brit. M. J. *1:*4, 1946.

Mollison, P. L., Veall, N. and Cutbush, M.: Red cell and

plasma volume in newborn infants. Arch. Dis. Child. *25:*242, 1950.

Moncrief, J. A.: Femoral catheters. Ann. Surg. *147:*166, 1958.

Moncrief, J. A.: Femoral catheters for intravenous therapy in the severely burned. (Personal communication.)

Moncrief, J. A., Coldwater, K. B. and Elman, R.: Postoperative loss of sugar in urine following intravenous infusion of fructose (levulose). A.M.A. Arch. Surg. *67:*57, 1953.

Moncrief, J. A., Weichselbaum, T. E. and Elman, R.: Changes in adrenocortical steroid concentration of peripheral plasma following surgery. S. Forum *4:*469, 1954.

Monsaingeon, A., Boureau, M. and Couturier, S.: Contribution à l'étude de l'histoire de l'operage. Ann. Chir. *11:*343, 1957.

Monsaingeon, A., Boureau, M. and Couturier, S.: Les variations de l'eosinophilie sanguine chez les brulés. J. Chir. *73:*173, 1957.

Moore, F. D.: Determination of total body water and solids with isotopes. Science *104:*157, 1946.

Moore, F. D.: Surgical nutrition. Nutrition Rev. *6:*161, 1948.

Moore, F. D.: Bodily changes in surgical convalescence. I. The normal sequence—observations and interpretations. Ann. Surg. *137:*289, 1953.

Moore, F. D.: Bodily changes in surgical convalescence. In Selye, H. and Heuser, G. (ed.): Fourth Annual Report on Stress. Montreal, Canada, Acta, Inc., 1954, p. 172.

Moore, F. D.: Bone sodium. Ann. Surg. *139:*253, 1954 (editorial).

Moore, F. D.: Isotope dilution; a theory, a method, a pathway to new horizons. (Lecture delivered on the occasion of receiving the Alvarenga prize, Nov, 4, 1953, College of Physicians of Philadelphia, Pa.) Tr. & Stud. Coll. Physicians Philadelphia *21:*106, 1954.

Moore, F. D.: Discussion on the endocrine response to trauma. Proc. Roy. Soc. Med. *48:*817, 1955.

Moore, F. D.: Hormones and stress—endocrine changes after anesthesia, surgery and unanesthetized trauma in man. Rec. Prog. Hormone Res. *13:*511, 1957.

Moore, F. D.: Common patterns of water and electrolyte change in injury, surgery and disease. New England J. Med. *258:*277, 325, 377, 427, 1958.

Moore, F. D.: Metabolism in trauma: the meaning of definitive surgery—the wound, the endocrine glands and metabolism. The Harvey Lectures 1956–1957. New York, Academic Press, Inc., 1958.

Moore, F. D.: Systemic mediators of surgical injury. Canad. M.A.J. *78:*85, 1958.

Moore, F. D. *et al.:* Body sodium and potassium. V. The relationship of alkalosis, potassium deficiency and surgical stress to acute hypokalemia in man. Presentation of experiments and review of the literature. Metabolism *4:*379, 1955.

Moore, F. D. and Ball, M. R.: The Metabolic Response to Surgery. (No. 132, American Lecture Series.) Springfield, Ill., Charles C Thomas, 1952.

Moore, F. D., Edelman, I. S., Olney, J. M., James, A. H., Brooks, L. and Wilson, G. M.: Body sodium and potassium. III. Interrelated trends in alimentary, renal and cardiovascular disease; lack of correlation between body stores and plasma concentration. Metabolism *3:*334, 1954.

Moore, F. D., Haley, H. B., Bering, E. A., Brooks, L. and

Edelman, I. S.: Further observations on total body water. II. Changes in body composition in disease. Surg., Gynec. & Obst. *95:*155, 1952.

Moore, F. D., Hammond, W. H. and Carter, R.: The effects of experimental venous hemorrhage in man. (Unpublished.)

Moore, F. D., Langohr, J. L., Ingebretsen, M. and Cope, O.: The role of the exudate losses in the protein and electrolyte imbalance of burned patients. Ann. Surg. *132:*1, 1950.

Moore, F. D., McMurrey, J. D., Parker, H. V., Davis, J. D. and Magnus, I. C.: Body Composition (monograph). In preparation.

Moore, F. D., McMurrey, J. D., Parker, H. V. and Magnus, I. C.: Body composition—total body water and electrolytes: intravascular and extravascular phase volumes. Metabolism *5:*447, 1956.

Moore, F. D., Peacock, W. C., Blakely, E. and Cope, O.: The anemia of thermal burns. Ann. Surg. *124:*811, 1946.

Moore, F. D., Steenburg, R. W., Ball, M. R., Wilson, G. M. and Myrden, J. A.: Studies in surgical endocrinology. I. The urinary excretion of 17-hydroxycorticoids and associated metabolic changes, in cases of soft tissue trauma of varying severity and in bone trauma. Ann. Surg. *141:*145, 1955.

Mörch, E. T., Avery, E. E. and Benson, D. W.: Hyperventilation in the treatment of crushing injuries of the chest. S. Forum *6:*270, 1956.

Morgan, H. C., Andrews, R. P. and Jurkiewicz, M. J.: The effect of thermal injury on insensible weight loss in the rat; preliminary report. S. Forum *6:*78, 1956.

Mosti, R.: L'azione dell'ormone testicolare sulla consolidazione della fratture. Ann. ital. di chir. *18:*281, 1939.

Moyer, C. A.: Recent advances in chemical supportive therapy of thermal injury. Texas J. Med. *45:*635, 1949.

Moyer, C. A.: Acute temporary changes in renal function associated with major surgical procedures. Surgery *27:*198, 1950.

Moyer, C. A.: An assessment of the therapy of burns: a clinical study. Ann. Surg. *137:*628, 1953.

Moyer, J. H., Morris, G. C., Jr. and Beazley, H. L.: Renal hemodynamic response to vasodepressor agents in treatment of shock. Circulation *12:*96, 1955.

Moyer, J. H., Skelton, J. M. and Mills, L. C.: Norepinephrine; effect in normal subjects—use in treatment of shock unresponsive to other measures. Am. J. Med. *15:*330, 1953.

Mudge, G. H. and Vislocky, K.: Electrolyte changes in human striated muscle in acidosis and alkalosis. J. Clin. Invest. *28:*482, 1949.

Muir, A.: Post-gastrectomy sindromes. Brit. J. Surg. *37:*165, 1949.

Mulholland, J. H., Co Tui, Wright, A. and Vinci, V. J.: Nitrogen metabolism, caloric intake and weight loss in postoperative convalescence. A study of eight patients undergoing partial gastrectomy for duodenal ulcers. Ann. Surg. *117:*512, 1943.

Muller, A. F., Riondel, A. M., Manning, E. L. and Mach, R. S.: Regulation of the secretion of aldosterone in man. J. Clin. Invest. *35:*725, 1956.

Munro, H. N.: The relationship of carbohydrate metabolism to protein metabolism. III. Further observations on time of carbohydrate ingestion as a factor in protein utilization by the adult rat. J. Nutrition *39:*375, 1949.

Munro, H. N.: Carbohydrate and fat as factors in protein utilization and metabolism. Physiol. Rev. *31:*449, 1951

Munro, H. N. and Chalmers, M. I.: Fracture metabolism

at different levels of protein intake. Brit. J. Exper. Path. *26:*396, 1945.

Murphy, R. J. F.: The effect of "rice diet" on plasma volume and extracellular fluid space in hypertensive subjects. J. Clin. Invest. *29:*912, 1950.

Myers, J. D. and Taylor, W. J.: An estimate of portal venous pressure by occlusive catheterization of an hepatic venule. J. Clin. Invest. *30:*662, 1951 (abstr.).

Myers, W. K. and Keefer, C. S.: Relation of plasma proteins to ascites and edema in cirrhosis of the liver. A.M.A. Arch. Int. Med. *55:*349, 1935.

Nachlas, M. M., O'Neil, J. E. and Campbell, A. J. A.: The life history of patients with cirrhosis of the liver and bleeding esophageal varices. Ann. Surg. *141:*10, 1955.

Nadell, J., Sweet, N. J. and Edelmann, I. S.: Gastrointestinal water and electrolytes. II. The equilibration of radiopotassium in gastrointestinal contents and the proportion of exchangeable potassium (K_e) in the gastrointestinal tract. J. Clin. Invest. *35:*512, 1956.

Najarian, J. S. and Harper, H. A.: A clinical study of the effect of arginine on blood ammonia. Am. J. Med. *21:*832, 1956.

Nakasone, N., Watkins, E., Jr., Janeway, C. A. and Gross, R. E.: Experimental studies of circulatory derangement following the massive transfusion of citrated blood. J. Lab. & Clin. Med. *43:*184, 1954.

Nanson, E. M.: Some respiratory responses to operative trauma. Ann. Royal Coll. Surgeons *7:*403, 1950.

Nardi, G. L.: "Essential" and "nonessential" amino acids in the urine of severely burned patients. J. Clin. Invest. *33:*847, 1954.

Natelson, S. and Alexander, M. O.: Marked hypernatremia and hyperchloremia with damage to the central nervous system. A.M.A. Arch. Int. Med. *96:*172, 1955.

Nealon, T. F., Jr., Haupt, G. J., Chase, H. F., Price, J. E. and Gibbon, J. H., Jr.: Inefficient carbon dioxide absorption requiring increased pulmonary ventilation during operations. J. Thoracic Surg. *32:*464, 1956.

Nelson, D H. and Samuels, L. T.: A method for the determination of 17-hydroxycorticosteroids in blood, 17-hydroxycorticosterone in the peripheral circulation. J. Clin. Endocrinol. *12:*519, 1952.

Nelson, D. H., Samuels, L. T., Willardson, D. G. and Tyler, F. H.: The levels of 17-hydroxycorticosteroids in peripheral blood of human subjects. J. Clin. Endocrinol. *11:*1021, 1951

Nelson, R. M. and Noyes, H. E.: Permeability of the intestine to bacterial toxins in hemorrhagic shock. S. Forum *3:*474, 1953.

Nelson, R. M. and Seligson, D.: Blood ammonia in normal and shock states. S. Forum *4:*511, 1954.

Nelson, T. G. and Bowers, W. F.: Fat embolism. A.M.A. Arch. Surg. *72:*649, 1956.

Nelson, W., Mayerson, H. S., Clark, J. H. and Lyons, C.: Studies of blood volume in the tetralogy of Fallot and in other types of congenital heart disease. J. Clin. Invest. *26:*860, 1947.

Nelson, W. P., III and Welt, L. G.: The effects of Pitressin on the metabolism and excretion of water and electrolytes in normal subjects and patients with cirrhosis and ascites. J. Clin. Invest. *31:*392, 1952.

Newman, P. H.: The clinical diagnosis of fat embolism. J. Bone & Joint Surg. *30-B:*290, 1948.

Nicholas, J. A., Burstein, C. L., Umberger, C. J. and Wilson, P. D.: Adrenocortical insufficiency during surgery. A.M.A. Arch. Surg. *71:*737, 1956.

Nicholas, J. A. and Wilson, P. D.: Adrenocortical response in operative procedures upon the bones and joints. J. Bone & Joint Surg. *35-A:*559, 1953.

Nicholas, J. A., Wilson, P. D. and Umberger, C. J.: Observations on adrenocortical function in patients undergoing operations upon the bones and joints. Surg., Gynec. & Obst. *99:*1, 1954.

Nicholas, J. A., Wilson, P. D. and Umberger, C. J.: A comparison of urinary neutral 17-ketosteroid excretion with other fractions in operations upon the bones and joints. Surg., Gynec. & Obst. *100:*387, 1955.

Nichols, G., Jr., Nichols, N., Weil, W. B. and Wallace, W M.: The direct measurement of the extracellular phase of tissues. J. Clin. Invest. *32:*1299, 1953.

Nichols, G., Jr. and Nichols, N.: The role of bone in sodium metabolism. Metabolism *5:*438, 1956.

Nickel, J. F., Smythe, C. M., Papper, E. M. and Bradley, S. E.: Study of the mode of action of adrenal medullary hormones on sodium, potassium and water excretion in man. J. Clin. Invest. *33:*1687, 1954.

Nickerson, M.: Factors of vasoconstriction and vasodilatation in shock. J. Michigan M. Soc. *54:*45, 1955.

Noble, R. P. and Gregersen, M. I.: Blood volume in clinical shock. II. The extent and cause of blood volume reduction in traumatic, hemorrhagic and burn shock. J. Clin. Invest. *25:*172, 1946.

Noble, T. B.: Paralytic ileus from peritonitis after appendicitis. Am. J. Surg. *84:*419, 1952.

Nunn, J. F.: The anesthetist and the emphysematous patient. Brit. J. Anesthesia *30:*134, 1958.

Ober, W. E., Reid, D. E., Romney, S. L. and Merrill, J. P.: Renal lesions and acute renal failure in pregnancy. Am. J. Med. *21:*781, 1956.

Oleson, K. H., Parker, H. V. and Moore, F. D.: Alterations in body composition with preparation of cardiac patients for surgery. S. Forum *8:*39, 1958.

Oliver, J., MacDowell, M. and Tracy, A.: The pathogenesis of acute renal failure associated with traumatic and toxic injury: renal ischemia, nephrotoxic damage and the ischemuric episode. J. Clin. Invest. *30:*1307, 1951.

Olsen, A.: ACTH in the treatment of severe burns. Acta Endocrinol. *9:*1, 1952.

Opdyke, D. F. and Foreman, R. C.: Study of coronary flow under conditions of hemorrhagic hypotension and shock. Am. J. Physiol. *148:*726, 1947.

Otis, A. B.: The work of breathing. Physiol. Rev. *34:*449, 1954.

Owen, K., Desautels, R. and Walter, C. W.: Experimental renal tubular necrosis—the effect of pitressin. S. Forum *4:*459, 1953.

Owen, R. A. C. and Murphy, A. F.: Surgery in old age Brit. M. J. *2:*186, 1952.

Owren, P. A.: The pathogenesis and treatment of iron deficiency anemia after partial gastrectomy. Acta chir. scandinav. *104:*207, 1952.

Pace, H. and Rathbun, F. N.: Studies on body composition. III. The body water and chemically combined nitrogen content in relation to fat content. J. Biol. Chem. *158:*685, 1945.

Palmer, J. D.: Effect of autonomic blocking drugs on experimental pancreatitis. S. Forum *2:*560, 1952.

Papper, E. M.: Renal function during general anesthesia and operation. J.A.M.A. *152:*1686, 1953.

Papper, E. M. and Ngai, S. H.: Kidney function during anesthesia. Ann. Rev. Med. *7:*213, 1956.

Paquin, A. J.: The rate of body weight loss following surgical stress of uniform intensity. Ann. Surg. *141:*383, 1955.

Parsons, F. M., Powell, F. J. N. and Pyrah, L. N.: Chemical imbalance following ureterocolic anastomosis. Lancet *2:*599, 1952.

Parsons, W. H. and Purks, W. K.: The surgical risk in elderly patients, South. Surgeon *11:*525, 1942.

Parsons, W. H. and Purks, W. K.: The elderly patient as a surgical risk; analysis of 322 operations performed on 244 patients 60 years of age and over. A.M.A. Arch. Surg. *58:*888, 1949.

Parsons, W. H., Whitaker, H. T. and Hinton, J. K.: Major surgery in patients 70 years of age and over—an analysis of 146 operations on 135 patients. Ann. Surg. *143:*845, 1956.

Parsons, W. H. and Williams, W. T.: Surgical problems in the aged Negro. South. Surgeon *16:*1163, 1950.

Paschkis, K. E., Cantarow, A., Eberhard, T. and Boyle, D.: Thyroid function in the alarm reaction. Proc. Soc. Exper. Biol. & Med. *73:*116, 1950.

Patterson, W. B. (ed.): Wound healing and tissue repair. Development Biology Series (1956). Chicago, University of Chicago Press, 1959.

Patton, T. B., Lombardo, C. R. and Lyons, C.: Experimental observations on meat intoxication, ammonia accumulation and hepatic coma. Ann. Surg. *143:*588, 1956.

Pawan, G. L. S.: Total body water in obesity. Biochem. J. *63:*12, 1956 (proc.).

Pearlman, D. M.: The effect of glutamate administration on blood ammonia level and its correlation with clinical status in patients with hepatic coma. S. Forum *6:*364, 1956.

Pearse, H. E. and Kingsley, H. D.: Thermal burns from the atomic bomb. Surg., Gynec. & Obst. *98:*385, 1954.

Pearse, H. E. and Morton, J. J.: The stimulation of bone growth by venous stasis. J. Bone & Joint Surg. *12:*97, 1930.

Peden, J. C., Jr. and Maxwell, M.: The anabolic effect of Nilevar on nitrogen metabolism following extensive abdominal surgery. In Proceedings of the Conference on the Clinical Use of Anabolic Agents, April, 1956 (G. D. Searle & Co.).

Peltier, L. F.: Fat embolism following intramedullary nailing: report of a fatality. Surgery *32:*719, 1952.

Peltier, L. F.: Fat embolism: the detection of fat emboli in the circulating blood. Surgery *36:*198, 1954.

Peltier, L. F.: The demonstration of fat emboli in tissue sections using Phosphin 3R, a water-soluble fluorochrome. J. Lab. & Clin. Med. *43:*321, 1954.

Peltier, L. F.: Fat embolism: the failure of lipemia to potentiate the degree of fat embolism accompanying fractures of the femur in rabbits. Surgery *38:*720, 1955.

Peltier, L. F.: The mechanics of parenchymatous embolism. Surg., Gynec. & Obst. *100:*612, 1955.

Peltier, L. F.: Fat embolism. I. The amount of fat in human long bones. Surgery *40:*657, 1956.

Peltier, L. F.: Fat embolism. III. The toxic properties of neutral fat and free fatty acids. Surgery *40:*665, 1956.

Peltier, L. F.: Fat embolism: the prophylactic value of a tourniquet. J. Bone & Joint Surg. *38-A:*835, 1956.

Peltier, L. F., Wheeler, D. H., Boyd, H. M. and Scott, J. R.: Fat embolism: II. The chemical composition of fat obtained from human long bones and subcutaneous tissue. Surgery *40:*661, 1956.

Perera, G. A.: The effect of significant weight change on the predicted plasma volume. J. Clin. Invest. *25:*401, 1946.

Perez-Tamayo, R. and Ihnen, M.: The effect of methionine in experimental wound healing—a morphologic study. Am. J. Path. *29:*233, 1953.

Perkins, J. G., Petersen, A. B. and Riley, J. A.: Renal and cardiac lesions in potassium deficiency due to chronic diarrhea. Am. J. Med. *8:*115, 1950.

Perman, E.: The so-called dumping syndrome after gastrectomy. Acta med. scandinav. (Suppl. 196): 361, 1947.

Perry, F. A., Deddish, M. R., Randall, H. T. and Roberts, K. E.: Evaluation of plasma electrolytes and renal function in patients with sigmoid urinary pouches. S. Forum *6:*599, 1956.

Perry, W. F. and Gemmell, J. P.: The effect of surgical operations on the excretion of iodine, corticosteroids and uric acid. Canad. J. Research *27:*320, 1949.

Perryman, R. G. and Hoerr, S. O.: Observations on postoperative pancreatitis and postoperative elevation of the serum amylase. Am. J. Surg. *88:*417, 1954.

Persky, L., Benson, J. W., Levey, S. and Abbott, W. E.: Metabolic alterations in surgical patients. VII. The relief of lower urinary tract obstruction. S. Forum *6:*608, 1956.

Persky, L., Benson, J. W., Levey, S. and Abbott, W. E.: Metabolic alterations in surgical patients. X. The benign course of the average patient with acute urinary retention. Surgery *42:*290, 1957.

Persky, L., Krieger, H., Levey, S. and Abbott, W. E.: Metabolic alterations in surgical patients. V. Cause and management of hyperchloremic acidosis following ureterosigmoidostomy. S. Forum *6:*496, 1956.

Peters, J. P.: Symposium on physiological aspects of convalescence. Fed. Proc. *3:*197, 1944.

Peters, J. P.: Effect of injury and disease on nitrogen metabolism. Am. J. Med. *5:*100, 1948.

Peters, J. P.: Diabetic acidosis. Metabolism *1:*223, 1952.

Petersdorf, R. G. and Welt, L. G.: The effect of an infusion of hyperoncotic albumin on the excretion of water and solutes. J. Clin. Invest. *32:*283, 1953.

Peterson, R. E. and Wyngaarden, J. B.: The miscible pool and turnover rate of hydrocortisone in man. J. Clin. Invest. *34:*956, 1955.

Pettet, J. D., Baggenstoss, A. H., Dearing, W. H. and Judd, E. S., Jr.: Postoperative pseudomembranous enterocolitis. Surg., Gynec. & Obst. *98:*546, 1954.

Phear, E. A., Ruebner, B., Sherlock, S. and Summerskill, W. H. J.: Methionine toxicity in liver disease and its prevention by chlortetracycline. Clin. Sc. *15:*93, 1956.

Phillips, G. B., Schwartz, R., Gabuzda, G. J., Jr. and Davidson, C. S.: The syndrome of impending hepatic coma in patients with cirrhosis of the liver given certain nitrogenous substances. New England J. Med. *247:*239, 1952.

Phillips, R. A., Dole, V. P., Hamilton, P. B., Emerson, K., Jr., Archibald, R. M. and VanSlyke, D. D.

Effects of acute hemorrhagic and traumatic shock on renal function of dogs. Am. J. Physiol. *145:*314, 1946.

Pickford, M. and Vogt, M.: The effect of adrenalin on secretion of cortical hormone in the hypophysectomized dog. J. Physiol. *112:*133, 1951.

Pierce, V. K., Robbins, G. F. and Brunschwig, A.: Ultra-rapid blood transfusion; clinical and experimental observations. Surg., Gynec. & Obst. *89:*442, 1949.

Pillemer, L., Blum, L., Lepow, I. H., Ross, O. A., Todd, E. W. and Wardlaw, A. C.: The properdin system and immunity. I. Demonstration and isolation of a new serum protein, properdin, and its role in immune phenomena. Science *120:*279, 1954.

Pincus, G., Romanoff, L. P. and Carlo, J.: Excretion of urinary steroids by men and women of various ages. J. Gerontol. *9:*113, 1954.

Pirani, C. L., Stepto, R. C. and Sutherland, K.: Desoxy-corticosterone acetate and wound healing. Medical Nutrition Laboratory Report No. 75, 1951.

Plough, I. C., Iber, F. L., Shipman, M. E. and Chalmers, T. C.: The effects of supplementary calories on nitrogen storage at high intakes of protein in patients with chronic liver disease. Am. J. Clin. Nutrition *4:*224, 1956.

Plzak, L. F., Fried, W., Jacobson, L. O. and Bethard, W. F.: Demonstration of stimulation of erythropoiesis by plasma from anemic rats using Fe⁵⁹. J. Lab. & Clin. Med. *46:*671, 1955.

Pohle, E. A., Sevringhaus, E. L. and Davy, L.: Studies of systemic effect of Roentgen rays. I. Blood chemical changes in dogs following exposure to filtered Roentgen rays of short wave length. Am. J. Roentgenol. *23:*291, 1930.

Pollock, A. V.: Antitryptic substances in experimental acute pancreatitis. Surg., Gynec. & Obst. *102:*483, 1956.

Pollock, A. V. and Bertrand, C. A.: Electrocardiographic changes in acute pancreatitis. Surgery *40:*951, 1956.

Pollock, G. A.: The effect of theelin on fracture repair. Proc. Staff Meet., Mayo Clin. *15:*209, 1940.

Poppell, J. W., Cuajunco, F., Jr., Horsley, J. S., III, Randall, H. T. and Roberts, K. E.: Renal arteriovenous ammonium difference and total renal ammonium production in normal, acidotic and alkalotic dogs. Clin. Res. Proc. *4:*137, 1956.

Popper, H. L. and Necheles, H.: Pancreatic injuries; experimental studies. Surg., Gynec. & Obst. *93:*621, 1951.

Porter, C. C. and Silber, R. H.: A quantitative color reaction for cortisone and related 17, 21-dihydroxy, 20-ketosteroids. J. Biol. Chem. *185:*201, 1950.

Porter, H. W. and Claman, Z. B.: Preliminary report on the small stoma. Ann. Surg. *129:*417, 1949.

Post, J. and Patek, A. J., Jr.: Serum proteins in cirrhosis of the liver. Relation to prognosis and to formation of ascites. A.M.A. Arch. Int. Med. *62:*67, 1942.

Post, J. and Patek, A. J., Jr.: Serum proteins in cirrhosis of the liver. II. Nitrogen balance studies on five patients. A.M.A. Arch. Int. Med. *69:*83, 1942.

Poth, E. J.: Intestinal antisepsis in surgery. J.A.M.A. *153:*1516, 1953.

Poth, E. J. and Wolma, F. J.: The treatment of recurring acute pancreatitis by decompression of the biliary tract. Am. Surg. *20:*270, 1954.

Powers, S. R., Jr. and Brown, H. H.: Studies on serum proteolytic activity in patients with spontaneous fibrinolysis. S. Forum *6:*100, 1956.

Prendergast, J. J., Fenichel, R. L. and Daly, B. M.-Albumin and globulin changes in burns as demonstrated by electrophoresis. A.M.A. Arch. Surg. *64:*733: 1952.

Prentice, T. C., Berlin, N. I., Hyde, G. M., Parsons, R. J., Lawrence, J. H. and Port, S.: Total red cell volume, plasma volume, and sodium space in congestive heart failure. J. Clin. Invest. *30:*1471, 1951.

Prentice, T. C., Olney, J. M., Jr., Artz, C. P. and Howard, J. M.: Studies of blood volume and transfusion therapy in the Korean battle casualty. Surg., Gynec. & Obst. *99:*542, 1954.

Pringle, H., Maunsell, R. C. B. and Pringle, S.: Clinical effects of ether anaesthesia on renal activity. Brit. Med. J. *2:*542, 1905.

Prohaska, J. V., Govostis, M. C. and Taubenhaus, M.: Postoperative pseudomembranous enterocolitis. J.A.M.A. *154:*320, 1954.

Prudden, J. F.: The stimulation of wound healing with heterologous cartilage. Transplantation Bull. *5:*14, 1958.

Prudden, J. F., Nishihara, G. and Baker, L.: The acceleration of wound healing with cartilage. Surg., Gynec. & Obst. *105:*283, 1957.

Prudden, J. F., Pearson, E. and Soroff, H. S.: The influence of growth hormone on the nitrogen balance of the severely burned. S. Forum *6:*76, 1956.

Prudden, J. F., Pearson, E. and Soroff, H. S.: Studies on growth hormone. II. The effect on the nitrogen metabolism of severely burned patients. Surg., Gynec. & Obst. *102:*695, 1956.

Pulaski, E. J.: Medical progress. War wounds. New England J. Med. *249:*890, 1953.

Purks, W. K.: The cause of death of patients with organic heart disease subjected to surgical operation. Ann. Int. Med. *7:*885, 1934.

Pyrah, L. N.: Uretero-colic anastomosis. Ann. Roy. Coll. Surgeons, England *14:*169, 1954.

Pyrah, L. N., Care, A. D., Reed, G. W. and Parsons, F. M.: The migration of sodium, chloride and potassium ions across the mucous membrane of the ileum. Brit. J. Surg. *42:*357, 1955.

Quinby, W. C., Jr. and Cope, O.: Blood viscosity and the whole blood therapy of burns. Surgery *32:*316, 1952.

Raab, W., Humphreys, R. J. and Lepeschkin, E.: Potentiation of pressor effects of nor-epinephrine and epinephrine in man by desoxycorticosterone acetate. J. Clin. Invest. *29:*1397, 1950.

Raab, W., Humphreys, R. J., Makous, N., DeGrandpré, R. and Gigee, W.: Pressor effects of epinephrine, nor-epinephrine and desoxycorticosterone acetate (DCA) weakened by sodium withdrawal. Circulation *6:*373, 1952.

Raab, W., Lepeschkin, E., Starcheska, Y. K. and Gigee, W.: Cardiotoxic effects of hypercatecholemia in renal insufficiency. Circulation Res. *14:*614, 1956.

Radakovitch, M., Dutton, A. M. and Schilling, J. A.: Effect of total body irradiation on wound closure. Ann. Surg. *139:*186, 1954.

Radford, E. P.: Clinical use of nomogram to estimate

proper ventilation during artificial respiration. New England J. Med. *251*:877, 1954.

Rains, A. J. H.: Experience in the measurement of blood and fluid loss at operation. Brit. J. Surg. *43*:191, 1955.

Raker, J. W. and Rovit, R. L.: The acute red blood cell destruction following severe thermal trauma in dogs; based on use of radioactive chromate-tagged red blood cells. Surg., Gynec. & Obst. *98*:169, 1954.

Ralli, E. P., Robson, J. S., Clarke, D. H. and Hoagland, C. L.: Factors influencing ascites in patients with cirrhosis of the liver. J. Clin. Invest. *24*:316, 1945.

Ralston, E. L.: Fracture of the femoral neck following irradiation of the pelvis. Surg., Gynec. & Obst. *103*:62, 1956.

Ramey, E. R., Goldstein, M. S. and Levine, R.: Action of nor-epinephrine and adrenal cortical steroids on blood pressure and work performance of adrenalecto-mized dogs. Am. J. Physiol. *165*:450, 1951.

Randall, H. T., Habif, D. V., Lockwood, J. S. and Werner, S. C.: Potassium deficiency in surgical patients. Surgery *26*:341, 1949.

Randall, R. E. and Papper, S.: Mechanism of postopera-tive limitation in sodium excretion: the role of extra-cellular fluid volume and of adrenal cortical activity. J. Clin. Invest. *37*:1628, 1958.

Rapoport, S.: Hyperosmolarity and hyperelectrolytemia in pathologic conditions of childhood. Am. J. Dis. Child. *74*:682, 1947.

Rappaport, H., Raum, M. and Horrell, J. B.: Bone marrow embolism. Am. J. Path. *27*:407, 1951.

Raventos, A.: Mortality due to x-ray in splenectomized mice. Am. J. Physiol. *177*:261, 1954.

Raventos, A.: Wound healing and mortality after total body exposure to ionizing radiation. Proc. Soc. Exper. Biol. & Med. *87*:165, 1954.

Rawson, R.: The binding of T-1824 and structurally related diazo dyes by the plasma proteins. Am. J. Physiol. *138*:708, 1943.

Reddy, W. J.: Modification of the Reddy-Jenkins-Thorn method for the estimation of 17-hydroxycorticoids in urine. Metabolism *3*:489, 1954.

Reddy, W. J., Haydar, N. A., Laidlaw, J. C., Renold, A. E. and Thorn, G. W.: Determination of total 17-hydroxycorticoids in plasma. J. Clin. Endocrinol. *16*:380, 1956.

Reddy, W. J., Jenkins, D. and Thorn, G. W.: Estimation of 17-hydroxycorticoids in urine. Metabolism *1*:511, 1952.

Reed, G. W. and Care, A. D.: Studies on the migration of Na^{24}, Cl^{38}, K^{42}, across bladder and intestinal mucosa. Proc. 2nd Radioisotope Conf., Oxford *1*:147, 1954.

Reeve, E. B.: Methods of estimating plasma and total red cell volume. Nutr. Abstr. & Rev. *17*:811, 1948.

Regan, T. J., Talmers, F. N. and Hellems, H. K.: Myo-cardial transfer of sodium and potassium: effect of acetyl strophanthidin in normal dogs. J. Clin. Invest. *35*:1220, 1956.

Reid, J. D., Brooks, J. W., Ham, W. T. and Evans, E. I.: The influence of x-radiation on mortality following thermal flash burns: the site of tissue injury as a factor determining the type of invading bacteria. Ann. Surg. *142*:844, 1955.

Reid, L. C. and Brace, D. E.: Irritation of respiratory tract and its reflex effect upon heart. Surg., Gynec. & Obst. *70*:157, 1940.

Reid, L. C., Stephenson, H. E., Jr. and Hinton, J. W.: Cardiac arrest. A.M.A. Arch. Surg. *64*:409, 1952.

Reifenstein, E. C., Jr.: The relationship of steroid hor-mones to the development and the management of osteo-porosis in aging people. Clin. Orthop. *10*:206, 1957.

Reifenstein, E. C., Jr. and Albright, F.: The metabolic effects of steroid hormones in osteoporosis. J. Clin. Invest. *26*:24, 1947.

Reilly, W. A., French, R. M., Lau, F. Y. K., Scott, K. G. and White, W. E.: Whole blood volume determined by radiochromium-tagged red cells. Circulation *9*:571, 1954.

Reiner, L., Schlesinger, M. J. and Miller, G. M.: Pseudo-membranous colitis following aureomycin and chlor-amphenicol. A.M.A. Arch. Path. *54*:39, 1952.

Reiss, E., Pearson, E. and Artz, C. P.: The metabolic response to burns. J. Clin. Invest. *35*:62, 1956.

Reiss, E., Pulaski, E. J., Amspacher, W. H. and Contreras, A. A.: Penicillin sensitivity of staphylococci New England J. Med. *246*:611, 1952.

Reiss, E., Stirman, J. A., Artz, C. P., Davis, J. H. and Amspacher, W. H.: Fluid and electrolyte balance in burns. J.A.M.A. *152*:1309, 1953.

Rekers, P. E., Pack, G. T. and Rhoads, C. P.: Metabolic studies in patients with cancer of the gastrointestinal tract, disorders in alimentary digestion and absorption in patients who have undergone total gastrectomy for carcinoma of the stomach. Surgery *14*:197, 1943.

Relman, A. S., Etsten, B. and Schwartz, W. B.: The regulation of renal bicarbonate reabsorption by plasma carbon dioxide tension. J. Clin. Invest. *32*:972, 1953.

Relman, A. S. and Schwartz, W. B.: The nephropathy of potassium-depletion; a clinico-pathologic entity. J. Clin. Invest. *34*:959, 1955 (abstr.).

Relman, A. S. and Schwartz, W. B.: The nephropathy of potassium depletion; a clinical and pathological entity. New England J. Med. *255*:195, 1956.

Remington, J. W., Hamilton, W. F., Boyd, G. H., Hamil-ton, W. F., Jr. and Caddell, H. M.: Role of vasocon-striction in the response of the dog to hemorrhage. Am. J. Physiol. *161*:117, 1950.

Renner, W. F.: Postoperative acute pancreatitis and lower nephron syndrome. J.A.M.A. *147*:1654, 1951.

Renold, A. E., Jenkins, D., Forsham, P. H. and Thorn, G. W.: The use of intravenous ACTH: a study in quantitative adrenocortical stimulation. J. Clin. Endo-crinol. *12*:763, 1952.

Renold, A. E., Quigley, T. B., Kennard, H. E. and Thorn, G. W.: Reaction of the adrenal cortex to physical and emotional stress in college oarsmen. New England J. Med. *244*:754, 1951.

Reynolds, L. E., Brown, C. R. and Price, P. B.: Effects of local chilling in the treatment of burns. S. Forum *6*:85, 1956.

Rhinelander, F. W., Langohr, J. L. and Cope, O.: Ex-plorations into the physiologic basis for the therapeutic use of restrictive bandages in thermal trauma—an experimental study. A.M.A. Arch. Surg. *59*:1056, 1949.

Rice, C. O., Orr, B. and Enquist, I.: Parenteral nutrition in the surgical patient as provided from glucose, amino acids and alcohol. Ann. Surg. *131*:289, 1950.

Rice, C. O., Strickler, J. H. and Azeris, H.: The relation-ship of an elevated blood sugar to an electrolyte imbalance. A.M.A. Arch. Surg. *72*:508, 1956.

Rich, A. R. and Duff, G. L.: Experimental and patho-logical studies on the pathogenesis of acute hemorrhagic pancreatitis. Bull. Johns Hopkins Hosp. *58*:212, 1936.

Richards, D. W.: The circulation in traumatic shock in

man. The Harvey Lectures 1943–1944, Lancaster, Pa., Science Press Printing Co., 1944.

Richards, R. C. and Hansen, F. L.: A comparison of intra-arterial and intravenous transfusion in the treatment of hemorrhagic shock. S. Forum *4:*478, 1954.

Richardson, W. R.: Metabolic studies on infants with enterostomies. S. Forum *7:*75, 1957.

Ricketts, W. E., Eichelberger, L. and Kirsner, J. B.: Observations on the alterations in electrolytes and fluid balance in patients with cirrhosis of the liver with and without ascites. J. Clin. Invest. *30:*1157, 1951.

Rickham, D. P.: The Metabolic Response to Neonatal Surgery. Cambridge, Mass., Harvard University Press, 1957.

Riegel, C., Koop, C. E., Drew, J., Stevens, L. W. and Rhoads, J. E.: The nutritional requirements for nitrogen balance in surgical patients during the early postoperative period. J. Clin. Invest. *26:*18, 1947.

Rienhoff, W. F., Jr.: Ligation of the hepatic and splenic arteries in the treatment of portal hypertension with a report of 6 cases: preliminary report. Bull. Johns Hopkins Hosp. *88:*368, 1951.

Rini, J. M.: Traumatic pancreatitis. Am. Surgeon *18:*596, 1952.

Rivera, J. A., Artz, C. P. and Contreras, A.: The role of antibiotics in thermal injury. I. Evaluation of results of antibiotic sensitivity tests during a five year period. In Welch, H. and Marti-Ibañez, F. (eds.): Antibiotics Annual. New York, Medical Encyclopedia, Inc., 1956, p. 810.

Robbins, M. H., Klein, E. C. and Geller, L.: Observations on the eosinophil count. New York J. Med. *52:*709, 1952.

Roberts, E.: Inhibition of bacterial and brain glutamic acid decarboxylases. Fed. Proc. *11:*275, 1952.

Roberts, K. E. and Magida, M. G.: Electrocardiographic alterations produced by a decrease in plasma pH, bicarbonate and sodium as compared with those produced by an increase in potassium. Circulation Res. *1:*206, 1953.

Roberts, K. E., Magida, M. G. and Pitts, R. F.: Relationship between potassium and bicarbonate in blood and urine. Am. J. Physiol. *172:*47, 1953.

Roberts, K. E., Randall, H. T., Bane, H. N., Medwid, A. and Schwartz, M. K.: Studies of the physiology of the dumping syndrome. New York J. Med. *55:*2897, 1955.

Roberts, K. E., Randall, H. T. and Farr, H. W.: Acute alterations in blood volume, plasma electrolytes and electrocardiogram produced by oral administration of hypertonic solutions to gastrectomized patients. S. Forum *4:*301, 1953.

Roberts, K. E., Randall, H. T. and Farr, H. W.: Acute alterations in blood volume, plasma electrolytes, and the electrocardiogram produced by oral administration of hypertonic solutions to gastrectomized patients. J. Clin. Invest. *32:*597, 1953 (abstr.).

Roberts, K. E., Randall, H. T., Farr, H. W., Kidwell, A. P., McNeer, G. P. and Pack, G. T.: Cardiovascular and blood volume alterations resulting from intrajejunal administration of hypertonic solutions to gastrectomized patients: the relationship of these changes to the dumping syndrome. Ann. Surg. *140:*631, 1954.

Roberts, K. E., Randall, H. T., Sanders, H. L. and Hood, M.: Effects of potassium on renal tubular reabsorption of bicarbonate. J. Clin. Invest. *34:*666, 1955.

Roberts, K. E., Randall, H. T., Vanamee, P. and Popell,

J. W.: Renal mechanisms involved in bicarbonate absorption. Metabolism *5:*404, 1956.

Roberts, S.: Influence of adrenal cortex on serum and liver protein regeneration in the partially hepatectomized rat. Fed. Proc. *10:*237, 1951.

Roberts, S.: The influence of the adrenal cortex on the mobilization of tissue protein. J. Biol. Chem. *200:*77, 1953.

Robertson, H. R., Colbeck, J. C. and Sutherland, W. H.: Some aspects of hospital infection. Am. J. Surg. *92:*233, 1956.

Robertson, R. L., Trincher, I. H. and Dennis, E. W.: Intra-arterial transfusion—experimental and clinical considerations. Surg., Gynec. & Obst. *87:*695, 1948.

Robin, E. D. *et al.:* A physiologic approach to the diagnosis of acute pulmonary embolism. New England J. Med. *260:*586, 1959.

Robins, R. E., Robertson, H. R. and McIntosh, H. W.: Fecal fat and nitrogen studies in postgastrectomy patients. Surgery *41:*248, 1957.

Robinson, K. W., Hawker, R. W. and Robertson, P. A.: Antidiuretic hormone (ADH) in the human female. J. Clin. Endocrinol. *17:*320, 1957.

Robinson, K. W. and Macfarlane, W. V.: The influence of environmental temperature on the level of plasma antidiuretic substances in the rat. Australian J. Biol. Sc. *9:*130, 1956.

Robson, J. S., Dudley, H. A., Horn, D. B. and Stewart, C. P.: The metabolic response to adrenalectomy and hypophysectomy. Clinica chimica acta *1:*533, 1956.

Robson, J. S., Horn, D. B., Dudley, H. A. and Stewart, C. P.: Metabolic response to adrenalectomy. Lancet *2:*325, 1955.

Roche, M., Hills, A. G. and Tho n, G. W.: The level of circulating eosinophils as an indicator of adrenal cortical adequacy following major surgery. J. Clin. Endocrinol. *9:*662, 1949.

Roche, M., Thorn, G. W. and Hills, A. G.: The levels of circulating eosinophils and their response to ACTH in surgery—their use as an index of adrenocortical function. New England J. Med. *242:*307, 1950.

Rogers, H. M., Keating, F. R., Jr., Morlock, C. G. and Barker, N. W.: Primary hypertrophy and hyperplasia of parathyroid glands associated with duodenal ulcer; report of additional case, with special reference to metabolic gastrointestinal and vascular manifestations. A.M.A. Arch. Int. Med. *79:*307, 1947.

Ronzoni, E.: Ether anesthesia. I. The determination of ethyl ether in air and in blood, and its distribution ratio between blood and air. J. Biol. Chem. *57:*741, 1923.

Ronzoni, E.: Ether anesthesia. II. Anesthetic concentration of ether for dogs. J. Biol. Chem. *57:*761, 1923.

Ronzoni, E., Loechig, J. E. and Eaton, E. P.: Ether anesthesia. III. Role of lactic acid in the acidosis of ether anesthesia. J. Biol. Chem. *61:*465, 1924.

Root, W. S., McAllister, F. F., Oster, R. H. and Solarz, S. D.: Effect of ether anesthesia upon certain blood electrolytes. Am. J. Physiol. *131:*449, 1940.

Rosenberg, M. L.: Physiology of hyperchloremic acidosis following ureterosigmoidostomy: a study of urinary reabsorption with radioactive isotopes. J. Urol. *70:*569, 1953.

Rosenburg, S. A. and Akgun, S.: Serum amylase test in differential diagnosis of freely perforated ulcer and acute pancreatitis—a reevaluation. A.M.A. Arch. Surg *75:*41, 1957.

Rosenthal, S. R., Samet, C., Winzler, R. J. and Shkolnik, S.: Substances released from the skin following thermal injury. I. Histamine and proteins. J. Clin. Invest. *36:*38, 1957.

Rosoff, C. B. and Walter, C. W.: The controlled laboratory production of hemoglobinuric nephrosis. Ann. Surg. *135:*324, 1952.

Ross, J. F., Chodos, R. B., Baker, W. H. and Freis, E. D.: The blood volume in congestive heart failure. Tr. A. Am. Physicians *65:*75, 1952.

Rousselot, L. M.: Combined (one-stage) splenectomy and portacaval shunts in portal hypertension, with observations on venous shunts in postsplenectomy patient with recurring hemorrhage. J.A.M.A. *140:*282, 1949.

Rubin, A. L. and Braveman, W. S.: Treatment of the low salt syndrome in congestive heart failure by the controlled use of mercurial diuretics. Circulation *13:*655, 1956.

Rudy, N. E. and Crepeau, J. L.: The role of intermittent positive pressure breathing postoperatively. J.A.M.A. *167:*1093, 1958.

Rush, B. and Cliffton, E. E.: The role of trypsin in pathogenesis of acute hemorrhagic pancreatitis and the effect of antitryptic agent in treatment. Surgery *31:*349, 1952.

Sachar, L., Walker, W. and Whittico, J.: Carbohydrate tolerance, blood ketone levels and nitrogen balance after human trauma (fractures). Arch. Surg. *60:*837, 1950.

Sack, T., Gibson, J. G., II and Buckley, E. S., Jr.: Preservation of whole ACD blood collected, stored and transfused in plastic equipment. Surg., Gynec. & Obst. *95:*113, 1952.

Sadove, M. S., Wyant, G. M., Julian, O. C. and Dye, W. S.: Cardiac arrest. Am. Surgeon *20:*5, 1954.

Saikku, L. A.: Fat embolism in connection with the treatment of fractures. Acta chir. scandinav. *108:*275, 1954.

Sako, Y., Artz, C. P., Howard, J. M., Bronwell, A. W. and Inui, F. K.: A survey of evacuation, resuscitation and mortality in a forward surgical hospital. Surgery *37:*602, 1955.

Salassa, R. M., Bennett, W. A., Keating, F. R., Jr. and Sprague, R. G.: Postoperative adrenal cortical insufficiency; occurrence in patients previously treated with cortisone. J.A.M.A. *152:*1509, 1953.

Salisbury, P. F.: Coronary artery pressure and strength of right ventricular contraction. Circulation Res. *3:*633, 1955.

Salzberg, A. M. and Evans, E. I.: Blood volumes in normal and burned dogs. A comparative study with radioactive phosphorus-tagged red cells and T-1824 dye. Ann. Surg. *132:*746, 1950.

Sandberg, A. A., Eik-Nes, K., Migeon, C. J. and Samuels, L. T.: Metabolism of adrenal steroids in dying patients. J. Clin. Endocrinol. *16:*1001, 1956.

Sanderson, P. H.: Renal failure following abdominal catastrophe and alkalosis. Clin. Sc. *6:*207, 1948.

Sarnoff, S. J., Case, R. B., Waithe, P. E. and Isaacs, J. P.: Insufficient coronary flow and myocardial failure as a complicating factor in late hemorrhagic shock. Am. J. Physiol. *176:*439, 1954.

Sayers, M. A., Sayers, G., Engel, M. G., Engel, F. L. and Long, C. N. H.: Elevation of plasma amino nitrogen as an index of the gravity of hemorrhagic shock. Proc. Soc. Exper. Biol. & Med. *60:*20, 1945.

Scalettar, R., Rubini, M. E. and Meroney, W. H.: Gastrointestinal hemorrhage in uremia—report of 2 cases of massive hemorrhage resulting from causes other than uremic enterocolitis. New England J. Med. *257:*211, 1957.

Schaefer, J. H.: Whiplash injuries of the neck. (Comment on Gay and Abbott's article.) J.A.M.A. *153:*974, 1953.

Schatten, W. E.: Intraperitoneal antibiotic administration in the treatment of acute bacterial peritonitis. Surg., Gynec. & Obst. *102:*339, 1956.

Schenk, W. G., Jr., Stephens, J. G., Burke, J., Hale, H. W., Jr., Eagle, J. F. and Stewart, J. D.: Treatment of mass civilian burn casualties; care of Cleveland Hill School fire victims. A.M.A. Arch. Surg. *71:*196, 1955.

Scherf, D.: Cardiac reflexes originating in respiratory tract. New York J. Med. *45:*1647, 1945.

Schlegel, J. U.: A new approach to the treatment of electrolyte disturbances in shock and severe stress. Surgery *35:*449, 1954.

Schlegel, J. U.: Return of sodium loads in normal subjects following restricted sodium intake. Surgery *35:*848, 1954.

Schlegel, J. U., Anderson, F. W., Madsen, P. O. and Betheil, J. J.: The altered response to sodium loading in several severely burned individuals after initial treatment with hypertonic sodium-containing fluids. Surg., Gynec. & Obst. *99:*187, 1954.

Schlegel, J. U., Eldrup-Jorgensen, S. and Stone, H.: Studies in metabolism of trauma. I. Maintenance of homeostasis during antidiuresis. Ann. Surg. *145:*12, 1957.

Schlegel, J. U., Parry, W. L., Betheil, J. J. and Bloch, A. L.: Study of relationship between pH of the urine and sodium and potassium excretion. Proc. Soc. Exper. Biol. & Med. *84:*223, 1953.

Schloerb, P. R., Friis-Hansen, B. J., Edelman, I. S., Sheldon, D. B. and Moore, F. D.: The measurement of deuterium oxide in body fluids by the falling drop method. J. Lab. & Clin. Med. *37:*653, 1951.

Schloerb, P. R., Friis-Hansen, B. J., Edelman, I. S., Solomon, A. K. and Moore, F. D.: The measurement of total body water in the human subject by deuterium oxide dilution; with consideration of the dynamics of deuterium distribution. J. Clin. Invest. *29:*1296, 1950.

Schmid H.: Zur Beeinflussung der Kallusbildung durch Perandren. Schweiz. med. wschr. *76:*538, 1946.

Schmidt, L. A., III, Iob, V., Flotte, C. T., Hodgson, P. E. and McMath, M.: Blood volume changes in the aged. Surgery *40:*938, 1956.

Schoen, I., Strauss, L. and Bay, M. W.: An evaluation of the eosinophil count in patients undergoing major surgery. Surg., Gynec. & Obst. *96:*403, 1953.

Schoolman, H. M., Dubin, A. and Hoffman, W. S.: Clinical syndromes associated with hypernatremia A.M.A. Arch. Int. Med. *95:*15, 1955.

Schram, W. R. and Fosdick, L. S.: Studies in bone healing. J. Oral Surg. *7:*191, 1943.

Schreiber, S. S., Bauman, A., Yalow, R. S. and Berson, S. A.: Blood volume alterations in congestive heart failure. J. Clin. Invest. *33:*578, 1954.

Schreiner, G. E., Smith, L. H., Jr. and Kyle, L. H.: Renal hyperchloremic acidosis; familial occurrence of nephrocalcinosis with hyperchloremia and low serum bicarbonate. Am. J. Med. *15:*122, 1953.

Schwachman, H., Dooley, R. R., Guilmette, F., Patterson, P. R., Weil, C. and Leubner, H.: Cystic fibrosis of the pancreas with varying degrees of pancreatic insufficiency. A.M.A. Am. J. Dis. Child. 92:347, 1956.

Schwartz, M. K., Bodansky, O. and Randall, H. T.: Metabolism in surgical patients. III. Effect of drugs and dietary procedures on fat and nitrogen metabolism in totally gastrectomized patients. Surgery 40:671, 1956.

Schwartz, M. K., Bodansky, O. and Randall, H. T.: Metabolism in surgical patients; fat and mineral metabolism in totally gastrectomized patients. Am. J. Clin. Nutrition 4:51, 1956.

Schwartz, M. K., Medwid, A., Roberts, K. E., Sleisenger, M. and Randall, H. T.: Fat and nitrogen metabolism in patients with massive small bowel resections. S. Forum 6:385, 1956.

Schwartz, R., Gabuzda, G. J., Jr. and Davidson, C. S.: Antidiuresis and hyponatremia in cirrhosis of the liver. Clin. Res. Proc. 1:111, 1953.

Schwartz, R., Phillips, G. B., Seegmiller, J. E., Gabuzda, G. J., Jr. and Davidson, C. S.: Dietary protein in the genesis of hepatic coma. New England J. Med. 251:685, 1954.

Schwartz, W. B.: The role of electrolyte balance in the response to mercurial diuretics in congestive heart failure. Bull. New England Med. Center 12:213, 1950.

Schwartz, W. B.: Potassium and the kidney. New England J. Med. 253:601, 1955.

Schwartz, W. B., Bennett, W., Curelop, S. and Bartter, F. C.: Studies on the mechanism of a sodium-losing syndrome in two patients with mediastinal tumors. J. Clin. Invest. 35:734, 1956 (abstr.).

Schwartz, W. B., Bennett, W., Curelop, S., Bartter, F. C.: A syndrome of renal sodium loss and hyponatremia probably resulting from inappropriate secretion of antidiuretic hormones. Am. J. Med. 23:529, 1957.

Schwartz, W. B., Jenson, R. L. and Relman, A. S.: The disposition of acid administered to sodium-depleted subjects: the renal response and the role of the whole body buffers. J. Clin. Invest. 33:587, 1954.

Schwartz, W. B., Levine, H. D. and Relman, A. S.: The electrocardiogram in potassium depletion. Its relation to the total potassium deficit and the serum concentration. Am. J. Med. 16:395, 1954.

Schwartz, W. B., Orning, K. J. and Porter, R.: The constant relationship between extracellular and intracellular buffering with varying degrees of metabolic acidosis. J. Clin. Invest. 34:918, 1955 (abstr.).

Schwartz, W. B., Orning, K. J. and Porter, R.: The internal distribution of hydrogen ions with varying degrees of metabolic acidosis. J. Clin. Invest. 36:373, 1957.

Schwartz, W. B. and Relman, A. S.: Metabolic and renal studies in chronic potassium depletion resulting from overuse of laxatives. J. Clin. Invest. 32:258, 1953.

Schwartz, W. B. and Relman, A. S.: Electrolyte disturbances in congestive heart failure. Clinical significance and management. J.A.M.A. 154:1237, 1954.

Schwartz, W. B. and Relman, A. S.: Acidosis in renal disease. New England J. Med. 256:1184, 1957.

Schwartz, W. B. and Wallace, W. M.: Observations on electrolyte balance during mercurial diuresis in congestive heart failure. J. Clin. Invest. 29:844, 1950 (abstr.).

Schwartz, W. B. and Wallace, W. M.: Electrolyte equilib-rium during mercurial diuresis. J. Clin. Invest. 30:1089, 1951.

Scott, R., Jr. and Crosby, W. H.: Changes in the coagulation mechanism following wounding and resuscitation with stored blood. A study of battle casualties in Korea. Blood 9:609, 1954.

Scott, R., Jr. and Crosby, W. H.: The hemostatic response to injury; a study of the Korean battle casualties. Ann. Surg. 141:347, 1955.

Scott, R., Jr. and Howard, J. M.: Hepatic function following wounding and resuscitation with plasma expanders. Ann. Surg. 141:357, 1955.

Scott, R., Jr., Howard, J. M., Shorr, E., Lawson, N. and Davis, J. H.: Circulatory homeostasis following massive injury, studies of vasodepressor and vaso-excitatory substances in the circulating blood. Ann. Surg. 141:504, 1955.

Scott, W. J. M.: Postoperative massive collapse of the lung. A.M.A. Arch. Surg. 10:73, 1925.

Scribner, B. H. and Burnell, J. M.: The effect of respiratory alterations of pH on the internal equilibrium of potassium. J. Clin. Invest. 34:919, 1955 (abstr.).

Scribner, B. H. and Burnell, J. M.: Interpretation of the serum potassium concentration. Metabolism 5:468, 1956.

Scuderi, C. S.: Fat embolism: a clinical and experimental study. Surg., Gynec. & Obst. 72:732, 1941.

Sealy, W. C., Young, W. G., Jr. and Harris, J. S.: Studies on cardiac arrest: the relationship of hypercapnia to ventricular fibrillation. J. Thoracic Surg. 28:447, 1954.

Sealy, W. C., Young, W. G., Jr. and Hickam, J. B.: Postoperative respiratory acidosis. A.M.A. Arch. Surg. 75:57, 1957.

Seeley, S. F.: Intra-arterial transfusion in profound shock. Anesth. & Analg. 30:195, 1951.

Seeley, S. F.: Intra-arterial transfusion. U. S. Armed Forces M. J. 5:229, 1954.

Seeley, S. F. and Nelson, R. M.: Collective review; intra-arterial transfusion. Internat. Abstr. Surg. 94:209, 1952.

Seevers, M. H., Cassels, W. H. and Becker, T. J.: The role of hypercapnia and pyrexia in the production of "ether convulsions." J. Pharmacol. & Exper. Therap. 63:33, 1938 (proc.).

Seibert, F. B., Pfaff, M. L. and Seibert, M. V.: A serum polysaccharide in tuberculosis and carcinoma. Arch Biochem. 18:279, 1948.

Seibert, F. B., Seibert, M. V., Atno, A. J. and Campbell, H. W.: Variation in protein and polysaccharide content of sera in the chronic diseases, tuberculosis, sarcoidosis and carcinoma. J. Clin. Invest. 26:90, 1947.

Seldin, D. W., Welt, L. G. and Cort, J. H.: The role of sodium salts and adrenal steroids in the production of hypokalemic alkalosis. Yale J. Biol. & Med. 29:229, 1956.

Seligman, A. M., Frank, H. A. and Fine, J.: Traumatic shock. XII. Hemodynamic effects of alterations of blood viscosity in normal dogs and in dogs in shock. J. Clin. Invest. 25:1, 1946.

Seligman, A. M., Frank, H. A. and Fine, J.: Traumatic shock. XIV. The successful treatment of hemorrhagic shock by viviperfusion of the liver in dogs irreversible to transfusion. J. Clin. Invest. 26:530, 1947.

Selkurt, E. E., Hall, P. W. and Spencer, M. P.: Influence of graded arterial pressure decrement on renal clearance of creatinine, P-aminohippurate and sodium. Am. J. Physiol. 159:369, 1949.

Selye, H.: General adaptation syndrome and diseases of adaptation. J. Clin. Endocrinol. *6:*117, 1946.

Selye, H.: Testicular diseases of adaptation, systemic stress, ionizing radiations. In The Physiology and Pathology of Exposure to Stress. Montreal, Canada, Acta, Inc. *1:*362, 1950.

Selye, H.: "Conditioning" vs. "permissive" actions of hormones. J. Clin. Endocrinol. *14:*122, 1954.

Selye, H. and Horava, A.: Third Annual Report on Stress. Montreal, Canada, Acta, Inc., 1953.

Sengstaken, R. W. and Blakemore, A. H.: Balloon tamponage for control of hemorrhage from esophageal varices. Ann. Surg. *131:*781, 1950.

Sevitt, S.: Post-traumatic adrenal apoplexy. J. Clin. Path. *8:*185, 1955.

Seymour, W. B., Pritchard, W. H., Longley, L. P. and Hayman, J. P., Jr.: Cardiac output, blood and interstitial fluid volumes, total circulating serum protein, and kidney function during cardiac failure and after improvement. J. Clin. Invest. *21:*229, 1942.

Shachman, R., Graber, G. I. and Melrose, D. G.: The haemodynamics of the surgical patient under general anaesthesia. Brit. J. Surg. *40:*193, 1952.

Shaffer, P. A. and Coleman, W.: Protein metabolism in typhoid fever. A.M.A. Arch. Int. Med. *4:*538, 1909.

Shands, A. R., Jr.: Studies in bone formation: the effect of the local presence of calcium salts on osteogenesis. J. Bone & Joint Surg. *19:*1065, 1957.

Sheehan, H. L.: Pathological lesions in the hypertensive toxemias of pregnancy. In Toxemias of Pregnancy. Ciba Foundation Symposium. Philadelphia, The Blakiston Co., 1950, p. 16.

Sheehan, H. L. *et al.:* Discussion on symmetrical cortical necrosis of the kidneys. Proc. Roy. Soc. Med. *44:*399, 1951.

Sheehan, H. L. and Moore, H. C.: Renal Cortical Necrosis and the Kidney of Concealed Accidental Hemorrhage. Springfield, Ill., Charles C Thomas, 1953.

Shen, S. C. and Ham, T. H.: Studies on destruction of red blood cells: mechanism and complications of hemoglobinuria in patients with thermal burns; spherocytosis and increased osmotic fragility of red blood cells. New England J. Med. *229:*701, 1943.

Sherman, M. S.: Oestrogens and bone formation in the human female. J. Bone & Joint Surg. *30A:*915, 1948.

Sherman, M. S.: Bone changes following bilateral ureterosigmoidostomy. Surg., Gynec. & Obst. *97:*159, 1953.

Sherman, W. B.: Hazards of therapy in respiratory disease. J.A.M.A. *168:*1866, 1958.

Shingleton, W. W. *et al.:* Studies on postgastrectomy steatorrhea using radioactive triolein and oleic acid. Surgery *42:*12, 1957.

Shingleton, W. W. and Anlyan, W. G.: Chronic relapsing pancreatitis. South. M. J. *47:*451, 1954.

Shingleton, W. W., Anlyan, W. G., Neill, K. C. and Vance, T. D.: Observations of changes in blood coagulability in patients with pancreatic disease. S. Forum *3:*522, 1953.

Shingleton, W. W., Anlyan, W. G., Salem, M. E. and Sanders, A. P.: Studies on intravenous fat emulsions. S. Forum *6:*18, 1956.

Shingleton, W. W., Wells, M. H., Baylin, G. J., Ruffin, J. M. and Saunders, A.: The use of radioactive-labeled protein and fat in the evaluation of pancreatic disorders. Surgery *38:*134, 1955.

Shipley, R. A., Dorfman, R. I., Buchwald, E. and Ross, E.: The effect of infection and trauma on the excretion of urinary cortin. J. Clin. Invest. *25:*673, 1946.

Shipley, R. A. and MacIntyre, J.: Effect of stress, TSH and ACTH on the level of hormonal I^{131} of serum. J. Clin. Endocrinol. *14:*309, 1954.

Shoemaker, W. C. and Wase, A. W.: Absorption patterns of isotope labeled dietary constituents in postgastrectomy patients. Surg., Gynec. & Obst. *105:*153, 1957.

Shohl, A. T.: Mineral metabolism (table showing mineral content of the whole body at different ages). Monograph series No. 82, New York, Reinhold Publishing Corp., 1939, p. 19.

Shooter, R. A., Taylor, G. W., Ellis, G. and Ross, J. P.: Postoperative wound infection. Surg., Gynec. & Obst. *103:*257, 1956.

Shorr, E.: Recent findings concerning the role of the liver and kidney in circulatory homeostasis. Transactions of the Eighth Conference on Liver Injury. New York Josiah Macy, Jr., Foundation, 1950.

Shorr, E. and Carter, A. C.: In Transactions of the Second Conference on Metabolic Interrelationships. New York, Josiah Macy, Jr., Foundation, 1950, p. 144.

Shorr, E., Zweifach, B. W. and Furchgott, R. F.: On the occurrence, sites and modes of origin and destruction, of principles affecting the compensatory vascular mechanisms in experimental shock. Science *102:*489, 1945.

Shorr, E., Zweifach, B. W. and Furchgott, R. F.: Hepatorenal factors in circulatory homeostasis. III. The influence of humoral factors of hepato-renal origin on the vascular reactions to hemorrhage. Ann. New York Acad. Sc. *49:*571, 1948.

Shorr, E., Zweifach, B. W., Furchgott, R. F. and Baez, S.: Hepatorenal vasotropic factors in experimental shock and renal hypertension. Tr. A. Am. Physicians *60:*28, 1947.

Shorr, E., Zweifach, B. W., Furchgott, R. F. and Baez, S.: Hepatorenal factors in circulatory homeostasis. IV. Tissue origins of the vasotropic principles, VEM and VDM, which appear during evolution of hemorrhagic and tourniquet shock. Circulation *3:*42, 1951.

Shumacker, H. B., Jr. and Hampton, L. J.: Sudden death occurring immediately after operation in patients with cardiac disease, with particular reference to the role of aspiration through the endotracheal tube and extubation. J. Thoracic Surg. *21:*48, 1951.

Siker, E. S., Lipschitz, E. and Klein, R.: The effect of preanesthetic medications on the blood level of 17-hydroxycorticosteroids. Ann. Surg. *143:*88, 1956.

Silber, R. H. and Porter, C. C.: The determination of 17, 21-dihydroxy-20-ketosteroids in urine and plasma. J. Biol. Chem. *210:*923, 1954.

Simpson, S. A., Tait, J. F. and Bush, I. E.: Secretion of salt-retaining hormone by mammalian adrenal cortex. Lancet *2:*226, 1952.

Simpson, S. A. *et al.:* Konstitution des Aldesterons, des neuen Mineralocorticoids. Experientia *10:*132, 1954.

Simpson, S. A., Tait, J. F., Wettstein, A., Neher, R., von Euw, J. and Reichstein, T.: Isolierung eines neuen kristallizierten Hormons aus Nebennieren mit besonders hoher Wirkzamkeit auf den Mineralstoffwechsel. Experimentia *9:*333, 1953.

Sims, E. A. H., Welt, L. G., Orloff, J. and Needham, J. W.: Asymptomatic hyponatremia in pulmonary tuberculosis. J. Clin. Invest. *29:*1545, 1950.

Sinclair, I. S. R.: Observations on a case of external pancreatic fistula in man. Brit. J. Surg. *44:*250, 1956.

Sinclair-Smith, B., Kattus, A. A., Genest, J. and Neuman, E. V.: The renal mechanism of electrolyte excretion and the metabolic balances of electrolytes and nitrogen in congestive cardiac failure, the effects of exercise, rest and aminophyllin. Bull. Johns Hopkins Hosp. 84:369, 1949.

Singer, B. and Wener, J.: Excretion of sodium-retaining substances in patients with congestive heart failure. Am. Heart J. 45:795, 1953.

Skanse, B. and Widen, T.: Potassium deficiency syndrome following bilateral ureterosigmoidostomy. J. Urol. 73:62, 1955.

Skerlj, B., Brozek, J. and Hunt, E. E., Jr.: Subcutaneous fat and age changes in body build and body form in women. Am. J. Phys. Anthropol. 11:477, 1953.

Sleisenger, M. H. and Freedberg, A. S.: Ammonium chloride acidosis; report of 6 cases. Circulation 3:837, 1951.

Smith, C. A.: The physiology of the newborn infant. 2nd ed. Springfield, Ill., Charles C Thomas, 1951.

Smith, D. W. and Lee, R. M.: Nutritional management in duodenal fistula. Surg., Gynec. & Obst. 103:666, 1956.

Smith, F. M.: Fracture of the femoral neck as a complication of pelvic irradiation. Am. J. Surg. 87:339, 1954.

Smith, J. C., McNealy, R. W. and Zaus, E. A.: Effect of hepatic artery ligation on ascites due to Laennec cirrhosis; report of 2 cases. A.M.A. Arch. Surg. 66:344, 1953.

Smith, J. R. and Howland, W. S.: The endotracheal tube as a source of infection. J.A.M.A. 169:343, 1959.

Smith, L. L., Williamson, A. W. R. and Moore, F. D.: The effect of acute addition acidosis in experimental hemorrhagic hypotension. S. Forum 8:43, 1958.

Smith, M. D. and Mallett, B.: Iron absorption before and after partial gastrectomy. Clin. Sc. 16:23, 1957.

Smith, S. W., Barker, W. F. and Kaplan, L.: Acute pancreatitis following transampullary biliary drainage. Surgery 30:695, 1951.

Smolik, E. A., Brown, S. and Nash, F. P.: Use of transfusion in the management of closed head injury; preliminary report. South. M. J. 44:592, 1951.

Smolik, E. A., Muether, R. O., Nash, F. P. and Konneker, W.: Blood volume changes in cases of cerebral trauma as determined by radioactive isotopes. Surg., Gynec. & Obst. 102:263, 1956.

Smolik, E. A., Nash, F. P. and Ninecurt, J.: Blood diastase activity in cerebral trauma. Ann. Surg. 138:863, 1953.

Smolik, E. A., Ninecurt, J. and Nash, F. P.: Eosinophil circulating response in cerebral trauma. Surgery 38:539, 1955.

Smythe, C. M., Gilmore, J. P., Maloney, J. V., Jr. and Handford, S. W.: Analysis of direct hydraulic effect of intra-arterial transfusion. Am. J. Physiol. 178:412, 1954.

Soberman, R. J., Keating, R. P. and Maxwell, R. D.: Effect of acute whole-body x-irradiation upon water and electrolyte balance. Am. J. Physiol. 164:450, 1951.

Sohval, A. R. and Soffer, L. J.: The influence of cortisone and adrenocorticotropin on urinary gonadotropin excretion. J. Clin. Endocrinol. 11:677, 1951.

Sohval, A. R., Weiner, I. and Soffer, L. J.: The effect of surgical procedures on urinary gonadotropin excretion. J. Clin. Endocrinol. 12:1053, 1952.

Solomon, A. K.: Equations for tracer experiments. J. Clin. Invest. 28:1297, 1949.

Soroff, H. S., Pearson, E., Reiss, E. and Artz, C. P.: The relationship between plasma sodium concentration and the state of hydration of burned patients. Surg., Gynec. & Obst. 102:472, 1956.

Spence, H. Y., Evans, E. I. and Forbes, J. C.: The influence of a special high protein diet on protein regeneration in the surgical patient. Ann. Surg. 124:131, 1946.

Spiegl, R. J., Long, J. B. and Dexter, L.: Clinical observations on patients undergoing finger fracture mitral valvuloplasty. I. Auscultatory changes. Am. J. Med. 12:626, 1952.

Spiegl, R. J., Long, J. B. and Dexter, L.: Clinical observations on patients undergoing finger fracture mitral valvuloplasty. II. Electrocardiographic observations. Am. J. Med. 12:631, 1952.

Sprunt, D. H.: The influence of roentgen rays on the acid-base equilibrium. J. Biol. Chem. 92:605, 1931.

Squires, R. D., Singer, R. B., Moffitt, G. R., Jr. and Elkinton, J. R.: The distribution of body fluids in congestive heart failure. II. Abnormalities in serum electrolyte concentration and in acid-base equilibrium. Circulation 4:697, 1951.

Stahl, R. R., Artz, C. P., Howard, J. M. and Simeone, F. A.: Studies of response of the autonomic nervous system following combat injury. Surg., Gynec. & Obst. 99:595, 1954.

Stamey, T. A.: The pathogenesis and implications of the electrolyte imbalance in ureterosigmoidostomy. Surg., Gynec. & Obst. 103:736, 1956.

Stanbury, S. W. and Thomson, A. E.: The renal response to respiratory alkalosis. Clin. Sc. 11:357, 1952.

Starr, K. W.: The Causation and Treatment of Delayed Union in Fractures of the Long Bone. London, Butterworth & Co., 1947.

Steenburg, R. W.: A study of the free 17-hydroxycorticoids in the peripheral blood of surgical patients. S. Forum 4:593, 1954.

Steenburg, R. W. and Ganong, W. F.: Observations on the influence of extra-adrenal factors on circulating 17-hydroxycorticoids in the surgically stressed, adrenalectomized animal. Surgery 38:92, 1955.

Steenburg, R. W., Lennihan, R. and Moore, F. D.: Studies in surgical endocrinology. II. The free blood 17-hydroxycorticoids in surgical patients; their relation to urine steroids, metabolism and convalescence. Ann. Surg. 143:180, 1956.

Steffanini, M.: Mechanism of blood coagulation in normal and pathologic conditions. Am. J. Med. 14:64, 1953.

Steffanini, M., Mednicoff, I. B., Salomon, L. and Campbell, E. W.: Thrombocytopenia of replacement transfusion: a cause of surgical bleeding. Clin. Res. Proc. 2:61, 1954.

Stein, M., Schwartz, R. and Mirsky, I. A.: The antidiuretic activity of plasma of patients with hepatic cirrhosis, congestive heart failure, hypertension and other clinical disorders. J. Clin. Invest. 33:77, 1954.

Stephenson, H. E., Jr., Reid, L. C. and Hinton, J. W.: Some common denominators in 1200 cases of cardiac arrest. Ann. Surg. 137:731, 1953.

Sterling, K., Lipsky, S. R. and Freedman, L. J.: Disappearance of curve of intravenously administered I[131] tagged albumin in the postoperative injury reaction. Metabolism 4:343, 1955.

Stevenson, J. A. F., Shenker, V. and Browne, J. S. L.: The 17-ketosteroid excretion in damage and convalescence. Endocrinology 35:216, 1944 (abstr.).

Stewart, H. J., Shepard, E. M. and Horger, E. L.: Electrocardiographic manifestations of potassium intoxication. Am. J. Med. 5:821, 1948.

Stewart, H. J. and Smith, J. J.: Changes in the electrocardiogram and in the cardiac rhythm during the therapeutic use of potassium salts. Am. J. Med. Sc. *201*:177, 1941.

Stewart, J. D. and Alfano, G. S.: Surgery of the elderly. J.A.M.A. *154*:643, 1954.

Stewart, J. D., Cosgriff, J. H. and Gray, J. G.: Experiences with the treatment of acutely massively bleeding peptic ulcer by blood replacement and gastric resection. Surg., Gynec. & Obst. *103*:409, 1956.

Stewart, J. D. and Rourke, G. M.: Changes in blood and interstitial fluid resulting from surgical operation and ether anesthesia. J. Clin. Invest. *17*:413, 1938.

Stewart, J. D. and Warner, F.: Observations on the severely wounded in forward field hospitals: with special reference to wound shock. Am. Surg. *122*:129, 1945.

Stewart, W. J.: Experimental bone regeneration using lime salts and autogenous grafts as sources of available calcium. Surg., Gynec. & Obst. *59*:867, 1934.

Stock, R. J., Mudge, G. H. and Nurnberg, M. J.: Congestive heart failure; variations in electrolyte metabolism with salt restriction and mercurial diuretics. Circulation *4*:54, 1951.

Stoerk, H. C., Eisen, H. N. and John, H. M.: Impairment of antibody response in pyridoxine-deficient rats. J. Exper. Med. *85*:365, 1947.

Stoner, H. B., Whiteley, H. J. and Emery, J. L.: The effect of systemic disease on the adrenal cortex of the child. J. Path. & Bact. *66*:171, 1953.

Stormont, R. T., Hathaway, H. R., Shideman, F. E. and Seevers, M. H.: Acid-base balance during cyclopropane anesthesia. Anesthesiology *3*:369, 1942.

Strauss, A. A. *et al.:* Physiological and clinical study of patients after subtotal gastrectomy. Am. J. Digest. Dis. *4*:32, 1937.

Strawitz, J. G., Howard, J. M. and Artz, C. P.: Effect of intravenous calcium gluconate on post-transfusion hypotension—clinical observations. A.M.A. Arch. Surg. *70*:233, 1955.

Strawitz, J. G. *et al.:* The healing of battle wounds—bacteriological and histological studies. Preliminary report to the Army Medical Service Graduate School, 1953.

Strawitz, J. G., Wetzler, T. F., Marshall, J. D., Lindberg, R. B., Howard, J. M. and Artz, C. P.: The bacterial flora of healing wounds. Surgery *37*:400, 1955.

Sturgis, S. H., Robey, H., Pierson, H., Gates, P., Plaut, T. and Menzer-Benaron, D.: Anesthesia recovery patterns after elective hysterectomy. Prognostic significance. Obst. & Gynec. *7*:363, 1956.

Summerskill, W. H. J., Wolfe, S. J. and Davidson, C. S.: The metabolism of ammonia and alpha keto-acids in liver disease and hepatic coma. J. Clin. Invest. *36*:361, 1957.

Sunderman, F. W.: Studies in serum electrolytes. XIV. Changes in blood and body fluids in prolonged fasting. Am. J. Clin. Path. *17*:169–180, 1956.

Suter, C. and Klingman, W. D.: Neurological manifestations of magnesium depletion states. Neurology *5*:691, 1955.

Svec, M. H. and Freeman, S.: Effects of impaired hepatic circulation on plasma free amino acids of dogs. Am. J. Physiol. *159*:357, 1949.

Swan, H.: Pharmacology of the heart. In Allen (ed.): Extracorporeal Circulation. Springfield, Ill., Charles C Thomas, 1958.

Swan, H., Jenkins, D. and Helmreich, M. L.: The adrenal cortical response to surgery. III. Changes in plasma and urinary corticosteroid levels during hypothermia in man. Surgery *42*:202, 1957.

Swan, H. and Montgomery, V.: Pharmacology of the heart. In Allen (ed.): Extracorporeal Circulation. Springfield, Ill., Charles C Thomas, 1958.

Swan, R. C., Madisso, H. and Pitts, R. F.: Measurement of extracellular fluid volume in nephrectomized dogs. J. Clin. Invest. *33*:1447, 1954.

Swan, R. C. and Merrill, J. P.: The clinical course of acute renal failure. Medicine *32*:215, 1953.

Swan, R. C. and Pitts, R. F.: Neutralization of infused acid by nephrectomized dogs. J. Clin. Invest. *34*:205, 1955.

Swank, R. L. and Dugger, G. S.: Fat embolism; a clinical and experimental study of the mechanisms involved. Surg., Gynec. & Obst. *98*:641, 1954.

Swanson, W. W.: The composition of growth II. The full-term infant. Am. J. Dis. Child. *43*:10, 1932.

Swanson, W. W. and Iob, L. V.: Loss of minerals through the skin of infants. Am. J. Dis. Child. *45*:1036, 1933.

Sweet, N. J., Nadell, J. and Edelman, I. S.: Gastrointestinal water and electrolytes. III. The equilibration of radiobromide in gastrointestinal contents and the proportion of exchangeable chloride (CLe) in the gastrointestinal tract. J. Clin. Invest. *36*:279, 1957.

Sweet, W. H., Cotzias, G. C., Seed, J. and Yakovler, P. I.: Gastrointestinal hemorrhages, hyperglycemia, azotemia, hyperchloremia and hypernatremia following lesions of frontal lobe in man. A. Res. Nerv. & Ment. Dis. Proc. *27*:795, 1948.

Swift, M. N., Patt, H. M. and Tyree, E. B.: The effect of adrenal cortical extract on adrenal response to total body x-irradiation. Fed. Proc. *7*:121, 1948 (abstr.).

Symington, T., Currie, A. R., Curran, R. C. and Davidson, J. N.: The reaction of the adrenal cortex in conditions of stress. Ciba Foundation Coll. Endocrinol. *8*:70, 1955.

Taffel, M., Donovan, A. J. and Lapinski, L. S.: The effect of trauma on wound healing. Yale J. Biol. & Med. *23*:482, 1950.

Tagnon, H. J., Levenson, S. M., Davidson, C. S. and Taylor, F. H. L.: The occurrence of fibrinolysis in shock, with observations on the prothrombin time and the plasma fibrinogen during hemorrhagic shock. Am. J. M. Sc. *211*:88, 1946.

Tagnon, H. J., Robbins, G. F. and Nichols, M. P.: The effect of surgical operations on the bromsulfalein-retention test. New England J. Med. *238*:556, 1948.

Talbot, N. B., Albright, F., Saltzman, A. H., Zygmuntowicz, A. and Wixon, R.: The excretion of 11-oxycorticosteroid-like substances by normal and abnormal subjects. J. Clin. Endocrinol. *7*:331, 1947.

Tarail, R.: Electrocardiographic abnormalities in a case of uremia manifesting hyperpotassemia. Am. Heart J. *35*:665, 1948.

Taylor, F. H. and Roos, A.: Disturbances in acid-base balance during ether anesthesia with special reference to changes occurring during thoracic surgery. J. Thoracic Surg. *20*:289, 1950.

Taylor, R. A. R.: Aetiology, pathology, diagnosis and treatment of acute pancreatitis. Hunterian lecture. Ann. Roy. Coll. Surgeons, England *5*:213, 1949.

Templeton, J. Y., III, Finley, R. K., Jr. and Gibbon, J. H., Jr.: Observations on thiocyanate space, serum electrolytes and acid base equilibrium in patients with intra thoracic disease. S. Forum 2:589, 1952.

Teschan, P. E. *et al.:* Post-traumatic renal insufficiency in military casualties. I. Clinical characteristics. Am. J. Med. *78:*172, 1955.

Thal, A. P., Perry, J. F., Molestina, J. E. and Egner, W. E.: Pancreatitis. V. A clinical and morphological study of acute fatal pancreatitis. Univ. Minnesota Med. Bull. *27:* 1955.

Theron, P. H. and Wilson, W. C.: Blood changes in peritonitis. Lancet *1:*172, 1949.

Thomas, P. O. and Ross, C. A.: Effect of exclusive parenteral feeding on the closure of a pancreatic fistula—study made after duodenal pancreatic resection for carcinoma of the ampulla of Vater. Arch. Surg., *57:*104, 1948.

Thomsen, V.: Studies of trauma and carbohydrate metabolism with special reference to existence of traumatic diabetes. Acta med. scand. (suppl.) *91:*1, 1938.

Thorn, G. W. *et al.:* Medical progress: pharmacologic aspects of adrenocortical steroids and ACTH in man. New England J. Med. *248:*232, 284, 323, 369, 414, 588, 632, 1953.

Thorn, G. W., Jenkins, D. and Laidlaw, J. C.: The adrenal response to stress in man. Rec. Progr. Horm. Res. *8:*171, 1953.

Thorn, G. W., Jenkins, D., Laidlaw, J. C., Goetz, J. C. and Reddy, W.: Response of the adrenal cortex to stress in man. Tr. A. Am. Physicians *66:*48, 1953.

Thorn, G. W. and Laidlaw, J. C.: Studies on the adrenal cortical response to stress in man. Tr. Am. Clin. & Climatol. A. *65:*179, 1954.

Tileston, W. and Comfort, C. W., Jr.: The total nonprotein nitrogen and the urea of the blood in health and in disease, as estimated by Folin's methods. A.M.A. Arch. Int. Med. *14:*620, 1914.

Tobian, L. and Fox, A.: The effect of nor-epinephrine on the electrolyte composition of arterial smooth muscle. J. Clin. Invest. *35:*297, 1956.

Topley, E. and Clarke, R.: The anemia of trauma. Blood *11:*357, 1956.

Topley, E. and Fisher, M. R.: The illness of trauma. Brit. J. Clin. Practice *10:*770, 1956.

Tovell, R. M. and Little, D. M.: Utility of fog as a therapeutic agent. Anesthesiology *18:*470, 1957.

Traeger, H. S., Gabuzda, G. J., Jr., Ballou, A. N. and Davidson, C. S.: Blood "ammonia" concentration in liver disease and liver coma. Metabolism *3:*99, 1954.

Troen, P. and Rynearson, E. H.: An evaluation of the prophylactic use of cortisone for pituitary operations. J. Clin. Endocrinol. *16:*747, 1956.

Tucker, F. R.: Arterial supply to the femoral head and its clinical importance. J. Bone & Joint Surg. *31-B:*82, 1949.

Tucker, F. R.: The use of radioactive phosphorus in the diagnosis of avascular necrosis of the femoral head. J. Bone & Joint Surg. *32-B:*100, 1950.

Turnbull, R. B.: Postoperative staphylococcal enteritis. Am. J. Surg. *92:*781, 1956.

Tyler, F. H., Schmidt, C. D., Eik-Nes, K., Brown, H. and Samuels, L. T.: The role of the liver and the adrenal in producing elevated plasma 17-hydroxycorticosteroid levels in surgery. J. Clin. Invest. *33:*1517, 1954.

Udenfriend, S. and Wyngaarden, J. B.: Precursors of adrenal epinephrine and norepinephrine. Biochim. et Biophys. Acta *20:*48, 1956.

Udupa, K. N. and Dunphy, J. E.: The effect of ascorbic acid on metachromasia in solutions of protein and acid polysaccharide. J. Histochem. *4:*448, 1956.

Udupa, K. N., Woessner, J. F. and Dunphy, J. E.: The effect of methionine on the production of mucopolysaccharides and collagen in healing wounds of protein-depleted animals. Surg., Gynec. & Obst. *102:*639, 1956.

Ullman, T. D.: Hyperosmolarity of the extracellular fluid in encephalitis with report of case. Am. J. Med. *15:*885, 1953.

Uricchio, J. F. and Calenda, D. G.: The failure of hypertonic saline in the treatment of hyponatremia and edema in congestive heart failure. Ann. Int. Med. *39:*1288, 1953.

Uricchio, J. F., Calenda, D. G. and Cutts, F. B.: Ulceration of the skin following intravenous use of arterenol. J.A.M.A. *152:*607, 1953.

Urist, M. R., Budy, A. M. and McLean, F. C.: Transactions of First Conference on Bone and Wound Healing. New York, Josiah Macy, Jr., Foundation, 1942, p. 79.

Urist, M. R. and Johnson, R. W., Jr.: Calcification and ossification. IV. The healing of fractures in man under clinical conditions. J. Bone & Joint Surg. *25:*375, 1943.

Valk, A. deT. and Price, H. L.: The chemical estimation of epinephrine and norepinephrine in human and canine plasma. I. A critique of the ethylenediamine condensation method. J. Clin. Invest. *35:*837, 1956.

Vandam, L. D. and Burnap, T. K.: Problems in anesthesia for operations on the heart. New England J. Med. *255:*110, 1956.

Van den Brenk, H. A. S.: Studies in restorative growth processes in mammalian wound healing. Brit. J. Surg. *43:*525, 1956.

VanDyke, H. B., Ames, R. G. and Plough, I. C.: The excretion of antidiuretic hormone in the urine of patients with cirrhosis of the liver. Tr. A. Am. Physicians *63:*35, 1950.

Van Goidsenhoven, G. M. T., Gray, O. V., Price, A. V. and Sanderson, P. H.: Effect of prolonged administration of large doses of sodium bicarbonate in man. Clin. Sc. *13:*383, 1954.

VanSlyke, D. D.: The effect of shock on the kidney. Ann. Int. Med. *28:*701, 1948.

VanSlyke, D. D., Phillips, R. A., Hamilton, P. B., Archibald, R. M., Dole, V. P. and Emerson, K., Jr.: Effect of shock on the kidney. Tr. A. Am. Physicians *58:*119, 1944.

Van Slyke, K. K. and Evans, E. I.: The paradox of aciduria in the presence of alkalosis caused by hypochloremia. Ann. Surg. *126:*545, 1947.

Venning, E. H., Beck, J. C., Dyrenfurth, I. and Giroud, C. J. P.: Studies on the excretion of the sodium-retaining corticoid. J. Clin. Endocrinol. *15:*853, 1955 (abstr.).

Venning, E. H., Hoffman, M. M. and Brown, J. S. L.: The extraction of cortin-like substances from human postoperative urine. Endocrinology *35:*49, 1944.

Verel, D., Bury, J. D. and Hope, A.: Blood volume changes in pregnancy and the puerperium. Clin. Sc. *15:*1, 1956.

Verney, E. B.: Absorption and excretion of water; the antidiuretic hormone. Lancet *2:*739, 1946.

Verney, E. B.: Agents determining and influencing the functions of the pars nervosa of the pituitary. Brit. M. J. *2:*119, 1948.

Verney, E. B.: Water diuresis. Irish J. M. Sc. *6:*377, 1954.

Verney, E. B.: Some aspects of water and electrolyte excretion. Surg., Gynec. & Obst. *106:*441, 1958.

Virtue, R. W., Helmreich, M. L. and Gainza, E.: The adrenal cortical response to surgery. I. The effect of anesthesia on plasma 17-hydroxycorticosteroid levels. Surgery *41:*549, 1957.

Visscher, M. B., Fetcher, E. S., Jr., Carr, C. W., Gregor, H. P., Bushey, M. S. and Barker, D. E.: Isotopic tracer studies on the movement of water and ions between intestinal lumen and blood. Am. J. Physiol. *142:*550, 1944.

Visscher, M. B. and Roepke, R. R.: Osmotic and electrolyte concentration relationships during absorption of salt solutions from ileal segments. Am. J. Physiol. *144:*468, 1945.

Visscher, M. B., Roepke, R. R. and Lifson, N.: Osmotic and electrolyte concentration relationships during the absorption of autogenous serum from ileal segments. Am. J. Physiol. *144:*457, 1945.

von Euler, U. S.: Adrenalin and noradrenalin; distribution and action. Pharmacol. Rev. *6:*15, 1954.

von Euler, U. S.: Stress and catechol hormones. In Selye, H. and Heuser, G. (eds.): Fifth Annual Report on Stress. New York, MD Publications, 1956, p. 125.

von Euler, U. S., Franksson, C. and Hellstrom, J.: Adrenalin and noradrenalin output in urine after unilateral and bilateral adrenalectomy in man. Acta physiol. scandinav. *31:*1, 1954.

von Euler, U. S., Franksson, C. and Hellstrom, J.: Adrenalin and noradrenalin content of surgically removed human suprarenal glands. Acta physiol. scandinav. *31:*6, 1954.

von Hevesy, G. and Hofer, E.: Der Austansch des Wassers im Fischkörper. Ztschr. f. physiol. Chem. *225:*28, 1934.

Waddell, W. R. and Wang, C. C.: Experimental studies in gastric physiology. I. The effect of fat upon gastric evacuation after partial gastrectomy. Am. New York Acad. Sc. *56:*83, 1952.

Wakeley, C. P. G.: Treatment of war burns. Surgery *10:*207, 1941.

Walker, W. F., Shoemaker, W. C., Kaalstad, A. J. and Moore, F. D.: The effect of hemorrhage on adrenocortical function—the influence of blood volume restoration and tissue trauma on the concentration and output of corticosteroids in the adrenal vein of dogs. (In preparation.)

Walker, W. F., Zileli, M. S., Reutter, F. W., Shoemaker, W. C. and Moore, F. D.: The effect of hemorrhage on adrenal medullary function. I. The influence of immobilization, anesthesia, pain and tissue trauma on the "resting" secretion of the adrenal medulla. (In preparation.)

Walker, W. F., Zileli, M. S., Reutter, F. W., Shoemaker, W. C. and Moore, F. D.: The effect of hemorrhage on adrenal medullary function. II. Acute and chronic hemorrhage including observations on blood replacement and infusion of norepinephrine. (In preparation.)

Wallace, A. B.: Treatment of burns: a return to basic principles. Brit. J. Plast. Surg. *1:*232, 1949.

Wallace, A. B.: The exposure treatment of burns. Lancet *1:*501, 1951.

Wallenstein, S.: The relation between sideropenia and anemia and the occurrence of postcibal symptoms following partial gastrectomy for peptic ulcer. Surgery *38:*289, 1955.

Walshe, J. M.: Disturbances of amino acid metabolism following liver injury. Quart. J. Med., Oxford *22:*483, 1953.

Walter, C. W.: A new technic for collection, storage, and administration of unadulterated whole blood. S. Forum *1:*483, 1951.

Walter, C. W., Bellamy, D., Jr. and Murphy, W. P.: Mechanical factors responsible for rapid infusion of blood. Surg., Gynec. & Obst. *101:*115, 1955.

Warner, G. F., Dobson, E. L., Rodgers, C. E., Johnston, M. E. and Pace, N.: The measurement of total "sodium space" and total body sodium in normal individuals and in patients with cardiac edema. Circulation *5:*915, 1952.

Warner, G. F., Sweet, N. J. and Dobson, E. L.: "Sodium space" and body sodium content exchangeable with sodium-24, in normal individuals and patients with ascites. Circulation Res. *1:*486, 1953.

Warren, J. V. and Stead, E. A., Jr.: Fluid dynamics in chronic congestive heart failure. A.M.A. Arch. Int. Med. *73:*138, 1944.

Warren, K. W.: Acute pancreatitis and pancreatic injuries following subtotal gastrectomy. Surgery *29:*643, 1951.

Warren, K. W.: Management of pancreatic injuries. S. Clin. North America *31:*743, 1951.

Warren, R. and Belko, J. S.: Deficiency of plasma prothrombin conversion accelerators in the postoperative state with a description of a simple method of assay. Blood *6:*544, 1951.

Warren, R., Lauridsen, J. and Belko, J. S.: Alterations in numbers of circulating platelets following surgical operation and administration of adrenocorticotropic hormone. Circulation *7:*481, 1953.

Wasmuth, C. E.: Anesthesia for mitral commissurotomy. Cleveland Clin. Quart. *20:*346, 1953.

Waterhouse, C., Kentmann, E. H. and Fenninger, L. D.: Studies on the mechanism of edema formation in patients with low serum electrolytes. J. Clin. Invest. *30:*681, 1951 (abstr.).

Waters, R. M. and Gillespie, N. A.: Deaths in operating room. Anesthesiology *5:*113, 1922.

Watkins, E., Jr.: Experimental citrate intoxication during massive blood transfusion. S. Forum *4:*213, 1954.

Watson, C. J. and Hoffbauer, F. W.: The problem of prolonged hepatitis with particular reference to the cholangiolitic type and to the development of cholangiolitic cirrhosis of the liver. Ann. Int. Med. *25:*195, 1946.

Watts, D. T.: Epinephrine in the circulating blood during ether anesthesia. J. Pharmacol. & Exper. Therap. *114:*203, 1955.

Webb, W. R.: Crushing injuries of the chest. Clin. Med. *3:*941, 1956.

Webster, L. T. and Davidson, C. S.: The effect of sodium glutamate on hepatic coma. J. Clin. Invest. *35:*191, 1956.

Weichselbaum, T. E. and Margraf, H. W.: Determination in plasma of free 17-hydroxy and 17-desoxy corticosteroids and their glucuronic acid conjugates. J. Clin. Endocrinol. *15:*970, 1955.

Weichselbaum, T. E., Elman, R. and Margraf, H. W.: Potentially active adrenocortical steroids in plasma after various stresses. J. Clin. Endocrinol. *17:*1158, 1957.

Weigel, A. E., Artz, C. P., Reiss, E., Davis, J. H. and

Amspacher, W. H.: Gastrointestinal ulcerations complicating burns; a report of 5 cases and a review of 17 cases reported from 1942 to 1952. Surgery 34:826, 1953.

Weil, W. B. and Wallace, W. M.: The role of connective tissue in body fluid physiology. J. Clin. Invest. 34:970, 1955 (abstr.).

Weil, G. P. and Webster, D. R.: Studies on the bleeding tendency following dextran infusion. S. Forum 6:88, 1956.

Weil-Malherbe, H. and Bone, A. D.: The adrenergic amines of human blood. Lancet 1:974, 1953.

Weimer, H. E., Redlich-Moshin, J. and Nelson, E. L.: Comparative effects of infection and of immunization on serum glycoprotein concentrations. J. Immunol. 74:243, 1955.

Weinstein, J. J. and Roe, J. H.: The utilization of dextrose, levulose and invert sugar by normal and surgical patients. Am. J. Proctol. 4:21, 1953.

Weismann, R. E. and Twitchell, E. B.: Acute pseudomembranous enterocolitis in the postoperative patient. Ann. Surg. 144:32, 1956.

Welch, C. E.: The treatment of combined intestinal obstruction and peritonitis by refunctionalization of the intestine. Ann. Surg. 142:739, 1955.

Welch, C. S.: Surgery in the aged. Shattuck lecture. New England J. Med. 238:821, 1948.

Welch, C. S.: Medical progress; portal hypertension. New England J. Med. 243:598, 1950.

Welch, C. S.: Management of patients with mass hemorrhage from esophageal varices and cirrhosis of the liver. Surgery 41:1029, 1957.

Welch, C. S., Kiley, J. E., Reeve, T. S., Goodrich, E. O. and Welch, H. F.: Treatment of bleeding from portal hypertension in patients with cirrhosis of the liver. New England J. Med. 254:493, 1956.

Welch, C. S. and Ramos, A. G.: Results of portacaval shunts in the treatment of portal hypertension. Surgery 41:756, 1957.

Weller, J. M. et al.: Effects of acute removal of potassium from dogs—changes in the electrocardiogram. Circulation 11:44, 1955.

Wells, C. and Welbourne, R.: Post-gastrectomy syndromes: a study in applied physiology. Brit. Med. J. 1:546, 1951.

Wells, R. E.: The use of high humidity environment in the therapy of upper and lower respiratory disease: experiences in a fog room. Dis. Chest, 1959 (in press).

Welt, L. G., Seldin, D. W., Nelson, W. P., III, German, W. J. and Peters, J. P.: Role of the central nervous system in metabolism of electrolyte and water. A.M.A. Arch. Int. Med. 90:355, 1952.

Werner, S. C.: Some effects upon nitrogen balance of the independent variation of protein and calories in man. J. Clin. Invest. 27:561, 1948 (abstr.).

Werner, S. C., Habif, D. V., Randall, H. T. and Lockwood, J. S.: Postoperative nitrogen loss—a comparison of the effects of trauma and of caloric adjustment. Ann. Surg. 130:688, 1949.

Wesson, L. G., Jr. and Anslow, W. P., Jr.: Effect of osmotic and mercurial diuresis on simultaneous water diuresis. Am. J. Physiol. 170:255, 1952.

West, C. D., Damast, B. L., Sarro, S. D. and Pearson, O. H.: Conversion of testosterone to estrogens in castrated, adrenalectomized human female. J. Biol. Chem. 218:409, 1956.

West, C. D., Traeger, J. and Kaplan, S. A.: A comparison of the relative effectiveness of hydropenia and of Pitressin in producing a concentrated urine. J. Clin. Invest. 34:887, 1955.

West, J. P.: Cardiac arrest during anesthesia and surgery. An analysis of 30 cases. Ann. Surg. 140:623, 1954.

Weston, R. E., Escher, D. J. W., Grossman, J. and Leiter, L.: Mechanisms contributing to unresponsiveness to mercurial diuretics in congestive heart failure. J. Clin. Invest. 31:901, 1952.

Weston, R. E., Hanenson, I. B., Borun, E. R., Grossman, J. and Wolfman, M.: Production of water retention and acute hyponatremia without sodium loss by administration of Pitressin tannate to patients in congestive heart failure. J. Clin. Invest. 31:672, 1952 (abstr.).

Weston, R. E., Hanenson, I. B., Grossman, J., Berdasco, G. A. and Wolfman, M.: Natriuresis and chloruresis following Pitressin-induced water retention in non-edematous patients: evidence of a homeostatic mechanism regulating body fluid volume. J. Clin. Invest. 32:611, 1953.

Weston, R. E., Hanenson, I. B., Grossman, J., Borun, E. R., Wolfman, M. and Leiter, L.: Water retention and hyponatremia produced in edematous cardiac patients by Pitressin tannate administration. Fed. Proc. 12:153, 1953.

Wettstein, A.: Advances in the field of adrenal cortical hormones. Experientia 10:397, 1954.

Wexler, I. B., Pincus, J. B., Natelson, S. and Lugovoy, J. K.: The fate of citrate in erythroblastotic infants treated with exchange transfusion. J. Clin. Invest. 28:474, 1949.

Whipple, A. O.: The problem of portal hypertension in relation to the hepatosplenopathies. Ann. Surg. 122:449, 1945.

Whipple, A. O.: The rationale of portacaval anastomosis. Bull. New York Acad. Med. 22:251, 1946.

White, J. R. and Roberts, K. N.: In Youmans, J. B. (ed.): Symposia on Nutrition of the Robert Gould Research Foundation. Vol. II, Plasma Proteins. Springfield, Ill., Charles C Thomas, 1950.

White, A. G., Rubin, G. and Leiter, L.: Studies in edema. III. The effect of Pitressin on the renal excretion of water and electrolytes in patients with and without liver disease. J. Clin. Invest. 30:1287, 1951.

White, A. G., Rubin, G. and Leiter, L.: Studies in edema. IV. Water retention and the antidiuretic hormone in hepatic and a cardiac disease. J. Clin. Invest. 32:931, 1953.

Whitelaw, M. J.: Physiological reaction to pituitary adrenocorticotropic hormone (ACTH) in severe burns. J.A.M.A. 145:85, 1951.

Whitelaw, M. J. and Woodman, T. W.: The treatment of severe burns with ACTH. J. Clin. Endocrinol. 10:1171, 1950.

Whiteley, H. J.: The relation between tissue injury and the manifestations of pulmonary fat embolism. J. Path. & Bact. 67:521, 1954.

Whittenberger, J. L. and Ferris, B. J.: Impairment of the mechanics of respiration: paralytic conditions. In Gordon, J. R.: Clinical Cardiopulmonary Physiology. New York, Grune & Stratton, 1957, p. 180.

Widdowson, E. M. and McCance, R. A.: The effect of development on the composition of the serum and extracellular fluid. Clin. Sc. 15:361, 1956.

Widdowson, E. M., McCance, R. A. and Spray, C. M.: The chemical composition of the human body. Clin. Sc. 10:113, 1951.

Wiener, A. S.: Intra-arterial transfusion. J.A.M.A. *146:*57, 1951 (Correspondence).

Wiener, A. S. and Wexler, I. B.: The use of heparin when performing exchange blood transfusions in newborn infants. J. Lab. & Clin. Med. *31:*1016, 1946.

Wiggers, C. J.: Present status of the shock problem. Physiol. Rev. *22:*74, 1942.

Wiggers, C. J.: Myocardial depression in shock; survey of cardiodynamic studies. Am. Heart J. *33:*633, 1947.

Wiggers, C. J. and Werle, J. M.: Cardiac and peripheral resistance factors as determinants of circulatory failure in hemorrhagic shock. Am. J. Physiol. *136:*421, 1942.

Wight, A., Hopkirk, J. F., DeMuylder, E. and Cope, O.: Metabolic derangements imperiling the perforated ulcer patient. II. Derangements and shifts of intracellular electrolytes; the need for potassium. A.M.A. Arch. Surg. *71:*839, 1955.

Wight, A., Raker, J. W., Merrington, W. R. and Cope, O.: The ebb and flood of the eosinophils in the burned patient and their uses in the clinical management. Ann. Surg. *137:*175, 1953.

Wight, A., Taylor, S., Minor, C. L., Lohnes, W., Hopkirk, J. F. and Cope, O.: Metabolic derangements imperiling the perforated ulcer patient. III. Derangements and shifts of sodium and chloride. A.M.A. Arch. Surg. *72:*166, 1956.

Wight, A., Weisman, P. A., Rovit, R. L. and Cope, O.: Adrenal hormones and increased capillary permeability of burns—an experimental evaluation. A.M.A. Arch. Surg. *65:*309, 1952.

Wilansky, D. L. and Schneiderman, C.: Renal tubular acidosis with recurrent nephrolithiasis and nephrocalcinosis. New England J. Med. *257:*399, 1957.

Wilkinson, A. W.: Biochemical changes after ureterocolic anastomosis. Brit. J. Urol. *24:*46, 1952.

Wilkinson, A. W.: Alcohol in intravenous feeding. Proc. Nutrition Soc. *14:*124, 1955.

Wilkinson, A. W.: Unpublished data.

Williams, F.: Plasma volume changes in egg-white injected rats. Effect of cortisone. Proc. Soc. Exper. Biol. & Med. *86:*77, 1954.

Williams, J. A., Belko, J. S. and Warren, R.: Thrombocytogenesis in surgical patients. Circulation Res. *3:*285, 1955.

Williams, J. A., Belko, J. S. and Warren, R.: The effect of ACTH on megakaryocyte activity: implications concerning postoperative thrombophilia. S. Forum *6:*112, 1956.

Williams, R. H., Jaffe, H. and Kemp, C.: Effects of severe stress upon thyroid function. Am. J. Physiol. *159:*291, 1949.

Williams, R. H. and MacMahon, H. E.: Gastroenterocolitis; carcinoma of pancreas; "clear-cell" nephrosis. Bull. New England M. Center *9:*274, 1947.

Williamson, M. B. (ed.): The Healing of Wounds. New York, McGraw-Hill Book Co., 1957.

Williamson, M. B. and Fromm, H. J.: Utilization of sulphur amino acids during healing of experimental wounds. Proc. Soc. Exper. Biol. & Med. *83:*329, 1953.

Williamson, M. B. and Fromm, H. J.: The incorporation of sulphur amino acids into the proteins of regenerating wound tissues. J. Biol. Chem. *212:*705, 1955.

Williamson, M. B., McCarthy, T. H. and Fromm, H. J.: Relation of protein nutrition to the healing of experimental wounds. Proc. Soc. Exper. Biol. & Med. *77:*302, 1951.

Willner, C. E.: War wounds of the thoracic respiratory apparatus. Surg., Gynec. & Obst. *97:*735, 1953.

Wilson, B. J., Reisman, D. D. and Moyer, C. A.: Fluid balance in the urological patient: disturbances in the renal regulation of the excretion of water and sodium salts following decompression of the urinary bladder. J. Urol. *66:*805, 1951.

Wilson, G. M.: In Moore, F. D. *et al.:* Discussion on the endocrine response to trauma. Proc. Roy. Soc. Med. *48:*819, 1955.

Wilson, G. M., Edelman, I. S., Brooks, L., Myrden, J. A., Harken, D. E. and Moore, F. D.: Metabolic changes associated with mitral valvuloplasty. Circulation *9:*199, 1954.

Wilson, G. M., Olney, J. M., Brooks, L., Myrden, J. A., Ball, M. and Moore, F. D.: Body sodium and potassium. II. A comparison of metabolic balance and isotope dilution methods of study. Metabolism *3:*324, 1954.

Wilson, H., Lovelace, J. R. and Hardy, J. D.: The adrenocortical response to extensive burns in man. Ann. Surg. *141:*175, 1955.

Wilson, J. V. and Salisbury, C. V.: Fat embolism in war surgery. Brit. J. Surg. *31:*384, 1944.

Wilson, W. C., MacGregor, A. R. and Stewart, C. P.: The clinical course and pathology of burns and scalds under modern methods of treatment. Brit. J. Surg. *25:*826, 1938.

Winfield, J. M., Fox, C. L., Jr. and Mersheimer, W. L.: Etiologic factors in postoperative salt retention and its prevention. Ann. Surg. *134:*626, 1951.

Winkler, A. W., Hoff, A. E. and Smith, P. K.: Electrocardiographic changes with concentration of potassium in serum following intravenous injection of potassium chloride. Am. J. Physiol. *124:*478, 1938.

Winkler, A. W. and Smith, P. K.: Renal excretion of potassium salts. Am. J. Physiol. *138:*94, 1942.

Winzler, R. J.: Determination of serum glycoproteins. In Methods of Biochemical Analysis, vol. 2. New York, Interscience Publishers, Inc., 1955.

Wissler, R. W.: The effect of protein-depletion and subsequent immunization upon the response of animals to pneumococcal infection. J. Infect. Dis. *80:*250, 1947.

Wohl, M. G., Reinhold, J. G. and Rose, S. B.: Antibody response in patients with hypoproteinemia. A.M.A. Arch. Int. Med. *83:*402, 1949.

Wolf, A. V. and McDowell, M. E.: Apparent and osmotic volumes of distribution of sodium, chloride, sulphate and urea. Am. J. Physiol. *176:*207, 1954.

Wolf, J. and Loeser, J. A.: Testosterone therapy for fractures. J. Clin. Endocrinol. *14:*107, 1954.

Wollaeger, E. E.: Disturbances of gastrointestinal function following partial gastrectomy. Postgrad. Med. *8:*251, 1950.

Wollaeger, E. E., Comfort, M. W. and Weir, J. F.: The total solids, fat and nitrogen in the feces—a study of persons who had undergone partial gastrectomy with anastomosis of the entire cut end of the stomach and the jejunum (polya anastomosis). Gastroenterology *6:*93, 1946.

Wollaeger, E. E., Comfort, M. W., Weir, J. F. and Osterberg, A. E.: The total solids, fat and nitrogen in feces—a study of normal persons and of patients with duodenal ulcer on test diet containing large amounts of fat. Gastroenterology *6:*83, 1946.

Womersley, R. A. and Darragh, J. H.: Potassium and

sodium restriction in the normal human. J. Clin. Invest. *34:*456, 1955.

Woodward, F. D.: Medical criticism of modern automotive engineering. J.A.M.A. *138:*627, 1948.

Wright, R. B.: Fat embolism. Ann. Surg. *96:*75, 1932.

Wrong, O.: The relationship between water retention and electrolyte excretion following administration of anti-diuretic hormone. Clin. Sc. *15:*401, 1956.

Wyngaarden, J. B., Peterson, R. E. and Wolff, A. R.: Physiologic disposition of radiometabolites of hydro-cortisone-4-C¹⁴ in the rat and guinea pig. J. Biol. Chem. *212:*963, 1955.

Wynn, V.: Electrolyte disturbances associated with failure to metabolise glucose during hypothermia. Lancet *2:*575, 1954.

Wynn, V.: A metabolic study of acute water intoxication in man and dogs. Clin. Sc. *14:*669, 1955.

Wynn, V.: Water intoxication and serum hypotonicity. Metabolism *5:*490, 1956.

Wynn, V.: The osmotic behaviour of the body cells in man. Significance of changes of plasma-electrolyte levels in body-fluid disorders. Lancet *2:*1212, 1957.

Wynn, V. and Houghton, B. J.: Observations in man upon the osmotic behavior of the body cells after trauma. Quart. J. Med. (n. s.) *26:*375, 1957.

Wynn, V. and Ludbrook, J.: A method of measuring the *p*H of body-fluids. Lancet *1:*1068, 1957.

Wyse, D. M. and Pattee, C. J.: Effects of the oscillating bed and tilting table on Ca, P, and N metabolism in paraplegics. Am. J. Med. *17:*645, 1954.

Yoshimura, H. *et al.:* Dehydration of the human body; some remarks on physiological effects of prolonged complete starvation. J. Biochem. (Japan) *40:*361, 1953.

Youmans, J. B.: Nutritional Deficiencies: Diagnosis and Treatment. 2nd ed. Philadelphia, J. B. Lippincott Co., 1943.

Young, P. C., Burnside, C. R. and Knowles, H. C., Jr.: The effect of the intragastric administration of whole blood on the blood ammonia, blood urea nitrogen and non-protein nitrogen in patients with liver disease. J. Clin. Invest. *35:*747, 1956 (abstr.).

Young, W. F., Hallum, J. L. and McCance, R. A.: The secretion of urine by premature infants. Arch. Dis. Child. *16:*243, 1941.

Young, W. G., Jr., Sealy, W. C. and Harris, J. S.: Role of intracellular and extracellular electrolytes in cardiac arrhythmias produced by prolonged hypercapnea. Surgery *36:*636, 1954.

Young, W. G., Jr., Sealy, W. C., Harris, J. S. and Botwin, A.: The effects of hypercapnia and hypoxia on the response of the heart to vagal stimulation. Surg., Gynec. & Obst. *93:*51, 1951.

Ziegler, R. F.: Cardiac mechanism during anesthesia and operation in patients with congenital heart disease and cyanosis. Bull. Johns Hopkins Hosp. *83:*237, 1948.

Zileli, M. S., Walker, W. F., Reutter, F. W., Shoemaker, W. C. and Friend, D. G.: The effect of hemorrhage on adrenal medullary function. III. Acute hemorrhage followed by replacement with saline or dextran. (In preparation.)

Zilva, S. S.: The influence of deficient nutrition on the production of agglutinins, complement and ambocep-tor. Biochem. J. *13:*172, 1919.

Zimmermann, B.: Endocrine mechanisms concerned in postoperative electrolyte changes. S. Forum *1:*447, 1951.

Zimmermann, B., Casey, J. H. and Block, H. S.: Mecha-nisms of sodium regulation in the surgical patient. Surgery *39:*161, 1956.

Zimmermann, B., Casey, J. H., Block, H. S., Bickel, E. Y. and Covrik, K.: Excretion of aldosterone by the post-operative patient. S. Forum *6:*3, 1956.

Zimmermann, B. and Freier, E. F.: The occurrence in surgical patients of severe hypernatremia without exogenous dehydration. Surgery *31:*373, 1952.

Zintel, H. A., Riegel, C., Peters, R., Rhoads, J. E. and Ravdin, I. S.: Intravenous administration of dextrose in the treatment of patients with disease of the biliary tract. A.M.A. Arch. Surg. *49:*238, 1944.

Zollinger, R. M. and Boles, T.: The problem of pancreatitis. Rocky Mountain M. J. *50:*554, 1953.

Zollinger, R. M. and Ellison, E. H.: Nutrition after gastric operation. J.A.M.A. *154:*811, 1954.

Zweifach, B. W.: Peripheral circulatory changes as criteria for hemorrhagic shock therapy. Circulation *1:*433, 1950.

Zweifach, B. W., Abell, R. G., Chambers, R. and Clowes, G. H. A.: Role of the decompensatory reactions of peripheral blood vessels in tourniquet shock. Surg., Gynec. & Obst. *80:*593, 1945.

Zweifach, B. W., Chambers, R., Lee, R. E. and Hyman, C.: Reactions of peripheral blood vessels in experi-mental hemorrhage. Ann. New York Acad. Sc. *49:*553, 1948.

Zweifach, B. W., Lee, R. E., Hyman, C. and Chambers, R.: Omental circulation in morphinized dogs subjected to graded hemorrhage. Ann. Surg. *120:*232, 1944.

Zweifach, B. W. and Metz, D. B.: Regional differences in response of terminal vascular bed to vasoactive agents. Am. J. Physiol. *182:*155, 1955.

Zweifach, B. W., Shorr, E. and Black, M. M.: The influence of the adrenal cortex on behavior of terminal vascular bed. Ann. New York Acad. Sc. *56:*626, 1953.

Clinical Procedures and Case Histories:
Reference Lists

CLINICAL PROCEDURES
Reference List*

---

* As repeatedly emphasized, these clinical procedures are based on events in a number of cases and are designed to show how the principles of metabolic care are applied to surgical problems. The reader is again cautioned against undue generalization from a single example.

CASE HISTORIES
Reference List*

* This list of diagnoses and operations is provided for reference should the reader wish to look up specific events or employ the case histories for teaching.

Index

Index

NOTE: The parenthetical expressions used in this index have the following significance:
(case) indicates the content of case histories
(illus.) indicates the content of illustrations
(literature) indicates discussions of reviews of the literature
(procedure) indicates presentations of specific clinical procedures
(table) indicates tabular matter

ABDOMEN, distention of, as cause of decreased vital capacity, 744
Abscesses, peritoneal, drainage of, 554
Absorption defects of gastrointestinal tract, 569–575, (literature)575
    in chronic pancreatitis, 635
Accumulation, bronchopulmonary, in surgical patients, 735–741. See also *Bronchopulmonary accumulation*.
ACD, formulas for, 253
Acid, excretion, by lungs, 330
    in urine, 328
Acid-base balance
    body buffers in relation to, 331
    disorders of, 324–338
        patterns of, 362–368
        range of values in, 330
        treatment, 339–344
            solutions for, 339
        urine in, 328
    effects of anesthesia on, (literature)388
        of extrarenal fluid loss on, 304
        of infusions on, (literature)388
        of potassium chloride on, 320
        of sodium and chloride on, 328
    methods of study, 325
    regulation of, 18
    restoration of, in water and electrolyte disorders, 341
    subtraction or addition of hydrogen in relation to, 334
    terminology of, 324
    types of disturbances in, 328

Acid-citrate-dextrose, formulas for, 253
Acidosis
    addition, 334
        in acute renal failure, 664
        postoperative, findings in, 337
    as result of anesthesia, (literature)113
    blood changes in, 328
    compensations for, effect of trauma on, 269
    diabetic, in surgical patient, 638
        prevention and treatment, 641
        potassium deficit in, 321
    hypoxic, during extracorporeal circulation, 718
    in newborn, 69
    in unresponsive shock, 815
    range of values in, 330
    relation to hyperkalemia, 319
        to potassium concentration, (literature)393
    renal compensation for, 329
    renal tubular, post-traumatic, 665
        urine in, 329
    respiratory, acute, 364, (illus.)365
        in surgical patients, 745
        treatment, 366
    chronic, 367, (illus.)367
        in surgical patients, 746
        treatment, 368
    unsuspected, discovery of, 272
    subtraction, 334
        postoperative, findings in, 338
    treatment of, 341

ACTH
    administration, in burns, 893
        unhealed, 906
        in surgical patients, 473
    effects of, compared to operation effects, (illus.)87
        on adrenals, 22
    importance of, 20
    response to, effect of operation on, (illus.)89,90
Adrenal cortex
    control of tissue protein by, (literature)102
    early changes after trauma, (literature)74–82
    effect of burns on, (literature)907
        of hemorrhage on,(literature)113
        of shock on, 174
        of surgical trauma on, 29
    lipid depletion in after trauma, (literature)82
    neuroendocrine activation of, after injury, 121
Adrenal cortical hormones
    after complicated appendectomy, (illus.)95
    after complicated gastrectomy, (illus.)91, 93
    classification of, 21
    effects of ACTH vs. those of operation, (illus.)87
        of ether anesthesia on, (illus.)76
            plus operation, (illus.)79
        of surgical trauma on, 30
        on nitrogen excretion, 33

Page 991